The Penguin Encyclopedia

EDITED BY

SIR JOHN SUMMERSCALE

PENGUIN BOOKS

Penguin Books Ltd, Harmondsworth, Middlesex, England
Penguin Books Inc., 3300 Clipper Mill Road, Baltimore 11, Md, U.S.A.
Penguin Books Pty Ltd, Ringwood, Victoria, Australia

—

First published 1965

—

Copyright © Penguin Books, 1965

—

Made and printed in Great Britain
by Hazell Watson & Viney Ltd
Aylesbury, Bucks
Set in Linotype Times

Drawings by Wolf Spoerl

FOREWORD

The Penguin Encyclopedia is small. For that we make no apology. Large, heavy encyclopedias usually have to be housed out of immediate reach: this one is designed to live on the desk, for quick and frequent reference.

The necessary compression has been effected in several ways. For a start, we have assumed the reader to be a reasonably educated, intelligent person who at least knows what 'every schoolboy knows', and have omitted obvious and banal information. In addition, extensive and judicious use of cross-references has saved space without sacrificing material. Moreover, we have deliberately excluded mere 'dictionary definitions' from what is strictly an encyclopedia of useful knowledge.

Further space has been saved by our treatment of biographical and geographical entries. Such as can be said to lie on the fringe of general knowledge – the theories of Marx or Einstein, for instance, or the politics and economics of Brazil or Yugoslavia – are covered here. For the rest we have accepted that facts about people and places are appreciably different in kind from other knowledge. To complement this volume we shall therefore be publishing a gazetteer and a dictionary of biography later.

The Penguin Encyclopedia takes full account of the very real shift in emphasis, as between different kinds of knowledge, which has occurred in this century. For the average man in western society (if he exists) it has become of the first importance today to understand the increasingly complex world of science and technology. Accordingly, in this work, much of the dead wood which clutters up so many encyclopedias has been compressed or dropped to make room for subjects of live interest.

Those fields of science, technology and research in which great strides have been made in recent years are covered thoroughly, and specialists of the younger generation – from the universities, the professions and industry – have contributed individual articles. We have also dealt similarly with the arts and humanities so as to ensure an up-to-date approach.

In short, our intention throughout has been to focus *The Penguin Encyclopedia* as sharply as possible on the real needs of the second half of the twentieth century.

NOTES FOR USE

Considerable use of cross-references has been made: words in the text in italics, preceded by either a single or a double arrow can be found as entries in their own right.

The single arrow ⟡ indicates that the supplementary information under the cross-referenced entry is closely relevant to the subject matter and in some cases essential for understanding it.

The double arrow ⟡⟡ (equivalent to 'see also') refers to entries whose information, though less immediately relevant, is connected.

Entries are listed under alternative spellings where this seems essential, but not where the reader can be assumed to know both forms.

Compound entry words appear in their customary or natural order; for example, **Association Football,** not **Football, Association.** However, a few compound words appear only under the heading of the word which is obviously the main component, e.g. Safety Glass is under **Glass.**

SYMBOLS AND ABBREVIATIONS

◊	see	Lat.	Latin
◊◊	see also	lb.	pound(s)
<	from	m.	mile(s); million
Ar.	Arabic	min.	minute(s)
at. no.	atomic number	mm.	millimetre(s)
at. wt	atomic weight	m.p.	melting point
Aug.	August	m.p.h.	miles per hour
b.	born	N.	north, northern
b.p.	boiling point	NE	north east
c.	*circa*, about	no.	number
C	centigrade	Nov.	November
cap.	capital	NW	north west
c.c.	cubic centimetres	Oct.	October
cent.	century	p.a.	per annum, annually
Co.	Company	P.M.	Prime Minister
d.	died	pop.	population
Dec.	December	pt	pint(s)
E.	east, eastern	qt	quart(s)
e.g.	for example, such as	rel.	religion
esp.	especially, in particular	S.	south, southern
f.	fathom	SE	south east
F	Fahrenheit	sec.	second(s)
Feb.	February	Sept.	September
fl.	*floruit*, flourished	SOED	Shorter Oxford English
f.p.	freezing point		Dictionary
Fr.	French	sp. gr.	specific gravity
ft	foot (feet)	Sp.	Spanish
gal.	gallon(s)	sq. m.	square miles
Ger.	German	SW	south west
gm.	gramme(s)	U.A.R.	United Arab Republic
Gr.	Greek	U.K.	United Kingdom
Gt	Great	U.N.	United Nations Organization
i.e.	that is	U.S.A.	United States of America
inc.	includes, including	U.S.S.R.	Soviet Union
Jan.	January	vel.	velocity
kg.	kilogram	vol.	volume
km.	kilometre	W.	west, western
lat.	latitude	wt	weight

A

Abacus. Calculating device of very ancient origin, used in China in the 6th cent. B.C. and in Egypt, Greece, and Rome. The earliest form was a tray of sand, divided into strips for units, tens, hundreds, etc. on which marks were made to record the numbers under manipulation. Later a frame strung with wire, on which beads are moved as a mechanical aid to performing additions and subtractions, was used. Simple multiplications can be obtained through a series of additions. The abacus is still widely used in the Near and Far East and in U.S.S.R.

Abbasids. A line of caliphs. In A.D. 750 the Abbasids massacred the Ommayad family which then held the ◊ *Caliphate*, and moved their capital from Damascus to Bagdad. Both Persian and Greek influence, and the enlightened rule of Harun al Rashid and his son Mamun, led to a brilliant flowering of Muslim civilization, which later spread westward to a then backward Europe. After 100 years of Abbasid glory, however, the incursions of the Seljuk Turks led to disorder and decline. The grandson of Jenghis Khan (Hulagu) destroyed Bagdad in 1258. One Abbasid escaped to Cairo, where his descendants for centuries enjoyed the title of Caliph but little of the power. ◊ *Ommayads.*

Abbevillian ◊ *Palaeolithic.*

A.B.C. Powers. Term formerly applied to Argentine, Brazil, and Chile, and still occasionally used: after 1910 cordial relations were established among them and a treaty was signed with the object of securing hegemony in S. America and maintaining peace. The treaty was never ratified, and differences in forms of government have caused the gradual dissolution of the entente.

Abdomen. Region of trunk below the diaphragm, comprising an upper part – abdomen proper – and a lower part, the pelvis. The abdominal cavity is bounded by the muscular abdominal wall in front and by the vertebral column and attached muscles behind. It contains the stomach, intestines, liver, pancreas, and spleen. These organs and the inner aspect of the cavity are covered by a thin, smooth membrane – the peritoneum. Within the abdomen, but immediately outside the peritoneum, are the aorta (◊ *Circulatory System*) and inferior vena cava, the kidneys and adrenal glands. In the pelvis are the bladder and some reproductive organs.

Aberration of Light. In astronomy, an apparent change in the position of a heavenly body caused by movement of the observer relative to the source of light. It results in a small angular displacement of a stellar image in telescope as the latter moves with the earth, and was discovered by the English astronomer James Bradley 1693–1762.

In optical instruments, aberration is a term applied to imperfections of lens and mirrors.

CHROMATIC ABERRATION: The formation of an image with coloured fringes by a lens whose refractive index differs for light of different colours.

SPHERICAL ABERRATION: The formation of a blurred image by a lens or mirror that imperfectly focuses the light from an object.

Abominable Snowman (Yeti). Sherpas and explorers in the Himalayas have reported seeing in the snow the footprints (12 in.) of a large flat-footed animal. Sighting reports have also been made. The Sherpas have woven around this spoor much ingenious and fearful mythology, but its real nature, if any, remains undetermined.

Abortion. Medically, the expulsion of a foetus before the viable age of 28 weeks, spontaneous expulsion being usually described as miscarriage. Legally, the expulsion of a foetus at any time before gestation is complete. In most countries the procuring of an abortion is a criminal offence, except after medical certification of its desirability, for which specific procedures exist in Scandinavian countries and some U.S.A. states. In U.S.S.R. the

---

A single arrow before a word or phrase indicates a cross-reference to another main entry. A double arrow means *See also.*

1920 legalization of abortion was revoked 1936 but restored 1955, provided the operation is carried out in hospital. Abortion by means of purgatives or other herbs is practised by many primitive peoples.

Clandestine abortions are frequent, but statistics are not available. Religious opinion is opposed to abortion, even at the risk of suffering or death for the mother.

Aboukir Bay. 1798. Naval action in the ◊ *Napoleonic Wars*, off the coast of Egypt, also known as the Battle of the Nile, in which after a long search Nelson came upon a French fleet at anchor, superior in size, under Brueys. By the daring manoeuvre of sailing close to the shore, he captured or destroyed all but 4 of the 17 French ships. As a result Napoleon's army in Egypt was isolated and Napoleon himself left Egypt for France.

Absolute. 'The Absolute' is used variously and vaguely in ◊ *metaphysics*, notably by Fichte, Schelling, and Hegel, for the universe conceived as a satisfyingly related or organic whole, the reality underlying its appearances, or its continuing source. The Absolute was seen as self-caused, eternal, and spiritual or mental, and sometimes as a cosmic person or 'self-thinking thought'; some said it was ultimately unknowable, others that it is known through mystical insight.

Absolutism. Government by a person or institution recognizing no limitation upon his or its powers e.g. absolute monarchy, at its height in Europe from the 16th to the end of the 17th cent. Louis XIV of France is the supreme example (although even his powers were limited by custom and by the Church). The most famous philosophical defence of absolutism was that of Thomas Hobbes, who held that men, selfish and aggressive, surrendered their natural rights to an absolute ruler in return for protection from their fellows. Attempts at absolute monarchy came to an end in Britain with the ◊ *Glorious Revolution* of 1688. In continental Europe during the early 19th cent. the central conflict was that between absolutism and the liberal ideas inspired by the ◊ *French Revolution*, and absolutism persisted in the German and Italian princedoms and in Russia until the end of the 19th cent.

Absorption. 1. Penetration of the molecules of one substance into the spaces of another so that the one is 'swallowed up' by the other. Many solid substances will absorb liquids and gases in this way. The absorption may be on a microscopic scale (as with activated charcoal) or macroscopic (as with cotton wool).

2. The absorbing, as distinct from reflecting or transmitting, of radiant energy by a surface on which it falls. Dull black surfaces absorb more readily than bright polished ones, and are also better radiators of energy. Absorption of energy is accompanied by a rise in temperature. The absorption lines that appear in a spectrum when a substance is placed between a light source and a spectroscope result from absorption by the substance of light of certain wavelengths – in general, of the wavelengths it would itself emit when heated. The position of these absorption lines in a spectrum is characteristic of the absorbing substance and identification of the lines is the basis of much spectrochemical analysis. ◊ *Fraunhofer Lines.*

Abstract Art. Non-representational paintings and sculptures, produced mainly by artists of the School of Paris in the 20th cent. Although motifs without figurative or symbolic meaning had been employed in ornament since the earliest times, abstract art in the usual sense of the term is the last stage of the late 19th-cent. reaction against naturalism. Relying for their effect solely on line, colour, and texture, abstract works may have a merely decorative appeal but are usually intended to convey impressions of balance, harmony, repose, etc., akin to those of the other abstract arts of music and architecture. Kandinsky 1910 and Mondrian 1917 developed the purest abstract styles in painting. Among the leading exponents today are Ben Nicholson, Poliakoff, and Magnelli. ◊ *Action Painting, Constructivism, Cubism, Mobile.*

Abyssinia ◊ *Ethiopia.*

A.C. (Alternating Current) ◊ *Electric Current.*

Acacia. ◊ *Leguminosae*; a large tropical and subtropical genus, usually a tree, esp. common in Australia (often called wattles). The flowers are typically fluffy balls with a large number of stamens, as in the yellow 'mimosa' of florists, an Australian species of acacia grown extensively on the Riviera. Many acacias are of commercial importance, providing timber and tannin extracts. They are valuable in regions of low rainfall which unlike many trees they tolerate. False acacia (black locust) is *Robinia pseudacacia*.

Academic Degree. Rank in scholarship, conferred usually by a university to mark the satisfactory completion of normally 3 or 4 years of study in a given subject and the passing of stipulated examinations; or, at higher levels, on evidence of research and advanced scholarship. Other institutions confer a certificate or diploma. There are three levels: Bachelor, Master, Doctor; these represent different standards of achievement in different universities. In Scotland, the master's is the normal first degree; in Germany, only the doctor's is left. At Oxford and Cambridge, bachelors may proceed to the master's degree without further study or examination; elsewhere this promotion may need two years' study and research. Possession of a degree confers the privilege of adding initials to one's name e.g. B.A. or B.Sc. In Britain and U.S.A. the degree of Doctor of Philosophy (Ph.D.) is granted in most faculties after a period of research and the submission of a thesis. Honorary degrees are conferred by universities upon eminent persons without examination, as a mark of honour, sometimes for academic and sometimes for civic distinction.

Académie Française. Originated in Paris 1629, Cardinal Richelieu becoming its patron; it received letters patent in 1635; it started work 1639 on the Dictionary of the French language, the first edition of which appeared in 1694. Disbanded 1793 after the Revolution, it was reconstituted 1796. It is limited to 40 members (the 'Immortals'), persons of intellectual distinction who need not be writers, and membership is regarded as a high honour. However, many very distinguished French writers, including Molière, Rousseau, Balzac, Stendhal, Flaubert, Zola, and Proust, have not qualified for membership.

Accelerator (Electronic) ◊ *Particle Accelerator*.

Acculturation ◊ *Culture*.

Accumulator. Storage battery; a device for storing ◊ *electricity*; one type consists of two lead plates in a vessel filled with dilute sulphuric acid. Current is passed between the two plates, causing chemical changes; the accumulator is then charged and will discharge electric energy as required. During discharge the chemical charges are reversed, and the accumulator may then be recharged.

Acetate Rayon ◊ *Cellulose*.

Acetic Acid. A pungent-smelling colourless liquid, b.p. 118° C; the vapour is irritant to the eyes and nose, the liquid to the skin. Freely soluble in water, as a weak solution it is familiar in the form of vinegar. It reacts with alkalis and carbonates e.g. soda or chalk, and although not one of the strong acids it will slowly corrode many metals. Industrially it is a source of acetic esters, including ◊ *cellulose* acetate, used in the manufacture of rayon; biochemically it is important as a product of sugar metabolism and as the starting-point, in plants and animals, for the synthesis of many important natural products. It is made from ◊ *ethyl alcohol* or from acetylene, and also occurs in the watery distillate from heating wood; alcohol is oxidized to acetic acid by bacteria in the conversion of wine or malted barley into vinegar.

Acetone ◊ *Ketones, Olefines*.

Acetylene. A hydrocarbon, C_2H_2, more unsaturated than ethylene, having a triple bond between its ◊ *carbon* atoms $HC\equiv CH$. It is a colourless, insoluble, highly inflammable gas, obtained when ◊ *calcium* carbide reacts with water. (The calcium carbide is made by heating lime and coke in an electric furnace.) Acetylene decomposes with liberation of ◊ *energy*, the decomposition being explosive if the gas is compressed. It can however be safely stored in cylinders if dissolved in acetone. In the oxy-acetylene torch it gives an extremely hot flame useful for cutting or welding metal. Acetylene is chemically versatile and is a valuable starting point for the manufacture of many synthetic chemicals, e.g. if combined with water, with the help of a catalyst it gives acetaldehyde CH_3CHO, and from this, by oxidation, acetic acid CH_3COOH. The vinyl plastics are derived from acetylene, the best known being polyvinyl chloride (P.V.C.) $(H_2C= CHCl)_n$.

Achaeans. In Homer, the Greeks in general, and in the classical period the inhabitants of a district on the N. coast of the Peloponnese; now sometimes esp. the Greeks of the Mycenaean period, about 1600–1100 B.C.

Achaemenids ◊ *Persia*.

Acheron ◊ *Hades*.

Acheulian Culture ◊ *Palaeolithic*.

Achilles. Greek legendary hero, principal

character in Homer's *Iliad*. Son of Peleus, king of the Myrmidons of Thessaly, and the sea-goddess Thetis, he was a pupil of the centaur Chiron. With his friend Patroclus he led his Myrmidons as part of the Greek army against Troy, performing many mighty deeds: but in the 10th year of the war, having been compelled to surrender his concubine Briseis to ◊ *Agamemnon*, he withdrew and sulked in his tent. With his permission, Patroclus took his place in the fight and was killed; Achilles resumed fighting to avenge his friend, killed Hector, the Trojan hero who had slain Patroclus, and dragged the body at his chariot-wheels to the Greek fleet, but himself was killed by the Trojan Paris before the Greek capture of Troy. Legend says that his mother had tried to make him immortal by immersing him in the river Styx, but the heel by which she held him was not immersed, and a wound in the heel caused his death; hence the term 'Achilles heel'.

Acids and Bases. Broadly, acids are substances which when dissolved in water give a solution with a vinegary taste, which change the colour of indicator dyes (e.g. turn blue litmus red), and which neutralize bases. Bases give alkaline solutions in water, having a bitter taste and reversing the colour changes produced in indicators by acids (e.g. turn red litmus blue).

Acidic properties, normally only apparent in solution, are due to ◊ *hydrogen* ions or protons, H^+, which in water exist in chemical association with water molecules; acids are thus substances capable of releasing protons. Strong acids (e.g. hydrochloric, nitric, sulphuric) have a stronger tendency to split off ◊ *protons* than weak acids (e.g. acetic and carbonic). Metals such as zinc and iron usually release gaseous hydrogen from dilute solutions of strong acids. Acids also dissolve metallic oxides and carbonates. Reaction of acids with metals, bases, and oxides produces salts.

Conversely, a base is a substance capable of combining with protons (e.g. ammonia and the caustic alkalis). Bases can also be weak or strong. In water, bases liberate hydroxide ions (OH^-); the process of neutralization of acids by bases to produce salts is thus the combination of hydrogen and hydroxide ions to produce water molecules (H_2O).

Acis ◊ *Galatea*.

Acquired Characteristics. Also known commonly as acquired characters. Those features of an organism that result from individual experience and are not common to similar organisms, e.g. the darkening of a light skin by constant exposure to sunlight. Biologists have been much concerned with the neo-Lamarckian theory (of which Lysenko has been the outstanding modern advocate) that acquired characteristics may be inherited by offspring. Lysenko's suggestion has been rejected by western biologists on grounds of inadequate experimental rigour and his unawareness of the considerable information (◊ *Mendelism*) now available on biochemical genetics. Nevertheless cases (not ◊ *mutations*) are known in which genetic characters previously obscured have been uncovered by environmental influence. In one case, the presence of a particular sugar in the environment of bacteria results in their being able to utilize it as a food, although their parents lacked the mechanism for this; this and other similar types of genetic change result from recognized cytoplasmic and nuclear interactions, but other experiments await explanation, e.g. the fact that transfusion of blood from coloured to white fowl subsequently results in coloured offspring. ◊ *Adaptation, Darwinism, Evolution, Natural Selection*.

Acre (1191) ◊ *Crusades*.

Acropolis ◊ *Athena*.

Actinides. The series of rare metallic ◊ *elements* from ◊ *actinium* (at. no. 89) to the last element of the Periodic Classification, ◊ *lawrencium* (103); actinium, thorium, protactinium, uranium, neptunium, plutonium, americium, curium, berkelium, californium, einsteinium, fermium, mendelevium, nobelium, lawrencium. They constitute the second inner-transition series of the Periodic Classification (◊ *Lanthanides*): in them the outer electronic configuration is very similar and the elements change, in the order given, by the filling of the 5f shell of electrons. ◊ *Uranium* (at. no. 92) was the last element of Mendeleev's Periodic Table, and all those following are sometimes known as the 'Transuranium elements'; these do not occur in nature but are produced in laboratory experiments.

Actinium. ◊ *Actinides*; an element produced in trace quantities from uranium-235 by the successive loss of an α-particle and β-particle, which gives protactinium followed by the loss of a second α-particle. This is the commonest isotope (half life 22 yrs); there are some others, all radioactive. Debierne found it in the lanthanide fraction from pitchblende 1899. Much less abundant than ◊ *radium*, it is a silverywhite metal which emits a feeble blue glow in the dark. In chemical properties it resembles lanthanum.

Action Painting. A form of ◊ *abstract art*, originating in America, where Hans Hofmann, Jackson Pollock, and Willem de Kooning were among its most notable exponents. Like abstract art, action painting is non-representational, but it tends also towards automatism. Action painting is probably not wholly irrational, and some subconscious feeling for form and coherence may direct the apparently impulsive dripping and splashing of paint. The movement was short-lived, but it had considerable influence outside America. In France e.g. Karel Appel and Soulages may be said to have derived their techniques from action painting.

Actium. 31 B.C. A promontory in Greece, scene of the sea and land battle of Octavian (later Augustus) against the forces of Antony and Cleopatra. When the latter fled in panic in her ship, Antony followed her, leaving his fleet to fight on until it was overwhelmed by Octavian, who was then left master of Rome.

Act of Settlement. 1701. Provided that the succession to the British throne should devolve on the Protestant heir, Sophia of ◊ *Hanover* (whose son became George I), after the death of William III and of Queen Anne, both childless. It also limited the rights of the Crown in certain respects, e.g. consent of Parliament was necessary before war could be declared or a judge removed from office. ◊◊ *Bill of Rights.*

Act of Union. 1. 1536, the Act uniting ◊ *Wales* to England; abolished all Welsh law differing from the English, and made English the legal language.
2. 1707, the Act uniting ◊ *Scotland* to England and Wales, thus forming Gt Britain; passed during the ◊ *War of the Spanish Succession* to allay mutual suspicions, the English suspecting the ◊ *Jacobite* Scots of French sympathies and the Scots mistrusting the Hanoverian succession which already seemed likely. The Act gave Scotland 45 Members in the House of Commons and 16 (chosen as their representatives by the Scottish peerage) in the House of Lords, but did not amalgamate the ecclesiastical and legal systems (◊ *Church of Scotland, Scots Law*).
3. 1800, the Act uniting ◊ *Ireland* to Gt Britain, thus forming the U.K. Projected throughout the 18th cent. it was not passed until the suppression of the 1798 Rebellion, and then only by dint of massive and unparalleled bribery with money (nearly £3 m.), government positions, and peerages (over 50 new creations) to induce the Dublin Parliament to vote its own extinction. The Act gave Ireland 28 'representative peers' (on the Scottish model) and 100 Members in the House of Commons who might include both peers not chosen for the Lords and also holders of government office in Ireland; it resulted in almost total economic stagnation in Ireland. ◊◊ *Church of Ireland, Easter Rebellion, Irish Famine, Home Rule, Orange Society, Sinn Fein.*

Adaptation. Evolutionary changes in living organisms which enable them to survive better in a given environment; e.g. bats are conspicuously well adapted to flight and seals to swimming, although both had terrestrial ancestors. Adaptation is believed to be a consequence of ◊ *natural selection* acting upon inherited variation. ◊◊ *Acquired Characteristics, Darwinism, Evolution.*

Adder ◊ *Snake, Viper.*

Addiction ◊ *Drug Addiction.*

Aden. Area 112,075 sq. m. Pop. 1.2 m. Cap. Aden (a free port). British colony (75 sq. m.) and protectorate, on the Arabian coast of the Red Sea. The port is a great oil-tankering and coaling station on the Suez Canal route.

Adenine ◊ *DNA.*

Adhesion. In physics, the tendency of matter to cling to other matter, due to the attractive forces between the surface molecules. This force increases as the surfaces come closer together, until at very short distances the force becomes repulsive and prevents interpenetration. Adhesion is similar to cohesion, the mutual attraction between adjacent molecules of the same body. Examples of adhesion are the way a film of water remains on a solid surface, and the enormous forces required to separate optically flat surfaces.

Administrative Law. The principles and rules of law concerning the relationship of the individual to public authorities. Dicey, a 19th-cent. British jurist, insisted that administrative law was a Continental phenomenon and that in Britain officials were subject to the ordinary law; but as the area of government regulation increases, the powers of officials are constantly extended and administrative law expands. Acts of Parliament delegate to Ministers wide power to make regulations, and tribunals may be established outside the judicial system to decide the rights of individuals against public authorities, or even as between various authorities; this development is often deplored as unduly extending the powers of the Executive. In Denmark, a public official with powers of interrogation and investigation, the Ombudsman, has been appointed and specifically charged to watch the interests of the individual as against government agencies, as some check against abusive exercise of administrative powers. ◊ *By-laws*.

Admiralty. In Britain, the body responsible for naval matters since Stewart times under the First Lord of the Admiralty. In 1964 it was transformed into the Ministry of Defence for the Royal Navy.

Adonis. < Semitic *Adon*, lord. In Greek legend, a youth whose name has become synonymous with male beauty; when ◊ *Aphrodite* and ◊ *Persephone* contended for his love, Zeus ordained that each should have him for one third of each year, the remaining being his own, but Adonis spent his third, too, with Aphrodite. He was killed by a boar when hunting, and Aphrodite caused the anemone to spring up at the spot; after death, he divided his time equally between Persephone in ◊ *Hades* and Aphrodite on earth, symbolizing the half-yearly course of vegetation. His images were surrounded with 'gardens of Adonis' containing flowering plants which both grew and withered rapidly. ◊ *Tammuz*.

Adoption. Assuming the functions of a parent in respect of a person, a practice (known to ◊ *Roman Law* but not to English ◊ *Common Law*) which in Britain did not become statutory until 1926, when the Chancery Division of the High Court, County Courts, or Magistrates' Courts were authorized to make adoption orders. Any unmarried person under 21 may be adopted. In practice, most adopted children are illegitimate and are adopted while still very young. A child may be adopted by relatives, including step-parents, or by the natural mother or father if illegitimate. Courts may now dispense with the consent of parents who fail to carry out their obligations; the rights and obligations of the parents cease and pass to the adopter. The courts act on a report from the Children's Officer of the local or county authority, who thoroughly investigates the suitability of the prospective adopters. There are various societies which arrange adoptions; these must fulfil regulations prescribed in the 1958 Act. Some 1300 children are adopted each year.

Adowa. 1896. Battle during the Italian invasion of Abyssinia (◊ *Ethiopia*). The Italians advanced on Adowa, were defeated heavily by the Emperor Menelik, and lost 8000 men. The memory of this defeat was a factor in impelling Mussolini to invade Abyssinia in 1935.

Adrenalin. One of the hormones of the body produced by the gland of that name, in quantities increased at times of stress or danger by an involuntary reaction which increases the heart beat and blood pressure. Once prepared from animal glands, it is now synthesized and used mainly by injection for the relief of asthma and severe allergies.

Adrianople. A.D. 378. Battle in Thrace in which a Roman army under Emperor Valens was routed by the ◊ *Goths* (Visigoths), whose cavalry, having adopted the stirrup, ended the invincibility of the Roman foot soldier; it marked the beginning of the end of the Roman Empire.

Adsorption. Type of ◊ *adhesion* that results in a concentration of a substance on a surface separating it from another substance; e.g. the molecules of a gas or of a substance in suspension tend to accumulate on the surface of a solid with which they are in contact.

Adult Education. Available in U.K. through various evening institutes and adult-education centres, some publicly assisted e.g. extra-mural university courses, some largely voluntary e.g. the Workers' Educational Association, the Federation of Women's Institutes, and some commercial e.g. correspondence colleges, secretarial colleges. The range of subjects varies from handicrafts and vocational studies up to university-degree level. Nonvocational courses are taken by over 200,000 students (1960).

FURTHER EDUCATION: A wide variety of vocational and other courses, provided in technical, commercial, and art colleges and in evening institutes, by local education authorities, as required under the 1944 Act, for those desiring full-time or part-time education after leaving school. In England and Wales there are 125,000 full-time and 1.5 m. part-time students at over 400 full-time and about 200 part-time colleges (1960), and several university-level colleges of advanced technology (◊ College).

Adultery. Sexual intercourse by a husband or a wife with a third person; not a criminal offence, but may be a ground for divorce or judicial separation, for the making by a magistrates' court of a separation and maintenance order, and for the award of damages to a husband against the adulterer. Adultery may be inferred from circumstantial evidence which satisfies the court.

Adventists. Protestant sect (mainly in English-speaking countries) which expects the imminent second coming of Christ and his reign for 1000 years on earth. Their origin is usually ascribed to William Miller 1782–1849, who prophesied the end of the world in 1843, though they may be obscurely descended from the 17th-cent. Fifth-Monarchy men. The most active group are the Seventh Day Adventists, who keep Saturday as their day of rest. They undertake wide-scale missionary work both religious and social esp. in Africa, and claim some 10,000 members in Britain and 350,000 in the U.S.A.

Advertising. Expenditure on advertising has risen considerably in many countries since 1946 and in e.g. Canada, Sweden, Switzerland, U.K., and U.S.A. now exceeds 2 per cent of annual national income; in 1960 over £400 m. was spent (all media) in U.K. (2 per cent of national income) and £4260 m. (2.9 per cent) in U.S.A. Most advertising is designed to promote the sale of specific products by creating a mass market esp. for goods e.g. cigarettes, cosmetics, detergents, in which the differences between competing brands are often minimal. Institutional advertising – to enhance the prestige of corporations (both public and private) and political parties – has recently increased. In communist countries advertising is virtually non-existent.

A.E.C. (Atomic Energy Commission). The American equivalent of the ◊ Atomic Energy Authority, founded 1946.

Aegean Civilization ◊ Minoan Civilization, Mycenae.

Aegospotami. 405 B.C. Final battle of the ◊ Peloponnesian War. The Athenian generals had unwisely drawn their ships up on the beach at Aegospotami on the Hellespont while they went foraging; Lysander's Spartans attacked, and were able to capture the ships with scarcely a blow.

Aeneas. Trojan hero of Virgil's Aeneid; legendary ancestor of the Romans, he escaped from Troy and reached Italy after an eventful voyage during which he loved and abandoned Dido, Queen of Carthage, who committed suicide. Traditionally, this began the enmity between Rome and Carthage.

Aeolus. In Greek mythology, ruler of the winds, living in Aeolia, one of the Lipari Islands near Sicily; reputed to keep the winds in a mountain and to have invented the use of sails for ships. Greek and Roman authors give the winds various names, the best-known being Boreas (N.), Eurus (E.), Notus (S.), and Zephyrus (W.).

Aerodynamics. A branch of ◊ fluid mechanics treating the behaviour of gaseous fluids when a body moves through them. Mechanical ◊ flight is based on the reaction that occurs when a particular shape is caused to move through the air. When it is a wing or aerofoil, the reaction may be divided into two components, lift and drag. Both increase as the speed of the relative air-flow increases, but with a suitable shape the lift will be greater than the drag, and the aircraft to which it is attached will climb. F. W. Lanchester's book Aerodynamics, 1907, analysed the means by which a wing develops lift when placed in an airstream, and provided a starting-point for modern theory. Because the performance of an aircraft depends so greatly upon the relationship between lift and drag, a vast range of different shapes for wings, fuselages, engine pods, and other aircraft parts have been tested in wind tunnels. The objective always is to keep the drag to a minimum, and this is done by so designing the part that the air molecules are parted smoothly as they meet it and are then allowed to come together again smoothly as they leave it. They move in streamlines, and the body is then said to be streamlined. But as a perfectly streamlined body will not necessarily give all the lift that is required, wings may be cambered or given a curvature above and below, in order to deflect the relative air-flow downwards and so obtain an upward reaction or lift. Cambering a wing, or setting a streamlined wing at a positive angle to the air-flow, causes the air-flow to be accelerated on top of the wing and decelerated below it; this produces a reduction in pressure on top and an increase below, which is the origin of the lift. About two thirds of the lift comes from the reduced pressure on top of the wing. In ordinary level flight the aircraft is in a state of balance, with the engine thrust counterbalancing the aerodynamic drag

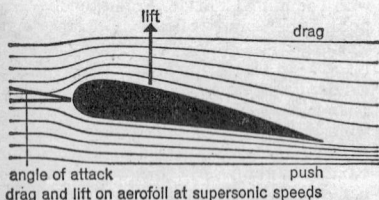

angle of attack   push
drag and lift on aerofoil at supersonic speeds

and the aerodynamic lift counterbalancing the aircraft weight, so the efficiency of an aircraft must be profoundly affected by the lift/drag ratio. In most circumstances of flight the objective will be to ensure that the air flows smoothly and does not become turbulent. Several methods have been devised for preventing or delaying turbulence, which increases the drag at the expense of the lift, from the Handley Page wing-slots to systems for sucking air into the wings or blowing air over them. The objective is always the same, to hold the air down in streamlines and to prevent it from becoming turbulent. At speeds above Mach 1 (the speed of sound, ◊ Mach Number), a new aerodynamic factor has to be taken into account, compressibility, which mostly can be ignored at low speeds. It is partly in order to postpone the onset of compressibility difficulties that the wings of high-speed aircraft are swept back. The shock waves formed by supersonic aircraft produce the sonic 'bangs' which can be heard on the ground, the main bang coming from the shock wave at the leading edges of the wings, followed by others from different parts of the aircraft. The term 'hypersonic flight' is now being used to denote flight at speeds of Mach 5 and

above, five or more times the speed of sound.

Aerolite ◊ *Meteor.*

Aeroplane. A heavier-than-air flying machine (◊ *Flight*). In the late 19th cent. man-lifting kites and gliders were steps towards the realization of powered flight. In France Clément Ader built a model whose engine lifted it off the ground 1890, but the Wrights' *Flyer*, a biplane carrying its pilot in a prone position, which first flew at Kitty Hawk U.S.A. 1903, is considered the first real aeroplane. Designers in America and France concentrated upon the biplane form until Blériot designed a monoplane in which he flew the Channel 1909, but there was a long period before the monoplane attained its later preeminence, during which triplanes were built (by Sopwith and by Fokker) and were used for military purposes. In the First World War the biplane was the form most generally adopted, both for fighters and bombers, and it was in a Vimy biplane that Alcock and Brown were the first to make an aeroplane flight non-stop across the N. Atlantic, June 1919. Between the two World Wars, commercial aviation began to develop (◊ *Aviation*), and single-plane aircraft became predominant. In the Second World War the Spitfire and the Hurricane (both powered by Rolls-Royce liquid-cooled engines) brought the piston-engined fighter to the peak of its development. ◊ *Aircraft engines* underwent a radical change with the advent of the gas-turbine engine, either for driving airscrews, as in the turbo-prop liner, the Viscount, or driving as jets, as in the first ◊ *jet-propulsion* airliner, the Comet, which carried its passengers in a pressure cabin at a speed close to that of sound and inaugurated the first passenger jet airliner service between London and Johannesburg 1952. The four-jet American Boeing 707 followed the Comet on the main airlines. In the 1950s military jet aircraft demonstrated the possibility of speeds beyond that of sound, first by diving and later by increased engine thrust. With the higher speeds, straight wings gave way to swept-back wings. The delta-plan form was adopted by some aircraft makers, and was used in the first large-size delta bomber, the Avro Vulcan. Rocket drive, introduced first by the Germans in a fighter and later experimentally by the French and the Americans, gave a fresh impetus to speed development, and the North Americans x-15 research aircraft achieved a speed of over 4000 miles an hour November 1961; this aircraft, with its ability to reach great heights and speeds, represented a transition between aircraft and spacecraft ($\diamond$ *Space Exploration*).

Aeschylus $\diamond$ *Athens, Drama, Tragedy*.

Aesculapius. Gr. Asklepios; in Greek and Roman mythology, god of medicine, son of $\diamond$ *Apollo*. His worship was possibly derived from a pre-Greek serpent cult, and his commonest symbol is a serpent twined round a staff. Cocks were sacrificed to him (as mentioned by Socrates in his last moments), and it was a custom (*incubatio*) for the sick to sleep in his temples in hope of dreams revealing curative advice; in Rome the special seat of his worship was an island in the Tiber, where a hospital still stands.

Aesir. In Scandinavian mythology, a group of 12 chief gods, presided over by $\diamond$ *Odin* or Woden (> Wednesday), who lived in Asgard, their celestial home. They are usually enumerated as Odin; Thor (> Thursday), Odin's son, god of thunder, whose emblem is a hammer; Tiw (> Tuesday), Odin's son, wisdom; $\diamond$ *Balder* ('the beautiful'), a sun-god; Hoder, a blind god; Loki, the god of mischief and destruction; Hermoder, Odin's messenger; Bragi, the god of poetry; Vidar, the god of silence; Hoenir, who helped to create mankind; Vali, Odin's youngest son; and Odnir. The goddesses, inc. Frigga (Odin's wife and 'mother of the Gods') and Freya or Freyja (> Friday), another wife of Odin and goddess of love and beauty, were not counted among the Aesir. Heimdall (a god of light, who guarded the bridge protecting Asgard and finally slew Loki) was associated with another group of gods, the Vanir.

Aesthetics. In philosophy, consideration of the nature of works of art and their definition and of human response to them and to 'beauty' in general, and the formation of criteria for artistic judgement. It has tended to be an abstract discussion of beauty – or art criticism lacking the generality and neutrality of philosophy – and often has been psychological inquiry issuing in e.g. the theory that aesthetic experience involves projection of one's own feelings on to a work of art. In many definitions art is in essence a symbolization of emotion, e.g. to Croce a real work

of art is a vision or sensuous intuition which the artist reproduces so that others may share it; another view is that no definition covering all art forms is possible, judgements being allegedly only of a work's 'objective' qualities e.g. beauty, or based solely on convention, or expressive only of the critic's attitudes and emotions.

In art history, a 'philosophy of beauty' or 'aesthetic' emerged when works of art acquired a significance beyond the simply utilitarian, decorative, symbolic, or magical – e.g. in the 5th cent. B.C. in Athens and the 9th cent. A.D. in China – and was extended from art to nature esp. landscape. Plato's theory that all art imitates either nature or supranatural ideas was the basis for most later aesthetics, and later periods esp. the 19th cent. echoed his preoccupation with the influence of art on society. However, though e.g. changes in taste and style, religious and social effects of art, development of art theories, may be studied dispassionately, aesthetic appreciation depends on individual subjective judgement. Before the Second World War Berenson's theory based on tactile values, or Fry's and Bell's concerned with significant form, were popular, but they are now as widely discredited as the 18th-cent. theories of Winckelmann, Lessing, Burke, Kames. More recent theories from e.g. Sir Herbert Read, André Malraux have been based on the study of anthropology and psychology.

Afghanistan. Area 250,000 sq. m. Pop. about 12 m. (about 2 m. nomadic tribesmen). Cap. Kabul. Rel. mainly Muslim. The government is a constitutional monarchy. Governmental powers are vested in the Council of Ministers, nearly all the members of which are relatives of the king. There is a Senate of 50 members nominated by the king, a National Assembly of 171 elected members, and a Grand Assembly summoned at irregular intervals to make important decisions on policy matters. The reigning king is Mohammed Zahir Shah. The official languages are Persian and Pushtu.

Only about five per cent of the land is cultivated, but Afghanistan is virtually self-supporting in foodstuffs and there is a flourishing export trade in Persian lamb skins. Oil has been discovered near the Soviet border; recently hydroelectric and irrigation schemes have been started with U.S. help. In 1956 the U.S.S.R. granted a credit of $100 m. A large U.N. Technical Aid Mission has been assisting the government in technical and medical projects since 1950.

AFL/CIO ◊ *American Federation of Labor.*

African Languages. Apart from ◊ *Arabic* and Coptic (◊ *Copts*), there are four main groups.

BERBER-CUSHITE: Berber languages include *Tuareg* (spoken by the Bedouin of the Sahara), *Shluh* (the vernacular of S. Morocco), and *Kabyl* (in the mountains of Algeria and Tunis); Cushite languages include *Somali, Galla,* and *Beja* (widely spoken in Ethiopia and the E. horn of Africa between the Nile and the Red Sea).

SUDANESE-GUINEAN: A medley of Negro languages covering a wide belt across the Sudan from Gambia to Kenya, e.g. *Ewe* (Togoland and part of Ghana, also as an extensive ◊ *lingua franca*), *Ibo* (SE Nigeria), *Hausa* (central Sudan and N. Nigeria, recently of increased importance as a commercial medium), *Efik, Mandingo, Mende, Nubian, Twi,* and *Yoruba.*

BANTU: S. of the 'Bantu line' crossing the Congo jungle obliquely W. to E. from the Gulf of Cameroon to Mombasa, probably containing an unknown admixture of non-Negro elements; by far the most important is *Swahili* (Ar. *Suahiliyi,* of the coasts), originally the speech of Zanzibar and the adjacent mainland and long a commercial medium throughout central Africa, which has acquired prestige as the medium of instruction in the schools of Kenya, Tanganyika, and parts of the Congo.

HOTTENTOT-BUSHMAN (Khoin): *Nama* (Hottentot) and *San* (Bushman), spoken in the sparsely populated desert and scrub of SW Africa; distinguished by suction sounds or clicks, of which San has 7 and Nama 4.

African Peoples and Cultures. The indigenous population of Africa may be roughly divided into four groups, by race and language. North of a line from Senegal to Somalia most of the population consists of peoples of Caucasoid (Europiform) race, speaking Hamitic or Semitic languages; they include Arabs, Berbers, Tuareg, and other Saharan peoples and the Somali and Galla in E. Africa, and most of them are Muslims. In the far SW of the continent are the Bushmen and Hottentots, speaking 'click' languages and today numbering only a few thousands. Between these groups is the bulk of the population, consisting of various Negro peoples, speaking Sudanic, Nilotic, Bantu, and other languages and varying considerably in physical features and cultures; with them may be included the few remaining Pygmies of the Congo forests. Lastly there is the Malaysian population of the island of Madagascar. None of these groupings is completely pure in any 'racial' sense: there has been continual physical intermingling for millennia, through migration and conquest and consequent wide dispersal of cultures and languages.

The economies, political and family organizations, and religions of Africa vary immensely. Bushmen and Pygmies are hunters and gatherers only. In the arid parts of the Sahara, Somalia, and other parts of E. Africa live pastoralists keeping cattle or camels. Elsewhere are agriculturalists, in the forested areas growing yams and other root crops and elsewhere growing grains (millets, maize, and some rice). Settlement is typically of small scattered ◊ *kinship* villages, although occasional towns are found, mainly in the large trading centres of W. Africa which were the seats of kings.

The most common traditional form of political organization is that of clans; a tribe consists of many clans related only by allegiance to a common mythical founding-ancestor and lacking centralized political authority. However, some African societies have kings, notably in W. Africa, Uganda, and S. Africa; some of these societies number several million and are often compared to large feudal states.

The indigenous religions include ancestor worship and cults of the earth and of various deities. Beliefs in a creator High God are virtually universal, as are beliefs in the powers of witches and sorcerers. Today Christianity and Islam are widespread and increasing in importance, weakening the traditional faiths, which are based largely on clan and tribal units which are now breaking down.

Traditional patterns of African life are changing rapidly today, especially with the growth of industrial towns: movements of labour from rural to urban areas affect indigenous life seriously, and although tribalism is still a strong force it is on the wane, with class and nationality becoming ever more important. ◊ *African Languages.*

Afrikaans. Variant (Taal) of Dutch, spoken by some 3 m. Boers in the Union of S. Africa, developed from the 17th-cent. Dutch of the early settlers, which became simplified as a result of isolation and through contact with other languages (Portuguese, French, German, English). The definite article has become invariable, as in English, the verb inflexions have been simplified, and parts of speech have been interchanged, but the vocabulary remains predominantly Dutch. ◊ *Germanic Languages.*

Agamemnon. In Greek legend, king of Mycenae; son of Atreus; husband of Clytaemnestra (sister of ◊ *Helen*); father of ◊ *Iphigenia*, Electra, and ◊ *Orestes*; brother of Helen's husband Menelaus. He led the Greek forces against the Trojans; his quarrel over Briseis caused ◊ *Achilles* to withdraw for a time from the war; he took ◊ *Cassandra* to Greece, where Clytaemnestra (who in his absence had taken his cousin Aegistheus as her lover) murdered him.

Agar ◊ *Gelatin.*

Agate. Form of chalcedonic ◊ *silica* filling cavities in lavas, cut and polished for brooches, snuff-boxes, etc. It usually has bands of different colours, occasionally well marked but sometimes changing imperceptibly from one colour to another. Sources of supply are S. Germany, India, and Perthshire (where the stones are called 'Scotch pebbles'). ◊ *Obsidian.*

Agave. Of the *Amaryllidaceae*; a large genus of tropical and southern American plants including the century plant or American aloe. They have short thick stems crowned by a rosette of fleshy waxy leaves. During the vegetative period they store reserves and eventually produce a large inflorescence up to 20 ft tall. After fruiting the plant dies. Under poor conditions the plants grow slowly and take years to mature (hence 'century plants'). They were introduced to Europe in the 16th cent. The Mexican drink pulque is produced by fermenting the sap exuding usually from the young decapitated inflorescence stalk. Mescal is a spirit distilled from pulque; tequila is a type of mescal. Various species are important as fibre plants esp. *A. sisalana*, the sisal-hemp.

Agency for International Development (A.I.D.). U.S. government agency set up in 1961 to organize U.S. economic aid to other countries.

Age of Reason ◊ *Encyclopédie, Enlightenment, Physiocrats.*

Agglutinins, Agglutinogens ◊ *Blood Groups.*

Agincourt. 1415. English victory over the French in the ◊ *Hundred Years War* which ensured Henry V's conquest of France. Although short of supplies and greatly outnumbered, the superiority in tactics and discipline of Henry's troops and their use of the long bow against armoured knights proved decisive.

Agnosticism ◊ *Atheism.*

Agriculture. Cultivation of the soil as pasture and for the production of crops, including grass for hay as well as e.g. wheat, maize, rice, tea, coffee, sugar-cane, and non-food crops e.g. cotton, flax, jute, and tobacco. In modern usage agriculture is understood to mean the entire science, art, and practice of farming, embracing both tillage and the rearing of livestock, and even forestry and fur-farming.

Prehistoric man first advanced beyond the role of hunter and food gatherer during the Neolithic age, when he began to till the soil and domesticate animals. By Roman times agriculture had passed through thousands of years of trial and error, and embodied advanced techniques such as crop rotation, without having evolved any scientific explanation for them. In England during the Middle Ages farming was based on the 'three-field' system: arable land was divided into units of three fields, which followed a fixed rotation, two of them carrying different crops while the third lay fallow. Outstanding improvements were made in the 18th cent. Jethro Tull showed the importance of thorough cultivation of the soil, sowing in drills or rows instead of broadcasting seed; the 'three-field' system was replaced by the Norfolk or four-phase rotation of crops. Leguminous crops, e.g. clover, and root crops, e.g. turnips, played their part in raising productivity, and crop yields were more than double those of the medieval farms. Robert Bakewell demonstrated how to improve livestock by selective breeding, which led later to the export of British cattle and sheep to new farming lands in the Americas and Australasia.

In the first half of the 19th cent. farming had begun to progress along scientific lines. Productivity was increased by the use of fertilizers such as guano, nitrate of soda, and superphosphates. Other developments included the preparation of animal feeds, the improvement of cereals and other crops by plant breeding, the treatment of plant and animal diseases, the manufacture of new types of agricultural machinery, and the application of new methods of land drainage. The keynote of modern agriculture, mechanization, was first introduced on a large scale in U.S.A. The tractor has replaced the horse or ox as the basic power-unit; new types of ploughs, planters, cultivators, fertilizer-distributors, and harvesters have been invented and manufactured; aircraft are employed to spray chemicals on growing crops to protect them from pests and diseases. Nevertheless, on millions of peasant holdings throughout the world there has been no agricultural progress for centuries. ◊ *Calcium, Fertilizers, Insecticides, Irrigation.*

Ainu. Aboriginal people of Hokkaido Island, N. Japan, Caucasoid in ◊ *race.* Apparently a long-isolated offshoot of the main Caucasoid stock, they have long been in close contact with the Japanese and are largely incorporated into the main Japanese population. They are famed for their hairiness and for their dances and rituals in which men portray the bear, a sacred animal in their cosmology.

Aircraft-carrier. Large warship which to some considerable extent has taken the place of the battleship in modern naval strategy, employing bomber aircraft as its main striking power instead of heavy guns. The largest aircraft-carrier afloat is the U.S.S. *Enterprise,* completed 1961, overall length 1101 ft and displacement 83,350 tons, with nuclear-powered engines of 280,000 S H P giving a speed of 33 knots.

Aircraft Engines. In its early stages the development of aircraft was based on internal-combustion engines using petrol; later on gas turbines using paraffin or petrol. French engine-makers were the leaders in the pioneer period, and most of the early constructors, including eventually the Wright brothers, took advantage of the light weights and relatively high powers of the French designs. Rotary petrol engines, e.g. the Gnôme, with crank-case and cylinders rotating about a fixed crank-shaft, were extensively used in the ◊ *First World War.* Then came the radial and in-line engines, of the stationary types and either air-cooled or liquid-cooled. The gas turbine (outcome of the work of

e.g. Ernst Heinkel, Dr A. A. Griffith, and Sir Frank Whittle) gave aviation a new power system used to drive airscrews in turbo-prop versions and to provide direct jet thrust in turbo-jet versions. A variant of the turbo-jet is the dual-flow or by-pass engine used in some large airliners; air entering the engine is divided into two streams, one flowing along an annular duct around the central engine and the other through the central engine, which join at the efflux. For experimental aircraft and for some standard fighters, rocket motors were developed, differing from other kinds of engine in that they carry their own oxygen supply. ◊ *Jet Propulsion, Rocket.*

Airship. Balloon provided with a means of propulsion and steering. There are three types: non-rigid; semi-rigid i.e. with a keel; fully rigid, in which a frame contains a number of gas bags. After Giffard's moderate success with steam-powered dirigibles, German and French designers turned to the internal-combustion engine. A young Brazilian, Santos-Dumont, did much to publicize the airship in the early 1900s. In the ◊ *First World War* the Germans made extensive use of large rigid airships of the ◊ *Zeppelin* type, but the vulnerability of its hydrogen-filled gas bags made them a military failure. Britain developed non-rigid airships, which proved of value for coastal patrol and anti-submarine work, and later built large rigid airships, the R 33 and R 34, based on German designs; the R 34 was the first aircraft to cross the Atlantic from Britain to America, July 1919. Britain's most ambitious airship ventures were the R 100 and the R 101, launched 1929–30, but the R 101 crashed in France on its maiden voyage and was destroyed. In spite of using non-inflammable helium in place of hydrogen, U.S.A. experience followed a similar disastrous pattern, with the loss of the *Akron* 1933 and the *Macon* 1935, since when no large rigid airships have been built.

Ajax (Ajas). In Greek mythology, the name of two heroes of the Trojan war. **1.** The Telamonian Ajax. After the death of ◊ *Achilles,* Ajax disputed with ◊ *Ulysses* for the possession of the dead hero's armour; when it was awarded to Ulysses, in a fury Ajax slaughtered a flock of sheep under the impression that they were his enemies who had made the award, and afterwards, ashamed, he committed suicide.

2. The Locrian (or Lesser) Ajax. He violated ◊ *Cassandra* after the fall of Troy; shipwrecked on his homeward journey, he swam to a rock and boasted that he was safe in spite of the gods, whereupon ◊ *Poseidon* struck the rock with his trident, the part on which Ajax stood fell off, and he was drowned.

Akkadians. Semitic people of the northern part of ancient Babylonia, named after their city of Akkad (Agade); in the 3rd millennium B.C. Sargon I, King of Akkad, established control over the whole of Mesopotamia. Akkadian was for long the chief commercial and diplomatic language in the Near East. ◊ *Babylon.*

Alabaster. Fine-grained form of ◊ *gypsum,* calcium sulphate; usually snow-white or very light-coloured, sometimes yellow or reddish. Used in statuary, light-fittings, and as a stone for interior decoration, being easy to carve and susceptible of a high polish.

ORIENTAL ALABASTER: Stalactitic calcium carbonate (◊ *Stalactite*) extensively used by the ancient Egyptians in temples and sarcophagi.

Alamein. 1942. In the ◊ *Second World War,* Rommel's Afrika Korps had driven the British 8th Army back to El Alamein, 70 miles from Alexandria. Here the British under Montgomery were able to build up a superiority of ground and especially of air forces. The battle began on 23 Oct. After fierce fighting British tanks finally broke through the enemy line on 5 Nov. and destroyed half Rommel's tank force, taking 30,000 prisoners. It was the first major British victory of the war, and the turning point in German fortunes in N. Africa.

Albania. Area 10,700 sq. m. Pop. 1.5 m. Cap. Tirana. Rel. mainly Muslim. Independent republic ruled by the Communist Party, of which Enver Hoxha has been the undisputed leader since 1945.

ECONOMY. Albania is a hilly, backward country with primitive agriculture but endowed with some mineral resources (copper, petroleum, coal) so far little developed.

HISTORY. In the 15th cent. despite a heroic stand by Skanderbeg Albania fell under Ottoman rule until it became an independent princedom in 1913, a republic 1918-28, and a kingdom under King Zog 1928-39. Invaded by Italy in 1939, from then until 1945 it was under Italian and German control. After 1945 it emerged as a people's democracy. Britain broke off relations after an incident in which a British destroyer was sunk by an Albanian mine in 1946. After 1954 Albania failed to follow the pattern of 'destalinization' and has remained in ideological opposition to Moscow with the full support of communist China. The present government is probably the first in Albanian history to establish its authority throughout the country.

LANGUAGE. Albanian, the smallest extant branch of the ◊ *Indo-European languages.* Its origins are in doubt, since no literature other than religious documents survives older than the 17th cent.

Albedo. In astronomy, the ratio of the light that a planet or satellite reflects to the amount of sunlight falling on it, and thus a measure of the reflecting power of the body and its atmosphere.

Albigenses. A sect, taking its name from Albi in France, not strictly Christian but deriving from the Cathari (pure ones) of the dualist and gnostic Manichaean creed, practising abstemious life and strict chastity, the full initiates (Perfecti) being bound by severe ascetic rules. They proselytized widely in Italy and France in the 11th and 12th centuries, and were denounced for ◊ *heresy* but supported by local magnates esp. the counts of Toulouse. In 1208 Pope Innocent III proclaimed the Albigensian Crusade (led by the elder Simon de Montfort), and the legal investigations led to the ◊ *Inquisition.* After 100 years the movement as such was finally crushed, but its puritan ideals were not without influence in the beginnings of the ◊ *Reformation.* ◊ *Dualism, Gnostics, Manichaeism.*

Albino. Person suffering from a marked deficiency of pigment in the skin, hair, and eyes; in the latter the blood vessels of the iris show through and give a pinkish appearance. Albinism, which is inherited as a recessive characteristic, also occurs in animals and plants; races of albino animals have been experimentally produced. In some countries albino animals are regarded as sacred e.g. white elephants in Thailand.

Albumin ◊ *Blood.*

Alcestis. In Greek legend, the wife of Admetus, king of Pherae and a hero of the Argonaut expedition (◊ *Golden Fleece*). The ◊ *Fates* agreed to postpone the death of Admetus if he could find someone to die in his place; Alcestis agreed to do so, and subsequently was brought back from ◊ *Hades* by ◊ *Hercules* and restored to her husband. The legend is the subject of a play by Euripides.

Alcohol. A class of organic compounds having the general formula R–OH, where R is the radical containing carbon and hydrogen in varying proportions and where OH stands for one of several hydroxyl groups; alcohols are described as primary, secondary, tertiary according to the number of radicals involved. Alcohols differ considerably in their properties, and at normal temperatures range from volatile liquids to solids. ◊ *Ethyl Alcohol, Methyl Alcohol, Proof Spirit.*

Alcoholism. Poisoning by drinking alcohol in great quantity. If methyl (wood) alcohol is taken blindness may ensue. Alcoholism may be a temporary disorder produced by a short drinking bout, or a chronic ailment due to the effects on the organs and tissues of continued excessive drinking. The latter may lead to delirium tremens and degeneration of the liver, and is a serious illness difficult to cure. Social rehabilitation is all-important. A lay organization known as Alcoholics Anonymous (founded 1934 in U.S.A.) has proved effective in helping alcoholics.

Aldehydes. < *Al*cohol *dehyd*rogenated, a class of organic compounds obtained when primary alcohols are oxidized. Further oxidation converts them into acids. Each has in its formula the characteristic group —CHO. Aldehydes are used in the preparation of a variety of industrial and commercial products, including synthetic resins and plastics, dyestuffs, disinfectants, and drugs. The simplest of them, formaldehyde, is a gas, but formalin, its solution in water, is a well-known preservative. Some aldehydes e.g. vanillin (vanilla) are useful as flavouring agents.

Alder. *Alnus glutinosa*; a common catkin-bearing tree growing in wet ground in the British Isles and Europe. The wood is soft and easily worked and at one time was extensively used for clogs and any object required to withstand immersion in water. It was also used for smoking herrings, and its charcoal for gunpowder.

Ale ◊ *Brewing*.

Alexandrine ◊ *Hexameter*.

Algae. Plants of the group *Thallophyta*, including pond scums, ◊ *plankton*, and seaweeds; the characteristic vegetation of the seas. They are photosynthetic, but may have brown, red, or blue-green pigments masking the ◊ *chlorophyll*; most are aquatic. Some are motile; others have diverse shape, size, and structure, but most have motile ◊ *spores* or ◊ *gametes*. Seaweeds are predominantly brown algae e.g. wrack and kelps in shallow waters. The largest are the giant kelps and sargassum weeds, many yards long, a source of ◊ *iodine*. Some red seaweeds (growing in deeper water) are used medicinally, as a culture medium, or in certain gelatinous food products e.g. ice-cream. Brown seaweeds are used as ◊ *fertilizers*. Green (predominantly freshwater) algae are the most varied in form and structure. There are several other groups, some of which esp. ◊ *diatoms* occur as plankton, a major food source for marine life. The flagellates (swimming by flagella) are notable as being intermediate between primitive animals and primitive plants, with chlorophyll but no cell wall.

Algebra. A method of generalizing mathematical statements by substituting symbols (letters) for numbers and evolving formulae which lead to the solution of problems of a practical or theoretical nature; foremost amongst these is the solution of ◊ *equations*.

Regarded in this sense, the quantities concerned in algebra obey fundamental laws: (1) Commutative (a) addition $a+b=b+a$; (b) multiplication $a\times b=b\times a$. (2) Associative (a) addition $a+(b+c)=(a+b)+c$; (b) multiplication $a\times(b\times c)=(a\times b)\times c$. (3) Distributive $a\times(b+c)=a\times b+a\times c$.

Algeria. Area 855,000 sq. m. Pop. 10.5 m. Cap. Algiers. Rel. Muslim. Independent N. African republic, between Morocco, Tunisia, and Libya.

ECONOMY. Chiefly agricultural, main exports cereals, edible oils, fruits, tobacco, wine; but industries are developing, with rising exports of iron and zinc ores, natural methane gas, petroleum, and phosphates. A new oil pipeline is planned. The large rural population is illiterate and barely self-supporting, with a very high birthrate.

HISTORY. In early times the area shared the history of the rest of the fertile Mediterranean coast of Africa, and was in turn held by the Romans, Vandals, Arabs, and

Turks. As the Barbary Coast it was a haven for pirates in the 18th cent. When conquered by France in 1830 it was sparsely populated and had no political entity. Under French rule the population increased rapidly, and during the Second World War a strong nationalist movement developed which rejected the established French policy of gradually assimilating Algeria to France, under which (since 1870) Algerian deputies and senators sat in the French Parliament. The French settlers (*colons*) were insistent that Algeria remain 'indissolubly linked' with France. Active rebellion broke out in 1954; until 1959 the French poured men and resources into combating the rebels. When de Gaulle came to power he offered to negotiate with the rebel organization but they refused. A year later he renewed his offer, this time agreeing to a referendum on independence or a link with France. The *colons* organized the O.A.S. (Organisation de l'Armée Secrète), which with the connivance or help of French generals tried by terrorism and disobedience to sabotage any agreement between de Gaulle and the Algerian nationalists. Nevertheless, agreement was reached at Évian in 1962, after a referendum overwhelmingly in favour of independence, and Ben Bella became the first Prime Minister of the Algerian republic, the French retaining military and naval bases, and agreeing to share the oil gas of the Sahara and to finance a three-year plan of technical aid and development. Of the million and a quarter French in Algeria, over a million have left in the past few years; the large estates have been nationalized. The economic situation has consequently deteriorated and would be still worse without massive French assistance.

Alien. Resident in or visitor to a country where he or she is not legally regarded as a subject. Under U.K. law an alien may not hold public office, be employed in government services or armed forces, vote at elections, or own a share in a British ship or aircraft; resident aliens are required to register. The Home Secretary, at his discretion or on the recommendation of a court, may order any alien to be deported. An alien may not land in the U.K. without leave of an Immigration Officer, or elsewhere than at an approved port (except when serving in a ship or aircraft).

Alienation. 1. Term used in psychiatry to refer to loss of memory, feelings of unreality, and states of depersonalization. Physicians dealing with such states used to be known as alienists.

2. *Verfremdung,* 'alienation', 'estrangement'; a theatrical term much used in connexion with the plays of Bertolt Brecht. It is a principle which – contrary to the Aristotelian idea of *catharsis* or purging – insists on 'distancing' the audience from the events shown on the stage in such a way as to preserve the spectator's sense of judgement and to encourage a desire to change the course of life outside the theatre. Alienation is achieved by various writing, acting, and production effects and techniques. ✧ *Berliner Ensemble, Epic Theatre.*

Alimentary Tract ◊ *Digestion, Intestine.*

Aliphatic Compounds. The study of organic chemistry was earlier divided into that of the aliphatic (fatty) bodies and that of the aromatic (fragrant), a division which for various reasons is still retained, the aliphatic being mainly compounds containing carbon atoms joined in straight or branched open chains and derived from natural ◊ *petroleum,* and the aromatic mainly ring-structure compounds formerly derived from coal-tar and a large number of them derivatives of ◊ *benzene.* Many aromatic compounds are now synthesized from materials provided by the petrochemical industry, and the two branches overlap considerably, but the general properties of aromatic substances e.g. nitration, sulphonation, etc. are distinct from those of the aliphatics.

Alizarin. Colouring-matter derived from madder root, in which it occurs as a ◊ *glucose* derivative (✧ *Carbohydrates, Indigo*); one of the anthraquinone group of dyestuffs, its synthesis was an early triumph of 19th-cent. chemistry. It is used with a mordant (◊ *Dyes*); the shade of colour obtained depends on the metal oxide used.

Alkali. A substance which dissolves in water to give a solution with a caustic soap-like taste, changes the colour of indicator dyes e.g. litmus and neutralizes ◊ *acids.*

ALKALI METALS: Group 1A of the Periodic Classification (◊ *Elements*): ◊ *Lithium, Sodium, Potassium, Rubidium, Caesium, Francium.*

ALKALINE EARTH METALS: Group 2A of the Periodic Classification (◊ *Ele-*

ments): ◊ *Calcium, Strontium, Barium, Radium.* Their oxides ('earths'), except that of radium, were recognized long before the metals were produced.

ALKALI INDUSTRY ◊ *Sodium.*

Alkaloids. Nitrogenous organic bases, usually of somewhat complex structure, extracted from certain parts of plants. Alkaloids are derived from vegetable sources, and botanically related plants commonly yield similar alkaloids. Many alkaloids provoke a physiological reaction when ingested by man or animals. In man, particular alkaloids may be poisonous or medically useful according to dosage. Cocaine from leaves of *Erythroxylon coca* is a local anaesthetic, atropine from deadly nightshade (*Atropa belladonna*) is a mydriatic. Emetine from ipecacuanha root is used in amoebic dysentery, morphine from juice of the opium poppy is analgesic. Quinine from the bark of the cinchona (S. America) is an anti-malarial drug. Strychnine from seeds of an Indian tree *Strychnos nux vomica* is poisonous or in small amounts acts as a stimulant.

The alkaloids have been the subject of chemical and physiological investigation since the early 19th cent. The first problem was their isolation, and some members of the opium group were obtained in a pure condition at an early date. Work on these compounds became the basis of the chemistry of the principal ◊ *nitrogen*-containing ring systems. The study of their modes of origin in the plant is a rapidly developing aspect of biochemistry. The medicinal value of quinine, morphine, and cocaine stimulated the search for similar synthetic drugs both more readily available and possessing more suitable balanced properties.

Allah. < Ar. *al-ilah*, the god; Muslim name for the Supreme Being (◊ *Islam*).

Allegory. A figurative narrative or description in which one or more meanings are embodied parallel to but distinct from the literal sense. The form may be either literary or pictorial (as in allegorical painting) and may be said to include the Fable, in which a moral is pointed from the conduct of animals. Allegory at its most formal is to be found in the secular and theological literature of the Middle Ages, notably in the 13th-cent. French poem *Roman de la Rose*, and the 14th-cent. English *Piers Plowman*, which can be regarded, at least in part, as a 'fourfold

allegory' (open to interpretation at four levels). Apart from Spenser's *Faerie Queene*, Bunyan's *Pilgrim's Progress*, and some of the poems of George Herbert, most later allegories which are still read are satirical; the best-known examples of the 17th and 18th centuries are Dryden's *Absalom and Achitophel* and Swift's *Gulliver's Travels* and *Tale of a Tub.* These, in their looseness of form and the variety of their satirical targets, are remote from the continuous allegorical narrative of the medieval type. Among 20th-cent. novels, George Orwell's *Animal Farm*, T. F. Powys's *Mr Weston's Good Wine*, and Franz Kafka's *The Trial* and *The Castle* can all be described as allegorical.

Allergy ◊ *Histamine.*

Alligator. Reptile of the same family as the ◊ *crocodile* and closely resembling it in appearance, development, and habit. Distribution is limited to tropical America (where it is called caiman) and China. The female lays up to 80 eggs, about the size of a duck's, in large nests. At maturity the male may measure 15 ft, the female 8.

Alloys. Metals each consisting of a single element e.g. iron or aluminium may not always possess the properties of strength, heat insulation, electrical conductivity, weldability etc. required for a particular use; the addition of other elements may meet these requirements, and the metal is then known as an alloy. Aluminium in its pure state is a metal of low strength; when alloyed with copper and magnesium, it becomes very strong. The elements added are usually other metals, but a few nonmetals such as carbon, silicon, and phosphorus are often used e.g. in steel. An alloy may be a compound, a solid solution, or a mixture of both. Sometimes the presence of very minute quantities of alloying substances greatly modifies the properties of a metal.

ANTIMONIAL LEAD: Lead containing 7–14 per cent antimony. Resistant to the action of sulphuric acid, and therefore used for accumulator plates.

BELL METAL: Copper with 20 per cent tin. Sonorous but brittle.

BRASS: Most brass is copper with 20–35 per cent zinc, but proportions vary.

BRITANNIA METAL: Tin with 5 per cent antimony, 1 per cent copper.

BRONZE: Most bronze is copper with 5–8 per cent tin. Phosphorbronze contains also up to 0.5 per cent phosphorus, used for castings and bearings. Aluminium bronze is copper with 3–10 per cent aluminium.

CUPRONICKEL: Copper with 25 per cent nickel. Now used for 'silver' coinage in the U.K.

DURALUMIN: One of the first aluminium alloys. The metal is hardened with 4 per cent copper and 0.5 per cent each of magnesium and manganese.

DUTCH METAL: A brass that in leaf form looks like gold-leaf.

ELEKTRON: Light magnesium alloy with 4.5 per cent zinc, 0.5 per cent copper.

FUSIBLE ALLOYS: These have very low melting points – usually below 100° C. Chief ingredients are lead, tin, bismuth, and sometimes cadmium. Wood's metal has 50 per cent bismuth, 25 per cent lead, the rest cadmium and tin in roughly equal proportions. Melts between 60° and 70° C.

GERMAN SILVER: Also called 'nickel silver'. Has copper with 10–30 per cent nickel and a little zinc. Commonly used for latchkeys and as a base for silver-plated articles. E.P.N.S. stands for 'electroplated nickel silver'.

GUNMETAL: Copper with 8–10 per cent tin, 2–4 per cent zinc.

MONEL: Nickel with about 30 per cent copper and small quantities of iron and manganese. Very tough, and resists corrosion.

NICHROME: Nickel with about 20 per cent each of chromium and iron. Has high m.p. and is commonly used for the elements of electric fires.

PEWTER: Formerly contained tin with 20 per cent lead and perhaps a little antimony. Modern pewter is more like Britannia metal (see above). It contains no lead, but 5–20 per cent antimony and a little copper.

SILVER STEEL ◊ *Iron and Steel Industry.*

SPECULUM: Copper with 30–40 per cent tin. Polishes well, and was formerly used for mirrors of reflecting telescopes.

TYPE-METAL: Lead with 11–20 per cent antimony and a little tin. Has a low melting point, and the molten alloy expands when solidifying. Thus it takes a sharp impression from a mould. ◊ *Bismuth.*

WHITE GOLD: Gold alloyed with nickel or tellurium. Looks like platinum.
◊ *Metallurgy.*

Almond. Kernel obtained from the fruit of a tree, *Prunus amygdalus*, resembling the peach and bearing very decorative blossoms. One variety gives sweet almonds, another bitter. From the latter is extracted almond oil used as a flavouring. Sweet almonds are grown in quantity in Italy, Spain, and the U.S.A.

FLOWERING ALMOND: Several varieties of the same family, widely grown as a decorative shrub or tree.

Almoravides ◊ *Ommayads.*

Aloe ◊ *Agave.*

Alpaca ◊ *Llama.*

Alphabet. System of representing speech sound by means of characters. The Roman alphabet of western Europe is descended, by way of Greek, from the Phoenician alphabet, which itself developed from the Egyptian hieroglyphs; these were originally conventionalized pictograms (signs representing things) and later ideograms (representing ideas), and from about 1600 B.C. came to be associated with sounds e.g. the conventional picture of the sun was used to represent also the spoken syllable *re*, which then might form part of a word. (A similar process took place in Babylonian and Assyrian ◊ *cuneiform*, 'wedge writing'.) The northern Semitic peoples took over these syllable-symbols and adapted them to form the Phoenician syllabary. The next was the decisive step: the syllable symbols became associated with only the first sound of each syllable, thus *aleph* (ox), *beth* (house), *grimel* (corner, or camel), and *daleth* (door) became sound-symbols i.e. letters. From this Phoenician alphabet of 22 consonants came all alphabets: Arabic, Cyrillic (Russian, Bulgarian), Greek, Hebrew, Hindi, Latin, Urdu, and the rest, however different they may now appear.

The Greeks took their alphabet from the Phoenician traders, adapting it to their own needs: half of the 22 letters (b, g, d, z, k, l, m, n, p, r, t) stood for sounds that Phoenicians and Greeks had in common, and these were adopted with little change. However, since the 22 Phoenician letters were all consonants, the Greeks adapted or invented A, E, I, O, Y to denote vowels. According to Herodotus, it was ◊ *Cadmus* who brought the Phoenician alphabet to Greece, soon after 1400 B.C. Extra letters were invented by Palamedes (the 'handy' or 'contriving' man), who served with ◊ *Agamemnon* in the Trojan

cuneiform characters	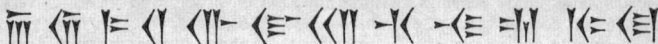
hieroglyphics	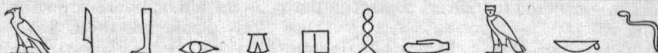
phoenician	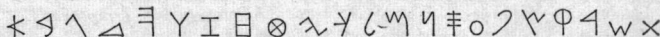
runic	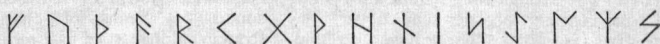
cyrillic (russian)	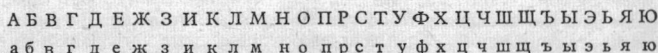
arabic	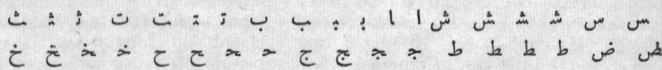
greek	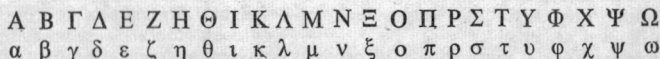

War 1193–1183 B.C. Like Phoenician, the earliest Greek script was written from right to left; later it was written *boustrophedon* ('as the ox turns' i.e. in ploughing), right to left and left to right in alternate lines. In both styles the letters sometimes began at the bottom and ran upwards.

The first Latin alphabet of 21 letters (our present alphabet without G, J, V, W, Y), the basis for half the alphabets now in use in the western world, came from Greek by way of Etruscan; the Ciceronian (classical) Latin alphabet (23 letters, with no J, V, W) was brought to Britain first by Imperial legionaries and later by Roman missionaries; in early times the Common Germanic futhorc (◊ *Runes*), a modification of Greek and Latin letters straightened for carving on beech-wood, was used in Britain.

INITIAL TEACHING ALPHABET: An interesting recent innovation of 44 symbols ('augmented Roman alphabet') devised by Sir James Pitman for facilitating the teaching of reading English for beginners. ◊ *Phonetics*.

Alpha Particle. Composite particle consisting of two ◊ *neutrons* and two ◊ *protons* tightly bound together. Alpha particles are emitted when certain radioactive nuclides decay. Each alpha particle has a positive charge of 2e (e is the magnitude of the charge on the electron) and is identical with the nucleus of the Helium atom $_2^4$ He. ◊ *Beta Particles, Radiation*.

Alpheus ◊ *Arethusa, Augean Stables*.

Alps. Mountain system in Switzerland and parts of neighbouring countries, extending from the Gulf of Genoa into Austria and Yugoslavia; an 'alp' is specifically a high mountain-pasture below the snowline, extensively used during the summer for grazing livestock. From late June to late Sept. the huts on the alp are occupied by villagers, who tend the cattle, make cheese and butter, returning to the villages with the livestock and produce when the snows begin.

Alsace and Lorraine. A fertile borderland west of the Rhine which became a centre of Charlemagne's Empire; after the dissolution of this in A.D. 870 it passed to Louis the German. It remained under German influence until the ◊ *Thirty Years War*, after which Alsace was ceded to France. Lorraine too came under French control and was finally incorporated in 1766. After the ◊ *Franco-Prussian War* Germany annexed both Alsace and East Lorraine in 1871. They reverted to France after the ◊ *First World War*. ◊ *Lotharingia*.

Altaic Languages. Perhaps related to the Uralian; named after the Altai mountains in central Asia.

MONGOL: Spoken by about 3 m. in Mongolia and by scattered communities elsewhere in U.S.S.R.

TUNGUS: A rapidly diminishing language mainly in Manchuria; can no longer compete with Chinese.

TURKIC: Spoken by about 40 m. and includes Turkish proper and several related languages (Turki) spoken across N. Asia e.g. *Azerbaijani* in NW Iran and the Caucasus; *Kazakh, Kirghiz*, and *Uzbek* in central Asia (U.S.S.R.); and *Yakut*, an isolated language still in use in the far N. of Siberia.

Altamira. Village in N. Spain famous for the ◊ *palaeolithic* paintings discovered in the Altamira Cavern in 1879 by Don Marcelino de Sautuola, which were not generally accepted as genuine until many years later. The paintings, chiefly of bison, are life-like, richly coloured, and remarkably well-preserved. ◊ *Cave Art, Lascaux*.

Alternating Current (A.C.) ◊ *Electric Current*.

Alternation of Generations. Biological phenomenon in both plants and animals (e.g. ferns, jellyfish, tapeworms) in which a generation which reproduces sexually alternates with a generation which reproduces asexually. The two forms may differ considerably.

Alternative Vote ◊ *Proportional Representation*.

Alternator. Electric ◊ *generator* producing alternating current. Alternators are mainly used for large power supplies, and are generally driven by steam or water ◊ *turbines*. Their speed is accurately controlled to produce alternating current of the required frequency.

Alum. A double sulphate of potassium and aluminium, used in dyeing (as a mordant), fireproofing, leather manufacture, sizing paper, and clarifying water. In chemistry the term includes any double sulphate containing a monovalent and trivalent metal.

Alumina ◊ *Aluminium*.

Aluminium. An element forming 7.45 per cent of the earth's crust, mainly in the form of ◊ *igneous rocks* which weather to give the mixture of hydrated silicates called ◊ *clays*; the raw material from which the metal is extracted commercially is ◊ *bauxite*. The presence of the element aluminium in these materials was first recognized 1809 by Davy, who named it aluminum; it was first isolated 1827 by Wöhler, and Deville discovered a cheaper extraction method 1854. The important electrolytic process was developed 1886 by Héroult (France) and Hall (U.S.A.): pure aluminium oxide is dissolved in molten cryolite (Na_3AlF_6) containing a little ◊ *fluorspar* (CaF_2) and electrolyzed in a graphite vessel (cathode) with graphite anodes. Aluminium separates, and being denser than the electrolyte it forms a liquid layer below it. The process calls for great quantities of electricity, and consequently production of the metal centres in areas where hydroelectric power is available e.g. Canada, Norway, Scotland, U.S.A. Aluminium is an extremely light silvery-white metal; immediately it is exposed to air, a thin film of transparent oxide is formed on the surface, which protects it from further oxidation. It can be cast, forged, extruded, and rolled, welded under an inert atmosphere of ◊ *helium* or argon, or brazed by means of an alloy of aluminium with silica. Although attacked by alkalis and certain acids, it shows remarkable resistance to corrosion by air and by many chemicals. Its electrical and heat conductivity are high, approaching those of copper. The tensile strength of pure aluminium is low, but it can be very much higher in the alloys. Its properties render it a suitable metal for cooking utensils, food containers and wrapping, since it is non-toxic. Stranded about a galvanized steel wire, it has entirely displaced copper for high-tension overhead cables. Various alloys are used increasingly in bridges, ship superstructures, building construction, vehicle bodies, tanks, chemical plant, aircraft and engine parts, and a vast range of metal products where lightness and strength are desirable. The chief alloying elements are magnesium, silicon, manganese, nickel, copper, and zinc; in various proportions and combinations, these give a great range of physical properties. The oxide alumina is Al_2O_3; it has a very high m.p. which makes it suitable for refractory ware. As ◊ *corundum* it is used as an abrasive; ruby and sapphire are almost pure alumina, and can be produced artificially. Aluminium sulphate is used as a mordant in the dyeing industry.

Amaryllidaceae ◊ *Narcissus.*

Amateurs. Persons who take part in sport for enjoyment and not for money; the ◊ *Olympic Games* definition of an amateur is 'one who participates and always has participated in sport as an avocation without material gain of any kind'. The term arose in the 19th cent. when 'gentlemen sportsmen' sought to dissociate themselves, particularly in athletics, from those who ran for prize-money. Cricket and Association Football were the first sports to permit amateurs and professionals to contest with each other (and they do also in golf and horseracing), but in lawn tennis, athletics, rugby football, and boxing the division is still maintained; official subsidies to 'amateurs' (notably by communist governments and American universities) have, however, created growing disputes in the international governing bodies. The decline of the former leisured classes has so altered the position of the genuine amateur in sport that in 1962 the governing body in cricket abolished all distinctions in the game; this has been widely advocated as the future pattern for all sport.

Amazons. In Greek legend, a race of women warriors living near the Black Sea, who cut off their right breasts for greater efficiency in archery. They fought against the Greeks in the Trojan war; ◊ *Achilles* killed their Queen Penthesilea. ◊ *Theseus.*

America ◊ *United States of America.*

American Architecture. The early colonists tended to build in the style of their homeland. In New England the clapboard house became popular and has remained characteristic of much American domestic building. It was not till the 18th cent. that increasing prosperity and skilled craftsmen brought architecture of distinction – adaptations of Georgian models suited to American conditions, such as can be seen in Charleston, Williamsburg, and Boston or in the elegant interpretations (often in wood) of English churches of the style of Wren and Gibbs. The interest in architec-

ture of Jefferson and other prominent leaders led to the neo-classical style, followed by 19th-cent. imitation Gothic. Jenney of Chicago devised the skyscraper 1884, entirely carried on columns and girders of steel, a peculiarly American contribution to modern architecture; his disciple Sullivan was responsible for an original development of frame construction based on his maxim 'form follows function', in his office and public buildings mainly in Chicago. Sullivan's ideas were carried further by Frank Lloyd Wright, whose imaginative and flexible approach greatly influenced the development of modern architecture in Europe. Wright was however obscured in U.S.A. in the academic reaction represented by the 1895 Chicago Exhibition, and remained a prophet without honour in his own country. During the 1930s eminent modern architects such as Gropius and Mies Van der Rohe came from Europe, first to teach, and after the war to carry out a series of influential buildings. A second generation of theorists and builders, Kahn, Saarinen, Rudolph, Johnson, and others, and such organizations as Skidmore, Owings & Merrill, have continued the pioneering work of the European innovators. The post-war building boom in U.S.A. has produced many recognized masterpieces. Apart from these, the influence of Buckminster Fuller, engineer and inventor, is strong and growing, particularly in the field of structural techniques. (S. American architecture ◊ *Brazil.*)

American Art. Prior to the 20th cent. American painting tended to follow European fashions. Notable exceptions were the Primitive Edward Hicks; Audubon, the exquisite watercolourist of birds; and George Catlin, whose subject matter was the American Indian. Otherwise, American painting from Benjamin West (d. 1820) to Winslow Homer (d. 1910) and Thomas Eakins (d. 1916) rarely rises above the merely competent, and tends always to the provincial.

During the late 19th cent. several American artists of note worked in Europe, chief among them James Whistler, Mary Cassat, and John Singer Sargent. In 1914 there was an exhibition of modern European art in New York which was highly influential for the subsequent development of art in U.S.A. It fortified the 'modernism' of a man like John Marin whose work, with that of Max Weber, Charles Demuth, Stanton Macdonald Wright and, above all, Stuart Davis, laid the foundations for an exuberant, muscular, metropolitan, wholly American and underivative modern art which has wrested the initiative from the School of Paris. Concurrently, America has rung the changes on varying forms of realism (fantastic, lyrical, folksy, expressionist, surrealist, etc.) in the work of George Bellows, Thomas Hart Benton, Grant Wood, Edward Hopper, Ivan Le Lorraine Albright, Peter Blume, Ben Shahn, and the strongly atmospheric precision of Andrew Wyeth. During the 1950s Jackson Pollock, Mark Rothko, Franz Kline, Willem de Kooning, etc., working in various styles roughly termed Abstract or Expressionist, came to dominate American and European painting alike. Subsequently, the impetus – or at least the publicity – has passed to painters like Robert Rauschenberg, Larry Rivers, or Jasper Johns, whose material is the *objets trouvés* of contemporary civilization – cigarette packs, Old Glory, strip cartoons, cars, etc. In the 20th cent. U.S.A. has produced two important sculptors, David Smith and Alexander Calder.

American Civil War. 1861-5. War between the States of U.S.A. precipitated by the secession of S. Carolina (which with 10 other southern states formed the Confederacy), caused by a complex of differences which reached a climax with the election of Abraham Lincoln as President. Widely divergent opinions are held as to its fundamental causes, but certainly sectional, commercial, and political rivalry as well as moral issues contributed to produce a position in which resort to secession by the Southern States, and the arbitrament of war, became inescapable. The one clear-cut issue, to which the Missouri Compromise of 1820 had not proved a sufficient answer, was the extension of slavery to the new States of the growing West (◊ *Mason-Dixon Line*). The Union forces were backed by superior industrial power and a larger population than the Confederacy, against whom they also established a naval blockade; nevertheless the outcome was not a foregone conclusion, and the bitter struggle lasted over four years and cost half a million lives. The Civil War was notable for new

tactics and improved weapons, for the beginnings of trench warfare, and for the great importance that railways and steamships assumed for the first time in military strategy. The military campaigns were a story of fluctuating fortunes, until the tenacity of Lincoln enabled the superior potential of the north to carry the Union to victory. The ruthlessness of the closing campaign (Sherman's march to the sea), the economic ruin that the sudden end of slavery brought to the south, and the activities of the ◊ *'carpetbaggers'* after the war left a legacy of bitterness in the South which to some extent still persists a century later. The freeing of the slaves did not lead to their integration in the community. ◊ *Bull Run, Chattanooga, Gettysburg Address, Merrimac and Monitor, Race Relations, Slavery, United States (History).*

American Federation of Labor. A loose organization of craft unions formed in 1886, opposed to the political and rather socialistic ideas of the Knights of Labor, an earlier organization whose influence gradually diminished. Under the leadership of Samuel Gompers the A.F. of L. did not enter into politics and concentrated upon securing higher wages, shorter hours, and other specific benefits. By the 1930s it had a membership of 10 m. but its policies were not entirely relevant to the large industry-wide unions, and dissident factions emerged which set up the Committee for Industrial Organization (C.I.O.) organized on an industry basis. This rapidly grew into a movement of some 6 m. members under the militant leadership of John L. Lewis (head of the mineworkers) and of Walter Reuther (of the automobile workers). However, the split was held by many to be inimical to the interests of American trade unionism, and in 1955 a merger between the A.F. of L. and C.I.O. was agreed. ◊ *Trade Union.*

American Football. An 11-a-side game played on a field 300 ft by 160 ft, dating to 1875 and derived from Rugby football, from which it differs mainly in that the ball may be passed in any direction and that the side in possession loses it if they fail to make 30 ft progress in four 'downs' (plays); tackling is rough, protective clothing is worn, and substitutes are allowed at any juncture. There are a number of important post-season play-off matches between winners of major leagues, known as Bowl Games from the names of the stadiums e.g. 'Rose Bowl'.

American Indians. Peoples of Mongol race, believed to have crossed from Asia by the Behring Straits about 60,000 years ago, who spread over the entire continent. When discovered by Europeans the Americas had an Indian population estimated very roughly at 13 m., the bulk in Mexico and Peru. Their languages and cultures differed widely, from the completely primitive societies of Tierra del Fuego and the jungles to the advanced civilizations of the Aztecs and Incas. Today the only largely untouched Indian groups are those of the remote Amazon jungles. The remainder have been influenced by European cultures, although the large Indian populations of Bolivia and Peru still retain much of their old community organization and customs.

LANGUAGES: Over a thousand languages survive in the American continent, descendants of the speech of the original Mongol stock which spread from Asia to populate the Americas in prehistoric times. Now widely differing, many are spoken by small and dwindling groups, have never been recorded in writing, and are destined to vanish. In N. America there are four main groups still spoken by about half a million people, while in Mexico and Central America some 4 m. speak Nahuatl, or Maya, the language of the ancient Aztec and Mayan civilizations. In S. America 8 m. people of Indian stock speak native languages, of which Kechuan (the ancient Inca tongue) in Peru, Araucanian in Chile, and Tupi-Guarani in Brazil are the most important. ◊ *Eskimo, Pueblo.*

American Revolution (War of Independence). 1775–81. The revolution by which the 13 original American colonies secured independence of Britain was caused initially by the colonists' resistance to 'taxation without representation' (i.e. representation in Parliament). After the heavy burden of the ◊ *Seven Years War,* the British government sought to increase revenue by introducing into the colonies such tax measures as the 1765 Stamp Act. This Act, which particularly roused ill feeling, was eventually repealed, but in 1773, in an effort to save the East India Company from bankruptcy, Parliament levied the tea tax on the colonists which resulted in the ◊ *Boston Tea Party* of 1773. Parliament retaliated in 1774 with

the Boston Port Act, which deprived Boston of its port revenues until the damage had been made good, and in the same year passed the Quebec Act which inflamed the Protestant colonists by granting toleration to Canadian Catholics.

A ◊ *Continental Congress,* convened at Philadelphia to secure redress for American grievances, was quickly dominated by a group anxious to break altogether with Britain. A clash of arms first occurred in April 1775, and in May the Congress decided to place the colonies in a state of defence and appointed George Washington commander-in-chief of an American army. It was not, however, until 1776 that the Congress finally issued its Declaration of Independence. Though compelled to abandon Boston, the British took New York in 1776 and Philadelphia in 1777. In 1777 too they planned a move south from Canada and New York state to meet the army based on Philadelphia and isolate the New England colonies. But the British commander remained in Philadelphia, while the troops from Canada were isolated and forced to surrender at ◊ *Saratoga.* With the subsequent intervention of France and Spain on the American side, the British, hemmed in by both land and sea, surrendered at ◊ *Yorktown* in 1781. Britain's military reverses arose from lack of liaison between the command at home and the generals in America, and because she used an army composed largely of German mercenaries against a people fighting on their own territory and imbued with a strong sense of purpose. America was the first colony to break away from the mother country. ◊ *Lexington, Minutemen.*

America's Cup. The New York Yacht Club's schooner *America,* 170 tons, defeated 14 British yachts 1851, in a race round the Isle of Wight for a £100 silver cup offered by the Royal Yacht Squadron; since then the U.S.A. has been challenged 17 times by Britain (most recently 1964, when *Sovereign* (U.K.) was beaten by *Constellation*), twice by Canada, and once by Australia (1962), but the cup has not been won back. The races must be held in the waters of the country holding the cup. **Americium** ◊ *Actinides.* A metal discovered 1944 during the neutron bombardment of plutonium-239.

Amerindians, Amerindian Languages ◊ *American Indians.*

Amethyst. Semi-precious gem-stone; transparent purple form of ◊ *quartz*. ORIENTAL AMETHYST: Form of ◊ *corundum*. ◊ *Silica*.

Amharic ◊ *Ethiopia, Semitic languages.*

Amiens (Peace, 1802) ◊ *Napoleonic Wars.*

Amino-acids. Organic compounds which are fundamental constituents of living matter; at least 60 have been isolated. Although they all contain an amino (basic) group and a carboxylic (acid) group, they show a wide variety of chemical groupings, which determine their individual characteristics. Linked together chemically in long chains, some of the amino-acids form ◊ *proteins*. Some hundreds or thousands of amino-acid molecules go into making each protein molecule.

Ammeter ◊ *Galvanometer.*

Ammonia. Pungent-smelling gas, lighter than air; very soluble in water, giving a weak base (ammonium hydroxide) also called 'ammonia'. The simplest hydride of nitrogen (NH_3), it is synthesized in large quantities from its elements, much being used for the further production of nitric acid, nylon, urea, and ammonium salts. The solution is used as a cleanser and water-softener. The gas is easily liquefied, and in this form is used as a refrigerant and as a convenient provider of hydrogen. Toxic in any concentrated form. ◊ *Nitrogen.*

Ammonite. Group of marine cephalopods abundant 150 m. years ago. ◊ *Fossils* show that they had limestone shells arranged in a flat spiral, similar to those of their present-day descendant Nautilus. The abundance of ammonite fossils helps petrologists to date sedimentary rocks of the Jurassic period (◊ *Geological Time Scale*). Many specimens are found in the cliffs of Dorset and Yorkshire. ◊ *Gault.*

Amnesia. Loss of memory, e.g. as a result of concussion, in which case the loss extends backwards in time (retrograde) for a period dependent on the severity of the injury. It also occurs in acute alcoholism and irregularly in chronic alcoholism and old age. Temporary loss can result from hysteria, in emotional crises, or after a major epileptic attack.

Amoeba. Microscopic, unicellular, or rather non-cellular, animalcule found in ponds and streams; has an irregular shape owing to the formation of blunt and transitory outgrowths from its surface, pseudopodia, which enable it to move and to trap food particles, digestion taking place in the temporary cavities formed by the engulfing pseudopodia. Reproduction is by simple cleavage, the body dividing into two more or less equal halves which eventually reach full size and again divide.

Amphibia. Class of vertebrate animals including the frogs, toads, newts, salamanders, and gymnophiona, a group of tropical worm-like animals. The amphibians were the first vertebrate animals to emerge on land; surviving amphibia lay their eggs in fresh water but as adults live on land. The reptiles evolved from early amphibian stock.

Amphitheatre. An oval arena surrounded by rising tiers of seats, invented by the Romans for gladiatorial and other displays, the Colosseum in Rome being the best-known example. Other well-preserved examples exist at Verona and Capua in Italy, Nîmes and Arles in France, and Cirencester in England. The form survives in Spanish bull-rings and modern sports stadiums.

Amplifier. Device for increasing the magnitude of a weak electrical signal. The name is usually applied to electronic devices in which a weak input signal (current or voltage) is used to convert local battery or mains power into magnified but similar signals of current or voltage at the output of the amplifier. Modern amplifiers are capable of increasing very weak signals, e.g. the voltage waves from the human brain, more than a million times without serious distortion of the original signal. Even greater amplification of the weak signals from remote radio stars can be obtained with ◊ *maser* amplifiers. Amplifiers are an essential part of all radio and television receivers, record-players, recorders, and many industrial and scientific instruments.

Amylase ◊ *Digestion, Pancreas.*

Anabaptists. Christian sectaries of the ◊ *Reformation* era, mainly in Germany, who rejected infant baptism and bore some resemblance to the earlier ◊ *Albigenses*. One group in Germany attempted in 1534 to form quasi-communistic theocratic communities, which aroused bitter opposition, and were savagely put down (◊ *Münster, Peasants War*). In Britain in the 17th and 18th centuries the name was applied to a number of puritan sects, esp. the Baptists (who repudiated it). On the

Continent the anabaptists were absorbed into e.g. the ◊ *Mennonites*.

Anabolism ◊ *Metabolism*.

Anaconda ◊ *Snake*.

Anaemia. A reduction in the blood's ◊ *haemoglobin* and therefore of its oxygen-carrying capacity. This leads to lassitude and in severe cases to breathlessness and ◊ *heart* failure. It may result from loss of red cells from bleeding, their destruction by toxins (haemolytic anaemia), insufficient iron, or by a deficiency of certain maturing agents without which the red cells will be reduced in number or imperfectly developed (pernicious anaemia). ◊ *Leukemia*.

Anaesthetics. Drugs which depress the ◊ *central nervous system* and bring about unconsciousness, given by inhalation of a vapour e.g. chloroform, ether, ethyl chloride, trichlorethylene, or of a gas e.g. nitrous oxide, cyclopropane; alternatively as a liquid injected intravenously e.g. barbitone preparations such as thiopentone. The intoxicating effect of nitrous oxide was observed by Davy in 1795 and that of ether shortly after. By the 1840s experiments in the use of ether in operations were being made in U.S.A. and Britain. In Edinburgh Simpson introduced ◊ *chloroform* in 1847; it long remained the main anaesthetic, but other types are now preferred. Great advances have been made in the techniques of administering anaesthetics. ◊ *Analgesia*.

Analgesia. Abolition or reduction of sensitivity to pain without loss of consciousness. General analgesia may be induced by inhaling diluted anaesthetic vapours e.g. a weak solution of nitrous oxide and air, and is commonly used in midwifery. Regional analgesia is produced by injecting non-toxic cocaine substitutes into trunk nerves to reduce sensitivity in the whole area they serve, and local analgesia by using the drugs directly on small branches and endings of nerves so that they affect only limited areas on which minor operations are to be performed. In spinal analgesia (commonly called spinal anaesthesia) drugs are injected into the spinal column and induce analgesia of all the body below the point of injection.

Anarchism. The doctrine that man is free only when unruled, and that political authority ought therefore to be discarded and replaced by freely associating communities. In the writings of Godwin, Proudhon, Bakunin, and Kropotkin there is a common assumption that men are all socialists by nature; that the State is a coercive machine perpetuating economic inequalities; and that if it is superseded (Godwin, Proudhon) or overthrown by violence (Bakunin, Kropotkin), then voluntary cooperation can be relied on to usher in a Golden Age. Anarchism had adherents, chiefly in Russia and Spain, in the late 19th and early 20th centuries. ◊ *Syndicalism*.

Anatomy. The study of the structure of the body, involving the consideration of 10 distinct systems, both individually and in their position relative to one another: the skeletal, muscular, integumentary (skin), circulatory, respiratory, alimentary, urinary, nervous, endocrine, and reproductive systems. Microscopic anatomy is known as histology.

The science of anatomy was founded in the 16th cent. by Vesalius in Padua, and advanced by Harvey and John Hunter. Progress in microscope technique in the late 19th and 20th centuries has enabled great advances to be made, esp. in ◊ *embryology* and the study of the brain and spinal cord.

Anchovy. Small bony marine fish related to the herring. There are numerous tropical species; the Mediterranean *Engraulis encrasicholus* has soft bones, oily flesh, and a distinctive flavour, which have long made it a highly regarded relish, and is preserved in oil or by salting in casks, and commonly made into sauce or fish-paste.

Andorra. Area 180 sq. m. Pop. 12,000. Cap. Andorra la Vella. Independent principality in the Pyrenees, between Spain and France. Its co-princes are the President of the French Republic and the Spanish Bishop of Urgel.

Andromache ◊ *Hector*.

Andromeda ◊ *Galaxy, Perseus*.

Anemone. Widely distributed genus in the *Ranunculaceae* (Buttercup family). Some are cultivated, e.g. the St Brigid and giant French types, with purple, pink, red, or white flowers with sooty black centres. Two species are native in Britain. The wood anemone (windflower) grows in open woods and hedge banks with a single white flower and three divided leaves. *A. pulsatilla* (pasque flower) grows on chalk grassland and has violet-blue hairy flowers with showy plumes. *A. apennina* and *A. blanda* are often grown in gardens and are

similar to the wood anemone but have
numerous bright blue petals.

Aneroid ◊ *Barometer*.

Aneurin ◊ *Vitamins (B)*.

Angel. < Gr. 'messenger'. In Christian,
Jewish, and Mohammedan belief a spiritual being superior to man who transmits
God's commands, usually depicted in
beautiful human form, but winged, often
holding a harp. Four angels are prominent
in Christian tradition: Michael, leader of
God's armies and conqueror of Satan;
Gabriel, who brought the news of Christ's
incarnation to Mary and in Islam revealed
the Koran to Mohammed; Raphael,
'God's healer', mentioned in the Apocryphal book of Tobit; and Azrael, angel of
death and of the soul's immortality. The
hierarchy of angels runs: Seraphim,
Cherubim, Thrones, Dominations, Virtues, Powers, Principalities, Archangels,
Angels. ◊ *Devil*.

Angina. *Angina pectoris*, a suffocating
pain in the chest caused by insufficient
blood reaching the heart; commonly a result of disease of the coronary arteries e.g.
◊ *arteriosclerosis*. An attack is usually
occasioned by overstrain.

Angiosperms. The most complex group of
◊ *plants* with flowers and seeds enclosed
within a fruit, very diverse in form and
growing in a wide variety of habitats.
There are two main groups. (1) Dicotyledons, i.e. with two cotyledons (seed
leaves); the flowers usually have their
parts in broad stalked leaves with a fine
network of veins e.g. pea, rose, foxglove.
(2) Monocotyledons, i.e. with one cotyle-
don; the flowers usually have their parts
in groups of three, and have narrow leaves
with parallel veins. Most of them are
herbs e.g. grasses, lilies, irises, narcissus,
but ◊ *palms* and bamboos are woody.

Angkor. Ancient capital of the Khmer
Empire which flourished in what are now
◊ *Cambodia, Laos*, and *Thailand* between
A.D. 600 and 1434, when it was over-
thrown. It produced remarkable buildings
and sculpture.

ANGKOR THOM: The walled city, believed to have been over five sq. m. in
area, which became the capital in the 9th
cent. A.D. and was abandoned about 1450,
now ruins, mainly of temples and palaces, discovered by French explorers in
1861.

ANGKOR VAT: A single temple of the
Khmer period one mile south of Angkor

Thom of vast size and architectural grandeur built about the 12th cent. A.D.

Anglicanism. Form of ◊ *Christianity*
represented by the established ◊ *Church
of England* and the various churches in
communion with it in Scotland, Wales,
Ireland, U.S.A., and other English-speaking countries, most of which recognize the
Archbishop of Canterbury as their
honorary president or general spokesman,
and meet periodically in the ◊ *Lambeth
Conference*.

Angling. Fishing with rod and line;
known to the ancient Egyptians, in Britain
the sport goes back to the Middle Ages,
and was widely popular in the 17th cent.
when Izaak Walton published his *Com-
pleat Angler*. Angling methods vary
according to the fish pursued; major
categories are fly-fishing (with artificial
flies), fishing with a spinner (simulating a
small fish), and fishing with natural bait
(e.g. worms). In dry-fly fishing the fly is
floated; in wet-fly fishing it is immersed.

There are recognized national and international records for weight of fish caught;
national freshwater-fishing and sea-fishing
championships are held by the National
Federations in many countries, and world
championships are held by the various
international confederations. Deep-sea
fishing for shark and tarpon enjoys great
popularity amongst Americans.

Anglo-catholicism ◊ *Oxford Movement*.

Anglo-Dutch Wars ◊ *Navigation Acts*.

Anglo-Irish 'Troubles'. After the self-
appointment of Dail Eireann in 1918 (◊
Easter Rebellion) there followed attempts
at forcible suppression by military and
police, known as the Anglo-Irish War
1918–20, in which the 'Black-and-Tan'
auxiliaries and the republican forces became involved in reprisal and counter-
reprisal. During the 1920 truce the suspended ◊ *Home Rule* Act was amended
to exclude six of the nine ◊ *Ulster*
counties, and (under Lloyd George's
threat of 'immediate full-scale war') in
November 1921 the Irish delegates unwill-
ingly signed the Treaty establishing ◊ *Partition* and making the remaining 26 counties of Ireland into the Irish Free State,
with the U.K. retaining certain ports and
harbours. At once civil war broke out between Republicans (under De Valera) and
'Free Staters' (under Collins). The Republicans called the cease-fire in 1923,
turning to political action as the Fianna

Fail party (though a rump continued in arms as the 'Irish Republican Army' (◊ *I.R.A.*)); Fianna Fail became the government of the 26 counties in 1932 and (with one brief interval) has remained in power ever since. In 1938 a new Constitution was ratified by popular referendum and the U.K. relinquished the 'Treaty ports'. ◊ *Ireland, Sinn Fein.*

Anglo-Saxon Architecture. Earliest known English architectural style; no domestic buildings have survived, and the few churches are small and very simple. Anglo-Saxon builders made rough copies of Roman and contemporary Carolingian architectural details, but the style may

Earl's Barton,
Northamptonshire

also show the influence of timber building e.g. in the characteristic 'long and short work' (as shown in the illustration) and the triangular headed openings. The earliest examples (from about the 7th cent.) have no towers in the accepted sense, but may have west porches; towers, transepts, and aisles appear from about the 10th cent. There are examples at Worth, Brixworth, Earl's Barton (about A.D. 1000), Wickham, Greenstead, Bradford-on-Avon, Escomb, and Canterbury (St Martin). The style

gave way in the 11th cent. to the equally robust but more evolved Norman style (◊ *Romanesque Architecture*).

Anglo-Saxon (language) ◊ *English Language.*

Anglo-Saxons. The Germanic peoples who began to settle in England from about A.D. 450 after the departure of the Romans. The Angles probably came from what is now Schleswig-Holstein and settled in areas which later became the kingdoms of E. Anglia, ◊ *Mercia*, and Northumbria. Their neighbours the Saxons had been attacking the English coast as pirates from about the 3rd cent. A.D. and now settled in what became Sussex, ◊ *Wessex*, and Essex. The Jutes, who probably came from around the mouth of the Rhine, settled in Kent and the Isle of Wight. ◊ *English Language.*

Angola. Area 488,000 sq. m. Pop. 4.2 m. (85 per cent African). Cap. Luanda (cap. designate Nova Lisboa). Technically an 'overseas province' of ◊ *Portugal*, by which it has been administered since 1500. The official policy is racial assimilation, and since 1962 Africans may qualify as Portuguese citizens; but they may not vote unless of comparable social and educational standard (*assimilados*) to the Portuguese settlers, and lack of schools means that literacy is low. There is no legal colour bar, however, and intermarriage is frequent. Educational facilities for Africans are beginning to extend.

ECONOMY. Largely an agricultural subsistence economy, with small exports of sisal, cotton, and coffee.

HISTORY. Revolts and guerrilla war broke out in 1961; considerable local grievances esp. over the oppressive system of contract labour caused massacres and counter-massacres before Portuguese troops restored order. ◊ *Mozambique.*

Angora ◊ *Wool.*

Angstrom. Unit of length, equal to one hundred millionth of a centimetre, in which the wavelength of light and other short-wave electromagnetic radiation is usually expressed; named after Anders Jonas Ångström, 1814–74, a Swedish physicist famous for his studies on light.

Anhydrite ◊ *Gypsum.*

Aniline ◊ *Dyes.*

Animism. Term for what many ethnologists consider to have been an original and once universal form of religion; first used by Sir Edward Tylor, who concluded that early man tried to explain dreams or visions by attributing a soul to living people which would continue after death. Animism is thus closely related to ancestor worship. Tylor maintained that later a soul was attributed to inanimate objects also, owing to men's failure to distinguish the animate from the inanimate; religion then came to include the worship of nature spirits. Tylor's views were taken up by Sir James Frazer, and although they are purely speculative they have exerted immense influence in general thinking about the origins and development of religion.

Aniseed. *Pimpinella anisum* (◊ *Umbelliferae*), a herb native to the Middle East, and containing, esp. in the seeds, aromatic oils used for flavouring foods and liqueurs and also medicinally.

Annam ◊ *Indo-China, Vietnam.*

Annelida ◊ *Earthworm, Worm.*

Annihilation. In physics the term does not have the literal meaning of 'utter destruction', because the total energy is conserved. Rather it describes a process in which a particular form of matter disappears, the energy reappearing in another form. Thus, when an ◊ *electron* meets its anti-particle (a positron) the two particles disappear, with the emission of two photons whose combined energy (E) is the same as that of the mass (m) which has disappeared, and is given by Einstein's relation $E = mc^2$ where c is the velocity of light.

Anode ◊ *Electrode, Electrolysis.*

Anschluss ◊ *Austria.*

Antarctica. A land mass of about the same size as Europe surrounding the S. Pole, perpetually ice-covered; it has an average height of 6000 ft, with some peaks of over 15,000 ft. Captain Cook first crossed the Antarctic circle in 1773, but the mainland was not discovered until later, probably by the Englishman Biscoe in 1830 when he sighted Enderby Land. Subsequently other explorers established that Antarctica was a land mass and not frozen sea like the N. Pole. Nevertheless the only animal life is aquatic – penguins and seals. Shackleton almost reached the S. Pole in 1908; in 1911 the Norwegian Amundsen first reached the Pole a few weeks before Scott, who with his companions died on the return journey. The American Admiral Byrd organized several important expeditions, especially that of 1946–8. Dr

Fuchs was the first to cross Antarctica in 1957–8. Many claims have been made to the land areas at different times, notably by Britain, Germany, and Argentina, but in 1959 a 30-year treaty was made by all interested countries which suspended all territorial claims and left the continent free for scientific work (excluding nuclear explosions).

Anteater. Mammals which feed on ants or termites e.g. the great and lesser anteaters of America and the banded and spiny anteaters of Australia. The pangolin and aardvark have a similar diet.

Antelope. A wide genus of ◊ *ruminants* with cloven hoofs, of which the greatest variety of species is found in Africa; they inhabit both equatorial forest and mountain regions, and are very graceful, nimble, speedy, and able to leap great distances. Characteristically they have branching horns, which are permanent, but they are not ◊ *deer*. They include the springbok, eland, impala, and gnu in Africa; gazelles are a large variety of small fleet fawn-coloured antelope.

Anther ◊ *Stamen.*

Anthracite. Form of coal containing up to 95 per cent of carbon; hard, lustrous, difficult to kindle, burns slowly with little flame or ash, and is used in closed stoves or where a smokeless fire is required. S. Wales and Pennsylvania (U.S.A.) are the leading world producers. ◊ *Coal and Coal-mining.*

Anthrax. Serious bacterial disease of animals and sometimes humans, caused by *B. anthracis*, which in its resting (spore) stage is very resistant to heat and to disinfectants; it can persist indefinitely in soil and in grain, which will infect animals to which it is fed. In Britain cases usually result from spores in food, grain, hide, and other animal products from Asian countries. The spores can enter the body through abrasions or mucous membrane, or be inhaled; in man, anthrax can now be cured by the injection of an anti-anthrax serum, whereas formerly it was often fatal.

Anthropoidea ◊ *Primates.*

Anthropology. The study of man, as an animal (physical anthropology), and as a member of a society (social and cultural anthropology); with the latter are usually included ethnology (study of the past history of peoples), ethnography (descriptive study of peoples), and archaeological and linguistic studies.

Social anthropology was originally (in the 19th cent.) devoted to tracing the origins of human ◊ *cultures* and the stages of their development. It was thus closely linked to physical anthropology, prehistoric ◊ *archaeology*, and folklore. With the discovery of 'primitive' peoples with stone age technologies, it was assumed that their types of ◊ *family* organization, ◊ *religion*, and so on would be similar to those of prehistoric men, which may or may not be the case. Morgan, Tylor, Frazer, and many others tried to trace the stages of cultural evolution by almost haphazard comparison with still existing primitive cultures. At the turn of the century workers such as Boas in America and Rivers and Seligman in England began to make first-hand studies of primitive societies, and soon realized that the search for origins could lead only to unprovable conjecture, and that contemporary small-scale societies have evolved complex social systems which deal effectively with the problems common to all societies, those of economy, politics, law, family, religion, etc. Radcliffe-Brown and Malinowski, inspired by Durkheim and others, insisted upon the functional interrelationship of all the institutions of a particular society ('functionalism') and held it more important to understand the present workings of a social system than to try to guess its original form; anthropology was called 'comparative sociology', and it was hoped to establish general sociological laws applicable to all societies. British social anthropological fieldwork has produced many intensive studies of small-scale societies, particularly in Africa. American anthropology, devoted largely to ◊ *American Indian* peoples, has understandably devoted more attention to Indian cultures, which are now largely destroyed, and so has remained closer to ethnology and ethno-history. Recently some anthropologists e.g. Evans-Pritchard have insisted that anthropology must take historical factors into account to explain the present. Today anthropologists are turning to literate and large-scale societies for study, and the distinction between anthropology and sociology is growing less clearly defined. ◊◊ *Race*.

Anthropometry ◊ *Race*.

Anthroposophy. Mystico-religious system with followers in Britain, the Germanic countries, and U.S.A. Based on the teachings of Rudolf Steiner 1861–1925, who founded it early in the 20th cent. after a breach with the Theosophical Society, whose eastern bias he rejected. By a special system of education and an elaborate mythology of human history, with much use of eurhythmics and the arts, it attempts to evoke a new appreciation of the spiritual world from which modern materialism has estranged man. The 'Goetheanum' at Dornach in Switzerland is the headquarters. ◊◊ *Gnostics, Mysticism, Theosophy*.

Anti-aircraft Missiles ◊ *Rocket*.

Antibiotics. Chemical substances produced by fungi or bacteria (or by synthetic processes) which are toxic to certain other micro-organisms. The first discovered was ◊ *penicillin*. There is now a wide range of antibiotics e.g. streptomycin (effective against some forms of tuberculosis), chloromycetin (against typhus), aureomycin (against pneumonia and several other diseases). Their effectiveness is limited by the emergence of antibiotic-resistant strains of bacteria: penicillin-resistant bacteria are now common. For this reason constant efforts are made to develop new antibiotics. ◊ *Deafness*.

Antibodies ◊ *Immunity*.

Anticlericalism. Antagonism to the influence of the Church, esp. the Roman Catholic, in politics and education. Such a feeling (esp. as regards education) existed in France from at least the 14th cent. and became increasingly strong in the 18th cent. under the influence of the ◊ *Encyclopédie* and Voltaire. French radical parties continue to agitate for the complete exclusion of the Church from the school system. Similar movements in other countries led to the ◊ *Kulturkampf* in Germany and to the Lateran Treaty in Italy (◊ *Papal States*).

Anticyclone. Region where atmospheric pressure is high compared with the surrounding areas, with pressure highest at the centre and decreasing outwards. The winds circulate clockwise in the N. and counter-clockwise in the S. hemisphere, and are usually less strong than in a ◊ *depression*; there may be a calm, or a light variable wind near the centre, the wind strength increasing somewhat towards the edges. In winter anticyclones develop over continents; one becomes established over Siberia and frequently extends influence over N. Europe, giving extremely cold dry weather. In contrast to the unsettled weather in a depression, quiet conditions are characteristic of an anticyclone, which usually covers a larger area and moves more slowly. In summer an anticyclone brings clear skies and warm weather, in winter frost or fog and low cloud. Besides the temporary anticyclones of the middle latitudes there are two belts of prevailing anticyclones, mainly over the oceans about lat. 30° N. and 30° S.; one of these, round the Azores, sometimes extends over NW Europe in summer, bringing a fine sunny spell.

Antifreeze. Preparations used to prevent water from freezing in car radiators; effective additives are methanol, ethanol, or ethylene glycol (◊ *Olefines*), which mix intimately with water, do not evaporate, and are non-corrosive. A 50-50 by weight ethanol-water mixture freezes at −37° C; in Britain a smaller proportion of antifreeze is usually adequate.

Antigens ◊ *Immunity.*

Antihistamine ◊ *Histamine.*

Antimonial Lead ◊ *Alloys.*

Antimony. A white metallic element about twice as abundant in the earth's crust as silver, occurring principally as the sulphide stibnite, from which the metal is produced by reduction. When added to other metals, it generally increases hardness and resistance to corrosion; it is alloyed with lead for electrical storage-battery plates and corrosion-resistant piping, with lead and tin in type-metal, and with tin, copper, and lead in bearing-metal. Its alloys with aluminium and indium are semi-conductors. The oxide is employed in vitreous enamels, as a pigment, in the preparation of the tartar emetic used in medicine, and as a mordant in dyeing and calico printing.

Antipodes. Places on opposite sides of the globe, an imaginary straight line between which would pass through the centre of the earth, e.g. Antipodes Island (SE of New Zealand) and London (England) are approximate antipodes; sometimes a whole region, e.g. in Gt Britain 'the Antipodes' may mean Australia and New Zealand. Exact antipodes must be distant from each other by 180° longitude and be an equal number of degrees N. and S. latitude respectively.

Antirrhinum. *Antirrhinum majus* is a European perennial, usually treated as an annual for garden purposes. There are now varieties varying from the six-inch

Tom Thumb to those two or three ft high, in every colour except blue. Some years ago their cultivation declined, because of attacks by a disfiguring fungus (rust), but resistant varieties have now been bred.

Antisemitism. ◊ *Jews* have been discriminated against in Europe on religious grounds ever since the Christianization of the Roman Empire. Throughout the Middle Ages rumours that Jews performed ritual murders of Christian children, or were responsible for the spread of the plague, resulted in brutal massacres. Although conducted in the name of religion, the persecution of Jews seems usually to have been an outlet for feelings of terror or insecurity and thus presented an irrational phenomenon recognized in many different societies by anthropologists (◊ *Witchcraft*). The term antisemitism is applied particularly to the anti-Jewish movement based on the racist theories of Houston Chamberlain, and his belief in the superiority of the ◊ *'Aryan'* race, which took root in Germany about 1873 and spread in a virulent form to Russia and to France (◊ *Dreyfus Affair*); it was revived in Germany after 1918, supported by Alfred Rosenberg, Julius Streicher, and others, and was one of the emotional mainsprings for Hitler and the Nazi movement (◊ *Nazism*). Several million European Jews were exterminated by the Nazis, during the ◊ *Second World War,* as Hitler's 'Final Solution'. The Vatican General Council of 1963 drafted an authoritative condemnation of antisemitism, ratification of which is expected.

Antiseptics. Chemicals which can kill or inhibit growth of micro-organisms. Their use in surgery was generalized by Joseph Lister, who used powerful disinfectants e.g. lysol, iodine, both as direct disinfectants and as sprays. In modern practice sterilization of surgical instruments by heat and recently by gamma radiation and of other surfaces by disinfectants replaces the older methods: the aim is to asepsize i.e. to remove and exclude from the operation theatre all pathogenic organisms. ◊ *Infection.*

Antitoxins ◊ *Immunity.*

Ants. Family of social ◊ *insects* of the *Formicoidea*, belonging (with the bee and wasp) to the *Hymenoptera*; the earliest fossils date from the Eocene period 60,000 years ago. There are some 5000 species, each comprising three castes: shortlived males; fertile females or queens; and sterile females, which may be workers or soldiers. In July and August the winged males and females swarm in the nuptial flight; once fertilized, the females tear off their wings and either return to the original nest or begin a new colony. The males do not generally survive long after the nuptials. The eggs give rise to larvae and pupae which metamorphose into adults. Primitive ants are carnivorous; some have stings. The more highly social ants may cultivate fungi in their nest as food, and some keep herds of ◊ aphids which they 'milk'. The carnivorous tropical Dorylinae travel in armies which destroy every living thing they meet. The ant-hills of S. America are esp. large, often as much as 12 ft high. ◊ Termite.

Anubis. In Egyptian mythology, son of ◊ Osiris and Nephthys, represented as a man with the head of a jackal; exposed by his parents at birth, he was found by ◊ Isis with her watchdogs, and became her attendant and guardian of the dogs (hence his name, 'dog-watcher'). It was his function to lead the dead to judgement; the Greeks and Romans identified him with ◊ Hermes.

Anzio. Small port 33 m. S. of Rome where Allied troops landed in 1944 in an attempt to by-pass the stubborn German resistance around Cassino. The Germans contained the bridgehead in fierce fighting and the hoped-for breakthrough to Rome was not effected although the campaign contributed to the final Allied advance in Italy.

Aorta ◊ Circulatory System.

Apache. 1. Several American Indian tribes, in New Mexico and Arizona, noted for long, fierce resistance to Spanish and American conquest; now numbering only about 6000. **2.** Parisian criminals in the early 20th cent.

Apartheid. Policy introduced in S. Africa in 1948 when the Nationalist Party came to power, based on the view held by the vast majority of Boers (supported by the tenets of the Dutch Reformed Church) that the future of S. Africa depends upon strict segregation of the races, through laws prohibiting sexual relations between them, the denial of common facilities for travel, sport, entertainment, and worship, and the establishment of autonomous and separate African enclaves (including educational facilities) of a tribal nature, known generally as Bantustan, outside which Africans (who provide essential manpower in S. African industry) are required to carry a pass. Resultant tension and disturbances have not inclined the S. African government to modify the policy, which it defends as beneficial and benevolent.

Mild criticism from the opposition United Party has not prevented the Nationalist Party from steadily improving its electoral position. There has been increasing criticism from outside S. Africa. The ◊ United Nations objected to the introduction of apartheid into SW Africa, a ◊ League of Nations mandated territory for which it considered it has a special responsibility, and S. Africa's intransigence on this issue led to a vote of condemnation by the U.N. in 1951; a general resolution expressing 'concern and regret' over apartheid was passed in 1959. The critical attitude of other ◊ British Commonwealth countries towards apartheid led the S. African government to renounce membership of the Commonwealth during the Conference of Commonwealth Prime Ministers in 1961. Opposition to apartheid in the United Nations became even stronger in the next two years; in spite of the rule of non-interference in internal affairs, in Nov. 1962 the General Assembly passed resolutions condemning this policy, requested member states to impose sanctions (◊ Boycott), and asked the Security Council to consider the possibility of expelling S. Africa from the U.N. ◊ Race, Race Relations.

Apatite (Rock Phosphate) ◊ Calcium, Phosphorus.

Ape. Name now usually restricted to those ◊ primates with no external tail (anthropoid apes) e.g. ◊ Chimpanzee, Gibbon, Gorilla, Orang-outang; they have a common ancestor with man, but have been distinct since the Miocene period. Mainly tree-dwellers, their arms are larger than their legs; they can stand semi-erect. Their brain is similar to that of man but smaller. ◊ Monkey.

Aphasia. Strictly, loss of power of speech; more specifically that due to a defect in the brain's function of symbolism of thought in speech, and inevitably involved with those of reading and writing. Usually caused by brain injury, tumour, or cerebral thrombosis.

Aphids. Greenfly, Blackfly; family of parasitic ◊ *insects*, some winged and some wingless, with needle-like sucking mouthparts through which the sap is extracted from young leaves. In many species the host plants are alternated, e.g. the common Blackfly, *Aphis fabae*, produces its living young on the broad bean during the summer and lays its winter eggs on the spindle tree. Many aphids cause great economic loss by transmitting plant viruses. The common peach aphis, *Myzas persicae*, is known to be the vector for at least twenty-four virus diseases including Potato Mosaic; *Phylloxera vastatrix* was responsible for the near-destruction of the vineries of Europe in the 19th cent.

Aphrodite (Venus). In Greek mythology, goddess of love and beauty, sprung from the sea-foam (◊ *Uranus*); from her close connexion with Cyprus, often called 'the Cyprian', but also 'the Cytherean' from the island of Cythera, off Laconia, a principal seat of her cult. Though the wife of ◊ *Hephaestus* (Vulcan), she welcomed the advances of ◊ *Ares* (Mars): Hephaestus caught her with Mars in a net and exposed them to their fellow gods as a laughing-stock. She plays a part in many Greek myths. Later, a distinction arose between Aphrodite Urania (heavenly Venus) and Aphrodite Pandemos (everybody's Venus), roughly corresponding to the spiritual and sensual concepts of love; ◊ *Eros* (Cupid) was her son.

Apis. In Egyptian mythology, a bull god; a manifestation of ◊ *Osiris*; depicted as a bull bearing the sun disk between his horns. A living bull representing Apis was honoured esp. at Memphis on the great festival of his birthday; if the bull reached the age of 25 he was ritually killed, buried, and nationally mourned. The Persian conqueror of Egypt, Cambyses, who slaughtered the Apis bull with his own hands, according to tradition went mad as a result.

Apocrypha. 1. Those parts of the Old Testament not contained in the Hebrew Masoretic text but which appear in the Vulgate, which is a translation of the Septuagint. They are not regarded as canonical by the Jews or by most Protestants, but are accepted by Roman Catholics as having equal authority with the rest of the O.T. After the Reformation they were placed in a separate section by the translators of the Authorized Version of the Bible as carrying less authority than the other writings. They include the books of Esdras, Tobit, Judith, Maccabees, the Wisdom of Solomon, Ecclesiasticus, etc. ◊ *Bible*.
2. Numerous writings (pseudepigrapha), some pre-Christian, others Christian, never accepted as authoritative by the Christian Churches, inc. pseudo ◊ *Gospels* e.g. Thomas, Philip, According to the Hebrews; pseudo Acts, of Paul and Thecla, of John, of Peter, of Andrew; pseudo Epistles; and pseudo Revelations. Among the best known is the ◊ *gnostic* Gospel of Thomas, parts of which were discovered in a Coptic text 1947.

Apollo. In Greek and Roman mythology, god of light and the sun, of prophecy, of oracles, of plagues, and of ideal male beauty (e.g. the statue of the ◊ *Belvedere* Apollo in the Vatican Museum); son of ◊ *Zeus* and Leto, and (with Zeus and ◊ *Athena*) a member of the threefold group of principal gods in Greece. Music and pastoral concerns were also his province. Delphi (where he presided over the Delphic ◊ *oracle*) and Delos were principal seats of his cult. In modern times, 'Apollonian' has frequently been used for the more sober and rational aspects of life and art as opposed to the 'Dionysian' (◊ *Dionysus*) or more unorganized and intuitive elements. ◊ *Midas*.

Apostles ◊ *Creed, Jesus Christ*.

Appeasement ◊ *Munich Pact*.

Appendix ◊ *Vestigial Organs*.

Apple ◊ *Fruit*.

Applejack ◊ *Brandy*.

Approved Schools. Residential single-sex schools to which young offenders under 17 may be sent on the recommendation of a Juvenile Court; other children may be sent to approved schools as being in need of care or protection. The schools provided by local authorities or welfare committees, or by voluntary welfare organizations, must be approved by the Home Secretary in England and Wales and by the Secretary of State in Scotland. Numbering about 150 throughout Gt Britain, they provide education similar to that of ordinary schools; delinquents are usually committed for 3 years, though they may be released on licence earlier. ◊ *Borstal Institutions, Child*

Aquamarine. Gem-stone, blue variety of ◊ *beryl*. ◊ *Emerald*.

Aqua Regia ◊ *Gold*.

Aquatint. A print emulating the washes of ◊ *watercolour*, printed from an etched plate (◊◊ *Engraving, Etching*). Jean-Baptiste le Prince (first aquatints 1768) seems to have invented the process, which became very popular in the early 19th cent. Goya was the greatest exponent of the method, which in the 20th cent. has been revived by Picasso, Miró, and several English artists.

Aquila ◊ *Eagle*.

Aquitaine. A former independent duchy in SW France stretching from the Pyrenees to the Garonne and at times almost to the Loire. After the Roman occupation it was controlled by the Visigoths until conquered by the Franks under Clovis in A.D. 507. Created a kingdom by Charlemagne for his son, it later became an influential duchy owing allegiance to the French crown, and gained Gascony in the 11th cent. In 1152 it passed to the English crown when the sole heiress, Eleanor, married Henry II. Thereafter it was held by the English kings, as vassals to France, causing constant strife over ownership. By the end of the ◊ *Hundred Years War* England had lost all Aquitaine, Bordeaux falling in 1453.

Arab Federation ◊ *Jordan*.

Arabia. Peninsula at the south-western extremity of Asia. Area 1.2 m. sq. m. mainly desert. Pop. about 10 m. In the 7th cent. in the city of Mecca, already famous as a religious centre, Mohammed established the religion of ◊ *Islam*, the inspiration of the remarkable Arab conquests that spread the new religion as far as Spain and India and transferred the centre of the Arab world to cities outside Arabia itself, where the importance of Mecca lay only in its role of holy city, object of the annual pilgrimages (Hajj) of Muslims from all parts of the world. After being conquered by the Turks, Arabia remained part of the ◊ *Ottoman Empire* from the 16th cent. until Lawrence led the Arab Revolt in the ◊ *First World War*; Arabia then split up into various independent states and sheikhdoms, of which Saudi Arabia became the largest and most influential. Arabia, esp. those parts bordering the Persian Gulf, assumed a new importance with the discovery and exploitation of rich oilfields. ◊◊ *Aden, Gulf Sheikhdoms, Muscat and Oman, Yemen*.

Arabian Nights. An Arabic collection of tales held together by the device of having Scheherezade put off her execution, ordered by her husband, by telling him a story each night, postponing the climax until the following night; hence the Arabic title *The Book of the Thousand and One Nights*. The stories derive from a variety of sources – Indian, Persian, Arabian, and Egyptian – and are of many different kinds and dates, from at least the 9th to the 15th centuries. The work has frequently been translated, first into French by Antoine Galland (Paris 1704–17, 12 vols.); this inaccurate and artificially coloured translation was frequently reprinted and translated into other European languages. Later translations into English include those by E. W. Lane 1839–41, scholarly and annotated, by John Payne 1882–9, accurate and full, and by Sir Richard Burton, 16 vols., Benares 1885–8, the most complete. An expurgated version of Burton's translation was brought out by Lady Burton, 6 vols., London 1886–8.

Arabic. One of the ◊ *Semitic languages*, spoken in its colloquial forms by over 70 m. from Iraq westwards through Syria, Egypt, the Sudan, and along the northern littoral of Africa to Morocco; it appears to have developed from earlier Semitic languages spoken in the Arabian peninsula. There are no early records, and the first inscriptions date to the early 4th cent. A.D. By the time of Mohammed it had emerged as a highly expressive, poetic, and rich language of the desert Arabs; as the vehicle for the ◊ *Koran* it acquired a religious and almost divine status, which to a great extent preserved its classical form from change. It shares many characteristics of other Semitic languages e.g. basic word-roots of three consonants, and classical Arabic developed word-formation into a pattern of great elaboration and symmetry; the verb has ten different forms, of set pattern, to indicate variants e.g. causative, repetitive action, reflex. Modern literary Arabic (used by present-day writers and journalists) has deviated only slightly from the language of the Koran, although it has many neologisms and much of the old vocabulary is not used. Spoken ('colloquial') Arabic varies in the several countries, in differing degrees; illiterate speakers of extreme variants would find difficulty in communicating, though any educated Arab could converse with another. Arabic script

(◊ *Alphabet*), descended from the Nabatean and remotely from the Phoenicians, consists of 28 consonants, the vowels being indicated by signs below or above the letters where necessary; it has been adapted with great effect to serve decorative purposes. In the course of the Arab conquests and the spread of ◊ *Islam*, the script was imposed on or adopted by peoples for whose languages (e.g. Persian, Turkish) it was not well adapted; Turkish substituted Roman script in the 20th cent.

Arab League. Voluntary association of sovereign Arab states, founded 1945, with the general aim of strengthening the ties binding them and furthering their common interests, with a Secretariat in Cairo. Original members were Egypt, Iraq, Jordan, Lebanon, Saudi Arabia, Syria, Yemen. Libya, Morocco, Sudan, Tunisia joined later. One activity of the Arab League is the organization of an economic boycott of ◊ *Israel*. In addition to the embargo on trade between Arab states and Israel, firms in other countries trading with or in Israel are refused access to Arab markets.

Arabs. Semitic-speaking peoples who originated in ◊ *Arabia* whence they erupted from time to time to conquer nearby Mediterranean regions. Originally they were nomads (◊ *Bedouin*), and nomadic tribes still exist, but an urban culture developed at Mecca and Medina and in the Yemen and Hadramaut. Neither the Persians nor the Romans ever overcame the desert barriers to make a complete conquest of the Arabian Peninsula. The Arabs were from early times skilful sailors and traded with India and Africa and founded settlements. With the coming of Mohammed and the unifying and inspiring influence of ◊ *Islam*, the Arabs established a vast empire from India to the Atlantic – larger than that of Rome at its peak – which lasted from about A.D. 650 to 850 and was accompanied by a flowering of Arab achievement in literature, philosophy, mathematics, and medicine which contrasted with the cultural stagnation of the 'Dark Ages' in W. Europe. Wherever they went the Arabs introduced their religion, language, and writing; though the Arab Empire disintegrated, from Morocco to the borders of Persia some 70 m. people still speak Arabic and are almost exclusively Muslim. This common bond of language and religion gives the Arabs an urge towards unity and federation which has, however, so far not overcome the differences and antagonisms which divide the various Arab states. ◊ *Caliphate, Muslim Architecture.*

Arachnida ◊ *Scorpion, Spider.*

Aragon. Kingdom created in 1035, based on the Ebro Valley, expanded in the 12th cent. at expense of the Moors, and ultimately equated with a confederation of territories: Aragon, Catalonia, Majorca, and Valencia. In the 13th cent. Aragon had possessions in Sicily and at Athens. It became united to Castile in 1469 by the marriage of King Ferdinand to Isabella of ◊ *Castile.*

Aramaic. Language closely related to ◊ *Hebrew*, forming the western branch of a group of ◊ *Semitic languages* whose E. branch is Syriac; used extensively in the later Babylonian empire, and under Darius I became the official language of the Persian empire (◊ *Persia*) and the ◊ *lingua franca* of its W. provinces; it was the language of ◊ *Jesus Christ*. Parts of the biblical books of Daniel and Ezra were recorded in Aramaic (the rest of the Old Testament being written in Hebrew). Aramaic is still spoken in small communities on the slopes of Anti-Lebanon. ◊ *Hamito-Semitic Languages.*

Araucanian ◊ *American Indians (Languages).*

Arbitration. Settlement of disputes without recourse to courts of law or, in industrial disputes, to strikes or lockouts; in the U.K. any dispute may be submitted to arbitration except one arising in criminal proceedings. Even where there is no arbitration agreement, in civil proceedings (except a jury action) the Court may refer a specific question, or the whole matter in dispute, to an arbitrator. Arbitration in labour disputes is sometimes but not always binding on both sides; a number of trade unions and employers' associations have standard negotiating machinery which provides for compulsory arbitration to settle their differences, which can be referred to an arbitrator chosen for the purpose or to the Industrial Court, a permanent tribunal established under the Industrial Courts Act. International arbitration is one method by which members of U.N.O. are required to settle their disputes. ◊ *International Court of Justice.*

Arbutus ◊ *Ericaceae.*

Arch. Construction in blocks or brick to

span an opening: the blocks are frequently wedge-shaped and the arch can support a load the thrust of which is transmitted to the supporting piers. The arch was known to the Babylonians and much used by the Assyrians and Etruscans in vaulted buildings, but its ultimate development came with the Romans who made use of it in a wide variety of applications. The Roman arch was semicircular. Islamic

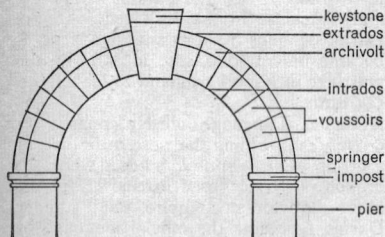

keystone
extrados
archivolt
intrados
voussoirs
springer
impost
pier

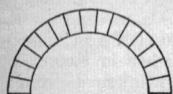

semicircular

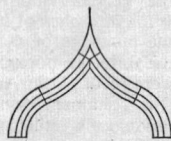

ogee

lancet (gothic)

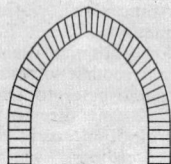

pointed saracenic

architects developed arches of horse-shoe and pointed shape, and either by contact with the Near East or as an independent means of solving structural problems, European architects adopted the pointed arch, which is capable of distributing the thrust of masonry over a greater area, thus making it possible to construct buildings in which windows occupy a considerable proportion of the wall-space. The ogee arch, popular in the late Gothic period, is a further refinement in which the two arcs of a Gothic arch are replaced by S-shaped curves. ◊ Architecture.

Archaeology. The study of man's past through surviving artefacts e.g. tools, weapons, pottery, buildings, tombs. For prehistory, i.e. happenings before the beginnings of literate civilization in a given area, archaeology is our only source of knowledge; for later times, it supplements history by supplying evidence of aspects of life not covered by the written records. The picture of ancient life provided by archaeology is necessarily partial and uncertain; it deals with broad cultural and historical developments of societies and communities rather than with specific events or individuals. Many important aspects of human life e.g. beliefs, institutions, social organization can only be inferred from scanty traces, and only a minute proportion of all that man made or built has survived decay and destruction: cases where almost a whole material culture has been accidentally preserved, as at Pompeii, are rare. Organic materials e.g. wood and textiles are the most short-lived (although exceptional finds have been made in the acidic soil of peat bogs), and the archaeologist depends chiefly on objects of stone, bone, metal, and pottery, esp. the last, which is virtually indestructible and with its variety of shapes and decoration provides considerable precise evidence about the past. Man has long been fascinated by his own past. Until recently, most scholars were interested only in the more superficially exciting finds. Early antiquaries believed with Dr Johnson that it was impossible to know more of history than was told in written records, and archaeology as an organized and scientific study emerged only in the 19th cent. largely through the stimulus of the theory of evolution and ◊ biological classification, and increasing knowledge of living primitive societies. An evolutionary view of human society gave rise to many false theories, but also stimulated such early attempts at broad classification as J. C. Thompson's 'Three Age System' (Stone Age, Bronze Age, Iron Age), which however changed remains the basis of modern archaeology. The dating of pre-historic finds by stratigraphy and typology of artefacts was for long only relative, except in cases where a link could be traced with contemporary literate cultures. Very recently, however, such methods as ◊ radio-carbon dating have enabled archaeologists to provide reasonably accurate absolute dates, and archaeology has had the assistance of e.g. biology, botany, and physics and also air photography. Attention has now shifted from the great cities of Egypt and Mesopotamia to sites which e.g. provide evidence of the beginnings of agriculture and urban civilization.

Archbishop ◊ *Bishop.*

Archeopteryx. The oldest ◊ *bird* found in fossil form; it is about the size of a crow, and combines specialized avian and primitive reptilian features. There are indications that it had an archosaur (◊ *Pterodactyl*) as its ancestor, and that it represents the transition from cold-blooded reptile to warm-blooded bird.

Archery. The use of bows and arrows for hunting and warfare probably dates from before 35,000 B.C. They appear to have been an invention of the later Old Stone Age (◊ *Palaeolithic*), the earliest arrowheads being made of flaked flints. Bows are of three main types: composite i.e. formed of two or more elements e.g. wood with horn, sinew, or whalebone; compound i.e. made by fastening several pieces of different woods together; and single i.e. a simple shaft of a single wood e.g. the English long bow, a decisive factor in 14th-cent. wars against the French; but the introduction of efficient firearms in the late 15th and 16th centuries made the bow obsolete as a military weapon. Charles II revived archery as a sport in the 1670s, the Royal Toxophilite Society was founded 1781, and world championships began 1931, about 30 countries now practising officially. In Britain the Grand National Archery Society, founded 1861, has over 600 clubs, and the Royal Company of Archers (the sovereign's bodyguard in Scotland) has records dating to 1676. For ranges of up to about 100 yds bows of up to 60 lb. may be used; women's bows average a pull of 28 lb. Modern bows are usually made of three laminated strips of wood, for greater pliancy; standard targets are four ft in diameter, with a gold centre and concentric rings of different colours and scoring values.

Architectural Orders. An order in ◊ *architecture* is a column of standardized proportions, with base, shaft, and capital, surmounted by an ◊ *entablature.* The Greeks evolved the three 'true' orders, Doric (without base), Ionic, and later Corinthian, and the Romans the Tuscan and the Composite. They were described by Vitruvius (1st cent. B.C.); the ratio of diameter to height of column was prescribed, as also the form and proportion

of base, capital, and entablature. The Doric was used at the Parthenon, the Ionic at the Erechtheum, and the Corinthian at the temple of Olympian Zeus in Athens.

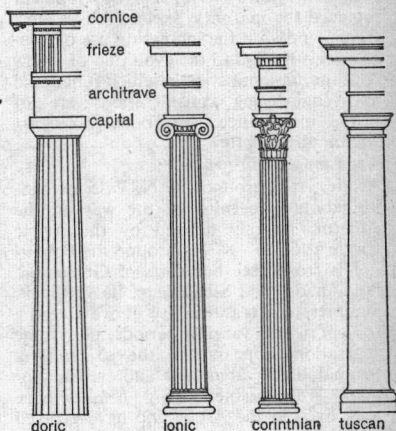

doric   ionic   corinthian   tuscan

Architecture. The art of building, as opposed to mere construction; implies an attempt to furnish a practical and also aesthetic solution to the problem of enclosing spaces for living, worship, and work. Climate and culture, and the materials, labour, and technique available combine to determine development; 'styles' of architecture, in the wider sense, are the result not of fashion or fantasy but of trends determined by a variety of formative causes. There have been three basic formulae in building: the post-and-lintel (trabeated) system, the earliest and simplest; the arch system; and the modern steel frame. ◊ *Egyptian architecture,* in the first great school, employed the post-and-lintel method, which ◊ *Greek architecture* brought to its highest perfection, creating the ◊ *architectural orders.* The Assyrians, building with brick, early developed the arch. The Romans copied and combined pillar and arch, invented ◊ *concrete,* and engaged in vault construction on a grand scale; but it remained for their successors the Byzantines to discover how to support their vaults not upon vast masses of masonry but by the transference of thrust to external supports e.g. buttresses, and to carry the cupola to an immense height, as in Haghia Sophia. This departure led through ◊ *Romanesque* *architecture* to the ◊ *Gothic* development of a style in which piers, vault ribs, and buttresses provided a skeleton for a building in which walls became curtains. The 19th cent. third and latest development replaced the masonry 'skeleton' by a steel frame, and with the increasing use of concrete this has led to the evolution of a new and international style in which functional and engineering considerations are of prime importance. ◊ *French/German/Indian Architecture*, etc.

Arc Lamp ◊ *Electric Arc.*

Arctic. Area around the N. Pole, extending about one third of the way to the equator, roughly defined by the Arctic Circle at 66° 17′ 8″ N. Around the Pole itself is frozen sea but parts of Greenland, N. Canada, and Siberia etc. lie within it. Summer temperatures rise above freezing for short and varying periods, and some vegetation appears in the ◊ *tundra*. Animal life is abundant and the furs of many are valuable. The ◊ *Eskimo* have long lived in the Arctic and have evolved a way of life compatible with their harsh surroundings. The earliest known Europeans to enter the Arctic were the ◊ *Vikings*, followed in the 16th and 17th centuries by explorers seeking a N E or N W passage to the Orient, e.g. Frobisher, Hudson, and Barents. Their hardships and meagre success discouraged further attempts until a fresh series of explorations began in the 19th cent. with Franklin, Ross, and others. Amundsen accomplished both the N E and N W passages (1903–6), and expeditions by American, British, Canadian, Norwegian, and Russian parties have thoroughly explored the area. The Arctic has assumed importance since the development of ◊ *great-circle* air routes and as being the shortest air distance between places in the U.S.S.R. and N. America.

Ares. In Greek and Roman mythology, god of war; son of ◊ *Zeus* and ◊ *Hera*, but plays comparatively little part in Greek legend. The Romans identified him with Mars (probably originally a Latin vegetation deity), invoked when fields were prepared for sowing; he was the father of ◊ *Romulus* and Remus, and his sacred animal was the wolf. His name is preserved in the month of March (Martius). ◊ *Aphrodite.*

Arethusa. A fountain on the island of Ortygia in Syracuse harbour; also the legendary nymph who dwelt there, an attendant of ◊ *Artemis*; while resting near the river Alpheus she was improperly approached by the river god who chased her until Artemis, answering her prayer, turned her into a fountain; but Alpheus mingled his waters with hers, and the combined stream went underground, to emerge in Ortygia where her fountain still flows, surrounded by papyrus plants.

Argentina. Area 1.1 m. sq. m. Pop. 22 m. (predominantly European in origin). Cap. Buenos Aires. Rel. 93 per cent Roman Catholic. Language Spanish. A republic with a President elected by popular vote for a term of six years, and a National Congress consisting of a Senate and a House of Deputies. Argentina occupies the southern wedge-shaped part of S. America; the climate is largely temperate. ECONOMY. Basically agricultural. The ◊ *pampas* are amongst the greatest areas of meat and wheat production in the world; in the southern extremity great flocks of sheep are raised. A good deal of industrialization has taken place in recent years, but the Argentine is poor in mineral resources, except oil, which is being successfully developed.

HISTORY. After a long struggle for freedom, led by José de San Martín, Argentina proclaimed its independence from Spanish rule in 1816, but it was not until 1853 that a stable government was established, with a constitution based on that of U.S.A. Argentina remained neutral in the First World War and in the Second declared war against Germany only in 1945. President Juan Perón ruled as a dictator 1946–55; he and his wife Eva had great popular following among industrial workers, in whose favour they introduced important social reforms. His regime led to economic disruption and was overthrown by a revolt of the armed forces in 1955, when General Eduardo Lonardi became Provisional President. Lonardi quickly fell after a further coup d'état; his successor General Pedro Aramburu failed to restore the country's economy, and in 1958 the radical Dr Arturo Frondizi was elected with a substantial majority. In 1962, after signs of a Peronist recovery, the armed forces arrested Frondizi, and Dr Guido became President. Dr Arturo Illia was elected President in 1963.

Argon ◊ *Inert Gases.*

Argonauts. 1. Those taking part in the

expedition of the Argo in search of the ◊ *Golden Fleece.*
2. ◊ *Octopus.*
Argus. 1. Legendary Greek hero with 100 eyes (of which two only were asleep at any given time) and therefore set by ◊ *Hera* to watch Io; ◊ *Hermes* slew him after lulling all his eyes to sleep with the music of his lyre, and ◊ *Juno* took his eyes to adorn the tail of her sacred bird, the peacock.
2. The dog of ◊ *Ulysses*, which welcomed him home after his 20 years' absence at the Trojan war.
3. The builder of the Argo (◊ *Golden Fleece*).
Ariadne ◊ *Minos, Theseus.*
Arianism. Christian ◊ *heresy* named after Arius, about 256–336, a priest of Alexandria who taught that Jesus was not coeternal with God the Father but created by him and therefore in some sense inferior. Condemned by the Council of Nicaea A.D. 325 and bitterly opposed by Athanasius (later Bishop of Alexandria), it was embraced by many pagan converts to Christianity esp. among the Goths and Germans, but from the 6th cent. gradually died out, though held by individuals (inc. allegedly Milton) at various times throughout Christian history; its catchword that Jesus is *homoiousios* (of like substance) not *homoousios* (of the same substance) gave rise to the taunt that the difference between Arians and orthodox depended on a single letter. ◊ *Creed.*
Aristocracy ◊ *Oligarchy.*
Aristotelianism. A magnificent attempt to organize human knowledge into departments and investigate each; primarily the work of the Greek philosopher Aristotle, 384–322 B.C. He inquired into logic, metaphysics, ethics, politics, natural science, biology, psychology, and literary art, and for many medieval scholars (◊ *Scholasticism*) his writings were dogma, amended only by Christian theology. Aristotelianism contains the foundations of logic, sets out fundamental categories in human thought about the world, argues to the existence of a Prime Mover or God, and in general expresses a dispassionate and analytical spirit of inquiry. Perhaps the part most read today is the *Nicomachean Ethics*, which describes the good life for man as a rational life and includes acute discussions of such topics as human freedom.

ARISTOTELIAN ELEMENTS: Aristotle assumed all matter to consist of the 4 'elements' earth, air, fire, water (not elements in the modern sense), an idea persisting till the late 18th cent. For instance, burning a damp log gave smoke (i.e. fire) and ash (i.e. earth). The concept is echoed in the phrase 'the elements' for the weather. ◊ *Humours.*
Armada. Fleet of 130 vessels carrying 20,000 soldiers sent by Philip of Spain to attack England in 1588. Its first objective was to embark a further 20,000 men of Parma's army in the Spanish Netherlands. During its course up the Channel it was harried for several days by an English fleet under Howard, and sought refuge in Calais. Eight fireships were sent against the Spanish fleet, which slipped its moorings and stood out to sea, abandoning the strict formation previously maintained. The next day every available English ship went into the attack and decisively outfought the Spaniards. A change of wind enabled the Spaniards to avoid being forced on to the Flemish coast, and they fled north on a perilous route round Scotland and Ireland. Less than half the Armada returned home. The English victory was due to the superior manoeuvrability of their ships and to the tactical skill of captains such as Drake, Hawkins, and Grenville. It removed completely the threat of invasion by Spain and the danger that Elizabeth I might be replaced by a Roman Catholic sovereign.
Armadillo. Member of the small mammalian order *Edentata* having an armour of horn-covered bony skin plates; nocturnal and omnivorous, it escapes from enemies by rolling into an armoured ball or burrowing rapidly. A remnant of an ancient group having fossils already differentiated in the Eocene period of 60 m. years ago, related to the ◊ *sloth.*
Armagnac ◊ *Brandy.*
Armenia. Area 11,306 sq. m. Pop. 1.8 m. Cap. Erevan. Rel. Armenian Christian. One of the 15 constituent republics of the ◊ *Soviet Union*; the Armenian S.S.R. was formed in 1920 and belonged to the Transcaucasian Federation 1922–36, when it was incorporated into the U.S.S.R. There are, however, Armenians living in Turkey and Persia.
ECONOMY. Mainly agricultural esp. grain and wine; also large deposits of copper ore, molybdenum, and other minerals.

HISTORY. The Armenians, a distinct ethnic group, have lived for many centuries in part of Asia Minor, but Armenia has been independent only for short periods. After the conquests of Alexander it fell successively under the Romans, Arabs, and Turks (◊ *Ottoman Empire*). The Armenians became Christian A.D. 300, and cling stubbornly to both their language and religion. In 1878 the ◊ *Berlin Congress* divided their country between Turkey and Russia. The attempts of Russia to increase her share by exploiting her role as protector of the Christians led to savage massacre of Armenians by the Turks in 1895 and again in 1915. After the ◊ *First World War*, an independent Armenia was projected, but Russia's proclamation of the Soviet Republic left the Armenians still divided between Turkey, Persia, and U.S.S.R.

LANGUAGE. Armenian, one of the smallest of the living branches of the ◊ *Indo-European languages*.

Arminianism. < Arminius (Jacob Harmesen), 16th-cent. Dutch theologian; Protestant theological doctrine opposed to ◊ *Calvinism*. It held that Jesus died not only for the 'elect' but for all men, that man by his free will can accept or reject the offer of divine grace, and that Calvin's view of ◊ *predestination* was unscriptural; it exercised much influence in the Netherlands, and in England has been held by many theologians of the Anglican Church e.g. during 17th-cent. struggles. Early ◊ *Methodism* was marked by the theological cleavage between the views of its two founders, the Arminian John Wesley and the Calvinist George Whitefield. ◊ *Anglicanism, Covenant, Puritans.*

Armorica ◊ *Breton.*

Armorican. Period of intense mountain-building at end of Carboniferous period (◊ *Geological Time Scale*), which raised a chain of mountains running E. across Europe from SW Ireland through S. Britain and Brittany (the Roman Armorica) to the Ukraine. The mountain chains are now reduced to their stumps, but many parts have been re-elevated and form plateaux, e.g. in central France and Bohemia. The Harz mountains in central Germany show the same typical structural trend: 'Hercynian' is synonymous with Armorican.

Army. An organized armed body, as distinguished from a horde of warriors. The Egyptians were the first to organize armies, which like those of the Assyrians and Persians were composed of paid soldiers. The Greeks made service compulsory for their citizens, and the Romans at first similarly relied on citizen armies. Later, however, their standing armies were largely of non-Italians from the provinces, who on discharge were rewarded with Roman citizenship. The Romans carried both ◊ *strategy* and ◊ *tactics* to a high level. They made the legion the basic unit, and the troops were intensively drilled, trained, and disciplined. Throughout this period the principal arms were the javelin, sword, and bow and arrow; cavalry, usually local levies or auxiliaries, were secondary to the foot soldier. Armour was used but was not so heavy as to impede mobility.

In the early Middle Ages the army was based upon the feudal rights of the king and was an assembly of the personal forces of the feudal lords. It was typically composed of heavily armed mounted knights, lightly armed infantry, and archers. The advent of ◊ *firearms* brought about a complete change in warfare: the importance of the knight and the castle disappeared and that of the infantry and artillery increased. Soldiers were in the main professional mercenaries, and control of the army was indisputably in the hands of the ruler. Cromwell's New Model Army, the iron discipline of Frederick of Prussia's troops, and the standing army of Louis XIV represented steps towards the well-trained and organized military forces typical of modern times. With the ◊ *French Revolution* the concept of the 'Nation in Arms' led to the emergence of the national army based on conscription and to the committing of the whole energies and resources of a country to 'total war'. A large conscript force with a cadre of professional soldiers became the typical army of continental Europe in the 19th cent. though Britain and U.S.A. continued to maintain only a small professional army and a territorial militia. Whilst the organization of armies continued on the traditional regimental basis, the Industrial Revolution and technological advances of every kind gradually changed their nature. Parade-ground drill and the discipline and morale associated with mass formations, which called for little individual initiative or education, were increasingly superseded as more elaborate weapons, rapid movement, and mechanization called for different qualities and training. A modern army depends in great measure upon technicians and specialists capable of dealing with equipment of growing complication. ◊ *British Army.*

Aromatic Compounds ◊ *Aliphatic Compounds.*

Arsenic. An element with non-metallic and metallic forms which sublimes at 616°C and can be melted only under pressure. About 20 times as abundant in the earth's crust as silver, it occurs in arsenical ◊ *pyrites* and as an impurity in many ores; it is recovered as white arsenic (arsenous oxide) in smelter flue-dusts, from which the element is easily obtained for use in certain copper and lead ◊ *alloys.* Soluble arsenic compounds are very poisonous to all forms of life; they have been used as insecticides, but organic compounds with specific toxicities are taking their place. Detecting arsenic in food and in pathological specimens is easy because under the right conditions it forms a volatile hydride which gives a dark stain when passed through a heated glass tube. In conjunction with ◊ *selenium* and sodium nitrate arsenious oxide is used for decolorizing glass.

Artemis. In Greek mythology, daughter of ◊ *Zeus* and Leto, twin sister of ◊ *Apollo,* goddess of wild nature and of childbirth, identified with the moon, specially associated with bears. At Ephesus, a great centre of her cult, she took over the attributes of the old Asian fertility goddess, and representations often show her as many-breasted. The Romans equated her with Diana, an old Latin goddess of nature and fertility specially worshipped by women; at her temple on Lake Nemi, near Rome, by tradition her priest was a runaway slave who plucked a branch from a certain tree, killed his priestly predecessor in single combat, and held office until he was killed in his turn (see Frazer, *The Golden Bough*). Both Artemis and Diana were sometimes identified with ◊ *Hecate.*

Arteriosclerosis ◊ *Sclerosis.*

Artery ◊ *Circulatory System.*

Arthritis ◊ *Cortisone.*

Arthropoda ◊ *Centipede, Crustacea, Insects, Spider.*

Arthurian Legend. At most a shadowy figure (although probably a historical British warrior of the 5th or 6th cent.) King Arthur as portrayed in medieval romance is not part of Celtic Britain's history or literature, but an invention of later centuries. There are numerous references to him from about A.D. 800 (e.g. Nennius), but the earliest fully developed account of his exploits is found in the *Historia Regum Britanniae,* about 1135, of Geoffrey of Monmouth, who drew on old British traditions to give a picture of the Danish and Saxon invasions from the point of view of the retreating Britons. Here Arthur figures as a British hero who after many successful campaigns refuses to pay tribute to Rome and sets out to conquer it, but is recalled by the treachery of his nephew Mordred and the disloyalty of his wife Guinevere, and meets his death in the great Last Battle in the West; the outline of the main Arthurian story is here, with Uther Pendragon and ◊ *Merlin* but without ◊ *Lancelot* or ◊ *Tristram.* Wace's *Roman de Brut* (about 1150) translates and elaborates Geoffrey, introducing the Round Table; its translation into English by Layamon appeared in the early 13th cent. Further development of the Arthurian legend in French romance concentrates more and more on the exploits of particular knights, with Arthur presiding vaguely in the background. The popular 12th-cent. French romancer Chrestien de Troyes wrote five romances dealing with the adventures, in love and action, of Arthurian knights; only Yvain (as *Ywain and Gawain*) was translated into English. Chrestien's *Conte du Graal* first introduces into Arthurian legend the ◊ *Holy Grail* theme, which was developed by later romancers who represented the Grail as the holy vessel brought to England by Joseph of Arimathea. In the early 13th cent. the Arthurian stories emerge as a vast French prose cycle with five main branches: the *Estoire del Graal, Livre Artu, Merlin, Lancelot, Queste del Saint Graal,* and *Mort Artu.* Sir Thomas Malory (d. 1471) drew on this cycle as well as on other French and English Arthurian romances to produce his cycle of prose tales, notably the final one, *The Most Piteous Tale of the Morte D'Arthur,* where the end of the Round Table and the deaths of Arthur, Lancelot, and Guinevere are presented with vivid nostalgic feeling as the end of a heroic phase of British life. Later English writers (e.g. Spenser, Tennyson,

Arnold, Morris, Swinburne) got their Arthurian material from Malory. Other European countries produced their own versions of French Arthurian stories; of these, only Wolfram von Eschenbach's *Parzifal* (which inspired Wagner's opera) is of any great significance (◊ *Parsifal*). The greatest Middle-English romance dealing with Arthurian material is the late 14th-cent. *Sir Gawain and the Green Knight*, written in the NW Midland dialect.

Artichoke. 1. Globe. *Cynara scolymus* (◊ *Compositae*). A perennial plant producing large flower heads. The closely packed fleshy leaves (bracts) surrounding the very young flower heads are edible. Grown extensively in Brittany.

2. Jerusalem ◊ *Jerusalem Artichoke*.

Artificial Insemination. The fertilization of an ovum by the artificial introduction of spermatozoa, a method widely used for the insemination of cattle and horses. It can also be used in cases of human infertility, where biological or psychological obstacles can be overcome by introducing semen either from the woman's husband (A.I.H.) or from another donor (A.I.D.). The legal questions involved in the latter case are complicated and largely undetermined.

Artificial Satellite. A body projected away from the earth at a speed of over 25,500 m.p.h. escapes the earth's effective gravitational field; at lesser speeds, if aimed correctly, it continues to orbit the earth indefinitely, its centrifugal force offsetting the pull of gravity; the shape of the orbit is determined by speed control, circular orbit requiring a lower speed than eliptical. Very high speeds turn the ellipse into a parabola and allow the body to escape from the earth's gravitational field completely. In general the life histories of most earth satellites follow the same pattern: the orbital period is longest immediately after launching, when the orbit is most elliptical; even at great heights there is still a small amount of atmosphere, the retarding effect of which is greatest when the satellite is nearest to the Earth (perigee) and least at the furthest point (apogee). Consequently, the orbit steadily shrinks, becoming more circular and nearer to the earth's surface, and the orbital period decreases; the satellite enters dense atmosphere (unless provided with retro-rockets) and burns out. The

scientific objectives of the satellites have been investigation of the upper layers of the earth's atmosphere and of the particles of interplanetary space, astronomical observations, photographing the reverse side of the moon, terrestrial weather plotting, and establishment of a satellite communications system. ◊ *Radar, Space Exploration, Satellite Astronomy.*

MAJOR ACHIEVEMENTS

1957	Sputnik I (U.S.S.R.) First earth satellite
1958	Explorer I (U.S.A.) Discovered the ◊ *Van Allen belts.*
1959	Lunik II (U.S.S.R.) Circled the moon.
1961	Vostok I (U.S.S.R.) Major Gagarin; first manned orbit.
1963	Telstar I & II (U.S.A.) Communication satellites made possible television broadcasts between U.S.A. and Europe.
1964	Voskhod (U.S.S.R.) First satellite to carry crew of three.

Manned orbits of increasing duration have been made by several American and Soviet astronauts.

TYPICAL FLIGHT DETAILS

	Major Nikolayev U.S.S.R. 1962	Major Cooper U.S.A. 1963
Orbits	64	22
Altitude	141–100 miles	165–100 miles
Distance travelled	1.5 m. miles	597,000 miles
Top speed	18,000 m.p.h.	17,500 m.p.h.
Duration	94 hours	34 hours
Size of craft	about 5 tons	3,035 lb.

Artillery. Originally the throwing of missiles e.g. by slings and catapults; subsequently applied to large weapons using explosive charges as propellants. Its development is intimately connected with the technology of ◊ *iron and steel* and of ◊ *explosives*. The early cannon of the 15th cent., primitive though they were, soon demonstrated their efficacy against fortifications. In 1450 French artillery dislodged the English from their strongholds in France; in 1453 the Turkish bombards quickly destroyed the great walls of Constantinople. Improvements in artillery came rather slowly. A better granular gunpowder permitted greater ranges and accuracy in the 16th cent. and more effective guns were an advantage that the English had over the Spanish ◊ *Armada*. Gustavus Adolphus was the first general to devise and exploit a lighter, more mobile field artillery, and Napoleon believed in the rapid massing of guns from an artillery reserve to deliver the final stroke in battle. But it was not until rifling became possible in large guns (1859) that artillery in modern shape emerged; such guns were used in the American Civil War. The first really modern field gun was the French '75' of 1898. The variety of artillery has increased rapidly in the 20th cent. New explosives have added to its destructive power and methods of fire control to its accuracy. The highly mobile tractor-mounted gun and the heavily gunned tank represent a mobility of the first order. Heavy artillery can now be used to fire shells with nuclear warheads of unprecedented force, and ◊ *rockets* introduce a range far beyond normal artillery: these developments present a whole new range of possibilities which were demonstrated only to a marginal extent in the Second World War. ◊ *Ballistics*.

Artiodactyla ◊ *Camel, Deer*.

Art Nouveau. An extravagant movement employing plant forms in an exotic linear style, known in Germany as *Der Jugendstil* and in Italy as *Liberty* (from the *art nouveau* fabrics of the London shop), of wide currency at the end of the 19th cent. Its earliest manifestation is the title page of a book by A. H. Mackmurdo (London 1883), and its largest monument the fantastic buildings by A. Gaudí in Barcelona; also the Métro stations by Guimard in Paris, and schemes of interior decoration by V. Horta in Brussels, C. R. Mackintosh in Glasgow, and Louis Sullivan in Chicago. On a smaller scale are glassware by Gallé and Tiffany, drawings by Aubrey Beardsley, and furniture by Mackintosh. The style is also reflected in much of the painting of the period, notably that of Gauguin, Munch, and Hodler. Despite their revolutionary intention, Art Nouveau works nearly all have the same rarefied *fin de siècle* atmosphere as the writings of Huysmans and Maeterlinck and the music of Debussy.

Arts Council of Gt Britain. Established 1946 under Royal Charter, it has 16 honorary members, serving for five years appointed by the Government. It seeks to bring the fine arts to the public by subsidizing opera, ballet, and drama (particularly the Royal Opera House, Covent Garden) and by arranging exhibitions, concerts, etc. It cooperates with the government and local authorities, and receives an annual grant from the Treasury.

Arum. A genus of plants native to Europe and the Mediterranean, characterized by a showy part (spathe) which is not the flower but a modified leaf; the inconspicuous flowers are carried on a club-like body (spadix), partly hidden by the spathe, which may be green, white, yellow, or lurid purple. The berries are usually orange, as in 'lords and ladies' or cuckoopint, *A. maculatum*. The leaves are often handsomely marbled with white or cream.

'Aryan'. Properly, a linguistic term < Sanskrit *Arya*, the name taken by the tribes who conquered India 1800–1500 B.C. to distinguish themselves from the original inhabitants; these invaders were fairskinned, spoke ◊ *Indo-European languages* (chiefly Sanskrit and Iranian), had a mobile culture combining a pastoral and agricultural economy with a military way of life (the present Hindu ◊ *caste* system reflects their social structure), and with their swift horse-drawn chariots rapidly overwhelmed the city-dwelling peoples of the ◊ *Indus civilization*. The recognition of the affinities between the Indo-Aryan (or Indo-Iranian) and other Indo-European language groups led to the hypothesis (now largely discarded) of an original 'Aryan race'; from the 19th cent. onwards extreme racialists seized on this idea and developed from it the theory of 'Aryan' supremacy, generally equating 'Aryan' with the fair-haired Nordic type. It has constantly been emphasized that this theory has no validity in fact, that the Caucasoid race – including the Semitic peoples (speakers of ◊ *Semitic languages* e.g. the ancient Babylonians and Phoenicians, the Arabs, the Jews) – include Nordic, Alpine, and Mediterranean stock, and that the term 'Aryan' can be applied only to a language group and cannot be equated with any particular race or culture.

Asbestos. Fibrous form of amphibole, one of the rock-forming silicates in ◊ *metamorphic rocks*, which when rubbed breaks up into silklike threads and is resistant to chemical action and to fire.

Long fibres are spun into fireproof cloths or made into brake-linings, short fibres are used in the manufacture of asbestos sheets and 'felt', fireproof paints, and insulating materials; asbestos cement (made up by impregnating the fibre with cement) is extensively used for roofing and pipes. Canada and S. Rhodesia are leading suppliers. ◊ *Serpentine (Chrysolite)*.

Ascorbic Acid ◊ *Vitamins (C)*.

Asdingians ◊ *Vandals*.

Asepsis ◊ *Infection*.

Ash. *Fraxinus*; deciduous tree valued for its timber, much used for articles requiring toughness and resilience e.g. oars, cricket bats, tool handles, etc.

Ashanti. A people of ◊ *Ghana*, numbering almost 1 m. and consisting of many small principalities whose Chief acts as King (Asantehene) of the Ashanti confederacy, renowned for their goldworking. Today the Ashanti are prosperous through gold exports and cocoa-growing; in the years following Ghana's independence they were associated with the opposition to President Nkrumah's policies, as they felt the position of the Asantehene was threatened by modern developments, but they are now largely reconciled.

Ashes. Australia beat England in a test ◊ *cricket* match on English soil for the first time 1882, by the narrow margin of seven runs, and next day the *Sporting Times* published a comic obituary: 'In affectionate remembrance of English cricket, which died at the Oval 29 August 1882. Deeply lamented by a large circle of sorrowing friends and acquaintances. R.I.P. (N.B. The body will be cremated and the ashes taken to Australia.)' When England beat Australia in Melbourne the following year, a group of Australian women presented the England captain with an urn containing the ashes of a burnt stump, and since then the winners of the England-Australia Test series are said to hold 'the Ashes': the urn is now in the Imperial Cricket Memorial at Lord's cricket ground.

Ashkenazim ◊ *Jews*.

Asoka ◊ *Mauryas*.

Asparagus. Developed from *Asparagus officinalis*, a wild plant on salt steppes of E. Europe and coastal areas of S. Europe and Britain. It was valued as a vegetable in ancient Rome and has been grown in Britain for at least 350 years. It is grown on a large scale in France and U.S.A. Much of the crop is canned. ◊ *Liliaceae*.

Asphalt. Natural form of bitumen, chemically a mixture of ◊ *hydrocarbons*. Obtained chiefly from the lake of pitch in Trinidad. A similar substance is obtained as a by-product of the ◊ *petroleum* industry. It is used for surfacing roads, as an alternative to macadam, and will stand up to heavy traffic. Waterproof floors and roofs are also surfaced with asphalt.

Aspirin. Common name for a mild analgesic and fever-reducing drug, probably the most widely used of all; chemically, acetylsalicylic acid, in which the acid is neutralized as a salt.

Ass ◊ *Horse*.

Assassins. < Ar. 'hashish-eaters'; secret Muslim sect founded A.D. 1090 by Hasan i-Sabah, the Old Man of the Mountains, who systematically resorted to assassination to further his ends, and rewarded his followers with bouts of luxurious living. In the 12th cent. the sect extended its power to Syria, where it came into contact with the ◊ *Crusades*. Hulagu Khan destroyed the Persian Assassins in 1256 and the ◊ *Mamelukes* wiped out the Syrian branch.

Assault. The use or threat of unlawful violence by one person against another; a misdemeanour punishable by a fine or by imprisonment for up to one year, unless grievous bodily harm results, when it is a ◊ *felony*. Self-defence, or force used to arrest a felon or evict a trespasser, are grounds for defence at law provided that no more force than was reasonably necessary was used.

Assizes. In England and other countries, the regular visits of judges to provincial centres ('assize towns') for the hearing of important criminal and civil cases. For this purpose England and Wales (except London) is divided into 'circuits', to each of which different High Court judges go each term, in rotation.

Association Football. An 11-a-side game played on a field of maximum size 130 yds long by 100 yds wide, with a goal at either end towards which a round ball is kicked or headed (but not handled except by the goal-keeper), it derives from crude 'mob' games (played with animals' bladders), which survived various royal edicts prohibiting them. In the 19th cent. these rough games began to take on a more organized form, the public schools adapted the 'kicking' games to their own liking (◊ *Rugby*), and by 1863, when the Football Association was formed, uniform rules had emerged; professionalism, though resisted, had become widespread by 1885. The growth of 'soccer' in the 20th cent. has been remarkable; still mainly a British game in 1900, it is now played in about 100 countries which are members of the international federation (F.I.F.A.), and at various times different national teams have had their spell of supremacy in international competitions, of which the most important are the World Cup (dominated in recent years by S. American countries) and the European Champions' Cup. In Britain, apart from the home international matches begun 1872, interest focuses mainly on the annual competitions for the Football Association and Scottish F.A. Cups and on the respective league programmes. The fall in attendance at league games in recent years has prompted much discussion, by the Football League and the Scottish League, of ways to stimulate both competitions e.g. a 'Super League'; some of the fall in attendance, however, is attributable to the counter-attraction of television and the failure of managements to improve the standards of comfort offered to spectators. Besides the appeal of professional football as a spectacle, soccer is played by millions of amateurs esp. in Europe and S. America; in Britain alone the existence of over 20,000 clubs indicates its popularity.

Association of Ideas. In seeking an explanation of how one idea suggests another, how simple ideas are combined to form complex ideas, and of learning in general, two major processes have been singled out as significant: association by contiguity (e.g. lightning suggests thunder) and association by similarity (e.g. a stranger reminds us of someone we have known). An important distinction is made between Free Association, in which the subject of the experiment is asked to produce any idea suggested by a given idea, and Constrained Association, in which he is asked to produce an idea in a logical relation to the idea given, e.g. its opposite or its synonym. As used in psychotherapy, Free Association reveals unconscious thoughts and motives, an important and logical connexion being thought to exist in the patient's unconscious mind. Constrained Association involves the higher thought processes, and is used in many mental tests (◊ *Intelligence Quotient*).

Assumption ◊ *Mary*.

Assyria. Ancient state of ◊ *Mesopotamia*, at different times in its history varying in extent and power from the territory around its principal cities (Assur, ◊ *Nineveh*, Nimrud, Erbil) to control over a large part of W. Asia and Egypt. Until the 2nd millennium B.C. Assyria was dominated by the ◊ *Sumerians* and Akkadians to the south, but in the 14th cent. B.C. it began to grow in power and to challenge the ◊ *Hittites*, the Babylonians, and the Egyptians for supremacy in the Tigris-Euphrates valley. Under Ashur-nasir-pal 884–859 B.C. began Assyria's great period of expansion over the countries of the E. Mediterranean, which reached its apogee in the 8th and 7th centuries B.C. under Sennacherib and Ashur-bani-pal. Their own records largely confirm the Old Testament portrait of the Assyrians as a nation of ruthless oppressors capable of the most abominable cruelty, but the later kings at least seem also to have been men of some culture. The widespread empire came to an end with the revolt of the Medes and Babylonians and the fall of Nineveh 612 B.C. ◊ *Babylon, Semitic Languages*.

Astarte ◊ *Ishtar*.

Astatine. Radioactive ◊ *element*, whose isotopes are short-lived (◊ *half-life* period seven or eight hours) which appears to resemble the ◊ *halogens*.

Asteroids. Minor planets, mostly with orbits between those of Mars and Jupiter. Many thousands have been photographed but only some 1500 orbits computed. The smallest asteroid detectable is about one m. in diameter, the largest (Ceres) about 430 m. ◊ *Solar System*.

Asthma. A condition characterized by attacks of breathlessness caused by spasmodic contractions of the air passages. It may be the result of allergy to a foreign substance e.g. animal hair, pollen, or house dust, or it may arise from psychological factors.

Astrolabe. Astronomical and navigational instrument for determining the position of planets and stars; probably of Greek origin. It was superseded by the quadrant (◊ *Sextant*).

Astrology. Pseudo-science of ◊ *divination*, based on a belief that the heavenly bodies and their conjunctions influence events on earth. It had its origins in ancient Chaldea, Egypt, and Assyria, but the form found in Europe made use of the Roman deities Mars, Venus, etc., who were said to exercise influence on the planets bearing their names. Divination is based on the horoscope, a plan of the heavens at the time of the subject's birth, showing the relations of the planets to the 'houses' (signs) of the ◊ Zodiac in the circle of the 'fixed stars'. Astrology was influential in medieval Europe, despite opposition from the Church, and enjoyed a revival in popularity during the Renaissance; it was officially condemned by Pope Sixtus V in 1585. In the 17th cent. it continued to flourish despite the growth of scientific astronomy, and it still has its followers catered for by popular newspapers; Hitler was a prominent adherent.

Astronomy. The study of everything beyond the confines of the earth. The older part of the subject, positional astronomy, has been largely concerned with the angular positions and motions of the planets and nearer ◊ stars relative to their background of distant stars. The first systematic observations of the heavenly bodies were made by the Egyptians, Chinese, and Chaldeans; by Greek times the movements of the sun and planets in the ◊ Zodiac and the ◊ Saros cycle of eclipses were known, the idea of a spherical earth was current, the distance of the sun from the earth had been estimated, and stars were classified in magnitude according to their brightness. In A.D. 150 in his *Almagest* the astronomer Ptolemy explained the movements of the heavenly bodies by postulating that the earth was the centre of the universe and that the planets and sun moved around it. The Ptolemaic theory, which agreed with the philosophy of Aristotle (◊ *Aristotelianism*), was made the keystone of much Christian and other theology, and thus went unchallenged until in the 16th cent. Copernicus formulated the theory that the sun was at the centre of the universe and that the earth and the other planets orbited around it. Opposition by the Church prevented this theory being fully accepted until the later 17th cent. In 1609 Kepler announced the laws of planetary motion he had deduced from the careful observations made by Tycho Brahe 1546–1601; these were later shown by Newton in his *Principia* 1687 to be a consequence of the law of gravitation.

The refracting telescope (attributed to Lippershey, although Galileo in 1609 was the first to use one) and the reflecting telescope (Newton 1668) brought a rapid advance in astronomical knowledge and realization of the earth's minuteness in the immensity of the universe. It was not until 1838, however, that the distance of a star was first measured (by Bessel) and useful theories on the significance of the sun among the stars became possible. The great advance that came with the use of photography in astronomy, 1840, has led directly to our current theories of the universe. Many branches of astronomy other than positional astronomy have now been developed, and ◊ *astrophysics* in particular has become an important and fruitful science methodically investigating the physics of both our own and the external galaxies. Cosmology, the study of the universe as a whole, is revealing more and more about cosmic development, and particular attention is being paid to the evolution of stars – how they are born and their life history. Astronomers are now able to use equipment and techniques unknown to their predecessors, e.g. spectroscopy has provided a means of studying the physical and chemical state of distant bodies, ◊ *radioastronomy* has opened up new possibilities for studying solar activity and the structure of the ◊ *Milky Way*, and ◊ *radar* has brought greater precision to measurements within the ◊ *solar system*.

The use of rockets and ◊ *satellite astronomy* seem likely to revolutionize all aspects of astronomy. The stationing of instruments above the earth's atmosphere will mean that the universe may be viewed in all the wavelengths of the electromagnetic spectrum. Ultraviolet observation of the sun is already well advanced, and the technique is now being applied to the stars. Gamma-ray and X-ray astronomy similarly have possibilities that cannot yet be assessed. ◊◊ *Space Exploration.*

Astrophysics. Modern branch of ◊ *astronomy* dealing with the physics and chemistry of heavenly bodies and interstellar space; much of its information is derived from the study of stellar spectra and data obtained from instruments carried by ◊ *artificial satellites*, and from ◊ *radioastronomy*.

Atalanta. In Greek mythology, a heroine who preferred hunting and athletics to married life and refused to marry unless a suitor could defeat her in a race, unsuccessful entrants being killed; Hippomenes raced carrying the three golden apples of the ◊ *Hesperides*, which he dropped at intervals, and she could not resist pausing to pick them up, so that he won. Atalanta also took part in Meleager's hunting of the boar ravaging Calydon, and was the first to wound it.

Athanasius ◊ *Arianism, Creed.*

Atheism. Denial of the existence of any god or Supreme Being (to be distinguished from agnosticism, which leaves the question open). Hinayana ◊ *Buddhism* and Jainism (◊ *Jains*) are atheistic religions. Atheism is now officially though not always in fact a part of the creed of communists. In U.S.A. an American Association for the Advancement of Atheism (the '4 A'), founded 1925, conducts intensive propaganda on missionary lines for the spread of the belief.

Athena (Athene). In Greek mythology, patron of Athens; born from the head of ◊ *Zeus* (when ◊ *Hephaestus* opened it with an axe): goddess of just war and of the sciences and fine arts; parallel with the Roman ◊ *Minerva.* The meaning of her title 'Pallas' is unknown; the name 'Palladium' was given to an image of her which fell from heaven, was carried off by the Greeks from Troy, and eventually reached Rome. From her title 'Parthenos' (the maiden) came the name of the Parthenon, her great temple on the Acropolis of Athens. She was represented as a female of severe beauty, armed, with Medusa's head (◊ *Gorgons*) on her shield (the aegis).

Athens. The most important city-state of Ancient Greece, where democracy in its Greek form first developed in the 5th cent. B.C. (◊ *Delian League*). Athens became the leading Greek state after playing the chief role in defeating the Persian invasions 500–449 B.C. (◊ *Marathon*). In the Age of Pericles and the century that followed she enjoyed her greatest period of intellectual, artistic, and political activity. The Parthenon was built, sculpture flourished, and philosophers (Anaxagoras and Socrates) and dramatists (Aeschylus, Sophocles, and Euripides) helped to create and were themselves sustained by what was perhaps the first truly secular civilization, in which knowledge and intellectual inquiry were no longer the preserve of a priestly class. This period of splendour ended with the ◊ *Peloponnesian War*, when ◊ *Sparta* at length conquered Athens,

which later fell into the hands of Philip of Macedon and Alexander the Great. But even in times of political eclipse Aristotle, Plato, and Aristophanes added to the reputation enjoyed by Athens, whose contribution to the development of civilization and learning in the Western world is without parallel. ◊ *Greece, Plataea, Salamis.*

Athletics. Track and field events, the sport with the longest recorded history (◊ *Olympic Games*); amateur athletics developed rapidly in the early 19th cent. partly as a result of athletics meetings held at the Royal Military Academy at Sandhurst; then the universities followed suit, and the first English championships were held 1866. The Amateur Athletic Association of England and Wales was formed 1880, setting the pattern for the similar organizations which soon arose in more than 100 other countries, the Olympic Games, revived 1896, being recognized as the world championships. The full programme is as follows. MEN: 100, 200, 400, 800, 1500, 5000, and 10,000 metres; marathon, 26 m. 385 yds; 4×100-metre and 4×400-metre relays; 110- and 400-metre hurdles; 3000-metre steeplechase; high jump; pole vault; long jump; hop, step, and jump; shot-put; discus-throw; javelin-throw; hammer-throw; 20- and 50-km. walks; decathlon. WOMEN: 100, 200, 400, and 800 metres; 4×100-metre relay; 80-metre hurdles; high jump; long jump; shot-put; discus-throw; javelin-throw; pentathlon. Two notable athletics records in recent years have been running the mile in under four minutes, and high jumps above seven ft. Professional athletics on a small scale still exist, principally in Australia, Scotland, and northern England.

Atlantic Charter. 1941. A declaration by the President of U.S.A. (F. D. Roosevelt) and the Prime Minister of the U.K. (Winston Churchill) that their two countries sought no territorial advantages, would support only changes that accorded with the wishes of the peoples concerned, respected the right of all peoples to choose their own form of government, have access to trade and raw materials, and enjoy improved standards of life, and aspired to security for all nations in the post-war world through disarmament and international cooperation.

The declaration was widely acclaimed as a statement of Anglo-American aims, and was received in many parts of the world as a promise that after the war self-government would be extended to all peoples.

Atlantis. Mythical island, said to have lain in the Atlantic off Gibraltar and to have been submerged by the gods before 9000 B.C. for the wickedness and impiety of its inhabitants; first mentioned by Plato.

Atlas. 1. In Greek mythology, one of the ◊ *Titans,* brother of ◊ *Prometheus* and father of the Hyades and the ◊ *Pleiades.* When ◊ *Zeus* had repulsed the attack of the Titans, Atlas was condemned to hold up the heavens with his head and hands for ever, from a position near the garden of the ◊ *Hesperides.* Homer makes him support the pillars which hold apart the earth and the heavens. The Atlas mountains, N. Africa, and the Atlantic derive their name from him, as did ◊ *Atlantis.*
2. A collection of ◊ *maps.*

Atmosphere. The mixture of gases surrounding the earth and other planets. The atmosphere of the earth consists of 78 per cent nitrogen, 21 per cent oxygen, and the

remaining one per cent of argon and other rare gases. It becomes more and more tenuous with height and is still present at 600 m. up, although at a density less than that of any man-made vacuum. The pressure of the atmosphere at sea level is equivalent to that of a depth of water of 34 ft or of 30 in. of mercury (◊ *Barometer*). The temperature of the air at sea level varies with the latitude. It decreases with altitude about 1 degree C per 500 ft, reaching minus 60° C 7 m. up, and then follows an irregular pattern. Nine tenths of the mass of the atmosphere occurs in the layer up to 10 m. Beyond 70 m. the atmosphere, on the evidence obtained from ◊ *artificial satellites,* consists first of a layer of atomic oxygen extending to about 600 m. up, for the next 1000 m. the main constituent is helium, and finally hydrogen predominates, growing more and more rarefied in outer space. ◊ *Meteorology.*

Atoll ◊ *Coral Reef (3).*

Atom. The smallest part of an ◊ *element* which can retain the characteristic properties of the element and enter into a chemical reaction. The dense central core (nucleus) of each atom is made up of positive protons and neutral neutrons, and thus carries a net positive charge dependent on the number of protons in it. The atom as a whole, however, is normally electrically neutral, because the nucleus is surrounded by as many negative electrons as it has protons; it becomes charged (ionized) only if this electrical balance is upset by losing or gaining electrons. The electrons rotate about the nucleus in a series of orbits, grouped in shells of increasing radius, rather like a planetary system. The innermost shell can have two electrons, the next eight, the next 18, such that the nth shell has room for $2n^2$ electrons. The simplest naturally occurring atom is that of ◊ *hydrogen,* which consists of a nucleus of one proton and one planetary electron; at the other end of the scale, ◊ *uranium* has 92 electrons arranged in seven shells not all completely filled. The chemical properties of an element depend on the total number of electrons in each of its atoms.

Atoms which vary only in the neutron content of the nucleus still belong to the same element, but to different isotopes of that element. Uranium ^{235}U and ^{238}U are typical examples of isotopes. ^{235}U

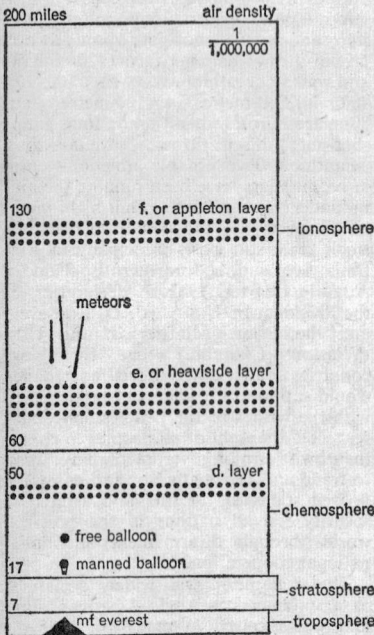

(Figure: atmospheric layers)

200 miles — air density — $\frac{1}{1,000,000}$

130 — f. or appleton layer — ionosphere

meteors

e. or heaviside layer

60

50 — d. layer — chemosphere

● free balloon

manned balloon

17

7 — stratosphere

mt everest — troposphere

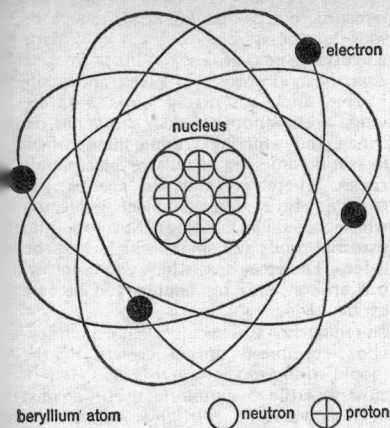

beryllium atom   ◯ neutron   ⊕ proton

contains 92 protons, 143 neutrons and 92 electrons; ^{238}U has the same number of protons and electrons, but has 146 neutrons in its nucleus. Chemical reactions consist of a regrouping of electrons between neighbouring atoms and are governed largely by the electron configuration in the outermost shell. Atoms with similar structure in this shell resemble each other in their chemical behaviour.

Atom Bomb. More properly called a nuclear bomb; a device which relies for its explosive force on the rapid release of ◊ *nuclear energy*. Obtained by bringing together, very quickly, pieces of fissile material (e.g. ◊ *isotopes* of plutonium or uranium) which are too small to explode on their own. The reason why the combined mass explodes is that the surface area per unit mass is reduced when the pieces are together and consequently, provided the combined size is correctly chosen, the loss of neutrons from the surface is proportionally less and the ◊ *chain reaction* is divergent.

The so-called hydrogen bomb has a central core similar to that described above, surrounded by light elements which by a fusion process, triggered off by the high temperature produced by the central core, release even greater explosions of energy than the fission process. Atom bombs were used against Japan at ◊ *Hiroshima* and Nagasaki in 1945, with devastating effect.

Atomic Clock. Very accurate clock in which the time-scale is determined by the period of vibration of certain atoms, this rate of vibration being very great but constant. The caesium clock in the National Physical Laboratory (◊ *Dept of Scientific and Industrial Research*), which uses excited caesium atoms, is accurate to about one sec. in 1000 years, and is used to check other clocks used as international time standards.

Atomic Energy ◊ *Nuclear Energy*.

Atomic Energy Authority. A state organization, under the Minister for Power, established 1954, responsible for atomic energy research and development; up to 16 members, divided into five groups for research, reactors, production, engineering, and weapons. The U.S.A. equivalent is the Atomic Energy Commission, founded 1946. ◊ *Nuclear Energy/Reactor*.

Atomic Number. The integer denoting the number of ◊ *protons* in the nucleus of the atom of a particular ◊ *element*; this is the same as the number of ◊ *electrons*. The simple ◊ *hydrogen* atom, with only one electron and one proton, has 1 as its atomic number, and ◊ *helium*, with two electrons and two protons, has 2 as its atomic number. Atoms of the heavy elements have much more complex electronic patterns and correspondingly high atomic numbers; e.g. ◊ *uranium* has 92. Elements with still higher numbers can be produced by nuclear reactions, but do not occur in nature; they are known as transuranium elements and include neptunium 93, plutonium 94, americium 95, and curium 96.

Atomic Physics ◊ *Atom, Nuclear Energy, Radiation, Subatomic Particles*.

Atomic Weight. For many scientific purposes, rather than consider the actual weight of an atom of a particular element, it is more convenient to consider the weight of the atom relative to say that of ◊ *hydrogen* (taken as 1) or, as for many years, that of ◊ *oxygen* (taken as 16). In 1960–1 it was recommended by the appropriate international bodies of physics and chemistry that the weights should be expressed relative to the principal isotope of ◊ *carbon* ($^{12}_{6}$C), with an assigned relative mass of exactly 12. 'Atomic weight' generally refers to the mixture of ◊ *isotopes* corresponding to the element, to 'atomic mass' or 'nuclidic mass' to a particular nuclide. ◊ *Avogadro's Law*.

Atonality. In music, the absence of tonality, as in composition which gives no sense of keys or modes, a phenomenon glimpsed in certain works of Debussy and occasionally in earlier composers, and adopted as a principle notably by Schoenberg and his followers. As a systematization within atonality, to replace the order imposed by keys, from about 1923 Schoenberg developed the '12-note' (in U.S.A. '12-tone') technique of composition, also sometimes called 'serial technique'.

Atreus ◊ *Agamemnon.*

Atrium ◊ *Circulatory System.*

Atropine ◊ *Alkaloids, Belladonna.*

Attar of Roses ◊ *Perfume.*

Attis (Atys). In eastern mythology, a Phrygian god, son and lover of ◊ *Cybele.* When he wanted to marry, his goddess mother made him mad; he castrated himself, and his spirit passed into a pine tree, violets springing up at its foot from his blood. His feast (conducted by similarly self-mutilated priests) was a scene of grief changing into joy. Like that of ◊ *Adonis* (with whom he has much in common), his myth represents the vegetation cycle; it spread from the east to Rome under the Roman Empire, and his cult is the subject of a remarkable poem by Catullus.

Attorney-General. The chief Law Officer of the Crown, assisted by the ◊ *Solicitor-General*; normally a Q.C. and M.P. and usually a member of the ◊ *Privy Council* but not generally of the Cabinet. His duties are to advise government departments on matters of law, represent the Crown in courts of justice, supervise the Director of Public Prosecutions (◊ *Public Prosecutor*), and speak for the Government on legal matters in the House of Commons and as head of the English Bar.

Aubade. A 'dawn-song'; more especially, a song of lovers parting at dawn, one of the established modes of Provençal lyric (◊ *Troubadours*), which spread into medieval European literature generally and is also to be found surviving in a variety of forms in ◊ *Renaissance* literature.

Auerstädt (1806) ◊ *Jena.*

Aufklärung ◊ *Enlightenment.*

Augean Stables. In Greek legend, kept by Augeas, king of Elis, for his 3000 cattle; after 30 years neglect, ◊ *Hercules* cleaned them out in one night (as one of his 12 labours) by running the rivers Alpheus (◊ *Arethusa*) and Peneus through the yard. Augeas refused to pay the promised fee (one tenth of the cattle); Hercules later returned to Elis and killed all the king's sons but one.

Augustan Age ◊ *Rome.*

Auk. Several species of black and white marine duck-like diving birds 8–13 in. long, with stubby necks, short narrow wings, and whirring veering flight, which live in colonies on islands or inaccessible rocks. There are various species e.g. ◊ *puffin*, little auk, and black guillemot, which breed in holes or burrows, and razorbill and guillemot, which nest on ledges. The great auk, which could not fly, was an easy prey for hunters and became extinct 1844.

Aureomycin. Chemically, chloro-tetracycline; produced during growth of the mould *Streptomyces aureofaciens*, it is a most versatile ◊ *antibiotic*, useful against bacteria where ◊ *penicillin* is ineffective.

Aurignacian ◊ *Palaeolithic.*

Aurochs. Name for the large wild ox of Europe (*Bos primigenius*) from which domesticated European cattle were bred. It became extinct in the 17th cent. By 'back-breeding' the Munich zoo has bred a form of ox closely resembling it. ◊ *Buffalo.*

Aurora. 1. Luminous display, usually in the form of streams of coloured light, often seen in the night sky in high latitudes. In the N. hemisphere it is known as Aurora Borealis, Northern Lights, in the S. hemisphere as Aurora Australis, Southern Lights. Streams of charged particles from the sun are attracted towards the earth's magnetic poles and when they strike the upper atmosphere ionize some of the gases and make them glow, in much the same way as an electric discharge lights a neon tube. Auroras have been shown to be linked with sunspot activity and magnetic storms on earth. ◊ *Ionization, Magnetism.*

2. In classical mythology, goddess of dawn or of the day, sister of Helios (the sun) and daughter of the Titan ◊ *Hyperion*; she crossed the sky daily in a rosy robe to announce to the gods the coming of the day.

Auschwitz (Oświęcim) ◊ *Genocide, War Crimes.*

Austerlitz. 1805. Town in Moravia 10 m. east of Brno, site of the 'Battle of the Three Emperors' in which Napoleon heavily defeated Francis II of Austria and Alexander I of Russia, though the two armies were of about equal size. Austria made peace by the Treaty of Pressburg, but Russia continued to take part in the ◊ *Napoleonic Wars*.

Australia. Area nearly 3 m. sq. m. Pop. 11 m. Cap. Canberra. Smallest of the continents, about the size of U.S.A. Much of central Australia is arid and many areas are subject to drought. The climate varies from tropical in the north to cool-temperate in Tasmania. The population is largely concentrated in towns on the south and south-east coasts.

Australia is a member of the ◊ *British Commonwealth*, organized as a federation of the states (New S. Wales, Victoria, S. Australia, Queensland, Northern Territory, W. Australia, and Tasmania), originally colonies, which in 1901 became the Commonwealth of Australia. The Federal Parliament consists of a Senate of 60 members and a House of Representatives of 122 elected by universal adult suffrage. Its competence is largely limited to defence, foreign policy, and financial policy. Voting is compulsory. Each state retains extensive powers of government.

ECONOMY, HISTORY. Originally discovered by the Dutch, Australia was not settled till Captain Cook discovered the more fertile east coast in 1770; it was then first used as a penal colony. The discovery of gold in 1850 led to a great increase of immigration; the basis of the economy, however, remained agricultural, sheep-rearing being the main activity, though there are rich supplies of iron ore, lignite, lead, and zinc. Australia is the leading world producer of wool, 50 per cent of its area being suitable for pasture. There is also a large production of meat (mainly mutton), dairy produce, wheat, wine, and fruits: over one m. workers are employed in the growing industries, based on a steel production of over two m. tons a year. The population is mainly of British and Irish stock, with a recent immigration from Europe ('New Australians'). In recent years a distinctive school of Australian art (Sid Nolan) and literature (Patrick White) has developed.

Australia is a very old land. It has a fauna unlike that of the other continents, of which the ◊ *kangaroo*, the ◊ *duck-billed platypus*, and the ◊ *koala* bear are examples. Its commonest tree is the ◊ *eucalyptus*, of which there are several hundred varieties.

Australian Aborigines. The indigenous inhabitants of Australia, racially classified (◊ *Race*) as Proto-Caucasoid because their physical features resemble those of the Caucasoids rather than of any other racial group; long isolation has left their traditional technology resembling that of the Middle Stone Age elsewhere, and they are popularly regarded as the most primitive of all peoples. They are renowned for the elaborateness of their religion (◊ *Totemism*) and mythology, the complexity of their marriage and ◊ *kinship* system, and their weapons the spear-thrower and boomerang. Before the white men came to Australia they numbered about 300,000; disease and slaughter have reduced them to some 50,000 full-blooded and 25,000 half-caste Aborigines, the former living mainly in the arid northern parts of the continent, mostly on ranches and mission stations. The very similar aborigines of Tasmania became extinct in the late 19th cent.

Australopithecus ◊ *Palaeolithic, Primates*.

Austria. Area 32,376 sq. m. Pop. 7 m. Cap. Vienna. Rel. predominantly Roman Catholic. A Federal republic, established 1918, with an elected President and a National Assembly of 165 elected members.

ECONOMY. Besides agriculture the most important activity is iron and steel production, four or five m. tons annually. There are also engineering and metal industries. The resources include iron ore, oil, brown coal, and hydroelectric potential.

HISTORY. Before 1918 the history of Austria is that of the Hapsburg dynasty (◊ *Holy Roman Empire*) and of ◊ *Austria-Hungary*. After the defeat of the central powers in the First World War Austria became a republic, the early years of which were a period of economic hardship, riots, and political disorder. Dollfuss, Chancellor in 1932, established a virtual dictatorship and in 1934 foiled a Nazi coup (◊ *Nazism*) in which he lost his life. Faced with the pressure and intrigues of Hitler, the next Chancellor, Schuschnigg, was powerless to prevent annexation by Germany in 1938, in an *Anschluss* welcomed by a large majority of Austrians. In the Second World War, Austria was occupied by Soviet forces and subsequently divided into four allied zones. In 1955 the Western Powers and the U.S.S.R. made a peace treaty with Austria which restored her independence and her 1938 frontiers and declared her neutral.

LANGUAGE. German.

◊ *Italy, Papal States.*

Austria-Hungary. The 'Dual Monarchy', a union of ◊ *Austria* (including ◊ *Bohemia*, much of ◊ *Poland*, and what is now ◊ *Yugoslavia*) and ◊ *Hungary* under a single ruler. After his defeat in the Austro-Prussian War of 1866, Franz Joseph created a new empire, united in the person of the Emperor, which contained two ethnic groups, Germans and Magyars, as equal partners with numerous minorities e.g. Czechs, Poles, and Rumanians; receiving scant consideration, the minorities became dissatisfied and divisive. It was the dissatisfaction of the Southern Slavs which led to the assassination of Franz Joseph's heir at Sarajevo in 1914 and so to the ◊ *First World War.* In 1916 Franz Joseph died and was succeeded by his great-nephew Karl. The minorities grew increasingly disaffected as the prospects of victory faded, and on its defeat in 1918 the Dual Monarchy disintegrated, its territories being divided between Austria, Czechoslovakia, Hungary, Poland, Rumania, and Yugoslavia. ◊ *Berlin Congress, Holy Roman Empire, St Germain Treaties, War of the Austrian Succession.*

Autogiro. A ◊ *rotorcraft* moved forward through the air by an ordinary airscrew but deriving lift from a freely rotating windmill; the invention of Don Juan de la Cierva. After a period of successful development, the autogiro was overshadowed by other forms of rotorcraft esp. the ◊ *helicopter*, but the autogiro principle was used in special craft e.g. esp. the Rotodyne. Although an autogiro cannot hover, it can fly slowly and descend almost vertically, and it has shown top-speed capabilities as great as or greater than those of other forms of rotorcraft.

Automatic Data Processing. Modern largely electronic methods of handling and organizing the vast flow of data involved in the conduct of an increasingly complicated and mechanized industrial society; there are five basic operations. (1) An input device, to feed in the data and instruct the system, using magnetic tape, punched tape or cards, or automatic reading machines. (2) A central processing unit, for doing sums and logical operations at lightning speed. (3) A storage or memory unit, often made up of a main

store for 'permanent' data and a temporary store which can be prepared and replaced very rapidly. (4) An output unit, for printing results. (5) A control unit, for regulating and routing the traffic between the other units.

Automation. The control of machines without human supervision. This has domestic applications, such as the thermostat of a refrigerator, no less than industrial ones where the development of ◊ *electronics*, which provided the necessary means of refining automatic control, has revolutionized the mechanization which began with the ◊ *Industrial Revolution.* The need to mass-produce led to the development of machines which could perform operations more quickly and economically than a man, and the constant pressure to increase production with smaller manpower has resulted in refinements in the theory and practice of automatic control in which ◊ *cybernetics* is playing an increasing role. Full automation, where the entire factory is run by machines while calculation and paper work is done by ◊ *automatic data processing*, is not yet a reality, though it is technically feasible. At such a level of complexity, where many individual machines have to be coordinated and controlled, the ◊ *computer* becomes an essential element in full automation.

Automobile Association. Founded in 1905, originally to warn motorists of 'police speed traps'; it developed into an organization to provide a wide variety of assistance to motorists, and now has a membership of well over a million. Similar associations have been formed in many other countries.

Autonomy. Self-government; the degree of self-government denoted, however, may fall well short of complete political independence, e.g. in the Tatar Autonomous Republic, U.S.S.R. When autonomy is qualified, e.g. administrative autonomy, self-government is always partial; thus Scotland has a large degree of administrative autonomy, within the framework of the laws passed by the Parliament at Westminster.

Auxins. Plant hormones; substances which affect the growth of plants. They can be made synthetically and used in horticulture. ◊ *Hormones.*

Avebury. Village in Wiltshire (England) famous for its concentration of prehistoric monuments esp. the stone circle, the largest known in Europe, which comprises about 100 massive stones enclosing over 28 acres, and with outer bank 25 ft high; it is thought to have been built by the ◊ *Beaker People* about 2000–1700 B.C. and was discovered in the 17th cent. by John Aubrey.

Aviation. Regular civil aviation transport services developed after the First World War; the first daily service opened was one between London and Paris 1919. Several British companies joined to form Imperial Airways 1924, which in 1931 acquired the Handley Page aircraft, capable of carrying 40 passengers at 100 m.p.h. Other countries set up air services, often with government support, esp. the Dutch K.L.M. and the German Lufthansa (using Fokker and Junkers aircraft). In U.S.A. after a slow start commercial aviation developed rapidly, aided by government subsidies in the form of mail contracts; Pan American Airways instituted a trans-Pacific service 1935 and a mail-and-passenger service across the N. Atlantic 1939. The Boeing 247, built 1933, a low-wing all-metal aeroplane, was the prototype of the modern passenger liner. It was followed by the Douglas DC 2 and DC 3, the latter one of the most successful aircraft ever designed, of which some 13,000 were built, for commercial as well as war-transport purposes. After the Second World War civil aviation entered a more intensive phase, with the large aircraft developed during the war; aircraft became very much more costly and rapidly obsolescent, and the high-performance propeller aircraft were superseded by turbo-prop and pure jet machines. B.O.A.C. introduced the Comet pure jet 1952; it was quickly followed by the American Boeing. Supersonic passenger aircraft are in the course of development. As a result of intensive competition on international routes, air companies of most countries have incurred heavy operating losses, since few services are operated at economic capacity. With the increase in the speed of aircraft and the number of passengers, the size and cost of airports grew enormously, mainly at the expense of governments. The longest runway at London airport increased to 11,000 ft. At the same time traffic control required ever more elaborate equipment e.g. radio, radar, blind-landing aids,

meteorological services. In countries of great extent, esp. U.S.A. and Brazil, internal air services have largely displaced the railways for passenger transport. Whilst the duration of journeys in the air has been progressively reduced, the time spent in reaching airports and entering and leaving aircraft have remained unchanged and disproportionately time-consuming. The cost of passenger air transport has been made competitive with other forms of transport, but at the price of commercial losses by the operators and of massive government subsidies of various kinds. A network of air routes now covers the world, so that rapid communication between the most distant places has become in most cases a matter of hours.

Scheduled Commercial Aviation International and Domestic Traffic (in millions)

Year	Km. flown	Hours flown	Passengers carried	Passenger km. flown
1948	1270	4.6	24	21,000
1958	2920	8.7	87	85,000
1961	3110	7.9	111	117,000

North Atlantic Scheduled Flights East and West

	1952	1957	1961
Passengers	448,000	1,018,000	2,175,000

Fatal accidents in all scheduled flights

	1950	1955	1961
Total	551	407	794
Per 100 m. passenger miles	3	1.8	1.15

MILITARY AVIATION: Aircraft were used in the First World War first for reconnaissance and later for bombing attacks and were differentiated into fighters and bombers. Dirigibles were also used, unsuccessfully, by the Germans. ◊ *Zeppelin*. In the Second World War military aviation played, if not the completely decisive role some theorists had predicted, an indispensable part in all major sea and land campaigns, and the air forces particularly of the U.S.A. and Britain expanded to vast proportions. Command of the air by the Allies was a vital factor in the cross-Channel invasion of German-held France and in the subsequent land battles. The combination of tank and tactical air force was the dominating aspect of the operations. At sea, aircraft played an important part in operations against surface craft and submarines; the battleship proved vulnerable to air attack and the aircraft carrier emerged as the primary striking force at sea. The guided missile in the shape of the German V2 rocket ushered in a new phase of air warfare which in conjunction with nuclear explosives has radically affected the role of military aviation. ◊ *Rocket, Royal Air Force.*

Avocado Pear. *Persea gratissima*; a tropical American tree existing in several races and with various characteristics of leaf and fruit. The most common fruits imported into England are pear-shaped and green, with greenish-yellow flesh round a large stone. The flesh is very rich in oil.

Avogadro's Law. The hypothesis, first enunciated by Italian physicist Amedeo Avogadro, 1776–1856, that, at the same temperature and pressure, equal volumes of all gases contain equal numbers of ◊ *molecules.* Although the hypothesis was put forward in 1811, its importance was not realized until 1858, when Cannizzaro pointed out that it could be used to determine atomic weight, and it became a basis of chemical classification. Avogadro's number or constant is the number of molecules in a gram-molecule of a substance. ◊ *Gas.*

Axis. The alliance between Germany, Italy, and Japan in the late 1930s, first publicly proclaimed by Mussolini in Nov. 1936. Germany and Italy later signed the Anti-Comintern Pact (◊ *Internationals*), to which Italy adhered in Nov. 1937. In May 1939 Axis cooperation between Germany and Italy was embodied in a comprehensive military and economic pact.

Axolotl ◊ *Salamander.*

Azalea. One of the groups into which the vast genus of rhododendrons is divided, popularly associated with those which lose their leaves in winter, e.g. the common yellow scented *A. pontica.* Many of the Japanese azaleas, however, esp. the group

known as Kurumes, are evergreen. The plants grown in gardens are hybrids of wild azaleas found in Japan, China, Formosa, and N. America. ◊ *Ericaceae.*

Azilian ◊ *Mesolithic.*

Aztecs. A wild aggressive central-American tribe which settled around Lake Tenochtitlan in Mexico about A.D. 1325; during the next century, by war and treachery, they established their supremacy over the other peoples of the valley of Mexico, and achieved the peak of their power and culture by about 1450. They were sporadically at war with neighbouring tribes esp. the Tlaxcala, partly to satisfy the mounting call for victims to sacrifice to their gods. The Aztec state was based upon three ruling classes: the aristocracy, headed by the king; the priesthood; and the military and merchants. Their religion was to feed and maintain the sun by human sacrifice, for which the priests demanded as many as 20,000 victims on an occasion such as the coronation of Montezuma; in return, the sun-god would assure Aztec supremacy over all other peoples. This savage cult did not prevent their reaching a high artistic and social culture, based on the arts of earlier Toltec and Mixtec cultures, which they assimilated. Their architecture was massive, dramatic, and impressive, with monstrous gods, jaguars, serpents, and death as motifs; in carving, pottery, weaving, and painting they achieved works of great beauty, and they were skilled in agriculture, botany, medicine, and surgery, while their capital, Tenochtitlan, was larger, more spacious and hygienic, and better planned than the contemporary cities of Europe. Cortès and his band of Spaniards entered Mexico 1519, and by war, stratagem, and the support of other Mexican tribes overthrew the last Aztec rulers (Montezuma II and Cuauhtemoc), pillaged the capital, and completely destroyed the Aztec empire.

B

Baal (Bel). Originally a Semitic fertility god; later, in combination with other words (often the names of places or things), almost a generic name for 'god', e.g. Baal-Zebub (Beelzebub) 'Lord of Flies', the Devil in the New Testament (◊ *Bible*); Baal-hermon (god or lord of Mount Hermon); etc. In 'Bel and the Dragon', Bel was probably ◊ *Marduk*, the principal deity of ◊ *Babylon*. ◊ *Ishtar.*

Ba'ath. Arabic, 'resurgence'; Arab socialist party, founded 1940, strongly attached to the idea of Arab unity, with moderate socialist aims and a belief in democratic processes. The majority is anti-Nasser, judging his regime too authoritarian. The Ba'ath party has been in power for short periods in Syria and Iraq.

Babel ◊ *Babylon.*

Baboon. Long-snouted ◊ *primate* monkey, with lion-like head and mane, found in Africa and the Middle East; they are the size of a large dog, omnivorous, can be fierce, and like ◊ *gorillas* live in polygynous groups.

Babylon. Ancient city of Mesopotamia which under Hammurabi about 1750 B.C. became the capital of a flourishing empire (Babylonia), the greatest of the Semitic states which succeeded the ◊ *Sumerians*; King Hammurabi devised a code of law and organized the administration and irrigation of the whole Tigris and Euphrates region. The religion of Babylonia, with its god ◊ *Marduk* (or ◊ *Baal*) and its artificial hills (ziggurats) for temples, is reflected in the story of the Tower of Babel. Babylonia's wealth tempted the neighbouring ◊ *Hittites* and Kassites, who attacked it repeatedly until it became part of the ◊ *Assyrian* empire. An uprising against the Assyrian king Sennacherib led to the destruction of Babylon about 689 B.C. Later rulers became independent, and helped the Persians to bring about the fall of Assyria; Nebuchadnezzar about 600 B.C. brought New Babylon (the Chaldean empire) to the peak of its splendour, and the terraced 'hanging' gardens of his rebuilt Babylon were one of the Seven Wonders of the ancient world. Fragments of the famous walls of Babylon still exist. The Persians under Cyrus the Great captured Babylon 539 B.C. and Babylonia became part of the Persian Empire. ◊ *Akkadians, Babylonian Captivity, Semitic Languages.*

Babylonian Captivity. According to tradition the period of seventy years after Nebuchadnezzar captured Jerusalem and exiled the Jews to Babylon. Also the period 1309–77 when the Popes lived in Avignon.

Baccalaureate. Obsolete term for the first degree awarded by a university, generally after the student has successfully completed three or four years of study; in France, the *baccalauréat* is the qualifying examination for admission to a university.

Baccarat. Gambling game much played in casinos. There are a variety of forms, and some clubs have their own rules. Usually it is played with a club official acting as banker, using three packs of 52 cards. Bets are made that the player sitting on the banker's right (or left) will beat him. The banker twice deals a card each face down to himself and then to the two players flanking him. The players then see how near they are to 8 or 9. If they have exactly 8 or 9 they must show their cards at once. Cards from the king down to 10 count nothing; all other cards have their numerical value. The banker if he has not an equal number himself must pay 8 or 9, but if he has he wins everything on the table against any other score. Any player holding nothing but court cards or a combination of cards which add up to ten is 'baccarat' i.e. nothing. Any player may propose 'Banco', meaning that he will bet as much as there is in the bank on one round. If the banker loses, the bank is 'broke'.

CHEMIN DE FER: A similar game in which six packs are used; each player in turn to the left becomes the banker, and the deal passes as soon as the banker loses a round.

Bacchus ◊ *Dionysus.*

Bacillariophyceae ◊ *Diatoms.*

Backgammon (Tric-trac). A game for two, involving skill and luck, played on a special board with counters, each player having 15, moved according to the throws of a pair of dice taken alternately by each player. The aim of each player is to be the first to bring his counters round to his home territory and then to 'throw' them off the board. If there are two adverse men upon any point, that point is 'covered' and a man of the opposite colour cannot stop upon it. If there is only one man there it is called a 'blot' and can be hit, the piece then being removed and placed on the bar. This piece must be entered again before any other man on his side can be moved, the point of entry being decided by the throw of the dice. There are various rules concerning the throw of doubles and treys. The game is widely played in the east and is of great antiquity. A board of very similar design was found in Ur of the Chaldees, and the Greeks and Romans played a version which has remained almost unchanged. The rules which are fairly involved were codified by Hoyle in 1743. A similar game, which can be played by four, is parchesi.

Bacteria. Microscopic single-celled organisms, generally classified as plants of the *Thallophyta*, which multiply by division; some are capable of motion by flagella. They are universally present in soil, water, and air, and important in the soil as the agents which produce the ◊ *nitrogen* necessary for plants. Bacteria which feed on other living things are called pathogenic forms. Some of these cause diseases e.g. ◊ *anthrax, diphtheria, pneumonia, tuberculosis.*

Bacteriology. Study of ◊ *bacteria.*

Badlands. Originally parts of SW South Dakota, U.S.A.; difficult to cross, with little vegetation or animal life. Now similar regions elsewhere. Characteristic features of these arid regions are the deep gullies and the fantastic ridges, columns, and pinnacles into which the rocks have been carved. The ◊ *erosion* is caused by the occasional heavy cloudbursts which wash down the bare slopes and carry away any plants that may have secured a temporary foothold.

Badminton. A game for individuals or pairs; a feathered shuttle of cork is volleyed with light gut-string rackets across a 5-ft-high net, on a court 44 ft by 20 ft (doubles) or 17 ft (singles). Probably originating in the East, it was first played in Britain at Badminton Hall, Gloucestershire, in the 1860s; the All-England Championships began 1899, and 43 coun-

tries are now affiliated to the International Federation, founded 1934, which holds triennial tournaments for both men and women.

Bagasse ◊ *Paper.*

Bagdad Pact ◊ *Central Treaty Organization.*

Bagpipe. Family of reed instruments using a bag to store wind-pressure; widely found in Europe, mainly in rustic communities. The bag may be mouth-filled, as in the Scottish Highland pipes, or filled by a bellows under the player's arm, as in the Irish Uillean pipes. The effect of the bagpipe's 'drone' (a long note sustained right through the concomitant melody) has been widely simulated by composers, often with reference to the French bagpipe (*musette*).

Bahaism. Religion based on the teachings of the Persian Ali Mohammed (known as the 'Bab') who was executed in 1850, and his successor Baha-ullah, proclaiming one God who progressively reveals himself to man, the essential harmony of all religious beliefs (Abraham, Moses, Christ, Mohammed, and the 'Bab' all being regarded as prophets), and human brotherhood; the sect carries on active propaganda in many languages; its headquarters are at Haifa. ◊ *Gnostics, Mysticism, Theosophy.*

Bahamas. Large group of islands extending from Florida to Haiti. Pop. 112,556. Cap. Nassau, on New Providence Island. Of the 700 islands only 22 are inhabited. A British colony with a few agricultural exports, and a highly developed tourist industry catering for Americans.

Bahrain ◊ *Gulf Sheikhdoms.*

Bailey Bridge. A lattice girder bridge made for rapid assembly from prefabricated panels. By using these in various combinations, a wide range of spans is available. Devised by Sir Donald Bailey, the system was used for military purposes during the Second World War and is now used for temporary ◊ *bridges* and other civil-engineering works.

Bakelite ◊ *Plastics.*

Baking-powder ◊ *Tartaric Acid.*

Balaclava. 1854. Indecisive battle during the ◊ *Crimean War.* The Russians, advancing to relieve Sevastopol, captured the Vorontsov ridge from the Turks and came down towards Balaclava. In a charge lasting five minutes the Heavy Brigade routed them, while at the same time the fire of the 93rd Highlanders turned back another Russian attack; owing to a mis-interpretation of orders, the Light Brigade then gallantly but uselessly charged the Russian batteries on the ridge, suffering heavy losses.

Balance of Payments. The balance, usually struck yearly, between all payments made to foreign accounts (debits) and all re-ceipts (credits) from sources abroad. A major item is the trade balance between imports and exports. Others are 'invisible' items e.g. tourist expenditure; interest on loans paid and received; payments for banking, shipping, and insurance services. These may be called current account. There are also long-term capital-account movements. The balance of payments is said to be 'favourable' when the credit side is larger. A simplified statement of the U.K. balance of payments for 1962 and 1963 is:

U.K. BALANCE OF PAYMENTS IN
£ MILLION

	1962	1963
Current account		
Imports	4059	4318
Exports	3991	4274
Deficit on visible trade	−68	−44
Balance of invisibles	+170	+165
Balance on current account	+102	+121
Capital account		
Balance of long-term capital movements	−89	−147
Balance of short-term mone-tary movements*	+13	−26

*including errors and omissions.

Balance of Power. The policy of keeping the power of different states or groups of states roughly equal, so that no one state is able to dominate another. Wolsey main-tained such a balance between France and Spain in the 16th cent. and the policy be-came traditional to England, who by shift-ing friendship or alliance sought to maintain the continental balance of power. In the 19th and 20th centuries the Triple Alliance and the Triple Entente were late examples of attempts to keep a balance between rival blocs.

Balder (Baldur). In Scandinavian and Teutonic mythology (◊ *Aesir*), god of light; son of ◊ *Odin* and Frigga. Harm done to him would involve the doom of the gods; his mother made all living crea-tures and inanimate things swear not to harm him, but the mistletoe was over-looked, and the bad god Loki induced the blind god Hoder to throw a branch of it at Balder, who was killed. Hel, god-dess of the dead, offered to restore Balder to life if every living thing wept for him; but Loki refused.

Baleen ◊ *Whale*.

Balkan Wars. 1912–13. Two short wars in-volving the Balkan States and Turkey. In the first, Bulgaria, Serbia, Greece, and Montenegro jointly and successfully at-tacked the Turks (◊ *Ottoman Empire*) in Thrace, Macedonia, and Salonika: Euro-pean Turkey was reduced to an area round Constantinople (including the Gallipoli peninsula). In the second, Serbia (cut off from the sea by the new boundaries of Albania) demanded more of Macedonia from Bulgaria, who attacked her. Ru-mania, Greece, and Turkey soon defeated Bulgaria, who had to cede territory to them. The wars prepared the way for the ◊ *First World War*, by satisfying some Serbian aspirations and encouraging Ser-bia's desire to annex parts of ◊ *Austria-Hungary*, while alarming and stiffening the latter and making Bulgaria and Turkey dissatisfied.

Ballad. Originally, a song to accompany a dance; in the 15th cent. any light simple song, from which comes the modern use for the (usually sentimental) words to a 'pop' tune. The most common literary meaning (from late 17th cent.) is an anonymous poem, usually in stanzas set to a well-known tune, vigorously relating a popular story, and at first handed down by oral tradition. There is a particularly fine body of Scottish ballads, generally of the 15th or early 16th centuries.

Ballade. A poem of three stanzas and a separate conclusion, the 'envoy', all end-ing with the same line, the 'envoy' often addressed to a real or imaginary prince. The great master of the form is François Villon, b. 1431. Revived in the 1870s, with other late-medieval forms, by Théodore de Banville in France and by Andrew Lang and Swinburne in England, the ballade enjoyed a considerable vogue until about 1930, mainly for light verse. The most usual ballade stanza, eight lines rhyming *a b a b b c b c*, is very common through-out French and English verse of the 14th and 15th centuries.

Ball-bearings ◊ *Bearing*.

Ballet. Loosely, almost any kind of danced dramatic presentation in costume with music; more accurately, a type of dance whose technique and convention were established at the French court from the late 16th cent. onwards. The *Ballet comique de la reine* in 1581 for the marriage of Margaret of Lorraine, sister of Henri III, was an early important example. Louis XIV founded the Royal Academy of Dance in 1661 and himself danced; so did Lully, chief composer at his court. Noverre 1727–1810, French choreographer and author of a treatise on the dance, collaborated with Gluck and Mozart and established the five-act ballet as an independent form of entertainment. Dancing on the toes (*pointes*) dates from about 1820: Marie Taglioni 1804–84, the first great exponent, represents the romantic age in ballet. The most famous ballet of this age is *Giselle* 1841, written for Taglioni's rival Carlotta Grisi and presenting a typical 'ethereal' heroine. The story is by the French poet Théophile Gautier, the music by Adolphe Adam. Ballet was a regular ingredient of 19th-cent. opera, but was reinvigorated as an independent form in the second half of the century at the imperial court in Russia, with the aid of the choreographers Marius Petipa (French) and Enrico Cecchetti (Italian). Its great achievements were the three full-length ballets of the 1890s with music by Tchaikovsky, *Swan Lake, The Sleeping Beauty,* and *The Nutcracker.* A later Russian school was the creation of the impresario Serge Diaghilev, who worked in Paris from 1909. His chief choreographer, Mikhail Fokine, collaborated with the composer Stravinsky in *The Firebird* 1910 and *Petrushka* 1911. Among Diaghilev's most celebrated dancers were Vaslav Nijinsky and Léonide Massine (also a choreographer), and briefly Anna Pavlova. Picasso also collaborated as a designer.

Two former members of Diaghilev's company, Marie Rambert (b. 1888) and Ninette de Valois (b. 1898), were chiefly responsible for the flowering of British ballet. In 1931 the Vic-Wells Ballet (Old Vic and Sadler's Wells Theatres) was formed, with de Valois as director, a post she retained through the transformations to Sadler's Wells Ballet and (1956) Royal Ballet till 1963, when she was succeeded by Frederick Ashton, who with Robert Helpmann has been a notable dancer-choreographer; outstanding ballerinas are Alicia Markova and Margot Fonteyn. Rudolf Nureyev joined the Royal Ballet in 1961.

Under the inspiration of Constant Lambert as musical director of Sadler's Wells Ballet, works by major British composers were commissioned for ballet. The Royal Ballet's *The Prince of the Pagodas*, 1957, with music by Benjamin Britten b. 1913 and choreography by John Cranko, is one of the rare 20th-cent. examples outside Russia of a ballet of a full evening's length. Since the war British ballet has maintained its standing; Kenneth MacMillan is its most admired new choreographer.

The so-called 'modern dance' using free movement (and thus not strictly ballet), developed by the American dancer Isadora Duncan in Europe, flourished in pre-Hitler Germany with Rudolf von Laban (who devised a much-used system of dance notation) and Kurt Jooss, and later in America itself, where its great exponent has been the choreographer Martha Graham, e.g. *Appalachian Spring* 1944 with music by Copland. The impulse to free movement characterizes the choreography of Jerome Robbins, who has revitalized the dance element in the Broadway 'musical' e.g. Leonard Bernstein's *West Side Story*. Another major and more classical influence in American dance is wielded by the Russian-born George Balanchine, choreographer with Diaghilev 1925–9, in U.S.A. from 1933, artistic director of New York City Ballet since its inception in 1948.

In U.S.S.R. ballet like the other arts has been kept less experimental than in the west. Its chief companies, those of the Bolshoi (Moscow) and Kirov (Leningrad) theatres, enjoy a reputation for technical proficiency rather than artistic imagination.

France remains a ballet centre, though not of its former importance. The Royal Danish Ballet is also of international standing.

Ballistics. The study of the trajectories of missiles, the basic calculations being relatively simple applications of Newton's equations of motion. The velocity with which a projectile emerges from a gun-barrel is determined primarily by the mass of the projectile and the energy released by the explosive charge. It is, however, also dependent on the energy lost as heat, on frictional losses in the barrel, and on the energy taken up by the gun's recoil. The emergent velocity for a particular gun and missile is therefore usually determined experimentally. The bore of gun barrels is rifled to impart a rotary motion to the projectile and so stabilize its motion gyroscopically and keep its nose pointing forward. The trajectory of the missile after leaving the barrel is determined by the downward force of gravity and the air resistance. If air resistance is neglected, the trajectory is always part of a parabola; the range (horizontal and vertical) and the flight time (total or to apex) can be calculated from four basic trigonometric formulae linking them with the angle of elevation of the barrel, the emergent velocity of the missile, and the gravitational constant of acceleration (g). These formulae show that maximum horizontal range is achieved when the barrel is at an angle of 45° to the horizontal. The basic formulae are applicable neither to self-powered projectiles e.g. rockets nor (because they assume a flat earth) to projectiles long enough in range to be affected by the curve of the earth's surface. For very accurate gun-laying, air resistance must be taken into account, and much more complicated calculations are necessary, the appropriate corrections usually being determined semi-empirically and the results presented to the gun-layers in graphic or tabular form. The branch of ballistics sometimes referred to as interior ballistics deals with the processes that take place within the gun, and is concerned with such problems as ignition of the propellant, gas pressures, rifling of the barrel, and the designing of the mechanism to withstand the sudden stresses. Bullets discharged from a small firearm can generally be identified by characteristic deformations imparted by that firearm, and ballistics thus sometimes plays a big part in crime detection. ◊ *Artillery, Firearms*.

Balloon ◊ *Airship*.

Balsa. Corkwood; very light soft timber from a tree belonging to the *Malvaceae* native to the W. Indies and tropical S. America, where balsa logs are extensively used for rafts, esp. in Peru. The ◊ *Kon Tiki* was a reproduction of the large ocean-going balsa raft of the ancient Peruvians.

Baltic Exchange. In full, the Baltic Mercantile and Shipping Exchange, in London; the principal market for the chartering of ships of all nationalities, dating to the 17th cent. when shipbrokers and merchants met in a coffee-house to arrange shipment and sale of goods.·

Baltic States. Collective name for Lithuania, Latvia, and Estonia, on the E. shore of the Baltic. Rel. Estonia and Latvia are Lutheran, Lithuania Roman Catholic. These former Russian provinces became independent in 1918, but in 1940 they were occupied by Soviet troops and incorporated into the U.S.S.R. as member republics. The annexation has not been formally recognized by U.S.A. and several other countries.
ECONOMY. The area is largely agricultural but also produces oil, timber, fish, textiles, and machinery.
HISTORY. In the 14th cent. Estonia and Latvia were both ruled by the German order of Livonian Knights, who introduced Christianity. In the 17th cent. both were annexed by Sweden and then by Russia (1721), which emancipated the Latvian serfs in 1819. Lithuania in the 13th cent. formed an independent pagan state which expanded rapidly and in the 14th cent. accepted Christianity and formed a close alliance with Poland, followed by full union in 1569. With the partition of Poland in the late 18th cent., Lithuania passed to Russia.
LANGUAGES. Lithuanian and Latvian belong to the Baltic branch of the ◊ *Slavonic languages* and are both highly inflected archaic tongues. Estonian belongs to the Finno-Ugrian group; its literary existence began only in the 16th cent.

Baluchi ◊ *Indo-European Languages, Persia*.

Bamboo. Woody-stemmed grasses belonging to three genera of the *Gramineae*, named after a Malayan variety. They vary greatly in size, from dwarf varieties to some which have stems or canes six in. thick and 100 ft high. The tropical species, which are most numerous, grow very rapidly. Some species are hardy in temperate climates. In the Far East they are used for many purposes: bridges, rafts, water pipes, building, etc. The young shoots are a popular Chinese vegetable and also the main food of the ◊ *panda*. Some bamboos flower annually, others at long intervals.

Banana. Species of *Musaceae*, giant monocotyledonous herbs native in the old world which grow widely throughout tropical and sub-tropical regions, in appearance resembling palms. The common banana, *M. paradisiaca*, grows up to 20 ft tall; the overlapping bases of its large leaves form a false trunk from which the true stem emerges to carry a single flower head with 6 to 9 clusters (hands) of 10 to 20 bananas. The cultivated banana has been developed by long selection; its seeds are sterile. After flowering the plant dies; new plants grow from suckers. There are very many varieties, of which the Canary banana is the smallest found in the export trade. The large variety, the plantain, is much eaten in the tropics either cooked or made into flour. In cultivation the new shoots bear fruit in under a year and the crop yield per acre is high. The main banana exporting areas are Central America, Brazil, the W. Indies, and the Canaries. Another important species of *Musa* is the Manila hemp plant, valued for its fibre.

Banking. Simple forms of banking existed in Greece and Rome, but after the breakup of the Roman Empire there was little banking until it revived in the 13th and 14th centuries. It grew in part from money-lending to rulers – the Medici for the papacy, Fuggers for the Holy Roman Empire – whilst the banks of Venice and Genoa were more direct ancestors of modern commercial banking. In England the goldsmiths for long discharged the function of banks. It was not until 1694, with the founding of the ◊ *Bank of England*, that modern forms of banking began to develop. The commonest are the joint-stock banks doing general business with the public and serving as repositories for deposits and sources of credit and loans, their activities varying slightly in different countries; a feature of such banks is that they can create credit by making more loans than they receive deposits. In Britain they seldom act as suppliers of long-term capital, though they function in this way in Germany and most continental countries. As not many of their customers will wish to withdraw their deposits in cash, but will transfer them to someone else by cheque, such banks consider it safe to create credit in the ratio of

eleven to one. In Britain such banks are expected by the Bank of England to keep 8 per cent of their total deposits in cash and 30 per cent on call or short notice. The remainder is put either into Government stock (U.K. banks do not buy shares) or is advanced to customers; these advances are usually for one or two years at most. The rate of interest on these advances is related to the Bank Rate.

CENTRAL BANK: A repository for the excess funds of commercial banks, and banker to the government; essential to a modern banking system, it can control the volume of bank credit and the rates of interest, implements government monetary policy, and nowadays is the only bank authorized to issue bank notes. In most countries the central bank, though not a government department, is closely controlled by the government, e.g. the Banque de France. The ◊ *Bank of England* in the U.K. and the Federal Reserve System in U.S.A. preserve a certain degree of autonomy.

Bank of England. The central bank (◊ *Banking*) for the U.K. It acts as banker to the government and to other banks, is the note-issuing authority, manages the National Debt, and operates Exchange Control (◊ *Foreign Exchange*). It is largely responsible for implementing monetary policy through the bank rate, which influences the general level of interest rates, and through its right since 1962 to call upon commercial banks to deposit with it, in cash, a certain percentage of their assets, thus regulating the amounts available for lending to the public. It also acts as the Government's agent in giving any instructions to the commercial banks about the permissible level of advances or the purposes for which they may properly be made. It was established by Royal Charter as a private bank in 1694; in 1946 its entire capital was acquired by the government by Act of Parliament. It is run by a Governor and Board of Directors.

Bankruptcy. A bankrupt is a debtor declared by a court of law to be unable to meet his debts. The appropriate court first makes a receiving order placing the debtor's property in charge of the Official Receiver; if the creditors then do not agree to an alternative arrangement, the court issues a bankruptcy order and a trustee in bankruptcy is nominated to distribute to the creditors the assets of the bankrupt, who is normally released from further liability, though in some cases his discharge may be suspended, when he remains subject to certain liabilities as an undischarged bankrupt.

Bannockburn. 1314. Battle in which the Scottish army under Robert Bruce defeated Edward II's greatly superior army on its way to the relief of Stirling. Edward's cavalry attacked the Scots in a prepared position behind the Bannock burn, with a narrow front protected by concealed pits. The English were unable to penetrate the Scottish pikemen, the second line could not join the battle, and the archers were put out of action by the Scottish cavalry. The lesson of the battle was later turned to advantage at ◊ *Crécy* and ◊ *Poitiers*. ◊ *Falkirk*.

Bantu ◊ *African Languages, Peoples, Basutoland.*

Bantustan ◊ *Apartheid.*

Baptism. Rite of admission to the Christian church, usually administered to infants soon after birth (except by ◊ *Baptists* and some smaller sects); in the Anglican, Roman Catholic, and Eastern Orthodox churches water is poured or sprinkled over the head and a fixed formula recited, but some Protestant sects prescribe complete immersion. ◊ *Anabaptists, Original Sin.*

Baptists. A Protestant Free Church which rejects infant baptism and practises adult baptism by immersion; arose in England in the 17th cent. (possibly remotely derived from the ◊ *Albigenses*); soon divided into General Baptists (◊ *Arminianism*) and Particular Baptists (◊ *Calvinism*), finally reunited 1891. Strict Baptists admit to ◊ *Holy Communion* only persons baptized as adults, open Baptists admit all who have been baptized, even if as infants. Baptist belief was introduced into America in 1639 by Roger Williams, founder of Rhode Island; the most famous of English Baptists is John Bunyan. The Baptist Missionary Society, founded 1792, was the first English organization for foreign ◊ *missions*. Today there are about 24 m. Baptists throughout the world, within the Baptist World Alliance. ◊ *Nonconformists.*

Barbiturates. Salts of barbituric acid having a powerful sedative action on the ◊ *central nervous system* but tending to be habit-forming. ◊ *Pharmacology.*

Barbizon School. A group of painters, associated with Théodore Rousseau and J.-F. Millet, who settled at Barbizon in the forest of Fontainebleau in the 1840s and produced unsentimental on-the-spot pictures of landscapes and peasant life, and though making no violent departure from tradition, prepared the way for ◊ *Impressionism.*

Bar Cochba ◊ *Messiah.*

Bard. A member of one of the guilds or families of Celtic poets who celebrated heroes to the accompaniment of the harp and also preserved genealogies. Welsh bards competed in ◊ *eisteddfod* tournaments, a custom revived in the 18th cent. Irish bards (◊ *Finn*) were honoured members of the community, with priestly functions. The word often connotes the poet's prophetic function, as in Gray's *The Bard*, 1757.

Barium. A silvery-white metal, the most electro-positive (◊ *Metals and Non-metals*) of the alkaline earth elements. It is found naturally as its sulphate (◊ *barytes* or heavy spar) and as the carbonate (witherite). It liberates ◊ *hydrogen* from water and is rapidly oxidized by the air; hence its use as a 'getter' for removing the last traces of oxygen during the manufacture of radio vacuum tubes and in the refining of other metals. Many of its compounds are insoluble in water, but the soluble ones (including hydroxide, chloride, and nitrate) are very poisonous. The most important compound is the sulphate, which is white, heavy, and very insoluble, used as a filler in the making of paper and rubber goods, in the gruel ('barium meal') given to patients whose digestive organs need to be X-rayed, and as a pigment either alone ('*blanc fixe*') or with zinc sulphide ('lithopone'). The nitrate and chlorate are used in fireworks to give green colour. As with the other alkaline earth elements, the valency state of barium in its compounds is two.

Bark. Non-technical term for tissues in woody plants outside the cambium. Bark is easily peeled off twigs and logs; it usually contains a lot of cork, but includes the phloem (◊ *Bast*) and a variety of other tissues. It often contains ◊ *tannins*, resins, ◊ *latex*, and other complex substances which can be used for tanning and dyeing and as a source of drugs and various fibres. ◊ *Elm.*

Barley. *Hordeum vulgare*; an ancient

◊ *cereal* probably originating in Asia. Huskless barley existed in Europe in the Stone Age (about 4000 years ago), but by the Bronze Age modern types predominated. As with wheat, there are several summer and winter varieties. Barley was the principal bread flour till the 16th cent. in Europe. Its chief use now is for fodder and straw and as malt for ◊ *brewing* and malt extracts. Malt is made by allowing the grains to germinate until the shoot is about one third the length of the grain. During germination much of the starch in the endosperm is converted into sugars. The grains are then kiln-dried and known as malt, the colour depending upon the drying temperature.

Barnacle. Marine crustacean; the acorn barnacle, *Balanus balanoides*, the best known, found limpet-like on rocks, driftwood, and hulls. Barnacles feed by drawing a current of water to the mouth by means of legs or 'feelers'; some have fleshy stalks by which they attach themselves to hard surfaces, some are parasites. The classification of the barnacles (Cirripedia) is complex and was one of Charles Darwin's major contributions to biology.

Barometer. Instrument for measuring changes in atmospheric pressure; essentially, a tall narrow tube containing mercury, which rises or falls according to the weight of the atmosphere and is affected by variations e.g. moisture content, so that the barometer indicates ◊ *weather* trends. The first barometer was invented 1643 by Torricelli, a pupil of Galileo.

ANEROID BAROMETER: A bellows-like box of thin metal, the sides responding to air-pressure changes; can be fitted with a mechanical device to make a continuous record. ◊ *Isobar*.

Baroque. Misshapen (form) or tortuous (idea); a term originally applied to art and architecture as abuse in the 17th cent. Some writers now use it as a synonym for '17th-cent.' but more correctly it is reserved for an artistic style which succeeded ◊ *Mannerism* in early 17th-cent. Rome and persisted throughout Europe until the emergence of ◊ *Rococo*. Anticlassical, emotional, Baroque is characterized by fondness for voluptuous movement, three-dimensional forms (in paintings marked by strong effects of light and shade and deep perspective), ◊ *trompe l'œil* effects, richness of materials, and

grandeur of scale; it found its finest expression in Bernini's ecstatic religious statues and sumptuous church interiors (notably St Peter's in Rome), Borromini's complicated *mouvementé* architecture, and the deeply emotional religious paintings of Rubens; and though somewhat outside the main current of the movement, Rembrandt and Velasquez were also influenced by the style. From Italy it spread to Spain, where is was very popular with church architects, and to Germany

Ss. Vincenzo ed Anastasio, Rome

and Austria about 1680; in France it was acceptable only in a classicized form, and in England it had even less success.

In music, Baroque is the somewhat monumental and ornate style of composers from about the early 17th cent. (Monteverdi) to the mid 18th cent. (Bach); and to the contemporary conventions for performing this music.

Barracuda. Large bony marine fish similar to the pike, with a formidable armament of teeth set in deep sockets, those on the roof of the mouth being particularly large and knife-like and well-adapted to its voracious habits. There are several species inhabiting all warm seas; they occasionally swim inshore and attack bathers.

Barracuta. A fierce voracious fish found

in Australian waters; not related to the ◊ *barracuda*.

Barrage. A low ◊ *dam* across a wide river, with sluice gates to control the flow. The object is to raise the level of the river so that water can be diverted into a system of irrigation canals. The plain of the River Indus and its tributaries has been extensively developed in this manner, the best known barrage being that at Sukkur, 4725 ft long. The Nile system has five barrages below Cairo and three between Cairo and Aswan, of which the Assiut, 2750 ft long, is the most notable.

Barrier Reef. Chain of ◊ *coral* rocks lying parallel to the coast, at or near the ocean surface; the Great Barrier Reef extends for about 1000 m. along the E. coast of Australia, separated from the shore by deep water from 20 to 150 m. wide.

Barrister. Member of the advocacy branch of the legal profession, having the right to address any superior court (i.e. higher than a magistrates' court in England); referred to as 'counsel' in court. To become a barrister a student must join one of the four ◊ *Inns of Court*, 'keep terms' by dining there, attend lectures, and pass examinations, after which he may be 'called to the Bar'; the professional conduct of barristers is supervised by the General Council of the Bar, and a barrister's services in court can be engaged only through a ◊ *solicitor*. A Queen's Counsel (QC) is a senior barrister permitted by the ◊ *Lord Chancellor* to 'take silk' i.e. wear a silk gown instead of a stuff one; by custom, he or she thereafter appears in court only when accompanied by another barrister, and his or her practice is confined to important cases carrying high fees. A barrister not a QC is known as a 'junior' irrespective of his or her age. The distinction between barrister and solicitor is peculiar to Gt Britain; in other countries, though lawyers may specialize, there is no formal division between advocates and other lawyers. ◊ *Dock Brief*, *Legal Aid*.

Barrow. Tumulus; a prehistoric burial mound. In Europe barrows of the ◊ *Neolithic* period are generally long (up to 300 ft) but those of the ◊ *Bronze Age* are round and as a rule contain only one primary grave. Round barrows were also constructed in the Romano-British and pagan Saxon periods.

Barytes. Mineral, ◊ *barium* sulphate, sp. gr. 4.5; usually called heavy spar. Commonly found in lead veins, e.g. in the carboniferous ◊ *limestone* of the S. Pennines; also occurs as nodules in the fuller's-earth beds of Surrey and as the cementing material of some Triassic sandstones (◊ *Geological Time Scale*). Usually white; used in white paint and added to wallpaper to give weight.

Basalt. Dark-coloured ◊ *igneous rock*, usually fine-grained crystalline but occasionally glassy; of basic composition, containing the minerals ◊ *felspar*, augite, and sometimes olivine, and found in ◊ *lava* flows or intruded into other rocks in dykes or sills. On cooling, it may develop hexagonal joints and form perfectly shaped columns separated into short sections by ball-and-socket joints, as at Giant's Causeway or Fingal's Cave. Basaltic rocks form the lowest layers of the earth's crust. ◊ *Sima*.

Baseball. The U.S.A. national summer game, evolved from old English bat-and-ball games esp. rounders; the earliest known match took place 1845. There are nine players a side (with substitution allowed), and the diamond-shaped pitch is 90 ft square, the pitcher's box being 60 ft 6 in. from the 'home plate' (batting position); the batting side attempt to score runs by completing circuits of the 'bases' at the four corners of the diamond. The ball, which is hard and weighs 5 oz., is delivered 'full toss' and the catcher (behind home plate) wears protective clothing. A game has nine innings, each being completed when three men are out. Baseball has spread to Canada, Japan, Mexico, and Australia, where it is competing in popularity with ◊ *cricket*. The two main U.S.A. professional leagues are the National and the American, each with eight clubs; league games are played every day in the April–Oct. season, each club playing 154 games, and the two league winners meet in a 'World Series' of seven games. An attempt has been made to introduce amateur baseball to Britain, with some success.

Bases ◊ *Acids and Bases*.

Basic Slag ◊ *Fertilizers*.

Basilica. A rectangular hall with colonnaded aisles and a semi-circular apse, used by the Romans for public administration, e.g. the Basilica of Maxentius at Rome. The early Christians adopted the form for

section of St Paul's, Rome

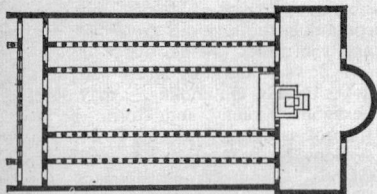

ground plan of St Paul's, Rome

their churches, e.g. S. Clemente at Rome, and the term is now applied to churches generally. ◊ *Roman Architecture.*

Basilisk. Central-American member of the iguana family, with an erectile crest along its back and a crested head reminiscent of a cock-fowl's; insectivorous, and extremely agile both in water and on land, where it lives chiefly among trees.

Basin ◊ *Catchment Area.*

Basketball. Indoor game resembling ◊ *netball,* except that players may move with the ball whilst bouncing it, but with five players to a side and up to seven substitutions allowed; primarily a men's game. It has spread from U.S.A. to nearly all countries, including Britain, and became an Olympic sport 1936.

Basques. A people of the W. Pyrenees living in both N. Spain and SW France; a social and linguistic rather than racial group, whose origin, long debated, is still unknown. Some cultural features – games, certain ceremonies, types of house – are quite distinct from those of their neighbours and of other peoples; they may be last survivals of an Upper Palaeolithic culture.

LANGUAGE: Like ◊ *Burushaski,* Basque is apparently related to no other language; the Basques call it Euskara, 'clear speaking', and it may be the sole surviving remnant of a pre-Roman Iberian or Aquitanian tongue used in S. France and Spain in remote antiquity. Various dialects are spoken by about 1 m. Basques in the W. Pyrenees; many place-names in Aragon, and the name 'Gascony', are Basque. The language is agglutinative; nouns have fifteen cases and verbs many complex auxiliaries but no active voice ('by John a house is built' for 'John builds a house').

Bass. Marine and freshwater bony fish, belonging to the ◊ *perch* family; the giant sea bass of tropical waters reach an enormous size. In America, bass are common freshwater fish valued as food-fish and cultivated in State hatcheries. The beautifully coloured small aquarium sunfishes are related to the freshwater bass. Their introduction as game-fish into many parts of the world has led to a serious depletion of the indigenous fish, which they eat.

Bassoon. Double-reed musical instrument, the bass counterpart of the ◊ *oboe*; a standard component of the symphony orchestra and military band. It evolved from the mid-16th-cent. 'curtal'. The lower-pitched double-bassoon appeared in the 18th cent. After Beethoven's *Choral Symphony* of 1824 it came to be regarded as normal in large orchestras.

Bast. Phloem; living vascular tissue which conducts soluble food materials throughout the plant. The process of conduction is known as translocation. In most woody plants the phloem is outside the ◊ *wood* and separated from it by the ◊ *cambium*; it is a component of ◊ *bark.* It often contains commercially important fibres e.g. flax, hemp, jute. It may also contain ◊ *tannins,* resins, ◊ *latex,* alkaloids (quinine), and spices (cinnamon).

Bastille. One of the forts in the old walls of Paris, used as a prison for political prisoners under the ◊ *Bourbons* and regarded as a symbol of royal oppression. It was singled out and stormed by the Paris mob on 14 July 1789; the tricolour flag of the Revolution was hoisted above it. The Fourteenth of July subsequently became the national day of France.

Basutoland. Area 11,716 sq. m. Pop. 0.6 m. (Bantu). Cap. Maseru. A British territory, an enclave geographically within ◊ *South Africa.* It is an African territory without white landowners. The Basuto nation was formed by the ruler Moshesh (*c.* 1810–70), partly by conquest but mainly by accepting and protecting the remnants of the many small tribes of the region scattered by the conquests of the ◊ *Zulu* king Shaka. The high mountain country gives an agrarian cattle-raising and agricultural economy. Many Bantu go as migrant labour to towns in S. Africa, and often settle there.

Bat. Of the *Chiroptera*; the only truly flying mammal. The wing is a sheet of skin between the forearm and hand, flank, and leg and thus inhibits walking. Bats vary in their diet; some eat fruit, some insects, some fish, and others are blood-suckers. Their body temperature falls rapidly when at rest. Their senses of smell and hearing are very acute; some bats can fly through a dark room and avoid wires stretched across it, by means of an ultrasonic echo-location mechanism. British bat species are roughly the size of a mouse, but the tropical fruit bats may have a wing span of five ft. Bats are a widespread and successful group distributed throughout temperate and tropical regions.

Bataan. 1942. Peninsula on an island in the Philippines, to which in the ◊ *Second World War* General MacArthur's American and Filipino troops withdrew to avoid encirclement by the Japanese. They held out for three months with inadequate food and munitions, against forces five times as strong, before being overrun. Their prolonged stand gave the Americans time to regroup their forces at a critical juncture.

Bathyscaphe, Bathysphere ◊ *Diving.*

Battle of Britain. 1940. In the ◊ *Second World War*, after the defeat of France Germany launched heavy air attacks upon Britain as a preliminary to possible invasion; for three months the Luftwaffe made daylight attacks upon London and other large cities, esp. those with docks. With a perilously small force of Spitfire and Hurricane fighters, but aided by the new device of ◊ *radar*, the R.A.F. inflicted such serious losses on German fighter and bomber planes that daylight raids were abandoned in favour of night-bombing (the Blitz); the risk of invasion was virtually eliminated. Heavy losses in aircraft and pilots were suffered by both sides; the exact figures remain in dispute. During these attacks some 44,000 civilians were killed and more than 50,000 seriously injured.

Battle of the Nations ◊ *Napoleonic Wars.*

Battleship. The most heavily armoured naval vessel, with guns of the largest calibre; until the advent of the ◊ *aircraft carrier* the largest of all naval craft, apart from a few battle-cruisers (similar vessels of greater speed but less heavily armoured and gunned). The forerunner of the battleship was the large line-of-battle ship of the 18th and 19th centuries, replaced from 1860 by ironclad warships. The British ◊ *Dreadnought*, launched in 1906, was the first of a class of huge heavily armoured vessels, soon copied by other naval powers.

Bauxite. Principally aluminium hydroxide; chief ore of aluminium. Usually found impure; probably formed by the ◊ *weathering* of ◊ *igneous rocks* in equatorial conditions. The chief suppliers of the world's bauxite are Jamaica (the world's biggest supplier), British and Dutch Guiana (together producing almost half the total of 9 m. tons), France, and U.S.A. The name derives from Les Baux in France, where the earth was first mined.

Bavaria. Area 27,000 sq. m. Pop. about 10 m. Cap. Munich. The southernmost German state; formerly an independent kingdom (◊ *Palatinate*), and always predominantly Catholic. Duke Maximilian I of Bavaria led the Catholic League during the ◊ *Thirty Years War*; in the ◊ *War of the Spanish Succession* Bavaria sided with France, and it was in Bavaria that Marlborough defeated their allied forces at ◊ *Blenheim*. After the ◊ *Napoleonic wars* Bavaria for a time kept the balance of power between Austria and Prussia. The 'mad King' Ludwig II built a number of extravagant palaces and castles, now of outstanding touristic value. Joining the German empire in 1871, Bavaria maintained a strong sense of identity; in the ◊ *First World War* its Crown Prince commanded a separate Bavarian army. In 1918 a Bavarian Socialist coup resulted briefly in a seizure of power by communists, but in the 1920s Munich became the cradle of ◊ *Nazism*. Bavaria is mainly agricultural, with some industry and considerable banking and insurance business in Munich and Nuremberg. S. Bavaria has splendid mountain scenery.

Bay ◊ *Daphne, Laurel.*

Bayeux Tapestry. Not a tapestry, but a strip of linen 19 in. wide and about 200 ft long, embroidered in coloured wool with scenes from the life of King Harold, traditionally supposed to be the work of Matilda, wife of William the Conqueror, but more probably executed by Norman craftsmen for his half-brother Odo, Bishop of Bayeux. It is in the Bayeux Museum, near Caen.

Bayou. Marshy creek, or offshoot to river or lake, containing sluggish or stagnant water; chiefly in southern U.S.A. and often meaning an ◊ *ox-bow lake*, e.g. in the lower basin of the Mississippi.

Beaker People. Of the early ◊ *Bronze Age*, named after their characteristic pottery; they spread all over central and W. Europe, probably from S. Spain, and about 2000–1800 B.C. arrived in Britain, where they introduced metal tools and weapons, although they also used ◊ *flint* implements. Their weapons and ornaments of copper and gold may perhaps have been limited for the most part to chieftains. They built round ◊ *barrows* for burials, and seem to have been responsible for at least part of the stone circles at ◊ *Avebury* and ◊ *Stonehenge*. Nothing is known of their domestic buildings.

Bean. Various species of *Leguminosae*; important varieties of edible beans are: (1) Broad bean, an annual derived from *Vicia faba*, probably native to the Near East, where it has been cultivated from time immemorial, being well known to the Egyptians and Romans. It was grown in Britain by Chaucer's time. (2) French or kidney bean, developed from the S. American *Phaseolus vulgaris* cultivated by the Incas, introduced in Europe in the 16th cent. (3) Scarlet runner bean, derived from the perennial *Phaseolus multiflorus*, a climbing plant from S. America first introduced as an ornamental climber early in the 17th cent. and now grown as an annual. (4) Soya bean, *Glycine soja*, rich in proteins, is an important crop in the Far East where it is used in a variety of forms for food and fodder.

Bear. 1. *Ursus*; large mammal, almost exclusive to the northern hemisphere. Although classed as carnivores, most bears are mainly herbivorous. One type, the white polar bear, a strong swimmer, has re-evolved a carnivorous dentition and preys on other animals e.g. seals as well as fish. The largest is the Alaskan brown bear, which may weigh up to 1500 lb. At one time the common brown bear was found in Britain, but it disappeared, and for the bear-baiting popular up to the 17th cent. it had to be imported. ◊ *Koala.*

2. In finance, a speculator who hopes to profit by a fall in the prices of stocks or commodities e.g. by selling for future delivery shares which he does not yet own (selling short), in the hope of buying and delivering them when the price has fallen and profiting by the difference; hence 'bear market', in which prices are falling or expected to fall. ◊ *Bull, Stag, Stock Exchange.*

Bearing. A means of supporting a revolving shaft. The simplest bearing is merely a hole in the supporting structure; usually it is provided with a renewable lining ('bush') of a suitable ◊ *alloy* of low frictional resistance. In ball or roller bearings the rubbing friction is greatly reduced by using hard steel balls or rollers held in 'races' which rotate when the shaft rotates. Ball or roller bearings call for utmost precision in their manu-

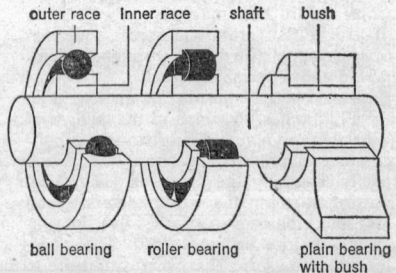

ball bearing   roller bearing   plain bearing with bush

facture, which is a very specialized process. Plain bearings are made of anti-friction alloys, consisting essentially of a soft metal as matrix containing harder particles of other metals. All bearings must be lubricated by an either closed or continuous system, to spread a film of oil over the surfaces in contact. More modern self-lubricating bearings are made by sintering together two metal powders e.g. copper with tin or lead; an oil lubricant can be incorporated into the resulting porous structure.

Beaufort Scale ◊ *Winds.*

Bechuanaland. Area 220,000 sq. m. Pop. 0.3 m. (of various African tribes). Cap. Mafeking. A British protectorate in southern Africa. The economy is pastoral, with extensive cattle-rearing.

Bedouin. < Ar. *bedawin*, desert dwellers; nomadic tribesmen still numerous in the uncultivable arid areas of Syria, Iraq, Arabia, and N. Africa, all Muslims and almost all Arabs. They live in tents of black goat's-hair and raise sheep and goats (their principal source of food), camels, and horses. They follow a strict traditional code of conduct which includes the obligation of hospitality to travellers. All members of a tribe are equal under the leadership of a sheikh, whose office is not necessarily hereditary. ⟡ *Senussi*.

Bee. Insect of the order *Hymenoptera*; there are over 20,000 species, of which about 95 per cent are solitary or show only incipient social behaviour. The solitary bees (in this resembling ⟡ *wasps*) build their nests of materials other than wax, e.g. leaves or mud. Of the social bees, the bumble bee and the ⟡ *honey* bee are best known, the latter being of considerable economic importance. The typical bee colony consists of a queen, a few hundred drones (fertile males), and thousands of workers, sterile females who do all the work of the nest. Workers are equipped with long tongues for lapping up nectar and with hair-covered limbs modified for pollen gathering. The wax, used in making the cells, is secreted in their bodies. The sting is a modified ovipositor, no longer used in egg-laying; its use almost invariably results in the death of the worker.

In the nuptial flight the new queen is inseminated by one of the drones, swarming after her. On return to the nest she lays the eggs in comb-cells. The size of the cell and the type of nutrition determine the caste of the offspring: workers result from fertilized eggs; queens arise from larvae housed in enlarged cells and fed entirely on royal jelly; drones develop from unfertilized eggs by ⟡ *parthenogenesis*.

Bees have colour vision, and sense ultraviolet light invisible to human beings. They detect the plane of polarization of daylight, and hence can navigate by determining the sun's position. Communication e.g. of the location and amount of pollen is effected by the pattern and intensity of the bee 'dance'.

Beech. *Fagus sylvatica*, of the *Fagaceae*; a large tree native in Europe. It has silvery bark, a dense spreading crown, and oval leaves with rather wavy edges. The edible fruit (mast), a flattened pyramidal nut in a spiny cupule, is produced copiously every few years. Various ornamental forms are known e.g. copper beech with purplish leaves, and the cut-leaved beech. In England the beech forms extensive woodlands, esp. on chalky soils.

Beelzebub ⟡ *Baal*.

Beer ⟡ *Brewing*.

Beet ⟡ *Sugarbeet*.

Beetle. Insect of the largest order, *Coleoptera*, comprising 250,000 species. They have four wings, of which the first two form hard covers (elytra) for the second pair. In some, e.g. the devil's coach-horse, the elytra are small, not covering the abdomen, so that intricate folding is required to tuck the wings beneath them. The male stag beetle has 'antlers' formed by the enormously enlarged mandibles which, as in other beetles, can be used for biting. The order includes ladybirds, weevils, which are pests attacking stored food and causing extensive damage, and the ⟡ *Colorado beetle*. The primitive aquatic *Dytiscidae* are large beetles that trap air beneath the elytra, so forming an artificial gill. Beetles develop in an egg-larva-pupa-adult cycle, some larvae e.g. those of the ground beetle being active mobile carnivores whilst others are maggot-like. Most beetles are harmless or beneficial; many e.g. the scarab are very beautiful.

Behaviourism ⟡ *Psychology*.

Belemnite. Pencil-like ⟡ *fossil* of the internal bones ('pen') of a cephalopod, a species of shellfish something like a modern cuttlefish, now extinct; common in Mesozoic rocks (⟡ *Geological Time Scale*).

Belgium. Area 11,780 sq. m. Pop. 9.5 m. of which just over half, the Flemings, live in the N. The rest, French-speaking Walloons, live in the S. Cap. Brussels. Constitutional monarchy (present king Baudouin) with a chamber of deputies (212) and a Senate (varying membership). There is tension between the Flemings and the Walloons.

ECONOMY. The most densely populated country in Europe, it is highly industrialized, textiles, engineering, iron and steel, and shipbuilding being most important. Dairy farming, beet and potato, and flax production are leading agricultural activities. ⟡ *Benelux*.

HISTORY. In the Middle Ages the great textile towns were virtually independent; the area came under ⟡ *Burgundy* and later Charles V (⟡ *Holy Roman Empire*). It was united with the ⟡ *Netherlands* in 1815 but broke away in 1830. Part of the 'cockpit of Europe', Belgium's neutrality did not save her from war in 1914, and she was again overrun by the Germans in 1941. Belgium established an important overseas Empire (◊ *Congolese Republic*) to which independence was granted in 1959. LANGUAGE. Both French and Flemish are official languages.

Belladonna. Extract of the leaves and roots of the plant *Atropa belladonna*, used as an anti-spasmodic drug in whooping-cough and asthma and externally as an ingredient of certain liniments. The active principle, atropine, is a nervous-system stimulant, diminishes glandular secretions, relieves spasm, and is used to dilate the pupil to facilitate examination of the eye.

Bellerophon. 1. British ship which carried Napoleon to exile in St Helena after the ◊ *Napoleonic Wars.*

2. ◊ *Pegasus.*

Bells. Percussion instruments, usually sounded by an interior clapper, of metal (the favoured being an alloy three-quarters copper and one-quarter tin). In an ◊ *orchestra*, bell sounds are generally provided by suspended tuned metal tubes ('chimes').

The traditional English method of sounding a set of bells is by change-ringing, where the ringers (one to each bell) follow mathematical patterns of succession. The largest bell in Britain is in St Paul's Cathedral (nearly 17 tons); in 1733 a bell of 180 tons was cast in Moscow but broke before it was used.

CARILLON: A set of bells played by a single player at a keyboard, esp. practised in Belgium and Holland.

Beltane. The great spring feast of the Celtic peoples at the beginning of May (still sometimes a name for 'May Day' in Scotland); modern May-day rites (e.g. dancing round the Maypole) probably derive from it, as similar autumn rites e.g. lighting bonfires do from the autumn feast Samhain in early November.

Beluga ◊ *Sturgeon.*

Belvedere. A turret or 'lantern' on the top of a house, or a summer-house on an eminence commanding a view; a courtyard in the Vatican, the Cortile del Belvedere, has given its name to certain classical statues shown in the rooms surrounding it e.g. the Apollo Belvedere.

Bends. Body pains resulting from too rapid decompression after deep diving (or from too rapid ascent to high altitudes), caused by infiltration into the tissues of bubbles of ◊ *nitrogen*, best removed by again subjecting the sufferer to pressure and then reducing it more slowly.

Benedictines. Christian religious order tracing its origin to St Benedict of Norcia A.D. 480–543 and following the Rule drawn up by him; specially devoted to learning, and largely responsible for the preservation of classical culture through the Dark Ages. Their principal activity is the *opus Dei*, work of God, i.e. the solemn celebration of the eight daily offices of liturgical prayer; also they conduct schools, assist the parish clergy, and do literary and foreign missionary work. Today they number about 12,000; some houses (both of men and of women) follow the Benedictine Rule but are members of the Church of England. ◊ *Monasticism.*

Benelux. A customs union established between Belgium, the Netherlands, and Luxemburg in 1947 as the result of a convention concluded in London in 1944. Common customs tariffs were fixed in 1948, and attempts were then made to unify excise and indirect taxes. It was found, however, that further integration and reconciliation of the separate countries' economies would be necessary. In 1958 a treaty establishing an economic union was concluded at the Hague; this provided for a free flow of capital, labour, goods, services, and traffic between the countries concerned, and a common commercial policy towards other countries. The Treaty came into force on 1 Nov. 1960.

Benzene. Volatile liquid ◊ *hydrocarbon* produced during the carbonization of coal and by ◊ *petroleum* cracking. Of formula C_6H_6, it is the simplest aromatic hydrocarbon. Benzene is used commercially in motor fuels as a solvent, and as a raw material for the production of ◊ *dyes, insecticides, plastics.*

Benzine. Mixture of ◊ *hydrocarbons* of the ◊ *paraffin* series, used as a solvent and in dry-cleaning.

Beowulf. One of the earliest Old English poems (probably A.D. 8th cent.) and the longest (about 3000 lines); the only known Old English ◊ *epic*. The first part deals with Beowulf's vanquishing of the monster Grendel and his dam, the second with his half century of rule over the Geats, and his death after defeating a ravaging dragon; it ends with the old hero's funeral, when 12 warriors circle his barrow praising his valour and virtue. Far from being a crude versification of marvels and violence, of historical interest only,

Beowulf is a great poem in its own right, with a complex and subtle organization, of true epic value. It throws much light on Old English moral and religious heroic ideals and their confrontation with Christian teaching.

Berbers. The indigenous inhabitants of N. Africa, who originally occupied all the area N. of the Sahara, from Egypt to the Atlantic; a 'white' race, they are generally still distinct from the Arab or mixed population, though Muslim. Berbers often form only isolated minorities, notably those of the North Atlas mountains, the Kabyle tribesmen of South Algeria, and the ◊ *Tuareg* of the Sahara. The settled Berbers engage mainly in agriculture and village handicrafts. Their languages are Hamitic.

Bergschrund. Major crack or ◊ *crevasse* at the head of a ◊ *glacier* where it begins to move down the mountain, between the descending glacier and a non-moving névé or snowfield, or between it and the rock wall of a cirque (an armchair-shaped hollow on the mountainside); frequently a major obstacle in the path of a mountain climber. ◊ *Moraine*.

Beri-beri. Deficiency disease caused by insufficient Vitamin B, common among orientals living on 'white' rice from which the vitamin-rich husk has been removed during polishing.

Berkelium. ◊ *Actinides*; a metal identified 1949, with at. no. 97. Isolated by bombarding ◊ *americium*-241 with alpha particles accelerated in a cyclotron.

Berlin. Originally a fishing village on the River Spree, Berlin grew in importance as a city of the ◊ *Hanseatic League* and later as the capital of ◊ *Brandenburg* under the ◊ *Hohenzollerns*, growing further under Frederick William after the ◊ *Thirty Years War* and the kings of Prussia in the 18th cent. During the ◊ *Seven Years War* it was occupied in 1760 by the Russians, and again by the French in the ◊ *Napoleonic Wars* in 1805. It was chosen as the capital of a united Germany in 1871. During the ◊ *Second World War* Berlin was almost totally destroyed. Following the ◊ *Potsdam Conference* 1945 the Allies placed it under a joint military government divided into four separate allied zones, 'pending the reunification of Germany by a peace treaty'. After friction between Soviet and Western commandants, the former withdrew from the quad-ripartite administration and in 1948 cut the rail and road communications to W. Berlin. The West countered the 'Berlin blockade' with an air-lift to bring in supplies, until the blockade ended in 1949. Disagreement over Berlin persisted. The E. German authorities, with Soviet approval, assumed substantial control over E. Berlin and in 1961 erected a wall to divide the city, in disregard of the Potsdam Agreement.

Berlin Congress. 1878. Congress of the signatories of the Treaty of Paris 1856 (◊ *Crimean War*) called to revise the terms of the Treaty of San Stefano after the ◊ *Russo-Turkish War*. Present were Great Britain (represented by Disraeli), France, Austria, Turkey, and Russia, with Bismarck as mediator. The resultant treaty recognized the independence of Montenegro, Serbia, and Rumania; Bulgaria was divided, the N. part falling under Turkish suzerainty (◊ *Ottoman Empire*). Austria-Hungary was authorized to occupy Bosnia and Herzegovina, and Britain Cyprus.

Berliner Ensemble. Theatre company founded by Bertolt Brecht in E. Berlin after the Second World War, devoted to the presentation of plays by dramatists like Ostrovsky, Gorki, Hauptmann, and Synge, and to Brecht's own plays and adaptations e.g. *The Good Woman of Setzuan, The Caucasian Chalk Circle*. It offered performances at low prices (heavily subsidized) to predominantly working-class audiences. Except *The Days of the Commune*, Brecht wrote few new plays during this period.

Bermuda. Chief of a group of some 100 islands off the S. coast of U.S.A. Pop. 47,230 (60 per cent Negro). Cap. Hamilton. British colony. Enjoys a pleasant climate and tourism is the main industry. St George harbour was used as a privateer and blockade-running base in the war of 1812 and the American Civil War, and as a naval base in the Second World War.

Bermuda Rig. The modern yacht rig, in which all the sails are triangular, a shape which has a longer leading edge and consequently better aerodynamic qualities than the older rigs with quadrilateral sails. ◊ *Sails and Sailing*.

Berne Convention ◊ *Copyright*.

Berry. A fleshy ◊ *fruit* with several seeds and usually formed from numerous ◊ *carpels*, e.g. grape, orange, gooseberry, currant, cucumber. Also, loosely, small fleshy fruits in general, e.g. strawberry, raspberry, which botanically are not strictly berries.

Beryl. Aluminosilicate mineral found in ⟡ *igneous* and ⟡ *metamorphic rocks*, from the coarse opaque types of which the element ⟡ *beryllium* is obtained. Rare crystalline varieties are the gemstones emerald (coloured green by traces of chromium) and aquamarine (coloured bluish perhaps by traces of iron). Beryls may also be pink, yellow, or white. ⟡ *Silica.*

Beryllium. A very light white metallic element of high tensile strength; when cast, the metal is brittle, but powder-fabricated metal has much better mechanical properties. Beryllium is transparent to ⟡ *X-rays* and has a low absorption of ⟡ *neutrons*, hence its use as windows in X-ray tubes. Non-magnetic parts e.g. springs can be made from its ⟡ *alloy* with copper, which is extensively used in the electrical industries. Chemically it resembles ⟡ *magnesium* (immediately below it in the Periodic Table, ⟡ *Elements*), but the properties of its compounds more closely resemble those of ⟡ *aluminium*. The element and its compounds are poisonous. ⟡ *Atom.*

Bessemer Process. Henry Bessemer introduced a method of making steel from crude iron in 1856; the molten metal is poured into a 'converter' which is then swung upright, and a blast of air under pressure is blown upward through the molten metal: the impurities oxidize, producing great heat, the spectacular 'blow' lasting about 20 minutes. The L.D. (Linz Donawitz) Process recently developed in Austria hastens the purification of iron by blowing oxygen through a lance on to the surface of the molten metal. ⟡ *Blast Furnace, Iron and Steel Industry, Siemens-Martin Process.*

Bestiary. A medieval popular literary form in which descriptions of real or (more usually) fabulous natural history are followed by an allegorical application to Christian morality. Many of them derive from the Old English *Physiologus*, attributed to Cynewulf but itself deriving through a Latin translation from a 2nd-cent. Greek original. Many were illustrated with coloured woodcuts. Allegories like those of the medieval Bestiary are to be found in Bunyan's *Pilgrim's Progress*,

suggesting that they continued to be used in sermons until the 17th cent.

Beta Particles. β-particles. Rapidly moving negative (negatron) or positive (positron) electrons emitted by radioactive substances.

Beta Ray ⟡ *Radiation.*

Betatron. Type of ⟡ *particle accelerator* used in nuclear research for accelerating electrons. The electrons are kept on a constant circular path by means of a magnetic field, whose intensity increases as they accelerate.

Betting and Gambling. Ancient and worldwide pastime in which money is placed to win or lose on events in which the outcome is a matter of chance. In English-speaking countries most betting is on horse-racing, greyhound-racing and (through the pools) football. In horse-racing and greyhound-racing, one can bet either with bookmakers (on or off the course) or with the official Totalizator. The 'Tote' originated in France in the 1860s but was not legalized in Britain until the 1928 Racecourse Betting Act. Profits from the horse-racing Tote are used for charities and for the improvement of racing, breeding etc. Bettors in many countries forecast results of soccer matches in the football pools. In some countries (but not Britain) money derived from the pools (in profits or tax) is used to benefit sport and recreation. Sometimes pools are run by the state, sometimes by the sporting authorities themselves. In Britain they are private enterprises.

Since the 1960 Betting and Gaming Act gaming is not in itself a criminal offence in the U.K. provided that: (a) the chances are equally favourable to all players; (b) no money staked is disposed of otherwise than by payment as winnings; and (c) no payment is required to take part other than a single sum previously determined. It is an offence to frequent public places for the purpose of making, paying, or receiving bets or to act as a bookmaker without a magistrate's permit. The Act authorized the opening of 'betting shops', subject to permission from local authorities. Since the 1954 Pools Betting Act it is lawful to conduct and advertise a ready-money pool betting business, provided that the promoter is registered and complies with the conditions laid down; 'fixed-odds' betting is excluded from the Act, but may be conducted from a betting shop.

In law, no claim can be maintained for payment of a wager, except in the case of football pool and totalizator winnings, which are normally recoverable at law.

Bezique. A card game for two players using two packs of 32 cards each containing ace down to seven. Each player receives eight cards, the 17th is turned up to show trumps, and the remainder are used as stock. The aim is to win tricks, especially those of particular combinations e.g. ace and ten; the most important of these are the Queen of Hearts and the Jack of Diamonds. Each player takes a card from the stock after each trick until it is exhausted.

The game became popular in France about 1860 and in London in 1868. The name probably comes from Spanish *besico*, 'little kiss', that of the Queen and Jack.

Bible. < Lat. *biblia*, Gr. *biblios*, book; a collection of religious books divided into the Old Testament (the Bible of ◊ *Judaism*) and the New Testament, which together comprise the sacred books of ◊ *Christianity*, the two terms representing a Latin rendering of the old and new 'covenants'.

The Old Testament, the record of the religious and historical thought of the people of Israel, and one of the most influential books in the world, was written in Hebrew (except for a few portions in Aramaic), and the New Testament (◊ *Gospels*) in Greek; the development of the Bible was a long slow process through 1000 years. Traditionally the OT is divided into (1) the *Pentateuch* (the Torah, law, i.e. the five books of Moses, from Genesis to Deuteronomy); (2) the *Prophets* (Former i.e. Joshua to II Kings, and Latter i.e. Isaiah to Malachi); and (3) the *Writings* (i.e. Psalms, Proverbs, Job, Song of Songs, Ruth, Lamentations, Ecclesiastes, Esther, Daniel, Ezra, Nehemiah, I and II Chronicles). There are many historical layers and internal references to older sources; the great variety of subject-matter and style includes historical, narrative, lyrical (e.g. Psalms, Song of Songs), hortatory, ethical, visionary (e.g. the Prophets), and proverbial or didactic material (e.g. Ecclesiastes, Proverbs). References to historical events provide clues to the date of composition of various parts, but that of the oldest portions of the Pentateuch remains uncertain; in general,

the OT may be said to contain material from about 1000 to about 150 B.C. The earliest Hebrew MSS extant date to about A.D. 900, but there are fragments of earlier date; existing texts vary little, Jewish authority having fixed a standard (Massoretic) text about A.D. 100, after which no others were perpetuated. To get behind the Massoretic text to often important earlier versions scholars must go to pre-Masoretic translations e.g. the Septuagint (see below). ◊ *Talmud*.

The New Testament – the story of ◊ *Jesus Christ* and his teaching, with some account of the very early Christian church – consists of the four Gospels; the Acts of the Apostles; the Epistles attributed to St Paul; the Epistle of St James; I and II Peter; I, II, and III John; the Epistle of Jude; and the Revelation of St John the Divine. The books were written in the late 1st and early 2nd cent. A.D. and only gradually acquired canonical status, the shape not being finally established until the 5th cent. after a series of Church synods; the oldest Greek MSS date to the 4th cent. and (unlike the OT Hebrew MSS) show many variations, making the establishment of a text very intricate.

There are also the books of the ◊ *Apocrypha*, bridging the gap between OT and NT, accepted as canonical by the Roman Catholic church but not by Protestantism.

The translation of the OT into Greek by the Jews of Alexandria, the Septuagint, was begun by the 3rd cent. B.C. and became the Bible of the early Christians; Jerome's great translation into Latin, the Vulgate, about A.D. 400, drew on the original OT Hebrew and NT Greek, became the accepted text of medieval Christianity long before it was officially authorized in 1546, and remains the authoritative Roman Catholic text. Translations into vernacular languages were not encouraged by the medieval church; but heretical (and later, Protestant) movements made the Bible available to the layman in his own tongue, Wycliffe's translation of the Vulgate into English (late 14th cent.) being a pioneer example. Tyndale published a translation of the NT from the original Greek into English in 1525 and later translated parts of the OT from Hebrew; Luther's great translation from the Hebrew and the Greek into German appeared in 1534, Coverdale's complete English Bible in 1535 and 'Great Bible' in 1540. Protestant exiles produced the Geneva Bible in 1557; under Elizabeth I Bible translation flourished in England, culminating after her death in the 1611 Authorized Version, commissioned by James I in 1604. The new Protestant attitude to the Scriptures (◊ *Reformation*), and the new Hebrew and Greek scholarship (◊ *Humanism, Renaissance*), made these 15th and 16th cent. translations possible. A Roman Catholic translation of the Vulgate into English appeared in 1582 (NT, Rheims) and 1609–10 (OT, Douai). Modern English translations include the Revised Version (NT 1881, OT 1885), Moffatt's version in ordinary modern English (NT 1913, OT 1924), Knox's Roman Catholic translation 1945–9, the American Revised Standard version (NT 1946, OT 1952), and the New English Bible, by committees of scholars representing English and Scottish denominations (NT 1961, OT in preparation).

Bibliothèque Nationale. The national library of France; housed in Paris and containing nearly 5 m. items, including maps, engravings, and the collections of manuscripts and books made by several French kings esp. Louis XIV.

Bicycle. A type of hobby-horse on which the rider 'walked' himself along was introduced into Britain from France in 1818; in 1834 McMillan constructed the first mechanically propelled bicycle, driven by treadles. Pedals were first used in France, about 1870, on Michaux's velocipede (the 'boneshaker'). The 'penny-farthing' (large pedal-driven front wheel, very small rear wheel) was introduced about 1870 and remained popular until 1885, when the Starley safety bicycle, basically similar to today's model, superseded it. The introduction of pneumatic tyres, invented by Dunlop in 1888, led to a rapid increase in popularity and to improvement in design. Since the Raleigh all-steel bicycle, 1900, there has been little outward change until the Moulton model of 1963, but a steady decrease in weight has been achieved.

Biedermeierstil. The name derives from two fictitious German philistines, Biedermann and Bummelmeier, and is applied to the cosy middle-class style of interior decoration and furniture popular in the Germanic countries 1815–48, and also to pictures, especially anecdotic ◊ *genre*

paintings similar to those popular in early Victorian England.

Biennials. Plants which take two years to complete their life cycle from ◊ *seed* to seed; in the first year they produce roots and leaves, frequently in the form of a rosette on the top of a thickened carrot-like main root, and in the second year the flowering shoot, after which they die. Common examples are Canterbury bells, honesty, forget-me-nots.

Billiards. A game for individuals, played with long cues and three hard heavy balls, on a table 12 ft by 6 ft, the aim being to score points by 'potting' the balls into the table's six pockets or by striking two balls with the third (a 'cannon'); originally an English 14th-cent. game derived from lawn ◊ *bowls*, it was modernized in the 18th cent. by a Frenchman while in prison. As a professional game, virtually replaced by ◊ *Snooker*, but has world and national amateur championships.

Bill of Rights. 1689. Enactment as law of the Declaration of Rights assented to by William and Mary when they accepted the English throne in 1688 (◊ *Glorious Revolution*), designed to preclude abuses of royal power such as had occurred under James II. The Bill prohibited the monarch from suspending or abusing the laws and from raising money or troops by his sole prerogative, and guaranteed freedom of speech and of elections and the right of petition. It also laid down the succession and debarred any Roman Catholic from the throne. It was amplified in 1701 by the ◊ *Act of Settlement*.

Binary Scale. System of calculation on the base 2 in which the only digits needed are 0 and 1. The commonest base is 10 ◊ *decimal system*, but there is nothing sacrosanct about this and it is possible to construct systems on other bases e.g. 12 ◊ *duodecimal system*, or 20 (which the Mayans chose). In the binary system the digits represent powers of 2, thus 1011 in the scale of two represents $1 \times 2^3(8) + 0 \times 2^2 (0) + 1 \times 2(2) + 1$ equals eleven. The scale of two is simple but cumbersome. It has assumed special importance since electronic devices came into use for computation, for since it has only two digits any number can be represented by a series of switches which are either 'on' for one or 'off' for nought. ◊ *Computer*.

Binary Stars ◊ *Star*.

Bindweed ◊ *Convolvulaceae*.

Biological Classification. The study of animal and plant life necessitates classifications, which remain to some extent subjective, however scientific; it was not until the Swedish naturalist Linnaeus published his 1758 (10th) edition of *Systemae naturae* that a logical scientific nomenclature emerged (which in its broad lines is still the same), with the object of establishing an arrangement of groups of diminishing scope, to enable an exact identification of organisms. The form of classification established by Linnaeus has survived, but the principles have changed, since his belief in the fixity of species has been replaced by the more fluid concept of ◊ *evolution.* A species is the basic unit, comprising all the individuals which are like one another and in general cannot breed successfully outside it; each species has a double Latin name, on the Linnaean model, first that of the genus and second that of the species e.g. the cat is *Felis domestica*, the dog rose *Rosa officinalis*. Many species also have common names, but some have only the Latin names. The following table shows examples of the major classifications now in use for animals and plants.

Kingdom	*Animalia:* cat, lion, cheetah, dog, horse, trout, oyster.
Phylum	*Chordata:* cat, lion, cheetah, dog, horse, trout.
Class	*Mammalia:* cat, lion, cheetah, dog, horse.
Order	*Carnivora:* cat, lion, cheetah, dog.
Family	*Felidae:* cat, lion, cheetah.
Genus	*Felis:* cat, lion.
Species	*domestica:* cat.

Kingdom	*Plantae:* all flowering plants and trees, ferns, mosses, seaweeds.
Phylum	*Tracheophyta:* all flowering plants and trees, ferns.
Class	*Angiospermae:* all flowering plants and most trees excluding conifers.
Order	*Dicotyledon:* rose, apple, foxglove.
Family	*Rosaceae:* rose, apple.
Genus	*Rosa:* various types of rose.
Species	*canina:* wild dog rose.

Biologists also recognize a third 'kingdom', *Protista*, comprising organisms in the indeterminate zone between animal and vegetable life, e.g. the ◊ *amoebae* and the flagellates (◊ *Protozoa*).

Biological Variation. All individuals of any species differ from one another (with the exception of monozygotic (identical) twins, derived from a single egg); this genetic variation is one of the sources of evolutionary change. Variations may also arise from environmental factors e.g. climate or diet, but these are not transmissible. ◊ *Reproduction.*

Biology. The science of life; its two main divisions are zoology (study of animals) and botany (study of plants), sub-divided into such studies as morphology (study of forms), ◊ *physiology, embryology, cytology*, histology (study of tissues), genetics (study of ◊ *heredity*), and ◊ *palaeontology.* In recent years it has increasingly combined with other sciences and some of the most important advances have been in the fields of biochemistry (chemistry of living matter) and biophysics. ◊ *Enzymes, Evolution, Mendelism, Radiobiology.*

Birch. *Betula*, of the *Betulaceae*; a small northern-temperate and Arctic genus. They form graceful trees and shrubs, many with ◊ *bark* separating into papery layers of various colours. The flowers are in ◊ *catkins*. The bark of *B. papyrifera* is used by N. American Indians for birch-bark canoes etc. Two British species, *B. alba* and *B. pubescens*, are trees and form woods, esp. on sandy soils. The dwarf birch is found in Scotland and also extends to the Arctic northern tree limit as a creeping shrub. Birch wood is used in furniture and in plywood, and also for high-grade ◊ *charcoal*. Distilled bark of *B. lenta* is used to prepare Russian leather.

Birds. *Aves*; class of warm-blooded vertebrates highly adapted for flight, probably evolved from primitive tree-dwelling reptiles. The only well-known fossil bird, ◊ *Archeopteryx*, shows primitive reptilian features but is a true bird possessing feathers, which are important both for flight and for the maintenance of constant body-temperature. Flight probably originated from gliding; it necessitates a large surface-to-volume ratio, so most birds are small-bodied. They are characterized by light bones (which contain air spaces), brains which are large in proportion to body size (possibly because they store complex instinctive behaviour patterns), and large eyes (which confer keen eyesight). They show their reptilian ancestry by laying shell-clad eggs, usually in nests; they hatch the eggs by brooding, and feed the young till they can fly. Whilst birds are alike in essentials, they have evolved many peculiarities in powers of flight, feeding, and nesting habits. A few, the *Paleognathae*, are large and incapable of flight, e.g. ◊ *ostrich*, ◊ *emu*, and the extinct dodo. The *Impennae*, ◊ *penguins*, are also incapable of flight, but are excellent swimmers. All other birds are classified as the *Neognathae*, comprising an immense variety of widely differing sub-orders. ◊ *Flight*; and under names of species.

Birth Control. The control of conception; currently approved methods are a mechanical barrier (diaphragm or cap for women, sheath for men) plus a spermicidal cream, or oral contraceptives for women (see below). Contraceptive devices were known to ancient peoples and to many primitive tribes. The first attempts to spread knowledge of birth control began in England early in the 19th cent. and resulted in the trial of Bradlaugh and Mrs Besant in 1877 for republishing an American pamphlet on birth control, for which Bradlaugh was sentenced to a fine and imprisonment (later quashed). In 1878 Bradlaugh and Mrs Besant founded the Malthusian League, and the movement soon spread. Owing largely to the efforts of Dr Marie Stopes, a birth-control clinic was opened in London in 1921, and further clinics followed in several cities. Clinics for medical cases are now conducted by some local health authorities and hospitals under the National Health Service; others refer patients to the Family Planning Association, founded 1930, a voluntary organization which provides advice on birth control, fertility, and sex difficulties in marriage, charging fees broadly relevant to income (waived in necessitous cases). Reliable data on the use of birth control are difficult to obtain, but recent sampling suggests that between 60–70 per cent of married couples in Gt Britain practise it. In underdeveloped countries, the use of contraceptives is limited by ignorance and by religious and traditional beliefs; in such areas high infant mortality acts as some check on population increase. The Roman Catholic Church remains opposed to birth control unless by abstinence and the so-called 'safe period' method; in most Roman Catholic countries and in some American states with large Roman Catholic populations birth control is illegal.

ORAL CONTRACEPTION: Pills containing certain synthetic hormones can inhibit ovulation by an action through the pituitary and produce temporary sterility in women. In the U.K. their use is now approved by the Family Planning Association. Although they have proved effective in some underdeveloped areas of the world, they are probably not the final answer to excessive rate of population increase because of expense and the need to ensure medical supervision.

Birthrate. Number of births per 1000 in a given year, as recorded in most countries. From about 1760 there was a remarkable rise in the birthrate in W. Europe, due partly to a decline in infant mortality. The birthrate fell off in the years 1880–1939 (from 33 to 15 in Britain) and began to rise steadily from 1946, and stands at present at about 18. In the underdeveloped countries a decline in infant mortality has resulted in recent years in a striking rise in ◊ *population*.

Bishop. Official in certain Christian churches exercising general supervision over a local area (his 'see' or 'diocese') and its lesser clergy; a bishop alone can perform certain religious functions e.g. ordination and ◊ *confirmation*. In the Church of England appointed by the Crown, but in its sister churches outside England generally elected by fellow bishops or by the clergy, and among Roman Catholics appointed by the ◊ *Pope*; 24 Anglican bishops sit in the British House of Lords, some by right of their sees and some by seniority. Some other Protestant churches also have bishops, e.g. Methodists (in America but not in Britain), Lutherans (in Germany and Scandinavia), and ◊ *Moravians*.

Bismuth. A metallic ◊ *element* which has lowest thermal conductivity at room temperature and an electrical conductivity which doubles on melting; it occurs as sulphide Bi_2S_3 associated with the sulphide ores of lead and copper, and also with limestone, and the principal source is the flue dust from the smelting of these metals. It is an important constituent of low-melting ◊ *alloys* e.g. Wood's Metal (m.p. 71° C) and type-metal, some of which are used for automatic sprinkler-heads in fire-protection systems and as fusible safety plugs for containers of compressed gases, to prevent explosion on overheating.

Bison ◊ *Buffalo.*
Bitumen ◊ *Petroleum.*
Black and Tans. Reinforcements for the Royal Irish Constabulary recruited mainly from ex-servicemen during the ◊ *Anglo-Irish Troubles* of 1920. They wore khaki jackets and trousers and almost black caps; hence their nickname.
Blackbird ◊ *Thrush.*
Black Death. Plague, mainly the bubonic type, characterized by glandular swellings, which reached Europe from the Far East in the 14th cent. and spread to England in 1348. One third to a half of the population died; the consequent demoralization among the survivors found expression not only in religious frenzy but also in increased crime and debauchery. Legislation against economic tendencies accelerated by the plague, e.g. rising wages and the loss of traditional labour services on the lord's demesne, led to much social unrest, of which the ◊ *Peasants Revolt* was an indirect result. Outbreaks of plague continued until the Great ◊ *Plague* of 1664–5 in London.
Black Earth. Dark soils rich in organic matter, which develop under ◊ *steppe* grasslands in a cool-continental climate; the aristocrats of soils. The parent rock is usually wind-blown loess. Most famous are the typically fertile and easily tilled grain-growing lands of S. Ukraine.
Blackfellows ◊ *Australian Aborigines, Race.*
Black Hole of Calcutta. 1756. During the ◊ *Seven Years War* Calcutta was captured by Siraj-ud-dowlah, the Nawab of Bengal; 146 English prisoners were put in the jail of Fort William, a room 18 ft by 14 ft with two small windows; only 23 were still alive next day. ◊ *Plassey.*
Black Muslims. In U.S.A. a separatist Negro movement which demands that the whites hand over to the Negroes sufficient land and capital for the establishment of a separate Negro state. Members uphold strict moral standards and are noticeably law-abiding citizens. They boycott white tradesmen, and as far as possible avoid contact with the whites, whom they regard as inferior. They give up their surnames ('slave names') and frequently adopt Muslim names instead, though the movement has no valid connexion with ◊ *Islam.* The leaders were Elijah Mohammed and Malcolm X until 1964, when the latter broke away to head an even more extreme faction.

Black Rod. The Gentleman Usher of the Black Rod; an official, one of whose duties is calling members of the House of Commons to the House of Lords and who is also Usher of the Order of the Garter (◊ *Heraldry*).
Bladder. Pear-shaped muscular organ acting as a reservoir for urine, which passes to it from the ◊ *kidneys* via two tubes (ureters) and is passed out of the body through another tube (urethra).
Bladderwort ◊ *Carnivorous Plants.*
'Blanc Fixe' ◊ *Barium.*
Blank Verse. Any unrhymed verse in any metre, but esp. the English unrhymed iambic pentameter, first used by Surrey about 1540 and later the standard metre of Elizabethan drama esp. that of Shakespeare. Also used e.g. by Milton in *Paradise Lost*, it was displaced in the late 17th and 18th centuries by the heroic couplet, revived by Wordsworth in *The Prelude*, and much (though self-consciously) used in the 19th cent. It is the most direct English ancestor of ◊ *free verse.*
Blast-furnace. Used to manufacture crude iron from iron ore. It consists basically of a tall hollow cylinder in which a mixture of iron ore, limestone, and coke is introduced at the top. A blast of hot air at the bottom ignites the coke, chemical reactions occur, and molten iron and slag accumulate in the bottom of the furnace. These are then tapped off. The hot gaseous products of the reaction are known as blast furnace gas, which may be used to drive the associated machinery. The resultant product is known as pig iron (as it used to be largely cast in small blocks or 'pigs'), now seldom used in that form but processed from the molten state into steel (◊ *Iron and Steel Industry*).
Blaue Reiter. A group of expressionist painters working in Munich 1911, from Kandinsky's painting *Der Blaue Reiter*; the group also included Münter, Klee, Franz Marc, Macke, and the composer Schoenberg. In opposition to traditional art forms, they aimed at a more direct and personal expression, combining the colour of ◊ *Fauvism* and a Cubist arrangement of form.
Blenheim. 1704. Scene of one of the decisive battles in the ◊ *War of the Spanish Succession*, when Marlborough and Prince Eugene of Savoy defeated the French and Bavarian armies under Marshal Tallard,

the victory ending the run of French successes.

A Baroque mansion in Oxfordshire designed by Vanbrugh and given by Queen Anne to Marlborough as a reward for the above victory, is named Blenheim Palace.

Blind-worm ◊ *Slow-worm.*

Blockade. A naval operation designed to cut off commerce by sea between the blockaded country and its allies or neutral countries; to be effective it must apply to the ships of neutrals, and thus it creates difficult problems in ◊ *international law* esp. as regards the Right of Search, and may also cause serious tensions between a belligerent and an otherwise friendly neutral e.g. between Britain and America during the ◊ *American Civil War.* Thanks to her maritime supremacy Britain effectively blockaded France in the ◊ *Seven Years War,* and the ◊ *Napoleonic Wars,* and Germany in both World Wars. One of the most telling blockades was that imposed by the North against the South in the American Civil War.

Blood. Fluid composed of two roughly equal parts, corpuscles and plasma, which convey oxygen and nutritive and other products of metabolic importance to the tissues of the body and simultaneously carry away carbon dioxide and metabolic waste products to the lungs, kidneys, liver, and spleen for disposal. The body of an adult contains about five litres of blood, composed of (a) red cells (about five m. per cubic mm. of blood), containing a complex iron-protein pigment ◊ *haemoglobin,* whose function is to carry oxygen from the lungs; (b) white cells (leucocytes, about 7000 per cubic mm. of blood), of various types, of which one group (phagocytes) performs the vital function of combating infection by destroying bacteria and removing impurities and diseased tissue; another group (lymphocytes) helps in the process of immunization. The plasma is a yellowish fluid 90 per cent water and seven per cent protein (mainly albumin) which maintains the osmotic pressure of the blood, together with globulins (concerned with immunity) and fibrinogen (essential for blood coagulation, a complex process in which a clot is formed to seal bleeding vessels). Plasma also contains ◊ *salts, glucose,* hormones, antibodies, and enzymes with metabolic functions. ◊ *Anaemia, Embolism, Leukemia.*

Blood Groups. Every human has ◊ *blood* which belongs to one of four major groups (A, B, AB, O) differentiated by the presence or absence, in the corpuscles and serum, of certain substances (agglutinogens and agglutinins). When blood from incompatible groups is mixed, agglutination (sticking together of red corpuscles) occurs, with possibly fatal results. A compatible transfusion is ensured by using blood from the same blood group or from group O (which has no antibodies). Group O is present in 46 per cent of the population of the U.K. and thus there is a large pool of potential universal donors. Group A (47 per cent) is the other large group. The ◊ *Rhesus factor* must also be taken into account. Blood groups are easily determined by a simple test.

Blood Pressure. The force which blood exerts within the arteries; it varies during the cardiac cycle (◊ *Circulatory System*). When the ◊ *heart* is pumping the blood into the aorta, pressure rises to a maximum (systolic pressure); this is measured to give the 'blood pressure', which in normal cases has the following range: infancy and childhood, 70 to 100; adolescence and young adults, 90 to 125; thereafter, 130 to 150.

Blood Transfusion ◊ *Blood Groups, Rhesus Factor.*

Bloody Assize ◊ *Sedgemoor.*

Bloomsbury Group. A literary circle meeting in London about 1906, all of whom were to make significant contributions to the intellectual and artistic life of the 1920s and 1930s. They included the novelists E. M. Forster and Virginia Woolf, the painters Vanessa Bell and Duncan Grant, the art critics Clive Bell and Roger Fry, the essayist Lytton Strachey, the economist Maynard ◊ *Keynes,* and the political journalist Leonard Woolf. Their intellectual and moral approach is represented in such works as Forster's *Two Cheers for Democracy.*

Blue Babies. Those with poorly oxygenated and hence bluish blood, resulting from any form of congenital heart disease that allows much of the blood to by-pass the lung. Operations to remedy such defects are now being successfully performed.

Blue Peter. A rectangular flag having a blue border surrounding a white rectangle, the letter 'P' in the International Code of Signals (hence 'Peter'), flown at the foremast by vessels about to sail.

Blue Riband. The liner holding the record for the fastest crossing of the N. Atlantic is said to hold the Blue Riband. In 1935 a silver trophy was presented to the French liner, *Normandie*, which lowered the record previously held by the Italian *Rex*; the *Queen Mary* won the trophy from *Normandie*, but lost it in 1952 to the present holder, *United States*, which made the passage in 3 days 10 hrs 40 min.

Blues. Slow sad American Negro song which became widely known through ◊ *jazz* and its derivatives from about 1911; strictly a 12-bar form with a fixed harmonic pattern. The term is often used loosely.

Boa Constrictor. Non-poisonous S. American ◊ *snake*, which kills its prey by crushing between the coils of its powerful body; some species are desert living, others both arboreal and aquatic. Some are nocturnal; these locate their warm-blooded prey with heat-sensitive pit-organs situated along the margin of the upper jaw. The python, which swallows its prey whole, is another similar snake of great size, in Asia, Africa, and Australia.

Board of Trade. The oldest government Department concerned with industry, derived from the Committee of the Privy Council set up in the 17th cent. to deal with 'Trade and Plantations'. Many former branches of the Board have now become separate departments. The Board's main responsibilities today are overseas trade relations, export promotion, the supervision of home industry (e.g. company law, patents, and bankruptcy), the location of industry, monopolies, and restrictive practices. It is headed by the President of the Board of Trade, a Cabinet Minister.

Boat. Any small craft, usually undecked, however propelled. For greater definition most types have descriptive names e.g. dinghy, punt, pinnace. The two main types of wooden-boat construction are 'clinker' (fore-and-aft planks with overlapping edges) and 'carvel' (fore-and-aft planks with edges which meet and do not overlap). The types of boat known throughout the world in ancient and modern times are innumerable, ranging in size, complexity, and seaworthiness from the coracle, dug-out-canoe, and gondola to the Chinese sampan and the Viking boats of the N. Atlantic. ◊ *Ship*.

Bodhisattva ◊ *Buddhism* (*Mahayana*).

Bodleian Library. The old library of Oxford University (destroyed mid 16th cent.) was restored by Thomas Bodley, 1545–1613. It houses very important MSS and rare books, and is one of the five 'copyright libraries' i.e. under the Copyright Act it receives two free copies of every book published in the U.K. and the Republic of Ireland. ◊ *Libraries*.

Boer War. 1899–1902. War in S. Africa between Britain and the Boers of the Transvaal and the Orange Free State, caused chiefly by Boer resentment of British encroachments and aggravated by the discovery of gold in the Witwatersrand, which resulted in a rush of prospectors, mainly British, whom the Boers taxed heavily although denying them citizenship, and by the ◊ *Jameson Raid* of 1895.

At first numerically superior, the Boers scored early successes, capturing ◊ *Mafeking* and laying siege to Ladysmith. Heavy reinforcements were sent to S. Africa under Roberts and Kitchener; Ladysmith and Mafeking were relieved and Bloemfontein, Johannesburg, and Pretoria captured. President Kruger of the Transvaal sued for peace, and Roberts returned to England; many Boers continued to resist, however (although now outnumbered by five to one), under leaders such as Botha, De Wet, and Smuts. The British gathered Boer women and children into camps and divided the country into sections, with lines of forts, in order to stamp out this guerrilla resistance. The war ended with the Treaty of Vereeniging in 1902, the Boers accepting British sovereignty with the promise of responsible government, and the British granting £3 m. in compensation for damage to Boer farms. ◊ *South Africa*.

Bog. An area of damp ground with a high water level, on which mosses esp. ◊ *sphagnum* and shrubs chiefly of the family ◊ *Ericaceae* form the dominant vegetation. The growth of these plants and their subsequent decay results in the accumulation of their remains as ◊ *peat*, and so bog surfaces are soft and treacherous. Unlike most others, bog plants tolerate a water supply deficient in nutrients and often acidic. Two main types of bog are the raised bog or peat-moss of the lowlands, where the growth of peat gives a convex surface, and the blanket bog of the uplands, which forms a layer of peat often several feet thick, concealing all the underlying rocks.

Bog Iron. Earthy form of brown ◊ *haematite*, hydrated iron oxide, found in lowlying swamps, with vegetable matter often embedded in loose deposits; the deposition of the iron suspended in the water may be caused by bacteria. A layer seven inches thick accumulated in a Swedish lake in 26 years.

Bohemia. Province of ◊ *Czechoslovakia*; once a kingdom named after the Celtic Boii, who were displaced by the Czechs, a Slavic people, in the first centuries A.D. Christianity was introduced in the 9th cent. The early Kings Ottocar I and Ottocar II (d. 1278), whose encouragement of German immigration had far-reaching effects, secured Bohemia's greatest expansion; these gains were subsequently lost after defeat by the ◊ *Hapsburgs*. Charles IV 1346–78 was elected Holy Roman Emperor, and his 'Golden Bull' of 1356 established the Bohemian rulers as Electors. Religious and social discord and the preaching of John Hus (burnt 1415 ◊ *Moravians*) led to the Hussite Wars and to subsequent serfdom for the Czech peasants under the nobles. The crown was held by Hapsburg or Hungarian rulers until 1526, when the Hapsburg domination was finally established under the Emperor Ferdinand I. In 1618 the Emperor rescinded the promise of freedom of worship; the Bohemians offered the throne to the Calvinist Frederick of the ◊ *Palatinate*, son-in-law of James I of Britain (the 'Winter King'). His acceptance precipitated the ◊ *Thirty Years War*, in which Bohemia was devastated. Maria Teresa and Joseph II incorporated it entirely into the Austrian Empire. In 1848 a nationalist rising in Bohemia was crushed by the Austrians. Bohemia was incorporated in Czechoslovakia in 1918.

Bohemians. Those (esp. artists and writers) who reject conventions and responsibilities accepted by the rest of society, mainly as a reaction against middle-class values. The name was adopted from the French *bohème*, applied to gipsies since the 15th cent. (from a belief that they originated in Bohemia). Bohemianism is particularly associated with the flamboyant and irregular life of artists and writers in the Paris of the Second Empire, of which Murger's *Scènes de la Vie de Bohème* (the basis of

Puccini's opera *La Bohème*) is a romantic portrait.

Boiler. Device used for producing highpressure steam, which may be required either to drive a steam engine or turbine, or for use in steam process plant e.g. in the manufacture of chemicals or paper. In early ◊ *steam engines* steam pressures of 20 or 30 lb. per sq. in. were considered high. The boiler then consisted of a large shell with an internal flue. In modern steam plant much higher pressures and temperatures are in use. At one recently built station the boilers are capable of steam pressures of 1600 lb. per sq. in. and temperatures of 1060° F. Each boiler is also able to supply over 800,000 lb. steam per hour. Shell boilers have been superseded by banks of tubes (inside the boiler), heated on their exterior by the hot gases of combustion. Oil or coal is normally burnt to produce the heat required, though in nuclear power plant it is produced by nuclear fission in the reactor.

Boiling Point. The b.p. of a liquid is the temperature at which its saturated vapour pressure becomes equal to the external pressure on the liquid, e.g. 100° C for pure water at standard atmospheric pressure. If the rate at which heat is supplied is increased, the temperature remains constant but the liquid boils away more rapidly.

Bolivia. Area 415,000 sq. m. Pop. about 3.5 m. Cap. La Paz. Rel. mainly Roman Catholic. Republic in the NW of S. America, with a President elected for four years and a National Congress consisting of an elected senate (27 members) and Chamber of Deputies (74 members).

ECONOMY. A barren mountainous country in the Andes, with few fertile areas. The most important industry is mining, tin being the principal mineral; the three largest tin producers, Patiño, Hochschild, and Aramayo, were nationalized in 1952. Petroleum has been discovered and is being rapidly developed. The principal city, La Paz, lies at an altitude of nearly 12,000 ft; its airfield, at 13,000 ft, is the highest civil aerodrome in the world.

HISTORY. Once part of the ◊ *Inca* Empire, Bolivia came under Spanish rule till it gained independence in 1825. It lost its only port in the Pacific War of 1879. Two thirds of the people are Indian, the rest white or mixed.

LANGUAGE. Spanish, and Indian languages.

Boll Weevil ◊ *Cotton*.

Bolsheviks. < Russian *bolshinstvo*, majority; the left-wing majority, led by Lenin, at the Russian Social-Democratic Party Congress in London 1903, when there was a split into radical and moderate (◊ *Mensheviks*) sections. In Oct. 1917 (Nov. in western calendar) the Bolsheviks, leading the Workers and Soldiers Soviets (councils), overthrew the Menshevik Provisional Government and established a Soviet Socialist Republic. 'Bolshevism' subsequently became a synonym for ◊ *communism*. ◊ *Brest-Litovsk Treaty*.

Bonding ◊ *Chemical Bonding*.

Boom. Period of rapidly rising general economic activity (◊ *Trade Cycle*); the opposite of slump (◊ *Depression*). Locally, a sharp rise in the demand for or price of any particular product e.g. a boom in rubber or in property shares.

Boomerang ◊ *Australian Aborigines*.

Borage. *Borago officinalis*, of the *Boraginaceae*; an annual herb about 18 in. high with bright blue flowers up to ¾ in. across. Attractive to bees.

Borax. Hydrated sodium borate, a mineral deposited when alkaline lakes evaporated, occurring as crystals in the mud or as a surface efflorescence; found in semi-desert areas in California, in Nevada, and in Tibet (as 'tincal'). It is used as an antiseptic and for some industrial purposes. ◊ *Boron*.

Bordeaux Mixture ◊ *Copper*.

Bore ◊ *Tides*.

Boreas ◊ *Aeolus*.

Borneo. Area 286,969 sq. m. Total pop. about 3 m. Largest island of the Malay archipelago, between Java and the Philippines. Its division is a cause of international friction.

NORTH BORNEO. Area 29,388 sq. m. Pop. 454,421 (75 per cent Malayan, 24 per cent Chinese). Cap. Jeselton. A former British colony, adjacent to Sarawak; now part of ◊ *Malaysia*. Chief products cocoa, manila hemp, palm oil, rubber, tobacco, and timber esp. camphor, cedar.

INDONESIAN BORNEO: The remaining nine tenths of the island; part of ◊ *Indonesia*.

Borodino. 1812. The last battle before Napoleon entered Moscow, notable chiefly for its carnage; the Russians lost 42,000 out of 121,000 men, but Napoleon also lost 32,000 of his 130,000 and gained nothing but the empty triumph of the capture of deserted Moscow. ◊ *Napoleonic Wars*.

Boron. A non-metallic element similar in properties to ◊ *silicon* but having a valency of 3; the chief sources of boron and its compounds are kernite (rasorite) and ◊ *borax* (a similar compound, but with more water in its formula). Boron can be obtained fairly pure by reducing its oxide with ◊ *magnesium*, but more elaborate methods are needed to obtain the pure element. It is used in the manufacture of hard steels and hard borides, for cutting edges; since it strongly absorbs neutrons, metal rods of high boron content are used for neutron control in atomic reactors. Borates are important constituents of glasses with a low coefficient of expansion, used in the manufacture of ovenware (borosilicate glass). Low-melting fluxes often contain borates. Sodium perborate has the alkaline properties of borax and also oxidizing power, and is much used in washing-powders, denture-cleaners, etc. Boric (boracic) acid, obtained from borax by the action of hydrochloric acid, is commonly used as a mild antiseptic. Boron nitride, BN, is very stable; the variety borazon has the structure of diamond and is claimed to be equally hard. One of the hydrides, diborane, is used as a propellant for underwater rockets: when it reacts with water, it liberates large quantities of ◊ *hydrogen*. ◊ *Trace Elements*.

Borstal Institutions. Establishments for educating and training young offenders between 16 and 21; named after the Kent village where the prototype was set up, they are of various types. Some are 'open' institutions with a minimum of confinement, others are 'closed' or 'special' Borstals for second-offence inmates or those who persistently escape. The period of detention (from 6 months to 2 years) is followed by supervision for 2 years after release. There are about 23 Borstals for youths in England and Wales, and one open Borstal for girls; they are under the control of the Home Office, which appoints the staff. The Borstal population 1938 (daily average) was 2100, in 1950 had risen to 2904, and in 1960 was 4115; the proportion of boys reconvicted within 3 years of release has shown a sharp rise recently, from about 40 per cent before the war to about 65 per cent today. With girls the numbers are very much smaller and recidivism is about 35 per cent.

Bort. Crystalline form of pure ◊ *carbon*, a variety of the gem diamond, equally hard but occurring in granular aggregates of lump-sugar appearance; of no great use for gems but used for the cutting edges of rock drills and for dressing emery polishing-wheels (◊ *Abrasive*). The chief suppliers are Brazil, the Congo, and S. Africa.

Bosnia-Herzegovina ◊ *Berlin Congress, Yugoslavia.*

Boston Tea Party. 1773. In 1767 the British Parliament passed legislation imposing duties on various imports into the American colonies, which led the latter to proclaim that there should be 'no taxation without representation'. In 1770 the offending duties were repealed except for that on tea, retained in the interests of the ◊ *East India Company.* To show their uncompromising opposition to any duty levied without their consent, the colonists staged a demonstration, boarded British ships in Boston harbour, and threw overboard their cargoes of tea: ◊ *American Revolution.*

Bosworth. 1485. Last battle of the ◊ *Wars of the Roses,* resulting in a new dynasty on the English throne. Henry Tudor, Earl of Richmond, landed at Milford Haven; collecting supporters on his way he marched nearly to Leicester before he was met by Richard III's superior force. The battle swung in Henry's favour when Lord Stanley deserted to him; Richard was killed fighting. Richmond was crowned Henry VII soon afterwards: ◊ *Tudors.*

Botanic Garden. A garden laid out with the prime purpose of advancing and diffusing a knowledge of plants. Botanic gardens have collections of living plants cultivated both outdoors and in glasshouses, arranged to demonstrate the classification and variety of plant life. The oldest botanic garden in Britain is that at Oxford, founded by the University in 1621 with the object of growing plants for the advancement of medicine; the largest is the Royal Botanic Gardens at Kew, founded 1759, which covers 288 acres and has the largest herbarium in the world, a result of active plant collection from all parts of the world, an activity begun by the first curator of the gardens, William Aiton.

Botany ◊ *Angiosperm, Biology, Carpel, Epiphytes, Flower, Fruit, Fungi, Plants,* etc.

Botulism. Rare and fatal poisoning caused by contamination of food (esp. imperfectly canned meat and vegetables) with *Bacillus botulinus.*

Boulder Clay (Till). Ground ◊ *moraine* of ice sheets of Pleistocene Ice Age (◊ *Geological Time Scale*) deposited when the ice melted. Usually very tough and unstratified; contains an abundance of stones of all sizes, many scratched. In some parts of Britain 100 ft thick (thinner over hills, thickening where it fills-in a pre-glacial valley); the evening-out of the inequalities of the relief produces a monotonous flattish landscape.

Bounty Mutiny. 1789. On the homeward voyage of H.M.S. *Bounty* from an expedition to Tahiti, the second in command, Fletcher Christian, led a mutiny against Captain Bligh who with 18 loyal members of the crew was set adrift in a longboat, and after an arduous and remarkable voyage of 4000 m. reached Batavia. *Bounty* returned to Tahiti; some of the mutineers went further to Pitcairn Island, which was not visited again until 1808, when only one of the original settlers, John Adams, was still alive. Other mutineers were captured and three were executed. Bligh – who has been generally, and perhaps unjustly, regarded as a cruel martinet – was exonerated by a Naval Court of Inquiry; he later became Governor of New South Wales.

Bourbons. Branch of the Capet dynasty, the family which ruled France from the accession of Henry of Navarre (Henri IV) in 1589 until the French Revolution in 1789, and again 1814–30 and (in the cadet branch of Bourbon-Orleans) 1830–48. In 1700 Louis XIV's grandson became king of Spain, where Bourbons ruled until Alfonso XIII's flight in 1930. Members of the Spanish line also ruled for a time in the 18th and 19th centuries the Kingdom of the Two Sicilies, Parma, and Lucca. ◊ *Absolutism, Counter-Reformation, France (History).*

Bourgeoisie ◊ *Marxism.*

Bowdlerism. The prudish editing of literary texts to remove such passages as might cause embarrassment however remotely; from Thomas Bowdler 1754–1825, physician and philanthropist, who undertook the expurgation of all 'indecencies' from the works of Shakespeare, 'chiefly with a view to the moral improvement of society'; the *Family Shakespeare* appeared in 1818 and went into four editions in seven years. Bowdler similarly expurgated Gibbon's *Decline and Fall of the Roman Empire* (his own version appeared in 6 vols. after his death), removing all suggestions of 'hostility to our holy religion'.

Bowls. A game (usually on turf) for individuals, pairs, triples, or fours (rinks) in which biased bowls ('woods') weighing 3½ lb. are rolled at a smaller ball ('jack'). A rink is not more than 21 ft wide by 120 ft long. A form of bowls may have been played in Egypt 7000 years ago; the game was known in Britain by the 13th cent. and was banned by various monarchs as being a menace to archery practice, but Henry VIII was a keen player, and Drake is said to have been playing as the Spanish Armada approached Plymouth 1588. Scottish bowlers prepared the present rules about 1850, and the first national association was Scotland's, founded 1892. Today the International Bowling Board, founded 1905, has nine members, mainly British Commonwealth countries, plus U.S.A.

In England bowls is played on flat greens or on sloping (crown) greens. The men's English Bowling Association, founded 1903, is the biggest flat-green body; some 10,000 enter its singles championships, and the game is no longer confined to the elderly and middle-aged of both sexes.

Box. *Buxus sempervirens*; an evergreen native bush widely found in chalk areas in Europe, N. Africa, the Caucasus, and the Himalayas. It may remain as a dwarf bush or grow into a tree 20 ft high. At one time it was used for topiary work and as an edging to formal beds in the garden. The wood is very dense and used for engraving etc.

Boxer Rebellion. 1899–1900. An attempt by the Chinese to drive all foreigners out of China; 'Boxer' is a rough translation of the Chinese name for a militant secret society, which in resistance to the settlement after the ◊ *Opium Wars*, and with the connivance of the Dowager Empress, organized the assault on foreign residents in Peking, who were besieged in the legation area until relieved by an international force. China was obliged to pay a large indemnity and give concessions to the foreign countries.

Boxing. A form of boxing was known in ancient Greece and was included in the old ◊ *Olympic Games*. Leather thongs were used to protect the hands; later the more brutal *caesti*, studded with nails, were favoured esp. in the Roman circus. Bare-fisted prize-fighting (pugilism) began in England over 250 years ago, 'modern' boxing being generally dated to 1719, when James Figg, a former fencing master, claimed the championship. Broughton, to whom is attributed the introduction of gloves, devised the first set of rules. New rules, which included the use of gloves, a roped-off ring, and rounds of three minutes, were introduced by the Marquess of Queensberry in 1866, and these were soon accepted throughout the world. The main differences in rules between professional and amateur boxing are that professionals fight up to 15 three-minute rounds, while amateurs are normally restricted to three rounds. Gloves must weigh not less than 4 oz. Boxing is an Olympic Games event. There is growing medical criticism of boxing (esp. in its professional form) for its damaging effect, immediate or delayed, upon boxers. In U.S.A. (partly owing to television) the sport has been further vitiated by the emphasis upon 'knock-outs'.

Boycott. Organized withdrawal of services from a person, business, or nation in order to enforce demands. The term originated as part of the Irish ◊ *Land League* campaign against absentee landlords and their agents: Parnell urged the complete isolating of any landlord or agent evicting the tenantry, and this was first proved successful against a certain Captain Boycott in Mayo.

'Economic sanctions' (some countries cutting off the supply of goods to another) are a form of international boycott; they were attempted ineffectually against Italy during her 1935–6 campaign in Abyssinia (◊ *Ethiopia*).

Boyle's Law ◊ *Gas.*

Boyne. 1690. Victory in Ireland of William III (◊ *Glorious Revolution*) over the deposed James II at the River Boyne where William's army (mainly Dutch and Germans) attacked James's smaller army of Irish holding a prepared position and eventually dislodged them. James fled to France, and the accession of William and Mary (James's daughter) was secure; Louis XIV's plans for intervening in Ireland were frustrated, and Ireland was subjugated. ◊ *Orange Society.*

Boys' Brigade. Founded 1883 by Sir William Smith, the oldest organization of its type; in the British Isles there are over 100,000 members and over 75,000 in the junior organization, the Life Boys.

Boy Scouts. Robert (Lord) Baden Powell founded the Boy Scout Association in 1908, on a non-military and non-political basis, with the motto 'Be Prepared' and the aim of training boys, in their spare time, to be resourceful, useful, and helpful members of society; they are expected to perform 'good turns' whenever possible. The organization caters for Wolf Cubs (aged 8–11), Scouts (11–18), and Rover Scouts (over 18). The Girl Scout Association (Girl Guides) has similar aims, and there are in the U.K. about a million Boy Scouts and about the same number of Girl Guides. The movement has become worldwide, and some 7 m. members are affiliated, international rallies ('Jamborees') being held periodically; the first was in London 1920.

Bracken. *Pteridium aquilinum*, of the *Polypodiaceae*; a ⬦ *fern* with long tough underground rhizomes. The leaves (fronds) appear singly at intervals and are two to six ft tall, usually with five deeply subdivided segments. They turn a rich brown in autumn and persist through the winter. The ⬦ *spores* are produced in late summer all round the edges of the fronds. Bracken is common throughout Britain and is often dominant on light acid soils. As animals do not eat it, it invades heath and moorland pastures, its deep rhizomes making it difficult to eradicate.

Bract. Modified form of ⬦ *leaf*; a scale or sheath, protecting an undeveloped flowering shoot, a bud, or a leaf. In some species the bracts are more conspicuous than the real flowers. ⬦⬦ *Euphorbiaceae*.

Brahma. Supreme god of the Hindu pantheon, with ⬦ *Vishnu* and ⬦ *Shiva* forming the Trimurti (Trinity), Vishnu and Shiva being themselves specialized manifestations of him; father and creator of all beings, the manifestation of the divine power inherent in the universe, he is said to have developed the world from a cosmic egg. In modern ⬦ *Hinduism,* Brahma-worship plays very little part.

BRAHMAN: 1. The ground of all being; the absolute universal spirit, union with which is sought by asceticism and meditation. (The distinction between Brahma (masc.) and Brahman (neut.) is compar-

able to that between God and the godhead.) 2. A member of the highest ⬦ *caste* (properly, Brahmins), providing priests and scholars. ⬦⬦ *Buddhism, Mysticism, Nirvana, Theosophy.*

Braille. A method of printing and writing for the use of the blind developed about 1830 by the blind Frenchman Louis Braille; letters, numerals, musical notation, etc. in 63 different combinations are represented by embossed dots identifiable by touch. A Standard English Braille was officially adopted 1932 and further clarified 1957; many books have been produced in Braille, and there are Braille writing machines (something like typewriters). For certain purposes Braille books can be replaced by 'talking books' i.e. gramophone and tape recordings.

Brain ⬦ *Nervous System.*

Brain-washing. Methods of treating prisoners so as to produce alterations in their political views or confessions to crimes of which they are innocent, applied particularly in communist countries. In Communist China brain-washing is mainly concerned with ideological re-education and is known as 'thought reform'. The methods include isolation from social contacts and sensory stimuli, fatigue, and other privations aimed at disorientation and loss of the sense of identity, followed by prolonged interrogation, threats, and finally rewards for 'improvement'. The methods are probably neither so new nor so ingenious as has been supposed, being largely developed from police procedures. There is no evidence that acceptance of the imposed doctrines persists when the individual returns to his normal environment, unless he was already susceptible of conversion.

Brake. In its simplest form, a friction pad pressed against a wheel or shaft by levers actuated by hand or pedal, to slow down or stop the movement e.g. the drum brake with internally expanding shoes widely used on motor cars. The pressure may also be transmitted by air, e.g. with Westinghouse brakes on trains, or by fluid pressure as in hydraulic brakes on cars. A recent development has been the disc brake, in which a thin disc on the wheel is gripped on both sides by pads, ensuring smoother and very effective braking.

Brandenburg. One of the Marks (frontier territories) set up in the 10th cent. to protect the eastern frontier of the ⬦ *Holy*

Roman Empire. Later its area was expanded eastwards and the native (Slav) Wends were merged with the German settlers; it became a Hohenzollern possession in the 15th cent. Devastated during the ◊ *Thirty Years War*, it became an important military power under Frederick William, the Great Elector, 1640–88. Frederick III became king of Brandenburg-Prussia in 1701, and the Mark's subsequent history is merged in that of ◊ *Prussia.* Bach wrote his six Brandenburg Concertos for one of the Margraves in 1721.

Brandy. < Dutch, *brandewyn,* burned wine (i.e. distilled); a spirit made from grape juice. It can be made in any wine region, but the most famous is cognac, a name limited by French law to brandy produced in a small region around the town of Cognac, made by the double distillation of local wine matured for at least three years in oak casks. The finest cognac comes from two localities known as Grande and Petite Champagne. Three Star brandy is a very ordinary quality; VSOP (Very Special Old Pale) is in itself no guarantee of high quality. Napoleon brandy is merely a name, and does not indicate any date. Armagnac, a brandy made in Gascony, is darker than cognac and has a distinctive flavour from the black-oak barrels in which it matures. Other brandies are made in Spain, Portugal, S. Africa, and Australia.

Fruit brandies are distilled from fermented fruit juice other than grape, e.g. kirsch from cherries (Germany and Switzerland); calvados is apple brandy (applejack) from cider, a speciality of Normandy. Marc, made in many wine districts by distilling the residue of skins, pips, and stalks after the wine has been run off, is a rough, potent spirit.

Liqueurs are brandies which are sweetened, flavoured (usually with fruit), and coloured, e.g. Benedictine, Chartreuse, Cointreau; there are many varieties, differing widely in alcoholic content.

Brass. ◊ *Alloys*; contains mainly copper and zinc, in varying proportions. Highly malleable, readily cast and machined; much used for machinery and for ornamental purposes (less today than in the 19th cent.) and scientific instruments. Ordinary yellow brass is 70 per cent copper, 30 per cent zinc. Dutch metal, Mannheim gold, and pinchbeck (introduced by Christopher Pinchbeck 1732) resemble gold.

BRASSES ◊ *Monumental Brasses.*

Brassica Family ◊ *Cabbage, Cruciferae.*

Brass Instruments. The term 'brass' is applied to the large group of metal wind instruments, of which the standard modern orchestral forms are the horn, trumpet, trombone, and tuba. The length of the tube determines the fundamental note and hence the ◊ *harmonic series* available; this in turn can be varied e.g. by the use of either a slide (trombone) or valves (trumpet). Valves were gradually introduced from about 1815; they are also found in the cornet (resembling the trumpet, but with a conical instead of cylindrical bore, thus yielding a mellowed tone) and in the saxhorn family (named after A. Sax 1814–94, inventor of the saxophone also). Cornets, saxhorns of various sizes, trombones, and percussion form the British brass band, much cultivated by amateurs esp. in the industrial north since the mid 19th cent. Unlike the military band, the brass band has no woodwind.

Brazil. Area 3.3 m. sq. m. Pop. 66.3 m. (63 per cent of European descent, the remainder Negro or mixed, with a few Indians). Cap. Brasilia (Rio de Janeiro until 1960). Rel. mainly Roman Catholic. Language Portuguese. A republic in the NW of S. America, with a President and Vice-President elected for five years, a Senate elected for eight years, and a Chamber of Deputies elected for four years. Voting is compulsory. Freedom of speech and of the press is complete. Although there is a high rate of illiteracy, Brazil has produced literature and art of distinction and several modern architects of world repute.

ECONOMY. The largest country in S. America, Brazil occupies most of the E. half of the continent, from the tropical ◊ *rain forest* of the Amazon basin through a vast tableland of varying climate and landscape to the more temperate southernmost states. The whole coast is hot and humid, but the plateau inland is drier and more favourable; tropical diseases have been virtually eliminated. Brazil has successively depended upon one main product for its riches – first sugar, then gold, and finally ◊ *coffee*, of which it produces half the world supply and which accounts for 60 per cent of Brazilian exports. There is considerable production of sugar, cotton, cattle, and rice. Mineral resources are varied and valuable, including about one quarter of the known world deposits of iron ore. Development of the vast potentialities of Brazil is handicapped by inadequate communications. The main centres of population lie along the coastal fringe. The oil industry is a national monopoly; production meets only a third of consumption, but refining capacity is adequate. There is enormous hydroelectric potential, and several large-scale projects have been completed. Industry has grown rapidly under the impetus of the Second World War and government encouragement. Steel production is rising above three m. tons per year, and there are extensive textile and engineering industries mainly around Rio and São Paulo, their chief centre and the fastest growing city in S. America.

HISTORY. Brazil was discovered in 1500 by the Portuguese, who after contesting possession with the French and Dutch emerged as the sole colonial power. In 1808, the Portuguese king fled from Napoleon and set up his capital in Rio de Janeiro. On his return to Portugal, he left as Regent his son Pedro, who in 1822 declared Brazil's independence and set up an Empire. Brazil became a Republic in 1889. Her politics were dominated 1930–54 by Getulio Vargas, who ruled for part of that time as a dictator with a programme for improving the lot of the workers. His successors Juscelino Kubitschek and Janio Quadros in some measure continued the Vargas tradition. Brazil was the one Latin American country which actively joined in the Second World War in support of the Allies.

Brazil Nut. Fruit of *Bertholletia excelsa*, a tropical tree which flourishes in the Amazon basin. The nuts, which are very rich in oil, grow in clusters of 8 to 24, enclosed in hard woody capsules which are difficult to break. Brazil nuts are a valuable export crop.

Brazil-wood. Varieties of *Sappan*; a wood giving a red dye. It was first known from India and Malaya and called bresel wood; the name was transferred to a similar wood from S. America found by the Portuguese, who extended the name to the country ◊ *Brazil*.

Bread. Baked foodstuff made from flour, the crushed ground grains of ◊ *cereals* e.g.

barley, millet, rye, maize, but today the flour is predominantly wheaten. Originally a mash of flour and water without yeast (unleavened) baked in thin wafers or pancakes, a practice still widely followed in many eastern countries. Subsequently yeast was introduced: this causes the mixture to swell ('rise') by generating carbon dioxide. Until the 20th cent. bread was largely made at home or in small bakeries; in industrialized countries it is now made on a commercial scale in large specialized bakeries (◊ *Milling*). Most bread is now made from white flour; brown bread includes the wheat germ. Vitamins and other substances are often added to white bread. Rye bread and pumpernickel, once in widespread use, remain popular with a minority. Bread was widely used in ancient Egypt, and the Bible mentions both leavened and unleavened bread.

Breccia. Conglomerate rock of angular fragments with sharp edges and unworn corners cemented together, e.g. the brockram of Permian age (◊ *Geological Time Scale*) of the Vale of Eden in Cumberland. FAULT BRECCIAS: Rocks crushed along ◊ *fault* planes.

VOLCANIC BRECCIAS: Those round the craters of volcanoes.

Breeding. Artificial selection for desirable traits in domestic animals and plants has been practised by man since neolithic times, but has been placed on a scientific basis only in the last 100 years, esp. since the discoveries of Mendel (◊ *Heredity, Mendelism*). Individuals from the same breed may be selected and mated to produce generations having a favourable characteristic (size, food-bearing qualities, etc.) or the favourable characteristics of two different breeds may be combined by cross-breeding, e.g. cattle bred from Western and Indian strains so as to combine the good meat quality of the former with the disease-resisting qualities of the latter. Recently ◊ *artificial insemination* has been introduced, esp. for cattle, sheep, and pigs. A more recent development is the transfer of fertilized ova from a donor dam to a recipient dam of the same species; the services of recipient dams of less value than either parent can be utilized so as to allow speedier and more economical breeding of valuable types.

Brest-Litovsk Treaty. 1918. Peace Treaty signed in March 1918 between the Central Powers and the new Soviet Russian government ($\diamond$ *Bolsheviks*). The latter was represented at first by Trotsky (who refused to sign) and then by Sokolnikov; on Lenin's instructions, Russia ceded large areas of her territory, including Poland, and recognized the independence of the Ukraine and Georgia. The treaty became void on the defeat of Germany on the western front later in 1918.

Breton. Brythonic or P-Celtic language ($\diamond$ *Celts Language*) of Brittany, still spoken by about 1 m. Bretons. Not (as might be supposed) a survival of Gaulish, the Celtic speech of pre-Roman Gaul, but an overspill from $\diamond$ *Cornish* (which became extinct as late as the 19th cent.); $\diamond$ *Celts* fled from the Saxon invaders of Britain to Armorica (Brittany) about A.D. 600, and founded the duchy of Brittany, which remained practically independent of France until the 15th cent.

Bretton Woods Conference. 1944. The United Nations Monetary and Financial Conference in U.S.A. at which the U.K. (represented by $\diamond$ *Keynes*) and U.S.A. (represented by Henry White of the U.S. Treasury) played prominent roles; only two major U.N. members dissociated themselves, Argentina and U.S.S.R. The conference laid the foundations for postwar monetary policy and led to the establishment of the $\diamond$ *International Monetary Fund* and the $\diamond$ *International Bank for Reconstruction and Development*, which started operations in 1946. These two institutions were instruments for working towards expansion and liberalization in international trade and finance, and the attainment of a high level of employment and improved living-standards, aims which have been realized in a remarkable measure in many member-countries. $\diamond$ *General Agreement on Tariffs and Trade*.

Breviary. Official manual of prayers containing the formulas for the eight daily offices every Roman Catholic priest and religious is bound to recite (Matins, Lauds, Prime, Terce, Sext, None, Vespers, Compline); made up of the $\diamond$ *Psalms* (recited in full once a week), daily Scripture readings ($\diamond$ *Bible*), and various $\diamond$ *hymns* and prayers arranged according to the Church's year and $\diamond$ *religious festivals*. Continually enriched during the centuries by new formulas; reorganized and simplified by the authority of Pope John XXIII 1960. The daily services of the Anglican $\diamond$ *Prayer Book* are a simplified and adapted form of the Sarum Breviary in use in England before the $\diamond$ *Reformation*. $\diamond$ *Liturgy*.

Brewing. Production of alcoholic malt beverages by fermentation; they contain two to seven per cent alcohol. Barley is allowed to germinate, the germination stopped by kiln-drying, and the 'malt' made into a mash ('wort') with water and boiled with hops for flavour. On cooling, it is fermented with yeast for a period depending on the percentage of alcohol desired; most of the yeast rises to the top ('top fermenting') and the liquid is finally filtered through kieselguhr to obtain beer. If fermentation is carried out at a lower temperature, about 7° C, the yeast sinks to the bottom: this process is used for lager. Ale once meant beer without hops, but is now only an alternative name for beer. In U.S.A. it is pale and highly hop-flavoured. Bock is a heavy dark beer of Prussian origin, similar to porter. Stout, even darker, usually has an alcoholic content of six to seven per cent. Beer is among the oldest of alcoholic beverages, and was known to the ancient Egyptians. In Europe it was first made in households and monasteries; in the later Middle Ages it was made commercially, and today there are large brewing industries in most countries, esp. Britain, Germany, Denmark, Czechoslovakia, and U.S.A.

Briar $\diamond$ *Brier*.

Briar pipes $\diamond$ *Ericaceae*.

Bridge. Card game for four players based on $\diamond$ *whist* and introduced into England at the end of the 19th cent. The origin of its name is uncertain. It developed from 'dummy whist', played by Englishmen in India. In its earliest form, the dealer (or his partner) could nominate the trumps; it was not until 1910 that there was an 'auction' (i.e. competitive bidding) to determine which pair of partners undertook to make a defined number of tricks with a chosen suit as trumps (or in no trumps). The play is similar to whist except that one hand is exposed ('dummy'). About 1920 the French version *plafond* introduced further refinements, the most significant being that scores below the line were limited to the number of tricks contracted for. This was incorporated in Contract Bridge, which emerged in U.S.A. in 1927 and rapidly won world-wide popularity, remaining virtually unchanged. The first theoreticians and popularizers of the game were Americans (esp. Milton Work and Culbertson); they introduced systems of evaluating hands and bidding to enable partners to cooperate effectively. A famous bridge match between Colonel Buller (England) and Culbertson (U.S.A.) in 1930 gained immense publicity for the game. Many rival systems of bidding have been developed. The luck of the deal plays a considerable part in the short run, but bridge possesses a more elaborate technique and affords more scope for intellectual exercise than any other card game.

The laws of bridge, determined by the Portland Club, London, the European Bridge League, and the U.S.A. National Bridge Organization, acting in concert, were revised in 1963. There is a World Bridge Federation, and each country has its own associations, which organize national and international tournaments.

Bridges. Until recent times the commonest form of bridge was the masonry arch. The

The Tamar bridge, 1961 1100 ft, and the Forth road bridge, 3300 ft, are of this type. Notable American suspension bridges are the George Washington, 3500 ft, and the Golden Gate, 4200 ft. Other long-span steel bridges employ a steel latticed arch to support the deck: Sydney Harbour 1932, 1650 ft, Runcorn–Widnes 1961, 1082 ft. ◊ *Caisson*.

Brier (Briar). *Rosa canina* (dog rose) and *R. eglanteria* (sweet briar); the former provides the 'briar' rootstock on which most garden roses are propagated by the method known as budding.

Bright's Disease ◊ *Nephritis*.

Brimstone ◊ *Sulphur*.

Brinell Hardness. A method devised by Brinell in 1900 for determining the hardness of a material. The method involves pressing a hardened steel ball into the surface of the material, causing an indentation. The hardness number of the material is then calculated by dividing

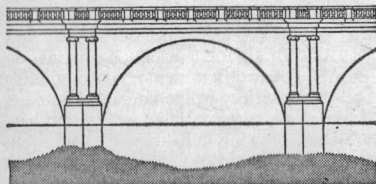

arch bridge.

cantilever bridge

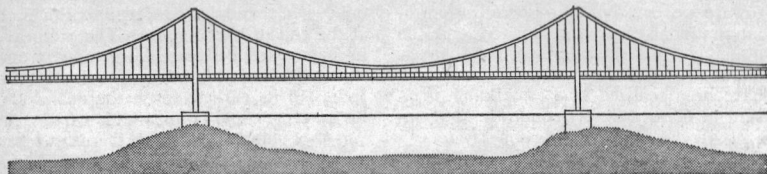

suspension bridge

introduction of cast iron, wrought iron, and steel during the ◊ *Industrial Revolution*, and of reinforced concrete, has resulted in a wide variety of forms to suit different circumstances. The suspension bridge has often been chosen for long spans. In the early ones the deck was suspended from chains of massive wrought-iron links (Menai 1826, main span 579 ft). Suspension cables made of many strands of steel wire were introduced in America and extensively used there by Roebling.

the applied load by the surface area of the indentation.

Britain ◊ *United Kingdom*.

Britannia Metal ◊ *Alloys*.

British Academy. Founded 1901, with the object of promoting humanistic studies; it receives an annual grant of £5000 from the Treasury.

British Army. The first standing ◊ *army* in Britain was Cromwell's New Model Army. Under Charles II a small part was retained, but it was not until 1689 and the

◊ *Bill of Rights* that Parliament recognized a standing army. The army was raised by contract between the crown and the colonels until 1783, when control of all army matters became the responsibility of the Secretary of War. Enlistment was voluntary, but in time of war men were pressed, while large numbers were obtained from the militia. After the Napoleonic wars the army and the militia were both greatly neglected and the army administration severely hampered by lack of funds. Its deficiencies were glaringly revealed by the ◊ *Crimean War*. Reforms introduced by Lord Cardwell in 1871 formed the organizational basis for the modern regular British Army. ◊◊ *Conscription, Ministry of Defence, Territorial Army, Uniform.*

British Association. Society for the advancement of science founded 1831. Of esp. interest is the Annual Meeting when an address is given by the President. It cooperates closely with other scientific institutions.

British Broadcasting Corporation (BBC). Incorporated under Royal Charter in 1926, to succeed the British Broadcasting Company formed in 1922. It has a Chairman and eight Governors appointed by the Crown, its chief executive officer being the Director-General, and its finance comes mainly from wireless and television licence fees and from its publications the *Radio Times*, the *Listener*, etc. Licences issued in 1964 rose to nearly 16 m. The BBC has the monopoly of sound broadcasting but shares television broadcasting with the ◊ *Independent Television Authority* (which supports itself by selling time to advertisers). Its overseas services, for which Parliament makes a grant, are broadcast in nearly 40 languages.

British Commonwealth of Nations. Free association of independent states which has slowly evolved since the grant of self-government to Canada in 1840. At first confined to those areas inhabited primarily by people of European stock (Canada, Australia, New Zealand, South Africa), membership of the Commonwealth has, since the grant of independence to India in 1948, been extended to a number of former British colonies in Asia and Africa. The Statute of Westminster, 1931, which gave legal status to the concept of the Commonwealth developed at the Imperial Conference of 1926, describes the members as 'autonomous communities within the British Empire, equal in status, in no way subordinate one to another, but united by a common allegiance to the Crown and freely associated as members of the British Commonwealth of Nations'. Certain countries e.g. India, Ghana have since become republics, and do not owe allegiance to the Queen; nevertheless they accept the Crown as the symbol of the free association of states which make up the Commonwealth. It has no written constitution, no central parliament or executive, and no united and centralized defence policy or military forces. Its members are bound only by certain historical ties and by broadly similar political ideals and judicial and governmental institutions. The Commonwealth is undergoing a period of transition and adaptation, as a result of the emergence of many new sovereign members, some of which have important relationships (notably with other African countries) outside the Commonwealth.

Consultation is by means of periodic meetings of Commonwealth Prime Ministers and other Ministerial meetings, and in day-to-day matters between the Commonwealth Relations Office and Commonwealth representatives in London. At the diplomatic level, members of the Commonwealth exchange representatives known as High Commissioners (not ambassadors). At the head of the government of each member of the Commonwealth (except in such as are republics) is a Governor General representing the Queen, appointed on the recommendation of the member country. In the economic field the members of the Commonwealth and the U.K. grant certain reciprocal tariff preferences. The Republic of ◊ *Ireland* has not belonged to the Commonwealth since 1937; ◊ *South Africa* left it in 1961; ◊ *Burma, Somalia, Sudan* declined offers of Dominion status. ◊◊ *Imperial Preference, Commonwealth Institute, Commonwealth Relations Office.*

British Council. Founded in 1934 to promote overseas knowledge of the English language and of British life and culture, it disseminates information on British thought and achievement through offices in many parts of the world, by means of libraries, periodicals, and films, sends British experts, lecturers, orchestras, teachers, and theatre companies (both drama and ballet) to many countries, organizes courses in English language and literature, and in the U.K. arranges study programmes for scholars, teachers, scientists, and professional visitors, besides looking after Commonwealth and other students from overseas. Government grants to the British Council amount to £10 m. annually, a much smaller sum than that spent on similar activities by e.g. France, U.S.A., or U.S.S.R.

British Guiana (Demerara). Area 83,000 sq. m. Pop. 0.6 m. (mainly Indians and Negroes whose antipathies have led to frequent disturbances and chronic political instability). Cap. Georgetown. British colony on the N E coast of S. America, between Venezuela, Surinam, and Brazil. The Legislative Assembly of 35 is elected for four years by direct universal adult suffrage; there is an appointed Senate of 25, who elect the President, a 10-man Council of Ministers, and a British Governor. The constitution has twice been suspended since 1953 because of grave political unrest. The strongest political party is People's Progressive Party, headed by Dr Jagan and of decided communist leanings. There is difficulty in finding work for the rapidly growing population.

ECONOMY. The country is mainly under forest; only the coastal strip is cultivated, growing rice and sugar, but the interior has vast deposits of bauxite (the world's largest source), and some diamonds, gold, manganese, mica.

HISTORY. Guiana was discovered by Ralegh in 1595 but first settled by the Dutch. The region was disputed throughout the 17th and 18th centuries, until the Vienna Congress of 1815 settled the division into British, Dutch, and French Guiana.

British Legion. Founded 1921 by Earl Haig to help ex-service men and women, most of the funds being raised by the sale of 'Flanders poppies' (as memorial emblems of the First World War) on or about 11 Nov. (Armistice Day). The Legion runs workshops, schools, and hospitals for its members.

British Museum. Founded 1753 on the basis of private collections, it has become the principal museum in the U.K. and one of the great museums of the world, with a rich collection of archaeological and ethnographical material from all over the world, and a wide variety of art treasures. It is also the national library for books and periodicals and under the Copyright Act is one of the five libraries which receive two free copies of every book printed in the U.K. and the Republic of Ireland. A reading room makes the vast resources of the library available for research.

British Standards Institution. Various engineering bodies combined in 1901 to form a joint Engineering Standards Committee, which was granted a charter in 1929; it prepares and publishes voluntarily agreed standards for manufacturing processes and also analyses etc. for both industrial and consumer products. Other countries maintain similar organizations, and e.g. the International Wool Textile Organization and the International Bureau of Standards help to advance universal standards.

British Thermal Unit ⟡ *Heat.*

Broad Beans ⟡ *Vetch.*

Bromides ⟡ *Halogens.*

Bromine. ⟡ *Halogens*; a dense brown liquid element derived from certain salt deposits and also from sea water (from which it is liberated by means of chlorine). Both liquid and vapour are toxic and produce dangerous burns. Its chemistry is similar to that of ⟡ *chlorine*, but it is a little less reactive. Its most important compound is potassium bromide (KBr), used in the manufacture of photographic film and paper and as a sedative in medicine.

Bronchitis. Acute or chronic inflammation of the mucous lining of the air passages of the ⟡ *lungs.* ⟡ *Larynx.*

Brontosaurus (Apatosaurus). Enormous ⟡ *dinosaur* living in the shallow Jurassic sea of 150 m. years ago (⟡ *Geological Time Scale*). A quadruped, its gigantic legs mainly functioned as anchors; its weak jaws, with small teeth crowded at the front, suggest a diet of some very nutritious plant to maintain its 40-ton bulk.

Bronze. An ⟡ *alloy* (copper with 5–8 per cent tin) used since very early times as an artistic medium; the two main methods of working it – by sand casting and *cire-perdue* casting – are recorded from at least the 3rd millennium B.C. It was extensively used for sculpture in ancient Greece and Rome. The secret of its working, lost in the Middle Ages, was recovered in 13th-cent. Italy. In 15th-cent. Italy it became the normal medium for statuettes, usually of mythological subjects, which are among the masterpieces of ⬦ *Renaissance* sculpture, notably those by L'Antico, Riccio, Bertoldo, and Bellano. The medium was also used for larger statues and reliefs, notably by Donatello, Ghiberti, Verrocchio, and in the late 16th cent. by Giovanni Bologna. It later became usual to entrust the casting to specialist craftsmen. Among later sculptors in bronze, Rodin is probably the greatest. In the present century it has been used by such sculptors as Epstein, Marino Marini, and Henry Moore. Bronze is sometimes gilded or given an artificial patina to imitate the natural effects of weathering. ⬦⬦ *Copper, Primitive Art*.

Bronze Age. Stage in the development of a ⬦ *culture* at which tools of bronze but not of iron were used; often preceded by a 'Copper Age'. This demanded an economy sufficiently advanced to permit some specialization of labour, and also widespread trade relations for the metal ores. It is associated in the Near East with the beginnings of urban civilization and of literacy, but obviously occurred at various dates in different regions, while some societies have never had a Bronze Age. The peoples of the ancient Near East moved into the bronze 'stage' in the 4th millennium B.C. and bronze working was introduced into S. Britain by the ⬦ *Beaker People* or their successors about 2000 B.C.

Brownian Motion. Random unceasing movement, on a microscopic scale, of small particles suspended in a fluid. The phenomenon was first noted by the Scottish botanist Robert Brown, 1773–1858, while studying the behaviour of pollen grains in water. Brownian movement is now known to result from molecular bombardment of the suspended particles.

Brownshirts ⬦ *Nazism*.

Bryophyta ⬦ *Plants*.

B.T.U. (British Thermal Unit) ⬦ *Heat*.

Buchmanism ⬦ *Moral Rearmament*.

Buddhism. Philosophico-religious system based on the teaching of Guatama Buddha 563–483 B.C. with the fundamental tenet that salvation from the suffering inherent in existence and the continual round of rebirths (⬦ *Transmigration*) can be attained through enlightenment reached by following the Eightfold Path (right views, motive, speech, action, way of life, effort, mindfulness, and concentration) which

leads to ⬦ *Nirvana*. In its first 1000 years Buddhism spread peacefully throughout E. Asia; it soon differentiated into two main schools, each with a separate collection of sacred writings, many of which have been translated into English.

MAHAYANA: In China, Japan, and Tibet (⬦ *Dalai Lama*). More social in outlook, the ideal being the Bodhisattva, who seeks enlightenment for others' sake. Mahayana is divided into numerous schools, including ⬦ *Zen*. ⬦⬦ *Burma*.

THERAVADA (HINAYANA): In Ceylon and Burma; the ideal is the Arhat, who finds the truth for himself.

Today Buddhism has about 300 m. at least nominal followers, and recently has found some response in Europe and America. ⬦⬦ *Gnostics, Jains, Karma, Mysticism, Nirvana, Pantheism*.

Budding ⬦ *Brier, Reproduction (Animal)*.

Budgerigar ⬦ *Parrot*.

Budget. Detailed plan of future receipts and expenditure for a definite period of time, most usually proposals by a government for taxation and expenditure; in Britain, an annual statement by the Chancellor of the Exchequer to the House of Commons, usually in early April, the first part giving the past year's income and expenditure and the second an estimate of both for the coming year and proposals for changes in taxation, forming the basis for the Finance Bill the government introduces to give effect to the proposals. In most western countries the Budget is presented and approved in one piece, but in U.S.A. it is a more general declaration of intentions, and the process of authorizing and appropriating expenditure continues throughout the legislative year. Up to 1939 the function of the Budget in Britain was simply to raise money, but since the Second World War it has become also one of the most important instruments by which governments seek to control the economy: by altering the size of the Budget surplus or deficit a government can add to or reduce the total demand for goods and thus stimulate or restrain the economy, and governments have increasingly tended to seek powers to change taxation between Budgets so that they are not limited to a once-a-year operation.

Buffalo. Animal of the ox family, *Bovidae*, often known as the water buffalo, which from time immemorial has been a domestic animal in India. It was later introduced into Egypt and parts of Europe. Indian and African buffalo are horned and larger than the ox; the female gives nourishing milk of peculiar flavour. Their favourite habitat is marshland. When wild they are among the most dangerous of big game, and the adult is quite a match for a tiger. The American buffalo (correctly bison), which once roamed in vast numbers over the prairies, is now protected. It has never been domesticated. The European bison (sometimes wrongly called aurochs, the primitive European cattle now completely extinct) is almost extinct, but small protected herds survive in Poland.

Buganda. Autonomous kingdom in federal relationship with ◊ *Uganda*. The ruler, the Kabaka, once regarded as semi-divine, was traditionally an autocratic king, but his power is now tempered by a landed aristocracy and an educated middle class. After his return from deportation in 1955 the affairs of Buganda were placed under a council of ministers and he became a constitutional monarch. The native Gandas number 850,000 out of a pop. of 1.3 m. The remainder are Asians.

Bugs. Members of the hemipterous insect family *Cimicidae*, with beak-like piercing and sucking mouth appendages; they may infest leaves and flowers; the bedbug, which is nocturnal in habit and chiefly attacks man, is not a disease carrier, although its bite produces swelling and irritation. ◊ *Louse.*

Bulb. A short stem bearing a tight mass of thick fleshy leaves, in which food materials are stored for use when growth begins again, e.g. onion, narcissus, lilies. Most bulbs are nature's response to adverse growing conditions e.g. great heat and drought. Whilst this lasts, the bulb remains dormant, but as soon as rain or melting snow provides moisture, roots develop and the plant grows. When cultivated in countries e.g. the British Isles where these conditions do not occur naturally, many bulbs are able to adapt themselves. Those which cannot must receive special treatment, the resting period being simulated by lifting the bulbs and storing them. Bulbs vary very much in the intensity of the adverse conditions required to cause cessation of growth and initiation of the resting period. ◊ *Corm.*

Bulgaria. Area 43,000 sq. m. Pop. 8.1 m.

Cap. Sofia. Rel. about 85 per cent Eastern Orthodox, with a Muslim minority. A socialist people's republic; the 1947 Constitution provides for a single-chamber National Assembly elected by universal suffrage, which elects a Presidium of 18 with a president and two vice-presidents. ECONOMY. Still essentially agricultural, with tobacco, grapes, and attar of roses as important products; but industrial output is increasing esp. coal, lead, zinc, copper, steel, and cement. Since 1947 private enterprise has been replaced by state ownership; collectivization of agriculture (about 95 per cent) is more advanced than in other communist-bloc countries.

HISTORY. For centuries the area was occupied by Turkey (◊ *Ottoman Empire*). The 1878 ◊ *Berlin Congress* and Treaty created a Principality of Bulgaria, which was enlarged in 1885 and became an independent kingdom 1908. Bulgaria joined the Central Powers in the First World War, and in 1919 had to cede territory to ◊ *Greece* and the newly-created ◊ *Yugoslavia.* Occupied by Germany in the Second World War, she proclaimed her neutrality but under subsequent Soviet occupation declared war on Germany in 1944. The communist-controlled Fatherland Front coalition (which later became the Communist Workers Party) seized power and proclaimed the Bulgarian People's Republic 1946.

LANGUAGE. Bulgarian, spoken also in parts of Bessarabia, Dobruja (Rumania), and Macedonia (Greece); the oldest and simplest of the ◊ *Slavonic languages*, with a considerable admixture of Turkish vocabulary. Old Bulgarian (Church Slavonic) dates to the 9th cent. when the Cyrillic alphabet was invented, and is still in use in church services.

Bull. 1. In finance, a speculator who hopes to profit by a rise in the price of shares or commodities, buying them on account in the hope of selling them at a higher price before settling day and profiting from the difference; hence bull market, in which prices are rising or expected to rise. ◊ *Bear, Stag, Stock Exchange.*
2. ◊ *Cattle.*

Bull-fighting. A blood sport dating to pre-Roman times and still practised (in rich costume and to traditional music) in Spain and Mexico; the bull (bred for speed and ferocity) is first goaded by horsemen with lances (*picadores*), followed by men on foot (*banderilleros*) who plant ornamental darts in the back of the bull's neck, and finally the enraged bull faces the *matador*, whose skill is judged by the risks he takes and by the perfection of his movements as he 'plays' the bull closer and closer with a red cloak stretched on a *muleta*, a stick held in the left hand, until he makes the kill with a sword. In Portugal and S. France killing the bull is not permitted, the object being to place a rosette between his horns.

Bull Run. 1861, 1862. The first major battles of the ◊ *American Civil War*. The determined defence of the Southern general 'Stonewall' Jackson halted the Northern Union troops, who had been accompanied by crowds of spectators from the city, and on the second day drove them back in disorder behind the Washington defences; but he was unable to exploit his success and occupy the capital. The battle shocked the North into a realization that the war would call for their utmost efforts. The second battle, a year later, was a longer and more complicated engagement, in which the Union forces were badly defeated; but again the Confederates were halted before they could capture Washington.

Buoys. Floats moored in waters used by shipping, to mark channels and warn against shoals, rocks, and other hazards, sometimes carrying a light or bell. Around Britain the lateral system is used, the shape and colour of the buoy indicating which side a ship should pass; in the cardinal system, the shape and colour of the buoy indicate the compass direction of a danger to navigation. Buoys are indicated on charts, with notes as to their shape, colour, lights, etc.

Burgundy. Region in E. France around the Saône valley. The duchy of Burgundy was formed in the 9th cent. and became rich and powerful under the dukes of Valois in the 14th and 15th centuries, when it included most of the Low Countries as well as vast territories in France and was famed for the brilliance of its court. In the early 15th cent. Philip of Burgundy supported England in the ◊ *Hundred Years War*, but in 1435 he gave his allegiance to France again in the Treaty of Arras. His son Charles the Bold dreamed of uniting the duchy with his ◊ *Netherlands* territories, but the attempt failed. After his defeat and death at Nancy in

1477, his daughter Mary married the Emperor Maximilian I (◊ *Holy Roman Empire*), taking to him the Burgundian possessions; the depleted area was annexed by Louis XI of France and formed into the province of Burgundy. It is now a noted wine-growing area (◊ *Wine*). ◊ *France (History)*, *Lotharingia*.

Burlesque. 1. A ◊ *parody* composition, usually literary or theatrical, in which serious matter is imitated in such a manner as to make it ridiculous by the incongruity between style and subject. The term was first applied to the mock-heroic parodies of Paul Scarron, 1610–60. The element of imitation is essential to burlesque, and distinguishes it from satire. Thus, while all burlesque could be called satirical, not all satire is burlesque; Pope's *Dunciad* is both satire and burlesque, but his *Epistle to Dr Arbuthnot* is satire only. Burlesque reached its zenith in the 18th cent. with Fielding's *Shamela* and Pope's *The Rape of the Lock*.
2. In America, a form of light entertainment centring on sex and striptease.

Burma. Area 262,000 sq. m. Pop. 21.5 m. Cap. Rangoon. Rel. mainly Buddhist. The second city, Mandalay, is the acknowledged centre of Buddhist scholarship, and as a result of the prevalence of schools run by Buddhist monks the Burmese level of literacy is high. A republic with a president elected for five years, a chamber of Deputies and a Chamber of Nationalities; but since the military coup d'état of 1962 a council of army officers has ruled. ECONOMY. Burma consists of three distinct regions; the largest is the eastern plateau, the most important the basin of the Irrawaddy river running down the centre of the country, in the delta of which is grown the rice which accounts for 75 per cent of Burma's exports. Oil has been found in the northern dry belt; other products include rubber, teak, some silver and lead (from the eastern mountains) and jade.
HISTORY. Until 1937 Burma formed part of British India; it then became a separate territory with a measure of self-government. It was under Japanese occupation in the ◊ *Second World War*. On attaining independence in 1948 Burma opted to leave the ◊ *British Commonwealth*; in 1951 the Anti-Fascist Freedom League, a left-wing coalition, gained a majority in the Chamber of Deputies and

remained in power till 1962. Under the constitution private property and private enterprises are guaranteed, but nationalization with compensation of owners is provided for, and the state is the ultimate owner of all land. The government is pursuing a policy of industrialization, land reform, and social welfare.

LANGUAGE. Burmese; one of the Tibeto-Burman language family. Also various Indian and Chinese dialects, and English.

Burnham Committees. National Committees established 1919 under the chairmanship of Lord Burnham, on which the Local Education Authorities and their staff (e.g. teachers, inspectors) are represented, and which, under a chairman appointed by the Minister of ◊ *Education*, make 3-yearly recommendations to the Minister on teachers' salaries; the Minister may accept or reject their proposals. The official scale of salaries is commonly known as the Burnham Scale; its equivalent in Scotland is the Teviot Scale. The Minister's rejection of the 1963 proposals aroused fierce opposition among teachers and caused a crisis leading to new arrangements.

Burundi. Area 10,747 sq. m. Pop. 2.8 m. (mainly Hutu and Tutsi). Cap. Kitega, but chief town Usumbura. Kingdom in central Africa, independent since 1962, formerly a part of the Belgian Congo colony and more recently a Belgian trusteeship under the U.N. (as part of Ruanda-Urundi).

ECONOMY. Wholly agricultural; main crop coffee, exported chiefly to U.S.A. Also large output of hides from extensive livestock-rearing.

HISTORY. ◊ *Rwanda*.

Burushaski. Apparently unrelated to any other tongue; it may be a survivor of an Asian tongue earlier than the ◊ *Indo-European languages*. Scholars have tried without success to prove it distantly related to the ◊ *Caucasian languages*. Spoken in Hunza and other parts of extreme N W India. ◊ *Basques*.

Bushmen. Aboriginal hunting and gathering people of S. Africa, today living in the Kalahari desert; once distributed over all central, southern, and probably eastern Africa, but pushed into their present arid and difficult habitat by Bantu Negroes from the north. They are slight and of yellowish complexion, physically distinct from the Negroes (◊ *Race*), and

their technology is of the simplest: they do not practise cultivation or domesticate animals. They worship the moon and have an elaborate and beautiful mythology. Today they work as herdsmen: only about 30,000 remain. ◊ *African Languages, African Peoples and Cultures.*

Butane ◊ *Paraffins.*

Butler Act ◊ *Education Acts and Reports.*

Butter ◊ *Milk.*

Butterfly. One of the two main divisions of the insect order *Lepidoptera* (the other being ◊ *moth*), including 80,000 species of world-wide distribution; usually diurnal, slender in body, and coloured, holding their wings perpendicular when at rest (whereas moths are nocturnal, faintly coloured, and settle with outspread wings). The brilliant colour of butterflies arises usually from minute coloured scales, but the metallic iridescent effects common in tropical butterflies are caused by refraction; their coloration is often protective, but sometimes mimics creatures unpalatable to their enemies. Their life-cycle is the typical one of egg-larva(caterpillar)-pupa-adult, the life-span of the adult being only a few days.

Buttress. A support built against a wall to strengthen it or to resist the pressure of an arch or vault on the other side of

romanesque   early english   flying buttress

it; this became a prominent feature in
◊ *Gothic architecture*, esp. the 'flying
buttress' consisting of an arch starting
from a detached pier and abutting against
a wall to take the thrust of the vaulting
within. ◊ *Architecture*.

Buzzard ◊ *Eagle*.

By-laws. Rules made by county councils,
metropolitan and county borough councils, and national undertakings e.g.
British Rail, under authority delegated by
Parliament; they are recognized by the
courts only if reasonable and strictly in
accordance with the authorizing Act. ◊
Administrative Law.

Byzantine Empire. The importance of Byzantium, founded as a Greek city in 657
B.C., dates from A.D. 330 when Constantine
rebuilt it as the capital of the Roman Empire and renamed it Constantinople. After
the fall of Rome a flourishing civilization
continued at Byzantium and under the
Macedonians expanded into Armenia and
Mesopotamia in the 9th and 10th centuries. Political and religious differences
between the Byzantine Empire and the
rest of Europe were symbolized by the
crowning of Charlemagne as head of the
◊ *Holy Roman Empire* in A.D. 800, and
when the Byzantines were compelled
to summon help against the Seljuk Turks,
the Crusaders proved more interested in
setting up independent kingdoms in Palestine than in succouring the Empire. The
antagonism between East and West became so strong that the Fourth Crusade
(1204) turned against Byzantium itself,
and a Latin kingdom was set up in the
East, lasting until 1261. The position of
Byzantium was by now so weak that after
a brief revival it fell a victim to the
Turkish ◊ *Ottoman Empire* in 1453. Constantinople was succeeded as capital of
Turkey in 1923 by Ankara and in 1930
Kemal Ataturk changed its name to Istanbul.

ART AND ARCHITECTURE: Byzantine
art stemmed from Hellenistic and Roman
traditions, but was directed predominantly
to religious purposes. By the 6th cent.
these influences had merged with others
from Asia and the Near East to create a
new and independent style best illustrated
by Haghia Sophia, Constantinople (532–
37) and S. Vitale, Ravenna (about 547). In
the 7th and 8th centuries the iconoclastic
movement encouraged a more spiritual
and less realistic rendering of the human
figure in paintings, mosaics, and sculpture.
For nearly a century only geometric and
foliage decorations were tolerated. In the
9th cent. the typical Byzantine domed
and apsed church was established, decorated with a mosaic or painted half-figure
of Christ Omnipotent in the eastern apse,
with a screen dividing the altar area from
the rest of the building. This form underwent no significant change in subsequent
centuries. The representations of Christ
and the Saints, whether painted or in
mosaic, were hieratic, expressionless, and
sombre. A similar style and spirit also
impressed Byzantine lay art, which found
its expression mainly in ceramics and textiles. Byzantine art continued to influence
European art until the Renaissance and
was influential in Russia until the 17th
cent. ◊ *Eastern Orthodox Church, Icon*.

C

Cabbage. Broccoli, brussels sprouts, cabbage, cauliflower, kale, savoys, and sprouting broccoli have all been derived, over a long period of cultivation, from the biennial coast plant *Brassica oleracea*, a native of central Europe widely cultivated in Mediterranean countries in ancient times. How the varieties developed is not known; the cauliflower is thought to have been introduced from Cyprus, and brussels sprouts were grown in Belgium in the early 15th cent. White and black mustard, ◊ *rape*, turnips, etc. also belong to the brassica family ◊ *Cruciferae*.

Cabinet ◊ *Parliament, Prime Minister.*

Cabotage. Coastal trading, esp. the conveyance of cargoes and passengers from one point to another within a country's borders; now applied also to aviation. The right to permit cabotage is a jealously guarded national prerogative: the negotiation of cabotage rights is of special importance in internal aviation. ◊◊ *International Civil Aviation Organization.*

Cactus. About 2000 species from three families of succulent plants with fleshy, flat, round, square, or triangular stems, which are photosynthetic and store water and often have spines and scales instead of leaves, thus reducing transpiration. They range in size from small globes ½ in. across to fantastic branched varieties 30 ft tall. True cacti are the family *Cactaceae*, native mostly in America, with beautiful flowers like waterlilies. Some have edible fruits e.g. the prickly pear. Many succulents are loosely called cacti (◊ *Euphorbiaceae*).

Caddis Fly. Dun-coloured moth-like member of the order *Trichoptera*, which frequents streams and pools at night, varying in size from that of a midge to that of a house-fly; lays its eggs in a jelly-like mass. The larvae are the common caddis worm sometimes used by anglers; they have glands supplying silk, with which they line an inhabitable tube made from sand, leaf fragments, etc. The tube is closed at the ends during the chrysalis stage preceding metamorphosis into a fly.

Cadmium. A rather rare metallic element found in zinc ores and isolated by fractional distillation. Like zinc, it is not attacked by moist air, and is used for electroplating, as a component of bearing and low-melting ◊ *alloys*, and to control atomic reactors. Rods of cadmium in atomic piles control the rate of atomic fission, because of their high efficiency in absorbing neutrons. In the 'Nife' type of storage cell, cadmium can be used in place of iron. Its sulphide (yellow) is a constituent of some pigments.

Cadmus. In Greek legend, son of the Phoenician king Agenor; sent by his father to recover his sister ◊ *Europa.* Unable to find her, he visited the Delphic ◊ *oracle*, which told him to follow a certain cow until it sank tired, and to settle there. He did so on the site of Thebes in Boeotia, where he slew a dragon and sowed its teeth, from which sprang armed men who killed one another, except five who became the ancestors of the Thebans. Cadmus is also said to have introduced the alphabet to Greece; this reflects the Phoenician origin of Greek script and perhaps of other arts.

Caesar. Originally the name of a patrician family of the *gens Julia* in ◊ *Rome*, claiming to be descended from Aeneas. Augustus, adopted son and heir of Julius Caesar, included 'Caesar' in his name; it became the second title of the Emperors until the time of Hadrian, when it was transferred to the Emperor's heir. From it derived the titles Tsar (borne by the king of Bulgaria and the Emperor of Russia) and Kaiser (the name used by the Holy Roman Emperors and rulers of Austria-Hungary until 1918 and by the rulers of Germany after 1871).

Caesarean Section. Removal of a child from the uterus by an abdominal operation; named after Julius Caesar, so delivered. (Roman law required the opening of the body of a woman dying in pregnancy in the hope of extracting a living child.) Modern surgical methods have greatly reduced the danger of the operation, which is often used when obstruction or pelvic deformity interferes with normal birth. It is being increasingly used on domestic animals in veterinary science. ◊◊ *Childbirth, Surgery.*

Caesium. A rare alkali metal which is

the most electro-positive of all the ◊ *elements*. It was discovered by Bunsen about 1860, using the new tool of ◊ *spectrum* analysis. ◊ *Atomic Clock, Metals and Non-Metals, Photoelectric Effect.*

Caffeine. An alkaloid present in small amounts in tea, in coffee beans, and in other sources e.g. the kola nut. It is readily soluble in water and is a mild stimulant.

Cainozoic ◊ *Cenozoic Era.*

Caisson. An open-ended cylindrical or rectangular box sunk to the bottom of a river. There are various types; some are simply sunk and filled with concrete to form piers, others are chambers from which the water is prevented from entering by compressed air, in which men can work while excavating etc. resembling the diving-bell in principle. The work is arduous and may lead to ◊ *bends.*

Calcite. Carbonate of lime, generally colourless or white but sometimes tinted, usually translucent, crystallizing in a variety of forms, all of which are distinguishable by their readiness to decompose with effervescence of carbon dioxide when treated with dilute acids.

CHALK: A soft earthy type.

ICELAND SPAR: A transparent crystal, not very common.

LIMESTONE: General term for lime carbonates in compact form.

MARBLE: A limestone crystallized by heat and pressure.

TUFA: ◊ *Stalactite.*

Calcium. An alkaline earth ◊ *metal* which is readily oxidized and releases ◊ *hydrogen* from water. The element forms 3.4 per cent of the earth's crust, occurring as the carbonate in limestone, chalk, and marble, as the phosphate in apatite, and as a major constituent of many silicate minerals. Heating the carbonate $CaCO_3$ gives the oxide quicklime, which water slakes to hydroxide $(CaO + H_2O \rightarrow Ca(OH)_2)$. This mixed with sand gives mortar. Calcium hydroxide, slaked lime, is the cheapest industrial alkali; it is much used in agriculture for dressing acid soils. Heating calcareous rocks or mixtures containing clay produces ◊ *cement*, a mixture of silicates which sets by combining with water and thus consolidates under water. ◊ *Gypsum* $CaSO_4.2H_2O$ when moderately heated loses some water and becomes plaster of Paris; this when moistened sets by re-hydration to gypsum. While setting it slightly expands and thus gives sharp casts of surfaces with which it is in contact. Lime heated with ◊ *coke* in an electric furnace produces calcium carbide; this with water gives ◊ *acetylene*, important as a fuel and as a starting material in organic synthesis. ◊ *Fluorspar* provides fluorine and fluorine compounds; because of its low melting point it is a valuable metallurgical flux. Apatite, or rock phosphate, furnishes phosphorus and its compounds, especially the fertilizer superphosphate; to produce this it is finely ground and treated with 70 per cent sulphuric acid. The metal, extracted electrolytically, has some use in metallurgy. Its relatively simple chemistry is based on a valency state of two. Calcium is of great biological importance; for instance, it is deposited by invertebrates as carbonate in shell and by vertebrates as phosphate in bone. ◊ *Oxalic Acid.*

Calculus. 1. < Lat. *calculus*, pebble (used in counting). In higher mathematics, methods for solving problems which involve variables or rates of change; also useful in calculating the area of curved and irregular figures, volume, pressure, etc. Newton and the German mathematician Leibnitz both made the discovery at about the same time; the belief that the one had stolen his idea from the other led to enmity between the two, but historians are now satisfied that the discoveries were in fact quite independent.

2. In medicine, a concretion of solid inorganic matter mainly ◊ *cholesterol* around a matrix of organic matter; commonly called 'stones'. It is liable to form in any of the secretions stored in the body's reservoirs, or in passages carrying these secretions. Stones have been found not only in gall bladder, urinary bladder, and prostate but in ducts of the tear and salivary glands. They are likely to cause serious obstruction; if not passed spontaneously they can be surgically removed.

Caldera. Shallow hollow remaining as the basal wreck of a ◊ *volcano* when an eruption blows off the former cone, much larger than a normal crater; new cones may develop within it, e.g. Vesuvius has grown in a caldera, the remains of the mountain which exploded and destroyed Pompeii in A.D. 79, the relics of whose former cone surround the modern volcano as a broken rim of highland called Monte

Somma. In some cases, the cone seems to have collapsed and disappeared into the underground ◊ *magma* chamber.

Calendar. System of reckoning time, usually by relating the day to the solar year and the lunar month. Complications arise because the year is not exactly divisible into months and days, so that odd days and months have to be added periodically, to preserve a correct relationship between date and season. Accurate calendars developed in Mesopotamia, and ancient Egypt had a year of twelve 30-day months and five extra days (six every fourth year). The Julian calendar, established by Julius Caesar 45 B.C. on the advice of the astronomer Sosigenes, was similarly based on 365-day years and 'leap' years, but gave arbitrary lengths to the months; it is the basis of the calendar now generally used. The true year is, however, 11 minutes, 14 seconds less than the 365¼ days usually assumed; by the 16th cent. the Julian calendar was 10 days out of step with the seasons. In 1582 on the advice of the astronomer Clavius, to remedy this discrepancy, Pope Gregory XIII decreed that century years, though divisible by four, should not be leap years; despite opposition from non-Catholics the Gregorian calendar was gradually accepted. The Jewish calendar has 12 months of 29 and 30 days alternately (354 days) and adds a 13th month every third year. The Muslim calendar is similar to the Jewish, but without the extra month; it thus bears no relationship to the seasons and has about 34 years to our 33. New but short-lived calendars devised during the French and Russian revolutions divided 360 days of the year into equal monthly and weekly units and used the surplus five or six days as holidays outside these units. Modern schemes for calendar reform are somewhat similar; the reform most widely advocated would ensure that a given date always fell on the same day of the week, and that every month had the same number of working days, by dividing the year into quarters made up of one 31-day month and two 30-day months, i.e. 364 days; the 365th day would follow the 12th month as an extra holiday, and every fourth year would have a 'leap year' holiday at the end of the second quarter. ◊ *Astronomy, Time.*

Californium ◊ *Actinides.*

Caliphate. < Arabic *Khalif*, successor; the caliphs were the heirs to the temporal kingdom of Mohammed and the spiritual heads of ◊ *Islam*, and the reigning Caliph came to be known as 'Commander of the Faithful'. Abu Bekr, Mohammed's father-in-law, was chosen in Medina as the first caliph, and by vigorous military action he consolidated the new faith throughout the Arabian Peninsula. He was succeeded by Omar (under whom the explosive expansion of Islam took place), Othman, and Ali, last of the Caliphs in Medina, who was opposed by a rival faction led by Muawiya. From this clash resulted the permanent division of Islam into ◊ *Shiahs* (partisans of Ali) and ◊ *Sunnis*, who set up the ◊ *Ommayad* caliphate in Damascus in A.D. 661. In 750 the ◊ *Shiahs* overthrew and massacred the Ommayads and established the ◊ *Abbasids* as caliphs in Bagdad, where under Harun al Rashid and Mamoun the finest flowering of Islamic civilization ensued, with the fusion of Greek and Persian influence. Thereafter the caliphate split up and decayed; rival caliphs arose, and the caliphate as an effective and unifying institution was over, although individual caliphs, e.g. Saladin in Syria and Abdul Rahman in Spain, still wielded great influence. By 1518 the Ottoman Turks had conquered almost all the Arab lands and thus virtually ended the caliphate, the caliphs in Egypt being their puppets. Later the title was assumed by the Ottoman Sultans in Constantinople; it was finally abolished in 1924.

Calorie. 1. In biology, the amount of heat needed to raise 1 kg. of water from 15° to 16°C. It is, in fact, a kilocalorie, 1000 times larger than the calorie of physics, and is used to measure the heat-equivalent content of food. ◊ *Metabolism.*

2. In physics, a unit of heat, equal to the amount required to raise the temperature of 1 gram of water through 1°C. This unit is being superseded by the more general unit of energy, the Joule.

Calvados ◊ *Brandy.*

Calvinism. Protestant Christian theological system based on the *Institutes* of Jean Calvin 1509–64, distinguishing the Reformed from the Lutheran churches; emphasizes God's sovereignty and 'otherness' and is esp. identified with the doctrine of ◊ *predestination*. It remains the official teaching of the ◊ *Presbyterians* and some other Protestant churches, but though some Calvinist influence is apparent in the Anglican ◊ *Thirty-Nine Articles*, its full implications are seldom accepted by Christian communions in the 20th cent. It has been an important influence on the theologian Karl Barth and his followers. ◊◊ *Arminianism, Covenant*.

Calypso. 1. In Greek legend, daughter of ◊ *Atlas* (or of the ocean), residing on the mythical island of Ogygia where ◊ *Ulysses* was shipwrecked. She promised Ulysses immortality if he would remain permanently on Ogygia; but after seven happy years, and the birth of two sons, ◊ *Hermes* ordered Ulysses to resume his homeward journey and Calypso was left inconsolable.

2. In music, an extemporized and ephemeral ballad, of W. Indian origin, usually improvised to the guitar, celebrating and commenting on some topical event.

Calyx ◊ *Flower*.

Cambium. A group or layer of plant ◊ *cells* which divides repeatedly to form new tissues, primarily to increase the thickness of a plant. Cambium cells often develop for special purposes e.g. in ◊ *cork* formation in ◊ *bark* or wound tissue.

Cambodia. Area 70,000 sq. m. Pop. 5.8 m. (mostly a mixed race, Indian and Malay). Cap. Phnom-Penh. Rel. Buddhist. An independent state in S W Indo-China, formerly under French rule, its present status being agreed by France in 1954 after negotiations in Geneva. The country, entirely agricultural, is self-supporting; because of the large numbers of celibate priests the birthrate is low. ◊◊ *Angkor*.

Cambrian System. Rocks laid down at the beginning of the Palaeozoic Era (◊ *Geological Time Scale*) over a period of 100 m. years, the name deriving from Wales, where these rocks were first studied; slates of Cambrian age are found in the Snowdon district. Limestones with Cambrian fossils appear in N W Scotland; earlier rocks are almost devoid of fossils. ◊◊ *Geology (Petrology)*, *Palaeontology*.

Cambridge ◊ *Universities of Oxford and Cambridge*.

Cambridge Platonists. Philosophical theologians of the 17th century, including Benjamin Whichcote, Ralph Cudworth,

and Henry More, all at Cambridge; their doctrines, many of them unscholarly and inconsistent, are derived from ◊ *platonism* and ◊ *neoplatonism* and, among other things, stress religious. experience and mysticism against creed and ritual.

Camel. ◊ *Ruminant* of the order *Artiodactyla* (even-toed ungulates) related to the deer and giraffe. One species – the dromedary – has one hump, the Bactrian camel, two. These serve as food stores and, together with a stomach adapted to store water, enable the camel to exist in desert-like areas. They are widely distributed in the Old World, from China to N. Africa. The Bactrian camel is sturdier and has a heavy coat, the dromedary has a short coat and is more speedy; the two species can interbreed. The ◊ *llama* of the New World is also of the camel family.

Camellia. Evergreen shrub with large decorative flowers; the wild species from which most garden camellias were developed is *C. japonica*, a native of Japan. The camellia was brought to Europe in the late 18th cent. but it had been cultivated in Japan and probably China for many centuries. Tea, also known in China for very many centuries, comes from *C. sinensis*, originally a native of Assam but now grown in other hilly areas of the tropics and sub-tropics, esp. Ceylon, China, India, Japan, Java, and Kenya.

Camera ◊ *Photography*.

Camera Obscura. The forerunner of the photographic camera; a darkened chamber with a lens or pin-hole through which light rays enter to throw an image on the opposite wall. Several 18th-cent. painters, notably Canaletto, used this device in drawing architecture.

Cameroon. Area 432,000 sq. m. Pop. 4.9 m. Cap. Yaounde. Originally German, this colony was granted to France under a ◊ *mandate*. It became an Associated Territory of the French Union, but progress towards independence was slow, and the Union des Populations du Caméroun began active resistance to the French in 1956. In January 1960 the country became independent, and a year later, by a U.N. plebiscite, the S. Cameroons (formerly a British Trust Territory) voted to join Caméroun. The republic did not join the ◊ *French Community*, but signed agreements with France on defence, aid, and trade relations.

Camomile. *Anthemis nobilis*; a perennial herb with much-branched stems, finely divided leaves, and flower-heads like large daisies, native in England and found on sandy soils. It is grown as a medicinal herb, infusions being used for digestive ailments. It is planted along paths and occasionally as lawns, as it survives trampling and gives a pleasant aroma when crushed. ◊ *Compositae.*

Camouflage. 1. Military: the disguising of vehicles, ships, emplacements, industrial plant, etc. in such a way as to make them blend with their surroundings, developed esp. in the two World Wars as protection against aerial bombing. Camouflage painting in irregular patches of green and brown became familiar, but more ingenious devices were also adopted: dummy airfields and complete false landscapes were built, factories were made to look like fields, etc. It has been estimated that the wastage of bombs due to these decoys was considerable on both sides. An early form of camouflage was the dark green uniform of the Rifle Corps introduced in 1797. The British khaki adopted in 1899, the German field grey, and the French blue were further developments of the same type.
2. In animals ◊ *pigmentation.*

Camperdown. 1797. British naval victory over the Dutch, the allies of France (◊ *French Revolution*). De Winter set sail to invade Ireland (◊ *United Irishmen*) but was intercepted and routed by a superior English fleet. Nine Dutch ships were captured. Coming after the naval mutinies of Spithead and the Nore, this victory re-established the reputation of the navy and raised the country's morale at a critical time in the French Revolutionary Wars.

Camphor. A white aromatic crystalline solid, usually distilled from the leaves and wood of the tree *Cinnamomum camphora*, native to Japan, China, and Formosa, or *Dryobalanops*, native to Malaya; camphor trees are now widely cultivated in the warmer parts of the world. Camphor, which crystallizes from a complicated mixture of oils secreted by oil cells in the tissues of the trees, was introduced to Europe as a medicine by Arab traders in the 1st cent. A.D. It is now also used as a plasticizer for celluloid and cellulose nitrate, and this has led to its industrial production by a chemical process starting from pinene, a principal constituent of turpentine oil.

Campion. Several members of the *Caryophyllaceae*. The red campion has deep rose-pink flowers and leaves often tinged with red. The white campion hybridizes freely with the red campion, giving a range of fertile pink intermediates. The bladder campion and sea campion both have white flowers with large inflated calyces and greyish-green leaves.

Campos ◊ *Savanna.*

Canada. Area 3.9 m. sq. m. Pop. 18 m. Cap. Ottawa. A federal union of 10 provinces within the ◊ *British Commonwealth.* The Executive is a federal Cabinet, the legislature bi-cameral: a Senate of 102 life members and a House of Commons of 265 members. Each province has a similar local government with considerable powers, but provincial legislation may be disallowed by the federal authority. In matters of taxation, control of the economy, and social welfare the powers of the central government have steadily increased. Roughly 30 per cent of the people are French-speaking and Roman Catholic (mostly in the Quebec province). Both English and French are official languages. The U.S.A. exerts a powerful economic and cultural influence, but Canada remains strongly attached to her Commonwealth link and wholeheartedly supported Britain in both World Wars, contributing large forces. Canada is a member of NATO and an active supporter of the United Nations. The judicial and legal systems resemble those of the U.K.

ECONOMY. Although one of the largest countries in the world, much of Canada is unfitted for habitation and less than 10 per cent of its area is cultivable. Most of the population lives in a long irregular strip north of the Canadian-U.S. border ('the longest undefended frontier in the world'). Nevertheless its resources are varied and rich. Its great forests make it the world's leading supplier of timber, pulp, and newsprint; on its prairies are raised vast crops of wheat and herds of cattle, and fruit-growing, fishing, and fur-farming are also important. In the production of nickel, asbestos, and platinum Canada ranks first in the world, and in gold and uranium second; copper, iron ore, and petroleum are also valuable products. Canada takes a leading part in international trade, chiefly in raw or semi-processed materials. Her main customer is U.S.A. and her second the U.K. (with whom a preferential-tariff system is maintained).

HISTORY. Canada was discovered by John Cabot in 1497 and first settled by the French, from 1604. The founding of the ◊ *Hudson's Bay Company* brought the British and French into conflict, ended after the ◊ *Seven Years War* by the cession to Britain of all Canada. In 1791 Canada was divided into Upper (British) and Lower (French); in 1840 the two were joined under one government, and in 1867 Canada became a self-governing Dominion. At first federal authority was emphasized, and transcontinental railways were built to unite the country. From the 1890s provincialism was to the fore, but the depression of the 1930s and the Second World War made the Canadians more conscious of the need for central planning and of their common nationality. Recently the French Canadians have shown increasing restiveness.

Canal. Artificial waterway, usually for navigation but sometimes for irrigation or drainage. A famous ancient canal was the Grand Canal constructed in the 13th cent. to cross the Great Plain of China, and in Roman times a canal linked the Rhine and the Meuse. Canals were practicable only across level country until the invention of ◊ *locks* in the 15th cent. One of the earliest (with 119 locks in 148 m.) was the Canal du Midi, between the Mediterranean and the Bay of Biscay, rising to 600 ft above sea level. In Britain the improvement of rivers began about 1600; after the completion of the Sankey Navigation Canal 1757 a network of similar canals spread over the country and were important traffic arteries until the coming of railways. Inland waterways have been intensively developed and are still important in France, Germany, and U.S.S.R. (esp. the White Sea Canal and the Volga-Don Canal). In the 19th and 20th centuries several great ship canals were made:

	Opened	Length (miles)
Corinth (Greece)	1893	4
Kiel (Germany)	1895	61
Manchester (England)	1894	35
Panama (C. America)	1914	50
Suez (Egypt)	1869	100

The longest inland waterway is the St Lawrence Seaway, completed in 1959 as a result of extensive canal and lock works, between Montreal and Lake Ontario, permitting the passage of ships of 9000 tons for over 2000 m. from Quebec to Duluth.

Canary. Small grey-brown finch, native of the Canary Islands; domestication and selection of yellow and other bright colours began in Italy in the 16th cent. but Germany is now the centre of canary breeding. The birds are trained to sing by proximity to music or to birds of marked ability. The canary produces three or four broods a year in captivity.

Canasta. An elaborate version of ◊ *rummy*, played with two packs of 52 cards and usually four jokers; normally played between two pairs, but there are versions for two and three players. Canasta originated in Uruguay in the late 1940s. It became a very popular game throughout S. America, where it has been largely superseded by Samba, a version in which more packs are used. The game had a world-wide vogue in the early 1950s.

Cancer. A group of diseases characterized by uncontrolled and purposeless proliferation of ◊ *cells*, giving rise to tumour formation at the primary site of the disease, and spreading into the surrounding tissues as well as to distant parts, by dissemination of tumour fragments. It affects all members of the animal kingdom, with fairly high incidence in man and other species all over the world, and occurs most frequently in the latter half of the normal life-span of a species. Cancers are divisible into two groups: (a) those arising in the tissues of skin, glands, and lining-membranes of internal organs; and (b) those arising in muscle, bone, and other connective tissues.

The nature of the malignant change in cancer remains unknown. The finding that nucleic acid is increased in cancer cells has led to the suggestion that a clue may be found in deoxyribonucleic acid (◊ *DNA*), a vital chemical constituent of ◊ *chromosomes* and therefore closely associated with the passing-on of hereditary characteristics from one generation of cells to another. It is established for many animal species that viruses may cause cancer, but only recently has evidence emerged that some human cancers may be virus-induced. Hereditary factors undoubtedly influence susceptibility to cancer in man in the same way as they do in other animal species, and dietary and other environmental factors influence the incidence of cancer of some organs, e.g. skin cancer of coal-tar workers, lung cancer of nickel and chrome workers. There is a positive correlation statistically between incidence of cancer of the lung and cigarette smoking. Exposure to various type of ionizing radiation also predisposes to cancer; as the ⋄ *X-ray* martyrs bear witness. Many forms of cancer may be attributed to specific chemical or physical agents, but this is only half the picture; the nature and significance of individual susceptibility remains a mystery. The diagnosis of cancer may be made by clinical examination, with or without the use of X-rays and instruments for examination of body cavities, but certain diagnosis can only be made by microscopic examination of a small piece of suspected tissue, surgically removed. Early diagnosis is facilitated by the study of cells cast off from the surfaces of organs e.g. lungs, bladder, and the cervix of the uterus.

As a rule cancer is treated by the complete removal of the affected part or organ, with as much as possible of the surrounding tissue and the lymph glands draining the affected area. However, radiation therapy is appropriate in some cases of cancer, even in the early stages. There is considerable chance of success when growth is confined to the organ of origin; but less so when the local lymph glands are affected. When spread beyond these glands has occurred, radiation therapy or chemotherapy, alone or in combination with surgery or with each other, give the best chances of success. In the case of radiotherapy, very high-voltage X-rays or radioisotopes e.g. cobalt[60] are usually employed. Treatment of cancer depends on the selective destruction of cancer cells whilst normal cells are left unharmed. Unfortunately, in many cases it is not possible to give doses sufficiently high to destroy all the cancer cells present without at the same time interfering drastically with normal body functions by the destruction of normal cells.

The use of hormone treatment has been found helpful, though not often curative, in cancer of secondary sex glands. The removal of all ovarian hormones from the body, by excision or destruction by radiation of the ovaries, has often been followed by relief of pain and sometimes by regression of cancerous growth in the breast. The removal of male sex hormones, or their neutralization by administration of female sex hormones, has had an even more satisfactory effect in cancer of the prostate. ⋄ *Carcinogens.*

Cannae. 216 B.C Victory of Carthaginians under Hannibal in S. Italy, in which the Roman army of 70,000 was practically wiped out. ⋄ *Punic Wars.*

Cannel. Bituminous coal, readily igniting, splinters of which can be used like candles (hence the name), containing less carbon but more hydrocarbons than ordinary coal, burning with a smoky flame, and yielding oil on distillation. It originates from organic oozes rich in spores, from waxy and resinous remains, and from algal residues, its very considerable ash-residue being the mud of the ponds into which the spores and resin fell. ⋄ *Coal Measures, Coal and Coal-mining, Fuel.*

Cannibalism. Eating human flesh, usually for magical purposes e.g. to incorporate the spirit of the victim, either to prevent his vengeance for his killing or to absorb his virtues and valour. There is some evidence of cannibalism among prehistoric men, but except in times of famine it does not appear to have been widely practised in historic times.

Canoe. Boat propelled by paddles which have no fulcrum provided as in a rowboat; amongst primitive peoples usually made by hollowing out a tree-trunk or covering a framework with skins or bark. Normally a small river craft, but sometimes (e.g. with the Polynesians) elaborate seagoing craft capable of carrying up to 50 people. The American Indians developed the birch-bark canoe, to meet the requirements of waterways where a very light portable canoe was necessary. The Eskimos make light watertight canoes of sealskin, in which they make remarkably long journeys in rough seas. In the Pacific the outrigger was developed to give added stability, the shape of the main hull being ingeniously modified to counteract deviation when a single outrigger was in use. Sails were sometimes also employed.

CANOEING. The modern sport began 1865, when John MacGregor built his 'Rob Roy' canoe for travelling abroad, 14 ft long, 26 in. wide, weighing 72 lb. and with a 7-ft paddle; the British Canoe Association, formed 1887, was revived as the British Canoe Union 1936. World championships were begun 1933, 19 nations competed in the 1936 Olympic canoeing events. The main competitive forms are canoe-paddling, canoe-sailing, canoe-slalom (paddling an obstacle course on fast broken water), and wild-water canoeing.

Canon and Fugue. A canon is a musical composition in which one statement of a melody is overlapped in time by one or more repetitions at the unison, i.e. each statement is at the same pitch, as in the English round, e.g. *Three Blind Mice,* which is a perpetual canon (it may go on *ad infinitum*). The oldest known example is the medieval English *Sumer is icumen in,* about 1240.

Fugue, from the Latin for 'flight', is the systematic use of such musical overlapping. The classic examples of fugal technique are Bach's *Well-tempered Clavier* and *Forty-Eight Preludes and Fugues,* but the device is found in many works not called fugues, e.g. the 'Amen' chorus of Handel's *Messiah.* Canon (from *fuga per canonem,* fugue according to rule) may be regarded as an esp. rigorous type of fugue.

Canonization. Official process by which in the ◊ *Roman Catholic Church* persons of esp. holy life are declared worthy of general public veneration as saints; in the early church the title was accorded by the general consent of the faithful, but since about the 10th cent. the right has been reserved to the ◊ *Pope,* who proclaims the new saint in a solemn ceremony, after a detailed and lengthy inquiry, often lasting many years, into the candidate's life and writings. In the ◊ *Eastern Orthodox Church* canonization is less formal; some branches of the Anglican Church, e.g. in Canada and S. Africa, have recently accorded a semi-official canonization by including the names of e.g. Alfred the Great, Archbishop Laud, the poet George Herbert, and William Wilberforce in the Kalendars of their Prayer Books.

Canon Law. System of regulations governing the organization of Christian church affairs, administered by special church courts and based on the decisions of the General Councils, local synods, and the ◊ *Pope.* The first complete code was compiled by Gratian of Bologna in about 1150; a new and exhaustive *Codex Juris Canonici* was promulgated 1917 by Pope Benedict XV. The ◊ *Church of England* issued a collection of Canons 1603; a revisionary Commission was appointed 1939, but the revision is still under consideration (1963).

Cantata. Literally, a musical piece wholly or partly sung, as distinct from one which is only played, ◊ *sonata*; in the 19th and 20th centuries, usually an extended choral work not susceptible of a more precise definition e.g. ◊ *oratorio,* but earlier sometimes an extended composition for only a single voice with accompaniment. Bach's church cantatas (nearly 200 are preserved) filled much the place of the modern anthem.

Canyon (Cañon). A gorge or narrow steep-walled river valley, characteristic of rivers in the vigorous youthful stage and occurring in resistant rock (where the valley sides are eroded only slowly) or in arid climates (where lateral ◊ *erosion* is negligible but the rivers are fed from melted snows in distant mountains and cut their beds vertically). The Grand Canyon of the Colorado river in U.S.A. is 300 m. long, and the river has cut down to a depth of 6250 ft through horizontal beds of different rocks.

Cape Colony ◊ *South Africa (History).*

Cape Coloured People. Racially mixed community of almost 1.5 m. living in farming areas of Cape Province in S. Africa, for which they provide the unskilled and semi-skilled labour; descendants of Europeans (mainly Dutch), ◊ *Hottentots,* and East Indians, the Negro element being slight. They speak ◊ *Afrikaans* and are Christian except for 60,000 Muslims (Cape Malays). Traditionally they regarded themselves as affiliated with the Whites (many light-skinned Coloured 'passing' into the White group) and considered the Negroes inferior, but by disfranchising them (◊ *Apartheid*) the Nationalist government has recently driven them to align themselves politically with the Negroes.

Caper. Buds of the Mediterranean shrub *Capparis spinosa,* or fruits of the caper or the garden nasturtium, preserved and pickled and used in piquant sauces.

Capetians ◊ *Carolingians, France (History)*.

Capillaries ◊ *Circulatory System*.

Capital. 1. In economics, an individual's wealth or 'net worth' in money or goods, e.g. bank deposits and shares as well as land and property. Nationally, capital consists essentially of the country's actual fixed assets, the houses, factories, roads, schools, etc. together with the total stocks of raw materials and finished goods as yet unconsumed; the only money counting as part of the nation's capital is its net holdings of gold and foreign currencies.

CAPITAL GAINS: Rise in the capital value of property or of industrial shares esp. in periods of prosperity and inflation. The 1962 U.K. ◊ *Budget* introduced a short-term capital-gains tax on sales of land or property if the period from acquisition to disposal is up to three years, and on other property e.g. stocks and shares if the period is up to six months or less, capital gains within these periods being taxed as ordinary income. In U.S.A. there is a tax on all capital gains whether short-term or long-term.

CAPITAL GOODS: Those used in the production of other goods and of services.

CAPITAL LEVY: A tax on individually-owned capital; distinct from ◊ *income tax* or ◊ *death duties*. A capital levy called a 'special contribution' was introduced in the U.K. by Sir Stafford Cripps in the 1948 ◊ *Budget* and raised £110 m. In Sweden an annual capital duty is levied at the rate of one per cent on all individually-owned capital.

GROSS FIXED INVESTMENT: The amount added to the total of fixed capital in any country in one year.

NET FIXED INVESTMENT: The addition to the capital stock after allowance has been made for the year's using-up of the existing capital.

2. In architecture, the crowning feature of a column or pilaster, the form and decoration being extremely varied (◊ *Architectural Orders*).

Capitalism. A form of production of goods dependent upon the accumulation of capital. It existed in a limited way in ancient and medieval societies, but the term is now applied to the system developed since the ◊ *Industrial Revolution*, in which massive amounts of capital are required to acquire and operate the large-scale and increasingly costly equipment necessary for modern production. The term is more narrowly applied to those capitalist systems which are based on private enterprise, i.e. on private ownership and operation, the profit motive, and the play of supply and demand; ◊ *socialism*, in its economic aspect, is also capitalist, taking the form of state capitalism in which the ownership and planned use of the means of production are in the hands of the State not of private enterprises. The word 'capitalist' came into use about the time of the Industrial Revolution and preceded the word capitalism, which (esp. in the works of Marx) acquired implications additional to its purely economic meaning, to label a system in which the organization of society is favourable to the capitalists and detrimental to the interests of the workers, who are exploited. In theory the free-enterprise system is subject only to the 'invisible hand' of 'natural economic forces' (◊ *Free Trade, Laissez-faire*); in practice the State early intervened to regulate trade and industry, and subsequently social legislation and trade union activity have substantially reduced the area of complete freedom of the western capitalist system. ◊ *Marxism*.

Capital Punishment. The death penalty, retained in English law for ◊ *treason*, certain categories of murder or ◊ *piracy*, and setting fire to H.M. ships. A pregnant woman or a person under 18 at the time of the offence may not now be sentenced to death. Until the 19th cent. the death penalty was inflicted in most countries for a wide variety of crimes of which many would now be considered petty; Blackstone 1723–80 estimated that there were 160 statutes imposing capital punishment in the U.K. In 1814 a man was executed for cutting down a tree; in 1833 a boy of nine was sentenced to death for stealing twopennyworth of paint, but reprieved. Gradually a more humane attitude prevailed; in 1830 over 1000 bankers signed a petition requesting the abolition of the death penalty for forgery, juries being reluctant to convict. Today capital punishment has been abolished in many countries, including Portugal 1867, Netherlands 1870, Sweden 1921, Switzerland 1942, Italy 1944, W. Germany 1949, New Zealand 1961; and also in six states of U.S.A. and in several S. American countries. In a number of countries it exists in law but is never applied in practice; it has not been carried out in Belgium since 1863. In Poland, Yugoslavia, U.S.S.R. and some other countries it is still applied though not in fact mandatory (as it is in Britain) for any offence. Statistics before and after abolition are available in some cases, but in changing conditions they are not reliable indications. A U.N.O. survey 1962, however, concluded that there was no case in which abolition had been followed by a notable rise in the number of crimes previously capital; it appears that speed and certainty of discovery are greater deterrents than severity of punishment. The method of execution varies: in Britain it is hanging, in France the guillotine, in U.S.S.R. shooting. In U.S.A. in such states as retain the death penalty execution is variously by hanging, gassing, or electrocution.

Caporetto. 1917. A spectacular Austro-German victory on the Italian front during the ◊ *First World War*, in which the Italians lost 320,000 men and 3000 guns. Nevertheless, the front was held until British and French reinforcements arrived.

Capsicum ◊ *Pepper (2).*

Caraway. *Carum carvi*, of the ◊ *Umbelliferae*; a branched biennial aromatic herb native in Europe, cultivated for its seeds, which are often used as a flavouring not only in the familiar caraway-seed cake but also (esp. in Europe) in bread, rolls, cheese, and liqueurs e.g. Kümmel. It is also used medicinally for digestive ailments.

Carbides. Binary compounds formed from ◊ *carbon* and another element. There are four main types : (a) salt-like e.g. calcium carbide CaC_2 which gives ◊ *acetylene* on treatment with water; (b) interstitial e.g. ◊ *tantalum* carbide and ◊ *tungsten* carbide, which are high-melting very hard materials used for facing cutting tools; (c) iron type e.g. those of iron and manganese, important constituents of steels (◊ *Iron and Steel Industry*); (d) covalent e.g. the ◊ *hydrocarbons*, carbon disulphide CS_2, carbon tetrachloride CCl_4, and the ◊ *abrasives* carborundum SiC (◊ *Silicon*), and ◊ *boron* carbide B_4C.

Carbohydrates. An important group of organic compounds; during the process of ◊ *photosynthesis* plants can build them from carbon and water, but it is not so far possible to do this in the laboratory. The group includes sugars (saccharoses), soluble in water and sweet to the taste, and more complex polysaccharoses e.g. starch, glycogen, inulin, cellulose, whose formulae have not been established, insoluble in water and tasteless. An important group of isomeric sugars, the hexoses, include ◊ *glucose* (dextrose) and fructose (fruit sugar). Another group includes sucrose (cane or beet sugar), lactose (milk sugar), and maltose (malt sugar). Of the polysaccharoses, starch is stored as a reserve-food carbohydrate in the fruits, seeds, and tubers of many plants e.g. cereals, potatoes. Similarly glycogen is a reserve carbohydrate of the animal organism found in muscle and the liver (◊ *Digestion*). Inulin (rather similar to starch) is stored in dahlia tubers. Cellulose is the main constituent of the cell walls and skeletal tissues of plants. Cotton contains about 90 per cent cellulose; flax, hemp, and jute also contain a high proportion. By a process of fermentation, starch or sucrose can be broken down into final products of alcohol and carbon dioxide, though large quantities of alcohol are now made from ethylene in the petrochemical industry.

Carbolic Acid ◊ *Phenol.*

Carbon. A non-metallic element occurring almost pure in diamond and fairly pure in graphite, both of which are crystalline allotropes of it, and also in ◊ *peat*, ◊ *lignite*, ◊ *coal*, and ◊ *anthracite*, products of vegetable matter which has lost successively increasing amounts of methane, carbon dioxide, and water under a variety of geological conditions. Large amounts occur chemically combined in natural oil (consisting of a great variety of ◊ *hydrocarbons*), in carbonate rocks e.g. limestone and chalk (◊ *Calcite*), and as atmospheric carbon dioxide. The ability of carbon atoms to form stable chains and rings results in an exceedingly large number of organic compounds, many of which are essential constituents of vegetable and animal tissues and fluids; the study of these constitutes organic chemistry. The normal valency of carbon is 4.

A single arrow before a word or phrase indicates a cross-reference to another main entry. A double arrow means *See also*.

Although known from antiquity, the various forms were recognized as modifications of the same element only when in 1797 Tennant proved that they all burned in oxygen to give carbon dioxide and nothing else.

Diamond, used as an ◊ *abrasive*, is very hard because the carbon atoms are held by covalent bonds in a uniform 3-dimensional framework. Graphite, by contrast, has a greasy feel and is a lubricant, the atoms being bonded into sheets which are held together by weak forces allowing them to slide on one another. When the volatile part of wood or coal is expelled, in the absence of air, ◊ *charcoal* or ◊ *coke* result. According to the original material and temperature employed, the products vary from bulky porous charcoals, used for absorbing gases or for purifying liquids, to hard metallurgical cokes, used to produce iron in blast furnaces, or ◊ *petroleum* cokes, which give the dense carbons used to fabricate chemical plant, for electrodes, and in nuclear reactors.

Carbon usually forms four strong covalent bonds, and its simpler compounds are either gases or volatile liquids, e.g. the oxides carbon monoxide and carbon dioxide, the hydrides methane and ethane, the chloride carbon tetrachloride. Combustion of carbon at high temperatures gives mainly carbon monoxide, an odourless lethal gas which burns with a blue flame to carbon dioxide and is used for removing oxygen from many metallic oxides, reducing them to the free metal. At lower temperatures, carbon combines with oxygen in ample supply to give non-poisonous carbon dioxide, which dissolves in water to produce carbonic acid, which forms two series of salts, the hydrogen carbonates (sodium bicarbonate, used in baking powder, and calcium bicarbonate) and the normal carbonates (soda ash, washing soda, and calcium carbonate). Iron carbide is soluble in molten iron, and its presence allows the properties of steel to be modified by heat treatment. Calcium carbide gives acetylene on treatment with water.

Carbonate ◊ *Calcium*.

Carbon Dioxide. Carbonic acid gas. Colourless, heavier than air of which it constitutes 0.03 per cent by volume. Fairly soluble in water giving a weak acid (◊ *Carbon*). Dissolved under pressure

gives 'soda-water' and other aerated waters. Easily solidified, and the resultant 'snow' is used in small-scale refrigeration. Produced when carbonaceous material burns or decays and by animal respiration, it is utilized by plants through ◊ *photosynthesis*. The gas is used for fruit storage and in one type of fire-extinguisher.

Carbon-14 Dating ◊ *Radiocarbon Dating*.
Carboniferous System. Rocks laid down in the last of the Primary Periods (◊ *Geological Time Scale*), the concluding 75 m. years of the Palaeozoic Era; of outstanding importance because of their valuable mineral content, esp. coal.

CARBONIFEROUS LIMESTONE: Mountain limestone; calcareous deposits in seas. ◊ *Calcite, Coal Measures, Millstone Grit*.
Carbon Monoxide. A colourless, odourless gas, occurring in coal gas and in motor-vehicle exhaust fumes. It is highly poisonous, as it combines with the haemoglobin of the blood and prevents it from carrying oxygen. ◊◊ *Carbon, Haemoglobin*.
Carbon Tetrachloride. A dense non-inflammable liquid, used in fire extinguishers since its vapour is heavy and smothers flames. Being also a good grease solvent, it is used as a dry-cleaning agent.
Carbonyls. Compounds of ◊ *elements* with carbon monoxide. Typical of the non-metals are carbonyl chloride (phosgene) $COCl_2$ and carbonyl sulphide COS, and of the metals, nickel tetracarbonyl $Ni(CO)_4$ and iron pentacarbonyl $Fe(CO)_5$. The nickel compound is used in the industrial purification of nickel. Iron combines with carbon monoxide at 200°C and 100 atmospheres pressure; by heating the compound at ordinary pressures, iron of high purity required for special purposes is produced (◊ *Iron and Steel Industry*).
Carborundum ◊ *Carbides, Silicon*.
Carburettor. Ancillary device used primarily on a petrol engine to ensure that the combustible drawn into the combustion chamber is correctly mixed. The fuel, fed from a container, is vaporized in the carburettor by mixing with air. The needle valves, of various sizes, ensure that the correct quantity of fuel can be fed into the combustion chamber, by coming into operation automatically to meet the different driving conditions.
Carcinogens. Chemical substances prolonged or repeated exposure to which pro-

vokes malignant tumours (◊ *Cancer*) in animal tissue.

Cardboard ◊ *Paper*.

Cardinal. Member of the College of Cardinals, which elects the ◊ *Pope* and under him is responsible for the government of the ◊ *Roman Catholic Church*; in theory the College numbers 70, but Pope John XXIII raised the figure to 82. Cardinals are appointed by the reigning Pope at Conclaves; some remain permanently *in Curia* at Rome, as the Pope's privy council; others are archbishops or bishops of important provinces and sees throughout the world. The principal insignia are the red hat, conferred by the Pope but not subsequently worn, and the red biretta; a cardinal is addressed as 'Eminence'. The Congregations of Rites, of Propaganda (i.e. foreign ◊ *missions*), of Ceremonies, of the Holy Office (◊ *Inquisition*), of the ◊ *Index Librorum Prohibitorum*, of ◊ *Bishops* and Regulars, etc. are committees of Cardinals acting as the supreme administrative bodies for the various departments of church work. Nominally Cardinals may be Cardinal Bishops (taking titles from the six sees bordering on Rome) or Cardinal Priests and Cardinal Deacons (taking titles from churches in the city), but Pope John XXIII ruled 1962 that all must be bishops by consecration (◊ *Holy Orders*).

Cargo Cults. Recent cults mainly among the ◊ *Melanesians* whose adherents believe that the equipment they have seen unloaded from aeroplanes and ships (esp. during the Second World War) was being sent to them by their ancestors but intercepted by the Whites; in order to regain their inheritance, they build crude simulated airstrips, radio masts, and ports, and keep watch for the ancestors, who are expected to return in aeroplanes and initiate the millennium.

Caribou ◊ *Reindeer*.

Caricature. < Ital. *caricare*, exaggerate; a portrait in which features are critically or ludicrously exaggerated, to stress character and peculiarities; grotesque designs and statuettes were popular from classical times until the ◊ *Renaissance*, as epitomized by Hellenistic terracottas, medieval gargoyles, and Leonardo da Vinci's grotesque heads, but portrait caricature as such does not appear until the late 16th cent. in Italy, Annibale Carracci 1560–1609 being credited with the foundation of

the school. By the 18th cent. it was established in England and transformed from a dilettante amusement into a vigorous political weapon; Hogarth's prints included mild caricature, but with Gillray 1757–1815 and Rowlandson 1756–1827 the art reached a peak of lusty and brilliant satire. In the 19th cent. English caricature declined into drawing-room gentility, but in France Daumier 1808–79 was influenced by the Gillray tradition, raised caricature to new heights, and was imprisoned for it. Among later English caricaturists Max Beerbohm was outstanding; more recently the work of David Low, 'Vicky', and 'Papas' in England and Sennep, Siné, and Jean Eiffel in France is notable. ◊ *Cartoon*.

Caries ◊ *Dentistry*.

Carillon ◊ *Bells*.

Carmelites. Christian ◊ *religious order* founded in the mid 12th cent. but traditionally descended from a community set up on Mt Carmel by the prophet Elijah; devoted to contemplation and foreign ◊ *missions*. A reform led by St Teresa of Avila and St John of the Cross 1562 divided the Calced (shod) Carmelites from the Discalced (barefoot). Today about 7000 friars and over 10,000 nuns, following a very strict rule. ◊ *Monasticism*.

Carnac. Village in Brittany remarkable for what is probably the richest group of ◊ *megalithic monuments* in W. Europe, esp. the long avenues of menhirs (standing stones) stretching for several miles, thought to have been associated with ritual processions to the near-by megalithic tombs. They probably date to 2000–1500 B.C.

Carnation. Plant developed from the wild single *Dianthus caryophyllus*, also the ancestor of the garden pink. Introduced into England by the Norman monks for flavouring wine, hence its old name 'sops and wine'. The clove pink is a specially fragrant form. The double carnation was evolved in the 16th cent.

Carnivorous Plants. Several genera of flowering plants with leaves modified to catch small animals e.g. insects and to absorb nutrients esp. nitrogenous substances from them. All these plants photosynthesize, and with good soil they can live without insects. Various forms of trap include pitchers (sarracenia), leaf traps (Venus fly-trap, sundew, butterwort), submerged bladders (bladderwort). Some aquatic ◊ *fungi* are carnivorous.

Carol. In the original medieval sense, any song with a regular burden or refrain; in the modern sense, a song for Christmas (or very occasionally for other religious seasons). A number of English Christmas carols survive from the 15th cent. but many of the most popular today are 19th-cent. e.g. *Hark the Herald Angels Sing*, with music by Mendelssohn adapted to words by Charles Wesley.

Carolingians. Descended from Pepin II, who supplanted the ◊ *Merovingians* as ruler of France. His illegitimate son Charles Martel continued the line, which took its name from its most famous member, Charlemagne (ruled A.D. 768–814). The Carolingians ruled until 987, when they were ousted by the Capetians, and disappeared from history about 1000.

Carotenes. A group of three red-coloured pigments originally obtained from the carrot but now recognized to be present in a wide range of plant materials e.g. grass, leaves. The carotenes are complex ◊ *hydrocarbons*; with the ◊ *chlorophylls*, they were the first groups to be separated by ◊ *chromatography*, in the early 20th cent.

Carp. Bony freshwater fish originating in S. Asia, probably introduced into Europe in Roman times; their great hardiness encouraged their cultivation for food purposes from the earliest times, and they are still bred in Europe on special fish farms, the water being manured to encourage a prolific growth of freshwater plants and invertebrate animals on which the carp can feed. They may grow to a length of 2 ft, live for 40 years, and are easily tamed.

Carpel. Female reproductive organ of a ◊ *flower*; a modified ◊ *leaf* (sporophyll), on which the ovules develop. At the top of the carpel is the stigma, a sticky surface which traps ◊ *pollen* at pollination. The carpel has its edges joined together, or is joined to other carpels, to form an ovary which encloses the ovules. The fertilized ovules become seeds and the ovary becomes a fruit. A pea-pod is a single carpel which opens down the joined edges and the midrib to shed the seeds. A poppy-head is formed from several joined carpels, the seeds being shed through pores in the top. A berry is a fleshy fruit formed of several carpels, with no special method for shedding the seeds.

Carpet. Hand-woven carpets date to very early times; evidence is found in carvings of 2500 B.C. The art of carpet-making reached its height in the uplands of Turkey, Persia, and China, where fine wool from sheep, goats, and camels was plentiful, the Persian carpets of the 15th and 16th centuries A.D. being the most famous. Hand-weaving involves the enormous labour of tying thousands of knots about the warp threads, quality depending on the number of knots to the square inch (40 to 1000) and on the materials and dyes used. Machine-made carpets were first produced in Flanders, on looms, and shortly afterwards in 1735 at Kidderminster in England; the 1850 introduction of Bigelow's power loom for manufacturing Brussels and Wilton carpets made mass production possible. Modern carpets are woven by highly complex specialized machines: Brussels carpet has a linen warp and weft with a worsted-yarn pile; Chenille (Chenille Axminster) is made on a different principle producing a very thick pile. Oriental hand-woven carpets have been debased by the influence of machine methods and the replacement of vegetable dyes by aniline.
RUGS: Woven more like ◊ *tapestry*, with no pile, e.g. those of the American Indians (◊ *Navaho*) and the kilims of Persia.

Carpetbagger. 1. In the southern states of U.S.A. after the ◊ *American Civil War*, northern financial and land speculators, most of them unscrupulous adventurers, carrying only carpet-bags as luggage. **2.** Later and pejoratively, northern politicians who gained power by canvassing the Negro vote.

Carrot. A hardy biennial developed from the wild *Daucus carota*, a native of Europe; it appears to have been grown in Elizabethan gardens. It is valued for its ◊ *vitamin* content as well as its flavour.

Cartel. Agreement between independent producers to fix prices, share markets, and limit production or further investment in a given industry, for the protection of their interests; particularly common in Germany before 1939, it differs from a ◊ *monopoly* in being an arrangement between separate firms, but the aim and results are similar. Cartels are illegal in U.S.A. and subject to scrutiny of the Monopolies Commission in the U.K. The Common Market countries purpose to control cartels to protect consumers' interests.

Cartesianism. The philosophy of Descartes and those influenced by him. Descartes shaped modern philosophy by beginning with a sceptical examination of our ordinary claims to knowledge. The foundation of his system of ◊ *rationalism*, intended to accommodate both religion and science, was that although he could doubt many of his beliefs, he could not doubt that he was thinking in so doing. If so, then he existed as a thinking substance. He went on to establish the existence of God by traditional arguments which, it was said, he ought in consistency to have subjected to doubt. Since God exists, he continued, the world must exist – we believe it does and God would not deceive us. Descartes' world-view, that there exist minds or thinking substances, and bodies or extended substances, is the most familiar of dualisms. The relation between the two, in men, is finally a mystery.

Carthage. According to tradition, founded 814 B.C. by ◊ *Phoenician* settlers from Tyre. After Nebuchadnezzar's destruction of Tyre, Carthage became the foremost city of the Mediterranean. In the 3rd cent. B.C. her power and wealth alarmed Rome, and the long series of ◊ *Punic Wars* ensued. Despite the conquest of Spain and the brilliant victories of Hannibal in Italy itself (◊ *Cannae*), Carthage was totally defeated, and the city was destroyed in 146 B.C. An attempt by the Romans to revive it in 122 B.C. failed, but Julius Caesar rebuilt it and it quickly rose to be a provincial capital and an important Christian centre. In A.D. 439 it was taken by the Vandals, who made it their capital. In 533 it was won for the Eastern Empire by Belisarius, but it finally fell into ruin after its capture by the Arabs in 698. Its site is close to modern Tunis.

Carthusians. Christian religious order, strictly enclosed, founded in the 11th cent. by St Bruno of Cologne at La Chartreuse near Grenoble; devoted to prayer and penance. The monks pray, eat, and sleep in individual cells, meeting only for certain church services and for communal meals and recreation on Sundays and ◊ *religious festivals*. England had several Carthusian priories (Charterhouses) before the ◊ *Reformation*, but has now only one, at Parkminster in Sussex. The order claims to be 'never reformed because never deformed'. ◊◊ *Monasticism*.

Cartography ◊ *Map*.

Cartoon. Originally a preparatory design for a painting or tapestry; the now more common meaning, a politico-satirical drawing founded on ◊ *caricature*, derives from the 1843 *Punch* parodies of painting-cartoons for the design of the new ◊ *Houses of Parliament*. Today the word covers several forms of graphic satire: the political cartoon, at which e.g. David Low excelled and which is a regular feature of most newspapers; the social-satirical or purely humorous drawing in periodicals and books; and the films composed of animated drawings e.g. those of Disney.

Carvel-construction ◊ *Boat*.

Caryatid. A sculptured female figure used in place of a column (as in the Erechtheum at Athens), traditionally representing one of the women of Caria, who sided with the Persians against the Greeks and were made slaves.

Casablanca Conference. 1943. Meeting between President F. D. Roosevelt (U.S.A.) and Prime Minister Winston Churchill (U.K.); a declaration was issued that the ◊ *Second World War* would end only with the unconditional surrender of Germany, Japan, and Italy. The rivalry of de Gaulle and Giraud for leadership of the Free French forces remained unresolved.

Cascara. *Rhamnus purshiana*; a tree native to N. America, from the ◊ *bark* of which a laxative is prepared.

Casein. The chief ◊ *protein* of cows' milk, a valuable food and the basis of a number of invalid-food preparations. When blended with a plasticizer and dye, it can be moulded and hardened to make plastic objects esp. buttons.

Cashmere ◊ *Wool*.

Casket Letters. Eight letters (no longer in existence) supposedly from Mary Queen of Scots to James Hepburn, Earl of Bothwell, the alleged murderer of her husband Lord Darnley in 1567. If genuine, they prove Mary's complicity in the murder, but until recently they were thought to have been forged, as Mary herself said. The balance of the evidence is now slightly in favour of their genuineness, however. ◊ *Scotland, Stewarts*.

Cassandra. In Greek legend, daughter of ◊ *Priam* and ◊ *Hecuba*; she offered her favours to ◊ *Apollo* in return for the gift of prophecy, but when he conferred it on her she refused to keep her bargain, whereupon he ordained that though her prophecies would be true no one would believe them. The Trojans thought her mad, and disregarded her predictions; after the Trojan war, ◊ *Agamemnon* took her to Greece, also disbelieved her, and in consequence was murdered with her by his wife Clytaemnestra, as she had predicted.

Cassava ◊ *Manihot.*

Cassowary. Flightless bird 5 ft high, found only in the forests of New Guinea and the neighbouring islands, covered in thick loose black feathers, but with brightly-coloured neck and the head crowned by a horny 'helmet'; the powerful legs are armed with a clawed inner toe. The adult bird is shy but pugnacious.

Caste. < Portuguese *casta*, breed, race, kind; one of a series of hierarchically arranged ranks in a socially stratified system, typical of endogamy, caste membership being by birth and not alterable during an individual's lifetime. The classic caste system is that of Hindu India, developed by the Aryans, derived from four classes, the first three (the 'Twice Born') practising ◊ *initiation rites* at which they are ritually reborn (◊ *Transmigration*) and which are forbidden to the castes below them. Each caste contains many sub-castes, also usually endogamous; each is associated with a given occupation, and members of one caste may not eat food prepared by those of lower caste, eat with members of any other caste, or have sexual relations outside their own caste. The five castes are as follows: BRAHMIN: The highest caste; priests and ritual celebrants. ◊> *Brahma.* KSHATRIYA: Rulers, nobles, warriors. VAISYA: Farmers, merchants. SUDRA: Servants and menials. 'UNTOUCHABLES': The lowest class, social outcasts, condemned to the most despised occupations, any physical contact with whom was considered a pollution by the other castes. Gandhi renamed them Harijan (children of God). Neither Gandhi's efforts nor the regulations of 1947 aimed at ending the caste system have been very effective, although caste is becoming obscured amongst urban populations.

Castile. Originally Old Castile, a small territory in N. Spain strongly fortified with *castillos*, forts, against the Moors at whose expense it gradually expanded southwards till it occupied the whole of central Spain. Key points in this process

were the union with León under Ferdinand I 1035–65, and the capture of Toledo in 1085, marking the foundation of New Castile. In 1072 Alfonso VI had assumed the title Emperor of Spain; in 1469 the heiress of Castile, Isabella, married Ferdinand, king of ◊ *Aragon*, and thus created a unified country of ◊ *Spain.*

Casting Metal. Casting was probably the earliest method used to work metals into the required shape; iron, steel, brass, copper, aluminium, etc. and magnesium ◊ *alloys* are poured in the molten state into moulds, usually of sand, made from wooden patterns to the same form as the finished product. Fine limits on dimensions cannot be obtained by this process, so that where these are required additional machining is necessary. Another method, die casting, can be employed to give greater accuracy in dimensions.

Castle. A construction designed for defence; at its simplest, a series of earthworks as at the prehistoric Maiden Castle in Dorset, but more generally it is the medieval fortress found throughout Europe and the Levant. The castle of western Europe was developed by the Normans, first as an artificial mound surmounted by a blockhouse and palisade, succeeded by the massive keep surrounded by walls as in the Tower of London. From experience of Muslim ◊ *fortifications*, and the need to counter improved siege techniques, the castle developed in the 12th and 13th centuries into an elaborate complex of concentric walls, bastions, and flanking towers. Outstanding examples are the castles built by Edward I e.g. Harlech and by the Crusaders in Syria e.g. Crac des Chevaliers. With the advent of gunpowder the castle rapidly lost its importance. Its place was taken by a different type of fortification designed to resist artillery bombardment, which changed with advances in the range and destructiveness of heavy artillery. In the ◊ *First World War* the French fortifications around Verdun stood against massive attack; in the ◊ *Second World War* the vast and elaborate Maginot Line proved of little value.

Castor and Pollux or Polydeuces. In Greek mythology, the Dioscuri, twin sons of ◊ *Zeus*, brothers of ◊ *Helen*, born with her from the eggs of ◊ *Leda*; Castor (a horseman) was mortal, Pollux (a boxer) immortal. When Castor was killed, Pollux asked to die with him; Zeus agreed that both should spend alternate days in ◊ *Hades* and in heaven. Special protectors of sailors, they appeared over ships as 'St Elmo's fire'; esp. popular in Rome, they were said to have headed the Roman army in the battle against Rome's Latin neighbours at Lake Regillus.

Castor Oil. An oil from the endosperm of the seeds of *Ricinus communis* of the ◊ *Euphorbiaceae*, probably native to Africa, which grows to the size of a small tree in hot climates. In the past it was the primary illuminant throughout the East, where it was also used as a purgative and for anointing. Its chief uses are for paint, varnish, in dyeing, leather dressing, and as a purgative. The seeds themselves are highly poisonous, containing ricin, which coagulates the blood: one seed may cause serious illness and four can be fatal. Ricin is destroyed by boiling or roasting the seeds.

Cat. Large family (*felidae*) of predators including lion, tiger, panther, leopard. The European domestic cat, of the same family, is probably of Egyptian origin but crossed with Asiatic and wild European cats. There are several breeds, with considerable differences in colour and markings, but far less differentiated than the breeds of dogs in size and appearance. They are broadly divided into short-haired and long-haired: the former include the Siamese, the tailless Manx, and several British varieties; the latter the Tabby, the Persian, and the Angora.

Catabolism ◊ *Metabolism.*

Catacombs. Subterranean vaults and passages dating to the 2nd–5th centuries A.D. constructed by the early Christians for burial purposes, under cities in Italy, Asia Minor, and elsewhere, those at Rome being the most extensive and best-known; also used as places of refuge in time of persecution, and for religious services. Some of the larger chambers, often decorated with ◊ *fresco* paintings, became miniature underground churches and are of great importance for the study of the earliest Christian art.

Catalan. One of the ◊ *Romance languages*, almost identical with that of ◊ *Provence*: the official language of ◊ *Andorra* and spoken by about 6 m. in Catalonia (NW Spain) and near-by regions in France. The literature dates to the 12th cent. and is both vigorous and original. Before the ◊ *Spanish Civil War* over 1000 newspapers were published in Catalan, but under Franco the Catalan language has been banned in all publications and for official and educational use. There has been some relaxation for plays and poetry, but recently the Catalan Omnium Cultural has been closed down.

Catalyst. A substance the presence of which affects the speed of a chemical action but is itself chemically unchanged. Most catalysts are positive and are used to start a reaction which otherwise would not take place or would proceed very slowly; others (negative catalysts) retard the speed of the action. Catalysts are of major importance in many industrial processes e.g. in ◊ *hydrogenation* or in the catalytic cracking of ◊ *petroleum.* Knowledge of catalysis is almost entirely empirical, the way catalysts act being little understood. ◊◊ *Enzyme.*

Catamaran. Originally a ◊ *canoe* with one or sometimes two outriggers to provide stability, commonly employed by native sailors in the E. Indies and the Pacific Islands; also a yacht with two slender parallel hulls connected by a rigid bridge. Some racing yachts of this design are capable of speeds of over 20 knots.

Catapult. Ancient form of ◊ *artillery,* used in Roman and medieval times; a common type used in siege operations resembled a giant crossbow. In aviation, a device, usually powered by compressed steam, to accelerate an aircraft during the take-off run, esp. valuable on ◊ *aircraft carriers.*

Cataract. Degenerative change, occurring mainly in old age, which makes the crystalline lens of the eye opaque. When the condition reaches an advanced stage it is often relieved by operation.

Catchment Area. Drainage area, basin: region in which water drains towards a given river or stream, which carries it to a lake or the sea, the boundary being the ◊ *watershed* (beyond which the water flows in a different direction, to another stream).

Categorical Imperative ◊ *Kantianism.*

Caterpillar. Larva of ◊ *butterfly* or ◊ *moth,* representing an intermediate stage between egg and pupa. Caterpillars feed on leaves or timber. They moult about 10 times, increasing in size at each moult.

Catfish. Large group of freshwater bony fish, common throughout the world except in the coldest regions and most abundant in S. America and Africa; so named because of the feelers round the mouth. Bottom-living, and carnivorous or omnivorous in their habits, they range in length from 2 in. to 6 ft.

Cathari ◊ *Albigenses*.

Catharsis. Tragedy, according to Aristotle, arouses pity and fear, and thus purges the spectator of an excess of these emotions; he called this discharge of emotion 'catharsis'. In Freudian theory, excess of ◊ *emotion* e.g. anxiety follows repression of its cause, and under psycho-analysis the patient relives in imagination events of his life which he has repressed; the accompanying discharge of emotion, called 'abreaction', can be regarded as a special case of catharsis. Perhaps all or most expressions of emotion are 'cathartic'.

Cathedral. Principal church of a diocese, the seat (cathedra) of the ◊ *bishop*. The urge to build churches of excep-

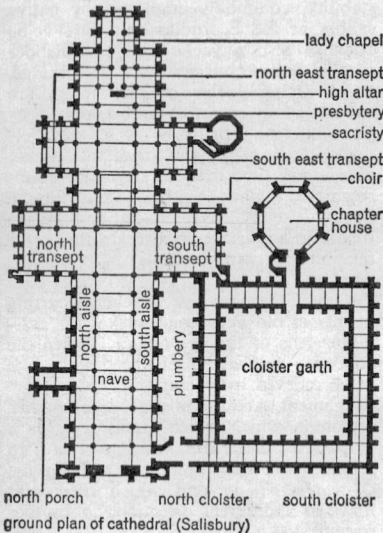

ground plan of cathedral (Salisbury)

tional size and magnificence began in the ◊ *Romanesque* period of the early Middle Ages and culminated in the 13th and 14th centuries in ◊ *Gothic architecture* with e.g. Chartres, Rheims, Notre-Dame (Paris) in France; Canterbury, Salisbury, Lincoln in England; Cologne and Strassburg in Germany (the latter is

now in France). The builders, few of whom are known by name, strove to build ever higher on more and more slender structures, in an effort to symbolize the spiritual aspirations of the age; the exteriors, aesthetically satisfying though they are, are essentially the structural necessities making possible the exalting effect of the interiors. The decoration, in ◊ *stained glass* and carvings, provided for the worshippers not simply a Bible but a medieval encyclopedia in stone, representing not only their religious beliefs but their assumptions about the nature of the world and every aspect of their daily lives. Most cathedrals took many decades to build, and scarcely any were completed in the form in which they were originally planned. Despite the ◊ *Renaissance* cathedral of Florence, St Peter's in Rome, and Wren's St Paul's, 19th-cent. architects regarded the Gothic as the proper style for cathedrals, as indeed for all churches; New York and Liverpool are examples of ◊ *Gothic Revival* cathedrals. In the rebuilding of Coventry Cathedral, completed 1962, Sir Basil Spence departed from traditional models to create a new style responsive to 20th-cent. trends.

Cathode ◊ *Electrode, Electrolysis*.

Cathode-ray Tube ◊ *Radar, Thermionic Valve*.

Catholic Emancipation. 1829. In the 1790s the titular hierarchy of the ◊ *Roman Catholic Church* in ◊ *Ireland* were promised the repeal of the ◊ *penal laws* in return for their denunciation of the ◊ *United Irishmen* and their support of the project for legislative union; after the 1800 ◊ *Act of Union* the promise was not implemented, however. A movement for the repeal of the Union began, but in 1808 Daniel O'Connell began to canalize it into that for Catholic emancipation only; he formed the huge Catholic Association in 1823 and became M.P. for Clare 1828. A great constitutional struggle over his admission to the House of Commons followed, and the Catholic Emancipation Act was passed in 1829. It was of direct benefit only to wealthier Catholics and to the priesthood, and the movement for Union repeal (closely associated with ◊ *Chartism*) was revived.

Catkin. Usually a unisexual spike of densely-packed small flowers separated by scaly ◊ *bracts*, cylindrical, and dropping off as a single unit. Most are pendulous, inconspicuous, and wind-pollinated but a few e.g. willows are erect and insect-pollinated, usually on shrubs or trees e.g. willow, poplar, walnut, beech, sweet chestnut.

Cattle. Domesticated animals of the bovine race, probably descended from the original Aurochs, now extinct. Selection and ◊ *breeding* throughout the world has produced many breeds; it was not till about 1700 in England that intensive experiments with cross-breeding led to much larger breeds, which fall into two main categories, for milk and for beef. Widely-spread breeds include the Ayrshire, Jersey, and Frisian. For hot and tick-infested countries, breeds of the humped zebu (*Bos indicus*) have proved useful, as in the Santa Gertrudis of U.S.A. Cattle-breeding remains an important industry in England and Scotland.

Caucasian Languages. Avar, Circassian, Georgian (official language of the Georgian S.S.R.), and others; they have no known affinities with other language groups, and may represent a substratum older than the ◊ *Indo-European languages* and akin to ◊ *Basque* and the language of the ◊ *Etruscans*.

Causation. There are two traditional views of the relationship between a cause and its effect. (1) There is some 'necessary connexion' or bond between them, somewhat like that between premiss and conclusion of an argument of ◊ *logic*; Hume argued that we can observe or discover no such thing as a necessary connexion, and claimed (2) that we regard two events as cause and effect simply because they always go together – one regularly follows the other. But many such sequences are not causally related. Neither theory, however elaborated, is generally accepted.

Caustic Potash ◊ *Potassium.*

Caustic Soda ◊ *Sodium.*

Cavalry. Soldiers who fought on horseback were first recorded in Egypt, and the Assyrians and Persians used light cavalry extensively. The Greeks made little use of cavalry, and whilst the Romans employed it to a greater extent, the foot soldier remained the dominant factor in most battles. The effectiveness of the mounted soldier was limited until the introduction of the stirrup, which came late to Europe, where the first expert and demoralizing use of cavalry in mass occurred in the invasions of the ◊ *Huns* and Magyars.

From them the Goths adopted the stirrup and developed the heavy mail-clad cavalry which was instrumental in the crushing defeat of the Romans in the battle of ◊ *Adrianople* in A.D. 378. In medieval warfare the heavily armoured knight remained the dominant figure until the English bowman, the Swiss halberdier, and the introduction of ◊ *fire-arms* put an end to his predominance. The role of cavalry came to be for the exploitation of tactical situations where rapid striking power was essential; they tended to remain a military élite even after ceasing to be the most important arm. The role of cavalry in the American Civil War and in the Franco-Prussian War of 1870 was limited, though in the form of mounted infantry it still played an important part in the Boer War. With the greater fire power of modern weapons, it was virtually useless in the First World War except in the Middle East. On the Western front it was held in reserve for a breakthrough which never came, and except for ceremonial purposes it is now obsolete.

Cave Art. The authenticity of paintings on the walls of Stone Age caves was proved by the 1879 discoveries at ◊ *Altamira*. Further discoveries made at ◊ *Lascaux* in the Dordogne, France, in the Pyrenees, and in S. Italy, and the artifacts and decorated bone objects associated with these paintings, indicate that they were made in the Upper ◊ *Palaeolithic* Era, and esp. during the Aurignacian and Magdalenian phases. The artists were almost certainly of the Cro-Magnon type; they had a fine sense of colour and were skilled, vigorous draughtsmen with a keen observation of animals in movement, using pigments of red, yellow, brown, and black earths, mixed with fat. For reasons that can only be guessed at, the human form is rarely represented, and then carelessly, with little attempt at realism. The motives behind the paintings are thought to have been at least partly magical or religious, possibly a form of sympathetic magic to induce increase of game and successful hunting. The artists often worked in the least accessible parts of the caves, necessitating the use of lamps. ◊ *Primitive Art.*

Caveat Emptor ◊ *Consumer Law.*

Caviar ◊ *Sturgeon.*

Cedar. Large ◊ *conifers* with spreading branches, not usually producing cones until they are 40 years old. The best known are the Atlantic Cedar *Cedrus atlantica*, an ornamental tree, the Deodar or Indian Cedar *C. deodara*, of value for timber, and the Cedar of Lebanon *C. libani*. The forests in ◊ *Lebanon* which once provided timber for ships have virtually disappeared. Magnificent cedars of great size and age are frequently found in English gardens.

PENCIL CEDAR ◊ *Juniper.*

Celery. The progenitor of the modern varieties is *Apium graveolens*, a biennial growing in Europe in marshland; in the Middle Ages it was called smallage and used in medicine, only the foliage being used as flavouring. Celery with blanched leaf-stalks was introduced in the 17th cent. as a salad herb called sallary.

Celestial Equator ◊ *Celestial Sphere, Equator.*

Celestial Sphere. Imaginary sphere, centred on the observer, on which the celestial bodies appear to lie. It is of infinite radius, and takes no account of distance but only of the angular position of the bodies. The pattern formed on it by the 'fixed' stars does not appear to change, but the nearer stars show slight move-

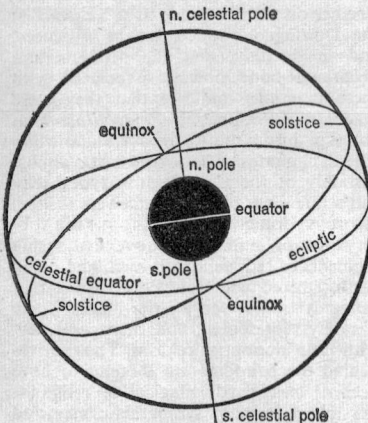

ments, owing to (a) their actual movements at right angles to the line of sight (proper motions), and (b) the earth's movement around the sun (◊ *Parallax*). The daily motion of the earth makes the celestial sphere appear to rotate once each sidereal day of 23 hours 56 min.

The celestial equator (equinoctial) is the

◊ *great circle* in which the plane of the earth's equator cuts the celestial sphere. The ecliptic, another great circle inclined at about $23\frac{1}{2}°$ to the celestial equator, is the apparent path of the sun among the stars as seen against the celestial sphere. The two points at which the ecliptic cuts the celestial equator represent the ◊ *equinoxes*, and the two points of the ecliptic farthest from the equator represent the ◊ *solstices*. The celestial poles are the points at which a line through the earth's poles would meet the celestial sphere. ◊ *Zenith.*

Cell. 1. In biology, the fundamental unit from which tissues and organs are built; even those parts of an organism which do not consist of cells, e.g. ◊ *hair* and ◊ *blood* plasma, are made by cells. Although cells vary greatly in size, shape, and function they are mostly very small; e.g. human liver cells are about a thousandth of an inch in diameter and there are millions of them in a piece of liver as big as a match-head. Each cell is enclosed by a thin membrane and has two parts, cytoplasm and nucleus; the cytoplasm is a fluid mass in which energy-storing particles of various sizes (mitochondria) can be microscopically detected, and the relatively large nucleus contains the ◊ *chromosomes* and within them the genetically-active deoxyribonucleic acid (DNA) from which the units of inheritance (genes) are formed. Cells reproduce by division, the process of mitosis producing a very exact division of the nucleus into two daughter nuclei each with the same number of chromosomes, which have doubled, so that each of the new cells has the same number as the original cell. The cytoplasm, however, does not appear to divide with the same precision, and the two daughter cells may thus vary in size and in some other respects. Tissue is a collection of similar cells, and can now be grown in culture tubes containing the nutrient necessary for cell development. ◊ *Cancer.*

In sexual reproduction, a cell from one parent fuses with one from the other parent to form a single cell, which becomes the founder-member of the cell population constituting the new individual (◊ *Meiosis*).

2. In electricity, a device in which energy is produced (primary cell) or stored (secondary cell) by chemical action (◊

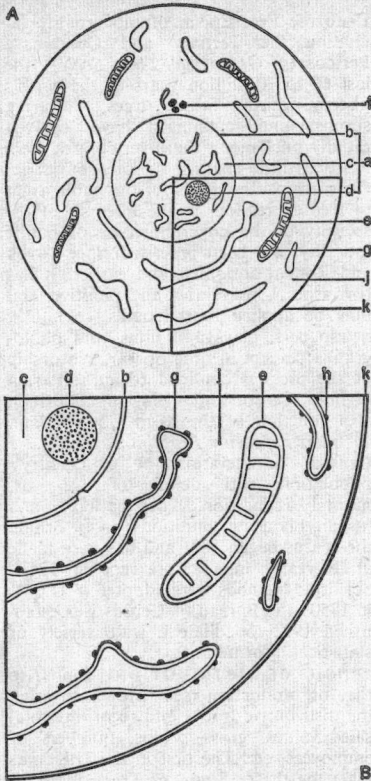

A shows a cell seen under an optical microscope. B represents part of the same cell photograped under an electron microscope.

a. the nucleus containing chromosomes and DNA, which codes instructions for cell type b. the porous, double nuclear membrane c. the nuclear sap d. the nucleolus e. the partitioned, double-membraned mitochondria in which cell respiration occurs f. golgi apparatus g. 'cytoplasm' containing a double-membraned endoplasmic reticulum with h. ribosomes, RNA-containing bodies which synthesize protein j. soluble RNA etc. in the cell sap k. the cell membrane.

material, discovered by Alexander Parkes in 1865; used as a substitute for tortoiseshell, ivory, etc. Now largely superseded by less inflammable synthetics.

Cellulose. A chain ◊ *polymer* of ◊ *glucose*, of high molecular weight, the common sources being cotton (almost pure cellulose fibre) and wood (about 50 per cent cellulose, separated from the ◊ *lignin* in making paper pulp). The long polymer chain is the basis of the fibre properties of cellulose and of its role as a structural material in plants; it is insoluble in water, but solvents have been found, and it has become the basis of the 20th-cent. man-made fibres called ◊ *rayon*. ◊◊ *Carbohydrates, Paper, Plastics.*

ACETATE RAYON: Cellulose is converted to the acetate derivative, which is dissolved in acetone for making the filaments by forcing the liquid through spinnerets.

CELLULOSE ACETATE: A non-inflammable thermoplastic; also used for making non-flame photographic film.

VISCOSE RAYON: Wood pulp is converted to cellulose xanthate by treatment with caustic soda and carbon disulphide; dissolved in dilute caustic-soda solution, this gives the 'viscose' from which the threads are made (see Acetate Rayon above). ◊ *Carbohydrates.*

Celts. Group of peoples probably from E. France and SW Germany who began to grow powerful and to spread across Europe from about 1200 B.C. Already skilled bronze-workers, they assimilated the developing craft of iron-working, and came to dominate central Europe during the Iron Age. Celtic tribes arriving in Britain in the 8th cent. B.C. and again about 250 B.C. had been in contact with the highly civilized peoples of the Mediterranean and learned the use of the chariot; their chieftains seem to have been fond of display and of superb workmanship in drinking-vessels, weapons, and personal jewellery. Celtic religion appears to have involved a belief in spirits and possibly the soul's immortality; its priests included the powerful ◊ *Druids.* Naming the small black-haired strain in the British population 'Celtic' is probably erroneous, this type being probably descended from the ◊ *Neolithic* Windmill Hill people; the influence of the Celts was cultural rather than ethnic. Their art, modified by contact with Mediterranean cultures and the

Electrolysis). Examples of a primary cell are the Leclanche cell, from which the dry battery used in radios and torches has been developed, and the Weston ◊ *cadmium* cell, used as a standard of voltage. Secondary cells, e.g. the lead-acid cells of accumulators and batteries, are used when high currents are required.

Celluloid. Colourless highly inflammable ◊ *plastic*, the first commercial synthetic

Orient and already highly developed before the Roman invasions of N. Europe, included stone carvings, bronze and silver objects, gold jewellery and coins, and shows a fondness for flat curvilinear ornament and a tendency to stylize or make symbols from representations of men and beasts, characteristics forming the basic elements in Anglo-Saxon and Irish art from the 7th to the 10th centuries, notably in the illuminated MSS produced in Ireland and Northumbria (e.g. the Book of Kells, the Lindisfarne Gospels, the Echternach Gospels) with their intricate many-coloured interlacing scroll decorations and stylized figures.

LANGUAGE. The Celtic languages form one of the eight living branches of the ◊ *Indo-European languages*; during the period of close association with Italic tribes a common Italo-Celtic language may have arisen about 1000 B.C. but remnants of the original purely Celtic tongue (Common Celt, Gaulish) are now recorded only in place-names, glosses, some brief inscriptions, graffiti found in Aveyron, and a fragmentary obscure calendar preserved at Coligny. Four forms of Celtic remain in daily use: Breton and Welsh (Brythonic, P-Celtic); Scottish Gaelic and Irish (Goidelic, Q-Celtic). ◊ *Breton, Cornish, Gaelic, Ireland, Manx, Wales*.

Cement. ◊ *Calcium* silicates with other compounds in powdered form, which when mixed with water set within half an hour or so and then harden to form a rock-like mass. Roman engineers used a cement made from *pozzulana*, a mineral of volcanic origin, both as mortar and as the binder in ◊ *concrete*. This type of cement was used in the 17th and 18th centuries for bridge construction. Smeaton experimented with artificial cement in building the Eddystone lighthouse, 1756, and 'Roman' cement was being manufactured from ◊ *London clay* late in the century. 'Portland' cement, invented by Joseph Aspdin 1824, is made by heating a mixture of chalk and clay. It is used extensively for concrete, and also, mixed with sand, as a mortar in brickwork and masonry. Cement mortar is used where high strength and resistance to water are required. High alumina cement, *ciment fondu*, made from ◊ *bauxite* clays, resists attack from sulphate-bearing waters and hardens rapidly.

Cenozoic Era. Epoch of modern life including the Tertiary and Quaternary Periods (◊ *Geological Time Scale*); the last 60 to 70 million years of the earth's history, during which trees, flowering shrubs, and mammals have evolved rapidly but among the invertebrates there has been little change. ◊ *Eocene System*.

Censorship. Restriction of the public right to free expression, in the interests of the security of the government or of public morality, has been practised since Greek and Roman antiquity, and earlier. It has two aspects, preventive and punitive, and may be applied to the mails, to books, newspapers, plays and films, and photographs; except in time of war, censorship of the press is confined to authoritarian regimes. Censorship of plays in Gt Britain is a function of the Lord Chamberlain. ◊ *Index Librorum Prohibitorum*.

Census. Enumeration of a country's population, with details of age, sex, marital condition, occupation, and (usually) housing conditions; in Gt Britain the census began 1801 and has been made at 10-yearly intervals (except in 1941). Scientific methods were adopted in U.S.A. in 1850; the Bureau of Census was established 1902 to collate a wide variety of statistical information.

CENSUS OF DISTRIBUTION: Similar to that of production (see below), covering the distributive trades and recording total sales values, gross profits, numbers of employees, etc. The first in the U.K. was taken by the ◊ *Board of Trade* in 1951; there was a sample census in 1957 and a second full census 1961.

CENSUS OF PRODUCTION: An estimate of the value of production, usually industrial only, normally compiled by the government on the basis of information supplied by all industrial establishments; in the U.K. it is conducted by the Board of Trade with an annual sample census and a full census every three years, usually including details of e.g. value of gross and net output, materials consumed, labour and power employed.

Centaurs. In Greek legend, a race of beings half horse, half man, living in Thessaly, who were defeated by a neighbouring race, the Lapithae. Chiron, the wisest of them, was a friend of ◊ *Hercules* (later killed by the centaur ◊ *Nessus*), who accidentally wounded him: in his pain, Chiron begged to lose his immortality, which ◊ *Zeus* transferred to ◊ *Prometheus*.

Centipede. Like the millipede, a member of the phylum Arthropoda, sub-phylum Myriapoda; it has a worm-like segmented body with numerous legs, set one pair to each segment. The first pair are modified to form poison claws, used to paralyse the insect prey.

Cento ◊ *Central Treaty Organization*.

Central African Federation ◊ *Malawi, Rhodesia, Zambia*.

Central African Republic. Area 234,000 sq. m. Pop. 1.2 m. Cap. Bangui. Republic (formerly Ubanghi Shari), bordered by the Congolese Republic, Congo, Cameroon, Chad, and Sudan; member of the French Community.

Central Bank ◊ *Banking*.

Central Criminal Court (Old Bailey). Built in 1834 (rebuilt 1900–7) where the old Newgate Prison once stood, in the street beside the former City wall (bailey); it now tries criminal offences committed within the City of London, and those in Middlesex and the surroundings of London which would normally be triable at Assizes.

Central Nervous System. That part of the ◊ *nervous system* which correlates the information available to the organism via the sensory nerves, and issues motor instructions to organs, limbs, and glands through the nerves of the peripheral nervous system. In all ◊ *vertebrates* the central nervous system consists of spinal cord and brain, is able to store information, and is dorsal i.e. situated along the back. In most invertebrates it consists of nerve cords containing nerve fibres and linking together ganglia (masses of nerve cell bodies) and is not dorsal, e.g. it may be along the belly and in the head, as in insects. A few invertebrates have no central nervous system, only an interlacing nerve network.

Central Treaty Organization (Bagdad Pact). Treaty signed in Bagdad by Turkey and Iraq in 1955 and joined shortly afterwards by Pakistan, Persia, and the U.K. In 1957 U.S.A. became a member of the economic and military committees although not acceding to the Bagdad Pact itself.

The parties agreed to cooperate in the interests of mutual security and defence, but there was no provision that each member should regard an attack on another as an attack on itself. Membership was open to any country concerned with promoting the peace and security of the Middle East and recognized by both the original signatories; Israel was thus excluded, not being recognized by Iraq.

After the revolution of 1958 Iraq formally withdrew in 1959, when the name was changed to Central Treaty Organization (Cento) and the headquarters transferred to Ankara. 'Cento' also has an economic programme for the development of road, rail, and air communications, medical research, and technical assistance.

Century Plant (Aloe) ◊ *Agave*.

Cephalopod. A large exclusively marine ◊ *mollusc*, with tentacles bearing suckers, and a well-developed head structure; the foot forms a funnel through which water is squirted, providing a means of rapid locomotion. The cephalopods include the ◊ *cuttlefish*, ◊ *octopuses*, and ◊ *squids*, all of which show a degree of organization in many ways (esp. in sensory and central nervous organization) comparable to that of vertebrates. In most cephalopods the shell is absent or vestigial; a well-developed shell is found only in *Nautilus*, which appears to be a living representative of the once dominant but now fossil Nautiloids. ◊ *Ammonite, Belemnite*.

Cepheid Variables ◊ *Star*.

Ceramics. Articles made from fired clay; the finest ◊ *porcelain* is made from the best ◊ *kaolin*, but poorer clays are used for cheaper articles. Most pottery is glazed by heating with a ◊ *silica* preparation, e.g. lead glaze (silica and litharge) or silica with alumina or ◊ *felspar*, but earthenware is glazed with common salt. When desired, pigments and modifiers are incorporated into the firing mixture. ◊ *Faience, Pottery*.

Cerberus. In Greek mythology, a monster of doglike form with three (or 50) heads and a body wreathed with snakes, guarding ◊ *Hades* from his kennel by the river Styx; as one of his 12 labours, ◊ *Hercules* borrowed him to show to Eurystheus.

Cereals. Grain-bearing grasses, cultivated for food since ◊ *Neolithic* times, the grain consisting largely of starch but also containing protein, minerals, and vitamins; mainly ◊ *maize*, ◊ *rice*, and ◊ *wheat*, the staple foodstuffs of the bulk of the world's population, though ◊ *barley*, buckwheat, ◊ *millet, oats, rye*, and *sorghum* are also important. In all early communities the sowing and harvesting of corn was associated with religious rites and magical practices. The word cereal derives from the Roman goddess Ceres. ◊ *Bread*.

Cerebellum, Cerebrum ◊ *Nervous System*.

Cerenkov Effect. The emission of electromagnetic radiation (light) when a charged particle passes through a medium at a greater velocity than the velocity of light in that medium. The effect, which is broadly analogous to the generation of shock waves by supersonic aircraft, has been used to determine the velocity of particles in nuclear physics research.

Ceres ◊ *Asteroids, Demeter*.

Cerium ◊ *Lanthanides*.

Certiorari. An order from the Queen's Bench Division of the High Court to a lower court for the removal of a case into the High Court so that a mistake in procedure or an excess of jurisdiction may be corrected; normally employed where there is no appeal procedure, it is (with ◊ *mandamus* and prohibition) one of the prerogative orders.

Cetacea ◊ *Dolphin, Porpoise, Whale*.

Ceylon. Area 25,332 sq. m. Pop. 10.6 m. Cap. Colombo. Rel. Mainly Buddhist. A large island off S. India, since 1948 a self-governing Dominion within the ◊ *British Commonwealth*. The only country in the world with a woman Prime Minister, Mrs Bandaranaike having been chosen after the assassination of her husband.

ECONOMY. Agricultural, with tea and rubber as the main crops, exports being of major importance. Rice is grown for local consumption.

HISTORY. The early history is mainly that of invasions from S. India and China after the Cinhalese had conquered the island about the 6th cent. B.C. The Portuguese landed in 1517, to be driven out later by the Cinhalese with the assistance of the British and Dutch, who were in turn expelled by the British in 1795, when Ceylon became a British colony.

Since independence Ceylon has been troubled with unrest amongst the Tamil minority, different in language and religion from the Cinhalese, and her policy of nationalization has brought friction with the U.K. and U.S.A.

Chad. Area 487,920 sq. m. Pop. 2.7 m. Cap. Fort Lamy. Republic in N. central Africa (between Cameroon, Central African Republic, Libya, Niger, and Sudan), formerly part of French Equatorial Africa; a member of the French Community since 1958, self-governing since 1960. In 1962 a new constitution was adopted and Mr Tombalbaye became President; five leading politicians were arrested for subversion in 1962.

ECONOMY. Similar to that of the ◊ *Central African Republic*. ◊ *Congo, Gaboon*.

Chalk. Soft white lime carbonate; one of the organically-formed ◊ *sedimentary rocks*, very thick beds of which are found in all parts of the world, consisting of the calcareous remains of foraminiferae, microscopic organisms deposited in clear salt water free from the discharge of sand and mud by rivers. Chalk is the uppermost series of the ◊ *Cretaceous* System, its deposition marking the close of the Mesozoic Era. ◊ *Calcite, Gault, Geological Time Scale*.

Châlons-sur-Marne. A.D. **451.** Roman victory over Attila the ◊ *Hun*, who had been driven from Orleans by the Visigoths and Romans and was retreating north when he was brought to battle by Aetius near Châlons. The victory was not followed up, however, and Attila escaped, to ravage Italy the following year.

Chalybeate Springs ◊ *Spring*.

Chamber Music. Literally, music suitable by its style and the small number of executants for performance in a private room. In practice, usually only instrumental music (though ◊ *madrigals* etc. are in fact vocal chamber music), and (purely for convenience) normally only that for more than one or two performers. Historically its two main forms are (a) the 17th–18th cent. suite and sonata e.g. of Purcell or Bach, in which a keyboard instrument accompanies one or more other instruments; and (b) the duet sonatas, trios, quartets, quintets, etc. of Haydn, Mozart, Beethoven, Schubert, and later composers, which formally correspond to the piano sonatas and orchestral symphonies of the same periods. Most later chamber music, e.g. Bartók's Six Quartets, needs highly skilled professional performers. 'Chamber Symphony' and 'Chamber Opera' indicate a complement of performers smaller than normal, with each performer used as a soloist rather than in massed effects.

Chameleon. A distinct family of lizards, the *Chameleontidae*, with 80 species in

Africa, Arabia, Ceylon, India, and Madagascar; the largest are six in. long, and they have prehensile (grasping) tails, split pincer-like feet, and an ability to change colour which has become proverbial.

Champagne. A sparkling ◊ *wine* made by a special and complicated process, *méthode champenoise*, which dates from the 18th cent. and produced only from the white and black grapes of the chalky region around Rheims. These produce a very distinctive dry wine. A first and crucial step in the making of champagne is to blend a mixture of these to produce the *cuvée*, which is bottled with small amounts of sugar and yeast; a secondary fermentation takes place within the bottle and makes the wine 'sparkling'. The final operation, after the wine has matured, is to open the bottles, remove any sediment, and add a 'dose' of wine appropriately sweetened to produce the various types of champagne to meet varying tastes, from *brut* (the driest) through *sec* (dry) to *doux* (sweet). Champagne, which all comes from the same region, is marketed under the names of makers (many of them world famous) and not by the name of a special locality. A still wine made in the same district is known as *champagne nature*.

Sparkling wine (red, white, or pink) is made in other districts of France by a similar method, but by French law cannot be called champagne. An inferior sparkling wine is also made, simply by charging ordinary wine with carbonic acid gas. Italy and Germany make sparkling wines called *Spumante* and *Sekt*, their champagne equivalents.

Chandragupta ◊ *Mauryas*.

Channel Tunnel. A company was formed in 1867 to build a tunnel between England and France from Dover to Calais, but it remained inactive. In 1930 the idea was revived, and recently a private enterprise has produced detailed plans for a modern channel tunnel to carry both road and rail traffic. Another company has plans for a channel bridge; neither scheme has yet been adopted

Chansons de Geste. Epic poems recited by French jongleurs (◊ *Troubadours*) from the 11th to the 14th centuries; some 70 or 80 survive, in three main groups, those on Charlemagne and Roland, those on Guillaume d'Orange and his fights against the Saracens, and those on the archetypal rebel Doön de Mayence, associated with the Charlemagne cycle on the false knights.

CHANSON DE ROLAND: Song of Roland; French *chanson de geste* of the Charlemagne cycle, about 4000 lines long, dating to the late 11th or early 12th cent. and dealing with Charlemagne's campaign against the Saracens in Spain. It centres on Roland and his death with his peers at Roncesvalles in the Pyrenees; Charlemagne later avenges his death. The poem inflates the Spanish campaign into a crusade, and may have been written to encourage pilgrimages and crusading piety.

Chapbooks. Small stitched pamphlets sold by travelling pedlars (chapmen) from the 16th cent. until newspapers and cheap magazines superseded them in the 19th cent. Printed all over Europe both in capital cities and in local centres, they were usually illustrated with woodcuts, and their contents (fairy-tales, hymns, sermons, old romances, jests, recipes, medical and astrological advice, and accounts of apparitions, disasters, travels, robberies, and executions) reflect the customs and reading-habits of successive periods. Various 20th-cent. miscellanies of prose or of verse have been called 'chapbooks'.

Charcoal. Form of ◊ *carbon* obtained by heating wood (◊ *Alder, Birch, Coconut*) with little or no air; in demand for the reduction of ores and the manufacture of gunpowder before coal was abundant, the charcoal-burner's woodpile being a feature of medieval times, and still used for ◊ *adsorption* of gases.

BONE CHARCOAL: Animal charcoal, made by destructive distillation of bones, and useful for medical purposes and for the adsorption of colouring-matter.

Charles's Law ◊ *Gas*.

Charon ◊ *Hades*.

Chart. A nautical ◊ *map*, usually constructed on the Mercator projection, showing only such details of the land as are necessary for navigation, but giving detailed information as to depth of water, nature of the sea-bed, lights, and buoys, etc. Charts are usually published by government authorities; in Britain by the Hydrographic Department of the Admiralty, which also publishes weekly *Notices to Mariners* giving the amendments necessary to keep the charts up to date.

Chartism. A political movement among the working class inspired by Owen and other reformers disappointed with the Whig reforms of the 1830s; the Chartist League demanded acceptance of the People's Charter, promulgated in 1838. The main points in the Charter were (a) universal manhood suffrage, (b) voting by ballot, (c) annual elections, (d) payment of Members of Parliament, (e) equal electoral districts, (f) abolition of the property qualification for Members of Parliament. It is indicative of the moderate nature of the Chartists' aims that all of these demands, except annual elections, were peacefully conceded in the subsequent 80 years. In its early days Chartism was handicapped by a difference between its leaders on the use of force. Lovett was for moral force, Frost for physical force, and O'Connor, the most successful demagogue, was undecided. The movement declined after the end of the 1830s, to revive in the mid 1840s in times of bad harvests. It faded away after the fiasco of the Chartist petition of 1848.

Charybdis ◊ *Scylla.*

Chattanooga. 1863. A key point in Tennessee commanding communications by rail and river between the eastern U.S. and the Mississippi in the ◊ *American Civil War*, which became the objective of a hard-fought campaign won by the Union forces after bitter engagements, known as the Battle above the Clouds and Missionary Ridge, in which two leading generals, Grant and Sherman, commanded the Union forces.

Cheese ◊ *Milk.*

Cheetah. *Acinonyx jubata*; member of cat family, found in Asia and Africa, long-legged and smaller than the leopard, which it resembles. The most rapid of all hunting animals, capable of up to 70 m.p.h., it can be domesticated and used in hunting.

Cheka ◊ *Secret Police.*

Chellean (Acheulian) ◊ *Palaeolithic.*

Chemical Bonding. Atoms can be linked to one another in at least five different ways – electrovalent, covalent, coordinate linkage (dative covalent), metallic, and hydrogen – and the bond formed between atoms usually involves a pair of electrons.

ELECTROVALENT BOND: An electron is transferred from atom to atom, as when sodium chloride is formed. Here the sodium atom loses an electron and the chlorine gains one, forming the ions Na+ and Cl-. In a crystal (giant molecule) of

common salt, the sodium and chloride ions are held together by electrostatic forces.

COVALENT BOND: Formed when each atom contributes one electron and the two are shared by the atoms concerned. In a truly covalent compound there is no unbalance of charge. The bonds are directional in character, and molecules of covalent compounds have a definite shape. Thus carbon dioxide is linear $O=C=O$, water is V-shaped, and methane is tetrahedral with the carbon atom in the middle and the hydrogens at the four corners.

COORDINATE LINKAGE: Similar to a covalent one, but in this case the electron pair comes from one atom only; the recipient atom therefore gains negative charge. The oxygen atom of the water molecule uses a pair of electrons in this way when it attaches itself to another atom in forming a hydrate.

METALLIC BOND: That which keeps the atoms in place in metallic elements, which are crystalline in nature. None of the three types so far mentioned can account for the special properties of metals e.g. high melting point, good conductivity, strength of structure, etc.

HYDROGEN BOND: Although hydrogen is nearly always univalent, it is possible for a hydrogen atom, with only one electron, to link two atoms of a very electronegative element e.g. fluorine or oxygen. The water molecules in the structure of ice are linked by hydrogen bonding between the oxygen atoms. ◊ *Valency.*

Chemical Warfare. The use of poison gases (and lethal bacteria) in war. Despite its proscription at the Hague Conference in 1899, poison gas was used by the Germans in April 1915 and later by the British and French. By the time more effective gases (e.g. the corrosive forms known as mustard gas and lewisite) and methods of delivery (e.g. the gas shell introduced by the French) had been developed, protective measures had been taken and gas had no decisive influence on the war. Gas warfare was banned at the Geneva Convention of 1925 but was used by the Italians in Abyssinia and by the Japanese against the Chinese, and the major nations continued to experiment with chemical warfare. Poison gas was not used in World War II, largely through fear of retaliation, but the Germans developed nerve gases and considerable progress was made in the development of biological methods (minute quantities of deadly germs which would kill whole populations) which however have not yet been put to use.

Chemin de Fer ◊ *Baccarat*.

Chemistry. Science dealing with the properties and changes of matter. It is divided into two sections, organic and inorganic. For organic chemistry ◊ *Aliphatic Compounds, Carbon, Hydrocarbons*. Inorganic chemistry deals with all other ◊ *elements*. ◊ *Acids and Bases, Alkaloids, Biology* (*Biochemistry*), *Chemical Bonding, Halogens, Ion Exchange, Salt* (2), etc.

Cherry. *Prunus*; a large genus common in the Old World. There are two main ◊ *fruit* types, Morello (sour) and sweet. Many cherries are cultivated for their beautiful blossom, esp. in Japan, where a national festival is held at cherry-blossom time. Cherry wood is highly esteemed for cabinet work. ◊ *Rosaceae*.

Chess. A game played by two opponents on a black and white chequered board of 64 squares. Each player has 16 pieces of contrasting colour (traditionally known as black and white), eight of which are pawns (from Sp. *peons*, peasants), which can only move one square forward at a time (except for the first move, which can be two squares). The first move is by white. A pawn which reaches the opposing black line can be transformed into any piece the player chooses, other than a king. The remaining eight pieces are two castles (or rooks), two knights, and two bishops (for their moves see diagram), a queen (which can move any distance in any direction), and a king (which can move only to an adjacent square). Apart from the knight, all pieces can move only over unoccupied squares: they can capture opposing pieces in their lines, by displacing them. When one player so moves a piece that at the next move he would be able to take his opponent's king, he must say 'check'; the king must then immediately be moved out of 'check' or else protected by the interposing of another piece: if this is impossible, the king is 'checkmated' and the game ends. Sometimes neither player can force a check-mate, and the game is drawn. If a player places his opponent in such a position that he has no other move open to him than moving his king into check, the position is 'stale-

mate' and the game is drawn. Chess is a very ancient game, which probably origin-

board and men   a. pieces b. pawns

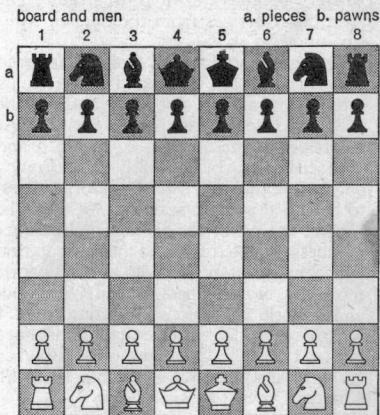

the moves

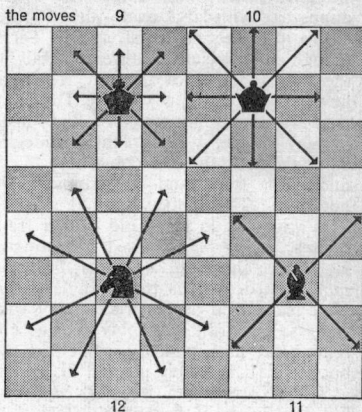

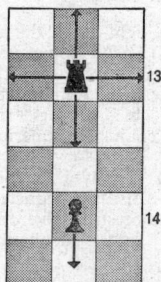

1. queen's castle or rook
2. queen's knight
3. queen's bishop
4. queen
5. king
6. king's bishop
7. king's knight
8. king's castle or rook
9. king
10. queen
11. bishop
12. knight
13. castle
14. pawn

ated in India, at an unknown date; in the 6th cent. A.D. it was introduced to Persia, where it became known as 'Shatrang'. The term chess derives from the Persian word for king.

The chequered board was introduced only in the 13th cent. and chess in its modern form did not evolve until the 16th cent. Spain and Italy were the first centres of modern chess, in the 15th and 16th centuries. In the 18th cent. French players became supreme; Philidor, the first to be called world champion, was also the earliest analyst of the game. The literature of chess is extensive and has a notation which makes it possible to record games move by move. Chess is widely played, and a world championship dating to 1851 is held annually; great champions have been Lasker (Germany), Capablanca (Cuba), Alekhine and Botvinnik (Russia).

Chester Cycle ◊ *Miracle Plays.*

Chestnut. 1. Sweet or Spanish chestnut, *Castanea sativa* of the *Fagaceae*; a deciduous tree with large oval toothed leaves, native to Greece, Albania, and N. Persia, though commercially France and Italy are the main sources of the nut. The male flowers are in long ◊ *catkins*. The edible nuts are usually in groups of three inside a spiny cupule. It was planted widely in S. England, both in parks, where it produces fine trees, and for coppicing for hop-poles. The timber is good and was used with oak in some old timber frame houses. The ◊ *bark* is used for tanning. **2.** Horse chestnut, *Aesculus hippocastanum*; a deciduous tree with large palmate leaves and upright racemes of white flowers. The fruit is a spiny capsule containing the nuts, which are not true nuts but seeds. It is widely planted in England as a large ornamental tree; *A. carnea* has red flowers and *A. octandra* yellow.

Chewing-gum ◊ *Gums.*

Chianti ◊ *Wine.*

Chiaroscuro. 1. Italian, 'light-dark'; the arrangement of light and shade in pictures, esp. the strong contrasts in works by 17th-cent. artists e.g. Caravaggio, Rembrandt. **2.** A ◊ *woodcut* print which renders various tones of a single colour by superimposed blocks.

Chickenpox. *Varicella*; highly infectious but usually mild virus disease characterized by the appearance of successive outbreaks of blister-like spots. Incubation period 14–16 days.

Chicory. *Cichorium intybus*, of the *Compositae*; a perennial herb native in Europe and the Mediterranean. It has a stout tap-root and a branching stem one to four ft tall, with many bright blue flower heads each lasting only a day. It grows wild in England and is common on chalky soils. The roots, dried, ground, and roasted, are used to mix with coffee. Its blanched leaves are used as a salad (known erroneously as ◊ *endive*: true endive, grown especially in Belgium, is *C. endiva*, sold as chicory).

Child. In law, the age at which a boy or girl ceases to be a child varies. In Britain, a child under 8 cannot be found guilty of any criminal offence; a child under 14, in the absence of strong evidence to the contrary, is presumed incapable of forming the intention to commit a crime; sentence of death may not be pronounced against anyone under 18 at the time of the offence; no one under 15 may be imprisoned; and no court may sentence anyone under 21 to imprisonment unless of opinion that no other treatment is appropriate (◊ *Approved Schools, Borstal Institutions*). An infant (i.e. a person under 21) is not normally bound by his or her contracts. It is the duty of parents to maintain their children, and an offence to neglect them or treat them with cruelty; the father is deemed to have custody of a legitimate child (◊ *Illegitimacy*), but if parents disagree either party may apply to the High Court or a magistrates' court for an order relating to custody, and in awarding it the court must have regard primarily to the child's well-being.

Childbirth. The process of giving birth has three distinct stages. (1) With the onset of contractions of the uterus (labour pains), the fluid-filled sac containing the child bulges downwards and dilates the opening (cervix) from the uterus to the vagina; the sac breaks and loses its fluid, so that the uterine muscles can press down more directly on the body of the infant. (2) Voluntary muscular effort by the mother is added to the expulsive contractions of the uterus, to force the infant through the cervix and vagina. The position of the child is usually head downward, with the back of its head to the mother's front; presentation buttocks-first may cause delay in a first labour in which the passages have not previously been dilated, and presentation of other parts e.g. face or shoulders may cause considerable difficulty in delivery. (3) After the child is born, rhythmic contractions of the uterus expel the placenta and minimize bloodloss by constricting ruptured blood vessels.

Chile. Area about 300,000 sq. m. Pop. 7.4 m. Cap. Santiago. Rel. Roman Catholic. A republic on the W. coast of S. America. Under the 1925 constitution legislative power is vested in the National Congress, consisting of a Senate of 45 members and a chamber of Deputies of 147, elected by proportional representation for eight and four years respectively, with a president elected for six years by direct popular vote and not eligible for successive terms. The present President is Eduardo Frei, elected 1964.

ECONOMY. Chile has a coastline about 2800 m. long and covers a narrow strip of land between the Andes and the Pacific; it has not many fertile areas and is subject to disastrous earthquakes, e.g. in 1960, but has large deposits of nitrates, coal, and copper. The chief problem is inflation, esp. since 1931 when owing to increasing world use of synthetic fertilizers the nitrates industry collapsed, and 1953 when world copper prices fell. Chile is also handicapped by an outdated landownership system.

HISTORY. Discovered in the 16th cent. by Spanish adventurers, Chile remained under Spanish rule until a war of liberation established its independence in 1818. The population consists of four ethnic groups, the indigenous Indians, the Spanish descendants of the early settlers, mixed Spanish-Indians, and European immigrants.

LANGUAGE. Spanish, and Indian dialects.

Chiltern Hundreds. The office of Steward of the Chiltern Hundreds is nominally still one of 'profit under the Crown' and as such cannot be held by a member of the House of Commons; therefore to apply for the Chiltern Hundreds is a Parliamentary device by which an M.P. gives up his seat, since he cannot simply resign.

Chimaera. In Greek mythology, a firebreathing dragon-lion-goat monster which ravaged Lycia and was killed by Bellerophon (◊ *Pegasus*). Hence, an illusory or fanciful idea. The myth may have originated from a volcano of the same name.

Chimpanzee. Anthropoid ◊ *ape*, similar to the ◊ *gorilla* but smaller, about 4 ft,

and less muscular; found in tropical Africa, where it lives in family groups, nesting in trees. Chimpanzees are highly intelligent, possessing considerable learning ability and even, it has been suggested, a rudimentary aesthetic sense. ◊ *Primates*.

China. Area about 4.3 m. sq. m. (inc. Inner Mongolia, Yunnan, Manchuria, Sinkiang, and Tibet). Pop. 656.6 m. Cap. Peking. Rel. Buddhism, Confucianism, Taoism. A people's republic; the sole legislative authority is the National People's Congress, with a permanent Standing Committee as effective administrative organ. Chairman (President) of the Republic, Liu Shao-chi; Chief of Council (Prime Minister), Chou En-lai; Chairman of Standing Committee, General Chu-Teh; Chairman of Communist Party Central Committee, Mao Tse-tung. The Chinese People's Republic is recognized by a majority of countries, but U.S.A. regards Chiang Kai-shek's former government as rightful, refuses to recognize the Republic, and blocks China's applications for admission to the United Nations. Recently China has engaged in increasingly bitter ideological controversy with U.S.S.R. over matters of war and peace, accusing the Soviet communists of ◊ *revisionism* and disputing Soviet claims to leadership of world communism.

ECONOMY. Despite abundant coal, copper, lead, zinc, tungsten, antimony, tin, and iron, China remains predominantly agricultural. Vast industrialization programmes, a massive drive for increased agricultural output, and intensive mass education have been undertaken at extreme speed since the establishment of the communist republic, for which remarkable results are claimed but hotly disputed; there has undoubtedly been considerable industrial development, but agricultural success is more dubious.

HISTORY. The largest Asian country, China has the world's longest continuous civilization; often invaded, ruled by many dynasties, China and the Chinese people constantly survived. The earliest records date to the Shang dynasty, 18th to 12th centuries B.C. The Chou dynasty of the 12th to 3rd centuries B.C. developed a social system resembling European feudalism. The Ch'in and Han dynasties, 3rd cent. B.C. to A.D. 300, ruled an area roughly that of modern China, administered by civil servants (the Mandarins being the

highest grade) recruited by a competitive examination system lasting till the 19th cent. The central-China Sung dynasty A.D. 960–1279 was an epoch of artistic and literary brilliance. Genghis Khan, 12th to 13th centuries, overran N. China, which remained in the Mongol Empire until the Ming Dynasty of the 14th cent. The Manchus infiltrated, conquered China in the 16th cent. and continued in power till 1912, but were completely absorbed by the Chinese. A new phase began in the 16th cent. with the coming of Europeans; the Chinese tried to exclude or isolate the westerners, allowing them to trade only through Canton, but at last were obliged in the 19th cent. (◊ *Boxer Rebellion, Opium Wars*) to grant trading concessions and open the ports. Pressure and then invasion by Russia and then ◊ *Japan* followed (◊ *Manchuria*). After a revolution 1911, Sun Yat-sen formed the ◊ *Kuomintang* party; later, as communism became a rising force, the right wing split away under Chiang Kai-shek 1927, while Mao Tse-tung organized and led the left-wing marxists, but when Japan invaded China 1937 the two factions agreed a truce pending victory over the invaders. After Japan's defeat in the ◊ *Second World War* 1945, and in China 1946, civil war broke out; despite Soviet recognition and substantial aid from U.S.A. the Kuomintang lost ground to the communists, Mao Tse-tung set up the People's Republic 1949, and Chiang Kai-shek sought refuge 1950 in Taiwan (Formosa), whence his party continues to claim authority. ◊◊ *Mongolia.*
LANGUAGE. One of the Sino-Tibetan languages, first developed along the Yellow River; the present standard form (Mandarin or N. Chinese) has changed little since the 13th cent. Non-alphabetic, its script consists of 30,000 ideographs; to read a newspaper one must know at least 3000, and 6000 to understand literature. Several dialects, differing so widely as to preclude mutual understanding, are each spoken by over 100 m. but the ideographs are common to all. Attempts are being made to devise a Roman-alphabetic script, though this would mean either the imposition of a standard language or the enhancement of linguistic differences owing to the loss of the non-variable common written medium. The language is uninflected, monosyllabic, and tonal: the spoken tone of a monosyllable conveys its meaning, e.g. *ma* level tone, mother, but *ma* rising tone, flax. It is the difference in the four tones that makes alphabetization a complicated problem, though identification is aided by about 50 'classifiers' as in English 'piece of', 'length of', etc. Whether the 1956 decision to introduce a 30-letter alphabet into school curricula has been implemented is not known.
China. A name for ◊ *porcelain*, the first examples of which were brought to Europe from China and in England named 'Chinaware'. Although Chinese porcelain reached Europe in the Middle Ages, it was not imported in quantity until the Chinese began to make wares expressly for the western market in the 16th cent. The porcelain exported to Europe was of inferior quality to that made for home use, more richly decorated in much brighter colours. The Japanese also exported porcelain to Europe from the 17th cent. and in the 19th cent. produced the over-decorated Satsuma wares, which were particularly popular though despised in their country of origin.
China Clay ◊ *Kaolin.*
Chinese Art. The Chinese at a very early date began to produce very fine work in ceramics (2nd millennium B.C.) and during the Shang-Yin period about 1500–1027 B.C. brought the art of working jade and bronze for ritual vessels and instruments to an astonishing peak of elegance; these materials (pottery, jade, bronze) assumed far greater importance in China than they have ever had in the west. In the Han period 206 B.C.–A.D. 220 silk-weaving and lacquer painting were also brought to a high pitch of refinement, and the art of figure painting was established. The earliest Chinese stone sculptures, mostly shallow-relief panels carved with numerous figures, also date from this period. Figure sculpture in the round came with Buddhism in the 1st cent. A.D., and remained a predominantly Buddhist rather than Chinese art. China entered her golden age in art with the 7th–10th-cent. T'ang dynasty, famous for its beautifully modelled and glazed pottery and porcelain vessels and figurines, for its superb naturalistic figure paintings, and for the vast high-relief sculptures in Buddhist cave temples. The Sung period 960–1279 saw the highest achievements in scroll painting: atmospheric ◊ *landscape paintings* of mountains and trees, spirited

studies of birds and beasts, exquisite sketches of flowers and foliage. Under the Ming emperors 1368–1644, Chinese arts enjoyed their last prolific flowering. Porcelain, with more elaborate forms and colour, surpassed pottery and stoneware: Europe developed a taste for Chinese art, and the Chinese were quick to cater for the Western market, whilst at home they continued to produce close imitations of the works of previous epochs (esp. Sung and T'ang); during the long Ch'ing dynasty 1644–1912 no departure was made from the traditional themes.

Chiron ◊ Centaurs.

Chivalry ◊ Heraldry, Orders of Chivalry.

Chlorates ◊ Chlorine.

Chlorides ◊ Halogens (Polyvinyl Chloride ◊ Plastics).

Chlorine. ◊ Halogens; a greenish-yellow toxic gas, 75 per cent chlorine-35 and 25 per cent chlorine-37 isotopes, forming about 0.2 per cent of the earth's crust, chiefly as sodium chloride in rock salt and sea water. Discovered by Scheele 1774, shown to be an element by Davy 1810; largely produced in the electrolytic manufacture of sodium hydroxide from brine and of metallic sodium from fused sodium chloride, and for industrial purposes stored and transported under pressure in iron cylinders. It was the first 'poison gas' used by the Germans in the First World War. Early recognized as a disinfecting and bleaching agent, it is still so used. It is very active chemically, combining with many elements and compounds at room temperature, sometimes violently; it very readily combines with hydrogen, and the oxidizing, bleaching, and disinfecting action of moist chlorine is due to its displacing hydrogen from water and producing active hypochlorous acid; it is not only the basis of an extensive chemical industry (producing hydrochloric acid, bleaching materials, chlorates, and other chemicals) but also has many applications in the organic field. In the form of common salt it is an essential item in the diet of men and animals.

Chloroform. A heavy sweet-smelling liquid, formula $CHCl_3$; not easily inflammable. Exposed to light and air, it oxidizes to generate phosgene. Formerly much used as an anaesthetic, it has been superseded by others of less toxicity, but has industrial use as a solvent of resins. ◊◊ Hepatitis.

Chloromycetin. Chloramphenicol, an ◊ antibiotic, the first to be synthesized; first obtained from cultures of a variety of streptomyces. It had early success against typhus and typhoid.

Chlorophyll. Green pigment found in most plants (except ◊ fungi), a key substance in ◊ photosynthesis. There are three types, a and b (found in green plants) and bacteriochlorophyll (in photosynthetic bacteria). They are all similar in structure and are complex compounds containing ◊ magnesium. Except in bacteria and blue-green algae, chlorophyll is found in cytoplasm in discrete bodies called chloroplasts which have a definite and complex structure. It is often masked by other pigments e.g. in brown and red algae, and is broken down in leaves in autumn, leaving yellow and orange pigments which give the typical autumn colours. It is used as a deodorant and has some medical value in treating infections. ◊◊ Protozoa.

Cholera. Acute infectious disease, caused by Vibrio cholerae, occurring in hot regions where standards of sanitation and cleanliness are low, and characterized by vomiting, diarrhoea and severe dehydration. Its incidence has been reduced by vaccination and the boiling of drinking water.

Cholesterol. Solid (fatty) alcohol which occurs widely in animal tissues and is manufactured in the liver. Excess of cholesterol may be deposited in the body in gallstones (◊ Calculus) and in the arteries.

Choral Music. Until the 18th cent. the maintenance of choirs and the provision of a regular repertory for them were matters exclusively of ◊ church music, though church choirs were sometimes used to maintain secular prestige, e.g. at the Field of the Cloth of Gold in 1520 the singers of the English Chapel Royal and its French equivalent performed in attendance on their respective sovereigns. Handel's invention of English ◊ oratorio allotted a principal part to the chorus, as representing 'the people'. Though Handel's own choirs were of professionals (with boy sopranos and adult male altos), the subsequent rise of massive mixed-voice amateur choirs (esp. in Protestant Britain, America, and Germany) was linked with the impulse to perform Handel's oratorios and their successors esp. Haydn's *The Creation* 1798 and Mendelssohn's *Elijah* 1846. Institutions such as the Three Choirs Festival (founded 1724 and achieving major importance in the 19th cent.) regularly brought forward ambitious new works, and thousands of smaller works were also written for mixed, all-male, and all-female choirs of moderate attainments. The combination of large choir and large symphony orchestra was employed by 19th cent. composers with particularly forceful effect, e.g. . Beethoven *Choral Symphony* 1824, Berlioz *Requiem* 1836–7, Verdi *Requiem* 1873, Mahler '*Resurrection*' *Symphony* 1894, etc. In the 20th cent. the multiplication of orchestral concerts and the rise of mechanical reproduction has assisted in bringing a decline in the number of choirs and in the importance of composers of choral writing.

Christianity. Religion based on the teachings of ◊ *Jesus Christ* and on the writings of his early followers, preserved in the New Testament (◊ *Bible, Gospels*). Persecuted for the first three centuries A.D. by the civil powers, it spread rapidly underground and early in the 4th cent. was adopted as the State religion of the Roman Empire under Constantine, soon becoming almost universal in Europe, N. Africa, and SW Asia, until faced by the spread of ◊ *Islam*. Since the 16th cent. it has been carried through the world with other Europeanizing influences, and today has probably about 1000 m. adherents. Its traditional beliefs (◊ *Creed*) include the virgin birth of Jesus (◊ *Mary*), bodily resurrection of the dead, and the divinity of its founder and his eternal coexistence with ◊ *God* the Father and the ◊ *Holy Ghost* in the ◊ *Trinity*. Disagreements on doctrine and discipline have divided Christianity into three main branches: the ◊ *Roman Catholic Church*, the ◊ *Eastern Orthodox Church*, and ◊ *Protestantism* (itself subdivided into a large number of sects). The high standards of Christian ethical teaching still influence many (esp. in the western world) who no longer or only vaguely accept the theology. ◊ *Ecumenical Movement, Heresy, Missions, Religious Festivals*, etc.

Christian Science. Religious cult founded by Mary Baker Eddy 1821–1910, an American; a system of spiritual healing based on the belief that matter has no real existence and that sickness and evil are illusions which can be overcome, teachings set forth in *Science and Health* 1875. After the opening in Boston (Mass.) in 1879 of the First ('Mother') Church of Christ Scientist, the cult spread rapidly in U.S.A. and Britain, but it issues no statistics of membership, though it publishes an international newspaper, *The Christian Science Monitor*. The activities of its healers and lecturers are closely supervised by the Boston 'Mother' Church.

Christmas. Festival commemorating the birth of ◊ *Jesus Christ*, observed by all Christian churches except the Armenian; the choice of 25 Dec. as Christmas Day may have been due to its marking the winter solstice, to its pre-Christian observance as the birthday of pagan gods e.g. ◊ *Adonis, Dionysus*, and of *sol invictus*, the unconquered sun, and also to the influence of the Roman festival of the Saturnalia celebrated at this season. Many of the British customs e.g. the Christmas tree and Christmas cards were imported from Germany in the 19th cent. The exchange of presents is a transference from the feast of St Nicholas, Santa Claus, 6 Dec. ◊ *Religious Festivals*.

Chromatic Aberration ◊ *Aberration of Light, Telescope*.

Chromatography. A technique, now of great practical importance, used to separate nearly-related elements or compounds very difficult to resolve by chemical means. Simple column chromatography was introduced by the Russian botanist Tsvett 1906 to separate the pigments of plants e.g. ◊ *carotene, chlorophyll*; several methods are now employed, but in all a fluid mixture is passed through a stationary bed of adsorbent material: the components of the mixture have different adsorbabilities, so that the one least adsorbed will pass through the column first, the others following in order. In column chromatography, a liquid mixture percolates downward through e.g. specially prepared alumina. As the substances separated in the early days were all coloured, the technique was named chromatography, but nowadays colourless liquids can be detected by staining or by the use of ultraviolet light. The procedure has proved of great use in the separation of the ◊ *lanthanides*, and ion exchange columns, e.g. the permutit water-softener, are in many ways similar. Paper chromatography, even simpler, has proved of great value in separating delicate organic compounds such as the amino-acids. In gas ('vapour phase') chromatography the gas mixture to be analysed is borne by an inert 'carrier' gas (commonly ◊ *nitrogen*) through ◊ *carbon* or an absorbing liquid dispersed over kieselguhr or ground firebrick. As they come through the gases can record themselves automatically by means of some physical detector e.g. a thermal conductance cell, and thus make possible the automatic control of petroleum refining.

Chromium. A silvery metallic ◊ *element*, corrosion-resistant because of an insoluble oxide film; the natural source is chrome ironstone, which is smelted to ferrochrome for steel-making (◊ *Iron and Steel Industry*). In chromium-plating, iron is first coated with nickel by ◊ *electrolysis*, and then a thin coating of chromium is plated above this, chromium metal alone being too porous. Chromium, with some nickel, is also alloyed with iron for stainless steel. Soluble chromates are used for tanning and as rust inhibitors, and insoluble ones e.g. lead ('chrome yellow') as pigments.

Chromosomes. Minute bodies consisting largely of deoxyribonucleic acid (DNA) and protein, in the nuclei of animal and plant ◊ *cells*; their appearance changes during various stages of the cell's life, and they are most easily seen microscopically during cell division, when they appear as tiny rods. Chromosomes contain the ◊ *genes* (the physical structures by which hereditary characteristics are handed on); the pattern in which the chromosomes from the two parents are distributed in the fertilized ovum during sexual ◊ *reproduction* is believed to determine what parental characteristics are impressed on the offspring.

The number of chromosomes in tissue tends to be constant for a particular species. Man has 46, in 23 similar pairs. The ◊ *gametes* in the sex cells in ova and spermatozoa have only half this number, the number 46 resulting from fertilization. In some species it has been possible to 'map' the chromosomes, i.e. to find on them the loci where genes of any particular characteristic are carried.

Chronometer. A specially accurate timepiece (◊ *Clocks and Watches*) used in ◊ *navigation*. The first dependable chronometer was invented about 1760 by John Harrison, and enabled navigators to establish their longitude with great accuracy, which had not previously been possible.

Chrysanthemum. A race of showy autumn flowering plants developed in China about 500 B.C. and introduced to Japan in the 9th cent. A.D. Varieties of every size and colour (except blue) in widely differing forms from single to most complicated doubles, and with short to long spidery petals, have been evolved. There are also chrysanthemums developed from wild plants of S. Europe and N. Africa e.g. marguerite, corn marigold, oxeye daisy and ◊ *pyrethrums*.

Church. The heathen temple was the dwelling place of the god; his altar and the place of worship were outside. The Christian church, however, was the meeting place of the worshippers, and the first form adopted was that of the Roman ◊ *basilica*, a secular public building to which later were added ambulatories, chapels, and transepts to give it the form of the cross. The walls and ceilings and capitals of ◊ *Byzantine* and ◊ *Romanesque* churches were covered with paintings (or mosaics) and carvings illustrating and narrating the stories of the ◊ *Bible* for the illiterate. The Byzantine form has persisted unchanged; the Western form developed a variety of plan, from the simplicity of the early Romanesque to the elaboration of the great Gothic churches and cathedrals. ◊◊ *Baroque, Gothic Architecture*.

Church Assembly. Body set up by Parliament 1919 (by an Enabling Act) to consider matters relating to the ◊ *Church of England* and prepare measures for Parliamentary approval, having no concern with theology; divided into the House of Bishops, the House of Clergy (all the members of the Lower Houses of ◊ *Convocation*), and the House of Laity (elected at 5-year intervals by Diocesan Conferences).

Church Music. The Christian church inherited psalmody from the Jewish synagogue, but early developed its own forms. With the divergence between the Byzantine and Western churches, their music also diverged: in the Eastern branch a tradition of chant now known as 'Byzantine' grew up, with a continued prohibition of instrumental music, as in the synagogue; in the west, ◊ *plainsong* became the accepted musical setting of the Latin ◊ *liturgy* and the organ became an accepted accompaniment from about the 8th cent. Musical settings of liturgical words more elaborate than plainsong are known from about A.D. 900, and from the period of Guillaume de Machaut in the 14th cent. come the earliest surviving full polyphonic settings of the ◊ *Mass,* which in all succeeding periods has been set in contemporary musical style, with a greater or lesser time-lag.

The era of the ◊ *Renaissance* brought a flowering of Roman Catholic church music (from Dufay, b. before 1400, to Palestrina, d. 1594), both in the settings of prescribed liturgical texts and in pieces to Latin religious texts of the composer's choosing. The Renaissance spirit is also seen in religious music in vernacular tongues, notably the Italian *Laudi spirituali* from the 14th cent. The Council of Trent 1545–63, with recommendations aimed at purifying church music from secular excesses, shows up a recurrent conflict between artistic and institutional demands, which has arisen in various forms. ◊ *Protestantism* gave decisively greater importance to congregational vernacular ◊ *hymn* singing (Luther himself was a writer of hymns and possibly composed the tunes) and made possible the extended devotional but non-liturgical works of J. S. Bach and his contemporaries. In the Church of England the two chief categories of music used are 'services' (Obligatory Texts) and 'anthems' (with the composer's choice of words). The late 16th cent. (Byrd, Tallis) is considered the golden age of English church (and secular) music. Purcell and his contemporaries exceptionally wrote anthems with string accompaniment for the Chapel Royal. Handel wrote similar works for a patron (the Chandos Anthem), but his ◊ *oratorios* are not church works. Later composers who have written notably for the church include Stanford, Vaughan Williams, and (not extensively) Britten.

Church of England. The established State church of England (but not of the rest of the U.K.); its doctrines are called ◊ *Anglicanism.* Tracing its origins from the mission of St Augustine of Canterbury from Rome, about A.D. 597, and the contemporary preaching of Celtic missionaries, it took its present form after the 16th-cent. breach with the Papacy, its formularies being broad enough to cover a range of interpretations from near

Roman Catholic to extreme Protestant. The Church of England 'by law established' is looked upon as the official Church of the State (◊ *Erastianism*), which in effect appoints its ◊ *bishops.* England is covered by a network of parishes, each usually in charge of a rector or vicar, organized into 43 dioceses under two archbishops and 41 bishops. The Church of England has large endowments administered by the Church Commissioners (income £16.4 m. 1961). Outside England the Anglican churches have the same status as other religious bodies, with no special relation to the State authorities. ◊ *Arminianism, Church Assembly, Convocation, Lambeth Conference, Methodism, Old Catholics, Oxford Movement, Prayer Book, Protestantism, Reformation, Sacrament, Savoy Conference, Thirty-Nine Articles.*

Church of Ireland. Protestant Episcopalian Church in Ireland. St Patrick converted the Irish to Christianity in the 5th cent. A.D. but the early relationship of the Church to papal authority was ambiguous. In the 16th cent. the majority of the Irish rejected the royal supremacy imposed on the Church by Henry VIII and have since then held to Roman Catholicism, the Church of Ireland then becoming that of a small minority. In 1869 it was disestablished. ◊ *Penal Laws.*

Church of Latter-day Saints (Mormons). Protestant Christian religious body founded in U.S.A. 1830 by Joseph Smith 1805–44, who claimed to have been guided by an angel to find and decipher a divinely-inspired account (*Book of Mormon*) of the settlement of America by Asian emigrants after the Tower of Babel, and of their subsequent history. After the mob-murder of Smith (accused of polygamy), Brigham Young led his followers across the continent to Utah, where they founded Salt Lake City and grew into a flourishing community. Polygamy, at first allowed by alleged divine revelation (though one section rejected it), was discontinued under State pressure. The 'Saints' claim about 1.75 m. members in U.S.A. alone, and enjoy a high reputation for their social work. Missions are carried on throughout the world. There is a British Temple of Latter-day Saints at Lingfield, Surrey.

Church of Scotland. Christian ◊ *Presbyterian* body, based on the teachings of

John Knox (*c.* 1505–72), the established form of Christianity in Scotland; a democratic body governed by a General Assembly meeting annually in Edinburgh. Under the Assembly are synods, district presbyteries, and kirk sessions (one in each parish) consisting of ministers and lay elders elected by the congregations. In the 18th and 19th centuries large bodies of clerical and lay members seceded, mostly over the method of appointing ministers; they were reunited to the Church in 1929. Much foreign missionary work is carried on, esp. in Africa (◊ *Missions*); membership is about 1.3. m.

Church, Slavonic ◊ *Bulgaria.*

Cicada. Insect common in Mediterranean countries and S. America; after hatching, the nymph buries itself in the ground for several years, but the life of the adult is only a few weeks. One of the longest insect life-histories, 17 years from egg to adult, is shown by the periodical cicada *Magicicada septendecim.* The males emit a shrill noise from vibrating drums in the abdomen.

Cider. Fermented juice of apples, containing from four to seven per cent alcohol. There are various kinds, sweet, semi-sweet, and dry. Sparkling cider is produced by charging with carbonic acid gas. Perry is a similar drink made from pears.

Cinema. The history of the cinema proper begins with the invention in 1895 of the Cinématographe by the Lumière brothers, and the opening of the first cinema houses in the early 1900s; thereafter it developed technically and aesthetically at an astonishing rate. The first films, those of Lumière or Pathé, could hold their audience through the sheer novelty of reality transported on to a screen in an auditorium; with the work of Georges Melies, a French magician, and of Edwin Porter, maker of *The Great Train Robbery,* 1903, the cinema acquired fantasy and narrative possibilities. From 1909 D. W. Griffith revealed something of the real narrative and dramatic potential of the cinema through the use of a selective, interpretative camera style. His *Birth of a Nation,* 1915, and *Intolerance,* 1916, also established a new scale of ambition for the cinema – huge sets, grandiose effects, a vast time-scale.

The First World War inhibited the film output of the European nations. U.S.A. gained a firm hold on the world market, and Hollywood became the undisputed centre of the film industry. In the 1920s there appeared such stars as Chaplin, Douglas Fairbanks, Buster Keaton, Mary Pickford, and Rudolf Valentino. Nevertheless many silent masterpieces were produced outside Hollywood, e.g. Robert Wiene's *Cabinet of Dr Caligari,* 1919, and the work of Fritz Lang and G. W. Pabst in Germany; René Clair and Jean Renoir in France; Eisenstein and Pudovkin in the U.S.S.R. Eisenstein's *Battleship Potemkin,* 1925, is one of the more famous films of the period.

In 1927 the first talking film appeared, *The Jazz Singer,* starring Al Jolson; and in 1932 colour was introduced, with *La Cucuracha.* In the 1930s Hollywood was responsible for about three quarters of the world's film production: 600 titles in 1937 alone. Major directors of this decade were Frank Capra, King Vidor, George Cukor, and Howard Hawks. Of the vast Hollywood output from the 30s and 40s, much is now forgotten, but a number of the finer films survive and command audiences to this day: e.g. the urbane, highly sophisticated comedies of Cukor, the very skilful and oddly compulsive gangster movies and thrillers of Otto Preminger, Howard Hawks, and Alfred Hitchcock, and Orson Welles's famous 'art' pieces *Citizen Kane,* 1941, and *The Magnificent Ambersons,* 1942.

During the 1950s television brought about a drastic fall in cinema audiences everywhere; the Hollywood studios began to close down or to turn to the production of television films. One response to this competition, partially successful, was the introduction of the wide screen and such technical devices as 3D, Cinerama, and 70 mm. film, continuing a trend towards an ever closer approximation to 'reality'. Associated with this tendency was the production of lavish spectaculars like *Cleopatra* and *55 Days at Peking,* much of whose attraction lay in their enormous production costs. Another response, particularly in Europe, was the creation of a truly international cinema, commanding smaller but more discriminating audiences throughout the world; in this connexion might be mentioned the work of Kazan, Kubrick, and Billy Wilder in U.S.A. and of Bresson, Chabrol, Godard, Franju, Resnais, and Truffaut in France, Antonioni,

Rossellini, and Visconti in Italy, Lindsay Anderson, Clive Donner, and Joseph Losey in Britain, Ingmar Bergman in Sweden, Polanski and Wajda in Poland, Satyajit Ray in India, and Mizoguchi, Ozu, and Kurosawa in Japan.

Cinematography. Making pictures photographically and projecting them so as to simulate movement, a process developed after the advent of celluloid film 1889; uses a camera carrying a moving film set to photograph the subject at a rate of 24 pictures per second. After development the film is projected on a screen, the pictures normally moving through the projector at the speed at which they were exposed in the camera. Colour cinematography, known 1897, was not introduced commercially till 1932. Sound was introduced by Warner Bros. 1927, by linking the film with a gramophone record; subsequently a sound-track was added to the film itself. Recent developments include the wide-projection screen, with Cinemascope and Todd-AO techniques, and the use of stereophonic sound.

The history of the cinema is that of many inventions in various countries, gradually combined to produce modern techniques. Two devices vital to good projection were making the film travel intermittently and cutting off the light after each 'frame'; these were successfully used in the first public film show, by the Lumière brothers, Paris 1895, and within a few weeks two Englishmen independently produced similar results. In 1898 a cameraman accompanied Kitchener's army in the Sudan. By the turn of the century cinematography was widespread; soon afterwards the 35 mm. width film became standard, and later the 8 mm. film was introduced for amateur cinematographers. ⬦ *Photography*.

Cinnabar ⬦ *Mercury*.

Cinnamon. A spice from the inner bark of the tree *Cinnamomum zeylanicum*, native in India and Ceylon, the latter producing the best cinnamon. The dried bark curls into the familiar sticks and may then be powdered; it is used for flavouring, and also medicinally.

Cinque Ports. Group of five (< French *cinq*) towns on the Kent coast which received privileges from the Crown in return for supplying ships, both before 1066 and under the Normans. Originally Hastings, Romney, Dover, Hythe, and Sandwich;

later Rye and Winchelsea obtained the same status. After the reign of Henry VII the towns declined in importance, esp. since most of them were cut off from the sea by the changing coastline. The office of Lord Warden is now almost wholly honorary and is held by distinguished men, such as Sir Winston Churchill.

C.I.O. (Congress of Industrial Organizations) ⬦ *American Federation of Labor*.

Cipher. Secret ⬦ *code* used for transmission e.g. of military or diplomatic messages for which secrecy is vital. Essentially it involves replacing one set of letters by figures or other letters to make the message incomprehensible to anyone not having the key. Many systems have been evolved; frequently the key has been discovered by careful analysis. Methods have been radically affected by ⬦ *computers*.

Circe. In Greek mythology, a sorceress living on Aeaea, an island near the ⬦ *Scylla* rocks visited by ⬦ *Ulysses* in his wanderings; by a magic potion she changed his companions into pigs, but it had no effect on Ulysses, who had eaten moly, a magic herb given to him by ⬦ *Hermes*, and he induced Circe, under threat of death, to change his friends into men again. He stayed with her for a year, begetting a child, and then, at her suggestion, left to visit ⬦ *Hades*.

Circulatory System. Earliest theories suggested that a kind of tidal flux kept blood in motion in the body. In the 16th cent. Servetus first described the lesser circulation through the lungs, but it was not till 1628 that William Harvey explained the system fully. It comprises the ⬦ *heart* (the pump), the arteries (conveying the blood from the heart throughout the body), the veins (returning the used blood to the heart), and the capillaries (where the replenishment of the oxygen supply and removal of waste matter takes place): the heart is divided into two sides, right and left, each further divided into two chambers, the auricle atrium (upper) and the ventricle (lower). The circulation of the blood has two courses: (a) from left ventricle to right auricle (systemic circulation); (b) from right ventricle to left auricle (pulmonary circulation). The systemic circulation leaves by the aorta (largest artery of the body); this subdivides into smaller arteries, which carry blood to all parts of the body, and these finally become the fine capillaries, which in turn unite into larger vessels to become the veins, which carry the blood back to the right auricle. The pulmonary circulation passes the blood into the right ventricle, which pumps it via the pulmonary artery into both ◊ *lungs*, whence the blood returns to the left auricle, from which it is pumped by the left ventricle into the aorta, completing the cycle. This cycle is repeated once every 28 heart beats when a

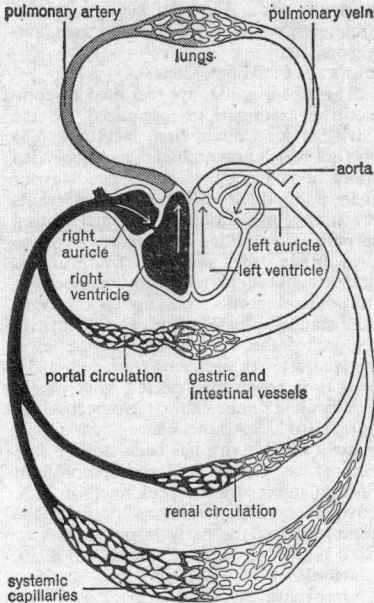

person is at rest, during which time about five litres of blood are moved and an equal volume is returned to the heart via the veins; this may rise to 20 or 25 litres per min. during exercise, when both the rate of beat and the volume of output per stroke are augmented.

Circumcision. Operation of cutting away part of the foreskin, usually in infancy but sometimes at puberty. In many religions, including Judaism and Islam, is is an important rite, probably originally associated with purification or initiation. In most modern countries circumcision is widely practised, for reasons of hygiene.

Cirrhosis. Progressive destruction of the tissue of the liver and its replacement by fibrous tissue; it may follow severe inflammation e.g. infectious hepatitis, or may result from chronic poisoning as with alcohol, organic solvents, or phosphorus.

Cirrus ◊ *Cloud.*

Cistercians. Christian religious order founded about 1100 by Robert of Molesme and the Englishman Stephen Harding at Cîteaux in France, with the intention of reviving the fervour of the primitive ◊ *Benedictines*; its most famous member was St Bernard. In the later 17th cent. a reform of the order by Abbot de Rancé, at La Trappe in Normandy, gave the name Trappists to those Cistercians whose severe rule enjoins almost perpetual silence. Largely employed in agricultural work, today the monks number about 6500 throughout the world. In England there are imposing Cistercian monastic ruins, e.g. Rievaulx, Tintern.

Citric Acid. A natural organic acid, present esp. in citrus fruits, which forms colourless water-soluble crystals. Chemical formula $(CO_2H.CH_2)_2.C(OH).CO_2H$. As a weak natural acid it is used in e.g. soft drinks or effervescent salts. Formerly extracted from citrus fruits, it is now manufactured by culturing suitable moulds on sugar. ◊ *Scurvy.*

Citrus ◊ *Grapefruit, Lemon, Lime, Orange.*

City-State. The characteristic political unit of classical Greece, a small autonomous community with an urban nucleus, idealized by Greek thinkers as the highest form of human association but resulting in a disunity which led to the collapse of the Greek polity. Political units of the same name and on a similarly small scale have also appeared occasionally in post-classical times, e.g. Florence and Venice in medieval Italy.

Civil Defence. Measures taken to protect civil populations from attack, esp. from the air. In the U.K. various Air Raid Precautions were established in 1937; they included air-raid warnings, lighting restrictions, evacuation, ◊ *camouflage,* shelters, emergency feeding and housing of the homeless, and the strengthening of normal fire-fighting, ambulance, and first-aid services. These arrangements were coordinated under the Home Office in 1941. The Civil Defence was disbanded in 1945, but was set up again in 1949 to face the new problems set by the possibility of atomic warfare.

Civil Disobedience. An act or series of acts deliberately performed in defiance of the civil authorities, but falling short of violence or insurrection, in pursuit of a declared aim; not isolated demonstrations by groups or individuals. The mass burning of pass-books by coloured S. Africans as a protest against ◊ *apartheid* was an act of civil disobedience. The term is associated with the American writer Thoreau, whose essay *Civil Disobedience* inspired Gandhi, but the latter's refusal to pay taxes to a government whose actions he abhorred falls rather under the heading of ◊ *Passive Resistance.*

Civil Engineering. Term coined in France in the 18th cent. to distinguish the work of State-employed civilian engineers. All branches of non-military engineering were regarded as civil engineering in the early 19th cent. and there were also close links with architecture. With the founding of the Institution of Civil Engineers 1828, civil engineering emerged as a separate profession, and it is now regarded as being distinct from mechanical and electrical engineering. Civil engineering includes the construction of roads, railways, bridges, dams, docks and irrigation works etc.

Civil Law. 1. The law governing claims for damages and other private remedies in respect of contracts, torts, and breaches of trust, as against the criminal law.
2. Law internal to a particular state, as against ◊ *international law.*
3. ◊ *Roman law,* and those systems descended from it, as against e.g. ◊ *common law.*
4. Law applicable to both soldiers and civilians, as against ◊ *military law.*

Civil List. The annual sum paid to the Sovereign (and other members of the royal family). The amount is fixed at the beginning of each reign. This practice dates from the first Hanoverian reign of William and Mary (1689–1702). The Civil List Consolidated Fund (Appropriation) Act 1952 fixed the amounts provided to Her Majesty the Queen (£475,000) and to other members of the royal family.

Civil Service. In the U.K. paid servants of the Crown employed in civil capacities; so defined, there are about a million civil servants, but half or a third of these are employed in dockyards, ordnance factories, the Post Office, etc. The Civil Service falls into various classes, all administered by the Treasury, the more important being:

ADMINISTRATIVE: About 2500, predominantly university graduates, who advise the Ministers of Departments; known as higher civil servants.

EXECUTIVE: About 70,000, working in conjunction with the administrative class in the day-to-day conduct of government business.

SPECIALIST: About 100,000, including architects, medical experts, engineers, surveyors, etc.

CLERICAL: About 120,000.

The higher grades are recruited by competitive examinations organized by the Civil Service Commission, instituted 1855 (before which appointments had depended more upon patronage and special favour than upon qualifications). Civil servants are subject to restrictions on participation in political activities, varying according to their grade; they may join trade unions and are not debarred from membership of political parties, but no civil servant may stand for Parliament. The distinctive feature of the British civil service, as it evolved after the reforms started in 1855, is that it serves the elected government loyally and impartially, irrespective of party. In U.S.A. the concept of a permanent civil service has been slow to find acceptance, and in part the composition of the administrative personnel of U.S. government departments still reflects the complexion of the party in power.

Civil War (England) ◊ *English Civil Wars.*
Clactonian ◊ *Palaeolithic.*
Clairvoyance ◊ *Extra-sensory Perception.*
Clam. Bivalve mollusc found inshore in mud or sand; the hinged shell valves close powerfully when exposed to air or physical shock. Clams feed by filtering food particles from a current of water washed through syphons; the largest, found in the Indian and Pacific Oceans, may weigh up to 500 lb. They are eaten in America, and are used for bait. The name is also applied to freshwater mussels.

Clan. Group of people claiming descent from a single ancestor, reckoning either through men only (patrilineal) or women only (matrilineal). In modern anthropological usage, clan members may not be able to reckon their genealogical relationship; if they can, the group is a lineage.

Clans and lineages are important units in many societies, from most African peoples to the Chinese. A clan was often the basic land-holding unit. In most pre-literate societies only a few generations may be remembered, but among the Chinese and other literate peoples dozens of generations may be known and a clan may number many thousand persons. Clans are usually exogamous. Clanship was the basic principle of early Teutonic and British society, and the clans continued to be effective groups in Scotland until the 18th cent. ♦ *Exogamy*.

Clarendon Code. Legislation after the ♦ *Restoration*, by which ♦ *Anglicanism* was re-established in England: unjustly attributed to Clarendon, who opposed it as shortsightedly repressive. The ♦ *Savoy Conference* having failed to produce a workable compromise between Anglicans and Independents, four Acts of Parliament were passed. CORPORATION ACT 1661: Required local government officials to take ♦ *Holy Communion* by Anglican rites and to abjure ♦ *Presbyterianism*. ACT OF UNIFORMITY 1662: Required all ministers to use the Anglican ♦ *Prayer Book* and subscribe to its tenets (thus causing the ejection of 2000 divines). CONVENTICLE ACT 1664: Prohibited more than five persons from meeting for non-Anglican worship. FIVE-MILE ACT 1665: Prohibited every non-Anglican preacher and teacher from being at any time within five miles of any corporate town and of any place where he had ever preached or taught. ♦ *Nonconformists, Test Act, Uniformity*.

Claret ♦ *Wine*.

Clarinet. Woodwind instrument, with a single reed and body normally of wood, in use since about 1750. The B♭ and A clarinets are the standard orchestral sizes, with a range of 3½ octaves from C♯ or D below middle C. Other clarinets are the high E♭ clarinet and the bass clarinet, an octave below the standard B♭.

Class. In the sense of social stratification, class depends upon birth, occupation, education, and wealth. In early civilizations class derived chiefly from birth or occupation and class barriers were very rigid. With the growth of trade and the spread of wealth, class came to depend also upon other criteria. Class-consciousness varies from country to country. In new countries where mobility between occupations and changes in fortune are frequent, class consciousness is reduced. In the U.S.A. the concept of 'income bracket' largely replaces that of 'class'. The result of increased equality of educational and economic opportunity, however, has not been a classless society, either in the capitalist or in the communist world. In the United Kingdom, using occupation as the best single criterion, the Census of 1951 distinguished five social classes:

Social Class	% of occupied males England and Wales 1951
Higher professional and managerial	3
Lower professional and managerial	15
Skilled manual, supervisory and routine clerical	53
Partly skilled	16
Unskilled	13

Classical Education. Studies centred on ancient Greek and Latin literature (and occasionally Sanskrit, Pali, Hebrew, etc.), until recently considered to have a unique value in training and disciplining the mind. ♦ *Grammar School, Public School*. CLASSICS: Greek and Latin literature, also any literature of acknowledged merit which has survived the age in which it was written.

Classicism. The practice of seeking standards in art and letters among the great works of the past, esp. in the literature and art of Greece and Rome; at its best, it leads to simplicity, elegance, and economy of means, but those who find in the past not standards but models risk becoming mere genteel copyists.

In architecture, 'classicism' refers to the style evolved in ancient Greece (of which the Parthenon is the most perfect expression) and later transmitted to Rome, and to revivals of this style in later times. It was the remains of Roman architecture rediscovered and studied during the ♦ *Renaissance* that inspired the 15th and 16th cent. neoclassical Italianate style, which emphasized harmony of proportions and the unbroken horizontal, and made use of the classical ♦ *architectural orders*. From then until the 20th cent. classicism (with its near-antithesis ♦ *Gothic*) was a main stream in European architecture, whether as Palladian, Georgian, Regency, Greek Revival, or 19th cent. Italianate.

In music, 'classicism' applies particularly to the works of Haydn, Mozart, and their age, implying such characteristics as compact form, regularity of rhythm, moderation in musical resources used, and avoidance of excessive emotionalism.

In painting and sculpture, 'classicism' aspires to an ideal beauty in human form, and makes no attempt to portray individual men and women.

In literature, 'classicism' at its narrowest meant rigid adherence to a set of 'rules' and 'unities' (see below) established from the works of the classical Greek and Roman authors, esp. Aristotle's *Poetics*; in a wider sense, it means application of the classical virtues of clarity and economy in expression and elegance and urbanity in manner. In England, Ben Jonson's 'classical' plays perhaps rank among instances of over-conscious imitative classicism, but in his odes and other short poems he (and some of his followers) attained a true classicism, in the tradition of English ◊ *humanism*. In 17th-cent. France the greatest classical critic was Boileau, and the elevated and lucid manner of Racine, Molière, and La Fontaine is the supreme achievement of French classicism. In England, the diverse strength of neoclassicism at its best is represented by Pope, Hume, Johnson, and Gibbon. In 18th-cent. Germany also, Lessing and Winckelmann advocated classical principles in art. The tendency towards decorum and narrow virtuosity, at the expense of spontaneous and affirmative impulses, however, provoked a reaction which eventually ushered in the Romantic Revival (◊ *Romanticism*). In the past 100 years, such diverse writers as Arnold, Yeats, Valéry, Pound, and Eliot have again appealed to classical models and standards, in protest against an exhausted romanticism. A similar process may be detected in music and architecture.

UNITIES: Unity of action, unity of time, unity of place; ideal aims developed by inference from various passages in Aristotle's *Poetics*, by Italian Renaissance critics esp. Scaliger and 17th-cent. French critics and dramatists esp. Racine. Only the unity of action (organic coherence and logical connexion) has much warrant in Aristotle. The unity of time meant that a

drama's action should occur within the time taken by the stage presentation, but this was often stretched to mean 24 hours, while the unity of place meant restriction normally to one scene, or sometimes to one house or one town. This conception dominated French neoclassical drama, the first great example being Corneille's *Le Cid*; but apart from e.g. Jonson's *The Alchemist* 1610 or Addison's *Cato* 1713, it had little influence in England. Dryden's Crites, in *An Essay of Dramatic Poetry* 1668, defends the unities, but the unity of time and the unity of place were cheerfully demolished by Farquhar in the *Discourse upon Comedy* 1702, and magisterially so by Johnson in *The Rambler* 1751 and the *Preface to Shakespeare* 1765.

Classification (biology) ◊ *Biological Classification.*

Clavichord ◊ *Keyboard Instruments.*

Clay. Fine-grained impermeable sedimentary rock formed by the deposit in a sea of tiny flakes of mud; largely aluminium silicates, but usually with other minerals and organic matter. As the clays become hardened and consolidated they form shales; both clay and shale have little resistance to erosion, and usually floor valleys and lowlands.

Cleavage. Splitting along certain definite planes, rather than breaking haphazard; a property of many crystalline minerals, owing to the arrangement of the atoms of the crystals, and of other rocks e.g. slate, ◊ *mica*, which split into thin sheets not from the rock's inherent formation but as the result of the intense stratifying pressure of other rocks.

Clerestory. Clear-storey; a range of windows in the upper part of a building, admitting light from over adjacent roofs, a feature of basilican churches taken over and adapted by ◊ *Romanesque* and ◊ *Gothic architecture.*

Climate. Weather over the whole year in a given place or region; < Gr. *klima*, a slope, probably referring to the varying angles at which the sun's rays strike the earth. Depends much on latitude. At the equator sunshine is considerable throughout the year and temperatures are high; as distance from the equator increases, the sun's rays become more oblique and weaker: in polar regions they are very oblique even in summer, and the sun disappears completely for part of the long winter, temperatures are always low and snow and rain light. In middle latitudes climate is maritime-temperate near the sea and cold-continental inland. Climate depends also on altitude (air temperature decreases with height, on average about 1° F per 300 ft) and on position relative to ocean and land masses, proximity to the sea being often very influential. Certain world zones are generally recognized, and though geographers do not all use the same terminology, the following are commonly met.

CONTINENTAL CLIMATE: That found in middle latitudes to the east side of continents or well inland, with prevailing winds from the land. Here there are hot summers, cold winters and moderate rainfall.

MARITIME CLIMATE: This is also found in middle latitudes on the west side of continents, where prevailing winds are from the ocean, which is warmer than the land in winter and cooler in summer. Such regions have mild winters, cool summers, and plentiful rainfall.

MEDITERRANEAN ZONE: Found on the west side of land masses, with hot dry summers and mild moist winters.

EQUATORIAL ZONE: A belt of tropical rain forests with high humidity and temperature.

MONSOON ZONE: On the east side of land masses, esp. in Asia, with pronounced wet and dry seasons.

Clipper. An extremely fine-lined sailing vessel built for speed, designed in the 19th cent. and the fastest type of sailing cargo-vessel ever built. The first British clipper was the *Reindeer*, built 1848 by Alexander Hall of Aberdeen, which set a pattern ultimately perfected in the *Thermopylae* and the *Cutty Sark*. Many fine clipper ships were built both in Britain and America during the second half of the 19th cent. and mainly employed in the China tea trade, U.S.A. east coast to California, and the Australia trade, in which the *Marco Polo* completed a round trip in 5 months 21 days, beating the steamer *Australia* by a clear week on both the outward and the homeward passages. The record day's run by a sailing vessel is 465 m. by the clipper *Champion of the Seas* averaging over 19 knots. In the 1860s, as steamships developed, the clipper gradually fell out of use.

Clocks and Watches. Water clocks and ◊ *sundials* existed from about 1300 B.C.

but the first weight-driven mechanical clocks were not invented until the 13th cent. in central Europe. One of the earliest still surviving is that at Salisbury Cathedral, 1386. When spring drive was applied to clocks, about 1450, they could be made of portable size. Christian Huygens 1629–95 made the first pendulum clock, 1656; John Harrison 1693–1776 produced the first dependable ship's ◊ *chronometer* about 1760. Towards the end of the 17th cent. the introduction of the balance-wheel and the hair-spring made watches more reliable. Domestic clock-making became firmly established in the late 17th and the 18th centuries, and clocks of great beauty and superb workmanship were constructed by Tompion 1639–1713, Ellicott 1706–72, Vulliamy 1780–1854, and many others. In the Victorian era, with mass production, the clock became a universal household article. Electric clocks next appeared, the earliest examples being electromagnetic; they are now usually driven by a synchronous motor, but transistor-battery clocks and watches have been produced. In scientific time-measurement the latest development is the caesium ◊ *atomic clock*, working to an accuracy of one part in 3×10^{10} (equivalent to an error of 1 sec. per 1000 years). ◊ *Time.*

Cloisonné ◊ *Enamel.*

Cloud. Mass of small water-drops or ice-

1. cirrostratus 2. cirrocumulus 3. cirrus 4. cumulonimbus (thunder cloud) 5. altostratus 6. altocumulus 7. nimbostratus 8. cumulus 9. stratocumulus 10. stratus

crystals, formed by the condensation of water vapour in the atmosphere. Almost invariably the cooling which causes condensation is brought about by upward air movement, so that clouds form at some height above the earth's surface. In meteorological classification there are 10 principal classes of cloud, usually grouped in three categories: (a) low, up to 10,000 ft; (b) medium, between 10,000 and 25,000 ft; (c) high, between 25,000 and 35,000 ft. Clouds assume a great variety of shapes, two predominant types being cumulus or 'heap' clouds, and stratus or 'layer' clouds; cirrus are fleecy clouds occurring at great height. ⟡ *Rain, Weather*.

Clover. A pasture plant of the genus *Trifolium*, one of the ⟡ *legumes*, with high protein and mineral content and valuable in stock feeding; the roots act as hosts to the micro-organism *Rhizobium*, which forms nodules on the roots and fixes atmospheric nitrogen, supplying the host plant and the surrounding soil with the excess nitrates formed. Unlike other plants, all legumes replenish the soil with nitrates and are thus valuable in ⟡ *crop rotation*. ⟡ *Nitrogen Cycle*.

Cloves. A ⟡ *spice* consisting of the dried flower-buds of *Eugenia aromatica*, a small tree native in Malaysia. Following the trade routes it spread gradually through Asia to the Mediterranean and was much valued in Europe in the 17th and 18th centuries. Most of the supplies now come from ⟡ *Zanzibar*. The oil can be used to alleviate toothache.

Clytaemnestra ⟡ *Agamemnon, Cassandra, Helen, Orestes*.

Coal and Coal-mining. Coal has been formed in stages, by the decay and then compression of residue from primeval forests: vegetable matter > peat > lignite > coal > anthracite. Less than 59 per cent carbon, lignite range; over 90 per cent carbon, anthracite range; between these, various grades of bituminous coal. Widely distributed, but relatively scarce in Africa, S. America, and Oceania; about one third of the world's output comes from U.S.A. In Britain the main coalfields are Yorkshire, Nottinghamshire, N. Derbyshire, Durham, Lancashire, Northumberland, S. Wales, and Lanarkshire (Scotland); most of the deposits are well below ground, but some opencast coal has been profitably worked. In modern practice, the coal seam is undercut with mechanical cutters and then either an explosive charge or a hydraulic ram is used to shatter the coal above; the broken pieces are screened and cleaned. Destructive distillation gives four main products: coke; coal tar; an aqueous distillate containing ammonia; gas. Low-temperature carbonization produces useful fuels of the 'Coalite' type. The British coal industry was nationalized and the National Coal Board set up in 1946. Coal now has to meet fierce competition from the rapidly expanding ⟡ *petroleum* industry, not only as an alternative fuel but also from by-products which formerly came only from coal.

Coal was mined in Britain in Roman times; from the reign of Elizabeth I coal-mining grew steadily, and by the 18th cent. it was a well-established industry. In 1770 Britain produced about six million tons; 100 years later, output was 10 times higher. A peak of 227 m. tons was reached in 1938. Leading world producers of coal (in round figures of m. tons) are: U.S.A. 440; U.S.S.R. 330; U.K. 220; W. Germany 120; Poland 90; France 70. ⟡ *Coal Measures, Gas Industry, Geological Time Scale, Mines and Mining*.

Coal Measures. Uppermost series of ⟡ *Carboniferous System* (name first used 1815, by William Smith, the 'father of geology'); consist chiefly of shales and sandstones, in which are bands of iron ore and fireclay as well as seams of coal. The shales and sands are the seat earths in which the coal-forming rushes, ferns, and trees grew in hot and swampy conditions not unlike those of the Ganges delta today. The decaying vegetation, slowly turning into ⟡ *peat*, was repeatedly buried under thick masses of mud or sand when the area subsided; any long halt in the general sinking of the land would allow much accumulation of peat and the creation of a thick coal seam, but in a total thickness of 10,000 ft there may be as little as 100 ft of coal, separated into 40 different thin seams. ⟡ *Fuel, Lignite, Oil Shales*.

Coal Tar. A major raw material obtained by the destructive ⟡ *distillation* of coal. It is a by-product of the coal-gas industry and contains many aromatic compounds e.g. ⟡ *benzene*, toluene, xylenes, and ⟡ *naphthalene*; also a number of ⟡ *phenols*. Its many uses include insulating, pipe-coating, roofing, waterproofing, road-making. From it are manufactured disinfectants, drugs, ⟡ *dyes*, ⟡ *explosives*, pesticides: but the petrochemical industry by producing by-products of similar properties has lessened its importance as a raw material. ⟡ *Cancer, Carcinogens*.

Cobalt. A grey metallic element, not very abundant, occurring chiefly as smaltite and used in corrosion-resistant and other special steels (⟡ *Iron and Steel Industry*) and for the manufacture of permanent magnets. Many of its compounds are used as pigments for paint and others for colour in porcelain and other ceramics; in agriculture it is an important ⟡ *trace element*.

Cobra. ⟡ *Snake* of the family *Elapidae*, which contains many other highly poisonous snakes, most of which are slender and swift e.g. the ⟡ *mamba*; their venom is a very fast-acting respiratory poison, ejected through the hollow fangs at the front of the upper jaw. Some cobras can spit venom several feet. There are two genera, to one of which, Naja, belongs the king-cobra or hamadryad, up to 18 ft long. ⟡ *Sea-snake*.

Cocaine. ⟡ *Alkaloid* obtained from the dried leaves of *Erythroxylum*, a shrub cultivated in Bolivia, Peru, and Java. It has been used as a local anaesthetic, particularly in dentistry, and as a surface anaesthetic for eye surgery. Nowadays it is seldom given internally, because of its high toxicity and habit-forming tendencies. Its use was discovered from the American Indians, who for centuries have chewed the leaves to alleviate the effects of fatigue and hunger; a majority of Bolivian and Peruvian Indians are addicted to the habit.

Cochineal. A natural red ⟡ *dye*-stuff obtained from the dried bodies of the females of the insect *Coccus cacti*, which lives on a cactus native to Mexico. Cochineal was formerly used for dyeing wool and silk and is still used as a colouring agent in cookery.

Cockatoo ⟡ *Parrot*.

Cockcroft-Walton Generator. Type of ⟡ *particle accelerator* named after Sir John Cockcroft and Ernest Walton, who developed and used it to accelerate ⟡ *protons* during their work on the transmutation of ⟡ *elements*. It is essentially a voltage-multiplying circuit in which a series of condensers are charged to a very high potential (up to about half a million volts) to accelerate the particles.

Cock-Fighting. A blood-sport popular in the East and in Latin America and still sometimes practised illegally in Europe; specially-reared cocks are fitted with sharp steel spurs and matched in a fight to the death.

Cockles ⟡ *Molluscs*.

Cockroach ⟡ *Insects*.

Cocoa. Product of *Theobroma cacao*, a small tree originally found in restricted areas of tropical America. It flowers directly from the trunk and branches, and has podlike fruits containing 40–60 seeds (cocoa beans). The ripe seeds are slightly fermented, dried, roasted, and ground to an oily paste (raw or bitter chocolate). Chocolate was known as a beverage to the ⟡ *Aztecs* and introduced to Europe in 1526 by the Spaniards, who kept the secret for a century. When it became generally known in the 17th cent. chocolate houses became popular in England and France. It was not until the 19th cent. that eating chocolate and powdered cocoa were developed. In modern practice the two products are interdependent: to make cocoa powder about half of the cocoa butter in raw chocolate has to be extracted; to make chocolate some cocoa butter has to be added to balance the sugar. Cocoa butter is also used in cosmetics and medicines. Cocoa is produced in Africa (Ghana and Nigeria) and Brazil, to a yearly total of about 1 m. tons. Chief importers are U.S.A. and W. Europe.

Coconut. Palm of great economic importance, up to 100 ft tall. Originating in the East, and originally dispersed by its floating fruits, it is now widely distributed in favourable tropical areas esp. near the sea. The 'coconut' is really a stone fruit (like plums or almonds). The outer fibrous husk gives coir used for matting, ropes, etc. and the hard shell makes high-grade ⟡ *charcoal*. The white meat (⟡ *endosperm*) contains about 50 per cent of oil and the central cavity a milky fluid. Coconut oil, usually pressed out of dried coconut meat (copra), is used in margarine, cosmetics, and soap, and the residue (cake) as cattle food. The milk, esp. of unripe nuts, is rich in ⟡ *vitamins* and minerals. The leaves are used for thatching, baskets, mats, etc. and the ribs and stalks for posts and canes. The terminal bud is eaten. Toddy is the sweet sap exuding from cut inflorescence-stalks.

Cocoon ◊ *Pupa.*

Cod. A marine fish often growing five ft long and weighing 50 lb. A voracious eater of other fish, it is itself one of the most important food fish, abounding in the N. Atlantic, where about 500 m. are caught each year. The liver yields a valuable medicinal oil rich in vitamin A.

Code. System of signs or signals used for letters, words, or phrases to secure brevity and sometimes secrecy and economy (in commercial codes).

MORSE CODE: Consists of patterns of dots, dashes, and spaces, each representing a letter or a figure; long and short flashes are substituted in lamp signalling. It was invented by Samuel F. B. Morse 1791–1872, an American electrician.

SEMAPHORE: Uses seven radial positions of human or mechanical arms to denote letters and numerals, a simple method of visual signalling devised 1794 by Chappe, a Frenchman. By means of repeater stations, it was used to relay messages rapidly overland, until the invention of the electric telegraph; it is still used at sea, mainly by the navy, though largely replaced by Morse. ◊ *Cipher.*

Codeine ◊ *Opium, Poppy.*

Code Napoléon (Code Civil). 1804. Revision of the French penal code, begun under the *ancien régime*, finally published by Napoleon, who had acted as chairman of the meetings of the Council of State at which it was discussed, though he took little part in the actual formulation of the code. A skilful combination of old French law with Revolutionary law, it was used as a model in many countries in the 19th cent. including Egypt and Japan.

Coeducation. Teaching both sexes together in the same school or college; comparatively new (except at primary level). Until about 100 years ago few girls went on to secondary schools and none to universities, but now most universities and professions are open to both sexes; it is argued that there is no more sense in having separate schools at secondary level than at primary, and that since men and women live and work together they should learn together. Against this it is urged that mixed schools encourage a precocious interest in sex at adolescence and that at this stage the rates of maturation of boys and of girls are so different that they should be separated, and that this caters more adequately for their different social

and vocational needs. In all communist countries, in the older Dominions, and in U.S.A. most schools are coeducational, Britain has both coeducational and single-sex schools, in Roman Catholic countries secondary schools are usually single-sex, and in Muslim countries social feeling is strongly opposed to coeducation and admits it at universities only reluctantly.

Coelacanth. Survivor of an otherwise extinct group of fish found as fossils in rocks of the Devonian period 300 m. years ago (◊ *Geological Time Scale*); one of these, Latimeria, was caught in very deep water off Madagascar 1952, and palaeontologists' forecasts, based on fossils, of the structure of their soft parts were largely confirmed. The coelacanth is closely related to present-day lung-fish and to the ancestors of all terrestrial vertebrate animals.

Coffee. Several species of *Coffea*, of the *Rubiaceae*; an evergreen shrub or small tree which produces fruit resembling cherries, the dried seeds of which are known as coffee beans. Coffee grows wild in the highlands of Africa, and the most widely cultivated variety, *C. arabica*, was probably introduced from Abyssinia into the Arabian peninsula about A.D. 1500. Coffee drinking became prevalent amongst the Arabians and soon spread to Europe, where coffee houses became popular in the 17th cent. The Dutch tried to establish coffee plantations in Ceylon and the Dutch Indies. It was introduced into the Caribbean about 1720; and it was from this area that coffee was introduced into Brazil, where soil and climatic conditions proved to be ideal for its cultivation and which with some three billion coffee trees remains by far the largest producer, although its share of world production, once as high as 70 per cent, is now below 50 per cent. Colombia is an important producer of high-grade coffee, and plantations are increasing rapidly in Africa. World production has risen as high as 7000 m. lb. in a single year. Yields fluctuate and there is recurrent over-production. Attempts have been made to establish an international coffee organization to control output. The U.S.A. turned to coffee drinking after the ◊ *Boston Tea Party* and is by far the greatest consumer of coffee in the world.

Coffer Dam. A wall enclosing part of the bed of a river to create an area which can be kept dry by pumping so that construction work can be done. The commonest method is to drive interlocking piles, usually of steel, into the river bed. Records of the use of timber piles for this purpose go back about four centuries. In the construction of the Kariba ◊ *dam* concrete coffer dams were used. ◊◊ *Caisson*.

Cognac ◊ *Brandy*.

Coke. By-product of the ◊ *gas industry*; up to 90 per cent carbon; it burns smokelessly at intense heat and is usually used in blast furnaces and closed stoves. It bears the same relation to coal as ◊ *charcoal* does to wood. ◊◊ *Ammonia, Coal Tar*.

Cola (Kola). *Cola acuminata*; a tropical African tree producing nuts of high caffeine content. Their use as a stimulant to appease hunger and stave off fatigue parallels the chewing of coca leaves in S. America (◊ *Cocaine*).

Coleoptera ◊ *Beetle*.

Collage. A picture made partly or wholly from pieces of paper, cloth, or other material stuck to the canvas or panel. The practitioners of ◊ *Cubism* (Braque, Picasso) made the first collages by incorporating pieces of newspaper in their oil-paintings. Collages of cut paper were later produced by many painters, notably Hans Arp and (in his last years) Matisse.

Collagen ◊ *Tannins*.

Collective Unconscious. In Jung's analytical psychology, the part of the ◊ *unconscious mind* which contains the inherited experiences of the human species, and which each member of the species shares with other members; the inherited contents are considered to be not actual memories but predispositions, based on the past history of the race, which influence the individual to deal with life in typically human ways. Among the contents of the collective unconscious are the 'archetypes', ideas or images common to the human race e.g. fear of the dark.

Collectivization of Agriculture. The amalgamation of small-holdings into large units, collectively owned and worked, a process fostered by communist states. In Russia the peasants who became smallholders on the expulsion of the landowners in the 1917 Revolution resisted collectivization; after the disastrous decrease in production and opposition which the policy engendered, Lenin suspended the programme. In the late 1920s Stalin ruthlessly imposed collectivization, which involved the death or deportation not only of the rich peasants (kulaks) but of perhaps 2 m. peasants. Agricultural production has remained the weakest element in the Soviet economy. In most communist-bloc countries collectivization has been persistently resisted and not completely carried out; in Poland it has been abandoned.

College. Institution of higher education, sometimes giving training in one particular sphere e.g. agriculture, teacher training, sometimes offering a wide variety of courses e.g. within universities. Exceptionally, a secondary school e.g. Eton College (◊ *Public School*) or a technical school.

COLLEGE OF ADVANCED TECHNOLOGY: Specializes in technical courses closely related to the needs of industry, at university-degree standard; directly financed by the Ministry of Education.

UNIVERSITY COLLEGE: Of university level but without a Royal Charter empowering it to grant degrees, and thus able to award diplomas only, but often federated into a university for degree-examination purposes.

Collotype. A planographic (flat-surface) printing process suitable for very accurate reproduction, e.g. of drawings and paintings. Printing is carried out from glass plates coated with gelatin in two colours, to which the image is transferred by a photo-mechanical process. The process depends on the hardening of gelatin on exposure to light, and ink is accepted by the plate in proportion with exposure, thus making possible exceedingly fine gradations of tone. The disadvantage of the process is the limited number of reproductions possible from a single plate.

Colombia. Area 461,606 sq. m. Pop. 15.1 m. Cap. Bogotá. Rel. Roman Catholic. A republic in the NW of S. America, with both Atlantic and Pacific coastlines. Legislative power is normally vested in a Congress of two houses, a Senate of 80 members and a House of Representatives of 152, elected for four and two years respectively. In 1953, however, when the dictatorship of President Gómez was finally displaced, the Congress was suspended in favour of a National Constituent and Legislative Assembly. The president is normally elected by direct popular vote for a term of four years and is not eligible for successive terms. The present President is Guillermo-Leon Valencia, elected 1962.

ECONOMY. Colombia is the world's second largest producer of coffee, which accounts for some 85 per cent of its exports. It has also considerable reserves of gold, silver, platinum (the largest deposit in the world), copper, coal, and petroleum. Of the foreign investment in the oil industry, American companies control 85 per cent and British companies about 15 per cent.

HISTORY. Discovered by Columbus in 1502 and conquered by Spain in 1536, Colombia remained under Spanish rule until the 1811–24 revolt of the Spanish-American colonies under Simon Bolivar, who in 1829 established a republic consisting of the territories which now are Colombia, Ecuador, Panama, and Venezuela. Ecuador and Venezuela seceded at once, and the remainder became New Granada, adopting the name Colombia in 1863; Panama seceded in 1903.

LANGUAGE. Spanish, and some Indian dialects.

Colombo Plan. 1950. Project for co-operative economic development in S. and SE Asia, devised at a conference in Ceylon by the ◊ *British Commonwealth* Foreign Ministers to provide a framework for the development programmes of the Asian member countries, i.e. India, Pakistan, Ceylon, Burma, Nepal, Thailand, Viet-Nam, Laos, Cambodia, the Philippines, Malaya, Singapore, Indonesia, and Borneo. A Council for Technical Cooperation, with headquarters at Colombo, was set up to plan public administration and organize health services, scientific research, etc. ◊ *International Bank for Reconstruction and Development, Point-Four Programmes.*

Colonial Office. British government department, in existence since 1854, supervising the affairs of colonial territories, the administration of which is usually conducted through governors and local governments, assisted by officers of the colonial service; now a rapidly contracting department, since on becoming independent such territories come within the competence of the ◊ *Commonwealth Relations Office.*

Colorado Beetle. Order *Coleoptera*; small beetle of bright metallic appearance, of N. American origin. It changed from its natural food to the leaves of the potato, became a serious agricultural pest, was accidentally introduced into Europe 1922, and has sporadically appeared in Britain, where it has so far been successfully controlled. Its striking wing-covers with ten black stripes gave it its zoological name, *Leptinotarsa decemlineata.*

Colour. The sensations produced on the ◊ *eye* by light rays, i.e. a limited range of rays from those which make up the whole electromagnetic spectrum of ◊ *radiation* between ◊ *infrared* and ◊ *ultraviolet.* ◊ *Spectrum, Vision.*

Colour-blindness. Congenital defect characterized by abnormal perception of any one of the three colours red, green, blue, or blindness to any one of them; or inability to distinguish any colours so that everything appears grey.

Columbine. Common name of the wild aquilegia, *A. vulgaris,* a native of Europe, from the supposed resemblance of the flower to a cluster of doves (Lat. *columba*). Columbines grow in most parts of the N. hemisphere and vary in height from a few inches to two or three ft, the latter being meadow and woodland plants. The popular long-spurred hybrids have been developed from several wild species from N. America.

Columbite, Columbium ◊ *Niobium, Tantalum.*

Coma. 1. State of unconsciousness from which the sufferer cannot be aroused. It may be caused by injury to the brain e.g. concussion, cerebral haemorrhage, meningitis, and encephalitis, by constitutional diseases e.g. diabetes, by heatstroke, and by many kinds of poison.
2. ◊ *Comet.*

Combination Acts. Several Acts of Parliament to prohibit the activities and formation of trades unions passed in 1799 and 1800 under the impact of war and fear of subversive political activities encouraged by the French Revolution; they were not repealed until 1824. In practice they were little used, since the ◊ *common law* against conspiracy in restraint of trade was a handy and more severe weapon. ◊ *Tolpuddle Martyrs.*

Comecon. Council for Mutual Economic Assistance. Formed in 1949 by Albania, Bulgaria, Czechoslovakia, the German Democratic Republic, Hungary, Poland, Rumania, and the U.S.S.R. as a counterpart of the economic organization of the Western European countries set up to administer the ◊ *Marshall Plan*. Its aim is to rationalize and coordinate production, research, and planning in the member countries. Its effectiveness has not been notably demonstrated.

Comédie Française (Théâtre Français). One of the foremost theatre companies in the world, founded in Paris in 1680, when it incorporated many of Molière's actors, and originally known as La Maison de Molière; later it was called the *Comédie Française* to distinguish it from the *Comédie Italienne*. It was made the state theatre of France by Napoleon in 1803. Today it consists of two theatres with a permanent company of artists; the most senior (*sociétaires*) receive pensions on retirement. The Comédie is subject to occasional purges and upheavals, but it represents a virtually unbroken line to the past. It is fully State-financed.

Comedy. As now used, the term cannot be limited to plays which are light and humorous in character; rather, it applies to works less boisterous than farce, less exalted than tragedy, and generally more realistic than both, since its starting-point is the actuality of life, however it may distort that actuality. It has included political satire (Aristophanes, Capek), moral satire (Ben Jonson), social comedy (Molière, Shaw), comedy of manners (Terence, Congreve, Wilde), and many other forms more difficult to label. Its view of human conduct varies from genial irony (Molière, Shakespeare's *Twelfth Night*) to bitter cynicism (Shakespeare's *Troilus and Cressida*, Jonson, Dürrenmatt). Comedy may also be regarded as including the work of such novelists as Fielding, Jane Austen, Balzac (*La Comédie Humaine*), and Dickens. ◊ *Drama, Farce.*

Comet. Celestial body consisting of a starlike head (nucleus), a surrounding haze (coma), and usually a tail. The head is believed to be relatively solid and composed of meteoric material, together with ice, frozen methane, and ammonia. The coma consists of gases liberated from the head and made up of simple molecules, involving hydrogen, carbon, nitrogen, and oxygen. At a distance from the sun the coma appears diffuse but has no tail. As it approaches the sun it becomes hotter, more gases are liberated, and the

coma grows. Pressure of sunlight forces some of these gases away to form the tail. About a dozen comets are seen each year, perhaps half being predicted. Comets are now believed to belong to the solar system and it is thought that there may be great numbers in the space between the sun and points half-way to the nearest stars. Some comets have very elongated elliptical orbits around the sun and periodically reappear; others move in parabolas or hyperbolas and having once been seen disappear forever into space. Halley's Comet is the most spectacular of those that periodically come close to earth. Halley observed it in 1682, identified it with earlier appearances of a great comet, and correctly predicted its next return. This comet is now known to have appeared in 1066, and is shown on the ◊ *Bayeux Tapestry*. It was last seen in 1910 (with a 37-million-mile tail) and is due again in 1986.

Cominform, Comintern ◊ *Internationals.*

Commando. Originally a raiding party used by the Boers in the Boer War; the name was adopted in the Second World War for mobile highly-trained raiding units raised from the Royal Marines and Army. Commandos fought in the Dieppe raid, the Normandy landing, the Rhine crossing, etc. Four Brigades, each of four Commandos, existed in June 1944.

Commedia dell'Arte. An improvised and stylized theatrical entertainment practised by Italian comedians in the 16th and 17th centuries, the cast limited to a set of stock characters inc. Punch, Pantaloon, Columbine, Scaramouche, and Harlequin; each member of a troupe, distinctively masked and costumed, specialized in one of these, the author providing a scenario from which the players improvised dialogue and action. The *commedia dell'arte* was seen widely in Europe, influencing the French classical comedy of Molière and Marivaux as well as dramatists like Lope de Vega. The conventions and characters survive in debased form in the harlequinade which traditionally rounded off the British pantomime at Christmas and in the Punch-and-Judy show.

COMMEDIA ERUDITA: Written comedies, like Machiavelli's *Mandragola*, as distinct from improvised ones.

Commodity Agreements. International trade agreements to regulate the production and the marketing of raw materials and foodstuffs; usually sponsored by the governments of the producer countries, but frequently including government representatives of the main importing countries too. Their object is to ensure stable and remunerative prices for producers by restricting production and regulating marketing by agreed prices or quotas. Commodity agreements have operated for rubber, tin, wheat, tea, and sugar. Prices of primary products have tended to fall in the 20th cent. in relation to the cost of manufactured goods, to the disadvantage of many underdeveloped countries. ◊ *Terms of Trade*.

Common Cold. Infection due to some agent which has the properties of a virus, of which so far no identifiable culture has been isolated. Research into the cause of the common cold has been carried out intensively at the Research Institute at Salisbury. The incubation period is about three days; resistance to colds lasts for about three months after recovery. The value of prophylactic inoculation is dubious. The increased incidence of colds in winter appears to be due more to overcrowding and indoor living than to wintry conditions; susceptibility of certain persons to colds generally reflects an allergic tendency. There is no specific treatment. Although normally a mild complaint, the common cold can be lethal to isolated communities e.g. primitive tribes not conditioned by previous exposure to infection.

Common Law. The term was first used in the 13th cent. when from the various local customs the king's travelling justices formulated a body of law common to the whole kingdom; it now describes (a) the law of England, and those systems descended from it, based upon precedent, as against other legal systems; (b) rules arising from precedent, as against those prescribed by statute; (c) rules developed in the Courts of Queen's Bench, Common Pleas, and Exchequer, as opposed to equity.

Common Market ◊ *European Economic Community*.

Common Salt ◊ *Chlorine, Salt (1), Sodium*.

Common Sense. The 'philosophy of common sense' was the doctrine of a group of 18th- and early 19th-cent. Scottish thinkers, led by Thomas Reid, who opposed the claim (◊ *Idealism, Phenomenalism*) that ordinary sense-experience is not of

material objects but of subjective impressions 'in the mind'.

Commonwealth and Protectorate. 1649–60. The Interregnum between the ◊ *English Civil Wars* and the ◊ *Restoration*. The Commonwealth was the Parliamentary republic of 1649–53, during which the 'Rump' Parliament (consisting of the purged House of Commons only) legislated under a State Council headed by Oliver Cromwell as Protector (styled His Excellency). The Protectorate dates from Cromwell's dismissal of the 'Rump' and his becoming Lord Protector. He nominated a ◊ *Puritan* House of Commons, called the Parliament of Saints; he was disgusted by their conduct, and they voluntarily resigned all power to him in 1655. He then ruled only through the State and Army Councils in 12 regions each governed by a Major-General. Though the promotion of men of merit irrespective of social status improved local government, the abrogation of Parliament (which the wars had been fought to preserve) was deeply resented. After an attempt on Cromwell's life in 1656 the Councils offered him the crown: he refused, but agreed to be Lord Protector for life, with the power to nominate his successor. When his son succeeded him in 1658, the Councils rebelled and recalled the 'Rump' Parliament; the nation, however, esp. London, demanded a free Parliament, and the State Council summoned General Monk from Scotland to restore order. When he arrived, Monk was secretly prevailed on to negotiate for the return of Charles II; within five weeks the ◊ *Restoration* was effected.

Though commonly associated with gloom and oppression, the Interregnum was in fact a period of prosperity and success, during which trade was considerably expanded and England's prestige restored almost to Elizabethan heights. Music and the sciences flourished. Cromwell's Court at Whitehall was not dismal but gay without being licentious. ◊ *Levellers*.

Commonwealth Institute. Founded 1887 as the Imperial Institute; now houses permanent ◊ *British Commonwealth* exhibitions, shows films, arranges lectures, and provides study facilities for Commonwealth students.

Commonwealth Relations Office. U.K. government department created 1947 in place of the Dominions Office when India and Pakistan became independent. It conducts diplomatic relations with the independent members of the British Commonwealth, and its sphere of responsibility has gradually increased. The department is headed by a Secretary of State.

Commune. Medievally, a town having a charter of liberties granted by its feudal overlord, governed by an elected council of magistrates, who were usually prominent in the craft guilds and corporations. In Italy the ◊ *Lombard League* was an aggregation of independent communes. In Germany many communes became free cities subject only to the Emperor, and in the Netherlands the communes very early enjoyed extensive privileges. Toulouse in France and Barcelona in Spain were outstanding examples of local self-government. In England the charter cities and boroughs corresponded to the communes, esp. the Corporation of the City of London; the attempt of James II to cancel all the charters and abolish local self-government was an important factor in his deposition (◊ *Glorious Revolution*). In France since 1792 the commune has been a unit of local government roughly corresponding to the English urban district council; strictly it was the commune of Montmartre, outside Paris proper, which began the ◊ *Paris Commune* rebellion.

Communism. Theory that property (other than personal chattels) should be held in common and that all labour should be applied for the joint benefit of the whole community; Plato's *Republic* may be said to have a strong communist element. More specifically, ◊ *marxism* as interpreted by Lenin and other theoreticians. Marx himself at first used the word interchangeably with Robert Owen's 'socialism' but later he distinguished socialism as a necessary stage on the way to communism, the ultimate classless society. Rousseau and Babeuf in the late 18th cent. had attacked private-property systems (◊ *Capitalism*); opponents of the society which was emerging as a result of the ◊ *Industrial Revolution* (e.g. Saint-Simon, Shelley) turned to utopian and anarchic ◊ *idealism*, and many short-lived 'communalist' societies were set up e.g. by Proudhon, Louis Blanc, and Blanqui in France, by Feargus O'Connor (◊ *Chartism*) in England, and

by Robert Owen in the U.K. and U.S.A. The *Communist Manifesto* of Marx and Engels 1848 put forward vividly expressed new ideas which led to the formation of the International Working Men's Association (the First International) and dominated the 19th-cent. syndicalist-socialist-communist movements, arousing vehement protracted controversies e.g. with Kautsky, Bernstein, etc. which resulted in the formation of the anti-marxist Second International of moderate social-democratic 'reformist' parties. Modern communism dates from the 1903 London conference of the Russian Social Democratic Party, when the Bolsheviki (i.e. majority), advocating immediate violent revolution, split from the gradualist Mensheviki (i.e. minority). With the 1917 victory of the Bolsheviks in the Russian revolution, the ascendancy of their ideas was established; the Third International (Communist International, Comintern) 1920 called for action by the workers of the world to bring about revolution, the dictatorship of the proletariat, and the creation of a classless society in which (as predicted by Engels) the state would wither away ('government of persons giving way to administration of things'), and there would be universal peace and plenty. The left wings of socialist parties in many countries thereupon formed communist parties. Lenin, Stalin, and others later developed various specialized applications of marxist theory and practice. Albania, Bulgaria, China, Cuba, Czechoslovakia, E. Germany, Hungary, N. Korea, N. Vietnam, Poland, Rumania, U.S.S.R. (◊ *Soviet Union*), and Yugoslavia are now communist states. Communist parties exist in various other countries, but in some (e.g. W. Germany, U.S.A.) are illegal; there are substantial communist parties in France and Italy, and about 30,000 communists in the U.K. (but no M.P., the British Communist Party being mainly active in the trade-union movement). Ideological differences between the Soviet and the Chinese parties have recently caused divisions in the world movement.

Communist International ◊ *Internationals*.

Communist Manifesto. 1848. A political tract written jointly by Marx and Engels, first published in France as a programme for the Communist League, a society mainly of German political émigrés; it expounds briefly and passionately the central ideas of ⋄ *marxism*, and has exerted great influence, containing notably an exposition of the marxist concept of history, an analysis of the contemporary capitalist society and its 'inevitable' class struggles, and a prophecy of the overthrow of the capitalist system.

Commutator. Multiple-way switching arrangement used in electrical machines for altering the direction of an electric current. It is usually a cylindrical system of copper bars, insulated from each other, so fitted in a dynamo or motor that they provide synchronized connexion with different parts of the armature during its rotation, thereby allowing a dynamo or motor to produce direct current or a motor to use it.

Company Law. Law relating to groups of persons recognized as a single legal entity with a specific set of purposes; English law relating to companies is contained principally in the 1948 Companies Act. The liability of a member of a limited liability company for its debts is only the amount he has paid or guaranteed for shares. The powers, rights, and duties of the members of the company are set out in the Memorandum and Articles of Association, which must be registered with the Registrar of Companies. A company which limits its membership to 50 and restricts the transfer of its shares is known as a 'private company' and is exempted from some of the provisions relating to public companies.

Compass. A device for indicating the direction of the N. and S. Poles; in its simplest form, the magnetic compass is a magnetized needle, free to rotate in the horizontal plane, which will come to rest in line with the earth's magnetic field, and the mariner's compass, employing this principle, has been in use since the Middle Ages. Now several magnets are generally used, and the compass is housed in a binnacle, which incorporates devices to reduce the magnetic effect of the ship's steel; the compass card (face) is marked with 32 directional 'points' and usually in degrees also.

GYRO COMPASS: First introducd 1908; employs the principle of gyroscope inertia and precession, being so ballasted that under the influence of the earth's rotation and the force of gravity the axle of a rapidly spinning wheel takes up a N.-S.

line. It has been used in the Royal Navy since 1915, being esp. useful in warships, and has also been extensively adopted in merchant vessels as it is unaffected by magnetism.

GYRO-MAGNETIC COMPASS: Produced for use in aircraft in the Second World War; has a gyroscope stabilizer and (instead of magnets) a set of coils which respond to the earth's magnetism. In polar regions it is much more efficient than the magnetic compass.

Complex. In psychology, generally a morbid emotionally-charged idea, wholly or partly repressed, usually in conflict with conscious beliefs and wishes; in Freudian psychology, esp. stages of infantile sexual development e.g. the ⋄ *Oedipus complex* and the castration complex, in which a boy fears loss of his genital organs and a girl may believe that this has actually happened to her. In Freudian theory the formation of such complexes is inevitable, and they must be successfully resolved if the child is to reach emotional maturity. ⋄ *Unconscious Mind*.

Compositae. Daisy family; the largest family of flowering plants (about ten per cent of the total), of wide distribution. Most are herbs, but some are trees and shrubs. They have small flowers (florets) aggregated into a head (capitulum): the daisy head or 'flower' is really an agglomeration of florets. Well-known flowers of this family are the dandelion and thistle. The fruits are plumed for wind dispersal, e.g. dandelion, but a few are animal-dispersed by spines or hooks, e.g. burr marigold, or the whole head has hooked bracts, e.g. burdock. The massing of florets into heads gives a conspicuous structure with easy cross-pollination. Many garden flowers, e.g. dahlia, chrysanthemum, belong to this family, and a few are edible, e.g. lettuce, chicory, artichoke.

Compound. Product of the chemical interaction of two or more ⋄ *elements* in definite proportion by weight, with resultant properties quite different from those of its components; e.g. common salt (a compound of sodium and chlorine) is neither metallic like sodium nor gaseous and poisonous like chlorine. The outermost (valency) atoms of the elements concerned determine the propensity to combine: if during the combination energy is released, the compound formed is exothermic, and if energy is absorbed, endothermic. ⟡ *Chemical Bonding, Valency.*

Comprehensive School. Provides all types of secondary education for all the normal children of the appropriate age group in its neighbourhood. Most comprehensive schools in Britain (unlike other countries) group the pupils either into 'streams' according to general ability or into 'sets' for special abilities. Such schools range in size from 200 to over 2000 pupils, 900 to 1500 being the most common. A large school offers many optional subjects in the sixth form, and so does a system foreshadowed in the 1964 Education Act (paralleled in parts of N. America and Sweden) of junior comprehensive schools, which feed pupils into senior schools or sixth-form colleges, facilitating the speedy incorporation of existing schools economically into a comprehensive system.

Computer. Machine for solving problems that are essentially mathematical. Although many ingenious mechanical computers have been designed, modern computers are electronic and of two main types – analogue and digital. Analogue computers operate by accurately simulating physical quantities e.g. speeds, rotations, amount of heat, frictional forces, etc. in terms of varying electrical currents or voltages, which can be much more conveniently and rapidly manipulated and measured; in this way complicated scientific and engineering problems which might occupy skilled mathematicians for many weeks can be solved in a few minutes. Digital computers (of which the ⟡ *abacus* may be regarded as a remote ancestor) deal directly with numbers, data being fed to the machine in the form of units of information, which it can store in its 'memory' cells and process on a binary (as opposed to decimal) scale by simple on-off electronic switches, of which there may be several hundreds in powerful machines, each capable of operating in less than a millionth of a second; any problems which can be resolved into sequences of mathematical calculations (from preparing a payroll to analysing weather prospects from data provided by artificial satellites) can be dealt with. Computers are being increasingly used for processing business and scientific data and for industrial calculations. They are also used by psychologists to throw light on problems of human behaviour, the ⟡ *central nervous system*, the nature of memory, etc. ⟡ *Automation, Cybernetics.*

Conceptualism ⟡ *Universals.*

Concerto. Musical term of disputed etymology, with two main meanings. In the 17th and 18th centuries the form called Concerto (or Grosso) was a piece in several movements for a substantial body of instruments, contrast often being achieved by the special use of soloists or (concertino) of a small instrumental group; works of this type include Bach's *Brandenburg Concertos* 1721, and concertos by Handel and Vivaldi. From the late 18th cent. (especially with the work of Mozart, regarded as the great establisher of the concerto in the second and more common meaning) the form concentrated on the contrast between one soloist (rarely more) and the orchestra. This form developed along with the ⟡ *symphony*, but usually retained three movements as against the symphony's four. The instruments for which concertos are most commonly written are the violin and piano, but there are also concertos for horn, clarinet, 'cello, viola, etc.

The earlier use was revived in the 20th cent. for certain works e.g. Bartók's *Concerto for Orchestra* which have prominent interplay between the full orchestra and a smaller group or groups (corresponding to the older concertino).

Conchubar. In Irish legend, king of Ulster, uncle of ⟡ *Cuchullin* and betrothed to ⟡ *Deirdre*; ruled from Emain Macha (near Armagh), a great *rath* (fort) whose ruins may still be seen, with a warrior host called the Red Branch (from the berries of the magical rowan tree), and is said to have had supernatural foreknowledge of the crucifixion of Jesus and on that day to have demonstrated what he would have done to prevent the death so vigorously that he himself died.

Concordat. Agreement, tantamount to an international diplomatic treaty, between the Pope and a national government on matters concerning relations between the ⟡ *Roman Catholic Church* and the State, e.g. mutual rights and obligations, the status of the clergy, state contributions to the Church, the position of Catholic schools; esp. that between Pius VII and Napoleon 1801, re-establishing the Church in France after the Revolution. Where a concordat is not attainable, it is

sometimes replaced by an informal agreement known as a *modus vivendi*, e.g. that
betwen Bismarck and the Papacy 1887.

Concrete. Made from broken stone or
gravel, sand, and ◊ *cement*, typically in
the proportions 4:2:1 by weight. Historically the use of concrete depended
upon the availability of cement; the
Romans made much use of it, and their
massive concrete domed roofs are especially noteworthy, but after them concrete
fell into disuse until the 17th cent.

PRE-STRESSED CONCRETE: Reinforced
concrete (see below) in which the steel,
often in the form of wires, is stretched
before the concrete is subjected to its
working load. The stretched wires give the
concrete a compressive stress, to counteract the tensile stress which the working
load would otherwise cause. Pre-stressing
enables concrete members to be light and
slender.

REINFORCED CONCRETE: In which steel
bars have been embedded to give increased
strength; reinforcement is placed esp.
where tensile stresses are likely to occur,
as concrete is weak in tension. Reinforced
concrete, particularly in its pre-stressed
form, has offered architects and engineers
new ways of building. Outstanding is the
work of the Italian engineer-architect
Nervi.
◊ *Architecture.*

Conditioning. In popular usage, the modification of behaviour by experience; in
psychology, several kinds are recognized,
all forms of learning by ◊ *association of
ideas.* In 'classical conditioning' (first
demonstrated by Pavlov) a buzzer is repeatedly sounded just before food is presented, and eventually the buzzer alone
causes salivation; the 'unconditioned'
stimulus is the food, which produces saliva
reflexly, and the 'conditioned' stimulus is
the sound of the buzzer, producing saliva
as a 'conditioned response'. In 'operant
conditioning' an animal is 'reinforced' by
a reward for carrying out a given action
e.g. pressing a lever; typically, food is
given to a hungry animal as a reinforcement.

Condor ◊ *Eagle.*

Conduction (Conductors). The transfer of
heat or electrical energy from one part of
a substance to another. With heat, this
transfer is attributed to colliding ◊ *molecules,* which pass kinetic energy to others
of lower energy in a direction away from

the source. The loose molecular structure
of liquids and gases makes them poorer
conductors than solids, which also vary
greatly in conductivity according to their
structure; in general, metals are good
conductors of heat and non-metals e.g.
wood and ceramics are poor conductors.
The transfer of electrical energy is attributed to free ◊ *electrons* which move between ◊ *atoms* under the influence of
difference in potential. Metals which are
good conductors of heat are generally
also good conductors of ◊ *electricity.*
Some substances e.g. rubber and glass are
such poor conductors that they are used
as insulators to prevent or direct the flow
of electricity; their lack of conductivity
is explained in their electrons being less
free to move between atoms.

SEMI-CONDUCTORS: Materials whose
conductivity at room temperature lies between that of metals and insulators, but
increases at high temperature and vice
versa. They include germanium, silicon,
selenium, copper oxide, and play an important role in many electronic devices
e.g. ◊ *transistor.*

Confederacy, Confederate Army ◊
American Civil War.

Confession. 1. Declaration of sins to a
priest, in order to obtain absolution, on
condition of contrition and intention to
amend, through the sacrament of penance; since the 1215 General Council
(Lateran 4), obligatory to Roman Catholics at least once a year and before taking
◊ *Holy Communion,* which is forbidden,
until after confession and penance, to
anyone guilty of mortal sin (sin incurring
eternal punishment). In no circumstances
may a priest divulge confessional revelations. Confession is usually made in
church, in a special confessional, a partition concealing the penitent from the
priest, who absolves him or her on condition of performing some good work, or
saying prayers, in token of sincere repentance. In the Anglican church, confession
is optional. Other Protestant bodies reject it.
2. Basic statement of essential religious
belief e.g. Augsburg Confession 1530
(◊ *Lutheranism*), Westminster Confession
1547 (◊ *Presbyterianism*).

Confirmation. Rite in various Christian
churches invoking the ◊ *Holy Ghost,*
generally by the laying-on of the hands
of a ◊ *bishop,* with or without anointing;

the baptismal vows are renewed and the recipient is rendered admissible to ◊ *Holy Communion*. In the ◊ *Eastern Orthodox Church* the rite is administered immediately after ◊ *baptism*, in the ◊ *Roman Catholic Church* and the Church of England (◊ *Anglicanism*) usually in later childhood or at adolescence. By Roman Catholic and Eastern Orthodox Christians confirmation is numbered among the ◊ *sacraments*, but not by Anglicans. The name is sometimes given also to a corresponding rite, Bar Mitzvah, by which at the age of 13 a Jewish boy (◊ *Judaism*) is first called to read the Law in the ◊ *synagogue* and assumes adult religious responsibilities.

Conflict of Laws (Private International Law) ◊ *International Law*.

Confucianism. Beliefs and practices based on the teaching of Confucius (Kung Fu-tse) about 550–480 B.C. and in China (at least until recently) equivalent to a national religion, but not involving belief in a personal god, though its founder reverenced Heaven (Tien) as a supernatural power; it places great stress on filial piety and reverence for ancestors, and on moderation and harmony in all things. A set of writings is reverenced (the five King and four Shu), including a book of aphorisms attributed to Confucius, the *Analects* (Lun Yu).

Congo. Area 129,960 sq. m. Pop. about 800,000. Cap. Brazzaville. Formerly the French Congo; since 1960 an independent republic within the ◊ *French Community*.

ECONOMY. A poor country (lacking the rich mineral deposits of the former Belgian Congo, ◊ *Congolese Republic*). The principal exports are lumber, palm oil, peanuts, and tobacco.

HISTORY. Colonization of the Congo began only after Stanley's discovery of the course of the Congo River 1875–8; the territory became a French colony in 1888 and later part of French Equatorial Africa. In 1963 violent anti-Government demonstrations forced the resignation of the President, Abbé Youlou.

Congolese Republic. Area 905,582 sq. m. Pop. 14 m. Africans (divided among 150 tribes, mainly Bantu, and 30,000 Europeans, mainly Belgian). Cap. Leopoldville. ECONOMY. The wealth of the country lies mainly in the minerals e.g. copper and uranium of the interior province of

Katanga; it is the world's chief supplier of ◊ *cobalt*, and also exports coffee, cotton, palm oil, and rubber.

HISTORY. From 1885 under the personal control of Leopold II of Belgium, the Congo became a Belgian colony in 1908. Maladministration and uncontrolled exploitation gave place after the First World War to orderly development, but political progress was blocked by a policy of paternalism. After 1957 the Belgian Government began to plan for a 30-year advance towards self-government, but the impatience of the Africans revealed itself in riots, and Belgium decided on an election in May 1960 to be followed by independence, for which the Congolese were ill prepared. A precarious administration under two leaders Lumumba and Kasavubu was defied by the secessionist Tshombe in Katanga. Disorder was rife. The U.N. sent a force to help keep order and to forestall possible intervention by rival foreign powers. It was successful in the latter aim, but less so in the former. In 1964 the U.N. forces were withdrawn and Tshombe joined the government which recruited mercenaries to strengthen its army. Unrest and sporadic revolts continue.

Congregationalists. Protestant Christian body in Britain and America, originating about 1640 as the Brownist sect of the Independents (◊ *Nonconformists*); the chief distinguishing principle is the autonomy of each congregation, which chooses its own minister and his assistant ◊ *deacons* and lay preachers. Since 1831 there has been federation in an advisory Congregational Union with an elected Chairman. Their beliefs resemble those of the ◊ *Baptists*, but without insistence on adult baptism. Congregationalists have been prominent in educational work, and founded the universities of Yale and Harvard in U.S.A.

Congress, U.S.A. Two-chamber legislature. (a) House of Representatives, 435 members (Congressmen) apportioned between the States according to population; elected every two years. Since the Presidential term is four years, the party majority may change and the President may then find his own party in a minority after mid-term Congressional elections. (b) Senate, 100 members (Senators), two for each State regardless of its population, elected for six years, of whom one third stand for election every second year (this again can affect the balance of party strength in Congress during a President's term of office). In addition to its legislative function, the Senate ratifies (or rejects) Presidential appointments (including members of his Cabinet, officers, and ambassadors) and foreign treaties; it is thus powerful in its treaty-making aspect, though the actual conduct of foreign affairs is handled by the State Department, under a Cabinet minister appointed by the President. Legislation may originate in either Chamber, except that finance bills must originate in the House of Representatives. There are various standing committees of both Chambers (Finance, Foreign Affairs, Agriculture, etc.). Bills are discussed, in the appropriate committee, first in one Chamber and then in the other. Amendments are returned to the Chamber where they originated for approval; in case of disagreement a committee of both houses evolves a compromise. Enactment can be delayed or prevented by ◊ *filibuster*, and chairmen of committees (elected by seniority, and often reactionary) exert powerful influence. The President has no means of expediting a Bill; he can, however, veto a Bill, after which it needs a two-thirds majority in each house to override his veto.

Congress of Industrial Organizations ◊ *American Federation of Labor.*

Conifers. A group of ◊ *gymnosperms*, mostly evergreen trees usually growing in N. temperate areas and in mountains up to the tree line. They are able to withstand severe weather conditions, their leaves being tough and often scale-like. Some of the oldest and largest trees in the world are conifers, e.g. ◊ *sequoia* and ◊ *metasequoia*. They do not produce flowers in the accepted sense, but have the female reproductive parts always in cones and the male parts usually but not exclusively so. When the female cones are ripe the scales open and shed the seeds. Conifers include pine, fir, Douglas fir, spruce, cedar, cypress, swamp cypress, sequoia, metasequoia, thuja, monkey puzzle, juniper, and larch. Larches and metasequoia are deciduous. Conifers, esp. pine and spruce, are very important commercially as timber (softwoods) and for turpentine and resins. A few species of pine have edible seeds (pine-kernels or pine-nuts).

Conjunction. In astronomy, the phenomenon by which as a result of their individual motions two or more heavenly bodies appear to come together in the sky; strictly, the moment of conjunction is when the bodies have the same celestial longitude. When a planet is merely said to be 'in conjunction', conjunction with the ◊ *sun* is implied; between the sun and earth it is in 'inferior conjunction', beyond the sun in 'superior conjunction'.

Conscience. The faculty in human nature through which primitive impulses are controlled, and action directed, in accordance with received moral or social principles. Apart from purely religious explanations of its existence are such views as McDougall's that it is an overflow of self-love ('self-regarding sentiment') and Freud's concept of the super-ego (◊ *Ego*).

Consciousness. To be conscious is the normal waking condition of an organism; some philosophers and psychologists have regarded this as the defining quality of mind, and the observation of consciousness by introspection as the basis of scientific ◊ *psychology*, but these views are contested by behaviourists and psychoanalysts. ◊ *Unconscious Mind.*

Conscription. Compulsory enlistment of troops for national defence. It was introduced in revolutionary France in 1793 and systematic conscription was made law in 1798, every citizen being liable for five years' service; the enormous armies the French were thus enabled to raise forced the other continental nations to follow suit. Conscription was abandoned after 1815, but was revived by Prussia in the latter half of the 19th cent. and became the rule in Europe, although in Britain and U.S.A. voluntary enlistment into regular standing armies was maintained. Britain finally introduced conscription in 1916 and again in 1939; compulsory military service for men reaching the age of 18 remained in force 1946–60, when recruiting reverted to a voluntary basis.

Conservation of Energy ◊ *Energy.*

Conservative Party. The former ◊ *Tory* party, renamed by Disraeli, now consisting of associations in each parliamentary constituency, with women's sections and 'young Conservative' branches, combined in the National Union of Conservative and Unionist Associations (Unionist being the party name in N. Ireland and Scotland, ◊ *Act of Union*). When the party is in opposition, the leader is chosen at a meeting of Conservative M.P.s and accredited candidates. The executive is called the Central Office. The party has no fixed doctrine, and adopts policies it judges practical and suitable to circumstances. In general, Conservatives believe in keeping government intervention to a minimum in the development of society in all its aspects. The party draws its support from all sections of the population. In the 20th cent. it has been in office under Balfour 1902–6, under Bonar Law and Baldwin 1922–4 and 1922–9, in the National and Coalition Governments under Baldwin and Chamberlain and Churchill 1935–45, and under Eden, Macmillan, and Home 1951–64. ⟡ *United Kingdom.*

Constantinople ⟡ *Byzantine Empire.*

Constellation. The patterns of the bright stars have been named after gods, animals, and so on since ancient times. Ptolemy's *Almagest* listed 48 constellations, including the 12 of the ⟡ *Zodiac.* In later years names were added, others dropped, and the outlines of individual constellations were left ill-defined. In 1930 the International Astronomical Union defined constellation limits by arcs of circles parallel or perpendicular to the celestial equator and named 88 constellations covering the whole sky.

The brightest stars of a constellation are given Greek letter prefixes, usually in alphabetical order according to their magnitude ('alpha' for the brightest). When the alphabet is exhausted, numbers are used, e.g. Beta Canis Minoris (βCMi) is the second brightest star in the constellation of Canis Minor (little Dog), and 27 Ori is a relatively faint star in the constellation of ⟡ *Orion.*

Constitution. The fundamental principles concerning the government of a nation. These may be embodied in a number of laws, as in Britain, or in a single document, as in the United States; in both cases there are usually also a number of unwritten practices ('conventions'). A single document is natural where the government, instead of gradually growing up on a traditional basis, is deliberately reorganized on a national one. It is also essential where the form of government is agreed on as a compromise between various conflicting groups or states (⟡ *Federalism*). The U.S. Constitution was established in 1789 with a Preamble and Seven Articles to which 21 Amendments have since been added. A constitution may either be flexible i.e. alterable in the same way as any other law, which makes it impossible to tell which laws are constitutional, or rigid i.e. alterable only by following some special procedure e.g. submission to a public vote.

Constructivism. Art movement founded in Moscow 1920, led by Kazimir Malevich, the brothers Gabo, and Pevsner, with roots in ⟡ *Cubism* and ⟡ *collage.* Constructivist sculpture employs materials such as glass, wire, celluloid, and sheet metal, and methods such as welding, and is concerned primarily with the way an object defines space and less with the plastic qualities of mass and volume. The movement was banned in Russia 1921.

Consubstantiation, Transubstantiation ⟡ *Holy Communion.*

Consumer Goods. In economics, goods which are rapidly used up, as against ⟡ *capital* goods; sometimes consumer 'goods' e.g. food, clothes are distinguished from consumer 'durables' e.g. refrigerators, cars.

Consumer Law. The general rule of English law on the purchase of goods is *caveat emptor,* let the buyer beware; except where some specific duty is established by statute, and provided he does not positively assert what is not true, there is no obligation on the seller to disclose defects in the article. Where a warranty (⟡ *Guarantee*) is given, whether in writing on the packets, orally by a salesman, or by implication, the purchaser is entitled to claim damages if the goods do not correspond with it, but except in certain circumstances he is not entitled to return the goods. If the purchaser accepts goods offered on terms (printed on the packet or an enclosed note) excluding these rules, he waives his rights; documents purporting to be guarantees frequently include terms waiving the purchaser's rights. ⟡ *Contract, Hire Purchase.*

Contempt of Court. Defiance of a court, or behaviour likely to prejudice the fair trial of proceedings, e.g. (a) wilful refusal to obey the order of a court; (b) interrupting proceedings in court; (c) publishing scandalous comments concerning a judge's conduct in court; (d) conduct calculated to prejudice the trial of pending proceedings, as by publishing scandalous matter about one of the parties (this does not apply if, having taken all reasonable care, the offender was not aware and had no reason to suspect that proceedings had been instituted).

Contempt of court is punishable by a fine or by imprisonment.

Continent. Large continuous land mass; the six generally recognized are (in order of size): Asia, Africa, N. America, S. America, Europe, and Australia. (Antarctica is often regarded as a seventh.) Australasia is Australia with New Zealand, and adjacent islands. Oceania is Australasia and the numerous scattered islands of the SW Pacific.

CONTINENTAL DRIFT: According to the widely-held and recently part-confirmed Displacement Theory (Wegener's Hypothesis), first advanced in 1920, the continents were once joined together in one great land mass which fractured, the parts drifting away to form separate continental islands. The present shape of the coast of S. America suggests that it may once have been joined to the W. coast of Africa, and geologists have discovered a marked similarity between the rocks and fossils of the two areas.

CONTINENTAL SHELF: Submerged outer edges of a continent extending from the coastline to the 100-f. line, where a 'continental slope' to the ocean deeps begins, varying greatly in width; the British Isles lie on that of Europe. All continental shelves considerably increase the effect of tides and are important fishing grounds.

Continental Congress. 1774-5. Meeting of delegates from all the American colonies except Georgia, to organize resistance to Britain's attempts to force the colonists to pay taxes (◊ *Boston Tea Party*). It first met at Philadelphia in 1774, but as it had no constitutional standing, its protests were ignored. After a second meeting in 1775, it raised an army and appointed George Washington commander (◊ *American Revolution*). In 1776 it approved the ◊ *Declaration of Independence* and assumed executive powers pending the adoption of a Federal Constitution.

Continental System. 1806-12. Napoleon's policy of forbidding all the countries under his influence (including Russia, Spain, and Italy) to receive British goods. Britain retaliated by the Orders in Council of 1807 prohibiting any trade with these countries, and proceeded to exercise a right of search over neutral ships, which was a major cause of the ◊ *War of 1812* with U.S.A. The Continental System became progressively less effective, though it caused Britain considerable hardship, and by forcing Napoleon to try to seal Europe off completely, e.g. in the ◊ *Peninsular War*, it overstrained his resources and ultimately proved disastrous to him.

Contour. Line drawn on a map through all points at the same height above sea level; most topographical maps carry a series of contours to show land relief. Besides giving altitudes, by their distances apart the contours indicate the steepness of slopes. Intervals between contours may represent height differences of as little as 50 ft (as on the 1 in. to 1 m. British Ordnance Survey maps) or several thousand ft (as e.g. on small-scale maps of continents).

CONTOUR PLOUGHING: A technique in which on hilly land the furrows follow the contours, to counteract the increased danger of ◊ *erosion* if they run up and down hill.

ISOBATH: Lines drawn on a map through all points at the same depth of water, to indicate the level of the seabed.

Contraception ◊ *Birth Control.*

Contract. Any agreement enforceable at law, whether made orally, in a formal document, or in a series of informal documents e.g. an exchange of letters; a contract is concluded when one party unconditionally accepts an offer made by the other. A conditional acceptance is a counter-offer; if the original offerer accepts the conditions, there is a contract. Once it is concluded, both parties are bound by the agreement, but until then neither party is bound. No contract other than a contract by deed is binding unless there is a 'consideration' i.e. something of value which the promisor obtains. The fairness of the bargain is irrelevant. A person may be sued for breach of contract, and damages may be awarded to the plaintiff; if damages would not be an adequate remedy, e.g. if the contract is to sell a unique article, the court may compel the other party to perform his contract by an order of the court. ◊ *Consumer Law*.

Convention. 1. International agreement, frequently of a non-political nature and often of wide scope e.g. Geneva Convention, Postal Convention.

2. Meeting for some specific purpose e.g. to draw up a constitution, like the American constitutional convention of 1787, or to nominate a candidate for political office, esp. in U.S.A. The process of electing an American President involves the nomination by each of the contending political parties of a single candidate, who is chosen at a convention. Delegations are sent from each State, their size determined on a population basis. In the first few ballots delegates are bound to vote for the candidate to whom the delegation as a whole promised their vote, either by the decision of the local party officials, or, increasingly, by a State 'primary election'. Primaries allow the rank and file of party members to nominate party candidates for political office, rather than leaving it to party officials. Although essentially party affairs, primaries are arranged, supervised, and paid for by the States and regulated by legislation. Both political parties require a two-thirds majority in the convention to elect a candidate. After the first ballots ('roll calls'), political manoeuvring may take place in which delegations may be released from previous obligations and 'swing' to another candidate more likely to secure the majority.

Converters. In electricity, the interconnexions between a.c. and d.c. systems (◊ *Electric Current*) or between systems of different voltage. In a.c. systems voltages are changed by ◊ *transformers*; a.c. to d.c. conversion is done by ◊ *rectifier* or by motor-generator systems in which the power from an a.c. motor is used to drive a d.c. generator. Conversion from d.c. to a.c. and from one voltage to another in d.c. systems can be similarly effected by using rotating machinery or special circuits known as inverters.

Conveyancing. The branch of law relating to the creation and transfer of rights in ◊ *property*; a very common form is the deed executed by the vendor of land or buildings which transfers the property to the purchaser.

Convocation. Assembly of Anglican clergy: one for the Province of Canterbury, one for that of York, each consisting of an Upper House of ◊ *bishops* and a Lower House of proctors (elected by the lesser clergy) under a presiding Prolocutor. An elected House of Laity is associated with each Convocation. ◊ *Church Assembly, Church of England, Lambeth Conference*.

Convolvulaceae. A dicotyledonous family of herbs and shrubs; many are climbers, including the several native British species. They have showy regular trumpet or bell flowers. Bindweed, esp. the large type with white flowers about two in. long, is a noxious and persistent weed. Smaller bindweed with pink or white flowers occurs in cultivated fields and roadsides. Many species are cultivated ornamentally e.g. the morning-glories (Ipomoea) with large blue, purple, or red flowers. ◊ *Dodder, Sweet Potato*.

Cooking. Primitive people evolved only the simplest forms of cooking, which became more elaborate with agriculture and a varied food supply and more decisively with the introduction of flour, yeast, and sugar in the E. All the cereals and many of the vegetables known today were already in use at the ◊ *Neolithic* stage of agriculture. The Egyptians baked bread, roasted and boiled meat and fish, and brewed beer; the wealthier Greeks elevated cooking to an art (gastronomy), and the later Romans e.g. Lucullus 110–56 B.C. were famous for their luxurious banquets. With the Dark Ages the art of cooking declined in Europe, but it re-emerged in the monasteries, with their gardens, fishponds, and well-appointed kitchens. The style of oriental cookery was influenced by and largely based on rice and spices, with less emphasis on meat and fish; eastern influence on European cooking was not felt till the Arab conquests and the Crusades. With the Renaissance came a revival of interest in the art of cooking, which spread from Italy to France (where Catherine de' Medici fostered it) and belatedly to England; the invention of the fork (still scorned in Elizabethan England) made possible sophisticated dishes unsuited for eating by hand, while the introduction of sugar (in medieval Europe honey had been the only sweetening) led to further developments. Fine cooking was a feature of the reign of Louis XIV in the 17th and early 18th centuries; Napoleon's chefs in the early 19th were famous and spread the renown of French cooking throughout Europe.

Climate, crops, the extent of trade and communication, and religious taboos have largely determined the development of national dishes; cooking techniques and utensils have not changed significantly throughout the ages, although the advent of new fuels and materials have altered and facilitated some processes (greater changes have been occasioned by ancillary developments such as canning, ◊ *refrigeration,* and dehydration).

COOKERY BOOKS: That of Hannah Glasse was the first widely printed in England (1757); in France the most famous was Brillat-Savarin's *Physiologie du Goût* 1826; Mrs Beeton's *Household Management* appeared 1859; its U.S.A. equivalent is Fannie Farmer's *Boston Cook Book* 1896. ◊◊ *Calorie, Diet.*

Cooperatives. Groups of producers or consumers who organize their production, selling, or buying jointly; in the U.K. consumers' cooperatives are the most important, deriving from that started at Rochdale 1844 with capital contributed by a few working-class members. Most cooperative stores sell at competitive market prices and distribute profits in the form of dividends; the return on share capital is fixed, and each member usually has only one vote however many shares he or she owns. The various retail cooperative societies in Britain own the Cooperative Wholesale Society (CWS), which manufactures a variety of goods, acts as a wholesaler, and owns a bank, a building society, and an insurance company, the two last among the big units in their own fields. In the last 100 years the British cooperative movement has grown from a few thousand members in 1844 to 12 or 13 million, but its share in the total of retail trade has recently declined.

In Europe, producers' cooperatives (esp. in agriculture) are more important than in Britain, e.g. Danish agriculture is largely organized on a cooperative basis; the cooperatives advise farmers, help to maintain standards, market the produce, and distribute the profits.

Copernican Theory ◊ *Astronomy.*

Copper. An ◊ *element* 300 times as abundant as silver, found as sulphide, oxide, and carbonate ores, all readily reduced to the crude metal, which is refined electrolytically to give metal of the high conductivity necessary for the electrical industry; it resists corrosion by water, is used for domestic boilers, pipes, and circulating tanks, is suitable for steam systems, and is a component of several important ◊ *alloys* e.g. the bronzes (with tin), the brasses (with zinc), and the flexible beryllium-copper from which non-magnetic springs are made. It has two sets of compounds, the cuprous (valency state 1) and the cupric (valency state 2). The cupric salts are the important ones, and aqueous solutions of them are usually blue e.g. copper (cupric) sulphate. Copper salts readily become basic ones which are insoluble, and the patina which appears on the surface of bronze statues is mainly due to the basic carbonate. Cuprous oxide is used for ruby glass and for red glaze in pottery, cupric oxide gives green and blue glasses and glazes. Copper salts are toxic, and the sulphate is used in preparing fungicides, of which Bordeaux Mixture (slaked lime, copper sulphate, and water), used for spraying potatoes, is a typical one.

'Copper Age' ◊ *Bronze Age.*

Copperhead ◊ *Snake, Viper.*

Copra ◊ *Coconut.*

Copts. < Ar. *Qibt,* from Gr. ai-*gupt*-ios: name given in the 16th cent. to the Christians in Egypt; direct descendants of the ancient Egyptians, and today about one tenth of the population of Egypt. The Coptic language, spoken as a vernacular A.D. 300 to 700, survives only for liturgical purposes in the Coptic Church (autonomous Christian church of Egypt), which split off from the main body of Christian churches when the monophysite doctrine (◊ *Nestorianism*) was declared a ◊ *heresy* A.D. 431 and 553. ◊◊ *Ethiopia.*

Copyright. A form of property, in respect of every original literary, dramatic, musical, and artistic work, consisting of the sole right to publish, perform, or record the work. Copyright vests in the author, compiler, or performer of the original, but it may be sold by him. A licence to produce the work in part or whole, or in any specific way, may be sold or otherwise transferred, while the copyright remains in the original owner. Copyright normally continues until 50 years after the death of the author. In England the first copyright act, 1710, provided for registration and a period of copyright of 14 years renewable once. Certain types of infringement of copyright are criminal offences; and all are actionable. The

Berne Convention of 1886 made the first arrangements between various countries for the protection of copyright and these have been ordered by the Convention of 1911 and the Universal Copyright Convention of 1958.

In Soviet law translation into another language does not constitute infringement of a copyright. In American law, works by American citizens published outside the U.S.A. are not protected by copyright within the U.S.A. ◊ *Libraries*.

COPYRIGHT LIBRARIES ◊ *Libraries*.

Coral. One of the ◊ *sedimentary rocks*, formed by reef-building marine organisms living in colonies in warm salt water, usually within 30° of the equator; each tiny polyp grows by extracting food and lime from the sea and building a calcareous skeleton. There are two distinct types of coral: the Aleyonarian group (which includes the precious Mediterranean red coral), and the reef-building corals, which form immense colonies. A bore-hole (1947) in Bikini atoll in the Pacific showed calcareous matter at a depth of some 2000 ft.

CORAL REEF: Three types are recognized. (1) *Fringing Reef*: built out from the shore, forming a rough platform at the level of low water. (2) *Barrier Reef*: at a distance from the shore, separated from it by a deep lagoon (the Great Barrier Reef off the NE coast of Australia is about 1000 m. long and its lagoon is up to 70 m. in width). (3) *Atoll*: a ring-shaped or horseshoe-shaped island of coral surrounding a lagoon; the Maldive Islands are a group of atolls about 400 m. SW of Ceylon, with a population of about 90,000.

Coral Sea. 1942. Air battle between the Americans and Japanese in which the Americans halted the southward thrust of the Japanese forces. ◊ *Pacific War, Second World War*.

Corbel. A block of stone projecting from a wall and supporting a roof-beam or other feature; a primitive form of cantilever. In ◊ *Gothic architecture* they are often elaborately carved with figures, grotesque heads, or foliage.

Cordillera. Originally, Spanish term for the parallel mountain ranges in S. America; now the entire Andes. The similar ranges in N. America, including the Rocky Mountains, the Sierra Nevada, and the Coast and Cascade ranges, are named the W. Cordillera by American geographers.

Cordite ◊ *Explosives*.

Coriander. *Coriandrum sativum*; a fragrant herb with round oily seeds, used as a spice and in medicine in the E. from early times. It was once extensively grown in English herb gardens. The seed is used for flavouring liqueurs and confectionery, in curries, and as an ingredient in mixed spice. ◊ *Umbelliferae*.

Corinthian Order ◊ *Architectural Orders*.

Cork. Protective tissue of closely-fitting dead cells with wax-impregnated walls, replacing the epidermis in the older stems of woody plants and forming a waterproof layer which serves to restrict water loss and the entry of pests. A component of ◊ *bark*, cork is produced from a ◊ *cambium* which either develops afresh each year in successively deeper layers of the plant, or persists intact from year to year as in cork oak; here it produces a very thick layer of pure cork, which can be removed every few years (leaving the cambium undamaged) and used for bungs, bottle corks, mats, insulation, etc.

Corm. A solid swollen plant-stem in which is stored food material, mainly starch. In e.g. a crocus corm, at the top is the bud containing the flower and future leaves, from the base come the roots, and on the side will be seen scars which are the remains of the previous season's leaf stalks. Like ◊ *bulbs* corms are plants that require or are forced by drought to undergo a period of rest until suitable conditions of moisture occur. The food reserve then supports the rapid growth of leaves and flowers. The old corm shrivels in this process and a new one is formed on the top of the old. Gladiolus and montbretia are other typical corms.

Corn ◊ *Cereals, Maize*.

Corn Belt. Region S. and SW of the Great Lakes in U.S.A. (Illinois, Indiana, adjacent parts of S. Dakota, Kansas, Minnesota, Missouri, Nebraska, Ohio, and esp. Iowa, the leading producer) where corn i.e. ◊ *maize* is the principal crop, the climate and soil being particularly favourable.

Cornice ◊ *Entablature*.

Cornish. Branch of Brythonic (P-Celtic), more closely related to ◊ *Breton* than to Welsh (◊ *Wales*), which died out in the

19th cent. The 6th-cent. Anglo-Saxon invasions separated the ◊ *Celts* of Cornwall from their Welsh kinsmen; after the Norman Conquest, Breton overlords helped to preserve the Cornish language, which developed its own literature of ◊ *miracle plays* and Biblical poems.

Corn Laws. From the 15th cent. attempts were made to protect English farmers by regulating the price at which corn was imported and exported. The fall in corn prices after the ◊ *Napoleonic wars* upset all previous legislation, and a new Act was passed in 1815 prohibiting the import of corn under 80s. a quarter; in 1828 a new sliding scale of import duties was imposed. But even then the interests of the poor were still subordinated to those of the farmers. Opposition to the Corn Laws became linked with the ◊ *free trade* movement of the manufacturing interests, as against ◊ *Chartism*, a purely working-class movement; it was principally led by Richard Cobden and John Bright, who formed the Anti-Corn Law League 1839 and achieved repeal of the Corn Laws in 1846.

Corolla ◊ *Flower.*

Corona ◊ *Sun.*

Coroner. Official appointed to inquire (◊ *Inquest*) into violent, accidental, or unexplained deaths and into treasure trove, to deputize in certain cases for the sheriff, and in London to investigate outbreaks of fire; appointed by the ◊ *Lord Chancellor* from among barristers, solicitors, or medical practitioners of at least five years' standing. Coroners were originally appointed in each county by the king in the 12th cent. to watch the sheriffs, esp. in respect of the royal revenues.

Corporal Punishment. Originally applicable to misdemeanours (◊ *felony* being punishable by death, ◊ *capital punishment*); the whipping of females was abolished 1820, and for a time whipping was forbidden altogether. It was reintroduced by a private member's Bill 1863, and till 1948 took two forms: (a) the cat o'nine tails (flogging), normally reserved for adults; (b) the birch, for juvenile offenders. The 1948 Criminal Justice Act abolished whipping as a sentence but retained it as a disciplinary measure in prisons, to punish attacks on warders. After this Act there was a considerable decrease in cases of robbery with violence (the principal offence for which whipping

had been prescribed); a Home Office investigation 1951 among 738 men convicted for it 1931–40 found that 51.8 per cent of those whipped had subsequently been convicted for another similar offence, while of the others only 44.7 per cent were convicted again.

Most European countries had abolished corporal punishment before 1948. There have been demands for its reintroduction in Britain; a private member's Bill for the purpose (after a resolution from the Magistrates' Association calling for such legislation) in 1953 was defeated.

Corporative State. One in which workers and employers in particular are formed into officially-recognized corporations for the purposes of industrial self-government and promoting social harmony, and in which Parliament is elected not by territorial constituencies but by the corporations. The system has become discredited by its association with the fascist regime in Italy, because the corporations then formed were primarily designed to buttress the power of a dictatorship. A corporative state need not be bureaucratic and authoritarian, and it can be claimed that by excluding 'party politics' it could lead to a more realistic conduct of public affairs. A more liberal conception can e.g. be found in embryonic form in the 1931 ◊ *encyclical* of Pope Pius XI, *Quadragesimo Anno.* ◊◊ *Portugal, Spain.*

Corpuscles ◊ *Blood.*

Corrosion. Destruction of a metal either by direct chemical attack or by an electrolytic process (the more electropositive the metal the more easily it corrodes); noble metals e.g. gold do not corrode. The most common form is rust on iron and steel, which causes grave losses in industry and buildings. Methods of preventing or retarding it include coating with an oil film; painting; plating (hot dip or electrolytic deposition); alloying (e.g. stainless steel); chemical treatment of the surface (e.g. phosphating); and where water stands in contact with iron, the addition of inhibitors to the water (e.g. in car radiators). ◊◊ *Alloys.*

Corrosive Sublimate ◊ *Mercury.*

Cortisone. One of a group of hormones produced in the cortex of the adrenal gland, which influences some body-processes e.g. carbohydrate-protein conversion and the balance of sodium and potassium in the body. The use of cortisone against rheumatoid arthritis, though of disputed value, stimulated research which resulted in cortisones being produced synthetically for wider clinical use. Adrenal cortical hormones are steroid derivatives. ◊ *Cholesterol.*

Corundum. Aluminium oxide; occurs in coloured varieties which are gem stones, and as stones not of gem quality used as abrasives. The hardest mineral known, except diamond.

EMERY: A greyish-black impure variety used for smoothing hard surfaces.

Cosmetics. Materials applied to the body and face. From the earliest time painting of the body for magical or religious purposes was practised by many peoples; later, cosmetics for personal adornment were much used in the East, and in 4000 B.C. Egyptian women were using kohl and henna; cosmetics were used extensively in Greece and Rome, and again in ◊ *Renaissance* times, many of the preparations containing arsenic and lead compounds, which attacked the skin and damaged the health. In Victorian England a 'painted face' was considered the badge of a 'loose' woman, but the 20th cent. has seen a vast increase in demand for cosmetics; manufacturing methods are precisely controlled and great care is taken to eliminate harmful ingredients.

Cosmic Rays. Particles which are continuously bombarding the earth from outer space. The energy of the primary cosmic radiation, which consists of ◊ *protons* and other particles of high energy, is shared with atmospheric ◊ *molecules* with which it collides; the radiation thus has a different character at the earth's surface, where it sometimes takes the form of electronic showers of many thousands of particles. Cosmic rays can be used as a source of high-energy particles for nuclear research, but although some of the rays have much greater energy than can be achieved with particle accelerators, as there is no control over the direction or moment of impact on the equipment exposed, the method is too random to be of great value.

Cosmology ◊ *Astronomy, Space Exploration.*

Cossacks. Russian ◊ *cavalry,* organized from the 17th cent. as semi-autonomous communities, notably those of the Don and Kuban; the descendants of fugitive serfs, they were superb horsemen and ferocious fighters. Under the tsars they received special privileges in return for military service between the ages of 18 and 38. After the ◊ *Bolshevik* revolution of 1917 what remained of their special privileges and organization was terminated, but they continued as military units.

Costa Rica. Area 19,653 sq. m. Pop. 1.3 m. (many of pure Spanish descent). Cap. San José. Rel. Roman Catholic. The most southerly republic of central America, W. of the Panama Canal on the Caribbean; government is by a president elected for four years, who appoints a cabinet.

ECONOMY. Wholly agricultural, esp. high-quality coffee; also bananas, cocoa, hemp, maize, potatoes, rice, sugar-cane. Cattle-raising is increasing. Ports and airfields are well developed. The standard of living is the highest in central America.

HISTORY. Part of the Spanish dominions 1530–1821, Costa Rica gained independence in the revolution led by Simon Bolivar in the 1820s and since then has established a tradition of stable, democratic, peaceful government. There is a Civic Guard, but the army was abolished 1948. Education is compulsory and the literacy rate the highest in Latin America.

Cost of Living. Cost of the goods and services needed by a family to maintain a certain standard of living in a specified area, normally calculated by supposing a fixed 'basket' of goods purchased by a typical family. To show changes in the cost-of-living index, index numbers based on any norm of 100 show the rise or fall of the cost of living in any particular year or month compared with the base-year. In Britain, the first such investigation was made in 1914 by the ◊ *Board of Trade,* calculating an index figure for an average family of five or six persons. Subsequently, the Ministry of Labour took over the work, and the index was reorganized 1918 to cover three types of family (skilled, semi-skilled, and unskilled workers), and this continued throughout the inter-war period; during the Second World War it was an unreliable indicator of price movements because the government subsidized the index items to prevent the index from rising. Since the war there have been a number of revisions, on the basis of budget surveys, and the index now includes e.g. the cost of a second-hand car. In a number of industries there is a fixed link between wage rates and increases in the cost of living; where there is no such established link, increases in the cost of living are almost invariably put forward in wage negotiations as an argument for increases. International comparisons of the cost of living in different countries are difficult, because of differences in the patterns of consumption, but in the major industrial countries it is possible to make reasonable comparisons of any changes.

Cotton. *Gossypium,* a plant of the mallow family, of uncertain origin, cultivated from time immemorial in the Orient and by the ancient Peruvians (◊ *Incas*) in S. America; a small shrub with seeds, covered with long white fibres, in capsules (bolls), perennial but in cultivation treated as an annual, and widely grown in tropical and sub-tropical countries, major producers being Brazil, China, India, U.S.A., and U.S.S.R. Picking is still mainly by hand, though mechanical pickers have been devised; the fibres used in spinning (staple fibre) are from $\frac{3}{4}$ to $2\frac{1}{2}$ in. long, shorter fibres (linters) being a main source of ◊ *cellulose.* American cotton is mainly of the upland variety *G. hirsutum*; Egyptian and sea-island cotton, *G. barbadense,* is valued for its smoothness and long staple. Cotton is subject to a number of pests, the boll weevil being the most dangerous. An important by-product is cottonseed oil, used both as an edible oil and industrially; its residue, cottonseed cake, is a valuable cattle food.

Long before the Christian era, cotton provided the staple clothing of China, India, and Egypt; it was woven with great skill in India, and the names of the first cotton fabrics introduced into Britain (calico, madras, muslin) attest their origin. ◊ *Spinning and weaving* remained hand processes until the first successful spinning-machines were developed in England in the 18th cent.

World consumption of raw cotton is still increasing, and accounts for about two thirds of the total world consumption of all fibres, mainly because of the intrinsic virtues and astonishing versatility of the cotton fibre; extremely absorbent, strong, durable, easy to launder, cotton is the most satisfactory apparel fabric for hot and humid climates and is esp. suitable for many surgical, industrial, and household purposes.

Cotton Industry. After the mechanization of ◊ *spinning and weaving,* for about a century and a half Lancashire was predominant in cotton manufacturing, and by 1913 was the largest manufacturing industry the world had seen, producing 8000 m. yards of cloth a year, of which 7000 m. were exported, two thirds of the total world trade in cotton goods. Raw-cotton consumption in the U.K. in 1780 had been about 4 m. lb. but by 1913 it was 2178 m. lb. Other countries started to build their own cotton industries, often behind high tariff walls; they first met their own needs and then began to export. After 1918 there was a drastic reduction in U.K. output as a result of competitive manufacturing in other countries. Subsequently there has been a great increase in cotton manufacture in e.g. Hong Kong, India, Pakistan, where labour costs are low, and the U.K. share of total world trade has declined. During the last 40 years various schemes to eliminate redundant capacity in the U.K. have been introduced, e.g. since 1959 a great deal of old and idle machinery has been eliminated and the industry is now re-equipping with the most advanced machinery and techniques, so that far fewer mills and a much smaller labour force are able to meet home and export requirements.

Council of Europe. Founded 1949 (original members Belgium, Denmark, France, Ireland, Italy, Luxemburg, the Netherlands, Norway, Sweden, and the U.K.) to examine European political and economic problems; its Committee consists of Foreign Ministers (or their deputies) and it has a Consultative Assembly, meeting in Strasbourg. More recently Austria, Cyprus, W. Germany, Greece, Iceland, and Turkey have been admitted.

Counterpoint. The simultaneous combination of melodies is one element in most forms of western music. It is particularly strong in the music of the ◊ *Renaissance* period e.g. such 16th-cent. masters as Byrd, Lassus, and Palestrina, and in the music of such ◊ *'baroque'* composers as Bach and Handel. A basic contrapuntal technique is that of inverting a melody i.e. preserving the shape but presenting it upside-down. ◊ *Canon and fugue* are applications of such contrapuntal techniques, rigidly systematized in the 18th cent.

In later music more emphasis was placed on ◊ *harmony*, and on the structural forms deriving from it, than on contrapuntal forms as such; but contrapuntal interest is still seen in e.g. the finale of Brahms's Symphony No. 4 with its bass theme many times repeated while other themes are developed above (the technique known as *chaconne* or *passacaglia*). In the 20th cent. counterpoint has to some extent been restored to its older primacy. In particular, modern serial technique, stemming from Schoenberg, rejects the harmonic conventions of consonance and dissonance and adopts a construction based on the permutations of a 'given' melody, using the contrapuntal devices of inversion etc. ◊ *Progression (Harmonic)*.

Counter-Reformation. In the late 16th cent. Roman Catholic doctrines and practices having been clarified and reformed by the Council of ◊ *Trent*, the Papacy renewed its struggle against ◊ *Protestantism*, esp. by means of the Congregation for Propaganda on Faith, founded in 1622, and led by the Jesuits, with the dual purpose of converting the pagans of the New World (◊ *Missions*) and re-converting the seceders of NW Europe, esp. Britain. The re-conversion policy rapidly involved the papacy in direct politics e.g. in France, Piedmont, the Netherlands, Britain, Bavaria, Poland, etc. and its political rather than religious aspects caused long-lasting anti-papal suspicions and hostility. After the failure of the political Counter-Reformation in Britain and the Netherlands, the movement became mainly associated with elaborate art forms e.g. ◊ *rococo* architecture. The 19th-cent. ◊ *Oxford Movement* was a late non-political recrudescence. ◊ *English Civil Wars, Glorious Revolution, Gunpowder Plot, Huguenots, Jacobites, Popish Plot, Thirty Years War*.

Counter-Trades ◊ *Trade Winds*.

Coursing. Hunting the hare with greyhounds (which run by sight, not scent), a sport said to be 4000 years old; the first rules were drawn up in Elizabeth I's reign, 16th cent. Two dogs are released simultaneously, and a judge awards them points for speed and good work; the hare does not have to be killed for a decision on the dogs to be given. The National Coursing Club was founded

1858, and Britain's classic event is the Waterloo Cup, founded 1836.

Courtly Love. A medieval European literary convention developed by the ◊ *troubadours* in 12th-cent. S. France, which produced an extensive body of poetry idealizing the 'lady' in a series of love situations; its roots are obscure, but it seems to owe something to the poets of Moorish Spain, to Plato's thought (assimilated independently or perhaps transmitted by the Moors), and to Ovid, and it has also been suggested that the obscurer troubadour poems are linked with the Cathar heresies (◊ *Albigenses*). The convention was developed and modified by the 13th- and 14th-cent. trouvères in N. France, who institutionalized the role of the knight in the love situation. The convention – which laid down that true love was outside the marriage bond, the knight being a secret and loyal obedient servant of his lady – had a religious counterpart in the development of the cult of the Virgin (◊ *Mary*), and its expression of the feelings of chivalric and romantic love has been of incalculable importance in European literature and life. The work most influential in English literature was Guillaume de Lorris's part of the ◊ *Roman de la Rose*, but the convention was never dominant in England.

Court Martial. Tribunal to try members of the armed forces for offences against discipline or (if the accused has not been brought before the civil courts) against the civil law. Military and Air-Force courts martial are of three kinds: (a) district (at least three officers of two years' standing); (b) general (at least five officers of three years' standing); (c) field-general (normally at least three officers). A Naval court martial consists of from five to nine officers. The court is usually advised by an officer with legal qualifications, from the Judge Advocate General's department; appeal from a court martial lies to the Courts Martial Appeals Court. Courts martial have jurisdiction over civilians only under ◊ *martial law*.

Court of Appeal. The Court which hears appeals from the High Court, in civil cases, and with the High Court forms the Supreme Court of Judicature, founded 1873; it consists of the ◊ *Lord Chancellor*, any former Lord Chancellor or former Lord of Appeal in Ordinary who consents to act, the ◊ *Lord Chief Justice*, the Master of the Rolls (who acts as president), the President of the Probate Divorce and Admiralty Division, and 8–11 Lords Justices of Appeal. The Court may sit in one division or more; normally the Master of the Rolls and the Lords Justices sit, three forming a quorum for most purposes.

Court of Criminal Appeal. The court which hears appeals against conviction or sentence, from the Central Criminal Court, the Assizes, and the Quarter Sessions; founded 1907, it consists of the ◊ *Lord Chief Justice* and the judges of the Queen's Bench Division, three forming a quorum but five sitting in difficult cases. It may dismiss an appeal even where a mistake has been made (if satisfied that no substantial miscarriage of justice has occurred), but has no power to order a retrial and must either allow an appeal or dismiss it.

Court of Star Chamber. A court not bound by formal rules of procedure, and exercising the criminal jurisdiction of the ◊ *Privy Council*, used by the Tudors for dealing with nobles powerful enough to intimidate ordinary courts and by the early Stewarts to evade normal processes of law; with the ecclesiastical High Commission court, it was abolished 1641 by the Long Parliament, and, whether deservedly or not, is of evil reputation.

Covenant. 1. In English law, a contract under seal or agreement by deed.
2. A treaty of agreement, or a constitution e.g. the Covenant of the ◊ *League of Nations*.
3. In the Judaic and Christian religions, promises from God; e.g. the rainbow is the sign of a covenant never again to overwhelm the world by flood. ◊◊ *Bible*.
4. In Scottish history, a series of Protestant agreements esp. in defence of ◊ *Calvinism* and the ◊ *Presbyterian* mode of church organization. In 1643 the Solemn League and Covenant demanded Presbyterianism as the State Church in England, Scotland, and Wales. The Scots took part in the ◊ *English Civil Wars* only after Parliament accepted the Covenant. The England of the ◊ *Commonwealth and Protectorate* rejected the Covenant in favour of Independency. After the ◊ *Restoration* all attempts to impose episcopacy on Scotland were met with bitter and violent resistance, bloodily suppressed

esp. 1679–80. The struggle ended with the ◊ *Glorious Revolution* of 1688.

Cow ◊ *Cattle.*

Cowpox. One of several pock diseases affecting animals, related to smallpox in humans. Prevalent among cattle a century ago, but now rare; it induced a mild infection on the hands of people milking infected cows, and was believed to give some protection against smallpox, which led Jenner to experiment successfully with the cowpox virus as the basis of antismallpox vaccination. ◊◊ *Scheduled Diseases, Sheep Pox.*

Crab. ◊ *Crustacean* distinguished by its prominent carapace, usually broader than it is long, e.g. in the edible and common shore crabs, though departures from this form are seen in the spider and hermit crabs. The first pair of legs are modified to form claws, often of large size; in most crabs the remaining four pairs of legs are used for walking, but in some the last pair are modified to facilitate swimming. The largest crab is the Giant Spider Crab of Japan, whose claws may span up to 11 ft.

'Cracking' (Fractional Distillation) ◊ *Catalyst, Petroleum (Refining).*

Cranium. The bone that forms the vault of the skull and protects the brain. ◊◊ *Skeleton.*

Craps ◊ *Dice.*

Crayfish (Crawfish). Small decapod freshwater ◊ *crustacean* resembling a ◊ *lobster*, common in the streams and rivers of Europe; related genera are found in Asia, Australasia, and America. The red-clawed species *Astacus fluviatilis* is eaten.

Cream of Tartar ◊ *Tartaric Acid.*

Creation ◊ *Evolution.*

Crécy. 1346. Battle in the ◊ *Hundred Years War* when Philip VI of France engaged the English under Edward III as they retreated towards the Low Countries. The defeat of the French cavalry by a largely plebeian English army of pikemen and archers marked the end of the military superiority of heavily-armed mounted knights. ◊◊ *Bannockburn.*

Creed. Official summary of Christian belief, used at baptism or in public worship.

APOSTLES CREED: Used only in the western churches; attributed to the 12 Apostles of ◊ *Jesus Christ* and extant from the 4th cent. in a form resembling that used today.

ATHANASIAN CREED: A hymn on the Trinity, not the work of Athanasius but possibly by St Ambrose.

NICENE CREED: That drawn up by the General Council at Nicaea A.D. 325 and enlarged at the Council of Constantinople A.D. 381, used by the Roman Catholic and Anglican churches at Mass or Holy Communion, and in slightly varied form by the Eastern Orthodox church. The earliest and possibly the ancestor of following creeds was the 'Old Roman', perhaps used in the 2nd cent. A.D., of which no sure record has survived.

Cremation. Disposal of the dead by burning; the normal procedure in much of the ancient civilized world (and in India and elsewhere today) but frowned on by early Christians because of belief in bodily resurrection; fell into disuse in Europe until the 19th cent., but has since become frequent.

Creoles. Originally persons of Spanish ancestry in the S. and central American colonies. The term is now used of descendants of non-aboriginal peoples, esp. French, including persons of mixed ancestry, in the West Indies, parts of America (e.g. Louisiana), Mauritius, Réunion, and some other colonies. In W. Africa creoles are the descendants of freed slaves repatriated from the New World. Creoles who have some Negro ancestry are sometimes called Creole Negroes. In the U.S.A. the term is applied to French-speaking people of mixed ancestry in Louisiana.

Also a debased form of French (◊ Pidgin) spoken in e.g. ◊ Haiti.

Creosote, Cresols ◊ Phenol.

Cresta ◊ Tobogganing.

Cretaceous Period. Geological period, lasting 120 m. years, concluding the Mesozoic Era (◊ Geological Time Scale); a relatively quiet period in the earth's history, during most of which the climate was generally mild. At first most of the British Isles was land, the lower cretaceous formations being ◊ delta deposits; a gradual subsidence followed, and ◊ chalk, which gives its name to the period, was deposited in shallow seas covering most of NW Europe. ◊◊ Calcite, Eustatic Movements, Gault, Isostasy.

Crete. Area 3235 sq. m. Pop. 483,258. Cap. Canea. Island in the E. Mediterranean, scene of the ◊ Minoan Civilization, part of ◊ Greece since 1913 (after the ◊ Balkan Wars). During the ◊ Second World War British and Greek forces retreated there 1940–1, when the Germans overran Greece; but they were defeated in the first mass parachute-landing in history, carried out by the Germans in 1941.

Crete (Ancient) ◊ Knossos, Minoan Civilization.

Cretinism. Condition of retarded mental and physical development in infants due to congenital lack of the hormone thyroxine, normally produced by the thyroid gland in the neck. Endemic cretinism occurs in regions where the water supply is deficient in iodine (e.g. the Alps). In its effort to utilize the small amount of iodine available, the thyroid enlarges and causes swelling of the neck (goitre). Sporadic cretinism occurs anywhere and is due to congenital absence of the thyroid gland. In this case, thyroxine given regularly from a very early age can ensure normal development.

Crevasse. Deep gaping crack in a ◊ glacier, occurring wherever the ice is stretched; transverse where the ice falls down a slope of increased steepness, longitudinal where the ice fans out in a widened part of the valley. Other crevasses result from the fact that the ice moves faster in the middle of the glacier than at the edges. If several crevasses intersect, the ice is broken up into a maze of ice pedestals known as séracs. ◊ Bergschrund, Ice Sheet, Moraine.

Cribbage. A card game for two or more players, scored on a board with 61 pegs. Each player receives five or six cards, and after two from each hand have been put aside to form the 'crib' (concealed hand), the remainder are laid down one at a time until either a count of 31 is reached or all have been played. Points are awarded for combinations e.g. making pairs, and for playing the final cards to make up totals 15 and 31. Each hand also scores for various combinations it contains. The dealer receives the crib. The game was invented by Sir John Suckling in the 17th cent. It may be descended from the older game 'Noddy', since the Jack in the crib used to be known as 'Knave Noddy', now corrupted to 'His Nobs'.

Cricket. An English summer game, played with bat and ball on a pitch 22 yards long; in turn, each team's batsmen aim to score 'runs' against the fielding side, who try to bowl, catch, or stump them out. Certainly as early as the 13th cent. in origin, cricket grew up in S. England, and by the mid 18th cent. the Hambledon (Hampshire) club was famous. Laws of cricket existed by 1744; the Marylebone Cricket Club (MCC), founded 1787, has revised them several times and still introduces minor improvements every few years, its authority remaining internationally accepted. The exact start of the County Championship is disputed, but Nottinghamshire are quoted as champions in 1853, by which time the game had spread abroad. The first overseas touring team left in 1859 for N. America, and an English touring team toured Australia 1861, paving the way for the first Test matches 1876–7; the ◊ '*Ashes*' resulted from England's defeat by seven runs at the Oval Cricket Ground in London, 1882, by which time teams had been standardized at 11 men and overarm bowling legalized. The Advisory County Cricket Committee was set up in 1904 and the Board of Control for Test Matches in England 1898. The Imperial Cricket Conference, founded 1909, comprises the Test-playing countries: England, Australia, West Indies, New Zealand, India, and Pakistan (S. Africa ceased to be a member 1961 on leaving the Commonwealth). Minor cricket countries include Holland, Canada, Malaya, Ceylon, U.S.A., and several African countries. Australia's states compete in the Sheffield Shield, founded 1892, corresponding to the English County Championship; New Zealand's trophy is the Plunket Shield, and the W. Indies have a Triangular Tournament, India the Ranji Trophy, Pakistan the Quaid-I-Azam Trophy, and S. Africa the Currie Cup. Amateur 'one-day' cricket flourishes in schools and clubs in all these countries, and professional league cricket in the N. of England. The distinction between ◊ *amateurs* and professionals in English county cricket was ended 1962. Recent attempts to halt falling attendances (at all but Test matches) have included bonus points for fast scoring in County games and the 1963 introduction of a 'knock-out' trophy competition.

Crime. A wrong against the community, for which punishment is prescribed (as opposed to civil injury i.e. a wrong against an individual, for which the remedy is normally compensation); an act may be both a crime and a civil wrong. Normally, to establish guilt, it must be proved not only that the act was done but that it was done with *mens rea* (a guilty mind) i.e. an intention to do that act. Criminal offences are indictable (i.e. must be tried before a jury) or summary (i.e. triable before a magistrates' court); certain indictable offences are triable summarily if the accused consents.

A person who actually commits a ◊ *felony* is a principal in the first degree; one who is present aiding and abetting e.g. by keeping watch, is a principal in the second degree; one who counsels or instigates a felony, but is not present when it is committed, is an accessory before the fact; one who knowingly assists or harbours the felon, or aids his escape, is an accessory after the fact.

In 1962 the number of persons convicted of indictable offences in England and Wales was 203,775, of whom 66,222 (32.5 per cent) were juveniles; 11,986 persons were convicted of violence, 1787 of them juveniles (15 per cent). The number of persons convicted for non-indictable offences was 1,062,821, of whom 54,715 were juveniles, five per cent. In all courts, 28,702 persons (exc. juveniles) were sentenced to imprisonment, corrective training, or preventive detention; of these 1081 were females and 1832 under 21. Fines were imposed on 80,893 persons, of whom 12,434 were females and 29,974 were under 21, and 41,657 persons were placed on probation, 7048 of them females and 30,353 under 21. ◊ *Central Criminal Court, Criminology.*

Crimean War. 1854–6. Caused mainly by Russia's aim of controlling Constantinople (◊ *Ottoman Empire*). Turkey declared war in 1853, and Britain entered the war with France as ally. After Constantinople had been secured, the Allies set out to besiege Sevastopol, Russian naval base in the Crimea. The British army, badly equipped and led, suffered enormously from cold and disease and, until Florence Nightingale intervened, from appalling hospitals. In spite of poor cooperation, the allies succeeded in defeating the numerically superior Russian forces, and the Paris Treaty of peace was concluded in 1856. The only significant effect of the war was to deny passage of the Dardanelles to Russian warships. ◊ *Bala-*

clava, Berlin Congress, British Army, Inkerman.

Criminology. The study of the causes and treatment of ◊ *crime.* It is doubtful whether criminology can claim to be a distinct science; rather it is the application of scientific methods and knowledge drawn from biology, medicine, psychology, and law. In Britain, the Cambridge Institute of Criminology is the only academic institution solely concerned with the subject. Until recently, criminology concentrated on the question: 'What is the cause of crime?' Cesare Lombroso, mid 19th cent., related crime to a kind of 'moral insanity' and sought to define the type of person who becomes a criminal, but it is now generally recognized that there is no one cause of crime and that to speak of a 'criminal type' is as fallacious as to refer to the 'criminal classes'; it thus becomes relevant to inquire what conditions are correlated with a high incidence of any particular crime, and what characteristics, if any, are frequently associated with a particular type of conduct.

The results of investigation in the field of penology appear in the Criminal Justice Act of 1948, but the legal profession as a whole has not familiarized itself with this study. ◊ *Capital Punishment, Corporal Punishment.*

Croatian (Serbo-Croat) ◊ *Slavonic Languages, Yugoslavia.*

Crocodile. Member of the *Crocodilia,* an order which evolved in the Mesozoic period some 150 m. years ago, adapted to an aquatic existence and retaining many features of their earliest ancestors. The blunt-nosed alligator found throughout the tropics, and the caiman of S. America, are flesh-eaters; the long-snouted fish-eaters are represented only by the gharial of India and one other Indian genus. The biggest are 20 ft long; normally sluggish, they can on occasion run for short distances. True crocodile skin furnishes a hard-wearing and decorative leather.

Crocus. The best known of plants grown from a ◊ *corm;* there are about 80 wild species, found only in a limited area, S. Europe, N. Africa, and the Near East. The flowers usually rise only a few inches above the ground, in winter, autumn, or spring, depending on the species, and appear with or without the leaves, open-

ing in the sun to bright-coloured stars. In gardens the Dutch Yellow of spring has been in cultivation since 1597; the white, mauve, and bluish ones were subsequently derived from the wild European *C. vernus.* The orange stigmas of *C. sativus* produce saffron (< Arabic, yellow), once extensively used for colouring and flavouring, as it still is in some countries. The place-name Saffron Walden arose from the cultivation of the plant there in the 14th cent. ◊ *Iridaceae.*

Croesus. King of Lydia 560–546 B.C. and in his early years a rich and powerful ruler who made many conquests. But on his asking whether he was not the happiest of men, the Greek philosopher Solon replied: 'Call no man happy till after a happy death.' When Croesus sent to the Delphic ◊ *oracle* to ask whether he should attack Persia, the reply was that by so doing he would overthrow a great empire. He was ingloriously defeated by Cyrus, the 'great empire' being his own; condemned to death, he called Solon's name. Cyrus asked why, and on hearing the story spared his life.

Cro-Magnon Man. Variety of *Homo sapiens,* of the upper ◊ *Palaeolithic* period, named after the rock shelter in the Dordogne (France) in which his remains were first found. Unlike ◊ *Neanderthal man,* Cro-Magnon was tall and slender in build, and had an entirely 'modern' skull with a brain capacity at least equal to that of modern man. He was responsible for the fine flint work and the polychrome paintings of the upper Palaeolithic in W. Europe. ◊ *Cave Art.*

Cronos ◊ *Titans, Uranus.*

Crop Rotation. System in agriculture whereby different crops are grown in a regular succession so as to avoid soil exhaustion and the plant diseases likely to occur with repeated culture of one crop. Some form of rotation probably arose in early times as a result of experience showing that a heavier crop was obtained after the growth of clover or beans, but systematic crop rotation began with the 18th-cent. agrarian revolution; the Norfolk four-course rotation (introduced by Lord Townshend) is clover pasture, oats (or wheat), roots, barley; the E. Lothian six-course rotation is roots, barley, seeds (grass and clover mixture), oats, potatoes, wheat.

Croquet. A lawn game for individuals or pairs in which wooden balls are struck with mallets through small hoops on a court 35 by 28 yds; possibly evolved from the 13th-cent. Languedoc game of *paille-maille* (pell-mell). Croquet became popular in England in the 19th cent. and the first Open Championship, 1868, led to men's and women's championships, inter-county matches, and a periodic International Trophy match involving England, New Zealand, and Australia.

Cross-breeding ◊ *Breeding, Hybrid*.

Crown Jewels. The jewels used by the sovereign on state occasions, including crowns and sceptres. The British crown jewels are kept in the Jewel House at the Tower of London; most of the old crown regalia were broken up by the Queen in 1644 and sold in France to raise funds for the King's Army in the Civil Wars, and only the ampulla and anointing-spoon are of great age. The chief crowns are St Edward's Crown, made for Charles II and used at all coronations, the Imperial State Crown, made for Queen Victoria and containing many famous jewels, and the Imperial Crown of India made for George V but no longer used.

Cruciferae. Wallflower family; dicotyledons, usually herbs with simple spirally-arranged leaves, flowers with four sepals, four petals, and six stamens. The fruit is a specialized capsule usually opening into two valves. Widely distributed, mostly in N. temperate zone, many are valuable food plants (shoots and seeds) e.g. ◊ *cabbage* (broccoli, cauliflower, cress, swede, turnip, etc.) and others ornamental (alyssum, arabis, aubretia, candytuft, honesty, stocks, wallflowers). Various species e.g. charlock, rocket, commonly grow wild in Britain.

Cruiser. A ◊ *warship* of medium size, about 5000 to 10,000 tons displacement, with a main armament of 5-in. to 8-in. guns and a speed of 30 knots or more. A famous cruiser action in the Second World War was the defeat of the German pocket ◊ *battleship* the *Graf Spee* by three British cruisers in the Battle of the River Plate. The latest British cruiser is the 8000-ton *Lion*, 1960.

Crusades. Military expeditions undertaken by European powers between the 11th cent. and the 14th to recover the Holy Land from its Muslim rulers.

The First Crusade, preached by Pope Urban II at the Council of Clermont in 1095, was undertaken with enthusiasm and from a variety of motives: genuine piety, land hunger, and a desire for trade, travel, and adventure. The armies, led by Godfrey of Bouillon, Raymond of Toulouse, Bohemond, Tancred, Robert of Normandy, and Robert II of Flanders, took Antioch in 1098 and Jerusalem in 1099 and set up the Latin Kingdom of Jerusalem under Godfrey. This was the only Crusade to achieve substantial results.

The Second Crusade, preached by Bernard of Clairvaux after the Turks took Edessa in 1144, ended in quarrelling among the leaders and in complete failure.

The Third Crusade, undertaken by Richard I of England, Philip II of France, and the Emperor Frederick I, after Saladin's capture of Jerusalem, ended with the capture of Acre in 1191 and a truce with Saladin permitting Christians free access to the Holy Sepulchre.

In the Fourth Crusade, 1202–4, devout motives gave way entirely to those of territorial expansion. The armies did not reach the Holy Land, but turned aside to sack Constantinople and depose the Byzantine Emperor Alexius III. The Crusaders shared the enormous wealth they gained with the Italian merchants who had prompted the expedition, and set up the Latin Kingdom of Constantinople. This disgrace marked the end of the great crusading period. ◊ *Byzantine Empire, Venice*.

Subsequent crusades were directed mainly at Egypt and were largely futile. The most pathetic was the Children's Crusade, 1212, which ended in the death and enslavement of large numbers of children from France and Germany.

The term Crusade is applied also to military expeditions sponsored by the Pope against non-Christians other than the Muslims, non-papal Christians e.g. the Slavs (◊ *Orders of Chivalry* (*Teutonic Knights*)), and heretics e.g. the ◊ *Albigenses*.

Although the political and territorial gains of the Crusades were short-lived, their results in other directions had an immeasurable importance in the growth of European civilization, through increased trade and the growth in knowledge and sophistication which resulted from contact with the Byzantine and Muslim civilizations.

Crustacea. Arthropods with many paired appendages, modified for sensory, feeding, motive, swimming, and sexual purposes, ranging from minute water-fleas to ◊ *crabs* and ◊ *lobsters*. In many species the head is fused with the thoracic segments to form the cephalothorax, and crustaceans possess an exoskeleton which may be hardened by calcification to form a series of prominent and segmentally arranged plates (sclerites) joined by other flexible plates. They are mostly aquatic, inhabiting fresh and sea water, but some e.g. woodlice are terrestrial. Many of the decapod crustaceans are edible e.g. shrimps, prawns, ◊ *crayfish*, etc.; the minute pelagic crustacea serve man indirectly as the food of economically important fish and of the baleen ◊ *whales*.

Crystal ◊ *Crystallography, Glass, Quartz.*

Crystallography. The study of the shape of crystals and of the geometric relationships between their planes. In general, the shape of a crystal results from a systematic arrangement of the atoms of which the substance is composed, a basic structure of atoms peculiar to that substance being repeated throughout the crystal. The structure of crystals can be studied with ◊ *X-rays* whose wavelength is of the same order of magnitude as the spacing between the planes of atoms. Crystallography has important applications in the metallurgical, ◊ *transistor*, and other industries in which a knowledge of crystal structure is required. ◊◊ *Optics.*

Cuba. Area 44,178 sq. m. Pop. 6.5 m. Cap. Havana. A Caribbean island; a socialist republic under a President and a Council of Ministers. Prime Minister Dr Fidel Castro.

ECONOMY. The means of production and distribution are nationalized; all foreign trade, 90 per cent of industrial production, and about 50 per cent of small commercial companies are State-controlled. About half the cultivated land is in co-operatives or State farms. Sugar accounts for 80 per cent of exports, though production 1963 was only about 3.6 m. tons as against 5.6 m. 1960. Other agricultural products are tobacco (especially cigars), bananas, rice, coffee, cocoa, maize, cotton. Cattle-raising is also important. Education is free and compulsory, and there are two universities. Broadcasting, television, and press are under government control.

HISTORY. Discovered 1492 by Columbus and conquered by Spain early in the 16th cent. Cuba remained a Spanish colony until the fierce war of independence in 1898, when U.S.A. intervened against Spain (◊ *Spanish-American War*), and then was under U.S. military rule 1899–1902 and again 1906–9. A republican system lasted till 1933, when General Batista seized power. In 1940 he introduced a constitution providing for a popularly elected president, a Senate of 54 members, and a House of Representatives of 140 members, and promulgated some limited reforms; but the regime remained essentially a dictatorship, the apportionment of land was grossly unjust, and there was serious unemployment and near-starvation of the peasantry. In 1959 Batista was forced to abdicate by the revolution of Fidel Castro, who inaugurated large-scale reforms in land-holding, education, industry, commerce, and finance. His severe repressive measures against opponents, and the close ties he formed with the Sino-Soviet bloc, alienated the U.S.A. and many of his former Cuban supporters. In 1961 a counter-revolutionary invasion openly supported by U.S.A. failed to overthrow his regime. In the same year he announced that he had long been a marxist, and in 1962 he permitted the construction of Soviet rocket bases, ◊ *Cuba Crisis.*

Cuba Crisis. 1962. In October 1962 President Kennedy announced the detection of Soviet rocket sites in ◊ *Cuba*. He instituted a blockade of Cuba to prevent delivery of offensive weapons and insisted that any already delivered should be withdrawn. On 28 October Khrushchev announced that the bases would be dismantled and the most acute international crisis since the ◊ *Berlin* blockade was brought to an end.

Cubism. The most influential style in 20th cent. painting; though not strictly non-representational, it sprang from a reaction against the preoccupation of ◊ *Impressionism* with visual appearances, and led towards ◊ *Abstract Art*. Its leaders Braque and Picasso followed Cézanne in a quest for a manner of painting to represent form and space without recourse to illusionism; natural forms were transformed into fragmented sculptural arrangements of transparent planes, which overlapped one another. Heralded by Picasso's *Demoiselles d'Avignon* 1907

(Museum of Modern Art, N.Y.) in which a group of nudes were transformed into a semi-abstract composition, the movement became established 1909–14. Braque declared: 'Painting is a means of representation. It is wrong to imitate what one wants to create. One does not imitate appearances; appearances are results. In order to achieve pure imitation, painting must disregard appearances. Working from nature is improvisation.' Braque and Picasso attracted many followers, but few adopted their empirical approach to the problems of representation. Juan Gris developed 'synthetic' cubism, and his severe forms and restrained colours greatly influenced non-figurative art.

Cuchullin (Cuchulain). In Irish legend, a great hero, nephew of ◊ *Conchubar* and central figure of the epic *Tain bo Cuailgne* (The Cattle-raid of Cooley). The warrior queen of Connaught, Maeve (Medhbh), raided Ulster to capture a coveted bull, but Cuchullin long held off her whole host single-handed; to his great grief, he slew (with many other warriors) his sworn brother Ferdiad. Though (with Conchubar's help) Maeve captured the bull, her army was driven out of Ulster; she again attacked, and there was a heroic struggle in which Cuchullin's horse the Grey of Macha fought the enemy with his hooves and Cuchullin fought tied to a post so as to die standing. His death was known when a raven alighted on his head to pluck out his eyes.

Cuckoo. Migrant bird which winters in Africa, India and S E Asia and in the breeding season spreads over Europe and N. Asia; much larger than the other birds in whose nests the female lays a small white egg about the size of a sparrow egg. Although the cuckoo fledgling rapidly throws out the other young, the involuntary foster parents continue to feed it until it flies away. The parent cuckoos migrate south before the young, leaving them to find their way alone.

Cucumber. *Cucumis sativus*, of the *Cucurbitaceae*, an annual climbing plant, from the warmer parts of Asia, cultivated in Mediterranean countries in very early times. Only a few varieties are hardy enough to fruit in the open in the U.K. Gherkins are small cucumbers produced by a special variety. ◊ *Gourds.*

Culloden. 1746. Decisive battle in which the English defeated Prince Charles Edward and his Highlanders and brought an end to the ◊ *Jacobite* rebellions against the Crown.

Culture. In anthropology, 'culture' does not connote any refinement or advanced civilization, but simply refers to the standardized learnt patterns of social behaviour of the members of a human society. It includes not only manners and customs but beliefs, morals, language, music, art, and the material objects and techniques in use and transmitted as a social heritage to succeeding generations. They may be wiped out or modified by war and conquest, and most rapid and radical changes in cultures have usually occurred as a consequence of influences external to the culture itself; modern technological developments, however, can generate rapid changes within a given culture.

ACCULTURATION: Process of accepting and absorbing elements of an external culture.

Cumulus ◊ *Cloud.*

Cuneiform. Wedge-shaped writing for inscriptions on soft clay, made with a stylus or pointed stick, the characteristic arrowheads being produced by the first touch or impression; used about 3500 B.C. by the ◊ *Sumerians* in the inscriptions (still preserved at Uruk) now regarded as the earliest recorded language. Later it was used by the Assyrians and the ◊ *Hittites* and in the 6th–7th cent. B.C. records of the Achaemenid kings (◊ *Persia*) Darius, Cyrus, and Artaxerxes, and remained in use until the Christian era. ◊ *Alphabet.*

Cupid ◊ *Aphrodite, Eros, Psyche.*

Cupronickel ◊ *Alloys.*

Curare. A vegetable extract used as an arrow-head poison by the Amazon Indians; an ◊ *alkaloid* which acts by paralysing motor-nerve endings in muscle, causing failure of respiration. The purified alkaloid is used in surgery to relax tense muscle; this can now be synthesized.

Curie. Unit of radioactivity. One curie is defined as the quantity of any radioactive nuclide in which the number of disintegrations per second is 3.7×10^{10}. It is approximately equal to the radioactivity of 1 gm of ◊ *radium.*

Curling. A type of ◊ *bowls* on ice, with four players to each team, using flattish round 44-lb. stones fitted with handles, thrown to slide nearest to an assigned mark on a rink 138 ft long; of ancient origin, the game has spread from Scotland to Canada and Switzerland. The international body is the Royal Caledonian Curling Club.

Currants ◊ *Ribesaceae.*

Curriculum. The range of subjects taught formally in a school. Until about 1900, elementary schools taught mainly the 'Three Rs' (writing, reading, 'rithmetic), while secondary schools concentrated on mathematics and classics; the curriculum at all levels has since become broader. In the U.K. a school curriculum is planned by the head teacher in consultation with his or her staff, and is subject only to advice from inspectors and to the influence of public examinations; in other countries e.g. France and U.S.S.R. it is planned in detail by the central authority and the schools must accept it. ◊ *Education.*

Cushites. Speakers of E. Hamitic languages in NE Africa e.g. the Somali, the Denskil, and many peoples in Ethiopia and Eritrea. ◊ *African Peoples and Cultures, Hamito-Semitic Languages.*

Customs and Excise Board. U.K. government department which collects the customs and excise duties enacted by Parliament. Customs duties are taxes levied on a wide range of imported goods; excise tax is levied on certain goods produced within the country e.g. spirits, beer, matches, petrol. The Board also collects purchase tax.

Cuttlefish. Marine invertebrate mollusc, class *Cephalopoda*, related to the ◊ *octopus*, the most characteristic feature being an internal calcified shell, cuttle-bone, which is used as an agricultural manure and as bird-food; about 100 species are known. In some countries e.g. Japan, Greece, the cuttlefish is considered a delicacy.

Cyanide ◊ *Sodium.*

Cybele. In Asian mythology, goddess of nature and fertility, the Great Mother (Magna Mater), mother and mistress of ◊ *Attis*; identified by the Greeks with Rhea (◊ *Titans*) the sister and wife of Cronos (◊ *Uranus*) and mother of ◊ *Zeus*, ◊ *Hera*, and other great gods; often represented crowned, and accompanied by lions. The main seat of her worship was Pessinus in Galatia (where her castrated priests, the Galli, worshipped her as a rough stone block); it was universal in Phrygia, and she was specially honoured

at Mt Ida in Crete. Her cult became widespread in Rome in the later days of the republic.

Cybernetics. The study of control and communication in the machine or in the animal. It is concerned with how living and non-living systems regulate and reproduce themselves, evolve, and learn. As an applied science, cybernetics makes extensive use of ◊ *electronic* techniques and seeks to create machines that can plan and make decisions (◊ *Automation, Computer*).

Cyclone. Region where atmospheric pressure is low. There are two types: one common in temperate latitudes is usually called a ◊ *depression*; the other, which occurs in the tropics, is known as a tropical cyclone or typhoon, the latter being specific to the China Seas. All tropical cyclones, including typhoons, have winds of tremendous violence and torrential rain, and often cause widespread destruction. ◊ *Anticyclone.*

Cyclopes. In Greek legend, offspring of ◊ *Uranus*, giants with one eye in the centre of the forehead, living in caves in Sicily, rearing sheep and eating human flesh; ◊ *Ulysses* and his companions fell among them on their voyage home from Troy, and were seized by their king Polyphemus (◊ *Galatea*), who ate two men a day until Ulysses got him drunk and in his sleep burned out his single eye with a flaming brand. Awakened by the pain, Polyphemus blocked the exit from his cave, but Ulysses tied his men under the bellies of sheep brought in for shelter and let out again for pasture, passing himself off as the shepherd Nemo (nobody). In other legends, the Cyclopes assist ◊ *Hephaestus* in mining and metalwork; their single eyes may derive from the use of head-lamps by Sicilian metal-miners.

Cyclotron. Device for accelerating atomic particles so as to provide a beam of high-energy protons or deutrons. The particles are made to execute a nearly circular orbit by the magnetic field produced by large electromagnets, and are accelerated by the voltage delivered by a radio-frequency oscillator as they pass between two semicircular ◊ *electrodes*, called 'dees' because of their shape. ◊ *Particle Accelerator.*

Cynicism. The attitudes and doctrines of Diogenes and his followers in the Graeco-Roman world, for whom the virtuous life was the life of happiness to be gained through self-sufficiency, that is freedom from all conventions and ordinary values, from the desire for money or property, from the ties of family or friends. The Cynics, often deliberately paupers, were biting critics of conventionality.

Cyperaceae. Sedge family; a widespread family of marsh plants, distinct from true ◊ *rushes*, usually perennial with grasslike shoots and narrow leaves but solid stem, which is triangular in some genera. Some sedges are used for baskets. The papyrus of ancient Egypt was made from strips of stems of *Cyperus papyrus* pressed together when wet. 'Tiger nuts' are the tubers of *Cyperus esculentus*, very popular in Spain, where a drink called *horchata de chufas* is made from them.

Cypress. An ornamental but not very hardy genus of ◊ *conifers*, widely found in Europe, Asia, and N. America, usually of a pyramidal habit with globular cones. The wood is used for building and cabinet work.

Cyprus. Area 3572 sq. m. Pop. 590,000. Cap. Nicosia. Island in Mediterranean; an independent republic, member of the Commonwealth. Some three quarters of the population are Greek-speaking members of the ◊ *Eastern Orthodox Church*; the remainder are Turkish Muslims (◊ *Islam*).

ECONOMY. Agriculture is the main occupation, but minerals form the chief export industry.

HISTORY. Settled in early times by Greeks, Cyprus had a succession of Assyrian, Egyptian, Roman, Byzantine, and Arab rulers. Richard I of England captured it in 1191; subsequently it was ruled by Venice until 1570. It was conquered in 1570 by the Turks (◊ *Ottoman Empire*), who continued in control, despite revolts, until Britain took over the administration in 1878 (◊ *Berlin Congress*). During the ◊ *First World War* it became a British colony. A movement for union with ◊ *Greece* (Enosis), fostered by the Church, gathered strength, and after the Second World War its organized body E.O.K.A. instituted a terrorist campaign against the British, and conflict between the Greek and Turkish communities also broke out. Archbishop Makarios was deported. In 1959 an agreement making Cyprus an independent republic was concluded between Greece, Turkey, and

Britain and accepted by the Greek and Turkish Cypriots. Archbishop Makarios was elected President and in 1961 Cyprus became a member of the ◊ *British Commonwealth*. Serious Greek-Turkish disturbances again broke out in 1964. ◊> *Partition*.

Cyrillic ◊ *Alphabet, Bulgaria*.

Cytology. The study of ◊ *cells*; classical cytology, based on the study of dead cells with the light microscope, established the essential similarity of cells whose bodily functions might give them widely different shapes and sizes, and also the method of cell reproduction i.e. by division of existing cells. The development of the electron microscope has permitted extension of these studies to intricate intracellular structures. Modern cytology has also concentrated on the behaviour of living cells in tissue culture and on the chemical activities of different parts of the living cell.

Cytoplasm ◊ *Cell, Gametes, Genes*.

Czechoslovakia. Area 49,000 sq. m. Pop. 1961, 13.7 m. Cap. Prague. The Czechoslovak Socialist Republic, a People's Democracy within the Soviet bloc. Its organs are the National Assembly, the Slovak National Council, and the National Committee, but power is in the hands of the Communist Party Politburo. The majority of the population is Roman Catholic; all churches are subject to state control, clergymen being paid by the state, and 90 per cent of the Roman Catholic priesthood had taken an oath of allegiance to the State by 1950.

ECONOMY. A well-endowed country with good agricultural land, forests, and coal and iron deposits, it was industrially well-advanced before 1939. Industry and trade are nationalized and agriculture is organized in state and collective farms; increases in industrial but not in agricultural production have been made under Five-Year Plans.

HISTORY. (◊> *Bohemia*.) Formerly part of ◊ *Austria-Hungary*, Czechoslovakia became independent 1918. Its first presidents, Masaryk 1918–35 and Beneš 1935–8, established good relations with France, which formed the ineffectual Little Entente with Czechoslovakia, Rumania, and Yugoslavia. The existence of a German minority in the Sudetenland gave Hitler a pretext for stirring up trouble: the 1938 ◊ *Munich Pact* handed over the

Sudetenland to Germany, Czechoslovakia not being consulted. (Poland and Hungary seized other ethnic minority areas at the same time.) Hitler occupied the whole country 1939; a government in exile, under Beneš, was set up in London. Prague fell to the allies 1945 and came under Soviet occupation; the Sudeten Germans were expelled. With Soviet backing, the Czech Communist Party obtained a majority in the 1948 elections; President Beneš resigned and Czechoslovakia became a member of the Soviet bloc.

LANGUAGE. Czech, a flexible and efficient means of expression with a near-phonetic alphabet of 29 letters, spoken by 9 m. in Bohemia and Moravia; and Slovak, spoken by 3 m. in Slovakia; both of them are ◊ *Slavonic languages.* ◊ *Locarno Pact.*

D

Dadaism. An extremist anti-art movement, rooted in the nihilism caused by the First World War, originated with Arp and others in Zurich in 1916 and spread to France, Germany, and (with Marcel Duchamp) U.S.A. Its members set out to shock a bourgeois public with productions which outraged all accepted literary and artistic traditions, e.g. its productions included a urinal obtained by Duchamp and exhibited as *The Fountain* under the manufacturer's name. Max Ernst, Picabia, and the painter-photographer Man Ray were among the prominent Dadaist artists. Betrayed by its own nihilism, the movement dissolved in the early 1920s; by contrast, ◊ *Surrealism*, which grew out of it, had a constructive philosophy.

Daedalus. In Greek legend, a sculptor and craftsman who for murdering a rival, Talus, was condemned to exile by the Areopagus, went to Crete, and constructed the Labyrinth for ◊ *Minos*, but later was himself imprisoned in it with his son Icarus. He made waxen wings, with which they flew away, but Icarus got too near the sun, his wings melted, and he was drowned in the Aegean. Daedalus landed in Sicily.

Daffodil. Common name for Trumpet ◊ *Narcissi*, applied to two natives of the British Isles, the Lenten Lily, *Narcissus pseudonarcissus*, and the Tenby Daffodil, *N. obvallaris*. The large modern trumpet narcissi have been bred from wild species native to S. France and N. Spain.

Daguerreotype. An early process in ◊ *photography*.

Dahlia. Tuberous-rooted plants, the original wild species coming from Mexico, now existing in many garden varieties with a wide range of colour and shape. They were named after Dahl, a Swedish botanist.

Dahomey. Area 47,000 sq. m. Pop. 1.9 m. Cap. Porto Novo, but chief town Cotonou. Republic in W. Africa (between Niger, Nigeria, Togo, and the Voltaic Republic); member of the ◊ *French Community* since 1958 and self-governing since 1960, when the Dahomey Unity Party won a large majority in the elections. The 1961 Constitution provides for a President, a single-house National Assembly, and a Supreme Court.

ECONOMY. Exports 80 per cent palm products; also coffee, nuts. There are small deposits of chromium, gold, iron ore. Thickly populated, with a high level of education.

HISTORY. France signed a treaty with a local king in 1851 and took over the administration in 1892. In 1963 an Army coup deposed President Maga, suspending the Constitution.

Dail Eireann. The House of Representatives in the Republic of ◊ *Ireland*, under the 1949 Constitution consisting of 140 members elected by universal suffrage on a system of proportional representation. The Dail is the primary centre of political power, since the Prime Minister and Cabinet are responsible to it and the Senate can amend but not veto its legislation. Laws are, however, open to review by the courts where they are contrary to the Constitution.

Dairy Farming. Branch of agriculture which produces milk and milk products e.g. butter, cheese. Its development into a major and organized industry dates to about 1860, when pasteurization, improved milk cattle, and greater recognition of the value of milk as a food combined to increase its importance. It is an important industry in Canada, Australia, New Zealand, Holland, Denmark, and U.S.A. which are large exporters of dairy products, and of importance in most W. European countries, mainly for home consumption.

Daisy ◊ *Compositae*.

Dalai Lama. In ◊ *Tibet*, head of the Mahayana Buddhists (◊ *Buddhism*); believed to be an incarnation of the *Bodhisattva* Avalokiteshvara, and after death to be reborn in the body of a child, who after identification by a body of monks is trained to reassume his office. Traditionally the Dalai Lama was the temporal ruler of Tibet, but the present (14th) Dalai Lama, installed 1940, has since 1959 resided in India, where he fled after the communist Chinese occupation of Tibet.

Dalton Plan. A method of education devised in U.S.A. by Helen Parkhurst, first put into practice in 1920 at Dalton, Massachusetts, but now seldom employed: children work individually or in groups at units of work given to them by the teachers, and are encouraged to show initiative in planning their own work and recording the results.

Dam. Construction which serves to store water, permits flood and river control, and facilitates irrigation and generation of power. The simplest type is the earth embankment, in which a core of impervious clay prevents leakage. A gravity dam consists of a triangular block of masonry or concrete whose weight is sufficient to prevent the thrust of water from causing it to overturn or slide. The Furens Dam in France, 184 ft high, built 1806, is an early example. Buttress dams require less concrete and are often cheaper than gravity dams. For canyon sites, the arch dam is the usual choice: a relatively thin wall of concrete is curved so as to transmit the thrust to the rock of the valley sides. The first such was built in Provence in 1843, and the type is now common; Kariba on the Zambesi, 1959, 420 ft high and 2025 ft long, forms a lake 2000 sq. m. in extent. Some other notable dams are the Aswan dam in Egypt, the Dokan Dam in Iraq, the Grand Coulee and Hoover dams in U.S.A. The Aswan High Dam in Egypt is expected to be completed in 1970. ⬦ *Barrage.*

Damocles. In Greek legend, a courtier of Dionysius I, ruler of Syracuse (Sicily) 405–367 B.C. In response to his flattering congratulations on the happiness power and wealth must bring, Dionysius invited him to a banquet, at which a naked sword was suspended above his head by a single hair to symbolize the ever-present risks of a ruler's life; hence the proverbial 'sword of Damocles'.

Damon. Pythagorean philosopher; friend of Phintias (erroneously, Pythias). When Phintias was condemned to death for a plot against Dionysius I of Syracuse (⬦ *Damocles*), Damon offered himself as hostage while Phintias went on a journey to arrange his affairs, agreeing to be executed in his place if he did not return at the agreed time. Phintias did return; impressed by such altruistic affection, Dionysius pardoned Phintias and asked to be their friend. Hence 'Damon and Pythias' (Phintias), the proverbial self-effacing friendship.

Danaë. In Greek legend, daughter of Acrisius, king of Argos; an ⬦ *oracle* foretold that she would bear a son who would kill her father, who therefore kept her isolated in a brazen tower. But ⬦ *Zeus* visited her as a shower of gold, and she gave birth to ⬦ *Perseus,* who ultimately fulfilled the prophecy.

Danakil ⬦ *Cushites.*

Dance. The earliest dances were invariably accompanied by beating time with hands or drums. Associated with religion (as they still are among primitive peoples), they were performed to invoke or thank tribal gods, to exorcize evil spirits, to re-enact events in tribal myth or history; they often resulted in ecstasy in the dancers e.g. the dancing Dervishes. Both in classical Greece and India, dancing was intimately linked with the development of the ⬦ *drama,* as it was also in the 14th-cent. Japanese ⬦ *Nō* plays. Folk dances, of pagan descent, similarly celebrated seasonal festivals (⬦ *Morris Dance*) and persisted in Europe in spite of the disapproval of the early church. In the 16th cent. the *danses basses* of the court and the livelier *danses hautes* of the country were the beginnings of a more sophisticated type of social dancing e.g. the minuet and gavotte, which became very fashionable esp. under the patronage of Louis XIV. Although the earlier *lavolta* of Provence had been a twirling dance with a partner, it was not till the polka (from Prague) and the waltz (from Vienna) were introduced early in the 19th cent. that dancing in couples became usual. In England, where dancing became very popular, country dances similar to e.g. the Sir Roger de Coverley and the later Lancers dominated balls and assemblies. Scotland had its reels and strathspeys; Spain, where there was a long unbroken tradition, evolved the fandango and bolero, Poland the mazurka and polonaise, Hungary the czardas, and Latin America contributed the tango, samba, and rhumba. Many of these dances, with modifications, found their way to the ballroom.

Oriental dancing – Arabic, Indian, Far Eastern – tended to extreme formality with stress on body and hand movements e.g. with the dancers of Bali and Siam, the nautch girls of India, and the geisha of Japan, dancing was a professional exhibition rather than a social activity.

In U.S.A. after 1900 the music of ◊ *ragtime* and ◊ *jazz* brought a new sort of dance in the turkey-trot, from which developed the smoother foxtrot. The later Charleston was the forerunner of the more athletic jive, rock-and-roll, and twist of later decades, with its tendency to become an individual rhythmic exercise. In the U.K. dancing is the foremost active pastime, weekly attendances at dance halls throughout the country being several million, and its popularity is growing throughout western Europe. ◊ *Ballet*.

Dandelion ◊ *Compositae*.

Danes ◊ *Denmark, Vikings, Wessex*.

Danzig (Gdańsk) ◊ *Poland, Polish Corridor*.

Daphne. In Greek legend, the daughter of a river-god; ◊ *Apollo* fell in love with her and chased her, but she prayed for help and was changed into a laurel bush (or was swallowed up by the earth, which produced a laurel in her place). The laurel or bay (Gr. *daphne*) was sacred to Apollo.

Dardanelles (Hellespont). Straits joining the Aegean Sea to the Sea of Marmora. In the 19th cent. Russia wished to control them in order to give her fleet access to the Mediterranean; Britain and the Western powers succeeded in preventing this. In 1915 during the ◊ *First World War* the British (mainly Australian and New Zealand troops) made an attack on the Gallipoli Peninsula with a view to opening a new and less static front against the Central Powers. After a series of costly failures, over several months, to extend the initial beach-heads, the troops were withdrawn. In 1923, despite Russian protests, Turkey was given virtual control of the Straits in return for allowing restricted rights of passage to warships. By the ◊ *Montreux Convention* 1936 warships were forbidden to enter the Black Sea.

Dark Ages. Roughly the period of European history from the fall of the Western Empire in 476 A.D. until the rise of Charlemagne in 768. An imprecise term, now largely fallen into disfavour, since whilst it correctly implies that little is known about the period, it suggests a break in the continuity of European civilization which in fact did not occur.

Darts. British indoor game for two individuals or two teams played by throwing metal-pointed flighted darts at a circular wooden or cork dart-board marked in numbered segments, the aim being to achieve the best score, to hit certain divisions on the board, or various combinations of the two. Darts is played almost exclusively in public-houses, and local 'house' championships play a major part in community spirit.

Darwinism. Theories of ◊ *evolution* based on ◊ *natural selection*, elaborated by Charles Darwin in his *Origin of Species* 1859 and *Variations of Animals and Plants* 1868. Although bitterly opposed during his lifetime, Darwin's theory of man's descent from the lower animals is now widely accepted, as (with some modification) is natural selection. ◊ *Acquired Characteristics, Adaptation*.

Date Line ◊ *International Date Line*.

Dawes Plan. 1924. A U.S. plan to revise the amount of German ◊ *reparations* imposed after the ◊ *First World War*, fixing the payments as annuities, eventually to total £123 m. A further settlement was produced by the Young Commission in 1928, which reduced the amount of the annuities to £101 m. But Germany defaulted on payments in 1931, and since the allies refused to countenance the more lenient terms proposed by the Lausanne Agreement, she was able to suspend them indefinitely.

Day of Atonement. Hebrew *Yom Kippur*; Jewish solemn day of penitence and prayer on 10 Tishri (tenth day of the Jewish New Year, in Sept. or Oct.) observed by a 24-hour absolute fast from sunset to sunset, abstinence from work, and an almost continuous series of ◊ *synagogue* services culminating in the solemn sounding of the shofar (ram's horn). In pre-exilic ◊ *Judaism* it was marked by solemn sacrifices and the sending forth of the scapegoat; see Lev. 16.

D.C. (Direct Current) ◊ *Electric Current*.

D-Day. 1944. During the ◊ *Second World War* the largest seaborne invasion ever mounted put Allied forces ashore in Normandy, between Cherbourg and Le Havre, on 6 June 1944, after a period of intensive air bombardment of the German coastal defences and railway centres in France. The forces, under the supreme command of General Eisenhower, included 903,000 Americans, 600,000 British under General Montgomery, and a Free French Expeditionary Force under General Delattre de Tassigny. By 7 June, the Allies had consolidated their bridge-heads. Allied casualties during the landings are estimated at 11,000. The actual date of landing remained unknown till the last moment; so in the military planning it was referred to as D-Day, before and after being designated 'D minus' and 'D plus'.

Deacon. 1. Order of the Christian ministry (◊ *Holy Orders*) immediately inferior to the priesthood; originally (Acts 6) the deacon's duties were to distribute alms; today he assists the ◊ *priest* in administering the ◊ *sacraments*, in preaching, and in other functions. In the Roman Catholic and Anglican churches today the status of deacon is invariably a stage in preparation for the priesthood, but in the Eastern churches the diaconate is usually life-long. **2.** In some Protestant churches, a layman supervising a congregation's business concerns and occasionally preaching.

Deadly Nightshade. *Atropa belladonna*; a herb up to 5 ft tall, with dull green oval pointed leaves, dark purple-brown bell flowers, and black shiny berries. All parts are highly poisonous; they contain the alkaloids atropine and hyoscyamine, used for diseases of the nervous system, heart, and muscles. Belladonna juice has long been used medicinally; its property of dilating the pupils of the eyes is produced by atropine.

Dead Reckoning. A corruption of 'deduced reckoning'; a method of estimating a ship's position by using the distance run (as indicated by the ◊ *log*) together with the compass courses steered from a known position, after making due allowance for tidal streams, leeway, etc.

Dead Sea ◊ *Lake.*

Dead Sea Scrolls. A large collection of ancient Hebrew, Aramaic, and Greek manuscripts found in caves near the Dead Sea in Palestine. The earliest finds were made by a shepherd in 1947; nearly 100,000 fragments were found in one cave alone in 1952. About one third of the manuscripts are of the Old Testament (◊ *Bible*), the remainder being portions of the ◊ *Apocrypha*, commentaries, and devotional and instructional works. The archaeological evidence (based mainly on coins found in proximity to the manuscripts) suggests that the scrolls were part of the library of a religious community which lived near the caves from about 125 B.C. to A.D. 68, when it was suppressed by the Romans. The community has been identified with the sect known as the Essenes, and the chief importance of the scrolls has been to reveal the extent to which this sect anticipated the teachings of Christ. It is possible that John the Baptist was a member of the Essene community.

Deafness. Total or partial inability to hear; the most common causes include obstruction of the outer ear by wax, infection of the middle or inner ear, damage (as by repeated noise) to the eardrum and conducting ossicles, and lesion of the auditory nerve. Toxic deafness, usually temporary, may be due to drugs, especially quinine; permanent toxic deafness is apt to follow treatment of tuberculosis with streptomycin. ◊ *Hearing.*

DEAF-MUTISM: Speech does not develop, owing to congenital or (more rarely) acquired deafness. There are special institutions for the education and training of deaf-mutes, of whom there are some 40,000 in the U.K.

Death Duties. The only form of duty now arising on a death is estate duty, on property passing at death, at rates graduated according to the net value of the property, including not only the deceased's own property but interests ceasing or changing hands on death e.g. under settlements. This duty (1894) marked the beginning of the element of progressiveness in British taxation. Estates not exceeding £5000 are exempt, after which duty is payable at varying rates according to the value of the estate; gifts made by the deceased within five years of death are dutiable, but gifts made to certain bodies e.g. the National Trust, for the public benefit, are exempt. Rates of duty are reduced by 45 per cent for agricultural property and certain industrial premises; assets which pass on two successive deaths within five years are taxed on a reduced scale. In the U.K. and U.S.A. the death duties do not vary according to the inheritor, but in most Continental countries they are inheritance taxes rather than estate taxes, and vary according to the relationship between the deceased and the beneficiary.

Decadence. In literary history, specifically a movement originating in mid 19th-cent. France, and issuing a review, *Le Décadent* (1886–9), the title taken from a poem by Verlaine ('Langueur'). Essentially an extreme reaction against bourgeois standards in art and literature, it stressed the independence of art from morality and social concern, and was preoccupied with form as against content, beauty as against morality, and, to a greater or lesser extent, with the morbid, perverse, and occult; it combined an extreme ◊ *romanticism* with an admiration for 18th-cent. elegance and patrician values. Its origin is generally attributed to the poetry of Théophile Gautier, *Émaux et Camées* 1852, and Baudelaire, *Les Fleurs du Mal* 1857; Leconte de Lisle, leader of the Parnassians, developed Gautier's doctrine of 'art for art's sake'. The most striking aspect of the movement is its doctrinaire quality; the same dicta and prepossessions are repeated in numerous works, most of them being contained in J.-K. Huysmans' novel *À Rebours*. When the movement reached England, through Swinburne's admiration for Baudelaire and George Moore's *Confessions of a Young Man*, it strengthened the aesthetic movement begun by Ruskin and Pater, to produce the characteristically decadent work of Oscar Wilde (*The Portrait of Dorian Gray* derives from *À Rebours*), Ernest Dowson, and Aubrey Beardsley; it was called by Symons 'a new and beautiful and interesting disease'.

Decameron. Collection of 100 *novelle*, or tales, supposed to be told during 10 days by young Florentines taking refuge in country villas while the city is plague-stricken, compiled 1348–53 from various often traditional sources by the Italian poet and prose-writer Boccaccio; the pattern is formal and the mainly humorous tales, frequently coarse, are characteristic ◊ *Renaissance* products in their straightforward non-allegorical treatment and realistic preoccupation with secular life. Their influence on European literature (quite apart from their intrinsic merit) was immense; Chaucer in particular made considerable use of them.

Decathlon. A competition involving ten events at Olympic and National level, comprising 100, 400, and 1500 metre runs, 110 metre hurdles, long jump, high jump, shot-put, discus-throw, javelin-throw, and pole-vault.

Decca Navigator. A system of radio-navigation which depends on the reception by apparatus in the aircraft or ship of continuous radio signals from several synchronized radio stations, which are translated on coloured dials; special charts are used, with a lattice of similarly coloured lines, and the navigator can find his exact position by plotting the intersection of the coloured lines bearing the figures indicated by the dials.

Decimal System. Based on the scale of 10, representing numbers by means of 10 different symbols 0,1,2,3,4,5,6,7,8,9 and by their relative positions. Thus 123 represents $1 \times 10^2 + 2 \times 10 + 3$. The decimal point, invented early in the 17th cent. by the Scot, John Napier, enabled decimal fractions to be represented by placing them to the right of the point e.g. 0.1 means 1/10, $0.55 = 55/100$ etc. Multiplication and division by 10 and powers of 10 is accomplished by moving the point to the right or left, adding any necessary 0's. The decimal system has been adopted in a vast majority of countries for their coinage, the U.K. and some Commonwealth countries being the chief exceptions. ◊ *Binary Scale, Duodecimal System, Metric System.*

Declaration of Independence. 1776. Written by Thomas Jefferson and issued by the ◊ *Continental Congress* during the ◊ *American Revolution.* Its political philosophy was crystallized in the famous sentence: 'We hold these truths to be self-evident, that all men are created equal, that they are endowed by their creator with certain inalienable rights, that among these rights are life, liberty, and the pursuit of happiness.' It subsequently proved a potent inspiration in European politics.

Declaration of the Rights of Man. 1789. Basic statement of the rights of the citizen adopted by the Constituent Assembly in 1789 and incorporated in the French Constitution of 1791 (◊ *French Revolution*). It enumerates certain 'inalienable rights' and guarantees the right to liberty, property, and security and freedom of speech and of the press. It exerted great influence on political thought.

Declination. 1. In ◊ *astronomy*, the angular distance of a heavenly body from the celestial equator.

2. In ◊ *magnetism*, the angle between the magnetic meridian at any point on the earth's surface and the geographic meridian at that point i.e. the angle between compass N/S and true N/S. Magnetic declination varies even at a given point, because of movement of the earth's magnetic poles in the course of time.

Decorated Style. The middle phase of English ◊ *Gothic architecture*, between the ◊ *Early English style* and the ◊ *Perpendicular*. Beginning about 1290, it lasted into the second half of the 14th cent. and is characterized mainly by the ogee (a double or S-curve in arches or window tracery) and also by lavish surface decoration. Spatially, the style favours the unexpected vista, esp. diagonally; and it is well illustrated in Bristol Cathedral Choir and in the Octagon and the Lady Chapel at Ely.

Deduction. In ◊ *logic*, an inference whose conclusion must be true if its premiss is true, e.g. if all desks are furniture and some are ugly, then some furniture is ugly. An inductive inference, usually contrasted, is one whose conclusion is not necessarily true even if the premiss is true; scientific laws, which claim something about all entities of a certain kind, but are based on observation of only limited number, are said to be conclusions of inductive inferences, which are examined in the philosophy of science.

Deer. Graceful agile animals, ◊ *ruminants* of the mammalian order of *Artiodactyla*, even-toed ungulates; the males only (except in ◊ *reindeer*) bear antlers, annually shed and replaced by a larger size (as much as 24 lb. of bone growing in about 10 weeks) and used in the contests of the rutting season. Some species lack antlers entirely; instead, the upper canines are long and curved e.g. in musk and water deer. Those of the British Isles are the fallow deer and in Scotland the ◊ *red deer*. ◊ *Antelopes* (which, however, are not deer).

Defamation. Publishing to a third person, or to the public, any statement or comment tending to bring someone into hatred, ridicule, or contempt. It is a defence to an action for defamation to show that the statements of fact were true ('justification'); that they were made without malice upon a matter of public interest ('fair comment'); or that they were privileged e.g. statements in court by a judge, advocate, party, or witness ('absolute privilege'), in Parliament by a member ('Parliamentary privilege'), or by a legal adviser to his client or vice versa, provided there is no malicious publication ('qualified privilege'). ◊ *Libel and Slander*.

Defence ◊ *Ministry of Defence*.

Defence Mechanisms. In psychology, as postulated by Freud, measures whereby, involuntarily and unconsciously, the individual defends his consciousness from painful experiences arising from unpleasant situations, memories, or impulses; e.g. repression enables people to forget or ignore anything tending to bring into consciousness unacceptable motives, without their realizing that they have done so. A key concept in psycho-analytic theory, it contributes to the explanation of apparently unmotivated behaviour in everyday life e.g. 'slips of the tongue' or missed appointments.

Deflation. Either contraction of economic activity, or government action designed to produce it or to prevent expansion (◊ *Trade Cycle*); more specifically, the fall in prices which before the war used to accompany contractions of this kind. ◊ *Inflation*.

Deirdre. In Irish legend, daughter of Fedlimid, whose wife bore her during a feast he was giving to ◊ *Conchubar*; a druid foretold that she would bring ruin on Ireland and destruction to the Red Branch Knights, but Conchubar ordered her to be handed to a foster-mother as his betrothed wife. In girlhood she met Conchubar's nephew Naoise and persuaded him and his brothers Ainnle and Ardan to elope with her to Scotland, where they lived happily for several years, until Conchubar sent Feargus to bring them home, with a promise of pardon. On their return, Conchubar treacherously attacked them; after a desperate fight, Naoise and his brothers were killed and Deirdre died lamenting upon Naoise's body. Many of Conchubar's best warriors, disgusted by his treachery, deserted him for Queen Maeve of Connaught (◊ *Cuchullin*); thus the prophecy was fulfilled.

Deism. The belief, which took shape in the 17th and 18th centuries, that ◊ *God* created the universe and man but now has nothing to do with them, and coupled with this 'absentee landlord' view, the claim that God's existence can be shown by reason alone. ◊ *Theism*.

Déjà Vu. An illusion of recognition, in which a place or situation perceived for the first time appears familiar; a form of 'paramnesia' (a term covering many forms of error in recognition or memory). *Déjà vu* differs from ordinary mistakes in recognition in that it is accompanied by an eerie feeling, possibly because in certain crucial details the situation resembles events or dreams now forgotten.

Delian League. 478–404, 377–338 B.C. A confederacy of Greek states, with its centre on the Aegean island of Delos, organized and led by ◊ *Athens*, formed after the defeat of Xerxes in order to continue the war against Persia. Since the other states preferred to contribute money rather than ships, Athens rapidly became the mistress of an empire instead of the head of a federation. Defeat by ◊ *Sparta* in the ◊ *Peloponnesian War* ended Athenian supremacy in 404 B.C. The league reformed for a short period in opposition to Sparta, but came to an end finally on Philip II of Macedon's victory at Chaeroneia in 338 B.C. It is noteworthy as the first attempt at cooperation between autonomous and highly developed states.

Delirium. State of mental confusion accompanied by restlessness and hallucinations, a symptom of fevers and various states of intoxication.

DELIRIUM TREMENS: An acute psychosis liable to occur in the course of chronic ◊ *alcoholism*.

Delphinium. Garden perennial developed from the wild *D. elatum*, a blue-flowered plant native to an area stretching from the Pyrenees to Siberia, introduced into Britain in the 18th cent. Larkspurs are annual delphiniums derived from two European wild species introduced into Britain in the 15th cent.

Delta. Deposit of silt, sand, or gravel made by a river when it reaches the sea or a lake, and its speed of flow decreases: the term derives from the Greek letter *delta* *Δ* which is roughly the shape of a typical river-delta e.g. that of the Nile. The peculiar 'bird's-foot' delta of the Mississippi is due to an exceptional amount of lime in solution and to the fine-grained nature of the river's load. The deltas of many W. European rivers have filled in former arms of the sea, e.g. the Fenland delta of the Great Ouse (which has greatly reduced the area of the Wash) and others.

Delta Wing. A triangular wing-plan form resembling the Greek capital D (delta); advocated for aircraft on grounds of simplicity and suitability for high-subsonic and supersonic speeds.

Demeter. In Greek mythology, goddess of crops, vegetation, and marriage; mother of ◊ *Persephone*, and equivalent to the Roman Ceres.

Democracy. < Gr. *demos*, people, and *kratos*, power; ◊ *government* by the people for the people. Direct democracy, i.e. rule by popular assemblies or by plebiscites on all proposed laws, was possible in the small Greek states; states with large and scattered population have recourse to indirect democracy, i.e. rule by representative institutions to which power both legislative and executive is delegated, as evolved in England and introduced by formal constitutions in France and U.S.A. after their revolutions. Democracy is usually held to involve the ◊ *separation of powers* and free choice of elected representatives. Associated with democracy are freedom of speech, of the press, and of political association, and the rule of law.

PEOPLE'S DEMOCRACY (or REPUBLIC): A description used by several countries of the communist bloc. Their claim to be democratic rests upon the theory that communism faithfully represents and secures the real interests of the citizen, rather than upon the attributes of democracy as defined above.

Democratic Party (U.S.A.). The party traces its lineage to the followers of Jefferson, who upheld States Rights against the centralizing tendency of the Federalists. Under President Andrew Jackson in 1828 the Democrats strengthened their position, and during the next 30 years, with two exceptions, they won every presidential election. The issue of slavery caused a rift and led to the election of Abraham Lincoln, leader of the new ◊ *Republican Party*. After the ◊ *American Civil War*, the party became further identified with the South, and in the later 19th cent. with the poorer farming States and the immigrant masses in the large industrial centres. This alliance of conservative southerners, poor farmers, and industrial workers carried the presidency on only four occasions between 1866 and 1932, twice by Grover Cleveland (1884, 1892) and twice by Woodrow Wilson (1912, 1916). The post-war reaction in 1920 removed the Democrats from office, but the ◊ *depression* and the personality of Franklin Roosevelt swept them back to power in 1932. They retained power throughout the Second World War and the presidency of Harry Truman 1945–52.

General Eisenhower proved an overwhelming Republican candidate in the two subsequent elections, but in 1960 by a narrow margin the Democrats returned J. F. Kennedy (the first Roman Catholic to become President), who identified himself with the liberal wing of the party and risked losing Southern support by pressing for racial integration. He was assassinated in 1963. The Vice President Lyndon Johnson who succeeded him secured the passage of Civil Rights Bill to implement the policy of integration, which further antagonized the Southern States. In the 1964 election Lyndon Johnson was elected President by a large majority although the traditionally Democratic Southern States swung to the Republicans.

The party consists of the aggregate of the local party machines and their leaders, the only national organization being the four-yearly convention to choose the presidential candidate, and a national committee appointed by him.

Denmark. Area 16,000 sq. m. Pop. 4.6 m. Cap. Copenhagen. Rel. mainly Lutheran. Named after a seafaring Scandinavian people, the Danes. Most of the country consists of islands, notably Zealand and Funen. An independent constitutional monarchy; the Parliament (Folketing) consists of one chamber with 179 members elected by ◊ *proportional representation* for four years. Denmark is a member of N.A.T.O. and also a member of E.F.T.A.

ECONOMY. The standard of living is high; there is an excellent educational system and a comprehensive social security scheme. The country is largely agricultural, with a highly efficient co-operative marketing system; much of its dairy produce is exported to Gt Britain. There are important shipyards and a sizeable merchant marine.

HISTORY. Denmark was united with England under Canute 1016–35. Upon union with ◊ *Norway* and ◊ *Sweden* in 1397, all Scandinavia came under Danish leadership, the acquisition of Copenhagen giving Denmark control over shipping entering the Baltic. Attempts to maintain the union led to numerous wars with Sweden, who decisively defeated Denmark in the 17th cent. though Norway remained under the Danish crown. Nelson's bombardment of Copenhagen in 1801 brought Denmark into the ◊ *Napoleonic wars* on the side of France; as a result Norway was separated from her in 1814. Denmark lost Schleswig-Holstein, with its largely German population, to Prussia 1864 but recovered N. Schleswig in 1919. ◊❯ *Thirty Years War.*

LANGUAGE. Danish belongs to the northern division of the ◊ *Germanic languages*; it derives from Old Norse, the common language of Scandinavia about A.D. 1000, which influenced English through the Danelaw. For many centuries Denmark and Norway were one; the Dano-Norwegian tongue was the medium used by Ibsen and Björnson in the 19th cent. Modern Danish has been influenced by ◊ *German.* ◊❯ *Vikings.*

Dentistry. The science of care of the teeth. Dental decay (caries) was common even in prehistoric man, and the earliest civilizations of China and Egypt attempted dental remedies. The Romans developed considerable skill in dentistry, most of which was lost in the Middle Ages. Modern dentistry developed after the introduction of ◊ *anaesthetics*; at first not distinguished from medicine, it has become a separate field. Increasing attention is paid to the prevention of caries, and the ◊ *fluoridation of water supplies* has had beneficial results.

Deodar ◊ *Cedar.*

Department of Scientific and Industrial Research (D.S.I.R.). U.K. government department to promote research. It operates several research stations inc. the National Physical and Chemical Laboratories, Teddington, and road and building research stations and supports research work in universities. The work of the D.S.I.R., by recommendation of the Trend committee, is likely to be directed by three new bodies: a Science Research Council, an Industrial Research and Development Authority, and a Natural Environment Research Council.

Depression. 1. Serious slackening in economic activity, more severe than a recession; the Great Depression after the widespread bank failures in Europe and U.S.A. and the 1929 collapse of the Wall Street ◊ *boom* led in U.S.A. and U.K. to mass unemployment, which persisted, though mitigated by remedial measures, until the outbreak of war 1939. The view that low wages, under-consumption, and too much saving are inimical to high employment has been reflected in the economic policy of most western nations since the Second World War. ⟡ *Inflation, Keynes, New Deal.*

2. In ⟡ *meteorology,* a region of low atmospheric pressure sometimes known as a ⟡ *cyclone.* They are believed to originate where tropical air meets cold polar air resulting in the formation of cold fronts and warm fronts. The movement of depressions affects the weather which is unsettled by their passage. The rainfall which accompanies them results from the warm air rising over the cold air and forming extensive cloud.

3. ⟡ *Manic Depression.*

Deprivation. Many child psychologists and psychiatrists believe that uninterrupted care of a child by the mother (or some other woman) is necessary if he or she is to achieve satisfactory emotional relationships in later life; a child who experiences long separations (or who is cared for by a succession of different women, as in some institutions) is said to suffer maternal deprivation. There is some evidence that paternal deprivation also has adverse effects.

Derris. Insecticide powder from roots of various species of *derris,* small trees and climbers of the ⟡ *Leguminosae* family growing throughout the tropics; the active material is primarily *rotenone.* Powdered derris root was known to the Malays for killing lice, and was first used against agricultural pests in 1848 by Oxley, a Singapore surgeon. It was also used in Indo-China, Malaysia, Australia, and tropical S. America for killing fish.

Dervish (Faqir) ⟡ *Dance, Sufis.*

Desert. Area where vegetation is absent, or so sparse that it is uninhabitable except by nomads; mean annual rainfall usually below 10 in. Some desert areas may have a higher rainfall, but in violent showers and rapidly lost by evaporation. A desert completely devoid of vegetation is uncommon, however; typical desert plants such as cacti and the common camel-thorn are specially adapted to long periods of drought and heat. A desert may have a rocky or stony surface as in Arabia or Syria, or it may be an area of shifting ridges of sand (dunes) as in the Sahara. In addition to the dryness of the atmosphere, a characteristic of the desert climate is the great daily range of temperature. Extensive deserts may occur in the interior of continents, e.g. the Gobi and Turkestan

deserts. Others occur on the W. sides of land masses in the Trade Wind belts, where dry offshore winds prevail, e.g. the Sahara, Arabian, Kalahari, Atacama, and central Australian deserts.

Destroyer. A fast ⟡ *warship,* about 1500 to 3000 tons displacement, originally evolved to counter the ⟡ *torpedo* boat, which it eventually replaced; the first British destroyer was the *Havock,* 1893. In the Second World War destroyers were extensively used for convoy-escort, antisubmarine, and auxiliary duties. Modern destroyers are equipped with torpedo tubes, 4-in. or 4.5-in. guns, and either depth-charge throwers or 'squid' antisubmarine devices.

Detergent. Cleanser soluble in water, derived not directly from animal and vegetable oils and fats, as ⟡ *soap* is, but from mineral oils. The most important are the sodium alkyl benzene sulphonates produced by the petrochemical industry. Detergents are surface-acting agents (surfactants) and derive their cleansing properties from a molecular structure which reduces the ⟡ *surface tension* of water and gives it greater 'wetting' power. Because they do not react like soap with ⟡ *calcium* and ⟡ *magnesium,* they function well in hard water. Though experimentally produced in France in the mid 19th cent. and developed to some extent in Germany during the First World War, large-scale commercial production of detergents did not begin until the 1930s. Soap is still preferred for toilet use, but detergents are now widely used for domestic and industrial cleaning. Discharge of detergents into rivers and streams causes a deleterious accumulation of foam: non-foaming detergents are now available.

Determinism ⟡ *Free Will.*

Dettingen. 1743. Village near Frankfurt; scene of a battle, notable as being the last time a king of England led his army in the field. George II's Austrian and English troops defeated the French and drove them across the Main. Frederick of Prussia, alarmed by the Austrians' success, entered into a secret alliance with Louis XV.

Deuterium ⟡ *Heavy Water, Hydrogen.*

Development Area. In the U.K. an area of particularly high unemployment, to which government assistance is given through special commissioners, first appointed 1934. By 1938 £21 m. had been spent on social rehabilitation, e.g. improving water supplies, clearing sites, establishing trading estates. The special areas were renamed Development Areas by the 1945 Act, and in the early postwar years building licensing was used to channel new factories into them, but in 1958 they were replaced by smaller Development Districts: any area with an unemployment rate of 4 per cent or more became eligible. Assistance consists of grants and loans for new factories, and under the 1963 ◊ *Budget* firms in Development Districts are allowed to write off the depreciation of new plant at whatever rate they wish.

Devil (Satan). In traditional Christian teaching, Lucifer, spirit of light and chief of the archangels, who through pride revolted against God and was punished by eternal banishment in a place or state called ◊ *Hell*, whence he continues the contest by tempting men to sin and thus share his fate. The concept may derive from Persian influence (◊ *Zoroastrianism*) upon ◊ *Judaism*, and in England has rested largely upon its poetic dramatization in Milton's *Paradise Lost*, 1667. Today many Christians consider 'the Devil' as simply a personification of the idea of evil.

Devil's Island ◊ *French Guiana*.

Devonian Period. Fourth period of the Paleozoic era (◊ *Geological Time Scale*), marked by a great flood which inundated large areas of N. America and Europe, and in Europe by considerable volcanic activity. In Europe two major rock systems were laid down: the marine deposits and the old red sandstone. Various species of fish appeared and there are traces of early amphibia.

Dew. Moisture deposited at night: as the earth's surface cools, the lower layers of air also cool and eventually the water-vapour condenses into water drops at the 'dew-point' temperature. A warm day followed by a calm clear night favours dew formation, the daytime warmth increasing the amount of water-vapour in the air by evaporation and lack of wind and clear sky contributing by radiation to a marked fall in temperature.

Dextrose ◊ *Glucose, Honey*.

Diabetes. Any disease whose chief symptom is the passing of excessive amounts of urine: usually *diabetes mellitus*, caused by a deficiency of the hormone ◊ *insulin*

secreted by islets of specialized cells in the ◊ *pancreas*; there is a high level of sugar in the blood, sugar in the urine, and gross metabolic disturbances, which unless treated are likely to culminate in coma and death. Treatment in severe cases is by regular injections of insulin. *Diabetes insipidus*, caused by a lesion in the ◊ *pituitary*, is characterized by the passing of large amounts of urine of low specific gravity and free from sugar. ◊ *Endocrine System*.

Dialect. Variety of speech used by a particular community, in a defined area or among a given class or group, distinguished by divergences in pronunciation, grammar, idioms, and vocabulary; the difference between a language and a dialect is one of degree, not of kind, the practical test being intelligibility. Every civilized community tends to develop a standardized written language, but a 'standard' is itself a selected and regularized dialect; e.g. in Middle English, before the rise of London English in the 14th cent., all five dialects (N., E. Midland, W. Midland, SE, SW) stood on a level, and each produced its own literature. Today dialect and ◊ *slang* meet and mingle in London Cockney, a dialect both regional and social.

Dialectic. < Gr. 'discussion'; term used by philosophers for a variety of procedures. (a) Proving a statement false by showing that it leads to self-contradiction, the basis of the ◊ *Socratic Method*. (b) Showing that a definition is correct or incorrect by examining particular cases (also a part of the Socratic Method). (c) Reasoning from opinions or hypotheses, by way of criticism and cross-examination, to justified conclusions, as in Plato and Aristotle. (d) Reasoning which moves from an initial statement or thesis to considering the opposite claim or antithesis and hence to a reconciliation or synthesis, a triadic process which according to ◊ *Hegelianism* and ◊ *marxism* repeats itself endlessly in the universe and in history.

Dialectical Materialism. Theory developed by Marx and Engels and now the philosophy of communism, differing from Hegelian dialectical ◊ *idealism* in postulating that matter preceded mind; it rejects all supernatural explanations of the universe, and holds that matter, and all phenomena, develop by processes in which the succession of thesis, antithesis, and synthesis is typical, the last occurring as a sudden or revolutionary leap rather than by gradual evolution. As applied to history, the theory produced the interpretation that society developed from primitive communism to slavery, feudalism, and capitalism, each stage being the result of the contradictions of the preceding one, which it finally negates. Thus the marxist view is that capitalism and the class struggle will give way to the dictatorship of the proletariat and this in turn to a classless society. In modern marxism the theory has been interpreted as applying to processes of change in virtually every field, physical, social, and intellectual.

Dialogue. Literary form in which matter is presented as a conversation between speakers representing either conflicting opinions or knowledge and ignorance; the form has been much used by philosophers (◊ *Dialectic*) including Plato, Aristotle, Berkeley, and Hume. Medieval dialogues were pious and didactic, but during the ◊ *Renaissance* (and later the ◊ *Enlightenment*) the satirical and sceptical dialogues of Lucian were much admired and imitated, notably by Erasmus, 1466–1536. In English the most important literary dialogues are Dryden's *Essay of Dramatick Poesy* 1668 and Landor's *Imaginary Conversations* 1824–9.

Diamond ◊ *Carbon.*

Diana ◊ *Artemis.*

Dianthus ◊ *Carnation.*

Diatoms. A class of microscopic aquatic and unicellular ◊ *algae*, the *Bacillariophyceae*, living either singly or in colonies; they have a cell-wall impregnated with ◊ *silica* and often beautifully sculptured, and their chloroplasts contain ◊ *chlorophyll* and the brown pigment isofucoxanthin. Diatoms are an important component of the marine and freshwater ◊ *plankton.* Sedimentation of dead diatoms in geological time has led to the formation of deposits of kieselguhr (diatomaceous earth), chiefly used as an absorbent for nitroglycerine in the manufacture of dynamite and as a filtering agent.

Diborane ◊ *Boron.*

Dice. Small cubes of different materials, usually bone or wood, with dots on each face from one to six, used in many games either to determine the moves of counters as in ◊ *backgammon* or by themselves as in craps (two dice), poker dice (five dice),

or cameroons (10 dice). The dots on opposite faces always total seven. The game of 'craps' (highly popular in U.S.A.) developed from the old English hazard game (i.e. throwing dice). Dice are one of the oldest methods of gambling, and they have been found in Egyptian tombs of 2000 B.C. Probably their first uses were religious e.g. for ◊ *divination*, and for lotteries.

Dicotelydon ◊ *Angiosperms.*

Dictatorship. Government by absolute authority; the term may correctly be used to describe rule by a group or class but is generally confined to circumstances in which absolute power is wielded by a single person, under the form of a republic. Also, authority similarly wielded by any corporate body or community.

Dictatorship of the Proletariat ◊ *Communism, Proletariat.*

Dictionary. There were word-lists of Latin, Greek, etc. into English from the 13th cent. but Robert Cawdrey's *A Table Alphabeticall* 1604 is usually called the first English dictionary; like others in the 17th cent. it contained only 'difficult' words (about 3000). The first comprehensive work, that of John Kersey 1702, had some 28,000 entries. The admirable dictionaries of Nathaniel Bailey, esp. the 60,000-word *Dictionarium Britannicum* 1730, paved the way for Samuel Johnson's great 40,000-word 2-vol. *Dictionary* 1755, the excellence of which lay in the careful discrimination and definition of different usages and the copious use of illustrative quotation. Johnson's American counterpart was Noah Webster, whose *American Dictionary* appeared in 1828. The great modern English lexicon the *Oxford English Dictionary* appeared in 12 vols 1884–1928 (supplementary volumes appeared later); it originally contained 414,825 entries and nearly 2 m. illustrative quotations. The American equivalent is Webster's *New International Dictionary*, 3rd ed. 1962, which contains pictorial illustrations.

Dido. In Middle-Eastern legend, originally a Phoenician goddess (also named Elissa), and later the foundress and queen of ◊ *Carthage*; a native of Phoenicia, after her husband's murder she went to Africa and by a local king, Iarbas, was granted as much land as a bull's hide would 'cover'. By cutting the hide into narrow thongs to form a boundary, she gained enough land to build a city (Carthage), but when Iarbas wished to marry her she stabbed herself on a funeral pyre to escape him. In Virgil's *Aeneid*, however, she stabs herself in grief at being deserted by ◊ *Aeneas*.

Die-casting ◊ *Casting Metal*.

Dien-Bien-Phu. French garrison in Tonkin which after a gallant and protracted defence was overwhelmed by the forces of Vietminh in 1954, after which the French withdrew from ◊ *Vietnam*.

Diesel ◊ *Internal Combustion Engine*.

Diet. For the human body, an adequate diet must include ◊ *proteins*, ◊ *carbohydrates*, fats, salts, water, and ◊ *vitamins*. Proteins contain carbon, hydrogen, oxygen, and nitrogen, this last being of fundamental importance for maintaining and building the structure of the body (muscle, bone, hair, etc.); carbohydrates (compounds of carbon, hydrogen, and oxygen) are the main energy producers and fats have a similar function. Salts (such as those of calcium, phosphorus, iron, and copper) are essential for the growth of bones. Water forms about 60 per cent of the body weight. A balanced diet must also contain ◊ *trace elements*, a deficiency of which causes ill-health and stunted growth. Proteins are provided by lean meat, eggs, milk, and leguminous vegetables. The chief carbohydrates are sugar and starch, of which sugar itself, ◊ *cereals*, and potatoes are major sources. Fats come from meat, butter, and vegetable oils, and green vegetables and fruit are important as sources of vitamins. A varied diet including all these foods should be adequate for health. Since it is now possible to make synthetic vitamins, these can be used as supplements. The amount of energy (or heat, the two being interchangeable) obtainable from specific amounts of food can be calculated and is expressed as ◊ *calories*. The daily calorific needs of different workers are: heavy workers 5000, sedentary manual workers 3000, sedentary clerical workers 2700. ◊ *Metabolism*.

Diffusion. The passage of one substance into another as a result of continuous movement of their ◊ *molecules*. Diffusion can occur in gases, liquids, and even solids. If two gases of differing density are brought together, each will diffuse into the whole available space, the rate at which each diffuses being inversely proportional to the square root of its density (Graham's Law). The same occurs with miscible liquids, but more slowly. Diffusion of solids has been observed but is extremely slow; e.g. gold will diffuse into lead.

Digestion. Conversion of food into products suitable for absorption into the blood (◊ *Metabolism*), the first agent being the saliva produced by ◊ *glands* in the mouth, whose activity is under reflex control and activated by the thought, sight, or smell of food as well as by taste (◊ *Conditioning*); salivary digestion persists for a time after food has entered the stomach and is followed by the action of the gastric juice, secreted by about 30 m. glands in the stomach wall, which contains hydrochloric acid; mucin to protect the stomach lining from the acid and the acid-dependent ◊ *enzymes*; pepsin, which converts ◊ *protein* into proteoses and peptones; and rennin, which curdles milk so as to prevent its too rapid passage through the stomach (this enzyme is not found in any quantity after infancy). The secretion of gastric juice, like that of saliva, is under reflex control, but in addition is stimulated by gastrin, a hormone which the stomach wall produces in response to the presence of food. Stomach contents are propelled into the small ◊ *intestine* by waves of muscular contraction. In the duodenum, pancreatic secretion provides three enzymes: trypsin, which breaks down any undigested protein and reduces proteoses and peptones to amino acids; amylase, which reduces ◊ *carbohydrates* to simple sugars, ◊ *glucose*, fructose, and levulose; and lipase, which reduces fats to fatty acids and glycerol. This last process requires the presence of bile, a greenish-yellow alkaline fluid secreted by the ◊ *liver* and concentrated and stored in the gall-bladder. The absorption of digested food takes place in the small intestine; very little digestion occurs in the large intestine or colon, but further reduction in bulk occurs as a result of fermentation and putrefactive action by bacteria. Faeces (of which on an average diet about 200 gr. are produced daily) contain about 75 per cent of water: the maintenance of this water content is an important function of the large intestine (◊ *Excretion*). ◊ *Pancreas*.

Diggers. An anti-enclosure group during the ◊ *English civil wars*, connected with but distinct from the ◊ *Levellers*, whose

Agreement of the People they strongly supported. Not army men like the Levellers, but poor civilians, they claimed a 'children of Adam' right to own land for cultivation. In 1649 they took possession of some waste land in Surrey and farmed it; soon forcibly ejected, they scattered and disappeared, but their song 'Stand up now' remained popular and the very moving essays of their leader Winstanley have survived.

Digitalis. Drug extracted from the dried leaves of the purple foxglove, *D. purpurea,* used in the treatment of heart complaints. It acts by slowing down the heart beat, lowering the blood pressure, and improving the oxygenation of the blood by assisting circulation through the lungs.

Diminished Responsibility. Insanity is not of itself normally a defence to a charge of crime unless it falls within the definition given in the ◊ *M'Naghten Rules*; but under the 1957 Homicide Act it is a defence to a charge of murder to show that the offender was 'suffering from such abnormality of mind (whether arising from a condition of arrested or retarded development of mind or any inherent causes or induced by disease or injury) as substantially impaired his mental responsibility for his acts', the application of this section of the Act being essentially a matter for the jury. An action which would otherwise be murder but which falls within this section is reduced to manslaughter; this is probably the only recognition in English criminal law that mental abnormality may take the form of absence of control rather than of understanding.

Diminishing Returns. Economic concept elaborated in the 18th cent. based on the observation that when additional capital and labour are applied to a constant element, e.g. agricultural land, a point is reached after which further increases yield diminishing returns of produce; the same phenomenon occurs in industrial production. The point at which the 'law' begins to operate varies with the development of productive techniques.

Dingo ◊ *Dog.*

Dinosaur. Extinct reptiles of the Mesozoic era, whose fossil remains have been found throughout the world. The largest were about 90 ft in length, their brain capacity being very small in proportion to their size. They varied considerably in structure and in diet, some being carnivorous bipeds and others herbivorous quadrupeds. The dominant animals during the Jurassic period, they became extinct in the Cretaceous, owing to climatic and geological change and failure in competition with the rising class of mammals. ◊ *Brontosaurus, Geological Time Scale.*

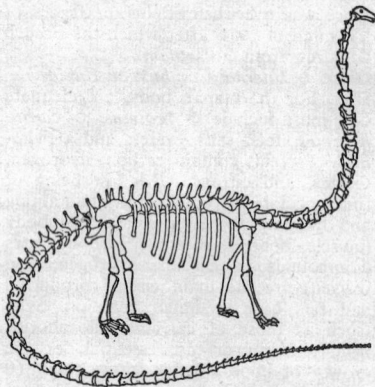

Dionysus (Bacchus). In Greek and Roman mythology, originally a vegetation god, and god of wine and revelry, patron of the drama, son of ◊ *Zeus* by Semele, who was killed by lightning at the request of ◊ *Hera,* Zeus placing the unborn child in his thigh, from which Dionysus was born; brought up by nymphs on Mt Nysa, he was made mad by Zeus and wandered about the world, on one journey marrying Ariadne (◊ *Minos, Theseus*); he is credited with introducing the culture of the vine and other arts of civilization. His worship, esp. the great feasts called Dionysia, was conducted largely by women votaries, the Bacchantes or Maenads, whose orgies involved intoxication, wild dancing, and the tearing apart of living creatures; his many cult legends include descent to the underworld and resurrection, and Greek tragedy and comedy were intimately linked with his festival celebrations. ◊ *Apollo.*

Diphtheria. Infection caused by the virulent bacillus *Corynebacterium diphtheriae*; although any mucous surface may be attacked, the organism usually establishes itself first in the throat, where it may obstruct breathing and necessitate ◊ *tracheotomy.* The incidence and severity of diphtheria have been markedly reduced by widespread immunization (◊ *Immunity*). ◊ *Larynx*.

Diplomacy. The art of representing one state to another, and the conduct of negotiations; in general, the process of conducting international affairs. It involves the government department responsible for foreign affairs, together with those public servants forming the personnel of permanent missions serving in foreign countries, usually referred to as the Diplomatic Service. By international usage, the residence and offices of the head of a diplomatic mission are immune from entry; he and his staff may not be arrested, and enjoy certain other local privileges. An embassy may not, however, be used as an asylum for political refugees, though the attempt to assert such a right is occasionally made.

DIPLOMATIC IMMUNITY: The representatives and ambassadors of foreign sovereign states are exempt from legal proceedings in the English courts; the privilege extends to members of embassy staffs if claimed for them by the ambassador. All countries follow the custom.

Diptera ◊ *Fly*.

Direct Current ◊ *Electric Current*.

Direct-grant School. Usually a long-established ◊ *grammar school*; one which receives money grants direct from the Ministry of Education and is therefore financially independent of the Local Education Authority and charges fees (varying from school to school). In return for the Ministry grant, such schools are required to reserve at least 25 per cent of their places for non-fee-paying pupils, and to accept Ministry inspection.

Director of Public Prosecutions ◊ *Public Prosecutor*.

Dirigible ◊ *Airship*.

Disarmament. An essentially 20th-cent. concept which envisages the reduction or abolition of weapons throughout the world. The ◊ *Hague Conferences* held before the First World War were the first attempts towards this end. Between the World Wars several conferences were held: the Washington Conference 1921–2 (which achieved some limitation on naval expansion), the Soviet proposals by Litvinov 1928, and the first World Disarmament Conference 1932, which were inconclusive. After the Second World War fresh attempts were made to reach inter-

national agreement on the reduction of armaments. The United Nations Organization set up the Atomic Energy Commission 1946, for the elimination of the destructive use of atomic energy, and the Commission for Conventional Armaments 1947 'for the general regulation and reduction of armaments and armed forces'. Limited progress was made; the Western Powers insisted on the importance of inspection and control from the outset, the U.S.S.R. proposed immediate prohibition and destruction of atomic weapons and proportional cuts in armed forces. The two Commissions were merged into the U.N. Disarmament Commission 1952. The U.S.S.R. now sought the abolition of U.S. bases in Europe and the Far East; the West rejected this and stressed adequate inspection and exchange of information. Talks were abandoned, and in 1957 the U.S.S.R. withdrew from the Commission, alleging that it was fruitless, but offering to continue discussions. In 1958 Marshal Bulganin proposed a summit conference at Geneva to discuss four major possibilities: (1) a temporary cessation of nuclear tests; (2) the renunciation of the use and manufacture of nuclear weapons; (3) a non-aggression pact between the ◊ *North Atlantic Treaty Organization* and the ◊ *Warsaw Pact* countries; (4) ◊ *disengagement*, i.e. the creation of an atom-free zone in central Europe, similar to that proposed in the ◊ *Rapacki Plan*. The U.S.A. rejected the proposal and stated that it was not willing to hold discussions outside U.N.O. In 1960 Canada, France, Italy, the U.K., and U.S.A. proposed an international disarmament organization to supervise general disarmament and a separate agency, to be closely associated with U.N.O. for the purpose of preventing aggression and preserving world peace and security. Soviet counter-proposals were rejected by the Western Powers, since the U.S.S.R. continued to insist on the abandonment of the nuclear deterrent and bases in Europe at what was thought to be too early a stage. The signing of a nuclear-test ban by Britain, U.S.A., and U.S.S.R. 1963 represented one positive advance.

Disengagement. Various plans for creating a neutral belt of territory to keep the forces of the ◊ *Warsaw Pact* and ◊ *North Atlantic Treaty Organization* from directly confronting each other across a common border. These schemes e.g. the ◊ *Rapacki Plan* have usually concentrated on keeping on the one hand W. Germany, and on the other Poland, Czechoslovakia, and perhaps Hungary, disarmed and neutral. ◊◊ *Disarmament*.

Disestablishment Acts. Although only one in seven people in Ireland were members of the Episcopal ◊ *Church of Ireland*, the Roman Catholic majority had to pay tithes towards its support. This remained a grievance until the Gladstone government disestablished the Church of Ireland in 1871. An Act to disestablish the Welsh Church, passed in 1914, became effective only in 1920.

Disinfectants ◊ *Antiseptics*.

Dispersion. Variation of the refractive index of a medium-width wavelength; e.g. glass has a higher refractive index for 'blue' light than for 'red' light, which is longer in wavelength. The colour components of a beam of white light incident on a prism are thus 'bent' different amounts and split up (dispersed) to form a ◊ *spectrum*.

Dissenters ◊ *Nonconformists*.

Distemper. Several infectious diseases of animals; usually a serious virus infection of young dogs, more easily prevented, by a suitable vaccine, than cured. Mortality in unprotected cases is high and the disease is likely to leave permanent damage.

Distillation. Boiling a liquid to produce vapour, and condensing it, either to purify it or to separate the various components of a mixture of liquids with different boiling-points. The process of fractional distillation is of great importance in the ◊ *petroleum* industry. Liquids which decompose on heating are distilled under reduced pressure: insoluble liquids can sometimes be distilled in steam. ◊◊ *Naphtha*.

DESTRUCTIVE DISTILLATION: Involves decomposition by heat and the recovery of the volatile constituents in e.g. coal, wood (◊ *Gas Industry*).

Divination. Foretelling of the future by a diviner believed to possess spiritual powers enabling him or her to see beyond the boundaries of ordinary human knowledge, often through the interpretation of portents or signs e.g. the aspect of the entrails of a sacrificial animal. In ancient Rome special priests (augurs) interpreted the 'auspices'. In primitive societies both ◊ *oracles* and diviners (the distinction often being confused) are commonly consulted also to discover reasons for disaster and ill-health if these are believed to be caused by spirits, gods, or human enemies (◊ *Witchcraft and Sorcery*), the sufferers suggesting possible agents from his own experience and himself interpreting the response; foretelling the future by such means is less common. ◊◊ *Shaman*.

Divine Right. The direct derivation of authority from God. The claim to Divine Right was based upon the theory that the ruler enjoyed a unique relationship with God and had received from him a commission for which he was not answerable to any human power. Bishops claimed it against the Pope, and also against the law and the constitution; kings first claimed it against the Pope and then against the Estates of their kingdoms.' The Divine Right of kings and bishops as expounded by James I of England (◊ *Stewarts*) was designed to emancipate the monarchy and the Church from control or criticism by the nobility and gentry assembled in ◊ *Parliament*.

Diving. Men have dived and swum under water from the earliest times, but without apparatus the time spent beneath the surface was minimal. The invention of the air-pump was followed by that of the diving bell, a bell-shaped tank, lowered into the sea, in which sufficient air pressure was maintained to repel the water, thus enabling men to work on the bottom for long periods. This was followed by the pressurized rubber diving suit, developed from that invented by Augustus Siebe in the early 19th cent. and consisting of a one-piece suit, weighted with lead, and a metal breastplate and helmet to which an air-line is attached. The air pressure within the flexible suit must equal the external water pressure, and there are limits to the pressure the human body can withstand, so that such apparatus is serviceable only in comparatively shallow water. Rigid metal diving suits have enabled men to descend to greater depths, but they hamper the diver.

A further development was the bathysphere, designed by Otis Barton, a hollow sphere with portholes, designed to resist great pressure, lowered from a ship; a descent to a depth of 3028 ft was made near Bermuda 1934. A more elaborate device is the bathyscaphe, which has its own buoyancy and sinking devices; one designed by Prof. Piccard descended to a depth of 35,800 ft in the Challenger Deep 1960.

Divorce. The dissolution of a ◊ *marriage*. In so far as it is a matter of religious, as distinct from civil marriage, the conditions applicable differ considerably from religion to religion and from sect to sect. Where it is governed by civil law the grounds for divorce differ from country to country (and in the U.S.A., from State to State).

The Roman Catholic church does not recognize divorce, and most Anglicans also hold that marriage can only be dissolved by death and that though in some circumstances separation may be justified neither party may remarry while the other lives. The Eastern Orthodox Churches, the Jews, and most Protestants permit divorce in certain cases; in Muslim law a husband may divorce his wife by threefold repetition of his intention to do so. In U.S.S.R. divorce by simple declaration before an official by either spouse was in force between 1926 and 1944 since when divorce is granted only if a court is satisfied that there is no prospect of reconciliation. Before 1857 divorce was possible in England only by private Act of Parliament; one of the bases of the current law is the Matrimonial Causes Act 1950 under which divorce may be granted for a variety of reasons, including adultery, cruelty, desertion, and incurable insanity. A decree of divorce and presumption of death may be granted where one party has not been heard of for seven years. A petition for divorce may not be presented within three years of the date of marriage, unless the Court gives leave, granted only in exceptional cases. An order entitling one spouse to live apart from the other may be given by a magistrates' court upon certain grounds such as desertion, persistent cruelty, assault upon the complainant or a child of the family, sexual offences against a child of the family, habitual drunkenness, or drug addiction. The husband may be ordered to make a weekly payment towards the maintenance of the wife and of children. The court may also give directions as to the custody of any children, the prime consideration being the welfare of the child. In Scotland the legal provisions are broadly similar. A divorce granted in a

foreign court is normally recognized in England, provided that the parties were domiciled in the foreign country; a decree granted to a wife in a foreign country where she has been living for 3 years or more will also be recognized; divorce based on a short period of residence e.g. in Reno, will not be recognized at all.

DNA. Deoxyribonucleic acid; the chemical basis of the ◊ *gene*, found in the cell nucleus; the largest naturally occurring molecule known. Living things are self-reproducing self-maintaining mechanisms whose growth, development, and reproduction are based on chemical information conveyed between generations of cells and of organisms. This information takes the form of a sequence of the sub-molecules composing the DNA, and is comparable to the arrangement of the signs (dot, dash, short and long pauses) of the morse code. The conveyance of DNA between generations involves a DNA copying mechanism that is partially understood and in which point ◊ *mutations* are comparable to a morse-code telegraphist's errors. Two of the main problems as to how this message controls the development of living things have now been solved in outline. First, the 'symbols' of the DNA code are known to be four organic molecules, adenine, thymine, guanine, and cytosine, arranged in a series of pairs similar to the rungs of a spiral ladder. The 'uprights' of the ladder are formed of molecules of carbohydrate and phosphoric acid. Groups of three neighbouring rungs form a 'letter'. There are about twenty letters in the DNA 'alphabet', and each 'means' a specific ◊ *amino-acid*. The second problem relates to the mechanism by which the amino-acids are linked to form ◊ *enzymes*, and involves another nucleic acid, ribonucleic acid (RNA). Several types of RNA are involved. One carries the 'message' from the DNA to ultra-microscopic particles in the ◊ *cell* cytoplasm called ribosomes. Another 'transfer' RNA arranges the amino-acids on ribosmal RNA in a sequence controlled by the messenger RNA and thus corresponding with the original DNA 'word'. In this way ◊ *protein* enzymes are manufactured, which control the synthesis of cellular materials and hence of cells. Although nucleic acids have been known since the 19th cent. our modern knowledge of their structure and function, a most fundamental biological discovery, originated in 1953 in the work of Crick, Wilkins, and Watson at King's College, London.

Dock Brief. In English courts, the traditional right of anyone indicted for a criminal offence to require (for a small fee) the service of any counsel present in court and not otherwise engaged; less used since the 1930 Poor Prisoners Defence Act (◊ *Legal Aid*).

Docks and Harbours. The use of moles and breakwaters to enclose a harbour from the open sea and provide a safe anchorage has been practised from early time; e.g. the Roman Empire had a number of artificial harbours. Where ports are sited on river estuaries, moles (usually banks of massive blocks of masonry or concrete) have often been provided at the mouth of the river, for protection and to guide the flow of water so that the need for dredging is reduced. In places where the tidal range is large, the loading of ships is facilitated by docks, large basins excavated along the shore, with locks (◊ *canal*) and gates to keep the inside water level constant. Dry docks (graving docks) are for the inspection and repair of ships; after the ship has been floated in, it is supported and the water pumped out.

Dodder. About 100 tropical and temperate species of *Cuscuta*, of the ◊ *Convolvulaceae*; there are three British species, total ◊ *parasites* with no roots, small-scale leaves, and small clusters of pink bell flowers on threadlike pinkish twining stems attached to the host stem by suckers. Hosts are commonly nettles, hops, flax, gorse, and heather.

Dodo ◊ *Birds*.

Dog. *Canis familiaris*; of the order *Carnivora*. The domestication of the dog occurred so early in prehistoric times that its descent is uncertain. Egyptian carvings show that by 3000 B.C. several distinct breeds had been developed. It is generally agreed that the domesticated dog was descended from the wolf, though one authority holds that this is true for certain northern breeds only, and that the rest developed from the jackal, this accounting for the widely differing natures of various breeds e.g. the fierce undemonstrative dog faithful to one master only (the wolf type) and the more playful, submissive, indiscriminately friendly type. The sledge dog

of the Eskimo does interbreed with the wolf, but no instance of interbreeding with jackals has been established. Dogs have a keen sense of smell and hearing, but in most dogs sight is not particularly well developed. They respond to training and have considerable intelligence. The great variety of types, e.g. such contrasting examples as the Pekinese and the Labrador or the bull dog and the Saluki, is a result partly of environment but mainly of selective breeding, which essentially had a definite end-purpose in view; but modern breeding for pets often results in bizarre and scarcely viable breeds. Dogs have been bred for hunting and herding, as watchdogs and draught animals, and even (in China and Mexico) for food. Some breeds still fulfil useful functions e.g. as sporting dogs, guide dogs, police dogs, sheep dogs, but the majority today are pets; expenditure for their food alone amounts in Britain to some £30 m. annually. The mongrel masterless pi-dogs of the East do not revert to the wild; wild dogs include the so-called 'hunting dog' of Africa (a ruthless predator hunting in packs which threatens the whole ◊ *antelope* family with extinction) and the dingo of Australia.

Dogwood. *Cornus florida*; one of the most beautiful of E. American flowering trees, with large white leaflike bracts surrounding the clusters of insignificant greenish flowers. It will grow 12 to 15 ft high, but its Californian relative *C. nuttallii* grows to 50 ft. The English dogwood *C. sanguinea* has no beauty of flower but its autumn foliage and red stems in winter are colourful.

Doldrums ◊ *Trade Winds*.

Dolomite. Carbonate of calcium and magnesium; ◊ *sedimentary rock* formed by chemical precipitation. A crystalline granular form found in NE England, magnesium limestone, is extensively used as a building stone e.g. in the Houses of Parliament; dolomite is also used for lining refractory furnaces. The name derives from the Dolomite Alps. ◊ *Geological Time Scale, Serpentine*.

Dolphin. *Delphinus delphis*; any aquatic mammal similar to the ◊ *porpoise* but with a beak-like snout. The common dolphin found in temperate and tropical waters is about eight ft long and may swim in schools of hundreds; there are numerous anecdotes of its intelligence and its affection for man. In captivity, dolphins may be taught to perform feats for reward, seem capable of communication with one another, and according to one claim can be trained to answer human speech. Several freshwater species are known.

Dome. A spherical roof placed like an inverted cup over a circular, square, or multi-angular apartment; if the curve is very flat it is called a saucer-dome. For visual effect, the dome is sometimes double, e.g. St Peter's in Rome, or even triple, e.g. St Paul's in London. The dome was used about 700 B.C. in Assyria, by the Romans e.g. in the Pantheon, and by the Byzantines e.g. in Haghia Sophia in Constantinople, but not in ◊ *Gothic architecture*; the ◊ *Renaissance* used the dome frequently, as have all subsequent architects.

Domesday Book. 1086. The record of an exhaustive survey of most of England carried out after the ◊ *Norman Conquest* at the orders of William the Conqueror. It records the amount of land held by the king and the magnates in each shire; the number of people and animals on each manor; the value of the manor in 1066 and in 1086; and the amount at which it had previously been assessed for tax e.g. Danegeld (◊ *Vikings*). William's object seems to have been chiefly to ascertain how much tax he could levy; for this reason the survey was greatly resented. It provides the historian with a unique record of social conditions under ◊ *feudalism* in 11th-cent. England.

Domestication. The method by which man has brought certain animals and plants into his service; by selecting and breeding qualities useful to man, many characteristics necessary for life in the wild may be lost, so that the domesticated variety can only survive under man's care, e.g. cereal crops, pigs. Many domesticated animals will breed at all times of the year, and their reproduction is no longer under the influence of seasonal changes. ◊ *Neolithic*.

Dominance. If a ◊ *gene* expresses itself i.e. produces the character for which it is responsible, whether received from one parent or from both, it is said to be dominant; if it does so only when received from both parents, it is said to be recessive.

Dominica ◊ *West Indies Federation.*

Dominican Republic. Area 19,322 sq. m. Pop. 3 m. Cap. Santo Domingo (Ciudad Trujillo). Formerly the Spanish colony on the island Hispaniola (which it shares with ◊ *Haiti*).

ECONOMY. Mainly agricultural, esp. sugar, also bananas, cocoa, coffee, groundnuts, honey, maize, rice, sisal. Some light industry, esp. rum, also glass, matches, paper, rope.

HISTORY. Discovered in 1492 by Columbus, whose brother founded the city of Santo Domingo, it is the oldest European settlement in the Americas. During the revolt of the Spanish colonies in the 1820s it became briefly independent but was annexed by Haiti until it regained independence in 1844. It was occupied by U.S. Marines 1916–24, and then self-governing except for U.S. administration of customs duties and foreign commitments. The Trujillo dictatorship of 1930–61 ended with his assassination; there was a provisional State Council 1961–3, after which a military coup d'état set up a triumvirate. There has been renewed friction with Haiti.

Dominicans. The Order of Preachers founded by St Dominic in 1216. The members (friars) devoted their lives to study and preaching, and were of great importance in the medieval universities; St Thomas Aquinas was a Dominican. The Dominican order was largely responsible for the ◊ *Inquisition.*

Dominions ◊ *British Commonwealth.*

Dominoes. A game for two to four players, normally using 28 'dominoes' (small rectangular pieces often of wood, ebony, and ivory): one side is divided into two squares containing dots in every combination from 0–0 to 6–6. Play usually proceeds by placing one domino at a time so that one square of the dots is against a corresponding free square of a piece already played; if this cannot be done the player forfeits his turn and in some games draws another piece from a central pool. The game is won by the person who places all his pieces first. Dominoes appeared in Italy and France in the mid 18th cent. and was introduced to England by French prisoners from the Napoleonic wars. The name may derive from a black cloak called a domino, the dominoes always having been coloured black and white.

Don Juan. The prototype of the rake and seducer, based on the gay but heartless hero of Spanish legend; since his appearance in a play by 'Tirso de Molina' (Gabriel Tellez) in 1630, the subject of countless literary and musical works, including Molière's *Don Juan ou Le Festin de Pierre* and Mozart's *Don Giovanni*. By the 18th cent. treatments were becoming more lighthearted; by the 19th cent. (esp. in Germany) he is more romantic, idealistic, and restless; in some versions he is sentimentalized and even allowed repentance and salvation.

Don Quixote. Hero of the satirical romance by Cervantes, Part 1 1605, Part 2 1615, which began as a burlesque of the then fashionable novels of chivalry (the reading of which turned Don Quixote's head); gradually the author's sympathies changed, and the book developed into a deeper, broader, and more compassionate account of the adventures of an eccentric idealist in a hostile, greedy, and cynical world, which leads the reader to the conclusion that if Quixote is a fool it is because the world does not live up to his ideals. Its main theme apart, the book is loosely constructed and contains a variety of humorous episodes, conversations, and digressions; a lengthy sequence describes the governorship of Sancho Panza, Quixote's peasant squire, and the wisdom of his judgements. It was translated almost immediately into most European languages, and has remained extremely popular ever since, each subsequent age interpreting it according to the prevailing taste. The first English translation was made 1612–20 and had considerable influence on 17th-cent. English comedy and the form of the 18th-cent. novel.

Doppler Effect. Change in the observed frequency of a wave source caused by variation in the distance between source and observer; the frequency appears to increase as the source approaches and vice versa. A common example in sound is often provided by the whistle of a train, higher in pitch (frequency) when it is moving towards the hearer than when stationary, lower in pitch when it is moving away. With light, the approach of the source similarly causes a shift towards the higher-frequency or violet end of the spectrum ($\Diamond$ *Dispersion*), and its recession a shift to the lower-frequency or red end. In $\Diamond$ *astronomy* this effect plays an important part in determining the speed at which celestial bodies are moving towards or away from the earth; e.g. with some galaxies a pronounced 'red shift' of lines in their spectrum indicates a high speed of recession. When the components of binary stars are too close to be seen separately, they may often be detected and have their individual orbits measured by observing the spectral displacement caused by Doppler effect. $\Diamond$ *Star*.

Dorians. Traditionally, the last of the migrant peoples to arrive in Greece from the north, about the 12th cent. B.C. They defeated the $\Diamond$ *Achaeans*, destroyed $\Diamond$ *Mycenae* and other important cities, and settled chiefly in Crete ($\Diamond$ *Minoan Civilization*) and in $\Diamond$ *Sparta*. The Spartans of later times spoke the dialect of the Dorians, from whom also they are thought to have inherited their severe and militaristic temperament.

Doric Order $\Diamond$ *Architectural Orders*.

Dormouse. Various small Old World nocturnal $\Diamond$ *rodents* three or four in. long, belonging to the family *Muscardinidae*; the common name refers to their daily sleep. They live in nests built in trees and bushes, and the northern species hibernate.

Double-bass $\Diamond$ *Stringed Instruments*.

Doukhobors. Christian religious body, of unclear origin, founded in Russia about 1750. Ruled by a community of elders, they teach the equality (in love and universal brotherhood) of all believers, see no need for secular authority, and claim to be directly guided by the divine spirit, interpreting the $\Diamond$ *Bible* allegorically and believing that the soul of $\Diamond$ *Jesus Christ* (whose divinity they do not recognize) has on various occasions been reincarnated ($\Diamond$ *Transmigration*), sometimes in one of their own elders. Persecuted in the 19th cent. by the Tsarist government, they were defended by Tolstoy; just before the end of the century most of them emigrated to Canada, settling mainly in Manitoba, where they have often collided with the State authorities owing to their $\Diamond$ *civil disobedience*.

Dowsing. A method of discovering water or metals below ground, in which a person believed to be specially gifted carries a forked rod or branch (divining rod) which twitches when he passes over the correct spot; though entirely lacking in scientific validation, the method is used quite extensively.

Dragonfly ◊ *Fly*.

Dragon's Teeth ◊ *Cadmus*.

Drama. Various forms of dramatic creation have existed since the earliest times, but the dramatized narrative of character and conflict which is the essence of European drama was the creation of the Greeks of the 5th cent. B.C. esp. Aeschylus 525–456, Sophocles 496–406, Euripides *c.* 480–406, and the comedian Aristophanes *c.* 445–388. The Romans, who learned dramatic art from the Greeks, added little to it, although the comedies of Plautus *c.* 250–184 and Terence *c.* 190–159, and the tragedies of Seneca 5 B.C. to A.D. 65, had considerable influence on dramatic theory and practice from the 16th cent. onwards. The theatre degenerated in later Roman times, and practically disappeared in face of the opposition of the early Christian Church.

Of early medieval drama little is known, apart from the religious comedies of the German nun Hroswitha in the 10th cent., until the mystery plays (◊ *Miracle Plays*) grew out of the rituals of the church and began to be performed by the guilds in the 13th cent. In England the Elizabethan and Jacobean ages saw an unparalleled upsurge of theatre-building and dramatic writing. Catering for all sections of society, the Elizabethan theatres mounted a succession of great plays and get-penny entertainments, including the work of Christopher Marlowe, William Shakespeare, and Ben Jonson. In Spain the 17th cent. witnessed the drama of Lope de Vega 1562–1635 and Calderón 1600–81, and in France the classical tragedies of Corneille 1606–84 and Racine 1639–99, and the comedies of Molière 1622–73. In England, reaction from the severities of the Interregnum produced the cynical and generally bawdy Restoration comedy of Buckingham, Etherege, Sedley, Wycherley, and later the urbanely licentious comedy of manners of Congreve, Vanbrugh, Farquhar in the reigns of William III and Anne. Dryden's heroic tragedies, often adaptations from Shakespeare e.g. *All for Love* (*Antony and Cleopatra*), remained a staple of the English theatre for 100 years.

The 18th cent. was an age of great comedy, with Goldsmith and Sheridan in England, Beaumarchais and Marivaux in France, Goldoni in Italy, but the tragedies of the period have not survived in the repertory. The German theatre, long dependent on imported works, developed a national drama at the end of the 18th cent. in the plays of Lessing, Goethe, and Schiller; Austria's 'classic' dramatist Grillparzer, the Romantic Prussian Kleist, philosophically gloomy Hebbel, and Büchner (with his masterpiece *Dantons Tod*) gave it a rich repertoire.

In the late 19th cent. sentimental romance and melodrama were replaced by a new psychological realism, a change largely wrought by the Norwegian Henrik Ibsen 1828–1906 and his followers the Swede Strindberg 1849–1912 and the Russian Chekhov 1860–1904. One of the most notable of Ibsen's followers in England was the Anglo-Irishman G. B. Shaw 1856–1950; it is noticeable that it was the Anglo-Irish (Congreve, Farquhar, Goldsmith, Sheridan, Wilde, Shaw, Yeats, Synge, O'Casey) who made the richest contribution to the English theatre from the late 17th cent. to the early 20th.

The divergence between 'commercial' and 'serious' drama in the 20th cent. and the diversity of its manifestations make it difficult to describe its main trends succinctly. Social and political comment remains an important preoccupation, esp. in the work of the impressive line of American playwrights who followed Eugene O'Neill 1888–1953, including Clifford Odets, Arthur Miller, and Tennessee Williams. Strenuous attempts were made to revive the tradition of verse drama, in England by T. S. Eliot, W. H. Auden, and Christopher Fry and in America by Maxwell Anderson 1888–1959, and in France the poetic impulse is strong in the work of dramatists as varied as Paul Claudel 1868–1955, Jean Cocteau 1891–1962, Jean Giraudoux 1882–1944, and Jean ·Anouilh (b. 1910), but perhaps the only wholly convincing 20th-cent. poetic dramatist was the Spaniard Federico García Lorca 1898–1936. Luigi Pirandello 1867–1936 introduced an intellectual note into the theatre, discussing such philosophical questions as the nature of actuality and of identity; his investigations into the dramatic illusion itself have had considerable influence on 20th-cent. writing. The influence of Bertolt Brecht 1878–1956 has only recently begun to be felt; his fiercely political plays, combining poetry, song, mime, and naturalistic dialogue, have largely been discovered since the 1950s, though most of his major work was written long before. Another group of dramatists, led by Samuel Beckett (b. 1906) and Eugène Ionesco (b. 1912), have taken a more extreme path; for them the breakdown of values, codes, and beliefs, and the general meaninglessness of life, summed up in the idea of the Absurd, entail a total clearing-away of the remaining debris (whatever the cost) if man is to survive his own lunacy. Other playwrights e.g. Harold Pinter and the American Edward Albee present divergent but related examples of such writing. John Osborne's *Look Back in Anger*, 1956, brought English drama out of the drawing-room, where it had for the most part been languishing, and ushered in a period of real if often exaggerated vitality in the British theatre. Arnold Wesker, John Arden, and Robert Bolt have, in their very different ways, also achieved a considerable reputation. ◊ *Comedy, Theatre, Tragedy*, etc.

Draughts (Checkers). A game for two played on a checker-board of 64 squares identical to that used in chess, of which it is possibly the fore-runner. Each player has 12 pieces, known as white and black, both sets being moved on the dark squares only. Play is on the same coloured squares: each player initially arranges his pieces on the three rows nearest to him. Moves are made forwards only one space at a time, diagonally, until pieces which reach the far side of the board are crowned and become kings: these can then move both backwards and forwards. Pieces are captured by jumping over any adjacent opposing piece if the square beyond is vacant: under a recent rule such capture is compulsory. Previously a player could choose not to effect the capture and have his own piece taken or 'huffed' if he judged it more advantageous. The game ends when all the pieces of one colour have been taken. The game was known in Egypt and adopted by the Romans, who learnt it from the Greeks. It was described in a Spanish book of 1547 and for the first time in an English book in 1756. The first British/U.S. match was in 1905.

Dravidian Languages. Antecedents not certainly identified; descended from the aboriginal tongue probably spoken over most of India before it was overrun by Indo-European invaders in the second millennium B.C. Now spoken by over 100

m. south of a line running obliquely across the Dekkan from Goa to Puri. The Dravidian tongues of the Dekkan include four notable literary languages, now recorded in modified Devanagari alphabets. TAMIL: By far the most important by virtue of its rich literature, dating to the 2nd cent. A.D. and surpassed by ◊ *Sanskrit* alone; still spoken by 27 m. in the S. of the Madras presidency, in the N. and E. of Ceylon, and by settlers in the Malay peninsula, it preserves an ancient and copious vocabulary, and has contributed cheroot, corundum, curry, pariah, and mulligatawny to English.

TELUGU: Spoken by 33 m. in the N. of the Madras presidency and neighbouring Hyderabad, and the W. coastal regions from Karvar to Mangalore.

KANARESE: Spoken by 15 m. in Mysore, S W Hyderabad, and the W. coast regions from Karvar to Mangalore.

MALAYALAM: Almost a dialect of Tamil, spoken by 14 m. in the states of Cochin and Travancore.

Drawing. The linear art underlying most forms of pictorial expression, usually in pen and ink (often with the addition of washes), charcoal, coloured chalk, or pencil, on paper or parchment. There is a distinction between drawings executed as ends in themselves and those made as sketches for works in other media. A list of the masters of draughtsmanship would include nearly all the great ◊ *Renaissance* and later painters: among the most notable are Leonardo da Vinci, Michelangelo, Raphael, Annibale Carracci, Rembrandt, Claude Lorraine, Watteau, Ingres, Degas, Picasso.

Dreadnought. 1. A ◊ *battleship*; H.M.S. *Dreadnought*, launched 1906, was the first of a class, of 17,900 tons displacement, with a main armament of ten 12-in. guns in five turrets, and a speed of 22 knots, the most powerful ◊ *warship* then afloat, which ushered in a new era of naval construction by the great powers of the day. **2.** A ◊ *submarine*; the *Dreadnought*, Britain's first nuclear-powered submarine, of 3400 tons displacement, was launched 1960 at the Barrow yard of Vickers-Armstrong Ltd.

Dream. A series of events vividly imagined during sleep, recall of a dream on waking being the only direct evidence for its occurrence; the time of dreaming is roughly indicated by movements of the sleeper's eyes and changes in the brain-rhythm. The vividness of dreams led primitive people to regard them as real events in which the sleeper was transported in space and/or time or was visited by supernatural beings. Dreams show in an exaggerated form some of the features of fantasy, and modern explanations come largely from Freud; by explaining them as expressing repressed wishes in a symbolic form, he established a scientific basis for the belief that dreams have a 'meaning' and admit of interpretation.

Dreyfus Affair. 1894–1906. In 1894, on flimsy evidence, a French officer of Jewish descent was condemned to life imprisonment on Devil's Island for betraying secrets to Germany. Émile Zola, by his open letter *J'Accuse!* and a sustained press campaign, forced a retrial in 1899, at which further trumped-up evidence was offered by the French Army authorities, to shield a gentile officer, Esterhazy, and to conceal their own guilt in faking evidence. Dreyfus was again convicted, but President Loubet immediately pardoned him. In 1906 the Court of Appeal quashed the 1894 judgement, and Dreyfus was reinstated in the Army. The Affair was a test of strength between radical ⟡ *anticlericalism* and the narrow sectionalism, illiberalism, and ⟡ *antisemitism* of the French officer corps.

Drift. General term in geology for the superficial deposits e.g. glacial debris which in many areas cover the solid rock formations. Chief among the drift deposits of the British Isles is ⟡ *boulder clay*. H.M. Geological Survey publishes many 1-in. geological maps in two editions, one showing the solid rocks and the other the drifts which overlie them.

Drifter. A fishing vessel for catching surface-swimming fish e.g. herring, by means of a wall of nets hanging vertically in the water; having 'shot' her nets, the vessel drifts with the tide at their lee end, and the fish are trapped by the gills in trying to extricate themselves. Drifters are stoutly built vessels, 60 to 80 ft long, usually of wooden construction, powered by diesel engines but also carrying a small sail aft to help them lie head-to-wind.

Drogheda. 1649. After the execution of Charles I some royalist forces still held out in Ireland; ordered to go there, part of Cromwell's army mutinied (⟡ *Level-*

lers), but after quelling the mutiny Cromwell landed an army at Dublin and marched to besiege the royalist stronghold at Drogheda. Having breached the walls with artillery, he ordered 'No Quarter' for anyone found in arms, which resulted in the slaughter of almost all the men in the city; some were burned alive. Having dealt similarly with Waterford, he returned to England, leaving first Ireton and then his own son Henry in charge of Irish affairs, which remained quiet throughout the Commonwealth and Protectorate. ⟡ *Poynings Law*.

Dromedary ⟡ *Camel*.

Drosophila ⟡ *Fruit Fly, Heredity*.

Drug Addiction. Chronic intoxication produced by repeated consumption of a narcotic drug, characterized by an overpowering desire to continue taking the drug and to obtain supplies regardless of cost, and by detrimental psychological or physical dependence upon it; sudden withdrawal of the drug causes serious distress. The addict has usually been a person of unstable personality before becoming addicted, and treatment is largely psychiatric, initially in hospital, with intensive after-care to prevent relapse. The percentage of complete cures is disappointing.

Drugs of addiction are subject to international control, and their prescription and sale are regulated by the 1951 and 1953 Dangerous Drugs Acts; they include opium, morphine, heroin, cocaine, cannabis indica (hashish, marijuana), pethidine, a number of synthetic narcotics, and more recently some of the barbiturate drugs. In the U.K. the free supply of the drug to registered addicts obviates drug peddling and its vicious results.

Addiction should be distinguished from habituation, in which there is desire to continue the use of a drug, for the sense of well-being it provides, but no compulsion; tranquillizers and stimulants are examples of drugs habituation to which is widespread and increasing. ⟡ *Alcoholism*.

Drugs ⟡ *Pharmacology*.

Druids. The priesthood of Celtic Britain, Ireland, and Gaul, described in Caesar's *Commentaries* and elsewhere. Little is known of them or of their religion, but they were men of rank and considerable political power who combined the functions of priest, judge, and sage, and led Gaulish resistance to the Romans. They did not (as was once thought) build Stonehenge and other megalithic monuments. Their places of worship were in oak groves. The practice of human sacrifice gave the Emperor Claudius reason to suppress them, and they declined into mere magicians, though surviving in Ireland as wandering bards.

Drumlins. < Irish, 'little hills'; made of ◊ *boulder clay*, rising any height up to 300 ft, varying in length from a few yards to a mile or more, they usually occur in swarms e.g. in N. Ireland, N W England, and central Scotland, their long axes marking the line of movement of the ◊ *ice sheet* which carved them out of the mass. Geologists are by no means agreed on their mode of origin. ◊◊ *Drift*.

Druses. Adherents of an esoteric religion comprising Muslim, Jewish, and Christian elements, living in the mountains of Syria and the Lebanon; they believe in a series of divine incarnations and in ◊ *transmigration*, follow a strict ethical code, and mix as little as possible with unbelievers, but as they are permitted to conform outwardly to other religions it is difficult to know their numbers (probably about 100,000). Their 19th-cent massacre of Christians helped to bring about French intervention; in 1925 they rebelled against French rule, and in the Second World War they supported the British and Free French forces against the Vichy French. The name Druses derives from Ismail ad-Darazi, a Persian preacher and disciple of the founder, the 11th-cent. Caliph Hakim of Egypt, who proclaimed himself an incarnation of God.

Drying Oils. On exposure to air certain vegetable oils dry to form a tough skin or film; the drying is a complex process of resinification due to a polymerization induced by the oxygen of the air (◊ *Polymers*). Linseed oil is used in the manufacture of paints, varnishes, linoleum; here the drying process can be accelerated by the addition of suitable catalysts. Drying oils are glycerides of highly unsaturated fatty acids such as linoleic.

Drypoint ◊ *Engraving*.

Dry Rot. Fungus infection by *Merulius lacrymans*; the spawn (mycelium) lives in wood and feeds by secreting ◊ *enzymes* which attack and destroy wood. Damp wood is particularly liable to infection, but once the fungus is established in such wood, it can spread to drier wood. The fungus can spread by strands (rhizo-

morphs) up to $\frac{1}{4}$ in. thick, which can travel several feet without nourishment over and through brickwork. Thus the woodwork of a whole house may become rapidly infected. The fruiting body, pale yellow or white, flat, and spongy, is clearly visible and disseminates myriads of ◊ *spores*.

Dry rot can be avoided by prevention of the damp conditions, i.e. by good ventilation and insulation of wood from the earth, or alternatively by treatment of wood with preservatives e.g. creosote before building. Once wood has been infected it is normally impossible to kill the fungus.

Dualism. Any doctrine dividing reality into two independent kinds of thing, or describing two forces at work in the universe. Descartes expressed in his philosophy (◊ *Cartesianism*) the traditional separation of reality into mind and matter; ◊ *Zoroastrianism*, like many religions, claims the existence of a good and a bad cosmic spirit. ◊◊ *Monism, Pluralism*.

Dubai ◊ *Gulf Sheikhdoms*.

Duchy of Lancaster. Created in 1351 by Edward III for Henry Wryneck, it passed on his death in 1361 to his son-in-law John of Gaunt and then in 1399 to his son Henry IV, who kept it separate from the other Crown lands. In medieval times it included castles and manors all over the country, and formed an important source of royal revenue. The ◊ *Stewarts* sold much of it, but what remained (some 52,000 acres) was kept by George III when all other Crown lands were surrendered. It is still administered by the Chancellor of the Duchy.

Duck. A world-wide family of freshwater and saltwater birds, domesticated for many centuries, nesting in reeds or on low muddy banks; many breed in cold areas and migrate to warmer regions in the winter, flying in V-shaped formations. The Chinese developed highly ornamental species which have been introduced to Europe. The wild eider duck furnishes fine feathers for eiderdowns.

Duck-billed Platypus. Strange mammal (more strictly, a monotreme) retaining several reptilian features, in which the beak of a duck is attached to a body covered with fur, somewhat like an ◊ *otter*; found in S. Australia and Tasmania, where its fossil remains show that it has existed unchanged for over 100 m.

years. It lays eggs, but suckles its young.

Dugong. Aquatic mammals belonging not to the *Cetacea* (◊ *Whale*) but to the *Sirenia*, resembling ◊ *porpoises* and found only inshore in the Indian Ocean. There are two species, *Halicore* (*Dugong*) *dugong* and *H. australis*. They give birth to single offspring which they suckle at the breast in human fashion, thus probably giving rise to the legend of the mermaid.

Duma. 1905–17. The Russian House of Representatives, set up by Nicholas II. Its first two meetings were short-lived, and the electoral machinery was then altered to favour the upper classes. The third Duma ran its full term 1907–12, and the fourth was in progress when the ◊ *Bolshevik* revolution occurred. Theoretically the Duma had wide powers, but in practice these were restricted by the extensive use of the Tsar's prerogative, the removal of much expenditure from its control, and the conservative nature of the upper house. ◊ *Soviet Union* (*History*).

Dumbarton Oaks. 1944. Scene of talks between the U.K., U.S.A., U.S.S.R., and Nationalist China, at which the outlines of the ◊ *United Nations Organization* were formulated. They were later adopted by the San Francisco Conference 1945.

Dunbar. 1650. After subduing the Royalists in Ireland (◊ *Drogheda*) Cromwell marched on Scotland (◊ *Covenant*). He soon encountered difficulties of supply and retired to Dunbar, where his retreat to Berwick was blocked by a Scots force twice as strong; but benefiting by an ill-conceived manoeuvre of their commander's, he defeated the Scots, of whom half were either killed or taken prisoner. Except for the rout of another Scots army under Charles II at ◊ *Worcester* in 1651, Dunbar was the final engagement of the Cromwellian civil wars.

Dunkirk Evacuation. 1940. The bulk of the British Expeditionary Force and other allied troops were encircled in a small area around Dunkirk by the rapid German advances of May 1940; vessels of every sort, naval and private, were mustered in English harbours, and crossed the Channel in a remarkable operation, which (with air support) succeeded in saving over 300,000 troops from a desperate position. Practically the whole of the heavy equipment of the British forces was lost, however. ◊ *Second World War*.

Duodecimal System. Various systems of counting exist of which counting in tens (◊ *Decimal System*) is the most widely used. In Britain and U.S.A. many measurements of length, weight, and time are based on groups of twelve, e.g. 12 in. to a foot, 12 months to a year, 60 min. to an hour and seconds to a minute. A duodecimal system, which would fit such measurements neatly, has some advocates. It would entail two extra digits; these are usually written as t for 10 and e for 11. The positional principle still applies: thus $10 = 1 \times 12$, $100 = 1 \times 12^2$, and $2t3e$ would represent $2 \times 12^3 + 10 \times 12^2 + 3 \times 12 + 11$, i.e. 4943. The major advantage of a duodecimal system is that the base 12 has more factors (2, 3, 4, 6) than 10 (2, 5).

Duralumin ◊ *Alloys*.

Dustbowl ◊ *Erosion, Tennessee Valley Authority*.

Duststorm ◊ *Sandstorm*.

Dutch Art. Up to the 17th cent. Dutch art is almost indistinguishable from Flemish, the masters of the 15th cent. being Dirk Bouts and Hieronymus Bosch. In the 17th cent. the influence of Caravaggio was brought back from Italy e.g. Terbrugghen and Honthorst, the Baroque style current in Rome being imported into Holland through Utrecht, which had close ties with Italy, as well as indirectly through the influence of Rubens, the greatest Flemish painter of the period, and the great age of Dutch art began. In the absence of patronage from the Protestant church, artists turned to largely secular subjects and esp. to ◊ *landscape painting*. The two Ruisdaels, Hobbema, van Goyen, and Koninck all painted realistic landscapes, while others – notably Cuyp – painted imaginary Italianate landscapes which reveal the additional influence of Claude. Portrait painting also flourished – Franz Hals being the outstanding exponent – particularly in the form of portrait groups, a genre which arose from commissions from the Civic Guards, who wished to commemorate themselves in the Halls they maintained in each town. At the same time many painters e.g. Steen, Ostade, de Hooch, and Vermeer – the greatest of them all – turned to subjects taken from everyday life. Most of these trends were summed up in the work of Rembrandt, the greatest of all Dutch artists, painter, draughtsman, and etcher; principally a portrait painter, he also introduced a great many Biblical themes (mostly from the Old Testament) not previously used by painters. Towards the end of the 17th cent. fashionable artists e.g. Rembrandt's pupil Maes began to be influenced by contemporary French ideas; this tendency continued during the 18th cent. No other major artist appeared till in the middle of the 19th cent. a number of painters of the so-called Hague School began to practise a rather sentimental genre form, which was taken up and transformed by Van Gogh, the greatest of modern Dutch painters; he worked mainly in France, however, and Mondrian, the leading 20th-cent. Dutch painter, also worked outside Holland.

Dutch Guiana ◊ *Netherlands West Indies.*

Dutch Wars ◊ *Navigation Acts.*

Dyes. Colouring matters, usually organic, which can be absorbed from solution by natural or synthetic fibres. If light and water have little effect on them, 'fast'; otherwise 'fugitive'. Dyes made from mineral, animal, or vegetable substances (e.g. umber, cochineal, wood) have been in use since earliest times; the invention of aniline ◊ *coal-tar* dyes in England by Perkin 1856 (◊ *Mauvine*) revolutionized dyeing. The important dyestuffs industry is one of the activities of such giant firms as I.C.I. in Britain, I.G. Farben Industrie in Germany, and Dupont in U.S.A. The synthetic dyes have a wide range of colour and great permanency, and have displaced natural dyes almost completely. Dyes are classified into various types according to the method needed to apply them, e.g. direct, mordant, vat. Though many of the original discoveries about synthetic dyes were made in Britain, their manufacture was at first almost a German monopoly; under the protection of an Act passed 1921 prohibiting the import of dyes into the U.K. except under licence, the British industry has developed rapidly.

Dynamite ◊ *Explosives.*

Dynamo ◊ *Generator.*

Dysentery. Inflammation of the mucous membrane of the large intestine resulting in the passage of loose stools with mucus and blood, commonly due to a protozoon, *Entamoeba histolytica* (amoebic dysentery), or to bacterial infection with organisms of the *Shigella* group (bacillary dysentery).

E

Eagle. *Aquila*; bird of prey with large hooked bill, keen eyesight, strong talons, and powerful soaring flight. There are several varieties, of world-wide distribution, some very large e.g. the American bald eagle found widely in U.S.A. and the golden eagle of the Old World which can kill hares and ptarmigan. Eagles live near mountains, forests, and rocky shores, and have families of from one to three a year. Similar to the eagle but smaller is the buzzard. The vulture also resembles the eagle, but always has a bald head, feeds on carrion, and is confined to warm climates; some e.g. the condor of S. America are extremely large. Hawks are smaller related birds of prey with less soaring flight. ◊ *Falcon*.

Ear. Receptor apparatus for the sense of ◊ *hearing*, consisting of (a) the external ear with its ear-drum, beyond which lies (b) the middle ear, a bony cavity shaped like an oblong box, in which are three small articulated bones, the malleus, the incus, and the stapes, which transmit movements of the drum to (c) the inner ear, a labyrinth of bone in front of which is the cochlea, shaped like a minute spiral snail shell, in which lies the organ of Corti (the actual organ of hearing). The mechanism of hearing is actuated by sound waves, which cause the ear-drum to vibrate, the vibrations being transmitted by the three bones in the middle ear to the organ of Corti, whence the auditory nerve carries the impulses to the brain, where the sensory stimuli are appreciated as sound.

Early English Style. The first phase of English ◊ *Gothic architecture*, followed by the ◊ *Decorated* and the ◊ *Perpendicular* styles. Beginning with the adoption of French Gothic, it lasted until 1300, characterized by less vertical emphasis than in the French style, by the retention of much English Norman usage (◊ *Romanesque Architecture*) e.g. galleries instead of triforia, and by a preference for two sets of transepts and for lancet windows, stiff-leaf capitals and vault bosses, and complex schemes of rib-vaulting. The cathedrals at Wells, Lincoln, Salisbury, and Westminster Abbey illustrate the style.

Earthing. The connecting of parts of electrical systems to the earth in order to prevent the build-up of large voltage differences between them and it. Exposed metal parts of electrical equipment are 'earthed' to make them safe in the event of their coming into contact with the supply lines during a breakdown.

Earthquakes. Vibrations or tremors in rocks, generally caused by a sudden earth movement along the line of a ◊ *fault*. Violent at the source of the disturbance; die down only slowly, spreading out in all directions. Can be detected, and their intensity measured, by seismographs (◊ *Seismology*). There are three regions where earthquakes are of considerable frequency: Japan; a belt across S. Europe and S. Asia; the W. coast of S. America. Earthquakes have taken a toll of lives over the centuries which runs into several millions, including 1755 Lisbon, 60,000 dead; 1906 San Francisco, city destroyed; 1923/4 Tokyo and Yokohama, 180,000 dead; 1939 Chile, 20,000 dead. Recently there have been disastrous earthquakes in Morocco 1960, Chile 1960, Skopje (Yugoslavia) 1963, and Alaska 1964.

Earthworm. A ◊ *hermaphrodite* invertebrate of the phylum Annelida, of worldwide distribution; the rings along the body indicate a serial repetition not only of external features but also of many internal organs, a feature which is found greatly modified in man. The swollen smooth part, the 'saddle', one fifth of the total length from the head, secretes a cocoon within which the eggs develop. There are more than 20 species and several genera in Britain, varying in length from one to nine in. An Australian worm may be several yards long. If they are bisected, death ensues, but damaged portions can be regenerated. Worms feed on soil micro-organisms, but also browse on leaves at night; they have photo-receptive cells enabling them to react instantly to light. They were closely studied by Charles Darwin, who showed their importance in aerating and in introducing humus to the soil, their activity benefiting 15 tons of soil per acre annually.

Easter. Principal feast of the Christian year, in commemoration of the resurrection of ◊ *Jesus Christ* from the dead; kept on the first Sunday after the 14th day of the new moon on or next after 21 March, i.e. a Sunday between 22 March and 25 April; preceded by the 40-day fast of Lent culminating in Good Friday, the anniversary of the crucifixion. There has recently been a movement to fix the date (e.g. the Sunday after the second Saturday in April) by agreement between the churches and the civil authorities. ◊ *Religious Festivals.*

Easter Island. Small volcanic island, one of the loneliest in the world, about 2000 m. off Chile, remarkable for the immense stone figures along its shores and their as yet indecipherable rock inscriptions; the figures, carved from a grey volcanic stone, are as much as 30 ft high, and all of them at one time seem to have had 'hats' of red tuff and to have stood on platforms of hewn rock. Captain Cook described the stonework as better than the best masonry in England, and archaeological investigations suggest that the figures were carved by a culture, possibly of S. American origin (◊ *Kon Tiki*), which was brought to a sudden end by warfare about A.D. 1680. In native tradition, the ancestors of the present population (mainly ◊ *Polynesian*) massacred an earlier population who had fair skins and reddish hair.

Eastern Orthodox Church. Incorrectly called 'Greek'; a federation of Christian churches in Asia and E. Europe claiming historical continuity with the Apostles (◊ *Jesus Christ*), differing from the ◊ *Roman Catholic Church* on certain points of discipline and doctrine, rejecting the authority of the ◊ *Pope*, and giving primacy to the see of Constantinople. Accepts the decisions of the first seven Councils and the seven ◊ *sacraments*; generally uses an archaic form of the local vernacular (e.g. Old Slavonic, Hellenic Greek) for the ◊ *liturgy*; rejects sacred statues (on the basis of the 'graven images' Commandment) but makes great use of sacred pictures (icons) and has an elaborately developed ritual; and permits pre-ordination marriage of the clergy. In Europe this church is dominant in Greece and still has a large following in the Balkan states and the U.S.S.R. As a result of emigration it has recently grown considerably in U.S.A. Its world member-

ship is about 150 m. There are also small eastern churches (e.g. Coptic, Abyssinian, Armenian, Syrian-Jacobite) deriving mainly from early ◊ *heresy.*

UNIATE CHURCH: A separatist body, reconciled to papal authority but retaining its own languages and liturgy.

Easter Rebellion. 1916. An abortive rebellion in Dublin led by the ◊ *Sinn Fein* Irish Volunteers and the trade-union Citizen Army. Sixteen leaders were executed. Subsequently, in the 1918 General Election, almost all the Irish constituencies returned Sinn Fein members; they refused to go to Westminster, and constituted themselves Dail Eireann under the leadership of De Valera. ◊ *Anglo-Irish 'Troubles'.*

East India Company. 1600–1858. English trading company, granted a charter by Elizabeth I in 1600, which founded its first 'factory' on the Indian mainland in 1610. Driven out of Malaysia by fierce competition from the Dutch, it concentrated on India, where by 1689 it had established its rule as well as trading rights. French attempts to challenge its position were finally crushed by Clive in 1751. It retained its privileged position, in return for loans to the government, but after the defeat of the French in the ◊ *Seven Years War* Pitt placed it under the supervision of a Board of Control and a Governor-General. The first Governor-General, Warren Hastings, however, was impeached in 1788 for oppressive rule, and his sensational trial continued for eight years. In 1813 the Company's absolute monopoly of Indian trade was abolished, and in 1833 its powers were limited to administration. After the ◊ *Indian Mutiny* it ceded all its powers to the Crown in 1858. ◊ *Boston Tea Party, Plassey.*

East Indies ◊ *Indonesia.*

Eau de Cologne. Perfume first prepared about 1710 by Johann Farina at Cologne, by a process long kept secret; made by dissolving various essential oils (e.g. bergamot, citron, lavender, etc.) in alcohol, and distilling the mixture.

Ebony. The heartwood of many trees of the genus *Diospyros* (family *Ebenaceae*) growing in warm regions; the sapwood is white and soft, but the heartwood, very hard and blackened by deposits of gum resin, is valuable and decorative. The wood also yields a poisonous substance used in Malaya for narcotizing fish. The fruits of some species can be eaten, the persimmon, *D. virginiana*, native to N. America, being the best known. After the establishment of ocean trade routes to the East by the Portuguese in the 16th cent. India became Europe's chief supplier of ebony.

Echo. In Roman legend, a nymph who distracted the attention of ◊ *Juno* by continually talking while ◊ *Jupiter* seduced other nymphs; when Juno discovered the reason, she deprived Echo of her voice, leaving her only the capacity to repeat what was said to her. Echo fell in love with ◊ *Narcissus*, but he did not respond; her grief turned her into a stone which retained the power of repeating what was said to it.

Eclipse. In ◊ *astronomy*, the total or partial obscuring of one heavenly body by another.

LUNAR ECLIPSE: When the earth's shadow, cast by the sun, passes across the face of the moon; thus only at full moon. Three lunar eclipses at most can occur in a year. Unlike solar eclipses, they can be seen from anywhere on the dark side of the earth. Even during a total eclipse, some sunlight is refracted and scattered into the shadow-cone by the earth's atmosphere and makes the moon visible. A lunar eclipse lasts up to three hours and is total for half the time. Although lunar eclipses are astronomically of less interest than solar eclipses, they make possible studies of the rate of heat-loss from the moon and of the absorption of sunlight in the earth's atmosphere.

SOLAR ECLIPSE: When the moon passes between the earth and the sun and obscures the sun; thus only at new moon, but it does not occur at every new moon, because the moon's orbit is not in the same plane as that of the earth. The cone of the moon's shadow is so narrow when it reaches the earth that a total eclipse can be observed only along a narrow belt (the path of totality), the width of which can never be more than 167 m. Totality at any point cannot exceed $7\frac{2}{3}$ min. A partial eclipse will be seen for some 2000 m. on either side of this path. Nearly similar eclipses recur at intervals of 18 years and 10 or 11 days (◊ *Saros*). The path of totality changes, however, and on the average a total solar eclipse occurs at a given place only once in about 360 years; the next one in the U.K. will be in 1999. Apart

from its impressiveness as a spectacle, a total solar eclipse is of particular interest to astronomers because the cutting-off of direct light from the sun allows the corona and prominences to be studied.

a. eclipse of the sun

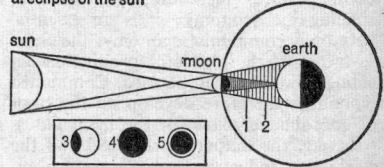

b. eclipse of the moon

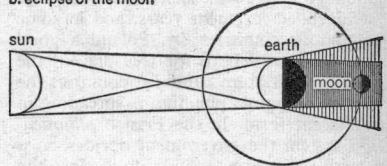

1. umbra 2. penumbra 3. partial eclipse
4. total eclipse 5. annular eclipse

Ecology. The study of plants and animals in relation to their natural environment, e.g. the effect of differences of soil and climate upon the growth, size, and colour of animal and plant life, and the interrelationship between plant and animal communities. It includes investigations into how much the needs of species living in the same region interact with each other by competition for food or in predator/prey relationships and into the effect of changes in the environment and of geographical location, climate, food supply, degree of shelter, and presence of predators. In botany it is the study of how the form, structure, reproduction, and distribution of plants are related to the conditions of the environment, and includes the study of the distribution of plants, both particular species and major vegetation types.

Econometrics ◊ *Economics.*

Economic Planning. Some kind of planning is needed in any economic activity however primitive, if only to hold back seed-corn for next year's sowing or to save in times of plenty for times of scarcity; in modern industry, most large firms necessarily plan ahead in considerable detail. Economic planning usually means planning by the government not in the ordinary run of government intervention in economic activity but in the working-out of some integrated plan of the economic future, including proposals for shaping the economy; it is an essential part of a communist economy, the State as owner of the means of production deciding how they shall be used. Communist economies therefore develop on the basis of coordinated plans for the main industries, e.g. the output of the steel and the steel-using industries are planned to increase in appropriate proportions. The amount of detail in such economic plans has declined in recent years, and in some communist countries e.g. Poland a good deal has been left to the free play of the market. In western capitalist countries the idea of economic planning is spreading in a different form. In the French *planificacation* system the government decides on a growth-rate target, and it is for the Commissariat du Plan to work out the implications in detail with industry and to make recommendations e.g. as to the amount to be allocated to education or to health. In the U.K. the government set up the National Economic Development Council (Neddy) in 1961; it has examined the implications of a growth rate of 4 per cent and has made some recommendations (on education and apprenticeship) for reaching it, but there is as yet no detailed industrial plan. W. Germany rejects planning, and government and industry have pinned their faith to a ◊ *free market* economy as the best economic regulator.

Economics. The study of how man's physical needs and wants are supplied, from a Greek word referring to household management; originally termed 'political economy', it was first discussed in early 17th-cent. France, but as a systematic subject of academic study it dates to Adam Smith's *Wealth of Nations* 1776. In the 19th cent. economics was more a philosophic defence of the ◊ *laissez-faire* system than an empirical science; economists tried to show that by relentlessly pursuing his own advantage, 'economic man' brought about the greatest happiness of the greatest number (◊ *Utilitarianism*). Subsequently attention shifted from these essentially ethical questions to analyses

of how whole economies behave. ◊ *Free Trade, Keynes, Marxism.*

ECONOMETRICS: Using the method of empirical science in processing the increasing volume of statistics, and attempting to establish significant relationships between economic series (e.g. how demand for cars increases as incomes rise and the price of cars alters in relation to other prices) on which predictions can be based. Some success in analysing and predicting short-term fluctuations in industrial economies has been achieved, but rather less in finding satisfactory theories to explain the longer-term processes of economic growth.

Ecuador. Area 226,000 sq. m. Pop. 4.5 m. (about one third Indian). Cap. Quito. A republic on the Pacific coast of S. America both N. and S. of the equator, at present governed by an army junta.

ECONOMY. Largely agricultural (exporting balsa wood, bananas, castor oil, cocoa, coffee, ivory, 'panama' hats, pyrethrum, rice), but rich in unexploited minerals e.g. gold, lead, petroleum, silver. Elementary education is free and compulsory, and voting rights are conditional upon literacy.

HISTORY. A Spanish colony from the early 16th cent. until the 1820–2 war of liberation, then part of ◊ *Colombia*, from which it seceded in 1830. The constitution of 1946, providing for government by a president elected for four years, a House of Representatives, and a Senate, has been suspended since the accession of President Arosemena in 1961.

LANGUAGE. Spanish, and some Indian dialects.

Ecumenical Movement. Movement directed towards attaining the greatest possible measure of unity between Christian Churches; prominent in the mid 20th cent. largely through the work of the ◊ *World Council of Churches*, the convening of the Second Vatican Council 1962 by Pope John XXIII to consider possible steps towards Catholic-Protestant-Orthodox understanding, and conversations between certain Protestant bodies, e.g. Anglican, Methodist, and Presbyterian, to examine ways of reconciling their standpoints. Successes already gained include the reunion of the Methodist Churches in Britain 1939, the union of the Scottish Free Church and the Church of Scotland 1929, and the federations of the Methodist-Congregational-

Presbyterian United Church of Canada 1925, and the Anglican-Methodist-Presbyterian Church of South India 1947.

Eczema. Inflammation of the skin, generally with itching or burning sensations, characterized by eruptions ranging from dry and scaly to weeping and pustular. Sufferers are usually constitutionally predisposed to the disease; attacks are often induced by unsuitable food or by contact with an irritating substance.

Edda. Two collections of Old Norse literature.

ELDER (POETIC) EDDA: Once erroneously attributed to the Icelandic historian Saemund, d. 1133, hence sometimes called Saemund's Edda; a collection of lays of gods and heroes, forming the earliest existing Norse literature (the oldest dating probably to the 9th cent.) and transmitted orally until written down about 1200.

YOUNGER (PROSE) EDDA: A collection of Norse myths, a handbook for the aspiring 'skald' (Icelandic bard), and an original example of the skald's celebratory art; by Snorri Sturluson, d. 1241.

Edelweiss. *Leontopodium alpinum*; a common European alpine plant with curious flannel-like flower-heads and white woolly leaves, usually growing in stony pastures or on grassy slopes. Other species similar in general appearance occur in Asia and S. America. ◊ *Compositae.*

Edict of Nantes. 1598. In 1572 the leader of the French ◊ *Huguenots* and of Protestant Europe, Henry of Navarre, had escaped murder in the massacre of ◊ *St Bartholomew* by declaring himself a convert to Roman Catholicism; after three years' imprisonment he had escaped, revoked his 'conversion', and again led the Huguenots in the Wars of Religion. In 1589 he had become legally King of France, but had remained unable to gain the throne until in 1593 he again declared himself a Roman Catholic ('Paris is well worth a Mass'). In 1598, as soon as he had achieved peace with Spain, he decreed full civil rights for the Huguenots, as well as liberty of conscience, and State subsidies to Huguenot cities and schools: in 1610 he was assassinated by a Jesuit agent.

His Edict, however, remained ostensibly in force (though constantly flouted) for 32 years, until Cardinal Richelieu ended the self-government of the 200 Huguenot cities, from 1629 onwards. Finally, after 55 years of increasingly violent anti-Huguenot persecutions, Louis XIV rescinded the Edict of Nantes altogether, in 1685.

Edinburgh Review. 1. The first of the great nineteenth-century critical quarterlies, started Oct. 1802 by Francis Jeffrey, Henry Brougham, and Sidney Smith as an independent periodical. Although Tories like Walter Scott contributed at first, it became strongly Whig, using the party colours on its cover until its demise 1929. Its attacks on the ◊ *Lake Poets* are well-known: Brougham's article on Byron provoked *English Bards and Scotch Reviewers*; Jeffrey's on Thomas Moore resulted in a duel. Contributors included Macaulay, Carlyle, Hazlitt, Lord John Russell, Matthew Arnold, J. S. Mill, Gladstone.

2. An earlier *Edinburgh Review*, run by Adam Smith, Alexander Wedderburn, and other *literati*, appeared July 1755 and Jan. 1756, but did not survive.

Education. Essentially a process by which the material, mental, moral, and cultural inheritance of society is transmitted to each new generation, it tends to be traditional and conservative, but also has a creative function and can selectively transmit what is good and worth-while. Among primitive peoples, practical skills are taught largely by imitation, but the elders often instruct the young in the laws and traditions of the tribe, such instruction being almost invariably hedged about with religious beliefs and ritual. 'Schools' in the modern sense evolved with the growth of urban civilization. From the 13th cent. onwards the need for an educated merchant class was met by schools maintained by municipalities e.g. Strasbourg, Geneva, in which such secular subjects as arithmetic were taught as well as religious doctrines. By the 17th cent. the Czech patriot Comenius was talking of a national system of schools in which 'all things' (i.e. not only those of religious importance) 'would be taught to all people', and after 1750 this idea was being discussed in detail in France, Poland, Prussia, Russia, and the American colonies, and universal free compulsory education was proposed. It became usual to think of three stages: elementary, secondary, and higher. The ◊ *Industrial Revolution* made such schools practicable by creating the necessary financial and human resources, and by the late 19th cent.

elementary education up to 13 was compulsory and free in most advanced nations. The facilities for secondary education were gradually enlarged, private fee-paying schools were replaced or supplemented by State-controlled or State-aided secondary education, the flow to universities was increased, and the universities themselves expanded. During the last 50 years education has ceased to be the privilege of the rich and become more and more accessible to all. Nearly two thirds of the world now insists upon at least four years of primary education, and in industrialized countries most children receive secondary education up to 15 or 16; grants are available to help poor students who are capable of advanced studies at universities or elsewhere, and a growing proportion of national resources (4 or 5 per cent) goes to finance the educational system. Local and national authorities usually share the responsibility for finance and administration; in some countries e.g. France, U.S.S.R. education is centralized, the national authorities providing most of the money needed and specifying what is to be taught, while in others e.g. U.S.A. it is decentralized, the central authority paying as little as one third and leaving the rest to be raised by the local authorities. Normally public authorities are secular or at least undenominational; schools are much less religious in atmosphere today than in the past.

The growing importance of education in modern societies has strengthened interest in educational theory; philosophers discuss and clarify aims and purposes, sociologists and economists consider policy in relation to social and economic structure, psychologists suggest improvements in the teaching process, students of comparative education compare and evaluate the systems of different countries. In all new and underdeveloped countries, interest in education is intense; those in charge see in it the best instrument available for social and economic improvement, and great efforts are made to build, equip, and staff schools and colleges. Between 1950 and 1960 China doubled her school population; similar achievements are recorded in other parts of Asia and in Latin America. ⟡ *Education Acts and Reports, Education and Science, Ministry of.*

Education Acts and Reports. The shape of education in the United Kingdom has been studied and influenced by a long series of reports by special committees many of which have been translated into terms of Education Acts starting with that of 1870 which was the basis of free and universal elementary education. In recent years one of the important developments has been the Butler Act 1944 which replaced the Board of Education by the Ministry of Education to coordinate the whole system, envisaged in three stages: Primary 5 to 11; Secondary 11 to 15; Further Education. At 11 children move to a Grammar, Secondary Modern, or Technical school according to intelligence and tests (⟡ *Intelligence Quotient*), Local Education Authorities being free to devise their own schemes for providing the three types of education, e.g. ⟡ *Comprehensive Schools*, Bilateral Schools; a majority have favoured separate Grammar and Secondary Modern schools, but the Comprehensive school seems to be increasing in popularity. The system of testing pupils at the age of 11 has come under increasing criticism and is likely to be generally abandoned. Increased attention has recently been given to Higher Education. The Crowther Report 1959 dealt with education between 15 and 18, and the Robbins Report 1963 dealt with the finance, structure, and expansion of higher education in universities, teacher-training colleges, and Colleges of Advanced Technology; and recommended thorough study of all aspects of higher education, the rapid increase in the number of university places, and the creation of numerous universities and other centres of higher education and technology.

Educational Subnormality. Apart from those so defective as to be unable to guard themselves against common physical dangers, educationally backward children fall into three categories: (a) Educationally subnormal (E.S.N.), with I.Q. (⟡ *Intelligence Quotient*) between 80 and 60; (b) Ineducable, with I.Q. below 60; (c) Morons, with I.Q. still lower. Borderline children may be required to undergo a statutory I.Q. examination. Parents may appeal against the resulting classification, but the final decision rests with the educational authority; factors other than strict I.Q. rating may sometimes affect this decision and many below-80 children continue in ordinary schools, with remedial teaching, although the majority are sent to Special Schools, where they are taught in small groups to a modified curriculum. Many benefit, and later return to ordinary schools. Ineducable children are sent to an Educational Training Centre, where efforts are made to teach them a trade. No attempt is made to educate the moron group, many of whom suffer from physical disabilities also.

Special Schools are also provided, without cost to parents, for other handicapped children e.g. the blind, partially blind, deaf, delicate, epileptic, and speech-defective; there are altogether 700 such institutions, catering for 57,000 children. The evidence is that the number of physically-handicapped children is decreasing and the need for E.S.N. schools growing; this may be due to improved child health and better methods of intelligence testing rather than to any actual decrease in the level of intelligence.

Education and Science, Ministry of. In 1944 the Board of Education was replaced by a Ministry, which controls all education in England and Wales (except at universities) but does not directly run any schools. It is the Minister's duty 'to secure the effective execution by the Local Education Authorities, under his control and direction, of the national policy for providing a varied and comprehensive education service in every area'; the Ministry decides the national educational policy, controls educational-buildings programmes, is responsible for the training of teachers, settles disputes, and distributes grants, the Minister being assisted by two Central Advisory Councils. In Scotland, education is under the control of the Secretary of State for Scotland and the Scottish Education Department.

Eel. Snake-like edible fish of the family *Anguillidae*; hatched in the Sargasso Sea as tiny transparent larvae, they migrate to their ancestral coasts, taking some 2½ years, during which time they turn into elver, small eels about six in. long. They stay in fresh water from 5 to 15 years (the period varies with their sex and whether they are European or American), and when sexually mature they migrate to their distant breeding grounds, reproduce, and die. The mystery of their migration, in which vast numbers perish, has not been solved.

Egg. The sex cell or gamete produced by a female; usually a large ◊ *cell* containing food resources (yolk) in addition to the normal constituents. In all higher animals eggs are produced by specialized organs (ovaries), of which mammals have two; in woman, one egg is normally shed from an ovary each month during reproductive life. On ◊ *fertilization* the egg begins to develop into an adult of its species; this involves cell-division. The egg is a single cell: the adult may contain millions or billions of cells, each of which is a lineal descendant of the egg cell and derived from it by successive cell-divisions. Specialization of these cells occurs, so that the various parts of the organism develop.

When the egg is laid, either before or shortly after fertilization, it is encased in a protective covering (jelly, egg-albumen, shell), from which the young later escapes at hatching. All mammals keep the eggs and embryos within the mother's body throughout their early life, with the exception of the ◊ *duck-billed platypus* and the Spiny ◊ *Anteater*.

Ego. Lat. 'I'; a distinction has been drawn between the 'empirical ego' (thoughts, feelings, etc. observable by introspection) and the 'pure ego' (unobservable, but postulated as the thinker rather than the thought). In Freudian psychology the ego is one of the three components of the total personality, id, ego, and super-ego. The id, composed of everything present in the mind at birth, including the primitive instincts, is the source of all psychic energy. The ego is the conscious mind, which plans to achieve the ends of the id. The super-ego (the last system to develop in human growth) is the primitive ◊ *conscience*, formed by the precepts and more esp. the behaviour of the parents, and controls action so as to ensure conformity with what they have approved and rewarded.

Egoism. In philosophy, primarily the view that my actions are right if they procure my own good or happiness; also the view that although sometimes disguised as altruistic, actions are always motivated by self-interest.

Egypt. Area 386,110 sq. m. Pop. 26.1 m. There are three ethnic elements: Fellahin (Hamito-Semitic), Bedouin (Arab), and Nubian (Arab-Negro). Cap. Cairo. Rel. predominantly Muslim (with Eastern

Orthodox and Coptic Christian minorities). A republic in NE Africa, between Libya and Sudan, bordering also on Jordan and Israel; the senior partner in the ◊ *United Arab Republic*.

ECONOMY. Largely agricultural, and conditioned by the flooding of the ◊ *Nile* and irrigation. Main crops in summer (July–Oct.) cotton, maize, rice, sugarcane, and in winter (Nov.–June) cereals, clover, onions, pulses. There are limited mineral resources: coal, gold, manganese, petroleum, phosphates, salt. Industry is developing, e.g. cement, chemicals, fertilizers, iron and steel. The Aswan High Dam will provide vast hydroelectric power and increase the arable land area by 30 per cent.

HISTORY. **1.** ◊ *Egypt (Ancient)*.
2. ◊ *Arabs, Caliphate, Ottoman Empire*.
3. In 1875 Ismail Pasha sold his shares in the ◊ *Suez Canal* to Britain; in 1879 Tewfik Pasha agreed to Anglo-French control of Egypt's finances. Rebellion in 1881–2 resulted in British bombardment of Alexandria, and France withdrew from administrative participation. British control was consolidated 1883–1907, and the Anglo-Egyptian ◊ *Sudan* was established. During the First World War Egypt was declared a British protectorate; in 1923 independence was granted and Egypt became a kingdom, but Britain continued to maintain troops in Egypt esp. in the Canal Zone, and in the Second World War undertook all defence (◊ *Alamein*). After the war Egypt's insistence on claiming Sudan caused the breakdown of all negotiations for a fresh treaty. Egypt bitterly opposed the creation of ◊ *Israel*, which it unsuccessfully invaded in 1948 (with other members of the ◊ *Arab League*). In 1952 a military coup under Colonel Neguib caused the abdication of King Farouk and abolition of the monarchy. During a period of martial law Colonel Nasser took power in 1954, and was elected President. In 1956 both Britain and Egypt recognized the independence of Sudan, and under a 1954 agreement British troops left the Canal Zone. When Britain and U.S.A. cancelled their financial aid to the Aswan High Dam project, Nasser announced the nationalization of the Suez Canal. Israel invaded Gaza and Sinai; Britain and France called on Egypt and Israel to withdraw from the Canal Zone, and upon Egypt's refusal to comply attacked her, but yielded to adverse world public opinion and ended hostilities. In 1958 Egypt and ◊ *Syria* formed the United Arab Republic, at once joined by ◊ *Yemen* also. Syria withdrew from U.A.R. in 1961 but returned in 1963, when ◊ *Iraq* also joined.

Egypt (Ancient). The territory in NE Africa comprising the Nile and the adjoining desert regions, centre of one of the great early civilizations based on cereal production; abundant wealth lay in the rich harvests from the fertile river silt, and the need for large-scale cooperative effort in drainage and irrigation stimulated the growth of urban communities and central organization. The pre-dynastic Egyptians from about 5000 B.C. introduced the use of copper, the beginnings of writing (leading to ◊ *hieroglyphs*), and sea-going ships. With the union of Upper and Lower Egypt (traditionally by Menes about 3200 B.C.) began the Dynastic period. The 1st and 2nd dynasties (Archaic period) saw the establishment of central government and led to the first great phase of Egyptian brilliance in the Old Kingdom (3rd–6th Dynasties, about 2780–2180 B.C.), to which belong magnificent sculptures and works of art in gold, copper, precious stones, ivory, alabaster, and wood, and the great monumental architecture of the ◊ *pyramids*. The main cities were ◊ *Memphis* and ◊ *Heliopolis*, the centre of the cult of the Sun God. Egyptian religion was dominated by the sun god Ra (with whom the Pharaoh identified himself) and ◊ *Osiris* the god of death, and there was also a large pantheon of other minor deities e.g. ◊ *Horus, Isis, Thoth*. After a period of decline and anarchy, a reunited Egypt entered a second period of greatness in the Middle Kingdom (11th–12th Dynasties about 2080–1785 B.C.); the chief cities were Thebes, Abydos, and Herakleopolis. A further disturbed phase followed, including a period of rule by Asian Semite kings, the Hyksos, who gained control either by conquest or infiltration. The next period, the New Kingdom, or Empire (18th–20th Dynasties, about 1570–1075 B.C.), was the great phase of Egyptian imperial expansion overseas. At its greatest the Empire extended to Nubia, Ethiopia, and Libya in Africa, to Palestine, Syria, and the Euphrates in Asia, and throughout the E. Mediterranean. The foreign possessions fluctuated greatly, in competition esp. with the Assyrians and ◊ *Hittites*, and according to the ability of individual pharaohs. The 20th Dynasty ended in cultural decline, political anarchy, and the loss of the territories in Asia. For the remainder of the Dynastic period, ruled by various petty kings, Egypt was invaded and conquered in turn by the Cushites from Ethiopia, the Assyrians, and the Persians. In 332 B.C. after Alexander's conquest of the Persian Empire, it fell to the share of his general, Ptolemy, and continued under the Ptolemaic rulers until 30 B.C. when it became a Roman province after the death of Cleopatra (◊ *Actium*). During the Ptolemaic period the new city of Alexandria again brought a degree of prosperity and fame to Egypt, the Pharos lighthouse being one of the Seven Wonders of the ancient world. In late Roman times Egypt developed into a major centre of ◊ *Christianity*, through the influence of the Coptic church, but it fell to the Arabs at the battle of Heliopolis A.D. 640, and much of the population adopted the faith of ◊ *Islam*.

Egyptian Architecture. The great scarcity of timber in the Nile Valley necessitated early resort to sun-baked and kiln-baked bricks, and to stone, for building materials. Domestic buildings were probably simple brick-built structures, and have not survived: ancient Egyptian architecture is known from pyramids, obelisks, tombs, and temples, all of massive proportions. The style remained remarkably unchanged through about 5000 years, from the Gizeh pyramids 3733–3566 B.C. to the temples at Karnak 2466 B.C. onwards, at Abu Simbel about 1330 B.C. and at Edfu about 230 B.C. Temples are all columnar and built on the post-and-lintel (trabeated) principle; they are characterized by sloping exterior walls, pillared halls lit mysteriously from high clerestories, and squat columns curved at the base like lotus stalks and crowned with capitals resembling lotus buds or palm leaves. Some columns resemble bundles of reeds, a reminiscence of earlier building methods. Walls are ornamented with incised reliefs and ◊ *hieroglyphs*. ◊◊ *Muslim Architecture*.

Egyptian Art. Egyptians began to produce fine pottery and stone vessels in the 4th millennium B.C. and sculpture by the time of the first Pharaoh, Menes, about 3200 B.C. During the succeeding 2500 years

their severely formalized style was gradually developed; Egyptian art was never merely decorative, being always linked with the religious cult, and statues were intended to ensure immortality for the persons represented, or to provide the gods with an earthly habitation. Tomb paintings and reliefs depicting people enjoying earthly pleasures were intended to secure their continuance for them after death. Some works e.g. the famous head of Queen Nefertiti (Berlin Museum) are astonishingly realistic, but in most naturalism is sacrificed to the symbolic aims of the religious cult; people and objects were represented not as they appeared to be but as they were known to be. Rigid conventions controlled the design of statues, which are always static and confined within the space of their bases. In the long history of Egyptian art three periods are outstanding. The Old Kingdom, the age of the pyramids, about 2780–2280 B.C. produced some of the finest statues; greater naturalism marks the Middle Kingdom period about 2130–1780, and a greater elegance the New Kingdom period about 1570–671. Paintings and jewellery of the latter period reveal a love for bright colours, also used in sculpture and on coffins. After the establishment of Christianity in the 4th cent. A.D., a new artistic style based on a fusion of ancient Egyptian with classical elements was developed by the ◊ *Copts*, the most notable products being portraits and decorative textiles.

Einsteinian Theory ◊ *Relativity*.

Einsteinium ◊ *Actinides*.

Eire ◊ *Ireland*.

Eisteddfod. Welsh, 'session'; a musical and poetic festival periodically held by ancient Welsh ◊ *bards*, or a derivative modern festival. Eisteddfodda are said to have been held as far back as the 7th cent. After a lapse, the great 'Eisteddfod of Carmarthen' took place in 1450. A further revival took place in the late 18th cent. with the aim of encouraging Welsh national tradition in verse, singing, harpplaying, etc. A Welsh National Eisteddfod is now held each August in one or other of the Welsh towns. The word is sometimes more broadly used, without the full Welsh connotations, notably at the International Musical Eisteddfod, held annually at Llangollen since 1947.

Elas ◊ *Greece (History)*.

El Cid. < Ar. *el Seyd*, lord; Rodrigo Díaz de Vivar, about 1040–90, a Spanish soldier of fortune who appears to have fought indiscriminately for both the Christians and the Moors but was elevated by subsequent legends into a hero of chivalric valour and courtesy and Christian virtue. He is the subject of the most famous of the Spanish ◊ *Chansons de Geste*, the *Poema de Mio Cid* (about 1140), of many Spanish ballads, and of plays by Lope de Vega, Guillén Castro, and Corneille.

El Dorado. A legendary country in S. America abounding in gold and precious stones, the search for which led to many fruitless expeditions, notably those of Diego de Ordaz 1531 and Sir Walter Ralegh 1595.

Electra ◊ *Orestes*.

Electra Complex ◊ *Oedipus Complex*.

Electrical Resistance. Opposition offered by a substance to the flow of ◊ *electricity*. It is measured in ohms. Low-resistance materials are used to conduct electricity, high-resistance materials (insulators) to prevent its flow, and semiconductors to regulate its flow. The flow of current always generates heat, the amount being proportional to the resistance multiplied by the square of the current. The resistance of a conductor varies with its temperature, usually increasing with rise in temperature (◊ *Conduction*). This characteristic is utilized in the resistance thermometer, in which the resistance of a spiral of platinum wire is measured and the temperature deduced from it. ◊ *Ohm's Law*.

Electric Arc. Discharge produced by continuously 'sparking' a current across two electrodes. It is used mainly for lighting, ultra-violet radiation, and welding. The arc lamp, a source of intense white light used for cinema projectors, flood lighting, searchlights, etc. requires constant maintenance of its carbon electrodes and has been superseded in many applications by ◊ *tungsten* and vapour lamps.

Electric Current. The flow of electrical charge from points of higher potential to points of lower potential in a circuit. Direct current (d.c.) flows continuously in the same direction, as in a circuit supplied from a battery. Alternating current (a.c.) flows temporarily in one direction, reduces to zero, and then builds up in the other direction, the frequency being the number of complete cycles of current variation per second, e.g. 50 cycles per second is the frequency of mains supplies in the U.K. ◊ *Converters, Electricity*.

Electric Eel. *Electrophorus*; S. American fish, related not to the true ◊ *eel* but to the ◊ *carp*. The tail forms four fifths of the length, which may be up to 8 ft, and the muscles near the tail are modified into a special organ capable of generating an electric current of several hundred volts, which the animal may use for defensive purposes or perhaps for stunning its prey.

Electricity. The phenomena associated with the forces between electrical charges. There are basically two kinds of force involved – those between two charges at rest (electrostatic forces) and those between two charges in motion (electromagnetic forces). Electric charges are arbitrarily labelled positive or negative, but differ only in that like charges repel and unlike charges attract each other. The basic law of electrostatics states that the magnitude of the force between two charges is proportional to the product of the magnitude of the charges and inversely proportional to the square of the distance between them. The basic repositories of electric charge in matter are the ◊ *proton* and ◊ *electron*; these carry numerically equal positive and negative charges respectively, and (together with uncharged ◊ *neutrons*) constitute all ◊ *atoms*. In electrically neutral matter there are equal numbers of protons and electrons, and an excess of either causes an object to become electrostatically charged, as when two dissimilar materials e.g. amber and silk are rubbed together so that electrons are transferred from one to the other. Substances can be very broadly classified into conductors of electricity and insulators (◊ *Conduction*); the former contain charged particles capable of diffusing through the substance, but in the latter the charged particles are more or less immobile. The movement of charges through a conductor constitutes an ◊ *electric current*. In a solid only the movement of electrons contributes to the current, but in a gas or liquid it may result from the movement of both positively and negatively charged molecular fragments known as ions. The phenomenon known as ◊ *electrical resistance* causes charged particles moving through a conductor to be subjected to forces akin to friction in mechanics, and it is the energy expended in overcoming these forces which gives an electric current its heating effect, as in an electric fire. Electricity and magnetism interact; a current-carrying conductor in a magnetic field is subjected to a mechanical force, and a potential difference is produced across the ends of a conductor if it moves in relation to a magnetic field. ◊ *Induction (1)*.

PHOTOELECTRICITY: The liberation of electrons from the surface of some metals by illumination. If the illuminated substance is included in a suitable circuit, the photoelectrons so released will constitute an electric current that can be used as a means of measurement, detection, or control. This is the basis of the photoelectric cell and allied electronic devices, including phototransistors. Applications are the measuring elements in exposure meters, the detecting elements in fire and burglar alarms, and the controlling elements on automatic doors. Photoelectric devices are now also widely used in the control of industrial processes and have become key instruments of ◊ *automation*.

PIEZOELECTRICITY: Some crystals e.g. those of ◊ *quartz* generate electricity when mechanical forces are applied to them; conversely, electric forces applied to them produce mechanical strains and vibrations. These effects are used in a wide range of crystal piezoelectric devices e.g. crystal microphones, crystal pick-ups for record players, and crystal-controlled oscillators for frequency standards.

Electric Motor. Machine for producing mechanical power from electricity – the reverse of a generator. Its operation is based on the fact that mechanical force is exerted on a current-carrying conductor if it is in a magnetic field (◊ *Conduction*). In its simplest form the electric motor consists of a coil (the armature) so placed between the poles of a strong electromagnet that it rotates rapidly whenever the passing of current subjects it to a mechanical force by virtue of the magnet. A central shaft allows the rotating armature to be harnessed to drive machinery. Electric motors are classed as a.c. or d.c. according to which form of ◊ *electric current* is used to drive them, and rated according to the horsepower they develop. In general d.c. motors can be more readily controlled and adapted to special

purposes but are usually more complex in structure; a.c. motors are widely used in industry because of their relative simplicity and strength. Small 'universal' motors (operating on either d.c. or a.c.) are often used to drive portable and small domestic appliances not requiring much power.

Electric Power ◊ *Electricity, Generator.*

Electric Spark. Discharge of ◊ *electricity* through a poor conductor when the potential difference becomes sufficiently high. The sparking plug used in internal combustion engines is a device in which such a spark jumps a very small gap and in doing so generates enough heat to ignite a mixture of air and petrol. Lightning is a very powerful spark between clouds of different potential, or between a charged cloud and earth, in which heating and sudden expansion of the intervening air produce both light waves and slower-travelling sound waves: hence a flash followed by thunder.

Electrode. The conductor through which an electric current enters (anode) and leaves (cathode) in the process of ◊ *electrolysis*, in the vacuum tube and ◊ *thermionic valve*. ◊ *Carbon.*

Electroencephalography. The study of the electrical activity (first described 1929) which can be recorded from the brain through electrodes placed on the scalp; used as a diagnostic aid in neurology and ◊ *psychiatry*, esp. in the study of ◊ *epilepsy.*

Electrolysis. The decomposition of certain ionized (◊ *Ionization*) chemical compounds by passing an ◊ *electric current* through them. Such compounds are usually first dissolved to form a current-carrying solution (the electrolyte) but some may be electrolyzed in a molten state. Passing of a current between two electrodes immersed in the electrolyte then has the effect of dissociating the compound into positive and negative ions which are attracted to the negative electrode (cathode) and positive electrode (anode) respectively. There the ions lose their electric charge and may be deposited on the electrode (electro-deposition), may be released, or may undergo chemical reaction with other substances in the electrode or electrolyte. Electrolysis has many applications in industry.

In medicine, electrolysis refers to the breaking down of fluid or tissue by passing an electric current through it; the process is used surgically, with a very strong current, to remove tumours from the bladder and other closed cavities of the body.

ELECTROPLATING: The depositing by electrolysis of a thin coating of one metal on another metal surface.

ELECTROREFINING: An electrolytic method of refining or extracting metals by depositing at one electrode pure metal drawn from an impure source, either dissolved in the electrolyte (as when aluminium is obtained from alumina) or used to form the other electrode (as in the refining of copper and the noble metals).

ELECTROTYPING: An electrolytic process for making duplicate printing-plates by depositing a film of metal on a wax impression of the original type or block; after plating, the wax is replaced by a substantial metal backing which allows the duplicate to be used in a printing machine.

Electromagnet. When ⟡ *electric current* flows through a wire, a magnetic field is set up around it. By winding the wire round a core of magnetic material e.g. iron, the effect is greatly increased and the core becomes an electromagnet. Electromagnets are used in machines to provide internal magnetic fields, in relays where switches are operated by the pull of the electromagnet on other magnetic material, and in cranes for lifting ferrous materials e.g. iron scrap.

ELECTROMAGNETIC INDUCTION: The production of a potential difference (e.m.f.) across the ends of a conductor if it either moves in a magnetic field or is stationary in a field of changing intensity. This interaction between magnetic field and electric circuit is the basic principle behind the induction coil and its application in transformers and generators. An associated effect, on which ⟡ *electric motors* are based, is that a force is exerted on a current-carrying conductor in a magnetic field.

The simple induction coil consists of a soft-iron core carrying two separate windings (an inner primary coil and an outer secondary coil). When a current is passed through the primary coil it creates a magnetic field through the core, and fluctuations in this field induce currents in the outer coil, the voltages in the two windings being proportional to the number of turns in each. When high voltages are required, the secondary coil has many more turns than the primary.

Electron. Elementary particle, and one of the basic constituents of matter, which contains the smallest known electric charge. The charge may be positive or negative, but the term electron is normally used for the negative particle (sometimes called negatron); positively charged it is known as the positron. Ordinary electric current is caused by the flow of electrons through a conductor, usually wire. Electrons determine the chemical properties of matter. ⟡ *Valency.*

Electronegativity ⟡ *Metals and Non-metals.*

Electron Gun. An essential part of many thermionic-emission devices, in which electrons emitted from a cathode are, by means of associated ⟡ *electrodes* to which voltages can be applied, concentrated into a beam and accelerated towards a particular target. If required, the beams can be shaped and deflected in much the same way as a beam of light.

Electronics. The study of, and techniques of manufacturing, devices and systems based on the phenomena of the ⟡ *conduction* of electricity in a vacuum, gas, or semiconductors (⟡ *Metals and Non-metals*). Of great importance has been the replacement of the bulky ⟡ *thermionic valve* by the ⟡ *transistor*, which has stimulated the search for similar bulk-saving substitutes for other components e.g. resistors, coils, and capacitors, which make possible very compact electronic devices. Two important techniques in this field are: (1) The thin-film technique, in which small parts are made by depositing (photographically or by evaporation) very thin layers of suitable metal or alloy, in accurately controlled shapes, on a thin wafer of glass or other insulator. Electrical connexions are similarly formed. (2) Molecular-circuit blocks, very thin slices of pure crystalline semiconductor (the basis of a transistor), a complete circuit being built into the structure of the crystal by delicate chemical, electrical, or mechanical processing. Microelectronics offers the prospect of increasingly small and densely-packed electronic devices – even a pocket-sized ⟡ *computer*; it is playing a key part in space research and missile development, by making possible the installation in artificial satellites and rockets of miniature but highly sensitive controlling and recording equipment.

Electron Microscope ◊ *Microscope*.

Electroplating. A process of ◊ *electrolysis* for covering a metal object with a thin layer of another metal to preserve it. The object to be coated is made the cathode of the electrolytic cell; the anode is formed from the pure metal to be deposited, and the electrolyte contains salts of this metal; thus in silver-plating by electrolysis the anodes are of pure silver and the electrolyte is a solution containing the double cyanide of silver and potassium. During electrolysis a thin coating of metal is transferred from the anode to the object to be coated. Metals applied by electroplating include zinc, tin, copper, cadmium, nickel, chromium, silver, and gold; examples of electro-plated products are the silver plate which has superseded ◊ *Sheffield plate*, and ◊ *tinplate* food containers. Chromium plating is widely used in industry, but because chromium on iron is often porous and does not prevent ◊ *corrosion*, the object is usually first coated with nickel or copper. Silver is usually plated on to German silver (◊ *alloys*); hence E P N S (electroplated nickel silver).

Electropositivity ◊ *Metals and Non-metals*.

Elegy. In Greek and Latin literature, the metre of a poem (alternating dactylic hexameters and pentameters), not its subject. Later, because of the popularity of meditative or melancholy poems written in this metre (e.g. Ovid's *Heroides* and *Tristia*), the term came to denote a reflective, melancholy, or commemorative poem. A tradition of pastoral elegy (a poem of lament over a dead person, supposed to be a shepherd, with imagery drawn from pastoral activities) derived from Greek models developed in Europe in the Renaissance, and was long popular, e.g. Milton's *Lycidas*, Shelley's *Adonais*, and Arnold's *Thyrsis*. Gray's *Elegy in a Country Churchyard* is an elegy in the more general sense of a meditative poem; Tennyson's *In Memoriam* is both a lament and a meditation.

Elektron ◊ *Alloys*.

Elements. From very early times men have speculated about the simple primal materials from which all substances are derived. Aristotle taught that the fundamental ele-

ments were earth, air, fire, and water (◊ *Aristotelianism*). Not one of these is an element in the modern sense, yet the four were accepted until the late 18th cent. The alchemists added mercury, sulphur, and salt. Boyle, in his *Sceptical Chymist*, 1661, tried to clarify the position, but it was left to Lavoisier in 1789 to give a list of what were then thought to be elements (about 33 of them), substances which as far as was then known could not be split into any simpler substances. In this atomic age, a reasonably good definition of an element is 'a substance which consists of atoms of one type and cannot be further decomposed by chemical means'. By the end of the 19th cent. there were believed to be about 90 elements, but recently, with the transuranium elements (◊ *Actinides*), the number has been extended to 103. From these an infinite variety of mixtures and compounds can be made.

PERIODIC TABLE OF ELEMENTS: If the elements are arranged in a table according to their ◊ *atomic number*, their chemical properties are found to repeat periodically. This periodicity was first noticed by Mendeleev, who arranged the elements according to their ◊ *atomic weights*; however, it is rather their atomic numbers which give the table its periodic pattern, because these are equal to the number of electrons circulating around the cores of the neutral atoms and it is the outermost of these which are primarily responsible for determining the chemical properties of a particular element: elements having atoms with outer shells of similar structure have similar chemical properties. Thus the ◊ *inert gases* all have outer closed shell of eight electrons. The elements immediately before or after the inert gases have one electron too few or too many to form such closed shells, and are chemically very active. Those immediately preceding the inert gases are known as the ◊ *halogens*, and those immediately after as the alkali metals (lithium, sodium, potassium, etc.). All the elements can be grouped in this way, and

A single arrow before a word or phrase indicates a cross-reference to another main entry. A double arrow means *See also*.

each 'family' has its characteristic properties. ⟡ *Metals and Non-metals*.

Elephant. Largest land mammal; order *Proboscidea*. Of the two existing species, the African is larger than the Indian; the latter has long been domesticated. In Africa the wild elephant is protected, its existence being threatened by ivory hunters; it reaches 11 ft at the shoulder, and the tusks weigh up to 200 lb. The elephant is herbivorous, and conveys food and water to its mouth by its trunk; adults browse the greater part of the day. They have a life of up to 60 years. Most circus elephants are Indian, but the most famous, Jumbo, was African and weighed six tons.

Elephantiasis. Swelling esp. of the limbs or genitalia caused by obstruction of the flow of lymph, which results in a fibrous overgrowth of skin and subcutaneous tissue. The disease is commonly caused by a small tropical wormlike parasite, *Filaria bancrofti*. ⟡ *Lymphatic System*.

Elgin Marbles. Reliefs and statues from the Parthenon, carved 447–438 B.C. and removed from the fabric and surroundings of the ruined building in 1803, in order to preserve them, by the British Ambassador Lord Elgin, who had them sent to London. After much discussion, they were acquired by Parliament in 1816 and deposited in the British Museum, where they remain. They are the most important examples of Greek sculpture outside Greece.

Elizabethan Style ⟡ *Tudors*.

Elm. *Ulmus*; widely distributed trees and shrubs. English elms are difficult to classify, as hybrids exist and are usually fertile. In general they form large trees, usually with suckers, and have heart-shaped toothed leaves, the leaf base often asymmetrical. The inconspicuous flowers are in clusters, and the fruit is a small nut surrounded by a circular papery wing. Elms are usually found in hedgerows and copses, and give a characteristic aspect to the countryside. In the ⟡ *Neolithic* period the inner parts of elm bark were eaten by both man and animals in time of famine. The wood is tough and is used in furniture-making, esp. for the seats of chairs.

Elysium (Elysian Fields). In Greek legend, a land where after death chosen heroes exist in conditions of blessedness, under the presidency of Rhadamanthus (⟡ *Europa*), passing their time in athletic contests and with music; traditionally in the far west, though Virgil places it in the

underworld and some in Africa or even on the moon. Celtic legends also tell of a western paradise (Hy Breasail, the Isles of the Blest) and Chinese Taoist and Buddhist mythology of western lands of perfection.

Embolism. Obstruction of a blood vessel, usually by a clot but occasionally by bubbles of air or by foreign substances introduced into the circulation; fat embolism may occur when particles of fat are released by broken bones. The consequences depend on the size of the affected artery and the importance of the area it supplies.

Embroidery. The decoration of textiles with needlework; not to be confused with woven ⟡ *tapestry*. One of the most ancient of the applied arts, it probably antedates weaving, although (apart from fragments in ancient Egyptian tombs) the earliest surviving examples are 4th-cent. B.C. Greek works, and in the Middle and Far East until the 13th cent. the textiles were usually decorated only with woven patterns, though splendid embroideries were produced in China. Those imported from the Orient, esp. China and India, influenced the style and technique of European needlework after the 17th cent. In Europe, fine embroideries were produced in 12th-cent. Sicily, where the Viennese Imperial mantle was worked, but the finest medieval embroideries are the vestments produced in England (Opus Anglicanum) and widely diffused throughout Europe, 16th-cent. English factories producing an abundance of rich secular embroidery for male and female costume and for domestic furnishings. In France, Louis XIV 1638–1715 established royal factories to keep up the supply for his court. With the advent of machinery, and a new simplicity in costume, embroidery declined; but it continued throughout the 19th cent. as an occupation for gentlewomen esp. in the production of samplers, and in its finer forms is still used for decorating women's clothes.

Embryo. In zoology, an animal in process of developing from the fertilized ovum to birth (⟡ *Reproduction*); it develops features similar to those seen in that of more primitive animals, e.g. vestigial ⟡ *gills*, but does not repeat the full process of evolution. It is contained in an external shell, e.g. fishes and birds, or within the mother, e.g. viviparous animals; in man the ⟡ *gestation* process takes about 280 days. During the first month the fertilized cell divides rapidly and repeatedly, building a solid mass of cells (morula) which enters the cavity of the uterus. Three weeks after fertilization it becomes embedded in the wall of the uterus, and the process of differentiation into three primary layers (entoderm, ectoderm, and mesoderm) takes place. From the fourth to the eighth week the main outline of the body develops from these layers, and the main system and organs appear. Three factors are at work in this process of development: growth in the form of cell-multiplication and increase in cell-size; differentiation, i.e. the creation of cells and tissues from previously undifferentiated cell masses; and organization i.e. the co-ordination of these newly-formed tissues into a functional whole. This development may be adversely affected by a number of factors (some of which are obscure), including maternal infection esp. German measles in the second and third months, syphilis, X-rays, and certain drugs e.g. thalidomide. ◊ *Endosperm*.

Embryology. The study of the development of living organisms; although originally restricted to embryonic development, now taken to include the study of the post-embryonic changes which help to create the adult. Until the beginning of the 20th cent. embryology was largely descriptive, but it has now become an experimental science seeking to establish the causes of developmental change, and throwing much light on not only the organization of the animal body but the evolutionary process as a whole. ◊ *Physiology*.

Emerald. Gem-stone; green variety of ◊ *beryl*.

ORIENTAL EMERALD: Green variety of ◊ *corundum*. ◊ *Amethyst, Ruby, Sapphire*.

Emery ◊ *Corundum*.

Emetine ◊ *Alkaloids*.

Emotion. In psychology, a response by recognizable physiological changes (e.g. increase in pulse and heart-beat and changes in glandular activity); it moves the individual to (usually) heightened awareness or activity of certain kinds. Fear and anger are clearly observable responses; love and envy, though less so, are none the less real. Emotions are usually aroused by external stimuli e.g. danger, but can also be engendered by reflection, memory, and desire.

Empire. < Lat. *imperium*, power, the term used by the later Romans for their empire and applied retrospectively to earlier great states e.g. Egypt, Assyria, Babylon; it implies the exercise of political power by a single authority over a number of territorially distinct units. Thus the term is incorrectly applied to the ◊ *Byzantine* and ◊ *Ottoman* empires, which did not constitute an empire in the strict sense, and the ◊ *Holy Roman Empire* was a title describing a claim to the heritage of the Roman Empire, rather than a reality. The title Emperor was also assumed by the rulers of Russia, Germany, Austria, Hungary, China, and Japan; and Napoleon styled himself Emperor of the French. The British Empire is a term loosely used to describe the complex of territories of different status at various times dependent upon the British Crown; Queen Victoria first assumed the title of Empress of India in 1877. ◊ *British Commonwealth, Hapsburgs, Hohenzollerns, Imperialism, Second Empire*.

Empiricism. In philosophy, the several views that human knowledge is limited to or founded upon human experience, usually sense experience: the core of the main tradition of British philosophy formed by Locke, Berkeley, and Hume, and opposed to continental ◊ *rationalism*. Empiricism usually has two main tenets: (a) There are no *a priori* truths about the world, no statements of fact known to be true on the basis of anything other than experience; and the only *a priori* truths (e.g. 'All bachelors are unmarried') and the arguments of ◊ *logic* are really definitions of words, and give us no new knowledge of the world; (b) All our particular concepts or ideas are derived from experience, and we have no 'innate' ideas.

Emu. Australian flightless bird related to the ◊ *cassowary* but differing from it in duller colour, feathered neck, and no 'helmet'; the second largest bird, slightly smaller than the ◊ *ostrich*. Emus inhabit open country, living in small groups and feeding on grass, fruit, and roots; in some areas they are increasing so much as to become a pest. They have a loud booming call in the breeding season; the male incubates the 9 to 13 eggs, which are laid in a hollow in the ground.

Enamel. A translucent vitreous material discovered in Egypt between about 2100 and 1700 B.C. and used for the decoration of glass, pottery, and metals ever since. There are two main processes for enamelling metals.

CHAMPLEVÉ: Made by pouring the molten enamel into troughs incised in the metal base; the process, practised most notably at Limoges, produces a surface without metallic outlines.

CLOISONNÉ: Made by shaping wires to outline the desired patterns, soldering them to a metal base, and filling the interstices with molten enamel in various colours; the process was transmitted to China in the 13th cent. and highly developed.

Encephalitis. Inflammation of the brain, usually caused by virus infection and sometimes by poisons e.g. lead, alcohol; likely to produce severe and often irreparable damage to the brain and to result in sleeplessness, mental depression, dementia, and blindness.

Enclosures. The open field system of medieval agriculture remained unchanged until the 14th cent., when the shortage of labour due to the Black Death and the profitability of sheep raising led to the extensive enclosure of much farm and common land. This continued through Elizabethan and Stewart times though discouraged under the Stewarts. In the 18th cent. improved farming methods and food shortages led to a new wave of enclosures encouraged by the Board of Agriculture set up in 1793. Between 1761 and 1844 several thousand private and government Enclosure Acts were passed affecting some 5½ m. acres. Though this agrarian revolution resulted in a more efficient agriculture it brought about the extinction of yeoman freeholders and transformed villagers into landless labourers, while the ruthless enclosures in the Scottish Highlands virtually depopulated large areas.

Encyclical. 1. Papal pronouncement in the form of a letter in Latin addressed to all the bishops of the ◊ *Roman Catholic Church* throughout the world, generally dealing with a question of faith or morals, and referred to by its opening words. Important recent encyclicals include Leo XIII's *Rerum novarum* 1891 on social questions, Pius X's *Pascendi* 1907 condemning modernism, and John XXIII's *Mater et magistra* 1961 on social questions and *Pacem in terris* 1963 on world peace.

2. Open letter issued by the Anglican episcopate at the conclusion of a ◊ *Lambeth Conference*.

Encyclopedia. The ancient world, the Chinese, the Arabs, and the Middle Ages possessed comprehensive works of reference, but the modern encyclopedia embracing all departments of knowledge and arranged alphabetically emerged gradually in the 17th cent., Pierre Bayle's *Dictionnaire historique et critique* 1697 being the first to attain independent intellectual force. The French ◊ *Encyclopédie*, 1751–65, with Voltaire, Diderot, and Rousseau among its contributors, codified and disseminated the science and philosophy of the ◊ *Enlightenment*. The *Encyclopaedia Britannica*, 1768–71, from its 9th ed. 1875–89, did the same for the Victorian and Edwardian age, up to its great 11th ed. 1910–11. The first notable British encyclopedia was Ephraim Chambers's *Cyclopaedia or Universal Dictionary of Arts and Sciences*, 1728; an important European encyclopedia was the Brockhaus *Konversations-Lexicon*, 1809, from which were adapted the *Encyclopaedia Americana*, 1829–32, *Chambers's Encyclopedia*, 1860–8, and the *Russky Entsiklopedichesky Slovar*, 1890–1905. Other notable modern encyclopedias are the *Bolshoya Sovetskaya Entsiklopediya*, 1928–47, the *Enciclopedia Italiana*, 1929–39, and the *Encyclopédie Française*, begun 1935.

Encyclopédie. The *Encyclopédie ou Dictionnaire raisonné des sciences, des arts et des métiers*, edited by Diderot and D'Alembert, with Voltaire, Rousseau, Montesquieu, and Buffon as contributors. The first volume appeared in 1751 and the work was completed 1765. It became the main vehicle for the empiricist thinkers of the ◊ *Enlightenment*, anxious to base their ethical and social arguments upon scientific grounds, and gave its name to a group of them, of whom the leaders were Diderot and D'Alembert.

Endive. *Cichorium endivia*; a hardy annual which probably originated in Egypt and was well known to the Greeks and Romans. It has been grown in England since the early 16th cent. The leaves are eaten as salad after blanching. There are two main types, the broad-leaved (Batavian) and the very curly-leaved. *C. intybus* is the ◊ *chicory*.

Endocrine System. Internal secretion by means of ◊ *glands* and tissues, in animals having a blood system. The endocrine glands secrete chemical messengers, hormones, and pass them directly into the blood. Glands are organs specialized for this purpose, but endocrine tissues are also present in organs which have other purposes, e.g. the stomach secretes a hormone affecting its own function. The various human endocrines are scattered throughout the body, with no particular anatomical relationship to the area of their activities, e.g. the male sex hormone, situated in the testis, affects the growth of facial hair, and the ◊ *thyroid* gland, situated in the neck, maintains the metabolic level of the whole organism.

Excess or deficiency of endocrine activity produces a number of abnormalities or diseases, e.g. ◊ *insulin* deficiency results in diabetes, excessive ◊ *pituitary* activity produces gigantism.

The following are examples of endocrines and their activities:

THYROID (hormone Thyroxin): maintains rate of metabolism, oxidation, etc.

ADRENAL MEDULLA (hormone Adrenalin): produces increase in blood pressure, pulse rate, and blood glucose in moments of stress or fear.

PANCREAS (hormone Insulin): maintains sugar balance in blood.

Endogamy ◊ *Caste, Exogamy.*

Endosperm. Food material stored in ◊ *seeds* to nourish the developing ◊ *embryo.* Some seeds have sufficient endosperm to support the embryo completely until it has enough leaves to produce its own food by ◊ *photosynthesis.* Endosperm may be mostly carbohydrate (◊ *Cereals*) or oil (◊ *Brazil Nut, Castor Oil, Coconut*) with ◊ *proteins*, acids, minerals, and many other substances in smaller amounts. Many seeds are economically important on account of the endosperm. In some seeds, however, by the time they are ripe the embryo has absorbed all the endosperm and is nourished by food reserves in the cotyledons, e.g. peas, beans.

Endothermic, Exothermic ◊ *Compound.*

Endymion. In Greek legend, a handsome youth loved by Selene (the moon, ◊ *Hyperion*), who cast him into a perpetual sleep except when she came down each night to his bed.

Energy. The potential energy of a body is the capacity to do work by virtue of its position or state; its kinetic energy is its capacity to do work by virtue of its motion. Energy can be classified as chemical, thermal, mechanical, electrical, radiant, and nuclear. The theory of the conservation of energy states that energy cannot be created or destroyed but only changed in form, any given amount of one form always transforming into an equal amount of other forms, e.g. a car obtains mechanical energy by the explosion of a petrol-air mixture (chemical energy) and uses some of it to overcome frictional and other forces opposing its motion; much of the energy will be dissipated as heat, and if the car climbs a hill some of it will be stored as potential energy, to be released as kinetic energy when the car descends; however complicated the processes involved, and however much energy may appear to be 'lost', the total is always maintained. Electrical energy is a particularly useful form, in that it can be conveniently and efficiently 'transported' on a grid system from the point of generation to where it is required. The generator which produces this electrical energy usually derives the necessary mechanical energy from steam (thermal energy) produced by burning coal or oil (chemical energy) or by releasing ◊ *nuclear energy* in a reactor; sometimes the generator's mechanical energy comes direct from another mechanical source such as a fast-moving stream of water (hydroelectricity). ◊ *Relativity.*

Engine. Originally, any mechanical device used to help man e.g. an 'engine of war' such as a catapult; a device to provide power, either for driving stationary machinery or for propelling vehicles. Most engines at the present time are heat engines, relying on the conversion of heat into mechanical energy. In e.g. an ◊ *internal combustion engine*, heat is released by the burning of a combustible mixture of liquid (or gaseous) fuel and air (or other oxygen source). The products of combustion at high temperature and pressure expand, producing power which can be harnessed. Thus in a steam engine, steam at high pressure and temperature produced in a boiler heated by burning fuel or by nuclear reaction is allowed to expand in a cylinder so as to drive a piston. This kind of motion is converted by crank and connecting-rod to the rotary motion of the crankshaft, and makes the energy more readily available for use. An alternative way to utilize the hot gases or steam is in a ◊ *turbine*. ◊ *Internal Combustion Engine, Steam Engine.*

England ◊ *United Kingdom.*

England (History). Pre 1066 ◊ *Anglo-Saxons, Vikings.* 1066–1485 ◊ *Norman Conquest, Domesday Book, Feudalism, Magna Carta, Peasants Revolt, Hundred Years War, Wars of the Roses.* 1485–1660 ◊ *Tudors, Reformation, Penal Laws, Armada, Stewarts, English Civil Wars, Covenant, Commonwealth and Protectorate.* 1660–88 ◊ *Restoration, Clarendon Code, Test Act, Exclusion Bill.* 1688–1815 ◊ *Glorious Revolution, Bill of Rights, Act of Settlement, Tory, Whig, Industrial Revolution, Napoleonic Wars.* 1815 onwards ◊ *Chartism, Crimean War, Poor Law, Boer War,* etc.

⟡ *Act of Union, Ireland, Scotland, Wales.*

English Architecture ◊ *Anglo-Saxon/ Georgian / Stewart Architecture, Decorated / Early English / Jacobean / Palladian Perpendicular/Queen Anne Style, Tudors.*

English Art. The earliest surviving examples are carvings and illuminated manuscripts of Celtic and Saxon inspiration produced in 7th-cent. Northumbria. Manuscript illumination remained the outstanding English art until after the Norman Conquest, and English painters, glass-stainers, and sculptors were still strongly influenced by French styles in the 11th cent. and throughout the ◊ *Gothic* period, the native genius being expressed in grotesque architectural carvings, amusing narrative scenes in manuscripts, exquisite embroidery, and small alabaster reliefs and statuettes carved at e.g. Nottingham and exported throughout Europe. An English school of painters began to form with the late 16th-cent. miniatures of Nicholas Hilliard and Isaac Oliver, but in the 16th and even 17th cent. the most prominent figures were foreigners brought in as Court portrait painters, e.g. Holbein, Van Dyck, Lely, Kneller; a notable exception was the sculptor Grinling Gibbons 1648–1721. The great age of English painting begins in the 1730s with William Hogarth; a little later, Reynolds, Gainsborough, and the Scotsmen Raeburn and Ramsay were producing fine portraits. Richard Wilson painted the first outstanding English landscapes; George Stubbs was outstanding as an animal painter. With ◊ *Neoclassicism* a school of English sculptors,

notably Nollekens and Flaxman, began to form. William Blake began to produce his visionary paintings in the late 18th and early 19th centuries, and Lawrence emerged as the leading portrait painter and Constable and Turner as the greatest of all English landscape painters. The most interesting Victorian artists were the ◊ *Pre-Raphaelites.* Under inspiration from the continent, the arts revived in the 1920s; several living artists e.g. Henry Moore, Ben Nicholson, Graham Sutherland, Francis Bacon have an international reputation. The English school has consistently shown a love of flowing linear patterns and a preference for portraiture and (later) landscapes; it has excelled in works on a small scale e.g. illuminations, portrait miniatures, and watercolours. ◊ *Landscape Painting.*

English Civil Wars. 1642–9. The conflict between Parliament and Charles I developed into a war over principles, for freedom in politics and religion as against royal and episcopal ◊ *absolutism* and ◊ *Divine Right,* as exemplified in the attempted arrest of the 'Five Members' of the House of Commons for having criticized royal actions. Unlike the later ◊ *French Revolution* and ◊ *American Civil War,* it was not a war of classes or of regions, but of parties. There was no widespread enthusiasm to fight, nor (with rare exceptions) was the fighting bitter or inhumane. Both sides had to improvise their armies: the Royalists from the Cavaliers (chiefly large landowners and Roman Catholics), the Parliament from town citizens and ◊ *Puritans* (though many wealthy peers fought on the Parliament side). The King made Oxford his headquarters, and at first local success went to the Royalists, who had a dashing cavalry leader in Prince Rupert and a more consistently successful one in Lord Wilmot (whom the King foolishly banished in 1644); but when Fairfax and Cromwell reorganized the Parliamentary forces they gradually obtained the upper hand, aided by the support of London and the Navy. After the battle of ◊ *Marston Moor,* 1644, where the Ironsides repelled Rupert's cavalry, Fairfax and Cromwell created the New Model Army, a devoted and highly disciplined force without equal in its time. At the battle of ◊ *Naseby,* 1645, the Royalists were decisively beaten, and Charles soon afterwards surrendered to the Scots army at Newcastle (◊ *Covenant*). In return for arrears of payment, the Scots delivered the King into the custody of Parliament, from which the Army Council under Cromwell removed him into their own hands, presently expelling all doubtful Members ('Pride's Purge') from the House of Commons and bringing him to trial for High Treason before the 'Rump' Parliament, which found him guilty and condemned him to death. After the ◊ *Restoration* his judges and the signatories to his death warrant were excluded from the Act of Oblivion as regicides, and 10 of them were hanged, drawn, and quartered. ◊ *Commonwealth and Protectorate, Diggers, Drogheda, Dunbar, Levellers, Worcester.*

English Language. Belongs to the W. division of the Germanic (Teutonic) branch of the ◊ *Indo-European languages*; most closely related to W. Germanic (Frisian, Flemish, Dutch, and German), somewhat more distantly akin to N. Germanic (Icelandic, Norwegian, Danish, and Swedish). Three related tribes, the Jutes, Angles, and Saxons, speaking three varieties of Anglo-Saxon (Old English) settled in Britain in the late 5th cent.; their language was not so highly inflected as Sanskrit, Greek, and Latin, but still possessed a complex system of declensions and conjugations: nouns had no less than 25 'mutated' plural forms, of which seven have survived (feet, geese, teeth; men, women; lice, mice). Many nouns belonged to *n*-stem (weak) declensions, e.g. brethren, children, oxen. (Such weak plurals were considerably extended in the S. dialect of Middle English, where e.g. 'treen' (trees), 'housen' (houses) were common; if this dialect (instead of E. Midland) had become the basis of Standard English, plurals in *-en* might have been the regular forms today, but 's' prevailed.) Nouns were of strong or weak declension according to their stems; adjectives showed both strong and weak forms according to function and position (as in Modern German), but with rare exceptions the weak forms – still significant in Chaucer – did not survive beyond the 15th cent. Since then adjectives have shed all their variations, apart from the demonstratives (this, these, that, those) and the terminations -er, -est (greater, greatest). Otherwise only nouns, pronouns, and verbs are now inflected; and in this respect no other Indo-European tongue has gone farther from synthesis towards analysis (◊ *Inflexion*).

SCANDINAVIAN INFLUENCE: The Scandinavian Vikings, related in race and language to the Angles, Jutes, and Saxons who had crossed the North Sea three centuries before, began raiding England in the late 8th cent. and soon conquered all England N. and E. of Watling Street. These men of the Danelaw left permanent marks not only on manorial organization and local government but upon the English language; many of the commonest words are from the Scandinavian (nouns e.g. leg, skull, anger, boom, gap, sky; adjectives e.g. happy, rotten, ugly; verbs e.g. call, cut, die, lug, rid). Undoubtedly Scandinavian influence hastened the shedding of inflexions, which slowly spread from N. to S. with a gain in directness, clarity, and strength.

FRENCH INFLUENCE: For 150 years after the Norman Conquest the main influence came from Normandy and Picardy (catch, warden, warrant, wage, reward); later the Central French of Paris made its impact (chase, guardian, guarantee, gage, regard).

LATIN INFLUENCE: Latin was the language of learning. For three centuries the literature of England was trilingual in French, Latin, and English, and from 1154 to 1254 English was threatened with extinction; but Parliament was opened in English for the first time 1362, and Chaucer (then a young man in his twenties) decided to write his poems in English not French (though half the words he used were of Romance origin). The present-day vocabulary is roughly half Germanic (English and Scandinavian) and half Romance (French and Latin).

MODERN ENGLISH: The revival of classical learning in the 15th cent. and its dissemination by means of printed books led to a literary reawakening, which found its centre in London (where Chaucer and Gower had lived and died). The speech of London belonged mainly to the E. Midland dialect, which also covered the most densely-populated areas of England, from Leicester to Norwich, and the two universities, Oxford on its W. border and Cambridge at its centre. In Shakespeare's London there was probably a diversity of pronunciation, but a 'received standard' speech won gradual acceptance in the 17th and 18th centuries, and within Dryden's lifetime (1631–1700) the language reached maturity. Today R S (Received Standard English) has 44 phonemes (speechsounds), 12 vowels, 9 diphthongs, and 23 consonants, represented by only 26 letters; the ◊ *alphabet* is thus inadequate, only 23 effective letters being available to express nearly twice that number of sounds. Though even more unphonetic than French, English spelling nevertheless has three good features in its favour: the letters standing singly for consonant sounds are fairly unambiguous, and on the whole consonant clusters do consistently represent the same sounds in the same position; English spelling has dispensed with those diacritical marks and accents which encumber the writing of French, Spanish, Italian, German, and some Slavonic languages; and the present spelling shows the European connexions of numerous speech forms, so that anyone acquainted with classical Latin or any modern Romance tongue is immediately aware of the meanings of many thousands of words which would become completely unrecognizable if written as now pronounced.

CURRENT TRENDS: Among the most notable may be mentioned the growing use of verb-adverb units as nouns – e.g. show-down (disclosure of facts or intentions, originally 'laying down of cards on the table with faces up'); hold-up (obstruction, delay); set-up (organization, arrangement) – and the proliferation of compounds such as road-block, news-value, girl-friend, gaol-break, and the use of abstract nouns as verbs e.g. to condition, to service. These expressions are felt to be vivid and forceful by reason of their brevity. Alphabetic abbreviations of many kinds (whether pronounceable like U N O and U N I C E F or unpronounceable like D.S.I.R. and T.G.W.U.) meet the needs of the modern world. In spite of the standardizing influence of school and television, differing speech levels (rhetorical, literary, common, colloquial, slang) continue to revivify one another and to invigorate the language as a whole; more slang is used today than ever before, but only a few examples are incorporated at the 'common' level.

Chaucer used the language of only 4 m. people, who were reduced to half that number by the Black Death; Shakespeare addressed a potential audience of 5½ m.

It was remarkable that the language of so small a community had already reached early maturity when it began to expand with unparalleled speed and power. The language taken to Virginia by John Smith 1607, and to Massachusetts by the Founding Fathers 1620, was the English of Shakespeare and Milton: today English is the most widely-known language in the world. ◊ *Germanic Languages.*

Engraving. Incising a metal plate, esp. for the reproduction of prints. Various reproductive techniques derive from the practice of line-engraving (developed in the 15th cent.), in which the artist engraves his design with a burin on a highly-polished plate, so that the incised furrows will hold printing ink, which transmits the design to paper applied under pressure.

DRYPOINT ENGRAVING: Print taken from plate inscribed with a steel needle, which throws up a burr to hold the ink; Rembrandt was the first to use this technique.

MEZZOTINT: < Ital. 'half-tone': produced by a reverse process, discovered and popularized by Prince Rupert of the Rhine in the mid 17th cent. Now superseded by ◊ *photography.* ◊◊ *Aquatint, Etching, Printing.*

Enlightenment. Strictly, the *Aufklärung* of 18th-cent. Germany, but more commonly the whole of the Age of Reason, from the English Revolution of the 1640s to the French Revolution of the 1780s; the England of Hobbes, Locke, and Newton; the Scotland of Hume and Adam Smith (◊ *Laissez-faire*); the France of Montesquieu, Voltaire, Diderot, Rousseau, and the ◊ *Encyclopédie*; the Germany of Kant, Lessing, and Herder. In the 19th cent. used ironically, the term is now usually applied without irony to the untrammelled ◊ *rationalism* and ◊ *empiricism*, and the ready questioning of authority and tradition in religious, social, and political matters, which mark the period. The age of Enlightenment was also that of the 'enlightened despots' Peter the Great of Russia, Frederick the Great of Prussia, the Emperor Joseph II, who attempted to put the liberal reforms advocated by the philosophers into effect. ◊ *Physiocrats.*

Enosis ◊ *Cyprus.*

Entablature. The upper part of one of the classical ◊ *architectural orders*, consisting of architrave, frieze, and cornice, supported by a colonnade.

Entente Cordiale. A series of treaties signed between Britain and France in 1904 eliminating long-standing disagreements on colonial questions. The intention was to remove obstacles to common action in face of the Triple Alliance of Germany, Austria-Hungary, and Italy, and esp. of German ambitions. When Britain reached similar agreements with Russia in 1907 the Triple Entente was created, France and Russia having been allies since 1891.

Enteritis. Inflammation of the mucous membrane of the small intestine, usually caused by bacterial food poisoning. Gastro-enteritis also involves the stomach and entero-colitis the large intestine. ⟡ *Digestion.*

Entomology. The study of insects concerned with e.g. the physiology of insect hearing, flight, behaviour, development, ecology, evolution, comparative anatomy, and classification. Applied entomology investigates insect pests e.g. ⟡ *aphids*, weevils, and ⟡ *mosquitoes*, seeking to control them by finding a suitable predator or insecticide (as in the control of malaria through the destruction of the mosquito) or by interfering with the life cycle e.g. the liberation of sterile males into the habitat of the blowfly-like pest *Simulium.*

Entropy ⟡ *Thermodynamics.*

Enzyme. A biological ferment acting catalytically in a specific way, to produce a reaction in a particular molecule (the enzyme substrate); in the living cell, major chemical changes (e.g. oxidation of ⟡ *glucose* to carbon dioxide) are achieved in a series of small steps, none requiring much energy and each controlled by an enzyme. Enzymes extracted from plant and animal materials have been purified and crystallized whilst retaining their activity; they have proved to be ⟡ *protein* in nature, some wholly so and others comprising a protein carrying a non-protein molecule (co-enzyme). For some enzymes a supply of a particular metal ion e.g. ⟡ *magnesium* is also necessary. The structure of the non-protein part has in some cases been determined, but the protein part is generally too complex. Some co-enzymes detached from the protein are included among the ⟡ *vitamins* but others are not, e.g. an enzyme called carboxylase,

which converts pyruvic acid into ⟡ *acetic acid*, has aneurin or Vitamin B_1 as the non-protein part. Examples of enzymic reactions include the production of alcohol by fermentation, the synthesis of fatty acids, the synthesis and hydrolysis of proteins, and reactions of oxidation and reduction. Enzyme preparations are available, and are often employed commercially.

Eocene System. < Gr. 'dawn of the recent'; rocks laid down in the first 20 m. years of the Cenozoic (Tertiary) Era (⟡ *Geological Time Scale*). In Britain rocks of this period are restricted to S E England, particularly the London and Hampshire basins; they are mainly sands and clays.

E.O.K.A. ⟡ *Cyprus.*

Eoliths. Roughly chipped stones claimed by some archaeologists to be the first crude stone implements made by primitive man; widely distributed throughout the world. In England they have been found in a 'stone bed' at the base of the Norwich Crag rocks of Pliocene age (⟡ *Geological Time Scale*) in East Anglia and also in some high-level gravels on the N. Downs. If man-made tools (but there is no complete agreement on this point) they are evidence of human occupation of Britain in pre-glacial times, well over 1 m. years ago. ⟡ *Flint.*

Ephemeris ⟡ *Time.*

Epic. A long narrative poem dealing with heroic persons and events; the historical evolution of the form is normally from the oral poetry of reciters (⟡ *Bard*) to the bookish epic showing a learned awareness of literary tradition, as in Virgil or Milton. The classical concept, based on Homer's *Iliad* and *Odyssey* and Virgil's *Aeneid*, requires certain definite features e.g. an initial invocation, a descent into Hades, a catalogue of military forces, and an athletic contest; also typical is a device resembling the cinema technique of the flash-back, whereby characters narrate at length events deemed to have happened before the beginning of the poem's action. The English epic tradition (⟡ *Beowulf*) was at one time influenced by a very different conception, derived from Italy, characterized by a labyrinthine structure of brief stories; Spenser's *Faerie Queene*, owing much to Ariosto's *Orlando Furioso*, is a good example of the kind. Many countries have national epics: England the ⟡ *Arthurian legends*, Ireland those of

◊ *Finn* and ◊ *Cuchullin*, Wales the ◊ *Mabinogion*, France the ◊ *Chansons de Geste*, Finland the ◊ *Kalevala*, Germany the ◊ *Nibelungenlied*, Portugal the *Lusíadas*, Spain ◊ *El Cid*, etc. Modern literature has largely abandoned the epic, though in Poland the 19th-cent. *Pan Tadeusz* by Mickiewicz is a notably successful exception.

Epic Theatre. Although an epic or 'narrative' style may be traced in a large number of plays and novels from Greek times to the present day, its principal exponent was Bertolt Brecht; his epic theatre was designed to arouse in audiences a desire to alter the world towards a marxist ideal; Brecht opposed his epic form to the dramatic form, and followed a line of narration-objectivity-investigation-reason, as against action-involvement-unalterability-feeling. ◊ *Alienation, Berliner Ensemble, Tragedy.*

Epicureanism. In philosophy, the often misconstrued doctrines of Epicurus (3rd cent. B.C.), who taught that pleasure alone is good but stressed not sensual pleasures but those of the mind and spirit: to live wisely, virtuously, and soberly is the way to pleasure. Epicurus also held an early atomic theory of the universe.

Epigram. Originally, a form of words suitable for an inscription, < Gr. *epigraphein*, to inscribe; later, any brief pithy poem or sentence. As used by the 5th-cent. B.C. Greeks, an 'epigram' was not 'witty' in the modern sense, but grave or even majestic, e.g. the famous epigram by Simonides for the Spartan dead at Plataea. The 'pointed' epigram was developed later by the scurrilous but brilliant Latin poet Martial. The 'scorpion' epigram with a sting in the tail prevailed in the 18th cent. Famous English epigrammatists are Pope and Belloc in verse and Wilde and Shaw in prose.

Epilepsy. Affection of the ◊ *central nervous system*, in which temporary loss of consciousness occurs, with or without violent muscular convulsions. It exists in two forms: *grand mal* (with convulsions) and *petit mal*. On recovery the sufferer often retains no memory of the attack. The cause is usually unknown.

Epiphytes (Air Plants). Plants which grow upon others but are independent of them except for support, thus differing from ◊ *parasites*; they manufacture their own food in the same way as other plants, and often obtain moisture from the air. Most common in tropical ◊ *rain forests*, they occur among many families, esp. lichens, mosses, ferns, and orchids.

Episcopalian ◊ *Anglicanism, Bishop, Church of England.*

Epochs (Ages, Eras, Periods) ◊ *Geological Time Scale.*

Epsom Salts ◊ *Magnesium.*

Equality. The literal meaning 'condition of being equal' is without content unless qualified, e.g. 'equality of opportunity' or 'equality before the law', which are meaningful phrases even if the implications are vague. Used alone, the word has a purely subjective emotive quality. As a slogan of the 1789 ◊ *French Revolution*, it was first intended as an abbreviation for 'equality before the law' i.e. the abolition of privilege; it was used by some revolutionary leaders, however, to imply a redistribution of wealth, and has since been frequently used to imply a removal of social distinctions.

Equation. In mathematics, a statement of the equality of two quantities, expressed either in numbers $(5+2=7)$ or in symbols $(x+2=7)$. The symbols or letters in an algebraic equation are called unknowns or variables. In algebra, methods are evolved for the solution of equations. In general, the number of variables must not exceed the number of equations, if a unique solution is to be found, e.g. $x+3=7$ has one solution $(x=4)$ but $x+y=7$ has an infinite number $(x=1$ where $y=6$, $x=2$ where $y=5$, etc.). In physics, equations are means of expressing fundamental relationships, as in Einstein's equation defining the conversion of mass into energy, $E=mc^2$, where E is energy released when a mass of m grams is converted entirely into energy, and c the velocity of light. Some statements in physics entail an indication of direction, e.g. velocity or acceleration; this is indicated by a symbol such as P or AB. When the concept of direction is involved, the normal rules of arithmetic may no longer be valid.

Equations involving derivatives are differential equations, encountered in almost every branch of applied mathematics.

In chemistry, equations represent a chemical reaction, e.g. $2H_2+O_2=2H_2O$; this example is reversible, and so is usually written $2H_2+O_2 \rightleftarrows 2H_2O$. Another example (marble plus hydrochloric acid > spirits of salts) is not reversible, and is usually written $CaCO_3 + 2HCl \rightarrow CaCl_2 + H_2O + CO_2$.

Equator. The ◊ *great circle* in which the plane perpendicular to the earth's axis and equidistant from the poles would cut the earth's surface.

CELESTIAL EQUATOR: The great circle in which this plane cuts the ◊ *celestial sphere*.

◊◊ *Climate, Rain Forest, Savannah, Tropics.*

Equatorial Forest ◊ *Rain Forest.*

Equinox. The date when the noon sun appears to be directly overhead at the equator, and all places on the earth have equal day and night; about 21 March and 23 Sept. every year. Also, the position of the sun in the ecliptic at these times (◊ *Celestial Sphere*). In the N. hemisphere the March and Sept. equinoxes are called respectively spring and autumn, the order being reversed in the S. hemisphere. ◊ *Solstice.*

Equity ◊ *Common Law, Law.*

Erastianism. Affirmation of State supremacy in ecclesiastical matters, as e.g. the right of Parliament to legislate for and supervise the Church of England (◊ *Prayer Book*). Named after Thomas Erastus, a German Swiss, 1524–83. ◊ *Anglicanism, Nonjurors.*

Erbium ◊ *Lanthanides.*

Erg. Unit of energy or work in the centimetre-gramme-second scale.

Ergonomics. The study of the performance of workers and of the external factors which influence output, esp. the equipment, layout, conditions of lighting and heating, periods of rest, and pace of work, with a view to increasing the worker's well-being and efficiency.

Ergosterol. Extract from yeast; formerly isolated from ◊ *ergot.* By ultraviolet irradiation, ergosterol gave the first active preparation of Vitamin D (*calciferol*).

Ergot. *Claviceps purpurea*; a parasitic fungus living on grasses and cereals esp. rye. The fungus-fruiting bodies grow among the developing ears and look like blackish grains. The fungus contains alkaloids e.g. ergotamine now used medicinally, but bread etc. made with contaminated grain causes illness with hallucinations and delirium, and can be fatal. Ergot poisoning is now rare but was previously more common; in the Middle Ages the sufferers were thought to be mad, devil-possessed, bewitched.

Ericaceae. Heaths; a large dicotyledonous family, mostly woody plants ranging from a few inches high to medium trees. They are widely distributed throughout the world, esp. on acid soils. They form characteristic vegetation types in many areas, e.g. heathland and moors are often dominated by heather or ling (*Calluna vulgaris*) and species of *Vaccinium* (bilberry) and Mediterranean scrubland by *Erica* (heath) species and *Arbutus* (strawberry tree). Most of the flowers are globular or funnel-shaped, and the leaves waxy or hard and rolled. There are several ornamental types, e.g. some heaths, mountain laurel, rhododendron, azalea, arbutus. Some produce berries, of which the most important are the cranberry (widely cultivated in U.S.A.) and the bilberry or whortleberry or blaeberry (N. England and Scotland). The '*briar*' pipe is made from the rootstocks of some of the almost treelike Mediterranean Ericas (Fr. *bruyère*), esp. *E. arborea.*

'Ernie'. Electronic Random Number Indicating Equipment; a machine designed and produced by the Post Office Research Station, to find and print a long series of mathematically 'random' nine-figure numbers. ◊ *Premium Bonds* bearing these are awarded prizes. The source of the numbers is the random behaviour of very large numbers of charged particles in a gasdischarge electron tube, which are translated by electronic circuits into different numbers printed every $2\frac{1}{2}$ seconds. ◊ *Lottery.*

Eros (Cupid). In Greek mythology, god of love; often represented as a beautiful boy-child stringing a bow. In early Greek theology he represented the bond of affection uniting gods with men and men with one another, but the concept became more sexual with time. The beautiful fable of Cupid and ◊ *Psyche* seems to date only to the 2nd-cent. A.D. *Golden Ass* by Apuleius.

Erosion. Wearing-away of rocks; covers all processes, including ◊ *weathering*, by which a landscape is denuded, but strictly should apply only to the destructive work of the agents of erosion (water, ice, wind, waves).

EROSION CYCLE: Stages through which a land mass passes between its uplift into a highland area and its final reduction by the agents of erosion into a nearly flat plain. Three stages in the cycle are generally recognized. *Youth:* Stream erosion is active and river valleys are cut deep. *Maturity:* The land forms have become subdued, the sharp crests rounded, the narrow valleys widened, and the waterfalls and rapids smoothed out. *Old Age:* The land is almost flat, and has become a peneplain (before this happens, a new elevation often rejuvenates the streams and begins a fresh cycle).

SOIL EROSION: Serious problem in many countries. Some of the most spectacular examples have been seen in the 'Dustbowl' of U.S.A. Great Plains, where vast areas of cultivated land lost their topsoil through wind erosion; the Soil Conservation Service estimated 1934 that over 57 m. acres had already become useless for farming, and a major scheme of soil conservation and land reclamation was successfully carried out by the ◊ *Tennessee Valley Authority.*

Both in N. America and elsewhere, deforestation, overgrazing, and overcropping (all of which remove the vegetative cover and expose the soil to erosion by water and wind) have led to soil erosion; the following practices help to prevent it.

CONTOUR PLOUGHING: The land is ploughed along instead of across the contour, and the flow of water and loss of soil checked.

STRIP CULTIVATION: Narrow strips are cultivated across the slope, erosion-resistant crops alternating with other crops.

TERRACING: Terraces cut into the slope prevent rapid run-off.

Erysipelas. Acute inflammation of the skin, caused by streptococcal infection and often producing fever. Formerly regarded as a serious complaint, it usually responds rapidly to ◊ *antibiotics* and rest.

Eskimo. A Mongoloid people of the Arctic, found from NE Siberia (where they originated) through Alaska and Canada to Greenland. Today they number only some 54,000 in several distinct groups, each with its own dialect and way of life. They depend upon hunting e.g. seal, walrus, caribou, bear, and on fish and lichens; they have an extremely complex and specialized technology to deal with the conditions of the Arctic, esp. their snowhouses (igloos), built either of sticks covered with snow or made entirely of blocks of snow arranged as a dome, in which the temperature must be kept just

below freezing point. The igloos are often large and elaborate, containing many rooms linked by passages. Their canoes (kayaks) and harpoons are also very ingenious. They have suffered severely from contact with whites, who introduced diseases unknown to Eskimo in their near-sterile environment. In many areas the traditional economy has been destroyed and Eskimo are dependent on governmental assistance; many are also employed on the radar defence schemes in extreme N. Canada.

E.S.N. ◊ *Educational Subnormality.*

E.S.P. ◊ *Extra-sensory Perception.*

Esperanto ◊ *International Languages.*

Essay. A short relatively informal literary work on a particular topic, or a piece at least giving the impression of informality; Montaigne's *Essais* 1580–95 and Bacon's *Essays* 1597 were among the first of the genre. The development of periodicals demanded a steady supply from the early 18th cent. onwards, e.g. Steele and Addison's *Tatler* and *Spectator*. In the titles of longer works e.g. Locke's *Essay Concerning Human Understanding* 1690, the word emphasizes the author's exploratory or tentative purpose.

Essences ◊ *Dead Sea Scrolls.*

Essential Oils. ◊ *Oils* extracted from many plants which contain the characteristic perfume or flavour of the plants, e.g. oil of cloves, oil of lavender, oil of ginger, eucalyptus. They are obtained by solvents, by steam treatment, or by pressing.

Estonia ◊ *Baltic States.*

Etching. Inscribing a metal surface with acid; much used for the decoration of armour in the Middle Ages and developed in the 16th cent. as a method of making prints. The etcher inscribes his design with a needle on a wax-coated copper plate and immerses the plate in acid, which eats into the parts exposed by the needle and thus produces an incised design. Prints are taken by the same method as in ◊ *engraving.* The art of etching was brought to its highest achievement by Dürer, Rembrandt, and Goya.

Ethers. Organic compounds having the general formula R–O–R, where R represents some organic radical; the commonest is the very volatile and inflammable diethyl ether H_5C_2–O–C_2H_5, very useful as a solvent and as an anaesthetic. Mixed with air or oxygen, its vapour is dan-

gerously explosive, though otherwise
ethers are chemically fairly inert.

Ethics. In its long history as a part of ◊
philosophy, ethics has included the following separable parts. (a) What may be
called morals, the recommending of particular moral principles and attitudes. (b)
Claims about the moral views in fact held
by people and their psychological or
sociological origins. (c) Analysis of the
meanings and logical relations of moral
terms e.g. 'good' and 'ought'. Kant's principle (akin to the Golden Rule) that one
ought always to act on a principle one
would choose to have as a universal law
is a moral recommendation, as is the
Utilitarian principle that an act is right
if it is likely to produce more happiness
than other possible acts. Appeals to 'the
deliverances of our moral consciousness'
are empirical claims, as is Hobbes's view
that apparently altruistic views are motivated by self-interest. Many contemporary
philosophers eschew both moral instruction and factual reporting, and confine
themselves to the investigation of moral
concepts. Analytical views of this sort,
past and present, include those called
naturalistic: e.g. to say an act is 'right'
is to mean that it is approved by the community or will produce pleasure. Quite
different is the doctrine that to say an act
is 'right' is to say it has a 'non-natural'
quality (rightness) which is somehow in-
tuited by morally-developed persons.
Other views, most common recently, are
that to say an act is 'right' is merely to
express an emotion or attitude towards it
or to say that it satisfies certain criteria
and also to prescribe it. On the latter
view, moral judgements are in part something like commands or imperatives.

Ethiopia (Abyssinia). Area 400,000 sq. m.
Pop. 21.8 m. Cap. Addis Ababa. The
Empire of Ethiopia in NE Africa; ruled
by Haile Selassie I, who exercises supreme
executive power with two advisory bodies,
a Senate appointed by him and a Chamber of Deputies chosen by the nobility.
The dominant race, the Amharas, are
Christian (◊ *Copts*); about two thirds of
the population are Muslims, of various
tribes. Much of the country is a high
plateau.

ECONOMY. Mainly cattle-breeding and
agriculture, esp. barley, coffee (52 per cent
of exports), cotton, maize, oilseeds, potatoes, tobacco, wheat.

HISTORY. The distinguishing features of
the Empire have been its Coptic Christianity and its successful resistance to
European conquest. The landmark in this
struggle was the overwhelming defeat of
an Italian army at ◊ *Adowa*, 1896. In
1935 the Italians invaded from their neighbouring territory of Eritrea, and with the
use of aircraft and bombing obtained
control by 1937. The exiled Haile Selassie
was restored as Emperor in 1943, after
British troops had ejected the Italians;
the province of Eritrea remained under
British administration 1945–52. Despite
its backward condition and failure to implement modern democratic ideals, other
African states have always accorded
Ethiopia special respect, because of its
long history and determined resistance to
foreign domination.

LANGUAGE. Amharic in central provinces; Arabic and Somali in other parts.

Ethnography, Ethnology ◊ *Anthropology*.

Ethyl Alcohol. A colourless liquid freely
miscible with water; b.p. 78.3° C. Obtained by yeast, fermentation of starch or
from ethylene, it is important as a solvent,
a fuel, and a chemical raw material e.g.
as a source of ◊ *acetic acid* and ethyl
esters. As methylated spirits, it is rendered unpalatable by the addition of e.g.
pyridine, crude wood spirit, or ◊ *naphtha*.

Ethylene ◊ *Olefines*.

Etruscans. People of unknown origin who
at the height of their power (about the 6th
to 5th cent. B.C.) dominated NW Italy
and the islands of Elba and Corsica with
wide trade and cultural contacts throughout the Mediterranean and S. Europe.
They are known chiefly from their tombs,
whose furnishings and decorations reveal
that the Etruscan ruling class were a rich
and highly sophisticated people, having
skilled metal-workers in bronze, iron, and
gold; their gold work in particular was
prized throughout the ancient world.
Their stone-built towns, like those of the
Greeks, were self-governing; the political
weakness resulting from this disunity led
to their eventual defeat at the hands first
of the Gaulish tribes (about 450–350 B.C.)
and later of the Romans, the last of their
cities falling to ◊ *Rome* about 250 B.C.
Relations with Rome, however, had
varied: the last Roman kings were
Etruscan, and many features of Roman
civilization, including the essential plan of
their cities, were borrowed from Etruria.

ART. Most Etruscan works of art have been found in tombs; they comprise very spirited and brightly-coloured wall paintings, pottery vessels, large and small bronze sculptures, gold jewellery, bronze mirrors, helmets, and cinerary urns. Near-Eastern influence predominates at first, but later Greek influence prevails. The earliest date is the 7th cent. B.C. but probably the finest are the 6th and 5th cent. B.C. paintings in the tombs of the Lioness, the Triclinium, and the Baron at Tarquinia. A decline set in after about 400 B.C. but some fine works were still produced, notably the bronze Mars from Todi now in the Vatican Museum.

LANGUAGE. An extinct tongue of unknown ancestry, not Indo-European. Etruscan letters are like Greek or Latin, but no one has succeeded (although recently some advance has been made) in interpreting the meanings of the Etruscan inscriptions, of which no fewer than 9000 survive, most of them very brief.

Etymology. < Gr. *etymos*, actual, true; study of the origin and history of words, tracing them to their earliest ascertainable source within a given language group and showing their connexion with other words. This can be done by studying all the recorded forms of a given word, comparing them with those in related languages, and reconstructing the original form (◊ *Grimm's Law*). Thus English 'tooth' can be traced through Old English, Common Germanic, etc. to the Latin *dens, dentis* and the related Gr. *odons, odontos*.

Eucalyptus (Gum-tree). A very large genus, originally from Australia, characteristically with greyish-green evergreen leaves, peeling bark, and an aromatic scent. They are of great economic importance and widely cultivated all over the world; many species give valuable timber and eucalyptus oil of various kinds, from which thymol and menthol can be produced; many give a gum used medicinally and for tanning. The young shoots form the major diet of the ◊ *koala* bear.

Eucharist. < Gr. *eucharistia*, thanksgiving; name given (esp. in the Anglican Church) to the service of ◊ *Holy Communion*, esp. when celebrated with music and full ritual.

EUCHARISTIC CONGRESS: International gathering of clergy and laity of the ◊ *Roman Catholic Church*, devotionally and doctrinally concerned with the Real Presence. ◊ *Sacrament*.

Euchre. A card game for four, playing in pairs, with a pack of 32 cards (ace to seven). Each player receives five cards, the next being turned up for trumps. In turn the players say whether they will accept these trumps; if no one will, the first can name trumps or pass, and so with the rest. If all pass the second time, the hands are thrown in. If trumps are named, the cards are played one at a time, and tricks are won. The pair calling trumps receive two points if they make all five, one if they make three or four, but lose two if they make two or less. The Jack of trumps (the right bower) ranks as the highest card and the Jack of the other suit of the same colour (left bower) as second.

Eumenides ◊ *Furies*.

Eunuch. A castrated human male; eunuchs were used as harem slaves in the ancient Middle and Far East and as confidential royal advisers in ancient China, Persia, later Rome, Byzantium, often rising to great political eminence e.g. the Byzantine general Narses who reconquered Italy and ruled it as exarch. The trade in African eunuchs for Muslim harems of Arabia still continues, but the castration of boy singers to train them as adult soprani ended with the reign of Pope Leo XIII in the late 19th cent. There have been voluntary eunuchs at different times in Christian countries and in India.

Euphorbiaceae. Large cosmopolitan family of dicotyledons, having ◊ *latex* and with a very characteristic complex flower structure, the flowers being unisexual and inconspicuous but with showy bracts and often clustered together and giving the appearance of a single flower e.g. Poinsettias. Many are shrubs and trees, some are herbs (spurges); a large number are succulents, many 'cacti' being really euphorbias, recognizable by the latex. Several genera are important economically.

Euphuism. An Elizabethan fashion in writing and conversation popularized by John Lyly's romance *Euphues, the Anatomy of Wit* 1578, marked by the exaggerated use of antithesis, of mythological allusions, and almost every device of verse except ◊ *metre* and set rhyme-schemes; ridiculed in its own time and since, it probably helped towards the 17th-cent. development of more flexible and conscious English prose.

Eurasian. In India, Burma, and other eastern countries, a person of mixed ancestry esp. of a European father and Asian mother. They number about a quarter of a million in India, and have lived an urban life and supplied the lower echelons of government service, esp. the postal services and the railways. Today their position is difficult, their attachment to European culture, language, and religion placing them to a large extent outside Hindu society. The term 'Anglo-Indian', formerly often used for the British administrators and Army of long residence in India, is now coming to mean Eurasian.

Europa. In classical mythology, a beautiful Phoenician girl whom ◊ *Zeus* approached in the form of an unusually tame bull; Europa climbed on his back and he swam with her to Crete, where she bore him ◊ *Minos* and Rhadamanthus (two of the judges of ◊ *Hades*). Europe is said to be named after her.

European Coal and Steel Community. France, Italy, W. Germany, and the three Benelux countries established a common market for coal and steel in 1952, removing tariff and quota restrictions; the supervisory institutions of ECSC are not subordinate to the national governments, and in many respects they served as the model for the supranational institutional framework of the Common Market. The U.K. did not attempt to join ECSC.

European Economic Community. Came into being 1957, when France, Italy, W. Germany, Belgium, Holland, and Luxemburg (the 'Six') signed the Treaty of Rome which created the Common Market. Main features are: (1) A Customs Union; by 1966 all internal customs tariffs will be eliminated. (2) Unification of import tariffs; eventually there will be a single list of import duties. (3) Economic policy and commercial law will be harmonized. (4) Restrictions on the movement of capital and workers will be progressively reduced. (5) A common agricultural policy will be adopted; government intervention to be through central marketing boards for each product (but many difficulties remain to be overcome).

The institutions of the Common Market are: (1) *The Commission:* proposes Community policy and day to day administra-

tive authority. (2) *The Council of Ministers:* decides Community policy and has final executive responsibility. (3) *The Assembly:* appointed by the parliaments of the member states, with few powers at present, but can debate and recommend. (4) *A Court of Justice.* These institutions are not fully 'supranational', since decisions must be unanimous; but the distant objective of the Treaty of Rome is political unity and a United States of Europe.

Britain and some other European countries (◊ *European Free Trade Association*) advocated a looser and wider free-trade area. After the signature of the Rome Treaty, attempts to associate EFTA with EEC failed in 1958. Subsequently Britain negotiated to become a full member of EEC but though favoured by most of the members her application foundered 1962 on the opposition of General de Gaulle.

European Free Trade Association. Customs union and trading bloc formed by Sweden, Norway, Denmark, Austria, Switzerland, Portugal, and U.K. in 1960; also known as 'the Seven'. The EFTA agreement provides for progressive reduction of tariffs and quota restrictions between the members but does not envisage a single uniform tariff or operate under a supranational authority. The proposal that the EFTA should join the Common Market was rejected by France in 1962.

Europium ◊ *Lanthanides.*

Eurydice ◊ *Orpheus.*

Eurystheus ◊ *Cerberus.*

Eustatic Movements. Periodic worldwide rises and falls in the level of the sea, caused by changes in the amount of water in the oceans; during e.g. the Pleistocene ◊ *Ice Age* much water evaporated from the sea and fell on the land as snow, and as it piled up the level of the oceans fell. If the Greenland and Antarctica ice-caps melted there would be a eustatic rise of at least 20 fathoms, all the coastal lowlands of the world would be submerged, and one third of the world's population would be homeless. ◊ *Isostasy.*

Euthanasia. Deliberate termination of the life of a person suffering from a painful or severely disabling illness bound to be fatal. A Bill to legalize voluntary euthanasia was introduced in the House of Commons 1936; the general principle received approval, but the elaborate safeguards proposed, and the fear of the possibility of later abandonment of the voluntary principle, and of its being extended to include the senile and the mentally defective, led to its withdrawal. Information on the number of those suffering from intractable pain and wishing for euthanasia is lacking.

Evaporation. The process by which a liquid passes into the vaporous or gaseous state, not necessarily at ◊ *boiling point*; some liquids, e.g. ether, evaporate more rapidly than others, e.g. oil, and are said to be more volatile. The rate of evaporation increases with the temperature.

Everyman. The 15th-cent. typical and best-known English ◊ *morality play*; when summoned by Death, Everyman is abandoned by Fellowship, Beauty, Strength, his five wits, and all his other personified qualities except Good Deeds, who alone stays with him to the end.

Evesham. 1265. Final battle of the Barons War, between the forces of Simon de Montfort (the younger) – framer of the 'Mad' Parliament's Provisions of Oxford 1258 and of Westminster 1259, by which the king had agreed to govern under advice from a representative council – and those of Henry III, led by Prince Edward (later Edward I). De Montfort and his leading supporters were slaughtered; but the Provisions were reaffirmed in the Statute of Marlborough 1267 and by the 'Model' Parliament 1295; they laid the foundations of constitutional government, as ◊ *Magna Carta* in 1215 had laid those of the rule of law.

Evidence. Testimony given in a court of law; all relevant facts of a case must be proved by evidence properly given (normally by a witness under oath), except facts of which the court 'takes judicial notice' (i.e. matters of such common knowledge that everyone may be deemed to know them), and, in civil cases, facts admitted by the opposing party. A witness is asked questions ('examination-in-chief') by the party calling him, or by that party's counsel, then by the other side ('cross-examination') in order to establish whether he really knows the facts or is prejudiced or lying, and to obtain further evidence; he may then be re-examined by the party calling him, on matters arising from the cross-examination. During examination-in-chief and re-examination the advocate must not ask 'leading ques-

tions' (so framed as to suggest what answer is required). There are detailed rules governing the admissibility of evidence, e.g. normally a witness must speak from his own knowledge and not merely from hearsay. ◊ *Judges Rules, Trial.*

Evil Eye. ◊ *Witchcraft and Sorcery.*

Evolution. Concept of a process by which living things have developed, and are still developing, by gradual continuous changes from earlier forms, as opposed to the belief in special creation of immutable individual species. The present-day fauna and flora of the world are very different from those of 500 m. or 100 m. or even 10 m. years ago. Thus 500 m. years ago the only vertebrate animals were fish, and none of them had yet left an aquatic habitat for the land; 100 m. years ago, in addition to fish, there were amphibians, reptiles, birds, and mammals, but none of the mammals closely resembled the familiar ones of today, and none even remotely resembled man; 10 m. years ago monkeys and apes of many kinds existed, but there were no true men. Yet all living things, including man, are lineal descendants of things then alive, and ultimately of primordial protoplasmic matter. The concept of the mutability of species was suggested from about the 16th cent. onwards, by such philosophers as Bacon and Descartes; by the 19th cent. the sciences of ◊ *embryology*, taxonomy, and comparative anatomy had provided most of the arguments in support of a theory of evolution. These arguments were synthesized by Charles Darwin and Alfred Russel Wallace, and the case was presented in 1859, when Darwin published *The Origin of Species.* The fact of evolution was later confirmed by developments in ◊ *palaeontology* and by increasing knowledge of the mechanism of inheritance; it is now accepted by all competent to assess the evidence. Opinions still differ, however, about the way in which it occurs. The great majority of evolutionists follow Darwin in proposing ◊ *natural selection* as the major agent of evolutionary change, and believe that the variants upon which selection operates are provided by the genetic material carried on the ◊ *chromosomes* of the body cells, and by sudden ◊ *mutations* of this material. Other views, e.g. of the inheritance of ◊ *acquired characteristics* (neo-Lamarckism) or of innate evolutionary trends (orthogenesis), have not yet received support from experimental findings.

CONVERGENT EVOLUTION: The process by which some animals, in response to similar external conditions or stimuli, develop particular features or organs closely resembling those of other animals of totally different descent, e.g. the two groups of animals in which the eye is best developed are the ◊ vertebrates and the invertebrate cephalopods ◊ squid, octopus, which could not have had a common ancestor with this feature. ◊ Adaptation, Darwinism, Mendelism.

Examination. A testing process as a result of which some but not all are permitted to practise a trade or profession or to register as members of a school or institution, or are awarded a post, promotion (e.g. in the civil service), or honour. The Chinese invented examinations in the form of written answers to a series of questions 2000 years ago, to select administrators. An examination may include a practical side, as in driving tests. One purpose of examinations is to ensure the attainment of a standard of competence, the other is competitive selection. As societies become more democratic and egalitarian, entry to the professions depends more on competence and less on wealth or social advantages; thus the importance of examinations continually grows, as does the number of candidates, and the problem of devising effective and equitable examination methods has become increasingly difficult, as the British controversy over the 11-plus examination has shown. In the American educational system, where a large proportion of the pupils automatically proceed to a university or college, examinations do not weigh heavily on students until college level, where there is a high fall-out of first-year students. In U.S.S.R. the school-leaving examinations are exceedingly important, as are those within the universities. In England and Wales the whole system is punctuated by important examinations. The 11-plus examination decides for most children the type of secondary school they will attend; in the independent sector the corresponding Common Entrance examination, taken at about 13, serves a similar purpose. At 16 nearly all pupils in grammar schools take the General Certificate of Education at ordinary level; at 18 those who have remained at school take it at advanced level. The outcome of these examinations determines whether students are permitted to proceed to universities or enter the professions. At the higher-education level there are further examinations leading to degrees and diplomas, and also National Certificates in scientific and technological subjects, while many voluntary bodies e.g. the Royal Society of Arts, the College of Preceptors, etc. examine in a wide range of subjects, and almost every professional association e.g. the Royal Institute of Chemistry, the Pharmaceutical Society, etc. has examination requirements for candidate members. Parallel situations exist in most industrialized countries. In Germany the *Abitur* examination and in France the *baccalauréat* guarantee successful completion of secondary education. ◊ Academic Degree.

Excalibur. In ◊ Arthurian legend, Arthur's magic sword, which he obtained by drawing it from a stone in which it had been magically fixed, thus proving his right to be king, as against 200 knights who had made unsuccessful attempts; it had the power of preserving the wearer against loss of blood from wounds. When Arthur was dying, by his command it was cast into a lake and reclaimed by the 'lady of the lake' who is said to have made it.

Exchange Control ◊ Foreign Exchange.

Exclusion Bill. 1679. Alarmed by the intensified persecution of the ◊ Huguenots in France and the continued official flouting of the ◊ penal laws and ◊ Test Act, the newly-elected House of Commons introduced a Bill to exclude the Roman Catholic Duke of York from the succession. After unprecedentedly bitter and vehement debates esp. in the Lords, the exclusionists (Shaftesbury) were defeated by the middle-way limitationists (Halifax). ◊ Glorious Revolution, Popish Plot.

Exclusive Brethren ◊ Plymouth Brethren.

Excommunication. Formal exclusion of a church member from the rights and privileges of his membership, especially from the sacraments. In the Roman Catholic and Anglican Churches bishops only can (though in the latter they never now do) pass sentence of excommunication. In Great Britain it formerly involved civil penalties also. It is now seldom imposed except for heresy or schism.

Excretion. The disposal of the waste products of ◊ *metabolism*, essential for the health of the organism, by methods which depend on its size, environment, and metabolic rate. Small aquatic animals e.g. ◊ *protozoa* and ◊ *hydra* simply diffuse waste into the surrounding water, but larger animals with a higher metabolic rate require special excretory organs. The terrestrial ◊ *insects* limit water-loss by excreting insoluble urates; ◊ *vertebrates* have a kidney which is associated with the intestine only at the rectal termination; fish, amphibia, birds, and reptiles have a common urino-genital-defaecatory sac (cloaca). In man, excretion is by means of the skin (which eliminates water), the lungs (CO_2), the kidneys (urine), and the large intestine (solid wastes). ◊ *Digestion*.

Exfoliation. Kind of ◊ *weathering* which disintegrates crystalline rocks e.g. granite in hot deserts; exposed to a very hot sun, the surface expands slightly more than the interior a few inches down, and there is an outward pull. Curved layers or shells of crystalline rocks (which in a more temperate climate would be most resistant to weathering) readily peel off, sharp edges disappear from the landscapes, slopes become rounded, and peaks are dome-shaped. ◊ *Erosion*.

Exhibitionism. In general, behaving in a way that will attract attention; in ◊ *psychiatry*, a disorder in which sexual gratification is obtained by exposing the genitalia. The condition is most characteristic of men inhibited in other forms of sexual activity and having unstable or inadequate personalities.

Existentialism. Diverse modern philosophies and theologies, sharing little more than an attitude, including hostility to deterministic views of man, a concern with personal experiences of individuals rather than general theories, a distrust of reason as a guide, and a confidence that men do make perfectly free choices; existentialist philosophers include Kierkegaard, Jaspers, Heidegger, and Sartre. The label existentialism derives from two sources; (1) German philosophers after 1918 spoke of men 'existing' in the peculiar sense that they are not cogs in a system or subject to scientific laws, but rather the makers of their destinies; (2) more important, Sartre claims that for men 'existence precedes essence' – first they exist, and then they choose their own essence or nature, which is not laid down in advance. Sartre also holds that perfect

freedom and an absence of guiding rules make for total individual responsibility, which issues in *angoisse* (anxiety caused by the burden of choice) or else in 'bad faith', a refusal to admit responsibility.

Exobiology. Consideration of the possibilities and likely forms of life outside the earth. So far, the only evidence that such life may exist was reported in 1961 by Claus and Nagy, who claim to have found microscopic-sized particles, resembling fossil algae, in meteorites.

Exogamy. Rule whereby a man may marry only a woman from a kin group, clan, etc. other than his own (◊ *Kinship*). Clan exogamy in particular is widespread among primitive peoples; an important consequence of the rule is the creation of ties of kinship through marriage between various social groups.

ENDOGAMY: A rarer rule whereby a man must marry a woman of his own group; found esp. in ◊ *caste* systems e.g. in India.

Exothermic (Endothermic) ◊ *Compound*.

Explosives. Materials which by rapid chemical reaction release large amounts of energy in a rapid burst; used extensively in mining and quarrying as well as for military purposes. Most explosives need a detonator to start the reaction. The earliest, gunpowder (a mixture of saltpetre, charcoal, and sulphur), has been largely superseded by nitrogen compounds e.g. trinitrotoluene (TNT) and gelignite, of much greater power. Nitroglycerin absorbed in kieselguhr (◊ *Diatoms*) gives dynamite, first made by Nobel 1867. Great as is the power of modern explosives, it is dwarfed by the nuclear explosions of the ◊ *atom bomb*.

Expressionism. Like ◊ *Cubism*, an early 20th-cent. artistic style in reaction against 19th-cent. naturalism and esp. against ◊ *Impressionism*, deriving inspiration from Van Gogh and Gauguin and concerned with the representation of emotion. The movement was most successful in Germany and Scandinavia, and the most important figure was the Norwegian Edvard Munch, whose neurasthenic paintings and lithographs convey emotions of horror, pain, and loneliness and form the pictorial counterpart to the plays of his friend Strindberg, who was a painter also. The ◊ *Blaue Reiter* group, James Ensor, Emil Nolde, Kokoschka, Rouault, and Soutine are among other notable Expressionists. In literature there was an analogous movement. Some Expressionist devices are found in late 19th and early 20th-cent. drama, e.g. Frank Wedekind's *Frühlings Erwachen* and August Strindberg's *Dream Play* and *Ghost Sonata*, but the movement first became recognized as such shortly before the First World War, and flourished about 1915–25, influencing the German poet Johannes Becher and playwrights Georg Kaiser and Ernst Toller, the Austrians Franz Werfel in his early poetry and Franz Kafka in his novels, the American playwrights Eugene O'Neill and Elmer Rice, and the Irish playwright Sean O'Casey in his later work.

Extra-sensory Perception (E.S.P.). Term invented by the parapsychological investigator J. B. Rhine to include such phenomena as telepathy (direct communication from one mind to another) and clairvoyance (direct knowledge obtained without the use of the senses), for the occasional occurrence of which there appears to be some evidence; experimental investigation has taken the form chiefly of card-guessing under varying conditions. ⟡ *Psychical Research.*

Extravert, Introvert. The two human types postulated by Jung; the extravert is predominantly guided by his mind and his senses, and characteristically interested in people and events, whereas the introvert is governed by his feelings and intuitions, which do more to shape his judgements than do his rational processes, and consequently he tends to be more concerned with himself than an extravert does. According to Jung, however, the extravert is unconsciously introverted and vice versa, the ⟡ *unconscious mind* compensating for the characteristics missing in the conscious mind.

Eye. Organ that focuses light from external objects on a screen (retina), to produce distinctive responses that are transmitted to the brain for interpretation. Behind a transparent window (cornea) in the tough outer covering (sclera) of the human eye is a lens, whose curvature and hence focal length can be varied by muscles. This lens is curtained in front by the iris, which has as its centre a circular opening (pupil) able to enlarge or contract in order to regulate the amount of light passing through the lens to the retina. The

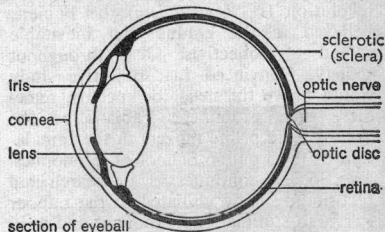

iris — cornea — lens — section of eyeball — sclerotic (sclera) — optic nerve — optic disc — retina

retina is composed of light-sensitive cells, from each of which nerve fibres lead to the optic disc, where they unite to form the optic nerve. The optic nerves from both eyes join at the base of the brain, where some fibres from the two retinas cross to the opposite sides and so link both eyes to both sides of the brain. Structural abnormalities of the eye impair the efficiency of the optical system, mainly by errors of refraction in focusing, e.g. shortsightedness results from a long eyeball focusing in front of the retina instead of on it, and longsightedness from a short eyeball focusing behind the retina. ⟡ *Optics, Vision.*

F

Fabian Society. Founded 1884 by a small group of socialists; named after Fabius, the Roman general famous for slow but sure strategy. Early Fabians e.g. George Bernard Shaw, Annie Besant, H. G. Wells, R. H. Tawney, and Sidney and Beatrice Webb contributed greatly to building the ◊ *Labour Party*. Rejecting the marxist concept of the class struggle and violent revolution (◊ *Revisionism*) the Fabians believed in the gradual but inevitable spread of collectivist ideas throughout society. Convinced that objective study would prove the need for socialist remedies, such prominent Fabians as the Webbs were prime movers in the foundation of the London School of Economics. The Society continues as a research and fact-finding body affiliated to the Labour Party, to stimulate new thought and writing among democratic socialists.

Fable. Now usually a brief prose or verse story designed to convey a moral or lesson; the characters are most often beasts, but may be gods, men, or inanimate objects. The earliest fables are those of Greece and the Orient; by the mid 5th cent. B.C. Greek fables (which have mainly come down through late medieval collections) had become associated with the semi-mythical Aesop. The principal sources are Sanskrit beast-fables transmitted via Persian and Arabic; more modern fables include medieval 'Ysopets' (versions of Aesop), Henryson's late 15th-cent. *Morall Fabillis*, the 12th to 15th cent. Reynard the Fox stories, and La Fontaine's *Fables Choisies* 1668–94 in 12 vols. Later fabulists include John Gay, Gotthold Lessing, Ivan Krylov, and more recently James Thurber.

Facsimile Transmission. Method of converting graphic material into electrical signals, which are reconverted into copies of the original. The original is usually placed on a rotating drum and 'scanned' by a thin pencil of light. The reflected ray is thrown on to a photocell, which converts the fluctuations in brightness into corresponding electric signals. The receiver, which may be on the spot or at the other end of a long telephone or radio link, includes a drum rotating syn-chronously with the sending drum and carries photosensitive paper on which a copy of the original is built up in sympathy with the transmitted signals. Although much slower than television, the system is very useful for long-distance transmission of still pictures, because it does not require such complex and expensive equipment.

Factory Acts. Legislation to remedy the many evils to which the ◊ *Industrial Revolution* had led in the absence of any national laws regulating working conditions. Various Acts were passed between 1802 and 1830, but they were not effective. Lord Shaftesbury's Act of 1833 banned the employment of children under 9 and limited the hours of work for those up to 18. The Act of 1844 limited women's hours to twelve a day. A series of other Acts gradually improved conditions of employment. The minimum age for employing children was raised to 12 in 1901 and 14 in 1920.

Faience. ◊ *Pottery* coated with a glaze rendered opaque by the addition of tin oxide; from Faenza, Italy, where tin-glazed wares have been produced since the 15th cent. Italian tin-glazed pottery is more usually called majolica, however, while that made in 17th-cent. Holland and England is known as delft. The term faience is normally reserved for French and German wares. ◊ *Ceramics, Porcelain.*

Fairy Rings. Circles, often several yards in diameter, of particularly green or lush grass, ◊ *toadstools*, or both; they usually begin with a fungus ◊ *spore* or spores, producing mycelium which grows outwards in all directions and may eventually form fruiting bodies. The breakdown of organic matter in the soil may supply extra nutrients and affect the growth of the grass.

Fairy-tale. Orally transmitted folk tale common throughout Europe, usually dealing with the fortunes of a hero or heroine and involving some degree of supernatural intervention e.g. metamorphosis or other enchantment; sometimes the hero or heroine must pass a series of tests in order to reach the desired goal, and may be aided by good supernatural creatures and hindered by bad. Its origin is uncertain: the widespread dispersion of similar or identical themes, and at the same time their numerous mutations and variations, might suggest an origin in common psychological drives; but fairy-tales are distinct from ◊ *mythology*, and in many cases may well derive from individually-invented stories. The brothers Wilhelm and Jacob Grimm were the first to collect traditional fairy-tales, in their *Kinder und Haus-Märchen* 1812 ff. The work of the Grimms must be distinguished from that of Charles Perrault 1628–1703, whose *Contes de ma mère l'oye* 1697 were original artistic creations (though based on folk material), and include 18 fairy-tales e.g. Cinderella, Little Red Riding-hood, Puss in Boots. Similarly the fairy-tales of Hans Christian Andersen 1805–75 e.g. *The Ugly Duckling, The Little Red Shoes, The Emperor's New Clothes* are not folk tales but original stories revealing the author's individual strain of imagination and combining pathos, masochism, and morality.

Falangist Party. *Falange Española*; founded 1933 by Primo de Rivera, son of the former dictator, emphasizing Spain's need for unity, to be achieved by unquestioning obedience to a centralized and authoritarian government; it claimed to be a militia, and urged the abolition of all parties. Most of its support came from the right, but it advocated some measures of anti-capitalist reform. It became the sole political organization under General Franco's regime. ◊ *Spain*.

Falcon. Long-winged ◊ *hawk*; the smallest of the birds of prey. They are shy, and nest in high trees or crags. Some species are world-wide. Beautiful birds, courageous, and powerful for their small size, they fly extremely fast, with rapid wing-beats, and kill their prey (birds and small animals) by 'stooping' on to them almost vertically at terrific speed. They have been trained by falconers since 2000 B.C. but easily revert to the wild state. The kestrel, peregrine, and hobby are also falcons.

Falkirk. 1298. Battle in which the Scots under William Wallace were defeated by Edward I, which opened the way for his conquest of Scotland; completed in 1305 with the execution of Wallace, it was undone by the defeat of Edward II at ◊ *Bannockburn*.

Falkland Islands. 1914. Important naval action in the ◊ *First World War*. Admiral Graf von Spee approached the Falkland Islands without realizing that the survivors of the British squadron which he had recently beaten at Coronel had been reinforced by the battle cruisers *Invincible* and *Inflexible*, which pursued and sank the German armoured cruisers *Scharnhorst* and *Gneisenau*, while the British armoured cruisers sank two of the German light cruisers. The battle eliminated German sea power from the S. Atlantic.

Fallout. The radioactive products from nuclear explosions or products which escape from nuclear power-plants. The amount of radioactive material in the atmosphere could be increased to levels of universal danger by excessive fallout, hence the general concern to put a limit to ◊ *nuclear tests*. ◊◊ *Radiation Sickness, Radiobiology*.

Family. The family group exists in all known human societies; in most primitive societies, the basic unit is larger than the single family of husband, wife, and their children. More usual is the joint family, consisting of several generations of related men with their wives and children, which persists over many generations and normally is not only a domestic unit but one with important economic, political, and religious functions. As cultures vary, so do family forms, though the incest taboo appears to be universal as a regulation of sexual conduct. The family group may be monogamous, polyandrous, or polygynous (◊ *Polygamy*) (with variations within each category). In European societies, the typical family unit has only recently become that of husband, wife, and children living together, the break-up of larger groups being largely an effect of industrialization. The 1946 U.K. census showed a sharp fall in family size: from 5.8 children per couple married in the 1870s to 2.2 for those married in the 1920s. ◊◊ *Biological Classification*.

Family Planning ◊ *Birth Control*.

Farce. Originally a popular medieval form, used to 'interlard' (< Fr. *farcir*, to stuff) mystery plays with crude satirical scenes; the players may have preserved the traditions of ancient Roman mimes. Now a form of dramatic entertainment securing the maximum comic effect by sacrificing probability and placing characters in extreme and embarrassing situations. Good farce-writing demands both inventiveness and supreme technical skill; the form has impeccable ancestry, e.g. Shakespeare's *Comedy of Errors* is a farce in which the situations come from Plautus. In 18th and 19th-cent. England farces were afterpieces which hilariously concluded an evening's entertainment; in late 19th-cent. London the full-length closely plotted productions of e.g. Labiche and Feydeau were given the genre label 'French farce' (with implications of 'naughtiness' and 'gay Paree'), and 20th cent. English descendants have been the 'Aldwych farce' of the 1920s and 1930s and the 'Whitehall farce' of the 1940s and 1950s. ⟡ *Comedy*.

Farming ⟡ *Agriculture*.

Faro. A gambling game using a full pack of cards, which are shuffled and placed face up in a special box: a cloth in front of the players has the 13 cards of the spade suit enamelled on it, and bets are placed for any particular number (of any suit) to win or to lose ('coppering', as in this case a copper coin is placed on the stake). The dealer removes the first card (joker) which is not used: the second card loses i.e. the bank collects bets placed for that card to win and pays those placed for it to lose, and the third card wins. This constitutes a turn, and the game continues in this way, every two cards making up the turn. The last card is called 'hock' and does not count. Bets on other numbers are not touched and can remain for subsequent turns.

Fascism. The authoritarian philosophy associated with the regime of Mussolini, under which Italy was governed 1922–43, the principal theoretical exponents being Rocco and Gentile. It asserted the absolute supremacy of the nation-state in the fields of morality and law, identified the will of the state with that of its ruler the Duce, and urged that the state be corporately organized (⟡ *Corporative State*) to maximize social harmony and national discipline; whilst developed as the antithesis to communism, in practice fascism differed little in methods from other dictatorial regimes, though it was unlike communism in its unconcealed belief in the 'leadership' principle, in its violent nationalism and ⟡ *antisemitism*, and in its exaltation of war rather than revolution as a means of national expansion. The leading fascist regimes in Germany (⟡ *Nazism*) and Italy disintegrated in defeat, but governments of somewhat similar type survive in Spain (⟡ *Falangist Party*) and Portugal.

Fat. One of the two animal energy stores, the other being the starch-like ⟡ *carbohydrate* glycogen. Fat, a compound of the alcohol glycerol with any of a number of fatty acids, which may be further combined with complex organic molecules, is deposited in adipose cells, apparently incapable of division, so that the obese adult has more fat in the same number of fat cells he possessed as a youth. The tendency to ⟡ *obesity* is inherited through the female line, and is associated with an impaired ability to move fat from cells to liver. It may also result from prolonged consumption of food in excess of the body's energy requirements. Normally adipose tissue is in a dynamic state of fat breakdown, exchange, and synthesis. Fat also plays a part in insulation and in body structure.

Fates. In Greek and Roman mythology, three goddesses (the Moirai, the Parcae), daughters of Erebus and Nox, governing the destinies of men and gods; Clotho (the youngest) held a distaff, presiding over the moment of birth, Lachesis had a spindle, to spin the thread of life and fix its length, and Atropos (the eldest) had shears, to cut the thread at the moment of death. There are three Fates in Scandinavian legend also, the Norns.

Fatigue of Materials. Under repeated load-reversals, materials and esp. metals suffer structural changes, which weaken them e.g. wire breaks when repeatedly bent backwards and forwards. Fatigue-failure of metals came into prominence with increasing aircraft speeds, the most spectacular example being the series of Comet accidents in 1954; fractures occurred in the pressurized cabins from being subjected to repeated load-reversals as the aircraft climbed and descended. Fatigue effects can be delayed by the avoidance of sharp angles in component design and by giving all parts a high surface finish.

Fault. Vertical or horizontal fracture or break in strata, where rocks on one side of the break have been displaced relatively to those on the other; a block of the earth's crust sinking between two parallel normal faults forms a ⟡ *rift valley* (graben), a block being raised between two faults forms a block mountain (horst). ◇ *Breccia, Earthquakes.*

Faust. The legend belongs to a long-standing Christian concern over 'forbidden knowledge', going back to the Biblical story of the Fall and perpetuated by Paul's 'take heed lest any man spoil you through philosophy and vain deceit'; it reflects clerical uneasiness as to the compatibility of knowledge and piety, and is associated with anti-heresy crusades and the belief in ◇ *magic* and ◇ *witchcraft*, which re-emerged strongly in the 16th cent. side by side with the rapid spread of printing and the rise of the ◇ *Reformation* anticlerical movements and then the ◇ *Counter-Reformation.*

Stories about a German scholar, probably Dr Georg Faust (*c.* 1480–1540), combined perhaps with the 6th-cent. legend of the Devil's pact with Theophilus of Syracuse, or the early Christian tradition of the Gnostic Simon Magnus performing miracles with the Devil's help, inspired the first written form of the myth, the *Historia von Dr Johann Fausten* by Johann Spiess 1587, a cautionary tale of the amazing life and horrible death of a wicked necromancer who had gained his magical powers by selling his soul to the Devil.

The 'Faustbuch' was Marlowe's source for *Dr Faustus* 1589, a typical ◇ *Renaissance* tragedy of the aspiring mind; subsequently the theme was used both satirically and tragically by the ◇ *Sturm und Drang* writers, and with philosophical and psychological depth involving total human destiny by Goethe in his much re-written and elaborated *Faust* (Part I 1775–1808, Part II posthumously 1832). In later 19th-cent. European literature the Faust theme was interlocked with the Don Juan legend and Byronism; the most striking 20th-cent. use is Thomas Mann's *Doktor Faustus* 1947, a complex symbolic novel probing *inter alia* the meaning of history and paradoxes in an artist's nature and life.

Fauvism. < Fr. *fauves*, wild beasts; a group of painters (Matisse, Marquet, Derain, Vlaminck, and Rouault) who exhibited together in Paris 1905, their work being marked by violent distortions, flat patterns, and strident colour schemes. Dufy, Braque, and Metzinger joined them 1906–7, but the group fell apart 1908.

F.B.I. ◇ *Federal Bureau of Investigation, Federation of British Industries.*

Feargus ◇ *Deirdre.*

Federal Bureau of Investigation. Established 1908 as the Investigation Branch of the U.S. department of Justice, with headquarters in Washington; the present name was adopted 1935. It is a federal body (the only U.S. police organization operating on a nationwide and not a State basis), with two chief duties: general criminal investigation, and security operations (◇ *Secret Police*). In 1963, however, the assassination of President Kennedy had to be investigated by the specially appointed Warren Commission, since murder, even of the President, is not a federal but a State matter and the Texas state authorities had declared the case closed with the murder of the alleged assassin. The Director of the F.B.I. is J. Edgar Hoover, who has held this position since 1924.

Federal German Republic (FGR) ◇ *Germany (Federal Republic).*

Federalism. A federal system is one in which there is 'a division of powers between one general and several regional governments, each of which, in its own sphere, is coordinate with the others; each government must act directly on the people; each must be limited to its own sphere of action; and each must within that sphere, be independent of the others' (K. C. Wheare). With the tendency of central governments to undertake economic planning and to offer conditional grants to regional governments, the last two points no longer apply to typical federal unions e.g. U.S.A. or India. It is accepted that in modern conditions there is a drift of power to the federal government. In U.S.A. the protection of 'States Rights' has always been and continues to be a major issue in national politics.

Federal Securities and Exchange Commissions ◇ *Stock Exchange.*

Fédération Aéronautique Internationale. Created 1905, with Prince Roland Bonaparte as its first President; formed of national aero clubs, the U.K. member being the Royal Aero Club. It exercises international regulation of aviation sport, including racing and record-breaking, its *Code Sportif* laying down the rules for the establishment of official international and world records. It also encourages air touring.

Federation of British Industries. Founded 1916 as the national association of British industry; about 8000 firms are members, and it provides wide economic and industrial advisory services, often acting as spokesman for industry on matters of broad interest. British Overseas Fairs Ltd is a subsidiary, responsible for organizing overseas British trade fairs.

Feedback. In chemical engineering, the return of part of the physical output of a process to the input; also applied to a widely used electronic control method in which part of the output of a system is returned to the input, where it may be either added or subtracted. If increase of output in the system corresponds to increase of input, as in the amplifier, subtracting the returned fraction from the input results in self-correction or control of the process, i.e. negative feedback, e.g. the distortion produced in a sound amplifier may be greatly reduced by the judicious application of negative feedback. In positive feedback the returned part is added to the input, and a runaway or out-of-control process may result.

Felony. Indictable offences (crimes triable before a ◊ *jury*, not summarily before magistrates) are divided into misdemeanours, felonies, and ◊ *treason*; originally, felonies were those crimes (other than treason) for which the punishment was death and forfeiture of all property to the Crown. Forfeiture, already virtually obsolete, was abolished 1870, and the death penalty (◊ *Capital Punishment*) has been considerably restricted; but the distinction remains, and there are still procedural differences. Statutes creating new offences normally state whether they are misdemeanours or felonies.

Felspars. Large class of rock-forming silicates and the chief mineral in ◊ *igneous rocks*, constituting a large part of the earth's crust; on ◊ *weathering*, the chief important residue is clay. ◊ *Silica.*

Fen. An area of swamp vegetation with a high water level in the soil. In contrast to ◊ *bogs*, the water supply is alkaline and rich in nutrients and there is a rich growth of sedges, rushes (reeds), and shrubs; ◊ *peat* accumulates by the growth and decay of these plants. In pre-medieval times the fenlands of E. Anglia were covered by fen vegetation, and its remains are seen in the fen peat now exposed by drainage and cultivation.

Fencing. The use of swordplay for sport is shown in an Egyptian temple mural of about 1190 B.C., and fencing became popular in Renaissance Italy; a 15th-cent. fencing school existed in England, but the sport remained primarily a training for duelling and warfare until the 19th-cent. standardization of the three weapons foil, épée, and sabre. The foil (light enough to be used by women) has a blunted point and is extremely flexible, the épée is stiff and sharp-pointed, and the sabre is a flexible 'cut-and-thrust' weapon. With the foil the target is the torso, with the épée the whole body, and with the sabre the torso, head, and arms. Face-masks of wire mesh are worn, and padded clothing according to the weapons used; the 'piste' (fencing area) is 12 by 2 metres for foils and 24 by 2 metres for épée and sabre. Scoring is by 'hits' recorded by four judges and a president, whose task is now simplified by electric foils and épées; a light records every hit. Over 400 clubs in Britain form the Amateur Fencing Association, founded 1902; 60 countries are in the International Fencing Federation (founded 1913), and the sport has ◊ *Olympic Games* status.

Fenians. After the ◊ *Irish Famine* and the ◊ *American Civil War* Irish immigrants in U.S.A. formed a society to continue action to oppose the British Government in its Irish policies, and named it after the legendary Gaelic hero ◊ *Finn*. They sent funds and organizers to Ireland, but were out of touch with developments; their 1867 attempt at insurrection failed. ◊ *Home Rule, Sinn Fein.*

Fermentation. Process by which organic compounds are broken down or changed by the agency of living organisms or of ferments (◊ *Enzymes*) produced by them; carbon dioxide is a usual by-product. The common case is the production of alcohol in brewing or wine-making, where a starch mash or solution of sucrose is fermented by yeast, which in its rapid development provides the enzyme invertase (which produces simple hexose sugar) and also zymase (which then converts the sugars to ◊ *ethyl alcohol* and carbon dioxide); however, although alcohol has for centuries been made by fermentation processes, much of it is now produced from ethylene in the petrochemical industry. Different organisms can produce different products by fermentation of the same starting-material; in the First World War Dr Chaim Weizmann produced much-needed acetone by fermentation of starch with *Bacillus butylicus*, the useful n-butyl alcohol being also formed. In vinegar-making the organism *Mycoderma aceti* oxidizes alcohol to ◊ *acetic acid*; if the process were allowed to go further, the final products would be carbon dioxide and water.

Ferns. *Pteridophytes*; primitive vascular plants, usually with feathery fronds, which reproduce by means of dust-like ◊ *spores* borne either on the underside of mature fronds or on special fertile fronds. They range in size from the inch-long e.g. wall spleenwort to the large tropical tree-ferns, which may grow up to 50 ft high. Most ferns live in damp shady places, but a few tolerate dry conditions e.g. on walls; others are alpines and many are ◊ *epiphytes*. Some are evergreen, but the widespread ◊ *bracken* dies down in autumn.

Ferret. Short-legged long-bodied domesticated variant of the polecat, used to flush rats and rabbits from their burrows, about 20 in. long and related to the smaller 10-in. weasel; originally a native of Africa.

Fertilization. The union of ◊ *gametes*, an essential feature of sexual ◊ *reproduction*. The union of sperm and egg results in a fusion of the cell nuclei, which carry genetic material from both parents; the ◊ *genes* are brought together, and recombine to produce a new hybrid nucleus, whose descendants will control important aspects of the development of the individual. ◊◊ *Flower, Fruit, Meiosis, Mendelism, Pollen.*

Fertilizers. Intensive cultivation of the land leads to soil impoverishment; to remedy this fertilizers which provide nitrogen, phosphorus, and potassium are applied. These may be either organic or inorganic. Of the former farmyard manure is the commonest, though guano, fish and bone manure, sea weeds, and compost are also valuable. Chemical fertilizers are used in increasing volume: minerals e.g. calcium phosphate are important sources, as are also industrial by-products such as basic slag from the iron and steel industry. Many nitrogenous fertilizers are now synthesized, the nitrogen being extracted from the atmosphere. ◊ *Humus.*

Fetish. < Portuguese *feitiço*, charm. Any object (whether natural or something made specifically to house a spirit or deity) with mystical religious power.

FETISHISM: In psychiatry, pathological sexual attachment to an object (e.g. underwear, handbags, shoes) usually associated with the opposite sex.

Feud. Institutionalized form of warfare on the principle of vengeance for an offence, a typical response to homicide in primitive societies; not unregulated warfare, but more a jural process (peace being expected once the original offence is avenged), and therefore tends to occur between neighbours and kin, not between distant peoples.

VENDETTA: Similar, but with no expectation of ultimate settlement; the term is used in Corsica and S. Italy.

Feudalism. Form of social and military organization prevailing in W. Europe from the end of the empire of Charlemagne to the rise of strong monarchies, roughly from the 10th to the 16th cent., although it has its roots in the disruption of European society in the late Roman Empire, and in Germanic institutions. Fundamental to the system was the holding of land in fief from the king (in theory the owner of all land), through a series of vassals, each of whom, in the ceremony of homage and fealty, undertook to serve his lord, who in return promised his protection; the barons, who received large grants of land, in turn created lesser vassals in fee to them. Division of society into nobility, clergy, and peasantry was a further feature. Besides military services at home, the vassal owed other duties to his lord. In principle, on the death of a vassal the lord could re-allocate his holding; in practice, succession became hereditary. In England (◊ *Norman Conquest*) the primacy of royal power over the feudal barons was seldom challenged, or with only brief success, but in France the feudal lords were for long powerful rivals of the king. The feudal nobility had gradations based both on military obligations and on landholding; at the base was the squire (originally the servant of the knight); above him the knight (the heavily armed mounted fighting man, who was the basis of medieval armies), and above the knight were higher ranks varying in different countries – counts, dukes, earls, barons, etc. The decline of feudalism in W. Europe was due to a variety of causes, but especially to the disrupting effects of the

◊ *Black Death*, to the growth of a money economy and of free commercial towns, and to the consolidation of royal power. Villeins and serfs began to give place to a free tenantry, landholding knights to a court aristocracy, and feudal armies to paid professional armies. The decline in feudal landholding was marked in England but less so in France and Germany, where elements of feudalism persisted until the late 18th and the 19th centuries. ◊ *Commune, Domesday Book, Evesham, Magna Carta, Manorial System, Peasants Revolt.*

Fianna Fail. Irish, 'soldiers of destiny'. The political party created by De Valera after he had ordered the 1923 cease-fire (◊ *Anglo-Irish 'Troubles'*); supported by Irish republicans generally and esp. by town workers and small farmers hit by the economic ◊ *depression*. It won the 1932 election, framed a new constitution abolishing the 'Irish Free State', and remained in power until 1948, when after the British ratification of the ◊ *partition* of Ireland the opposition parties Fine Gael and Clann na Poblachta were returned and formed a coalition government; but in 1957 Fianna Fail was re-elected. In 1959 De Valera (b. 1882) retired from active politics and was elected President of the Republic; Sean Lemass became leader of Fianna Fail and P.M. (*Taoiseach*).

Field of the Cloth of Gold. 1520. The last great political pageant of the Middle Ages, an incident in the rivalry between England, France, and Spain. Charles V of Spain was elected head of the ◊ *Holy Roman Empire* in 1519; François I of France wished Henry VIII to unite with him against Charles; Cardinal Wolsey wished on his own behalf to be elected Pope and on Henry's to hold the balance of power. Wolsey invited François to meet Henry at Calais (then an English possession); the two kings entertained each other, and the Cardinal both of them, in the utmost sumptuousness, with great jousts and lavish feasting. But the apparent friendship was at once disrupted by the intrigues of both sides with Spain.

Fifth Republic ◊ *Fourth Republic*.

Fig. Fruits of various species of *Ficus*, but mostly from *Ficus carica*, cultivated from early times in warm regions. The fruit is complex and develops from a large number of fertilized flowers enclosed in a pear-shaped common receptacle which is soft when ripe and may be green, brown, or black. The ◊ *latex* of some tropical species of fig was a source of rubber e.g. *Ficus elastica*, the indiarubber fig.

Fiji ◊ *Melanesians*.

Filibuster. Effort by one or more members of the U.S. Senate to obstruct business by protracted speaking, a tactic possible because Senate rules do not limit the time one man can speak, nor do they require speeches to be relevant. Some have lasted over 24 hours. A filibuster can be broken only by a two-thirds majority on a closure vote.

Filigree. Ornaments fashioned from fine wires of gold or silver, first produced in ancient Egypt, popular among the Greeks and ◊ *Etruscans* for the decoration of ◊ *jewellery*. These ornaments were attached to a solid base; self-supporting metal lace of filigree dates to the 17th cent.

Finland. Area 130,165 sq. m. Pop. 4.6 m. Cap. Helsinki. Rel. 93 per cent Lutheran. A republic in the N E extremity of Scandinavia; the President, elected for six years, appoints a Cabinet responsible to the House of Representatives, a single chamber of 200 members. The minority communist party is represented in the House and powerful in the trade unions. About 9 per cent of the pop. are Swedish by origin and speak that language.

ECONOMY. About 70 per cent forest; paper pulp and timber form the bulk of the export trade, and there are some exports of metal, manufactured goods, and dairy products. Domestic needs in manufactures are largely met by local production; the standard of living is high, with good educational facilities at primary and secondary levels.

HISTORY. Early occupied by 8th-cent. settlers from the south; the indigenous Lapps were driven north, where they still live, and until 1808 Finland remained under Swedish rule. The extensive wars of Gustavus Adolphus II in the 17th cent. were a drain on the economy but prevented absorption by Russia, to whom, however, Finland was ceded in 1809. Under Russian suzerainty the country enjoyed a measure of autonomy, but a russification policy after 1899 aroused mounting resistance, and in 1917 Finland declared her independence, gaining recognition by the new Soviet government in 1920. During the Second World War she fought against U.S.S.R. twice, in 1939 to resist Soviet demands and in 1941 in an attempt to regain her losses. By the 1947 peace treaty she had to pay a heavy indemnity and to cede Karelia, which involved resettling about half a million refugees.

LANGUAGE. Finnish (Suomi), spoken by about 3 m. in Finland and by small communities in Norway and Sweden; belongs to the Finno-Ugrian division of the Ural-Altaic language family and is closely related to Estonian (◊ *Baltic States*) and Lapp, distantly to Magyar (◊ *Hungary*), and yet more distantly to the ◊ *Altaic languages* e.g. Turkish, Mongol, Manchu. There was no written Finnish until the Bible was translated in 1548. The nouns have no gender but many cases, 12 in full use though only two in the plural; the verbs have singular and plural and three persons as well as a separate impersonal form and a complex set of infinitives and participles.

Finn (Fionn). In Irish legend, a great hero, son of Cumhail (hence Finn M'Cool) and father of ◊ *Ossian*; the leader of the Fianna warrior-hunters (from whom the 19th-cent. ◊ *Fenians* and 20th-cent. ◊ *Fianna Fail* derived their names). Apprenticed to a bard (also named Finn), he caught the Salmon of Wisdom in the river Boyne, cooked it, burned his thumb on it, sucked his thumb, and thus acquired wisdom. The elopement of his betrothed wife Grania (Grainne) with his nephew Dermot (Diairmuid), and their wanderings through Ireland (a legend much resembling that of ◊ *Tristram* and Yseult), ending in Finn's killing of Dermot, are the subject of many folk tales.

Finno-Ugrian ◊ *Finland*.

Fiord. Inlet of the sea; originally a valley cut by a river, then moulded by a glacier, and later flooded by a rise in sea level. Usually long, narrow, and steep-sided, deepest some distance from the mouth, where often there is a threshold bar. Examples occur along the coast of Norway and W. Scotland.

Firearms. Small portable firearms appeared soon after the introduction of ◊ *gunpowder*. First came the arquebus and the musket, clumsy heavy muzzle-loaders fired from rests; these were succeeded by lighter muskets fired from the shoulder, whilst the flintlock replaced firing by match. The 'Brown Bess' musket was used by the British army 1690–1840. The rifled

barrel, with greater range and accuracy, came into use about 1800, but it was only with the invention of the percussion cap in 1807 by a Scottish clergyman that breech-loaders became feasible and made firing from a prone position possible. Not till the Prussian needle gun (a breech-loader) routed the Austrians in 1866 was the British army equipped with breech-loading weapons, and eventually with the Lee Metford magazine rifle. Pistols were essentially a cavalry firearm. Multiple-shot pistols were devised in the 17th cent. but the first reliable revolver was the American Colt, invented 1835, in which the barrel was fixed and a revolving cylinder carried successive rounds into the breech. Various types were evolved, including pistols with magazines similar to those of repeating rifles.

In the U.K. and most other countries the possession of firearms is subject to licence, but in U.S.A. it is a constitutional right of all citizens. ◊ *Ballistics*.

Firefly. A tropical member of the family *Elateridae*, the Click-beetles; the eggs, larvae, and adult exhibit ◊ *luminescence*, the last two emitting the light from three small areas on thorax and abdomen. This light-emission plays a part in mating; it does not involve heat loss, but is effected by the oxidation of the substrate luciferin by the ◊ *enzyme* luciferase.

Though not closely related to the firefly, the glow-worm has a similar luminescence mechanism. ◊ *Phosphorescence*.

Fire of London. 1666. Extensive fire, lasting five days, which destroyed almost the whole of the medieval city; consequently only a few early buildings survived. It cleansed the area of ◊ *plague* infection, and gave rise to the first town-planning Act of Parliament. ◊ *Queen Anne Style*.

First World War. 1914–18. Owing to the tense state of Europe resulting from the desire of the Slavs in ◊ *Austria-Hungary* for self-government and Germany's ambition to become a world power, and the consequent arms race, the declaration of war by Austria-Hungary on ◊ *Serbia* touched off a general conflict in which the Central Powers (Germany, Austria-Hungary, Bulgaria, Turkey) were aligned against the Allies (Russia, France, Britain, and later Japan, Italy, U.S.A.). On the western front, following the ◊ *Schlieffen Plan*, the Germans advanced rapidly into France, violating the neutrality of

Belgium, and almost took Paris, but were checked at the battle of the ◊ *Marne*. Deadlock followed; both sides dug in from Switzerland to the North Sea. Years of almost static trench warfare ensued, with calamitous casualties in all major offensives e.g. the 1916 British attack on the ◊ *Somme* and long struggles for *Verdun*, and the costly battles of the Passchendaele campaign in 1917; on the eastern front the Germans routed the ill-equipped Russian army at ◊ *Tannenberg*. Though the Russians managed to continue resistance, their effectiveness declined; after the Bolshevik Revolution they made peace at ◊ *Brest-Litovsk* in 1918. The Italian attack on Austria was halted in 1917 by their rout at ◊ *Caporetto*; their front had to be saved by French and British reinforcements. The Turks successfully resisted a 1915 British attempt to capture the Gallipoli peninsula (◊ *Dardanelles*) and the first attack on Mesopotamia, but were eventually driven out of the Arab lands. The German colonies in Africa and the Far East were cut off by British sea power and fell to the Allies.

The war at sea was of vital importance; the British navy established undisputed control of the surface of the seas, and after the battle of ◊ *Jutland* 1916, in which both sides suffered heavy losses, the German fleet remained within its own waters and the British were able to maintain an effective blockade of the Central Powers. The German policy of unrestricted sinking of Allied shipping by submarines (◊ *Lusitania*) nearly brought disaster to Britain in 1917, when the flow of food and raw materials was critically reduced; but submarine sinkings brought U.S.A. into the war on the Allied side in 1917.

The Germans made a series of air raids on the U.K. by ◊ *zeppelin* (which proved impractical) and later by bomber aircraft on a small scale. Aircraft at the front were mainly useful for reconnaissance, and though of increasing importance were not a decisive factor.

In France the stalemate of trench warfare continued in terrible conditions; the introduction of the ◊ *tank* in small numbers by the British was an advantage, but not sufficient to break the deadlock. Early in 1918, relieved of fighting on the Russian front, the Germans mounted another offensive, but this too was halted short of Paris, on the Marne; the Ger-

mans and their allies were exhausted, and the arrival of the fresh American troops turned the tide. In a series of battles the Allies drove the Germans back out of France and Belgium; before the fighting reached Germany itself, an Armistice was signed on 11 November 1918.

Casualties on all fronts were estimated at over 8 m. dead. The British dead (including those of the Commonwealth) were nearly one million. ◊ *Balkan Wars, Marne, Verdun, Versailles Treaty, Ypres.*

Fish. A large and varied group of ◊ *vertebrates* adapted to aquatic life. Their common features include (a) ◊ *gills*, the chief and in most fish the only organs of respiration (although one class, e.g. ◊ *lungfish*, have nostrils and lungs); (b) fins,

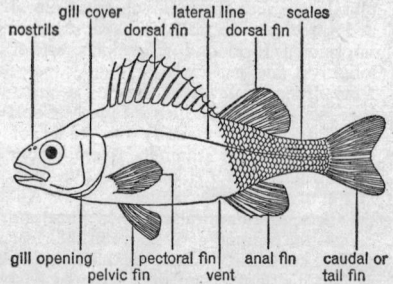

similar in purpose to the limbs of terrestrial vertebrates; (c) bony or cartilaginous skeletons e.g. esp. ◊ *shark*; (d) scales (although some fish possess these only in a very rudimentary form).

Fish are now divided into nine classes, several of which include only extinct species. Most extant fish belong to the *Actinopterygii* (characterized by a bony skeleton, delicate fin-rays, and external fertilization) or to the *Chondrichthyes* (e.g. sharks and rays) which have a cartilaginous skeleton. In the latter, fertilization is usually internal; some bear living young, although most lay eggs in tough cases, e.g. the 'mermaid's purse' of the dogfish. It is from the class of lunged fish that the terrestrial vertebrates evolved. (See also under names of species.)

Fishing. Practised with hook, spear, and net since earliest times (◊ *Angling*); the exploitation of the deep sea became possible only with the modern ◊ *trawler*. The most important fishing grounds are in the

N. Atlantic, where the fishing fleets of Britain, Norway, U.S.S.R. and Iceland are the most active; Japan has a large fishing industry in the N. Pacific. ◊ *Herring*, mackerel, and sprat swim near the surface, and are fished by set or drift nets (though herring is now also trawled). The flat fishes and ◊ *cod*, ◊ *haddock*, and whiting live near the bottom and are caught by trawls, seines, and long-lines. The open seas are free to all, but the coastal waters of each country are a preserve for their own national fishing industry: the extent of such ◊ *territorial waters* has become a subject of international dispute in recent years. Some 60,000 men are employed in the fishing industry of Gt Britain, and annual catch is worth around £20 m.

Fitzgerald-Lorenz Contraction. Hypothesis independently proposed by Fitzgerald 1893 and Lorenz 1895 to explain Michelson and Morley's failure to detect any motion of the earth relative to the ether. The hypothesis stated that a body moving through the ether at high velocity would be contracted in length in the direction of motion. A similar phenomenon is predicted by the modern theory of ◊ *relativity*.

Fives. A game in which two or four players hit a small hard ball against a wall or walls, with gloved hands in various types of court; principally Eton Fives (doubles) and Rugby Fives (doubles or singles).

Five Year Plan. 1928. The first of a series of economic State Plans (ending the ◊ *New Economic Policy*), introduced in U.S.S.R. by Stalin to speed industrialization and impose ◊ *collectivization of agriculture*. It was put into execution with great ruthlessness and lack of elasticity and caused untold suffering esp. to the peasantry, millions of whom died or were transported; it also resulted in the slaughter of millions of livestock. Declared 'fulfilled' in 1932, it was succeeded by other Five Year Plans. Since Stalin's death in 1953 the tendency has increasingly been to discard much of the centralization and rigidity of concept of the earlier plans. Other countries in the Soviet bloc adopted the State Plan system, as have also e.g. ◊ *Cuba, Egypt*. ◊◊ *Economic planning*.

Fixation. Sometimes termed 'affective fixation'; the continuation into later life,

in immature form, of an emotional attachment to a person or an object which existed in early childhood and was more appropriate to this earlier stage of development. In consequence, the person is unable to make new and normal attachments to other people, ideas, and things.

Fjord ◊ *Fiord*.

Flagellates ◊ *Protozoa*.

Flags of Convenience ◊ *Shipping*.

Flamboyant Style. < Fr. *flamboyant*, flaming; the last phase of French ◊ *Gothic architecture*, contemporary with the ◊ *Perpendicular style* in England, the name referring to the flame-like lines of the tracery; well illustrated at Rouen Cathedral.

Flanders ◊ *Belgium, Netherlands*.

Flax. *Linum usitatissimum*; the source of linen and linseed oil, an annual herb cultivated from prehistoric times. The fibres in the stem are tough and durable and are released from the softer tissues by retting. Linseed oil is extracted from the seeds and is a valuable ◊ *drying oil* extensively used in paint and varnish manufacture. The residual oil cake is used as cattle food.

Flea. Common name for small wingless laterally-compressed insects of the order *Siphonaptera* or *Aphaniptera*; the adults have well-developed legs enabling them to jump a horizontal distance of about 13 in. (50–100 times their own length) and mouthparts adapted for piercing and sucking; they feed exclusively on the blood of birds and mammals, and also transmit disease, e.g. bubonic plague and murine typhus, from rat to man. Their immature stages are non-parasitic and spent in the nest or habitation of the host; they have a typical insect life-cycle lasting 17 days or over a year according to species.

Fleet Air Arm. Carrier-borne and other airborne but entirely naval units; originally the naval wing of the Royal Flying Corps, but later the separate Royal Naval Air Service, taking its present name after the formation of the R.A.F. During the ◊ *Second World War* the R.A.F. Coastal Command was under ◊ *Admiralty* operational control.

Flemish ◊ *Belgium, Germanic Languages*.

Flemish Art. In the 15th cent. Flanders emerged as a centre of art second only to ◊ *Renaissance* Italy. The brothers Hubert and Jan van Eyck, whose masterpiece is the altarpiece of the Holy Lamb at Ghent, completed 1432, virtually created easel-painting, established the technique of oil painting, and developed a method of aerial or colour perspective parallel to the linear perspective of the contemporary Italians. Jan van Eyck's portraits attained a degree of intense realism never since surpassed. It was, however, Roger van der Weyden, working closer to the linear hard-edged medieval tradition, who created the Flemish style, followed by Hans Memling and Quentin Massys. Only Petrus Christus followed the style of the van Eycks closely. At the end of the 15th cent. Hieronymus Bosch's horrific visions typify the sense of doom that characterizes the end of the Middle Ages, and many similar grotesqueries are to be seen in the work of the greatest 16th-cent. Flemish painter, Pieter Brueghel, who was also, however, capable of earthy humour in his genre paintings and of a quiet serenity of vision in his ◊ *landscape paintings*. In the late 16th cent. Flemish art (◊ *Dutch Art*) was strongly influenced by Italian ◊ *Mannerism*. Early in the 17th cent. the versatile Rubens emerged as the greatest painter since Van Eyck and Brueghel, and his genius overshadows the subsequent history of the school; his portraits provided the point of departure for Van Dyck, his kermesse scenes for Teniers, his animal subjects for Snyders. In the 16th and 17th centuries Flanders produced the notable sculptors Giovanni Bologna, Adrien de Vries, François Duquesnoy, who worked mainly abroad. Flemish art languished in the 18th cent. but there was a revival in the second half of the 19th in the work of e.g. Henri de Brakelaer, Smits, Permeke, and James Ensor.

Flight. Probably the earliest practical consideration of the problem of mechanical flight is recorded in the numerous designs left by Leonardo da Vinci; but it was not till 1773 that the writings and experimental models of Sir George Cayley brought a technical engineering approach which eventually led to success. Both da Vinci and Cayley considered flight by moving wing (i.e. ◊ *helicopter*), by flapping wing (not achieved), and by fixed wing – the eventual choice. It was, however, by the lighter-than-air balloon (◊ *Airship*) that man first rose from the ground, when in 1783 Pilâtre de Rozier made an ascent in a Montgolfier hot-air balloon. Later, he went up with a pas-

senger and was carried across Paris at a height of 300 ft. The first controlled airship flight was made by Henri Giffard near Paris in 1852. Man-lifting kites and gliders led to the powered aeroplane and the first flights of the Wright Brothers. ◊ *Aviation*.

ANIMAL FLIGHT: In all flying vertebrates, the forelimb is modified to form a wing of large surface area, of feathers in birds and of stretched skin in bats, angled so that air currents support the animal; in insects the wing is a special chitinous outgrowth from the thorax. Birds are the most efficient and sustained fliers; flight can be soaring, gliding, or flapping, and the form of their wings varies according to the method most used. The speed of bird-flight varies from about 10 m.p.h. to the swift's 70–100 m.p.h. ◊ *Flying Fish*.

Flint. Crypto-crystalline rock, occurring most frequently in nodules but also in slabs and veins of diverse colours, in the bedding-planes or joints of the Upper Chalk. The outer part has turned white in a long slow ◊ *weathering* process, the inner part is opaque and varies in colour. Flints break with conchoidal fracture, giving sharp edges; for this reason, and because they fracture in a regular and controllable way, prehistoric man developed a wide variety of flint tools. They were made by chipping a nodule to shape (core tools), by working flakes or parallel-sided 'blades' struck from a nodule, by striking on an 'anvil', by chipping with a pebble, a bone, or a piece of wood, or simply by pressure with wood. In ◊ *Neolithic* times flints were often shaped by grinding and polishing. Before the introduction of metals (and for expendable implements until much later) flint was used for cutting, scraping, and piercing tools and weapons, e.g. knives, axes, saws, sickles, drills, arrowheads. In the ◊ *Palaeolithic* and ◊ *Mesolithic* periods flints are often the only artifacts to survive, and cultures and periods are defined by the different tool types and their techniques of manufacture. The finest flint tools come from the Solutrean phase of the Upper Palaeolithic, from pre-dynastic Egypt and Neolithic Scandinavia. Flint was usually obtained from surface nodules, but in Neolithic and possibly earlier times it was mined in Britain and NW Europe and a widespread trade was carried on in semi-worked objects. The craft still survives in the work of the flint knappers of Brandon, Suffolk.

Flintlock ◊ *Firearms.*

Flodden. 1513. Decisive defeat of the Scots by the English during the reign of Henry VIII. James IV of ◊ *Scotland* (Henry's brother-in-law), in alliance with the French, had crossed the border into Northumberland, but he was routed by the Earl of Surrey (2nd Duke of Norfolk) and his son (3rd Duke); 10,000 Scots, including James himself, were killed, and the threat from Scotland was at an end for the rest of Henry's reign.

Flood Plain. Part of a river valley over which the stream deposits alluvium when it floods. As the water spreads out over the plain, its velocity is reduced (its depth being much less over the plain than in the deep channel) and its load of silt is dropped. Most sediment is deposited near the banks; where flooding is most frequent, natural levees are raised on both sides and may reach 10 ft or more above the level of the flood plain of a great river e.g. the Mississippi. ◊ *Irrigation.*

Florence. A leading city of northern Italy which emerged as a republic in the 13th cent. rapidly enriching itself by trade and banking (hence 'florin'). Like other Italian towns, it came under the rule of one family, the Medici; it was an outstanding artistic and intellectual centre of the ◊ *Renaissance* under Lorenzo the Magnificent 1469–92, who acquired virtually despotic powers. The Medici were expelled in 1494, whereupon Savonarola, a religious reformer, restored the republic in 1498 and the Medici returned in 1512, to rule the city until 1737, although it was absorbed into the Grand Duchy of Tuscany. The dukes of Lorraine were in power 1737–1860.

Flower. A specialized reproductive structure characteristic of ◊ *angiosperms*; it consists of a simple axis, the receptacle (a) on which are borne typically four types of organs. The outermost type are sepals (b), which together form the calyx, which is often green and may protect the developing bud (e.g. roses, wallflowers). Within the sepals are the petals (c) collectively forming the corolla, which is often coloured and may secrete nectar. Petals may be separated from one another (buttercups), united into a tube at the

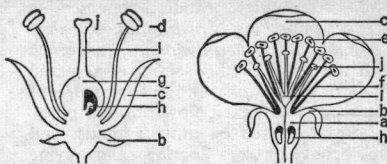

base only (jasmine), or more or less completely joined (foxgloves). The calyx and corolla together are called the perianth. In some flowers the petals and sepals are very similar in shape and colour, either coloured and petal-like (lilies, crocus, bluebell) or green and sepal-like (plantain, docks, nettle). Within the petals are the stamens (d) which are the male reproductive organs with ◊ *pollen* sacs called anthers (e) on filaments (f). The pollen grains within the sacs produce the sperm nuclei. The female reproductive organ (the ovary (g)) is in the centre of the flower and is formed of one or more carpels, small scales which are modified leaves (analogous to the cone scales in ◊ *gymnosperms*) and totally enclose the ovules (h) within which the female egg-cell develops. The carpels are elongated upwards to form the style (i) (a stalk which has a sticky end, the stigma (j), which catches the pollen during pollination). The pollen is either blown on to the stigma or brought by insects, esp. bees. Fertilization occurs when the sperm cells have passed down the style and one has united with the egg cell to form a zygote, which becomes the new embryo plant. A fertilized ovule becomes a seed and the ovary then develops into a ◊ *fruit.*

Not all flowers are complete with calyx, corolla, stamens, and ovary. Many flowers have no perianth and the reproductive structures are protected by small scale-leaves, e.g. in grasses, sedges, and catkins. Some plants have separate male and female flowers, which may be on different parts of the same plant (marrow, melon, hazel) or on different plants (willow, asparagus, holly). In some plants showy sterile flowers surround small fertile flowers in an inflorescence, making the whole more conspicuous for insect pollination (e.g. guelder rose, cornflower, sweet sultan, wild hydrangeas). In bougainvillea and poinsettias brightly coloured bracts surround the small flowers. ◊ *Leaf.*

Fluid Mechanics. Modern engineering science, embracing ◇ *hydraulics*, ◇ *hydrodynamics*, and ◇ *aerodynamics*, concerned with the study of fluids both at rest and in motion. It deals with the pressure of fluids on solids, their flow through pipes, the force exerted by moving fluids, and the behaviour of floating and flying objects. Fluid mechanics has important applications in ship and aircraft design, in hydraulic and chemical engineering, and in meteorology and oceanography; in design it makes use of scale models and simulated conditions and by a mathematical approach is able to predict the behaviour of the full-scale project accurately from that of the model. General laws are deduced from experimental results, and by the process of dimension analysis dimensionless ratios or 'numbers' are evolved which establish the relationship between the variable factors to be considered. ◇ *Mach Number.*

Fluorescence. The property of many substances of a particular molecular construction e.g. fluorspar (from which the name is derived) of being able, when a beam of light falls on them, themselves to radiate light, this light being of a different wavelength from that of the incident light and ceasing as soon as the incident beam is interrupted. ◇ *Phosphorescence* is a similar phenomenon, in which the radiation continues for some time after the incident light has been stopped. ◇ *Dyes* containing fluorescent material have an attention-catching brilliance which is e.g. used in tracing rafts at sea and in advertising signs. The same principle is used in the whitening agents employed in some domestic detergents. ◇ *Luminescence.*

Fluoridation of Water Supplies. Although an excess of fluoride can be harmful, it is now generally agreed that very small quantities (about one part per million) can be beneficial in preventing dental decay, esp. in young children (◇ *Dentistry*). Some natural waters already contain beneficial amounts of fluoride; where there is a deficiency, sodium fluoride or sodium fluorosilicate can be added, to raise the fluoride content to the permitted one part per million. Most foodstuffs, and some beverages e.g. beer and tea, contain minute amounts of fluoride, but children do not obtain enough from such sources. **Fluorides** ◇ *Halogens.*

Fluorine. ◇ *Halogens*; a pale yellow gas occurring principally in combination with calcium as the fluoride (◇ *Fluorspar*) first isolated by Moissan 1886, now produced on a large scale by electrolysis of molten potassium hydrogen fluoride at the carbon anode; the most electronegative of all the elements and a powerful oxidizing agent, its toxicity and high reactivity make it dangerous. Since 1940 it has been of increasing importance because large quantities are needed in the preparation of atomic explosives and in certain types of atomic reactors. The organic fluorocarbons (derived from ◇ *hydrocarbons*) are also of great significance, particularly for refrigeration ('freons'); polytetrafluoroethylene (PTFE) is a well-known ◇ *polymer*, and a chlorofluorocarbon is used as an aerosol propellent for the automatic spraying of perfumes, deodorants, and insecticides.

Fluorspar. Calcium fluoride; mineral found in metalliferous veins e.g. with tin in Cornwall and with lead in the Pennines, and used in enamelling, manufacturing opaque glass, as a flux in metallurgy, and in the nuclear energy industry.

Flute. 1. Generic name for various primitive and modern woodwind instruments without reeds.

2. The modern representative of this type, the transverse (side-blown) instrument standard in the orchestra and also used in ◇ *chamber music*, brass bands, etc. For ease of manipulation, keys began to be added to the flute from the mid 18th cent.

Of the same family are the piccolo (higher) and alto (sometimes miscalled bass) flutes.

Fly. Commonly the ◇ *housefly* (*Musca*) and the blowfly or bluebottle, *Calliphora*; but also a wide range of winged insects of different orders e.g. dragonfly, alder-fly, mayfly, ◇ *fruit-fly*, etc. The housefly and blowfly are members of the large order *Diptera*, with 80,000 species including gnats, midges, and ◇ *mosquitoes*; insects of the order typically have one pair of wings (the posterior pair being modified into balancing appendages), and the mouth-parts are in the form of a special sucking apparatus. The eggs develop through larval stages to pupae before the emergence of the adult; many of the *Diptera* are disease carriers, others are plant pests.

Flying Fish. Bony fish, belonging to several unrelated families, which can leave the water and become airborne for short periods; as they leave the water at speed, propelled by the tail, they spread their large fins and glide considerable distances. The fins do not beat as bird wings do. The purpose of the gliding seems to be escape from predators.

Flywheel. A heavy wheel, generally attached to rotating machinery, enabling the output speed of the machine to be kept within small limits of variation. The excess energy which the machine generates can be temporarily stored in the flywheel, in the form of kinetic energy, without a significant increase in its speed. Any falling-off in engine energy, which would otherwise cause a decrease of speed, is for a short time counteracted by the energy stored in the flywheel.

Focal Length ◊ *Optics.*

Fog. Dense mass of small water-drops (sometimes with smoke or dust-particles) formed on the earth's surface by the condensation of moisture in the atmosphere; resembles a cloud, and from above looks like a cloud layer. Technically, 'fog' means visibility of less than one km. When visibility is between one and two km. it is called 'mist' (caused by condensed water-particles) or 'haze' (caused by smoke or dust-particles). A fog may form at sea when warm air passes over the cooler water; land fogs are most frequent in autumn and winter, sea fogs in spring and summer.

SMOG: A fog heavily laden with smoke-particles. ◊ *Pollution, Weather.*

Föhn. Warm dry wind blowing down lee slopes of mountain ranges, esp. prevalent on northern slopes of the Alps; raises temperature by several degrees and quickly melts the snow. Also, e.g. on the E. side of the Rocky Mountains in N. America, a warm dry W. wind, the chinook.

Folk Literature. Traditional popular orally-transmitted literature consisting of songs, ◊ *ballads,* legends, stories, ◊ *fairytales,* plays, pseudo-historical anecdotes, and proverbs of pre-literate peoples, committed to writing only after their essential inspiration has ceased, either by a chance scribe or (more often and still later) by the scholar and antiquary. Folk literature began to claim the serious attention of European scholars in the 18th cent., but at first they did not always realize the difficulties of establishing the original texts and often 'improved' them in conformity with their own notions of literary propriety. Early collectors of folk literature were chiefly interested in ballads and songs; later came interest in legends and tales, both in collecting them from oral recital and in tracing them back to 'archetypal' themes. Folk literature survives into modern times chiefly in the remoter rural areas and particularly in the Celtic fringes of the British Isles. The great pioneer scholarly work of collecting and classifying English and Scottish ballads was that of the American Francis James Child, *English and Scottish Popular Ballads,* 5 vols. 1883–98. The more far-ranging task of tracking down and relating motifs in folk literature has been greatly helped by the monumental work of another American folklorist, Stith Thompson, *A Motif Index of Folk-Literature* 1932–7 and *The Folk Tale* 1946.

Folklore ◊ *Anthropology.*

Folk Music. Since the 19th cent. this has meant music apparently of anonymous composition, usually transmitted among a musically unlettered population, and thus subject to both variation and continuity. It is uncertain whether in general folksongs actually originate in this population or are adapted and modified from a literate composer's work. In Britain, the chief pioneer in the scholarly modern cultivation of folk music was Cecil Sharp 1859–1924; the English Folk Song Society (now the English Folk Dance and Song Society) was established in 1898. The investigation of both European (with collateral American) and non-European folk-song was greatly facilitated by gramophone recording.

The special melodic and rhythmical characteristics of folk music, esp. its usual adherence to the old 'modes' (which had largely disappeared from European art music by about 1600), proved stimulating to a number of 19th and 20th-cent. composers, esp. those concerned to revive a national tradition independent of the 'alien' German symphonic or Italian operatic tradition. Among composers so stimulated were Glinka and Mussorgsky in Russia, Granados and Falla in Spain, Vaughan Williams in England, Bartók and Kodály in Hungary. Jazz is recognized as having folk music elements both in certain basic forms (notably the 12-bar blues) and in its technique of improvisation. In the mid 20th cent. the revival of folksong itself, till then largely confined to aesthetic circles, spread conspicuously to the general world of light entertainment, both professional and amateur, and by the 1960s it had come to influence 'pop' songs.

Food ◊ *Diet, Nutrition.*

Food Adulteration. Laws have been passed in different countries to protect the consumer from bad or adulterated food; standards of purity for many foods have been set, and goods must be marked to show what they are made of or contain. In the U.K. there are Food and Drugs Acts for England and Wales, 1955, for Scotland, 1956, and for N. Ireland, 1958. The Ministries of Health and of Agriculture, Fisheries, and Food are the responsible central authorities, and authorized officers (usually of local government) can take samples for analysis. There are special regulations for various foods e.g. milk, meat, ice cream. In U.S.A. very stringent regulations are administered under the Food, Drug, and Cosmetic Act (1938).

Food and Agriculture Organization. A United Nations agency which grew out of the 1943 Conference on Food and Agriculture called by President Roosevelt, with permanent headquarters, now in Rome, and regional offices throughout the world, its objects being to maintain efficient distribution of food and to increase the world's food supply. The member nations meet every two years.

Food Preservation. Food decays because of ◊ *micro-organisms* and ◊ *enzymes* which multiply in certain conditions of heat, air, moisture, etc. It can be preserved by destroying or inhibiting such organisms by smoking, salting, or pickling, or by drying, heating, or refrigeration. Drying processes produce dried or dehydrated fruits, milk, eggs, etc. but often the character of the food is radically altered. Heating is used in canning and bottling; the canning process, which preserves food in hermetically sealed containers, was invented 1795 by a Frenchman, Appert, who used glass jars; later Durand in England used canisters of tinplate 1810, and a cannery was set up in Bermondsey 1812 to supply the British Navy. The process assumed real importance only when it became possible to make cans by machinery. By 1870, Armour had started the great meat-packing industry in Chicago. It was not till towards the end of the 19th cent. that the chemistry and technology of canning were fully developed; it has now grown into a vast modern industry, though frozen foods refrigerated by quick-freezing methods are becoming more and more popular. The latest method of preservation, still being developed, is accelerated freeze drying (AFD): the food is dehydrated, but when reconstituted it resembles the original form and flavour very closely.

Many ways of preserving food were discovered long before the reasons for food decay were understood. Drying was early used for keeping fruit (currants and raisins), fish, and meat (pemmican). The efficacy of adding salt was known in primitive times, as were various devices for excluding air e.g. by coating in fat or covering with oil. In recent times the addition of chemicals e.g. formalin, benzoic acid, boric acid, etc. was found to inhibit micro-organisms, and the excessive use of such chemicals led to legislation in most countries to control adulteration.

Foot-and-Mouth Disease. Virus disease of domestic and wild cloven-footed animals, causing blisters, particularly on the feet and mouth. In countries where the disease is endemic mortality is usually low, but its extreme infectiousness makes it one of the most economically serious agricultural diseases; it has at times caused enormous losses to the cattle industry. Once it is established, only ruthless slaughter of all infected and in-contact animals, with safe disposal of carcases and the quarantine and disinfection of affected areas, will provide control. Britain has rigid control measures (◊ *Scheduled Diseases*); most other countries normally free from the disease have strict regulations for dealing with outbreaks and for preventing the entry of infected animals or materials. The virus can be carried in the bone-marrow of carcases and introduced by the importation of chilled meat (◊ *Refrigeration*). Humans may carry the disease from one animal to another and may themselves sometimes contract it, but effects are not usually severe.

Football ◊ *American, Association, Gaelic, Rugby League, Rugby Union.*

Football Pools ◊ *Betting and Gambling.*

Foreign Exchange. Under the full gold-standard system, the transfer of the money of one country to another was entirely free, but the imbalance of international payments after the Second World War led to widespread restrictions on the transfer of currencies; by 1964 most industrial countries had returned to free transferibility for current transactions while still keeping some form of exchange control for capital transactions.

EXCHANGE CONTROL: Official control of the transfer of foreign exchange, to prevent depletion of a country's gold and monetary reserves. Widely adopted as a short-term measure to cope with a grave imbalance of payments in several countries esp. Germany during the 1930s depression and further developed during the Second World War, it is still widely used in many countries and to some extent in the U.K. under the 1947 Exchange Control Act controlling transfer of capital abroad. In any extensive form it involves the most strict official control of all trade transactions as well as financial dealings, and its dismantling has been a major objective of post-war economic policy. ◊ *Bretton Woods Conference, Gold Standard.*

Foreign Legion. Any regiment of soldiers serving in a country other than their own, but specifically the French Foreign Legion, created by Louis Philippe in 1831 and stationed in the former French territories in N. Africa. It fought in N. Africa and Indo-China. After the First and Second World Wars it recruited many Germans. The depot is now in Bastia, Corsica, with battalions in Somaliland, Madagascar, and Pacific islands.

Foreign Office. The U.K. government department responsible for the conduct of relations with foreign states and for the administration of the Foreign Service; it became a separate department 1782. The Minister in charge is the Secretary of State for Foreign Affairs, assisted by two Ministers of State and two Parliamentary Under-Secretaries. It serves as a channel of communication and discussion for all matters concerning international relations, through H.M. diplomatic missions abroad or the representatives of foreign governments in Britain, and as an agency for protecting British subjects and interests abroad and for promoting trade. A uni-fied Foreign Service was created 1943 from the Foreign Office, the Diplomatic service, and the Consular service, the members serving approximately two thirds of their time at posts abroad and one third in London; they are selected by competitive examination conducted by the ◊ *Civil Service* Commission. When the Foreign Secretary is a member of the House of Lords, the Foreign Office is represented in the House of Commons by the ◊ *Lord Privy Seal.*

Foreign Service ◊ *Diplomacy, Foreign Office.*

Forensic Medicine. The study of those aspects of medical science which relate to the giving of expert evidence in court; medical experts are frequently asked to offer opinons as to the cause of death, identification by physical characteristics, the causes and effects of wounds, or the comparison of ◊ *blood* groups.

Forest. The natural vegetation of trees where rainfall is sufficient both in summer and winter and where the summers are not too cold or the wind too strong. In many parts of the world, in both temperate and tropical regions, the natural forest has been cut down to make way for agriculture. This is esp. true of Europe, most of which (including Britain) was covered by forest in prehistoric times. There are many forest types in the world, growing under differing climatic conditions. The most luxuriant is the tropical ◊ *rain forest*, where seasonal changes in climate are negligible. Here trees with evergreen foliage grow to heights of 100 to 200 ft, and there is a wide variety of species. ◊ *Epiphytes* and climbers abound but there is little or no undergrowth. Where there are dry seasons in tropical or subtropical regions, monsoon forests occur. During the dry season foliage is shed, though the trees may flower at this time. In temperate regions with well-differentiated summer and winter seasons, two types of forest are formed: deciduous, and evergreen coniferous. The former are dominated by a small number of tree species e.g. oak, elm, beech, lime, hornbeam. The coniferous forests occur where the winters are more severe, e.g. in large areas of Siberia and Canada, and are dominated by a few species of conifers, mostly pines and spruces.

Forget-me-not. *Myosotis*; the popular name was originally applied to the European water forget-me-not *M. palustris*, a bright blue-flowered perennial, which grows in wet shady places. There are several other British species, of which the best are the wood forget-me-not *M. sylvatica*, a dwarf European alpine variety, and New Zealand varieties which are either white or yellow, never blue. Tradition has it that the name comes from the last words of a youth drowned in the Danube while picking the flowers for his sweetheart.

Formaldehyde. A gaseous substance of irritant odour, usually met with as a water solution ('formalin') containing about 40 per cent of formaldehyde; formula CH_2O. It is made by controlled oxidation of ◊ *methyl alcohol*, and used in the manufacture of bakelite and urea-formaldehyde ◊ *polymer* plastics, and as a disinfectant and a preservative for biological specimens.

PARAFORMALDEHYDE: A ◊ *polymer*, obtained, as a white powder, when 'formalin' is evaporated to dryness. It regenerates formaldehyde on heating.

PHENOL/UREA FORMALDEHYDES ◊ *Plastics*.

◊*Aldehydes*.

Formalin ◊ *Formaldehyde*.

Formic Acid. The simplest of the organic acids, generally similar to ◊ *acetic acid*; formula HCO_2H. A very irritant liquid which blisters the skin, it resembles ◊ *formaldehyde* in bactericidal action and is used as a disinfectant e.g. of wine casks. The stings of nettles and of some species of ◊ *ants* are due to formic acid, and in former days the acid was obtained from red ants. Hence the name, from Lat. *formica*, ant. The compound is now synthesized, starting from carbon monoxide and caustic soda, for use in the textile industry.

Formosa (Taiwan). Area 13,850 sq. m. Pop. 11.5 m. (mainly Chinese). Cap. Taipeh. An island 90 m. E. of China, with small islands (Matsu, Quemoy) very near the mainland (so-called 'offshore islands'). ECONOMY. Agricultural, esp. camphor; bananas, pineapples, rice, sugarcane, tea, tobacco, and considerable fisheries. Mineral resources coal, copper, gold, iron, petroleum, sulphur.

HISTORY. Originally settled by the Chinese, later colonized by the Dutch and Spanish, and under Japanese administration 1894–1945. On the collapse of the ◊ *Kuomintang* government in 1950,

in the face of communist attack, General Chiang Kai-shek withdrew to Formosa with half a million troops, and has since maintained his Nationalist Chinese regime there. The Peking government claims Formosa, but has not attempted to seize it by force. Chiang Kai-shek's government, whose delegates sit in the U.N. as representing China, is still recognized by the U.S.A. (which has furnished massive financial aid) as the *de jure* government of China, with the result that communist China (though recognized by e.g. Britain, France, U.S.S.R.) is not a member of the U.N.

Fortifications. Defensive fortifications have been in use since the beginnings of organized war, the earliest being simple earthworks and palisades. The earliest known permanent defences are the massive walls of the ◊ *Neolithic* town of Jericho, 7th millennium B.C. The unified Egyptian state had no need for defences of this kind, but the cities of ancient Mesopotamia were walled, and fortified citadels within city walls appeared early, as did isolated forts built to defend frontiers or to provide refuges for the local peasants. The characteristic fortification of Celtic Europe was the hill-fort, e.g. Maiden Castle in Dorset, a complex system of high earthworks and ditches around a hill camp. Roman cities were not walled until the troubled centuries of the late Empire, but Roman troops on campaign built semi-permanent camps, and to protect their frontiers in Britain and on the Rhine and Danube built systems of garrisoned forts linked by walls (◊ *Hadrian's Wall*). The Great Wall of China, 3rd cent. B.C., was a similar structure on a much greater scale. From the 4th cent. onwards walled cities and local ◊ *castles* became the rule in Europe, and the design of walls to give maximum firepower to the inhabitants and the minimum amount of cover to attackers became a recognized part of military science. At the same time special devices were introduced for the conduct of sieges, notably mining and the use of catapults, battering rams, and other siege engines originally invented by the Greeks. Artillery diminished the value of the medieval castle, and new kinds of fortifications had to be developed, notably bastions for defensive artillery positions. The tendency to widen city defences led eventually to the late

19th-cent. linear defences, consisting of lines of forts, fortified artillery positions, and pillboxes; the Maginot Line built by the French after the First World War was a defence of this kind, but since it had never been fully extended to the sea it was easily outflanked by the Germans in 1940. The German Siegfried Line held out much longer, but the fixed fortification was finally discredited in favour of temporary field fortifications.

Fortnightly Review. A periodical of mid-Victorian radical thought and humanitarianism, founded 1865 by a group including Anthony Trollope, a frequent contributor; at first it ran bi-monthly, later monthly until 1954, when it was absorbed by *The Contemporary Review*. Among the editors were G. H. Lewes, John Morley, T. H. S. Escott, Frank Harris, and W. L. Courtney, and contributors included J. S. Mill, George Meredith, Herbert Spencer, and T. H. Huxley.

Fossils. Shells and petrified remains of plants and animals found preserved in the earth; also imprints of skeletons, and trails of extinct creatures e.g. footprints of reptiles. Not until about 1800 was the importance of fossils recognized and the study of ◊ *palaeontology* begun. ◊◊ *Ammonite, Belemnite*.

Fourteen Points. President Wilson in Jan. 1918 listed 14 aims to be sought in a peace treaty after the ◊ *First World War*. (1) To renounce secret diplomacy. (2) Freedom of the seas. (3) Reduction of commercial barriers. (4) Disarmament. (5) Impartial settlement of colonial claims. (6, 7, 8) Evacuation and restoration of territory in Russia, Belgium, and France (with return of Alsace-Lorraine). (9) Readjustment of Italian frontier. (10) Self-determination for the peoples of Austria-Hungary. (11) Restoration of territory of Rumania, Montenegro, and Serbia (the latter to have access to sea). (12) Self-determination for the peoples of the Ottoman Empire and freedom of the Dardanelles. (13) Creation of an independent Poland with access to the Baltic. (14) Establishment of a League of Nations. These points were accepted by the Allies as a basis for discussion, although some of the Allies were bound by secret agreements made before U.S.A. entered the war.

Fourteenth of July ◊ *Bastille*.

Fourth Republic. 1944–58. After the liberation of France at the end of the Second World War, the discredited ◊ *Third Republic* was replaced by a new Constitution; the seeds of instability were present in the provision (aimed at curbing communist influence) that majorities of two thirds or three fifths were required for all important legislation. Lack of party solidarity, and the power of special lobbies (e.g. the French settlers in Algeria), led to increasing weakness. During the 14 years of its existence the Fourth Republic saw no less than 25 cabinets. A coup by French officers in Algiers led to a crisis during which General de Gaulle announced that he was willing to assume leadership as President; the Assembly accepted his offer in 1958. A new constitution for the Fifth Republic was adopted by referendum; under this the President wields very considerable powers, which he used to bring the Algerian war to an end and grant Algerian independence. ◊◊ *French Community*.

Fowl Pest (Newcastle Disease). Serious virus disease affecting fowls, pigeons, turkeys, pheasants, and some wild birds; spread by direct contact or by infected material, with 4–10 days' incubation period. Some outbreaks are very serious, but self-limiting in that they quickly kill off all susceptible birds; others are milder and can only be diagnosed by laboratory examination, but nevertheless spread rapidly. In Britain, a ◊ *scheduled disease*; infected and in-contact birds are destroyed, the owners being compensated. An effective vaccine has recently been developed.

Foxglove. *Digitalis purpurea*; a tall biennial or sometimes perennial herb, native in Britain in woods and heaths, usually having purple flowers, though some are white. Foxgloves have been used medicinally from early times, and are cultivated for their alkaloids, esp. digitalin, used for heart diseases. Garden foxgloves may be the British species, but recently 'excelsior hybrids' have been developed with less drooping flowers, in a range of shades of purple, pink, and cream.

France. Area 212,700 sq. m. Pop. 46.5 m. Cap. Paris. Under the constitution of the Fifth Republic, 1958, the President is elected for seven years by a special body of electors; he has great powers, one of which is that of appointing the Prime Minister, and may assume extensive emergency powers. Parliament comprises the

Senate and National Assembly, the latter elected by universal suffrage. Administratively France is highly centralized; the system of division into *Départements*, each under a *Préfet* responsible to Paris, has given France administrative order and stability even though the Parliamentary regimes of the ◊ *Third Republic* and the ◊ *Fourth Republic* showed grave weaknesses and the functions of French local government are very limited. With a very competent higher civil service, and progressive industries, France has made great economic progress since 1945; she took a leading part in the creation of the ◊ *European Economic Community*, and under President de Gaulle has pursued a policy of reconciliation and cooperation with Germany.

ECONOMY. France is one of the richly endowed countries, with great fertile areas, grazing land, and forests, 80 per cent of the territory being productive; it is the major wine producer. Nevertheless, the agricultural population (one third of the total) produces only some 15 per cent of the national product. In the N. there are extensive coal and iron deposits. France has excellent river and canal routes, a good railway system, and considerable hydroelectric potential, and is a modern industrial country, one third of all employment being in industry. The standard of living has risen substantially in recent years.

EDUCATION. Public education is highly centralized and is the responsibility of the Ministry at all levels, including universities. Children start school at six, and at 11 are transferred (chiefly according to examination results) to various types of secondary school, of which the most important are the *lycées* and *collèges*, which prepare pupils for the universities. In 1962 there were over 240,000 university students, and there will be 500,000 by 1970, when the school-leaving age will be 16. At all levels French education tends to be more formally academic than is usual in the U.K.

Private schools, chiefly Roman Catholic, are numerous, esp. at the secondary level, where they cater for nearly 30 per cent of the total.

HISTORY. The land of Gaul was conquered for Rome by Julius Caesar in 51 B.C. and remained a Roman province until overrun by ◊ *Vandals* and Visigoths (◊ *Goths*) in the 5th cent. A.D. The Franks, under Clovis, eventually became dominant, setting up first the ◊ *Merovingian* and then the ◊ *Carolingian* monarchies, the area having been part of Charlemagne's empire. The union of England and Normandy in 1066, the acquisition of ◊ *Aquitaine* by Henry II, and the quasi independence of the great feudal princes, were sources of division. The able Capetian King of Paris, Philippe Auguste, succeeded in conquering Normandy and used the Albigensian crusade to take control of most of Aquitaine. St Louis and Philip IV ruled an area roughly equivalent to modern France, and centralized the power of the state, a process intensified under Louis XI, though the long struggle with England and ◊ *Burgundy* in the ◊ *Hundred Years War* left France weak. She had scarcely recovered before plunging into ambitious wars in Italy in 1494. Again the country had only a brief respite (◊ *Field of Cloth of Gold*) before the religious wars between Guise and Bourbon in the reigns of François II and Charles IX again prostrated her. The acceptance of Roman Catholicism by Henry of Navarre, his accession as Henri IV, and his religious toleration (◊ *Edict of Nantes*) in 1598 ended this struggle. Under the guidance of Cardinal Richelieu and later Cardinal Mazarin the country gained advantage from the ◊ *Thirty Years War*, with spectacular growth of military prowess, ◊ *absolutism*, and also cultural influence, under Louis XIV 1643–1715. In the 18th cent. though French civilization dominated Europe, the rigid and autocratic administration brought increasing strain and discontent, which resulted in the 1789 ◊ *French Revolution* and Napoleon's rise to power in 1799. Before his defeat at ◊ *Waterloo*, Napoleon had raised France to a new pinnacle of influence, but the restoration of the ◊ *Bourbon* monarchy in the direct line and from 1830 in the Orleanist line proved unpopular. A revolution in 1848 led to the 1852 ◊ *Second Empire* under Napoleon III, ended by the ◊ *Franco-Prussian War* in which France lost ◊ *Alsace and Lorraine* to Prussia. After this defeat and the collapse of the 1871 ◊ *Paris Commune*, the ◊ *Third Republic* was founded. A period of economic and industrial growth at home and the establishment of a considerable overseas empire followed. France suffered enormous casualties and damage in the ◊ *First World War*, scarcely compensated by the return of Alsace-Lorraine. During the ◊ *Second World War*, France was occupied by the Germans in 1940; S. of the Loire a collaborationist government at ◊ *Vichy* was set up. Overseas the Free French forces continued to fight, under the leadership of General de Gaulle. After liberation, the ◊ *Fourth Republic* was set up; it encountered serious difficulties first in Indo-China and then in ◊ *Algeria*, and came to an end with General de Gaulle's accession to power in 1958. ◊◊ *French*.

LANGUAGE ◊ *French*.

Franciscans. Christian religious order founded by St Francis of Assisi 1182–1226. After the saint's death disputes arose in the order over the stricter or laxer interpretations of his Rule, and the Spirituals (Fraticelli) were suppressed as heretics. Today there are three main branches, Friars Minor and Capuchins wearing brown, and Conventuals wearing black; they preach, conduct home and foreign ◊ *missions*, and engage in social work. There are also Franciscan communities in the Church of England.

THIRD ORDER (Tertiaries). Lay men and women who follow a special Rule adapted for life in the world. The friars and the tertiaries together number about 45,000.

POOR CLARES. Nuns of the Franciscan order.

◊◊ *Monasticism*.

Francium. A very rare ◊ *element*, an alkali metal which has eight isotopes, all radioactive; first identified by Mlle Perey, 1939.

Franco-Prussian War. 1870–1. The rapid success of Prussia in conquering Austria in the Seven Weeks War of 1866 took by surprise the French Emperor Napoleon III, and he sought an opportunity of restoring the balance. In 1870 he tried to prevent an increase of German influence in Spain and, finding himself outmanoeuvred by Bismarck, declared war. The ill-organized French forces were quickly overwhelmed and the Emperor with 100,000 men was forced to surrender at ◊ *Sedan*. Paris withstood a siege of several months before capitulation, on terms which ceded ◊ *Alsace and Lorraine* to Germany. After the peace was signed, the Parisians (who considered the peace terms too humiliating) refused to disarm

and formed the ◊ *Paris Commune*, which defied the regime of Thiers.

Franks. One of the Germanic tribes which settled within the Roman Empire, occupying parts of Belgium and the Rhine valley and N. France. They were united by Clovis, who by his baptism in 496 brought about the alliance with the Church which ultimately resulted in Charlemagne's coronation as head of the ◊ *Holy Roman Empire* in 800. The Frankish kingdom was always a weak one, and rapidly collapsed after Charlemagne's death, finally breaking up in 887.

Fraternities. In American colleges, student societies, with secret initiation ceremonies. They provide meeting-places and usually living accommodation for members; only the Phi Beta Kappa fraternity reflects scholastic merit. In some colleges student opinion bans fraternities. The corresponding societies in women's colleges are sororities, but these are rare.

Fraunhofer Lines. The absorption lines in the solar spectrum by which atoms and ions comprising the gases at the surface of the sun are identified. The lines appear because each particular gas absorbs light of characteristic wave-lengths out of the continuous radiation coming from deeper in the sun. The lines are named after their discoverer, Joseph von Fraunhofer 1787–1826, who mapped some 600 of many thousands of lines now counted.

Free Association ◊ *Association of Ideas*.

Free Churches ◊ *Nonconformists*.

Free Enterprise ◊ *Capitalism*.

Free Fall ◊ *Weightlessness*.

Freehold. A form of holding land in Great Britain (and other countries) which offers the most complete possession, equivalent in practice to ownership, and in English law limited only by the theory that the Crown ultimately owns all land. Even freehold land can, however, be compulsorily acquired (expropriation) by the state or local authorities for certain statutorily defined purposes. ◊◊ *Leasehold*.

Free Market. The interplay of supply and demand, in fully competitive conditions, as the price-regulating mechanism, with no government intervention or very little; sometimes called the price mechanism, it plays the predominant role in settling price levels in capitalist countries, and even in communist countries there has recently been more inclination to rely on price mechanism rather than state planning and price-fixing (◊ *Economic Planning*). Since 1948 W. Germany has operated a more free-market economy than any other capitalist country.

Freemasons. International body of uncertain origin, claiming to date to the building of Solomon's Temple but more probably originating with medieval guilds of travelling stonemasons and builders; organized in 'lodges' using elaborate ritual, they undertake various kinds of benevolent and social work. At various times, esp. on the European continent (not in Britain), they have been accused of subversive activities, notably in connexion with the French Revolution. As a ◊ *secret society*, they are frowned upon by the ◊ *Roman Catholic Church*; in Britain their relations with Protestant religious bodies are friendly.

Free Port. Port (or zone within port) where goods may be trans-shipped without payment of customs duties. Free ports arose in the Middle Ages when certain cities, to encourage transit trade, waived levying customs duties. The Hanse towns of Hamburg, Bremen, and Lübeck were among the earliest (◊ *Hanseatic League*). When absorbed into the newly formed 19th-cent. nations, these extra-territorial units became inconvenient and most free ports lost their privileges, which have been replaced by the bonded-warehouse system. By their nature free ports usually have a considerable entrepôt trade; Hong Kong, Singapore, Hamburg, Copenhagen are surviving examples.

Free Trade. International commerce unhampered by tariffs or quotas, the basic argument for which is the territorial division of labour: each region should produce what it most cheaply can and exchange its products for those of other nations, rather than try to protect home industries by restricting the import of goods produced more cheaply elsewhere. Free trade was advocated by the Physiocrats in France and by Adam Smith in England, where Whig industrialists favoured it and Tory landowners did not: poor harvests and a population explosion led to the 1837 movement for cheaper imported food (◊ *Corn Laws*); the 1845–8 ◊ *Irish famine* converted the Tory leader Sir Robert Peel, and the restrictive laws were abolished 1849. Gladstone's budgets completed the establishment of free trade; whereas 1425 articles had been dutiable

in 1787, only 12 were in 1882. For 70 years Britain practised free trade, to abandon it in the ◊ *depression* and worldwide restrictions of the 1930s. Since 1946 high tariffs and quotas have been reduced mainly through the ◊ *Organization for European Economic Cooperation* and the ◊ *General Agreement on Tariffs and Trade*, and a partial return to free trade has been achieved, at least between industrial countries. Free trade appeals much less to underdeveloped countries, since infant industries can most easily be built up behind tariff walls.

Free Verse (*Vers Libre*). Although sometimes applied to older verse having no regular pattern (e.g. the choruses of Milton's *Samson Agonistes*), the term is best reserved for verse of the kind written by the Symbolists in France and Whitman in America, and taken up by many 20th-cent. poets (e.g. ◊ *Imagism*), having no set ◊ *metre* or rhyme scheme and depending for effect mainly upon cadence. D. H. Lawrence 1920 saw it as 'the direct utterance from the instant, whole man', a pruning-away of clichés of rhythm as well as of phrase. ◊ *Blank Verse*.

Free Will. In philosophy, the problem of reconciling the vague but entrenched beliefs that sometimes we make free choices, but that nevertheless all choices result in some way from our characters and environments. The latter assumption is part of the theory of determinism, that each event in the universe is the necessary effect of preceding causes, i.e. each event is subject to scientific law and in theory predictable. There can be no proof of determinism (since this would involve studying *all* events, an impossibility) and no disproof (because any allegedly undetermined event may have hidden causes). Three recurrent answers to the free-will problem are (1) the Determinist: choices, since often predictable, must be determined by character and environment; thus we are never free or responsible. (2) The Libertarian: if we reflect on the act of choosing, we must conclude that sometimes we choose freely, thus some choices are not determined by character and environment but are the work of an intervening and itself undetermined entity, the person's 'self'. (3) The Compatibilist: the determinist and libertarian conclusions are muddles born of oversight, for there is in fact no incompatibility in a choice being both determined and free; and it may be both; the opposite of a free choice is not a determined choice, but merely one performed against the agent's will, and free choices (those according to my will) may also be determined; thus there is no problem.

In theology the free-will problem usually takes this form: If God is omniscient, and therefore knows what I shall decide, my decision must be predetermined and thus not free; if so, I can never justly be held guilty of sin.

Freezing. Change of state from liquid to solid. For a given substance under given pressure, the change takes place at a constant temperature called the freezing point. The f.p. normally quoted is that for standard atmospheric pressure, but in general the effect of pressure is small.

French. A ◊ *Romance language*; spoken by about 65 m. people in France and parts of Belgium, Switzerland, Canada, Haiti, and former French possessions. The Gauls were Celts, but gave up their native tongue in favour of Latin, which had linguistic affinities with Gaulish; Vulgar Latin remained the language of Gaul and the ◊ *Franks* until about A.D. 500 when it had become so different as to be called Gallo-Roman. This was used in 842 in the text of the Strasbourg Oaths, which marked the beginning of Old French, destined to reach its heyday in the 12th and 13th centuries, in two forms, the *langue d'oïl* of the N. and the *langue d'oc* of the S. (◊ *Provence*). Francien, the language of Paris, was gradually adopted as the standard form. Modern French began with the 16th cent. when grammarians and poets shaped and codified it; after further refining in the *salons* and the Court, and by the ◊ *Académie Française*, it became the most polished and precise of all living tongues. From the 17th cent. onwards, French held an unrivalled position as the language of international intercourse and diplomacy, until in the 20th cent. its pre-eminence was successfully challenged by English.

French Architecture. France was the birthplace of ◊ *Gothic architecture*, which grew out of ◊ *Romanesque architecture* in the 11th cent. and reached its finest form in e.g. the cathedrals of Chartres, Rheims, Amiens; the late-Gothic French style is called ◊ *Flamboyant*. Classical architecture was introduced from Italy in the early 16th cent. and rapidly took on a characteristically French form, culminating in the work of the great architects of the 17th cent. Mansart (Val-de-Grâce), Perrault (the Louvre), and the Hardouin-Mansart (Versailles, Place Vendôme). In France as elsewhere in the 19th cent. classicism gave way to eclecticism; perhaps the greatest achievement of that time was Haussmann's replanning of Paris. In the 20th cent. Le Corbusier (a Swiss who has worked mainly in France) has exerted a tremendous international influence on modern architecture.

French Art. The earliest manifestations are associated with architecture, ◊ *Romanesque* sculpture e.g. at Moissac and Vézelay, ◊ *Gothic* sculpture (of which one of the finest and earliest examples is the Royal Portal at Chartres), and ◊ *stained glass*. Important schools of ivory carvers and manuscript illuminators were established in the 13th cent. but it was not until the early 15th that a truly national style emerged in the paintings of Jean Fouquet and the brothers Clouet. The arrival of Italian artists to decorate the Palace of Fontainebleau in the mid 16th cent. introduced ◊ *Mannerism*, naturalized by the sculptors Jean Goujon and Germain Pilon; Poussin and Claude, the two great painters of the 17th cent., worked mainly in Italy, and Georges de la Tour and the Le Nain brothers also worked outside court circles, but the dominance of court patronage was asserted by Louis XIV, who at Versailles and elsewhere employed an army of painters and sculptors to magnify his glory. Early in the 18th cent. a new note of lightness and elegance was introduced into painting by Watteau; later great ◊ *Rococo* artists include the painters Boucher, Fragonard, Chardin, and the sculptors Bouchardon, Falconet, Pigalle, Houdon, Clodion. Under the late 18th and 19th cent. Directorate and Empire ◊ *Neoclassicism*, introduced by David, was adopted as the official style and persisted later in the work of Ingres, though after 1815 the romantic painters notably Géricault and Delacroix were predominant. In sculpture Rodin was the greatest 19th-cent. master. The late 19th and early 20th centuries were a period of changing styles and great vitality which made Paris the unchallenged international centre of painting. ◊ *Abstract Art, Barbizon School, Cubism, Fauvism, Impressionism, Land-*

scape Painting, Post-Impressionism, Realism, Surrealism.

French Community. Association of former French overseas possessions and of Metropolitan France, created in 1958 by general plebiscite (◊ *Guinea*, however, voting against membership); in 1960 (by an amendment to the Constitution of the 5th Republic) it became an association of independent states. The President of France is Head of the Community; its organs are an Executive Council (the P.M. of France and the heads of the member states, together with the ministers responsible for affairs common to all members), the Senate (an assembly of delegates from the parliaments of all members), and a court of arbitration. It developed from the French Union established under the Fourth Republic in 1946. ◊ *Central African Republic, Chad, Congo, French Polynesia, French Somaliland, Gaboon, Ivory Coast, Madagascar, Mali, Mauritania, New Caledonia, St Pierre, Senegal.*

French Equatorial Africa. Until 1910, French Congo. Now four separate states: *Central African Republic, Chad, Congo, Gaboon.*

French Guiana. Area 34,370 sq. m. Pop. 33,000. Cap. Cayenne. Formerly a French colony, on the N. coast of S. America; since 1946 one of the departments of France proper.

ECONOMY. Almost wholly undeveloped; a subsistence economy.

HISTORY. The Guiana coast was first settled by the Dutch; the territories changed hands many times between British, Dutch, French, and Portuguese, the French intervening in the 1640s and 1780s, and French Guiana being created in 1815 by the Vienna Congress; it was a convict settlement (esp. on Devil's Island) 1792–1946. ◊ *British Guiana, Netherlands W. Indies.*

French Polynesia. Area 2500 sq. m. Pop. 77,000. Cap. Papeete (Tahiti). The Society Islands (Leeward and Windward), the Marquesas, the Gambier Isles, the Tubuai Islands: collectively a member of the French Community since 1958.

ECONOMY. Mainly agricultural; chief products arrowroot, breadfruit, coconuts, coffee, copra, mother-of-pearl, pearls, phosphates, rum, sugar, tobacco, vanilla. HISTORY. Tahiti was discovered by the British in 1767 and visited in 1769 by Capt. Cook and members of the Royal Society (hence the name Society Islands); ◊ *Bounty Mutiny*. France set up a Tahiti protectorate in 1843. The Marquesas were discovered by an American navigator in 1791 and named Washington Islands, and the people voted 1813 for U.S. incorporation, but no action was taken until they were ceded to France in 1842. The Tubuai Islands were discovered by Capt. Cook in 1777; annexing them in 1880, France declared these three groups of islands the French colony of Oceania, to which in 1881 the Gambier Islands were annexed. The population of all the islands esp. the Marquesas was drastically reduced by plague-like epidemics of European diseases, to which the Polynesians had no immunity.

French Revolution. 1789–99. Inspired by the writings of the ◊ *Enlightenment* philosophers, and by the example of the ◊ *American Revolution*, the culmination of a variety of causes financial, social, and historical, the Revolution broke out when the States General (a legacy of the medieval type of national assembly, not called since 1614), aspiring to the role of the English Parliament, refused to be dismissed. The fall of the ◊ *Bastille* was the signal for local revolutions throughout the country, and Louis XVI was forced to accept a constitution. In 1792 the First Coalition (Austria, Britain, Holland, Russia, Spain) declared war on France, but was broken up in a series of defeats, ◊ *Valmy*; a Second Coalition was formed 1798 (◊ *Napoleonic Wars*). Provoked by the King's attempted flight, and faced with foreign intervention, the revolutionaries set up the Convention in 1792; the King and Queen (Marie Antoinette) were executed in 1793. The Committee of Public Safety began the Reign of Terror, during which Robespierre made himself a dictator, executing his more moderate rivals the Girondins (including his former colleagues Hébert and Danton). In 1794 Robespierre himself went to the guillotine; with the advent of the Directorate, 1795–9, the government became more corrupt but less repressive (though the 1796 proletarian Conspiracy of Equals was savagely suppressed). Napoleon Bonaparte brought the period of revolutionary rule to an end with the coup d'état of 1799, establishing the Consulate with himself as First Consul; this was made a life appointment in 1802, but in 1804 he crowned himself Emperor of the French. ◊ *Camperdown, Declaration of the Rights of Man*.

French Somaliland. Area 9000 sq. m. Pop. 67,000. Cap. Jibuti. A NE African republic with a seaboard on the Gulf of Aden; member of the French Community since 1958.

ECONOMY. Considerable transit trade, esp. from Ethiopia. ◊ *Somalia*.

French Soudan ◊ *Mali*.

French Union ◊ *French Community*.

Frequency. The number of complete oscillations or cycles an oscillating system performs in unit time. Thus a tuning fork (middle C) is said to have a frequency of 256 cycles per second.

Fresco. A process of wall painting in which the colour (powdered pigment mixed with water) is applied to wet plaster, with which it unites to a depth of at least 1 mm. Esp. popular in Italy, but climatic conditions have prevented its use in N. Europe. Also (incorrectly), paintings on dry plaster (much less durable), and other types of mural painting. Fresco proper was used by most of the Italian ◊ *Renaissance* masters, and has been revived in the 20th cent. by e.g. Diego Rivera.

Freya ◊ *Aesir*.

Friars ◊ *Monasticism*.

Friedland (1807) ◊ *Napoleonic Wars*.

Frigate. Word of Mediterranean origin, first used to describe a small ◊ *galley*, later applied to small fast ◊ *warships*, and often used figuratively to indicate a trim sailing vessel e.g. the Blackwell Frigates, handsome London-owned ships of the first half of the 19th cent. The name was first used in the Royal Navy in the 18th cent. for a class of fast three-masted warships carrying 24 to 40 guns on one deck and used for scouting and convoy-escort duties; with the advent of steam, some of the lighter warships were designated steam frigates, but the term went out of use until the Second World War, when a new class of anti-submarine escorts, of 1000–2300 tons displacement and armed with depth-charges and 4-in. or 4.5-in. guns, were classed as frigates.

Frisian. The W. Germanic language most akin to English, spoken by $3\frac{1}{2}$ m. Old English and Old Frisian were so nearly allied that they formed one language, Anglo-Frisian, intermediate between W. Germanic and Anglo-Saxon (Old English), as spoken by the Angles and Saxons in the centuries immediately before their settlement in England. N. Frisian dialects survive on the Schleswig coast and on a few islands; W. Frisian developed a flourishing literature in the 17th cent. and is now the recognized speech of Dutch Friesland. ◊ *Germanic Languages*.

Frog. Tailless ◊ *amphibian*; with ◊ *toads*, frogs form the group *Anura*, of world-wide temperate and tropical distribution. *Rana temporaria*, common in Britain, lays its eggs in water in the spring, and development proceeds through a tailed or ◊ *tadpole* stage. The ◊ *metamorphosis* into a frog occurs after 3–4 months, and involves modifications e.g. the gill slits develop into lungs and the diet changes from plants to insects. Edible frogs, *R. esculenta*, are found in Europe, and other types in America; one species in Asia, the flying frog, uses its large webbed feet as parachutes when jumping from trees. The tree-frog is allied to the toad.

Fronde ◊ *Huguenots*.

Fruit. The fertilized ovary of a ◊ *flower*; the receptacle is frequently incorporated into the fruit, and the calyx may persist, but the other parts of the flower are lost as the fruit develops. The process of fertilization and hence ◊ *seed* production is

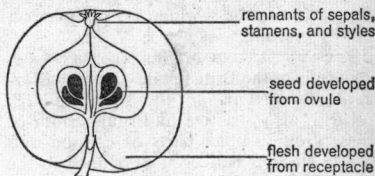

remnants of sepals, stamens, and styles

seed developed from ovule

flesh developed from receptacle

correlated with the production of plant hormones in the fruit, which encourage its enlargement; the commercial development of seedless fruits (esp. citrus) depends on the use of synthetic plant hormones to promote the swelling of the fruit. Fruits vary very much in size, shape, structure, and consistency, and these properties are influenced by both their genetic constitution and the environment. Fruits may be simple, formed from an ovary of one carpel (e.g. a pea pod) or from more carpels (e.g. wallflower, poppy); or they may be compound, developed from a flower with several separated carpels (e.g. strawberry), where the receptacle greatly enlarges, to form the bulk of the fruit. They may be dry or fleshy; when they ripen, they may open, to free the seeds (e.g. horse-chestnut), or remain closed (e.g. hazelnut). Dispersal may be by wind, by animals, or by an explosive mechanism. Wind-dispersed fruits are the most common (e.g. sycamore, with wings, or dandelion, with tufts of hairs); other means are by attachment to animals (e.g. by burrs) or by the passing of seeds through the digestive systems of animals. Explosive fruits (e.g. violet, balsam) are less common.

Many fruits are important as foods, or for oils (e.g. coconut), drugs, and spices. Cultivated fruits have been developed from wild species by selection of seedlings possessing the desired properties, and by interbreeding, to produce varieties larger in size, of better colour, and sometimes of better flavour, of good keeping quality, and of ability to withstand the rigours of transport. These qualities are not found all united in any one variety.

APPLE: The hard fruit of widest distribution, in cultivation for many centuries, probably developed from the wild *Malus pumila* of Europe, W. Asia, and the Himalayas. Canada, Australia, New Zealand, and U.S.A. are major commercial producers. It is of interest that the popular Cox's Orange Pippin was developed from the sowing of a pip or seed, not by grafting.

CHERRY: Of two origins, the sweet deriving from the British wild Gean or Mazzard, *Prunus avium*, the sour from *P. cerasus*, also a native of Britain. Both of these grow in other parts of Europe, and edible cherries had been developed in the Near East in much earlier times.

PEAR: The chief fruit of France and Italy, where it enjoys hot summers and where many varieties were already being grown in the 16th cent. It derives from the wild *Pyrus communis*, from the same areas as *Malus pumila*. Probably the best known is William's *Bon Chrétien*, widely used as 'Bartlett' in U.S.A. for canning.

PLUM: Derived from *Prunus domestica*, probably originating in the Caucasus, it was introduced into Britain in the 18th cent. Prunes are dried blue plums, from regions with hot summers e.g. Turkey, California, and S. Africa.

SOFT FRUITS: Common are gooseberry, raspberry, and strawberry, the last being the most modern development in fruit. The wild strawberry of Europe was grown in gardens from the Middle Ages onwards, but it remained small; the large modern berry is a cross between the N. American *Fragaria virginiana* and the Chilean *F. chiloensis* with relatively large fruits, developed in the 18th cent.

Fruit-fly. Small flies of the genus *Drosophila*, common in Europe and N. America, which attack fruit. *D. melanogaster* is of prime importance for genetics, as its reproduction cycle of only 14 days enables large numbers of generations to be studied; after the 1901 rediscovery of Mendel's work, the long life-cycles of the organisms used in research on genetics hampered progress, until T. H. Morgan started to use the fruit-fly. ⟡ *Fly.*

Frustration. The failure to achieve a desired goal, in consequence of physical or psychological barriers; in experimental psychology, frustration can be produced by preventing a hungry animal from reaching food, by removing toys from children, etc. It often leads to aggression (which according to the 'frustration-aggression hypothesis' is caused solely by frustration) and may also lead to stress symptoms.

Fuel. Any material (solid, liquid, or gaseous) whose combustion supplies useful energy. Principal solid fuel: coal. Common liquid fuels: ◊ *petroleum* derivatives e.g. diesel oil, paraffin (kerosene), petrol (gasoline). Gaseous fuels: e.g. acetylene, blast-furnace gas, butane, coal gas, methane, producer gas, propane, water gas. Oil is gradually replacing coal as the most important fuel; at present ◊ *nuclear energy* makes a very small impact on the world fuel position. ⟡ *Coal and Coal-mining, Gas Industry, Peat.*

Fugue ◊ *Canon and Fugue.*

Fuller's Earth. Commercially, any clay with high natural absorbent qualities; the name derives from the fuller of cloth, who used the material to remove grease from the wool. Now used as a bleaching agent in the refining of mineral oils and vegetable fats, from which it removes unwanted colours. Also used medicinally. Quarried in the Lower Greensand formations of Surrey and in the ◊ *oolites* near Bath. ⟡ *Silica.*

Fundamentalism ◊ *Jehovah's Witnesses, Plymouth Brethren.*

Fungi. Simple plants, usually ◊ *sapro-phytes* living on dead organic matter, or ◊ *parasites* of the group *Thallophyta*, reproducing by ◊ *spores*; they include ◊ *mushrooms*, ◊ *toadstools*, moulds, mildews, rusts, and ◊ *yeasts*, and never have ◊ *chlorophyll* (though some have other pigments). Except in yeasts, the body is of cellular threads like fine hairs, forming a tangled mass, the mycelium, which penetrates the medium (substrate or host) and draws nourishment from it. The mycelium of many parasites remains mostly within the host (except when spores are produced), showing as lesions or powder on the surface (rusts, smuts, mildew, black spot, blight); in others the mycelium forms a web over the surface (moulds), or in some a fleshy body (mushrooms, toadstools, puffballs). Fungi, like bacteria, are essential to all living organisms in that they break down and make assimilable all sorts of organic matter. They also cause most plant and some animal diseases, and, by attacking food and timber (◊ *Dry Rot*) cause much damage. ◊ *Mycosis*.

Fur. Since prehistoric times the fur of many animals has been used by man for clothing; it may be obtained from the skins of wild animals caught by trapping, but to meet a growing demand fur-farming has become a thriving industry in which e.g. fox, mink, wolverine, ermine, coypu, musk-rat, and special breeds of rabbit are bred in captivity. The trapping of animals for fur continues in Canada, Alaska, Mongolia, and Siberia; the staple fur of the great fur-trapping period in N. America was the beaver, but more prized furs are now marten, sable, mink, ermine, chinchilla, and blue and silver fox.

Furies (Erinnyes, Eumenides). In Greek legend, three beings (usually represented as winged snake-wreathed women), personifying the quest for vengeance on the guilty esp. in cases of e.g. patricide, and best-known in connexion with ◊ *Orestes*; said to have sprung from the blood of ◊ *Uranus*.

Furniture. The origins of furniture are unknown, since the chief material, wood, rarely survives the passage of time. The history of furniture until the 19th cent. in general reflects the needs and tastes of the rich and of the court; provincial furniture imitates metropolitan styles, and peasant furniture is usually crude, massive,

and of conservative design. The earliest articles of furniture known (either from pictorial records or from material remains) are the highly sophisticated products of the ancient Egyptian and Assyrian civilizations; their chairs and couches, inlaid with ivory and precious metals, and frequently with legs and armrests carved in the form of lions, bulls, or rams, were elegant enough to serve as models for some of the furniture designers of the early 19th cent. The ancient Greeks took their furniture styles from the East; the Romans copied the Greeks, but made their furniture more sumptuous and extended its range beyond the simple necessities of bed, table, and chair. Medieval European furniture returned to the barest necessities; it was chiefly of oak, simple and solid, but some pieces (esp. the chests in which clothes and valuables were stored) were often richly carved. Ornate highly-finished furniture in finer woods reappeared in Europe with the ◊ *Renaissance*; Italian craftsmen of the 15th cent. supplied their wealthy patrons with pieces which were conscious works of art, often carved with scenes from classical mythology and richly inlaid. At the same time the range of furniture extended again, to include e.g. cabinets and bookcases. Italian fashions were introduced into France and England in the 16th cent. but the great age of furniture in these countries is the 18th cent. esp. 1770–90. The great craftsmen-designers of 18th-cent. England, working in polished mahogany and walnut, were Chippendale (who popularized Gothic and Chinese styles) and Sheraton and Hepplewhite, whose styles belong to the classical revival; in France the major styles are those of Louis XV, a rococo style with fluid curves and ormolu decoration, and Louis XVI, the supreme neoclassical style, marked by elegant fluted verticals and unsurpassed lightness and restraint. Elegant furniture continued to be produced at the beginning of the 19th cent. but craftsmanship was declining and in the Empire period classical and archaic styles degenerated into a heavy ornateness. The shift in wealth in the 19th cent. was reflected in furniture, as in architecture; classical good taste gave way to vulgar eclecticism and ostentation, and comfort rather than elegance became a criterion for design. Moreover, the growth of machine pro-

medieval
chest

Egyptian

Italian
wedding chest
16th century

English: 17th century, Chippendale, Sheraton, Hepplewhite

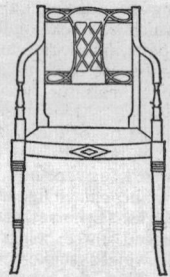

Louis XV
Louis XVI
Regency

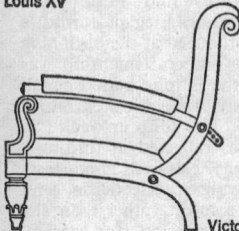
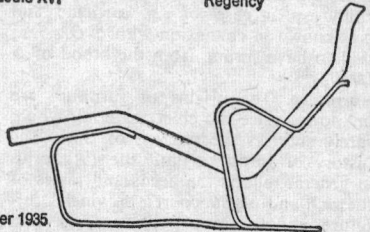

Victorian
Marcel Breuer 1935

duction resulted in a separation of design from manufacture, in which both design and manufacture suffered. Attempts were made towards the end of the 19th cent. (e.g. by William Morris) to revive the standards of the earlier craftsmanship, but despite superficial changes in taste the worst aspects of Victorian furniture design persisted into the 20th cent. Up till the Second World War the staple of mass-produced furniture was a bogus 'traditional' style, characterized by heavily upholstered suites and machine-turned 'Jacobean' table and chair legs; dissatisfaction with contemporary design was reflected in a widespread tendency to turn to antique furniture or to accurate reproductions of 18th-cent. or earlier styles. Attempts in the 1920s (by Marcel Breuer and others) to create a 'functional' style, using such non-traditional materials as glass, tubular steel, and plastics, were too austere to make a widespread impact on taste, and it was not until the post-war period that a satisfactory union between good design and mass-production began to emerge; the leaders in this were the Italians and Scandinavians. Outstanding in contemporary furniture design are Gio Ponti, Mies van der Rohe, Eero Saarinen, all of whom are primarily architects.

Futhorc ◊ *Alphabet*.

Futurism. An artistic style evolved 1910–15 by a small but voluble group of Italian painters, Carrà, Russolo, Balla, Boccioni, Severini, and the theorist Marinetti, who proclaimed that 'universal dynamism must be rendered as dynamic sensation'; that 'movement and light destroy the substance of objects'; and that 'a roaring motor car which runs like a machine-gun is more beautiful than the Winged Victory of Samothrace'. The futurists rejected tradition and set out to glorify and express the dynamism of the machine age.

G

Gaboon (Gabon). Area 101,400 sq. m. Pop. 450,000. Cap. Libreville. Independent republic in W. Africa, between Cameroon and Congo, with an Atlantic seaboard; formerly part of French Equatorial Africa (with Chad, Congo, and Central African Republic), and since 1958 a member of the French Community, self-governing since 1960.

ECONOMY. Underdeveloped, but with budget and overseas payments both balanced, owing to very valuable deposits of iron ore, manganese, petroleum, and uranium (of which Gaboon is France's prime source).

HISTORY. In early 1964 the popular discontent at increasing autocracy, and esp. at the postponement of even the single-list elections, resulted in a peaceful coup d'état deposing President Mba; a liberalized programme was announced. The same day, France intervened (with troops from Chad, Congo, Senegal, Central African Republic) and forcibly reinstated Mba, who again postponed the elections.

Gadolinum ◊ *Lanthanides.*

Gaelic. Strictly, Scottish Gaelic; a language belonging to the Goedelic (Q-Celtic) division of the ◊ *Indo-European languages,* spoken by about 100,000 in the Scottish Highlands and the Western Isles, and by some Scottish emigrants in Nova Scotia and Cape Breton Island; not autochthonous in Scotland, but taken there by immigrants from Ireland from the 16th cent. onwards; until the reign of Malcolm Canmore 1057–93 it was spoken at the royal court. ◊ *Celts.*

Gaelic Football. An Irish amateur 15-a-side game, of the ◊ *Rugby Union* type but played with a round ball on a 160-yd pitch and with the player retaining possession of the ball by bouncing it instead of carrying it. Modern rules were established by the Gaelic Athletic Association, founded 1884.

Gaelic Mod. The National Festival of the Highland Association, founded 1891; prizes are given for singing, piping, and written works.

Galahad. In ◊ *Arthurian legend,* son of ◊ *Lancelot;* the purest of the knights, who saw the ◊ *Holy Grail* and thus earned the seat at the Round Table to be occupied only by one who had seen the mystic vessel, called the Siege Perilous because the earth would swallow up any false claimant.

Galatea. In Greek legend (a) a sea nymph loved by Polyphemus (◊ *Cyclopes*) but preferring Acis; when the lovers overheard Polyphemus singing a love-song and were discovered by him, he killed Acis, but Galatea turned her dead lover into a river. (b) A statue made by ◊ *Pygmalion* and brought to life by ◊ *Aphrodite.*

Galaxy. In ◊ *astronomy,* a vast system of heavenly bodies and associated matter. That of which our solar system forms a minute part is known as the Galaxy or ◊ *Milky Way System,* but it is only one of millions of similar island systems forming the universe. There is clear evidence that they are not randomly distributed but form clusters. Since galaxies, being collections of stars, have ill-defined edges, they are often described as ◊ *nebulae.* Most of them appear to be rapidly receding from us, and this fact is the basis of the theory of the expanding universe. The nearest galaxies are the Large and Small Magellanic Clouds, which can be seen from the southern hemisphere on moonless nights; they are only about 150,000 light years away, relatively so close that they are regarded as satellites of the Milky Way. Our next nearest galactic neighbour, the great galaxy in Andromeda, is more than 10 times as far; although it is about 200,000 light years in diameter, to the naked eye it appears merely as a faint spot in the northern hemisphere, and even in fine-detail astronomical photographs only its brightest stars are individually distinguishable.

Galena ◊ *Lead.*

Galla ◊ *African Languages, Hamito-Semitic Languages.*

Galleon. Large ocean-going sailing vessel, developed by the Spaniards in the 16th cent. to maintain communications with their overseas possessions, with three or four masts, square-rigged on the fore and main masts, with lateen sails on the others; bow and stern were high and elaborately ornamented. Numerous guns were mounted, but the galleon was clumsy; its limitations were shown in the defeat of the ◊ *Armada*.

Galley. A ◊ *warship* propelled by oars, sometimes also carrying sail for occasional use; the standard warship in the Mediterranean (where it originated) from ancient times until the 18th cent. and also used in the Baltic. Until the 16th cent. galleys usually had two or more banks of oars on each side, each rowed by one man; then a single bank of oars each pulled by several men became usual. The galley's main fighting weapon was the ram, a forward-projecting extension of the stem, just above the waterline; guns were later fitted. A typical 17th-cent. Mediterranean galley would be about 160 ft long by 21 ft wide and rowed by 28 oars on each side. ◊ *Lepanto*.

Gallic Wars. 58–51 B.C. Series of campaigns in which Julius Caesar conquered all Gaul, from the Pyrenees to the Rhine. He first drove back the Helvetii into Switzerland, then defeated the Alemanni under Ariovistus, who had entered Gaul from across the Rhine. In 56 B.C. he built a fleet of ships in order to combat the Veneti in Brittany, and in 55 B.C. again threw back the German tribes across the Rhine. From Britain, which he visited twice, Caesar was recalled to put down three successive rebellions in Gaul, the last, under Vercingetorix, ending in 51 B.C. Caesar's 'Commentaries' (*De Bello Gallico*) provide a detailed account of the campaigns. ◊ *Rome*.

Gallipoli ◊ *Dardanelles*.

Gallium. A rare metallic ◊ *element*, m.p. 29.8° C, b.p. 2070° C, remarkable for the great temperature range (over 2000 degrees) through which it is liquid; in a ◊ *quartz* envelope, it gives thermometer readings up to 1000° C. It readily supercools, at room temperature frequently remaining liquid for long periods; it has a valency state of 3 and a chemistry similar to that of ◊ *aluminium*.

Gallo-Roman ◊ *French*.

Gallstones. Concretions (mainly of ◊ *cholesterol*) which form in the gall bladder or bile ducts, blocking them and causing jaundice; the stones may be passed spontaneously into the small intestine, after an attack of biliary colic, or may have to be surgically removed. 'Silent' gallstones give rise to no symptoms and

are revealed by radiography. ◊ *Calculus* (2).

Galvanizing. Coating iron or steel with ◊ *zinc* as a protection against ◊ *corrosion*, the zinc usually being applied either by a 'hot dipping' process similar to that used for ◊ *tinplate* or a process of ◊ *electrolysis* using a zinc-sulphate bath and a zinc anode (◊ *Electrode*). The electrolytic method gives a less brittle covering, which allows galvanized sheets to be bent. Galvanizing is widely used for the protection of wire, tanks, and roofing; even if the surface is scratched, this protection persists to some extent, because corrosive agents acting on the zinc tend to produce a durable zinc-iron ◊ *alloy*.

SHERARDIZING: A method of protecting iron or steel by applying powdered zinc to the surface and baking it to produce a corrosion-resistant alloy.

Galvanometer. Instrument for detecting very small electric currents and for determining the direction and strength of currents. Its operation depends on the interaction of a magnet and a current-carrying conductor (◊ *Conduction, Magnetism*). There are two main types: in one a magnet is suspended at the centre of a coil carrying the current; in the other (the moving-coil type usually used) a small coil carrying the current is suspended between the poles of a magnet. Deflection of the magnet or coil shows that a current is flowing, and if an indicating needle and graduated scale are attached the strength of the current can be deduced from the deflection. The galvanometer is the basis of several other instruments for making electrical measurements, e.g. the ammeter is a galvanometer graduated in amperes, shunts being used so that the same basic movement can measure currents of different magnitude to the same relative accuracy; this is a low-resistance device placed in series with the circuit. The voltmeter, a galvanometer moving in series with a high resistance, is used to measure the potential difference (voltage) between two points by connecting it in parallel with the circuit. Because of its high resistance, only a small current flows through the instrument, and the measurement hardly affects the circuit on which it is being made.

Gambia. Area 4003 sq. m. Pop. 316,000 (mainly Negro, with large W. Indian minority). Cap. Bathurst. Rel. mainly Muslim. British protectorate in W. Africa, between Guinea, Senegal, and Mali. Internally self-governed since 1962; full self-government 1965.

ECONOMY. Predominantly agricultural, esp. ground-nuts; also fruit, millet, rice, vegetables, and considerable livestock-breeding and fisheries. No mineral or other industries, except ground-nut processing. HISTORY. Discovered by the Portuguese in the 15th cent. and colonized by the British in the 17th; the scene of the 17th- and 18th-cent. fighting for possession between British, Dutch, and French.

Gambling ◊ *Betting and Gambling.*

Game. Wild animals and birds which are hunted or whose flesh is used as food; in Britain grouse, hares, partridges, and pheasants are principal game and are protected by legal closed seasons when shooting is prohibited. 'Big game' is e.g. lion, tiger, elephant. Game reserves are large areas of protected countryside, mainly in Africa and N. America, where wild life may live and breed unmolested. African game reserves cover thousands of square miles; Serengeti in Tanganyika is 4480 sq. m. and Kruger in Transvaal 8000 sq. m. Smaller areas e.g. the Ben Eighe Nature Reserve have been set up in Britain to preserve fauna and flora.

Gametes. The sex cells of animals and plants, arising in the sex organs by a process in which ◊ *meiosis* plays the most significant part. The result of this process (gametogenesis) is to provide from each primary sex cell four sperm nuclei in males, or in female vertebrates one egg nucleus and three others known as polar bodies. The egg proper contains all the cytoplasm (food material) accumulated during maturation; the polar bodies degenerate.

Gamma Ray. The quantum of electromagnetic energy which can be emitted by a radioactive atom as it decays and goes into a state of lower energy. Like ◊ *X-Rays*, gamma rays (γ-rays) may be extremely penetrating. ◊◊ *Radiation.*

Gangrene. Localized death of tissue, resulting from interference with the blood supply, severe inflammation, or injury e.g. crushing; bacterial infection and decomposition of the tissue follow. Gas gangrene is caused by bacteria (usually *Clostridium welchii*) which require an oxygen-free atmosphere for their development; they destroy tissue, liberating gas by fermentation of carbohydrates.

Ganymede. In Greek mythology, a beautiful youth who caught the eye of ◊ *Zeus* while tending sheep (or hunting) and was transported on the back of an eagle to Olympus to become cup-bearer in place of ◊ *Hebe.*

Garden City. The name was introduced by Sir Ebenezer Howard in 1898 to describe a planned city, in a country setting, of a limited size, but endowed with a wide range of amenities – schools, hospitals, recreational facilities, etc. To promote his concept an association built the first garden city (Letchworth 1903) and later Welwyn Garden City (1920) and Hampstead Garden Suburb. ◊◊ *New Towns Act.*

Garlic. Perennial herb *Allium sativum*, closely related to the onion, used for flavouring food since ancient times. It was introduced into England in the early 16th cent. ◊ *Liliaceae.*

Garnet ◊ *Silica.*

Gas. A state of matter in which the molecules move freely in all directions. A gas has no fixed shape or volume, and will occupy the whole space of any container in which it finds itself. The pressure of the gas is caused by the rebounding of molecules from the walls of the container. All gases can be liquefied by cooling, compression, and other means, hydrogen and helium offering the greatest difficulty, as these approach most nearly to the ideal state. Various laws describe their behaviour.

AVOGADRO'S LAW: Equal volumes of all gases under the same conditions of temperature and pressure contain the same number of molecules.

BOYLE'S LAW: At constant temperature the volume of a given mass of gas is inversely proportional to its pressure. (This law is strictly true only for an ideal gas.)

CHARLES' LAW: The volume of a given mass of gas at constant pressure is directly proportional to the absolute temperature i.e. its volume will increase by $\frac{1}{273}$ of its volume at 0° C for each 1° C rise in temperature.

GRAHAM'S LAW: Gases diffuse at rates that are inversely proportional to the square roots of their densities.

Gascony. The area between the Garonne, the Pyrenees, and the Atlantic. Known to the Romans as *Aquitanea tertia*. In ◊ *Carolingian* times it was semi-independent, but was united to ◊ *Aquitaine* in 1152, and was the only part of that duchy which remained consistently under English rule until 1453; it was a valuable possession on account of its wine exports. During the ◊ Hundred Years War it was reconquered by the French.

Gas Industry. The first successful application of ◊ coal gas for large-scale lighting was in the late 18th cent. by William Murdock; the German F. A. Winsor gave demonstrations in the Lyceum Theatre, London, 1804, and his company provided gas street-lighting for Pall Mall by 1807. The chartered Gas Light and Coke Co. was formed 1812, and within a few years gas lighting was common in London; Welsbach's invention of the gas mantle 1885 greatly increased the illuminating power. Coal gas is now made by the destructive distillation of low-ash-content coal in vertical retorts (coke ovens); useful by-products are coke, coal tar, and ammonia (usually converted to the fertilizer ammonium sulphate). The percentage composition of the piped gas is usually hydrogen 55, methane 30, carbon monoxide 10, with small quantities of other gases. By eliminating carbon monoxide and making more use of imported methane, gas undertakings hope soon to supply an improved non-toxic 'town gas'. In the U.K. the Lurgi process (burning coal in oxygen-enriched air in a rotary furnace) is of growing importance, and much of the country's gas is also made by the carburetted water process or by the steam reforming of light petroleum distillates. ◊ Coal and Coal-mining, Coke, Distillation, Fuel, Petroleum.

Gasoline (Petrol) ◊ Petroleum.

Gastritis. Inflammation of the gastric ◊ mucous membrane. Mild forms result from errors of diet and from infection, and may also be brought on by psychological causes e.g. worry and overwork. Some irritant and corrosive poisons will produce severe and often fatal gastritis.

Gastropoda ◊ Molluscs, Snail.

GATT ◊ General Agreement on Tariffs and Trade.

Gaul ◊ France, Gallic Wars, Goths, Vandals.

Gault. Stiff blue-grey clay underlying the chalk in S·E England; marine in origin (the fine-grained mud which accumulated in the Cretaceous Sea) and very fossiliferous, outstandingly rich in ◊ ammonites. Gault clays are extensively dug in S E England for the manufacture of bricks and tiles. ◊ Geological Time Scale.

Gawain. In ◊ Arthurian legend, nephew of Arthur, a pattern of knightly courtesy; possibly he derives from a Celtic solar deity. He took part in the quest for the ◊ Holy Grail, and was killed in a fight with ◊ Lancelot. He also appears in the 14th-cent. English romance Sir Gawain and the Green Knight, and as Gwalchmai in the Mabinogion.

Gazelle ◊ Antelope.

Gears. Devices to couple revolving shafts and to regulate their relative speed. The simplest form is the straight-tooth spun type (cog wheel). When meshed together,

driver 10 teeth   driven 30. teeth

One complete revolution of the driving gear (a) will engage 10 teeth of the driven gear (b) turning it 10/30 or ⅓ of its its cycle. Thus (b) revolves at one third of the speed of (a).

the wheel with the smaller number of teeth rotates more rapidly than that with the larger number, the ratio of the speeds thus being in direct but opposite relation to the number of teeth (see diagram); the direction of rotation is also opposite. There is a variety of types and arrangements (some extremely complicated), but all work similarly.

Geiger Counter. Early electronic device of great sensitivity, capable of detecting and counting radioactive particles. It has many applications e.g. as a check on dangerous levels of emanations in atomic power stations, etc. and in following the course of radioactive ◊ tracer elements for medical purposes in the human body. Now largely replaced by still more complex instruments.

Gelatin. A ◊ protein soluble in hot water, which turns to a jelly on cooling, manufactured from the hoofs, bones, and tendons of animals by boiling in water or dilute acid, as a by-product of the meat or tanning industries. In its most refined form it absorbs 5–10 times its own volume of water, and is used for the preparation of photographic emulsions and in cooking and food preparation; in less purified form, it is known as glue and size. A vegetable gelatin can be obtained from the Indian seaweed agar.

Gelignite ◊ *Explosives.*

Gems. Precious or semi-precious stones have been cut, polished, and frequently engraved for use as adornment or as ◊ *seals* at least since the Egyptian and Mesopotamian civilizations; the art of gemengraving was brought to a peak of excellence in 5th cent. B.C. Athens, portraits and mythological subjects being the most popular, while that of ◊ *cameo*-cutting seems to have been developed under Alexander. From about the 3rd cent. B.C. gems were carved in Rome, the most exquisite work being produced in the later Republican and Imperial periods; the most famous of the Roman gem-engravers is Dioscorides, in the reign of Augustus. During the Middle Ages the art seems almost to have been forgotten, but it was revived with great success in Italy during the ◊ *Renaissance*, and gems (especially imitations, adaptations, copies and sometimes fakes of antique examples) became very popular throughout Europe in the ◊ *Neoclassical* period. ◊ *Corundum.*

General Agreement on Tariffs and Trade (GATT). Concluded by 22 trading nations 1947, with a charter of rules for the conduct of international trade on liberalized lines, it negotiated reciprocal tariff concessions covering some £3,000 m. worth of trade; subsequent meetings have brought further tariff reductions, and there are now 60 members (including some of the Soviet-bloc countries), conducting about 80 per cent of the world's trade. The main objective is to remove barriers obstructing international trade e.g. quota restrictions and high tariffs, and to eliminate preferences. An International Trade Organization to replace GATT was projected, but U.S.A. failure to ratify it prevented its creation. GATT works by the voluntary observance of rules by its members, but is an effective instrument for tariff reduction.

General Strike. Cessation of work in all major industries, with the intention of paralysing the economic life of a country, either to redress an economic grievance (e.g. the British general strike of 1926, in sympathy with the locked-out miners) or to achieve a political objective (e.g. the Belgian general strikes 1893, 1902, for franchise reforms). Advocacy of the general strike as a method of securing reforms dates to ◊ *Chartism* in England, though a complete strike of all workers in Dublin had been attempted in the 18th cent. The movement (◊ *Syndicalism*) reached a peak in the writings of Georges Sorel in the early 20th cent. In the U.K. the Trade Disputes Act 1927 made general strikes illegal, until its repeal in 1946. There were general strikes in the 1950s in e.g. Hungary, British Guiana. Today they are usually short-term, as token demonstrations of ◊ *trade-union* solidarity.

General Will. A highly metaphysical concept, first formulated by Diderot and Rousseau, notably in the latter's *Du Contrat Social* 1762: an ideal and infallible Will, which sets the standard of right and which is revealed when each individual independently exercises his will as a fully enlightened citizen with nothing but the general good in view. Unanimity is mystically expected to result from this process, expressing the collective conscience of the society as a whole.

Generator (Dynamo). Rotary device for changing mechanical into electrical energy, based on electromagnetic ◊ *induction*. In its simplest form it consists of a series of wires coiled round an iron core (armature) which rotates between the poles of a stationary electromagnet. The current generated as the armature breaks the magnetic field is picked up from the armature by brushes of carbon or of copper wire.

The large-scale supply of electricity for industrial and public use is generated mainly by steam ◊ *turbines*, and secondly by water-power (hydroelectric power stations).

Genes. The unit of ◊ *heredity* resides in the nucleus of the sex cell, although a few traits are known to be inherited through the cytoplasm (◊ *Gametes*). The nuclear gene is known to consist of deoxyribonucleic acid, ◊ *DNA*. Genes may undergo spontaneous chemical changes called point- ◊ *mutations*; the chance of such a mutation may be increased by radiation ($\lozenge$ *radiobiology*), or the expression of the genes may be altered, independently of chemical gene alteration, during cell division. Genes influence traits either in single pairs e.g. albinism, or by several pairs influencing one trait e.g. human height, or again they may interact with one another, e.g. two gene pairs give four possible interactions controlling the production of the four types of cock's-comb found in fowls. It is now known that genes can be transmitted from one bacterium to another by virus infections, and it may be that this can happen among mammals.

Genetics $\lozenge$ *Heredity, Mendelism, Mutations.*

Geneva Conference. 1954. Meeting between representatives of Britain, France, Nationalist China, U.S.A., and U.S.S.R. with the aim of restoring peace in S E Asia. No agreement was reached over replacing the Korean armistice by a treaty. $\lozenge$ *Disarmament, Korea, Summit Conference.*

Geneva Convention $\lozenge$ *Red Cross.*

Genocide. The systematic extermination of a group, class, or race of people defined by the exterminators as undesirable. A new term in $\lozenge$ *international law*, it was coined in 1945 by the $\lozenge$ *War Crimes* Commission at the Nuremberg trials, to cover the 'Final Solution' policy of $\lozenge$ *Nazism*, which had resulted in the destruction of millions of persons in the gas-chambers at Oświęcim (Ger. Auschwitz) and by other methods elsewhere, e.g. in the concentration camps of Belsen, Buchenwald, etc.

Genre Painting. Picture of figures in contemporary costume engaged in some everyday pursuit, esp. popular in 17th-cent. Holland ($\lozenge$ *Dutch Art*). In 18th-cent. England and France e.g. Hogarth and Greuze used such paintings to tell moral or sentimental stories, and when works of this nature reached their peak of popularity in the 19th cent. they were usually expected to have some anecdotal content, e.g. 'When did you last see your father?'

Genus $\lozenge$ *Biological Classification.*

Geodesy. Measurement of the earth's size and shape, surveying such large areas that its curvature has to be considered. The first recorded investigation into the earth's shape and size was that of Eratosthenes of Alexandria (a Greek), about 276–194 B.C.; he measured the arc on the supposed meridian of $\lozenge$ *longitude* between Syene

(mod. Aswan) and Alexandria and also (assuming Syene to lie on the Tropic of Cancer) the sun's angular deviation from the vertical at noon on the summer $\lozenge$ *solstice* at Alexandria. The resulting calculation of the earth's circumference was remarkably accurate; not till the 18th cent. was it recognized (largely through the work of Newton and Huygens) that the earth is not spherical but approximately an oblate spheroid. The basis of modern geodetic $\lozenge$ *surveying* is the triangulation method: extremely accurate (a) measurement of a base line and (b) angular observation of a distant object from each end of this line, to construct a complete triangle, from which a chain of triangles can be constructed in any direction required. Geodetic surveying demands international cooperation; the International Geodetic Association was formed 1886. $\lozenge$ *Plane-table.*

Geography. Describes the earth's surface, natural and political divisions, physical features, climates, vegetation, soils, products, and population; the earliest geographers were Greeks, who at first believed the world to be a flat elliptical disk, but Aristotle in the 4th cent. B.C. was convinced it was spherical, and Eratosthenes calculated its circumference about 200 B.C. In Roman times Strabo travelled widely in the 1st cent. B.C. and left a description of the then known world, in the 17 books of his *Geography*, and about A.D. 150 Ptolemy of Alexandria ascertained the positions of important places in terms of latitude and longitude. Then the Arabs alone maintained an interest in the subject, until the journeys of Marco Polo (c. 1254–1324) in the Far East; the next advance came with the late 15th-cent. voyages of exploration, when the Portuguese explorers Diaz and da Gama discovered and rounded the Cape of Good Hope, the latter reached India, Columbus discovered America, and Magellan circumnavigated the globe. Mercator published the first modern $\lozenge$ *map* (on the projection named after him) 1568, and map-making was also improved by new instruments e.g. the $\lozenge$ *barometer* and $\lozenge$ *telescope*, and by new methods e.g. $\lozenge$ *contours* and triangulation ($\lozenge$ *Geodesy*). From then on, more and more of the till-then unknown world was discovered by explorers; Dutch and British navigators discovered Tasmania (Van Diemen's Land), New Zealand, and

sponges

coelenterates

brachiopods

molluscs

echinoderms

fish

protozoans

vascular plants

bryozoans

amphibians

arthropods

reptiles

birds

mammals

man

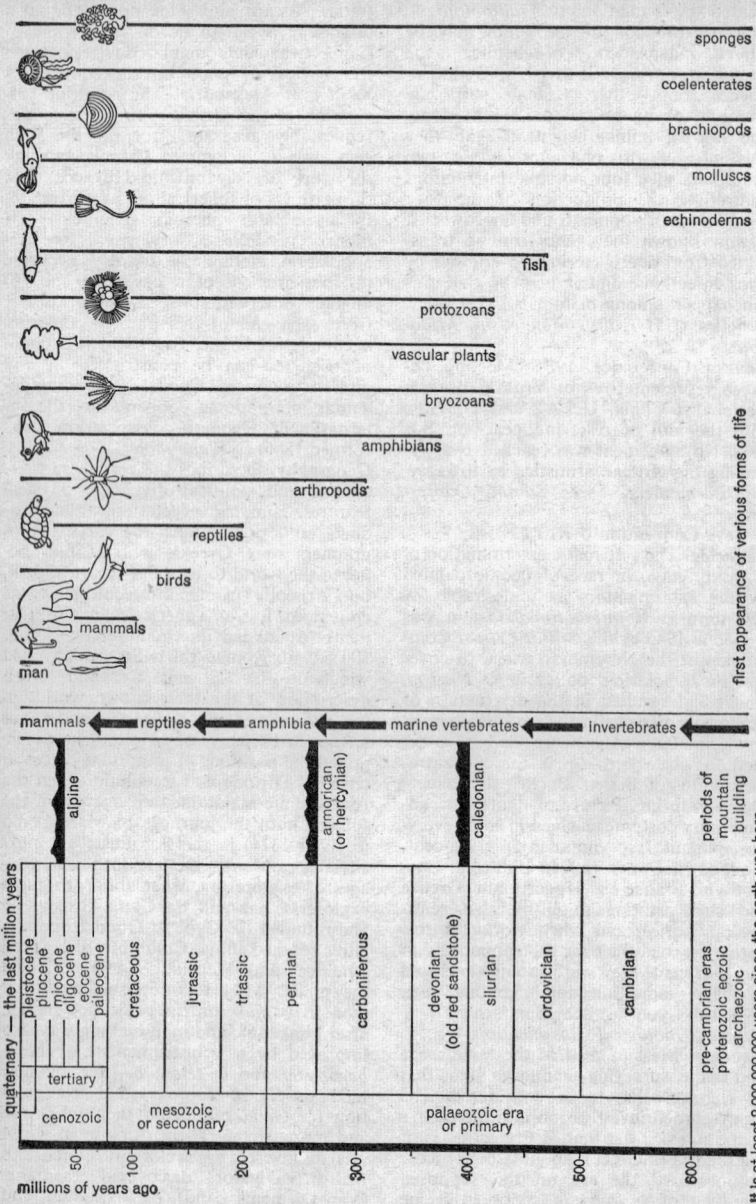

first appearance of various forms of life

mammals ← reptiles ← amphibia ← marine vertebrates ← invertebrates ←

alpine

armorican (or hercynian)

caledonian

periods of mountain building

quaternary — the last million years

pleistocene
pliocene
miocene
oligocene
eocene
palaeocene

cretaceous

jurassic

triassic

permian

carboniferous

devonian (old red sandstone)

silurian

ordovician

cambrian

pre-cambrian eras
proterozoic eozoic
archaezoic

tertiary

cenozoic

mesozoic or secondary

palaeozoic era or primary

50   100   200   300   400   500   600

millions of years ago.

It is at least 2,000,000,000 years since the earth was born

Australia, and the 17th–19th centuries saw many expeditions into the interiors of continents; S. America was penetrated by Humboldt, Africa by Livingstone and Stanley, Australia by Sturt and Eyre. More recently, exploration has often been concerned with the polar regions; early in the 20th cent. the N. Pole was reached by Peary and the S. Pole by Amundsen and Scott.

Geological Time Scale. Method of subdividing the immense period of time from the earliest known geological events down to the present day. The main divisions, though fixed largely in an arbitrary manner, have been recognized internationally (many of the names of the subdivisions have only local significance). Each of the major divisions, Eras, includes two or more Periods, divided into Epochs, further subdivided into Ages; and corresponding terms describe the rocks then formed: Era (Group); Period (System); Epoch (Series); Age (Stage, Formation). Thus, the rocks of the Carboniferous System were laid down during the Carboniferous Period.

The names of the Eras derive from Gr. *zoe* (life), prefixed by *kainos* (recent), *mesos* (middle), *palaeos* (old), *proteros* (earlier), and *eos* (dawn). The Eozoic Era and the Proterozoic Era are the longest as well as the oldest of the main divisions. During this vast extent of time (over 3000 m. years) many mountain-building movements occurred, and the rocks known as Archaean or pre-Cambrian were formed (◊ *Cambrian System*): these, almost entirely igneous or metamorphic, are structurally complex and yield many metallic ores; ◊ *fossils* are rare, and it is very difficult to correlate rocks in widely separated areas. The Palaeozoic Era, the second great division, is the first in which recognizable fossils are common, proving the existence of living things; the 380 m. years of this Era saw the appearance of fish, reptiles, and primitive plants. During the Mesozoic Era, ferns and evergreens flourished (◊ *Gymnosperms*) and in the swamps lived reptiles e.g. dinosaurs and pterodactyls; on the whole this was a calm Era with little mountain-building activity, in the warm Mesozoic seas deposition of sand, clays, and limestones was almost continuous (the ◊ *ammonite* is the characteristic fossil), and the first primitive mammals also developed. The earlier part

of the Cenozoic (Tertiary) Era lasted about 70 m. years, during which modern types of plants and mammals gradually evolved. The last million years of the earth's history forms the Quaternary Period (divided into the Pleistocene Epoch and the Recent Epoch). An older classification recognized four Eras: Primary, Secondary, Tertiary, and Quaternary; the last two names are still in general use (as subdivisions of the ◊ *Cenozoic Era*), but 'Secondary' and 'Primary' are less common: the name Primary suggests either the beginning of the world or the appearance of life on its surface, but it is now known that before this Era began the earth had already passed through three quarters of its long history, and a few fossils have been recognized in pre-Cambrian rocks, proving that life existed before the Primary Era. ◊ *Geology*.

Geology. Science concerned with the origin, evolution, structure, and composition of the earth (and its fauna and flora), as revealed by the rocks of the earth's crust, many subdivisions now being sciences in their own right.

The development of geology owes much to the work of non-professional observers. In no other science (astronomy and archaeology possibly excepted) has the keen amateur participated so actively or contributed so much. Experimental methods of investigation involving complicated apparatus typical of chemistry, physics, and biology are of only limited use in geology, for geological processes work slowly and depend on factors beyond human control; the advance of geological knowledge has depended on simple observations, patiently gathered, of the outcrops of rocks, their thicknesses, their tilt, their lithological character, and their fossil content. William Smith 1769–1839 (who drew the first geological map of England and Wales about 1800) is often called 'the father of English geology'. From very early times men had recognized the shapes of shellfish and plants in rocks; such fossils were variously interpreted as 'nature's ornaments' or as the Creator's early apprentice efforts in making shellfish, which he had rejected as not being good enough. Leonardo da Vinci offered a true explanation of fossils in the 15th cent. but learned clerics maintained as late as the 19th cent. that they had been placed in rocks by the devil, to deceive mankind.

Until the early 19th cent. it was generally believed that crystalline as well as sedimentary rocks had accumulated from deposits in the oceans. James Hutton 1726–97 (regarded as the founder of modern geology) demonstrated the igneous origin of these rocks, refuted the prevalent idea that earth features were the result of sudden cataclysms, and developed the view that the present is the key to the past; the canyon is not the sudden consequence of a mighty earthquake, but the exceedingly slow work of an eroding river.

Geology is useful in locating minerals of economic importance (coal, petroleum, building and road materials e.g. stone, clay for bricks, and lime for cement, metal ores) and water supplies (siting dams for purposes of irrigation, hydroelectricity, or drinking-water). Geological surveys also help to determine the position of roads and railways, bridges and tunnels; drift maps show the kind of soil likely to be present and its suitability for agriculture.

GEOMORPHOLOGY: Study of present-day landscapes and land forms, and the interpretation of their evolution.

GEOPHYSICS: The physics of the earth, esp. making and interpreting physical measurements e.g. seismic, gravitational, magnetic, and electrical methods used in e.g. the search for mineral deposits, petroleum, and underground supplies of water.

MINERALOGY: Deals with the minerals which form the rocks of the earth's crust.

PALAEONTOLOGY: Study of the fossil remains of plants and animals.

PETROLOGY: Deals with the rocks themselves, their formation and the changes they undergo (e.g. eruption, crystallization, metamorphism) and includes the classification of rocks and their mode of occurrence.

STRATIGRAPHY: A branch of historical geology dealing with rocks occurring in layers (strata), their age and distribution, the thickness of the deposits, and the changes to which they have been subjected, esp. the correlation of ore deposit with another by comparing fossils.

◊ *Drift, Geological Time Scale, Igneous/Metamorphic/Sedimentary Rocks, Seismology.*

Geometry. The surveying and architectural diagrams of the Babylonians and Egyptians developed into the axiomatic study of figures in the abstract, formulated by Euclid in a method still relevant to most practical and theoretical applications. Plane geometry is the study of figures drawn upon a flat surface, spherical geometry that of figures drawn upon a sphere, and solid geometry that of three-dimensional figures, e.g. cubes, cones, and spheroids. Euclid's geometry is presented in terms of a number of axioms, and his system depends directly upon the figures themselves, but Descartes evolved an analytical geometry in which the algebraic representations of the figures are studied. Euclid's geometry is based on an assumption (the famous 5th postulate) which is equivalent to the result that the angle-sum of a triangle is two right angles. There are consequently two other geometries, in which the angle-sum is either less (elliptic or Riemannian geometry) or greater (hyperbolic geometry) than two right-angles. In the theory of relativity, Einstein makes use of Riemannian geometry to postulate a 'space' in which his results may be represented.

Georgian ◊ *Caucasian Languages.*

Georgian Architecture. The English architectural style of about 1700–1830, beginning with the revival of Inigo Jones's ◊ *Palladian* style; the main architects are

Colen Campbell, Lord Burlington, and William Kent (while Gibbs continued in the Wren manner), and Palladianism persisted until gently modified by Robert Adam about 1760. Interiors are more elaborate than exteriors, being first richly Italianate under Kent, then ◊ *Rococo*, and finally Adamesque; mainly a domestic style, its most characteristic products are solid stone-faced country houses e.g. Houghton and Wentworth Woodhouse, usually with some form of temple front or portico on the main façade, and elegantly simple brick-built town houses such as still survive in London and Dublin, often arranged in terraces or crescents which form decorative units sometimes embellished with the classical ◊ *architectural orders*.

Georgian Poets. Strictly, the 36 contributors to the anthology *Georgian Poetry*, 5 vols 1912–22 (chief ed. Edward Marsh), the aim and achievement of which was bringing new poetry to a large popular audience; also other similar poets of the time. Georgian poetry was mainly lyric, celebrating 'beauty' esp. of nature, and often nostalgic, but sometimes sentimental and trivial; it was never 'difficult'. A. E. Housman has been called the 'spiritual father' of the group, which included Rupert Brooke, Walter de la Mare, John Masefield, W. H. Davies, J. E. Flecker, Harold Monro, J. C. Squire, Edward Thomas, and Edmund Blunden.

Geosyncline. Long, relatively narrow trough in the earth's crust; sinks slowly downwards as it continuously fills at the surface with more and more sediments, becomes stretched and weakened by melting as its base gets deeper into the earth's interior, and finally breaks under the strain. Molten ◊ *magma* rises from the earth's interior, and the sediments of the trough are crumpled and folded into mountains. It is estimated that the geosyncline of the Palaeozoic Era was over seven miles deep, filling slowly through the Cambrian, Ordovician, and Silurian Periods for about 175 m. years. ◊ *Geological Time Scale, Syncline.*

Geranium. The plants commonly known as geraniums are pelargoniums, probably derived from two species native to S. Africa, with a dark zone on the leaves. The true geraniums grow in most parts of the temperate world; the beautiful English meadow cranesbill, *G. pra-*

tense, is typical, and herb robert, *G. robertianum,* is an example of the small annuals. Many of the exotic species are valuable for their vigorous weed-smothering growth.

German. Part of the W. Germanic division of the Germanic branch of the ◊ *Indo-European languages*; spoken by about 90 m. in Germany, Austria, and German-speaking Switzerland (and as a second language in many other parts of the world). Standard German descends from Old High German, about A.D. 750–1100, the speech of the highlands of central and S. Germany; Low German was the speech of the N. plain (though the *platt* in Plattdeutsch has no reference to the flat lands but means 'downright' and hence 'popular'). The Middle High German period about 1100–1500 was followed by the New High German period, when the standard language was regularized. In 1534 Martin Luther used the E. Middle German *Kanzleisprache* of Meissen for his Bible, and unified the written language as *Neuhochdeutsche Schriftsprache*, which was widely spread by his Bible, hymns, and tracts, and ousted Low German from pulpits and from official use. From the 17th cent. onwards this literary language was further regularized by professional grammarians, by the rise as cultural centres of Halle, Leipzig, and Berlin, and by the writings of Klopstock, Lessing, and later Goethe, Schiller, and Wieland. Today German is the most uniform and highly-inflected (in nouns and in adjectives) of all living Germanic languages; in the invention of compounds and derivatives it shows astounding virtuosity, but is burdened by inflexions of noun and adjective almost as elaborate as those of the ◊ *Slavonic languages.* ◊◊ *Germanic Languages.*

German Architecture. Not till the 9th-cent. age of Charlemagne did a specifically German style e.g. the Palatine Chapel at Aachen grow out of Italian models. After 1100 Germany adopted a Central European form of ◊ *Romanesque architecture* e.g. St Michael's in Hildesheim, and in the 11th cent. German architects produced masterpieces e.g. the cathedrals and churches of Speier, Mainz, Worms, Laach; ◊ *Gothic architecture* was introduced from France about 1200, but a distinctively German style developed esp. in the East German redbrick churches. ◊ *Renaissance* architecture reached Germany late, about 1550, and (as in England) was largely based on high-gabled Flemish models, notably in the many late 16th- and early 17th-cent. town halls. Purely Italianate buildings are rare, but the Germans eagerly adopted the ◊ *Baroque* and ◊ *Rococo* styles, which became as successful in 18th-cent. Germany as did the simpler ◊ *Georgian* style in England. The magnificent churches of the Asam brothers are outstanding examples of German High Baroque. A stricter ◊ *Neoclassicism* was introduced about 1760 and culminated in the work of Gilly and Schinkel, about 1800, before the onset of 19th-cent. Gothic and Greek revivalism. Behrens and Gropius, under whose direction the Bauhaus became the source of many new architectural ideas, contributed to the development of the 20th-cent. functional style, until ◊ *Nazism* arrested modernist tendencies and drove many German architects abroad.

German Art. From its earliest examples (in Carolingian book covers and ◊ *Romanesque* carvings) German art exhibited a persistent duality, the conflict between classical influences and a native impulse towards fantasy and expressionism. German ◊ *Gothic* painting was not dissimilar from its counterparts elsewhere in Europe, and sculpture remained a more important art, until in the 15th cent. a specifically German School of painting appeared with Konrad Witz, Martin Schongauer, Stephen Lochner, who combined mysticism with a detailed naturalism. The works of Cranach, Altdorfer, Hans Baldung, and esp. Grünewald introduced an unmistakably German modification. Closest to the ◊ *Renaissance* aesthetic were Holbein the Younger, whose objectivity and firm draughtsmanship were distinguishing northern characteristics, and Dürer, who remained close to the Renaissance style which he introduced, but in his graphic work was not far from the late Gothic tradition. The long religious wars strangled artistic development, and it was not until the 20th cent. that German painting again made outstanding contributions (◊ *Blaue Reiter Group, Expressionism*).

Germanic Languages. A branch of the ◊ *Indo-European languages*; a common Germanic language was spoken in prehistoric times on the N. German plain, whence it expanded and split into three divisions.

EAST GERMANIC: Burgundian, Vandal (both early extinct), and Gothic, the earliest literary form of any Germanic language, preserved in the Biblical translation made from the Greek by Bishop Wulfila 311–83, a Visigoth.

NORTH GERMANIC: Now includes Danish (spoken by about 4 m.); Icelandic (little changed in the last 1000 years from the language of the Old Norse sagas); Norwegian (*riksmål*, closely resembling literary Danish, and *landsmål*); and Swedish, spoken by 6½ m.

WEST GERMANIC: Has split into ◊ *English*; ◊ *Frisian*; Flemish (spoken by about 4.5 m. in Flanders in and around Ghent); Dutch (the national language of the Netherlands); Low German; High German. Originally highly inflected languages like Latin, all except German (the least evolved of the group) have shed most of their inflexions.

AFRIKAANS (CAPE DUTCH): A variant of Dutch used in S. Africa.

PLATTDEUTSCH: A collection of Low German dialects descending from Old Saxon and retaining many features which distinguish them from Neuhochdeutsch, New High German.

SCHWEIZERDEUTSCH: A variant spoken in 19 of the 25 cantons of Switzerland.

Germanium. A rare silvery-grey brittle ◊ *element*, a by-product of the smelting of sulphide ores of zinc, lead, and copper; an important semi-conductor, used in transistors.

German Silver (Nickel Silver) ◊ *Alloys*.

Germany. The German Empire was created in 1871 (for previous history ◊ *Prussia*). Under Wilhelm I and his minister Bismarck Germany rapidly became an important industrial power, built up a powerful army and navy, and acquired extensive overseas possessions mainly in Africa. After the dismissal of Bismarck by Wilhelm II in 1890 the expansionist policies of the Kaiser drew Britain and France together into the ◊ *Entente Cordiale*. In 1914 the assassination of the Archduke Ferdinand in Sarajevo led Austria supported by Germany into war against Serbia which precipitated the First World War. After Germany's defeat in 1918 the Kaiser was forced to abdicate and a republic was set up (◊ *Weimar Re-*

public) for which neither the bulk of the electorate nor the army had any deep loyalty. Beset with economic difficulties and political unrest the young Republic and the old President Hindenburg succumbed to the tactics of Hitler and ◊ *Nazism*; the Republic gave way to the Third Reich and totalitarian rule (1933). Hitler pursued a foreign policy which reaped rapid early successes but culminated in the Second World War and total defeat for Germany. The peace treaty between the Allies and Germany envisaged in the ◊ *Potsdam* agreement of 1946 failed to materialize and Germany remains divided into the Federal Republic, the Democratic Republic, and an isolated ◊ *Berlin*.

Germany, Democratic Republic (E. Germany). Area (excluding E. Berlin) 41,479 sq. m. Pop. 17.3 m. Cap. E. Berlin. The former German states of Brandenburg, Mecklenburg, Thuringia, Saxony, and Saxony-Anhalt, which became the Soviet zone of occupation in 1945. A new constitution, abolishing these states, was drawn up in 1949 under Soviet supervision. Otto Grotewohl became prime minister of the one-party state, but Walter Ulbricht, first secretary of the Socialist Unity party, was effective leader. In 1953 the Soviet commander-in-chief was replaced by a civilian High Commissioner; the same year there were workers' riots, crushed by Soviet troops. Full sovereignty was granted in 1955, and E. Germany joined the ◊ *Warsaw Pact*, but Soviet troops remained. In 1961 the E. German government erected a wall across ◊ *Berlin*, sealing off a hitherto steady flow of E. Germans to the west. ◊» *Germany (Federal Republic).*

Germany, Federal Republic (W. Germany). Area (excluding W. Berlin) 95,744 sq. m. Pop. 59 m. (both figures being remarkably close to those of the U.K.). Cap. Bonn. When it became clear that Soviet acceptance of free elections in a united Germany would be refused, France, U.K., and U.S.A. terminated the military occupation in 1949, and in 1955 W. Germany regained full sovereignty and became a member of N.A.T.O., agreeing to the retention of American, British, and French troops within Germany. W. Berlin is technically not part of the Federal Republic, although it is in the closest possible association. Under the 1949 constitution, the legislature consists of an elected President, the *Bundestag* elected by universal suffrage, and the *Bundesrat* (Federal Council elected by the 10 states (*Länder*) of the Republic which enjoy some measure of local government esp. in education and religious matters). The strongest party is the Christian Democratic Union (C.D.U.), in power either alone or in coalition with smaller parties since 1949: the Social Democratic Party (S.P.D.) has consistently been the largest opposition party. Konrad Adenauer (leader of the C.D.U.) became Chancellor under the 1949 constitution, and remained in office until 1963, when he was succeeded by Ludwig Erhard, previously Minister of Economics, chief architect of the German industrial revival. ECONOMY. After financial reform in 1948 W. Germany enjoyed a rapid return to prosperity, with a ◊ *free market* economy, and successfully absorbed several millions of German refugees, to become the most powerful industrial country in continental Europe. Its cooperation with France within the European Economic Community is a notable feature of post-war policy. Principal products are coal, iron, and steel, industrial manufactures of a wide variety, particularly strong in the field of motor vehicles, machine tools, and chemicals. The agricultural production is important though much of it remains on a small-scale basis. ◊» *Berlin, Germany (Democratic Republic).*

HISTORY ◊ *Bavaria, Nazism, Palatinate, Prussia, Saxony, Silesia, Third Reich.*

Gestalt School ◊ *Psychology.*

Gestapo ◊ *Nazism, Secret Police.*

Gesta Romanorum. A miscellaneous collection of popular tales compiled in Latin in the 14th cent. and translated into English about 1450; the collector's object was didactic, to provide 'exemplae' (moral examples) for the use of the clergy, but the stories themselves belong to folklore, with only a nominal association with Rome.

Gestation. Period during which young animals develop within the mother's body; for man, usually about 280 days (but may be well over 300). The longest known gestation period is that of the African elephant (up to 650 days) and the shortest that of the opossum (less than 14 days). Mean periods (in days) are horse 340; Arabian camel 336; cattle

280; sheep and goat 148; pig 115; dog 63; cat 60; mouse 21.

Gettysburg Address. 1863. Dedication by Abraham Lincoln of the Civil War cemetery at the battlefield of Gettysburg; one of the most famous speeches of history, beginning: 'Four score and seven years ago our fathers brought forth on this continent a new nation, conceived in Liberty, and dedicated to the proposition that all men are created equal' . . . and ending: '. . . and that government of the people, by the people, for the people, shall not perish from the earth'.

Geyser. < Geysir, in Iceland. Spring intermittently ejecting hot water and steam in volcanic areas, where water reaches rocks hot enough to generate steam but the cracks are not wide enough to allow continuous ejection; most frequent in Iceland, New Zealand, and U.S.A.

Ghana. Area 92,100 sq. m. Pop. 6.7 m. Cap. Accra. Republic in W. Africa (formerly named the Gold Coast), between the Ivory Coast, Togo, Mali, and Upper Volta; member of the British Commonwealth. The legislature is the President and the National Assembly, 104 members elected by adult suffrage, plus 10 women's representatives; there are also advisory Houses of Chiefs. The regime is dictatorial, under President Nkrumah, who is also Prime Minister; dismissals of judges for 'unsatisfactory' decisions have aroused widespread criticisms.

ECONOMY. Predominantly agricultural; main product cocoa; also coffee, hardwoods, rubber, and considerable fisheries. Rich mineral resources esp. bauxite, diamonds, gold, manganese. The Voltariver hydroelectric scheme will supply power for producing aluminium from bauxite.

HISTORY. Discovered by Europeans in the 15th cent. At various times ◊ *Ashanti*, the Gold Coast, Toga, Volta, and the Northern Territories came under British control; the Gold Coast colony was established in 1874, others in 1901–2. The German colony of Transvolta-Togo became a British mandated territory after the First World War and as a result of a U.N. plebiscite in 1956 was integrated with the Gold Coast, and the whole became Ghana, independent within the British Commonwealth, in 1957. It adopted a republican constitution in 1960. ◊◊ *Ashanti, Mali.*

Ghetto. In early medieval cities, the quarter where Jews voluntarily lived together. In late medieval times compulsory ghettoes were instituted in Rome, Spain, and Portugal; though most of them disappeared by the 19th cent. they persisted in Russia and E. Europe. In the ◊ *Second World War* the Nazis strictly confined all the Jews in Warsaw in the old ghetto, which was destroyed with all its inhabitants in 1944.

Gibbon. Slender long-armed S E Asian ◊ *ape*, with two genera, Hylobates and Symphyla, and several species; their characteristic motion is by swinging from branch to branch, and they are gregarious, each family defending its own living-space.

Gibraltar. A rocky peninsula joined to the Spanish mainland only by a sand flat; in antiquity, part of the 'Pillars of Hercules'. It was settled in turn by Romans, Arabs, and Berbers before it became part of Spain in 1462. Sir George Rooke captured it in 1704, since when it has remained in British hands.

Gila Monster. One species about 18 in. long is among the few ◊ *lizards* known to be poisonous; found in U.S.A. (SW) and Mexico, of a mottled black and yellow appearance; the venom-carrying teeth are far back, and only rarely bite man deeply enough to be lethal.

Gilgamesh. Hero of a Babylonian epic known largely from tablets of the 7th cent. B.C. but dating to well over 1000 years earlier; he was a king of Erech (◊ *Sumerians*), but nothing is known of him historically beyond mention in the Sumerian king-lists. In the epic, he ruled Erech harshly until the gods created the savage man Enkidu, with whom he eventually became fast friends. Having offended the goddess ◊ *Ishtar*, Gilgamesh was punished by leprosy, and Enkidu was killed; seeking advice on how to cure himself and restore his friend to life, he went to the wise man Utnapishtim (the Babylonian Noah), who told him the story of the flood, and of the plant of life at the bottom of the sea, for which Gilgamesh dived, only to be forestalled by a sea-serpent which ate the plant. Later he was allowed to visit Enkidu in the underworld.

Gills. Respiratory organs of aquatic animals which (like lungs) increase the body surface across which gases may be exchanged; may be extensions of the body surface (as in marine lugworms, molluscs, and some aquatic insect larvae) or of the lining of the alimentary canal (as in the pharyngeal gills of fish). Stiff appendages (gill-rakers) filter the water, so that no solid food matter is passed over the gill-filaments which absorb the oxygen.

Gilt-edged Securities. Fixed interest stock, usually issued by the Government or by local government authorities, where the payment of interest carries a government guarantee. Hence there is no risk; but neither is there any prospect of capital appreciation, unless the general level of the rate of interest falls.

Gin. Alcohol diluted and flavoured with various herbs ('botanicals'), the principal of which has always been juniper, Ital. *ginevra*, hence 'gin'. Originally a Dutch drink, it was introduced into England some 300 years ago, when it quickly displaced French brandy as the drink of the poor, being sold so cheaply that drunkenness became and long remained a very serious social evil. Gin differs from most other spirits in that its taste is derived not from the base from which it is distilled but from the added flavouring; it can be distilled from a great variety of ingredients, but the most common is grain alcohol. In Britain it is usually sold at 70° proof. 'London' gin is an unsweetened gin; sweetened gin is known as 'Old Tom' or 'Old Geneva'; and sloe gin is ordinary gin flavoured with sloes. Probably more gin is drunk throughout the world than any other liquor.

Ginger. A spice from the dried rhizomes of the tropical herb *Zingiber officinale*, cultivated in India and China from the earliest times and then spread throughout the tropics. Crystallized and 'stem' ginger are made from the young rhizomes boiled in syrup.

Gipsies. A scattered people of Eurasia (originally a low-caste people of India) speaking a language related to Sanskrit (◊ *Romany*) and calling themselves Roma (the word gipsy deriving from 'Egyptian'), who left India in the 1st millennium A.D. and entered Europe by about 1300 and England by 1500. They were formerly centred on E. Europe, where there were perhaps 150,000; many were killed by the Germans in the Second World War. In Britain there are fewer than 2000 true Gipsies; many wandering tinkers etc.

often called 'gipsies' are repudiated by the true Gipsies. Everywhere Gipsies have been regarded as socially inferior, and even outcasts; they became craftsmen, musicians, fortune-tellers, etc. There have been various attempts to set up a Gipsy state (a Gipsy 'King' exists). Although there is much romantic writing about them (from George Borrow onwards), very little is really known of them and their way of life.

Giraffe. Tallest of all mammals, reaching a height of 18 ft, inhabiting ◊ *savanna* country and browsing on trees; their small horns are seldom used in defence, and they rely on their speed of 30 m.p.h. at a gallop to escape their enemies. Now confined to Africa S. of the Sahara, although formerly they inhabited S. Europe and India in large herds.

Girl Guides ◊ *Boy Scouts.*

Girondins ◊ *French Revolution.*

Glacier. Mass of ice moving down a valley or slope: a high collecting-ground of snow (the névé or firn) which recrystallizes as the air is squeezed out of the snowflakes, and a tongue of ice which flows slowly downslope under gravity, tapering to a narrow snout as it melts. The annual movement is rarely more than a few feet. ◊ *Bergschrund, Crevasse, Moraine.*

Glanders. Contagious bacterial ailment, one of the ◊ *scheduled diseases;* affects primarily horses, but also humans (to whom it is usually fatal). Formerly a great scourge of horses in all countries, in the early 20th cent. it was eradicated from Britain, Canada, and U.S.A. Caused by *B. pfeifferella*, it is characterized by the formation of nodules in the lungs and liver and of skin lesions and ulcerative sores in the ◊ *mucous membrane* of the nose.

Glands. Organs whose function is to provide secretions necessary for bodily functions, or to excrete waste products from the system; they vary in structure from simple unicellular secreting units e.g. those of the mucous membrane of the alimentary tract, through tubular aggregations of secretory cells e.g. those which help to form the lining of the uterus, to branching structures of great complexity. ENDOCRINE GLANDS: Those which secrete internally, i.e. discharge into the blood chemical substances which in turn influence other glands. ◊ *Endocrine System.*

EXOCRINE GLANDS: Those which secrete through a duct; sweat, tears, and bile are exocrine secretions, as is nectar in flowers. They sometimes serve defensive purposes e.g. the 'ink' discharged by ♢ *cephalopods*.

Glass. The art of making glass was invented before 1500 B.C. in Egypt and later transmitted to Europe and China; vessels were at first moulded, but the art of modelling by blowing into the molten glass through a pipe was discovered 1st cent. B.C. The Romans carried the art of glassmaking to a peak only recently regained. The Venetians 15th cent. rediscovered how to clarify glass with manganese, and became famous for ornamental and mirror glass. Later the French invented a casting method for plate glass (e.g. in the 17th cent. Palace of Versailles). An English contribution was a flint glass (containing lead oxide) esp. suitable for cut glass. In comparatively recent times, glassmaking became a mass-production industry and glass found very many different uses; the basic materials have remained unchanged, but manufacturing methods have become more efficient. Common glass is made by fusing together sand (silica), soda, and lime. It is essentially composed of sodium and calcium silicates ('soda-glass'). If potash is used instead of soda a 'hard' glass is obtained which softens at a higher temperature, though this is more expensive. Crude glass is coloured by traces of iron impurity, green (ferrous) or brown (ferric). To remove this colour the iron is oxidized to the ferric state and the brownish colour neutralized by a pink colour supplied by another element. This is done by adding small quantities of manganese dioxide or a mixture containing selenium. Ravenscroft, 1675, introduced lead oxide to the mixture instead of lime and obtained a much more brilliant product. In modern times, to produce tough heat-resisting glass the lime has been replaced by boric oxide (with aluminium oxide). The three chief types of glass now made are therefore: soda, lead crystal (made from silica, potash, and lead monoxide (32 per cent)), and borosilicate (ovenware) made from silica, soda, and oxides of boron and aluminium.

CRYSTAL GLASS: Originally a colourless ♢ *quartz* (rock crystal), now any high-quality brilliant glass.

FIBRE GLASS: Finely spun glass filament used for insulation, fireproof textiles, and mouldings e.g. hulls of boats.

PLATE GLASS: Produced in the form of a ribbon flowing from the tank on to metal rollers; on hardening, the opaque glass is ground on a line of grinders which treat both surfaces simultaneously, and then cut into lengths for polishing. The Pilkington 'float' process 1959 introduced a continuous method: the molten metal flows on to a bath of molten tin, ensuring a perfect undersurface, and heat applied above produces a similar upper surface.

SAFETY GLASS: If fractured, this gives fragments less liable to cause severe cuts than those from ordinary glass. *Heat-treated safety glass:* Two or more pieces of glass firmly united to and alternating with pieces of reinforcing material.

SHEET GLASS (e.g. for windows): Drawn continuously from large fireclay containers in which the 'metal' (molten glass) is prepared; the modern method is to draw it vertically between powered rollers.
  ♢ *Stained Glass.*

Glaucoma. Eye disease characterized by pressure and hardness in the eyeball, usually leading to impaired vision. It is often secondary to some other eye disease or injury, but may be congenital, resulting from defective drainage of the eye. Treatment is by drugs to relieve the tension in the eyeball, or by surgical drainage.

Glider. Motorless aircraft; the term often covers both gliders and sailplanes, the strict distinction being that gliders do not normally gain height after their launching (by winch or powered aeroplane) at an initial release height, while sailplanes use up-currents (caused by temperature differences in the air masses and by ground contours) to gain height. Gliders built and flown by Lilienthal, Chanute, and the Voisin brothers helped to pave the way for the powered aeroplane.

GLIDING: Developed early in aviation history, became popular as a competitive sport after Robert Kronfeld, an Austrian, had shown its possibilities 1928, and is controlled by the International Aeronautical Federation. The British Gliding Association, founded 1929, which controls the sport in the U.K. under powers delegated by the Royal Aero Club, has 49 clubs, and world and national championships comprise distance and speed events.

Globulin ♢ *Blood.*

Glorious Revolution. 1688. The 'bloodless revolution' i.e. the deposition of James II and the accession of William III and Mary to the British throne. There had been opposition to Charles II through suspicion of his leanings to ◊ *absolutism*, but it was James II's admitted Roman Catholicism (◊ *Exclusion Bill, Seven Bishops*) and the birth of a Catholic heir to follow him which united some leading ◊ *Tories* with the ◊ *Whigs* and led to their joint invitation to James's nephew and son-in-law the Protestant William of Orange to rule as sovereign. William landed at Torbay in 1688; James's forces deserted him and he fled first to Ireland (◊ *Boyne*) and then to France. William and Mary became joint rulers the following year. The Declaration of Rights 1688 established a constitutional monarchy, the Bill of Rights 1689 barred Roman Catholic succession to the British throne and admitted religious freedom for Scotland (◊ *Covenant*); but the ◊ *Penal Laws* were extended (◊ *Orange Society*). From then on the ascendancy of Parliament over Crown has never been successfully challenged in England. ◊◊ *Sedgemoor.*

Glow-worm ◊ *Firefly.*

Glucose (Dextrose). Colourless highly soluble crystalline sugar (◊ *Carbohydrates*) found in honey, grapes, etc. Other sugars are converted into glucose in the body to provide energy (◊ *Digestion*), and ingestion of glucose is thus a rapid source of energy. It is extensively used in confectionery and in brewing.

Glue ◊ *Gelatin.*

Glycerine. Chemically glycerol, < Gr. *glykys*, sweet; a viscous alcohol of b.p. 290° C, very soluble in water and also hygroscopic. It is obtained by hydrolysis of glyceride fats, mainly as a by-product of soap manufacture, but it may also be made synthetically from propylene produced by petroleum cracking. It is used in manufacturing perfumes, medicine, and explosives, and as an anti-freeze.

Glycol ◊ *Olefines.*

Glyndebourne Festival. An annual summer opera festival at a private estate in Sussex, founded 1934; now internationally renowned for its very high standards of music and production. Mozart operas are most frequently performed.

G.M.T. (Greenwich Mean Time) ◊ *Greenwich Observatory, Time.*

Gnat ◊ *Fly.*

Gneiss. Coarse-grained crystalline rock, a metamorphosed form of ◊ *granite*; under great pressures and at high temperatures, the original minerals have been rearranged in bands or 'foliated'. The Lewisian gneisses of N W Scotland are the most ancient rocks of Britain. ◊◊ *Metamorphic Rocks.*

Gnostics. < Gr. *gnosis*, knowledge. Early Christian teaching that man is a material being created not by the absolute godhead (which is unknowable) but by the demiurge (an emanation from the godhead), that therefore man's nature is imperfect and liable to follow evil, but that his spark of the divine essence can be redeemed and reunited to the godhead through the knowledge brought by ◊ *Jesus Christ.* Very numerous in Egypt, the Gnostics had various sects, and many fragments of their literature are extant, inc. apocryphal ◊ *Gospels.* Famous Gnostics include Marcion, fl. A.D. 100–65, Basilides, fl. A.D. 125, and Valentinus, fl. A.D. 136–60. ◊◊ *Albigenses, Manichaeism, Mysticism.*

Goa. Former colony of ◊ *Portugal*, founded 1510, in W. India, bordered by Bombay state. About two thirds of the population are Hindu and the remainder Christian. After 1953 by blocking communications etc. India attempted to exclude Portugal; tension mounted until in 1962 Indian troops marched in and assumed control.

Goat. *Capra* (*Bovidae*); horned ruminant related to the ◊ *sheep*, probably first domesticated in Persia and still widely bred for its milk, which differs in content from that of the cow. Voracious eaters, goats have been largely responsible for the deforestation of large areas in Persia, Syria, and Turkey. The Angora goat produces a fine wool called mohair. The wild goat, ibex, is found in the Alps and Apennines.

God. The Supreme Being, First Cause, or Creator, esp. as an object of religious worship. Many religions acknowledge a number of gods (polytheism), either as independent beings or as aspects of a single divinity; the monotheistic religions (◊ *Christianity, Islam, Judaism*) admit only one, and many of the early religions, e.g. of the ancient Egyptians and Greeks, also show a tendency towards monotheism. The chief of the names for the god of the Hebrews was J H W H (commonly transliterated as Jehovah or Jahweh), but this was considered inexpressible and other names e.g. Adonai (Lord) were substituted. Another name, *El*, is related etymologically to Allah, the name for God used by Arabs. Christians, Jews, and Muslims believe that God has revealed himself to man through inspired messengers (e.g. prophets) and sacred writings (◊ *Bible*, ◊ *Koran*); he is venerated by prayer, thanksgiving, and in many cases ◊ *sacrifice*, by conformity to a code of ethics, and often by ascetic practices e.g. fasting. He is generally regarded as omnipotent, infinite, and in some sense both transcendent (as infinitely removed from man) and immanent (as dwelling in the human spirit or soul). Of the several arguments for his existence, none is indisputable; many contemporary theologians choose rather to rest their case on religious experience. ◊ *Deism, Theism.*

COSMOLOGICAL ARGUMENT: Begins with the fact that ordinary things in the world have causes, which themselves had causes, and asserts that there must have been a First Cause i.e. God.

ONTOLOGICAL ARGUMENT: That God must exist, since 'God does not exist' is self-contradictory and hence false, because 'God' means, at least, 'most perfect being': to say he does not exist is to deny he is most perfect, since perfection presupposes existence.

TELEOLOGICAL ARGUMENT: Argument from design, i.e. that the universe gives evidence of being designed, which postulates the existence of God.

Goetheanum ◊ *Anthroposophy.*

Gog, Magog. In English legend, the last of a race of giants, compelled to guard the London Guildhall, where two large effigies of them still stand, earlier pairs of effigies having been destroyed in the Great Fire 1666 and in an air raid 1940. There are references to Gog in the Bible e.g. Rev. xx. 7–9, and also in the Koran.

Goitre. Enlargement of the ◊ *thyroid* gland, usually accompanied by a swelling on the neck, generally classified as congenital, cystic, or malignant; causes protrusion of the eyeball, increased nervous tension, and heart disorder. Endemic in certain areas e.g. Derbyshire and Switzerland, as a result of a deficiency of ◊ *iodine* in food and water. ◊ *Cretinism.*

Gold. One of the world's most valuable metallic elements, almost twice as heavy as silver, which occurs in the native state and has been known and sought for centuries, the quest for it having stimulated European exploration and conquest in the New and Old Worlds, whilst its discovery in quantity in Australia, Africa and America led to the 19th-cent. gold rushes. The finely-divided metal occurring in auriferous rock is now extracted by dissolving it in a very dilute solution of sodium cyanide and recovering the metal from this by throwing scrap zinc into the solution. An extremely malleable metal, it can be beaten into a leaf so thin as to be translucent, which is used for gilding. Gold does not tarnish, being quite unaffected by air, water, or any acid or alkali. A mixture of concentrated hydrochloric and nitric acids (*aqua regia*) will dissolve it, mainly because this mixture produces free chlorine, an element that does combine with gold. Too soft a metal for ordinary use, gold is usually alloyed with ◊ *copper*; pure gold is 24 carat; thus 18, 15, 12, and 9 carat gold indicate lower gold content, in descending order. Current uses of gold are for backing the paper currencies issued by the national central banks (◊ *Banking*) and for plate, jewellery, and commemorative coinage. ◊ *Gold Standard, Hallmark.*

Gold Coast ◊ *Ghana.*

Golden Fleece. Subject of a Greek heroic legend in varying versions. Jason, son of Aeson, a Thessalian king, set forth in the ship *Argo* to obtain the golden fleece of a ram which hung from a tree in Colchis (on the Black Sea), guarded by a dragon. (This may refer to a practice among tribes north of the Black Sea of putting sheep skins in rivers to collect alluvial gold.) He took with him some 50 Greek heroes, including ◊ *Castor and Pollux*, ◊ *Hercules*, ◊ *Nestor*, ◊ *Orpheus*, ◊ *Theseus*. After many adventures (Hercules left them on the way) they reached Colchis, where King Aeëtes promised them the fleece in return for performing various near-impossible tasks; his daughter Medea, an expert in magic, fell in love with Jason and for a promise of marriage assisted him to obtain the fleece. On returning to Greece, he deserted her for Creusa, the daughter of Creon, king of Corinth. Medea sent Creusa a poisoned garment (by which she and her father Creon were burnt to death), killed the two children she herself had borne to Jason, and escaped to Athens in a chariot drawn by flying dragons. Jason died of grief; or was killed by a piece of the *Argo* falling on him; or was reconciled to Medea, who returned to Colchis after attempting to poison Theseus.

Golden Hind. The sloop, previously named the *Pelican*, in which Sir Francis Drake circumnavigated the world 1577–80, the first Englishman to do so. Exact details are lacking, but from measurements of the retaining walls of a dry-dock at Deptford in which the *Golden Hind* was docked, it is believed that she was about 75 ft long and about 19 ft broad overall.

Golden Section. An ideal proportion used by architects and artists which cannot be resolved mathematically; expressed by a line divided so that the smaller part is to the greater as the greater is to the whole; very roughly, 8 : 13. In classical times and during the ◊ *Renaissance* it was supposed to provide a key to the harmony of the universe, and architects and artists sought to compose their works in accordance with it.

Goldfish. Bony freshwater omnivorous fish, not a variety of the golden ◊ *carp* but related to it, originally native to Chinese waters, where the wild form still exists; goldfish-breeding in China dates to A.D. 1000, but they were not introduced into Europe until the 18th cent. Their bright colouring (due to breeding) and their hardiness have made them favourites for house and pond. They may live up to 30 years.

Gold Rush. In 1848 gold was discovered in California; in 1849 prospectors of all nationalities flocked westwards hoping to make their fortunes. The 'forty-niners' set up chaotic and lawless settlements; the village of San Francisco became a town of 25,000 within a few months. Later 'gold rushes' include the Australian gold rush 1851–2, the 'Pike's Peak or Bust' rush in Colorado 1859, and the Klondike stampede of 1897–8.

Gold Standard. FULL GOLD STANDARD: Gold coins circulate and may be exported freely, and the central bank must redeem paper money in gold and at a fixed price. GOLD BULLION STANDARD: There is no gold in circulation, but the bank buys and sells gold at a fixed price and it may be exported.

GOLD EXCHANGE STANDARD: The bank sells and buys drafts only on the gold backing held.

Up to 1914, the full gold standard worked on an international basis; it was suspended by Britain 1914, and Britain was on the gold bullion standard 1925–34. Since 1945 the gold standard has not been generally restored, and a variety of systems have been in use, many involving exchange control and fluctuating exchange rates. ◊ *Foreign Exchange.*

Golf. A game in which clubs with wooden and iron heads are used to hit a small rubber-cored ball over a course (links) of 9 or 18 holes with the minimum of strokes. A first-class 18-hole course often exceeds 6000 yds, the holes varying from 100 to 550 yds in length; 14 clubs (4 or 5 woods, 8 or 9 irons, and putter for the green) make up a full set, both woods and irons being graded in loft from the almost perpendicular to 50° from the perpendicular (No. 9 iron). With a wooden club a good player will hope to hit approximately 200 yds and at the other end of the scale a No. 8 iron will carry roughly 70 yds. The ball weighs 1.62 oz. and is 1.62 in. in diameter (U.S.A. 1.68). The game is usually contested by two players (twosome) or four (foursome). Although 'four-ball foursomes' are common, a true foursome is played with one ball to each pair of partners, who hit it alternately. Games are by match-play (how many holes each player a side wins) and stroke-play (the least number of strokes for the round wins).

The earliest reference to golf is a Scottish law forbidding it 1457; until the 19th cent. it was almost exclusively a Scottish game. The name Royal and Ancient Golf Club, of St Andrews, reflects the game's status (James IV of Scotland certainly played it), and the R. & A. rules have long been accepted internationally. The British Open Championship dates to 1860, the British Amateur Championship to 1885, and the U.S.A. Open Championship to 1894. Of the Britain and Ireland *v.* U.S.A. matches, the Walker Cup (amateur) dates to 1922, the Ryder Cup (professional) to 1927, and the women's Curtis Cup (amateur) to 1932. Over 40 nations compete in the annual International Canada Cup. The U.S.A. has for many years dominated both amateur and professional competitions.

Goliards. < Old Fr. *goliard*, glutton; but possibly ultimately connected with Celtic words for denunciatory satire. Wandering 12th- and 13th-cent. scholar-satirists (*vagantes*), highly anticlerical, who parodied the most sacred portions of the Catholic liturgy and were banned by the Council of Trèves: *ut omnes sacerdotes non permittant Goliardos cantare versas super 'sanctus' et 'Agnus Dei'* etc. They were lay intellectuals competing with their clerical rivals for social prestige and power; many of their parodies of the Mass survive e.g. as hymns to Bacchus, and are mythically attributed to a licentious 'Goliardic order' founded by 'Golias'. Riotous or bawdy songs and poems are sometimes generically called 'goliardic'.

Gondwanaland. Large continent which in late Carboniferous times began to break up and drift apart; included E. parts of S. America, most of Africa, Arabia, the Deccan of India, Antarctica, and W. Australia. The movement was away from the poles; as the fragments pushed forwards the earth's crust was rucked up in front of them, forming the fold-mountain chains Andes, Atlas, Himalaya, etc. All these areas show striking similarities of rock structure and evidence of ice ages in places which now enjoy tropical climates. ⟢ *Continent, Geological Time Scale, Isostasy.*

Gonorrhoea ⟢ *Venereal Disease.*

Good Neighbour Policy ⟢ *Pan-American Union.*

Goose. Large waterfowl with heavy body and long neck, a powerful flier, breeding in the Arctic and migrating south in winter, flying in V-formations; commonest in the N. Hemisphere are the Whitefront, Greylag, Canada, and Barnacle geese. Diurnal in habit, they fly at dawn to feeding grounds by lakes or near the sea. Geese have been domesticated, and are unusual in that they can be used to keep grass e.g. lawns close-cropped, being largely grazing birds; they are less dependent on water for swimming than are ⟢ *ducks.*

Gordian Knot. Gordius, a peasant, becoming king of Phrygia, consecrated to Zeus his old farm-wagon, the pole of which was fastened to the yoke by a complicated knot; an ⟢ *oracle* foretold that whoever unfastened the knot should rule over Asia. Alexander the Great cut the knot with his sword and claimed the fulfilment of the oracle; hence 'to cut the Gordian knot' is to solve a problem by drastic measures.

Gordon Riots, 1780. Lord George Gordon, a rabid anti-Catholic, fomented demonstrations in London which turned into a series of riots and orgies lasting several days, in which some 300 people were killed or injured. Troops were called out to suppress the disturbances, and 21 rioters were executed.

Gorgons. In Greek legend, three loathsome sisters, their hair and waists entwined with serpents; they had brass claws, and shared one eye and one tooth between them, passing them round as needed; anyone who looked directly on their faces was turned into stone. Stheno and Euryale were immortal, but Medusa was mortal and was slain by ⟢ *Perseus* with the aid of a magic sword, mirror, winged sandals, and helmet; he presented her head to ⟢ *Athene*, who placed it on her shield (the aegis), where it retained its death-dealing quality. Drops of Medusa's blood fell on the ground and changed into snakes; the winged horse ⟢ *Pegasus* also sprang from them.

Gorilla. Large ⟢ *primate*, of two species, *Gorilla gorilla* and *G. beringei*, the former found in W. African forests, the latter (the largest of the ⟢ *apes*) on the E. African highlands; fruit-eating social animals forming polygynous social groups each with a number of females under the control of a single dominant male.

Gospels. The four accounts of the life and teaching of Jesus Christ contained in the New Testament (⟢ *Bible*), the only direct sources of information about him, dating to the 1st cent. A.D. The earliest, Mark, seems to have been used as one of the sources of Matthew and Luke, these three being called the Synoptic Gospels; the fourth, John, appears to be less a historical account than a pious meditation on Jesus Christ's message and its implications. A number of other 'gospels' (e.g. Thomas, Philip, According to the Hebrews) were compiled, mainly by ⟢ *Gnostics*, and are in part extant; these have little if any value as historical documents, but may contain trustworthy traditional details. ⟢ *Apocrypha.*

Gothic Architecture. Name given derogatively in the 17th cent. but subsequently adopted as a descriptive term for the style which succeeded ⟢ *Romanesque* and lasted till the 16th cent. It has no connexion with the Goths; the pointed arch was taken over from Sassanian architecture via the Arabs and Crusaders and introduced into the Romanesque, and became preferred to the round arch; but the great innovation was the cross-ribbed vault, which (with flying buttresses) made possible higher naves, larger windows,

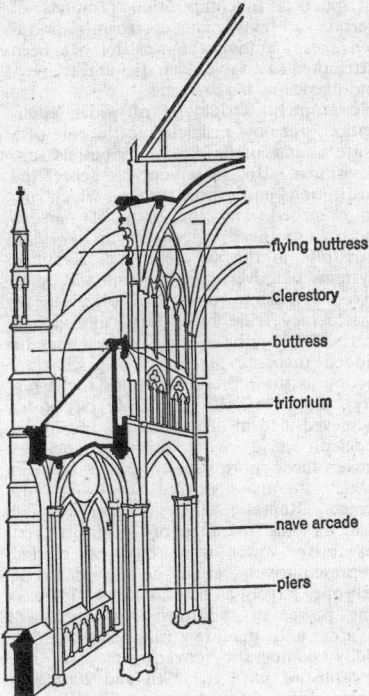

flying buttress

clerestory

buttress

triforium

nave arcade

piers

section of gothic cathedral (Amiens)

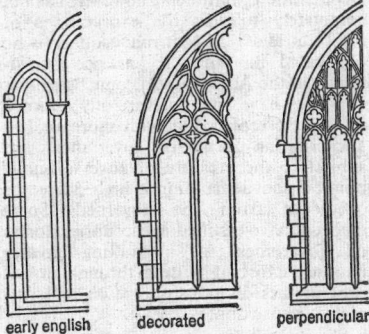

early english

decorated

perpendicular

and a light stone roof, leading to skeletal buildings in which the walls were curtains rather than supports. The Ste Chapelle in Paris is a perfect example of a skeletal building, all the space between the supporting ribs being filled with glass. The profusion of external decoration in the form of free-standing sculpture on the front and around the porch is a further characteristic differentiating Gothic from Romanesque. Examples of Gothic ecclesiastical architecture at its height are to be seen in Notre-Dame (Paris), Amiens, Chartres, Beauvais, Strasbourg, Ulm; the Italian Gothic at Pisa and the Doge's Palace in Venice reveal its Byzantine and Arab connexions. In England, Gothic was assimilated slowly and was moulded into a characteristic version at first known as ◊ *Early English*, e.g. Salisbury Cathedral, and then developed into the more ornate ◊ *decorated style*, e.g. Bristol Cathedral, and ◊ *perpendicular style*, e.g. King's College Chapel, Cambridge. ⟡ *Stained Glass, Vault.*

Gothic Revival (Gothick). An 18th- and 19th-cent. artistic style, mainly architectural, inspired by medieval church architecture and decoration and implying a conscious choice of Gothic forms, in contrast to Gothic survival or the unthinking continuation of the Gothic tradition. Rare before 1720, Gothic Revival became fashionable in England about 1750, with Horace Walpole's Strawberry Hill, the fashion for mock abbeys and castles, Chippendale's 'gothick' furniture, and esp. the 'Gothic novel' of mystery and terror, a genre inaugurated by Walpole's *Castle of Otranto*. The 18th-cent. quasi Gothic architecture was a gentleman's fancy, however, not seriously regarded as a challenge to classicism in architecture, and should be distinguished from 19th-cent. neo-Gothic. Of the many 'Gothic novels' of the late 18th cent. only Beckford's *Vathek*, Matthew Lewis's *The Monk*, and Mrs Radcliffe's *Mysteries of Udolfo* are remembered, though the genre interested e.g. Sir Walter Scott and was mildly burlesqued by Jane Austen in *Northanger Abbey*; the 'Gothic novel' was a precursor of and an influence on ◊ *Romanticism*. The 19th-cent. neo-Gothic architecture shows a further distinction, between the ecclesiastical and fairly accurate Gothic of such architects as Pugin (who regarded classicism as pagan and

Gothic as the only proper style for churches) and 'commercial' Gothic (merely an aspect of Victorian eclecticism, seen in its extreme form in St Pancras railway station and the Albert Memorial). The Houses of Parliament combines Pugin's authentic Gothicism with Barry's feeling for classical symmetry and good taste. America and most European countries were affected by the Gothic manner, which remained the accepted style for churches until well into the 20th cent.

Goths. Tribes from Gotland on the Baltic, who spread eastwards to set up an empire in Russia, and in the 4th cent A.D. adopted the Christian heresy of ◊ *Arianism*. When attacked by the ◊ *Huns*, the Goths moved S. in two groups.

The Visigoths defeated the Emperor Valens at ◊ *Adrianople* in A.D. 378 and settled in the Balkans. Under Alaric they sacked Rome in 410, withdrew from Italy in 418, and built up an empire extending from Gibraltar to the Loire. In 507 they were beaten by Clovis and expelled from ◊ *France*. They remained in Spain, where they gradually assimilated the civilization of the Hispano-Romans. After the battle of Cadiz in 711 they were overcome by the ◊ *Arabs*.

The Ostrogoths attacked Italy, but were turned back and moved into the Balkans. Under Theodoric, who ruled 488–526, they again invaded Italy and this time settled it; after his death, their extermination by Justinian's forces proved disastrous for Italy, which was easily overrun by the Lombards. ◊◊ *Lombard League, Vandals.*

Gouache. Watercolour mixed with Chinese white to provide an opaque pigment for painting on paper, having something of the quality of a pastel, drying lighter in tone than it appears when wet; and much used by manuscript illuminators and in the 18th cent. by landscape painters, esp. on the Continent.

Gourds. Plants of the family *Cucurbitaceae*, annual climbing herbs with tendrils; the fruit is a berry with a firm rind, which may become woody in some species esp. the bottle or calabash gourd, which is used for flasks, bowls, etc. The loofah (vegetable sponge, or dish-rag gourd) is the net of vascular tissue in the ripe fruit-wall of *Luffa cylindrica* after the soft parts have decayed away. Pumpkins, squashes, ◊ *marrows*, melons, ◊ *cucum-*

bers, gherkins, and watermelons are also types of gourd.

Gout. Disease, often hereditary, characterized by recurrent attacks of arthritis, esp. in the main joint of the big toe; as it progresses, many other joints may be affected. Gout results from a defective metabolism of puxines (decomposition products of certain proteins), and its former prevalence esp. among the wealthy has been attributed to an over-rich diet and to over-indulgence in ◊ *port* wine.

Government. Originally of wider application, but now restricted to the rule of a state or one of its semi-autonomous subdivisions; also, in a concrete sense, the institutions and offices through which rule is exercised, and the body of persons occupying these offices. In his *Politics*, Aristotle in the 4th cent. B.C. classified systems of government into monarchy or tyranny (rule by one man), oligarchy or aristocracy (rule by a few), and democracy (rule by the many). To these may be added theocracy (rule by a priest-class acting as the representatives of the divinity). Some of the Greek ◊ *city-states* achieved a form of democracy, but in the ancient world as in primitive societies government more usually took a form in which the mass of the people had no voice. Representative government, in which some measure of legislative and executive power was vested in elected representatives, grew up in medieval Europe, largely as a result of the increasing power of the towns and the mercantile and manufacturing classes; but fully democratic government was not established until the 19th and 20th centuries, when in many countries the franchise was gradually extended to all adults. Democratic government, however, has not completely fulfilled the expectations of the 18th- and 19th-cent. philosophers who advocated it. While it has been maintained in the Anglo-Saxon countries, other countries have either never fully adopted it or have replaced it with more or less authoritarian forms of government not subject to the pressure of adverse public opinion and demanding a high degree of obedience from the governed. Some theorists have justified authoritarian forms of government as permitting greater national effort in putting through urgent programmes of industrialization or large-scale construction.

Grafting. Transplanting organs or tissues. There is no special difficulty in grafting from one region to another of the same individual, or of identical twins or members of a highly inbred strain of animals. In other cases a graft may be apparently successful for up to two weeks and then be destroyed by antibodies produced by the recipient. Even so, the graft can be a useful temporary substitute allowing the patient's own tissues to recover. Corneal grafts taken from recently dead subjects are widely used to restore sight to patients whose own corneae have become opaque. In this exceptional case, antibodies are apparently not produced. Large doses of X-rays and some drugs e.g. cyclophosphamide suppress the formation of antibodies so that it is beginning to be possible to transplant whole organs (esp. kidney) from unrelated persons.

In horticulture, grafting is the joining of parts of two or more plants so that their ◊ *cambium* cells are in contact and they grow as one, a scion (bud or healthy twig) of delicate or exotic habits often being attached to a strong-growing rooted stock suited to the climate and soil. Grafting is also extensively used for propagating plants which do not seed or come true from seed, for dwarfing, and for increasing the productivity of fruit trees requiring cross-pollination.

Graham's Law ◊ *Diffusion, Gas.*

Gramineae ◊ *Grass.*

Grammar School. In the U.K. a secondary school providing an academic course from 11 to 16/18, to prepare pupils for entry to a university or profession; they were established in the Middle Ages to teach Latin and Greek. Many were closed as a result of the dissolution of the monasteries in the 16th cent., but large numbers were re-founded in the 17th. Until recently they continued to emphasize classical education. By the 19th cent. there were about 700 grammar schools some of which developed into ◊ *public schools* (mainly residential) while others survived either under Local Education Authorities (charging no fees) or as ◊ *direct-grant* fee-charging schools. The equivalents in France and Germany are the *lycée* and the *Gymnasium.* ◊> *Comprehensive Schools.*

Gramophone. First conceived by the French scientist Charles Cros in April 1877; later that year, working independently, Thomas Edison in New York achieved the first recording of the human voice. Early records were made on cylinders, but these were gradually replaced by the flat disc, introduced by Emile Berliner in 1888. Among early celebrities recorded were Caruso in 1902 and Melba in 1905. The first symphony to be recorded complete was Beethoven's Fifth (by the Berlin Philharmonic Orchestra) in 1909.

Electrical recording superseded the earlier non-electrical (known as 'acoustic') in the 1920s, but the sound continued to be recorded on to wax discs (from which the commercial shellac discs were produced) until 1947, when magnetic tape-recording came into use. This led to higher fidelity of sound and to higher standards of musical accuracy in performances transferred to commercial discs, as tape-recordings of different performances can easily be cut and joined.

In 1948 the microgroove ($33\frac{1}{3}$ r.p.m.) or 'long-playing' disc made of vinylite, a non-breakable plastic, was introduced in U.S.A. During the 1950s this and the 45 r.p.m. (also microgroove) disc effectively displaced the old 78 r.p.m. shellac disc. Stereophonic gramophone records (needing special reproducing equipment) were introduced in 1958, but in the first five years these captured only a minority share of the market from the older (so-called monophonic or monaural) type.

In 1962 the British output of gramophone records was estimated at 17,423,000; in March 1963 Beethoven's Fifth Symphony was available in Britain in 30 recordings, all microgroove, 20 of them in monophonic only, one in stereophonic only, and the remaining nine in both.

Granite. Coarse-grained crystalline rock with a high ◊ *silica* content. It is generally considered a typical igneous rock of plutonic origin, its large crystals of quartz, mica, and felspar being the result of slow deep-seated cooling. But many granites may be metamorphosed forms of other rocks, e.g. schists, which have been 'granitized' by the intrusion of molten ◊ *magma* which soaked into the rocks and added new constituents to them. ◊> *Gneiss, Metamorphic Rocks, Tantalum.*

Grape. The grapevine is *Vitis vinifera*, a climbing shrub with tendrils; its berries (grapes) are used extensively fresh, dried as currants, raisins, and sultanas, and for ◊ *wine* making. There are many wild species with fruit too acid to eat. *V. vinifera*, the wine grape, probably originated from a species growing wild in the Mediterranean and central Asia.

Grapefruit (Shaddock, Pomelo). A member of the *Citrus* family, *C. paradisi*, native to the E. Indies. In the last 50 years it has been much developed in U.S.A. and improved from the rather coarse original; it is now of great commercial importance.

Graph. A diagram to illustrate the relationship between two variable quantities, usually plotted between axes at right angles to one another; e.g. the variation of volume with pressure for a gas confined in a container (Boyle's Law). Graphs are useful not only to represent scientific formulae but also to illustrate e.g. the growth of plants or the cooling of a liquid in relation to the passage of time.

Graphite ◊ *Carbon*.

Grass. *Gramineae*; the largest and most widely distributed and important plant family, of over 4000 species, characterized by jointed stems, usually hollow and circular, from which grow narrow blade-like leaves. Its adaptability to diverse conditions is remarkable, and despite a basic similarity in structure it takes widely different forms e.g. from lawn grass to the giant ◊ *bamboo*. In temperate regions grasses are the dominant vegetation of prairies and steppes. The often inconspicuous wind-pollinated flowers are closely grouped into a small spike which produces seeds which in some cases (rye, barley, wheat) are valuable ◊ *cereals*. The bamboo, ◊ *maize*, and sugar cane are other grasses of commercial importance, whilst in agriculture grass is the basis of livestock rearing.

Gravettian ◊ *Palaeolithic*.

Gravitation. Every body in the universe, from the smallest particle to the largest star, attracts every other body. Newton's law states that this attractive force between two bodies is directly proportional to the product of the masses of the two bodies and inversely proportional to the square of the distance separating them. However, at very close range (intermolecular distances) strong repulsive forces are now known to exist, preventing matter collapsing into itself (which could be implied from Newton's Law) when distances are very small.

GRAVITY: Correctly, the force operating between the earth and other bodies; it is the gravitational pull of the earth which determines the weight of an object from its ◊ *mass*. Since the force of gravity varies at different points, so does the weight of a body measured at these points. ◊ *Weightlessness*.

Great Circle. Circle formed on the surface of a sphere when cut by a plane passing through its centre; such a circle on the earth's surface. Meridians of longitude form great circles, but of the parallels of latitude only the equator is a great circle. The shortest distance between any two points on the earth's surface is the arc of the great circle which passes through them.

Great Exhibition. 1851. The first great international exhibition, proposed by Prince Albert, organized by a Royal Commission, and held in the specially built Crystal Palace in Hyde Park. From May to October about 6 m. people saw the 19,000 exhibits, including raw materials, machinery, manufactures, and sculpture. After the social unrest earlier in Victoria's reign, the exhibition demonstrated the fruitful results of peaceful industrial expansion, and symbolized Britain's position as the 'workshop of the world'. Architecturally, the Crystal Palace was an outstanding example of a new technique, the erection of great buildings within a framework of steel, and was a precursor of the American skyscraper.

Greece (Ancient). After an early period of Mycenaean civilization (2000–1100 B.C.) Greece was invaded by ◊ *Dorians*, Ionians, and Aeolians, who gradually spread over the Aegean area. Colonies of Greeks sprang up in Asia Minor, and as far as Marseilles, in the 7th and 8th centuries B.C. There was at first little political unity between the Greek states, though they combined to take part every four years in the Olympic Games. In the face of expanding Persian power, ◊ *Athens* won the leadership of the Greek states from Sparta 480 B.C. by successfully resisting the Persian attack; the 5th cent. B.C. was the zenith of Greek and esp. Athenian civilization, the age of the Greek tragedies and of Pericles, Socrates, and Phidias. With the disasters of the Peloponnesian War 431–404 B.C. in which ◊ *Sparta* defeated Athens, Greece began a gradual decline. For a time the Boeotian League was dominant, soon to be overcome by Philip of ⟡ *Macedon*. Alexander the Great's widespread conquests brought Anatolia, Syria, and Egypt under Hellenic influence, but his empire quickly broke up. Roman power expanded over the whole area in the 2nd cent. B.C. and Greece became a political backwater, though Greek cultural influence was consolidated and spread by the Romans.

Greece. Area, mainland 41,328 sq. m. and islands 9854 sq. m. Pop. 8.5 m. Cap. Athens. Rel. chiefly Eastern Orthodox. Limited monarchy; legislature a single chamber of deputies, executive a prime minister.

ECONOMY. Only 15 per cent of the land is cultivable. Until recently, war and political instability have retarded industrial growth and any solution of economic problems, but Greece has a considerable merchant marine, and exports tobacco.

HISTORY. Greece was for a time overrun by ⟡ *Goths* and ⟡ *Vandals* in the 5th and 6th centuries A.D. but then settled down under ⟡ *Byzantine* rule until A.D. 1204, when the country was partitioned by the Crusaders, whose weak hold was easily supplanted by that of the Turks in the 15th cent. (⟡ *Ottoman Empire*). Venice retained much of the Peloponnese until 1715, but Turkish control of the rest of Greece continued until the 1821 rising. With Allied help at the battle of ⟡ *Navarino* 1827, an independent Greece came into being in 1832, with Otto of Bavaria as king; after his deposition in 1862 the present royal line came to the throne. Greece was a republic 1924–35; in 1934 she abandoned her traditional anti-Turkish policy and joined the Balkan Entente. General Metaxas made himself dictator of a semi-fascist state 1936–41. In the ⟡ *Second World War* an Italian invasion was repulsed, but the Germans then occupied the country until the 1944 liberation. By 1943 rivalry between communist (ELAS) and non-communist guerilla organizations had already produced virtual civil war, which continued after the liberation and the return of King George II 1946, and did not end until 1949. In 1946 the post-war right-wing government was replaced by a liberal/social-democrat coalition, but economic recovery was slow. Field-Marshal Papagos's promise of 'strong government' brought his right-wing Greek Rally a majority in 1952, but the National Radical Union became the majority party in 1956, under Karamanlis. In spite of differences over ⟡ *Cyprus*, Greece and Turkey maintained a friendly relationship 1946–63, but tension developed 1963–4. ⟡ *Macedonia*.

Greek. Greek (Hellenic) is one of the ⟡ *Indo-European languages*; the recent decipherment of Linear B Mycenean script has placed the beginning of recorded Greek as early as 1500 B.C. The Greeks moved into the peninsula from the north in separate waves of migration with different dialects. IONIC: The dialect of Homer and Hesiod. ATTIC: The speech of Athens; became the norm for classical Greek literature after 500 B.C. AEOLIC: the dialect of Alcaeus and Sappho. DORIC: The form chosen for the choruses in tragedy, interrupting the Attic of the dialogues. Classical Greek was highly inflected: the verb had three voices (middle as well as active and passive), four moods (optative as well as indicative, subjunctive, and imperative), ten declinable participles as well as two verbal adjectives, three numbers (dual as well as singular and plural), and an abundance of compound forms expressing widely divergent meanings. HELLENISTIC GREEK (KOINÉ): Became the ⟡ *lingua franca* of the E. Mediterranean countries from the death of Alexander the Great 323 B.C. to the foundation of Constantinople A.D. 330; was the language of the Septuagint and the New Testament and the first language of the Antonines, who ruled Rome in the 2nd cent. A.D. BYZANTINE GREEK: Remained the language of the eastern Empire throughout the Middle Ages, A.D. 330–1453. MODERN GREEK: Two varieties: literary and colloquial (Demotiké). A classical scholar can read either with ease. All vowels have the same length, and whether stressed or unstressed are clearly pronounced. Many common words, after thousands of years, remain substantially unchanged, e.g. *anthropos*, man; *arithmos*, number; *khronos*, time; *nomos*, law; *polis*, city; *potamos*, river; *topos*, place.

Greek Architecture. The architecture of the ancient Aegean may be divided into four distinct periods: Minoan, Mycenaean, Hellenic (largely independent of one another), and Hellenistic. Surviving buildings in the Minoan style at Knossos have elegantly painted walls and downward-tapering columns around a central patio. Buildings in the archaic Mycenaean style of 1300–700 B.C. at Argos, Mycenae, and Tyrins are characterized by immense irregular masonry, pillared great halls, and corbelled vaults. The Hellenic style is essentially an importation into Greece by the Dorians about 1000 B.C. and many of its most striking features, e.g. the fluted columns and the post-and-lintel (trabeated) structure (◇ *Architectural Orders*), almost certainly derive from the principles of building in wood. The high Hellenic period about 700–300 B.C. saw the development of the classical style, characterized by the use of the Doric and Ionic Orders and epitomized in the Parthenon, a one-storey rectangular columnar temple notable for its self-evident construction, harmony, and unity of effect and for the utmost simplicity and refinement of detail. To achieve these qualities of perfection, which have influenced architecture for 2500 years, the Greeks used traditional formulae on geometrical bases, and such devices as entasis (the substitution of curved for straight lines in order to correct the illusion of concavity in the columns); the buildings were probably painted and gilded, sculpture being also used for decoration, though sparingly and usually in pediments only. The Hellenistic style, a debased form showing Asiatic influences, flourished throughout the E. Mediterranean under Roman rule during the 1st cent. B.C.

Greek Art. The earliest examples of life-size ◇ *sculpture* are those of the Early Archaic period, 660–580 B.C., in which seated figures and '*kouros*' (youth) statues reflect Egyptian influence, an influence which was attenuated during the Middle Archaic Period, about 580–535 B.C., when the '*kouros*' achieves greater refinement and elegance and the figure becomes less stiff and less obviously related to the shape of the block from which it has been cut. In the Late Archaic Period, 540–480 B.C., a new degree of naturalism emerges in the treatment of the '*kouros*' torso and in the expressiveness of the features. Temple sculptures achieve motion, often violent, e.g. the fighting warriors on the temple of Aphaia at Aegina. The Early Classical Period, 480–450 B.C., achieves a new ease of posture, grace of movement, and realism of detail, of which the bronze

charioteer at Delphi (about 475), the Bronze Poseidon (about 470–450), and the famous Diskobolos (460–450) are outstanding examples. (The Diskobolos, like many other Hellenic sculptures, is known only from a Roman copy.) The second half of the 5th cent. brings the climax of classical Greek sculpture. The Parthenon sculptures, executed under the supervision of Phidias, reveal a perfect understanding of foreshortening, great technical skill in the handling of posture and draperies, almost infinite variation on certain repeated figure themes, and a complete mastery of narrative and dramatic effect. From the same period date the Caryatid figures on the Erechtheum, and on the Acropolis. Sculpture of the 4th cent. is in many respects similar to that of the preceding period. Praxiteles was perhaps the most famous sculptor of the age (Hermes and the Infant Dionysos, 350–330), though rivalled in reputation and capacity by Skopas, the probable executor of the Mausoleum frieze at Halikarnassos (355–330). The Hellenistic period intensified the realism of this last phase, and, in the manner of all ultra-naturalistic art, embraced extreme subject-matter such as drunkenness or deformity. Amongst the most celebrated works of this period are the Niké of Samothrace (about 200) in the Louvre, and the Laocoon group (160–130).

In the broadest sense Greek vase-painting is of two kinds – that which has figures in strong black silhouette against the red of the clay (black-figure), and that which leaves the figures the natural clay colour and has their surroundings painted black (red-figure). The first of these appeared 650–600 B.C. (the Daedalid period) and the second around 530 B.C. Vase decoration comprises both ornamentation (e.g. lotus, meander, palmette) and figure scenes, these latter pre-eminently mythological in inspiration, though later themes also included everyday activities (e.g. athletics or banquets). The major centres of vase-production were Attica, Corinth, and Rhodes. The delicacy of lines, the reproduction of movement and gesture, the combination of realism with elegance and style, and indeed humour, make the best of Greek vase-painting a form which remains unrivalled in its excellence.

Of Greek painting very little survives. From the 7th and early 6th centuries there are the terra-cotta metopes from Thermos, and some Attic terra-cottas illustrating a lying-in-state of the dead. From the 5th cent. and later even less survives, though some writers e.g. Vitruvius refer to the achievements of the great painters like Apollodorus (about 430–400), Zeuxis, or Apelles, the portraitist and favourite of Alexander the Great. But of necessity it is in vase-painting that we can best observe the technical development of the Greek artist, and his mastery by the second half of the 5th cent. of the principles of painting to suggest a third dimension.

Greek Church ◇ *Eastern Orthodox Church*.

Greek Philosophy ◇ *Aristotelianism, Cynicism, Epicureanism, Platonism, Stoicism*.

Greenwich Hospital. Group of buildings on the S. bank of the Thames at Greenwich; the oldest part, the Queen's house, was designed by Inigo Jones and completed 1635 as a palace, and further buildings were later added, some by Wren and some by Vanbrugh. It was first used as a hospital for pensioners 1705; this use continued till 1869, and it became the Royal Naval College 1873. Some of the buildings now house the National Maritime Museum.

Greenwich Observatory. Founded 1675 with a grant of £500 from Charles II, to correct the astronomical tables for the use of seamen. All ◇ *longitudes* are measured from the Prime Meridian 0° at Greenwich, as is standard world ◇ *time* (formerly named Greenwich Mean Time). Owing to noise and vibration affecting the apparatus, the observatory and the Astronomer Royal's department moved to Hurstmonceux, Sussex, in 1953.

Greyhound Racing. Sport in which greyhounds chase an artificial hare around a track, the dogs being released by opening trap-doors; it evolved in U.S.A. from ◇ *coursing*, which had been declared illegal. The perfecting of the mechanical hare 1919 widened the sport's popularity, and it spread to Britain 1926; there are about 60 tracks, under the Greyhound Racing Association, but attendances have fallen sharply esp. since the introduction of 'off-the-course' betting shops.

Grimm's Law. The occurrence of a regular sound-shift of groups of consonants in ◇ *Germanic languages*; formulated by Jacob Grimm in 1822. Grimm showed that

in the course of development the first shift was from the early phonetic values of consonants in Sanskrit, Greek, and Latin to fresh values in the early Germanic tongues, e.g. from Lat. *pater* to English 'father' and German *Vater*. The second shift was one which concerned only High German. ◇ *Etymology*.

Groundnuts ◇ *Leguminosae, Peanuts*.

Grouse. Well-camouflaged ◇ *game* birds of heathlands in the N. hemisphere; they lay six to ten eggs in a shallow depression in the ground, and large areas in Scotland and N. England are kept as game preserves, the shooting season being from 12 Aug. to 10 Dec. The ptarmigan and willow grouse are remarkable for their seasonal changes in plumage to blend with the background, ranging from pure white in winter to brown and black in the spring and summer.

Grünwald (1410) ◇ *Tannenberg*.

Guadalcanal. 1942–3. Battle of the ◇ *Second World War*. The Japanese occupied Guadalcanal in the British Solomon Islands; U.S. marines landed at Lunga Point and captured an airfield and three smaller islands. The Japanese struck back, but a U.S. naval victory enabled the Americans to consolidate their hold, and in Feb. 1943 the Japanese were driven out. The first American offensive against the Japanese, this victory gained the U.S. a base for future operations in the ◇ *Pacific War*.

Guanaco ◇ *Llama*.

Guano. The accumulation of the excreta of sea-birds, mixed with fish remains, dead birds, etc. which has dried in the sun; dug from the rocks on islands off the coast of S. America as a plentiful and valuable nitrogenous ◇ *fertilizer*. When aged, it is rich in phosphorus, with a little nitrogen content.

Guarani. Group of S. American Indians living mainly in Paraguay, N. Argentine, S. Brazil, and Bolivia. Originally primitive agriculturalists, renowned as cannibals, they came under strong Jesuit influence (◇ *Society of Jesus*) in the 17th and 18th centuries in ◇ *Paraguay*, where large and successful Christian Indian communities ('reductions') were established. When the Jesuits were ordered to leave the Americas in 1767, the 'reductions' were left to the mercies of slave-traders and were rapidly depleted. The Guarani language is still widely spoken.

Guarantee. In law, an undertaking by a person to answer for the debt, default, or miscarriage of another. In its popular sense it is used to mean a promise by the vendor or manufacturer of goods that they conform to a certain standard and/or an undertaking to carry out certain repairs or replacements should they be necessary. Such promises are often given in lieu of obligations imposed on vendors under the Sale of Goods Act, and very often they restrict rather than enlarge the purchaser's rights.

Guatemala. Area 42,042 sq. m. Pop. 4 m. comprising Indians (60 per cent), mestizos, and whites. Cap. Guatemala City. Independent republic in Central America. Guatemala has had a turbulent history and a long series of dictators of right and left since it gained its independence from Spain in 1821. In 1944 the Liberal, Arévalo, became president and inaugurated a programme of economic and social reforms. He was succeeded in 1951 by Jacobo Arbenz, who also carried out land redistribution, including the expropriation of land belonging to the American United Fruit Company. In 1954 a revolt by the right-wing opposition under Colonel Armas, supported by the U.S.A., overthrew the Arbenz regime and reversed much of his legislation (over 70 per cent of the cultivated land is now owned by 2 per cent of the population). Armas was assassinated in 1957 and succeeded as president by the Conservative General Ydígoras Fuentes who was driven out by an army coup in 1963. There is a long-standing dispute with the U.K. over British Honduras, and since 1960 Guatemala has had a dispute with Cuba over training of anti-Castro forces on its soil.

The chief products are coffee and bananas; 70 per cent of exports are to U.S.A.

Guelphs and Ghibellines. Medieval political factions of the 12th–14th centuries, deriving from the rival German families of Welf (dukes of Saxony and Bavaria) and Hohenstaufen (dukes and princes of Swabia). During the Hohenstaufen Emperor Frederick I's rivalry with the Papacy, papal supporters adopted the name of Guelph, while the imperial supporters became known as Ghibellines, supposedly the italianized form of their battle-cry *Hie Weiblingen* (from a Hohenstaufen castle). After the defeat of the Emperors the names lost their original significance and became simply those of two rival Italian factions, e.g. Florence was Guelph but Siena and Pisa were Ghibelline.

Guenevere (Guinivere) ◊ *Lancelot.*

Guernica. 1937. During the ◊ *Spanish Civil War* German 'volunteers' assisting General Franco heavily bombed Guernica, an ancient and historic town in the Viscaya province of the ◊ *Basque* country of N. Spain, with many casualties among the entirely civilian population. The attack, which profoundly shocked world opinion, was commemorated by Picasso (a Spaniard) in a powerful and savagely angry painting.

Guild Socialism. A variety of socialist doctrine influenced by William Morris, which originated in Britain in the early 20th cent. and reached its zenith immediately after the First World War, its best-known exponent being G. D. H. Cole; wishing every functional group in society to administer its own affairs co-operatively in a socially responsible guild, the movement was in large measure a revolt against the monotonous and boring nature of work in the modern industrial system. It saw guilds as the means by which work could be made more interesting and the spirit of creative pride revived.

Guillemot ◊ *Auk.*

Guinea. Area 96,865 sq. m. Pop. 3 m. Cap. Conakry. An independent republic (formerly part of French W. Africa) bordering on the Ivory Coast, Mali, Senegal, and Sierra Leone, governed by an elected President and Constituent Assembly. The sole political body, the Parti Démocratique de Guinée, founded and led by Sékou Touré – elected president in 1961 by an overwhelming majority – dominates and runs the country.

ECONOMY. Main exports are alumina, iron-ore, rubber, palm kernels, rice, coffee, bananas, pineapples, millet. There are rich bauxite and iron-ore deposits and large-scale mining.

HISTORY. In 1891 French Guinea was separated from ◊ *Senegal* and thenceforward administered as a separate colony until 1958, when at the referendum on membership of the ◊ *French Community* Guinea voted for separation. French administration, trade relations, and financial aid ceased; a degree of economic stability has been achieved with aid from Ghana, the Soviet bloc, and U.S.A. In world affairs Guinea has pursued a neutralist policy, willing to take aid from the West; but of all African states, it remains on the closest terms with communist countries. In African affairs, Guinea has been a consistent exponent of extreme radicalism and the desire for W. African federation. ◊ *Ghana, Mali, Portugal.*

Guinea-pig. Domesticated relative of *Cavia porcellus*, a wild S. American ◊ *rodent*; introduced into Europe in the 16th cent. It is tailless, nocturnal in the wild state, and very prolific, breeding every two months, and is much used in medical and biological experiments.

Guitar ◊ *Stringed Instruments.*

Gulf Sheikhdoms. The British-protected states of Kuwait, Bahrein, Qatar, and also the Trucial States on the Persian Gulf, all of which are in special treaty relations with the U.K. under which the British government is responsible for their foreign relations; local consultation and advice is provided through H.M. Political Resident in the Persian Gulf (headquarters in Bahrein) and Political Agents in the separate states. British treaty relations date to 1820, when a 'general treaty of peace' was concluded, after naval intervention to suppress piracy in the Persian Gulf. Since the discovery of oil in recent years, the rulers of several of these small states, esp. Kuwait, have become extremely rich. The Trucial States comprise seven small independent Sheikhdoms, of which Abu Dhabi has the largest area and Dubai the largest urban population, 45,000.

Gulf Stream ◊ *Ocean.*

Gums. Exudations from plants, which harden on drying but are soluble in water; chemically, a mixed group of acidic substances, but all contain sugar residues, which are removed by mild hydrolysis to leave a more resistant complex. There is no sharp division between gums and mucilages. Common gums are gum arabic, tragacanth, damson gum, cherry gum. CHEWING GUM: Chicle; not chemically a gum but a coagulated resinous ◊ *latex* insoluble in water.

GUM-LAC ◊ *Japanning, Lacquer.*

Gum-tree ◊ *Eucalyptus.*

Gunmetal ◊ *Alloys.*

Gunpowder. Oldest known ◊ *explosive,* of relatively low power; an intimate mix-

ture of 75 per cent nitre (◊ *potassium* nitrate), 14 per cent wood charcoal, 10 per cent sulphur, it fires when struck with sufficient force or when heated to about 300° C. Now little used for military purposes, but still in use for blasting. It was known to the Chinese (who used it for fireworks), and introduced by the Arabs to Europe, where by the 16th cent. it completely altered warfare.

Gunpowder Plot. 1605. Robert Catesby, angered by James I's refusal to repeal the ◊ *penal laws,* organized a Roman Catholic attempt to blow up the Houses of Parliament at the opening by James. One conspirator, wishing to warn his friend Lord Monteagle, accidentally gave the plot away; Guy Fawkes, who was to have exploded the barrels of gunpowder in the cellars, was arrested, tortured, and executed, with several other conspirators, including the Provincial of the Jesuits, Henry Garnett. The anniversary of the discovery and frustration of the plot (5 Nov.) was declared a day of public celebration in perpetuity; it is still marked by bonfires and firework displays. ◊ *Counter-Reformation.*

Guns ◊ *Artillery, Ballistics, Firearms, Gunpowder.*

Gurkhas. Properly, the dominant ethnic group in ◊ *Nepal*; the British long recruited regiments from among them, and the term came to mean Nepalese troops of the British and Indian armies. The weapon peculiar to the Gurkhas is the *kukri,* a heavy curved knife.

Gut. General term for the intestinal tract. Catgut, made from the submucous layer of sheep intestine, carefully sterilized, is used as a surgical ligature; as healing proceeds, it is slowly absorbed in the patient's tissues.

Gutta-percha. Obtained from the ◊ *latex* of large forest trees e.g. the *Palaquium* and *Payena* of Indomalaya; harder and less elastic than rubber, but softens on warming and can then be moulded, and is useful esp. for underwater insulation and for the manufacture of golf balls and special bottles.

Guy Fawkes Day ◊ *Gunpowder Plot.*

Gymnastics. Systematic athletic and physical exercises, originating probably in ancient Greece, revived in the 18th cent. and included when the ◊ *Olympic Games* were resumed 1896. The present Olympic programme includes team awards for both men and women, and the following competitions. MEN: Twelve exercises combined; floor exercises; horizontal bar; rings; long horse vault; parallel bars; pommelled horse. WOMEN: Eight exercises combined; beam; floor exercises; asymmetrical bars; vault.

Gymnosperms. Woody ◊ *plants*, with no true flowers, the seeds not enclosed within a fruit. ◊ *Conifers*, the largest group, have seeds naked on scales grouped into cones. Gymnosperms were the dominant vegetation in the Mesozoic era, but declined in importance after the ◊ *angiosperms* became established.

Gynaecology. The study and treatment of diseases of the female generative organs; it includes the repair of structural defects e.g. prolapse of the uterus after ◊ *childbirth*, the removal of benign cysts and fibroid tumours from the uterus and ovaries, and the surgical extirpation of malignant growths, and much non-operative treatment is devoted to disorders of ◊ *menstruation* and to the treatment of sub-fertility. A recent development is the regular examination of cells shed into the generative tract, in order to detect cancer esp. of the *cervix uteri* before it begins to invade the tissues and while it can still safely be dealt with by a relatively minor operation.

Gypsies ◊ *Gipsies*.

Gypsum. Hydrated ◊ *calcium* sulphate; usually formed on the evaporation of enclosed seas. Selenite, a crystalline form common in London Clay and Oxford Clay, results from the action of sulphuric acid on the limestone shells in the clay, the acid being derived from the decomposition of iron pyrites.

ANHYDRITE: The anhydrous form, mined in N. Yorkshire and at Billingham, Co. Durham; extensively used as a fertilizer and in the manufacture of cement, plaster of paris, and school chalk, as a filler in making paper, paint, and crayons, and as the basis of many chemicals.

Gyroscope. Invented by Foucault 1852; a rotating disc mounted in gimbals so that it is free to move in any direction, its axis having the important property of tending to remain constant in space (so that it can be used in ◊ *aviation* and ◊ *rockets*, for sensing any lateral or fore-and-aft changes in heading, or in azimuth and blind-flying instruments). Many automatic controls are based upon it. When linked to a magnetic compass in a ship or aircraft it can provide a steady source of reference for orientation. The gyro-compass was first brought to the practical stage by Dr Anschütz-Kämpfe. The first Anschütz single gyro compass underwent sea trials in the battleship *Deutschland* 1907. Gyroscopes are also used in ships to reduce rolling; at first large ones were used direct, but later as controls for anti-rolling fins mounted on the hull.

H

Habeas Corpus. In English law, a High Court writ which orders the gaoler to present the person detained before the court at a fixed time, for an inquiry into the legality of the detention; an effective way of ensuring that no one is kept in prison or otherwise deprived of his liberty otherwise than as provided by law. The Habeas Corpus Act, 1679, of vital importance in establishing the freedom of the citizen, reached the statute book only when in the House of Lords division one of the tellers deliberately miscounted; he later passed off the matter with a jest of having counted a fat peer as 10 men.

Habsburg ◊ *Hapsburg*.

Haddock. Bony marine fish related to the ◊ *cod*, one of Britain's most important food fishes; the haddock catch, about 100 m. per year, forms about half the total weight of fish caught by ◊ *trawlers* in the North Sea. When smoked it is known as Finnan Haddock. It is one of several fish species which has two black spots just behind the head, supposed to mark where St Peter's fingers held it.

Hades. In Greek and Roman mythology (1) ◊ *Pluto*, the god of the underworld; (2) the underworld itself, the dwelling-place of the spirits of the departed, except those who merit ◊ *Elysium* on the one hand or ◊ *Tartarus* on the other: the entrance is guarded by ◊ *Cerberus*, and Hades contains the rivers Acheron, Cocytus, Lethe, Phlegethon, and Styx, the ferryman Charon carrying new entrants across Acheron or Styx on return for a fee of one obol (hence the custom of placing a small coin between the lips of the dead), and the three judges Aeacus, ◊ *Minos*, and Rhadamanthus assigning each spirit to its appropriate place.

Hadrian's Wall. Defensive wall between Tyne and Solway built by Hadrian about A.D. 122–8; in its final form, 80 Roman m. long, stone-built throughout its length, and defended by 16 major forts and a large number of smaller mile-forts. Substantial though greatly damaged remains of this remarkable wall are still to be seen.

Haematite. Kidney ore of ◊ *iron*, a form of iron oxide, found in pockets or solution hollows of rocks e.g. the carboniferous limestone of the Furness district of N. Lancashire; the limestone has been dissolved and washed out of the rock and its place taken by iron oxides percolating from red sandstones lying above. The rich iron content makes haematite a valuable ore. Abundant in N. Spain, Brazil, and round the western end of Lake Superior in U.S.A. ◊ *Bog Iron*.

Haemoglobin. The red pigment of the ◊ *blood*, with the important property of combining in the lungs with ◊ *oxygen*, which in the course of circulation it distributes to the tissue cells, taking up in exchange carbon dioxide which it carries back to the lungs, whence it is expelled. The blood of mammals can carry up to a quarter of its own volume of oxygen; in birds, fishes, or reptiles the oxygen capacity of the blood is smaller. Carbon monoxide combines with the iron of haemoglobin more firmly than does oxygen; thus haemoglobin exposed to carbon monoxide is no longer able to carry oxygen, and it is for this reason that carbon monoxide is so lethal.

Haemophilia. Hereditary disease of the ◊ *blood*, characterized by a tendency to bleed excessively from even the slightest injury, owing to a deficiency of a specific anti-haemophilic globulin in the blood. A sex-linked disease, it affects only the males in a family; although immune to it, the females are capable of transmitting it to their male descendants.

Hafnium. A silvery metallic ◊ *element*, found in ◊ *zirconium* minerals, its chemistry similar to that of zirconium, from which it is separated with difficulty. It has as yet no important use.

Haggis. A famous Scottish dish (originally from France), consisting of the heart, liver, and lungs of a calf, sheep, or other animal minced and boiled with seasonings in a sheep's stomach.

Hague Conferences. International conferences called to halt the arms race. The first, convened by Tsar Nicholas II in 1899, was attended by 24 nations; it failed to achieve ◊ *disarmament*, but drew up the Hague Convention for the Pacific Settlement of International Disputes, and agreed on certain rules of war. The second conference (1907) similarly failed in its main purpose, but proposed the ◊ *International Court of Justice* (established 1920).

Hair. Essentially, a modified skin structure, keratin, growing from roots in the dermis and containing neither blood nor nerves, its function being protection against heat and cold; it grows (at a rate of two or three mm. a day) on most parts of the body and densely on the head, where the number of hairs varies from 100,000 (dark) to 140,000 (fair). Hair contains melanin, a pigment which determines its colour. In animals there is an undercoat of dense fine hair, the ◊ *fur*; in some, where it is rougher, it is called ◊ *wool*.

Haiti. Area 10,700 sq. m. Pop. 4 m. Cap. Port-au-Prince. A republic occupying half of the Caribbean island of Hispaniola (the other half being the ◊ *Dominican Republic*). The people are mostly Negroes, descendants of former slaves, with an influential minority of mulattoes, from whom an unenlightened exclusive governing class emerged; 85 per cent of the population are illiterate.

ECONOMY. Once the most prosperous of the French colonies, Haiti is now one of the world's most impoverished and backward countries. Its main export is coffee; also sugar, oils, bananas, cocoa, cotton, bauxite. There are U.N. and U.S. plans to provide hydroelectric and irrigation schemes and to improve education and agricultural techniques.

HISTORY. As St Dominique (San Domingo), it was a French colony 1697–1804, when it declared its independence after the 1791–1803 revolt and 'Black Republic' led by the former slaves Toussaint L'Ouverture and Jean-Jacques Dessalines (◊ *Louisiana Purchase*). It was occupied by U.S. marines 1915–34 and released from U.S. revenue control in 1947.

LANGUAGE. French; also ◊ *Creole*.

Hake. Bony marine fish related to the ◊ *cod* but having a large head resembling that of the ◊ *pike*, found in the Atlantic and the Mediterranean, normally at a depth of 100–300 fathoms, but moving to shallow waters to breed. Important as a food fish, it may reach a weight of 20 lb.

Half-life. The length of time taken for the number of radioactive atoms of a particular ◊ *nuclide* to fall to one half of the original number. The radioactive decay of atoms is statistical, and the half-life is used as an index of the disintegration rate. It may vary from several thousand years (e.g. carbon) to a fraction of a second (as in the transuranic elements). All atoms of radioactive nuclides will undergo radioactive decay into other nuclides of lower atomic weight, until a non-radioactive nuclide of an element results (e.g. an isotope of lead is the end product of the disintegration of uranium). ◊ *Radiocarbon Dating*.

Half-tone ◊ *Engraving (Mezzotint), Photo-engraving.*

Halibut. Bony marine fish found around Britain. The females often attain a length of over eight feet and a weight of 500 lb. Adapted to life on the sea bottom by its shape and the location of its eyes, the halibut is an active swimmer, feeding on other fish and crabs. It is an excellent food fish, and its liver yields an oil valued for its high vitamin content.

Halides ◊ *Halogens.*

Hallmark. Mark on objects of silver or gold to show official confirmation of the degree of purity of the metal. It was introduced by law in England in 1300 and carried out by the Goldsmiths' Hall, London (and later elsewhere). The marks indicate the genuineness of the gold or silver and the year of testing. Similar marks were introduced on the Continent and in America.

Hallstatt Culture ◊ *Iron Age.*

Hallucination. A subjective phenomenon common in some psychoses, but occasionally experienced by normal individuals, taking the form of 'visions' so real-seeming that their victims often react as if they were true. They occur in waking life, and the experiencer has no control over their occurrence or content; they are more frequently auditory in ◊ *schizophrenia* and visual in delirium tremens. There are hallucinations for which objective significance has been claimed. ◊ *Ergot*.

Halo. In astronomy, a ring of light round the sun (or moon) when shining through thin cloud, usually cirrostratus; results from reflection and refraction of light by ice crystals. May be small (22° radius) or large (46° radius).

PARHELION: A mock sun resulting from a concentration of light on one point of a small halo.

Halogens. The family of non-metallic elements making up Group VII of the Periodic Classification: ⬦ *astatine, bromine, chlorine, fluorine, iodine.* The word means 'salt former'; these elements readily combine directly with metals to form salts e.g. chlorine with sodium to give sodium chloride, common salt. The salts so formed (fluorides, chlorides, bromides, iodides) are collectively known as halides. The halogens also combine with hydrogen; the hydrides formed dissolve in water to give strong acids e.g. hydrogen chloride forms 'hydrochloric acid, commonly known as 'spirits of salt'.

Hamites. Peoples living in N. Africa; the Berbers, Tuareg, and other Saharan peoples, and the Somali and peoples of the Horn of Africa (⬦ *Cushites*). The ancient Egyptians were Hamites. 'Superior' culture traits in Negro Africa, esp. divine kingship, were once attributed to Hamitic invaders, but this theory, based mainly on faulty linguistic reconstruction and wishful thinking, is no longer tenable.

Hamito-Semitic Languages. Language family straddling Africa and Asia, inc. Egyptian, Berber, and Cushite in the Hamitic sub-family and ⬦ *Hebrew* and ⬦ *Arabic* in the Semitic.

BERBER LANGUAGES: N. Africa. Inc. Tuareg (spoken by the Sahara Bedouins), Shluh (vernacular of S. Morocco), and Kabyl (in the mountains of Algiers and Tunis).

CUSHITE LANGUAGES: Ethiopia and the E. Horn of Africa, between the Nile and the Red Sea. Inc. Somali, Galla, and Beja; are still spoken by large populations over wide areas. Since the typical word is basically of two consonants (as in Old Egyptian), their word-structure may be even more ancient than the now universal tri-consonantal pattern of the ⬦ *Semitic languages.* ⬦ *African Languages, Cushites, Egypt, Masai.*

Hamster. Member of the *Cricetainea*, a ⬦ *rodent* sub-family, of worldwide distribution (except Australia); with a gestation period of 16 days, and maturity attained in 11 weeks, its breeding is rapid. Omnivorous, before mastication the hamster stacks food in large cheek pouches extending back on to the shoulder. It is easily domesticated and widely used as an experimental animal. All the known specimens of one variant, the Syrian or golden hamster, derive from one original breeding pair, and consequently are genetically homogeneous.

Hanover. Formed by the union of the duchies of Calenberg and Göttingen in 1512; from 1634 ruled by the house of Brunswick-Lüneberg. Ernest Augustus's marriage to Sophia, granddaughter of James I of Britain, gave the house a claim to the English throne, to which George of Hanover acceded in 1714 on the death of Anne (⬦ *Jacobites*). The duchy was united with Britain 1714–1837 (becoming a kingdom after the ⬦ *Napoleonic wars*), but ceased to be so upon the accession of Victoria to the British throne, when her uncle the Duke of Cumberland became King Ernest of Hanover. Annexed by Prussia in 1866, after the ⬦ *Second World War* it became part of the province of Lower ⬦ *Saxony.*

Hanseatic League. After the German expansion into the previously Slav territories in the Baltic area, certain cities formed themselves into leagues for protection. The association of Lübeck and Hamburg in 1241 was joined by other cities, and for two centuries the League was virtually paramount, with establishments throughout N. Europe from London to Novgorod, until defeated by the Dutch. Thereafter the importance of the League gradually dissolved. Hamburg, Lübeck, and Bremen still call themselves Hansa towns. ⬦ *Free Port.*

Hapsburgs (Habsburgs). Family (named after the castle of Hapsburg in Switzerland) which first acquired importance when Rudolf I became king of Germany, 1273–91. Despite the loss of the crown in 1308, the family continued to expand its lands, adding ⬦ *Burgundy* when Maximilian married the daughter of Charles the Bold; their son Philip married Juana of Spain (daughter of Ferdinand and Isabella, sister of Catherine of Aragon). Philip's son by Juana, the Emperor Charles V, 1500–58, thus united vast territories. After 1521 Charles ruled only Spain and Burgundy (including the ⬦ *Netherlands*); his brother Ferdinand I thereafter ruled Austria where the family remained Emperors till 1918 (⬦ *Austria-Hungary*). Charles's son Philip II married Mary I of England and warred against Elizabeth I. Their line continued until the death of Charles II of Spain in 1700. The Hapsburgs were noted for close intermarriage, which resulted in the perpetuation of physical deformities, esp. the 'Hapsburg jaw' and ◊ *haemophilia*. ◊ *Bohemia, Holy Roman Empire, Thirty Years War, War of the Austrian Succession*.

Harappa ◊ *Indus Civilization*.

Harbours ◊ *Docks and Harbours*.

Hare-lip ◊ *Palate*.

Harmattan. Dry dusty N E or E. wind in W. Africa, blowing directly from the Sahara, so dry that it sometimes splits the trunks of trees, but along the Guinea coast relatively cool. Its extreme dryness promotes evaporation, providing such relief from the usual moist heat that it is named 'the Doctor'.

Harmonic Series. When a string or air column is set vibrating along its whole length, the note produced is said to be its 'fundamental'. The harmonic series consists of integral multiples of the fundamental frequency. The intervals between the notes become progressively smaller : octave, fifth, third, and so on. Harmonics are more or less audible in any musical note as overtones or 'partials'. Different instrumental tone colours are the result of the differing strengths of these overtones. The sound-production of brass instruments is governed by the physical law of harmonics.

Harmony. The musical effect of sounding more than one note at a time, which may be produced by the simultaneous sounding of two or more melodies each with a musical validity of its own (◊ *Counterpoint*); the supplementing of one melody by another one in parallel appears to have been its historical origin. Since about 1600 (and increasingly thereafter), however, composers have often made a single melody prominent and regarded harmony as a means of supporting that melody. Harmony thus draws attention to the vertical structure of music, while counterpoint refers to its horizontal aspect.

From about 1600 to about 1900 western music was firmly based on the system of harmony called tonality, using the major and minor keys with an ordered system of passing from one such key to another (modulation). The 18th- and 19th-cent instrumental forms of ◊ *sonata*, ◊ *symphony*, and ◊ *concerto* are based on key-structure, i.e. on the 'long-range' use of harmony, and Beethoven (who extended this 'long range') may be regarded as a harmonic innovator no less than say

Chopin (whose innovations were in the juxtaposition of individual notes and chords). During this period harmony was based on the differentiation between consonance (sounds implying stability) and dissonance (implying the necessity to move forward to a consonance). Gradually, however, more and more former dissonances came to be accepted as consonant, and in the search for new dissonances composers developed an ever wider harmonic vocabulary. Some 20th-cent. composers, notably the followers of serialism, have rejected the traditional differentiation between consonance and dissonance and adopted other structural principles.

Harpsichord ◊ *Keyboard Instruments*.

Harvard University. Founded 1636 as a college of higher education for men at Cambridge, Massachusetts, and subsequently endowed by a gift of money and books from John Harvard; as early as 1782 it included a graduate school of medicine, and by the 20th cent. it had become a leading U.S.A. university, accepting students from every State, offering graduate courses in every branch of education, and establishing a high reputation esp. in Law, Engineering, and Business Administration. The university is equipped with several observatories, museums, and agricultural and botanical research stations, one of the largest libraries in America, and the Harvard University Press. Undergraduates are resident in houses headed by a member of the college faculty, and owing to its enormous expansion the university is now widely dispersed throughout Cambridge and the environs, but the original buildings, surrounding the area known as Harvard 'Yard', are still the administrative centre. Officially the university is non-denominational. Affiliated to Harvard is Radcliffe College for women, whose students attend Harvard lectures but receive a separate degree.

Harvester ◊ *Reaper*.

Harvest Moon. The full moon which occurs nearest to the autumn ◊ *equinox*. As a result of the particular inclination of the moon's orbit to the horizon at this time, the moon rises only 20–30 min. later each night (instead of an average of 50 min.) for several consecutive nights. There is thus an unusual amount of moonlight in the early evening.

Hashish ◊ *Drug Addiction, Hemp.*

Hasidim (Chasidim). Followers of a Jewish pietistic movement in E. Europe, which arose on the basis of the teaching of the Ukrainian Baal-Shem Tob 1700–60 in reaction against the legalistic and intellectualistic tradition of the orthodox Rabbis. ZADDIKIM (Righteous Ones): Teachers whose lives and sayings have given rise to a large anecdotal literature, which has recently become widely known through the writings of the Jewish theologian and philosopher Martin Buber. ◊ *Judaism.*

Hastings (1066) ◊ *Norman Conquest.*

Hausa. Various peoples of N. Nigeria and neighbouring areas, numbering over 6 m. Basically a language group, they include a wide variety of cultures and physical types; almost all are Muslims. The original Hausa were organized into large kingdoms, which were conquered in the early 19th cent. by the nomadic Fulani, who took over the emirates and adopted the Hausa language; today the emirates (Kano, Zaria, Katsina, etc.) recognize the religious leadership of the Sultan of Sokoto. The Hausa language is a ◊ *lingua franca* over much of *Nigeria.*

Hawk ◊ *Eagle, Falcon.*

Hawking. The hunting of birds and animals with trained hawks or falcons; practised from very early times, it was an aristocratic sport in England for many centuries but declined in the 18th cent. and is now very rare indeed, except in Arabia.

Hazel (Cobnut). *Corylus avellana,* of the *Betulaceae*; a common shrub of woods and scrubland, often coppiced. In early spring it has pendulous male ◊ *catkins* and female flowers like small green buds. The fruit is a brown nut in a cup of green bracts. *C. maxima* is the filbert, cultivated for its larger nuts and native in S E Europe and Asia Minor.

Hearing. The sense by which many living things detect and interpret vibrations of certain frequencies (sound waves) in their environment, of which in man and most other animals the ear is the receiving organ; minute changes of air pressure act on the ear to produce characteristic vibrations, which are converted into electric impulses and passed to the brain for interpretation. Defective hearing may be congenital, or may result from injury or disease or from degenerations associated with age (e.g. osteoarthritis), and is fairly general among the elderly; it can usually be improved by the use of electronic devices, which amplify sound in a selective manner to compensate for the particular defects of the user. ◊ *Deafness, Ear.*

Heart. The organ which pumps blood throughout the ◊ *circulatory system* of multicellular animals; an indispensable feature of vertebrates, it exists in simpler form in most invertebrates also. During vertebrate ◊ *evolution,* the heart changed by folding and division from a muscular valve-tube (fish) to a four-chambered organ (birds and mammals) in which two chambers are concerned with pulmonary and two with systemic circulation.

Heat. A form of energy (kinetic or potential) which can be transmitted from one body to another by conduction, convection, and radiation. According to the kinetic theory of matter, heat is an increase in the state of agitation of the molecules. Degree of heat (temperature) is measured by means of a ◊ *thermometer,* and quantitatively either in terms of the ◊ *calorie* or the British Thermal Unit i.e. the heat required to raise the temperature of 1 lb. of water 1 deg. F. ◊ *Conduction, Thermodynamics.*

Heather. Common name for some shrubs of the ◊ *Ericaceae,* with tough wiry stems and very small leaves, which usually grow in the peaty soil of cold, damp, windy moorlands, where they are often the main vegetation. In Britain, usually *Calluna vulgaris* (Ling, 'Scotch' heather) or the 'bell' heathers *E. cinerea* and *E. tetralix.* A mountain heath of central Europe is *E. carnea,* which will grow on lime.

Heaviside Layer. Layer of ionized gas in the upper atmosphere which reflects or refracts wireless waves; discovered by the English physicist Oliver Heaviside and (independently) by Arthur Kennelly. ◊ *Ionosphere.*

Heavy Water. Formed from a stable isotope of hydrogen $^2_1$H known as deuterium, and similar to ordinary water, in which it is present in minute amounts. It is used as a moderator in ◊ *nuclear power stations.*

Hebe. In Greek mythology, goddess of youth, cupbearer of ◊ *Zeus,* his daughter by ◊ *Hera* (said to have conceived her after eating lettuce), and wife of ◊ *Hercules* after his deification; she is represented as a girl crowned with flowers and by the Romans was identified with the old Italian goddess of youth, Juventas.

Hebrew. One of the ◊ *Hamito-Semitic languages*, recorded before 1000 B.C. Its history falls into three broad periods: Biblical, post-Biblical or Rabbinic (the literature of the Diaspora or Dispersion), and Modern (the revived version spoken by the inhabitants of ◊ *Israel*). Classical Hebrew had 23 signs, which stood for consonants only. Most roots have three consonants; most words have two syllables, with stress on the second; verbs have aspects, not tenses. Apart from proper nouns, Hebrew has no compounds.

Hecate. In Greek mythology, a moon goddess sometimes identified with ◊ *Artemis*; the daughter of a Titan, esp. associated with crossroads, sorcery, magic, and the black arts, and attended by fearsome dogs; according to some writers she was the mother of Medea (◊ *Golden Fleece*). She is often represented in triple form facing three ways, and played a considerable role in medieval and later demonology.

Hector. In classical legend a Trojan hero, son of ◊ *Priam* and ◊ *Hecuba*, husband of Andromache, his parting from whom is one of the most moving passages in the *Iliad*; he killed Patroclus the friend of ◊ *Achilles*, who in turn killed him and then dragged his corpse round the city walls at the tail of his chariot, but at the command of ◊ *Zeus* handed it to Priam for burial.

Hecuba. In classical legend, wife of ◊ *Priam*, King of Troy, and mother of ◊ *Cassandra*, ◊ *Hector*, ◊ *Paris*, and other famous persons. After the Trojan war, in which most of her children were killed, she was carried off by ◊ *Ulysses*; on the journey to Greece, the ghost of ◊ *Achilles* demanded the sacrifice of her daughter Polyxena, and a local king murdered her son Polydorus. In revenge, she tore out the murderer's eyes, but was prevented from killing him; escaping, she was changed into a bitch and leapt into the sea.

Hedgehog. *Erinaceus europaeus*; the one of the five genera of the mammalian order *Insectivora* which is found in Britain, the others being distributed throughout the Old World. It feeds on insects, worms, and snails, and protects itself against enemies by rolling itself into a spiny ball. During winter it hibernates.

Hedonism. The moral view that we ought always to seek pleasure; the psychological view that men never in fact seek anything else. In the ancient world, hedonism took two main forms, Aristippus holding that pleasure was to be obtained by the gratification of sensual desires and Epicurus that it was better sought by the rational control of desires (◊ *Epicureanism*). In the modern world, hedonism took a more social form in ◊ *utilitarianism* i.e. 'the greatest happiness of the greatest number'.

Hegelianism. The philosophy of Hegel and his successors; his work (in 20 vols.) eludes summary, but among its leading ideas is a version of philosophical ◊ *idealism*. The natural world, and also mankind, are seen as manifestations or revelations of a cosmic spirit, the ◊ *Absolute*, while nature, history, intellectual development, all thinking, exhibit a kind of progression called dialectical: one stage of development, the affirmation, gives rise to an 'opposite' or 'contradictory' one, the negation, the two result in a synthesis, the negation of the negation, which becomes a fresh affirmation and the process begins again (◊ *Dialectic*). Hegel said that his philosophy marked the high point of human development until that time; it gave rise to a transitory Hegelianism in Britain, helped to engender ◊ *marxism* (Marx claimed that he 'found Hegel standing on his head, and turned him right side up'), and later influenced ◊ *Existentialism*.

Hegira. The flight of Mohammed from Mecca to Medina A.D. 622. It was adopted as a base date of the Muslim ◊ *calendar*. Muslim dates bear no relation to those in the Gregorian system: besides starting from a different base each year contains only twelve lunar months. .

Heidelberg Man ◊ *Primates*.

Helen. In classical legend, daughter of ◊ *Zeus* and ◊ *Leda*, supreme among women for her beauty and sought in marriage by many eminent Greeks, who at the suggestion of ◊ *Ulysses* at last agreed to accept her own decision; she selected Menelaus, brother of ◊ *Agamemnon* (husband of her sister Clytaemnestra), but her abduction by ◊ *Paris* of Troy caused the Trojan war. After the ten-year siege, she returned to Greece and was reconciled to Menelaus; another legend, however, says that Paris carried off to Troy only her wraith, her real body being in Egypt, where the king sheltered her pending her husband's return.

283   HENBANE

Helicopter. A rotorcraft deriving both lift and propulsion from one or more power-driven screws or rotors having their axes nearly vertical. Louis Breguet made the first man-carrying helicopter flight 1907, in France, but the first recorded helicopter design was by Leonardo da Vinci 1483, and the first to fly was probably the spring-operated model by Launoy and Bienvenue 1748, which was also the first powered heavier-than-air device to fly.. For search and rescue, helicopters have the advantage over other rotorcraft that they can not only take off and land vertically but can also hover.

Heliopolis. Ancient city in the Nile delta dedicated to the sun god Ra, the centre of Egyptian sun-worship; its priestly colleges of philosophy and astronomy were widely respected as late as the 4th cent. B.C. and were said to have been visited by Plato and other Greek philosophers, but it declined after the founding of Alexandria 332 B.C. and its buildings were largely destroyed to provide building-stone for later towns.

Helium. ◊ *Inert Gases*; a colourless odourless monatomic gas, twice as dense as ◊ *hydrogen*; m.p. −272° C, b.p. −269° C. The spectrum of an unknown element was identified in the sun's chromosphere 1868 by Lockyer and Frankland and named helium. The nuclei are produced during radioactive decay of some elements, and thus helium is the only non-radioactive natural element which has been produced since the earth left the sun. Liquid helium has remarkable properties: when cooled below −270° C it forms helium II, a liquid with a heat conductance 600 times that of copper, extremely low viscosity, and an ability to flow *up* the surface of a container. The commercial source of helium is natural gas from U.S.A. oil wells; it is chiefly used for obtaining low temperatures, since by rapidly boiling liquid helium a temperature within 0.7° of absolute zero can be reached. It has great promise as a means of heat transfer in gas-cooled graphite-moderated atomic reactors, as it neither becomes radioactive nor attacks graphite. Being less soluble than ◊ *nitrogen*, it is used with ◊ *oxygen* when men are working under pressure, to avoid caisson sickness caused by the release of bubbles of nitrogen in the blood as the pressure returns to atmospheric; in U.S.A. it is used (as argon is elsewhere) to provide an inert atmosphere when welding easily-oxidized metals e.g. magnesium, aluminium, titanium, and their alloys.

Hell. In Christian theology, a place of eternal punishment for the souls of the damned; the medieval conception of its nature is described in the *Inferno* of Dante. There are analogies in most other religions, e.g. Gehenna of the Jews in the New Testament epoch, the ◊ *Tartarus* of the Romans; but most non-Christian hells are places of gloomy half-life rather than of punishment, e.g. the Sheol or Tophet of the ancient Hebrews, the ◊ *Hades* of the Greeks, and the Dis or Avernus of the Romans. ◊◊ *Devil*.

Hemlock. 1. *Conium maculatum*; a biennial herb up to six ft tall, with bright green finely-divided leaves and small white flowers, the most striking feature being the furrowed pale stem blotched with purple, which grows throughout Britain in damp places, by ditches and in open woods. The plant is poisonous and contains alkaloids of the coniine group, narcotics and sedatives which produce paralysis of the muscles. It is commonly believed that hemlock was used to poison Socrates. ◊◊ *Umbelliferae*. **2.** Evergreen ◊ *conifers*, trees of the genus *Tsuga*, several species of which are widely distributed in N. America.

Hemp. Fibres derived from the annual herb *Cannabis sativa* (5–15 ft) grown in many countries e.g. China, India, Russia, and parts of Europe, mainly for ropemaking. The fibres, 3–6 ft long, are strong and durable, similar to those of ◊ *flax*, with which it is often blended; it is more expensive than ◊ *jute*. Its uses include the manufacture of canvas, sailcloth, and sacking; the tow is useful as cleaning waste and for packing joints. Tropical hemp produces a narcotic resin variously known as Indian hemp, hashish, and marijuana; as a narcotic drug it produces hallucinations, and prolonged use leads to illness and insanity. ◊◊ *Bast*.

MANILA HEMP ◊ *Banana*.

Henbane. *Hyoscyamus niger*; a foetid annual or biennial herb up to two ft tall, with a stout stem, sticky downy leaves, and dull yellow flowers with purple veins. It is native in England and occurs in scattered localities, but is cultivated for its alkaloids hyoscyamine and hyoscine, extensively used as sedatives; hyoscine is the 'twilight sleep' anaesthetic, and is used in some seasickness tablets. ⟡ *Solanaceae*.

Heparin. < Gr. *hepar*, liver; a tissue constituent, sometimes used in surgery, which has the property of retarding the clotting of ⟡ *blood*.

Hepatitis. Inflammation of the liver, often associated with jaundice. The most common form is infectious hepatitis (catarrhal jaundice), which is caused by a virus infection and usually occurs in epidemics. Hepatitis caused by poisoning, e.g. by chloroform or phosphorus, is likely to be severe and is often fatal. Chronic hepatitis may lead to ⟡ *cirrhosis*.

Hephaestus. Equivalent to the Latin Vulcan; god of fire, of smiths' work, and of the useful arts. Son of ⟡ *Hera* and husband of ⟡ *Aphrodite*, who frequently exposes him to ridicule as a cuckold. Traditionally lame, either congenitally (for which his mother cast him down from Olympus) or by breaking his leg when falling on the island of Lemnos after ⟡ *Zeus* had kicked him down from Olympus for taking his mother's part in a matrimonial quarrel; ⟡ *Wayland* and Völund, the smiths of English and Norse legend, were also lame. Volcanoes (esp. Etna) were supposed to mark the sites of his underground workshops; the ⟡ *Cyclopes* were his attendants. ⟡ *Athena*.

Heptane ⟡ *Paraffins (Octane)*.

Hera. In Greek mythology, sister and wife of ⟡ *Zeus*, mother of ⟡ *Ares*, ⟡ *Hebe*, ⟡ *Hephaestus*, etc. and patron goddess of women, identified with ⟡ *Juno* by the Romans.

Heraldry. All over the world – e.g. in China, Japan, among the Aztecs of Mexico – devices to denote clan or family or name have been used; in England, the use of personal emblems was established by the time of Richard I, who used a lion (for his nickname Lionheart) and a sprig of broom (hence the cognomen Plantagenet, *planta genesta*). Arms later became universal on shields, gloves, etc., and standard forms and colours were established: two metals – *or*, gold (yellow) and *argent*, silver (white) – with five other colours – *gules* (red), *azure* (blue), *vert* (green), *pourpre* (purple), and *sable* (black) – and two furs – *ermine* and *vair* (squirrel, stoat) – were used, and some animals were given standard positions e.g. the lion was usually *rampant* (one foot clawing the air), *passant* (prowling), *couchant* (sleeping,

lying down), or leaping, while the leopard (a lion image looking sidelong) was normally *passant*. Other animals used were the tiger, deer, and unicorn, as well as birds, fishes, reptiles, and insects. Often the shield was quartered e.g. when a man's arms were combined with his wife's. After 1600 engravers showed the heraldic colours, in uncoloured plates, by means of a system of lines and dots. The arms passed to the eldest son; younger sons used 'differences' i.e. symbols showing the degree of cadetship. The band sinister (from upper right to lower left) did not necessarily indicate illegitimacy, which was usually shown by a wavy band round the border of the shield.

Various tours of England were made (the first by John Leland in Henry VIII's reign) to draw up tables of genealogy, and in the late 17th cent. both William Prynne and William Dugdale made exhaustive genealogical examinations of old records in e.g. the Tower of London. The College of Heralds (made a corporation 1484 by Richard III), which is the final authority, consists of the five Kings-of-Arms – Garter, Clarenceux, Norroy, Lyon (for Scotland), and Ulster (for Ireland) – the six Heralds – Windsor, Chester, Richmond, Somerset, York, and Lancaster – and the four Pursuivants – Rouge Croix, Bluemantle, Rouge Dragon, and Portcullis.

Herb Robert ⟡ *Geranium*.

Herbs. Botanically, plants whose shoots do not become woody and perennial but die down and are replaced by fresh ones each year (hence 'herbaceous' border); also an arbitrary classification of a wide selection of plants whose stems, leaves, and frequently flowers are aromatic and contain ⟡ *essential oils*, used in cooking, beverages, and old-fashioned remedies. Those used in making soups, salads, sauces, etc. are known as sweet herbs, e.g. chives, mint, parsley, sage, thyme. Camomile is used for tea, and also in shampoos; tarragon flavours vinegar. Herb gardens were long in great favour, and many books describing the use of herbs (herbals) were published in the 17th and 18th centuries. Many herbs are still important sources of drugs.

Hercules (Heracles, Herakles). Legendary Greek hero renowned for strength and courage: son of ⟡ *Zeus* and Alcmene. His heroic career began in his cradle, where he strangled two snakes sent by ◊ *Hera* to kill him; of his numerous adventures, the chief are the 12 labours (◊ *Hydra, Augean Stables, Theseus, Amazons, Hesperides*) imposed on him by Eurystheus, king of Tiryns (at the command of the Delphic ◊ *oracle*) as a penance for having killed his wife Megara in a fit of madness. Many other such quests and adventures are attributed to him. For casting down the walls of Tiryns in a fit of madness, the Delphic oracle condemned him to a year of slavery to Omphale, a Lydian queen, during which he worked as a woman, while Omphale wore his special attributes, the lion's skin and club. At last, the pain caused by the shirt of ◊ *Nessus* led him to burn himself alive; becoming immortal, he married ◊ *Hebe*.

Heredity. The genetic relationship between parent and offspring. It was early observed that a child often resembled one (or both) of his parents, but it was not until recently that the mechanism for the transmission of characteristics was studied and understood in any detail: until the end of the 19th cent. the most common theory was that the individual simply

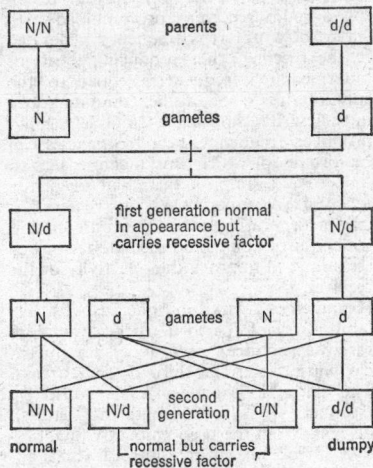

represented a merging of the characteristics of its parents.

The mechanism of heredity is dependent upon the fact that sexual ◊ *reproduction* consists in the union of two germ cells (◊ *Gametes*) to form a new cell (the zygote), which develops into the new individual. The nucleus of each germ cell (egg in the female, sperm in the male) contains a single set of ◊ *chromosomes*, on which are conveyed the ◊ *genes* which determine the characteristics of the individual inheriting them (◊ *Meiosis*). The new individual thus receives from its parents two sets of chromosomes, which maintain their integrity in its body cells and are again segregated and passed to a new generation when the individual reproduces. The new individual's characteristics are determined by this inheritance of two sets of genetic factors and by the ◊ *dominance* of certain factors over others.

The results of this process have been investigated by the observation in relatively simple organisms of alternative characters thought to be determined by a single pair of alternative genes (allelomorphs), e.g. Mendel's studies of the field pea (19th cent.) and Morgan and Bridges's experiments with *Drosophila* ◊ *fruit-fly*. Heredity is complicated by many factors e.g. ◊ *mutation* and chromosome crossing, but the essentials of the mechanism may be seen in the diagram, where *N* is the factor for normal wings in *Drosophila* (the dominant factor) and *d* is the factor for dumpy wings (the recessive factor). ◊◊ *Mendelism*.

Heresy. In ◊ *Christianity*, doctrine opposed to the generally accepted official teaching, esp. a deviation from the orthodox or Catholic form of the faith as held in the early centuries of the Church (e.g. Monophysitism held that ◊ *Jesus Christ* had only a single human-divine nature). ◊◊ *Albigenses, Arianism, Gnostics, Jansenism, Lollards, Manichaeism, Maronites, Moravians, Nestorianism, Pelagianism*.

Hermaphrodite. Individual with both male and female organs. Earthworms are hermaphrodite, but have to copulate in pairs in order to reproduce; many plants and some invertebrate animals e.g. tapeworms are self-fertilizing, however. In humans the condition known as unilateral hermaphroditism occasionally occurs (the doubling of sex characteristics occurs only on one side of the individual, i.e. there is an ovo-testis on one side and either an ovary or a testis on the other); true hermaphroditism is rare, and more often it is only the secondary sex characteristics that are duplicated.

Hermes. In Greek mythology, god of commerce, wealth, thievery, and messenger of Olympus as well as guide of the dead to ◊ *Hades*; son of ◊ *Zeus* and Maia, equivalent to the Roman Mercury. On the day of his birth he invented the lyre and then stole 50 of the cows of ◊ *Apollo*, driving them backwards so that their hoof-marks concealed the direction of their route; when the angry Apollo came to retrieve them, Hermes gave him the lute instead, and went back to his cradle. His attributes are winged sandals, a serpent-twined staff, and a wide-brimmed hat (petasus); the Egyptians identified him with ◊ *Thoth*, and the ◊ *neoplatonist* philosophers attributed to him the authorship, under the name of Hermes Trismegistus (thrice greatest), of certain occult writings, some of which still survive.

Hernia. The abnormal protrusion or rupture of a tissue or organ through an opening in the wall of the cavity in which it usually lies; it may be either congenital or acquired. Commonest is inguinal hernia, a protrusion of the omentum or the intestine into the inguinal canal through which ducts to the testicle pass through the abdominal wall.

Hero. In Greek legend, a beautiful priestess of ◊ *Aphrodite* at Sestos on the European shore of the Hellespont; Leander, a youth of Abydos on the Asian side, swam across to her nightly, guided by a torch which she held, standing at the top of a tower. One stormy night he was drowned, and she jumped from the tower to share his fate.

Heroic Couplets. In French verse, rhymed hexameters. In English verse, rhymed iambic pentameters; first developed by Chaucer, they became the chief narrative measure, and in the 17th–18th centuries were largely used in rendering classical hexameters, esp. by e.g. Dryden, Pope.

Heroin. Synthetic derivative of ◊ *morphine*, which it closely resembles in general effects although it is more toxic and depressant; a powerful and effective analgesic. Its use is prohibited in some countries because of its habit-forming characteristics. ◊> *Drug Addiction.*

Herpes. Blister-like eruptions, usually in clusters on the skin or mucous membrane; in *Herpes zoster* (shingles), the lesions follow the course of surface nerves esp. on the trunk, and the disease may be associated with severe constitutional upset.

Herring. Bony fish abundant in the North Sea and of great importance as human food; herring swim in enormous shoals, often miles wide and long, in numbers estimated at 3000 m. A million tons of herring are fished annually, by means of drift nets whose mesh is designed to catch the adult fish but let the young escape to mature; trawling for herring is prohibited by law, as being too destructive of young fish. About 70 per cent of the herring caught are cured, and become buckling, bloaters, red herring, or kippers according to the degree of salting and smoking.

Hesperides. In classical mythology, daughters of ◊ *Atlas*; maiden votaries of a garden in N. Africa where grew golden apples (given by Gaea, mother of the ◊ *Titans*, to ◊ *Hera* when she married ◊ *Zeus*), guarded by the never-sleeping dragon Ladon. As one of his 12 labours, ◊ *Hercules* was sent to collect some of the apples; he supported the world on his shoulders, while Atlas gathered the apples for him. The apples also appear in the story of Atalanta.

Heterodyne. Process whereby ◊ *radio* waves of a particular ◊ *frequency* reaching a radio receiver are combined with waves of a different frequency generated in the receiver, thus producing 'beat' or 'intermediate' frequencies equal to the sum or difference of the combining frequencies. By choosing a suitable locally-produced frequency, beat frequencies can be produced which are much easier to tune to and amplify than that originally received. A superheterodyne receiver is one incorporating an ◊ *electronic* circuit, which uses this intermediate-frequency technique to improve the selectivity of the receiver.

Hexameter. A six-foot line, usually five iambs (◊ *metre*) and a trochee (or more rarely a spondee), with a caesura (metrical pause) after the third or fourth foot. The classical hexameter was quantitative (scanned by syllable-length not stress), deriving from the predominantly quantitative Greek speech-rhythms; it first appeared in Homer's epics and later was adopted by the Romans esp. Virgil, and in the 17th cent. by the French, as the heroic metre. In English it is most commonly used as the last line in a 'spenserian' stanza and as a variant in ◊ *heroic* *couplets*. The alternative name 'Alexandrine' is from the 12th-cent. *Roman d'Alexandre*.

Hibernation. Mechanism which allows some animals to dispense with the high internal temperature required for full activity, and so to survive winter cold and food shortage; during hibernation, the glands of the endocrine system regress and the rates of metabolism, heartbeat, and breathing greatly decrease. In full hibernation, body temperature may drop to that of the environment, and the body become stiff, but even at a temperature of 0° C or lower the tissues do not freeze; a variety of stimuli bring about spontaneous rewarming. The physiology of hibernation is of interest for the understanding of surgical hypothermia.

Hieroglyphs. < Gr. 'sacred carvings' i.e. of ancient ◊ *Egypt*, incised or sculptured in raised relief on temple walls. These pictures of men, animals, and common objects began with the First Dynasty about 3000 B.C. and later developed into symbolic images or ideographs. Other forms of Egyptian writing were the hieratic (abbreviated hieroglyphic) written with reed-pen and ink on ◊ *papyrus* or potsherds, and the demotic (a later cursive script). The hieroglyphs were first deciphered in 1822 ◊ *Rosetta Stone*. ◊◊ *Alphabet*.

Hildebrandslied. *Lay of Hildebrand*; the only surviving example of a Germanic heroic poem, existing incomplete as 68 alliterative lines in a single MS dating to the late 8th cent. A.D. though the original may have been 6th-cent. The language is Low German, altered to conform to High German usage by the two copyist scribes, and the subject is the fight between Hildebrand and his son Hadubrand, ignorant of each other's identity (a widespread folk-literature motif); the ending is unknown, but external evidence and the tone of the MS suggests that the father kills his son.

Hinduism. Complex of religious and philosophical beliefs developed in India on the basis of the teachings of the ◊ *Vedas*; in its popular form an elaborate polytheism, the principal gods being Vishnu, representing the positive preservative principle, and Shiva, the principle of change and destruction. Marked by veneration of the cow (as milk-giving and ploughing animal), a social ◊ *caste* system, an elaborate temple worship (with a large sexual and fertility element), respect for personal holiness (manifested in ascetics), and belief in reincarnation (◊ *Transmigration*), it has no creed or body of compulsory dogmas and takes innumerable forms, from gross superstition to profound mystical devotion and the quest for union with the Absolute (◊ *Gnostics*). ◊◊ *Brahma, Mysticism, Pantheism*.

Hindustani (Hindi) ◊ *Indo-European Languages, Sanskrit*.

Hinterland. < Ger. 'back country'. Originally political as well as economic: when a colonial power occupied a coastal region in e.g. Africa, the 'hinterland' was politically and economically dependent on the coast; the absorption of the various hinterlands led to Africa's partitioning between European colonial powers. Later the term was adopted in economic geography to mean the area behind a seaport or seaboard supplying and receiving most of its exports and imports.

Hippolytus. < Gr. 'horse-destroyed'. In Greek legend, son of Hippolyta and ◊ *Theseus*, whose second wife Phaedra fell in love with her stepson; when he spurned her, she accused him of raping her, and then hanged herself. Theseus banished his son, calling to ◊ *Poseidon* for vengeance; and as Hippolytus was driving away in his chariot a sea-monster sent by the god terrified the horses, so that he was thrown and killed. Some versions attribute Phaedra's suicide to despair when Theseus, too late, discovered his son's innocence.

Hire Purchase. A method of acquiring goods by payments spread over a stated period, in which the legal title to the goods remains with the hirer until the purchaser has fulfilled the conditions in the agreement, usually between the purchaser and a finance company (not direct between buyer and seller); distinguished from purchase by instalments, in which title to the goods passes to the buyer on payment of the first instalment. The 1938 Hire Purchase Act as amended 1954 aims at ensuring that purchasers are properly acquainted with the terms, and gives the purchaser some rights in the goods after one third of the hire-purchase price has been paid. In all agreements where the hire-purchase price does not exceed £300 (for livestock £1000) the agreement cannot be enforced on the purchaser unless a statement of the price and instalments is signed by both parties and a copy given to the purchaser within a week. By altering the terms on which hire purchase may be done, e.g. the amount of down payment, the government can exert considerable influence on the trend of consumer demand esp. as regards furniture and electrical appliances. The total rate of hire-purchase debt in the U.K. (1964) is about £1000 m. but in U.S.A. hire purchase indebtedness, as a proportion of personal income, is much greater.

Hiroshima. 1945. The first atom bomb was dropped on Hiroshima by a single U.S. aircraft, as a result of a joint decision by President Truman and Prime Minister Attlee; 75–80,000 people were killed, and many more were severely burned or suffered later from radiation sickness, while the city was almost completely destroyed. A second bomb was soon after dropped on Nagasaki; Japan thereupon surrendered and brought the ◊ *Second World War* to an end.

Histamine. One of the amines, which occurs in the body in a combined form, and when liberated has a powerful action in causing dilation of blood vessels and reducing blood pressure. Some allergies are associated with the release of histamine within the body, and consequently are treated with anti-histamine drugs.

Histology ◊ *Anatomy.*

Hittites. Ancient empire in Anatolia and Syria about 2000–1200 B.C. of an Indo-European people probably from beyond the Black Sea; their culture shows strong foreign influences, notably Mesopotamian, esp. in art and religion. They sacked ◊ *Babylon* about 1595 B.C. and their empire was at its widest in the mid 14th cent. B.C. after Suppiluliumas had established control over N. Syria. The first references to iron-working occur in Hittite archives, and it seems certain that they were the first to exploit iron on a large scale; they kept the knowledge a closely-guarded secret because of its military and economic advantages, and iron-working did not spread widely until after the Hittites were expelled from Anatolia by invaders coming, it seems, by sea, and set up scattered kingdoms further south. The Hittite language became extinct and was not rediscovered until numerous ◊ *cuneiform* tablets were unearthed 1905 at Boghazköy, site of the Hittite capital, and decipherment showed the kinship of Hittite with Greek and Sanskrit; a Hittite ◊ *hieroglyphic* alphabet still remains largely undeciphered.

Hock ◊ *Wine.*

Hockey. An 11-a-side game played with curved sticks and a hard ball on a field 100 yds by 60 yds, closely resembling ◊ *Association Football* in general tactics; similar games existed in ancient Greece, Rome, and Mexico, but the modern game dates from the founding of the Hockey Association in England 1875. ◊ *Olympic Games* status was gained 1908 when the International Hockey Federation (47 members) was formed, the principal hockey nations being India, Pakistan, Holland, and the U.K. Both men and women play; the game is solely ◊ *amateur.*

Hohenzollerns. Leading German princely family, of Swabian origin, who acquired importance as Electors first of Brandenburg (1415) and later of Prussia. Outstanding were Frederick William the 'Great Elector' who built up Prussia, his son Frederick I who assumed the title of King in Prussia in 1701, Frederick II (the Great) who conquered Silesia in 1740 and seized West Prussia in the first ◊ *Partition of Poland* 1772, and William I who became Emperor of Germany in 1871. The last Hohenzollern was William II, Emperor from 1888 till his abdication in October 1918 (◊ *First World War*), after which he lived in exile at Doorn in Holland till his death in 1941.

Holly. *Ilex aquifolium*; a native of the British Isles, with handsome evergreen foliage and shining red berries, used for wind breaks and hedges and long associated with Christmas, although the origin of the usage is unknown. There are many varieties, some with silvery or golden variegated leaves, others with yellow or orange berries.

Holmium ◊ *Lanthanides.*

Holy Alliance. 1815. Treaty signed at the instigation of Tsar Alexander I between himself and the rulers of Austria and Prussia; declaring general agreement on vague Christian principles for the conduct of international affairs; it was signed by every European ruler except George IV and the Sultan of Turkey. Its effect was negligible, but the name became identified (erroneously) with the policies inspired by Metternich (◊ *Vienna, Congress of*).

Holy Communion. Christian rite in which bread and wine, blessed or consecrated by a minister or ◊ *priest,* are eaten and drunk by the believer after the example set at the last supper (◊ *Jesus Christ*) with his disciples before his crucifixion.

TRANSUBSTANTIATION (Real Presence): Roman Catholics believe that the elements so blessed are invisibly made into the real body and blood of Jesus.

CONSUBSTANTIATION: Protestants usually consider that the bread and wine coexist with the body and blood; many, however, believe that the elements remain unchanged and that the rite is purely commemorative. ◊ *Eucharist, Mass, Sacraments.*

Holy Ghost (Holy Spirit). Third member of the Christian ◊ *Trinity,* coequal with God the Father and God the Son and constituting with them one divinity in three persons; ◊ *Jesus Christ* promised his disciples that after his withdrawal from bodily existence the Spirit would be present with them, and is said to have manifested the presence visibly at Pentecost (◊ *Religious Festivals*) and thenceforward to have guided the Church in its life and teaching. The doctrine concerning the Holy Ghost was officially defined at Constantinople A.D. 381; the exact relation of the Holy Ghost to the Father and to the Son is a major point of dispute between the Eastern churches (the Spirit 'proceeds' from the Father alone) and the Western (the Spirit 'proceeds' from both the Father and the Son).

SEVEN GIFTS OF THE SPIRIT: Those enumerated in Isaiah xi. 2 (◊ *Bible*) with the addition of 'piety' (which the Vulgate mentions in that passage).

Holy Grail. In medieval belief and ◊ *Arthurian legend,* the chalice used by Jesus Christ at the Last Supper, brought to Britain by Joseph of Arimathaea, deposited at Glastonbury, and later lost; the knights of the Round Table went in quest of it, and it was eventually seen by Bors, ◊ *Galahad,* and ◊ *Parsifal.* A vast medieval and modern literature has grown up around the many forms of the legend and its connexions with other legends and folklore of 'food-providing vessels'.

Holy Orders. Various grades of the historic Christian ministry. The Anglican Church recognizes three: ◊ *bishop,* ◊ *priest,* and ◊ *deacon.* The ◊ *Roman*

Catholic Church (which numbers the conferring of these major orders among the ◊ *sacraments*) also recognizes the minor orders of subdeacon, acolyte, reader, exorcist, and doorkeeper; these involve no special duties, though they are still conferred on candidates for the priesthood. Ordination is conferred by the laying-on of a bishop's hands, to the accompaniment of decreed prayers.

Holy Roman Empire. Attempted continuation of the Roman empire (◊ *Rome*), founded by Charlemagne in 800 A.D. (◊ *Franks*) and revived by Otto I in 962 under papal sanction. Although the Holy Roman Emperor was in theory the temporal ruler of Christendom, the dream of a politically united Europe could not resist the growth of nationalism; his power never extended beyond Italy, Germany, the kingdom of Arles, Bohemia, Moravia, the Low Countries, and Switzerland, and in most of these was often purely nominal. Germany was divided among countless petty princedoms, and in Italy imperial authority was early challenged by the rise of rich and powerful city communes and by the popes. After the election of the Hapsburg Rudolf I in 1273 the Empire was a purely German institution, and from the 15th cent. it was identified with the house of ◊ *Hapsburg.* The ◊ *Thirty Years War* ended with the dissolution of the Empire at the Treaty of Westphalia, although the emperors continued to be powerful monarchs and retained their traditional ceremonial. In 1806, during the ◊ *Napoleonic Wars,* Francis II took the title of Emperor of Austria and renounced the title of Holy Roman Emperor; the Empire thus came to an end.

Holy Year ◊ *Papal Jubilee.*

Home Office. U.K. government department; created 1782. Its main duties concern the maintenance of law and order and of prisons, probation services, and provision for juvenile offenders, and control of immigration and resident aliens. Under the 1948 Civil Defence Act it is responsible for the Auxiliary Fire Service, and it is the ultimate authority in police affairs (although police forces are still county-administered). The responsible Minister is the Home Secretary.

Homeopathy. System of medicine introduced by Samuel Hahnemann 1755–1843, based on the theory that disease can be cured by administering minute doses of drugs which in a healthy patient would produce reactions similar to those produced by the disease.

Home Rule. The project of 'Irish autonomy in Irish matters' put forward in 1870, harking back beyond the 1800 ◊ *Act of Union* to Grattan's Revolution distinct from the Irish separatist demand for complete independent sovereignty. In 1875 Parnell became leader of the Irish Nationalist Party in the House of Commons, which held the balance of power between the Conservative and Liberal parties, and so successfully harassed all successive governments by his tactic of obstructionism that in 1886 Gladstone at last introduced a Home Rule Bill. Though very moderate, this failed to pass. Parnell and his party turned from compromise to separatism. In 1887 *The Times* attempted to implicate Parnell in the ◊ *Phoenix Park Murders* (an act of terror unconnected with Parnell), but the Parnell Commission vindicated him 1889. In 1890 he was cited in the O'Shea divorce case and his party split over his continued leadership. With his death in 1891 Home Rule was believed dead also, and a second Bill was defeated 1893, but in Ireland the Gaelic League and ◊ *Sinn Fein*-agitated, with increasing success, for separate sovereignty. A third Home Rule Bill in 1912 was passed, but threats of armed revolt (◊ *Orange Society*) caused the Lords to amend the Bill so as to exclude most of ◊ *Ulster*, and this, with the imminence of the First World War, caused its indefinite suspension; it was never implemented. ◊◊ *Anglo-Irish 'Troubles', Easter Rebellion, Partition.*

Hominids ◊ *Primates.*

Homology. The relationship between organs in different animals which have been shown to have similar ancestry and development. The wings of birds and bats are homologous, because they are both modifications of the fore-limb of land vertebrates; they are also homologous with human arms, but not with insect wings. ◊ *Anatomy.*

Honduras. Area 43,227 sq. m. Pop. 2 m. Cap. Tegucigalpa. Independent Central American republic. Under the 1957 constitution the government consists of a President, elected by popular vote for 6 years, a Council, and a single legislative chamber elected by universal adult suffrage.

ECONOMY: The chief industries are banana- and coconut-growing; banana-growing, which accounts for 60 per cent of exports, is dominated by American fruit companies. Silver exports are also important.

HISTORY: Honduras proclaimed its independence from Spain in 1821 and became fully independent in 1838. The dictatorship of General Carías Andino (1932-49) was followed by the enlightened rule of Juan Manuel Galvez (1949-54), who granted civil and political rights and attempted to develop the country's resources. Popular elections in 1957 led to the election of the Liberal Dr José Ramón Villeda, who carried on a programme of social reforms. He was deposed by an army coup in October 1963.

Honey. Sweet fluid produced by ◊ *bees*; 70 to 80 per cent sugar, in the form of dextrose and levulose. The worker bee collects ◊ *nectar* from flowers and carries it back to the hive, where it is placed in the hexagonal wax cells of the honeycomb; at least 20,000 trips are required to make one pound of honey. The cells are sealed, and the honey serves as food for the hive in winter. A minimum amount is needed by each hive; what is surplus can be removed by the beekeeper, and good husbandry can increase the quantity available. Different flowers produce differently flavoured honeys. Before sugar became available in Europe in the 16th cent. honey was virtually the sole sweetening agent.

Hong Kong. Area 398 sq. m. Pop. about 3.5 m. Cap. Victoria. British crown colony, comprising the island of Hong Kong (seized by the British in 1841), Kowloon (ceded in 1860), the New Territories (a mainland area leased in 1898 for a term of 99 years), and adjacent islands. There have been repeated demands from China for the return of Hong Kong. Since 1949 its population has grown greatly owing to the influx of refugees from Communist China, and there has been a rapid development of domestic industries, esp. cotton and a wide variety of consumer goods.

Hops. The ripened flowers of the female hop-plant, used to impart a bitter flavour to beer and, medically, as a tonic and a soporific. ◊ *Brewing.*

Hormones ◊ *Endocrine System.*

Horn. First used in hunting; about 1650,

probably in France, the spiral 'French horn' appeared, and from this evolved the modern orchestral horn. In the 19th cent. the addition of valves (◊ *Brass Instruments*) became standard, as did the use of four horns in the symphony ◊ *orchestra*. The instrument also appears in the military band, but not in the British brass band. ◊ *Oboe*.

Hornbeam. *Carpinus betulus*, of the *Betulaceae*; a tree up to 30 ft tall, with a fluted trunk and smooth grey bark, native to S. England. The leaves are oval and toothed, and the male and female flowers are in separate hanging ◊ *catkins*; the wood is very hard (hence the name horn-tree) and was used for various wooden articles, e.g. ox yokes, requiring great durability.

Horoscope ◊ *Astrology*.

Horse. *Equus caballus*, of the order *Perissodactyla* (◊ *Mammal*). The earliest horses were small swift animals resembling whippets, and abundant horse ◊ *fossils* provide one of the best demonstrations of ◊ *evolution* within an order, involving changes in teeth and limbs in response to changes in diet and habitat. The modern domesticated horse is the descendant of horses found around the Mediterranean and in Arabia, which probably originated and were tamed in central Asia. Although N. America was the cradle of its evolution, the horse spread into many other parts of the world; it was no longer found in America after its separation from Asia, in the ◊ *Pleistocene Epoch*. Horses were reintroduced by European settlers; the wild bands of mustangs and broncos were descendants of horses brought in by the Spanish. Horses are divided broadly into two groups, light horses for riding and for drawing vehicles at speed, and heavy horses e.g. the Clydesdale, Shire, Percheron, and Suffolk Punch used for heavy hauling; smaller breeds are known as ponies. The ◊ *gestation* period is about 11 months, and usually single offspring are born. Horses live up to 20 or even 30 years, and vary greatly in temperament, from the placid draught animal to the mettlesome racehorse (see below); apart from the ◊ *dog*, no animal has been bred in greater diversity. Closely related are the ass (found wild in Asia) and the untamable *zebra*. The only horse found wild today is the central Asian *Equus przewalskii*.

RACEHORSES: A special line of horses which by selection over the last 250 years have developed great speed and endurance; all are descended in the male line from an original crossing between the English 'running horse' (as developed to produce the royal mares owned by Charles II) and three sires, the Darley Arabian, the Byerly Turk, and the Godolphin Arabian (imported about 1700); they have been kept 'thoroughbred' by continued selection. Racehorses have increased in size (now 15–16 hands as against 13 in 1700), but it is impossible to demonstrate whether the best of today are superior to those of the past. A stud book has been kept in England since 1791, from which the pedigree of all thoroughbreds can be traced. Racing contests with horses date back to prehistoric times; horseracing began in England in Roman times, and was popular throughout the Middle Ages. The earliest regular annual meeting was at Chester, beginning before 1500. James I established royal support for the 'sport of kings'; under Charles II Newmarket became the headquarters of racing and breeding. The Jockey Club, founded about 1750, controls the sport in Britain and (indirectly) abroad. The five 'classics' of flat racing are the St Leger (1776), the Derby (1780), the Oaks (1779), the 2000 Guineas (1809), and the 1000 Guineas (1814): all are for three-year-olds; the Oaks and the 1000 Guineas are for fillies. Steeplechasing and hurdle-racing, which have cavalry and hunt origins, date from the 18th cent. and in Britain are governed by the National Hunt Committee; the most famous steeplechase is the Grand National (1839). Flat-racing predominates abroad; a strong challenge in British events comes from France, Germany, U.S.A., and recently U.S.S.R. In harnessracing, horses of a special breed draw driver-manned carts at a special 'trotting' gait; a form of trotting race existed in Asia Minor 3000–4000 years ago, and the sport featured in the ancient ◊ *Olympic Games*. Its modern revival came through British bloodstock in the 18th cent. and has most flourished in Australia, New Zealand, and esp. U.S.A. where there are over 500 tracks.

Horse-power. One horse-power is a rate of working of 33,000 ft-lb. per min. In the early days of steam it was found convenient to assess engines in terms of the number of horses it could replace; possibly the term was first used by James Watt.

BRAKE HORSE-POWER: A measure of the actual power output of an engine, reckoned by making the engine work against a brake and calculating the work done in a given time.

Horsetails. Scouring rushes; a small genus of perennial herbs in the *Pteridophyta*, most of which grow in damp places, with thin green ridged and jointed photosynthetic stems, usually branched, and leaves reduced to a sheath of small brown-tipped scales at each joint (node). The rough stems contain ◊ *silica* spicules, and were formerly used for scouring and polishing. They reproduce by means of spores, and are surviving examples of a group of plants which first appeared during the Devonian period and during the Carboniferous became one of the dominant species of plants, some of them growing as large as trees. *Calamites* and *Sphenophyllum*, both now extinct, were the commonest. The Calamites resembled modern horsetails but included trees possibly 60 to 90 ft high.

Horus. In Egyptian mythology, a sun-god not easily distinguishable from the older Ra; son of ◊ *Osiris* and ◊ *Isis*. Associated with the falcon or hawk, and represented with a falcon's head; his emblem is the sun's disk, winged. Horus the Elder is the daytime Sun, who avenged his father Osiris on Set, the evil god; Horus the Child (Gr. Harpocrates) is the rising sun, often represented with finger on lips to denote secrecy and silence.

Hottentots. People of S. and SW Africa (now almost extinct) encountered by the early Dutch in the Cape of Good Hope; herders of cattle and sheep, living in bands with hereditary chiefs. At first they were treated as equals by the Dutch, who interbred with them, but they were later driven from their lands and are now reduced to a few small groups mostly in SW Africa, known as Bastaards on account of their Dutch admixture; most of them have been absorbed into the Cape Coloured population. Hottentots were racially a mixture of ◊ *Bushmen* and possibly ◊ *Cushites*; the name may come from the Dutch for 'stutterer', on account of the click sounds in the Hottentot language. ◊◊ *African Languages, Race.*

Housefly. *Musca domestica* (◊ *Fly*); insect of the family *Muscidae* in the order *Diptera* (two wings), of world-wide distribution and found wherever man has established himself, abounding in the warm seasons and disappearing in winter. They feed on rotting vegetable matter, where the eggs are laid; usually a single female will lay 600–1000 eggs in her lifetime, and the life cycle is 10–12 days. They are carriers of diseases e.g. summer diarrhoea and typhoid.

House-leeks. Succulents of the genus *Sempervivum*, so called on account of its members' ability to survive for long periods in times of drought, thanks to the water stored in their leaves; from SE Europe, Himalayas, and Abyssinia. The common house-leek is most often seen on roofs.

House of Representatives. A popularly-elected house in a national (or regional) legislature, the members being returned from territorial constituencies on a population basis. The U.S.A. Lower House of Congress provides probably the best-known example, but the title is not uncommon; it is in use e.g. in Australia.

Houses of Parliament. The ancient palace of Westminster, used since 1547 for meetings of the Commons and of the Lords, was destroyed by fire 1834 (except ◊ *Westminster Hall*); the present Houses of Parliament were built on its site 1840–67 (opened 1843). The 320-ft high clock tower contains the famous 13-ton bell Big Ben. The chamber used by the Commons was destroyed in an air-raid 1941; the Commons sat in the chamber of the Lords until their new chamber was opened 1950. ◊◊ *Parliament.*

Housing. In Britain the Public Health Act, 1848, marked the beginning of modern public health and housing legislation in the U.K. and the first British legislation relating specifically to housing dates from 1851. Before the First World War government action was mainly directed towards the replacement of slum housing but later the State became concerned with expanding the supply of houses for rent. Between 1919 and 1939 over four million houses were built for local authority tenants or owner-occupiers, the latter aided by a remarkable expansion of building-society loans. In the decade following the Second World War local authorities made great efforts to overcome the shortage of houses. Once again subsidies and rent controls were the main financial instruments used. By the mid-fifties the emphasis in housing policy was shifted in favour of more privately owned housing and a more effective use of existing dwellings. Subsidies were granted more selectively and greater financial incentives were offered to private landlords to improve their property, or to use it more efficiently: the means adopted were increased improvement grants and a relaxation of rent controls. In the same period the slum clearance programme which had been interrupted by the war was resumed and attention began to focus on replacing obsolete housing.

The principal features of housing policy since the war have been the priority given to local authority building under the Labour government, subsequently revised by the Conservatives to favour more building for owner-occupation; the use of selective subsidies to promote local authority slum clearance programmes and special purpose housing; and the relaxation of rent controls. Of the 17 m. dwellings in the U.K., approximately 42 per cent are owner-occupied, 28 per cent are owned by local authorities, and the remainder are privately rented.

Hovercraft. Proprietary name for vehicles which travel slightly above land or water, supported by a volume of compressed air ('cushion' or 'ground effect') immediately beneath them, produced by large fans driving air downwards. Early development of the cushion-riding vehicle went on simultaneously in Britain and U.S.A.

Hudson's Bay Company. In 1670 a group of merchants received a charter from Charles II to import furs and skins into England. By 1821, when it combined with the NW Fur Company of Montreal, the Hudson's Bay Company exercised administrative control over all Canada except the Great Lakes basin and the Maritime Provinces. In 1869 it relinquished its administrative control and most of its land to the Canadian government; and in 1931 the remaining operations came under the administration of a Canadian committee.

Huguenots. The French ◊ *Calvinists*, severely persecuted from the time of their first synod in 1559, esp. by the Duke and the Cardinal de Guise and their followers the *Fronde*; the Wars of Religion broke out in 1562 and continued sporadically until 1589, with great loss of life, esp. in the 1572 massacre of ◊ *St Bartholomew*. The civil wars ended only with the final acceptance of Roman Catholicism and accession to the French throne in 1593 of the Huguenot leader Henry of Navarre (◊ *Edict of Nantes*). In the 1620s the Huguenots were again provoked into revolt and then suppressed by Cardinal Richelieu; Cardinal Mazarin in the 1640s continued the persecutions, moderated in the 1650s, however, owing to the influence of Cromwell (◊ *Commonwealth and Protectorate*). After the English ◊ *Restoration*, Louis XIV resumed the persecutions in 1665, and many Huguenots began emigrating, esp. to England; in 1685 (on the accession of James II in Britain) Louis finally revoked the Edict of Nantes, and a mass exodus began, esp. of skilled craftsmen (notably silk-weavers), whose loss severely damaged French industry. Those Huguenots who remained in France did not receive full civil rights until the ◊ *Code Napoléon* of 1804.

Humanism. The rediscovery, editing and reinterpretation of Latin and Greek literature begun by Italian scholars in the 14th cent. (◊ *Renaissance*), causing the questionings of medieval belief which contributed eventually to the ◊ *Reformation*. The early Italian humanists tended to make a mere cult of antiquity, pursuing erudition and a pure Latin style as ends in themselves; the later northern humanists, e.g. Budé, Erasmus, Vives, Colet, Linacre, and More, brought the new scholarship and the new critical spirit to bear on religious, political, social, and legal questions, preaching a more humane social ethic of education, tolerance, and peace. By discrediting medieval Latin without re-establishing classical Latin, the humanists opened the way for the modern European languages to become the media of educated discourse.

In its wider sense 'humanism' is a view of life rather than a coherent philosophical system. It includes the scepticism of Montaigne, the rationalism of Voltaire, Rousseau's faith in man's moral sense, and Comte's substitution of faith in human altruism for Christianity; what these beliefs have in common is their insistence on centring their world-view on man himself and on limiting it to the here-and-now. The two sides of humanism – social amelioration and the good personal life – diverge in the 20th cent. Some writers e.g. E. M. Forster emphasize personal relationships, while others e.g. Maxim Gorki believe that the individual is best fulfilled by cooperation with others for the good of all.

Humours. Medical and psychological theories prevalent in the Middle Ages, based on Greek philosophy, which stated that all nature consists of the four elements earth, air, fire, and water ($\Diamond$ *Aristotelianism*); the body was thought to be composed of the four corresponding humours black-bile (earth), blood (air), yellow-bile (fire), and phlegm (water), and illness to be the result of imbalance among the humours. The 'sanguine' temperament was the result of the predominance of blood, the 'choleric' of yellow bile, the 'melancholic' of black bile, and the 'phlegmatic' of phlegm.

Humus. Decayed organic material, a constituent of soil important for fertility. It is the result of the activity of microorganisms in decomposing organic matter ($\Diamond$ *Nitrogen Cycle*). While chemical fertilizers add nutrients to the soil only manures (including compost) add to the humus.

Hundred Days. The period when Napoleon was again Emperor of France from his escape from Elba to his surrender after $\Diamond$ *Waterloo* – from 20 March to 28 June 1815.

Hundred Years War. 1339–1453. Intermittent warfare between France and England, caused by the latter's possession of $\Diamond$ *Gascony*, her interests in Flanders, and Edward III's claim to the French throne ($\Diamond$ *Salic Law*). The English victory at $\Diamond$ *Crécy* in 1346 gained only Calais, but that of the Black Prince at $\Diamond$ *Poitiers* in 1356 made King John of France a prisoner and resulted in the Treaty of Brétigny in 1360. by which Calais and $\Diamond$ *Aquitaine* were ceded to England; after 1369, however, the guerrilla tactics of du Guesclin slowly won back these possessions. No further English conquests were made until Henry V won the battle of $\Diamond$ *Agincourt* in 1415, and in 1420 (with the assistance of $\Diamond$ *Burgundy*) forced on Charles VI the Treaty of Troyes, which secured the N. and E. of France for the English and gained for Henry V the hand of Charles's daughter Catherine; their son Henry VI succeeded to both France and England. After initial victories, the English Regent (the Duke of Bedford) gradually lost ground, however, and under Joan of Arc the French began to drive the English out; by 1453 they had lost all their French possessions except Calais, later lost by Mary I. $\Diamond$ *Bannockburn*.

Hungary. Area 36,000 sq. m. Pop. 10.1 m. Cap. Budapest. Rel. about one third Calvinist, two thirds Roman Catholic. Under the 1949 Constitution, a 'Republic of Workers and Working Peasants' with a National Assembly (deputies elected for four years) which elects a Council of Ministers and a Presidential Council, industry, transport, and agriculture being nationalized or run as cooperatives.

ECONOMY. A rich agricultural country, with 75 per cent of the farming on a cooperative basis and 14 per cent state-run. There is substantial coal, iron and steel, and bauxite production, with some light engineering and electrical industry.

HISTORY. Settled A.D. 896 by $\Diamond$ *Magyars*, a barbarian tribe which appeared out of Asia; their raids into Germany and Italy alarmed Europe until their defeat at the battle of Lechfeld A.D. 955. King Stephen adopted Christianity A.D. 1000 and began the organization of the state, which after the Mongol invasion 1241–2 became one of the most powerful in E. Europe. Defeat by the Turks at Mohacs in 1526 brought central and S. Hungary under Turkish and the rest under Hapsburg rule; the Hapsburgs resisted reforms and encouraged the Germanization of the country. A 19th-cent. nationalist movement led by Kossuth revived Magyar aspirations and caused the 1848 rebellion, which was suppressed. In 1867 Hungary obtained self-government in the dual monarchy of Austria-Hungary. After the First World War, by the 1920 Trianon Treaty, Hungary was compelled to cede 68 per cent of her historic area to Rumania, Czechoslovakia, Yugoslavia, and Austria, and became a kingdom with Admiral Horthy as permanent regent. An ally of Germany in the Second World War, Hungary was occupied by the Soviet forces, who sponsored a communist government. An anti-Stalinist revolution broke out October 1956; the government of Imre Nagy withdrew from the $\Diamond$ *Warsaw Pact* and asked U.N.O. to protect Hungarian neutrality, but János Kádár (a member of Nagy's government) formed a countergovernment with Soviet support. Soviet troops crushed the rebellion; Nagy and his ministers were lured from asylum in the Yugoslav Embassy and later executed. The Communist Party was reorganized, and changed its name to the Hungarian Socialist Workers' Party (First Secretary of the Central Committee and head of the Politburo, János Kádár, who is also President of the Council of Ministers). Since 1956 there have been improved economic conditions and some relaxation of police repression.

LANGUAGE. Magyar; no obvious connexion with any other European language, though probably related to Finnish. Spoken by some 13 m. in Hungary and near-by countries. It is clear and concise, uses the Latin alphabet, and is near-phonetic.

Huns. Nomads of unknown race who emerged from central Asia into Europe and India in the 4th century A.D. Their organization was in military 'hordes' of incomparably skilful horsemen, and they spread terror wherever they appeared. They achieved their furthest penetration under Attila, who sacked Rome before being driven out of Italy and Gaul in 453. They appear to have retired to southern Russia and settled there.

Hurling. Ancient Irish game, revived by the Gaelic Athletic Association 1884; the ball ('slitter') and sticks ('hurleys') resemble those of hockey, but the game is 15-a-side on a 160-yd pitch, with few of hockey's restrictive rules.

Hurricane. Any wind of Force 12 (◇ *Winds*) i.e. velocity over 75 m.p.h. More specifically, a tropical cyclone in the W. Indies and Gulf of Mexico; may cause loss of life and great destruction on the islands and Gulf mainland coasts, and also affects the Atlantic coasts of U.S.A. and the E. coast of central America, chiefly Aug. to Oct.

TYPHOON: Chinese for 'great wind'; a hurricane (cyclone) in the China seas esp. Philippines area, S. coasts of China, and Japanese islands.

Hussites. Jan Hus, a disciple of Wyclif (◇ *Lollards*), was burned for heresy by the General Council of Constance, 1415; there was a fierce reaction in his native Bohemia, his followers the Hussites driving out the emperor Sigismund when he tried to make good his claim to the throne, in 1420–31. After this victory, the division between the moderates (Utraquists) and extremists (Taborites) intensi-

fied; the latter were defeated at Lipany in 1434, and Sigismund was accepted as king in 1436 on condition that he tolerated the Utraquist church, which (◇ *Moravians*) was not supplanted by Roman Catholicism until 1620, when the ◇ *Hapsburg* monarchy ejected King Frederick, son-in-law of James I of Britain.

Hyacinth. An early-flowering sweet-scented bulbous plant, originally a wild species of the Near East; because of its pleasant scent and varied colours it has been in cultivation for many centuries, during which time the size and variety of colours has been improved. The modern hyacinth is largely due to the work of the Dutch growers, who (though normally the hyacinth flowers in spring) have recently produced bulbs treated to flower by Christmas. ◇ *Liliaceae*.

Hyaena ◇ *Jackal*.

Hybrid. The result of cross-breeding in plants or animals; a cross between two different species or genera produces hybrids which usually display greater vigour and resistance than pure strains, e.g. hybrid maize and barley, but in animals the hybrid is usually incapable of reproduction, e.g. the ◇ *mule*. Hybridization is much employed in horticulture and agriculture to produce plants which combine the desirable characteristics of different parents.

Hydra. < Gr. 'watery', i.e. water-snake. **1.** LERNAEAN HYDRA: In Greek legend, a serpent with 9 heads; one of them was immortal, and if any one of the others were struck off, two new ones replaced it. One of the 12 Labours of ◇ *Hercules* was to kill the Hydra, which was assisted by a monstrous crab. He and his servant Iolaus severed the mortal heads, cauterized the necks, and buried the immortal part under a rock; he then made his arrows fatal by impregnating them with the monster's venom-blood (◇ *Nessus*). The crab became the constellation Cancer. **2.** Small freshwater polyp, of the class Hydrozoa (phylum Coelenterates); like all coelenterates, consists fundamentally of two cell layers with an intervening cell-free mesoglea (very thin in the hydra); the five or six tentacles surrounding the mouth are well supplied with nematocysts, specialized stinging cells used for paralysing prey, a characteristic feature of the phylum. The hydra reproduces itself by budding, and possesses great powers of regeneration: if the body is cut up into a number of pieces, each piece will become a new polyp.

3. In astronomy, a long, slender, winding constellation (the Water Snake).

4. Island in the Aegean.

Hydrangea. A small genus of shrubs of the ◊ *Saxifragaceae* family mostly from the northern hemisphere; the true flowers are small and insignificant, but some species bear in addition large . sterile flowers, white or pink (or more rarely, in acid soils, bright blue). There are many garden varieties of the Japanese *H. macrophylla*, in which all the flowers are sterile and form large rounded heads. The more graceful wild species have recently become popular under the name of 'lace caps'.

Hydrate. Formed by the union of a compound, usually a ◊ *salt*, with one or more molecules of water; when the compound crystallizes from solution, it may retain water in its constitution (water of crystallization), which is usually lost when it is gently heated. A common example is washing soda which gives up some of its water of crystallization at room temperature, a process called efflorescence.

Hydraulics. The study of the mechanics of incompressible fluids e.g. water, oil. It is largely concerned with applying the laws of hydrodynamics to engineering problems, and in particular with the use of water pressure for driving machinery. ◊ *Fluid Mechanics.*

Hydrides. Compounds formed when ◊ *hydrogen* unites with a single other ◊ *element.* There are three types: (a) the salt-like, which conduct electricity when fused and evolve hydrogen when treated with water, e.g. those of the alkali and alkaline earth metals; (b) the covalent, usually gaseous e.g. methane (CH_4) hydrogen sulphide (H_2S); (c) the interstitial, where the small hydrogen atoms are packed into the spaces between the atoms that form the crystalline structure of a metal; here the hydrogen is said to be occluded by the metal, and elements that readily occlude the gas e.g. platinum, palladium, and nickel (all transition elements) are very useful as ◊ *catalysts* in hydrogenation processes. ◊ *Halogens.*

Hydrocarbons. Chemical substances composed only of ◊ *carbon* and ◊ *hydrogen*; the basis of all organic compounds. They are intrinsically combustible, oil-soluble, water-insoluble materials, their detailed properties depending on their molecular size and structure. Some hydrocarbons have their carbon atoms linked in open chains e.g. the ◊ *paraffins*; others e.g. ◊ *benzene* have a ring structure.

Hydrocephalus. Presence of an abnormally large amount of cerebrospinal fluid within the skull; it may be congenital and caused by structural malformation obstructing normal circulation of fluid, or acquired after inflammation e.g. ◊ *meningitis.* If unrelieved, in young children the condition leads to atrophy of the brain, with severe mental impairment and often blindness.

Hydrochloric (Hydrochlorous) Acid ◊ *Chlorine, Halogens.*

Hydrodynamics. The largely mathematical study of the motion, energy, and pressure of fluids in motion. From it is derived much of the theory used in ◊ *hydraulics* and in ◊ *fluid mechanics* generally.

Hydrogen. A gas without colour, smell, or taste; the element has two stable isotopes, $_1^1H$ (protium) and $_1^2H$ (deuterium), and a radioactive isotope, $_1^3H$ (tritium). Natural hydrogen (m.p. $-259°$ C, b.p. $-253°$ C) is the gas of lowest density, about one sixteenth that of oxygen. Although widely distributed, most hydrogen is contained in water (of which it forms one ninth of the weight), in mineral oil, and in other fuels; it is also found as an essential constituent in nearly all organic compounds. The alchemists called it 'inflammable air'; Cavendish recognized it as an element 1766, and Lavoisier named it hydrogen 1783. The molecule H_2 has two atoms held together by a strong covalent bond (◊ *Chemical Bonding*), and consequently hydrogen is not very chemically active at ordinary temperatures. With air or oxygen it forms mixtures which explode at red heat; it combines with heated sulphur to give hydrogen sulphide, but only extremely slowly (except in the presence of a catalyst) with nitrogen to form ammonia. Passing molecular hydrogen through an electric arc produces atomic hydrogen, very chemically active e.g. the 'hydrogen torch' for welding; the so-called 'nascent' hydrogen, from a metal dissolving in acid (early observed to have, at the moment of production, reducing properties absent from ordinary molecular hydrogen), is also atomic hydrogen.

The hydrogen atom consists of a proton and an electron, and is neutral; but when the electron is lost, the positively charged proton H$^+$ remains, which is the essential and common constituent of ◊ *acids*. Great quantities of hydrogen gas are produced industrially by (a) the electrolysis of brine; (b) the water-gas reaction, in which steam is reduced by white-hot carbon ($H_2O + C \rightarrow CO + H_2$), followed by passing the mixed gases with more steam over an iron catalyst ($H_2O + CO + H_2 \rightarrow CO_2 + 2H_2$) to give a mixture from which the carbon dioxide is easily removed; (c) the gas and coke industry, where it amounts to about half the gaseous product; (d) the 'cracking' of hydrocarbons in the petrochemical industry. Typical industrial uses of hydrogen are (a) as a fuel, in coal gas; (b) in the synthesis of ammonia (Haber process); (c) in many hydrogenations, mainly catalytic, of carbon compounds e.g. the methanol process $CO + 2H_2 \rightarrow CH_3OH$; (d) in the hydrogenation of unsaturated vegetable and animal oils, in the presence of finely-divided nickel, to produce hard fats for margarine.

Hydrogenation. A chemical process by which hydrogen is incorporated in a substance in the presence of a hydrogen carrier or ◊ *catalyst*, usually consisting of finely dispersed nickel. A most important hydrogenation-process is the hardening of glyceride oils in animal fats and vegetable oils in the manufacture of margarine; hydrogenation processes are also used to convert coal into liquid or gaseous fuels.

Hydrogen Bomb ◊ *Atom Bomb*.

Hydrolysis. A method of resolving a compound into two parts by the action of water, whereby one part combines with the hydrogen of the water and the other with the hydroxyl (the monovalent constituent OH or ion OH$^-$). Hydrolysis can be effected in various ways: by cold or hot water; by steam; by dilute acids or alkalis; and through enzymes.

Hydrophobia ◊ *Rabies*.

Hydroponics. The growing of food-plants without soil, either in water or in some other neutral medium, e.g. sand, gravel, to which nutrients are added; plants can be grown close together and yields increased. Experiments of a commercial nature were first made by Gericke 1929, and the technique is still in an experimental stage.

Hyena ◊ *Jackal*.

Hyksos. Nomadic Semitic people who invaded Egypt about 1675 B.C. (during the late Middle Kingdom) and ruled for about a century, although they do not seem to have established their rule fully in Upper Egypt.

Hymen (Hymenaeus). In Greek and Roman mythology, god of marriage, a beautiful effeminate youth whose name was invoked in ritual bridal songs; generally represented bearing a torch.

Hymenoptera ◊ *Ants, Bee, Wasp*.

Hymn. In general, a poem or song of praise; more specifically, a song of praise to God. Literary criticism distinguishes the hymn, for use in public worship, from the religious poem, which may be a highly personal wrestling with a religious experience or problem, e.g. the hymns of Isaac Watts, the poems of Donne. The Hebrew psalms (◊ *Bible*) include public songs of praise to God and also poems expressing highly personal religious, moral, or other feelings. In Greek literature, the Homeric hymns tell of the blissful life of the gods, often with humour and liveliness; the finest, the Hymn to ◊ *Demeter*, tells the story of the abduction of ◊ *Persephone* with remarkable poetic force. Medieval Latin hymns are important in the development of European verse away from classical quantitative ◊ *metre*, the later examples also using ◊ *rhyme*, with considerable elegance and sometimes power; the ◊ *Reformation* gave a new emphasis to hymns as a congregational utterance, and Luther himself wrote the words and possibly also the tunes of some. The 17th-cent. metrical versions of the psalms in England and Scotland made many of them into hymn-like songs e.g. the 'Old Hundredth'; though in strict puritan circles non-Biblical hymns were frowned on, the metrical psalms soon encouraged imitations, and Isaac Watts 1674–1748 produced over 500 hymns including some of the best-known. The other great English hymn-writer, Charles Wesley 1707–88, is said to have written 6500.

A good hymn must be uncomplicated in expression, strongly rhythmic, easily sung to its tune, and of simple devotional tone. Though some fine individual hymns have been written since Wesley, a growing sophistication of religious feeling and of poetic technique has contributed to the decline of the hymn in favour of the religious poem.

Hyperion. 1. In Greek mythology, one of the ◊ *Titans*, son of ◊ *Uranus* and Ge; father of Helios the sun, Selene the moon, and Eos dawn.

2. In astronomy ◊ *Saturn*.

Hypnosis. A trance-like state, physiologically different from ◊ *sleep*, in which suggestibility is greater than in the normal condition; the depth of the trance depends on e.g. past experience with hypnosis, the method of induction, and the length of the hypnotic session. Not all people can be hypnotized, and normally the cooperation of the person tranced is necessary. There is no completely satisfactory explanation of the facts, nor is there any good evidence that a normal individual (as distinct from one with criminal tendencies) can be made to commit criminal acts in this state. Operations can be performed on a hypnotized patient without anaesthetic, and psychiatrists have used hypnotic suggestion to treat cases of ◊ *neurosis*, though such treatment is frequently neither complete nor permanent.

Hysteria. A neurosis (generally known as a 'conversion neurosis') in which a psychological conflict develops into an actual illness (◊ *psychosomatics*); symptoms vary greatly, ranging from general nervous instability to emotional outbursts characterized by alternate laughing and weeping, and there may also be physical symptoms for which there is no organic basis. The name derives from the fact that in ancient times hysterical behaviour was attributed to displacement of the womb (Gr. *hystera*). Towards the end of the 19th cent. the recognition of the psychic basis of hysteria led to considerable progress in its treatment, one form of which involved the use of ◊ *hypnosis*, in which Josef Breuer, J. M. Charcot, Janet, and Freud were pioneers; later Freud abandoned the use of hypnosis, and used only his psycho-analytic techniques for the investigation and cure of hysteria.

I

Ibo ◊ *Nigeria.*
Icarus ◊ *Daedalus.*
I.C.B.M. ◊ *Rocket.*
Ice Ages. The earth has been subjected to unusual cold at least twice in its geological history (for reasons not entirely understood); the ◊ *solar system* may have passed through a cloud of interstellar dust cutting the earth off from some of the sun's heat, or explosions of gases on the sun's surface may have caused a great increase in 'sunspots'. The amount of carbon dioxide in the earth's atmosphere varies, and if vegetation using it greatly increased, more of the supply would be used up; since the gas acts as a blanket holding the heat received from the sun, the depletion could lead to a cold spell. A shift in the position of the earth's axis of rotation, or continental drift (◊ *Continent*), may have brought land masses into polar regions. The most recent glaciation, when layers of ice many thousands of feet thick were formed, was in the Pleistocene Epoch (◊ *Geological Time Scale*) and is often called the Great Ice Age; it lasted between 600,000 and a million years, until about 20,000 years ago. Since then (despite setbacks) the earth's climate has been generally getting milder, though Antarctica and Greenland still carry ice caps up to 8000 ft thick. The fossil glacial fauna of the Pleistocene Epoch indicate that the area covered by the ice sheet (now Canada, N. Europe including Britain down to the Thames, and Siberia) was several times repopulated as the ice retreated during the long false springs. In these interglacial periods (which lasted 100,000 to 200,000 years) modern man and horse originated, the elephant evolved, and other mammals (e.g. the sabre-toothed tiger, the woolly mammoth, the woolly and other rhinoceros, the great ox, bison, cattle, deer, sloths) either evolved anew, to leave descendants today, or (like many carnivores of the preceding Pliocene Epoch) were exterminated in competition with better-adapted species. Some geologists believe that we are living in another such interglacial period and that the cold will return; a temperature drop of 5° C (9° F) would be sufficient to create another ice age. ◊ *Eustatic Movements, Glacier, Isostasy.*

Iceberg. Mass of ice broken away from end of glacier or ice shelf, floating on the sea, only about one ninth of the mass being visible above water. When a glacier reaches the sea and is forced out into deeper water, its buoyed-up end portion breaks off and floats away; the iceberg may rise 200 or more ft above the surface and extend irregularly to some hundreds of yds in length. An iceberg broken away from an ice shelf is usually rectangular, flat-topped, and often much larger than a glacier iceberg. Icebergs originate mainly in the great ice sheets of Greenland and Antarctica, drift with sea currents, and are sometimes observed far from the polar regions. The Greenland glacier icebergs are carried S. by the Labrador Current towards the Newfoundland Grand Banks and the N. Atlantic shipping lanes; it was one of these that struck and sank the ◊ *Titanic* on 15 April 1912, after which disaster the International Ice Patrol was formed to warn shipping of the movements of icebergs.

Ice-hockey. Game in which teams of six skaters a side play hockey on ice in a rink about 190 ft long and 85 ft wide, in which a rubber 'puck' replaces the ball. Of Canadian origin it rapidly became popular throughout N. America in the last decade of the 19th cent. and was later adopted in Europe. The British Ice-hockey Association was founded in 1914, and by 1939 professional ice-hockey had become a major sport, but its popularity faded after the Second World War. Amateur ice-hockey has been a winter ◊ *Olympic Games* sport since 1920.

Iceland. Area 40,500 sq. m. Pop. 186,000. Cap. Reykjavik. Rel. Lutheran. Independent island republic in the N. Atlantic, close to the Arctic Circle. Since 1918 it has been an independent state, but remained united with Denmark through a common sovereign until proclaimed a republic by referendum in 1944. The Althing (Parliament) elects one third of its members to serve as an Upper House.

ECONOMY. The country is mountainous, with volcanoes and geysers, and three-quarters uninhabitable; the economy depends mainly on fish and fish products. The Government issued a decree 1958 extending the fishery limits off Iceland from 4 to 12 m. After disputes over British trawler fishing, Britain withdrew her objection to the 12-mile limit in March 1961, but continued to fish in parts of the outer six miles until 1964 (◊ *Territorial Waters*).

HISTORY. Iceland was discovered and settled A.D. 870 by the Norsemen; converted to Christianity, it was incorporated into the Bishopric of Norway 1152, and the recognition 1262 of the King of Norway ended prolonged internal strife. With Norway, Iceland passed to Denmark 1380. a relationship which lasted in some form till 1944. The standard of education and literacy is probably the highest in Europe. LANGUAGE. Icelandic, spoken by about 150,000; the most archaic of the northern ◊ *Germanic languages*. Contemporary Icelandic is almost the same as Old Norse, spoken and written at the date of Iceland's 9th-cent. colonization, which had close kinship with Old English (Anglo-Saxon), and during the Viking Age 750–1050 was spoken not only in Scandinavia but also in parts of Russia, Normandy, England, Scotland, and Ireland. An Icelander can still read classical Old Norse, the language of the Icelandic sagas 1150–1350, without special training. Icelandic has a remarkably pure vocabulary; substantives have three genders, and are declined in four cases according to various declensions. In the 13th and 14th centuries Iceland was the source of the earliest Scandinavian poetry ('Sagas').

Iceland Spar. Pure form of ◊ *Calcite*, first brought from Iceland. Transparent; used in the construction of Nicol prisms in petrological microscopes, because of its high double refraction. ◊ *Crystallography, Microscope*

Ice Sheet. Permanent mass of ice and snow of great thickness, such as covered much of the N. hemisphere during the great ◊ *Ice Age*. The largest ice sheets still in existence are those covering Antarctica and most of Greenland, in places several thousand ft thick.

ICE CAP CLIMATE: In the interior of e.g. Greenland, where the mean monthly temperature throughout the year is below f.p.

Ichthyosaurs ◊ *Reptiles*.

Icon. < Gr. *ikon*, an image or picture; a panel painting of a religious subject executed for or under the influence of the ◊ *Eastern Orthodox Church*. The earliest known icons date to the 6th cent. A.D. and icons include some of the best examples of the ◊ *Byzantine* style of painting. They are generally mask-like representations of saints painted in rich dark colours, often with a free use of gold.

Iconography. The study of the subject-matter of works of art, esp. portraits and allegorical paintings and sculptures; the aim may be purely systematic, or an attempt at the elucidation of meaning in such problematical fields as Egyptian wall-paintings, Byzantine and oriental religious art, or the symbolic works of Brueghel and Hieronymus Bosch (◊ *Flemish Art*). Recent students have thrown much light on the ideas of artists and patrons esp. during the ◊ *Renaissance* by revealing the iconographical programme or literary meaning of e.g. Botticelli's *Primavera* (an allegory illustrating an abstruse philosophical theory, not, as had been supposed, a fantasy about Spring). Similarly, elements of pagan symbolism have been revealed in many overtly Christian Renaissance works. **Id** ◊ *Ego*.

Idealism. In philosophy, the many doctrines opposed to ◊ *realism*; < idea, as against the other sense of 'idealism' < ideal. It involves claims that the physical world somehow depends for its existence, or at least for its form of organization, on mind or spirit, sometimes said to be the true reality. Starting from the fact that qualities of objects, e.g. colour, change with the conditions of our experiencing them, Berkeley concluded that they – and hence the objects – consist of 'ideas' in our minds or in the mind of God; ◊ *Kantianism* is idealism in a more restricted sense.

Igneous Rocks. < Gr. *ignis*, fire; volcanic rocks cooled from molten ◊ *magma*, fine-grained or glassy if cooled quickly on the surface but ◊ *plutonic* and coarse-grained if slowly solidified at depth. ◊ *Basalt, Granite, Lava, Mica, Obsidian*.

Iguana ◊ *Basilisk, Monitor (1)*.

Illegitimacy. Legal status of a child born out of wedlock (a bastard or natural child). The attitude of society towards such children has varied a great deal; in some societies they enjoy the same rights as legitimate offspring, in others they share inheritance from the mother equally with legitimate children, and under English ◊ *common law* they long suffered grave disabilities, most of which have been removed in recent legislation. The mother of an illegitimate child who can establish that a certain man is her child's father can obtain an affiliation order, in a magistrates' court, for him to pay her a weekly sum of up to 50s. for the child's maintenance; failure to maintain payments is punishable by prison. The evidence of the mother must be corroborated; if she is married, the evidence must be completely conclusive. The father has virtually no rights over the child, except that he may apply to a court for custody or may appoint a guardian. The child may succeed to his mother's property provided she leaves no legitimate issue, but not to his father's. A child born illegitimate may be legitimated if his parents subsequently marry, even though either parent or both were married to someone else at the time of his birth.

Illumination. The embellishment of a manuscript with coloured and gilt decorations; the art attained great beauty in the 8th cent. with the Lindisfarne Gospels and the Book of Kells (◊ *Celts*), and in the ◊ *Gothic* period sometimes assumed greater importance than the texts it adorned.

Illustration. Elucidation or embellishment of texts by means of drawings, prints, or reproductions. Manuscript books e.g. those of the Persians and Chinese, and of early medieval Europe, were often decorated with rich and intricate paintings (◊ *Illumination*), and the 15th-cent. earliest printed books were illustrated with ◊ *woodcuts* (occasionally coloured), but in the 16th and 17th centuries the woodcut was superseded by copperplate ◊ *engraving* and ◊ *etching*. At the end of the 18th cent. Bewick's revival of wood engraving and the introduction of ◊ *lithography* brought a new vigour and variety to book illustration. French and English books of the 18th and 19th centuries were often illustrated by leading artists of the day e.g. Hogarth, Blake, Daumier, Beardsley; in the early 19th cent. illustrations of superb quality by Redouté, Audubon, and T. S. Boys were included in books on botany, ornithology, and architectural antiquities. There was a brief revival in France in the

1920s when Ambroise Vollard published works illustrated by such artists as Maillol, Chagall, Picasso. Among the most famous English book illustrations are those of 'Phiz' (H. K. Browne) for Dickens, and Tenniel's in *Alice in Wonderland*. Illustration in works of fiction is now relatively uncommon except in children's books and in limited editions for bibliophiles. ◊◊ *Bestiary*.

Imagism. An Anglo-American poetic movement avowedly based on the philosophy of T. E. Hulme, inspired by classical and oriental lyric, and reacting against excessive ◊ *romanticism* and vaguely emotive verse; with Hulme, its founders were F. S. Flint, Amy Lowell, and Ezra Pound, and the group included Richard Aldington, Hilda Doolittle, and J. G. Fletcher. Four Imagist anthologies appeared 1914–17 and the movement's magazines were *Poetry* in U.S.A. from 1912 and *The Egoist* in Britain 1914–19, the 1915 credo emphasizing concentration, hardness, clarity, exact presentation of images, precise choice of words, freedom of subject-matter, and new rhythms, mainly ◊ *free verse*. Later poets showing Imagist influence include Wallace Stevens and Marianne Moore.

Imago ◊ *Insects*.

Immaculate Conception ◊ *Mary*.

Immigration. The deliberate transfer of residence to a selected destination; international movement of this kind is 'emigration' from the viewpoint of the country left behind and 'immigration' for the country entered. 'Internal' migration is movement within national boundaries and is often related to economic factors, e.g. in Britain to the rise of manufacturing in the late 18th cent. and to the decline of traditional industries (coal, shipbuilding) in the 1920s and 1930s. 'External' migration most frequently results from the emigrants' urge to improve their economic conditions, but occasionally from religious or political motives. The emigration of ◊ *Huguenots* to Britain and of Puritans to America stemmed chiefly from politico-religious grounds, but the mass

---

A single arrow before a word or phrase indicates a cross-reference to another main entry. A double arrow means *See also*.

emigration movements of the 19th and 20th centuries were largely economic. The greatest flow was from Europe to U.S.A. which received some 40 m. immigrants in the century before 1930. After 1920 immigration into the U.S.A. was limited to 100,000 a year and placed upon a national quota basis. Other countries to which there has been a large flow of immigrants are Australia, New Zealand, and Canada. People from Ireland and Britain have emigrated to all these destinations, and a substantial stream of emigration still continues. ⟡ *Population.*

Immunity. Protection developed by the body against disease, esp. infection: it may be natural and inherited (e.g. the immunity of man to many animal diseases) or acquired. When bacteria invade the body, they (and the toxins or poisons which they produce) are combated by the ⟡ *phagocytes* in the blood (which devour the invasive micro-organisms) and by the antibodies. Active immunity results from stimulation of a person's own body-cells against some specific infection, either naturally, by successfully fighting off an attack of an infection, or artificially by injection (sometimes ingestion) of a specific vaccine. Immunity is acquired by the entry into the body of a bacterium or virus known as an antigen, which stimulates the production of antibodies which fight the infection. The development of immunity is not immediate, but once it is established the reaction to infection is at once effective. Vaccines may consist of emulsions of killed bacteria or viruses (as in typhoid, paratyphoid, and in the Salk vaccine for poliomyelitis); of live organisms intended to produce immunity as a result of infection with a mild variant of the disease (e.g. in smallpox, to which immunity is provided by infection with the cowpox virus); of organisms of a greatly reduced virulence (e.g. BCG vaccine in tuberculosis, oral vaccine in poliomyelitis); or of toxins rendered harmless by chemical treatment i.e. antitoxins, which provide short-term assistance in diseases e.g. ⟡ *diphtheria* and tetanus in which the damage results principally from the toxins produced by the bacteria. Such passive immunity provides no stimulation to the antibody-forming mechanism; and since the antitoxins are soon destroyed in the body, it has no prolonged effect. ⟡ *Blood, Grafting.*

Imperial Conferences. First held under the name of colonial conference, in 1887, and thereafter in 1894, 1897, and 1902, they were meetings of representatives from the colonies to discuss defence. After 1907 (when they were renamed imperial conferences) four-yearly meetings were held, and their scope was widened to include economic affairs. An Imperial Economic Committee was set up in 1924, and remained a standing committee between conferences. They have now been replaced by Commonwealth Prime Ministers' meetings.

Imperialism. The rule, direct and indirect, of a dominant nation over subject communities. Empires e.g. Assyria and Egypt existed in very early times, when domination of the powerful over the weak was taken as a matter of course and culminated in the long-maintained Roman Empire. Imperialism as a conscious political concept emerged only in recent times. The younger Pitt's vision of empire gave an impetus to the administration and development of colonial possessions, which became a feature of the latter half of the 19th cent. when virtually every part of the globe hitherto independent was brought under the aegis of European colonial powers. At the same time began the growth of anti-imperialist sentiment amongst the liberal thinkers of the colonial powers and an urge to independence amongst the subject peoples. The First World War, and the doctrine of self-determination sponsored by President Wilson, brought a loosening of imperial bonds. Marxists, esp. Lenin, attacked imperialism as the mainstay of capitalism and the root cause of war. In Britain in the 20th cent. the concept of empire was transformed into that of a ⟡ *British Commonwealth of Nations,* in which the members are fully independent, a process which by 1964 was virtually complete. The extensive French colonies have evolved on similar lines.

Imperial Preference. System whereby Britain and Commonwealth countries reciprocally levy lower duties on goods passing between each other than upon goods of other countries, such lower duty being a 'preference'. There was little scope for the system so long as the U.K. adhered to ⟡ *free trade,* but on the introduction of extensive U.K. tariffs, after 1931, the Ottawa Conference of 1932 established an elaborate system of Imperial Preference, whereby goods from the ◊ British Commonwealth and the colonies imported into the U.K. enjoyed either free entry (e.g. most foodstuffs and raw materials) or lower rates of duty than those imposed on foreign goods; U.K. manufacturers enjoyed somewhat similar privileges in return. These preferences were reduced as part of a general lowering of tariffs after 1947 (◊ General Agreement on Tariffs and Trade) but their existence proved a major complication in the negotiations of the U.K. for entry into the European Common Market.

Impressionism. The most important movement in the late 19th-cent. painting. The term was first used in derisive reference to Claude Monet's picture Impression: Sunrise. exhibited in 1874 at a Paris exhibition which included Renoir, Sisley, Pissarro, Cézanne, Degas, Boudin, and Berthe Morisot. The aim of the Impressionists was to fix an instantaneous impression of space and surfaces dissolved in light and colour. In pursuit of so thorough-going a naturalism they conducted scientific research into the properties of light (for the artistic result of such intensive investigation see Monet's Rouen Cathedral sequence). Like the ◊ Barbizon school, the Impressionists painted landscape on the spot, yet they were not above learning from art as from nature. In this respect the pictorial effects of Constable and Turner and the systematic colour research of Delacroix were influential. Impressionism was widely followed even in U.S.A., but events were to indicate that Cézanne's study of the structure of objects, and not Monet's of their surfaces, provided the breakthrough to modern art.

Inca. Pre-Columbian empire in western S. America, a highly organized, despotic, and paternalistic state which assimilated earlier indigenous cultures already skilled in weaving, pottery, metalwork, and architecture and already cultivating cotton, maize, and potatoes. The Inca clan (whose legendary founder was Manco Capac) occupied the fertile valley of Cuzco in Peru, and their chiefs extended their rule over a wide surrounding area in the 15th cent. Under Topa Inca 1471–91, the Inca Empire covered much of what is now Ecuador, Bolivia, N. Argentine, Peru, and Chile. Huayna Capac (d. 1527), by dividing the Empire between his sons, plunged it into civil war, from which Pizarro with his handful of Spaniards profited to overthrow the whole empire in 1532, by removing the keystone of a totalitarian society in which a small core of divine king, nobles, and priests dominated every aspect of their subjects' lives.

The Incas did not use the wheel, did not know the use of iron, and had no system of writing. Their metalwork in gold, silver, copper, bronze, and tin was among the finest ever produced. Their buildings were built of immense blocks (some of them, as in the fortress of Sacsahuaman, weighing 100 tons) shaped and fitted together with incredible precision. They built an extensive system of roads, on which relays of runners carried messages 150 miles in a day. Their administration was elaborate and efficient: all property, except houses and household goods, was owned by the state. They divided the empire into provinces, and recorded statistical information on knotted cords, quipu, so that the economy could be minutely regulated. Production was conducted upon a collective basis, but distribution went according to rank. Although despotic in the extreme, Inca government was benevolent and provided security from want and hardship for all, by a system of state storehouses and regulation of labour which though onerous was not inhuman. After the Spanish conquest (◊ Peru), which eliminated the ruling classes, ruthless exploitation of the Indian workers in the mines and textile mills, and the growth of the cola-chewing habit, reduced them to a state of demoralization in which they have continued until today. The language of the Incas, Quichua (Kechuan), is still spoken over a wide area.

Incest. Sexual intercourse between close kin, esp. father-daughter, son-mother, brother-sister; in most societies sexual relations between other kin are also held to be incestuous, although not as serious as within the immediate family. Incest is almost invariably regarded as a sin, often with supernatural punishment; in some countries it is also a crime. Certain royal families (e.g. those of Ancient Egypt, the Inca Empire, and Hawaii) had to make incestuous marriages, the king marrying his own sister, because the king (considered divine) could mate only with another divinity.

Income Tax. A modern form of taxation of personal earnings or income, first introduced in Britain 1799 to finance the Napoleonic wars and finally made permanent 1842; in U.S.A. it was introduced during the Civil War of the 1860s and did not gain final acceptance as a Federal tax till 1913. It has become a graduated 'progressive' tax i.e. the rate becomes progressively higher for larger incomes; in Britain it is levied on company profits as well as personal earnings, and in U.S.A. the various States levy a lower State income tax also, in addition to the Federal Income Tax, comparable in its incidence to that in the U.K. Payroll tax-deduction was introduced in U.S.A. 1943 and in the U.K. 1944 as PAYE (pay as you earn).

Independent Labour Party. Socialist party founded in 1893 which played a major part in spreading socialist doctrine among trade unionists and the working class in Britain. It helped to found the Labour Representation Committee, 1900, which became the ◊ *Labour Party* in 1906. Most Labour Party leaders were members of the I.L.P. till the 1920s, when it tended to move to the far left. In the late 1920s the I.L.P. came under the influence of James Maxton and the 'Clydesiders', and persisted in bitter criticism of the Labour Premier Ramsay MacDonald and his policies. Disaffiliated from the Labour Party in 1932, it rapidly lost importance.

Independent Television Authority. Founded 1954 under the Television Act to provide an alternative TV service to that of the BBC paid for by the proceeds of advertising; consists of a Chairman, a Deputy Chairman, and eight members, appointed by the Postmaster General, with a Director-General as chief executive officer. The I.T.A. owns and operates the transmitting stations, but the programmes are provided under contract by some 15 commercial companies, who own the equipment and the studios and arrange for advertising. The I.T.A. has wide powers over the content and standard of programmes; its functioning was one of the subjects dealt with in the Pilkington Report 1962, which contained various criticisms and recommendations.

Index Librorum Prohibitorum. Official list of books which members of ◊ *Roman Catholic Church* are forbidden to read or to possess without special permission, on pain of incurring the penalties of sin. First issued 1559 after the Council of ◊ *Trent*, and occasionally reissued (with additions and deletions), most recently 1948 with a supplement 1961.

INDEX EXPURGATORIUS: Subsection, works sanctioned for reading after expurgation by the Congregation of the Index.

India. Area 1.2 m. sq. m. Pop. 434.7 m. Cap. Delhi. Rel. mainly Buddhist and Hindu. The republic covering 77 per cent of the Indian sub-continent; created a British Dominion in 1947, it declared itself a separate republic in 1950 but remains within the ◊ *British Commonwealth*. The constitution is federal, with a central two-chamber legislature and three categories of state government. At the general elections of 1952, 1957, 1962 the Congress Party under Pandit Nehru maintained a strong majority in the central parliament and in most of the states. India's policy has been largely determined by Nehru.

ECONOMY. Predominantly agricultural, with rice as the main crop, followed by sugar, and with tea as the main export crop. India has about 160 m. cattle, but their economic value is limited, as the cow is holy to the Hindus. Production of coal is about 50 m. tons annually, and a modern steel industry is being built; industrial production is growing. Manufactures of cotton yarn and textiles are important.

HISTORY. The sub-continent S. of the Himalayas has had a long and turbulent history. In about 2500 B.C. the flourishing urban ◊ *Indus civilization* emerged, to be destroyed about 1500 B.C. by Aryan invaders from the N W, who drove the Dravidian inhabitants south, and occupied the Ganges valley; they adopted ◊ *Hinduism* and introduced the ◊ *caste* system. In the 6th cent. B.C. the rival religions of ◊ *Jains* and ◊ *Buddhism* were introduced, and exerted a dominating influence in the kingdom set up 326 B.C. by Alexander the Great in the Punjab and later ruled by Asoka. After conquest by the ◊ *Huns* and later the ◊ *Arabs*, a period of stability ensued. Subsequently Baber the Turk set up the ◊ *Mogul* Empire, with its capital at Delhi; the Great Moguls, of whom the most famous was Akbar A.D. 1542–1605, were more powerful rulers than any hitherto. With their decline, and the death of Auranzeb in

1707, came further invasions. Delhi was sacked by the Persians in 1739, while European intervention in India was growing. By the 18th cent. the British ◊ *East India Company* had set up posts at Madras, Bombay, and Calcutta, the French at Pondicherry, and the Portuguese in Goa; after Clive's victory at ◊ *Plassey* in 1757, which gave control over Bengal, the British gradually eliminated French influence and brought the affairs of the Company under the supervision of a Board. After the ◊ *Indian Mutiny* in 1857 India was taken under the full control of the British Government, although two fifths of its area was still ruled by native princes. After 1880 the Indian nationalists demanded a share in political power; reforms in 1909, 1919, and 1935 were steps towards ultimate self-government but too slow to satisfy them. Mahatma Gandhi and Pandit Nehru advocated non-violent opposition to British rule. In 1942 the British offered full self-government after the war, but this was rejected; repeated in 1946, its realization on an all-India basis was stultified by Muslim-Hindu suspicions. Britain resorted to partition into two states, India and ◊ *Pakistan*, and the transfer of power took place in August 1947. Under Prime Minister Nehru the new state of India followed a policy of 'non-alignment' which led to acceptance of economic and even military aid from either N.A.T.O. or the Soviet bloc, without commitment to either, a policy called into question by the invasion of the N W frontier by ◊ *China* in 1962. Relations between India and Pakistan, strained by the massacres and turmoil which followed partition, degenerated further owing to the quarrel over ◊ *Kashmir*. Nehru died in 1964.

PEOPLES, LANGUAGES. Of extremely diverse origins, languages, and culture. The descendants of aboriginal peoples (usually termed 'pre-Dravidian') are found in the hills and jungles of central and S. India, and the Dravidian peoples (i.e. those speaking ◊ *Dravidian languages* e.g. Tamil) mainly in S. India. About the 2nd millennium B.C. the Dravidians were subjected to invasion by ◊ *Aryan*-speakers from N W India, who set up states and today form the bulk of the peoples of northern and central India, speaking ◊ *Indo-European languages*. In Assam and neighbouring N E areas there are also

small communities of Mongoloid origin e.g. Naga, Gurkha, Sherpa. ◊ *McMahon Line, Mauryas, Sikhs, Tibet.*

Indian Architecture. The first stone buildings in India were Buddhist shrines and temples, sometimes carved out of solid rock, from about 250 B.C. Their columns suggest Persian and Greek inspiration, but the profusion of animal and human figures in decoration is a purely Indian feature. Hindu temples generally have a shrine-cell crowned by a curvilinear or pyramidal tower, an entrance porch, a pillared hall, and a lofty gateway. The mingling of Buddhist and Jain styles produced what is most typical of Indian architecture, an excessive richness of carving and design, a profuse symbolic use of figures, the spire-like domes, and the vast size and elaboration of the buildings e.g. at Sadree and Tanjore. With the Arab conquest, many ◊ *mosques* were built in the Mogul style, a graceful fusion of Islamic and Indian tradition which produced outstanding buildings e.g. the Taj Mahal.

Indian Hemp ◊ *Hemp.*

Indian Languages ◊ *Dravidian Languages, Indo-European Languages, Sanskrit.*

Indian Mutiny. 1857–9. Amongst the native regiments, esp. those from Bengal, in British service, various causes had provoked unrest, such as an order making them liable to overseas service, and a rumour that cartridges were being coated with the grease of cows, an animal sacred to the Hindus (or with that of pigs, an unclean animal), which sparked off the mutiny. Some regiments murdered their officers and captured Delhi, and the rebellion spread; Lucknow was besieged, at Cawnpore the British garrison and their families were murdered. The revolt was confined to N. and central India; other Indian troops esp. the Bombay army remained loyal and helped to suppress the mutiny. Delhi was recaptured after four months, and by 1859 all the rebels had been rounded up or driven into Nepal. Reforms were carried out after the mutiny, the most important being that the ◊ *East India Company* was liquidated and the Crown took over all responsibility for India.

Indigo. A blue dye obtained originally from certain Indian plants; the natural dye is of ancient use, and was an early subject of chemical research. After its structure became known in 1883 methods were found of making synthetic indigo, which replaced the vegetable dye. The ancient colour Tyrian purple, obtained from the snail *Murex brandaris*, has also been found to be an indigo derivative. ⟡ *Paint*.

Indium. Rare metallic ⟡ *element* occurring in zinc-blende, recently used in O-rings for cold high-vacuum joints, and for tinting glass yellow; has a valency state of 3 and a chemistry similar to that of ⟡ *gallium*, and is a common impurity in commercial tin.

Indo-China. Former French dependency in S E Asia, formed in 1887 from the French colony of Cochin China and the protectorates of ⟡ *Cambodia*, Annam, and Tonkin; ⟡ *Laos* was added in 1893. After 1945 France proposed a new federation of Indo-China. Laos and Cambodia accepted, but Annamese nationalists demanded complete independence for Cambodia, Annam, and Tonkin, united as ⟡ *Vietnam*. War followed, and ended with French defeat at ⟡ *Dien-bien-phu*; the Geneva Conference of 1954 ended French control in the area. ⟡ *Thailand*.

Indo-European Languages. Spoken by about half the world's people. They are descended from the language spoken about 3000 B.C. by the nomads of S E Europe, which later spread into India and the rest of Europe. This language has been reconstructed and named Proto-Indo-European.

PROTO-INDO-EUROPEAN: A highly inflected language. Nouns had 8 case-forms in daily use (nominative, vocative, accusative, genitive, dative, locative, ablative, instrumental); verbs had numerous suffixes expressing manner of action or 'aspect' (perfective, imperfective, inceptive, iterative) rather than time of action or 'tense' (past, present, future), but separate forms only for the middle voice (forms for the passive voice developed later). Aspect was superseded by tense only gradually, being seen in classical Greek in the distinctions between the aorist, perfect, and imperfect tenses and in ⟡ *Latin* in the distinction between the perfect and imperfect; it is still preserved in the ⟡ *Slavonic languages*, esp. Russian. Word-order was fairly free, as in Greek, Latin, and Old English (Anglo-Saxon): since inflexions showed syntactic structure, verb or object might come before the subject. Counting was based on 10, not on 12

as in ancient Babylon (though traces of the duodecimal system are seen in 'dozen' and 'gross' and also in 'eleven' (one left) and twelve (two left) i.e. left over after counting on 10 fingers). The word for 100 was *dekmtém* (10 tens), which lost its first unstressed syllable and became *kmtém*; the initial k then showed notably divergent developments. In the four eastern branches of Indo-European (Indo-Iranian, Armenian, Balto-Slavonic, Illyrian-Albanian) it became s, whereas in the four western branches (Greek, Latin, Celtic, Germanic) it remained k; the former are therefore known as the Satem group (< Avestan *sat⟩m*) and the latter as the Centum group (< Latin *centum*, pronounced kentum).

HITTITE: The oldest Indo-European tongue; spoken in Anatolia (Asia Minor) until about 1300 B.C. AGNEAN, KUCHEAN (Tokharian A and B): Two other ancient tongues, brought to light in Chinese Turkestan. SANSKRIT (Old Indian): Survives as the sacred language of the Hindus; from Sanskrit came Hindi and Urdu, the official languages of India and Pakistan respectively (variations of Hindustani, written in different scripts). In the Indian sub-continent about 380 m. speak about 150 Indo-European languages, as against about 100 m. in S. India speaking ⟡ *Dravidian languages*.

ALBANIAN: The smallest group, spoken by only 1.5 m. people. Shows no clear affinities with neighbouring Serbian or Greek. ARMENIAN: A distinct branch of Indo-European although spoken by less than 4 m. people. BALUCHI: The language of Baluchistan. GREEK: For all its ancient glory, a small language with only about 8 m. speakers. Two varieties, the literary and the *demotiké* (colloquial), either of which a classical scholar can read. KURDISH: Spoken by the Kurds scattered over N W Iran and neighbouring parts of Turkey and Iraq. PERSIAN: Long the court language of India under the Moguls. Spoken in Iran. Its closely-related form PUSHTU is the official language of Afghanistan. ROMANY: Contains numerous borrowed words but remains basically Indian.

CELTIC LANGUAGES: Four survive: ⟡ *Breton* and Welsh; (Scots) ⟡ *Gaelic* and Irish. GERMANIC LANGUAGES: Now divided into N. Germanic, inc. Danish, Norwegian, Swedish (similar enough to

permit easy communication), and Icelandic; and W. Germanic, inc. English and its nearest connexion, Frisian, with Dutch, Flemish, German, and Plattdeutsch. ROMANCE LANGUAGES: The present-day descendants of Latin, inc. 5 national languages (French, Italian, Portuguese, Rumanian, Spanish) and 4 regional tongues (◊ *Catalan*, Galician or Gallego, ◊ *Provençal*, Rhaeto-Romanic or Rumansch, and Sardinian). They have spread widely in central and S. America, Spanish having undoubted supremacy except for Portuguese in Brazil. French is spoken by about 5 m. of the Canadians and by the more educated classes in Algeria and Tunisia and other African territories which were formerly French. In Angola and Mozambique there has been some penetration by Portuguese. SLAVONIC LANGUAGES: Old Prussian, extinct about 16th cent., belonged to the Baltic division and was related to Lithuanian (the most conservative of extant Indo-European languages) and Latvian or Lettish. The other main Slavonic tongues are Russian, Polish, Czech, Slovak, Slovene, Serbo-Croat, and Bulgarian.
◊ *Celts, Greece, Hittites, Ireland, Persia, Wales,* etc.

Indonesia. Area 887,000 sq. m. Pop. 103 m. Cap. Djakarta (formerly Batavia, in Java). Rel. predominantly Muslim. Independent republic comprising the large islands of Java, Sumatra, the Celebes, most of Borneo (N. Borneo being in Malaysia), and minor islands, including the Moluccas and Bali; known as the Netherlands East Indies until 1945, when Dr Soekarno declared their independence, finally recognized by the Dutch in 1949. The W. part of New Guinea was excluded from this transfer; its status was to be determined by negotiations within one year, but it was not finally transferred to Indonesia until 1963. Originally planned as a federation, the federal system was abolished in 1950 in favour of a centralized state administered from Djakarta; outbreaks of guerrilla activity by political or religious extremists in some of the remoter parts have occurred. There is friction with ◊ *Malaysia* over Borneo: ◊ *Partition.* Under the 1945 constitution, sovereignty is vested in the Provisional People's Consultative Assembly, inaugurated 1960, a nominated assembly.

ECONOMY. Indonesia has valuable mineral resources: tin, coal, bauxite, petroleum, large rubber production, coffee, tea, sugar, tobacco, copra, and rice. The government's violent nationalism has led to the withdrawal of foreign capital.

HISTORY. Until the Muslim invasions of the 13th cent. Indonesia was under Hindu priestly influence, but by the 15th cent. it was entirely Muslim. It was first visited from Europe by Portuguese traders, but the Dutch took possession by 1600; the British briefly seized the islands in the ◊ *Napoleonic wars*, but they remained under Dutch control until the ◊ *Second World War*, when they were occupied by the Japanese.

LANGUAGE ◊ *Malay.*

Induction. 1. Electromagnetic (inductor): the electrifying or magnetizing of one body by another electrified or magnetized body near it. Not only is magnetism induced in some materials e.g. iron by the presence of a magnetic field, but a voltage is induced in a conductor if it either moves in a magnetic field or is stationary in a field of changing intensity (◊ *Conduction*). This interaction between magnetic field and electric circuit is the basic principle behind the induction coil, transformers, and most types of ◊ *generator*. The simple induction coil consists of a soft-iron core carrying two separate windings, an inner primary and an outer secondary coil. When a current is passed through the primary coil it creates a magnetic field around the core; fluctuations in this field induce currents in the outer coil, the voltages in the two windings being proportional to the number of coils in each. When high voltages are required, the secondary coil is made of very thin wire and has many more turns than the primary.
2. The procedure of establishing conclusions not strictly deducible from the premisses. ◊ *Deduction, Logic.*

Indulgence. 1. In Roman Catholic practice, a grant, in God's name, of remission of the temporal punishment due for sins already committed and repented, the effect being conditional on contrition and on the receiver being in a state of grace. Plenary indulgence remits all such punishment incurred up to the time of granting, and indulgences may be obtained not only for oneself but for others whether living or dead who are in a state of grace; they are

normally granted subject to the performance of some act of devotion or pious
work. Putting indulgences up for public
sale in the 16th cent. (as a method of
raising funds for church-building in
Rome, esp. St Peter's) was an important
factor in provoking Luther's *Ninety-five
Theses* and in precipitating the ◊ *Reformation.* ◊ *Trent, Council of.*
2. After his ◊ *Restoration,* Charles II repeatedly attempted to override the ◊
penal laws and the ◊ *Clarendon Code* and
permit 'Indulgence' to those not belonging
to the ◊ *Church of England,* i.e. to give
them the right to purchase royal licences
entitling them to their own form of worship. His motive was probably more
financial than religious; but though the
system would have benefited the ◊ *nonconformists,* they preferred self-sacrifice
to any encouragement of the Roman
Catholics, and led the violent opposition
to his attempts. After the 1670 secret
Dover Treaty, in 1672 Charles stopped all
repayment of Exchequer debts and simultaneously issued his Declaration of Indulgence, on which he said he staked his
crown. Parliament replied with the ◊
Test Act, and the Indulgence was withdrawn. ◊ *Exclusion Bill, Popish Plot,
Seven Bishops.*
Indus Civilization. Ancient civilization in
the alluvial valley of the Indus in NW
India about 3000–1500 B.C. At its fullest
extent the Indus civilization stretched for
roughly 700 m. N/S and 950 m. E/W. Its
main cities were Harappa in the E. and
Mohenjo-daro in the W. both of which
still exist as gigantic mounds. Each was
divided into a raised citadel containing
immense and complex granaries and baths,
and a lower city with two-storeyed houses
and an elaborate system of sewers and
wells. The people had a simple picto-
graphic script and a standardized system
of weights and measures; they produced
delicate and sometimes superb art work
esp. in engraved seals and statuary, but
the remains suggest an austere and regi-
mented way of life. About 1500 B.C. the
culture was destroyed by barbarous but
perhaps more vital ◊ *Aryan*-speaking invaders, whose exploits are recorded in the
Rigveda; at Mohenjo-daro a large number of skeletons lying in the streets bear
witness to a massacre at this time. Many
of the elements of ◊ *Hinduism* are already
present in the Indus civilization, esp.

lustration and phallicism, reverence for
animals, and a prototypal ◊ *Shiva* as
Lord of the Beasts.
Industrial Design. When manufacture by
artisans was replaced by factory production design became entirely divorced from
the influence of the artist. It was not till
the second half of the 19th cent. that
attempts to improve industrial design
began in Germany when Peter Behrens,
architect and painter, was employed by
the leading German electricity combine
to raise the standards of design in industry. His influence was followed by that of
the Bauhaus which stressed the importance
of functionalism. These pioners avoided
useless ornamentation and sought beauty
in simple and functional design attuned
to the materials used and the purpose of
the product. The movement was carried
forward outside Germany by Mies van
der Rohe and Le Corbusier. In recent
years particularly good industrial design
has originated in Finland, Denmark, and
Italy. In Britain the Council of Industrial
Design was set up in 1944 to provide
courses in design; it holds exhibitions at
the Design Centre in London.
Industrial Revolution. The period about
1750–1850 in Britain, when a wealth of
inventions, esp. in steam power and in the
textile and iron-and-steel industries, replaced older methods of manufacture by
faster processes, and turned Britain from
a largely agricultural and hand-industry
society into an increasingly industrialized
one, owing to (a) a big rise in agricultural
productivity; (b) the freedom of agricultural labourers to leave the land, and a
plentiful supply of labour from an expanding population; (c) improvements in
communications e.g. roads, canals, railways; (d) a financial system favourable
to the development of ◊ *capitalism.* With
the Industrial Revolution came the factory
system; the growth of large industrial
towns; the emergence of a rich bourgeois
class of industrial and business owners
and of an urban ◊ *proletariat* or working
class; the development of trade unionism;
and the search for overseas markets, with
a consequent increase in the importance
of foreign trade. The population increased
rapidly; large migrations of people from
the land to the cities led to conditions of
squalor and hardship, which only gradually improved.
This transformation of society followed

the same pattern when it spread to western Europe and U.S.A. The process is not fundamentally different in communist countries, though capital is accumulated by the state and not by private persons. In many countries it has been necessary to increase capital by borrowing from abroad.

Inert Gases (Noble Gases). Six gases constituting Group 0 of the Periodic Table, helium, neon, argon, krypton, xenon, and radon. Chemically inert, they are monatomic i.e. their atoms remain single, and unlike those of most common gases do not combine to form polyatomic molecules. Radon is radioactive. The discovery of this group of elements (largely due to Sir William Ramsay) has led to an understanding of atomic structure and the nature of ◊ *chemical bonding.* The first to be isolated, by Rayleigh and Ramsay 1894, was argon, a gas which forms nearly one per cent by volume of the air; helium had been detected by Lockyer as early as 1868 in the spectrum of the sun's chromosphere, but Ramsay proved its presence on earth 1894. The rarer gases neon, krypton, and xenon were isolated 1898; at about the same time the work of Pierre and Marie Curie on radium identified a new gas (first known as the 'radium emanation') eventually named radon. That these gases may not be completely inert was shown by the preparation 1962, by the Americans Claasen, Selig, and Malm, of a tetra-fluoride of xenon, a reasonably stable white crystalline substance. In spite or perhaps because of their general chemical inactivity, these gases have found important uses.

ARGON: Gas-filled electric lamps; argon-arc welding.

HELIUM: Airships and balloons (usually mixed with ◊ *hydrogen*); it is non-inflammable and has only twice the density of hydrogen.

KRYPTON, XENON: Scarce and expensive, but can be used for gas-filling special electric lamps e.g. miners' cap-lamps and lighthouse lamps.

NEON: Advertising signs, giving a bright red glow in discharge tubes.

RADON: Treatment of malignant growths.
XENON: See Krypton above.

Inertial Guidance. Mechanism carried in a rocket incorporating a computer for comparing its flight with the predeter-mined course and keeping it on its correct path in powered flight, entirely independent of radio or other control from the earth, utilized in military rockets.

Infant ◊ *Child.*

Infection. Invasion of the body by disease-producing organisms. The external surfaces of the body and the surfaces of cavities open to the exterior have their own systems of defence against bacterial invasion (◊ *Immunity*); where tissues not ordinarily exposed are to be laid open e.g. by surgical operation, infection is avoided by asepsis, by which the immediate environment of the patient is kept free of disease-producing organisms. Asepsis is achieved by (a) heat, microbes being killed by boiling in water or exposure to saturated steam or by dry heat e.g. in an oven; (b) disinfectants i.e. chemical substances with the power to kill germs, varying from crude and relatively powerful antiseptics of the phenol group (lysol) to effective non-irritating substances for sterilizing the skin esp. the hands; liquids which cannot be sterilized by heat may be freed of bacteria by filtration through media whose pore-diameter is such as to hold back particles of the size of the smallest bacteria. A recent development has been the use of ◊ *gamma rays,* which may be applied to almost any substance without fear of causing deterioration; the apparatus is costly and large, so that the method is economic only on an industrial scale. ◊ *Lymphatic System.*

Inflammation. Response of body tissues to injury or infection; accompanied by redness and a sense of heat due to increased blood flow to the affected area, swelling, and pain due to exudation of fluid from the engorged vessels. Under the microscope it can be seen to involve emigration of leucocytes (◊ *Blood*) to immobilize and collect invading bacteria (◊ *Immunity*).

Inflation. Rising prices, or a fall in the purchasing-power of money; ◊ *unemployment,* the great defect of the capitalist systems in the inter-war years, has largely been solved, but in its place is the problem of continuously rising prices, and there is no peace-time parallel in Britain in the last 100 years to the price-rise since 1946. In the early post-war years, inflation was explained as 'too much money chasing too few goods' and driving their prices up (demand inflation); attempts to correct this simply by reducing the amount of money in the economy, or reducing purchasing power by taxation, have not been successful. The most potent cause of inflation is now considered to lie in manufacturers' prices and costs, and the main force behind it is seen in the tendency for wage-increase to exceed commensurate rises in production; if the wage-rise is bigger than the expected rise in productivity, as it usually is, prices will be raised accordingly. Certain Continental countries e.g. Sweden, the Netherlands have devised methods by which the size of wage-awards has to be agreed by a central body on which the national interest is represented. In the U.K. there have been various attempts to exert this direct influence on wages: Sir Stafford Cripps persuaded the unions to agree to a wage-freeze; Mr Thorneycroft set up the Council on Prices, Productivity, and Incomes 1957–61, and Mr Selwyn Lloyd (after an eight-month pay-pause in wage-awards in the public services) set up the National Incomes Commission. The Labour government 1964 also addressed itself to finding an incomes policy acceptable to the trades unions and employers.

Inflexion. Addition of an ending to a word, or a modification of its basic form, to denote number, person, case, tense, etc. e.g. day, days; work, worked. Some languages e.g. Latin, German, Russian retain a highly complicated system of word-endings, and are sometimes called synthetic as against those classified as analytic, which never possessed such endings (e.g. Chinese) or have almost entirely discarded them (e.g. English, French).

Influenza. Acute virus infection esp. of the respiratory tract, accompanied by fever and muscular pains and often followed by a period of mental depression; not serious in itself, but complications such as broncho-pneumonia can be fatal. There is a tendency for new forms of the virus arising in one area to spread rapidly throughout the world. After the First World War widespread epidemics killed millions of people and so-called Asian flu some years after the Second caused many deaths.

Infrared Rays. Electromagnetic ◊ *radiation* in wavelengths in excess of those of the visible red rays. Absorption of infrared rays produces heat. Although invisible to the eye, they affect photographic plates, and infrared photography can achieve very special results e.g. in long-range photography.

Inheritance Taxes ◊ *Death Duties.*

Inhibition. Restraint imposed upon instincts, feelings, or thoughts by fear or anxiety or the demands of society. Society imposes some degree of inhibition on all its members, but in extreme cases the repression of thoughts and feelings may result in functional mental disorder.

Initiation Rites (Rites de Passage). Ceremonies in most primitive societies marking changes in status undergone in a lifetime (e.g. boy to man, bachelor to husband), esp. entry into adulthood or a new group or community. Those at puberty (the most widespread and important) may consist merely of formal teaching about adult life, but are usually accompanied by temporary isolation from the rest of the tribe and by some physical operation e.g. circumcision or scarification; women may undergo analogous operations. The ceremonies accompanying the entry of novices into the church, medieval knights into orders, and freemasons into lodges are similar in kind.

Ink. Coloured liquid or grease used for writing and printing; known since prehistoric times, the earliest forms being mixtures of gum, soot, and water. Writing inks, formerly made mainly from iron salts with an infusion of gum and oak-gall, are now also prepared from aniline dyes, e.g. red ink. Printer's ink is a mixture of carbon-black with oil or varnish, and dries partly by oxidation and partly by penetrating the paper, various ◊ *drying oils* and ◊ *catalysts* being added to assist and control the action. Copying and typing inks contain glycerine to retard drying; marking inks are solutions of silver or copper compounds, sometimes with aniline dyes. Indian ink, intensely black and durable, is made in semi-solid form by mixing lamp-black with parchment-size or fish-glue and is then rubbed down in water. Ingredients can be added to make inks waterproof after drying, and special additives can make print luminous.

Inkerman. 1854. Battle in the ◊ *Crimean War* soon after ◊ *Balaclava.* The British army besieging ◊ *Sevastopol* was attacked on Inkerman heights by the Russian relieving army. In thick fog the British infantry, with French assistance, drove the

Russians slowly back. The battle was the last before the fall of Sevastopol the following year.

Inns of Court. The bodies responsible for the qualification and discipline of ◊ *barristers*, each under the control of 'Benchers', senior members of the Inn; the senior officer, the Treasurer, is appointed for one year by the Benchers from among their own number. The four Inns (Gray's Inn, Lincoln's Inn, Inner Temple, Middle Temple) all rank equally, having originated as colleges where aspirants to the legal profession lived and studied together.

Inoculation ◊ *Immunity*.

Inquest. Investigation by a ◊ *coroner* into a death occurring in unusual circumstances, or into treasure trove, with a ◊ *jury* of from seven to eleven members; anyone who desires to give evidence must be heard, and the coroner can compel anyone to attend whose evidence may be helpful. Anyone with an interest in the case may examine the witnesses, either himself or by his counsel (◊ *Barrister*), or by a ◊ *solicitor*; this right is often used by those expecting to be involved in a suit arising out of the death. If the jury is not unanimous, a majority verdict may be accepted, unlike verdicts in criminal proceedings.

Inquisition. The Congregation of the Holy Office (◊ *Cardinal*); ecclesiastical tribunal for the discovery and extirpation of ◊ *heresy* Founded by Pope Gregory IX 1233 to intensify the 'crusade' against the ◊ *Albigenses*. The object of the Inquisition was to obtain recantation and abjuration of heresy, but the accuser's identity was not revealed, and (despite intermittent and ineffective papal objections) 'the Question' i.e. physical torture was more and more frequently used to extract confessions. The ultimate penalty was burning alive, by the civil power; this was not invariably enforced, some persons being kept permanently imprisoned. Pope Paul III used the Inquisition against Italian Protestants 1542; in England under Queen Mary Tudor after her marriage to Philip of Spain (see below), the Inquisition-like methods of Cardinal Pole and Bishop Bonner, and the resulting hundreds of executions by burning alive, were a major cause of English militant ◊ *Protestantism* in the late 16th cent. and throughout the 17th.

SPANISH INQUISITION: An independent state tribunal, founded 1481 by Ferdinand and Isabella, originally to hunt out relapsed converts from ◊ *Islam* and ◊ *Judaism* and confiscate their property; and even harsher than the medieval anti-Albigensian Inquisition (see above). The first Grand Inquisitor, Isabella's confessor Tomas de Torquemada 1420–98, allegedly had about 2000 people burned alive at public *autos de fe* (acts of faith).

Insanity ◊ *Diminished Responsibility, M'Naghten Rules, Mental Health Service.*

Insecticides ◊ *Pesticides.*

Insectivorous Plants ◊ *Carnivorous Plants.*

Insects. The largest class of living organisms, with nearly 700,000 known species, varying in size from the microscopic to

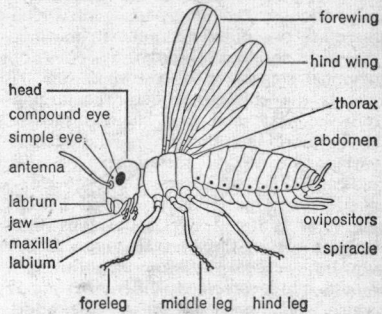

several inches. Despite their shorter evolutionary history (300 m. years) insects have developed into a far wider variety of forms than the ◊ *vertebrates*, whose fossils are known from the Silurian period 500 m. years ago. As members of the phylum Arthropoda, insects are related to (but do not include) scorpions, spiders, and centipedes. They have a 20-segment external (exo-) skeleton like a suit of armour, further subdivided into a head, a thorax, and an abdomen; the thorax bears three pairs of legs and sometimes two pairs of wings. There are some 25 living and nearly as many fossil orders. The mouth-parts, although primitively like that of the omnivorous grasshopper or cockroach, became modified in the wide adaptive proliferation of insects. Some insects lap with a long 'tongue' e.g. butterfly, others e.g. aphis pierce plant tissue. Ventilation is by a series of air-tubes (*tracheae*) conducting gases between the body surface and the cells, with no intermediary blood system, instead of which a heart circulates a colourless body-fluid for nutrition and excretion. Sensory ability may be very limited (as in ◊ *aphids*) or extremely acute; the *Pterygota* have compound eyes with a mechanism that gives accurate vision by adjustment to differing light intensity. The nervous system may be relatively generalized, as in the grasshopper, or highly condensed; in most insects the segmental arrangement results in the brain being less important than in vertebrates.

Insect behaviour is instinctive; within a single group, it varies from the independent individual to group cooperation e.g. ◊ *bees*.

Development is in two main ways, with or without ◊ *metamorphosis*, of which there are two different kinds. In the first the egg develops through a series of nymphal stages: each ◊ *nymph* (instar) moults the old cuticle before enlarging into the next; and each stage is successively more like the adult. The second variant, markedly metamorphic, with radically different instars, is the development of the most highly evolved insects e.g. the ◊ *fly*; the egg develops first through two or three larval stages, differing little except in size, and the last moults into a completely different ◊ *pupa*, which splits open to release the adult (imago).

Instinct. In biology, an innate or unlearned tendency of animals to behave in a certain way, e.g. hunting for prey; a given stimulus always produces the same response in all members of a species. However, most of the behaviour of the higher animals (and some of that of others e.g. birds) involves learning, even though the learning entails only one trial, e.g. bird flight. Some behaviour regarded as instinctive, e.g. bird migration, is very complicated and not fully understood. Much that is called 'instinctive' behaviour is better described as reflex action, indicating an automatic reaction of the nervous system without reference to the brain. Instinctive behaviour is distinguished from even the most complex of reflex actions by its modifiability. Psychology has been concerned with the study of the mental concomitants of such behaviour in man, i.e. the tendencies to

notice and respond emotionally to certain objects, and the felt drives towards certain goals. Psychologists such as McDougall and Freud have assigned a central place to instinct in the explanation of behaviour.

Insulator ◊ *Conduction.*

Insulin. A secretion of the ◊ *pancreas,* which controls sugar ◊ *metabolism.* It was established in 1922 that lack of insulin due to degeneration of the pancreas causes ◊ *diabetes,* and the active material from the pancreas was shortly afterwards isolated from animal organs. Being a ◊ *protein,* insulin is destroyed in the stomach, and when used medically it must be given by injection. ◊ *Endocrine System.*

Intaglio. Carvings esp. on ◊ *gems* in which the design is hollowed out of the stone. ◊ *Printing.*

Integration ◊ *Race Relations.*

Intelligence Quotient. Alfred Binet, a French psychologist, about 1904, investigated methods of finding out which children were unlikely to succeed in school, and devised tests to discover reasoning power and inherited ability (which he called the intelligence quotient) rather than acquired knowledge. If a child of eight gets marks equal to the average at ten, his mental age is said to be ten and his I.Q. ten divided by eight i.e. 1.25 (usually stated as 125), whereas if the score of a child of nine is only equal to the average at six, his mental age would be six and his I.Q. 66. The median I.Q. (100) is established by a careful test of a large group of children in a given age group, and is the average of the marks scored by the group as a whole. Most grammar-school children are of I.Q. above 110 or even 115. In the majority of children the I.Q. seems not to change by any very considerable amount after the age of six and after twelve to remain fairly constant. In schools, I.Q. tests are used to help grade pupils into ability groups and form part of the eleven-plus ◊ *examination* in England and Wales; they have been used to measure ability both in industry and in the armed forces. ◊ *Educational Subnormality.*

Intercontinental Ballistic Missile (I.C.B.M.) ◊ *Rocket.*

Interferon ◊ *Viruses.*

Interior Design. The architecture, decoration, and furnishing of interiors. In the classical and oriental civilizations, rooms in palaces and the houses of the rich e.g. at Pompeii were elaborately designed and adorned with painted decorations on walls and ceilings. In medieval Europe, with the exception of Muslim Spain, domestic interiors were in general crudely furnished, and tapestry hangings provided the only decoration; not until the ◊ *Renaissance* were rooms again treated as artistic units in which all decorations and furnishings were designed to harmonize, and in the 18th cent. new standards of domestic comfort and elegance spread from Italy throughout Europe. The best 16th-cent. example to survive is probably the Studiolo of Francesco I de' Medici in the Palazzo Vecchio in Florence, 1570–2. In the second half of the 17th cent. Louis XIV's artists created palatial interior designs at Versailles, where decorations and furnishings of the greatest richness were conceived as parts of an artistic whole and embellished with ornaments symbolic of the power and glory of the 'Sun King'. In the 18th cent. greater attention was paid to the design of smaller rooms in bourgeois as well as noble houses; a lighter and more delicate style developed. At this period notable architects e.g. William Kent and Robert Adam in England often designed not merely the wall decorations but the chairs, tables, lamps, and even such small objects as keyhole guards. This practice was followed in the early 19th-cent. First Empire period, when designs for wall decorations and furniture were inspired by classical prototypes. Most 19th-cent. designers concentrated on achieving effects of comfortable cosiness, to modern eyes somewhat stuffy and overcrowded. A return to a sparser style was made in 1859 by William Morris, in conjunction with William Webb, in the Red House at Bexley. Early in the 20th cent. Voysey and a few other architects applied themselves to the design of furniture as well as houses, but nowadays the interior designer is seldom an architect and is usually responsible for the choice rather than the design of decorations and furniture, but homogeneity of principles in design tends to produce the effect of an artistic unity, esp. in the Scandinavian countries.

Internal Combustion Engine. In general there are two types: (a) the spark-ignition engine, in which a sparking plug ignites the combustible mixture drawn into the cylinder, e.g. petrol and gas engines; (b) the compression ignition engine, in which air is so highly compressed in the cylinder before the explosive mixture is injected that the temperature is high enough to cause ignition, e.g. the diesel engine, in which oils heavier and cheaper than petrol are used. Internal combustion engines of both types may be made with one cylinder or a number of cylinders. The sequence of operation is normally either the four-stroke cycle or the two-stroke cycle.

Experiments with internal combustion engines began in the 18th cent. but it was not till 1876 that Otto built a four-sroke

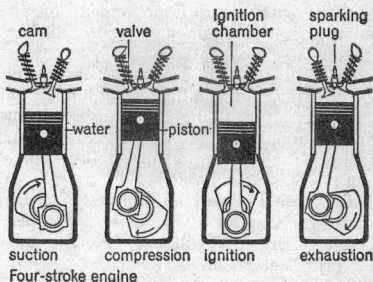

Four-stroke engine

suction · compression · ignition · exhaustion

gas engine still called after him. This ran at slow speeds; Gottlieb Daimler patented a high-speed petrol engine in 1885 which proved the most suitable power unit for motor cars. Whilst various refinements have been made the modern motor-car engine remains basically unchanged.

However, amongst many attempts to design alternative varieties, mention must be made of the rotary engine developed by the German Felix Wankel. Instead of a number of cylinders it consists of an eccentric curved triangular rotor which rotates in a combustion chamber something like an hour-glass in shape. It can run on a variety of fuels and produces greater power than a conventional engine of similar size.

International Bank for Reconstruction and Development. Institution created 1945 with a capital of $10,000 m. to make loans to member countries to promote their development and international trade: autonomous, but affiliated to the United Nations Organization and working closely with the ◊ *International Monetary Fund* (both bodies have their headquarters in

Washington), it is controlled by an annually elected council of 21. ⟡ *Bretton Woods Conference, Colombo Plan, Point-Four Programme.*

International Bureau of Standards ⟡ *British Standards Institution.*

International Civil Aviation Organization. Affiliate of the United Nations Organization which grew out of the 1944 Chicago Conference on the 'five freedoms of the air'; the first two, (1) to fly over the air space of another country without permission and (2) to land for non-traffic purposes, were the only ones included in an agreement generally accepted. The organization, with headquarters in Montreal and a membership of 97 states, works for the safety and improvement of air communications, air navigation, air-line documentation, standardization, air traffic control, accident studies, and the assembly of statistical information being among its activities. It is to be distinguished from International Air Transport Association, which is an association of air line representatives. ⟡ *Cabotage.*

International Court of Justice. Set up under the Charter of the United Nations. Its jurisdiction is voluntary i.e. depends on prior agreement between the parties; there is no power to compel attendance before it. Such agreement may be made as and when a dispute arises, in a treaty or convention which provides for disputes to be referred to the Court or by signature to the 'optional clause' of the Court's statute which means that the state signing accepts in advance the court's jurisdiction in (1) the interpretation of a treaty, (2) any question of international law, (3) breaches of international obligation, or (4) reparation to be made for such a breach. It consists of 15 judges elected by the U.N. General Assembly and Security Council, no two of whom may be nationals of the same state. Its judgement is final; if one party fails to carry out the ruling, the other party may bring the matter before the U.N. Security Council. The International Court is sometimes called the Hague Tribunal; a permanent international court was first proposed at the 1899 Hague Conference and set up 1920 by the ⟡ *League of Nations,* remaining in session 1922–45, when it was superseded by the present court.

International Date Line. The 180° meridian of longitude. Crossing it eastwards a traveller puts the date back by one day; westwards, forward by one day. Deviations have been agreed to allow Alaska and the Aleutian islands the same date as N. America, and certain S. Pacific islands the same date as Australia and New Zealand.

International Labour Organization. Created 1919, in association with the League of Nations; a specialized agency of the United Nations Organization since 1946. The governing body has 40 members, with headquarters at Geneva, and it organizes conferences to which countries send delegates representing governments, unions, and employers and is concerned with economic and social stability and general improvement of working conditions.

International Languages. Phoenician, Koiné (Hellenistic Greek), and Latin served as international languages for long periods in the ancient world. Phoenician, a Semitic tongue related to ⟡ *Hebrew,* was spoken by the people of Tyre and Sidon (the Canaanites of the Old Testament), who were enterprising seafarers and the founders of Carthage; it remained the ⟡ *lingua franca* of the E. Mediterranean until the time of Alexander 356–323 B.C. It was superseded by Koiné, which persisted as the speech of the E. Mediterranean even after the expansion of the Roman Empire; gradually, however, Latin expanded, and throughout the Middle Ages had no competitor as an international means of communication until French (the language of the Crusades) became more widespread and established itself as the language of the arts and diplomacy. Later ⟡ *English* was the first world language of trade and commerce, and with the emergence of U.S.A. as a great world power became indisputably the major medium for international use in most spheres.

ARTIFICIAL LANGUAGES: In recent times over 100 have been devised, of which two are outstanding. VOLAPÜK: 'World Speech', constructed 1879 by a Bavarian pastor, Johan Martin Schleyer, and hailed as the future universal language. ESPERANTO: a more flexible system invented 1887 by a Polish Jew, Lazarus Zamenhof (nicknamed Doktoro Esperanto, 'the hoping doctor'); in spite of competitors this remains the world's first auxiliary language and has an increasing number of adherents, esp. in U.S.S.R. and China.

International Law.
PRIVATE INTERNATIONAL LAW: Otherwise known as the Conflict of Laws. Rules of national or municipal law which regulate cases which have a foreign element (e.g. where an Englishman makes a contract abroad, or gets married abroad). In England, private international law deals with two questions: (1) have the English courts jurisdiction to try the case? (2) what system of national or municipal law applies?

PUBLIC INTERNATIONAL LAW: The rules which apply between sovereign states consisting partly of customary rules and partly of treaties and conventions.

International Monetary Fund. Independent organization founded 1946 with a capital of $8000 m. subscribed by member countries, to support their financial stability, advise and make loans to countries in need of assistance, and generally facilitate international trade and the stability of ◊ *foreign exchange* rates. ◊ *Bretton Woods Conference, International Bank for Reconstruction and Development.*

Internationals. FIRST INTERNATIONAL: The International Working Men's Association, founded in London 1864 as an instrument for cooperation between trade union movements in different lands. Karl Marx, who drafted its constitution, saw in it a means of creating an international working-class party which would help to advance the cause of proletarian revolution. It was much weakened by the ◊ *Franco-Prussian war* and the débâcle of the ◊ *Paris Commune*; a quarrel between Marx and Bakunin (◊ *Anarchism*) completed the process. Already moribund for some years, it was formally dissolved in Philadelphia 1876.

SECOND INTERNATIONAL: The Socialist International, founded in Paris 1889 for non-revolutionary socialist parties, of which the German and Russian Social Democratic parties were the most influential. Splintered by the ◊ *First World War* and the 1917 ◊ *Bolshevik* revolution in Russia, it was never effectively reconstructed.

THIRD INTERNATIONAL: The Communist International (Comintern); founded in Moscow 1919 under the auspices of the Communist Party of the new Russian Soviet Republic. It rapidly developed into a highly centralized Soviet-dominated league of communist parties in many lands; support for the foreign policy of the ◊ *Soviet Union* was enlisted, and was identified with support for the cause of spreading communism throughout the world, and at the same time the Comintern ensured that non-Russian communist parties took their impress from the Soviet party. It was disbanded 1943, as a gesture of good-will towards the capitalist allies of U.S.S.R. in the ◊ *Second World War*. The Communist Information Bureau (Cominform), founded 1947, was hardly a successor, being limited to the parties of eastern and central Europe, France, Italy, and U.S.S.R. It ceased to function after the 1956 Hungarian revolt.

The ◊ *Trotskyite* movement is sometimes loosely called the 'Fourth International'.

Interpol. The International Criminal Police Commission; an international police bureau to provide for cooperation between the criminal-investigation branches of the police of over fifty countries. Established 1923 with headquarters in Vienna, it was interrupted by the Second World War and re-established 1946 with headquarters and secretariat in Paris and a General Assembly meeting in a different capital each year; it provides a radio network for speedy communication between police forces and the interception and arrest of criminals.

Interstellar Matter. Within the ◊ *Milky Way* system of stars there is approximately as much matter (probably ◊ *hydrogen* or finely divided dust) in the 'empty' space between the stars as in the stars themselves. It is detectable in many ways e.g. radio waves at a wavelength of 21 cm. are emitted, and the matter may be lit up if it chances to be near a bright star. ◊ *Radioastronomy.*

Intervertebral Disc. One of the discs of fibrous cartilage between the surfaces of adjacent vertebrae in the spinal column. Each contains a high-elastic central nucleus (*nucleus pulposus*), which if the disc is damaged may extrude and press on the spinal cord, causing severe pain and sometimes muscular weakness and localized paralysis, the condition commonly known as 'slipped disc'. ◊ *Lumbago.*

Intestine. The alimentary tract, between stomach and anus. From the outlet of the stomach, the small intestine is made up of the duodenum (about 10 in. long in adults), the jejunum (8 ft), and the ileum (12 ft); the large intestine, about 5 ft long, consists of the caecum, the colon, the rectum, and the anal canal. ⟡ *Digestion*.

Introvert ◊ *Extravert*.

Investment Trust. A company whose business it is to invest its capital in a chosen range of investments; by acquiring shares in such companies, investors can spread their risks and obtain the benefit of skilled management. Investment trusts originated in Scotland about 100 years ago and today have holdings of over £2000 m. in the U.K.

UNIT TRUSTS: Whereas investment trusts have a fixed capital from which they invest, unit trusts differ in that they are 'open-ended' i.e. they invest (on behalf of those who buy their shares) all sums subscribed. Unit trusts began in U.S.A. and were introduced in the U.K. in 1931; their daily quotations are the result not of stock-exchange transactions but of a formula applied according to specific rules. They are of two types, (a) fixed, where the type of investment is predetermined and may not be changed; (b) flexible, where the management may invest as they think fit. The market value of unit trust funds is now over £300 m.

Invisible Trade. Receipts and payments arising between countries for services (not goods) e.g. shipping and aviation freight and fares, insurance, tourist expenditures, royalties, interest on investments, and so on; also for government expenditures abroad for diplomatic services and military establishments. ⟡ *Balance of Payments*.

Iodine. ◊ *Halogens*; an almost black crystalline element with a metallic lustre, much rarer than chlorine or bromine. The solid has a high vapour pressure and a smell resembling that of chlorine; the vapour is dark violet. Its solution in carbon tetrachloride and chloroform is purple, but in water and alcohol (solvents containing OH) it is brown. Extracted from Chilean nitrate deposits, from natural brines, and from seaweed, it is used in the organic-chemical industry, in photography, and esp. for pharmaceutical preparations. One of its ◊ *isotopes*, the radioactive iodine I-131, is a fission product from uranium in an atomic reactor; its release into the atmosphere is dangerous, because by contaminating herbage it may appear in cows' milk and affect children at an age when they are particularly sensitive to radiation injury. About three-quarters of the world's iodine production goes to make potassium iodide (KI). Iodine is only slightly soluble in water; 'tincture of iodine' is a solution of it in potassium iodide, water, and alcohol.

Ion, Ionization. An ion is an ◊ *atom* or group of atoms possessing an electric charge, whether positive or negative. An atom is normally neutral, since the positive and negative charges it contains are equal in number and cancel each other. The atom, however, may lose an electron and become positively charged, or gain an electron and become negatively charged. Either process requires energy, and changes the neutral atom into a charged ion. Ionization can be brought about by electrovalent combination between atoms, or by the effect of heat. Energetic subatomic particles from the nuclei of atoms e.g. radioactive nuclides or fragments of nuclear fission, lose their energy by causing ionization of the matter through which they pass. ⟡ *Nuclear Energy, Spectrum*.

Ion Exchange. The reversible exchange of ions between a solution and a solid, such as occurs typically in a water-softener. Salts of calcium and magnesium in water make it 'hard' and inhibit lather. By filtering it through sodium permutite (a zeolite), the calcium and magnesium ions are exchanged for ions of sodium, which do not affect the soap. The cycle can be reversed by flushing with a solution of common salt, and the device is ready to resume the process, the unwanted ions of calcium and magnesium being flushed away. This process has been greatly facilitated by the manufacture of more effective artificial zeolites and resins, and it is now possible to 'demineralize' water commercially and obtain potable water from sea water. Ion exchange is now widely used in purifying water for boilers producing steam at high temperatures and pressures, e.g. those in conventional power stations.

Ionians. Greek colonists in W. Asia Minor and the Aegean Islands from about 1000 B.C. Like the Athenians, they spoke Attic Greek. Their cities e.g. Chios, Ephesus, Erythrae, Miletus, Samos prospered, and they sent out traders and colonists as far as Spain and the Black

Sea, but in the early 6th cent. they came under Persian rule and after the Persian Wars in the 5th cent. they enjoyed only a brief period of political freedom. They continued to flourish, however, contributing much to Greek and later to Roman and Byzantine civilization, until their final destruction in the invasions of the Seljuk and Ottoman Turks of the 11th–14th centuries A.D.

Ionic Order ◊ *Architectural Orders.*

Ionosphere. Series of layers, lying about 50–80 m. above the earth's surface, ionized (i.e. electrically charged) by ultraviolet rays emitted by the sun. These layers have the property of reflecting radio waves back to earth and thus are important in making possible long-distance wireless communication. They are known as the E, F, and G layers; the name ◊ *Heaviside layer* (Kennelly layer) is applied both to the E layer and to the ionosphere as a whole. ◊ *Atmosphere.*

Iphigenia. In Greek legend, daughter of ◊ *Agamemnon* and Clytaemnestra. When the Greek fleet was on the way to the Trojan war, ◊ *Artemis* caused a calm preventing them from sailing from Aulis; the seer Calchas advised Iphigenia's father to sacrifice her, but Artemis substituted a stag and carried her off to Tauris, where she became a priestess. She saved her brother ◊ *Orestes* and his friend Pylades from being sacrificed as unwelcome strangers, and fled with them to Greece.

I.Q. ◊ *Intelligence Quotient.*

I.R.A. (Irish Republican Army). Originally the armed section of the Irish Republican Brotherhood i.e. ◊ *Fenians*; after the Irish Civil War (◊ *Anglo-Irish 'Troubles'*, *Easter Rebellion*), the irredentist rump which continued guerrilla activities despite the efforts of the governments of the Irish Republic, N. Ireland, and the U.K. It maintained sporadic raids across the N. Ireland border, and in 1938 carried out bomb attacks in Great Britain. It voluntarily disbanded itself 1962. ◊ *Ireland.*

Iran ◊ *Persia.*

Iraq. Area 172,000 sq. m. Pop. (1957) 6.5 m. Cap. Bagdad. Rel. Muslim. Language Arabic. A republic in the area once known as Mesopotamia in the basin of the Tigris and Euphrates.

ECONOMY. Potentially fertile, the region once supported a much greater population until the ruin of the irrigation system of the Babylonians. Today the main source of wealth is oil, the major field being that around Kirkuk, operated by the International Iraq Petroleum Co. Annual production has reached 50 m. tons. Half the revenue from oil royalties is allocated for irrigation, land improvement, social welfare, etc. Wheat, barley, cotton, and tobacco are grown, and Iraq is the major world exporter of dates. Its main port is Basra at the head of the Persian Gulf.

HISTORY. For long a backward province of the Ottoman Empire, Iraq after the First World War became a state under British Mandate, of which Faisal became king in 1921. Independence came in 1932. In 1958 General Kassem overthrew the regime, Faisal II and his Prime Minister Nuri-al-Said being murdered. The new republic at once repudiated the Bagdad Pact. In 1963 Colonel Arif, in a further military coup, overthrew Kassem who was executed. Iraq's relations with Syria and Egypt have swung from attempts to form a union to deep suspicion. Iraq has accepted Soviet aid and simultaneously banned the communist party. The Kurdish minority has sought to secure autonomy and has frequently been in revolt. ◊ *Kurds.*

Ireland. The Irish Republic (26 counties) and N. Ireland (6 counties).

1. REPUBLIC OF IRELAND: Area 26,600 sq. m. Pop. 2.8 m. (1961), 96 per cent Roman Catholic. Cap. Dublin. A parliamentary democracy; Dail Eireann and President elected by universal adult suffrage on a ◊ *proportional representation* system, the Senate part nominated and part indirectly elected, and the Cabinet responsible to the Dail. President, Eamonn de Valera. Citizens of the Irish Republic enter and leave the U.K. without passports; if resident there they have full voting rights.

ECONOMY. Lacks coal and iron, hence no heavy industry; in the last 10 years light industry has increased considerably but the country remains largely agricultural.

HISTORY. The ◊ *Neolithic* flint-users and Mediterranean bronze-users were followed about 300 B.C. by Gaels from France and Spain, whose 'golden age' was from the 6th cent. to the 10th. Ireland became Christian in the early 5th cent. under St Patrick, and Irish priests travelled widely as missionaries (◊ *Church of Ireland*).

English invasions after the 12th cent. brought about a very complex process of interpenetration between Anglo-Norman feudalism and the Gaelic clan-order. Between 1381 and 1495 the English enclosed the four most fertile counties (the Pale), within which Irish custom and law were banned (◊ *Penal Laws, Poynings Law*) but beyond which the English Crown did not enforce its jurisdiction until Stewart times. Between 1647 and 1652 Cromwell brutally suppressed both Royalists and Catholics in Ireland, settling English Puritans on land confiscated from the Irish. With the Renunciation Act 1782 England ceased to legislate on Irish matters, and several years of remarkably rapid commercial development followed; the revival of the project of legislative union provoked the Rebellion of 1798, and after wholesale bribery the Irish Parliament voted itself out of existence in the 1800 ◊ *Act of Union.*

The first movement for repeal of the Union was deflected into that for ◊ *Catholic emancipation,* finally granted 1829. Agitation was muted by the endemic potato dearth which in the 1840s became the ◊ *Irish Famine.* After a troubled period, the separatist Irish Nationalist Party under Parnell held a balance of power in the House of Commons, and Gladstone at last offered ◊ *Home Rule*; but Parnell's disgrace and death made its postponement possible, and when the Home Rule Act was finally passed in 1912, threats of armed revolt from ◊ *Ulster,* combined with the menacing situation in Europe, caused its suspension. After the First World War, following renewed ◊ *Anglo-Irish troubles,* 26 counties were established as the Irish State. In 1938 this was rechristened Eire and left the Commonwealth though retaining special trade and immigration arrangements with Britain. In the Second World War Eire remained neutral, but large numbers of her citizens joined the British forces as volunteers. In 1948 the title Republic of Ireland became the official name of the state.

LANGUAGE. Irish; a Goidelic (Q-Celtic) language. It was in common use till the late 17th cent. Ancient Irish literature dates to 5th-cent. ◊ *Ogam* inscriptions. Irish was harshly suppressed, and declined in the 18th and 19th centuries, but the Gaelic Revival movement saved it

from extinction. The Republic is officially bilingual, Irish and English, but though taught in the schools Irish has made little progress towards being the chief means of communication, except in the Gaeltacht of the west coast. Irish spelling is not phonetic, consonants varying in pronunciation according to the vowels following them, and both nouns and verbs are elaborately inflected.

2. NORTHERN IRELAND: Two thirds of the province of Ulster. Area 5451 sq. m. Pop. 1.4 m. Cap. Stormont (Belfast). Rel. 67 per cent Protestant (largely ◊ *Presbyterian*), 33 per cent Roman Catholic. The six counties return 12 members to the House of Commons as well as electing 52 members to the Stormont parliament. The Crown appoints a Governor, who is advised by nine ministers responsible to Stormont; the British government retains certain Reserved Powers e.g. defence, foreign affairs, some aspects of taxation and trade.

ECONOMY. Textile industries esp. linen, also engineering industries, aircraft construction, shipbuilding. Good agricultural output esp. eggs. Unemployment remains about 10 per cent.

HISTORY. In Gaelic times (see above) Ulster was the territory of some of the largest and most powerful clans (esp. O'Neill, O'Donnell), but it was systematically repopulated mainly from Scotland, and from the 17th cent. onward was much troubled by politico-religious disturbances. Proposals for reuniting the two parts of Ireland while granting the Belfast area considerable autonomy are frequently canvassed, but as yet inconclusively, though closer commercial and industrial relations between the two parts are developing. In 1963 the P.M. of the Republic publicly appealed to the British government to end the partition; the P.M. of N. Ireland replied in cautiously hopeful terms.

Iridescence ◊ *Pigmentation.*

Iridium ◊ *Platinum Metals.*

Iris. 1. Annular diaphragm of involuntary muscle separating the anterior and posterior chambers of the ◊ *eye.* It is composed of layers of radially and circularly arranged muscle fibres, the contraction or expansion of which adjusts the aperture (pupil) for the light entering the eye. Pigmentation of the iris gives the eye its characteristic colour.

2. *Iridaceae*; family of decorative flowering plants, in many widely distributed varieties, characterized by ◊ *bulbs*, ◊ *corms*, ◊ *rhizomes*, and swordlike leaves. The genus includes the wild flag and the garden iris as well as the crocus, gladiolus, and freesia.

Irish Civil War ◊ *Anglo-Irish 'Troubles', I.R.A., Ireland, Partition.*

Irish Famine. In ◊ *Ireland*, esp. after 1800, the single-cropping of the blight-prone 'lumper' potato over vast areas of the country, to provide literally a mono-diet for the rapidly expanding population living on tiny holdings of 'insanely fragmented' land, meant that partial dearth of potatoes everywhere or absolute dearth locally were endemic; under the ◊ *Act of Union*, the transfer of all administrative decision to Westminster and the immense increase in absentee landlordism intensified the problem. Partial famines occurred throughout the first four decades of the 19th cent. but in 1845–7 the potato famine was absolute all over the country; other crops were not affected, and exports of grain and meat continued while one third of the people died of hunger and 'famine fever' (typhus). In the next decade well over a million Irish emigrated to U.S.A. where the ◊ *Fenians* continued to agitate against the British Government.

Irish Free State ◊ *Anglo-Irish 'Troubles', Ireland, Partition.*

Iron. Metallic element, 4.7 per cent of the earth's crust, in widely-distributed ores smelted since very early times; rarely found as a pure metal, but the earth's core is thought to be mainly pure iron. It has two principal valency states, $+2$ giving ferrous compounds and $+3$ ferric compounds. Ferric oxide (rouge) is used as a polishing abrasive and an industrial paint pigment. Ferrous sulphate (green vitriol), known from antiquity, is used in the dye, tanning, and ink industries for making Prussian blue and oxide pigments. An essential item in human diet, iron is stored in the blood as a metallic constituent of haemoglobin. Many of its salts (sulphate, carbonate, citrate, phosphate) are used in medicine. Commercially iron is obtained by heating an ore e.g. haematite (ferric oxide) or siderite (ferrous carbonate) with coke and limestone in a blast furnace, the silica being removed in the slag that forms as a molten layer above the iron at the base of the furnace (the two are tapped

separately); in modern practice the air blast is oxygen-enriched. Some of the resultant pig-iron is converted into cast-iron, but most of the molten metal is immediately converted into steel, for which the iron has to be further purified and its carbon content refined well below the 4 per cent commonly present in cast-iron.

STEEL: May be manufactured in several ways (◊ *Bessemer Process, Siemens-Martin Process*); essentially, steel is formed when undesirable elements in pig-iron are oxidized (the carbon content being too large). The most important steel ingredient is iron carbide, imparting hardening and tempering properties.

ALLOYS: Formed by combination with e.g. chromium, nickel, and molybdenum; used where resistance to high temperatures or to corrosion is required. All steels contain some manganese. Special-purpose (e.g. tool) steels may also contain nickel 3.5 per cent, chromium 0.7–18.0 per cent, vanadium 0.5–2.0 per cent, molybdenum 0.2–8.0 per cent, tungsten 1.0–18.0 per cent, cobalt 1.0–8.0 per cent.

CASE-HARDENED STEEL: Designed to resist fracture; heated with sodium cyanide or in gaseous hydrocarbons, producing a hard long-wearing skin on a tough core.

MILD STEEL: Carbon content 0.06 to 0.25 per cent; used for boiler and ship plates, tubes, wire, forgings, rolled sections for building purposes; combines relatively high strength with considerable ductility and is easily workable.

STAINLESS STEEL: Contains chromium and nickel; protective surface layer of chromic oxide makes it almost immune to corrosion. Steels are generally subject to heat treatment e.g. reheating to defined temperatures and cooling at predetermined rate.

◊ *Alloys, Bog Iron, Metallurgy, Mines and Mining, Tantalum, Thermite.*

Iron Age. The last of the 'Three Ages' of human technology, as systematized by archaeologists in the 19th cent. Iron is much more widely distributed than copper, but the properties of iron ore are not so recognizable and not so liable to accidental discovery; hence probably the long interval between the beginning of the ◊ *Bronze Age* in the Near East and the beginning of the Iron Age. There is evidence of simple working of meteoric iron in Mesopotamia about 2500 B.C., the earliest finds being decorative objects. The first true iron industry, including the processes of carburizing, quenching, and tempering the metal, seems to have been developed in the second millennium B.C. by the ◊ *Hittites*, who kept a tight hold on the industry; finds of iron objects in other regions e.g. ◊ *Egypt* at this time probably indicate Hittite gifts. Iron-working did not spread until after the fall of the Hittite empire about 1200 B.C. when ◊ *Assyria* took over as a mass-production centre. Egypt did not have a fully developed iron-working economy until the 8th cent. B.C. and a true Iron Age did not begin in central Europe until 100 years later. The main European Iron Age cultures are known as the Hallstatt and the La Tène cultures.

Iron and Steel Industry. The ◊ *Hittites* are credited with the introduction of iron-smelting well before 1000 B.C. In Europe iron was made from about 800 B.C. In Roman Britain ore was smelted (chiefly in the Weald and the Forest of Dean) with charcoal obtained from the forests then existing in S. England; later iron production moved to the coalfields. Wrought iron gave way to steel in the 18th cent. Britain pioneered the use of coal in smelting. The Bessemer and Siemens-Martin processes of the 19th cent. led to cheaper and increased steel for the rapidly expanding requirements of industry. British ore comes mainly from the Lincolnshire–Northamptonshire beds; as the supply is no longer adequate, much is now imported from Sweden, S. America, Canada, and N. Africa, and the iron content of Swedish ore is at least twice that of the British. The other raw materials for the blast-furnace (coking coal and limestone) are still plentiful in Britain, which remains a large producer. Britain's centres of steel making are Wales (with special emphasis on steel sheet and tinplate), the Midlands, the N. of England, and Scotland; equipment has been thoroughly modernized in recent years. The iron and steel industry was placed under public ownership 1951, but the Act was repealed 1953 and most of the industry returned to private ownership, the Iron and Steel Board being established (its members appointed by the government) to exercise general supervision of the industry; this is distinct from the major trade association, the British Iron and Steel Federation.

STEEL PRODUCTION: 1962 (in m. tons) U.S.A. 87.8; U.S.S.R. 75.1; Germany 32.1; Japan 27.1; Gt Britain 20.5; France 17.0.

◊ *Alloys, Mines and Mining, Tantalum, Tungsten.*

Iron Curtain. Term which gained immediate currency after its use in a speech by Sir Winston Churchill at Fulton (U.S.A.) in 1946 to describe the virtual isolation of U.S.S.R. and its satellite countries (Albania, Bulgaria, Czechoslovakia, Hungary, Poland, Rumania) through their imposition of stringent restrictions upon travel and communication with other countries. Some slight relaxation has occurred since the death of Stalin in 1953, but the barriers between the Iron Curtain countries and W. Europe remain substantial.

Irrigation. Artificial distribution of water in order to cultivate crops on land deficient in rainfall; primitive forms were practised at least 4000 years ago, probably originating in Egypt, where the annual flood waters of the Nile were canalized to embanked fields, crops sown there growing and ripening without further water. This method is known as basin irrigation; its disadvantage is that it can be used only at the flood season, though it can be supplemented by various means e.g. in early times by hand-baling water and later by simple lifting devices e.g. shadoof and sakia to raise water from the river to the fields. The Babylonian civilization depended on an elaborate irrigation system based on the difference in level between the Tigris and the Euphrates. Modern systems make water permanently available; a dam or barrage may be built across a river to create a large reservoir from which canals lead water to the fields, under control, enabling irrigation of a larger area. A major advance in the development of irrigation schemes, the Aswan dam on the Nile, completed 1902, has twice been heightened to increase the storage capacity of its lake. The Sennar dam on the Blue Nile in the Sudan, completed 1925, provided irrigation water for cotton cultivation on the Gezira plain. Since ancient times the Indian sub-continent has been dependent on irrigation, and in NW India an elaborate system of canals takes the water from the Indus and Ganges river systems; in W. Pakistan the Lloyd Barrage scheme alone irrigates about $5\frac{1}{2}$ m. acres. Many schemes utilizing large dams have also provided power for generating electricity e.g. the U.S.A. Hoover Dam scheme on the Colorado irrigates a million acres and supplies electricity to much of S. California. The combination of electricity generation and agricultural improvement has led to many large combined projects in countries not traditionally using irrigation e.g. France. Irrigation has also long been important in e.g. Iran, Mexico, Japan, and in Far Eastern countries is the basis for growing rice, the staple grain, in 'paddy fields' alternately flooded and drained. ⟡ *Levees*.

Isault (Isolde, Isoud, Yseult) ⟡ *Tristram*.

Ishtar (Astarte). In Babylonian mythology, goddess of love and of war, identified with the planet Venus, wife of ⟡ *Baal*; she killed her lover ⟡ *Tammuz* but descended to the underworld to bring him back.

Isinglass. ⟡ *Gelatin* with special properties, used to clarify wines and beers, in pickling, and as a preservative; obtained from the swimming-bladders of certain fish esp. sturgeon.

Isis. In Egyptian mythology, goddess of fertility and identified with the moon, wife of ⟡ *Osiris*, mother of ⟡ *Horus*; often represented with the face of her sacred animal the cow, and with outstretched arms. Osiris fell victim to the plots of his evil brother Set, who quartered his body and scattered the pieces over the country; Isis built a temple over each fragment and urged Horus to avenge his father, but after he had captured Set she released him, and Horus beheaded her, ⟡ *Thoth* replacing her head by that of a cow. The worship of Isis became very popular under the late Roman republic, her special attribute being a rattle (sistrum).

Islam. The latest of the great monotheistic religions, based on the teachings of Mohammed, an Arab prophet A.D. 570–632 who considered himself a successor to Abraham and Jesus. The basic tenet is 'There is no God but Allah, and Mohammed is his prophet'; the principal duties of those who submit themselves to the will of Allah (Muslims) are prayer five times a day, fasting esp. in ⟡ *Ramadan*, alms-giving, and the pilgrimage (Hajj) to ⟡ *Mecca*. The ⟡ *Koran* is not merely a book of religious revelation but a guide to a way of life. Islam was the inspiration of the great 7th- and 8th-cent. Arab conquests, which carried the new religion as far as Spain westwards and India eastwards. Today it claims at least 400 m. adherents, in the Near East, N. Africa, Pakistan, Persia, and SE Asia. ⟡ *Caliphate, Shiahs, Sunnis.*

Isobar. Line drawn on map or chart to join places with equal atmospheric pressure, the actual pressure-readings usually corrected by reduction to mean sea level. On a climatological map, isobars show the average pressure distribution over a large area during a given period, and on a weather chart, pressure distribution at a given time on a given day, to indicate the positions of depressions etc. for forecasts.

Isomerism. Two or more ⟡ *compounds* may have the same formula but different properties, owing to different arrangements of atoms in the molecules. Thus ordinary alcohol C_2H_5OH is very different from dimethyl ether $(CH_3)_2O$, though the molecular formula of each is C_2H_6O. Such compounds are known as isomers, and the phenomenon as isomerism. There are other types of isomerism. One involves interchange of groups e.g. the ester ethyl acetate $CH_3.CO_2C_2H_5$ is different from the ester methyl propionate $C_2H_5.CO_2CH_3$. Another, geometrical isomerism, is associated with a double bond, two groups being fixed in space on one side of the carbon atom or the other and free rotation being prevented by the double bond (e.g. maleic and fumaric acids). A particularly interesting variety is optical isomerism, associated with optical activity. An optically active substance is one that can rotate the plane of polarized light. Such a substance will usually contain one or more asymmetric carbon atoms, and a carbon atom of this sort has attached to it four atoms or groups that are *all* different, e.g. lactic acid $CH_3.C*H(OH)CO_2H$. Here the four atoms or groups attached to the starred carbon atom are in fact all different: CH_3, H, OH, CO_2H, and it is therefore possible to have two isomers (with the atoms and groups in three dimensions) one being the mirror image of the other:

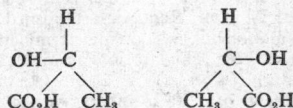

Thus if the first rotates the plane of

polarized light to the left (laevo), the other will rotate it to the right (dextro). An equal mixture of the two is optically inactive and is known as a racemic mixture. Many natural substances are optically active, including sugars, amino-acids, alkaloids, and this property plays an important part in their assimilation by the body. Optical isomers are very similar in chemical properties and are therefore difficult to separate. It was Louis Pasteur who found the best means of resolving them.

Isostasy. State of balance in the earth's crust; the continental masses (◊ *Sial*) are composed of rocks less dense than those under the oceans (◊ *Sima*) and stand up in the way icebergs float in water, the higher the continent above sea-level the greater being the depth of its roots. Under the mountain ranges, the lighter rocks extend 25 m. downwards, but under low-lying plains only six or seven miles, while there may be none at all under the oceans. If – by the formation of an ice-cap or the deposition of sediment – an extra load is added to the earth's crust, the fresh weight will cause the continental mass to sink, whereas the removal of such a load will be followed by a rise of the mass of lighter rocks.

Isotherm ◊ *Weather.*

Isotope. One of two or more ◊ *nuclides* belonging to the same element but differing in mass (i.e. having the same number of ◊ *protons* but different numbers of ◊ *neutrons*). The chemical properties of isotopes are therefore the same, and so are the physical properties except those that are determined by the mass of the atoms. Most elements have a mixture of isotopes. Uranium for example (atomic number 92) has several isotopes; in particular two with mass-numbers 235 and 238 respectively. The first contains $235-92 = 143$ neutrons, and the other $238-92 = 146$ neutrons. The term 'isotope' was introduced by Soddy, and means (from Greek) 'having the same place' i.e. in the Periodic Table of the elements. ◊◊ *Iodine, Tracer Elements.*

Israel. Area 7992 sq. m. Pop. 2.4 m. Cap. Jerusalem. Rel. about 88 per cent Judaic, the rest Muslim. Republic established by proclamation in 1948 on the termination of the British Mandate in Palestine. The legislature (Knesset) is a one-chamber parliament of 120 members elected by universal suffrage. Since 1961 the government has been a coalition under first David Ben-Gurion, then Levi Eshkol.

ECONOMY. Israel is not a country of great natural resources, and the cost of agricultural development is high. The most important production is citrus fruit. There are mineral deposits around the Dead Sea, which are exploited. There is a persistent deficit on balance of trade, redressed by gifts from Jews abroad, German compensation payments, and inflow of capital. Invisible exports include an increasing tourist traffic and the supply of Israeli experts to African and Eastern countries. Education is compulsory and facilities are wide. The University of Jerusalem has some 7000 students, and there is a large technical college at Haifa.

HISTORY. Set up as a Jewish state in 1948 on the recommendation of the United Nations General Assembly, which fixed its boundaries (◊ *Partition*), Israel was immediately invaded by neighbouring Arab states e.g. ◊ *Jordan*; fighting continued until 1949, by which time Israel had gained some Arab territory and lost the Gaza strip to ◊ *Egypt*. The Arab states do not recognize Israel, and the armistices have not been translated into peace. The U.N. maintains a mixed Armistice Commission to observe the frontiers. The Declaration of Independence of 1948 stated: 'Israel will be open to the immigration of Jews from all countries of their dispersion'; since then a million immigrants have entered, but in recent years the flow has slackened.

LANGUAGE. ◊ *Hebrew.*

◊◊ *Jews, Jordan, Judaism, Palestine.*

Issus (333 B.C.) ◊ *Phoenician.*

I.T.A. (I.T.V.) ◊ *Independent Television Authority.*

Italian. A ◊ *Romance language*, descended not from Classical Latin but from colloquial Vulgar Latin; spoken by some 63 m. persons in Italy, Switzerland, Corsica, Sardinia, Malta, and to some extent in NE Africa. The early Italian writers Dante, Petrarch, and Boccaccio all belonged to Florence; for this and other reasons (partly political) Standard Italian, regularized by the Accademia della Crusca founded in 1582, is based on the language of Florence rather than that of Rome. Italian is still rich in dialects, and Sardinian, which preserves many archaic features, is nearer to Latin than any other Romance tongue. Italian spelling is near-phonetic. Many Italian terms relating to music and the arts – *allegretto, andante, chiaroscuro, intaglio* – have international currency.

Italian Architecture and Art. Derived from the art of the Roman Empire, and modified from the 4th cent. on by the Christian ideals which produced ◊*Byzantine* art, a style which prevailed in Italy and in the whole of the west, with modifications, until about the 12th cent. Italian art proper is generally reckoned to begin with the sculpture of the 12th and 13th centuries, esp. the revived classicism of Nicola Pisano in his pulpits at Pisa and Siena; the return to classical models was easier for sculptors than for painters, because much antique sculpture had survived. The great Byzantine art of ◊ *mosaic* was gradually abandoned; early names in painting are Cavallini in Rome and Cimabue in Florence, but the new naturalistic art reached its climax in the 14th cent. with Giotto, whose style formed the basis of ◊ *Renaissance* painting and thus of European painting as a whole, having a dramatic and realistic quality which set it apart from the contemporary school of Siena founded by Duccio and continued by Simone Martini and the Lorenzetti. The Renaissance style was largely Florentine in inspiration and naturalistic and scientific in its aims; Masaccio, Donatello, and Brunelleschi were the three great early 15th-cent. artists, and Leonardo da Vinci in the second half of the century was the most characteristic example of a scientist and artist. The climax of the period was reached at the beginning of the 16th cent. when most of the works were produced in Rome (where Raphael, Michelangelo, and Bramante were active). The early 16th-cent. political catastrophies and the spiritual crisis of the ◊ *Reformation* produced a new and more introspective kind of art now generally known as ◊ *Mannerism*. This style – of which, after Michelangelo, the greatest exponents were Pontormo, Parmigianino, and Tintoretto – lasted until in the 17th cent. it was superseded by ◊ *Baroque,* the product of the new confidence of the Counter-Reformation, best exemplified in the works of Bernini. Venice, where the afterglow of the Renaissance lasted longer than anywhere else, was comparatively unaffected by Mannerism or Baroque, but in the 18th cent. the ◊ *Rococo* style produced the last great flowering of Venetian painting, with Tiepolo, Canaletto, and Guardi. The light-heartedness of rococo had little effect south of Venice, and from Rome in the mid 18th cent. came a revival of classical antiquity called ◊ *neoclassicism*; this spread to France and England, and was an international rather than an Italian movement. In the 19th cent. Italian art was at a low ebb and much influenced by France, and the principal early 20th-cent. Italian contribution was ◊ *futurism*, nearly as much French as Italian. Modigliani worked almost entirely in Paris, as have many modern Italian artists. Marini, Manzù, and Morandi are regarded as the leading Italian artists of the 20th-cent. international style, with Guttuso as the principal exponent of a ◊ *realist* art. ◊ *Palladian Style.*

Italy. Area (including Sicily and Sardinia) 131,000 sq. m. Pop. 50 m. Cap. Rome. Rel. Roman Catholic. A republic since 1946, the present constitution resulting from the 1946 referendum, which gave a narrow majority for a republic, and provides for a parliamentary system, a constitutional court, and a referendum on any major changes. Since the ◊ *Second World War*, governments have been coalitions dominated by the Christian Democrats. The Communist Party is numerically strong, but Italy's considerable economic progress has lessened its influence.

ECONOMY. A mountainous country, in which agriculture remains a chief activity, cereals, fruit, vegetables, wine, and olives being main crops, although in N. Italy, around e.g. Milan, Turin, there are regions of great industrial activity, motor-car, shipping, engineering, and textile manufacture, which have rapidly expanded since 1946. An important mineral resource is sulphur; recent discoveries of natural gas are of great value. S. Italy has long been a neglected and poor part of the country, but efforts to raise productivity and living standards are being intensified. The natural beauty and artistic treasures of Italy attract tourists, who have recently reached a total of 20 m. annually. In the field of industrial design and architecture Italy has made significant contributions, and Rome has become a major centre for the European film industry.

Education at primary level is free and compulsory; secondary schools are generally state-financed. Several Italian universities e.g. Bologna, Padua, Rome date to the 13th or 14th centuries.

HISTORY. From the collapse of the ◊ *Carolingian* empire in the 9th cent. until the 19th, Italy was not a unified nation but a number of independent states, in some of which stable republics were early established e.g. Venice, Genoa, while others were ◊ *Papal States*, ruled from Rome. In many, mercenary captains (*condottieri*) set up precarious dukedoms constantly at war with one another. The cities prospered in the period of peace which followed the Treaty of Lodi in 1454, and the ◊ *Renaissance* was able to reach its full flowering under the patronage of merchant princes esp. the Medici. There was no major change till the ◊ *War of the Spanish Succession* at the end of the 17th cent. when the ◊ *Hapsburgs* became dominant. In 1796 Napoleon established a unified kingdom in the north (◊ *Marengo*); although the old divisions were largely restored in 1815, nationalist feeling persisted (◊ *Risorgimento*). Revolts in 1821, 1830, and 1848 failed; but in 1859 Cavour, premier of Sardinia, with the support of Napoleon III, drove the Austrians from Lombardy. In 1860 Garibaldi and his 'thousand red shirts' took Sicily, and in 1861 Victor Emmanuel, King of Sardinia, became king of all Italy, except Venetia (regained from Austria 1866) and Rome (a Papal State until 1870). The new kingdom acquired colonies in Eritrea and Tripoli, but was badly defeated in Abyssinia (◊ *Ethiopia*) in 1896. Italy entered the ◊ *First World War* on the Allied side, and gained Trieste and Trentino. In 1922 Mussolini introduced ◊ *fascism*; he invaded and annexed Abyssinia in 1935 and aided General Franco in the ◊ *Spanish Civil War* 1936-9, the Rome-Berlin ◊ *'Axis'* being formed in 1937. In the ◊ *Second World War*, Italy declared war on the Allies in 1940, but in 1943 was defeated in N. Africa and invaded. Mussolini was overthrown (and later executed by partisans) and a democratic government was set up which supported the Allies. After serious difficulties in early post-war years Italy made impressive progress in productivity, living standards, and political stability.

Ivory Coast. Area 189,000 sq. m. Pop. 3.3 m. Cap. Abijan. Previously part of French W. Africa 1893-1958.

ECONOMY. Principal exports coffee, cocoa, bananas, timber; some diamond mining.

HISTORY. Political life in the Ivory Coast began with the formation of the Parti Démocratique de la Côte d'Ivoire in 1946, at first disliked by the French; later its leader, Félix Houphouët-Boigny, was a Cabinet Minister in Paris 1956-9. The Ivory Coast led the French territories which still wished to retain individual associations with France within the ◊ *French Community*; but when de Gaulle in 1959 allowed ◊ *Mali* to become independent within the Community, Houphouët-Boigny left the Community and established full independence. The new constitution gives complete executive powers to the President, who dominates the country through his highly organized party; a plot to assassinate him was foiled in 1963.

Ivy. A small group of evergreen climbers, which attach themselves to their support by aerial roots. The ivy which in Britain grows on trees, walls, etc. is *Hedera helix*, which has sported an extraordinary number of varieties, varying in the shape of the leaf and the markings, which may be marbling, blotching, or edging in white, cream, or yellow. ◊ *Poison Ivy*.

GROUND IVY ◊ *Labiatae*.

J

Jackal. *Canis aureus*; several species of foul-smelling ◊ *dog*, foraging nocturnally in packs, found in SE Europe, N. Africa, and Asia. They may rob farmyards or feed on carrion, often on scraps left by lions. The similar hyena is more closely related to the ◊ *cat*.

Jackdaw. Cunning acquisitive bird of the crow family; inhabits church towers and castles, but also trees and old rabbit burrows, where its nest for the four to six mottled eggs may be enormous. Its voracious feeding on insects is of great help to the farmer.

Jacobean Style. An English domestic architectural style, intermediate between the Elizabethan and the mature classical style introduced by Inigo Jones (◊ *Pal-*

porch of Hatfield House

ladian); characterized by a combination of Italian ◊ *Renaissance* forms, Netherlandish ornamental detail e.g. in gables, and a native late ◊ *Gothic* preference for large square mullioned windows. Though a bastard style, outside the main currents of European architecture, it produced many of the most picturesque English country houses, esp. Hatfield and Audley End.

Jacobins. Originally, the members of a political club, the Society of Friends of the Constitution, established in Paris 1790, which became known as the Jacobin Club because its headquarters were in a former Jacobin monastery; the first and by far the most influential of the political clubs of the ◊ *French Revolution*, it attracted the extreme radical elements, esp. in Paris. There were branches of the Jacobin Club all over France, and under the leadership of Robespierre the party controlled the country 1792–4.

Jacobite Church. A monophysite sect in Syria founded by Jacob Baradaeus, bishop of Edessa (about 500–78), and regarded by the papacy as heretical. Its head is the Patriarch of Antioch and it follows the Syrian rite. In the 17th cent. a group of Christians at Malabar in India adopted the Jacobite heresy, and they now outnumber the Syrian Jacobites. ◊◊ *Nestorianism*.

Jacobites. The supporters of James II after his deposition in 1688 (◊ *Glorious Revolution*) and of his son the Old Pretender ('James III') and grandson the Young Pretender (Prince Charles Edward). James II was defeated at the ◊ *Boyne* in Ireland, but his supporters remained influential in Scotland, where they supported the rebellions of the Earl of Mar, beaten at Sheriffmuir in 1715, and of Prince Charles Edward, beaten with great loss of life at ◊ *Culloden* in 1746. The last direct male descendant of James II, the Young Pretender's brother the Cardinal Duke of York, died at Rome in 1807. ◊◊ *Hanover*.

Jaguar ◊ *Panther*.

Jains. Followers of a religion originated or perhaps reformed by a contemporary of Buddha, Mahavira (Vardhamana) 599–527 B.C. Still professed in India by over 1 m. persons, it is atheistic and like ◊ *Buddhism* seeks as man's goal release from the cycle of existence and reincarnation (◊ *Transmigration*). Even more than Buddhism it emphasizes the virtue of ahimsa (harmlessness) and the sacredness and inviolability of all living things. Jain temples, often adorned with statues of their 72 jinas (saints), are renowned for their architectural and sculptural beauty. ◊ *Pantheism*.

Jamaica. Area 4411 sq. m. Pop. 1.6 m. (about 95 per cent of Negro origin). Cap. Kingston. Island in the Caribbean; independent within the British Commonwealth since 1962. The legislature is a House of Representatives of 45 members elected by direct universal adult suffrage, and a Senate of 21 nominated members.

ECONOMY. Agricultural, inc. bananas, cocoa, coconuts, coffee, ginger, pimentoes, sugar, tobacco. Industry is mainly food-processing and distilling; exports esp. rum but also bauxite (world's largest producer) and gypsum.

HISTORY. Discovered in 1494 by Columbus; the Spanish settlement founded in 1509 was attacked in 1596 and 1643 by the English, and finally captured in 1655 by the expedition sent by Cromwell (as part of the Dutch war). Ceded to Britain by the Madrid Treaty, 1670, Jamaica became a wealthy centre of buccaneering and the slave trade; but a series of earthquakes, hurricanes, slave revolts, and Indian wars greatly impoverished it during the 18th cent.

Jamboree ◊ *Boy Scouts*.

Jameson Raid. 1895. After the discovery of gold and diamonds in the Boer republic of Transvaal, many British went there; these *uitlanders* (foreigners) were not welcome to the Boers. Jameson dreamed (like Rhodes) of a S. Africa united under British leadership; he organized an armed raid into the Transvaal, but Kruger defeated and captured him. The incident contributed to the ◊ *Boer War*.

Jammu ◊ *Kashmir*.

Jams, Jellies. Preserves of fruit, containing about two-thirds their weight of sugar. All fresh fruits have a very large percentage of water, in some up to 80 per cent; unless most of this is removed, decomposition will occur. The fruit is boiled with an equal weight of sugar, to the required consistency, and then carefully sealed to prevent the growth of moulds. All kinds of fruit will make jam, but only those with enough natural pectin (a carbohydrate which can solidify to a gelatinous mass) will jellify.

Janissaries. Élite troops of the ◊ *Ottoman* Turkish army, founded in the 14th cent. and originally recruited from Christian boys and captives of war. From the 17th cent. Muslims were recruited, membership became hereditary, and they became a powerful and influential force. In 1826, after a mutiny, Sultan Mahmud II massacred them in their barracks.

Jansenism. Movement in the ◊ *Roman Catholic Church* in the 17th cent. based on the teaching of Cornelius Jansen 1585–1638, maintaining a form of determinism or ◊ *predestination*; after a long controversy, in which Jansen's views were bitterly opposed by the Jesuits (◊ *Society of Jesus*) and others, certain propositions alleged to be taken from his works were condemned as ◊ *heresy* by the papal bull *Unigenitus* in 1713. Numerous French Jansenists took refuge in the Netherlands, where they ultimately merged into the ◊ *Old Catholics*.

Janus. In Roman mythology, the god who guarded doors and gates; with two faces, symbolizing past/future or sunrise/sunset; his emblems were a staff and a key. His temples were open in times of war but closed in peace-time. January (opening) takes its name from him.

Japan. Area 182,700 sq. m. Pop. 98.4 m. Cap. Tokyo. Rel. Buddhism and Shinto. A group of islands in the Pacific, of which Honshu, Kyushu, Hokkaido, and Shikoku are the major parts. Under the 1947 constitution the Emperor is a symbol of the state but is divested of both political power and 'attributes of divinity'. Legislative power resides in the Diet, consisting of the House of Representatives (467 members) elected for a four-year term, and the House of Councillors (250 members, one half being elected every three years). Executive power is vested in the Prime Minister and Cabinet, the former elected by and from the Diet. Despite a provision of the Constitution that Japan should have no armed forces, there are ground, maritime, and air self-defence forces of over 250,000 men. The present majority party is the Liberal-Democratic Party, these parties having merged in 1955 in the face of joint socialist and communist opposition to rearming.

ECONOMY. The most highly industrialized country in Asia, with the whole range of light and heavy industries. Also highly-developed agriculture and fisheries. Since the ◊ *Second World War* the textile industry has been revived, and enormous strides have been made in shipbuilding and in the manufacture of electrical and electronic appliances, but Japan still faces problems of over-population and shortage of natural resources.

Japan is subject to frequent and destructive ◊ *earthquakes*, and up to the 20th cent. Japanese buildings were entirely of wood, but western methods of construction have now been widely adopted.

HISTORY. Japanese tradition (taught until 1945) held that the Japanese were of divine origin and the Emperor a descendant of the Sun Goddess. The early history is obscure, but organized government had emerged by the 8th cent. A.D. Chinese influence long predominated in culture and religion, but the native ◊ *Shinto* religion persisted. The history of the following centuries was one of inter-clan struggle within a quasi-feudal organization, until in the 12th cent. Yoritomo made his family supreme and assumed the title of Shogun, war-lord. For the next 700 years Japan was ruled by military dictators, the Emperor remaining an obscure figure. In the 17th cent. Portuguese traders and missionaries settled in Japan, but subsequently a policy of complete seclusion was enforced. Internally, a repressive feudal system based on the daimyo (lords) and the samurai (warriors) was maintained. In 1854 an American naval commander, Perry, forced the opening of trade with the West. In 1867 the Shogunate was suppressed and an Emperor 'restored'; the capital moved to Tokyo. Japan rapidly adopted western techniques, the myth of a divine Emperor was revived, and an aggressive, nationalistic, and ruthless policy of expansion followed. ◊ *Korea* was economically dominated by Japan from 1876 and incorporated into the Japanese empire in 1910. Japan acquired Formosa 1894, defeated Russia 1905, and joined the Allies 1914. The Allies disappointed her by not supporting her designs on ◊ *China*, a long aggression against which began in 1931 with the invasion of ◊ *Manchuria*. Japan joined the Italo-German ◊ *Axis* in 1936, and in the ◊ *Second World War* attacked U.S.A. in 1941 without declaring war (◊ *Pearl Harbor*). After sweeping initial success, the Japanese were driven back, and eventually succumbed after atom bombs had been dropped on ◊ *Hiroshima* and Nagasaki in 1945. After a U.S. military occupation, Japan was given a new constitution and in 1951 signed a peace treaty with the Allies.

Japanese. Language spoken by over 90 m. Being agglutinative, it was believed to be nearly related to Korean and more remotely to Uralic and East Altaic languages, but Japanese and Korean are now considered to be unrelated to each other or to any other languages. Japanese has no separate form for the plurals of nouns; its verbs have no infinitive forms and they are invariable for person and number. Japanese uses Chinese ideographic characters for the roots of words, and adds phonetic terminations called *kana* (somewhat like writing fifth as 5th); consonants and vowels usually alternate, as in *Fuji-yama* (peerless mountain), *Mi-kado* (majestic door), and all syllables are uttered with equal stress. Many words have been borrowed from Chinese continuously during the past 15 centuries.

Japanese Architecture. Though derived largely from older Chinese architecture, the Japanese developed on different lines and has a character of its own; examples more than 1000 years old still survive. It is characterized mainly by steep-curving roofs (gabled or hipped, or both) with wide projecting eaves. Until recently, buildings were entirely of timber to withstand ◊ *earthquakes*, but the traditional construction has now been largely replaced by concrete structures and styles introduced by the American Frank Lloyd Wright.

Japanese Art. From the 6th cent. A.D. onwards, Japan came under the cultural influence of ◊ *China*, from which it absorbed both ◊ *Buddhism* and the Buddhist aesthetic; among the finest works of this early period are the strongly Buddhistic 8th-cent. Nara sculptures and Horyuji frescoes. China continued to influence Japanese art esp. in the 14th and 15th centuries, when ◊ *landscape painting* shows a clear debt to the art of the Sung period, but Chinese styles were constantly modified in accordance with the Japanese temperament. The tendency to firm draughtsmanship, brilliant and clearly-defined colours, humour, and realism was most fully realized with the invention of colour-printing in 1742 and the 18th- and 19th-cent. development of the popular art of Ukiyo-e, the wood-block print (which had considerable influence on European art in the late 19th cent.) under the masters Outamaro, Hokusai, and Hiroshige. The opening of Japan to the West had a depressing influence on Japanese arts, but since 1945 an important school of non-representational painters, influenced by ◊ *Zen* Buddhism, has grown up.

Japanning. Imitations of oriental ◊ *lacquer*, made from gum-lac, ◊ *shellac*, or seed-lac, produced in Europe since the early 17th cent. and applied to all kinds of wooden, metal, or papiermâché objects esp. household furnishings.

Jasmine. *Jasminum*; a genus of about 200 species, mostly from warm regions in the old world, of which two are hardy in Britain. *J. officinale*, with clusters of very fragrant white flowers in the summer, grows rapidly on sheltered walls. In the East an essential oil is distilled from it. *J. nudiflorum*, winter jasmine, has yellow flowers through the winter and is native in China.

Jason ◊ *Golden Fleece*.

Jaundice ◊ *Hepatitis*.

Jazz. The term began to be used from about 1914 for a type of American popular music originating among the Negroes of New Orleans; it is characterized by simple forms (notably the ◊ *blues*), strong rhythms, syncopations, and improvisation. Such 'serious' composers as Milhaud, Stravinsky, and Weill have made use of it or of its commercial derivatives. Among the most celebrated jazz musicians are Duke Ellington, pianist-composer b. 1899, and Louis Armstrong, trumpeter b. 1900. The term 'modern jazz' has been appropriated for a relaxed ('cool') post-1950 style, harmonically sophisticated and aiming at an intimate 'chamber-music' sonority. ◊ *Dance*.

Jehovah's Witnesses. Protestant fundamentalist (i.e. based on literal inerrancy of the ◊ *Bible*) Christian sect, founded about 1879 in U.S.A. by 'Pastor' C. T. Russell and developed by 'Judge' J. F. Rutherford, spreading widely in Britain, Africa, and elsewhere; they reject all organization, and believe that after an imminent battle – in which Jehovah will overcome Satan – the armies of believers (surviving and also raised from the dead) will live on earth under direct divine rule. Many of them refuse to serve in the armed forces; ardent propagandists, they seek converts by house-to-house visiting. Active membership is estimated at about 600,000.

Jellies ◊ *Jams*.

Jellyfish (Medusa). Jelly-like umbrella-shaped marine coelenterate, with a single internal cavity for the digestion of food and stinging cells (nematocysts) for paralysing prey. Locomotion is generally by strong rhythmic pulsations. The body as a whole is 99 per cent water.

Jena. 1806. Decisive victory of Napoleon over the Prussians, followed immediately by a further battle at Auerstädt, where the French repulsed a large Prussian army, after which Prussia capitulated.

Jericho. In Palestine, 5 m. north of the Dead Sea; site of a succession of towns and cities dated from ◊ *Neolithic* to Muslim times, a span of some 8000 years; the oldest are represented by a mound over 60 ft high excavated in the 20th cent. chiefly by John Garstang (who tried without success to establish a date for the late ◊ *Bronze Age* city destroyed by Joshua) and later by Kathleen Kenyon, who continued Garstang's excavations of the lowest level and found the remains of a Neolithic walled town with a tower 25 ft high. For this level the ◊ *radiocarbon dating* method gave the astonishingly early date of about 7000 B.C.

Jerusalem Artichoke. *Helianthus tuberosus* (◊ *Compositae*) has edible ◊ *tubers* which bear some resemblance to potatoes, but instead of starch they store insulin, a polymer of fructose. ◊ *Sunflower*.

Jesuits ◊ *Society of Jesus*.

Jesus Christ. Founder and chief object of worship of ◊ *Christianity*; about 4 B.C. to A.D. 29. In orthodox Christian belief, an incarnation of God the Son (◊ *Trinity*), born to a Hebrew girl (◊ *Mary*) by the intervention of the ◊ *Holy Ghost*; after living 30 years in obscurity at Nazareth, he preached for about three years in Palestine, performing many miracles, and excited the enmity of the official classes and Jewish priesthood. Betrayed to them by Judas Iscariot, he was tried before Caiaphas the High Priest and Pontius Pilate the Roman Governor; condemned and crucified, he rose from the dead, and after 40 days ascended to heaven. His message was disseminated by the 12 Apostles whom he had converted and instructed. ◊ *Bible, Gospels, Messiah*.

Jet Propulsion. Operates on the principle laid down in Newton's Third Law of Dynamics that action and reaction are equal and opposed so that forward propulsion can be obtained by the thrust

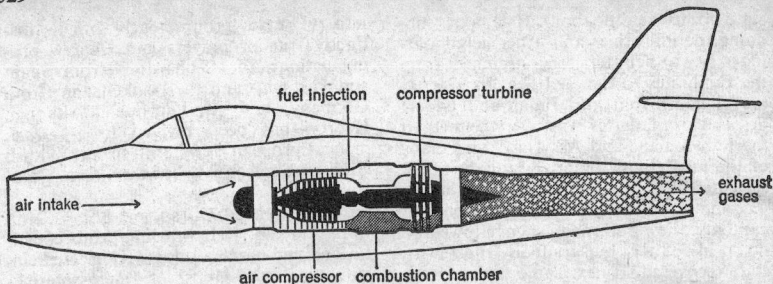

generated by the rearward escape of gases. The principle was indeed utilized in the first steam engine on record, that of Hero of Alexandria A.D. 300. Rocket-flight is also jet propulsion. A further type on which experiment is proceeding is the Ram Jet, suitable only for very high speeds, in which the combustion 'chamber' is simply a pipe. A jet engine is basically a shaped tube open at one end, in which fuel is burnt steadily, creating a forward drive by the reaction effect of the escaping gases. The diagram shows a simple form of such an engine: air is drawn into an air compressor and forced into a combustion chamber into which fuel is injected; the exhaust escapes at great speed from the rear nozzle. The technological problems of devising a practical form of reaction motor for aircraft were formidable. Pioneer work in this field was done after the ◊ First World War both in Germany and Britain, where Whittle patented his design in 1930. The German Heinkel 178, using a Heinkel S-3 jet engine, made its first flight in 1939 and the British Gloster E28/39, with a Whittle W1 engine, in 1941. Such aircraft were not in sufficient production to affect military tactics in the ◊ Second World War, although the V1 German flying bombs were examples of pulse jet propulsion. In the post-war period the application of jet propulsion to civil aircraft went ahead rapidly, both to power propellers (turbo-prop), as in the Britannia, and as a pure jet in the Comet. The supersonic speeds which became possible involve problems of stress and ◊ fatigue of materials. ◊ Aircraft Engines, Rocket.

Jewellery. Objects made of precious materials for personal adornment, produced since prehistoric times; magnificent examples of the 4th millennium B.C. have

been found at Ur (◊ Sumerians), and fine specimens of Egyptian, Greek, Etruscan, Roman, and Celtic jewellery also survive. In the ◊ Renaissance period it became usual for jewellers to enhance a single fine stone or strangely-shaped pearl by devising an elaborate setting for it. One of the last outstanding jewellers was Karl Fabergé, who worked for the Tsar's Court before the 1917 Russian revolution; the finest contemporary examples were produced by the French artist Braque in the 1960s. ◊ Gems.

Jewish Agency. World organization linking the state of ◊ Israel with ◊ Jews in the rest of the world, established under the terms of the League of Nations ◊ Mandate for Palestine. The Agency has extra-territorial rights and is responsible for the absorption of immigrants, land development, and all the problems involved in the cultural and economic progress of Israel in so far as they affect or interest Jewry outside the state.

Jews. The adherents of ◊ Judaism; the term applies both to a specific religion and to a dispersed people, since it includes people who have lapsed from Judaism and also members of other nationalities who have adopted the Jewish faith. The use of the term to connote a distinct 'race' is inaccurate; there are in fact Jews of all 'racial' types. The Jews of Palestine were a group of tribes, closely related to the other Semitic peoples of SW Asia. According to tradition, about 2000 B.C. Abraham led his people from Mesopotamia into Canaan and then into Egypt. The exodus from Egypt under Moses took place about 1445 B.C. and under Joshua the Jews conquered Palestine and divided the territory among their own tribes. Their first king was Saul, whose successors, David and Solomon, brought the Jewish state to its zenith about 1000 B.C., subduing the Philistines and other neighbouring tribes; their territory stretched from the Euphrates to the Red Sea. In 930 B.C. the kingdom split into Judah and Israel; in 721 B.C. the latter was overwhelmed by the Babylonians and Assyrians, and many of the inhabitants deported. Judah was in turn defeated by Nebuchadnezzar in 586 B.C. and again many Jews were taken into captivity. Few returned when allowed to do so in 538 B.C. but gradually the Jewish state recovered. It next came under Greek influence, with the invasion of Alexander the Great, and was ruled by the Egyptian Ptolemies. Many Jews emigrated to Alexandria, North Africa, and Ethiopia. Antiochus III of Syria brought Judea within the Seleucid empire, but it was freed by Judas Maccabeus in 166–160 B.C. and was virtually independent until the capture of Jerusalem by the Romans in 63 B.C. With the destruction of Jerusalem by the Romans in A.D. 70 the dispersion of the Jews began; they came to play an important part in the economic and cultural life of the European countries in which they settled, esp. Spain from the 9th to the 12th cent. Persecution of the Jews in Europe began about the 12th cent. when the General Councils of 1179 and 1215 revived old anti-Jewish legislation, devised by the early Church but almost dormant for several centuries. Ownership of land and many occupations were forbidden to Jews, and they became an almost exclusively urban population, living for the most part in ghettoes and periodically decimated by massacres. They were tacitly permitted to lend money at interest, which was forbidden to Christians. They were expelled from England 1290, from France 1394, from Spain 1492; the German Jews fled to Poland, where for a time they were welcomed. They were re-admitted to England by the Cromwellian Protectorate in the 17th cent. A more liberal attitude began to appear towards the end of the 18th cent. and their presence was tolerated, though in some countries (Russia, Rumania) equal political rights were not granted to them until the 20th cent. Before the ◊ Second World War the world Jewish population was estimated at about 16 m. Of these, at least six million were victims of the Nazi extermination campaign 1933–45 (◊ Genocide, Nazism). European Jews fall

into two main groups, each with its distinctive rite of prayers and Hebrew pronunciation: the Sephardim (from Spain and Portugal) and the Ashkenazim (from Germany and E. Europe). Although Hebrew has been revived in ◊ Israel, many European Jews still speak Yiddish (Jüdisch-Deutsch). ◊ Antisemitism, Zionism.

Jordan. Area 34,750 sq. m. Pop. 1.8 m. Cap. Amman. Rel. Muslim. Arab constitutional monarchy under King Hussein, with an elected House of Representatives (50 members), a nominated Senate, and an Executive Council; bounded by Iraq, Israel, Saudi Arabia, and Syria. Half of the city of Jerusalem lies in Jordan; ◊ Partition.

ECONOMY. Hilly but fertile E. of the Jordan, elsewhere eroded but potentially of agricultural value; there are large-scale irrigation plans esp. the Jordan Valley Plan.

HISTORY. Under Turkish rule till 1918; then under British ◊ mandate (as part of ◊ Palestine) until 1946, when it became independent. In 1958 Jordan and ◊ Iraq formed the Arab Federation, but the Iraqi revolution of the same year ended the union. There are about half a million refugees from ◊ Israel.

Joule. Electrical unit of work, named after the English scientist James Joule 1818–89, who first established the mechanical equivalent of heat: for practical purposes it is reckoned as the work done in one second by a current of one ampere in a resistance of 1 ohm, equal to 10 m. ◊ ergs. ◊ Magnetostriction.

J.P. (Justice of the Peace) ◊ Magistrate.

Judaism. The oldest of the monotheistic religions, from which both ◊ Christianity and ◊ Islam derives; it insists on the absolute unity and transcendence of God, and on the duty of ◊ Jews to witness to it by worship both domestic and congregational and by observing the ethical precepts of the Old Testament (◊ Bible), esp. the laws given to Moses (the Torah) as explained and supplemented by the ◊ Talmud and other authoritative commentaries. The Temple at Jerusalem was destroyed by the Romans A.D. 70; since then the place of worship has been a ◊ synagogue, but the ◊ Passover is held at home. The Jewish rabbis are religious teachers, not priests. In the 18th cent. Moses Mendelssohn began the Reform

Movement, and since that time Jews have been either Orthodox i.e. conservative (chiefly in E. Europe) or Reformed (Non-orthodox); the latter have given up many ceremonial observances e.g. the Saturday sabbath and the ban on eating pork, but observe Passover and practise circumcision. Judaism has a world membership of about 13 m. ◊ *Day of Atonement, Hasidim, Kabbalah, Religious Festivals.*

Judas Tree. *Cercis siliquastrum*; native of Near East and S. Europe, characterized by brilliant magenta flowers borne in bunches on the bare branches and trunk. According to legend it was on a branch of such a tree that Judas Iscariot hanged himself. ◊ *Leguminosae.*

Judges Rules. Rules (approved by the judges of the Queen's Bench Division) for the admissibility in court of statements made to police officers; first made 1912, and revised 1964, they are not strictly law but are normally followed. In brief: when a police officer has evidence affording reasonable suspicion that someone has committed an offence or where a person is charged or informed he may be prosecuted for an offence, before that person is questioned he should first be cautioned that he is not bound to say anything and that anything he says may be given in evidence; if he wishes to make a statement voluntarily, he should nevertheless first be cautioned; any statement made should be written down, and signed by the maker after he has read and corrected it. ◊ *Evidence.*

Judiciary. The whole body of judges and other officials who administer the law. The theory of the separation of powers (enunciated by Montesquieu and incorporated formally in the American Constitution) lays great emphasis upon the complete independence of the judiciary, who must be free from interference either from the legislative or the executive branch of the government, and although in the U.K. there is no written constitutional safeguard the independence of the judiciary is jealously guarded. Judges are appointed by the ◊ *Lord Chancellor*, a member of the Cabinet; those of High Court rank and above may be dismissed only for misconduct and upon an address from both Houses of Parliament, a power which has never been exercised in England or Scotland.

Judo. A sport derived from ju-jitsu, the Japanese art of self-defence; judo wrestlers attempt to obtain limb and body locks which compel surrender in order to avoid injury. Many of these utilize the opponent's own weight and strength, and this is therefore the only form of unarmed combat in which the winner's weight is seldom the deciding factor. The Japanese remain the masters of judo, but there is now an International Federation and a British Judo Association founded 1948. The standard of proficiency is shown by the colour of the belt worn; there are six novice belts (Kyus) and ten grades of Dans, the highest being the black.

Juggernaut (Jagannath). A Hindu god, an incarnation of ◊ *Vishnu*; honoured at Puri in Orissa, where at his yearly festival his image is drawn in a monstrous car pulled by pilgrims and devotees. The belief that many worshippers immolated themselves under the wheels, to be crushed by the god, probably derives from occasional accidents.

Ju-Jitsu ◊ *Judo.*

Julian Date. A date system used in astronomy, which has the day as its only unit. It was introduced 1582 by Joseph Scaliger, as a means of avoiding the uncertainty about dates which might arise from the use of different ◊ *calendar* systems. Julian date (which is quite independent of the Julian calendar) is expressed as the number of days since noon on the arbitrarily chosen 1 January 4713 B.C. Midday on 1 January 1962 was thus Julian day 2,437,666. The Julian Days are tabulated in the yearly *Astronomical Ephemeris.*

Jungle ◊ *Rain Forest.*

Juniper. A group of ◊ *conifers*, evergreen trees and shrubs, some erect, others prostrate, common over the colder parts of the N. Hemisphere. The berry-like cones have a 'bloom' or are coated with resin. The wood is fragrant and durable; that of *Juniperus virginiana*, of eastern N. America, is used for the casing of lead pencils. The berries of the common juniper are used in flavouring ◊ *gin.*

Juno. In Roman mythology, wife of ◊ *Jupiter*, identified with Gr. ◊ *Hera* (in origin a different goddess); guardian of women esp. wives, the Matronalia, her principal festival (1 March) being exclusively for women. Also guardian of finance: the temple of Juno Moneta (>

'money') contained the Roman mint. Originally (unlike Hera) probably a goddess of war, she retained that character.

Jupiter. 1. The largest planet; the fifth from the sun. The solid surface, if any, cannot be seen, but the outer layers of thick cloud show a band structure parallel to the equator. A few marks have appeared and lasted for a considerable time, and one (the Red Spot) is persistent. One theory explains this spot as the outpourings of a volcano; another as a solid island floating in a liquid atmosphere. 'Radio' emission is detectable on a frequency of 14–30 megacycles per second and is polarized, suggesting that the planet has an ionosphere and a magnetic field. Jupiter has twelve moons; the four brightest (Io, Europa, Ganymede, and Callisto) are known as the Galilean Satellites and are visible in a small telescope.

2. < Sanskrit *Dyaus-pitar*, sky-father; in Roman mythology, the principal god later identified with ◊ *Zeus* and given his attributes; husband of ◊ *Juno*. His emblems were the eagle, lightning, the oak-tree, and the colour white; protector of the state, he was honoured in the temple of Jupiter Optimus Maximus ('greatest and best') on the Roman Capitol.

Jurisprudence. The theory of law (as against the content of law itself); concerned to answer the question 'What is law?' and to analyse and compare legal principles and concepts, their relation to other studies, and the consequences, for a legal system, of certain moral, political, or religious premisses.

Jury. A body – usually of 12 persons – sworn to decide questions of fact according to evidence and to accept the judge's directions on matters of law; in English law, a jury's verdict must be unanimous, and if a jury fails to agree it is discharged and the case retried before a fresh jury. Lists of eligible persons are drawn up by local authorities; anyone on a jury list must serve if summoned. Juries are independent of both the executive and the judicial authorities and are free from any interference (even if their verdict apparently contradicts the evidence); it is a serious offence to attempt to bribe or intimidate or influence a juror. In England the jury system developed in the 13th cent. originally from requiring neighbours to declare the truth of a case out of their own knowledge or by popular belief; it has since been adopted in other countries, and in France was included in the Napoleonic Code at Napoleon's own insistence. The present system in England, however, in which jury panels are composed of 'householders', is criticized for excluding large numbers of people esp. married women, and there are proposals to make all voters between 25 and 60 (of a given standard of literacy) liable for jury service. ◊> *Not Proven*.

Justice of the Peace ◊ *Magistrate*.

Jute. The most important vegetable fibre after cotton; obtained from two species of Corchorus or 'gunny', annual herbs found throughout the tropics, growing for about 10 ft unbranched and yielding long, soft, lustrous but not very strong fibres used in manufacturing sacking ('gunny sacks'), bags, brown paper, carpets, linoleum, and twine; main exporter Pakistan. ◊> *Bast*.

Jutes ◊ *Anglo-Saxons*.

Jutland. 1916. Naval battle of the ◊ *First World War*, called by the Germans Skagerrak. The German High Seas Fleet, under Admiral Scheer, unintentionally came into contact with the British Grand Fleet off Jutland Bank. Admiral Jellicoe was unable to force the German battleships into a decisive battle; they eventually withdrew, having inflicted heavier losses than they had received, but the German fleet made no further attempt to challenge the British.

K

Kaaba ◊ *Mecca.*

Kabaka ◊ *Buganda.*

Kabbalah (Cabala). Jewish mystical philosophy (◊ *Judaism*) based on the *Zohar*, probably by Moses of Leon about A.D. 1300; pantheistic in tendency and concerned with the attributes and emanations of God and his relation to angels and to men, it developed into an elaborate number-and-letter symbolism finding hidden significances in almost every letter of the Pentateuch (◊ *Bible*), and though it influenced certain Christian scholars during the ◊ *Renaissance*, it declined into more or less a system of magic. ◊ *Gnostics, Pantheism.*

Kabuki ◊ *Nō.*

Kale. A number of species and varieties of the genus *Brassica*, with predominantly leafy growth; a few e.g. curly kale are used for human consumption, but most are used as green food for stock. *Cruciferae.*

Kalevala. 'The country of the Finns.' The national epic of Finland, assembled in the 19th cent. from ancient folk songs and heroic poems. The first edition, 1835–6, by Elias Lönnrot, contained some 12,000 verses in 32 cantos; a much-expanded second edition appeared in 1849. The Kalevala recounts the adventures of five heroes, of whom the principal is Väinämöinen, the poet and seer.

Kames. Scottish form of 'combs' (i.e. cocks' combs): sand and gravel hills up to 100 ft high formed by material carried by melt water issuing from the edge of an ◊ *ice-sheet* or deposited from the ice during its final waning stage; frequent roughly circular hollows ('kettles') mark where blocks of ice were left stranded, and are now filled with peat bogs or lakes.

Kanarese ◊ *Dravidian Languages.*

Kangaroo. Large herbivorous ◊ *marsupial* indigenous to Australia, the largest eight ft tall; travels rapidly over open ground, propelled by strong hind legs and tail. Wallabies are similar, but smaller. Some live in trees, some in scrub, and others among rocks.

Kantianism. The philosophy of Kant and his followers, combining ◊ *rationalism* and ◊ *empiricism*. Kant's views form a system and are in part a theory of ◊ *knowledge*: (1) Our experience is made up of sense impressions, upon which we impose a certain order; making sense of or organizing impressions by using ideas e.g. space, time, substance, cause, which are not obtained from impressions; (2) such *a priori* ideas make possible an important class of judgements called 'synthetic *a priori*' e.g. 'every event has a cause' which are necessarily true and yet not analytic or true by definition like 'all bachelors are unmarried'; (3) the synthetic *a priori* judgement central to morals is the famous Categorical Imperative that my action is right if it is according to a rule that I could agree should be a universal law.

Kaolin. White or off-white clay, a hydrated silicate of alumina formed by the weathering of the ◊ *felspar* crystal in felspar-rich granite where very hot gases have risen from great depths in the earth's crust; also contains ◊ *mica* and ◊ *quartz* crystals; these are removed from the deposits to produce commercial china clay. Occurs in widely scattered places, a main centre of production being St Austell in Cornwall, and used not only for making pottery but as a filler in cloth and paper manufacture, and in many chemical and pharmaceutical products. ◊ *Silica.*

Kapok. *Ceiba*; large tropical tree bearing capsules containing silky fibres resembling cotton, which have a long unfilled cavity down the centre making them very buoyant. Kapok fibres are used in lifebelts and similar equipment.

Karma. In ◊ *Buddhism* and ◊ *Hinduism*, the law or principle of ethical ◊ *causation*, by which the effects of every human action must be fully worked out in the present or some future existence; applying to groups (families, nations, states) as well as to individuals, it involves the doctrine of ◊ *transmigration* (reincarnation). ◊ *Yoga.*

Karnak. Village in Egypt, on the site of the ancient city of Thebes; the most notable of its many remains is the great Temple of Amon (sister-temple of that at ◊ *Luxor*) built mainly in the 18th Dynasty; standing in extensive grounds where an avenue of ram-headed sphinxes leads to the main gate.

Karst Region. Originally the limestone region of the Dinaric Alps, Yugoslavia; now similar topography elsewhere. Rainwater dissolves the calcium carbonate in the limestone, leaving only insoluble material; the thin soil supports very sparse vegetation in a bare uneven landscape with underground rivers, swallowholes, and caves. In the Yugoslavian karst region are the famous Postojna caves with their ◊ *stalactites* and stalagmites. Other European karst regions are the French Causses du Quercy, the Jura, and to a lesser extent the Pennines in Britain.

Kashmir. Officially Jammu and Kashmir. Area 81,000 sq. m. Pop. 4 m. Cap. Srinagar. Rel. mainly Muslim. A mountainous country, in the far N. of ◊ *India* at the foot of the Karakorum Mts. On the partition of India in 1947 the Hindu ruler opposed ◊ *Pakistan* troops, and recognized Indian suzerainty. The dispute was referred to the U.N. who recommended a plebiscite to determine whether Kashmir should adhere to India or to Pakistan, a procedure stubbornly refused by India. Economic as well as political interests were involved, as water from the Indus ◊ *catchment area* in Kashmir is vital to the W. Pakistan economy. The E. Punjab (Indian) Government laid exclusive claim to the rivers, while Pakistan maintained that by ◊ *international law* she had an equal right in their control. Mediation by the ◊ *International Bank* has largely solved the economic difficulty, but the political difference between Pakistan and India remains intractable.

Katanga ◊ *Congolese Republic.*

Kellogg Pact. 1928. Declaration inspired by the U.S. Secretary of State Frank B. Kellogg, first signed by U.S.A. and France, whereby signatories renounced war as a method of settling international disputes; it was later signed by 59 other countries. In practice its effect was nil.

Kennelly Layer ◊ *Heaviside Layer.*

Kenya. Area 224,960 sq. m. (5224 sq. m. of which are water). Pop. 8.6 m. (inc. 67,000 Europeans). Cap. Nairobi. Independent republic in E. Africa, a member of the ◊ *British Commonwealth.*

ECONOMY. Mainly agricultural, though industries are being developed esp. mining e.g. copper, diatomite, gold, salt, and production in general is increasing. Main exports are coffee, tea, sisal, pyrethrum, leather, tinned meats. Cotton, fruits, and cereals are also widely cultivated. There is a considerable Asian community, mainly Indian, as well as African (◊ *Masai*) and European.

HISTORY. A British protectorate was declared in 1895. In 1920, E. Africa was formally annexed as Kenya Colony. Political activity began among the ◊ *Kikuyu* in the 1940s; in 1951 the leader of the Kenya African Union, Jomo Kenyatta, demanded African representation and remedies for the land grievances of the Kikuyu. The latter formed a terrorist organization, the ◊ *Mau Mau,* which operated with great atrocity 1952–60; Kenyatta was imprisoned and the K.A.U. banned. By 1960 most of the leaders had been released, and despite the fears of the 67,000 European settlers, an African majority in the Legislative Council was granted. At elections held in 1961 the Kenya African National Union won a majority in the Council, and later in the year Kenyatta was released. Despite personal rivalries, the political leaders were united in pressing for independence, and at conferences in 1962 a new constitution for an independent Kenya was worked out; it was promulgated in April 1963, and at elections later in the year K.A.N.U. won 67 of the 112 seats and Kenyatta was designated P.M. Full independence was established later in the same year.

LANGUAGE. Swahili; also other African dialects.

Kepler's Law ◊ *Astronomy, Orbit.*

Keratin. The ◊ *protein* constituent of structural tissues such as ◊ *hair,* nails, horn, ◊ *wool,* the quill of feathers; it has a high sulphur content and is resistant to chemicals and ◊ *enzymes* that normally break down other proteins.

Ketones. A class of neutral organic compounds having the general formula RCOR′, where R and R′ may be the same or different groups of ◊ *aliphatic* or aromatic type. They are of generally agreeable odour, and some more complex ones e.g. civet and ◊ *musk* are used as perfumery materials; ◊ *camphor* is a ketonic substance. The simplest and best-known ketone is the volatile inflammable liquid acetone, a versatile solvent esp. useful in the manufacture of ◊ *explosives.* synthetic fibres, and ◊ *lacquers.* The important plastic 'perspex' (which might be described as an 'organic glass') is made from acetone, large quantities of which are now manufactured from propylene (◊ Olefines).

Keyboard Instruments. Keyboards allowing a choice of notes to be sounded, at a prearranged pitch, by the pressure of the fingers (or the feet) are used in three types of instrument, using wind, strings, and electronics. The historic organ or pipe-organ, developed from the Greek and Roman *hydraulus* or water-organ, has been chiefly used in Western Christian liturgies since the 8th cent. Wind is supplied to various sets of pipes, either by manual action or in modern organs mechanically, and by drawing a 'stop' the player selects the set of pipes and thus the tone he wishes. By the 15th cent. the organ had developed its standard equipment of two or more manual keyboards, a pedal keyboard, and a variety of stops; later enlargements and structural changes reflected mechanical advances and changes of aesthetic taste. J. S. Bach is regarded as the chief composer for the organ.

Of keyboard stringed instruments, the harpsichord normally has two manual keyboards (occasionally also a pedal keyboard) which sound the strings by a plucking mechanism; it and its smaller version the spinet were in prominent use 1500–1800 and has been latterly revived. The Elizabethan virginals are a small single-keyboard instrument of the same type. The clavichord of about the same time has a different action: its single keyboard actuates metal strikers which hit (not pluck) the strings and remain in contact with them. On the pianoforte, invented in the early 18th cent., the strings are hit by hammers which then rebound; favoured by such composers as Beethoven and Chopin, in the 19th cent. it became the 'universal' instrument of music.

In the 20th cent. it has become possible to synthesize musical tone electronically and to control the results by a keyboard. In particular the 'electronic organ' e.g. the Hammond Organ, invented 1934 in U.S.A., could approximately imitate the pipe-organ and was cheaper and more compact.

Keynes. *The General Theory of Employment, Interest, and Money* 1936, by J. M. Keynes 1883–1946, revolutionized economic theory. Although by the 20th cent. it was clear that the economic system was unstable, classic economics had furnished no satisfactory theory to explain this, and Keynes's exposition of the relationship between savings and investment propounded an answer. The classical economists had not envisaged that savings might disturb economic stability; in the days of Adam Smith (◊ *Laissez-faire*), the men who saved and the men who put those savings to use had been by and large the same: the capitalists themselves saved, and their savings went back into factory operation. But saving and investing gradually became divorced from one another, and the separation between the decision to save and the decision to invest introduced a new element. The economy is maintained by a flow of incomes which are spent in exchange for goods and become the incomes of their producers, and so on (◊ *National Income*); most people spend the bulk of their incomes on consumer goods, the producers of these goods in turn do the same, and so the wheel goes round. But any money saved is taken out of this flow, and only comes back in if these savings are borrowed by Government or business and spent. If the two sets of decisions to save and to invest are out of joint, and if businesses invest less than the community saves, the flow of income is reduced and the economy swings into a ◊ *depression*. This was the basis of the Keynesian analysis, from which the conclusion was drawn that if private investment spending is inadequate, governments should take action to supplement it. By acting accordingly, and by closer control over their economies, governments in the big industrial-capitalist countries have avoided slumps like that of the 1930s, and instability, the great defect of capitalism, has come under control. ◊ *Trade Cycle, Inflation.*

Khamsin. Hot S. wind in Egypt; < Ar. for 50, said to last 50 days April–June, blowing ahead of depressions moving E. along the Mediterranean or across N. Africa; often carries dust from the interior like the ◊ *sirocco*. In the E. Mediterranean, any hot dry wind blowing from the desert.

Khartoum (1885) ◊ *Mahdi*.

Khmer ◊ *Angkor, Thailand (History).*

Kidneys. Two excretory organs present in all mammals, situated in the abdomen, behind the peritoneum; they filter waste products from the blood, concentrate them as urine in the tubules, and pass this fluid via the ureters to the urinary bladder. At least one kidney must function to maintain life. ⟡ *Excretion, Lupus, Prostate.*

Kieselguhr ⟡ *Diatoms.*

Kikuyu. Bantu-speaking people of central Kenya, numbering some 1.25 m. Traditionally peasant farmers living in the high forested region south of Mount Kenya, they had no chiefs, their government being based on councils of elders. They have suffered much overcrowding and land pressure, with some loss of land to Europeans, and today about a quarter of the population live outside the tribal boundaries, mainly in Nairobi and as squatters on European farms. Dissatisfaction grew, especially amongst the younger men, and led to the ⟡ *Mau Mau* movement. Today the Kikuyu are still expanding and threatening to move into the tribal lands of other peoples, who much resent their superior political position in independent Kenya. ⟡ *Masai.*

Kinetic Energy ⟡ *Energy.*

Kinship. Recognition of common ancestry between two or more persons; among primitive peoples it is recognized over many generations and may be the basis for rights in land and property; usually either the paternal or the maternal line of descent is the more important. All the men of a man's own generation may be known as his 'brothers' and those of the preceding generation as his 'fathers', and rights and obligations be recognized accordingly. In industrial societies its importance outside the immediate family is minimal and does not usually extend beyond two or three generations.

Kite. Earliest form of artificial winged flight, used by many pioneers in the development of man-carrying aircraft. The Australian Hargrave devised the box-kite, used in Britain to lift a man 100 ft from the ground. It was thus a stepping-stone to the ⟡ *glider* which in turn led to powered aircraft. In a kite, the tethering line is the substitute for engine power, giving the kite its air speed relative to the natural wind. Kite-flying was a traditional sport in China and Japan, and Benjamin Franklin used a kite in his famous experiment for collecting electricity from a thundercloud.

Knights of St John ⟡ *Orders of Chivalry.*

Knossos. Palace and chief city of the ⟡ *Minoan civilization* in Crete; the site was occupied long before the first palace was built about 2000 B.C. The palace was several times destroyed by earthquakes before being sacked and burned by ⟡ *Achaean* invaders from the Greek mainland about 1400 B.C. (or possibly somewhat later). Knossos continued to flourish as an important Greek city, however, until the 4th cent. A.D. Sir Arthur Evans began to excavate and partially reconstruct the palace 1900; he revealed a throne room and a complex system of apartments, bathrooms, and storehouses, many of them decorated with vivid and lively frescoes of birds, animals, plants, and sporting scenes.

Knot. Nautical mile per hour; the unit of speed commonly used at sea and in aviation. A nautical mile technically is one 60th of a degree of latitude, and thus subject to variation. In practice, it is reckoned at 6080 ft, which is the distance adopted by the British Admiralty as the sea mile for speed trials.

Knowledge. The theory of knowledge, or epistemology, is that large part of philosophy which tries to explain the nature of human knowledge, to find its limitations, and to assess claims to knowledge, notably those based on sense experience. Partly because our senses may deceive us, ordinary beliefs based on sense experience do not have that certainty of logical and mathematical conclusions so long revered in philosophy as the mark of true knowledge; in ⟡ *Platonism* and ⟡ *Rationalism* this fact led to the disparagement of empirical belief and to claims that some kinds of *a priori* knowledge of the world are possible, while ⟡ *Empiricism* takes roughly the opposite position, and ⟡ *Kantianism* attempts the middle road that knowledge results from our imposing *a priori* concepts or organization on our sense experience. Contemporary theory of knowledge is on the whole empiricist and more concerned with specific problems e.g. the analysis of perception, memory, judgement, and truth. As for what it is to know something, older accounts having to do with special states of mind or with acts of knowing, and their objects, have given way to accounts sometimes based on what we actually mean when we say that someone knows something e.g. that he has the right to be sure of it.

Koala. Bear-like climbing ⟡ *marsupial,* native to Australia, living in eucalyptus trees; feeds on young green shoots, which are stored in cheek pouches. Koalas are two ft long, with ash-grey fur; threatened with extinction by over-hunting, they are now protected and may not be taken out of Australia.

Koh-i-nor. < Persian, 'mountain of light'; a large diamond first mentioned in the 14th cent. It was owned for a long time by the Great Mogul, and was acquired by the Persians but subsequently returned to India. After the annexation of the Punjab it became a British ◊ *Crown jewel.*

Kola ◊ *Cola.*

Kon Tiki. A raft of balsa logs, bound together with rope, on which the Norwegian Thor Heyerdahl and five companions set out from Peru 1947 hoping to show that the Pacific islands could have been colonized from S. America; they left from Callao and 100 days later drifted ashore in the Tuamoto Archipelago. (◊ *Easter Island.*)

Koran (Q'ran). Sacred book of the Muslims, written in ◊ *Arabic* in 114 *suras* (sections). While it echoes themes from the Old Testament (◊ *Bible*), the ◊ *Talmud,* and the ◊ *Apocrypha,* it possesses a quality wholly its own; its theological and legal teaching forms the basis of the religion of ◊ *Islam,* it is well suited to recitation, and its rhythmic language is considered a model of Arabic style and has greatly influenced the development of Arabic language and literature. The text, believed by Muslims to have been transmitted by God to Mohammed through the angel Gabriel, was revised and standardized by order of the Caliph Othman in the 7th cent. and all variant texts were destroyed.

Korea. Area 85,256 sq. m. Pop. 36 m. Cap. Seoul (S.) and Pyongyang (N.). A peninsula in NE Asia, bordering on China and U.S.S.R. At the end of the ◊ *Second World War* its promised independence from ◊ *Japan* took the form of partition into two states with the 38th parallel as frontier, N. Korea in the communist bloc and S. Korea under western influence. The latter, with area 37,426 sq. m. and pop. 26.3 m., is recognized by most nations outside the communist bloc.

ECONOMY. N. Korea is the chief supplier of ginseng, a medicinal root much used in China, and has deposits of coal, copper, gold, graphite, iron and tungsten. S. Korea exports anthracite, fish products, graphite, iron ores, rice, seaweed products, soya beans, raw silk, and tungsten, all mainly to Japan. In general there is a high level of literacy and of industrial development.

HISTORY. An ancient land with a distinct people, language, and culture, Korea has repeatedly been overrun by Chinese, Mongols, and Japanese. Invasions and internal rivalry between native ◊ *Shamanism* and foreign ◊ *Buddhism* and ◊ *Confucianism* left Korea unstable, but a native dynasty ruled from 1392 till 1910. From the early 17th cent. Korea came nominally under Chinese sovereignty, until it was declared independent after the 1894 Sino-Japanese war; Japanese penetration rapidly increased, and Korea was annexed by Japan in 1910, to be partitioned in 1945 after Japan's defeat. In 1950, after many border incidents, the N. Koreans invaded S. Korea, and had advanced to Pusan before a mainly American and British U.N.O. force drove them back to the Chinese border, after which a force of 200,000 Chinese volunteers reversed the tide and with the N. Korean forces occupied Seoul. A U.N.O. counteroffensive in 1951 made the front static along the partition frontier, and an armistice was signed in 1953. In 1960 Syngman Rhee, the president of S. Korea, had to resign. A more democratic government was elected and N. Korea proposed reunification, which S. Korea refused unless free elections were first held throughout Korea, a proposal which was rejected.

LANGUAGE. Korean; an agglutinative language, unrelated to any other. Its history before the 1446 invention of the Unmun alphabet is unknown. Much of the vocabulary is of Chinese derivation.

Kraken. In Norwegian legend, a monster haunting the northern seas, $1\frac{1}{2}$ m. in girth, with arms able to grapple the largest ships, creating dangerous whirlpools when it submerges. The legend (first recorded in the mid 18th cent. by Bishop Pontoppidan) may derive from the exceptionally large squids sometimes seen in these waters.

Kremlin. < Russian *kreml,* citadel; esp. that of Moscow, the historic centre from which the city grew, and the only part of old Moscow to have escaped the fires which have at various times (e.g. in Napoleon's 1812 invasion) destroyed the city. The Moscow Kremlin contains former Imperial palaces (now museums) and the splendid golden-domed 15th- and

16th-cent. cathedrals of the Assumption and the Annunciation; it is the seat of the U.S.S.R. Supreme Soviet.

Krishna. Hindu god of fire and light, eighth incarnation of ◊ *Vishnu*; one of the greatest objects of devotion in ◊ *Hinduism*. The name ('black') may indicate that the Indo-European invaders adopted his cult from the darker indigenous races. In legend, Krishna is a brave, beautiful, crafty youth brought up among cowherds to save him from relatives seeking his death; many stories describe his amours with the milkmaids. His exploits appear in the ◊ *Mahabharata,* and he figures in the Bhagavad Gita (◊ *Yoga*) as a god of salvation or indeed as the supreme deity.

Krypton ◊ *Inert Gases.*

Ku Klux Klan. Two U.S.A. southern-state ◊ *secret societies*; the first was organized 1865 in Tennessee by ex-Confederates after their defeat in the ◊ *American Civil War*, to maintain white supremacy, but was disbanded by its founder 1869, though locally it survived for many years. It was revived in Georgia 1915 as an organization not only anti-Negro but somewhat anti-Semitic and strongly anti-Catholic, closely resembling the 19th-cent. 'Know-nothing' secret societies. This second KKK was professionally promoted, spread rapidly in the southern and in some northern States, and in some – esp. Texas, Oklahoma, Indiana, Oregon, Maine – dominated politics even to controlling the election of many State officials and Congressmen. Its membership was estimated at 5 m. but during the 1930s it declined, though in some southern States it still exists as an active opponent of racial integration (◊ *Race Relations*).

Kulturkampf. A struggle between the Roman Catholic Church and the State in 19th-cent. Germany, instigated by Bismarck, who disliked and distrusted church influence in politics. The Jesuits were expelled in 1872, and the May Laws of 1873 aimed at controlling Church schools and seminaries, but in 1887 Bismarck reached a *modus vivendi* (◊ *Concordat*) with Pope Leo XIII, which left the church substantial control over its seminaries and schools.

Kuomintang. Chinese nationalist party, successor of the 1911 Revolutionary Alliance, founded by Sun Yat-sen in 1912.

Having taken part in the first Chinese revolution of 1911, it gradually gained political ascendancy. It was strongly under the influence of its communist left wing 1923–7, but Sun Yat-sen's successor Chiang Kai-shek broke with the communists; civil war between the two factions followed, but was suspended when both were engaged in China's defence against the Japanese invasions 1937–45. During the ◊ *Second World War* the Chiang Kai-shek wing received massive aid from U.S.A. and became the major anti-Japanese force; but when the civil war was resumed the communists defeated the nationalists in 1948, and Chiang Kai-shek withdrew to the island of Taiwan (◊ *Formosa*), where he set up the Chinese Nationalist Government. The reactionary right wing of the Kuomintang remained dominant; the Formosa regime has been criticized for inefficiency and corruption, and for not implementing its programme of social welfare and political democracy. It claims to be the legitimate government of all China, is so recognized by U.S.A. and some other countries, and is a member of U.N.O. and one of the five permanent members of the U.N. Security Council, although not recognized by Britain, which in 1949 gave recognition to the communist government of mainland China. France, having previously recognized only the Formosa regime, in 1964 extended the recognition to the mainland government also, and then withdrew recognition from Formosa.

Kurds. A small ethnic and linguistic minority numbering about 1.5 m. living in the mountainous border areas of Turkey, ◊ *Iraq*, Iran (◊ *Persia*), and U.S.S.R. For centuries they have resisted assimilation, whether by Arabs, Turks, Persians, or Russians, but have never succeeded in obtaining independence. They came nearest to success in 1919, but discussions were protracted and a revolt in 1925 was severely repressed by the Turks. Their religion is Shiite Muslim; it was in Kurdistan that the ◊ *Assassins* once held sway. In Iraq the Kurdish leader Barzani called for autonomy in 1962; a year later he led a full-scale revolt against the Iraq Government, which in 1963 granted the Iraqi Kurds quasi autonomous status. Fighting broke out again in 1964, the Kurds demanding complete autonomy.

Kuwait ◊ *Gulf Sheikhdoms.*

L

Labiatae. Mint family; a large widely distributed family esp. common in Mediterranean countries. Most are herbs, of which mint is typical, and many are strongly aromatic: the flowers are basically tubular, with a protruding lip. The family is important for the production of aromatic ◊ *essential oils* for flavouring and perfumes, as pot-herbs, and as ornamental plants. Well known are ◊ *lavender*, mint, sage, rosemary, thyme, bergamot, marjoram, basil, savory, balm. Common British wild species include deadnettles, woundworts, bugle, horehound, betony, and ground ivy.

Labour Day. The U.S.A. and Canadian workingman's holiday, the first Monday in September, started 1882 by the Knights of Labour; it became a national holiday 1894.

Labour Party. British political party, broadly committed to the principles of ◊ *socialism*. The first Labour M.P. was Keir Hardie, elected 1892; the first step towards an organization was the Labour Representation Committee, formed in 1900, which became known as the Labour Party in 1906. The party is headed by the leader of the Parliamentary Labour Party, who is also chairman of the National Executive, the governing body within the party, which is elected at an annual conference made up of two main groups of delegates, those of the constituency parties (i.e. the local Labour Party branches throughout the country) and those of the ◊ *trade unions*. The conference can lay down the broad lines of party policy. The financial backing of the party comes mainly from the trade unions, who raise a political levy from those of their members who do not 'contract out'.

In 1922 the Labour Party displaced the Liberals as the second major British party; in 1924 under Ramsay MacDonald it formed its first (and minority) government, which lasted a few months only. In 1929 a second (minority) Labour government was formed, which in 1931 collapsed in the face of mounting economic difficulties and gave way to a National Government, i.e. a coalition with the Conservative Party, in which MacDonald and other Labour leaders joined, Labour representation being enormously reduced by their defection. After the war, Labour won a decisive majority in 1945, and under the leadership of Clement Attlee was in office till 1951, during which time it introduced the National Health Service and nationalized the coal, steel, gas, electricity, and transport services. In 1950, its majority fell to six, and it lost the elections of 1951, 1955, and 1959. It returned to power in Oct. 1964 with an overall majority of five. ◊ *United Kingdom.*

The Labour Party policy aims at levelling-out economic and financial privilege and providing better educational opportunities and improved health and welfare services within a planned national economy. An attempt by Hugh Gaitskell, the leader 1955–62, to remove from the party programme the specific provision to work for these ends by way of nationalization of industry was rejected; but under his guidance the party steadily gained in strength and unity of purpose until his untimely death early in 1963; the leadership then passed to Harold Wilson, who became Prime Minister in 1964. ◊ *Fabian Society, Independent Labour Party.*

Laburnum ◊ *Leguminosae.*

Lace. An openwork fabric, usually of linen, silk, or cotton, wrought in decorative patterns; the chief kinds are needlepoint lace and bobbin lace. Loosely-woven network headdresses were produced in Coptic Egypt, and openwork trimmings of metallic thread were applied to clothes in the Middle Ages, but true lace was probably invented in the 15th cent. either in Flanders or in Italy; by the 17th cent. Venice was producing the finest of needlepoint lace and Flanders was noted for its exquisite bobbin lace. By this time lace had become an essential part of both male and female costume, and it was produced in most European countries. In France the lace industry was greatly encouraged in the 17th and early 18th centuries by Louis XIV and his minister Colbert, but the Flemish lace-makers esp. those of Valenciennes were regarded as the most expert. By the end of the 18th cent. machine-made lace had appeared; it developed rapidly, superseding the hand-made variety. Nottingham has long been a centre of the English lace-making industry.

Lacquer. An opaque, glossy, waterproof varnish, made from the resin of the *Rhus vernicifera* tree; applied in numerous coats to wooden objects esp. furniture, and used in China since about the 4th cent. B.C. and in Japan since the 3rd cent. A.D. Since the 17th cent. oriental lacquer has been much prized by Europeans, who have attempted to imitate it in ◊ *japanning*, with gum-lac, seed-lac, and ◊ *shellac*.

Lacrosse. In Britain, a 12-a-side team game (10 in Canada and U.S.A.) in which the object is to score with a 4½ or 5-oz. rubber ball through goals 6 ft square on a pitch 90–110 yds long. The ball is propelled and carried with a crosse (a curved stick with woven strings). There are many variants in the rules, particularly as between men's lacrosse and women's. Derived from an American Indian game, it was brought to Britain from Canada (where it is a major sport) in 1867 and is now widespread in British girls' schools.

Lactic Acid. Results from the ◊ *fermentation* of sugar under controlled conditions, using a suitable lactobacillus; also a product of sugar ◊ *metabolism* in the body, it accumulates in muscle during exercise, since conversion of glycogen to lactic acid is the means of releasing the chemical energy used in muscular contraction. The lactic acid extracted from muscle, and that from sugar fermentation, differ in their effect on plane-polarized light; these were early examples of optical isomers which (with others) led to the recognition of the importance of the spatial arrangement of the atoms in a molecule. ◊ *Isomerism*.

Lactoflavin ◊ *Vitamins (B₂)*.

Lactose. Sugar of milk; a colourless crystalline solid, a by-product of cheese manufacture. It has the same molecular formula as ordinary cane sugar (sucrose) $C_{12}H_{22}O_{11}$ but is less sweet. ◊ *Carbohydrates*.

Ladysmith ◊ *Boer War*.

Lager ◊ *Brewing*.

Laissez-faire. Theory developed in the 18th cent. that the regulation of commerce hampered rather than promoted prosperity; a reaction against ◊ *mercantilism*. The greatest British exponent was Adam Smith. It holds that the natural economic order, undisturbed by regulations, will make for the greatest good of the greatest number (◊ *Enlightenment*, *Physiocrats*): Bentham and John Stuart Mill erected it into the philosophy of ◊ *utilitarianism*; Richard Cobden and John Bright popularized the doctrines and gave it political expression in the anti-Corn-Law agitation (◊ *Free Trade*). The doctrine appealed to the factory owners and merchants of the ◊ *Industrial Revolution*, who found themselves hampered by out-of-date restrictions, and what had started as a radical belief became the orthodoxy of the late Victorian era, enshrined in the teachings of the classic Manchester school of economics. Since the early 20th cent. it has been increasingly recognized that state intervention in economic affairs is necessary; governments in capitalist economies have intervened in e.g. the regulation of working conditions, distribution of income, prevention of unemployment and the promotion of a high rate of economic growth. Most economies in the western world are now 'mixed' i.e. partly laissez-faire and partly subject to government regulation and control.

Lake. Sheet of water occupying a depression in the earth's surface and surrounded by land; called a 'sea' if exceptionally large, and a pond (pool, tarn) if very small. Some lakes e.g. Lake Nyasa and Lake Tanganyika, in the African part of the Great ◊ *Rift Valley*, occupy depressions formed by earth movements; others e.g. in the Alps occupy depressions formed by glacial erosion, by e.g. landslides or moraines damming up rivers, or form in the craters of extinct volcanoes. The amount of water entering a lake exceeds that lost by evaporation, and (given an outflow) the water remains fresh. In a region of low rainfall and great evaporation, if there is no outflow the lake forms an inland drainage area; the salts carried down by the inflowing rivers accumulate, and the lake becomes salt, e.g. the Dead Sea, the Great Salt Lake in U.S.A. Other lakes e.g. the Caspian Sea are salt because they were once part of the ocean. Where rainfall is seasonal a lake's area may considerably decrease in the dry season, e.g. Lake Chad (Africa), or during a long drought may dry up entirely, leaving a deposit of salt, e.g. Lake Eyre (S. Australia). The Caspian Sea (169,300 sq. m.) is the largest lake; Lake Superior (31,800 sq. m.) is the largest freshwater lake. Lake Titicaca (3200 sq. m.) between Bolivia and Peru is the highest, 12,500 ft above sea level. The Dead Sea in Israel is 1290 ft below sea level.

Lake Poets. Contemporary reviewers of the 'new poetry' of Wordsworth, Coleridge, and Southey (who all had some local associations with the English Lake District) called them the 'Lake poets' in derision; the term was also and even more misleadingly applied to some of their friends e.g. Lamb, but the poets thus labelled have little in common, and only Wordsworth could meaningfully be called a 'lake' poet. Reviewing Southey's *Thalaba* in the ◊ *Edinburgh Review* Oct. 1802, Francis Jeffrey spoke of the new 'sect' as being distinguished by affected simplicity and rusticity; in 1814 he referred to the 'Lakers', and the term was expanded in the *Edinburgh Review* Aug. 1817.

Lallans. < Dialectal 'lawlands' i.e. lowlands; the historic speech of the Scottish lowland counties, deriving mainly from the Northumbrian dialect of Old English (Anglo-Saxon). Also (as Middle Scots) the notable literature in it A.D. 1450–1630. A movement to recreate and enlarge the literary vocabulary of Lallans was begun 1940 by Hugh MacDiarmid and others.

Lamaism ◊ *Buddhism, Dalai Lama, Tibet.*

Lamarckism ◊ *Acquired Characteristics, Evolution, Natural Selection.*

Lambeth Conference. Assembly of bishops of the Anglican Church from all parts of the world, held periodically at Lambeth Palace, London (seat of the Archbishop of Canterbury, who presides). The first was held 1867, the most recent, attended by 310 bishops, 1958. A Lambeth Conference does not establish doctrine, but its resolutions are of weight as expressing the general views of the Anglican communion. ◊ *Anglicanism, Church Assembly, Encyclical.*

Lamp ◊ *Electricity, Gas.*

Lampreys. Eel-like animals not closely related to eels or other fishes, thought to be the relatively unmodified descendants of the earliest known true vertebrates.

Lancelot. Principal figure in the ◊ *Arthurian-legend* cycle; father of ◊ *Galahad*. Stolen from his parents as a child by Vivien (the 'lady of the lake') and hence surnamed 'of the Lake', and taken to King Arthur on reaching manhood, he took part in the quest for the ◊ *Holy Grail* but could only glimpse it from afar, because of his guilty love for Arthur's wife Queen Guinevere; this love, which caused Guinevere to enter a convent and Lancelot to become a religious recluse, ultimately led to the death of Arthur and the end of the Round Table company.

Land League. Irish tenants-defence organization founded in 1879 which organized rent strikes, the ◊ *boycott*, resistance to eviction, and assaults upon absentee landlords' agents. When Parnell was its President he obtained remission of rents and called off physical violence, and the 1881 Land Act at last gave Ireland a fair-rent tribunal. The League disbanded in 1890.

Landscape Gardening. Planning the landscape surrounding a house, to provide 'natural' walks and vistas, as distinct from laying out formal enclosed gardens; the practice developed in 18th-cent. England, where first William Kent and then 'Capability' Brown, Humphrey Repton, and others created what came to be known abroad as the 'English garden' i.e. a landscape essentially natural but skilfully managed so as to provide a pleasing effect. The magnificent grounds of Blenheim, Stowe, Longleat, Wilton, and Chatsworth are evidence of the landscape gardeners' success, and can rightly be regarded as works of art. In the 19th cent. there was a reaction towards more formal gardening, but the tendency of modern architects to integrate buildings into natural surroundings may be the sign of a revival.

Landscape Painting. Though popular for the decoration of rooms in Roman times, naturalistic landscapes are seldom found in European art until the 14th cent. During this and the next two centuries, landscapes (usually imaginary) often appeared in the backgrounds of pictures, but in Italy and France they were thought unsuitable subjects for pictures, even as late as the 17th cent. Great landscape painters e.g. Claude, Poussin usually added mythological or religious figures to their landscapes; but in ◊ *Dutch* and ◊ *Flemish art*, 17th-cent. artists esp. Rubens, Rembrandt, Hobbema, J. van Ruisdael began to paint identifiable landscape for its own sake. The second great period of landscape painting was in the 19th cent. with Constable and Turner in England and Corot, Courbet, Monet, Van Gogh, and Cézanne in France. In China landscape painting was a popular form of art from the 8th cent. onwards; many of the finest Chinese paintings being of impressionistic mountain scenes. Landscape painting has not in general engaged the attention of the most important 20th-cent. painters (unless the dream landscapes of e.g. ◊ *surrealists* like Dali or the semi-abstract landscapes of Paul Klee are included); Kokoschka and Vlaminck, and in England Paul Nash and Ivon Hitchens are notable exceptions.

Language. System of speech communication; every human community, however primitive, has language, and the theory of a single place of origin is now abandoned. Languages have close associations, but do not necessarily coincide with race, nationality, religion, and culture. The more primitive the culture the more complicated are the devices for exact definition: primitive languages have very elaborate case-endings and verbal forms, and the ability to formulate generalized concepts is still undeveloped. Probably the earliest recorded language is preserved in the ◊ *cuneiform* inscriptions at Uruk (Erech) in the lower Euphrates valley, dating to about 3000 B.C. These are in ◊ *Sumerian*, which died out about 300 B.C. It is estimated that about 2800 languages are still in use among the world's 3000 m. inhabitants; many belong to the Indo-European languages and the Sino-Tibetan languages, but the 'language-family' concept is applicable only to a few main groups; e.g. ◊ *Basque* and ◊ *Burushaski* on a small scale, and ◊ *Japanese* and Korean on a larger, are unrelated to any other known languages. Besides these, and the ◊ *Indo-European* and Sino-Tibetan languages, there are in the Old World the ◊ *Hamito-Semitic*, the Ural-Altaic, the ◊ *Caucasian*, the ◊ *Dravidian*, the south-Asian, the ◊ *Malayo*, and Polynesian; in Africa south of the Sahara there are Bantu, Khoin, and Sudanese-Guinean; in N. and S. America ('the philologist's happiest hunting ground') there are aboriginal ◊ *American Indian* languages. Only 13 languages are each spoken by more than 50 m. In numerical order these are Chinese, English, Hindustani (i.e. Hindi and Urdu), Russian, Spanish, German, Japanese, French, Malay, Bengali, Italian, Portuguese, Arabic. Only about 50 languages have notable literatures. ◊▷ *African Languages.*

Lanthanides. The fifteen metallic ◊ *elements* (formerly called the 'rare-earth' elements) of atomic nos. 57–71 inclusive: lanthanum, cerium, praseodymium, neodymium, promethium (artificially produced by nuclear reaction), samarium, europium, gadolinium, terbium, dysprosium, holmium, erbium, thulium, ytterbium, lutetium. They constitute the first inner-transition series of the Periodic Classification (◊ *Actinides*); their outer electronic configuration is very similar, and the elements change (in the order given) by the filling of the 4f shell electrons. They show a dominant valency state of 3, except cerium, which has compounds of Ce^{3+} and Ce^{+4}. The elements occur in the minerals cerite and monazite, are similar in chemical properties, and were difficult to separate before ion-exchange and solvent extraction methods became available. The readily-oxidized metals are used as 'flints'; their oxides are used as pigments in decorating porcelain; others are ingredients of certain oxide catalysts. 'Didymium' was once thought to be a rare-earth element but was eventually proved to be a mixture of praseodymium and neodymium.

Lanthanum ◊ *Lanthanides.*

Laocoon. In classical mythology, a Trojan hero, a priest of ◊ *Apollo*; while he was sacrificing to ◊ *Neptune*, two large serpents came from the sea, attacked his two sons, and crushed him to death when he attempted rescue, this being his punishment for having tried to persuade the Trojans not to admit the wooden horse. The Vatican Museum sculpture of Laocoon in the coils of the serpents gave Lessing the title for his work on poetry and painting.

Laos. Area 90,000 sq. m. Pop. about 2.5 m. Cap. Luang Prabang (royal cap.) and Vientiane. Independent kingdom in NW ◊ *Indo-China*, bordered by China, Vietnam, Cambodia, Thailand, and Burma; formerly part of the French Union. Since 1962 Laos has been governed by an uneasy coalition of the 'three princes' under Prince Souvanna Phouma. King Tiao Savang Vatthana is Head of State.

ECONOMY. The country is mountainous, communications are poor and the people are among the most primitive in SE Asia. Simple agriculture is practised, but mineral resources are not developed and there is no industry to speak of.

HISTORY. Laos became a French Protectorate in 1893 and an independent member of the French Union under Prince Souvanna Phouma, in 1949. In the Indo-China war, nationalist Pathet Lao forces under Prince Souphanou Vong collaborated with the Viet-minh and invaded Laos in 1953. The Geneva Agreement of 1954 recognized Pathet Lao's authority over the two northern provinces, and in 1957 the princes attempted re-unification of the country. In 1960 Prince Souvanna Phouma's government was ousted by right-wing forces under General Phoumi Nosavan, and a government was set up under Prince Boun Oum, with the support of U.S.A. Souvanna Phouma's forces counterattacked, with support from the Pathet Lao, and compelled a cease-fire. After the Geneva Conference of 1961 a coalition was set up under Souvanna Phouma, with Phouma Nosavan and Souphanou Vong as Deputy Premiers, and Laotian neutrality was guaranteed. Sporadic fighting continued. ◊ *Angkor*.

Lapis Lazuli. A blue rock, one of the ◊ *felspar* family of aluminium silicates, valued from ancient times for its beauty and used in mosaics, ornaments, and (formerly) as the pigment ultramarine.

Lapps. The inhabitants of Lapland, stretching across N. Norway, Sweden, ◊ *Finland*, and U.S.S.R. as far as the White Sea; of Mongoloid origin, from Siberia. Traditionally they are isolated hunters and fishers, and breed large herds of reindeer; the need for pasturage in the Arctic area has necessitated continual movement, and settlements even today are rarely permanent, but they are being increasingly affected by the peoples among whom they live and are adopting the customs and names of Swedes and Finns.

Lapwing ◊ *Plover*.

Larceny. Taking and carrying away property without the consent of the owner or fraudulently by a trick, with the intention to deprive the owner of it permanently; to keep a lost object without taking steps to restore it to its owner is larceny by finding. The offence is aggravated if the property is taken from the person or from a dwelling house; housebreaking is punishable by imprisonment for up to fourteen years, and between 9.0 p.m. and 6.0 a.m. it is burglary, which carries a maximum penalty of imprisonment for life.

Larch. *Larix*; one of the few deciduous ◊ *conifers*, with 10 species. The common *L. decidua* is a native of the mountain forests from the European Alps to as far E. as Siberia; its timber is used for fences, pit props, masts, etc. More recently the Japanese larch *L. leptolepis* has been grown as a timber tree; its growth is more rapid but its wood is not as strong as that of the common larch.

Lares. Roman (orig. Etruscan) tutelary household and familiar spirits, usually mentioned together with the roughly equivalent *Penates*; singular, *lar*. Kept in a special household shrine (*Lararium*), their images were given offerings at meals and esp. honoured on the Kalends, Nones, and Ides every month.

LARES COMPITALES: Propitiated at crossroads.

LARES FAMILIARES: Concerned with the home.

LARES PRAESTITES: Concerned with the whole of the State.

LARES RUSTICI: Concerned with the countryside.

Lark. A streaked brown bird; the English skylark is noted for its ability to sing and soar simultaneously. It lays a few small eggs among grass tussocks in rough open country. Other species include the wood lark and the shore lark, found in Europe, Asia, and N. Africa.

Larva. Form in which some animals are hatched from the egg; distinctly different from the adult form. Familiar larvae are those of insects (caterpillars and grubs) and amphibia (tadpoles); the larval phase frequently ends suddenly, with a drastic reorganization of structure (◊ *metamorphosis*) which results in the formation of the sexually mature adult. Occasionally a species reaches sexual maturity while still in a larval form, a phenomenon known as neoteny or paedogenesis. Larvae are widespread, forming an important element in the food supply of many fish and terrestrial animals, esp. birds. They are also an ever-present hazard to agriculture and horticulture.

Larynx. Organ in the windpipe composed of cartilage structures. Vibrations of two bands of fibrous tissue (the vocal cords) stretched across the cavity of the larynx produce vocal sounds, which are varied by delicate muscle movements that change the tension on the vocal cords and the distance between them. Laryngitis (inflammation of the larynx) is usually the extension of a catarrhal infection of the nose and throat, and may be the forerunner of ◊ *bronchitis*. ◊ *Diphtheria*.

Lascaux. Cave in the Dordogne region of France, with ◊ *Altamira* (which it probably antedates) the finest of the painted caves of the upper ◊ *Palaeolithic*; discovered 1940 by small boys, it was found to contain vivid, lively, astonishingly skilful paintings and engravings chiefly of oxen, red deer, and horses, reflecting the hunting economy of the men who painted them. It is thought that the cave was used over a period of many centuries as a religious shrine. Serious damage was caused to the paintings owing to the opening of the cave; it is now closed, and the preservation of the paintings remains in doubt.

Laser. Light Amplification by Stimulated Emission of Radiation; a device for the amplification and concentration of light waves. In one form of Laser a rod of synthetic ruby, silvered at one end, is subjected to bright flashes of ordinary light; these excite some of the chromium atoms in the ruby to an abnormally high level of energy, and as these excited atoms jump back to their normal state they release the extra energy as bursts of extremely-concentrated coherent red light, which after reflection from the silvered end of the rod escape from the other end to form an intense needle of infrared light, which can drill a hole through a steel plate. The Laser has been hailed in some quarters as the long-awaited 'death-ray', but its real importance may prove to be as an efficient means of communication over interplanetary distances. ◊ *Maser*.

La Tène Culture ◊ *Iron Age*.

Lateran Treaty (1929) ◊ *Papal States*.

Laterite. < Lat. *later*, brick. Relatively infertile red clayey soil consisting largely of aluminium and iron oxides and occasionally very rich in iron, an end-product of the weathering of basic ◊ *igneous rocks*, found in tropical regions e.g. Africa, Brazil, India; used in brick-making.

Latex. Milky fluid produced in special vessels or cells in the tissues of various plants, which exudes when the stem or bark is cut; it consists of particles suspended in a liquid medium, coagulates on exposure to the air, and is insoluble in water. Many common plants produce latex e.g. lettuce, poppies, dandelions. ◊ *Rubber*.

Latin. Closely related to the Italic dialects Oscan, Umbrian, and Venetic, more distantly to the Celtic and Germanic branches of the ◊ *Indo-European languages*, Latin was originally the speech of a small community which moved south into N. Latium about 1000 B.C. and later the official language of the Roman Republic and Empire. A highly inflected language, unlike Greek it had no articles (*homo*, man, a man, or the man), no dual number, no aorist tense, no emotive particles, and not many verbal particles; vigorous, orderly, and clear, it reflected the practical, lawgiving, administrative characteristics of the Romans, and for centuries after the fall of the Western Empire A.D. 476 it remained the language of learning (e.g. More's *Utopia* 1516 and Newton's *Principia* 1687) and of international communication and diplomacy. It survived as the sole liturgical language of the Roman Catholic Church (◊ *Mass*). The ◊ *Romance languages* descend from vulgar Latin (the colloquial forms used by ordinary people and the imperial legionaries); all the ◊ *Germanic languages* have borrowed from Latin (English both direct and through French, about half the vocabulary deriving ultimately from Latin).

CLASSICAL LATIN: The language of Rome 81 B.C. to the death of Augustus A.D. 14.

SILVER LATIN: From Tiberius A.D. 14 to the death of Trajan A.D. 117, when the Roman Empire was at its greatest extent.

Latitude. Angular distance N. or S. of the ◊ *equator*, taken as zero latitude; a degree of latitude equals about 69 m. but owing to the flattening of the earth's surface is slightly less at the poles.

CELESTIAL LATITUDE: Angular distance of heavenly bodies from the plane of the ecliptic.

HORSE LATITUDES: Zones of high atmospheric pressure, calms, light variable winds, and dry stable weather conditions, in both hemispheres, between the ◊ *trade winds* and the prevailing W. winds of higher latitudes, which move N. and S. with the seasons; one explanation of the name is that sailors had to throw horses overboard from becalmed ships.

PARALLELS OF LATITUDE: Imaginary

circles, parallel to the equator, joining places of equal latitude.

Latvia, Latvian ⟡ *Baltic States.*

Laurel. The true laurel (the bay) *Laurus nobilis* was sacred to ⟡ *Apollo* and is a native of the Mediterranean area. The pointed evergreen leaves were used for making crowns (chaplets) for triumphant heroes, and sprays of the berries were presented to distinguished poets (hence 'poet laureate'). The leaves of the bay are used for flavouring stews and soups. The shrubs commonly called laurels (whose leaves are poisonous), used for screens and shelter in shrubberies, are the cherry laurel *Prunus lauro-cerasus,* the Portugal laurel *P. lusitanica,* or the Japanese laurel *Aucuba japonica.*

Lausanne Conference. 1922-3. International conference, requested by Kemal Ataturk, to revise the Treaty of Sèvres, imposed on Turkey after the First World War. The treaty signed in 1923 restored full sovereignty and control of the ⟡ *Dardanelles* (which had been internationalized), but it was to remain demilitarized and subject to an international convention. ⟡ *Montreux Convention.*

Lava. Molten rock escaping from a vent in a ⟡ *volcano*; chemically very variable, some lava country being highly fertile and ᶜome barren. ⟡ *Basalt, Pumice, Sulphur.*

Lavender. *Lavandula*; a small grey-leaved aromatic shrub from the Mediterranean. *L. spica* has been grown in Britain since the 16th cent. Its flowers were at one time much used for scenting bedlinen. Oil of lavender, used in perfumery, is obtained from a special variety of *L. spica* formerly known as *L. vera,* grown on a large scale in the S. of France.

Law. A rule of conduct imposed by authority, or otherwise recognized as binding. Law may be either written or customary; it may be derived from the legislative edict of a ruler (Positive Law); from an accepted religious revelation (Divine Law); or from moral principles assumed to be inherent in natural man (Natural Law). Primitive law is not for the most part made systematically. Rules are followed because they are traditional, often because they are inseparable from superstition and magic, and frequently are kept a closely guarded secret known only to priests and judges. The earliest known rational code of law is the Code of Hammurabi, a king of Babylon about 2100

B.C. It has much in common with the Hebrew law found in the Pentateuch (⟡ *Bible*). ⟡ *Roman law* was carried to a high stage of development and forms the basis of all Western law. Up to the 12th cent. there was no such thing as a 'legal system' in England: the lord of the manor dispensed justice according to local custom, and the central government intervened only in matters affecting politics or the royal revenues. In the 12th cent. the king began to send royal officials experienced in judicial work on tour to dispense royal justice in local matters. They selected and adapted the various local rules and usages to establish a body of law common to the whole kingdom. Thus the ⟡ *common law* arose. English law consists of the rules of common law and Equity, embodied in precedents, changed or supplemented in parts by Acts of Parliament. ⟡ *Administrative Law, International Law, Martial Law, Military Law, Scots Law.*

Lawn Tennis. Game played on grass or hard courts, or covered wooden courts, with stringed rackets and a resilient rubber ball across a net on a court 78 ft long by 27 ft wide for singles and 36 ft wide for doubles. On the decline of ⟡ *real tennis* in the 19th cent. a Major Wingfield patented a somewhat similar outdoor game called 'sphairistike' in 1874, from which the modern game quickly developed. In 1877 the All England Croquet Club at Wimbledon added Lawn Tennis to its title and held a tennis tournament, where balls covered with white cloth were first introduced, on a court the dimensions of which have remained the same; the net was much higher at the sides than in the centre, and was not made almost horizontal until much later. The new game gained rapid popularity, to become the most widely played game in the world. Today almost every country has its national championships. Wimbledon remains the premier event of international tennis; the Davis Cup, in which a large number of countries compete annually, is the international team event for men, while the women of Great Britain and America compete annually for the Wightman Cup. Australia and America easily overtook England as leading tennis nations, although there have been outstanding players from a wide variety of countries. The International Lawn Tennis Federation (1912) is the ruling world body, which has had a difficult task in the recent years to preserve the major championships as amateur events, since most leading men players turn professional after a few seasons' success as amateurs.

Lawrencium. A radioactive metal, the ◊ *element* of the highest atomic number yet discovered and the last of the ◊ *actinide* series, produced by nuclear reaction.

Law Society. Professional body founded 1825, responsible for the education, admission, and professional conduct of ◊ *solicitors*, complaints about whom are heard by the Disciplinary Committee, which may e.g. strike the offender off the roll.

Lead. A grey metallic ◊ *element*, occurring as the sulphide galena and the carbonate cerussite, both easily reduced to the metal by simple metallurgical processes. The metal is soft, but can be hardened by adding ◊ *antimony* or ◊ *tellurium*; with ◊ *tin* it gives pewter and the low-melting alloy solder. Lead is not much attacked by air, water, or acids; it is used for the manufacture of accumulator plates, the 'anti-knock' compound tetraethyl lead, for sheathing electric cables, as sheet and tubing for building materials, and as a screen against radioactive emission. Industrial compounds are the yellow litharge used for making flint glass, lead glazes (◊ *Ceramics*), and lead salts. Controlled oxidation of lead oxide by air gives the pigment red lead. Lead salts oxidized under suitable conditions yield the dioxide, extensively used for filling the positive plates of lead storage batteries. White lead, a basic carbonate, is a pigment of great covering power; the chromates provide yellow-to-brown pigments. All these compounds are poisonous.

Leadership. As a cult, the belief that history is shaped and determined by the power and virtue of outstanding individuals; essentially a romantic doctrine, it was manifest in Carlyle's faith in the Hero, and in its most extreme form in Nietzsche's concept of the Superman. When applied to or exploited by a particular leader, the doctrine becomes a cult; it was so exploited by Hitler, as the 'Führer', and (although fundamentally opposed to marxist theory) by Stalin.

Leaf. A flat green organ growing laterally from a stem whose primary function is ◊ *photosynthesis*. Moss leaves are only one cell thick, but those of vascular plants consist of a variety of tissues and are covered by an epidermis broken at intervals (except in aquatic plants) by pores (stomata) through which water vapour and gases pass. The stomata are bordered by pairs of cells which alter in shape with

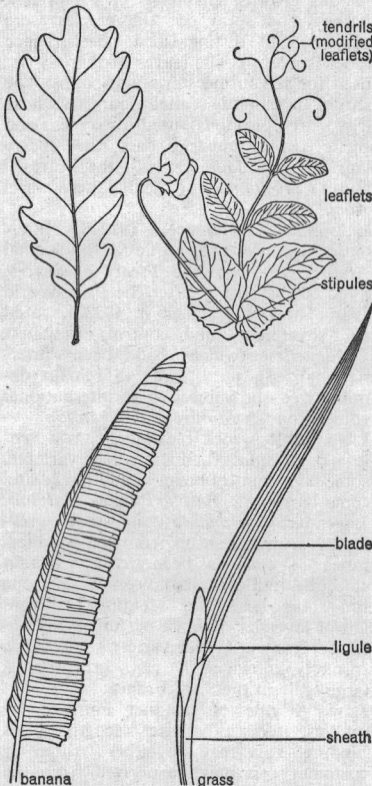

pinnately lobed leaf, oak   compound pinnate leaf, pea

tendrils (modified leaflets)

leaflets

stipules

blade.

ligule

sheath

banana   grass

monocot leaves with parallel veins

changes in their water content (turgor), and this opens and closes the stoma. The leaf blade is supported by veins, strands of vascular tissue. Most dicotyledons have stalked leaves with palmate (fanshaped) or pinnate (feathershaped) veins ending in a fine network, whilst most monocotyledons have long narrow leaves with parallel veins. Many monocotyledon leaves grow from the base e.g. grass, which enables the ends to be cut off without killing them.

Specialized leaves have other functions in addition to (or sometimes instead of) photosynthesis. Leaves may support the plant with e.g. tendrils (pea, bean), hooks (goosegrass, rattan palms), floats (water hyacinth), or long rigid leaf bases straight from the ground (banana). Leaves may absorb nutrients (submerged aquatics, ◊ *carnivorous plants*) or water (◊ *Epiphytes*). Leaves may be vegetative reproductive organs and develop buds (walking ferns, bryophyllum), or storage organs for water (agave, some succulents), or food (bulbs). Leaves may also be non-photosynthetic and reduced to small scales, to reduce transpiration or protect buds. Some ◊ *parasites* and ◊ *saprophytes* have scale-like leaves. Some flowers are inconspicuous, and leaves are coloured to attract insects e.g. poinsettias, bougainvillea. Vascular plants have leaves (sporophylls) on which reproductive bodies develop. In ◊ *angiosperms* they are called ◊ *carpels* and are folded or joined together to form an ovary. The other parts of a ◊ *flower* (sepals, petals, and stamens) are also thought to be modified leaves.

League of Nations. Body created in 1919 by the Treaty of ◊ *Versailles*, as a world authority to maintain international law and order and permit disarmament. The U.S.A. refusal to join, the exclusion of the defeated Central Powers, and the hostility of Soviet Russia weakened the League, but its primary problems were failure to agree whether peaceful settlement of international disputes required a willingness to surrender sovereignty to the League, and also failure to endow it with adequate power. As a result most nations continued their normal policies of alliance and self-defence. The League was unable to prevent the Japanese invasion of ◊ *Manchuria* in 1931 or the Italian invasion of ◊ *Ethiopia* in 1935, and was impotent against the aggressive policy of Germany under ◊ *Nazism*, e.g. in the ◊ *Spanish Civil War*. After the ◊ *Second World War* the League was replaced by the ◊ *United Nations Organization*.

Leap Year ◊ *Calendar*.

Leasehold. The right to exclusive possession, in return for rent, of land held under a lease for a limited period, after which it reverts to the owner; the usual term is 99 years for building land, while farms and large houses are often let on lease for 7 or 14 years. The lessor's pay-

ment is termed ground rent. ◊ *Freehold*.

Lebanon. Area 4300 sq. m. Pop. 1.8 m. Cap. Beirut. Rel. Muslim and Christian. Language Arabic. An E. Mediterranean republic; the legislature is a single chamber elected by universal adult suffrage, and the executive a President with a Prime Minister, who appoints the Cabinet. There is no highly developed party system, and deputies are allocated according to the religious distribution of the population. By convention the President is always a ◊ *Maronite* Christian and the P.M. a Muslim.

ECONOMY. The general standard of living is the highest among the Arab countries, based in part on emigrant remittances, on a large entrepôt trade, and a growing tourist industry, which supplement the agricultural assets of tobacco, fruit, and silk. Industry is limited to local needs.

HISTORY. The area, once the homeland of the ◊ *Phoenicians*, has long been inhabited partly by a Christian sect, the Maronites, and partly by the fiercely independent heretic Muslim sect, ◊ *Druses*. Under the Mamelukes and the ◊ *Ottoman Empire* it enjoyed a semi-independent status. After the ◊ *First World War* it was governed by France under a ◊ *mandate* until 1941. In the ◊ *Second World War* British troops removed the French garrison, which had rallied to Vichy France, and gave the country independence, with the approval of the Free French.

CEDARS OF LEBANON. Historic grove of trees, now greatly reduced, traditionally considered the source of the timber used in the building of the Judaic Temple and the House of Solomon.

Lech (1632) ◊ *Thirty Years War*.

Leda. In Greek mythology, daughter of Thestius, wife of Tyndareus King of Sparta, mother of ◊ *Castor and Pollux*, Clytaemnestra (◊ *Agamemnon*), and ◊ *Helen*. She received ◊ *Zeus* in the form of a swan, and from two eggs brought to her by Nemesis (Fate) hatched Helen and the heavenly twins (or in one version, only the twins).

Leech. Blood-sucking parasite, a branch of the Chaetopod worms; of the *Hirudinea*; in the past much used by physicians as blood-letting agents. In tropical countries the land leeches are capable of seriously injuring or killing people, and in the Near East *Limnatis nilotica*, which lives in streams and ponds, is a serious menace to man and animals: the parasite is swallowed in the drinking water and attaches itself to the larynx, epiglottis, and nasal cavities of the host, causing haemorrhages which may prove fatal if the leeches are not removed. Leech saliva contains the anticoagulant hirudin, much used in surgery during the First World War.

Leek. *Allium porrum*; a mild-flavoured onion, used as a culinary vegetable in ancient Rome and Egypt, found native in the Mediterranean and the Near East. It is a biennial, but the plants are used in the first year, after being blanched by earthing-up. The leek is the national emblem of Wales.

Legal Aid. The provision of legal advice and representation, on proof of need; legal aid in civil cases is regulated by the 1949 Legal Aid and Advice Act. All applicants for aid must show that they have reasonable cause for resorting to legal action in civil cases, the disposable income limits to qualify for aid being £250 for full assistance or £700 for partial. The scheme is operated in England and Wales by the ◊ *Law Society*, working through local committees. 70 per cent of all cases in which legal aid was granted in 1961–2 were divorce cases. Legal aid in criminal cases is regulated by the Poor Prisoners Defence Act 1930. A person is entitled to such aid if his means are insufficient to get legal aid otherwise, and the service is much used. The provision for aid has now been extended to cover civil cases in the Magistrates' Courts. ◊◊ *Dock Brief.*

Legal Tender. The sorts of money specified by law in which sums due may be paid. Bronze coin is legal tender up to one shilling, silver up to £2, £1 and 10s. notes for any amount (in Gt Britain and N. Ireland). Notes above £1 are legal tender in England and Wales only.

Legion. Unit of the Roman army, which varied in size at different periods; but typically of 3000–6000 foot, with additional cavalry (300) and auxiliaries. Originally a militia of the citizens of Rome, it later became a professional army recruited mainly in the provinces. In Julius Caesar's time each legion was commanded by a prefect, a legate, six tribunes, and 60 centurions. The standard was an eagle, inscribed with the number of the legion and the letters S P Q R (Senate and People of Rome). Highly

disciplined and trained, and more manoeuvrable than the Greek phalanx, the tactic of the legion remained basically that of shock frontal attack. The Roman legions remained effective until the heavy cavalry of the ◊ *Goths* brought about their destruction amid the general disintegration of the Roman Empire.

Legitimacy. 1. The conformity of a government to established principles of creation or succession; normally, the hereditary descent of a ◊ *monarchy*. As a technical term in political theory, it is the principle of lineal succession to the throne and therefore concerned rather with the incumbent than the office. Legitimist theory was of importance in English history in connexion with the ◊ *Jacobite* resistance to the Hanoverian succession. **2.** ◊ *Illegitimacy.*

Legnano. 1176. Town N W of Milan where the ◊ *Lombard League* defeated the emperor Frederick I (Barbarossa) who was endeavouring to make good his claim to rule N. Italy; it forced him to submit to the pope at Venice the following year.

Legume. Botanically, a fruit formed from a single ◊ *carpel*, a pod, which splits to shed the seeds, e.g. peas, beans. In general, members of the ◊ *Leguminosae* (pea family), esp. the edible parts.

Leguminosae. Pea family; a very large dicotyledon family, of great economic importance as foods, widely distributed as herbs, shrubs, and trees in all types of habitat, the ◊ *fruit* being typically a pod. The family is divided into three main groups, based on flower structure. (a) Mimosa type, with regular flowers e.g. ◊ *acacia.* (b) Cassia and cercis type, with regular or bilaterally symmetrical flowers. (c) Pea type, with typical pealike flowers. This last group is the most extensive in Europe; the second group is more important in the tropics. The seeds of many species are eaten, e.g. pea, ◊ *bean*, lentil, chick pea, soya bean, groundnut. A large number are valuable as fodder e.g. clover, lucerne, sainfoin. Many trees, mostly tropical and sub-tropical, give valuable timber; ◊ *gums*, resins, ◊ *tannins*, and ◊ *dyes* are produced from others. An important feature of most species are nodules on the roots which contain nitrogen-fixing bacteria (◊ *Nitrogen Cycle*); the nitrogen compounds produced in the nodules enrich the soil, and legumes are thus valuable in ◊ *crop rota-*

tion and are often ploughed in for green manure. The leguminosae are well known for their flowers e.g. ◊ *sweet pea,* gorse, broom, laburnum, ◊ *wistaria,* ◊ *lupin,* ◊ *vetch.*

Leipzig (1813) ◊ *Napoleonic Wars.*

Lemming. A small rodent, one of four genera of the rat family *Muridae,* of Arctic distribution from Scandinavia to Canada. Norwegian lemmings are remarkable for unexplained periodic mass migrations westwards, in which they are killed by predators or drowned in the Atlantic.

Lemon. 1. Fruit of *Citrus limonia,* which seems of relatively recent but unknown origin. Cultivated esp. in the Mediterranean area. Like the orange, it flowers all the year, so that ripe fruit is always available. The juice is used for 'soft drinks' and the peel for flavouring and the preparation of lemon oil. ◊ *Lime (1).* **2. 'Salts of Lemon'** ◊ *Oxalic Acid.*

Lemur. Omnivorous arboreal or rock-dwelling ◊ *primate* found in Madagascar, closely related to the insectivorous tree shrews; resembles the other primates in having opposable thumbs, but has a dog-like head, lacks stereoscopic vision, and has other primitive and non-primate characteristics.

Lend Lease. System devised by President Roosevelt by which U.S.A. provided arms and supplies to the Allies in the ◊ *Second World War.* As a result of isolationist opinion in U.S.A. Congress passed a law in 1939 which permitted the sale of arms only on the basis of 'cash and carry' i.e. payment to be made and transport effected by the purchaser. By 1940 Britain was at the end of her dollar reserves; Roosevelt thereupon agreed to lend or lease supplies, to be returned at the end of the war if unused. The total value of such supplies to all the Allies was $46,040 m. and the value of 'reverse Lend Lease' i.e. aid to U.S.A. $6300 m. In the settlement, U.S.A. virtually waived all reimbursement and thus avoided saddling Europe with an unbearable burden of debt. In return Britain and France undertook to cooperate with U.S.A. to expand and liberalize international trade and to pursue economic policies aimed at maximizing production and employment: ◊ *Bretton Woods Conference.*

Lenses ◊ *Optics.*

Leopard ◊ *Panther.*

Lepanto. 1571. Naval engagement in the gulf of Corinth, in which a combined Spanish, Venetian, and Papal fleet, commanded by Don John of Austria, destroyed the naval power of the Turks, with enormous casualties on both sides. The battle is notable as the last major engagement in which ◊ *galleys* were used.

Leprosy. A disease of great antiquity, endemic in many tropical and sub-tropical countries, characterized by nodules on the skin and atrophy of nerves, which if untreated result in deformities, caused by a bacterium *Mycobacterium leprae* related to that of tuberculosis but not highly communicable. The pattern of infection after contact is unpredictable. Possibly introduced from Egypt in the 1st cent. A.D. it gradually spread throughout Europe and by 1400 reached a peak, but laws for the segregation of lepers and the establishment of leper communities gradually reduced its incidence. The disease continued widespread in tropical Africa into the 20th cent. but its incidence has now been greatly reduced.

Lethe. In Greek mythology, one of the five rivers of ◊ *Hades;* all departed spirits are made to drink from it to bring forgetfulness of their past lives. Dante places it in ◊ *Purgatory.*

Letter of Marque. Authority from the Crown for a ◊ *privateer* to operate against foreign shipping, which distinguished this activity from ◊ *piracy.*

Lettuce. *Lactuca sativa;* a hardy annual, a native of Europe, known to the Greeks and Romans and grown in Britain since the mid 16th cent. There are two main types, the cos and the cabbage; the former has a tall habit of growth and is supposed to have been introduced from the Greek island of Cos.

Leucocytes ◊ *Blood.*

Leucotomy (Lobotomy). A neuro-surgical brain operation involving a division of the nerves passing between the thalmus and the frontal area of the cerebrum (◊ *Nervous System*), usually by introducing an ◊ *electrode* to the appropriate area of the brain and passing a current which destroys the nerve fibres. The operation has been successfully used for the treatment of otherwise incurable forms of insanity, and to relieve anxiety and acute pain. The patient subsequently displays marked changes in behaviour and personality, but is usually relieved from delusions and ◊ *hallucinations*.

Leukemia. Disease characterized by malignant increase of leucocyte-producing tissues in the bone marrow, so that the ◊ *blood* is flooded with immature white corpuscles, and the patient suffers from haemorrhages, ◊ *anaemia*, and swelling of the lymphatic glands. The disease may be either acute or chronic, and spontaneous remissions may occur. Treatment with drugs which destroy the proliferating cells in the bone marrow may bring temporary relief, but the disease is almost always fatal. ◊ *Radiation Sickness*.

Levalloisian ◊ *Palaeolithic*.

Levees. Low banks on each side of a river, built up by silt-deposition in flooding; the highest part of the ◊ *flood plain*, they are progressively raised by further flooding, until the levees and the river bed may be higher than the surrounding country, e.g. the lower Mississippi, the Po. Supplementary artificial levees are often constructed to help prevent flooding, e.g. along the Mississippi. ◊ *Irrigation*.

Levellers. Extremist party of the mid 17th cent. whose egalitarian programme aimed at levelling-out the sharper class divisions, which for a time was powerful during the ◊ *English civil wars*. In 1647 they obliged Cromwell and the other generals to sign the *Agreement of the People*, a forward-looking but very premature 'democratic constitution'; with the army's seizure of the king, the situation changed, and the Leveller regiments whose loyalty was suspect were ordered to Ireland in 1649. They mutinied, and were severely repressed. After the ◊ *Restoration* some reappeared as 'Fifth Monarchy men' and raised a brief rebellion. Many more reappeared in the 1670s as 'Country Party' ◊ *Whigs*. ◊ *Diggers*.

Lexington. 1775. The first skirmish and prelude to the ◊ *American Revolution*. The British had set out from Boston to seize a stock of arms at Concord, but the ◊ *Minutemen* (revolutionary militia), alerted by Paul Revere, engaged the column. A few Americans were killed, but the bridge at Concord was held and the British retreated to Boston.

Leyden. 1574. During the revolt of the northern ◊ *Netherlands* against Spain, Leyden was besieged by the Spanish for six months, and eventually relieved by William the Silent, who had the dikes cut:

the area round the town was flooded, and supplies could be sent in by water.

Leyte Gulf. 1944. Series of air and naval battles between U.S.A. and Japan during the ◊ *Second World War*. With the loss of only six ships, the Americans inflicted overwhelming damage on the Japanese fleet, and the engagement led to the recapture of the island of Leyte (Philippines).

Lianas. Woody climbing plants of many families found in tropical forests. The stems resemble ropes, and often attain lengths of over 100 ft.

Lias. Lowest strata of the Jurassic rocks (◊ *Geological Time Scale*); deposits chiefly of clays and sandstones with thin beds of clayey limestones.

Libel and Slander. ◊ *Defamation* in writing is libel; by the spoken word it is slander. Both are torts and actionable, provided in the case of slander that financial loss results or that the derogatory remark is an allegation of a criminal offence, a venereal or other contagious or infectious disease, unfitness for one's profession, or female unchastity. It is no defence to criminal proceedings to show that it was published not to a third person but only to the person defamed (although if so it would not be a tort and no damages could be claimed).

Liberal Party. The name, increasingly applied to the ◊ *Whig* party of the early 19th cent., became its official title in the 1860s under Gladstone's leadership. The party was in office for 23 of the 46 years 1868–1914, but in the later years of the period it had been losing working-class support to the new ◊ *Labour Party*, while men of wealth and middle-class elements had been moving over to the Conservatives (◊ *Tory*). These trends both caused and were intensified by splits first between the supporters of Lloyd George and H. H. Asquith in the 1920s and then over membership of the National Government of 1931. After 1918 the Liberals never held office and steadily lost support; in the 1945 election they could return only a handful of M.P.s, their traditional ◊ *laissez-faire* and ◊ *free trade* doctrines having become increasingly irrelevant, but in the 1960s their attraction as an alternative to both Labour and Conservative began to revive. ◊ *United Kingdom*.

Liberia. Area 43,000 sq. m. Pop. 1.25 m. Cap. Monrovia. An independent Negro republic in W. Africa, between the Ivory Coast and Sierra Leone, with a constitution similar to that of U.S.A. Since 1944 the president, W. Tubman, has endeavoured to draw into his administration men from outside the Liberian-American oligarchy and to use the proceeds of a 25 per cent tax on the profits of the Firestone Rubber Co. to institute social and economic reforms.

ECONOMY. Mainly agricultural, the chief exports being cocoa, coffee, palm kernels, and rubber; also some gold, diamonds, iron ore.

HISTORY. A settlement of freed American slaves, established near Monrovia in 1821 by the American Colonization Society, became independent in 1847; the administration remained in the hands of the descendants of the American Negroes, who had little in common with the indigenous tribes. In the 1920s the Firestone Rubber Company established large plantations, and since 1927 American finance has supported the regime.

The 'Monrovia Group' of African states consisted of Liberia together with most of the former French equatorial territories, Nigeria, and Sierra Leone; it was opposed to the more radical and Pan-Africanist group led by Ghana, Mali, and Guinea. These divisions were largely smoothed over at the Addis Ababa Conference of African States in 1963.

Libido. In psychoanalytic theory, the energy by which the life instincts (the psychological form of the physical needs concerned with survival and propagation) perform their work. Among the life instincts are thirst, hunger, and sex; Freud first applied the term 'libido' exclusively to sexual energy, but later he used it to cover the energy of all the life instincts. In Jung's psychology 'libido' has an even more general sense.

Libraries. The earliest were royal or religious archives in ancient Babylon, Egypt, and elsewhere; wealthy or learned Greeks e.g. Aristotle kept extensive private collections, and the first public library in Greece was founded 330 B.C. The most celebrated ancient library was that founded by Ptolemy I at Alexandria in the 4th cent. B.C. and said to have contained 400,000 volumes; it was destroyed by fire A.D. 272. The great public collections of the Romans, at first captured from the Greeks, were destroyed or dis-

persed in the early Middle Ages, but monastic libraries and *scriptoria* for MSS copying were set up from the 6th cent. A.D. onwards, while the libraries of the Arabs preserved a large part of the learning of antiquity. The ⟡ *Sorbonne* library in Paris was founded in the 13th cent. but the great age of European libraries came in the 14th and 15th centuries with the formation of many other university libraries e.g. Oxford (⟡ *Bodleian*), Heidelberg, and also the Vatican library and the private collections of Italian ⟡ *Renaissance* princes e.g. Lorenzo de' Medici. Other great libraries include the ⟡ *Bibliothèque Nationale*, the ⟡ *British Museum*, and the U.S. Library of Congress, founded 1800.

COPYRIGHT LIBRARIES: Under the Copyright Act, two free copies of every book published in the U.K. and the Irish Republic are sent to the British Museum, the Bodleian, the University of Cambridge, the National Library of Scotland, the National Library of Wales, and Trinity College, Dublin.

PUBLIC LIBRARIES: Under the 1850 Libraries Act these are maintained out of the rates by municipal and county authorities. By giving library buildings to many towns in the early 20th cent. the American philanthropist Andrew Carnegie greatly accelerated the growth of the system.

Libration. In its motion around the earth, the moon in general turns the same face towards us, but the geometry and mechanics of its orbit cause it to appear to swing slightly left and right and up and down; as a result of these inequalities (libration) about six tenths of the moon's surface can be seen from the earth.

Libya. Area 810,000 sq. m. Pop. 1.2 m. Cap. Tripoli. Rel. Muslim. Language Arabic. N. African kingdom between Egypt and Tunisia; a hereditary monarchy under King Idris I, with a Senate of 24 members 12 of whom are nominated by the King, and an elected House of Representatives of 55 members; the constitution allows considerable autonomy to the provinces. There are no political parties.

ECONOMY. The country is mainly desert, and agriculture is confined to the oases and the coastal strip; exports include wool, cattle, esparto grass, olive oil, sponges, and esp. petroleum, for which 22 oil companies are prospecting. The oil exports began in 1962, with the opening of the first pipeline; others are under construction, and output is rapidly increasing. HISTORY. Part of the Turkish empire until 1911, Libya was then occupied by Italy, which incorporated it into Italy proper in 1939. A battleground during the ◊ *Second World War*, Libya was under British and French administration 1945–51, but then became the first independent state created by the ◊ *United Nations*.

Li-chee ◊ *Litchi*.

Lichens. Small simple plants formed by the ◊ *symbiosis* of a ◊ *fungus* and an ◊ *alga*; world-wide and hardy, they often tolerate very dry conditions, grow e.g. on rocks, tree trunks, tiled roofs, and form the main vegetation in parts of the Arctic (Lichen-tundra) where some species are important as food for ◊ *reindeer*. Lichens are the source of many natural dyes and are used as a test for acids and alkalis, being turned red by acids and blue by alkalis.

Lie-detection. The observation of an individual's involuntary reactions as a guide to the degree of credence to be attributed to statements he makes; such reactions have been used since ancient times, but the 20th-cent. development of techniques for measuring physiological responses e.g. the inspiration-expiration ratio of breathing, and systolic blood-pressure changes, have placed the method on a less subjective basis. Lie-detection may be used either to scare the individual into confessing, by suggesting the infallibility of the techniques, or to discern whether the individual is in fact lying. Experience shows the general validity of such methods, but caution must be exercised in interpreting data obtained, as other and uncontrolled factors may affect the responses. Such tests are not admissible as evidence in English courts.

Life. Broadly, a substance may be said to live when it maintains its organization in a changing environment by responding to stimuli, exhibiting defence mechanisms, and obtaining material from its environment for its own structure and energy; living things possess both some reproductive mechanism and a term of life for the individual. The process of life is susceptible of investigation and elucidation: the origin of the earliest living organisms is a mystery.

Lifeboat. Special type of very seaworthy boat, for sea rescue, capable of righting itself if capsized and freeing itself of water. The first specially built lifeboat was that of Henry Greathead (1789); the first self-righting boat was built in 1851 and the first motor-driven lifeboat came into use in 1904. ◊ *Royal National Lifeboat Institute*.

Life Peers. Under the 1958 Act, commoners distinguished in public life, given the non-hereditary title of Baron or Baroness, and entitled to sit in the House of Lords.

Ligament. In general, any thickened fibrous band serving to unite two or more bones or forming the envelope keeping a joint stable; also, the fibrous structures supporting internal organs.

Light. Visible light is energy radiated in the form of waves occupying a small section of the full electromagnetic radiation spectrum. There have been many theories regarding the nature of light. Newton conceived it as minute particles from luminous sources travelling at great speed; Maxwell developed the theory of electromagnetic waves transmitted through the 'ether'; the concept of the ether was later abandoned, but the experiments concerning it led to Einstein's special theory of ◊ *relativity* and to the ◊ *quantum* theory of light as photons (quanta) of radiant energy, now accepted as the best explanation. All light, visible or outside the visible range, travels at about 186,000 m. per second through space, and nothing else travels faster. The velocity of light, however, varies through different media: less in air than in 'empty' space, less in water, and so on. ◊ *Optics, Spectrum, Vision*.

LIGHT-YEAR: In astronomy, a unit of distance, that which a ray of light travels in one year; about 6×10^{12} (6 million million) miles.

Lighthouse. A tower surmounted by a lantern, usually showing a white light (sometimes green or red), which has a particular pattern of flashing so that it may be identified; the colours are often arranged to show at certain angles from the lighthouse e.g. a light may have a red sector indicating a certain danger, which is avoided by the vessel's remaining in the white sector. The earliest lighthouse known was the Pharos built at Alexandria in the 3rd cent. B.C. to guide ships into the Nile; the Romans also built lighthouses, around the Mediterranean coast and on the English Channel. From medieval times the coasts of Europe have been marked with beacons, usually braziers but later candle-lanterns or oil-lamps. Since the early 19th cent. coal gas, acetylene, and electricty have been used, with refinements e.g. the Fresnel lens to focus the beam. In the most modern lighthouses radio signals are supplementing the light beam; remote-control lighthouses have been in existence since 1934. The chief U.K. authority for lighthouses is ⟡ *Trinity House.*

Lightning ⟡ *Electric Spark, Thunderstorm.*

Light-year. Unit of distance used in astronomy, being the distance travelled by light in one year, roughly six million million miles.

Lignin. With ⟡ *cellulose,* one of the structural materials of plant-cell walls, and the chief component of wood; lignin and cellulose are both ⟡ *polymers,* but are based on chemically very different structures. In preparing cellulose for paper-making, the lignin is extracted by means of sodium sulphite solution, with which it reacts.

Lignite. A soft coal, in which the alteration of the original vegetable remains has gone further than the ⟡ *peat* stage but has not produced true bituminous ⟡ *coal;* the plant-remains can be recognized in the brownish-black rock. Lignite rapidly crumbles on exposure to air, and travels badly; it is generally used to generate steam at the place where it is quarried. It cannot be made into ⟡ *coke.* East Germany produces over one third and U.S.S.R. a quarter of the world's annual output of 600 m. tons.

Ligny ⟡ *Waterloo.*

Lilac. Ornamental shrubs or trees of the genus *Syringa,* the common lilac with white or lavender sweet-scented flowers being the most popular cultivated form. Many hybrids have been bred. The ⟡ *mock orange,* of a different family, is sometimes misleadingly named syringa.

Liliaceae. Lily family; a very large cosmopolitan monocotyledonous family, containing some of the most beautiful plants of the world. Most are herbs, with rhizomes or bulbs, but a few are woody e.g. yucca. The family includes the true lilies (*Lilium*), hyacinth, red hot poker, lily of the valley, etc. Some plants give fibres e.g. New Zealand flax (*Phormium*) and yucca. Some are eaten e.g. onion, garlic, leek, asparagus (and lily bulbs in parts of China and Japan).

Lime. 1. Edible fruits from varieties of *Citrus medica,* of bitter and sweet varieties, similar to ⟡ *lemons* but greener and with a distinctive flavour. ⟡⟡ *Scurvy.* **2.** English lime (linden): Sub-species of tree in the *Tiliaceae,* with heart-shaped leaves and clusters of small whitish fragrant flowers. The bract at the base of the inflorescence adheres to it and gives a wing to the fruits. The timber was popular for wood carvings, and the flowers are dried for linden (lime-blossom) tea; lime-blossom honey is of esp. high quality. **3.** ⟡ *Limestone.*

Limerick. A five-line humorous verse rhyming a a b b a; said (without much evidence) to be named from a refrain 'We'll all come up to Limerick' sung after each improvised verse at parties, but possibly from 'Learic' after Edward Lear, whose *Book of Nonsense* 1846 popularized the earlier form in which the last line merely repeats the first (later limericks using it to clinch the anecdote or epigram). There are, however, early collections dating to 1820. Though often pseudo-topographical or biographical, most limericks nowadays are oral, ephemeral, and bawdy.

Limestone. One of the commonest ⟡ *sedimentary rocks,* 40–90 per cent lime carbonate, consolidated usually from fragments of shells or marine organisms, or from limey mud or calcareous sand. The principal forms are chalk, oolite, coral, and carboniferous or mountain limestone. As it is soluble in contact with rainwater acids, limestone landscapes are of a special kind (⟡ *Karst Region*).

Limited Liability Company ⟡ *Company Law.*

Linen. Cloth made from the fibres of flax, the first vegetable fibre spun by man; until the introduction of cotton, the only form of fine smooth cloth known (apart from silk). Has been found in early Egyptian tombs, and was much used by the Romans. The French Huguenots, expert at working flax, carried their skill to Britain, which became an important producer. Fine linens woven from long fibres are known as cambrics, lawns, and damasks; shorter fibres are used for coarser fabrics. Stronger than cotton, it is less elastic and much more difficult to work. The chief British centre of production is N. Ireland.

Lingua Franca. < Ital. 'Frankish tongue'; any mixed speech widely used for common currency among peoples of different native languages, esp. the Spanish-Italian-French-Greek jargon of the Levant.

Linotype. A type-composing and type-casting machine invented *c.* 1884 by Ottmar Mergenthaler. By pressing appropriate keys on a keyboard, matrices (metal moulds of individual characters) are assembled into words and lines; each line can thus be cast in one piece (slug). The matrices are automatically returned to their original position while the operator composes the next line. Recently the system has been adapted for use with punched tape produced on a separate keyboard; this speeds up the casting process. ◇ *Printing, Type.*

Linseed ◇ *Flax.*

Lion. *Felis leo*; of the cat family, originally of wide distribution but now extinct in Europe and much of its former range in Asia. It is found mainly in Africa and parts of Asia and India. Unlike most cats, the adult male differs from the female in having a mane. A formidable animal of prey, it hunts a wide variety of animals, large and small. Usually only old lions attack man.

Liquid ◇ *Molecule.*

Liquorice. *Glycyrrhiza glabra*, of the ◇ *Leguminosae*; a herb from the ◇ *rhizome* of which comes the juice which forms the basis of the black sticks of liquorice used in confectionery and for medicinal purposes. It was introduced into England in the 16th cent. at Pontefract, which became famous for its manufacture; 'Pomfret cakes' (liquorice tablets) became a well-known sweet. Spain is now the main source of the root.

Litchi (Li-chee). The fruit of *Litchi chinensis*, a tree native to S. China and long cultivated in the Far East, where it is a very popular fruit eaten fresh or dried. Both dried and tinned fruits are exported.

Literacy. Probably some two thirds of the world's population are illiterate. Available data (e.g. *World Illiteracy at Midcentury*, published by UNESCO) provide only approximate estimates; taking an average for 136 countries gave a literacy rate of 56 per cent, but 43 per cent of countries had rates of 25 per cent or less. The higher literacy rates were found mostly in N.

America, Europe, U.S.S.R. and Australasia, while illiteracy tends to be highest in sub-Saharan Africa. Great efforts are made in most countries of Asia, Africa, and Latin America to provide universal primary education for at least four years and to promote adult literacy campaigns; among the chief difficulties to be overcome are the apathy of peasant peoples and the immense difficulty of mastering the use of such scripts as Chinese. UNESCO has assisted literacy campaigns by providing information, skilled teachers, training colleges, and publishing specially prepared books; the U.S.S.R. claims virtually to have eliminated illiteracy since the 1917 revolution, when it was over 40 per cent in Russia proper and over 90 per cent in the provinces e.g. Uzbekistan.

Lithium. A fairly rare ◇ *element*, the hardest and least chemically active of the alkali metals, occurring in lithium mica and spodumene. It has two ◇ *isotopes*, lithium-6 and lithium-7; the separation of these has become important, because when the first is bombarded with neutrons ◇ *tritium* is formed.

Lithography. < Gr. *lithos*, stone; a planographic as distinct from relief or intaglio method of ◇ *printing*, invented about 1796 by Alois Senefelder of Munich, which exploits the antipathy of grease and water by using the surface of a stone prepared in such a way that it will pick up the ink only where it carries the image. It can render a wide variety of tones, from deep black to light grey, effectively reproduces work done with pencil, pen, crayon, or brush, and has been used by many leading artists, including Blake (who pioneered the process in England), Goya, Daumier, Toulouse-Lautrec, Bonnard, and Picasso. The preferred base is the original Bavarian limestone.

The invention of ◇ *photography*, with which it soon became linked, led to a wide application of lithography to printing; metal plates were substituted for stones and the rotary principle was introduced. In modern offset-lithography the image is transferred to the paper from a 'right-reading' curved metal plate via a rubber sheet called a 'blanket'. In web offset-lithography, a process which is beginning to be used for magazine and weekly newspaper production, the paper is fed into the press from a reel and passed between two rubber blankets, so that both sides are printed simultaneously. This important development may have far-reaching results in newspaper production and in colour printing at moderate cost. The development of film-setting, which eliminates the need to compose three-dimensional type merely for the purpose of photographically transferring one impression to the offset-lithographic plate, and facilitates the combination of text with illustrations in black and white or colour, will further promote the use of offset-lithography.

Lithuania ◊ *Baltic States.*

Litmus ◊ *Lichen.*

Little Entente ◊ *Czechoslovakia.*

Liturgy. Set of official formulas for Christian public prayer, esp. one for use at ◊ *Holy Communion.* Traces of fixed liturgies date to at least the 2nd cent. and those in use today preserve many early elements. The Roman Catholic liturgy is set forth in the Missal (for use at ◊ *Mass*), in the ◊ *Breviary,* in the Ritual for ◊ *baptism,* marriage, and other occasional rites. In the ◊ *Eastern Orthodox Church* the liturgy in most general use is that of St John Chrysostom; the small Eastern churches preserve other ancient forms (e.g. St Mark, St James). The Anglican liturgy is set forth in the ◊ *Prayer Book.*

Liver. The largest ◊ *gland* in the body, occupying the upper right side of the abdominal cavity; a very complex and vital organ, intimately concerned with ◊ *metabolism* of carbohydrates, proteins, and fats, with the regulation of blood-sugar, and the storage of glycogen and factors essential for the formation of red blood-cells. It synthesizes prothrombin, ◊ *heparin,* and the proteins of the blood plasma. It is also the chief detoxicating organ of the body, renders many toxic substances innocuous by chemical treatment, and secretes bile, important in the digestion of fats. ◊ *Cirrhosis, Hepatitis.*

Liver-fluke. Parasitic flatworm which may infest the bile-ducts of the liver. In sheep it produces liver rot, a fatal disease. In the Near East, particularly in Egypt where irrigation channels favour the breeding of secondary host organisms, the disease in humans is widespread, causing debility.

Lizard. Numerous and widely distributed species of reptile, belonging to the suborder Sauria; lizards differ from snakes in having well-developed limbs. Most are insectivorous; only the bearded lizard and the ◊ *gila monster* are poisonous. There are four small species in Britain.

Llama. Humpless S. American relative of the ◊ *camel* resembling a large sheep with a long neck; domesticated by the ancient Peruvians and probably descended from the wild guanaco; used as a beast of burden, but refuses to move if loaded much above 30 lb. The alpaca is a closely related variety, which yields a finer wool, and the entirely wild and smaller vicuña is prized for its silky fleece.

Llanos. Sp. 'plains'; loosely, plains in various parts of the world e.g. the Llano Estacado, staked plain, of Texas; but specifically the northern ◊ *savanna,* the extensive plains in S. America between the Andes and the Orinoco, about 600 m. long by 200 m. wide, largely grass-covered with scattered trees and suitable for cattle raising.

Lloyds. An association in London (named after the coffee-house where marine-insurance brokers met in the 18th cent.) whose members deal in all kinds of insurance including fire, accident, and aircraft, but are mainly concerned with marine insurance. Since 1734 Lloyds have published a daily report of the arrivals and departures of ships at every port in the world. A Lloyds policy binds only those members who underwrite the particular risk on which insurance is issued, the insurance being not with the association but with the individual syndicates. Lloyds have created standard policies used all over the world, the first dating to 1779, which greatly facilitate marine-insurance transactions.

LLOYDS REGISTER: The association classifies shipping of any nationality in accordance with rules as to construction and equipment; almost 40 per cent of world shipping is registered at Lloyds. Since 1834 the Register has been a separate organization; it also establishes safety rules and shipbuilding specifications, periodically conducts surveys of vessels, and publishes the annual *Lloyds Register of Shipping* with details of almost every merchant vessel in the world. A ship recognized as first-class in hull and equipment used to be designated 'A1 at Lloyds'. ◊ *Lutine Bell.*

Lobotomy ◊ *Leucotomy.*

Lobster. Large decapod marine ◊ *crustacean* of the genus *Homarus*, found and fished around the coasts of Europe and N. America. The first pair of legs are enlarged to form the characteristic claws, unlike in size and shape, one being adapted for crushing and the other for grasping. Injured limbs can be replaced by regeneration. Lobsters progress on the sea-bed mainly by walking, but are capable of swimming backwards at great speed.

Local Government. Administrative and executive bodies, popularly elected, in a defined locality, with the power to make by-laws. The system is of long standing in the U.K.; its present organization dates to the 19th cent. and takes the form of locally elected councils (e.g. county councils, county borough councils, borough councils, urban district councils, rural district councils, etc.) whose members are unpaid. The services administered by local authorities vary, usually including health and sanitary services, highways, street lighting, parks, public baths, housing, welfare, fire, and civil defence services. Primary and secondary education is also a matter for the Local Education Authorities, working in conjunction with the Ministry of Education. In 1964 the London County Council was reorganized into the Greater London Council covering a still larger area but sub-divided into newly grouped boroughs.

In the U.S.A. local government follows a similar pattern, but in most other countries (notably France, where a system of complete centralization of government was instituted during the Revolutionary period) all local administration is closely controlled by the central government and is only advisory in function. In communist countries local councils (known in U.S.S.R. as soviets < Russian 'council') have varying competence in certain limited fields.

Locarno Pact. 1925. Series of treaties which (a) guaranteed the 1919 Franco-German and Belgo-German frontiers, (b) provided for the peaceful settlement of all disputes between Germany, France, and Belgium, (c) provided that if (a) and (b) were broken other signatories (inc. Britain and Italy) would come to the help of the party attacked, and (d) committed France to helping Poland and Czechoslovakia

against an attack. Germany thus accepted the 1919 settlement in the west (but not in the east).

Lock. A basin with gates, to enable ships to be transferred from one level to another in a ◊ *canal*; also necessary between tidal waters and docks. The vessel enters the lock, and with the gates closed water is admitted or released through sluices, to raise or lower the water level. Locks were in use in the Netherlands by the end of the 14th cent. Leonardo da Vinci in the 15th cent. evolved the mitre gate, which uses the water pressure to keep the gates tightly closed.

Lockjaw. Disease of the ◊ *central nervous system* caused by toxins of the tetanus bacillus, which gains entry to the body through an abrasion or wound esp. when contaminated by soil. The earliest symptom is *trismus*, a spasm of the jaw muscle; later the spasms spread until all muscles are involved. Tetanus toxoid injections provide active immunization; anti-toxic serum gives brief passive immunity.

Lockout. Exclusion of workers from their employment by the employers (the counterpart of a ◊ *strike*) to force the employer's terms, sometimes used in the early days of industrialism but now virtually obsolete.

Locust. 1. Tropical insects of the order *Orthoptera*, to which also belong the cockroaches and grasshoppers; well-known are the African migratory locust and the desert locust. The third pair of legs, with which they jump, is very long; and when rubbed against the fore-wings the legs make a whirring noise. They have 'ears' on the front legs or the first abdominal segment. Locusts are vegetarian and usually solitary, but in certain conditions, as yet not fully understood, they increase rapidly in numbers and migrate in thick clouds, to devour everything vegetable in their path; they cause incalculable damage to agriculture. The young wingless 'hoppers' are also extremely destructive. Locust control, which limits the damage by poisoning breeding grounds and spraying the swarms in the air, is directed by an international organization. **2.** LOCUST BEAN (CAROB): *Ceratonia siliqua*; a tree from the Near East of which the pods, containing a large amount of sugar, are eaten as food (St John's

Bread) and also much used as fodder ◊ *Leguminosae*.

3. Trees of the genus *Robinia* (◊ *Leguminosae*), native to U.S.A. and Mexico; false acacia. The common locust produces a hard wood used for shipbuilding etc.

Lodestone. < Anglo-Saxon *lōd*, way. Naturally magnetic variety of black oxide of iron (magnetite), known in antiquity, from which the first form of ◊ *compass* was made. ◊ *Magnetism*.

Log. 1. A device for measuring a ship's speed or the distance run; the hand log was a triangular piece of wood, weighted so as to hang vertically in the water and thus remain stationary while the log-line reeled out during the period set by a sand-glass, knots in the line being so spaced that the number passing through the operator's hand indicated the vessel's speed in nautical m.p.h. (hence ◊ *knots*). The patent log, introduced in the mid 19th cent. and still in general use, employs a spinner on the log-line, the number of revolutions being recorded mechanically on a dial showing the distance run.

2. A ship's official diary; properly, the log book.

Logarithms. Early in the 17th cent. John Napier, a Scots mathematician, invented a way of doing multiplication and division which greatly reduced the labour involved by ordinary procedures, particularly where very large numbers are involved. His method is based on the addition or subtraction of indices e.g. $a^3 \times a^2 = a^5$ (the power to which a must be raised to give the result is obtained by adding the indices). Conversely $a^6 \div a^2 = a^4$. Every positive number has its 'logarithm', the power to which a third number (the base) must be raised to produce the given number, i.e. if $N = b^1$ then $\log_b N = 1$. Tedious calculations of multiplication (or division) or root extraction can be replaced by the simpler process of adding (or subtracting) the appropriate logarithms, which are obtained from tables. Napier published the first tables in 1614. Logarithms are usually to the base of 10 (thus the log of 100 is 2 to the base of 10) but other bases can be used. ◊ *Slide Rule*.

Logic. Traditionally part of ◊ *philosophy*, as founded by Aristotle, but now technically developed and as much the concern of mathematicians; basically the specification of forms of valid arguments, i.e.

those whose conclusions must be true *if* their premisses are true. Affirming the premisses and denying the conclusions results in self-contradiction, e.g. If no animals are altruists and all men are animals, then no men are altruists. The form of this argument – that characteristic which makes it valid, and is shared with similar arguments containing other terms in place of 'animals', 'altruists', and 'men' – can be set out as : If no A's are B's, and all C's are A's, then no C's are B's. Another argument, 'If it is raining, the grass is wet; it is raining; therefore the grass is wet', is of a different kind, such that its form can be set out by the use of symbols standing for whole propositions or assertions rather than single terms: If p then q; and p; therefore q. Although both these very simple forms of argument are intuitively recognizable as valid, more complex forms require special methods of determining whether or not they are valid. In a somewhat extended sense of the term, logic is also taken to cover the study of arguments where the truth of the premisses makes that of the conclusion not certain but only probable; these are inductive arguments in which a general conclusion about a kind of thing (e.g. all metals) is based on an examination of a limited number.

Logical Positivism. A recent philosophy, whose ideals and attitudes remain influential although its specific doctrines have been qualified or abandoned; founded on ◊ *empiricism* and modern ◊ *logic* and respectful of science, it originated in the 'Vienna Circle' about 1920 and was expounded in English by A. J. Ayer. Its central claim, that the only meaningful statements (except in logic and mathematics) are those which at least in principle are verifiable by sense experience, led to the notorious rejection of religious, metaphysical, and evaluative statements as meaningless.

Lohengrin. Hero of a medieval German poem; son of Parsifal (◊ *Holy Grail*). At the command of King Arthur he was carried in a boat drawn by a swan to Mainz, where he married Elsa, daughter of the duke of Brabant. She was enjoined never to ask his name; when she did so, the swan-drawn boat carried him away to the Grail.

Lollards. Reformist Christians in England in the 14th and 15th centuries, who followed the teachings of John Wyclif 1324–84. They rejected transsubstantiation (◊ *Holy Communion*), clerical celibacy, and other Roman Catholic beliefs and practices, and upheld the right of every believer to interpret the ◊ *Bible* for himself as the sole source of religious authority. Their advanced views on social reform led to civil disturbances, and their bitter persecution as heretical by the official Church and the State (some being burnt alive) drove them underground, but Lollardry was still influential in England at the time of the ◊ *Reformation*. ◊◊ *Hussites*.

Lombard League. 1167. League of towns in Lombardy against the emperor Frederick I (◊ *Holy Roman Empire*). Originally Cremona, Mantua, Bergamo, and Brescia; it grew rapidly until it included 36 cities, with Pope Alexander III as their leader. In his honour the league named its fortified city Alessandria. At the battle of ◊ *Legnano* the League defeated the emperor, greatly reducing his power in Italy. The League was revived in 1226 against Frederick II.

London Clay. Stiff intractable clay deposited as a fine-grained mud in a tropical sea in Eocene (Tertiary) times (◊ *Geological Time Scale*); bluish grey at depth but weathering to brown near the surface, found as subsoil in and around London. It affords poor farmland, and was often avoided in early times, the natural oak forests being cleared for agriculture only slowly.

Longitude. Angular E. or W. distance of the meridian of a given place from the standard Greenwich meridian (longitude 0°), degrees of longitude being about 69 m. at the equator and decreasing towards the poles. For every 15° longitude E. local time goes forward an hour, for every 15° W. back an hour, until there is 24 hours difference at points immediately on either side of longitude 180° (the International Date Line).

MERIDIAN: Half of a ◊ *great circle* passing through the poles and cutting the equator at right angles; a line through places of equal longitude.

CELESTIAL MERIDIAN: Half a great circle passing through the celestial poles and cutting the celestial equator at right angles.

◊◊ *Astronomy, Celestial Sphere, Map.*
Loofah ◊ *Gourds.*

Lord Advocate. The principal Law Officer in Scotland, corresponding to the ◊ *Attorney-General* in England but also performing the duties of ◊ *Public Prosecutor*.

Lord Chamberlain's Office. All plays, revues, sketches, and acts which are to be presented publicly in the U.K. must first be submitted to the Lord Chamberlain, who has the power to require deletion of words, actions, or gestures as he thinks fit. In practice he employs a staff of readers (who also attend performances). Any censorship of the theatre has been much criticized in modern times (notably and eloquently by Shaw), but the Office is now becoming more liberal. It is largely supported by theatre managers, since the Lord Chamberlain's approval guarantees that there is no risk of legal prosecution. Theatre clubs are outside the Lord Chamberlain's jurisdiction.

Lord Chancellor. The president of the House of Lords when it sits in full session as a branch of the Legislature; presides over the House when it sits as a final court of appeal, nominates High Court judges, appoints magistrates, and is entitled to sit in the ◊ *Court of Appeal* though he rarely does so. He is also a member of the Cabinet, and thus his position is the most obvious exception to the doctrine of ◊ *Separation of Powers*. ◊◊ *Judiciary*.

Lord Chief Justice. The president of the Queen's Bench Division of the High Court, and *ex officio* a member of the Courts of Appeal and of Criminal Appeal, where he presides; entitled to sit in the House of Lords, he is invariably appointed a Privy Councillor and is therefore a member of the Judicial Committee of the ◊ *Privy Council* and is sometimes called the permanent head of the Judiciary. Unlike the ◊ *Lord Chancellor*, he is not a member of the government and does not resign when it changes, his position being similar to that of a permanent secretary to the Minister in charge of a department.

Lord Lieutenant. Representative of the monarch, and therefore chief of the justices and chief of the militia, in each county of England, Wales, Scotland, and N. Ireland; a life appointment, first created in the 16th cent. Also, historically, until 1800 the monarch's deputy in and for Ireland (also called the Viceroy), after the office lapsed in 1920.

Lord President of the Council. In the U.K. used to preside over meetings of the

Privy Council; usually a member of the Cabinet, but often has no fixed departmental duties, so as to be free to carry out any special functions decided on by the Prime Minister.

Lord Privy Seal. A member of the government, in charge of no specific department; originally, the privy seal (one of the three royal seals) was used to legalize the private expenses of the Crown, and though this practice ceased 1884, the title of Lord Keeper was kept for one of the Cabinet.

Lotharingia. The Middle Kingdom (between France and Germany), comprising the present Low Countries, Alsace, Lorraine, and NW Germany. It was granted to Lothair I at the division of the ◊ *Carolingian* empire in A.D. 843, and for a short time also included Burgundy and Italy. In 870 it was divided between France and Germany, and a long struggle for its complete possession ensued, ending in 925 when the emperor Henry I was able to make it a German duchy. Bruno of Cologne divided it in two: the northern half (including the Netherlands and parts of modern Belgium and Germany) split up into many bishoprics and principalities, while most of the southern half became the duchy of Lorraine. The territories of Lotharingia have been for centuries a constant battleground between France and Germany.

Lottery. Allotting prizes, usually monetary, by drawing lots; illegal in the U.K. since 1826, with the exception of 'small lotteries' promoted by registered societies for non-commercial purposes in which no prize exceeds £100 and no ticket costs more than a shilling. However, many competitions in which there is a nominal exercise of skill, e.g. football pools, are virtually lotteries. In many countries a national lottery is run to raise money for the state. Sweepstakes – lotteries based on the results of horseraces – are also illegal in the U.K. The Irish Republic runs the flourishing Irish Hospitals Sweepstake. Lotteries are also illegal in U.S.A. but the 'numbers racket' is in effect a vast daily lottery. The British ◊ *premium bonds* are legally not a lottery.

Lotus. Popular name for several plants, esp. water lilies. The Egyptian lotus, *Nymphaea lotus*, is pink or white. *N. v caerulea* is blue and was a sacred flower in Ancient Egypt. Flowers were put in

tombs and used as a carved emblem. The sacred lotus of the old world esp. India is *Nelumbium speciosum*, pink-flowered, and introduced to Egypt about 700 B.C. Both have edible seeds. The lotus-eaters (*lotophagi*) of legend ate a quite different 'lotus', which was said to induce oblivion and happiness.

Loudspeaker. The most common type is the moving-coil speaker, in which a 'voice' coil of finely wound copper wire is so fixed in a paper cone that it is free to move across the pole-piece of a powerful magnet. When fluctuating current passes through the coil, the magnetic field created by it reacts with the field of the magnet to produce a to-and-fro piston-like motion of the coil and thus create a succession of sound waves corresponding to the current. Loudspeakers of modern design are capable of very faithful reproduction, when sufficiently large.

Louisiana Purchase. 1803. In the 1680s France claimed the drainage basin of the Mississippi, amounting to over one million sq. m. In 1762 and 1763 the area was ceded to Britain and Spain. When Spain gave back her part (west of the Mississippi and the 'Isle of Orleans') to France in 1800, the U.S. government grew uneasy and offered to buy the area; Napoleon, then busy with the 'Black Republic' revolt in ◊ *Haiti*, sold it for about $15 m. All or part of 13 States of U.S.A. were created from this land.

Lourdes. Town in Hautes-Pyrénées, France, where in 1858 Bernadette Soubirous (canonized 1933) had a vision of ◊ *Mary*. After a number of miraculous healings were alleged to have taken place at a spring which arose near the spot, sick and infirm persons began to visit Lourdes in large numbers, two great churches were built, and it became a pilgrim centre attracting millions of visitors hoping to be healed. Zola's *Lourdes* was an attack on haphazard management and wild claims, but the centre is now strictly supervised. Medical and ecclesiastical commissions investigate and report on the numerous claims of miraculous cures; relatively few are established.

Louse. Parasitic insect in the orders *Mallophaga* (biting lice) and *Anoplura* (sucking lice); the human body louse, a piercer, transmits relapsing fevers and typhus.

Lucerne. A ◊ *clover*-like plant, one of the ◊ *legumes*, widely grown as a feeding-stuff for stock (fed direct, as hay or silage, or artificially dried), preferring a continental to a maritime climate; named alfalfa in America.

Luciferase, Luciferin ◊ *Firefly, Luminescence.*

Lucknow (1857) ◊ *Indian Mutiny.*

Luddites. Workers of the late 18th and early 19th centuries who broke up the new machines introduced into factories (◊ *Industrial Revolution*), in protest against the resulting unemployment and reduced payments as compared with the former home-working handwork rates. The 18th-cent. Luddites were knitters, led by 'Captain Ludd' (from a legendary King Ludd of ancient Britain), who smashed the first knitting-frames esp. in Nottinghamshire. The main outbreaks were in 1811–16; Byron's House of Lords speech in defence of the protesting workmen is famous. Luddism continued sporadically, though harshly suppressed, until the 1840s.

Lumbago. Generic term for an attack of severe pain in the lumbar or lumbo-sacral region of the back. ◊ *Intervertebral Disc.*

Luminescence. Production of visible light by means other than heat, the basic mechanism being the conversion of a different form of energy (e.g. chemical) into light energy. Some substances possess the ability to absorb light of one wavelength and emit it at another; this was first observed in ◊ *fluorspar* (calcium fluoride), hence the term 'fluorescence'. Many living organisms e.g. bacteria, fungi, protozoa, crustaceans, insects, and a few fishes are able to emit light. ◊ *Firefly, Phosphorescence.*

Lungfish. Tropical freshwater fish whose chief characteristic is the possession of lungs, enabling it to breathe air when the pools in which it lives become foul during the dry season, with consequent reduction of oxygen; they have ◊ *gills* also.

Lungs. Organs of breathing; in mammals there are two lungs in the chest cavity surrounding the heart. The tubes carrying the air into the lungs divide and sub-divide a great number of times, finally reaching the thin-walled air sacs (*alveoli*) in which the air comes into very close contact with the blood over a very large area. Oxygen can readily diffuse from the air to replenish that of the venous blood flowing into the lungs; at the same time carbon dioxide can diffuse out into the *alveoli* to be exhaled. ◊ *Circulatory System, Respiration.*

Lunik. Soviet ◊ *rocket*; Lunik I was the first deep-space probe, Lunik II the first to achieve an impact on the moon, and Lunik III obtained the first photograph of the previously unseen side of the moon, in 1959. ◊ *Artificial Satellite, Space Exploration.*

Lupin. Large genus of the ◊ *Leguminosae*, of which but few wild species are in cultivation. For many years the only lupin in cultivation was the herbaceous perennial *Lupinus polyphyllus*, from N. America; later the shrubby yellow-flowered tree lupin was reintroduced from California. By crossing these two lupins and selecting seedlings, a very popular race has arisen known as 'Russell lupins'. Annual lupins e.g. *L. luteus* from S. Europe are frequently grown as green manure (◊ *Nitrogen Cycle*).

Lupus. *Lupus erythematosus* is a generalized disease unconnected with tuberculosis, in which inflammatory lesions appear not only in the skin but also in connective tissues generally, and in many organs, esp. the kidneys, which may be severely damaged.

Lusitania. Built on the Clyde 1907, the largest and fastest liner then afloat (with her sister-ship, the *Mauretania*); sunk without warning by a German ◊ *submarine* off the Irish coast, 7 May 1915, with the loss of 1198 lives, an event which aroused horror and indignation.

Lutetium ◊ *Lanthanides.*

Lutheranism. Form of Protestant ◊ *Christianity* based upon the Augsburg Confession 1530 (written by Melancthon, confirmed by Luther), widespread today in Germany, Scandinavia, and U.S.A. In Europe it usually has close connexions with the State, which often appoints its chief officials (◊ *Erastianism*). Emphasizes the sole authority of the ◊ *Bible*, and justification by faith; in the 19th and 20th centuries its doctrinal basis has considerably broadened, though recently the influence of Karl Barth and his associates has tended towards a return to first principles. ◊ *Calvinism, Creed, Peasants War, Reformation.*

Lutine Bell. The British frigate the *Lutine* was lost off the Dutch coast 1799 when carrying a large amount of bullion; during unsuccessful attempts to salvage the treasure, her bell was recovered and was hung in ◊ *Lloyds*, where it has been rung to announce important news ever since.

Lützen. 1632. A town in Saxony where the Swedish King Gustavus Adolphus fought a fierce and protracted battle during the ◊ *Thirty Years War* with the imperial troops under Wallenstein. Gustavus was killed, but the Swedish troops were eventually victorious.

Luxemburg. Area 1000 sq. m. Pop. 314,800. Cap. Luxemburg. Rel. Roman Catholic. Grand Duchy, bordered by Belgium, France, and Germany. Government is by a Chamber of Deputies elected by universal suffrage, and an upper Chamber appointed by the sovereign. The Head of State is the Grand Duchess Charlotte, but since 1961 rule has been delegated to her son Prince Jean.

ECONOMY. An important steel-producing country; headquarters of the European Coal and Steel Community. It has been a member of the Benelux Customs Union since 1947 and is a member of the European Economic Community.

HISTORY. Luxemburg was an important fief of the ◊ *Holy Roman Empire* in the Middle Ages and became a duchy in 1354. It passed to ◊ *Burgundy* in 1443 and to the house of ◊ *Hapsburg* soon afterwards, when it became part of the Austrian and Spanish Netherlands. Occupied by the French during the Napoleonic Wars, at the ◊ *Vienna Congress* 1815 it became both a Grand Duchy (in union with the ◊ *Netherlands*) and a member of the German Confederation. Its position was disputed throughout the 19th cent. and at the London Conference of 1867 the European powers declared it a neutral territory. This neutrality was violated by Germany in the First and Second World Wars. Luxemburg was liberated by the Allies in 1944, and with the Netherlands and Belgium formed the Benelux Union. Neutrality was formally abolished in 1948 and Luxemburg joined the North Atlantic Treaty Organization.

Luxor. Town in central ◊ *Egypt* (ancient), occupying part of the site of the ancient city of Thebes, notable for the Temple of Amon, 623 ft long, originally built in the reign of Amenhotep III but altered and added to by later Pharaohs. ◊ *Karnak*.

Lymphatic System. Comprises a very large number of thin-walled fine vessels which start blindly in the tissues of the body and unite to form progressively larger vessels as they go from the periphery to the central parts of the body. They eventually form two main trunks which empty lymph into the great veins at the base of the neck. Lymph is the clear fluid which exudes from the blood capillaries in the tissues and is picked up by the lymphatics together with bacteria and some cells and protein material. The lymph passes through lymph nodes on its way back to the blood stream and in these phagocytes deal with bacteria and foreign proteins. If the lymphatics are blocked or over-taxed, oedema results owing to accumulation of fluid in the tissues.

Lymphocytes ◊ *Blood*.

Lyre-bird. Australian bird; the male has a disproportionately large tail with three kinds of feathers, which suggest a lyre. It has an elaborate mating dance. Its nesting habit, a single egg laid in a nest often on the ground, exposes it to the risk of extinction.

Lyric. Originally a short poem, accompanied on the lyre; and hence poetry with a song-like quality, and more generally any short poem expressing personal thoughts and feelings. Lyric poems may be in a variety of forms e.g. ◊ *ballad, elegy,* folk-song, ◊ *hymn,* madrigal, ◊ *ode, sonnet.* The most celebrated lyric poets of the ancient world were Sappho, Alcaeus, Pindar, Horace, and Catullus; in medieval Europe there was a rich output of lyric poetry both in Latin and in the vernacular tongues, some of it exquisite; but the greatest periods of European lyric were probably about 1530–1660 (Shakespeare, Sidney, Donne, Marvell in England, Ronsard in France) and the late 18th and early 19th centuries (Burns, Wordsworth, Blake, Byron, Keats, Shelley, Lamartine, De Musset, Hugo, Goethe, Heine, Leopardi). Similar poetry is found in non-European literatures, notably those of China and Japan, where extreme brevity is the rule.

M

Mabinogion. Collection of Welsh tales in the White Book of Rhydderch (about A.D. 1300) and the Red Book of Hergest (about A.D. 1400). Some are old Welsh legends, others are romances about King Arthur and an important element in the ◊ *Arthurian Legend*. It was collected and edited by Lady Charlotte Guest and published with her translation between 1838 and 1849.

Macaroni. 1. Generic name for several kinds of food of dried paste made from hard wheaten flour. Macaroni is tubular, spaghetti and vermicelli like thin rods. Noodles are in the form of thin ribbons and often contain egg. Similar food pastes were long known in the Orient whence they were introduced into Europe about A.D. 1200 and became esp. popular in Italy.
2. Name for late 18th-cent. fops in England who affected extravagant fashions in dress and wigs (after their 'Macaroni Club' which introduced the dish to England).

Macedon. Country of the ancient world, N. of Greece. From the 6th cent B.C. its early independence was overshadowed by the Persians and Illyrians. Philip II 359–336 B.C. became the ruler of ◊ *Greece* and laid the foundations for the reign of Alexander the Great, when Macedonia was the centre of an empire stretching as far as India and Egypt. After his death there was a struggle for the throne and a time of foreign invasion. Alexander's successors brought about the spread of Hellenistic civilization, but Macedon itself declined. The Romans set up four independent republics there, which in 146 B.C. became the single province of ◊ *Macedonia*.

Macedonia. Mountainous region of the Balkan peninsula, of mixed population and complex history, smaller in extent than the Roman province (◊ *Macedon*), now divided between ◊ *Greece*, ◊ *Yugoslavia*, and ◊ *Bulgaria*. Ancient Macedonia was for a time under Byzantine rule until overrun by the Slavs in the 9th cent. After a period under the Bulgarian empire, it returned to ◊ *Byzantine* rule in 1018, but fell to the Turks in 1371. As the power of the ◊ *Ottoman empire* crumbled away, Macedonia's mixed population was disputed by Austria, Hungary, Russia, Greece, Serbia, and Bulgaria. The second Balkan War 1912–13 brought about the country's division, mainly between Greece and Serbia, and despite Bulgaria's efforts to reclaim it, after the ◊ *Second World War* it was again divided between Greece and Yugoslavia.

Machine-gun. Gun with automatic device for rapid and continuous bursts of rifle fire. An early mechanical version, invented by an American, Gatling, which fired six rounds in succession, was used in the ◊ *American Civil War*. Later versions were electrically driven. The French *mitrailleuse*, first used in the ◊ *Franco-Prussian war*, fired 37 barrels simultaneously. Further developments came with the Maxim gun (invented by the American Hiram S. Maxim), the first to use the recoil to reload, and the Vickers M.G. using a gas-trap recoil-cup to speed up the fire. Modern machine-guns fall into two classes: light weapons e.g. the Bren, fired from light mountings or from the shoulder; and heavier types supported by tripods. The former use clips or pans of ammunition, the latter work with belts. The tremendous increase in fire-power provided by the machine-gun radically affected tactics; it virtually ended the cavalry charge and contributed to pinning-down infantry warfare in the First World War.

Automatic weapons of above half-inch calibre, firing small shells (e.g. the Bofors 40 mm.), are known as cannon.

Mach Number. The relationship of the speed of an aircraft or rocket etc. to the speed of sound (Mach 1) in the same conditions. In terms of m.p.h. the Mach number varies with the air temperature and hence with the altitude: Mach 1 might be about 760 m.p.h. at sea level but 660 m.p.h. at 36,000 ft.

Mackerel. *Scomber scombrus*; handsome marine fish, common in the N. Atlantic, generally 10–12 in. long. The back is blue-green with black bars, the underside silvery. It is fished in great quantities for food.

McMahon Line. 1914. In 1913–14 a conference was held between China, Tibet, and Britain by which it was agreed between Britain and Tibet that a large part of the Indian-Tibet frontier should run along the crest of the Himalayas; this became known as the McMahon Line, after the British delegate. The Chinese delegate did not join in the negotiation, and although he initialled a draft tripartite convention, his government did not ratify it. After occupying Tibet in 1950, China made overtures to the Indian Government for a revision of the line; in September 1959 Chou En-lai withdrew his earlier acceptance of it, and in 1960 he negotiated frontier adjustments with Burma and Nepal. Clashes occurred on the Chinese-Indian border, and in 1962 Chinese troops advanced, driving back the Indian forces even after they were reinforced. Subsequently the Chinese withdrew from most of the occupied area.

M'Naghten Rules. Rules laid down by the judges in the case of Regina v. M'Naghten 1843, for the guidance of the House of Lords as to the extent to which insanity is a defence in criminal law: (a) Everyone is presumed sane until the contrary is proved; (b) insanity is a defence only if it is shown either that at the time of the offence the accused did not know what he was doing, or, if he knew, that he did not realize that it was wrong according to the standards of ordinary people; (c) an insane delusion must be treated as though it were true: if the belief would have justified the action had it been true, then it will equally do so when proved to be an insane delusion.

The appropriate verdict is 'not guilty by reason of insanity'. The prisoner is detained as a patient in Broadmoor, an institution for insane criminals. Although the special verdict is an acquittal, an appeal is now possible.

Madagascar (Malagasy). Area 228,000 sq. m. Pop. 5.7 m. Cap. Antananarivo (Tananarive). The fifth largest island in the world, in the Indian Ocean 240 m. from the coast of Africa; since 1960 an independent republic, but a member of the ◊ *French Community*, under a president and a National Assembly elected every four years.

ECONOMY. Mainly agricultural, principal exports being coffee (a third of the total), rice, vanilla, sugar, sisal, tobacco, cloves, ground-nuts, spices, raffia, pepper. Mineral resources include graphite and mica.

HISTORY. First visited by Europeans in 1500, it was claimed by France although active French attempts at colonization ceased in 1672. Despite British competition, the French declared it their protectorate in 1895, and suppressed the native dynasty. In 1957 constitutional reforms were introduced; Madagascar declared itself a republic in 1958 and a sovereign state in 1960, thereafter rejoining the French Community with special treaties of alliance. Now officially Malagasy.

Madrigal. Originally and etymologically a pastoral poem; later, a 16th-cent. verse form common in Italy. In music, a short polyphonic vocal composition requiring only one or two voices to each part, nearly always set to a secular text. A type of madrigal flourished in Italy in the 14th cent. and a new flowering in the 16th cent. produced the celebrated madrigals of Willaert, Arcadelt, and Lassus (all Flemings settled in Italy) and of such Italians as Marenzio. Under Italian inspiration, madrigals were also composed in England by Byrd, Weelkes, and others at the end of the 16th cent. and the beginning of the 17th. The form then died out in both Italy and England, except for later isolated imitations, not always stylistically close, e.g. Sullivan's 'madrigal' in *The Mikado*.

Mafeking. 1900. Town in S. Africa, besieged at the start of the ◊ *Boer War* by Cronje and defended for 218 days by Colonel Baden-Powell; its relief by Lord Roberts occasioned widespread celebration in England, the rejoicings on 'Mafeking Night' adding the word 'mafficking' to the language.

Mafia. A ◊ *secret society* in ◊ *Sicily*, highly organized and effective, using blackmail and intimidation in order to gain power over the peasants. It originated in the extensive influence gained by agents appointed by the landowners during Sicily's turbulent history, and spread through all classes in society. Mussolini attempted to stamp it out, but it is still in existence. With Italian immigration it also passed to U.S.A. where it underlay much of the gangsterism in major cities, and allegedly still does so.

Magdalenian ◊ *Palaeolithic.*

Magdeburg (1631) ◊ *Thirty Years War.*

Magenta. 1859. Village W. of Milan where the Franco-Sardinians under Napoleon III (◊ *Second Empire*) defeated Gyulai's Austrians (◊ *Italy*), the first decisive battle in the campaign which caused the expulsion of the Austrians from all their Italian possessions except Venetia, and led to the unification of Italy.

Magic. The performance of acts which are believed to influence events, where the link between cause and effect is mystical rather than scientific or 'common-sense'. It is often associated with a supernatural power ('mana') which pervades nature and may be manipulated by rites and incantations. The link between cause and effect is also associative, according to similarity (imitative magic) or contact (contagious magic). Some belief in magic is found in practically all cultures, diminishing with the advance of knowledge and technology. Magical beliefs were found in highly elaborated forms in the ancient civilizations esp. the Chaldean, Persian, and Egyptian. ◊ *Witchcraft and Sorcery.*

Maginot Line ◊ *Fortifications.*

Magistrate. A Justice of the Peace, appointed by the ◊ *Lord Chancellor.* Lay magistrates are unsalaried officials not trained as lawyers, acting in a part-time capacity; stipendiary magistrates are barristers or solicitors appointed to act fulltime. A magistrates' court takes criminal cases relating to any summary offence or to any indictable offence triable summarily (◊ *Crime*); matrimonial cases relating to separation, maintenance, and the custody of children; and a very limited class of civil claims. The clerk to the Court is legally qualified and advises lay magistrates in matters of law and procedure, but they are not bound to follow his advice.

Maglemosian ◊ *Mesolithic.*

Magma. Molten rock under the earth's crust which on cooling crystallizes into ◊ *igneous rocks,* the rate of flow varying with the quantity of steam and gases, and rocks in contact with the magma usually altering (sometimes completely) according to its temperature, pressure, and chemical composition. ◊ *Volcano.*

Magna Carta. 1215. The Great Charter of England, signed by King John at Runnymede under pressure from the barons and the Archbishop of Canterbury. As a statement of the law, the charter was chiefly intended to guarantee feudal rights against royal abuse and to maintain baronial privileges. By demanding reforms in local government, and insisting on the freedom of the Church and the right of merchants, it did provide safeguards for other sections of the community besides the baronage but its general provisions against oppression were few and vague. Its importance grew as it was reissued by later kings, and became a standard of appeal against injustice. In later years and esp. by Coke in the 17th cent. it was used, mistakenly but effectively, as the basis for increasing the power of the Commons against the Crown. ◊ *Evesham.*

Magnesium. Silvery metallic ◊ *element* which burns brightly when heated but resembles aluminium in its physical properties. It occurs in magnesite, dolomite, carnallite, and sea water from all of which it is commercially extracted. Its terrestrial abundance is nearly 2 per cent. Chlorophyll, present in all green plants, is a magnesium compound. Magnesium is a constituent of many light ◊ *alloys* e.g. magnalium and elektron. In powder form it is used in fireworks and flash powders. The properties of magnesium compounds resemble those of ◊ *calcium.* The oxide magnesia is used in metallurgical bricks and certain cements and in medicine. The carbonate has applications in the rubber, cosmetic, and pharmaceutical industries. The sulphate is known as Epsom salts.

Magnet. Originally a natural stone capable of attracting iron ◊ *lodestone*; also an electromagnet (permanent magnet) made by subjecting a suitable metal or alloy (◊ *Magnetism*) to an external magnetic field. A permanent magnet does not lose its strength through repeated use though frequent percussion or heating to a high temperature will dissipate it.

Magnetic Pole. Every ◊ *magnet* has a north-seeking and a south-seeking pole. Like poles repel and unlike attract each other. The earth, itself a magnet, has N. and S. magnetic poles, situated some distance from the geographical poles and liable to variation in position. Any magnet, freely suspended, will align itself with the magnetic poles and this is the basis for the ◊ *compass.* ◊ *Magnetism.*

Magnetism. All magnetic effects are apparently produced by moving electric charges, and by the fact that an atom possesses a magnetic moment due to the orbital motion of its electrons. The susceptibility of a substance to magnetism thus depends on how easily the magnetic moment of individual atoms can be brought into line. In this respect substances fall into three classes. PARAMAGNETIC: Substances which exhibit positive susceptibility to magnetism, such that when an external magnetic field is applied the magnetic moment of individual atoms becomes aligned along the magnetic field, causing the substance as a whole to acquire a magnetic moment. DIAMAGNETIC: Substances which have a small negative reaction to magnetism i.e. in them the application of an external magnetic field predominantly distorts the electron orbits. FERROMAGNETIC: Substances, notably iron, nickel, and cobalt, which have very pronounced properties. Whole regions of their microstructure (magnetic domains) have permanently aligned magnetic moments. In the unmagnetized state, the magnetic axes of individual domains are randomly oriented, but they become aligned when an external field is applied. The substance as a whole then acquires a magnetic moment far in excess of that obtainable with paramagnetic substances. Permanent magnetization results when the domains remain aligned after the external field is removed.

MAGNETIC FIELD: That space around a magnet or electric current showing special properties i.e. it will affect ferromagnetic materials, deflect another current or electrically charged particles.
◊ Lodestone.

Magneto. Permanent-magnet ◊ generator sometimes used on internal-combustion engines to provide the high-voltage supply to the sparking plugs.

Magnetostriction. ◊ Joule effect; slight change in the dimensions of substances on magnetization, and conversely a slight change in the magnetic properties of these substances when subjected to mechanical stress. This effect is used to produce small high-frequency vibrations for echo-sounding and vibration-testing of materials. Unwanted 'hum' in transformers results from the alternating magnetostriction in the core.

Magnetron. High-vacuum electron tube in which electrons are excited by crossed electromagnetic and magnetic fields, to produce power at high frequencies in the microwave region. The magnetron is at present the basis of ◊ radar transmitters.

Magnolia. A family of trees or shrubs native to N. America, China, Japan, and the Himalayas, many of which bear their flowers in early spring before the leaves appear, with very striking effect. Usually white, but some are in various shades of pink. *M. campbellii* from Sikkim and the glossy evergreen *M. grandiflora* from U.S.A. have flowers 10 in. across. The tulip-tree is one of the *Magnoliaceae*.

Magpie. Long-tailed bird with green, purple, and black plumage contrasting with the white belly and wing patches; common throughout the European countryside. It builds a massive domed nest in trees or bushes, rearing six to nine young.

Magyars. The people of ◊ Hungary. As a barbarian tribe, they appeared in Europe in the 9th cent. A.D. and occupied Hungary (under Arpad) 896; for a century they spread alarm in Europe by their raids into Italy and Germany, until they were Christianized under Stephen I (later canonized) in the 11th cent. Although synonymous with Hungarian, the name is now used to distinguish the Hungarian-speaking population from other racial minorities within the country.

Mahabharata. Indian epic, of enormous length (100,000 couplets), in its classical ◊ Sanskrit form apparently dating to about 300 A.D. and based on earlier tales or ballads. It deals with the strife between the Kauravas (the 100 sons of the blind king Dhritarashtra) and the Pandavas (the five sons of his brother Pandu); the Pandavas, in a game of dice, lose to the Kauravas everything they possess, retire for 12 years to the Kamyaka forest, and then return to claim their own in a great war, all the Kauravas being finally slain and the Pandavas winning back their kingdom, when the five brothers and their joint wife Draupadi renounce it, make a pilgrimage to Mount Meru, and ascend to heaven. Woven around this central story are many other episodes, tales, myths, and legends constituting an encyclopedia of Indian ideas on religion, morality, history, and other subjects. Most famous of the didactic and religious accretions is the *Bhagavad Gita*, Song of the Lord (◊ *Yoga*), in which ◊ *Krishna* reveals to the warrior prince Arujna the doctrine of ◊ *Karma* and the relation between illusion and reality.

Mahayana ◊ *Buddhism, Nirvana, Zen.*

Mahdi. An Islamic concept, not based on the Koran (Q'ran), of a redeemer who will appear at the end of time to establish a perfect kingdom. Many reformers have laid claim to be the Mahdi, one of whom, Mohamed Ahmed, arose in the ◊ *Sudan* to lead a revolt against the Egyptians, in the course of which in 1885 he captured Khartoum, where General Gordon was killed. His followers were finally overcome by an Anglo-Egyptian army under Kitchener at the battle of Omdurman, 1898, which resulted in British control of the Sudan.

Mah Jongg. A game for two or, more usually, four players, using 136 (formerly 144) decorated pieces of bamboo and ivory called 'tiles'. To start the game, the tiles are mixed and arranged in walls, face down, in front of each player. Each person selects 13, and in turn takes one and discards, aiming to make up four sets of threes – of a kind or in sequence – and one pair, when he can 'go out'. Points are given for these different combinations, and the score can be doubled several times for particular situations, making at times very large totals. The game probably originated in China· at a time unknown, and reached Japan in 1907. Constantly popular among the Chinese, it had its Western vogue in U.S.A. and Britain in the mid 1920s.

Mahogany. Strictly, the timber from species of *Swietenia*, of the *Meliaceae*, native to tropical America; more loosely, over 60 species of hardwoods from various continents. Mahogany was widely used as a cabinet wood in Europe in the 18th cent. The finest wood is of a rich red colour with a close grain, produced from slow-growing trees.

Mahrattas. People of central India who built up a powerful kingdom in the 17th cent. and constituted a considerable threat to the ◊ *Mogul* empire. Their power declined when they split up into five separate states, and especially after their defeat by Ahmad Shah of Afghanistan in 1761. The British fought a number of wars against them and by 1818 had brought all their territory under control.

Maiden Castle ◊ *Castle, Fortifications.*

Maize. *Zea mays*; a major ◊ *cereal*, of complex ancestry, native to S. America, where it has been cultivated since early times. There are many varieties, and in U.S.A. yields have been increased by the development of hybrid corn. The plant is a tall annual 3–15 ft high, with a tuft of erect male flowers; the cobs form from the lateral female flowers (with long, silky stigmas). The grain is usually yellow, but varies according to type, from soft and sugary (as in sweet-corn, usually· eaten unripe) to very hard (as in popcorn, which explodes when roasted). The ◊ *endosperm* is mainly starch; the germ is rich in oil. It is cultivated for making flour (polenta), or for fodder. Further uses are as a source of starch, glucose, alcohol, and oil. World production is about 200 m. tons annually, of which half is grown in U.S.A. (◊ *Corn Belt*). Other producers are Brazil, India, U.S.S.R. Smaller quantities are grown in Europe, mainly as fodder. In Italy and parts of U.S.A. and Mexico polenta is a staple of human diet.

Majlis. Ar. 'a session'; hence name for national assembly or parliament in several Arab States and in ◊ *Persia.*

Majolica ◊ *Faience.*

Maladjustment. A child whose behaviour causes concern, who suffers from a long-standing emotional difficulty, who is continually at loggerheads with his family, or who is excessively shy or apathetic, is described as maladjusted. Child Guidance Centres have been set up in most districts to help parents to deal with maladjusted children and to give treatment; in some cases, children may be sent to special day and boarding schools set up under the 1944 Education Act. The term is also applied to adults who suffer from similar emotional difficulties. ◊ *Neurosis.*

Malaga. A fortified wine from S. Spain, made by a process similar to that for ◊ *port*, except that there are additions of other ingredients derived from grape juice. The resultant wine is dark in colour with a very distinctive flavour. It is believed to have been made in somewhat the same fashion since Phoenician times.

Malagasy ◊ *Madagascar.*

Malapropism. A ludicrous misuse of words based on mis-hearing or incomprehension (i.e. Fr. *mal à propos*), exemplified by the verbal blunders of Mrs Malaprop in Sheridan's *The Rivals* 1775, e.g. 'Caparisons are odorous!' for 'comparisons are odious'.

Malawi. Area 36,686 sq. m. Pop. 3 m. 2.9 m. Africans). Cap. Zomba. Independent country of central Africa, member of the British Commonwealth, formerly Nyasaland. The elections of 1961, held under the 1961 constitution which extended the franchise, resulted in a clear majority for the African Malawi Congress Party under Dr Hastings Banda, who became Prime Minister.

ECONOMY. Malawi is predominantly agricultural; chief exports are tea, tobacco, and cotton. There are mineral deposits, but poor communications have hampered development; there is no outlet to the sea except through ◊ *Mozambique* or ◊ *S. Rhodesia*.

HISTORY. Nyasaland became a British protectorate in 1891 and in 1953 became part of the Federation of Rhodesia and Nyasaland. The British government granted a new constitution in 1961 and in 1962 the right to secede from the Federation. In 1963 Nyasaland became self-governing, and the Federation was dissolved. In 1964 she achieved full independence, as Malawi.

Malay. A widespread variety of the Malayo-Polynesian languages; as Bahasa Indonesian it has been adopted as the official language of an extensive region roughly from Formosa to New Zealand and from Easter Island to Madagascar. Pidgin or Bazaar Malay is used as a ◊ *lingua franca* in this entire Pacific area, which contains a population of over 100 m. Malay has been called 'the world's easiest language'. Its grammar, pronunciation, and word-forms are simple: nouns have no case inflexion, number, or gender; verbs are distinguished as transitive, passive, causative, etc. by affixes. It has long been written in an adapted ◊ *Arabic* alphabet, but recently Roman script has been introduced. English has borrowed many Malay words e.g. bamboo, bantam, raffia, sago. The national language of the ◊ *Philippines*, Tagalog, is Malayan.

Malaya ◊ *Malaysia*.

Malaysia. Area 128,703 sq. m. Pop. 10.3 m. (about half Malay, a third Chinese, the rest Indian, with some tribes of pre-Malay aborigines). Cap. Kuala Lumpur. Rel. Muslim. A sovereign member of the ◊ *British Commonwealth*; the Federation of Malaya since 1957, reconstituted 1963 to include N. Borneo (◊ *Indonesia*), Sarawak, and Singapore. The Head of the Federation is the Raja, with a Deputy Head, a President, and a Council of Rulers (of the 11 federated states) who are empowered to elect the Head and his Deputy.

ECONOMY. Malaya is the chief world supplier of rubber and tin (respectively 60

and 20 per cent of its total exports); also large exports of iron ore, palm oil, coconut oil, copra. An equatorial jungle country, 70 per cent of the territory is still undeveloped.

HISTORY. The Malays probably originated in S. China. In the first 12 centuries A.D. there was much trade and cultural penetration from India; Thai and Javan invasions began in the 13th cent. and brought Indo-Chinese influence, and in the 15th cent. the Malays were converted from Buddhism to Islam. The Portuguese and Dutch began European colonial conquest in the 16th cent. and in the 17th were followed by the British, who were dominant from 1786 onwards. In the ◊ *Second World War* the Malay States were occupied by Japan. A Union of Malay States was again set up by Britain in 1946; after a period of nationalist armed resistance, the Federation was formed. ◊◊ *Partition*.

LANGUAGE. ◊ *Malay*.

Maldive Islands. Pop. about 90,000. Cap. Malé. Rel. Muslim. Chain of 7000 coral atolls 600 m. long, SW of Ceylon, of which 200 are inhabited. An elective sultanate with an elected Parliament (Majlis); British protectorate.

ECONOMY. Chiefly fishing; large exports of dried fish to Ceylon.

LANGUAGE. Maldivian, related to old Sinhalese.

Mali. Area· 582,437 sq. m. Pop. 4.4 m. Cap. Bamako. An independent republic (formerly French Sudan) in NW Africa. Rel. mainly Muslim.

ECONOMY. Semi-desert; some gold-mining and salt-mining, but the mineral resources (iron ore, manganese, and phosphates) are largely unexploited. France and U.S.A. give economic aid.

HISTORY. In the Middle Ages the Mali and Songhai empires were powerful and Timbuktu a centre of learning and culture, but the Songhai empire fell to Moroccan conquerors in the 16th cent. and the Mali was swallowed up by Tuareg invaders in the 17th. French conquest began in the 19th cent. but Mali did not succumb until 1896; the area was named French Sudan from 1899. In 1958 the colony voted to remain a member of the ◊ *French Community* as the autonomous Sudanese Republic; it united with Senegal in 1959 (as the Mali Federation) but in 1960 the union was dissolved and the former

Sudan declared itself the completely independent Mali Republic, withdrawing from the French Community, becoming a member of U.N.O. and forming the Union of African States with Ghana and Guinea. With Morocco and Egypt, this Union forms the neutralist but strongly nationalist Casablanca group within the Afro-Asian bloc.

Malplaquet. 1709. Village in N. France near Mons, scene of the last pitched battle of the ◊ *War of the Spanish Succession*, in which the allies, under Marlborough and Prince Eugène, opposed the French under Villars. The French retreated from the field, but the allied casualties were the heavier and they gained little advantage from the battle.

Malt ◊ *Barley, Brewing.*

Malta. Area 122 sq. m. Pop. 330,000. Cap. Valetta. Rel. Roman Catholic. Small Mediterranean island of strategic importance, member of the British Commonwealth.

ECONOMY. Agriculture, esp. potatoes and onions for export; fishing; lace-making; important port of call for shipping.

HISTORY. Under foreign rule since Phoenician times, long linked with Sicily, occupied by Arabs in the 8th cent. and Normans in the 11th, and in the 16th given by the Emperor Charles V (◊ *Holy Roman Empire*) to the Knights Hospitallers, who won fame as the Knights of Malta by repelling a Muslim attack 1565 and ruled the island until it was taken by the French 1798. Ceded to Britain 1814, Malta became self-governing 1921, served as a British naval base during the ◊ *Second World War* (being awarded the George Cross in 1942 in recognition of its people's bravery under continual heavy bombing), reverted briefly to colony status 1959, and received a fresh self-governing constitution which came into force 1962, despite keen differences between the Socialists and the Catholic Church. Fully independent since 1964.

LANGUAGE. Maltese, a dialect of the ◊ *Semitic languages*, descended from that of the Phoenician colonists; it uses the Roman alphabet and is related to Arabic and Hebrew. Italian and English are also used.

Malta Fever ◊ *Undulant Fever.*

Malthusianism. The English economist Malthus 1766–1834 set against the growth of the human ◊ *population* the fact that land (unlike people) cannot be multiplied: while the number of mouths grows geometrically, the productivity of land does so only arithmetically. His pessimistic conclusion that the mass of the world's population must remain near starvation level stimulated the ◊ *birth-control* movement. Improvements in agriculture, and a falling birth rate in industrial countries, have in the present century been offset by a population explosion in many parts of the world which threatens to outrun world food production.

Mamba. Extremely poisonous African snake, related to the ◊ *cobra.*

Mamelukes. < Ar. *mamluk*, a slave. Originally a bodyguard of slaves for the caliph of Egypt, who became so powerful as to make one of themselves caliph in A.D. 1250. A line of Mamelukes reigned till 1517. After the Turks conquered Egypt they again became the palace guard and rose to power during Napoleon's occupation. They were exterminated by Mohammed Ali in 1811.

Mammal. Class of vertebrate animals which are warm-blooded and suckle their young, divided into three sub-classes. The monotremes, which survive only in Australia e.g. the duck-billed platypus, lay eggs, but suckle their young when hatched. The ◊ *marsupials* bear their young alive, but little developed, transferring them to a pouch until development is complete. They survive in Australia and S. America. In the placentals, mammals proper, the placenta maintains the embryo until full term; they have the potentiality of a large cerebral cortex, and hence of learned behaviour of great sensitivity, and are warm-blooded and hair-covered. There are 26 orders (of which 10 are known only from fossils) e.g. ◊ *Primates* (including man), Carnivora (e.g. ◊ *bear*, ◊ *tiger*), Insectivora (e.g. ◊ *hedgehog*), Perissodactyla (e.g. ◊ *horse*), Rodentia (◊ *mouse*), Cetacea (◊ *whales*), and Chiroptera (◊ *bat*).

Mammoth ◊ *Mastodon.*

Man ◊ *Primates.*

Manchester School ◊ *Laissez-faire.*

Manchuria. Mountainous region of NE ◊ *China*, the home of nomadic tribes who early invaded China and were gradually absorbed within the Chinese sphere of influence; in the 17th cent. it became a state powerful enough to impose on China the Manchu dynasty, which ruled until 1911. In its decline Russian influence increased,

the evolution of mammals

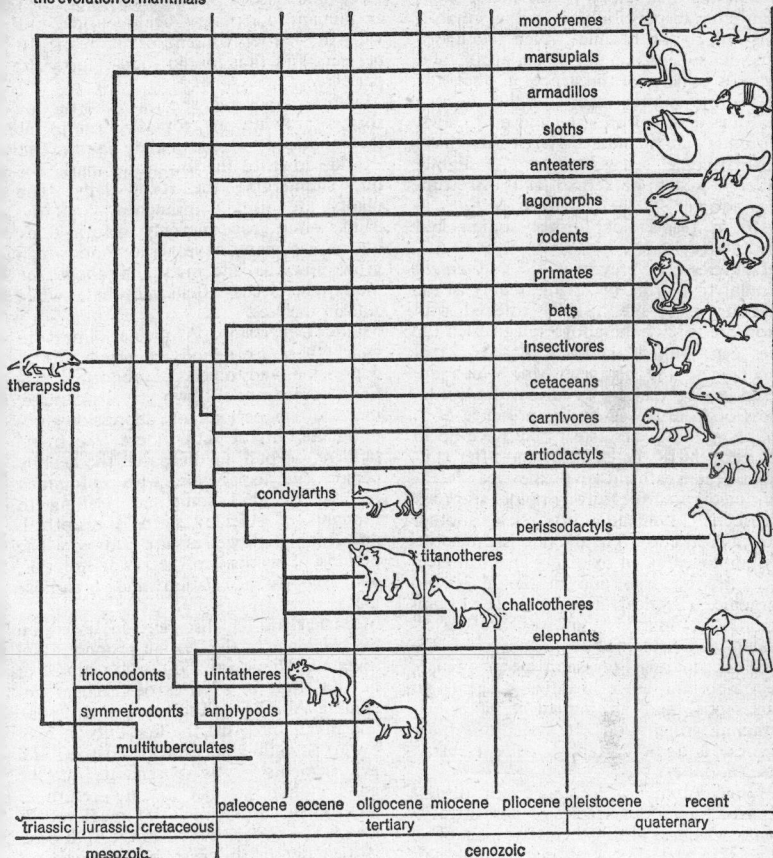

				paleocene	eocene	oligocene	miocene	pliocene	pleistocene		recent
triassic	jurassic	cretaceous				tertiary					quaternary
mesozoic							cenozoic				

as in the building of the Chinese Eastern Railway (a branch of the Trans-Siberian) and the lease of the Liaotung peninsula (including Port Arthur) to Russia. After the ◊ *Russo-Japanese War* Russia had to cede to ◊ *Japan* Port Arthur and S. Manchuria. In 1932 the Japanese occupied all Manchuria and set up the puppet state of Manchukuo under the restored Manchu emperor, but their defeat in the ◊ *Second World War* enabled U.S.S.R. to reoccupy Manchuria, which was returned to China after the victory of the Chinese communists in 1948. It is now a region of some 600,000 sq. m. with a pop. of 50 m.,

of great agricultural and industrial importance.

Mandamus. A prerogative order (◊ *Certiorari*) issued by the Queen's Bench Division of the High Court, commanding a judge or other official to perform a public duty which he has refused to perform e.g. because he erroneously believed that he had no power to do so.

Mandate. Trusteeship system established by the ◊ *League of Nations* after the ◊ *First World War*, for the administration of former German and Turkish possessions by appointed members of the Allied powers. It differed from a ◊ *protectorate* in that the mandatory power had obligations and responsibilities to the inhabitants and to the League (which retained a general supervision of mandates), and from a sphere of influence in that the mandatory power had a right to levy revenues, appoint officials, and make laws. Virtually all mandated territories have now become self-governing. A slightly different system of Territorial Trusteeships was adopted by the ◊ *United Nations* in 1946 in respect of former Italian and Japanese colonies.

Manganese. A grey metallic ◊ *element* similar to ◊ *iron*, occurring mainly as the dioxide pyrolusite, usually smelted with iron ore to give the alloys spiegeleisen (20 per cent Mn, 80 per cent Fe) or ferromanganese (80 per cent Mn) which are used in steel making to correct the brittleness of iron caused by the presence of ◊ *sulphur*. Manganese steel may have up to 26 per cent of the element, and after suitable heat treatment gives the wear-resistant metal used for railway points and rock crushers. Manganese bronze is another much-used alloy. The dioxide is extensively employed as an oxidizing agent in electric dry batteries and in the glass and organic chemical industry. The commonest compounds, however, are the divalent $+2$ (manganous) ones and the permanganates. Potassium permanganate is important as an oxidizing agent, an antiseptic, and an ingredient of wood-staining preparations. In agriculture manganese is an important ◊ *trace element*. ◊◊ *Thermite*.

Mange. Animal ◊ *scabies*, a skin disease caused by various species of parasitical ◊ *mite* which establish themselves on or in the skin esp. in sweat glands and hair follicles; in horses and sheep, one of the ◊ *scheduled diseases*. All types respond to drug treatment exc. follicular mange in dogs.

Mangel-wurzel ◊ *Mangold*.

Mango. *Mangifera indica*; native to India, but now extensively cultivated throughout the tropics for its edible fruits, oval and yellowish-orange when ripe, three or four in. long. The tissues contain resinous fibre, and inferior fruits have a marked flavour of turpentine. The unripe fruits are used in pickles and chutneys.

Mangold. < German *Mangelwurzel*, famine root; a specially developed variety of beet grown for animal feeding (esp.

sheep and cattle) but in emergency used as human food; very heavy yields, but with dry-matter content often below 10 per cent and thus low in food-value yield per acre.

Mangrove. Several species of trees or shrubs growing in tropical swamps at the mouths of rivers, mainly in the Old World, down to the low water mark, the tide submerging the roots daily. The plants are usually branched, and the trunks often grow unevenly to form thick buttresses; many have aerial roots which grow upwards and stick out above the mud. The seeds often germinate while still on the tree.

Manic Depression. A mental illness in which there are periods of severe mental depression and others of abnormal elation; sometimes the two states alternate, more often periods of depression predominate. In the latter there is extreme sadness, beyond anything that the healthy person can experience, with unfounded feelings of guilt sometimes leading to thoughts of suicide; sleep is disturbed, and bodily processes are slowed. The periods of mania are the reverse of this, with moods of elation and grandiose ideas.

Manichaeism. Dualist religion based on the teachings of the Persian prophet Mani (executed about A.D. 275), who claimed to be the latest in a series of teachers (including Abraham, Zoroaster, and Jesus), and maintained that the first duty of man – who is compounded of mixed good and evil elements – was to separate out the good in him, so that it could return to its source. Influential in medieval ◊ *heresy* (◊ *Albigenses*), after the 10th cent. it died out in the west, but survived till the 14th in central Asia.

ELECT: Lived secluded from the world in extreme asceticism.

HEARERS: Lived in the world (subject to certain rules of conduct) and supported the Elect.

◊◊ *Gnostics, Mysticism*.

Manihot. Tropical plants of the ◊ *Euphorbiaceae*, native in S. America. *M. utilissima* (cassava, manioc) is one of the major food plants of the world; its large tuberous roots, rich in starch, have long been the staple food of many S. American Indians, and the Portuguese carried it from S. America to many other tropical countries, where it is widely cultivated.

There are two main types, bitter and sweet, the former being easy to grow and a heavy cropper. The juice of the roots is highly poisonous, containing hydrocyanic (prussic) acid; this has to be pressed out of the roots, which are then further purified by heating. Tapioca is the resultant starch in pellet or flake form; when ground, it is called Brazilian arrowroot. The sweet variety may be eaten without special preparation, but is little cultivated except for cattle fodder. Some tree species of manihot yield ◊ *rubber*.

Manila Bay (1898) ◊ *Philippines (History)*.

Manila Hemp ◊ *Banana*.

Manioc ◊ *Manihot*.

Mannerism. A term of disputed meaning; often, the style of certain late 16th-cent. artists in Italy, extremely sophisticated and giving a disturbing impression of unease and forced self-tormenting artificiality. In such painting and sculpture, figures are elongated and contorted, and in architecture the classical rules are deliberately broken and motifs misused. It is a neurotic style, a product of the unsettling effects of the ◊ *Counter-Reformation* and also a reaction against the suave accomplishment of Raphael and the High ◊ *Renaissance*. From Italy it spread north, and enjoyed particular success at the French court and in the Netherlands. There are many great Mannerist works of art, notably Michelangelo's Laurentian Library in Florence, the Palazzo del Tè at Mantua by Giulio Romano, the 16th-cent. parts of the palace of Fontainebleau, statues by Giovanni Bologna and Vittoria, and paintings by Pontormo, Rosso, Parmigianino, Tintoretto, and El Greco.

Manorial System. The system of land tenure operative in feudal society. The basic characteristic was that the peasant held land from the lord in return for dues and services esp. a substantial number of days' work per year on the lord's land. Manors, which varied in size, consisted of land retained for the lord's own use (demesne), while the rest of the arable land, divided in strips, was allocated for the use of the peasants. The meadow land ('commons') was shared; the woods, hunting, and fishing belonged to the lord. The peasants were either villeins (personally free but attached to the land) or serfs (virtually the lord's property). The administration of justice and levying of taxes for local amenities (e.g. roads and bridges) were in the hands of the lord of the manor or his bailiff. As time went on, the substitution of money payments for services led to the gradual disappearance of villeinage, esp. in England. The system varied in detail from place to place and country to country, e.g. in France and in German principalities the status of serf persisted long after it had disappeared elsewhere. ◊ *Feudalism*.

Manslaughter. The ◊ *felony* of unlawful homicide falling short of ◊ *murder*, where death is caused unintentionally in the course of an unlawful act, by culpable negligence, or under strong provocation; punishable by imprisonment for life. ◊ *Diminished Responsibility*.

Manx. The Goidelic (Q-Celtic) language of the Isle of Man (*man*, a rock, highland), first peopled by Gaelic-speaking settlers from Ireland; many Manx words e.g. *sliaeaus* (mountains), *cronks* (hills), *glions* (valleys), *curraghs* (bogs) survive in daily use. A complete Manx Bible was published 1775, and Manx was spoken in the cottages of Cregneish (preserved by the Manx Museum) until the 20th cent., but it is now almost extinct.

Maori. The racially and culturally ◊ *Polynesian* indigenous people of New Zealand, divided into tribes, each with its own lands, a common ancestor, and a chief; they had a system of strongly marked ranks – chiefs, aristocrats, commoners, and slaves – although the last no longer exist. Much of their land was early lost to the English settlers; the Maori wars of the 19th cent. were conducted with remarkable restraint on both sides, and since the Treaty of Waitangi 1840 Maori lands and customs have been left to their own control. In recent years Maori have tended to become impoverished in the rural areas and to move into the towns, where although still intensely proud of being Maori, they have lost much of their tribal culture; they now number about 60,000 (with an increasing number of half-castes).
LANGUAGE: of the ◊ *Malay* group.

Map. Representation on a flat surface of all or part of the earth's surface, to a definite scale or projection according to the purpose in view. A true representation of a curved surface on a flat one is impossible (the only exact one being a globe); the curved surface has to be projected on to a framework on the plane surface, by two intersecting systems of lines corresponding to the parallels of ◊ *latitude* and meridians of ◊ *longitude*. Some projections are correct for direction, others for area or for shape, but in one way or another there is bound to be distortion.

Attempts at cartography were made in the 14th cent. B.C. in ancient Egypt. Eratosthenes (◊ *Geodesy*) about 276 to about 194 B.C. used Egyptian cadastral maps to calculate the earth's circumference. Ptolemy of Alexandria, fl. about A.D. 150, employed meridians and parallels in his map of the world, which still influenced cartographers 14 centuries later. The British Ordnance Survey was begun 1791. An international map of the world on the scale one to one million (La Carte du Monde au Millionième), proposed 1891, has been interrupted by the two World Wars.

ATLAS MAP: On a fairly small scale (e.g. 16 m. to 1 in.), showing the position of towns, rivers, mountains, and international or regional borders for continents, countries, or smaller units.

CADASTRAL MAP: On a large scale (e.g. 1 m. to 25 in.), for administrative and taxation purposes.

MERCATOR'S PROJECTION: A map made 1568 by Gerhard Kremer (Gerardus Mercator) 1512–94; the globe is projected from its centre on to an enclosing cylinder tangent to it at the equator, meridians and parallels becoming straight lines intersecting one another at right angles and all parallels being the same length as the equator, so that outlines are increasingly distorted, and size exaggerated, the further features are from the equator. The advantage of this projection is that true bearings can be read from it by joining two points, and it is extremely useful for marine ◊ *charts*.

ORDNANCE SURVEY MAP: The 1 in. to 1 m. O.S. map is the principal topographical map of the British Isles.

TOPOGRAPHICAL MAP: Showing relief and other natural or artificial surface features.

Maple. *Acer*; a widespread genus in the N. hemisphere, characterized by winged propeller-like seeds and often by the brilliant autumn colouring of the foliage. Several species provide valuable wood, while the American sugar-maple yields maple syrup, once extensively used by the Indians and early settlers but now an expensive product. In Britain two species are found, the sycamore and the hedge maple. ◊◊ *Fruit*.

Marabouts. Muslim holy men in N. Africa living usually as hermits and venerated as saints: also the name given to the domed shrines erected to commemorate them. ◊ *Senussi*.

Marathon. 490 B.C. Decisive battle of Greek history, in which, though inferior in numbers, the Athenian army under Miltiades outmanoeuvred and defeated the Persians, thereby stopping the invasion. Pheidippides ran the 22 m. to Athens at great speed to carry the news of the victory, and dropped dead from his exertions, an event commemorated by the Marathon of the ◊ *Olympic Games*.

Marble. Metamorphosed form of limestone (calcium carbonate) or dolomite (magnesian limestone); the original rocks have been subjected to intense heat and pressure, and the calcite or dolomite grains have recrystallized and regrown together. Pure marbles are white in colour, the bands and mottling usually present being due to impurities, esp. iron oxides. Valuable for statuary and architectural facing; statuary marble comes from Carrara, onyx from Algeria. ◊◊ *Calcite, Metamorphic Rocks, Silica*.

Marduk. In Babylonian mythology, god of war, identified with the planet Jupiter; son of Ea (one of the chief trinity of gods, with Anu and Enlil) and conqueror of Tiamat and the monsters she created, and later in history taking over most of the attributes of Enlil as ruler of light and fate. In the Old Testament Marduk appears as Merodach and as Bel (◊ *Baal*).

Marengo. 1800. Village in Piedmont, scene of a victory of Napoleon's army over an Austrian army under Melas. The French were on the brink of defeat when reinforcements arrived: Melas was killed and Napoleon was left in possession of a large part of ◊ *Italy*. ◊◊ *French Revolution, Napoleonic Wars*.

Margarine. A solid fat food used as a substitute for butter, consisting of about 80 per cent edible animal or vegetable fats, with skim milk and salt and different vitamins. Minimum standards are set for its manufacture. It was first developed in France in the late 1860s as a cheap alternative to butter, made from beef fat, known as oleo. Modern margarine, manufactured principally from vegetable oils (coconut, palm kernel, cottonseed, etc.) is similar to butter and contains about the same number of ◊ *calories*. In U.S.A. it is subject to various restrictions, to lessen its competitiveness with dairy butter.

Marijuana ◊ *Hemp*.

Marl. Soil containing high proportion of calcium carbonate grains; usually part clay, part sand, and part lime, but the term covers a wide range of materials, some marls being used for cement material, others for fertilizers or brickmaking.

Marne. 1914, 1918. The first battle stopped the German advance on Paris in the ◊ *First World War*; it was followed by an attempt to outflank the Allied armies between Paris and the Channel, and ended with both sides 'digging in' and the long years of trench warfare. In 1918 a final German offensive again reached the Marne, where it was halted; shortly followed by a series of Allied successes which led to the collapse of the German forces.

Maronites. Christian sect, chiefly in the Lebanon, tracing their origin to the 7th-cent. John Maro; at first holding that Jesus Christ did not have distinct human and divine wills but a single will (the Monothelite heresy, condemned by the Constantinople III General Council, A.D. 680), they were reconciled to the Pope in the 12th cent. but maintain the ancient Syriac liturgy and do not insist on clerical celibacy. They are governed by the Patriarch of Antioch (under the Pope) and number about 250,000. Their massacre by the ◊ *Druses* in the 19th cent. resulted in French intervention.

Marriage. The form of permanent association between persons of opposite sex approved and regulated by a society; exists in some form (usually initiated by a specific ceremony) in even the most primitive communities. By Roman Catholics (and some Anglicans) it is held to be an indissoluble union, although after the death of a spouse remarriage is permitted to the surviving partner. Roman Catholics acknowledge only those marriages entered into in the presence of a priest, although marriage did not become a religious ceremony in Christian countries until the 9th cent. Common-law marriage (i.e. simply by consent of the parties), once common throughout Europe, was abolished 1753 in England. Mohammed allowed his followers up to four wives, but in Islamic countries monogamy is now virtually the rule. In English law, to constitute a valid marriage, both parties must have reached the age of 16 and any previous marriage must have been terminated by death or divorce. They must not be within the prohibited degrees of relationship, as set out in the Book of Common Prayer (with certain modifications introduced by law). If either party is under 21 consent is required either of the parents or of a magistrate (◊ *Ward of Court*) but failure to obtain consent does not invalidate the marriage if in fact it takes place. Both parties must understand the purport of the ceremony and undergo it freely. ◊ *Divorce, Exogamy, Polygamy*.

Marrow. 1. *Cucurbita pepo*; a gourd-like vegetable of the same species as the large round pumpkin and the various forms known as squashes in U.S.A. The *courgettes* of France and *zucchini* of Italy (baby marrows) are similar. The family probably originated from the annual vine found wild in central America. ◊ *Gourd*. **2.** Bone-marrow; soft tissue in the hollow of long bones, a function of which is to produce the red corpuscles of the blood. ◊ *Leukemia*.

Mars. 1. Planet fourth from the sun, named after the god of war (see below) because of its blood colour, more closely resembling the earth than any other planet but having a much less extensive atmosphere. The so-called canals on Mars are almost certainly illusory, and result from the tendency of the eyes, when viewing patchy objects under difficult conditions, to join markings by straight lines. Under good seeing conditions, with a large telescope, the polar caps and a few ill-defined permanent markings can be seen, and also the daily rotation. Other markings, which change during the year, may be dust or mist. Although oxygen and water have not been detected, there is some spectroscopic evidence for plant life (but ◊ *Exobiology*). Mars has two small moons, Phobos (diameter about 10 m. with revolution period $7\frac{1}{2}$ hours) and Deimos (diameter about 5 m. with revolution period 30 hours). From a point on the surface of Mars the two moons would appear to move in opposite directions.

2. In mythology ◊ *Ares*.

Marsala. A fortified wine from Sicily, made from white grapes and fortified with brandy, matured from two to five years in casks. A dark very sweet wine, with 20 per cent alcohol and five or six per cent sugar content.

Marsh. A flat area of grassy vegetation subject to inundation by floods from rivers or by tides near the sea (salt marsh). Marshland is often valuable pasturage, but is too wet to cultivate. Salt marshes are characterized by a number of plants which are tolerant of high concentrations of salt and are rarely found in other places e.g. sea lavender, marsh samphire, sea aster, and thrift.

Marshall Plan. 1947. Proposed by George Marshall, U.S.A. Secretary of State, to remedy Europe's trade deficit and quicken her recovery after the ◊ *Second World War* by providing dollars free of interest and repayment. No communist country accepted aid, but 16 other countries, including Britain, France, Germany, and Italy, received about £10,000 m. 1948–51, distributed under the supervision of the ◊ *Organization for European Economic Cooperation*.

Marsh Gas ◊ *Methane*.

Marston Moor. 1644. Victory of the Parliamentarians over Prince Rupert and Lord Newcastle during the ◊ *English civil war*. Fairfax and Cromwell attacked unexpectedly, and their newly trained cavalry were largely responsible for the victory. Prince Rupert and Newcastle escaped, but the northern royalist army was destroyed.

Marsupials. Previously more widespread, living marsupials are now found almost exclusively in Australasia; the ovum develops in the uterus, without placenta, and the young, with well-developed forelimbs and heads, crawl from the vagina to the pouch of the female, where they attach to the teats and complete their development. Marsupials show superficial resemblance to many species e.g. there are marsupials which resemble the ◊ *anteater*, ◊ *rat*, mouse, ◊ *otter*, and ◊ *monkey*. ◊◊ *Kangaroo*, *Koala*, *Tasmanian Wolf*.

Martial Law. The suspension of ordinary law and the substitution for it of the discretionary powers of the Executive exercised through the military authorities, when owing to war or disaster ordinary courts cease to function. In Britain, martial law cannot be proclaimed unless the courts in fact cease to function, and there is some conflict of opinion whether martial law can ever exist; certainly it is impossible in time of peace, even in civil commotion. Martial law is to be distinguished from ◊ *military law*.

Marxism. The system evolved by Karl Marx as the senior partner and Frederick Engels as the junior, based on observation of capitalism in England in the mid 19th cent. and expounded in the three volumes of *Das Kapital*; now the credo of the communist parties. Basic to these doctrines is the theory of ◊ *dialectical materialism*, on which the marxist view of history rests. Historical stages succeed one another according to the dialectical concept that progress is based upon conflict. The economic basis of one historical stage gives rise to a stage of opposition, and the two then merge or synthesize into a third. Thus the bourgeoisie displaced the old feudal nobility. The stage is now set for the final struggle between the bourgeoisie and the working classes, the end of which is seen as the control of production and distribution by the proletariat, the withering-away of the state as we know it, and a classless society. Although this process is believed inevitable, marxists are expected to speed it up by working to unify the proletariat, by cooperating temporarily with any political party useful to them, and by eventually resorting to revolution.

A second major claim is that the economic system at each historical stage is the basis which conditions all else: class structure, institutions, and culture. Thus art and religion under capitalism are conditioned by the fact of capitalist ownership of the means of production and control of the economy.

Lenin, Mao Tse-tung, and other orthodox communist writers claim to develop the ideas of Marx and Engels. Their writings may thus be considered as part of marxist doctrine.

On the purely economic side Marx was essentially of the classical economic tradition, and his theory was a development of the 'iron law of wages' that all goods are worth the socially necessary labour which is embodied in them (the labour theory of value), and this is true of labour itself. A labourer's work is worth the amount of socially necessary labour it takes to keep him alive. This may be only, say, six hours' work a day, but in fact labourers are forced to agree to work for longer than this: so the value he produces per day will be greater than his wage. The margin is 'surplus value' which the capitalist appropriates. Capitalists compete, force up wages temporarily, reduce their surplus value, and produce business fluctuations. They turn from labour to machines, so as to cause unemployment, and force wages down. However, since profits come only from the surplus value of labour, this reduces the ratio of profits to output: and in time profits will dwindle to nothing, production will not pay, and there will be a capitalist crisis. The small men will go under; the stronger capitalists will start again – until the next crisis, bigger than the last. So the process continues till the final convulsion: the revolt of the working class. 'The expropriators are expropriated.'

On what happens after that, Marx has little to say. During a transitional period there would be a dictatorship of the proletariat; after that, pure ◇ *communism*, which needs no economics. There is nothing in Marx about central planning or about communism as it has in fact evolved. ◇ *Internationals, Paris Commune, Soviet Union.*

Mary. Mother of ◇ *Jesus Christ*, to whom in traditional Christian belief she gave birth parthenogenetically. The New Testament says little of her, but records her presence at the Crucifixion and at Pentecost. As Mother of God – a title officially accorded her at the Council of Ephesus A.D. 431 – she is the object of intense devotion in the ◇ *Roman Catholic Church* and the ◇ *Eastern Orthodox Church*, to such an extent that many Protestants accuse them of 'Mariolatry', A favourite devotion to her is the Rosary (repetition of certain prayers counted on a string of beads). Many devotees have claimed visions of her (◇ *Lourdes*), and she has countless shrines and places of pilgrimage in all parts of the world. In the Roman Catholic Church she is the subject of two dogmas (articles of faith binding upon all believers within the church): that of 1854, teaching that she was born free from ◇ *original sin* and incapable of sinning (the Immaculate Conception); and that of 1950, teaching that at death she was physically transferred to heaven (the Bodily Assumption).

Masai. Nilo-Hamitic-speaking nomadic people of Kenya and Tanganyika (racially a mixture of Nilotes and Europiforms) numbering about 125,000; their economy is based on cattle, which they venerate as their source of life, not killing them for food but making incisions in their veins and drinking the blood. Renowned for their fine physical appearance and strength, the Masai have resolutely opposed westernization and are traditional enemies of the politically stronger Kikuyu. ◇ *African Languages, Hamites, Hamito-Semitic Languages.*

Maser. A device to stimulate the radiation of energy in the form of microwaves, in order to amplify an electromagnetic field. Certain gases e.g. ammonia and some crystalline solids are used as the source of radiation, because their atoms or electrons can possess at least two levels of internal energy. The source is 'pumped' into its upper 'excited' level of energy by a stimulating electric field, and is then triggered back to its normal energy level by interacting with the electromagnetic field (e.g. the faint signal from a radio star) to be amplified. The energy released when the system returns to its normal state appears as an amplified form of the triggering waves.

When the frequency of the emitted radiation is so high that it approaches the frequency of light waves, the device is called a ◇ *laser* or optical maser.

Maser devices are used in ◇ *space exploration*, because they generate little internal noise and therefore do not mask the very faint signals from remote objects.

Mason-Dixon Line. The boundary line between Pennsylvania and Maryland in U.S.A. which was marked out in 1763–7 by the British astronomers Charles Mason and Jeremiah Dixon in order to end the boundary dispute between the two states; it later became known as the line dividing slave states from free (◇ *American Civil War*). In U.S. popular usage it still means the line between 'North' and 'South'.

Masque. A ◇ *Renaissance* form of court entertainment, allegorical, combining speech, music, dance, song, and spectacle, and usually complimenting an important spectator; imported to England from the Continent, it had a great vogue under Queen Elizabeth and at the courts of

James I and Charles I, Queen Henrietta Maria (a Frenchwoman) herself taking part in performances. Ben Jonson, the greatest English contriver of masques, added the Anti-masque, an Interlude of grotesque or bawdy comedy (◊ *Morality Play*). As scenic effects became more gorgeous and extravagant, Jonson's poetic contribution was eclipsed by the masques of his collaborator, the great architect and designer Inigo Jones. A notable example of the masque is *Comus* 1634, the text by Milton and the music by Henry Lawes. Masques continued in popularity at the Restoration court of Charles II, but were displaced by their derivative, ◊ *opera*.

Mass. In physics, basic property of matter, which can be regarded in two aspects (a) gravitational mass, and (b) inertial mass. The former may be ascertained by measuring an object on a beam-balance, the second by measuring the acceleration it undergoes when acted upon by a given force. Mass is distinct from weight, the measure of the force of gravity acting upon a given body, which may vary according to its location e.g. the same body on the earth and on the moon has the same mass but a quite different weight. The mass of bodies may be regarded as constant for terrestrial purposes, but in Einstein's special theory of ◊ *relativity* mass increases with speed. ◊ *Gravitation*.

The mass of an ◊ *atom* resides in the ◊ *nucleus* and is expressed as mass-number, the total of the nucleons (i.e. protons and neutrons) in the nucleus.

MASS-NUMBER: Number of nucleons (i.e. ◊ *protons* + ◊ *neutrons*) in the nucleus of an ◊ *atom*.

Mass. Celebration of the sacrament of the ◊ *Eucharist* or Lord's Supper; the chief act of Roman Catholic worship, generally performed daily by every priest, as a sacrifice commemorating and perpetually repeating Christ's sacrificial death. The Mass, the rites for which are set forth in the Missal, has for many centuries been said or sung in Latin (exc. in eastern churches in communion with Rome, where Greek, Old Slavonic, Syriac, or other Oriental languages are used), but the use of a vernacular language was sanctioned by the General Council (Vatican II) 1963. HIGH MASS: The officiant is assisted by a ◊ *deacon* and subdeacon, with musical accompaniment and elaborate ritual.

LOW MASS: Celebrated without music or clerical assistants.

REQUIEM MASS: Offered for the dead in purgatory.

In musical history, settings of the Mass form an important part of choral music, from the Middle Ages till today; composers have mostly set the 'Ordinary' or 'Common' of the Mass, leaving the 'Proper' (varying with the occasion) to traditional plainsong, except for the Requiem Mass, of which many settings have been composed. The first polyphonic mass traceable to a single known composer is one by Machaut 1364 or earlier; later celebrated composers of Masses for church use include Palestrina (who wrote nearly 100), Haydn, and Mozart. The Masses or Requiem Masses of Bach, Beethoven, Rossini, Berlioz, and Verdi are now mainly heard in concert halls.

Mass-Energy Equation. Einstein's equation of the equivalence of mass and energy: ◊ *Relativity*.

Mastersingers. Guilds of German poets of the 14th–17th centuries, largely artisans and craftsmen who regarded poetry as a craft governed by specific traditions and rules, the most famous among them being Hans Sachs 1494–1576. Later mastersinger guilds lingered until the 19th cent. ◊ *Troubadours*.

Mastitis. Inflammation of the breast. Acute mastitis usually results from infection during lactation; chronic mastitis, which is common in middle-aged women, is a benign overgrowth of the breast tissue, not always easy to distinguish from cancer.

Mastodon (Mammoth). Fossil mammal from which the ◊ *elephant* is thought to be descended; the earliest were little larger than pigs, the latest similar to elephants. Many had four tusks.

Matapan. 1941. Naval battle of the ◊ *Second World War*, a night action off Cape Matapan in Greece between the British and Italian fleets. The destruction of three Italian cruisers and two destroyers gave the British Navy command of the Mediterranean.

Maté. *Ilex paraguariensis* (Paraguay tea) or Yerba maté, an evergreen tree of the holly genus, from the young leaves and shoots of which the S. American Indians have made an infusion since antiquity. Maté, the main beverage of much of S. America, is a stimulant (containing caffeine), restorative, and more astringent than ordinary tea.

Materialism. Doctrine that all things, including minds, are physical matter, or that they depend upon it for existence; in both views matter is the ultimate reality. Democritus (4th cent. B.C.) was one of the earliest exponents of materialism; he explained all phenomena on the basis of atoms and their movements. Gassendi and Hobbes presented a materialistic system in the late 17th cent. and materialist views were widely held, esp. in France, until a reaction set in at the end of the 18th cent. ◊ *Dialectical materialism* is the most systematized form of 19th- and 20th-cent. materialism.

Mathematics. The study of the logical consequences which follow from any collection of assumptions; in the broadest sense, the study and classification of 'patterns', including that of number and the relationship between numbers, and in ◊ *geometry* the study of spatial quantities and relationships. Arithmetic is the most ancient form of mathematics; it was known to the Egyptians and the Greeks, but development in these civilizations was handicapped by the absence of a suitable system of numerals (◊ *Number*). The Greeks carried geometry (less involved with number) to an advanced stage, however.

The introduction of the ◊ *decimal system* into Europe in the 13th cent. led to great advances in mathematics, which accelerated still more rapidly after the 17th cent. with the development of algebra, ◊ *calculus*, and trigonometry.

Mathematics has become an essential tool in all sciences for the development of theory. By translating the result of experiments into mathematical terms, it is possible to develop assumptions and formulae of general application; further experimentation is often suggested in the process. In this way mathematics both clarifies and engenders knowledge of the physical world.

APPLIED MATHEMATICS: The application of mathematics to practical problems.

PURE MATHEMATICS: The study of mathematical logic and method in the abstract.

Matriarchy, Matriliny ◊ *Kinship.*

Matter. That which has substance and weight, as distinct from such phenomena as light, and other forms of energy, which appear to have no substance. Matter and energy are now held to be interchangeable. Matter is generally considered to be in one of three states – solid, liquid, gas – according to the state of the molecules of which it is composed. ◊ *Atom, Element, Molecule.*

Mau Mau. Politico-religious movement among the ◊ *Kikuyu* of Kenya, aimed at driving out Europeans and European culture; it arose about 1952 and was supported mainly by younger men and women esp. those without rights in ancestral land and so without close family ties, but was suppressed by 1957. Initiation to the movement was by oaths (some of which were obscene and bestial), the purpose being mainly to remove the initiate from ordinary human obligations and bind him to his new fellows, who stood outside normal society by having performed these traditionally forbidden acts; any breach of the oath would be followed by mystical retribution. By no means all Kikuyu supported Mau Mau and far more Kikuyu than Europeans were killed in the murder campaign.

Mauritania. Area 322,340 sq. m. Pop. 880,000. Cap. Nouakchott. In N W Africa, between Senegal and the Sahara; since 1958 an autonomous republic within the ◊ *French Community*, fully independent since 1960. The inhabitants are partly nomads and partly settled, mainly ◊ *Berber.*

ECONOMY. The rich deposits of iron ore are being exploited by the Société des Mines de Fer de Mauritanie, an international company, with the aid of a loan from the ◊ *International Bank for Reconstruction and Development.*

HISTORY. Originally, Mauritania was an area corresponding roughly to modern Morocco. In antiquity it was colonized by both Phoenicians and Romans; it did not become a French colony till 1920.

Mauryas. Indian warrior dynasty 320–184 B.C. founded by Chandragupta, whose grandson Asoka for the first time united most of India and Afghanistan under one rule and replaced ◊ *Hinduism* by a form of ◊ *Buddhism* as the national religion. Of the apparently rich artistic achievement of the period, only a few carved pillars of Asoka's reign have survived.

Mauveine. Aniline purple, the first synthetic dyestuff, obtained in small yield by

W. H. Perkin in 1856 from the oxidation of aniline. His aim was to make quinine, but he recognized the value of his coloured product and began to manufacture it. Mauve was the forerunner of many new ◊ *dyes* (which rapidly superseded it); its discovery is a landmark in chemical history and marks the beginning of a period of rapid development not only of the 'coal-tar' dyes but of aromatic chemistry for many other preparations e.g. aspirin, vanillin.

Maya. In ◊ *Hinduism* and Indianizing philosophies, and in ◊ *Buddhism*, 'illusion', 'appearance', 'unreality'. The world of phenomena is maya: its existence is solely an illusion, resulting from mistaken belief in the reality of an individual self.

Mayan Civilization. A pre-Columbian American civilization, centred upon the Yucatan peninsula and parts of Guatemala and Honduras; although a 'Stone Age' civilization in the sense that it did not possess metal tools, and although it never achieved the highly organized political structure of the ◊ *Incas* and ◊ *Aztecs*, in other respects Mayan civilization far surpassed the other American cultures, notably in the development of a form of picture-writing from as early as the 4th cent. A.D. and in the use of a calendar more accurate than the Gregorian and a system of numbering based on 20 (which for the first time in any civilization included a symbol for zero), and an advanced knowledge of astronomy. Mayan architecture, pyramidal in basic structure and (like that of the other American civilizations) lacking the arch, was less massive and more graceful in design than Inca and Aztec structures. There is some disagreement about the chronology of the Mayan civilization, but it may be said that the classic period began about A.D. 325 and ended in the 10th cent. with the mysterious abandonment of sites in the central region. About this time there was an invasion from Mexico, and for the next three centuries the Maya were strongly influenced by Mexican culture, adopting elements of Mexican religion (inc. the worship of Quetzalcoatl and human sacrifice) and becoming more militaristic. From about 1200 Maya culture was in decline, and it had virtually disintegrated before the Spanish conquest. The languages derived from or related to

ancient Mayan (◊ *American Indians (Languages)*) now number about 60 and are spoken in Yucatan and the adjacent parts of Mexico, Guatemala, Honduras, and Salvador.

Mayflower ◊ *Pilgrim Fathers*.

Mead. An alcoholic drink made by fermenting honey and water, sometimes spiced. It was drunk a great deal in medieval England, and is still manufactured and exported by Poland.

Meaning. Much recent philosophy has investigated or used different theories of meaning; the vague assumption that the meaning of a symbol is that which it stands for, or the class of things it can stand for, has been replaced e.g. by the view that the meaning of a symbol amounts to rules or conventions (often imprecise) for its use. When I am asked for the meaning of 'red', essentially my answer is a statement that 'red' is correctly used in such and such situations. Such rules or conventions may connect a symbol with things and qualities (descriptive meaning) or with the user's attitudes and intentions (emotive or prescriptive meaning). The use of an emotive term e.g. 'rabble-rouser' indicates by convention that the speaker feels in a certain way about what he is mentioning. ◊ *Logical Positivism, Pragmatism.*

Measles. Acute infectious disease caused by a filtrable virus and usually occurring in epidemics. The incubation period is 10–14 days and begins with a catarrhal phase (sneezing, coughing, watering of the eyes) and a high temperature; this is followed by a blotchy rash. Bronchopneumonia, ◊ *enteritis,* ◊ *eye* ulcers, and disease of the middle ◊ *ear* are possible complications.

Mecca. Chief city of Arabia, and home of Mohammed; in it stands the Kaaba, a cube-shaped building within which is the 'Black Stone' (a meteorite), an object of worship from the earliest times. After his flight to Medina A.D. 622 (◊ *Hegira*), Mohammed returned to Mecca to assert his growing political and spiritual ascendancy over the Arabs. On his death Mecca became the chief shrine of ◊ *Islam* and the object of pilgrimage (*al Hajj*) of millions of Muslims, despite the fact that after the effective centre of Islam moved to Medina with the Caliphate, Mecca fell under the control of first the Egyptian Mamelukes and later the Turks, for centuries. ◊ *Saudi Arabia.*

Mechanics. That branch of physics which deals with the effect of forces acting upon bodies, divided into statics (where the body is in equilibrium) and dynamics (where an excess of force leads to changes in speed or direction). Mechanics once represented the whole field of physics, but the explanation of ◊ *light* and ◊ *electricity* involved new concepts. ◊ *Motion.*

Medea ◊ *Golden Fleece, Tragedy (Greek).*

Medicine. The science and art of the treatment of disease. Prehistoric societies possessed some herbal remedies but resorted more often to ◊ *magic* and the medicine man to cure illness, as in primitive societies today. In the ancient civilizations of Mesopotamia and Egypt there was some medical knowledge, but the first great physician was Hippocrates, about 400 B.C., who freed medicine from superstition and the priests and laid the basis of an empirical art; the Hippocratic Oath remains an enduring formulation of the duties and ethic of doctors. He was followed A.D. 140 by Galen who by his extensive writings and skill in dissection became the undisputed authority for nearly 1500 years. The diffusion of Arabic works and retranslations of the Greek medical writings stimulated a fresh approach: independent thinkers e.g. Vesalius and Servetus and Paracelsus and finally William Harvey, with his discovery of the ◊ *circulatory system* of the blood, revolutionized medicine and set it on its modern development. Jenner introduced vaccination 1796, Virchow revolutionized ◊ *pathology* 1858 by his studies of the effect of disease on cellular structure, and within 20 years Pasteur and Koch had founded the science of ◊ *bacteriology*, while Claude Bernard placed the study of ◊ *physiology* on a firm basis of experiment. During the first half of the 19th cent. the notable feature of medicine was the descriptive work of physicians e.g. Bright and Addison, and in the second half, while German medicine flourished as never before or since, French medicine came to the fore with the foundation of neurology by the Paris school under Charcot. With the end of the century came the discovery of X-rays by W. C. Röntgen in Germany. The earliest years of the 20th cent. were marked by an enormous expansion of preventive medicine, based on the new knowledge of hygiene; the resulting fall in mortality from infectious disease has been one of the most spectacular 20th-cent. successes. Landmarks are: ◊ *vitamins*, Hopkins 1906; salvarsan (the first chemotherapeutic substance), Ehrlich 1910; the first ◊ *sulphonamide* drug, Domagk 1935; ◊ *penicillin*, Fleming 1929. During this time there was progress in many specialized branches of medicine, some from old roots e.g. ◊ *psychiatry*, and some entirely new e.g. endocrinology. Basic medical discoveries have enabled medicine to pass from 19th-cent. trial-and-error procedures to a science in which (if still handicapped in some respects by incomplete data) the approach is for the most part founded on a sound basis both of theory and experiment. It is sometimes felt that modern scientific medicine neglects consideration of the patient as a human being; on the other hand the 20th cent. has seen a deepening of interest, never before exhibited in the welfare of the individual, out of which has grown social medicine, partly preventive but also concerned to mitigate the social consequences of illness and physical disabilities. ◊ *Surgery.*

Mediums. Persons who claim to form a medium of communication, in trance or waking state, between the spirits of the dead and the living. ◊ *Extra-sensory Perception, Psychical Research, Spiritualism.*

Medusa. 1. ◊ *Gorgons, Pegasus, Perseus.* **2.** ◊ *Jellyfish.*

Megalithic Monuments. Burial and ritual structures of massive blocks of stone erected during the ◊ *Neolithic* and early ◊ *Bronze Age*, found along the coasts of the W. Mediterranean and in N W Europe. Of the ritual sites, those at ◊ *Avebury*, ◊ *Stonehenge*, and ◊ *Carnac* are among the best known. The tombs are associated with the practice of collective burial and possibly with the worship of a Mother Goddess, and are now generally regarded as deriving from the rock-cut and corbelled tombs of the higher cultures of the Mediterranean. Their builders were agriculturalists and presumably seafarers, some of them migrant peoples from the Mediterranean and others local imitators of the style.

Meiosis. One of the two types of cell division; in meiosis, while the cell divides twice:

gametes

the ◊ *chromosomes* within the ◊ *nucleus* (which carry genetic information) divide, or replicate, only once:

gametes

Thus, while the body cells which make up the adult organism contain two sets of chromosomes (diploid), the sex cells (◊ *gametes*) contain only one (haploid). In reproduction, the female gamete (egg) is fertilized by a sperm or other male gamete; the result of this fusion is called a zygote.

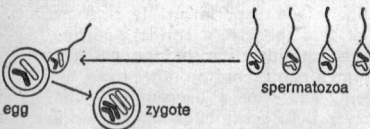

egg   zygote   spermatozoa

The zygote, which eventually produces the new organism, thus contains two sets of chromosomes, like its parents. In addition this process rearranges the genetic information transmitted from parents to offspring (one possible pattern is indicated in the diagram) and is thus a source of variation in living populations providing much of the new genetic material which permits evolution by ◊ *natural selection.*

Melanesians. Agricultural negroid peoples of New Guinea, Papua, the Solomon Islands, and Fiji; some of those of New Guinea were discovered by whites only in the 1950s. Their numbers were much reduced in the 19th cent. by the slave trade. ◊ *Cargo Cults, Race.*

Memory. In psychology, all forms of recall; there is evidence that no past experience is ever completely forgotten, i.e. that all experiences leave some permanent trace. Memory ability is in part innate, and individuals differ in endowment; there are, however, many ways in which it can be enhanced by training. Memory can be impaired by such things as shock, repression, and age. ◊ *Amnesia, Defence Mechanism.*

Memphis. Capital of ◊ *Egypt* (ancient) about 2700–2200 B.C. in the Old Kingdom, at the apex of the Nile delta, reputedly founded about 3200 B.C. by Menes, who first united Upper and Lower Egypt. It was superseded as capital by Thebes, but did not cease to be an important city and trade centre until the Arab conquest, when its buildings were dispersed for the construction of near-by Arab cities. The ruins of temples and other buildings have been revealed by excavations.

Mendelevium ◊ *Actinides.*

Mendelism. Theory of heredity. The Austrian monk Gregor Mendel 1822–84 made the first systematic experiments into the inheritance of single characters in plants. He used the garden pea to investigate the transmission from parent to offspring of such pairs of alternate characters as round or wrinkled seeds, green or yellow seeds, and tall or short plants, and concluded that the heritable characters of plants are represented by particles or factors in the cells (now known as the ◊ *genes* of the ◊ *chromosomes*). He put forward a number of conclusions: chiefly, that in each cell of the plant (except the germ cells) two of each factor are present, but during the formation of the germ cells members of each pair segregate from each other and are transmitted singly to the offspring (◊ *Meiosis*), and further that some factors are dominant over others (◊ *Dominance*). Mendel's work was published in 1865 and 1869, but its importance for the study of heredity was not realized until after 1900. His observations and laws, forming the system called Mendelism, became the basis of modern genetics.

Menelaus ◊ *Agamemnon, Helen.*

Menhirs ◊ *Carnac.*

Meningitis. Inflammation of the membranes of the brain or spinal cord; streptococcal, influenzal, meningococcal, tuberculous, and syphilitic infections are the most common causes. Formerly usually fatal or leaving serious mental impairment, its treatment has been revolutionized by chemotherapy and the use of ◊ *antibiotics.*

Mennonites (Swiss Brethren). Christian sect in central Europe, Canada, and U.S.A. which rejects sacraments and church organization, maintaining a strict puritan ethic with no special dogmas; named after the Dutch ◊ *anabaptist* Menno Simons 1496–1561. Pacifist and holding aloof from worldly affairs, they have split into a number of branches but have many members in U.S.A. (esp. in

Pennsylvania, Ohio, and Middle West) and in Canada.

'HOOK-AND-EYE' MENNONITES: A sub-sect forbidding its members to use buttons.

Mensheviks. < Russian *menshinstvo*, minority; the moderates of the Russian Social Democratic Party, led by Martoff, who from about 1900 opposed Lenin's radical majority the ◊ *Bolsheviks*, esp. in the 1917 Revolution, at the beginning of which (February Revolution) they formed the Provisional Government under Kerensky, until it was overthrown by the Workers Soviets (Councils) led by the Bolsheviks (October Revolution, but 7 Nov. according to the Western ◊ *calendar*).

Menstruation. The shedding of the mucous lining of the uterus (◊ *Reproduction*) at regular intervals of from 26 to 32 days throughout a woman's reproductive life; the end of a cycle of changes which prepare this lining membrane (endometrium) to receive and nourish a fertilized ovum. At the beginning of the cycle, some 10 days are occupied in the growth of the new endometrium; towards the 14th day, when an ovum is shed by the ovary, the endometrium becomes increasingly soft and well-supplied with blood, for the reception of the ovum should conception occur. In the absence of fertilization, the blood supply to the endometrium is interrupted; it dies, and is expelled during menstruation, after which a new cycle begins. The onset of menstrual cycles at ◊ *puberty* is termed menarche, their cessation menopause.

Mental Age ◊ *Intelligence Quotient.*

Mental Defectives ◊ *Educational Subnormality, Mental Health Service.*

Mental Health Service. Reorganized under the 1959 Mental Health Act, it is part of the National Health Service, provision for the care and treatment of mentally ill persons being the duty of the local health authority; they may attend psychiatric out-patient clinics free of charge, or if necessary may be admitted to mental hospitals for treatment. The majority of admissions are voluntary, but the local health authority is empowered to secure compulsory detention in serious cases, where the patient or his relatives fail to apply, and in an emergency a patient may be detained for 72 hours on the recommendation of a single doctor;

admission for longer periods must be recommended by two doctors. If such a patient escapes from hospital and remains at large for six months in the case of a ◊ *psychopath* or sub-normal adult, or otherwise for 28 days, he may not be retaken without a further application. Appeals by the patient or his relatives against compulsory detention may be made to a mental health tribunal in England and Wales or to the Sheriff in Scotland.

Mental Tests. Devices to measure human mental characteristics, abilities, aptitudes, attainments, interests, and personality traits; individual performances are measured under standardized conditions, and scores compared with a 'norm' or scale derived from the performances of a defined group. Some tests are intended to measure inborn traits e.g. intelligence, while attainment tests measure acquired knowledge and skill e.g. reading ability, and personality tests measure emotional or temperamental disposition. ◊ *Educational Subnormality, Intelligence Quotient.*

Menthol ◊ *Eucalyptus.*

Mephistopheles. Mocking evil spirit in various treatments of the ◊ *Faust* legend; usually but incorrectly supposed to derive from three Greek words meaning 'not loving the light'.

Mercantilism. The economic policy which superseded the medieval feudal organization in W. Europe, esp. in Britain, Holland, and France; mercantilist theories, based on the belief that what made a country powerful was 'men, ships, and money', dominated economic thinking about 1500–1800 until the ◊ *free-trade* doctrines of Adam Smith (◊ *Laissez-faire*) superseded them. Trading nations were impressed by the need for precious metals (bullion) to buy other commodities, and identified wealth with money; foreign trade to acquire bullion was therefore encouraged, at the expense of domestic trade; and making goods for foreign trade and ships to carry them was encouraged at the expense of agriculture and mining. High duties were imposed on imports except raw materials, treaties were made to obtain exclusive trading privileges, and the commerce of colonies was exploited for the benefit of the mother country; in Britain Henry VIII, Elizabeth I, and Protector Oliver Cromwell all followed mercantilist policies, while in France the chief exponent was Colbert.

Mercator's Projection ◊ *Map*.

Merchant Navy. The Merchant Marine, Merchant Fleet, or Merchant Service; British merchant shipping, its distinguishing flag the red ensign. About half of all U.K. trade is carried in British ships. Freight and other ◊ *shipping* earnings account for slightly over a quarter of U.K. invisible exports, but recently have been slightly exceeded by U.K. payments to foreign owners for such services.

Mercia. One of the kingdoms of Anglo-Saxon England. Probably originating in the upper Trent valley about A.D. 500, by the reign of King Penda in the mid 7th cent. it had extended its power over most of England S. of the Humber; Penda was killed in an attempt to bring Northumbria under Mercian overlordship. The kingdom reached the height of its power in the 8th cent. under Offa, who ruled as overlord in all the southern kingdoms except E. Anglia and Wales (the boundary of which was defended by his famous dyke). After his death Mercia declined; it succumbed to the Danes in 874 and was annexed by ◊ *Wessex* in the 10th cent. ◊ *Vikings*.

Mercury. 1. The smallest planet (diameter 3100 m.), the nearest to the sun (mean distance about 36 m. miles). Never being more than 28° in angular distance from the sun, it is difficult to see and must be observed either through a bright day sky or near the horizon just after sunset or just before sunrise, when definition is poor. Mercury always keeps the same face to the sun, and is very hot on that side (about 600° F). It has no moons, little or no atmosphere, and shows no surface features. ◊ *Solar System*.

2. A silvery metallic element, liquid at room temperature, occurring as the sulphide cinnabar; this is roasted in air, the sulphur is oxidized to sulphur dioxide, and the mercury vapour is condensed. Purified by distillation, it is extensively used in thermometers and barometers, and since it does not wet glass it is also used in research dealings with gases, and for high-vacuum pumps, mercury vapour lamps, and mercury electrical switches. It forms many ◊ *alloys* (amalgams) which have important industrial applications. The element shows valence states of 1 and 2, giving respectively mercurous compounds e.g. calomel and mercuric compounds e.g. corrosive sublimate. Calomel is used as a fungicide and in medicine; the sulphide is the pigment vermilion; many organo-mercury compounds are employed in medicine and agriculture. The fulminate is used as a detonator for cartridges. All mercury compounds are poisonous.

3. In mythology ◊ *Hermes*.

Meridian. The vertical plane, through a given locality, containing the north celestial ◊ *pole*. It cuts the ground in the true geographical N/S line. ◊ *Longitude*.

Merino ◊ *Wool*.

Merlin. In medieval romance e.g. ◊ *Arthurian legend*, born to a girl seduced by a devil, made human by baptism, and later a magician and seer; the enchantress Nimue enclosed him in a rock, and finally Vivien the 'lady of the lake' (◊ *Excalibur, Lancelot*) imprisoned him in a thornbush, to sleep there until it is necessary to recall Arthur to Britain. The legend is inextricably confused with tales of a semi-historical 6th-cent. Welsh bard Myrddin, associated with the putatively historical Arthur and said to have lost his reason and been killed in a battle between the Welsh and the Romanized British, perhaps the Last Battle of the West. Many and varied 'Merlin' prophecies in Welsh and English circulated in the Middle Ages and as late at the mid 17th cent.

Merovingians. The earliest dynasty in France, descended from the legendary Frankish chief Merovic. Under Clovis I and his heirs in the 5th and 6th centuries, they extended their rule to much of France and Germany, and the kingdoms of Austrasia in the east and ◊ *Burgundy*, ◊ *Aquitaine*, and Neustria in the west gradually evolved. These were reunited by Chlotar II in 613, but internal feuds disrupted the kingdom after his death. The Austrasian mayors of the palace, the ◊ *Carolingians*, seized power, displacing Childeric III, the last Merovingian, in 751.

Merrimac and Monitor. 1862. Warships famous in the ◊ *American Civil War*. *Merrimac*, originally a U.S. Federal steam frigate, was re-equipped by the Confederates with 4-in. armour plate and several 6-in. and 7-in. guns. *Monitor* was a smaller vessel, built for the Federal government by a Swedish designer, who introduced a revolving armoured turret mounting two 11-in. guns. The two vessels met and fought in 1862; neither was sunk, and no one was killed, but *Merrimac* was damaged. After this first action between armoured vessels, the navies of the world adopted armoured warships carrying big guns mounted in turrets.

Mesa. < Sp. *mesa*, table; mountain with a flat table-like top, falling away steeply, the remnant of a plateau reduced by river ⬦ *erosion*. In U.S.A. it is sometimes large enough to house a settlement of Indian tribes. BUTTE: Small mesa, only a fragment of the original surface.

Mescalin. An ⬦ *alkaloid* present in 'mescal buttons', the dried flower heads of a Mexican cactus; it produces vivid visual hallucinations in colour. The native form, peyote, is used by American Indians in their religious ceremonies.

Mesolithic. Middle Stone Age; in the development of human culture, transitional between the ⬦ *Palaeolithic* and the ⬦ *Neolithic*, and associated with the period immediately following the last of the ⬦ *Ice Ages*. In N. Europe the warmer climate and thicker forestation resulted in the departure of much of the large game previously hunted, the standard of living was probably lower in some areas than it had been in the Palaeolithic, and there was no major technological advance. The main European cultures of this time in N. and central Europe are the Azilian and the Tardenoisian (esp. associated with the development of microliths, tiny finely shaped ⬦ *flint* blades) and also the Maglemosian (esp. adapted to forest life).

In W. Asia the climate became gradually drier after the end of the Pluvials (corresponding to the northern glacial periods); the worsening conditions resulted in a movement of populations from the plateaux down into the alluvial valleys of great rivers e.g. the Nile and the Tigris-Euphrates, while the greater urgency of food production led eventually to the first domestication of plants and animals.

Meson. Elementary particle, larger in mass than the ⬦ *electron* but lighter than the ⬦ *proton*. One theory suggests that mesons are the forces holding together the nucleus of the atom.

Mesopotamia. (Now ⬦ *Iraq*); literally 'the land between the rivers', the country in and around the valleys of the Tigris-Euphrates river system. The extreme fertility of these lands when properly irrigated is thought to have been a major factor in the remarkably rapid rise of civilization in this part of the world. ⬦⬦

Akkadians, Assyria, Babylon, Sumerians.
Mesozoic ⬦ *Geological Time Scale.*
Messiah. In traditional ⬦ *Judaism*, a descendant of David who is to reassemble the Jews in Israel and set up a theocracy; false claimants have included esp. Bar Cochba, who led an anti-Roman rebellion in the 2nd cent. A.D. and Sabbatai Zevi, about 1620–76, who apostatized to ⬦ *Islam*. The Biblical prophecies of a Messiah are believed by Christians to have been fulfilled in ⬦ *Jesus Christ*. The Muslim ⬦ *Shiahs* expect a ⬦ *Mahdi*.

Metabolism. The complex of biochemical reactions which constantly renew all parts of living organisms including apparently permanent structures e.g. bone and cartilage. Metabolic processes fall into two groups, anabolic (synthetic) and catabolic (destructive): anabolism is the building-up of complex substances from simple components e.g. conversion of ⬦ *amino-acids* into complex tissue proteins; catabolism is the breaking-down of complex substances into simpler ones, with the liberation of energy, e.g. ⬦ *glucose* into carbon dioxide and water, accompanied by the production of heat. There are differing metabolic mechanisms for ⬦ *protein*, ⬦ *carbohydrates*, and fat. In protein metabolism, the basic amino-acids resulting from protein digestion may be used at once as a source of energy, built up into tissue proteins, converted into carbohydrate or fat, or stored. Carbohydrate may circulate as glucose in the blood as an immediate source of energy, or be converted into glycogen or fat for storage. Fat may be stored as such, or may be oxidized for the provision of energy. The metabolic rate of a body (rate at which metabolic turnover takes place) is expressed in terms of heat production; an adult doing sedentary work produces about 2000 ⬦ *Calories* a day, a labourer doing heavy work more than twice this amount.

Metallurgy. 1. The earliest metal-working consisted simply of hammering native ores of copper and gold; true metallurgy, the extraction of metal from its ores and the technique of casting, was first applied to copper in parts of W. Asia in the 5th millennium B.C. and reached Mesopotamia by about 4000 B.C. The alloying of tin and copper to produce the much more serviceable metal bronze was known from about 3000 B.C. in Mesopotamia. A further de-

velopment, the extraction of copper from deep-mined sulphide ores, resulted in a greater abundance of metal from about 1500 B.C. Bronze workers held a high status in early societies because of their special skills (◊ *Bronze Age*). The earliest iron objects, dating to the 3rd millennium B.C. in Egypt, Asia Minor, and Mesopotamia (◊ *Iron Age*) were made from meteoric or pure terrestrial iron; smelting of iron ores was first developed by the ◊ *Hittites* about 1400 B.C. Iron extraction involves more technical processes than copper and bronze working, but once these are mastered iron is a cheaper material, since the ores are more widespread and also it produces a superior cutting edge for tools and weapons; blacksmiths did not usually enjoy the same prestige as bronze workers. All iron was wrought (except for rare and probably accidental examples of cast iron) until the introduction of the ◊ *blast furnace* in the 16th cent. A.D. Only in China was this sequence reversed, cast iron being found from the 7th cent. B.C. and wrought iron not until the 3rd. In Roman and later times the Rhineland and Spain were noted for their high-grade steel. ◊> *Alloys, Iron and Steel Industry*.
2. The study of metals, e.g. the production from their ore, methods of processing them, their properties, and their behaviour in use.

Metals and Non-metals. In the early days of chemistry the ◊ *elements* were roughly divided into these two classes, i.e. those that looked and behaved like metals and those that did not (e.g. sulphur, phosphorus, carbon, oxygen). The classification was never satisfactory, as several elements seemed to have properties belonging to both types; in modern chemistry, the concept of electronegativity has proved much more useful. The atoms of electronegative elements, e.g. fluorine, oxygen, chlorine, readily accept electrons, and these are also the most typical of the non-metals. Electropositive elements, on the other hand, e.g. potassium, sodium, magnesium, have atoms that readily lose electrons, and these are the typical metals. Elements whose properties are intermediate between the two, e.g. germanium, selenium, are sometimes called semi-metals. Whereas metals should conduct electricity easily but non-metals should not, these semi-metals act as 'semi-con-

ductors' and are of vital importance in transistors (germanium) and photoelectric cells (selenium). ◊> *Conduction, Electricity, Electronics*.

Metamorphic Rocks. < Gr. *meta*, change, and *morpha*, form; rocks which under intense heat and pressure (◊ *Magma*) have undergone such complete structural changes as to become virtually new rocks, generally very resistant to denudation. Superheated steam and hot water with substances in solution add new materials to ◊ *igneous rocks* or ◊ *sedimentary rocks*, which become transformed in character and composition; clay > slate, limestone > marble, shale or sandstone > schist or quartzite, granite > gneiss.

Metamorphosis. Drastic transformation occurring in the body of some animals (usually with concomitant changes in physiology and way of life) when they reach a final stage of development, e.g. caterpillars into butterflies, tadpoles into frogs. ◊> *Pupa*.

Metaphysical Poets. First used by Dryden, and made contemptuous by Dr Johnson but laudatory by later critics, the term describes 17th-cent. poets e.g. John Donne, Richard Crashaw, Thomas Traherne, Henry Vaughan, who fused passion and intellect in original and witty imagery, often with mystical religious content.

Metaphysics. A traditional part of ◊ *philosophy*, roughly divisible into speculative and critical; the former, mainly attempting to set out the fundamental nature of the universe, often distinguishes this as 'the reality behind appearances' and sometimes calls it the ◊ *Absolute*, not empirically but characteristically by an *a priori* argument related to ◊ *rationalism*. Aristotle presents a doctrine of substances, entities basic to all things in that they are the bearers of all their perceptible qualities but not qualities themselves; Spinoza regards the universe as one substance, God or Nature; McTaggart concludes that fundamental reality consists in spirits, not all of them embodied. Sometimes a substitute for religion, speculative metaphysics was long revered, but it is now ignored at least by most English-speaking philosophers, though lesser problems sometimes assigned to it, e.g. ◊ *causation*, remain alive. Critical metaphysics, e.g. ◊ *Kantianism*, is near to the theory of ◊ *knowledge* and studies the presuppositions, nature, and limits of human knowledge; in this secondary sense metaphysics is the concern of several contemporary philosophers.

Metasequoia. A genus of deciduous ◊ conifers of the family Taxodiaceae. Metasequoia was first described from fossil leaves and twigs of the Tertiary Age by the Japanese botanist, Miki, and named for the resemblance of its foliage and that of ◊ sequoia. The frequency of fossil foliage finds suggest that this was common in the so-called Arcto-Tertiary forest. In 1943, after it was known as a fossil, one living species, Metasequoia glyptostroboides, was found in western China, and since then it has been widely planted as an ornamental tree. Under favourable conditions, it may grow as fast as three ft a year.

Meteor (Meteorite). Stony or metallic particle orbiting around the sun and becoming visible when it enters the earth's atmosphere and burns up as a shooting star or (if very bright) fireball. Meteors average only about one twentieth of an inch in diameter, and if even half an inch in diameter produce very bright trails. On a clear dark night the naked eye can see six or more meteors per hour, and it is estimated that as many as a million an hour may burn up around the earth; ◊ radar is detecting more and more from their ionized gas trails. Showers of meteors tending to recur about the same time every year are possibly the remains of a ◊ comet continuing in orbit through which the earth passes; it is merely perspective that makes the individual meteors of a shower appear all to diverge from the same point (the radiant). Large meteorites may strike the earth with such force that they bury themselves deep in the ground and then explode, scattering fragments and leaving a large crater. One such crater in Arizona is 570 ft deep and 4200 ft across. Meteorites are of two types as below.

AEROLITE: Of rock; one of the largest (60-ton) lies near Groot Fontein in SW Africa.

SIDERITE: Of iron and nickel.

Claims to have found traces of organic substances in some of them have recently been made by British and Soviet scientists.

Meteorology. Science of the atmosphere, esp. of weather. Among the earliest studies was the Meteorologica of Aristotle

384–322 B.C. but little or no progress was made until Galileo invented an air thermometer and his pupil Torricelli discovered the principle of measuring atmospheric pressure by a ◊ barometer 1643. Hooke invented the wheel barometer about 1670 and discussed using atmospheric pressure changes for weather forecasting. By the early 19th cent. French scientists had established observing stations and were making daily weather charts; networks of such stations were set up in other countries, and the London Meteorological Office came into being in 1854. Investigations of the upper air were made first by means of manned balloons and then by small balloons carrying instruments. The main use of meteorology is to assist weather forecasting, of particular importance for aviation. A network of observing stations, of which there are thousands throughout the world, is the basis of the meteorological service; simultaneously regular observations cover type and amount of cloud, atmospheric pressure, temperature, relative humidity, wind direction and speed, and visibility. Small hydrogen-filled pilot balloons rising at known speeds and observed with theodolites indicate wind speed and direction at various heights. Sondes carried by sounding balloons register temperature, pressure, and humidity and transmit the information by radio. Radar maps rainclouds and storms. The first meteorological satellite was launched 1960. All the information collected is passed to forecasting stations, where weather charts are drawn showing the isobars, depressions and fronts, and anticyclones, and weather forecasts are prepared. International cooperation is secured through the World Meteorological Organization founded in 1950. ◊ Atmosphere.

Methane. Marsh-gas. Colourless gas and simplest hydrocarbon (CH_4). Formed when carbonaceous material decays out of contact with air, and coal-gas contains about 25 per cent by volume (known as 'fire-damp' in mines). Natural gas is mainly methane and is widely sought as a cheap fuel and raw material for chemical industry. Often found close to natural petroleum, and in Europe valuable quantities have been found in Holland and S. France. Great Britain imports large quantities from Algeria. ◊ Gas Industry, Paraffins.

Methodism. Protestant Christian Church tracing its origins to the preaching of John Wesley 1703–91, whose unorthodox methods of evangelization led after his death to the expulsion of his followers from the Church of England. Closest to ⇨ *Anglicanism* of all dissenting bodies (it has ⇨ *bishops* in U.S.A. though not in Britain), it is governed by an annual Conference of half ministers and half laymen, and has a world membership of about 15 m. In England the healing of certain schisms led to the fusion of several separate Methodist bodies in the existing Church 1932, and conversations to explore the possibility of reunion with the Church of England began 1962 in connexion with the ⇨ *Ecumenical Movement.* ⇨⇨ *Arminianism, Nonconformists, Protestantism.*

Methyl Alcohol. CH_3OH; the simplest ⇨ *alcohol*, a colourless, water-soluble, somewhat volatile liquid, inflammable and toxic. Formerly obtained by distillation of wood (⇨ *Acetic Acid*); now made, as an industrial chemical and solvent, by catalytic ⇨ *hydrogenation* of carbon monoxide.

Methylated Spirit. ⇨ *Ethyl alcohol*, with disagreeable additives which make it unsuitable for drinking but do not interfere with its use as an industrial solvent. The principal addition is crude ⇨ *methyl alcohol* (wood ⇨ *naphtha*).

Metre. In verse, the recurrence of short recognized combinations of long-short or stressed-unstressed syllables (feet); not a rule but a norm for poets, whose finer effects often arise from conflict between the run of the words and the metre expected. In reading, the natural emphasis of meaning should prevail over the metrical pattern. Rarer metres include the tribrach (each foot consisting of three unstressed or short syllables and three stressed or long) and the amphibrach (each foot consisting of unstressed-stressed-stressed or short-long-long syllables). The symbol ¯ is used over vowels to denote stressed syllables (in accentual metre) or long syllables (in quantitative metre), the symbol ˘ to denote unstressed or short. Metres are described (whether accentual or quantitative) as dimeter, trimeter, tetrameter, pentameter, or hexameter, according to the number of feet in the line. The commonest types of metre are as follows.

ANAPAEST: A three-syllable foot (e.g. picturesque).

DACTYL: A three-syllable foot (e.g. strawberry).

IAMB: A two-syllable foot (e.g. delight); iambic verse is usual in English poetic drama, owing to its resemblance to normal speech-rhythms.

SPONDEE: A two-syllable foot (e.g. shoehorn).

TROCHEE: A two-syllable foot (e.g. quickly).

Metric System. A unified logical system for weights and measures, based upon the ⇨ *decimal* notation, invented in France and introduced at the time of the French Revolution; the unit was the metre (calculated as one ten-millionth of the distance from the equator to the pole, measured along the meridian through Paris), on which all the other measures are calculated. In practice, the legal metre is the length of a standard platinum bar, kept in Paris. The unit of volume is the litre (the cube of one tenth of a metre), and the unit of weight is the gramme (the weight of one cubic centimetre of water at 4° C). ⇨⇨ *Weights and Measures.*

	Principal Metric Measures	U.K. Equivalents
Length	1 centimetre	0·39 in.
	1 metre	1·09 yd.
	1 kilometre	0·62 m.
Weight	1 gramme	0·04 oz.
	1 kilogram	2·21 lb.
Area	1 hectare	2·47 acres
	1 sq. kilometre	0·39 sq. m.
Capacity	1 litre	1·76 pt.

For easy conversion, 8 km may be reckoned as 5 m. and a litre as 1¾ pt, 10 litres as 2¼ gal. ⇨⇨ *Weights and Measures.* The British Government in 1965 decided upon the introduction of the metric system over the next few years.

Mexico (United States of Mexico). Area 758,000 sq. m. Pop. 37.2 m. Cap. Mexico City. Rel. Roman Catholic. Language Spanish. A federal republic of 29 states each enjoying substantial autonomy, with a Chamber of Deputies elected by universal suffrage for three and a Senate for six years; the President is elected by direct popular vote for a term of six years.

ECONOMY. Mainly plateau between 4000

and 8000 ft high, but with large agricultural areas, where primitive methods are gradually being superseded by modern practices. Cotton and coffee are the main exports. Forestry and stock-raising are also important. Mineral resources are considerable: there are lead and copper mines (mainly foreign-owned) and a nationalized ◊ *petroleum* industry. Mexico is the most industrially developed of the Latin American countries, with considerable iron and steel production, textile, rubber, and many light industries. It has become a favoured resort for Americans, and tourism earns substantial sums. Education is free and compulsory, but illiteracy is still widespread though diminishing.

HISTORY. Two civilizations, the ◊ *Mayas* and Toltecs, preceded the ◊ *Aztec* empire, which was conquered for Spain by Cortés 1521. Spanish rule continued till 1810, when the Mexicans revolted. An era of disorder and maladministration ensued, until Juárez in 1855 instituted reforms, interrupted by revolt, French intervention, and the execution of Emperor Maximilian. From 1877 until 1911 Mexico was ruled by Porfirio Díaz, a benevolent dictator under whom political stability and general progress was attained except as regards land reform, dissatisfaction about which led to revolution and his resignation 1911. Succeeding presidents continued as virtual dictators without the efficiency of the Díaz regime, until President Cárdenas 1934–40 began to achieve the objects of the 1910 revolution: the big estates were divided up, irrigation and education increased, and industrialization was encouraged. The railways and the oil industry were nationalized. Even today the aims of the revolution have not been fully realized.

Mezzotint ◊ *Engraving.*

Mica. Family of rock-forming silicates; the different kinds vary in chemical composition, the common form being muscovite (silicate of aluminium, potassium, and hydrogen). Chief among many properties which make them valuable is a perfect basal ◊ *cleavage*, which enables them to be split into thin plates not only flexible and elastic but transparent, poor conductors of heat, used e.g. as the windows of domestic oil stoves. Owing to their high dielectric strength they are used as insulators in electrical apparatus e.g. condensers, telephones, and dynamos.

Large sheets of mica occur in acid ◊ *igneous rocks* (pegmatites and granites) in SE U.S.A. and India, which together supply over 90 per cent of the world's needs. ◊ *Quartz, Silica.*

Michaelmas Daisy. Autumn-flowering asters in numerous cultivated varieties, which originated from about a dozen species of wild plants native to N. America. They vary in habit, from tall large-flowered pyramids of blossom to graceful small-flowered sprays. One European species only has contributed, *Aster amellus*, giving dwarf large-flowered plants.

Micronesians. The inhabitants of the Pacific islands north of Melanesia, including the Mariana, Marshall, Caroline, and Gilbert islands; of mixed racial type, the ◊ *Polynesian* preponderating, they have been occupied and influenced by various colonial powers, and today Japanese and American influences are strong, much of the indigenous culture having died out.

Micro-organisms. Those whose anatomy can be studied only by microscopy or biochemistry; the smallest are ◊ *viruses*, varying from 10 to 200 millionths mm. in diameter; the largest are multicellular animals and plants e.g. small insects, mites, threadworms, algae, fungi, mosses, etc. The distribution of micro-organisms is very general; not only do they form much of the ◊ *plankton*, but they are also to be found in sea and fresh water, soil, and air. Although many, e.g. viruses, are ◊ *parasites*, the majority are harmless to man, and many are directly or indirectly beneficial. Plankton ultimately feed all fish, and some bacteria involved in the ◊ *nitrogen cycle* are essential for the maintenance of life.

Microphone. Device for converting sound into electrical energy, usually by means of a diaphragm that vibrates in response to sound waves and causes in an ◊ *electric current* a pattern of vibrations similar to the pattern of the sound waves. The diaphragm may exert its effect on the current by varying the pressure on granules of carbon and altering their resistance, by moving a coil of wire or conducting ribbon in the field of a magnet, by varying the capacitance between the diaphragm and a fixed electrode, or by deforming a special type of crystal (piezoelectricity). Good microphones frequently have very weak output signals, which have to be fed into amplifiers before they can be used. ⟡ *Electricity*.

Microscope. Optical instrument which, like a simple magnifying glass, increases the apparent size of very small objects; the term is now usually used for the compound microscope, the invention of which is generally attributed to a Middelburg spectacle-maker, Jansen, but sometimes to Galileo, who was using one in 1610. It consists essentially of a hollow tube with lenses so fixed at both ends that the lower lens or objective (nearest the object) produces a magnified but inverted image which is then further magnified and observed by means of the upper lens or eyepiece. The modern compound microscope gives magnification up to 18,000 diameters and permits the study of objects the size of the smallest bacteria.

ELECTRON MICROSCOPE: Beams of electrons are used instead of beams of light, and are so much shorter in wavelength that much greater magnification can be achieved; the electrons can be deflected by objects less than one 10-millionth of an inch in diameter (i.e. of dimensions approaching those of an atom), with the result that very fine detail is revealed. The electrons are obtained from a heated filament and the 'electron lenses', which are adjusted by varying electromagnetic fields, act on them in much the same way as optical lenses act on light waves. The space through which the electron beams travel must be highly evacuated, and because the electrons cannot be seen directly the final image is observed on a fluorescent screen, or is recorded on a photographic plate.

ION MICROSCOPE: A development of the electron microscope, in which the images are formed by ionized atoms of ⟡ *helium* gas. Detail is sharpened by working at low temperatures, and magnifications approaching 3 m. are possible. ⟡ *Optics*.

Midas. In classical legend, king of Phrygia, hero of several folk tales. In one of the best-known, he was granted the wish that everything he touched might become gold. Even his food became gold as his lips touched it, and he was allowed to get rid of the useless gift by bathing in the river Pactolus. In another tale he judged the flute-playing contest between ⟡ *Apollo* and ⟡ *Pan*; he declared for Pan, and Apollo changed his ears into

those of a donkey. Though he tried to conceal them, a servant saw, whispered the news into a hole in the ground, and filled it up; reeds grew over the hole, and their whispering in the wind told the world that Midas had donkey's ears.

Midway. 1942. Naval engagement of the ⟡ *Second World War*, in which a powerful Japanese fleet, sent against the U.S. base on Midway Island in the Pacific, was heavily defeated by American aircraft. It proved a turning point in the war at sea, and was followed by the American attack on ⟡ *Guadalcanal*.

Mignonette. *Reseda odorata*; an annual, or short-lived perennial, originally from Egypt, where it was strewn around mummies. It is scented and is commoner in cottage gardens. It was introduced into Europe about 1750. In the original plant the greenish flowers were insignificant, but varieties with brighter colours have been introduced, perhaps with loss of scent. An ⟡ *essential oil* derived from the flowers is used in perfumery.

Migration. The movement of large groups of animals, between breeding places and feeding-grounds, either seasonally e.g. birds, or at long intervals e.g. salmon and eels. The destination and general route are often the same from year to year for a particular species, but over a longer period there may be changes connected with some aspect of environmental change. The origin of migratory movements is unknown; their value lies in allowing a species to exploit a wider range of habitat than if it remained static. Many species migrate in summer to regions inhospitable in winter, where they can breed and feed with less competition than in the crowded winter feeding-grounds. The most conspicuous migrations are made by birds, which have remarkable powers of navigation; some species travel 4000 m. each year. Regular migrations are also known in a few mammals, amphibia, fish, and insects. Other animals e.g. ⟡ *lemmings* and ⟡ *locusts* undertake non-migratory random wanderings.

Military Law. The rules of law to which members of the armed forces are subject and which govern military discipline and the powers and procedure of a ⟡ *court martial*; to be distinguished from ⟡ *martial law*. The detailed code is contained largely in Queen's Regulations, made under the authority of various Acts of Parliament. Members of the armed forces do not cease to be citizens, and remain subject to ◊ *civil law*.

Milk. A fluid produced by female mammals to feed the young, consisting mainly of fat globules held in suspension in water, and containing calcium, phosphorus, and the vitamins A, B, C, and D. Man drinks the milk of many animals e.g. mares, sheep, goats, camels, but principally that of cows, which is about 3.5 per cent protein, 4 per cent fat, 5 per cent milk sugar, and 87 per cent water. Other milks have similar proportions; a pint of good milk gives 90 per cent of man's daily requirement of calcium, with 30 per cent of the riboflavin and 25 per cent of the protein requirements. As milk is easily contaminated, cleanliness in milking and handling is essential.

BUTTER: Made from cream, churned to combine the fat-globules; typically it contains about 80 per cent fat and about 13 per cent water, and the important Vitamin A. The white or yellow colour depends upon the type of pasturage. Australia, Denmark, and New Zealand are the chief exporters.

BUTTERMILK: The semi-liquid residue after butter has been churned.

CHEESE: Consolidated milk curd. Lactic acid and rennet (or pepsin) are added to coagulate the milk, the serum (whey) is removed, and the residue is shaped under pressure; 100 lb. of milk produces 8–16 lb. of cheese (according to hardness). There are hundreds of varieties of cheese, in three main classes: hard (e.g. Parmesan, Cheddar); soft (Brie, Camembert); and cream cheeses (to be distinguished from the similar cottage cheeses, made from sour milk, not cream). In the blue cheeses (e.g. Gorgonzola, Stilton), the veining is produced by fungus moulds. The characteristics of the milk and the types of manufacturing process give the distinctive consistencies, colours, and flavours of various cheeses.

CONDENSED MILK: Sweetened evaporated skim milk.

CREAM: The fattiest part of milk, which rises to the top and can be skimmed off.

CURD: The solid part of whole milk.

DRIED MILK: Skim milk, evaporated, dehydrated, and powdered.

EVAPORATED MILK: Tinned evaporated whole milk, unsweetened.

HOMOGENIZED MILK: Milk forced through small holes in order to break up the fat-globules and distribute the fat evenly.

PASTEURIZED MILK: Milk which has been heated to a critical temperature in order to kill disease-bearing bacteria.

SKIM MILK: The residue after the removal of the cream.

TUBERCULIN-TESTED MILK: From cows warranted free from tuberculous infection.

WHEY: The watery serum separated-off from the curd e.g. in cheese-making.

YOGURT: Milk fermented with a special bacillus; a semi-solid.

Milky Way System. The ◊ *Galaxy*, our island universe, a roughly lens-shaped system of some 100,000 m. stars (including the sun); rather less than 100,000 light years in diameter and about 5000 light years thick. The stars are denser towards the central plane of this 'lens' and densest in spiral arms lying in this plane. Between the stars are clouds of gas and dust, which obscure vast areas of the system and interfere with astronomical observation (◊ *Nebulae*). The system rotates in its plane, and the sun (about two thirds out from the centre) takes some 200 m. years to make its circuit. In popular usage 'Milky Way' is often limited to a broad band of the system's stars which seem to form a white pathway across the sky on clear moonless nights; in the northern hemisphere this is best seen in the evenings of late summer.

Millet. *Panicum miliaceum*, a cereal of importance in Asia and Africa which grows in poor soil and withstands heat. It produces small seeds in a tuft at the top of a long stem. It has been found in prehistoric settlements, e.g. those of the lake-dwellers of Switzerland.

Milling. Grinding grain to produce flour. Among the earliest evidences of the cultivation of plants (8th millennium B.C.) are stone querns in which grain placed in a hollow on the lower millstone was ground by hand with a smaller rounded stone; this simple device was adapted to water power by the Greeks and Romans. Windmills (thought to have originated in Asia Minor) were probably introduced into Europe after the Crusades. With the Industrial Revolution, steam power was introduced and large-scale milling became possible; millstones were replaced by steel rollers, and various cleaning and sifting processes have facilitated the production of flour of great whiteness and fineness but with loss of nutritive values. By extension, many manufacturing processes in which the original power was a water mill are called 'milling' e.g. saw mill, paper mill, textile mill. ◊ *Rolling-Mills*.

Millstone Grit. Mainly coarse sandstones deposited by a river in an enormous ◊ *delta* over most of N. Britain. The middle division of the ◊ *Carboniferous System*, and in the central Pennines over 6000 ft thick. Named 'millstone' from its once common use for grinding corn.

Mime. Speechless acting (or actor), using gesture, bodily movement, and facial expression; esp. important in oriental theatre and in ◊ *ballet*. Notable mimes of the European theatre include four Frenchmen, Debureau in the 19th cent. and Jean-Louis Barrault, Étienne Decroux, and Marcel Marceau in the 20th. The comedians of the silent screen were of course mimes, e.g. Chaplin, Buster Keaton, Harry Langdon, Harold Lloyd. ◊ *Pantomime*.

Mimicry. Resemblance of one animal to some object or other animal, which serves to protect it from predators; most common among insects e.g. stick insect, but occurs among other animals also (◊ *Snake*). In 'Batesian mimicry' a defenceless species comes to resemble another species having offensive or poisonous characteristics, e.g. the hornet clear-wings, which are ◊ *moths* which resemble ◊ *wasps* both in appearance and behaviour, and in S. America the numerous varieties of poisonous snakes which are duplicated by non-venomous mimics. The success of mimicry of this kind depends upon the mingling of both species in close association.

Mimosa ◊ *Acacia, Leguminosae*.

Mind ◊ *Consciousness, Psychology, Unconscious Mind*.

Minerva. In Roman mythology, goddess of artisans and their guilds; later equated with ◊ *Athena*, the third in the principal triad of Roman deities (with ◊ *Jupiter* and ◊ *Juno*).

Mines and Mining. Extraction of minerals both from the surface ('opencast') and below ground. As early as 3500 B.C. in the Near East simple shafts and galleries were dug to obtain copper ores; as knowledge of metals grew, a greater variety of ores

was mined, e.g. lead, tin, and from about 1500 B.C. iron. The Romans developed mining wherever they went, e.g. the Rio Tinto mines in Spain and the lead, tin, silver, iron, and rock-salt mines in Britain. Neolithic settlers mined ◊ *flint* in Europe from about 3000 B.C. and their mines reveal a remarkable knowledge of excavation techniques. Tin mines existed in Britain before the Roman invasions; rock-salt, mined in Cheshire and Worcestershire by the Romans, became important in the late 17th cent. Coal-mining developed during the reign of Elizabeth I and was well established by 1750. Throughout the history of mining men have been exposed to the hazards of flooding, subsidence, and imperfect ventilation, and in coalmines to dangers of explosion. Early mines were ventilated naturally, by convection currents due to the difference in temperature of the air above and below ground. Georg Agricola in *De Re Metallica* 1556 describes the use of surface windmills or even giant bellows below ground. Ventilation problems were largely solved by the introduction of centrifugal-type ventilators about 1850. Meanwhile the danger of explosion in coalmines had been much reduced by the introduction of the Davy safety-lamp 1816. Safety and humane conditions in mines were long neglected; in Britain the first law to prevent inhuman exploitation was passed in 1842, and led to a gradual improvement. Mining remains a hazardous occupation, in spite of all precautions and technical advances. ◊ *Coal and Coal-mining, Iron, Metallurgy*.

Ming ◊ *China, Porcelain*.

Miniature Painting. Originally, a painting in *minium* (red lead or vermilion), with no reference to size. In general, any small detailed painting (of which Indian and Persian works are among the finest), ◊ *illuminations* in medieval manuscripts, and esp. small portraits of a type first produced in Flanders in the early 16th cent. painted with watercolour and body-colour on parchment; miniatures by Jean Clouet, Hans Holbein, Nicholas Hilliard, and Isaac Oliver are among the most vivid of all 16th-cent. portraits. The genre remained popular into the 19th cent. but with changed character owing to the use of ivory or metal as a ground and of pigments other than watercolour, portrait miniatures often being framed to be worn as jewellery. The advent of ◊ *photography* brought the art virtually to an end.

Ministry of Defence. U.K. Ministry set up in 1964 to correlate the functions previously exercised by the Admiralty, War Office, and Air Ministry. The Minister is assisted by the Ministers for the Navy, Army, and Air Force.

Mink. Two species of semi-aquatic Carnivora, *Mustela lutreola* and *M. vison*, found in Europe, Africa, and N. America; they have dense under-fur with superimposed silky guard hair, which makes their fur of special value. Minks are now bred for the fur trade, and genetic study has resulted in the production of a wide variety of mutant furs.

Minnesingers. German poets and singers late 12th and early 13th cent. who composed and sang lyrics of ◊ *courtly love* in accordance with the traditions established by the Provençal love poetry of the ◊ *troubadours*; the best known are Wolfram von Eschenbach, d. about 1220, and Walther von der Vogelweide, d. after 1227.

Minnow. Freshwater bony fish seldom over four in. long, a member of the carp family; widespread in Europe in clear brooks and streams. It lays its eggs on the sandy bed in shallows in May and June. In Britain it is used as live bait for larger fish.

Minoan Civilization. The first European civilization (about 3000–1200 B.C.) and the first anywhere to be based on maritime trade, centred on the island of Crete, and named after the legendary king ◊ *Minos*. Crete was early colonized from Egypt and Asia Minor, and the growth of Minoan civilization was due in part to influences from the older eastern and southern civilization, but although Minoan culture in some ways (e.g. centralized political, religious, and economic organization) mirrored the oriental civilizations, it was in other respects strongly individual esp. in architecture, seen best at the royal palace of ◊ *Knossos*. The Minoans had an advanced ◊ *Bronze Age* technology, and by about 1700 B.C. were using a script known as Linear A, which is still undeciphered; the later script known as Linear B was recently demonstrated by Michael Ventris to be Greek. In the freshness and humanistic realism of Minoan art, and in the high degree of freedom from oppression which the Minoans seem to have enjoyed,

in contrast to their oriental neighbours, are discernible some of the sources of Greek civilization. Knossos was destroyed about 1400 B.C. (or later, according to a recent theory) by Mycenaean Greeks from the mainland, who assumed political and mercantile leadership in the E. Mediterranean. ◊ *Mycenae*.

Minos. In Greek legend, son of ◊ *Zeus* and ◊ *Europa*; king of Crete, he required from the Athenians a yearly payment of seven young men and seven maidens for the diet of the Minotaur, a part-bull and part-human monster living in the centre of the Labyrinth, a maze constructed by Daedalus. ◊ *Theseus* killed the monster, aided by Ariadne, daughter of Minos. Other legends represent Minos as a just ruler who after death became a judge in ◊ *Hades*; 'Minos' may have been a title or dynastic name for Cretan kings in general. The Theseus story may enshrine some memory of the bull-fighting frequently represented in surviving objects of Cretan art.

Mint ◊ *Herbs, Labiatae.*

Minuet. A dance in triple time, supposedly of rustic origin, introduced at the court of Louis XIV in the 17th cent. Musically it was one of the dance-movements which often formed part of the classical suite, e.g. Bach's, and later became a regular movement (usually light-hearted) of the classical type of symphony, e.g. Haydn's, Mozart's; as such it is the ancestor of the symphonic scherzo.

Minutemen. In the ◊ *American Revolution*, armed citizens or militiamen ready to serve at a minute's notice, esp. those from Massachusetts, who fought at ◊ *Lexington* and Concord.

MINUTEMAN: The name has also been given to a type of U.S. ballistic missile of intercontinental range located in widely scattered protected launching pits; a major element in U.S. nuclear armament.

Miracle Play. Medieval religious drama, in which episodes from the lives of the saints were presented in the vernacular; similar to a mystery-play presenting episodes from the ◊ *Bible*. In England, however, the terms miracle-play and mystery-play were interchangeable, both having developed from the illustrative liturgical drama incorporated into the ◊ *Mass* for worshippers who knew no Latin. Control passed to the trade guilds, and in larger English towns each guild mounted its appropriate episode in the great cycle of vernacular miracle plays beginning with the Creation and ending with Doomsday; in summer (at Corpus Christi) each episode was staged on a pageant waggon and played to bystanders at various 'stations' round the town. More or less complete cycles survive: York 48 plays, Wakefield 32 plays, Chester 25 plays; 'N-Town', the most remarkable dramatic writing, both comic and emotional, occurs in the Wakefield cycle and is attributed to the Wakefield Master.

Mirage. Optical phenomenon which may occur when the atmosphere is heated or cooled in horizontal strata and light is refracted when passing from one layer to another. Under certain conditions the light can be bent through such a large angle that there is the appearance of reflection by a mirror. An observer e.g. in a desert or on a hot smooth road may imagine he is looking at a sheet of water. Similarly when the 'mirror' conditions occur well above ground level an observer can see images of distant objects which are normally hidden over the horizon, e.g. the ships and icebergs which sometimes appear to be suspended over polar seas.

Misdemeanour ◊ *Felony*.

Missiles. ◊ *Rockets* carrying explosives (warheads) and capable of reaching distant targets. In the Second World War the German V2 rocket of 1944 established the possibility of long-range missiles. Later improvements in rocket performance, and the provision of atomic warheads made possible (1) the Intercontinental Ballistic Missile, with a range of 5000 m. (flight time about 30 min.) – such missiles need elaborate fixed launching sites; (2) the Intermediate Range Ballistic Missile, with a range of 1500 m. (flight time of 5–10 min.), which needs less elaborate launching (the Polaris type is mounted in nuclear submarines and can be adapted to other mobile launching media); (3) the smaller short-range missile, with various tactical applications e.g. as an anti-aircraft weapon, which may already be so efficient as to make bomber penetration a dubious method of delivering an attack. From the wide variety of such missiles it is possible that the 'anti-missile missile' may emerge. The large missiles are essentially weapons of mass-destruction, of overwhelming power. ◊ *Artillery, Ballistics, Firearms*.

Missions. Organized efforts to spread religious cults, esp. those of ◊ *Christianity* and ◊ *Islam*. Intensively carried on in the first centuries A.D., Christian mission work, however, practically ceased after the rise of Islam, until the discovery of America in the 15th cent. The ◊ *Roman Catholic Church* then took active steps to convert American Indians, and the Jesuits (◊ *Society of Jesus*) sent missions to the Far East also; the Congregation of Propaganda (◊ *Cardinal*) was created 1622 to organize and supervise foreign missions (and also to reconvert the Protestant countries). Protestant missionary work began in the 17th cent. e.g. the Society for the Propagation of the Gospel (SPG) 1701, and continued in the 18th e.g. the Baptist Missionary Society 1792 and the Church Missionary Society (CMS) 1799. Missions have been closely associated with hospitals and education, esp. in Africa, but 20th-cent. nationalism in Asia and Africa has in many cases led to missionary effort being superseded by the founding and consolidating of indigenous churches. Islamic missions have long been carried on with much success in Africa. Missions were sent out on a wide scale in the first centuries of ◊ *Buddhism*, and have again operated in Europe in the 20th cent. but ◊ *Judaism* does not proselytize.

Missouri Compromise (1820) ◊ *United States (History)*.

Mistletoe. *Viscum album*; a widely distributed plant semi-parasitic on certain trees esp. old apple-trees, deriving its food in part from the sap of the host. The seeds are spread by birds, which eat the very sticky berries. It was associated with the rites of the ◊ *Druids* although rare on their sacred tree the oak, and is a magical plant in Scandinavian mythology (◊ *Baldur*).

Mistral. Extremely strong, cold, and dry N. to N W wind in S. France and adjacent areas of Spain and Italy, mainly in winter when atmospheric pressure is high over Europe and low over the W. Mediterranean; the air sweeps S. from the French central plateau and is funnelled through the Rhône valley to the delta, often blowing in a cloudless sky but reducing temperatures to well below f.p.

Mite. Very small organism of the arachnoid class (◊ *Scorpion, Spider*), found in food or as an infesting ◊ *parasite*; some cause ◊ *mange* or ◊ *scabies* on animals or humans, others e.g. rust mite, red spider mite, are destructively parasitic on vegetation. Foods likely to become mite-infested include cheese, sugar, flour, grain.

Mithra (Mithras). Ancient Indo-European god; his cult, associated with caverns and the ritual slaughter of bulls, soon disappeared from India but developed greatly in Persia, where Mithra was the leader of the forces of light against darkness and good against evil (until ◊ *Zoroastrianism* reduced his status). A form of his cult spread to Rome and became extremely popular.

MITHRAEUM: Man-made cavern for Mithraic worship; a Mithraeum was excavated in London 1954.

MITHRAISM: A dualist religion postulating eternal war between the forces of good and evil (in a state of approximate equilibrium). Until the 3rd cent. A.D. Mithraism was a serious rival to ◊ *Christianity* (which it resembled e.g. in rites of ◊ *baptism* and ◊ *Holy Communion* and in postulating eternal reward or punishment and preaching salvation by ritual observance and ethical purity); esp. popular in the Roman armies, it was widespread throughout the imperial dominions.

Mitosis ◊ *Cell, Spores.*

Mobile. A type of sculpture invented in 1932 by the American Alexander Calder, consisting of pieces of metal, glass, wood, etc. fastened to the ends of pivoted wire rods so balanced that at a gentle touch each moves freely and the whole thus presents a sequence of forms.

Mock Orange. *Philadelphus*; originally, only the very strongly scented *P. coronarius*, from the Near East, which has been in British gardens since the 18th cent. Other species are valuable flowering shrubs, but not all are scented. The name 'syringa' (correctly ◊ *lilac*) has been erroneously applied to *Philadelphus*.

Moderator (physics) ◊ *Nuclear Reactor.*

Modulation. Every method of communication – speech, writing, musical instruments, smoke signals, radio, television, etc. – includes a vehicle, or carrier, e.g. the human voice or a selected band of radio waves, and also a method of varying or modulating it. In radio and television broadcasting the two principal methods of modulating carrier waves are amplitude modulation and frequency modulation.

AMPLITUDE MODULATION: Fluctuating signals derived from sound vibrations or picture variations are impressed on a carrier wave of constant amplitude, so that the resulting modulated wave varies in amplitude in sympathy with the modulating signals; when the modulated wave reaches the receiver, its amplitude variations are reconverted into sound or picture signals.

FREQUENCY MODULATION: The frequency of the radio wave at any instant depends on the modulating signal. This is being increasingly used; its important advantage over amplitude modulation is that it is less susceptible to interference from other transmitters and from many types of local electrical noise.

Moguls (Moghuls). A variant of Mongol; a Muslim dynasty founded in Delhi in 1526 by Baber, who claimed descent from Jenghis Khan. The Mogul empire reached its greatest territorial expansion under Shah Jehan and Aurangzeb, but was then harassed by the Sikhs and Marathas and was in decline when conquered by the British in 1803. Its art and literature flowered in the 17th cent. under Shah Jehan, who left the incomparable mosque of Taj Mahal as his monument.

Mohacs. 1526. Crushing defeat of Lewis II of Hungary by a Turkish army eight times as numerous, which placed Hungary under Turkish domination for 150 years. In 1687 in the same vicinity a victory of Charles V of Lorraine over the Turks paved the way for the liberation of Hungary.

Mohammedan ◊ *Islam.*

Mohenjo-Daro ◊ *Indus Civilization.*

Moho. The Mohorovičić Discontinuity (discovered by a Yugoslavian scientist). The earth's crust is a thin skin over the interior; under the crust is the mantle, and then a metallic core. At the dividing line between crust and mantle a marked change occurs in the velocity of earthquake waves, suggesting that the crustal rocks differ physically or chemically from those of the mantle and core.

MOHOLE PROJECT 1962: Attempt to bore through to the rocks of the mantle, at a place (off the coast of California) under the Pacific where the crust (generally 20–25 m. thick, but always more under the continents) is abnormally thin, 3–4 m. ◊ *Fault, Seismology.*

Molasses. A thick brown syrup produced

during the refining of cane and beet sugar, which is removed from the sugar crystals and used for various purposes; better grades are refined to make treacle or rum. Standard molasses contains up to 16 per cent sucrose.

Mole. Of the *Insectivora*, though the common mole *Talpa europea* feeds mainly on worms; its adaptation to underground life includes a conical head, oar-like fore-limbs which are digging tools, and fur set at right angles to the skin so that it does not impede forward or backward motion. Mole-hills may be the earth thrown out of an excavated tunnel, or a 'fortress' over the spherical nest.

Molecule. The smallest portion into which a substance can be divided while retaining its properties, made up of atoms either of the same kind or of different kinds, in chemical combinations which are indicated by chemical formulae. The form in which matter appears (i.e. solid, liquid, gas) is thought to depend on the distance between the molecules composing it and on their energy. Thus, in a liquid, the molecules are farther apart and are more energetic than in a solid. The application of heat or pressure to a substance affects the movements of its molecules and eventually produces a change of state, e.g. solid to liquid.

MOLECULAR WEIGHT: The sum of the weights of the atoms which constitute a molecule (◊ *Atomic Weight*).

Molluscs. Soft-bodied and unsegmented invertebrate animals, usually protected by a hard shell; one of the principal groups of invertebrates, exceeded in number of species only by the *Arthropoda*. A typical mollusc, e.g. snail, consists of a prominent muscular portion (head-foot), a visceral mass, and a shell which is secreted by the free edge of the mantle (the exterior of the visceral mass). In some molluscs, however, e.g. slugs, the shell is absent or rudimentary, and in others e.g. ◊ *cephalopods* the head-foot is greatly modified and forms tentacles. The majority of molluscs are included in three large groups: gastropods (e.g. slug), lamellibranchs (bivalves e.g. oyster, cockle, mussel), and cephalopods (e.g. octopus, squid).

Molybdenum. A silvery-white metallic element obtained from the sulphide molybdenite. The pure metal is used in electric lamps, in thermionic, X-ray, and television tubes, and as wire for heating-elements in high-temperature furnaces. Ferromolybdenum is used in alloy steels for cutting tools, and recently to replace ◊ *tungsten*. Ammonium molybdate is a common laboratory reagent.

Monaco. Area 350 acres. Pop. 20,000. A small principality, an enclave within French territory on the Mediterranean, which has been a semi-independent state under Spanish or French protection since the Middle Ages; most of its revenues are derived from the famous casino of Monte Carlo. The practice of registering companies in Monaco so as to avoid payment of French taxes brought the country into a dispute with France in 1962. The present ruler, Prince Rainier III, married the American film actress Grace Kelly in 1956; the birth of a male heir has prevented Monaco becoming a French protectorate, under a treaty of 1918.

Monarchy. Rule by a single person; it may be absolute (independent of all other authority) or constitutional, hereditary or elective. Many monarchs in the past were regarded as gods or the descendants of gods. Few absolute monarchies now remain; the majority are constitutional, the monarch being primarily a symbol of national solidarity, a hereditary alternative to the largely titular presidents of most republics.

Monasticism. Religious way of life in communities secluded from the world, and following a more or less ascetic rule of life, to which the members are bound by vow, such as have always existed among Buddhists, and since the 4th cent. among Christians both in Eastern and Western Churches (◊ *Benedictines, Carmelites, Carthusians, Cistercians, Dominicans, Franciscans*). Since the ◊ *Oxford Movement* monastic groups have been revived in the Church of England: their members are usually occupied in educational, literary, or social work as well as personal sanctification and liturgical worship.

Money. A token of value, accepted in exchange for goods or services, which may have some intrinsic value e.g. gold or silver coins or be valueless in itself e.g. paper money. It replaces the cumbersome process of barter, facilitates the exchange of goods, serves to establish a scale of values or prices, furnishes a unit of account and fund of value. Many forms of money have been used, some purely conventional e.g. cowrie shells, some of intrinsic value e.g. cattle or measures of gold or silver. The invention of coins, attributed to the Lydians in the 7th cent. B.C., was a further step leading to the expansion of trade. Gold and silver coinage remained prevalent until 1914 when paper money was first issued in quantity in Europe. Once paper money is not convertible into gold on demand (and most currencies are now inconvertible), its acceptability depends in the first place on its status as legal tender and in the last resort upon the users' confidence in it. ◊ *Gold Standard*.

Mongolia. Region of Asia, lying W. of Manchuria, S. of Siberia, and N. of the Great Wall of China. A mountainous country, unsuitable for agriculture, it was the home of the hordes of horsemen who for centuries swept across Asia, threatening Europe and establishing great empires such as that of Jenghiz Khan. After the 14th cent. its power declined and in the 17th cent. it came under the suzerainty of China. Outer Mongolia broke away from China in 1921 and in 1924 became the Mongolian People's Republic; China recognized its independence in 1945. Inner Mongolia remains an autonomous province of China.

MONGOLIAN PEOPLE'S REPUBLIC. Area about 604,000 sq. m. Pop. about 1 m. Cap. Ulan Bator. Rel. Lamaist-Buddhist. Independent republic closely associated with the U.S.S.R. Under the 1960 constitution there is a Great People's Khural (Parliament) elected by universal suffrage; seven of its members form the Presidium. Cattle-breeding is still the chief industry, despite five-year plans to introduce industry. Wool, hides, and gold are exported.

Mongolism. Mental deficiency characterized by the typical 'mongoloid' appearance of small skull, stiff hair, eyes slanting downwards and inwards, small depressed nose, high colour, and a fissured tongue. Mongols are usually cheerful, affectionate, and fond of music; they are, however, highly susceptible to infection and generally live only a few years. Statistics indicate that most mongols are born to mothers over 35; the cause is unknown.

Mongol Languages ◊ *Altaic Languages*.

Mongols. Asian race now numbering about 3 m. An obscure nomadic people, under their ruler Yesukai they suddenly emerged as a conquering army in the 12th cent. and under Jenghiz Khan swept across Asia in the 13th, setting up Khanates in Russia, China, Persia, and India. In Europe they reached Poland, Hungary, and Germany. In the 14th cent. Tamerlane created a new Mongol empire in India, Russia, and the Levant; but the Mongol supremacy proved ephemeral, they returned to their nomadic life, and in the 17th cent. Mongolia came under the suzerainty of the Chinese: ◊ *Mongolia*.

Mongoose. A member of the Carnivora, about twice the size of and similar in appearance and habit to the ◊ *ferret*; there are several genera, distributed throughout India, S. Spain, and Africa. The mongoose is ground-living, and its diet of rats, snakes, etc. has proved of value in the biological control of pests.

Monism. A type of philosophy contrasted with ◊ *dualism* and ◊ *pluralism* which views reality as one thing or one kind of thing: e.g. for Spinoza the universe is one substance, God or Nature; for materialists everything is material.

Monitor. 1. In biology, several varieties of ◊ *lizard* found in the tropics of the Old World; up to 10 ft long, with prominent eyes, long necks, and powerful defensive tails, their evolutionary history dates to the Mesozoic era. Many are desert species, with a diet of small mammals, reptiles, or fowl; they are sometimes erroneously called iguana.
2. Shallow-draft ◊ *warship* carrying large-calibre guns to provide artillery support from the sea for military operations ashore; the modern successor of the bomb ketch of Nelson's day. The only British monitor now afloat is H.M.S. *Roberts*, built 1941, displacement 7970 tons, carrying two 15-in. and eight 4-in. guns.
3. ◊ *Merrimac and Monitor*.

Monkey. Tailed member of the ◊ *Primates*, divided into the catarrhine (prominent-nosed) monkeys of the Old World and the platyrrhine (flat-nosed) monkeys of the New World, with prehensile tails and without cheek-pouches. ◊ *Ape*.

Monkshood. *Aconitum napellus*; a hardy perennial of the *Ranunculus* family, named for the shape of its flowers, extremely poisonous to both man and animals. Its roots contain the narcotic drug aconitine.

Monocotyledon ◊ *Angiosperms*.

Monopoly. Condition in which there is only one seller of a particular commodity, opposed to monopsony (where there is only one buyer) and to perfect competition (where there are so many sellers that no one individual can significantly influence the market); a modified form is oligopoly, where there are few sellers. Monopolies may pursue policies against the common interest, and in many countries the government takes powers to control them (often as part of legislation against restrictive practices in general); such powers are extensive in U.S.A. where under its Anti-Trust legislation the government can forbid mergers and divide up large companies. In the U.K. the Monopolies Commission, set up 1948, has power to investigate but none of enforcement; it can only make recommendations, and since 1956 has not concerned itself with matters coming under the jurisdiction of the ◊ *Restrictive Practices* Court. European countries are on the whole more tolerant of such arrangements (◊ *Cartel*), but there too the recent trends are towards stricter supervision.

Monotype. A type-composing and type-casting system invented in 1893 by Tolbert Lanston, consisting of two units: (1) a keyboard, somewhat like that of a typewriter, by which small round holes are punched into a paper ribbon by means of compressed air and steel punches; and (2) a caster, which (instructed by the perforated ribbon) casts single types from matrices and automatically assembles them into words and lines. Recently the system has also been adapted to film-setting. It is particularly valuable as a method of printing books with complicated tables and formulae.

Monroe Doctrine. 1823. A principle of U.S.A. policy enunciated by President James Monroe when the Spanish colonies in Central and S. America were in revolt to establish their independence. It declared 'that the American continents, by the free and independent condition which they have assumed and maintain, are henceforth not to be considered as subjects for future colonization by European powers'. He added that any interference with these republics would be regarded by the United States as the 'manifestation of an unfriendly disposition'.

Monsoon. < Ar. *mausim*, season; originally the winds of the Arabian Sea, now esp. the regular winds of the Indian Ocean, caused primarily by the seasonal differences in temperature between land and sea, the land being the warmer in summer and the sea in winter. From about April to Sept. the SW winds of the summer monsoon (originating as the SE trade wind in the Indian Ocean) blow towards India, saturated with moisture and bringing heavy rain to extensive areas esp. where mountain barriers e.g. the W. Ghats cause precipitation. Moving forward with a definite front, the monsoon reaches any given place at about the same date every year, the first rain being known as the burst; rain being essential to rice cultivation, monsoon failure causes food shortage and even famine. Violent tropical cyclones (◊ *tornado*) occur in the van and rear of the monsoon. In sharp contrast to the strong winds, heavy seas, overcast skies, and frequent rain of the SW monsoon are the winter conditions of the NE monsoon, when the land is cooler than the sea and cold dry air from the interior of Asia sweeps SW towards the Indian Ocean. The NE monsoon, advancing over India as the SW monsoon retreats, lasts from about Oct. to March.

Montenegro. One of the republics of ◊ *Yugoslavia*. Occupied by Slavs in the 7th cent. it formed part of ◊ *Serbia*, but in the late Middle Ages it achieved a certain independence, and was the only Balkan state to hold out against the Turks (◊ *Ottoman Empire*) for five centuries, under its prince-bishops, who organized the state on a military footing for continuous defence. From the 18th cent. Montenegro came under strong Russian influence and was a leading advocate of ◊ *panslavism* in the 19th cent.; its territory was enlarged in 1878 by the ◊ *Berlin Congress* and Treaty, and after the ◊ *Balkan Wars*. After 1918 King Nicholas was deposed and Montenegro became part of Yugoslavia.

Montreux Convention. 1936. International agreement reversing some of the provisions of the ◊ *Lausanne Conference*. It permitted Turkey to fortify the ◊ *Dardanelles*, and if at war to close the Straits to ships of all countries. It is still in force.

Monumental Brasses. Flat brass plates deeply engraved with figures, often of armed knights; popular in the Middle

Ages as sepulchral monuments, esp. in England, where the earliest example (in Stoke d'Abernon church) is dated 1277. Brasses are an important source of information on costume, armour, genealogy, ◊ *heraldry*, etc.

Moon. The earth's satellite (diameter 2160 m.) moving in an orbit varying between 253,000 and 221,000 m. from the earth's centre. In relation to the earth, it is appreciably larger than the moons of other planets, and the earth-moon system may almost be regarded as a double planet. The moon has negligible atmosphere; thus surface temperatures vary greatly during the lunar day, there is no protection from incoming meteorites, and the surface is unweathered and therefore likely to hold important information about the formation and history of the ◊ *solar system*. Mountains and circular craters are visible, and there is believed to be a layer of dust on the valleys and plains. There is no water, but possibly some ice in crevices. Until a small volcanic eruption was observed recently, the moon was thought to be a dead world. A Soviet satellite obtained pictures of the dark side of the moon in 1961; a U.S. capsule transmitted close-up photographs of the lunar surface in 1964.

Moorhen. Long-legged long-toed black freshwater bird living in lakes, ponds, and marshes, where it nests among reeds; swims jerkily, occasionally diving, and flies low and clumsily. The conspicuous white undertail coverts are used in warning and courtship displays.

Moors. The inhabitants of Mauretania and N. Soudan; forcibly converted to ◊ *Islam* in the 8th cent. and intermarried with the ◊ *Arabs* and ◊ *Berbers*, they became fanatical Muslims. In 711 they crossed into Spain and rapidly established themselves there; only their defeat at ◊ *Tours* prevented their spreading into France. In the cities of the south, notably Córdoba, they established a brilliant civilization which transmitted to medieval Europe ancient learning and Islamic skills, esp. in architecture, science, and medicine. Politically, however, Moorish Spain was weak, and in the 11th cent. the caliphate of Córdoba fell and was replaced by the stronger but sterner and more philistine rule of the Almoravides; the Christian reconquest of Spain had already begun; and the Moors, with the

◊ *Jews*, were driven out after the fall of Granada to Ferdinand and Isabella in 1492. Even converts to Christianity were allowed to remain only under the harshest restrictions. In 1569 the remaining Moors rose against the oppression, but were ruthlessly repressed; their last descendants were expelled by the ◊ *Inquisition* in 1609.

Moraine. Deposits left by a retreating glacier.

GROUND MORAINE: Areas formerly occupied by the ◊ *ice sheet*; generally ◊ *boulder clay.*

TERMINAL MORAINE: Marks the limit of the ice sheet; unsorted material of all sizes, from enormous rocks to fine silts. ◊ *Bergschrund, Drumlins, Kames.*

Morality Play. Allegorical didactic form of late medieval drama, in England usually showing a central representative character (Mankind, Everyman) in conflict with particular vices or virtues, the theme being human salvation; the Devil, or Vice, was traditionally a chief comic character. Out of the morality play, sometimes indistinguishable from it, grew the Interlude (◊ *Masque*), a short crude secular comedy with little if any moral or didactic intent. ◊ *Everyman, Miracle Play.*

Moral Philosophy ◊ *Ethics.*

Moral Rearmament. Movement founded by an American, Dr Frank Buchman, also known as the Oxford Group. It advocates the regeneration of society by 'complete honesty, purity, and love', the members seeking divine guidance in all their activities and meeting at house parties for mutual encouragement and 'sharing' (confession of failings). It refrained from denouncing Hitler's policies. It maintains headquarters in Caux, Switzerland.

Moravians (United Brethren). Protestant Christian body tracing its origins to the Czech reformer John Hus (*c.* 1370–1415) and reconstituted in Germany in the early 18th cent. by Count Zinzendorf 1700–60, agreeing in general with other Protestant bodies, but not demanding acceptance of any formal creed beyond the Scriptures (◊ *Bible*); have been extremely active in foreign missionary work. John Wesley's conversion (◊ *Methodism*) was a result of contact with them. Their influence is considerably greater than suggested by their small number, about 3000 communicant members in Gt Britain.

Morganatic Marriage. A man's marriage to a woman of lower social status, in which she and the children of the marriage are barred from inheriting the husband's estate or titles. It was customary principally in Germany, and was unknown in English law, though the term is colloquially used of marriages between royalty and commoners. Occasionally it was used of a woman's marriage to a lower-ranking man.

Mormons ◊ *Church of Latter-day Saints.*

Morocco. Area 180,000 sq. m. Pop. 13.1 m. (mainly ◊ *Berber*). Cap. Rabat. Rel. Muslim. An independent kingdom in NW Africa, with an elected two-chamber legislature with limited legislative powers, King Hassan II retaining considerable control of policy.

ECONOMY. Both agricultural and mineral; the construction of dams for irrigation and for electric power is hastening development. There is a growing tourist trade. Principal exports citrus fruits, cork, esparto grass, fish, leather, vegetables, and iron ore, lead, manganese, phosphates, zinc. Petroleum fields are being developed. HISTORY. Morocco remained isolated in the early centuries A.D. until in the 8th cent. the ◊ *Arabs* founded an empire centred on Fez. While the ◊ *Moors* occupied Spain there was considerable Spanish influence, but from the 16th cent. onwards Morocco relapsed into isolation. The mountain Berbers resisted the introduction of a quasi feudal system by the Sherif, and the coast-dwellers took to pirate raids upon Mediterranean shipping. French attempts to absorb and colonize Morocco in the 19th cent. were resisted by other European powers, but in 1906 the Algeciras Conference agreed to French and Spanish penetration. In 1912 Morocco was divided into a Spanish sphere of influence and a ◊ *protectorate* governed by France. In the ◊ *Second World War* the French protectorate supported the Vichy government; the Allies invaded Morocco in 1942. After the war there was protracted civil disturbance until 1956, when the two zones were united and granted independence under King Mohammed V, whose son Hassan II succeeded him in 1961.

Morphine. One of the opium ◊ *alkaloids*, a drug for the relief of pain. It is habit-forming, and effective analgesic non-habit-forming substitutes have been developed. ◊ *Drug Addiction, Opium.*

Morris Dance. English folk dance; originally a dramatic ritual dance, performed by young men chosen for their vigour and vitality, dressed in white with bells and ribbons and carrying handkerchiefs or sticks. In its earlier forms it came to Britain with very early settlers as part of their culture; it occurs elsewhere in other forms and is obviously an integral part of the early culture of all N. Europe. In recent years there has been a considerable revival in Morris dancing, stemming from the surviving traditional teams.

Morse ◊ *Code.*

Mosaics. A surface decoration (for walls, floors, or ceilings) formed of small cubes (*tesserae*) of marble, coloured stone, or opaque or gilt glass, embedded in cement and arranged to form ornamental patterns or pictures. In constant use from ancient times, mosaics became very popular for the decoration of early Christian and Byzantine churches, notably in Rome, Ravenna, Constantinople, Venice, Sicily, and Greece. After the 13th cent. ◊ *fresco* superseded mosaic in western Europe, being capable of more realistic representation; but in Islamic countries mosaics remained popular for the decoration of ◊ *mosques.* The art of mosaic has recently been revived in Italy and by Boris Anrep in England.

Moscow Conference (1812) ◊ *Borodino, Napoleonic Wars.*

Moslem (Muslim) ◊ *Islam.*

Mosque. A building for Muslim public prayer and study; usually square or rectangular, and originally a central unroofed court surrounded by an open or covered cloister. The wall on the side nearest Mecca (◊ *Hegira*) is marked by a niche, *mihrab*, to show which way worshippers should face at prayer. There is a pulpit, an enclosure for women, a tank or pool near the entrance for ritual ablutions, and a turret or minaret from which the muezzin calls believers to prayer at the set times. The first mosque built by Mohammed in Medina was simply a square walled enclosure. ◊ *Muslim Architecture.*

Mosquito. Insect (◊ *Fly*) of the order *Diptera* whose larval and pupal stages are spent in fresh water. Adults absorb their food in liquid form through tube-like mouthparts; those of the female are strong enough to pierce skin and take blood, and thus transmit diseases to man, harbouring the parasites in their own bodies, e.g. *Anopheles* transmits malaria, *Aedes* yellow fever, and *Culex* elephantiasis. The incidence of these diseases is reduced by killing the mosquitoes e.g. by spraying swamps with oil to suffocate the young.

Moss ◊ *Plants* (*Bryophyta*).

Motet. In music (1) a choral composition in Latin; for church service, but to words chosen by the composer, not fixed by the liturgy, i.e. corresponding to the Anglican anthem. (2) A medieval vocal composition based on a 'given' melody and verbal text, to which the composer added other melodies (with other words) in ◊ *counterpoint*.

Moth. Several thousand species of insect of the order *Lepidoptera*; most but not all fly at night. The ◊ *pupa* is protected by a cocoon, often of ◊ *silk*; that of the silkworm moth is of great commercial value. Some moths, esp. the clothes moth and the codling moth, do great damage at the larva stage.

Motion. In physics, the change of position of one body in relation to another. A body can be in motion relative to another body whilst also at rest in relation to a third body, e.g. a person in a train is moving in relation to the earth but is at rest within the train. Newton in his *Principia* was the first to put forward a general theory of motion. His laws state that (1) a body remains in a state of rest or of uniform motion in a straight line unless acted upon by an external force; (2) the rate of change in momentum is proportional to the force causing the change, and takes place in the direction in which the force is acting, the rate of increase or decrease in velocity (i.e. acceleration) being proportional to the force; and (3) to every action there is always an equal and opposite reaction, i.e. when one body exerts a force on a second, the second exerts an equal and opposite force on the first. The system of classical mechanics built on these fundamentals is that used in dealing with the motion of bodies at ordinary velocities. When extremely high velocities are involved recourse must be had to the concepts of ◊ *relativity*.

Motor Car. The earliest 'horseless vehicles' on roads were driven by steam, the first practical example being Trevithick's steam carriage of 1802. Subsequently many steam vehicles were built in Gt Britain, and the more advanced versions remained in use for heavy road transport even into the 20th cent. However, the lighter and more compact ◊ *internal combustion engine* proved much more suitable, and after Daimler's successful petrol engine of 1885 the motor car evolved rapidly in France and Germany, and slightly later in the U.K. once the Act of 1896 removed the legal restrictions on mechanized road transport. In 1910 the era of mass production of motor vehicles began, with methods introduced by Henry Ford, and led to the rise of great automobile industries esp. in France, Italy, Germany, U.S.A., and the U.K.

MOTOR RACING: The first motor race was from Paris to Rouen and back, 1894; in 1903 tragedies in the Paris–Madrid race forced the sport on to special closed circuits. The International Federation in Paris governs the sport and has many times changed the technical rules for the major Grand Prix events; the present maximum engine size is 1500 c.c. with a minimum car weight of 1100 lb. Drivers and manufacturers compete for the most prized titles, the annual Formula I World Championships, decided by results in the principal races, which are professional. Semi-professional are sports-car racing, rallies to test driving skill and ordinary car reliability over long distances (notably the Monte Carlo 2600-mile Rally), hill climbs, etc. The whole sport is heavily subsidized by industry for prestige purposes and as a test of fuels and of designs which may subsequently be used in commercial production.

Motor-cycling. Divisible into Grand Prix racing, Moto-Cross racing (over rough country), Reliability Trials, Hill Climbs and Scrambles, Speed Bids, Sprints, and the radically different speedway or dirt-track racing, introduced from Australia 1928. At the top it is a professional sport, often with manufacturers' backing, but the vast majority of riders are amateurs. Road racing is not permitted in Britain, but a road circuit is cleared annually for the Isle of Man Tourist Trophy races, founded 1907, the world's oldest and most famous motor cycle event. For world championships, riders compete in various Grands Prix, titles being awarded for 125, 250, 350, and 500 c.c. classes and for side-cars. The governing body is the International Motorcycling Federation (41 affiliations).

Mountaineering. A sport which has developed since about 1857, when the Alpine Club was founded in London; earlier climbers did not climb for pleasure but for some scientific or monetary motive. A Dr Paccard of Chamonix was the first to scale Mt Blanc, in 1786, to show that man could live above the snow-line, but it was the lectures of Albert Smith, who climbed the peak in 1851, that kindled English interest. In 1854 Wills climbed the Wetterhorn and eleven years later Whymper made his famous ascent of the Matterhorn. By 1880 all the major peaks of the Alps had been scaled and climbers went further afield, to the Andes and the Himalayas. Many attempts were made to reach the summit of the highest of these, Everest (29,028 ft) but it was not till 1953 that Hillary and Tensing succeeded. Present-day climbers have more elaborate equipment than the pioneers, e.g. pitons (spikes to be driven into the rock) and, at great height, oxygen supplies.

Mouse. Small widely-distributed rodent, genus *Mus*, e.g. house mice and ◊ *rats*. The house mouse, *M. musculus*, of Asian origin, is common in Britain, as are also the field mouse, *M. sylvaticus*, and the harvest mouse. All mice breed prolifically: white mice (albino house mice) are used as laboratory animals. Like rats, mice are disease carriers.

Mousterian ◊ *Neanderthal Man, Palaeolithic.*

Mozambique. Area 297,657 sq. m. Pop. 5.7 m. (almost wholly Bantu). Cap. Lourenço Marques. Portuguese E. Africa, technically an 'overseas province' of ◊ *Portugal.* Discovered by Vasco da Gama and colonized from 1505. There are about 100,000 Portuguese settlers. The official policy of racial assimilation has had somewhat more success here than in ◊ *Angola.* The economy is agricultural; Mozambique is commercially important mainly as an entrepôt for the trade of Malawi, Rhodesia, Zambia, and part of S. Africa. Lourenço Marques, a fine town, is a tourist centre.

Mucous Membranes. Moist lining of the alimentary canal and the respiratory, urinary, and genital passages. Although they vary in form in different structures, mucous membranes all consist of a super-ficial layer of mucus-secreting epithelium supported on a layer of connective tissue containing nerves, blood vessels, and lymphatics. The mucous membrane of the intestines is made velvety in texture by innumerable tiny projections (villi), through which the products of ◊ *digestion* are absorbed.

Mukden. 1905. The last battle of the ◊ *Russo-Japanese War*; the Russians were forced to retreat, but the Japanese were too exhausted to pursue.

Mulatto. A person of mixed white and Negro percentage; in many racially mixed societies e.g. those of the New World elaborate distinctions may be made, according to degrees or kinds of white or Negro ancestry.

MESTIZO: Mulatto whose white parent is Spanish or Portuguese.

OCTAROON: A person one eighth non-white.

QUADROON: A person one quarter non-white.

Mule. Offspring of a male ass and a mare (◊ *Hybrid*); a sterile animal, of great hardiness and strength esp. suited to pack-work in mountainous country.

Mullet. Two unrelated kinds of marine bony fish.

GREY MULLET: Breeds in-shore in warm or temperate seas; the roe is eaten as a delicacy.

RED MULLET: A Mediterranean fish resembling the perch; one sort reaches British waters.

Mumps. Swelling of the parotid gland, which mainly affects young people and is infectious; caused by a filterable virus and spread by direct contact or by air-borne droplets. The incubation period is 8–30 days, and the disease produces a mild temperature which lasts 3–5 days. Glands other than the parotid may be affected; acute orchitis (inflammation of the testicle) is a fairly common complication in men.

Munich Pact. 1938. Agreement between Germany, Italy, France, and Britain, signed by Hitler, Mussolini, Daladier, and Chamberlain – no representative of Czechoslovakia being present – which permitted the German occupation of the Sudetenland in Czechoslovakia and guaranteed the new frontiers thus created; the last of a series of concessions to Hitler made in the name of 'appeasement'. An Anglo-German non-aggression pact was signed at the same time. ◊ *Nazism, Second World War.*

Münster. 1533–5. While the reprisals for the ◊ *Peasants War* were still going on, the ◊ *anabaptists* occupied Münster (a town in Westphalia), deposed both religious and civil authorities, and established a 'democracy' of reformed religion and popular rule, proclaiming it the 'new Zion' and declaring all property communal (and polygamy legal, on Biblical authority). When the prince-bishop's forces entered the town, extremely severe reprisals followed.

Murder. Killing a human being with 'malice aforethought' i.e. the intention to kill or to do him grievous bodily harm; if the death is by misadventure, or in reasonable defence of oneself or others (excusable homicide), it is not murder (◊ *Manslaughter*).

CAPITAL MURDER: In the course of theft; by shooting; in the course of resisting arrest, or in effecting an escape from lawful custody; of a police officer on duty, or of anyone assisting him; of a prison officer on duty, by a prisoner; multiple murder if the murders are done on different occasions; and murder by anyone already convicted of non-capital murder in Great Britain.

NON-CAPITAL MURDER: Punishable by imprisonment for life. ◊ *Capital Punishment, Diminished Responsibility.*

Muscat and Oman. Area 82,000 sq. m. Pop. 750,000 (Arab with large Baluchi and Negro minorities). Cap. Muscat. Independent sultanate in E. Arabia.

ECONOMY: Largely desert, but with fertile areas; camel-breeding, date and sugar-cane cultivation, and exports of frankincense.

Muscular System. Muscles, the specialized tissues by which bodily movements are carried out, occur in three types: (1) Voluntary muscles, which are under the control of the subject. (2) Involuntary muscles, which carry out functions not under voluntary control. (3) Cardiac muscle, specialized for the functions of the heart and unique in possessing an inherent power of rhythmic contraction. The function of muscle ◊ *cells* is to contract in response to nervous stimuli; the energy for this contraction is supplied by ◊ *carbohydrate*. The cycle of chemical operations which brings about muscular contraction is extremely complex; the resulting mechanical effect is a shortening of the long molecular chains of which muscle ◊ *protein* is made up. Part of the energy of muscular activity is dissipated as heat; the mechanical efficiency of muscle is about 25 per cent.

Muses. In Greek mythology, the nine minor goddesses presiding over literature and song, associated with ◊ *Apollo*, god of the arts; daughters of ◊ *Zeus* and Mnemosyne (Memory), and born near Olympus in Pieria (the 'Pierian spring'). CALLIOPE: Epic poetry. CLIO: History. ERATO: Love poems; mime. EUTERPE: Lyric poetry. MELPOMENE: Tragedy. POLYHYMNIA: Sacred song. TERPSICHORE: Dancing. THALIA: Comedy; idyll. URANIA: Astronomy.

Museum. Repository for pictures, treasures, and objects of antique, scientific, and general interest. Collections of manuscripts, antiquities, and objects of art were made by the Ptolemies in Alexandria in the 3rd cent. B.C.; museums in the modern form, providing for the display of noteworthy objects, developed first in 16th-cent. Italy e.g. the Uffizi Palace 1581, and were followed by the great systematic collections e.g. the Vatican 1740, the ◊ *British Museum* 1753, the Prado in Madrid 1809, and the Louvre in Paris. Museums of every kind now abound, some concentrating on art e.g. the National Gallery and the Tate Gallery in London and the Museum of Modern Art in New York, some on science e.g. the Science Museum 1857 in London and the Deutsches Museum in Munich, and some on furniture and objets d'art e.g. the Victoria and Albert Museum in London. Other famous museums and art galleries are the Escorial in Madrid, the Belvedere and the Albertina in Vienna, the Hermitage in Leningrad, the Alte Pinakothek in Munich, and the Metropolitan Museum of Art in New York.

Mushrooms. The edible fruiting-bodies of various ◊ *fungi*; usually, species of *Psalliota*, esp. *P. campestris*, the common mushroom, found wild in grassland and

---

A single arrow before a word or phrase indicates a cross-reference to another main entry. A double arrow means *See also.*

meadows esp. where horses feed, generally appearing in moist weather in late summer and autumn, though mushrooms are now grown commercially throughout the year. Mushroom spawn consists of blocks of organic material in which grow the hyphae (mycelium), underground vegetative-fungus threads; when sown under the right conditions, the mycelium grows rapidly and produces the mushrooms. In many European countries a large variety of fungi are eaten. ◊ *Toadstools*.

Music. The fine art of combining sounds 'with a view to beauty of form and expression of thought or feeling' (SOED); essential elements are tone, rhythm, and melody (◊ *harmony* developing late in western music and not being present at all in oriental music). Chinese music subordinated melody and rhythm to the single tone, for reasons related to the nature of the language and of the instrument producing it; tones were grouped into six male and six female. Arab music is monodic and is based on a scale of 17 notes; it was influenced by Greek musical theory and itself influenced Hindu music and (through Moorish Spain) European music, into which it introduced the lute. Hindu music also is monodic, and divides the octave into 22 parts, each roughly equivalent to one quarter of a whole tone in western music; melody is based on a system of some 60 *ragas*, melodic types used as bases for improvisation, and similarly rhythm is based on variations on a set of rhythmic patterns, the *talas*. Like Hindu and Chinese music, Greek music was thought to have ethical and religious properties, and was judged by Plato to be good or bad according to its moral effect; it played an important role in Greek drama, esp. the choruses. The discovery of the mathematical basis of harmony is attributed to Pythagoras, and the modern theory of music dates to Aristoxenus in the 3rd cent. B.C. As well as being the chief basis of Roman music, classical Greek music was also a major influence on Byzantine (Eastern Orthodox) church music, as is shown by the surviving 3rd-cent. Greek Christian ◊ *hymn* on the Oxyrhyncus papyrus. In its turn, Byzantine music influenced the Latin ◊ *plainsong* of the western church, of which the hymns linked with St Ambrose A.D. 340–97 are an early famous example. In the Middle Ages professional composers

served the Church extensively, chiefly by varying or adding to traditional plainsong. The English round known as *Sumer is icumen in*, about 1240, also possesses a Latin religious text and is musically related to a plainsong antiphon. The earliest composers known by name are Léonin (active about 1160–80) of Notre-Dame in Paris, and his successor Pérotin. The most important contribution to secular music was that of the ◊ *troubadours* and trouvères in France and the ◊ *minnesingers* and ◊ *mastersingers* in Germany. The ◊ *Renaissance*, as far as music is concerned, may de dated from the 14th-cent. French and Italian polyphonic composers Vitry, Machaut, Landini. The 15th-cent composers include Dunstable (an Englishman who had considerable influence on the Continent), Dufay, Ockegham, and Obrecht, the three last belonging to the Franco-Flemish school, as did Josquin Desprès, about 1440–1521. Emigrant Franco-Flemish composers assisted the growth of a 16th-cent. Roman (Papal) school, including the Italian Palestrina, the Belgian Lassus, and the Spaniard Victoria.(◊ *Mass*).

A strong English Tudor school, influenced by Italy, included Byrd, Morley, Tallis, Weelkes, and Wilbye. With the exception of certain dance music, music up to this period had been mainly vocal, but now music for the virginals and other ◊ *keyboard instruments* flourished, as did music for the lute, in which the Englishman Dowland had a European reputation. In Germany, the ◊ *Reformation* greatly influenced music, from the simple hymns of Luther to the polyphony and organ music of Schütz and of J. S. Bach 1685–1750.

◊ *Opera* developed in Italy from about 1600, Monteverdi being the first major composer, and the Italian operatic example influenced Lully (himself Italian-born) in France and in England contributed to the unique and varied output of the short-lived Purcell 1659–95.

Among Bach's contemporaries were Domenico Scarlatti, the Italian virtuoso of and composer for the harpsichord, 1685–1757, Antonio Vivaldi, the prolific Italian composer of concertos, about 1685–1741, Rameau, the important French theorist and composer 1683–1764, and Handel, 1685–1759, who invented English ◊ *oratorio* after having failed to find commercial success with opera, a genre afterwards made dramatically stronger by Glück, 1714–87. The late 18th cent. and the 19th saw the rise of the ◊ *symphony*, the ◊ *sonata*, and the ◊ *concerto*. The illustrative orchestral tone-poem dates effectively from Liszt (equally important as the prototype of the piano virtuoso), who had been preceded by Paganini, the prototype of the modern violin virtuoso, 1782–1840. The massed choir of mixed male and female voices dates from 1784 (Handel Commemoration Festival in London), and the modern conductor and baton from Spohr and Mendelssohn in the early 19th cent.

Music of the period from Monteverdi to Bach is often characterized as ◊ *baroque*, most of the Haydn-Beethoven period as classical, and that of the Chopin-Wagner-Tchaikovsky-Puccini period as romantic, while the term neoclassical applies to certain 20th-cent. supposed revivals of old forms. In the second half of the 19th cent. music was increasingly marked by national divisions, and some composers e.g. Dvořák have been called 'nationalist'. In the 20th cent. and esp. with the practice of serialism European music has returned to a more international manner and has been subject to non-European influences such as those of jazz, American, Afro-Cuban, and Oriental music. ◊ *Atonality, Canon and Fugue, Chamber/Choral/Church Music, Counterpoint, Temperament.*

Musical Comedy. The type of light dramatic and musical entertainment (related to operetta) popular in Britain and America in the late 19th and early 20th centuries, e.g. *The Geisha* (music by S. Jones) 1896, *The Maid of the Mountains* (music by H. Fraser-Simpson) 1916. Later examples, more and more frequently of American origin, tended to be known as musical plays or simply 'musicals' e.g. *Oklahoma!* (Rodgers and Hammerstein) 1943, *West Side Story* (Leonard Bernstein) 1957.

Musical Instruments. Classified for the modern ◊ *orchestra* into (1) strings i.e. violin, viola, 'cello, double-bass (not usually harp); (2) woodwind (flute, oboe, clarinet, and bassoon, and their larger or smaller analogues); (3) brass (horn, trumpet, trombone, tuba); (4) percussion; and (5) extras (harp, pianoforte, organ, windmachine, etc.).

Types of instruments recognizably like our own are known from ancient Egypt, and the East was a source for European instruments (e.g. lute, kettledrums) up to the time of the Crusades. The basic forms of most instruments of western music were established by the 17th cent. By then the violin family had displaced the older viols; violin-making reached a peak in the era of Stradivari 1644–1737. The late 18th cent. brought the pianoforte into general use, and the mechanical advances of the 19th cent. greatly increased the constructional efficiency and facility of wind instruments, including the organ (◊ *Keyboard Instruments*). The electronic organ was invented in 1930. Latin-American percussion instruments e.g. maracas, claves have been the chief 'exotic' import into 20th-cent. music, which has also seen the deliberate revival of older instruments e.g. recorder, lute, harpsichord in the cause of a historically authentic style of performance. A pioneer in this revival was Arnold Dolmetsch 1858–1940. ◊ *Brass Instruments, Stringed Instruments.*

Musical Modes. Different types of ◊ *musical scales*; the major and minor scales are only two of the seven possible ways (each with a different sequence of intervals) in which the notes corresponding to the white keys of the piano can be ordered. If a melody, constructed on the white keys only, has its 'home' note on D it is in the Dorian mode; if on E the Phrygian; F the Lydian; G the Mixolydian; A the Aeolian (modern minor); B the Locrian (not used); C the Ionian (modern major). These modes apply to medieval music, including ◊ *plainsong*, and to most European ◊ *folk music*; the names are taken from Greek, but do not correspond to the classical Greek usage.

Musical Scale. < It. *scala*, ladder; this is based upon natural acoustic phenomena, esp. the fact that if the length of a vibrating string or air-column is halved the note is raised to another note which appears to be a higher reproduction of it. The interval between the original note and the 'reproduction' (which is that between the first and second notes of the ◊ *harmonic series*) is called an octave in western music, because it is commonly graded into eight notes; in non-European music there may be different gradations, of more or less than eight. The two chief ◊ *musical modes* of the octave (esp. for music composed 1600–1900) are the major scale (corresponding to the white notes of the piano from any C to the note C above or the note C below) and the minor scale (from any A to the A above or below).

CHROMATIC SCALE: Both the white and the black notes of the piano in continuous adjacent order.

Music-hall. From the mid 17th to the 19th cent. only three London theatres had royal charters enabling them to remain open at all times (Covent Garden, Drury Lane, and later Haymarket); other theatres often evaded the regulations by e.g. selling cups of tea or coffee at high prices and giving entertainment 'free'. Increasingly also, in the 19th cent. the taverns and eating-houses all over Britain offered their customers free musical and comic entertainment at mealtimes. In 1854 the Canterbury Music Hall, London, obtained a licence to charge admission fees for a variety entertainment at which refreshments were also sold, and the music-hall era had begun. The 'singing taverns' could not compete with the theatres, which gradually reduced the refreshments aspect to the interval. The music-halls lasted from 1854 to 1914, and then declined in face of competition from cinema and radio. In their heyday they produced stars like the male impersonator Vesta Tilley, the black-face vocalist Eugene Stratton, the clown Dan Leno, the 'emperor of mirth' George Robey, and the long remembered Marie Lloyd. Many radio and TV comedy programmes derive directly from music-hall 'patter' and 'cross-talk' and 'song-and-dance acts'. ◇ *Pantomime*.

Musk. A fixative material used in perfumery, extracted from an abdominal gland of the male musk deer, a native of the Himalayan and Central Asian mountains; similar materials are produced by other animals e.g. the musk rat, and by some plants. A cheap synthetic imitation has been evolved.

Muslim (Moslem) ◇ *Islam*.

Muslim Architecture. As there was virtually no architecture in Arabia when Mohammed built his first simple ◇ *mosque* at Medina A.D. 622, the Muslims elaborated the original plan by adapting the architectural styles of countries that they conquered, surrounding the open court by arcades and then constructing a large building and minarets within the enclosure. They often transformed existing buildings into mosques e.g. the church of Haghia Sophia in Constantinople, and variant forms emerged in Egypt, Turkey, Persia, India, and the Moorish lands, the Persian style (and the Indian, which derives from it) making spectacular use of glazed tiles to cover domes and decorate façades. Nevertheless, a certain broad similarity characterizes Islamic architecture: while the exterior is usually plain, the interiors are often highly decorated, with intricate tracery, stalactite ornaments, and marble and semi-

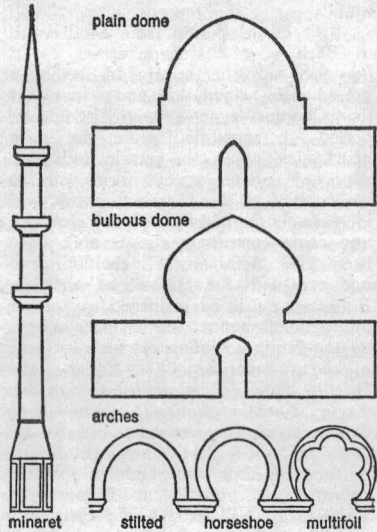

precious stones in contrasting colours. The geometric decorations of Islam were first designed by Byzantine artists of the iconoclast party, probably in the Omayyad Mosque at Damascus; religious precept, ornamentation is limited to such designs and to Koranic inscriptions in highly conventionalized and decorative Cufic and Nashi scripts. Characteristics of Islamic architecture are the horseshoe arch e.g. at Córdoba, delicate columns, and graceful bulbous domes; the pointed arch (copied from the Sassanians) antedated the ◇ *Gothic* arch of Europe, which derived from it. Outstanding examples of mosques are the Dome of the Rock in Jerusalem, the

Masjed-i-Shah in Isfahan, and the Taj Mahal in India.

Mustard Gas ◊ *Chemical Warfare.*

Mutation. An unpredictable and relatively permanent change in a gene, resulting in the emergence in the offspring of a character not present in the parents. Biological inheritance is based on the transmission of patterns within the cells (◊ *DNA*) which in general are passed on unchanged apart from the reshuffling or cutting of the 'pack' or chain of patterns which occurs in bi-parental reproduction. This brings some variety in individuals, but marked evolutionary change could not occur without some actual modification of the genetic material itself i.e. mutation. In some cases the change in the gene is so drastic that it is unable to propagate descendants (lethal gene); less extensive mutations are transmissible. Some which involve the loss of part of a chromosome or the rearrangement of damaged ones can be observed under the microscope. Others cannot be so detected, and probably result from subtle alterations in the genetic material caused by a variety of agents such as certain chemicals or ultraviolet and ionizing radiations, while others arise apparently spontaneously. Mutation occurs in both animals and plants; in the latter they are commonly known as 'sports'.

M.V.D. ◊ *Secret Police.*

Mycenae. One of several towns on the Greek mainland constituting the Mycenaean civilization, which flourished from about 1600 B.C. and superseded the ◊ *Minoan civilization* in the Aegean from about 1400 B.C. The Mycenaeans were possibly a Greek-speaking people (◊ *Achaeans*) who had arrived in the Aegean from somewhere in S. Russia as part of the Indo-European migrations of about 2000 B.C. Although subject to Minoan influences, their culture was strongly independent esp. in the plan of their palaces, which differs markedly from that of the Minoans, and their way of life was less settled. Their towns were built around strongly fortified citadels, their economy based partly on piracy and partly on trade with the civilizations of W. Asia and perhaps the uncivilized peoples of Europe as far north as Britain and the Baltic. Mycenae and several other towns were destroyed after 1200 B.C. possibly by ◊ *Dorian* invaders.

Mycosis. Any infection caused by one of the ◊ *fungi*; the commonest mycoses are those caused by the *Candida* species (which give rise to lesions in the mouth, ◊ *thrush*, and in cavities e.g. the vagina) and the dermatophytes, which cause the various forms of ◊ *ringworm.*

Myrtle. *Myrtus communis,* the common myrtle, an evergreen bush with fragrant white flowers, well known in Britain since the 16th cent. One of the flora of the Mediterranean maquis, though probably not native there. In classical legend the myrtle was sacred to ◊ *Aphrodite,* and a sprig of it long remained traditional in wedding bouquets. Bog myrtle (myrica gale) is an aromatic shrub native in Britain.

Mystery Play ◊ *Miracle Play.*

Mysticism. Religious experience of direct communion with the godhead or the Absolute; mystics are found in all the higher religions, and in Christianity outstanding examples are Denis the pseudo-Areopagite, St Teresa of Avila, St John of the Cross, Meister Eckhart, Richard Rolle, Jakob Boehme, and Swedenborg. Outside the Christian world the Egyptian Plotinus, the ◊ *Sufis,* and many Buddhist and Hindu writers have contributed to the universal mystical tradition. A non-religious 'nature' mysticism is represented by e.g. Wordsworth, Walt Whitman, and the Irish poet A. E. (G. W. Russell). ◊◊ *Gnostics, Karma, Swedenborgianism, Theosophy.*

Mythology. Body of traditional stories involving supernatural persons and events belonging to a particular people; also the study of such stories (myths). Since the subject began to be studied seriously in the late 18th cent. many theories on the origin of myths have been produced. Max Müller regarded them as 'linguistic corruptions' deriving from personification of natural phenomena; Frazer in *The Golden Bough* related them to fertility cults and to the natural cycle of birth, death, and resurrection; Jung saw them as the symbolic expression of a people's collective unconscious. Students no longer believe it possible to find one theory to fit all myths, but try rather to relate individual myths to the whole culture and history of the society producing them. In general there seem to be two kinds.

EXPLANATION MYTHS: How the world began (e.g. the creation myths found in practically all societies) and how it will end (e.g. ♢ *Ragnarok*); how a given city was founded; how a given craft was first practised.

JUSTIFICATION MYTHS: Rationalizing a people's customs, beliefs, or rituals.

Myths also reflect history: a nation's defeat by invaders may produce myths of one group of gods defeating another (♢ *Titans*); or the conquest of a matriarchal society by patriarchal invaders may be expressed in a myth of marriage between a moon goddess and a sun god or sky god. BABYLONIAN ♢ *Baal, Ishtar*, etc. BRITISH ♢ *Arthurian Legend, Lancelot*, etc. EGYPTIAN ♢ *Horus, Isis*, etc. GREEK ♢ *Adonis, Aphrodite*, etc. HINDU ♢ *Shiva, Vishnu*, etc. IRISH ♢ *Conchubar, Deirdre*, etc. ROMAN ♢ *Janus, Jupiter*, etc. SCANDINAVIAN ♢ *Aesir, Balder*, etc. WELSH ♢ *Merlin*.

Myxomatosis. Serious virus disease of rabbits, spread by direct contact or by biting-insects (in Britain usually by rabbit fleas), causing severe head and body swellings, and eye infection quickly leading to blindness. Deliberately introduced into Australia to kill off rabbits (a serious menace to crops and pasture land), it was rapidly spread by mosquitoes, and in many areas rabbits were temporarily almost exterminated; later, however, they developed a resistance and began to increase again.

N

Nagaland. Area of Assam near Burma where the tribes, differing in race, language, and religion from the rest of ◊ *India*, sought to obtain separate independence and resisted Indian rule after 1947. A partial concession, whereby a separate State within the Indian Republic was set up in 1963, has not obtained the support and loyalty of the Nagas.

Names. 1. PERSONAL NAMES. In many ancient ◊ *Indo-European languages* a person was identified by a single name of two elements e.g. Greek Aristo-cles, of best renown; Slavonic Bogu-slav, divine glory; Old English Ethel-red, noble counsel. The Romans evolved a threefold system: *praenomen*, given nine days after birth, e.g. Marcus; *nomen*, the inherited family name, e.g. Tullius; *cognomen*, an epithet or nickname, e.g. Cicero (chickpea). Hence Quintus Horatius Flaccus, Publius Ovidius Naso, etc. The Russians also evolved a threefold system: Christian name e.g. Lev; patronymic e.g. Nikolaievich (son of Nikolai); surname e.g. Tolstoy. Hence Anton Pavlovich Chekhov, Nikita Sergeievich Khrushchev, etc. The Christian name and patronymic e.g. Ivan Petrovich, Anna Petrovna are used in Russian when addressing acquaintances.

British surnames (apart from those which are simply Christian names e.g. Gilbert, James, Lawrence) fall into four main groups. *Descriptive:* Armstrong, Foot, Head, Long (or Lang), Short (or Little), Strong (or Strang); Cruikshank (crooked leg), Doggett (dog head); Doughty, Moody, Peacock (or Pocock). Some came from ownership of an inn, e.g. Dawe (jackdaw), or a part played in a pageant, e.g. Bishop, King, Pope. *Local:* Brook, Church, Field, Green (i.e. village green), Hall, Hill, Lane, Lea, Wood. More than 50 per cent of British surnames are local. *Occupational:* Archer, Baker (or Baxter), Butcher, Carpenter, Fletcher (i.e. arrow maker or seller), Horner (i.e. maker of horn spoons etc), Latimer (or Latiner, i.e. interpreter); sometimes regional, e.g. Fuller (S. and E.), Walker (W. and N.), and Tucker (S W) all mean 'cloth cleaner'. These names reflect the wide variety of occupations in the three centuries after the Norman Conquest, when heritable surnames first came into common use. *Patronymic:* Johnson, Peterson; Macdonald, Macmillan; O'Brien, O'Connor; Fitzroy, Fitzgerald; also C, K, Q prefixed e.g. (Manx) Cubbin, Kissack, Quail; and P, B prefixed e.g. (Welsh) Bryce, Price, ap Rhys.

2. PLACE-NAMES. The waves of Celtic, Roman, Irish, Jutish, Anglish, Saxon, Frisian, Danish, Norwegian, and Norman-French settlers in Britain are recorded in a rich variety of place-names e.g. Hatfield < *hǽþ-feld* not from 'hat' but 'heather field' i.e. open land; Smithfield < *smeðe-feld* not from 'smith' but 'smooth field'; Oxted < *āc-stede* is not from 'ox' but means 'oak-stead'; Milton may be *middel tun* (middle farm) or *mylen tun* (mill farm); Holton, Hooton, Houghton, Howton, Hutton, are all *hoh-tun* (a farm built on a *hoh*, heel of land, as a precaution against flooding); Startforth, Strafford, Stratford, Stretford, Trafford are all variants meaning a ford on a Roman road. Different languages often give place-names of identical meaning e.g. Land's End, Finistère (French); Blackpool, Dublin (Irish); Whitby, Casablanca (Spanish); Oxford, Bosporus (Latin). In long-distance communication the standardization of place-names is important; the Postal Union issues a full list in Roman script of all the post offices in the world including China and U.S.S.R.

Nancy (1477) ◊ *Burgundy.*

Nantes (1598) ◊ *Edict of Nantes.*

Nap (Napoleon). A card game using a full pack, for two to six players with five cards each, playing separately. Each must bid a minimum of two tricks in his trump suit or pass: the highest bidder then leads his trump suit, and all must follow suit if possible. The bidder is paid or pays according to whether he succeeds or fails in making his bid: to go 'Nap' means to bid and take all five tricks, and the other players must then pay double. A bid of misère, which is the next highest, is that no tricks will be won by the declarer.

Naphtha. A volatile inflammable liquid; comprising certain fractions of the ◊ *hydrocarbon* oils obtained from ◊ *distilla-*

tion of petroleum, coal, or shale as well as the crude ◊ *methyl alcohol* (wood naphtha) from dry distillation of wood. Petroleum naphtha is a fraction obtained just before the motor fuel. The naphthas are useful chiefly as solvents.

Naphthalene. The most abundant of the coal-tar aromatic ◊ *hydrocarbons*. It is important as the starting point for a number of ◊ *dyes* and also as a source of phthalic acid, which in turn leads to ◊ *indigo* and to certain resins used in very large quantities in paint (◊ *polymers*). It was formerly used as 'moth balls'.

Naples. In S. Italy; both the city and the kingdom of which it was the capital. Originally a Greek colony, the city was captured by the Romans in 328 B.C. Under ◊ *Byzantine* rule from the 6th cent. Naples enjoyed a period of independence from the 8th cent. until 1139, when it came under Norman rule as a part of the kingdom of ◊ *Sicily*. The Norman kingdom flourished, esp. under Frederick II who founded the University of Naples. After 1266 S. Italy passed to the Angevins; when Sicily passed to the Aragonese in 1282, a separate Kingdom of Naples was formed, and thereafter declined in the course of the long struggle between Anjou and Aragon. The ultimate victory of Spain in 1503 began a period of peace, but the heavy taxes imposed by the ◊ *Hapsburgs* and the huge estates maintained by the nobles and the Roman Catholic church drained the country's resources, and in 1734 the ◊ *Bourbons* inherited Naples as one of the most backward and impoverished states in Europe. In 1808 Napoleon established his brother-in-law Marshal Murat as King of Naples, but with the fall of the Napoleonic empire in 1815 the Bourbons returned; their reactionary regime continued until in 1860 Garibaldi's invasion united Naples with the newly formed kingdom of ◊ *Italy*.

Napoleonic Wars. 1800–15. General Bonaparte, leader of the victorious armies of the ◊ *French Revolution*, after making himself First Consul in 1799 continued the war against the Second Coalition (mainly Austria, Britain), defeating the Austrians heavily at ◊ *Marengo* in 1800. Austria signed the peace of Lunéville in 1801 and Britain that of Amiens in 1802, but when Bonaparte became First Consul for life as Napoleon, and obviously aimed

at crown and empire, Britain again declared war on France 1803. The 1803–14 campaigns are the Napoleonic Wars proper, in the course of which Napoleon, as Emperor of the French, made himself master of an empire which for a time included Austria, Germany, Italy, the Netherlands, Poland, Spain, Sweden, and Switzerland. He planned to invade Britain or Ireland, but could not win control of the sea routes, and his plan finally crumbled on the British victory over the French and Spanish fleets at ◊ *Trafalgar* in 1805. He had annexed ◊ *Spain*, but in the ◊ *Peninsular War* his armies suffered their first defeats, although he had broken the Third Coalition (Austria, Britain, Prussia, Russia, Sweden) and Britain alone resisted. By his victories of Ulm, ◊ *Austerlitz*, ◊ *Jena*, Friedland, he overcame the continental nations, induced Russia to become his military ally and Austria to ally itself with him by his marriage to the Emperor's daughter, and imposed on all Europe his ◊ *Continental System* in an attempt to starve Britain out. During two years of peace (1810–11) he organized the vast territories under his rule, but in 1812 his grandiose scheme of going overland into India ('trying to reach London via Calcutta') led him to invade Russia despite the alliance, and resulted in the disastrous Moscow campaign. During the winter retreat through Russia, which became a rout, two thirds of his huge army died of cold, hunger, and disease. The Fourth Coalition (Austria, Britain, Prussia, Russia, Sweden) declared a war of Liberation 1813, and defeated him heavily at Leipzig, the Battle of the Nations; he abdicated and was banished to Elba, but in 1815 returned to France and was again received as Emperor. After his ◊ *Hundred Days*, however, the Allies finally defeated him at ◊ *Waterloo*; he abdicated for the second time and was banished to St Helena, where he died in 1821. ◊◊ *Aboukir Bay, Borodino, Vienna Congress, Wagram, War of 1812*.

Narcissus. 1. A genus of ornamental plants in the *Amaryllidaceae*, characterized by the flowers, which have a corona, a funnel-shaped petal-like structure within the normal perianth.

2. In Greek legend, a beautiful youth, son of a river god, whose imperviousness to love led him to reject the advances of ◊ *Echo*, who died of grief. Another of his spurned lovers induced Nemesis to punish his coldness to female charms by making him fall in love with his own reflection in a spring; from this unrequited passion he pined away until he was changed into the flower named after him. Hence also the psychological term narcissism, obsessive or morbid self-love.

Narcotics ◊ *Alkaloids, Opium, Poppy.*

Naseby. 1645. Decisive victory of Cromwell's New Model Army over the royalist forces during the ◊ *English civil wars.* Prince Rupert's cavalry charged successfully on one wing but scattered to great distances in search of plunder; Cromwell's highly disciplined cavalry dispersed the royalist left, attacked their centre from the rear and destroyed most of the King's army, virtually ending the Civil War (the later defeats of the royalists at Preston 1648, ◊ *Dunbar* 1650, and ◊ *Worcester* 1651 were comparatively minor engagements).

National Anthem. Patriotic song played, and sometimes sung, on ceremonial occasions. The British national anthem *God Save the King* was first sung in 1745, after the defeat of the ◊ *Jacobite* rebellion; its authorship is unknown. The French national anthem the *Marseillaise* (named after the citizen soldiers of Marseilles marching to relieve Paris) was composed in 1792 during the ◊ *French Revolution* by Rouget de l'Isle. That of U.S.A. is *The Star-Spangled Banner*, its words written 1814 by an American prisoner-of-war, F. S. Key, and its music by J. S. Smith (d. 1836); adopted as the national anthem by forces and citizens, it did not become so officially until 1916, by executive order of President Wilson, confirmed by Act of Congress 1931.

National Chemical Laboratory ◊ *Department of Scientific and Industrial Research.*

National Debt. The total indebtedness of a government. In the U.K. it includes e.g. short-term borrowings (Treasury Bills), National Savings, and in sum all the gilt-edged securities or Government stock outstanding. The National Debt stood at £651 m. in 1914, rose to £7435 m. by 1918, and after the Second World War reached £23,637 m. It stood at about £30,000 m. in 1963; of this some £2,460 m. was owing to overseas lenders. Interest payments on the sterling part of the debt are merely transfers of money from one pocket to another; they represent no productive

assets but are a burden on the Budget and thus on every individual taxpayer. Interest on borrowings in foreign currencies are a burden on the U.K. balance of payments and must ultimately be met by the export of goods or services. ◊ *South Sea Bubble.*

National Economic Development Council ('Neddy'). Set up in the U.K. 1962 on government initiative; it includes government nominees and representatives of industry and of the T.U.C. Its general aim is to improve economic performance. After preliminary study, it set as target a four per cent annual increase in the ◊ *national income.* ◊ *Economic Planning.*

National Gallery. A collection of paintings owned by the State. In Britain Parliament granted money in 1824 to buy and exhibit the Angerstein picture collection; the present building in Trafalgar Square was opened 1838, and has since been enlarged. It contains a wide selection of the world's great masters. Famous national galleries in other countries include the Louvre in Paris, the Prado in Madrid, and the Hermitage in Leningrad.

National Guard. 1. French militia 1789–95, during the ◊ *French Revolution*; 1805–15 under Napoleon; revived in 1830–71 under the Orleanist monarchy, Second Republic, and Second Empire. In 1871 it was the National Guard in Paris which precipitated the ◊ *Paris Commune.* **2.** U.S.A. militia, under the jurisdiction of the various States with equipment and organization on the pattern of the U.S. federal army, and liable for national duty in time of war or emergency. Enlistment is voluntary and peace-time service is on a part-time basis.

National Health Service ◊ *Welfare State.*

National Income. Economic activity consists essentially of a circular flow which can be split up three ways: Spending (1) which leads to production, (2) which leads to incomes, (3) which in turn leads back to spending.

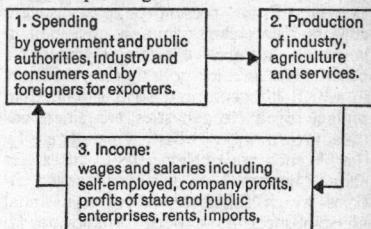

1. Spending	2. Production
by government and public authorities, industry and consumers and by foreigners for exporters.	of industry, agriculture and services.

3. Income:
wages and salaries including self-employed, company profits, profits of state and public enterprises, rents, imports,

Spending includes gross fixed investment i.e. replacement of or addition to the country's capital e.g. machinery, factories, buildings of all kinds, whether carried out by private industry or by public bodies e.g. coal and electricity authorities. Expenditure includes not only purchases by the general public but central and local government expenditure on goods and services e.g. roads, education and – the two largest items in the U.K. – defence and health services. The demand by foreigners for goods, i.e. the level of exports, is outside government control, though imports can be influenced by tariffs and quotas. Stockbuilding is an item which fluctuates considerably and with changes in investment is one of the causes of the ◊ trade cycle. Production consists of the net output of the various industries, including agriculture, fisheries, plus the sum of all the services e.g. transport, communications, personal services such as hairdressing, amusement facilities. The three main accounts are also three different ways of measuring a country's total output. Theoretically they should all produce the same result. The value of total output within the borders of a country is known as the Gross Domestic Product. Since many countries own overseas assets the annual income from these when added to the foregoing gives the Gross National Product. Both totals are gross because they include the investment which goes to replace outworn capital assets; if this figure is calculated and excluded the resultant sum is the net domestic (or national) product. What is referred to when growth rates in the economy are under discussion e.g. the 4 per cent growth rate target in the U.K. set by the ◊ National Economic Development Council is the gross annual rise in the real (i.e. calculated at constant prices) national product.

Nationalism. Awareness of and loyalty to a common interest on the part of men sharing, in the present or past, certain characteristics esp. common government, language, culture, religion. A loyalty so based gives greater cohesion to the state in which it occurs and so has tended to replace loyalty to dynasties, etc. There has thus grown up a belief, crystallized by the French revolution, that all states should be based on nations; earlier entities which failed to evolve a national consciousness have been broken up (◊

Ottoman Empire, Austria-Hungary). President Wilson at the Versailles Peace Conference 1919 championed the principle of allowing each group which felt itself to be a nation to have its own state.

19th-cent. theorists, particularly in Germany, popularized the idea that there could be no higher authority than the ◊ *nation state* whose interests were overriding. The practice of this doctrine esp. in face of economic difficulties (◊ *Depression*) led to the emergence of ◊ *Fascism* and ◊ *Nazism*. The assumption that state and nation ought to coincide combined with the lack in English of an adjective derived from the noun 'state' has led to the use of 'national' instead, e.g. nationalization.

Nationalization. Acquisition of private enterprises by the state; the nationalization of the means of production, distribution, and exchange is a fundamental aim of ◊ *socialism* and is enshrined in Clause 4 of the British ◊ *Labour Party* constitution. Nationalization of specific undertakings has been carried out by some non-socialist governments; in recent years the socialist parties of Germany, Sweden, Holland, and Australia have abandoned it as an object of policy; in communist countries all industries are nationalized. Nationalization has sometimes been used to expropriate foreign enterprises e.g. the oil-industry nationalization in Mexico 1938, the seizure of the Suez Canal by Egypt 1956. The word is not usually applied to concerns started by the state e.g. the Post Office, the Atomic Energy Commission, the B.B.C. There are several forms, varying from direct operation of an industry by a government department to the creation of one centralized board or a number of local boards, or simply the acquisition of sufficient shares to guarantee control.

National Labor Relations Act. 1935. Also known as the Wagner Act. A ◊ *New Deal* measure establishing in detail the right of U.S. workers to form trade unions and bargain collectively. It specified certain prevalent practices of employers to discourage unionization as 'unfair' and set up a Board to investigate complaints and secure compliance with the Act.

National Maritime Museum ◊ *Greenwich Hospital.*

National Physical Laboratory ◊ *Department of Scientific and Industrial Research.*

National Socialism ◊ *Nazism.*

National Society for the Prevention of Cruelty to Children. Incorporated 1884; it maintains inspectors and visitors to investigate reports of cruelty to or neglect of children in their own homes, and is a useful adjunct to similar official services. ◊◊ *Royal Society for the Prevention of Cruelty to Animals.*

National Theatre ◊ *Comédie Française, Old Vic.*

National Trust. Founded 1895 to preserve the countryside and later incorporated by Act of Parliament to preserve historic buildings, places of beauty, gardens, and bird and animal sanctuaries in England, Wales, and Ireland. It relies on gifts from individuals e.g. supporting members (100,000), administers 250,000 acres, and owns over 1000 properties, of which many have been presented to it as gifts. Since 1946 certain lands and buildings have been taken by the Treasury in lieu of ◊ *death duties* and then handed over to the Trust. The separate National Trust for Scotland is similarly run.

NATO ◊ *North Atlantic Treaty Organization.*

Natural Gas ◊ *Methane.*

Naturalism. 1. In works of art, close adherence to appearances and avoidance of stylization, artistic convention, ◊ *symbolism,* and distortion; whereas the term ◊ *realism* describes content, 'naturalism' describes the treatment or technique. Also, the quasi-scientific descriptive ambitions of Zola and his followers, who developed the objectivity of Flaubert's realism into a concept of the novel as the working-out of an 'experimental situation'; their squalid and sordid subject-matter influenced the meaning of the word naturalism in the third quarter of the 19th cent. though it had not quite lost the sense of 'fidelity to nature' in the general modern usage of the word realism, so that the two terms are sometimes confused.

2. In philosophy, two types of doctrine: (a) that the natural world alone exists, and that it can be explained without recourse to anything supernatural; (b) the ethical view that goodness or rightness consists in some natural quality e.g. that of producing general happiness.

Naturalization. Legal process by which a person becomes a national of a country to which he previously did not owe allegiance; in Britain the requirements are that an applicant has resided or served under the Crown for the previous 12 months and also for four of the previous seven years, and that he is of good character and has sufficient knowledge of English, application being to the Home Secretary, against whose decision there is no appeal.

Natural Law. A rule of conduct or set of guiding principles, based upon ethical instincts supposedly inherent in human nature. In political theory this concept has been used to provide a standard by which the acts of particular governments or the positive laws of particular communities may be judged. When the concept of justice is set above rather than beneath positive laws, it becomes equivalent to Natural Law.

Natural Selection. Term used by Darwin to describe the main mechanism controlling ◊ *evolution,* i.e. the tendency of individuals with certain 'survival' characteristics to reach maturity in greater numbers and thus to produce more offspring than those without such characteristics, a natural process which puts emphasis on ability to survive in a particular environment and hence is often termed 'the survival of the fittest'. It is now clear that a system of natural selection does operate throughout nature, to produce very complex evolutionary changes some of which, however, are not obviously related to survival requirements. Many thinkers maintain that man's mental development has made him dependent for survival on the development not so much of physical characteristics for competitive struggle as of an ability to cooperate. ◊◊ *Acquired Characteristics.*

Nautical Almanac. A book published annually containing astronomical information for the navigator four years in advance; the official publication is the *Admiralty Nautical Almanac,* issued since 1767; others issued by commercial publishers contain other information of use to the mariner.

Nautical Mile (Sea Mile). One 60th of a degree of ◊ *latitude;* varies between 6045 ft at the equator to 6092 ft at latitude 60°. For speed trials the nautical mile (Admiralty measured mile) is 6080 ft. ◊◊ *Knot.*

Navaho (Navajo). The largest Indian tribe in U.S.A. About 60,000, mainly in Ari-

zona and New Mexico; they adopted
cattle and sheep breeding from the early
Spanish settlers, and gave up the Indian
hunting life. Today they are progressive
and increasing in numbers, and their
brightly-coloured blankets and rugs have
become articles of commerce. Like other
Indian tribes of the region they are addicted to peyote, a drug whose effects resemble those of ◊ *mescalin*.

Navarino. 1827. Greece, then part of the
◊ *Ottoman Empire*, rebelled against Turkish rule in 1821. European sentiment supported the Greeks, and aid and volunteers
flowed to Greece. In 1827 Britain, France,
and Russia, after calling for an armistice,
intervened when the Turks refused; an
Allied fleet attacked the Turkish fleet at
Navarino, a bay on the W. coast of the
Peloponnese, almost totally destroying it.
Turkey conceded autonomy to Greece in
1829 and complete independence in 1832.

Navigation. At sea, the setting of a course
was originally dependent on observations
of the sun, moon, and stars esp. the N.
star (which furnished a fixed point),
making it possible to set approximate
courses across the seas. A simple ◊ *compass* and other navigational instruments
e.g. the ◊ *astrolabe* were introduced in the
late Middle Ages; ◊ *charts* and ◊ *maps*
were improved and mathematical reckoning aids developed. By the early 18th cent.
the quadrant (◊ *sextant*) and ◊ *log* were
in use, enabling mariners to establish ◊
latitude and distance travelled, with fair
accuracy; but it was not until the invention of the ◊ *chronometer* that the navigator could accurately ascertain ◊ *longitude*. The sextant, invented 1731, gave
greater accuracy in fixing positions. By
the 19th cent. the system of ◊ *dead
reckoning* had been refined and an efficient buoyage system and detailed charts
were available. All these devices were progressively improved, and in the 20th cent.
have been supplemented by radio and
radar. ◊◊ *Buoys, Decca Navigator, Radar,
Shipping*.

AIR NAVIGATION: Differs from other
kinds of navigation mainly in the more
extensive exploitation of radio, radar, and
ground aids. For military purposes it
tends to rely increasingly upon methods
not subject to jamming, e.g. Doppler and
inertial. By making use of the ◊ *Doppler
effect* instruments can provide a continuous measurement of an aircraft's ground

speed, and with the azimuthal information
from the compass this determines the
course. Inertial navigation depends upon
instrumental readings of the accelerations
to which the aircraft is subjected; it was
used in the German V2 rockets in the
Second World War.

ASTRAL NAVIGATION: Navigating by
the stars does not differ in aeronautical
use from its use on the sea, but there are
usually more automatic aids and a more
extensive use of ◊ *computers*.

Navigation Acts. English legislation, of
medieval origin, re-enacted under the ◊
Commonwealth in 1650–1 as an answer
to Dutch competition in the carrying trade
and in the W. Indies and E. Indies
colonies. All goods arriving at ports in
England (or her colonies), except those
carried direct by European ships from
their country of origin, were to be carried
by English ships. Four Anglo-Dutch wars
were fought over this issue; later Navigation Acts provided that all goods imported
into the English colonies be shipped from
English ports, and that colonial products
be shipped only to England, provisions
which were contributory to the outbreak
of the ◊ *American Revolution*. The Navigation Acts remained in force until
1849.

Navy. Lat. *naves*, a ship; originally, all
the ships of a state, but later fighting ships
only. Navies first appeared in the Mediterranean. The galleys of the Greeks,
Romans, and Persians, equipped with
rams, developed tactics other than those
of merely grappling and fighting as on
land, and the galley remained the typical
war vessel in the Mediterranean up to the
battle of ◊ *Lepanto* in 1571. Along the
Atlantic coast, the ◊ *Vikings* extended
their power by means of their 'long ships',
a type of vessel replaced in medieval
times by the 'round ship' of very broad
beam. Tactics at sea resembled those on
land: arrow fire was followed by grappling and boarding. With the advent of
guns, at first light weapons were mounted
in the 'castles' to repel boarders; but
later, when English ships adopted portholes, heavy guns led to ships of narrower
beam and lower in the water. Gunfire not
hand-to-hand fighting then became the
decisive factor. Up to the 17th cent.
navies were mainly made up from merchant ships as necessity arose; later, permanent navies of specialized battleships

were maintained by the chief maritime nations, Britain, France, Holland, and Spain. With the coming of steam and iron ships, the size and fire-power of naval vessels increased rapidly, while the invention of the ◊ *submarine* and later of the ◊ *aeroplane* brought new elements into naval warfare.

Sea power has exerted a great influence on the course of history. The 16th-cent. struggles between England and Spain, and those between the various Coalitions and Napoleonic France, were largely determined by command of the sea. The works of Mahan on naval strategy were closely studied, and the 19th cent. saw the rise of new naval powers (Germany, Japan, U.S.A.) and increasing competition in building powerful navies. In both world wars, war at sea between the Allies and Germany led only to one inconclusive clash between battle fleets (◊ *Jutland*), and its main feature was the prolonged struggle against unrestricted German submarine attacks, principally against merchant shipping. In the Second World War, however, large-scale naval battles occurred between U.S. and Japanese fleets (◊ *Pacific War*), in which the aircraft carrier played a decisive role.

Nazism (National Socialism). The political movement inspired and led by Hitler; its ideology, developed in his *Mein Kampf*, is a violently nationalist and antireligious creed based on the claimed superiority of the ◊ *'Aryan'* race and specifically of its 'best' exemplar, the German people. The object was to assert the primacy of the German *Herrenvolk*, 'master race' (whose mortal enemy was the Jewish people), through its leader (Führer) and to assure it ample living space (*Lebensraum*). The 'socialist' aspect was interpreted as harnessing the resources of Germany to national and largely military purposes, rather than as redistributing wealth more equitably. Like ◊ *Fascism*, nazism exalted discipline, power, and the Leader. The success of the nazi movement in Germany was a product of the post-war European depression of the 1920s (◊ *Weimar Republic*), the demagogy and violence of Hitler and his associates, the pusillanimity of the aged President Hindenburg, and the reluctance of the French and British governments to intervene forcibly (for appeasement ◊ *Munich Pact*). Hitler's first 'putsch' in

Munich 1923 was a failure, but after a short imprisonment he re-emerged to build up the Nazi Party. Twelve Nazis were elected to the Bundestag in 1928 and 230 in 1932; electoral success then declined slightly, but in 1933 Hindenburg appointed Hitler Chancellor. He immediately suspended the Constitution, made the Nazi Party the sole legal political party, and strengthened his hold on it by purging the left-wing elements and the mass 'Brownshirt' organization, retaining the more disciplined S.S. (*Schutz Staffel*, storm-troopers) as his personal army. He suppressed criticism by use of secret police (Gestapo) and concentration camps. In foreign policy he was able to achieve surprising success, aided by the British and French fear of and unreadiness for war. In 1938 he seized Austria (the *Anschluss*) and was allowed to absorb Czechoslovakia, and in 1939 he made a non-aggression pact with U.S.S.R. as a prelude to invading Poland, which aggression finally caused the outbreak of the ◊ *Second World War*. The brutality of the Nazi Party increased once the war began. Persecution of ◊ *Jews* and 'lesser races' was replaced by the 'Final Solution' i.e. mass extermination (◊ *Genocide*). The Nazi Party broke up in the hour of defeat and Hitler and his Minister of Propaganda, Goebbels, committed suicide. During the occupation of Germany the Allies carried out a policy of 'denazification' i.e. the dismissal of Nazi Party members in local government, the civil service, and other positions of influence. Since the establishment of the German Federal Republic there have been some cases of the appointment of ex-Nazis to positions of importance, but there is no evidence that this was systematic or extensive. ◊ *Genocide, Leadership, Third Reich, War Crimes.*

Neanderthal Man. *Homo neanderthalis*; primitive species of man, known from fossil remains of the later ◊ *Pleistocene* (30,000–150,000 years ago) and associated with flint tools of Mousterian type. In general, he was short in stature (about 5 ft) and slightly stooping in posture, with exceptionally thick arm and leg bones. The (male) brain capacity was as large as that of modern man, but the frontal region was relatively small and the skull was massive, with a low forehead and heavy brow ridges. Neanderthal man seems to have become extinct at the end of the Pleistocene period.

Neap Tides ◊ *Tides.*

Nebulae. In ◊ *astronomy,* two distinct types of celestial objects: (1) galactic nebulae, clouds of dust and gas within the ◊ *Milky Way;* (2) extra-galactic nebulae, vast systems of ◊ *stars* and interstellar matter similar to the whole Milky Way. The nebulae in the Milky Way are classified as bright (made luminous, e.g. like Orion Nebula, by nearby stars) or dark (revealing their presence, e.g. the Coalsack, by obscuring the star clouds behind them). The star-centred Crab Nebula in the constellation of Taurus is a cloud of bright gas still expanding at about 800 m.p. sec. and is a strong source of radio radiation; it is believed to be the result of a supernova explosion seen in A.D. 1054.

Nectar. Sweet secretions produced by some plants, used by bees for making honey; secreted by special cells, often grouped together as nectaries and usually within a flower, although some are outside e.g. on leaf stalks and leaves of *Prunus* species. The nectar attracts insects, which pollinate the flowers.

'Neddy' ◊ *National Economic Development Council.*

Negligence. In law, failure to take reasonable care, a ◊ *tort* in civil law. It has emerged as a separate tort only in the 20th cent. Those held to owe the duty of reasonable care include employers to their employees, manufacturers to persons who may consume their goods (where there is no probability of examination before use or consumption). Negligence may also arise through failure to perform contractual duties.

Negritoes ◊ *Pygmies.*

Negroes ◊ *African Peoples and Cultures, Race, Race Relations.*

Neoclassicism. A style which affected all the arts in the second half of the 18th cent. Partly a reaction to the extravagances of ◊ *Rococo,* partly an attempt to revive the classical style of antiquity, and partly an expression of a new seriousness of purpose; neoclassical painters adopted a flat linear manner and arranged their pictures according to rules of composition derived as much from Raphael as from the ancients. The most important were J.-L. David, who veered towards ◊ *romanticism* in mid-career, and Ingres, in whose

work the style persisted beyond the mid 19th cent. The sculptors, notably Canova and Thorvaldsen, were more obviously and directly inspired by classical prototypes, and abandoned the quest for ◊ *naturalism,* seeking to represent an ideal of beauty. Architects, e.g. Robert Adam, used classical motifs with greater archaeological accuracy than before. Towards the end of the 18th cent. Greek architecture began to exert a stronger influence than Roman.

Neodymium ◊ *Lanthanides.*

Neolithic. New Stone Age; mid 19th-cent. term for the last phase of the Stone Age cultures, in which tools of highly polished stone were used. It was notable for the development of ◊ *agriculture* and the domestication of animals, and thus for crop-raising and animal-breeding cultures instead of purely food-gathering and hunting communities. The concurrent development of ◊ *pottery* and weaving and a more settled way of life led eventually to the first urban civilizations. In the Near East the Neolithic lasted approximately from 7000 to 3500 B.C. (when the ◊ *Bronze Age* began), and in NW Europe from 3000 to 1800 B.C. The earliest traces of farming in Britain date to about 3400 B.C. In S. America the Neolithic may be placed at about 1500 B.C. with the introduction of ◊ *maize.* ◊ *Barrow.*

Neon ◊ *Inert Gases.*

Neoplatonism. The last of the Greek philosophies, derived from Plato and many other sources, classically formulated by Plotinus and elaborated by other thinkers from the 3rd to the 6th centuries A.D. Claiming that the universe emanates or flows from a supreme entity, the One, which is indescribable, it opposed and greatly influenced ◊ *Christianity* and was a religion as well as a philosophy. Its stress on asceticism and ecstasy has its origins in oriental practice.

N.E.P. ◊ *New Economic Policy.*

Nepal. Area 54,000 sq. m. Pop. 9.4 m. part Mongolian and part Indian. Cap. Katmandu. Rel. Buddhist and Muslim. A Himalayan kingdom, including Mt Everest; famous as the home of the ◊ *Gurkhas* and as the birthplace of Buddha, 560 B.C. A direct-rule monarchy, with an advisory State Council of 69 and no political parties.

ECONOMY. Few industries. Exports include considerable timber, also cattle, hides, jute, oil-seeds, rice. The illiteracy rate is believed to be about 90 per cent. HISTORY. Little is known of the early history, but in 1768 the Gurkhas, a hill tribe, became ascendant and established the present boundaries. In conflict with the ◊ *East India Company*, they were defeated and in 1815 signed a treaty of friendship with Britain. Later they helped to relieve Lucknow in the ◊ *Indian Mutiny*, and were rewarded by the restoration of lands they had lost. Jung Bahadur, Prime Minister 1846-77, made the premiership hereditary in his family, the Ranas, who remained in power until 1951. Nepal fought in alliance with Britain in the ◊ *First World War*, and in 1923 an Anglo-Nepalese treaty declared the country independent. Again allied with Britain in the ◊ *Second World War*, Nepal was later the scene of revolution and civil war 1950-60; the Ranas were deposed and the 19th-cent. monarchy restored, under King Mahendra. The state of emergency was declared over in April 1963.

Nephritis. Inflammation of the kidneys. Acute nephritis, first described by Richard Bright 1789-1858, and hence named Bright's Disease, usually occurs in the course of some general infection, especially streptococcal, or as the result of some toxic condition. The symptoms are fever, headache, the passing of albumin and blood in the urine, oedema, increased blood pressure, and the retention of abnormal amounts of nitrogenous waste in the blood (◊ *Urea*). Favourable cases usually respond to treatment after a few days; but others may become less acute and then develop chronic nephritis, an insidious progressive disease, at first not easy to detect, which results in cumulative damage to all parts of the excretory system and the blood vessels, and is likely to be fatal. ◊ *Digestion, Excretion*.

Neptune. 1. The planet eighth from the sun (mean distance 2793 m. miles). Invisible to the naked eye, it was discovered 1846 after its position had been mathematically predicted from perturbations to the orbit of ◊ *Uranus*. Although its diameter is 3.5 times that of the earth, it is so far distant that even a large telescope shows little detail. It has two moons, Triton and Nereid. ◊ *Solar System*.
2. ◊ *Poseidon*.

Neptunium. ◊ *Actinides*; a grey metal like ◊ *uranium*; the first of the transuranium

◊ *elements* to be discovered (McMillan and Abelson 1940), as the result of neutron bombardment of uranium. It is also found in minute quantities in pitchblende.
Nervous System. The human nervous system comprises the ◊ *central nervous system* (brain and spinal cord), the peripheral nerves (arising from the central nervous system), and the autonomic nervous system (governing bodily functions not under conscious control). The system is built up of supporting cells (neuraglia) and nerve cells (neurones). Each neurone consists of a cell body and an axon, or conducting fibre, which may be from a fraction of an inch to several feet in length. The brain consists of the cerebrum, the cerebellum,

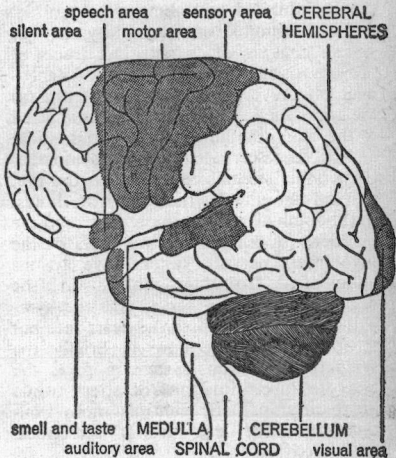

speech area | sensory area | CEREBRAL
silent area | motor area | HEMISPHERES

smell and taste | MEDULLA | CEREBELLUM
auditory area | SPINAL CORD | visual area

and the brain-stem. The cerebrum, a dome-shaped mass of nervous tissue divided into two symmetrical halves (cerebral hemispheres) by a longitudinal fissure, receives all the sensory impressions of the body and controls voluntary movements. It is also concerned with consciousness, thought, intellect, and memory, a specific area being predominantly involved with each of these functions (see diagram). The so-called 'silent area' of the cerebral hemispheres is thought to be the seat of the higher human faculties; damage to it has been found to produce moral degeneration. The cerebellum, below and behind the cerebrum, also divided lengthwise into halves, coordinates muscular movements and maintains posture and equilibrium. In the brain-stem are the centres controlling the heart and respiration; 12 pairs of cranial nerves coming from the base of the brain provide sensory paths for smell, sight, hearing, and equilibrium; sensation in face, head, and tongue; motor paths to the muscles of the eye, face, tongue, larynx, pharynx, and certain neck muscles. The spinal cord is composed of a bundle of communicating fibres from the brain to all parts of the body, and possesses the property of reflex activity; reflex movements e.g. withdrawal of hand from hot surface, often defensive in character, are more rapid than voluntary movements, since the impulses concerned follow a short path, by-passing the brain, and to some extent can be inhibited by voluntary control.

The autonomic or involuntary nervous system consists of two distinct tracts of nervous tissue, separate from but dependent on the central nervous system: (a) the sympathetic nervous system, connected to the heart, the lungs, and the abdominal and pelvic viscera; (b) the parasympathetic nervous system, connected to the eye, the salivary glands, the heart, the lungs, the abdominal viscera, the rectum, and the bladder. In general the two parts of the involuntary nervous system have actions antagonistic to one another in the organs they jointly serve, e.g. the sympathetic nerve increases the heart rate but the parasympathetic slows it. Briefly, the sympathetic nervous system prepares the body to meet situations of stress, while the parasympathetic controls more 'routine' functions e.g. gastric secretions, bowel activity.

Nessus. In Greek mythology, one of the ◊ *Centaurs.* Ordered by ◊ *Hercules* to carry his wife Deianeira across a river, Nessus tried to run away with her; Hercules shot him with an arrow poisoned with the blood of the ◊ *Hydra,* and in revenge Chiron gave Deianeira his shirt (impregnated with his own now poisoned blood), saying that if Hercules wore it she would keep his love. When Hercules put the shirt on, it clung to his skin and so tortured him that he threw himself on a funeral pyre and was conveyed to heaven by the gods; Deianeira hanged herself.

Nestor. King of Pyles; in classical legend, a Greek leader in the Trojan war, extolled by Homer as the wisest and most virtuous of the participants. He survived the war,

returned to his kingdom, and lived to an extreme old age (some say 300 years), thus becoming the typical 'wise old man'.

Nestorianism. Christian ◊ *heresy* based on the teaching of Nestorius, Bishop of Constantinople 428–31, maintaining that in ◊ *Jesus Christ* there were two separate 'persons' (a divine and a human) united in one body; though condemned by the General Council at Ephesus and at Chalcedon, it spread widely in Syria and Mesopotamia and sent missionaries to India and China, where a Nestorian church existed for many centuries. Remnants still exist in Iraq, Kurdistan, and in U.S.A.

Netball. British indoor or outdoor women's hand-ball game, played between teams of seven on a rectangular court with a circular open net suspended on a 10-ft post at each end. The ball, resembling an association football, is passed until one player can score a goal by throwing it to fall through the opponents' net. Players may not move with the ball, but must pass or shoot. Netball is a main winter game in British girls' schools, and is the origin of ◊ *basketball.*

Netherlands. Area 13,500 sq. m. Pop. 12.1 m. Cap. Amsterdam and The Hague. Rel. Protestant, with a substantial Roman Catholic minority. A constitutional monarchy, with government by a Premier responsible to the States-General, consisting of a Senate of 50 members elected by the Diets of the provincial states, for six years, and a second chamber of 100 members elected by universal suffrage, for four years. The voting age is 23 and voting compulsory. Since the general election of 1952 Dutch politics have been dominated by a Roman Catholic and Labour Party coalition.

ECONOMY. The maritime provinces are mainly agricultural, esp. dairy and market-garden produce, of which very large quantities are exported. Industry is centred in the inland provinces. Resources include coal and natural gas, an important recent discovery. Dutch interests control much of the world output of oil, tin, and diamonds. HISTORY. The Low Countries (roughly modern Belgium, N. France, Holland, and Luxemburg) were occupied in the first centuries A.D. by the Romans, who were expelled in the 4th cent. by Franks, Frisians, and Saxons. After forming part of the ◊ *Carolingian* empire, they passed to ◊ *Lotharingia* in A.D. 843 and in 925 to the ◊ *Holy Roman Empire*. Flanders, Brabant, and Holland developed as small states, and the S. Netherlands became a prosperous weaving area. Almost the whole area was united by Charles the Bold of ◊ *Burgundy* and passed to the ◊ *Hapsburgs* on the marriage of his daughter to Maximilian in 1477. By 1543 Charles V's rule extended to all the Netherlands besides Spain and Austria. During the ◊ *Reformation* the mercantile free cities of the north became Lutheran or Calvinist, as against the still Roman Catholic south. The long rebellion against Spanish rule led to the emergence of the northern independent United Provinces, but the south remained a Spanish dependency until 1700. After the Peace of ◊ *Westphalia* in 1648 the new republic rapidly became an important naval power, in colonial competition against Britain (◊ *Navigation Acts*), and acquired the Dutch East Indies, the Cape of S. Africa, Java, and other colonies (◊ *Indonesia*). In 1677 William of Orange married his cousin Mary, daughter of the Duke of York (◊ *Exclusion Bill*); when York became James II and was deposed, his daughter and nephew were invited to accept the crown (◊ *Glorious Revolution*), and until the death of William III in 1702 Britain and the United Provinces were closely associated. As a result of the ◊ *War of the Spanish Succession* 1701–14, and the ◊ *War of the Austrian Succession* 1740–8 the S. Netherlands passed in turn to Austria, France, and Austria again. Napoleon created a Netherlands monarchy, making his brother Louis King of Holland. After ◊ *Waterloo* the kingdom was retained, under the Prince of Orange (as William I); in 1830 what had been the Austrian Netherlands seceded and formed ◊ *Belgium*. During the 19th cent. Holland endeavoured to further the cause of international peace (◊ *Hague Conferences*). In the ◊ *First World War* she remained neutral and in the ◊ Second World War was under German occupation 1940–4.

◊◊ *Benelux, Counter-Reformation, Dutch Art, European Economic Community, Flemish Art.*

Netherlands West Indies. Area 54,394 sq. m. Pop. 0.5 m. Cap. Paramaribo (Surinam). The Dutch Antilles (Curaçao, Bonaire, etc.), with Surinam (formerly named

Dutch Guiana); a Dutch overseas possession, autonomous in domestic affairs since 1949 and since 1954 part of the Netherlands Crown Realm.

ECONOMY. Chief exports bauxite (almost wholly to U.S.A.), coffee, hardwood, timber, rum.

HISTORY. The Guiana coast was first settled by the Dutch 1597; a colony was established in 1616 (in what is now ◊ *British Guiana*) and the Dutch W. India Co. founded in 1621, but there was continual war with Britain and France for possession, and a serious slave revolt in 1762. The Vienna Congress settlement of 1815 allotted some Dutch colonial territories to Britain but ratified Holland's possession of Surinam and the Dutch Antilles.

Nettlerash ◊ *Urticaria.*

Neuritis. Inflammation of a nerve, causing pain, local tenderness, and often loss of feeling and of power of movement. Common causes of inflammation include infections, trauma, and vitamin B_1 deficiency, the last often associated with chronic ◊ *alcoholism.*

Neurosis. A mental illness, mainly psychological in origin, which does not produce the severe disturbances encountered in ◊ *psychoses*, so that contact with reality and insight into the condition are preserved; the most important types are anxiety states, obsessional and phobic states, ◊ *hysteria*, and certain of the less severe forms of depression. The causes of these illnesses are both constitutional and environmental, and childhood environment experiences are particularly important, as Freud emphasized.

Neutron. Electrically uncharged particle in the nuclei of all atoms except hydrogen. Its mass is approximately equal to that of the proton.

New Caledonia. Area 7200 sq. m. Pop. 68,000 (Melanesian and Polynesian). Cap. Noumea. W. Pacific island off Australia, with dependencies the Loyalty and Huon islands (formerly also the Wallis and Futuna Islands); a member of the ◊ *French Community* since 1958.

ECONOMY. Extensive resources, esp. chromium, cobalt, gold, iron ore, nickel, silver; chief crop, coffee.

HISTORY. Discovered 1774 by Capt. Cook; annexed by France 1853, a convict settlement 1864–94. During the ◊ *Second World War* it was occupied by U.S. forces

1942–5 to prevent invasion from Japan.

Newcastle Disease ◊ *Fowl Pest*.

New Deal. 1933–41. The social and economic policies introduced in U.S.A. by President F. D. Roosevelt, to combat the acute ◊ *depression* begun in 1929, which had led to 16 m. unemployed. Vast public works e.g. the ◊ *Tennessee Valley Authority*, the control and direction of ◊ *banking* and credit, and a series of *ad hoc* measures were introduced. These did not entirely eliminate unemployment, but the figures fell from 17 m. to 7 m. in five years. The New Deal also had a strong social mission to improve the lot of the common man, and one important result was the 1935 National Labor Relations Act, which strengthened the trade-union movement.

New Economic Policy (N.E.P.). Policy introduced by Lenin in 1921 to avert the breakdown of the Soviet economy esp. agriculture in the conditions of post-revolutionary dislocation. Trade in grain was freed, some industry was returned to private hands (the 'nepmen'), and the operation of a free market was restored. Under Stalin it was replaced 1928 by the First Five-Year Plan involving detailed industrial planning and the collectivization of agriculture.

New Guinea ◊ *Melanesians*.

New Hebrides ◊ *Pacific Islands (British)*.

New Model Army ◊ *Army, British Army*.

Newspapers. Julius Caesar had *Acta Diurna* displayed daily in Rome in the 1st cent. B.C. and medieval China had regular court gazettes. In early 17th-cent. England the hitherto intermittent printed broadsheets began to appear weekly in regular series, and advertising, illustration, and headlines emerged soon after the appearance of the first newspaper 1621. The first daily news-sheet, *The Daily Courant* 1702, was followed by the more literary periodicals associated with Steele, Addison, Swift, and Johnson (◊ *Essay*). Successive governments endeavoured vainly to check the press by direct repression in the 17th cent. and bribery and crippling taxation in the 18th, but the 17th-cent 'underground' press, and later Defoe, Junius, Wilkes, and Cobbett, established a tradition of outspokenness which under the stimulus of the French Revolution and the Reform Movement bore fruit in the great expansion of periodicals early in the 19th cent. (◊ *Edinburgh Review*,

Quarterly Review). *The Times*, founded 1785, early became influential, but it was not till improvements in printing, paper-making, and communications, the expansion of the electorate, the spread of literacy, and above all the lifting of the newspaper taxes (reduced 1836 and abolished 1855) that the newspaper emerged as a mass medium. In Victorian times content and treatment were serious, but in America Joseph Pulitzer developed tabloid presentation and in Britain Newnes and Harmsworth saw the possibilities of a more popular form; Harmsworth's *Daily Mail*, founded 1896, though conventional in format, broke with the Victorian tradition of serious content and immediately attained the highest daily sale then recorded; the *Daily Express*, founded 1900, adopted the *Daily Mail* news treatment and the American practice of front-page news. Today the mass-circulation field is almost equally divided between the comparatively conservative *Daily Express* and the leftish tabloid *Daily Mirror*, each with a circulation of four to five m. copies per day and a readership of 11 or 12 m. In contrast, *The Times* and the *Guardian* (the leading 'quality' newspapers) have circulations of only 0.25 m. The total circulation of the popular Sunday papers has remained stable at about 19 m. since 1952, with readership about double; the circulation of the 'quality' Sunday papers in the same period has increased by over 50 per cent. The concentration of ownership, the large scale of operation of modern newspapers, and their dependence on advertisement revenue have made the public aware that the old threat to freedom of expression from political pressures is now paralleled by direct and indirect commercial influence. The 1947–9 Royal Commission on the Press resulted in the formation of the Press Council 1953; it has not proved very efficacious in achieving the aims envisaged and is being reorganized. The British public buys more newspapers per head than any other in the world, about 570 copies per 1000 population, largely because the 'national' newspapers can be distributed throughout the U.K. on the day of printing; in U.S.A. circulations of individual papers are far less, and there are few 'national' dailies, but vast newspaper chains, of which the Hearst and Scripps-Howard are the most influential, control large numbers of New York and provincial papers. ⟡ *Censorship*.

Newt. An ⟡ *amphibian* related to the ⟡ *salamander*; has a life-cycle similar to that of the ⟡ *frog*, but has internal fertilization, the male opposing its cloaca (genital and excretory orifice) to that of the female. The male develops a crest along its back and tail at the breeding season, when both mature sexes return to water.

New Testament ⟡ *Bible, Gospels*.

'Newton's Rings' ⟡ *Optics*.

New Towns Act. 1946. Gives powers to the Minister of Housing to designate areas for new towns and to appoint a development corporation. The capital for developing new towns is advanced from public funds to be repaid on agreed terms. There are now fifteen such towns in Great Britain housing about half a million (of which Harlow and Basildon were early examples) and three in Scotland. They stem from and develop the ⟡ *Garden City* concept and represent the most successful example of town planning in Britain.

New Zealand. Area 104,000 sq. m. Pop. 2.5 m. Cap. Wellington. A member of the ⟡ *British Commonwealth*, comprising N. Island and S. Island, with the Ross Dependency and the Cook Islands. The sovereign is represented by a Governor General, guided by the advice of the Executive Council, and the House of Representatives consists of 80 members (including four ⟡ *Maoris*) elected for three years by universal suffrage. During the period of Labour government 1935–49 many economic and social reforms were effected, and New Zealand became virtually a socialist state, though by planning rather than nationalization. The moderate National Party has been in power since 1949, the Labour Party holding the remainder of the seats. ECONOMY. Sun and rain are plentiful; the climate is very similar to that of Britain in S. Island and that of Italy in N. Island. Only two thirds of the total area is cultivable, but 95 per cent of this is devoted to pastoral farming. Great quantities of meat, wool, and dairy products are exported to the U.K. since the home demand for food crops is small, the climate allows cattle to remain in the open all the year round, and the rolling land is unsuited to arable farming. Thanks to

the terrain and the high rainfall there is considerable hydroelectric power and also timber, one fifth of the land being under evergreen forest. All iron and steel for the large engineering industries is imported. HISTORY. The islands were discovered by Tasman in 1642 and explored by Cook in 1769, but extensive settlement took place only after 1840, when British sovereignty was declared. The original Maori inhabitants resisted the gradual absorption of their land, but eventually the differences were settled without rancour. In 1852 New Zealand received the most liberal constitution till then allowed to any colony. Maoris were admitted to representation in 1867 and Dominion status was granted in 1907; close contact with Britain was maintained. New Zealand troops fought in both world wars, notably at Gallipoli in 1915 (⟡ *Dardanelles*).

Niacin ⟡ *Vitamins* (B_4, B_5).

Nibelungenlied. Middle High German epic in 39 cantos, produced early 13th cent. but probably based on two earlier heroic lays. Having killed the possessors of the treasure of the Nibelungs, Siegfried woos the Icelandic princess Brunhild for King Gunther of Burgundy, and marries Gunther's sister Kriemhild, who later accuses Brunhild of having been Siegfried's mistress. As a result, Siegfried is slain by Gunther's henchman Hagen and the treasure is finally sunk in the Rhine. Wagner's opera cycle *Der Ring des Nibelungen*, The Ring of the Nibelungs, mixes Nibelungenlied and Norse-saga material.

Nicaragua. Area 57,000 sq. m. Pop. 1.7 m. (68 per cent mainly of mixed race, the remainder Indian, Negro, and white). Cap. Managua. The largest but most thinly populated of the central American republics, with both Pacific and Atlantic seaboards. Long political strife and protracted dictatorship have hindered Nicaragua's development.
ECONOMY. Predominantly agricultural, exporting coffee, cotton, maize, rice, sesame-seeds, sugar, bananas, beans. Gold and silver are mined and exported by Canadian and U.S. concessionaries, U.S.A. being the chief market for all products.
HISTORY. Discovered by Columbus in 1502, Nicaragua was occupied by Spanish forces in 1519 and formed part of the Spanish colony of ⟡ *Guatemala* until the revolt of all the Spanish-American colon-

ies in 1820–21, when it declared itself independent. There were long periods of civil war; armed U.S. intervention to preserve order lasted virtually from 1912 to 1933.

Nickel. A not uncommon grey metallic ◊ *element* showing a marked resistance to oxidation and chemical attack; the chief sources are sulphide ores, occurring in Canada, Norway, and China, and silicate ores from U.S.A. Generally obtained in the extraction of other metals, it is purified electrolytically or by the ◊ *carbonyl* process. Its chief use is as metal in the manufacture of chemical and food-processing plant and of nickel steels, cupronickel, and nickel coinage (◊ *Alloys, Iron and Steel Industry*); it is also employed in nickel electrical-storage batteries, and is very widely used as a ◊ *catalyst,* esp. in the hardening of fats by ◊ *hydrogenation* for the manufacture of margarine, and in other organic syntheses. The dominant valency state is 2, and the sulphate, the most important industrial compound, is largely used in electroplating baths for applying a protective and decorative coating to metals liable to rust or tarnish. Chromium plate usually has an undercoating of nickel. ◊◊ *Electrolysis.*

Nickel Silver (German Silver) ◊ *Alloy.*

Nicotine. The principal ◊ *alkaloid* of the tobacco plant; extremely poisonous. It is soluble in water and alcohol and is widely used as an insecticide. In tobacco smoke nicotine is largely converted into innocuous products.

Nicotinic Acid ◊ *Vitamins (B_4, B_5).*

Niger. Area 484,000 sq. m. Pop. 2.9 m. (largely Hausa and Tuareg). Cap. Niamey. A republic in central Africa, formerly a French colony, with a single-chamber National Assembly and a presidential system.

ECONOMY. The country is almost wholly desert or savannah; exports cattle, groundnuts. Deposits of copper, iron, petroleum, uranium, are being surveyed.

HISTORY. Colonized by France 1891–1914, a French colony 1914–58. Voted for autonomy within the French Community in 1958; in 1960 declared full independence outside the Community, but has special trade and technical agreements with France.

Nigeria. Area 357,000 sq. m. Pop. 40 m. (with three distinct African races, ◊ *Hausa,* Ibo, and Yoruba). Cap. Lagos.

Rel. Muslim (Hausa), Protestant Christian (Ibo, Yoruba); also African religions. A federal republic in W. Africa, a member of the ◊ *British Commonwealth* since 1960. The Federal Parliament consists of the Senate and a House of Representatives. In addition, each of the three Regions has its own Executive Council, House of Assembly, House of Chiefs, a Premier, and a Governor, as has Lagos also; a fourth Region is planned.

ECONOMY. The country is wholly tropical, very hot, and very humid near the coast, which is lined with ◊ *mangrove* swamps. Inland is a zone of ◊ *rain forest* and oil-palms, and the higher land is ◊ *savannah,* with near-desert in the extreme north. The economy is mainly agricultural, exporting large quantities of cocoa, cotton, groundnuts, hides, palm-kernels, palm-oil, timber, and also e.g. cassava, coffee, copra, gum, nuts, maize, millet, rice, rubber, tobacco, yams. Coal is mined for home requirements, tin and columbite (chief world producer, ◊ *Tantalum*) for export: a steel rolling-mill is in operation, and there is a wide range of industrial products e.g. beer, bicycles, canned foods, cement, ceramics, cigarettes, fruit juices, plastics, shoes, soap, etc. Railways, roads, and civil aviation are well developed. Education is a Regional responsibility, except for the six Federal universities: there is universal free education for children aged 6–12 in Lagos and in E. and W. Nigeria, with a school population of over 3 m.

HISTORY. Until 1914, two British protectorates; administered in two sections N. and S. In 1914 the two were amalgamated though the North continued to be ruled indirectly through the Emirs. The nationalist movement of the 1940s, led by Dr Azekiwe, gained progressive degrees of self-government after 1956, leading to the united Federation 1960, when it voted to remain independent within the Commonwealth. The Emirate was abolished in favour of a republic in 1963.

LANGUAGES. Until 1914, two British protectorates; administered in two sections N. Over 50 African languages are spoken; English is the unofficial *lingua franca.*

Nile. 1. The longest (about 4000 m.) and most important river of Africa, emptying through a delta into the Mediterranean, and the cradle of one of the earliest civilizations (◊ *Egypt (Ancient)*). The source of the Nile was for long unknown and many explorers – Bruce, Speke, Burton, etc. – finally traced it back through the Blue Nile to the Nyanza Lakes. Without the Nile and the irrigation systems from it, based on gigantic dams (e.g. Aswan, Assiut) ◊ *Egypt* would be incapable of supporting a large population.

2. Battle 1798 ◊ *Aboukir Bay.*

Ninepins ◊ *Ten-pin Bowling.*

Nineveh. On the river Tigris, capital of ancient ◊ *Assyria* from the 8th cent. B.C. Sennacherib (ruled 704–681) set out to make it an imperial city rivalling Babylon in splendour. Its two most magnificent buildings were the palace built by him and the one later added by Ashur-bani-pal. In 612 B.C. the city fell to the Medes and Babylonians and was destroyed. It is now represented by two mounds, the larger of which contains the ruins of the palaces and temples, the smaller the royal storehouses.

Niobium. A silvery metallic ◊ *element* (sometimes called columbium) occurring in columbite (a mineral containing another similar element ◊ *tantalum*). Obtained by the ◊ *electrolysis* of fused halides, it is used in special steels intended for nuclear-power reactors, in making ceramic-metallic compounds employed in rockets and jet engines, and in hard ◊ *carbides* for cutting-tools.

Nirvana. In ◊ *Buddhism*, the ineffable state which is the goal of human existence, the 'blowing out', extinction, of the round of reincarnations and suffering (◊ *Transmigration*). Buddha did not describe it, but clearly did not envisage mere annihilation. To Hinayana Buddhists it is a timeless condition of non-being and changeless peace, to Mahayana Buddhists the attainment of Buddha-nature in realizing by illumination that Samsara (existence, involving continual becoming) is itself Nirvana.

Nitrates ◊ *Nitrogen, Salt (2).*

Nitre ◊ *Gunpowder, Potassium.*

Nitric Acid ◊ *Nitrogen, Salt (2).*

Nitrogen. The gaseous element somewhat less dense and soluble in water than oxygen which makes up 78 vol. per cent of air and is found combined in saltpetre, Chile saltpetre, and many organic compounds of vegetable and animal origin e.g. ◊ *proteins*. It is obtained industrially by liquefying air and separating it from oxygen and argon by fractional ◊ *distillation*. Liquid nitrogen is used for cooling to low temperatures, for providing an inert atmosphere, and in the synthesis of ◊ *ammonia*, as a basis for the production of nitrogen compounds for ◊ *fertilizers*, ◊ *explosives*, ◊ *synthetic resins*, and chemicals. The inertness of nitrogen and the instability of its compounds with non-metals are due to the strong bonds holding the two atoms in the nitrogen molecule together; these have to be broken before a compound can be formed. Particularly unstable are the oxides, which are oxidizing agents supporting combustion and allowing molecular nitrogen to reform. Nitrous oxide, a colourless pleasant-smelling gas which supports combustion better than air, is used as an anaesthetic in short operations. Nitric oxide is formed in lightning discharges, which are an important natural means of 'fixing' large quantities of nitrogen, since the nitric oxide is at once oxidized to the dioxide, a brown gas which dissolves in rain and falls to the earth's surface as nitric acid. The principal acids are nitrous acid, which gives sodium nitrite (an important reagent in the dyestuffs industry), and nitric acid, used to produce nitrates for explosives and fertilizers, and for other chemical uses. From its compound, ammonia, come many industrially important salts: the chloride (salammoniac) used in fluxes and in medicine; the sulphate, some a by-product of the ◊ *coke* and gas industries and some from synthetic ammonia, is used as fertilizer; the nitrate is also a fertilizer and a constituent of many high explosives; the phosphate is used as a fertilizer and also for flame-proofing paper, wood, and textiles. Nitrogen combines with a number of metals to form nitrides, which are very hard and very stable: those of boron and titanium have industrial uses. Steel can be case-hardened by nitriding the hot metal in ammonia.

Nitrogen Cycle. The continuous circulation of ◊ *nitrogen* between living organisms and the environment (water, soil, atmosphere). Nitrogen is an essential element for life, but although air is 78 per cent gaseous nitrogen, only bacteria and blue-green ◊ *algae* can use nitrogen in its atmospheric ('free') form. All other living things can use it only in its compounds e.g. nitrates, ammonia. Green plants absorb these compounds through the roots and transform them into ◊ *proteins*, organic compounds necessary to animals, which can obtain them only by eating plants (or, at one remove, by eating other animals). This is the absorption side of the circle.

The return of nitrogen to the soil, water, or air proceeds by the discharge of ◊ *urea* and excreta and by the decay of dead animal and vegetable matter. Thus there is a cycle of soil-nitrate denudation by living plants and animals and its reconversion from animal and decayed matter by a complex chain of bacterial action. In countries in which animal dung is used for

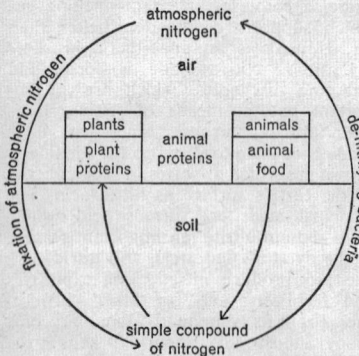

fuel, e.g. India, nitrogen depletion is a serious problem and a main cause of poor husbandry and human malnutrition.

A certain amount of nitrogen is also fixed through bacteria in the root nodules of leguminous plants (◊ *Leguminosae*), a feature which makes legumes important in ◊ *crop rotation*, while some nitrogen is fixed electrically in the atmosphere during electrical storms and is brought down in rainwater. The effect of nitrogen-fixing is partially offset by de-nitrifying bacteria, which reduce the available nitrogen by converting nitrogen compounds and freeing gaseous nitrogen into the atmosphere.

N.K.V.D. ◊ *Secret Police*.

Nō. A branch of Japanese dramatic art, which may date to as early as the 12th cent. A.D. though the first extant texts are from the 16th and 17th. Its form, drawn from ritualistic dance, myth, and scripture, and predominantly an upper-class lyrical art, has not changed greatly since the latter part of the 17th cent. The performance comprises actors, singers, dancers, musicians, and visible stage hands.

KABUKI: A popularization of the original Nō form.

Elements of bøth Nō and Kabuki have been adopted by many European dramatists as varied as W. B. Yeats and Bertolt Brecht. There are some excellent translations of Nō plays by Arthur Waley and Ezra Pound.

Nobelium. The name given in 1957 to a nuclide which was thought to have been an isotope of Element 102. Isotopes of Element 102 have since been discovered but as yet the element remains unnamed.

Noble Gases (Rare Gases) ◊ *Inert Gases*.

Nominalism ◊ *Scholasticism*.

Nonconformists (Free Churches). Protestant Christians in the U.K. who do not conform to the established Church of England or Church of Scotland; descended from the Dissenters, who under the ◊ *Clarendon Code* were for a generation banned from public use of their own form of worship and were in turn descended from ◊ *Puritan* and ◊ *anabaptist* Independents. The largest Nonconformist bodies, the ◊ *Methodists*, ◊ *Baptists*, ◊ *Congregationalists*, ◊ *Presbyterians*, and Quakers (◊ *Society of Friends*), with some others, are united in the Free Church Federal Council.

Nonjurors. Anglican clergy who lost their benefices for refusing to take the oath of allegiance to William III after the deposition of James II (◊ *Glorious Revolution*). Headed by Sancroft, Archbishop of Canterbury, with eight bishops and several hundred lesser clergy, they formed an unofficial church organization, to a greater or lesser extent involved in the various Stewart restoration movements (◊ *Jacobites*) and lasting until the early 19th cent. (when the last Stewart pretender died). ◊ *Anglicanism, Erastianism*.

Nore Mutiny. 1797. Bad conditions – poor food, infrequent leave, irregular pay – led the Channel fleet at Spithead to refuse to put to sea. Their demands were met; shortly afterwards the North Sea fleet at the Nore made similar but wider demands. This mutiny was suppressed and its leader hanged. At Camperdown four months later the fleet decisively defeated the Dutch.

Norman Architecture ◊ *Romanesque*.

Norman Conquest. 1066–87. The conquest of England by William, Duke of Normandy; he had been promised the throne by his cousin Edward the Confessor, on whose death the Witan chose Harold, Duke of Wessex, as King. While Harold was in the N. repulsing invasion from Norway, William landed unopposed at Pevensey; Harold hastened south, but was defeated and killed near Hastings. William was crowned King of England, put down rebellions in the S. and W. in 1068, and in 1069 devastated Yorkshire after an anti-Norman rising. He replaced Saxons by Normans in the greater earldoms and in the Church, bringing it into closer contact with the then rapidly developing papacy (which had assisted him in the invasion). Granting land throughout England to his Norman supporters, he strengthened the already-developing system of ◊ *feudalism*, but thanks to the advanced administrative techniques of the Saxons did not replace Saxon administrators. As a result of the Conquest, French became the language of the court and the law, much building was done in the Norman style, and continental methods of warfare based on cavalry superseded the Saxon style. Antagonism between Saxon and Norman persisted for several generations, but by the reign of Henry II it was negligible (although as late as the mid 17th cent. 'Norman' was popularly used for 'oppressive'). The two nationalities and languages fused into English. ◊ *Bayeux Tapestry, Domesday Book, Romanesque.*

Norse ◊ *Denmark, Germanic Languages, Iceland, Norway.*

Norsemen ◊ *Vikings.*

North Atlantic Treaty Organization (NATO). Association of European and N. American countries based on a pact signed in 1949 by the members of the Brussels Treaty Organization (Belgium, France, Luxemburg, the Netherlands, and the U.K.) and Canada, Denmark, Iceland, Italy, Norway, Portugal, and U.S.A. It was later joined by Greece, Turkey, and the Federal German Republic. It was inspired largely by fears that the Security Council of the ◊ *United Nations*, hampered by Soviet use of the veto, might be impotent to prevent Soviet aggression. The signatories declare their determination 'to safeguard the freedom, common heritage, and civilization of their peoples' and agree that an armed attack on one of them will be regarded as an attack on all

and that each will assist the one attacked by taking 'such action as it deems necessary', pending action by the Security Council. There is thus no automatic obligation to fight, the decision to do so being left to individual governments, but the treaty amounts to a formal military alliance, adherence to which was a significant step on the part of U.S.A. with its traditional mistrust of 'entangling foreign alliances'. The headquarters of the NATO Council are in Paris. Military forces in Europe are integrated under Supreme Headquarters, Allied Powers, Europe (SHAPE). ◊ *Warsaw Pact.*

Northern Lights ◊ *Aurora.*

Northern Rhodesia ◊ *Zambia.*

Norway. Area 125,183 sq. m. Pop. 3.6 m. Cap. Oslo. Rel. mainly Lutheran. An independent Scandinavian state, a constitutional hereditary monarchy with legislative power vested in the Storting, 150 representatives elected every four years (one-quarter of them forming an upper House) and executive functions carried out by the Prime Minister and Cabinet. Present monarch King Olaf V.

ECONOMY. 73 per cent of Norway is unproductive; its chief resources are timber and fish, some minerals (iron ores), and abundant hydroelectric power. It has a large merchant navy (6th in the world).

HISTORY. United with ◊ *Denmark* from the 14th cent. to 1814 and with ◊ *Sweden* 1814–1905. At Norway's independence, a Danish prince became King Haakon. After the German occupation in 1940 during the ◊ *Second World War*, King Olaf transferred his government to London until British troops liberated Norway in 1945.

LANGUAGE. Old Norse (◊ *Germanic Languages, Runes*) was the common Scandinavian language before A.D. 1000; owing to the long union with Denmark, Danish tended to be the written language, but a 19th-cent. revival of interest in Norwegian led to a synthetic-standard 'land speech' or *nynorsk* (New Norse), based on western dialects.

Not Proven. Like English law, ◊ *Scots law* holds that a person not proved guilty shall be deemed innocent; nevertheless if a Scots jury is neither satisfied as to an accused person's guilt nor convinced of his or her innocence, they may return the verdict 'Not Proven'. The effect is 'Not

Guilty', with the difference that retrial in the light of fresh evidence remains theoretically possible. The verdict is seldom given.

Nova ◊ *Star*.

Novel. The term was first used in the 17th cent. for a fictitious narrative in prose, of some length and complexity, dealing with characters and events similar to those of real life, as distinct from the ◊ *romance*, which tended to deal with a world of marvels and wish-fulfilment. The novel is largely a product of post-Renaissance European culture and (esp. in England) reflects the reading tastes of the middle classes, who produced most of the novelists. ◊ *Don Quixote* 1605–15 established a tradition of satiric realism, which the novel was to take up in many fruitful ways. Madame de La Fayette's *La Princesse de Clèves* 1678 introduced subtle psychological analysis of emotions associated with sexual love. Defoe's *Robinson Crusoe* 1719 pioneered a scrupulous realism in handling the material environment. Richardson's *Clarissa* 1748 combined psychological analysis with strong moral feeling, in a way which was to become characteristic of the English novel. *Les Liaisons Dangereuses* 1782, by Laclos, probes feminine sexual psychology with equal craft but ironic amorality, developing the tradition in a characteristically Gallic manner. The Gothic novel of the late 18th cent. reflected, however absurdly, the new 'sensibility' which was to be important for the Romantic Movement, of which Rousseau's *Nouvelle Héloïse* was the prototype. Scott's *Waverley* 1814 and subsequent novels inaugurated the historical-novel genre, the vogue for which both in England and on the Continent still continues.

The novel was the dominant literary form in 19th-cent. Europe. The cool elegance of Jane Austen's perfectly focused social vision, the exuberant imagination of Dickens, the social understanding and moral subtlety of George Eliot, or the elemental rhythms beneath Hardy's brooding explorations of human fate, represent only a few of the great achievements of the 19th-cent. English novel, while French achievements included the massive yet lively sociological fiction of Balzac, the psychological precision and political understanding of Stendhal, the documentary yet symbolic

realism of Zola, and the analytic craftsmanship of Flaubert. In Germany the novel was not a dominant form in the 18th or 19th centuries, and in Italy (in spite of the great achievement of the ◊ *Renaissance* story-writers) it was not until Manzoni's *I Promessi Sposi* 1827 that the novel achieved real literary stature. In Russia the novel developed remarkably in the 19th cent. with Gogol's grotesque satire, Goncharov's poetic irony, Turgenev's skill and delicacy, Dostoievsky's combination of social and psychological realism with intense visionary power and religious feeling, and Tolstoy's blending of moral investigation with panoramic social and historical vision.

The 20th-cent. novel has reflected uncertainties about traditional values. In France, Proust's great novel-sequence is preoccupied with a new interest in time and its relation to personality, an interest reflected in a very different way in the subtly poetic novels of Virginia Woolf in England. The Polish-born Joseph Conrad in his mature work embodied and projected some of the dilemmas about individual and social values thrown up by modern civilization. Behind James Joyce's artfully constructed experimental masterpiece *Ulysses* 1922 lies the problem of communication, resulting from the individual's sense of alienation from society, while D. H. Lawrence in his novels explored the possibilities of human communication and fulfilment, and the factors that hinder them, with a powerfully original symbolic use of events and objects.

The American novel, which had already produced some remarkable original forms in the 19th cent. (Melville, Hawthorne, Mark Twain), developed rapidly in the late 19th and the 20th centuries, Henry James exerting a wide influence with a new technical rigour and a deep sense of artistic responsibility.

The novel remains a major literary form in Europe and America, but also has long been a medium of popular entertainment; the latest form, science fiction, has an honourable lineage in Jules Verne and H. G. Wells, as has the detective or crime novel in Poe, Wilkie Collins, and Conan Doyle.

Novella. A short prose narrative, a form developed in Italy in the 14th and 15th centuries. Shakespeare took the plots of many of his comedies from Italian *novelle*, and the form was revived by some later writers, notably Henry James, as being midway between the ◊ *short story* and the ◊ *novel*.

Nuclear Bomb ◊ *Atom Bomb*.

Nuclear Energy. Obtained by releasing the binding energy which holds together atomic nuclei. There are two distinct processes, the first to be realized being nuclear fission. In this reaction the heavy nucleus, e.g. uranium in the form of its isotope $^{235}_{92}U$, splits into two parts releasing the binding energy holding the nuclei together. This takes place within the reactor core of a nuclear power station, and in the ◊ *atom bomb*. The second process is nuclear fusion, in which the nuclei of two light atoms fuse to form a new composite nucleus. At many millions of degrees C, two deuterons (an isotope of hydrogen of atomic mass 2) will fuse together to form an isotope of helium with the release of a neutron. In such a reaction, energy is released, as the mass of the resultant parts is less than that of the original two deuterons.

The fission process can be controlled and used in the generation of utilizable energy in ◊ *nuclear power stations*. The fusion reaction, so far, can be used only in an uncontrolled reaction, as in the hydrogen bomb. Although a great deal of effort has gone into research to produce a controlled self-sustaining fusion-reaction for the release of useful energy, the problem has so far proved insoluble. The vast energy thrown out by the sun is based upon the fusion process. ◊> *Atomic Energy Authority*.

Nuclear Power Stations. In these ◊ *nuclear energy* produces heat for generating steam. Britain has several such stations (Calder Hall, 1956, was the world's first). Power production cost is slightly above that of coal or oil fuel stations, but a new British design of gas-cooled reactor promising lower costs has been developed by the Atomic Energy Authority and chosen (1965) for the Dungeness B Station. Its compact design consists essentially of a hot uranium furnace surrounded by carbon dioxide gas which circulates round boiler tubes in a closed circuit to produce high-temperature steam to drive turbines, the cooled gas returning to the furnace area.

Nuclear Reactor. Device in which controlled nuclear fission generates heat. All nuclear reactors consist essentially of a heat-producing core and a cooling system, but there are now several types.

THERMAL REACTORS: The fuel is natural or slightly enriched uranium. The neutrons which bombard it have to be slowed down – 'moderated' – generally by water, heavy water, and graphite. Plutonium, produced as a by-product from uranium-238 in such reactors is itself a fissile material. This is the type of reactor used in the first nuclear power stations. Drawbacks are its great size and the necessity for specially designed steam generators, but these are overcome in a new gas-cooled U.K. reactor design which is compact and can use normal high-efficiency generators.

FAST REACTORS: Use pure uranium-235, uranium-238 or plutonium and no slowing down of the neutrons is necessary; there is thus no need for a moderator, and fast reactors are far less bulky than thermal reactors, but the fuel is much more difficult to produce. Fast reactors are the type being developed for transport purposes.

BREEDER REACTORS: Produce more fissile material than they consume, by production of plutonium.

Nuclear power has already been applied to marine propulsion in submarines, of which the American *Nautilus* was the first (1955), and in surface vessels; before it can be used in vehicles or aircraft, many formidable problems have to be overcome.

Nuclear Tests. In the process of developing more powerful nuclear bombs the U.S.S.R., U.S.A., and U.K. exploded at intervals devices of increasing destructiveness, the fallout from which threatened to become a serious hazard to health throughout the world. In 1958 there was a voluntary and temporary cessation of testing nuclear weapons by these powers, tests were resumed by the U.S.S.R. in 1961, and shortly afterwards by the U.S.A., both underground and in the atmosphere. France exploded test bombs in the Sahara in 1960. An agreement to suspend further tests was reached between U.S.S.R., U.S.A., and U.K. in 1963, but the graver problem of nuclear disarmament still remains. China exploded a nuclear device in 1964.

Nucleic Acid ◊ *DNA*.

Nucleus. Central core of the ◊ *atom*, consisting of roughly equal numbers of ◊

neutrons and ◊ *protons* and containing practically all the mass of the atom.

Nuclide. Any particular species of an atomic ◊ *nucleus*, determined by the number of ◊ *neutrons* and ◊ *protons* present. It is a recent and broader term which avoids the use of the term 'isotope' in its wrong context. ◊ *Isotope*.

Nuclidic Mass ◊ *Atomic Weight*.

Number. In arithmetic, a system of counting; numerals are symbols representing number. Counting started on the fingers, from which naturally developed the habit of counting in tens. The Greeks and Romans used letters to represent numerals, but their system of computation remained cumbrous; a crucial advance came in the Middle Ages in Europe with the introduction of the simple Arab numerals and the invention of an additional symbol for ◊ *zero*, which permitted a positional function for numerals, as contrasted with the clumsy ·cumulative function of the Greek or Roman figures. With the ◊ *decimal system*, mathematics rapidly developed into an instrument of great flexibility and complication, capable of dealing with large numbers, without which modern chemistry, physics, and astronomy would not have been possible.

Numbers were originally limited to expressing simple integers; then came fractions. Later elaborations were the 'irrational' numbers (e.g. the square root of two) and 'imaginary' numbers (e.g. the square root of minus one) and other refinements of modern mathematics. There is some difference between European and U.S. practice in the nomenclature of billion, trillion, etc. Both use million to denote a thousand thousand: but a billion in U.S.A. means a thousand million. The U.S. trillion etc. are similarly less by a thousand times.

Nuremberg Trials ◊ *War Crimes*.

Nut. A dry woody one-seeded fruit, formed from more than one ◊ *carpel*, which does not split open to release the seed, e.g. hazel, brazil, cob, cashew, pecan, pistachio. The ◊ *endosperm* in a nut is often oily. Walnuts and almonds are not strictly nuts, but stone fruits with a fleshy outer wall of the pericarp.

Nutrition. The various processes involved in obtaining, converting, and using food (◊ *Metabolism*). Food requirements of organisms vary according to their ability to synthesize their needs, e.g. plants make their cells from chemical compounds by ◊ *photosynthesis*, and certain bacteria are able .to prepare the complex molecules which they require from inorganic salts and ◊ *glucose*; animals, including man, on the other hand, have only a limited capacity to synthesize their own ◊ *proteins*, the bulk of which they must obtain 'ready-made' from plants or by eating other animals (which in their turn obtained them from plants). ◊ *Calorie, Diet, Vitamins*.

Nyasaland ◊ *Malawi*.

Nylon. Name given to the first completely ◊ *synthetic fibre* developed in 1938 by the U.S. firm Dupont de Nemours, after research into ◊ *polymers*. It remains an important member of the synthetic filaments group which now compete with, or supplement, natural fibres in textile manufacture, etc. ◊ *Plastics*.

Nymph (Instar). Developmental stage in the life-cycle of some ◊ *insects*, e.g. aphis, cockroach, dragonfly, earwig; the egg develops into a first nymph, a small edition of the adult but lacking wings, and on completion of each growth-phase moulting occurs and a new larger nymph emerges. There may be as many as a dozen nymphal stages, the last two or three developing wing-buds. An exception to this type of development is shown by the mayfly, whose last nymph is capable of flight.

O

Oak. *Quercus*, of the *Fagaceae*; a genus of N. temperate and Asian evergreen and deciduous trees and shrubs. The fruit is an acorn, the timber hard and durable, and the ◊ *bark* used for dyeing and tanning. *Q. robur* and *Q. sessiliflora*, the common native British species, grow esp. well on clay soil. The timber was much used for houses and in ship-building; for the latter the trees were carefully cultivated and thinned to 15 trees per acre, to produce large timbers for keels and for stem and stern posts. Acorns were valuable as pig-food.

Q. cerris, the turkey oak, has a spiny acorn cup. *Q. ilex*, the holm (evergreen) oak, is of decorative form. *Q. suber*, the ◊ *cork* oak, is cultivated in the Mediterranean, where *Q. coccifera*, the Kermes oak (grain tree), a shrub with spiny leaves, like a holly bush with acorns, is also very common.

Oasis. Area in a desert where there is water and vegetation; may be simply a clump of palms around a spring, or a larger area where cultivation of crops is possible. The existence of oases makes it possible for nomads to cross deserts in search of pasture for their flocks.

Oats. Valuable cereals of the genus *Avena*, with a higher protein and fat content than most food grains; used as oatmeal and rolled oats, and as cattle food. The origin is unknown, but the grain occurred in Europe in the late ◊ *Bronze Age* about 3000 years ago. *A. sativa* is now the most widely cultivated species; *A. fatua* (false oats) is a common weed.

Oberammergau. A village in Upper Bavaria famous for its Passion Play, first performed in 1634 and since produced every 10 years, with some breaks. The play deals with the passion of Christ and was originally in the style of the baroque theatre, but since the first printed version of 1662 there have been several later versions. The parts are still played exclusively by the inhabitants of the village, and the play has become a major tourist attraction.

Oberon ◊ *Uranus*.

Obesity. Excess ◊ *fat* in the tissues; usually caused by overeating and insuffi-cient exercise, but sometimes resulting from disorders of the ductless ◊ *glands*, especially the sex, pituitary, and thyroid glands. Water-retention may also be a factor. The dangers are extra strain on the heart and diminished resistance to the effects of disease. The state is easier to prevent than cure; straightforward cases are treated by restricting food and water intake, and by providing the sufferer with substances to satisfy the appetite without nourishing.

Oboe. < Fr. *hautbois*, high wood; a woodwind ◊ *musical instrument*, distinguished by the double reed (vibrated by the player's breath) and the nasal tone; it evolved (from earlier types) about 1660 at the court of Louis XIV, later was mechanically improved, and rapidly became standard in both the ◊ *orchestra* and the military band, as it still is. The English ◊ *horn* or *cor anglais* is the oboe's slightly lower-pitched and notably more sombre-toned relative; pitched between the two is the *oboe d'amore* (used by Bach).

Obscenity. In law, an article, book, sound recording, film, or picture the effect of which taken as a whole is such as to deprave or corrupt persons likely to see or hear it; to issue an obscene publication is an offence which may be punished by imprisonment for three years. It is a defence to show that the accused had not examined the article; thus a bookseller is not necessarily responsible for what he sells. It is also a defence if the publication is justified on the ground that it is in the interest of the public good, of science, literature, art, or learning.

Obsession. A recurring idea or impulse, which persists in the mind although it is recognized as false or unimportant, accompanied by a feeling of resistance to its presence which causes distress; obsessions can be experienced by normal people, but when numerous and severe they are often part of a ◊ *neurosis*. Sometimes the obsession can be temporarily dispelled by some action, e.g. an obsession that the hands are contaminated may be relieved for a while by washing, but the idea soon returns with its original force.

Obsidian. Volcanic rock with ◊ *granite* chemical composition, but glassy not crystalline in structure, owing to rapid cooling; usually black or very dark green (thin pieces are translucent). It was used in the Stone Age for tools and instruments esp. where flint was lacking, e.g. in the Andes.

ICELAND AGATE: A gem-stone obsidian found on Mt Hecla.

PITCHSTONE: A dull obsidian forming the sgurr of the island of Eigg off the W. of Scotland.

◊ *Metamorphic Rocks.*

Obstetrics ◊ *Childbirth.*

Occultation. In astronomy, the covering up of a star by the moon or a planet; also the disappearance of a satellite behind a planet. The moon's occultations of stars give accurate information about its orbit.

Ocean. The sea is divided by the great land masses into extensive identifiable parts covering 71 per cent of the earth's surface: the Pacific Ocean (the largest, remarkable for the number of islands); the Atlantic Ocean (narrower, with few islands); the Indian Ocean; the Arctic Ocean (round the N. Pole); and the Southern Ocean (round Antarctica). An ocean has four depth regions: the shallow continental shelf adjoining the land; the continental slope fringing the shelf; the deep-sea plain (wide, fairly level, forming most of the ocean floor and 12–18,000 ft deep); and the deeps (usually trough-like depressions). One of the deepest troughs is the Marianas Trench, nearly 36,000 ft. The temperature of the oceans varies from over 80° F (25° C) near the equator to below f.p. in polar regions; in all areas the temperature is low at great depth, about 30–40° F (−1 to 5° C) below 12,000 ft. Salinity also varies (over 4 per cent in the Red Sea, about 3 per cent in polar seas). Most sea water contains about 3.5 per cent of chemical salts; of these four-fifths is common salt.

CURRENTS: Among the chief causes are prevailing winds. In the Atlantic, currents driven by the ◊ *trade winds* combine to form a westward-moving equatorial current: off the Brazilian coast this divides, the N. portion forming the Gulf Stream, which continues towards Europe with the prevailing W. winds. Whether in the Atlantic or the Pacific, the main ocean currents flow clockwise in the N. and anticlockwise in the S. hemisphere. Ocean currents are also caused by temperature differences: warm water from the equatorial region flows to the polar region, cools, sinks, returns as a bottom current, warms, and rises again. Difference in salinity may cause currents: the less salty water of the Atlantic flows into the Mediterranean and vice versa.

Ocelot. *Leopardus pardalis*; tawny irregularly-striped S. American carnivorous cat, three to four ft long, arboreal, preying on birds and small mammals. ◊ *Panther.*

Octane ◊ *Paraffins.*

Octave ◊ *Musical Scale.*

Octopus. Marine mollusc with eight arms without shell, of the class *Cephalopoda* (◊ *cuttlefish, squid*); the arms drag the prey to the mouth, where it is destroyed by the horny beak. The genus *Eledone*, the one variety in British waters, shows a remarkable ability to change colour; black and white stripes move rapidly over its surface or it may 'blush' a suffused pink. The Mediterranean genus *Argonauta*, the pearly nautilus, shows an extreme of sexual dimorphism, the male being less than a tenth of the female size. The cephalopods show two clear examples of convergent evolution: although they have evolved quite independently of the vertebrates, they have complicated bioluminescent organs nearly identical with those of fish, and an eye differing from the vertebrate eye primarily in the lack of a sclerotic (hard) coat.

Ode. In English, a ◊ *lyric* poem, sometimes in the form of an address (. . . *to Autumn, . . . a Grecian Urn*), often of elaborate construction, and usually on a noble subject; supposedly in direct descent from classical prototypes e.g. choric odes in Greek ◊ *tragedy.*

PINDARIC ODE: Strictly, a close imitation of the Greek poet Pindar's irregular stanzaic patterns, but all irregular English odes since Cowley's *Pindarique Odes* 1656 have often been called Pindaric.

Oder-Neisse Line. Since 1945, the Western frontier of Poland along the rivers Odra (Oder) and Nysa (western Neisse). At the ◊ *Potsdam Conference* it was agreed that in return for ceding Lvov and Western Galicia to U.S.S.R., Poland should immediately administer all the area east of the two rivers. The U.K. and U.S.A. accepted this westward shift of Poland, with the proviso that final *de* *jure* delimitation was a matter for an eventual peace conference between a unified Germany and the ◊ *Second World War* allies.

Most of the 8 m. German inhabitants of the 'Polish Western Territories' left or were expelled in 1946 and the area has since been repopulated by Poles from Lvov and other regions. The German Democratic Republic and Poland agreed to regard the frontier as permanent in 1950; the German Federal Republic does not recognize it, and the U.K. and U.S.A. continue to maintain that final agreement can only be reached when a peace treaty is concluded with a united Germany.

Odin (Woden). In Scandinavian mythology, head of the pantheon, ◊ *Aesir*; god of wisdom, culture, and the dead. He was usually one-eyed, but could assume any form at will, often visiting the earth in disguise. He gained wisdom by drinking from the cauldron or fountain of Mimir and hanging pierced by a spear for nine days and nights on the tree ◊ *Yggdrasil*. Ravens and wolves were sacred to him, but the demon wolf Fenuris overcomes and swallows him at ◊ *Ragnarok*.

Odysseus ◊ *Ulysses*.

O.E.C.D. ◊ *Organization for European Economic Cooperation*.

Oedipus. In Greek legend, king of Thebes; son of Jocasta and Laius, who, warned by an ◊ *oracle* that his son would cause his death, exposed him at birth. He was found by a shepherd and brought up at Corinth. When told by the Delphic oracle that he was destined to kill his father and marry his mother, he fled, but on the way he met Laius and killed him in a quarrel, ignorant of his identity. After delivering his country from the ◊ *Sphinx*, he was rewarded by marriage with Jocasta; as a result of his unknowing incest, a plague ravaged the land, and the oracle declared that only the expulsion of the parricide would end it. Horrified to realize the truth, Jocasta hanged herself; Oedipus tore out his eyes, left Thebes with his daughter Antigone, and died at Colonus near Athens. Various aspects of the story were dealt with in Greek tragedy, and today it is well known owing to its use (◊ *Oedipus Complex*) in Freudian psychology. ◊› *Tragedy (Greek)*.

Oedipus Complex. In Freudian psychoanalytic theory, held to be a universal infantile experience, in which during the 'phallic stage' (age three to five) a boy has sexual tendencies towards his mother and hostility to his father (◊ *Oedipus*), which makes him fear that the jealous father will remove his offending sexual organs, so that a 'castration anxiety' develops (◊ *Complex*). Repression (◊ *Defence Mechanisms*) of the Oedipus complex leads to the development of the Superego (◊ *Ego*).

ELECTRA COMPLEX: A similar process in girls (◊ *Orestes*).

O.E.E.C. ◊ *Organization for European Economic Cooperation*.

Offa's Dyke ◊ *Mercia*.

Official Receiver ◊ *Bankruptcy*.

Ogam. < Gr. *ogmos*, furrow, straight line; ancient British and Irish writing on memorial stones, traditionally invented by a legendary Ogma. Lines (consonants) and points (vowels), one to five, are made in reference to a guiding line, e.g. as below:

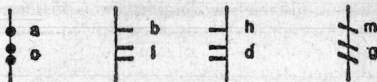

the vertical line represents the arris (edge) of the stone

The Ogam alphabet has only 20 letters. The inscriptions are found mostly in S. Ireland, but there are some elsewhere in Ireland, in the Isle of Man, in Wales, and in Cornwall.

Ohm's Law. Law of ◊ *electricity* formulated by the German physicist Georg Simon Ohm 1787–1854, which states that the current (I) passing through a conductor is proportional to the potential difference (V) between its ends, provided the temperature of the conductor does not change. The ratio V/I is known as the ◊ *electrical resistance* of the conductor. The ohm is the unit of resistance, defined as the resistance of a circuit in which a potential difference of one volt produces a current of one ampere.

Oil. Any liquid that has a high viscosity and a greasy feel. There are three main types. Mineral, e.g. natural ◊ *petroleum* (a complex mixture of ◊ *paraffins*). Fixed, e.g. the vegetable oils (linseed, olive, peanut etc.), and the fish oils (cod-liver, whale). Essential, i.e. volatile oils with strong aroma (e.g. clove, turpentine, wintergreen). Other classifications of oils sort them into 'drying' and 'non-drying' or 'edible' and 'inedible'.

Oil Industry ⟡ *Petroleum*.

Oil Painting. The medium most frequently used in Europe for easel pictures since the 15th cent. The pigments are ground and mixed with enough oil to produce a viscous paint, which may be applied in any number of layers to prepared canvas or to panels of wood or metal. Although known since classical times, this type of paint was not used for pictures until the early 15th cent. when an improved technique was evolved in the Netherlands whence it spread throughout Europe. By varying the amount of oil mixed with the pigments, artists can produce paints of greater or less transparency and also can vary the surface texture from the very smooth to the very rough, obtaining a greater range of effects than from any other medium.

Oil Shales. ⟡ *Sedimentary rocks* from which oils may be obtained by ⟡ *distillation*; originally muds in which considerable quantities of organic matter accumulated, found in a group of rocks in the Lower ⟡ *Carboniferous System* of central Scotland and other areas e.g. Germany. Oils have been distilled from them in Scotland since 1865; they yield motor fuels, lubricants, and paraffin wax. ⟠ *Geological Time Scale*.

Old Bailey ⟡ *Central Criminal Court*.

Old Catholics. Body of Christians originating in Holland early 18th cent. as a result of the refusal of some members of the ⟡ *Roman Catholic Church* to accept the papal condemnation of ⟡ *Jansenism*, and joined after 1870 by other Roman Catholic seceders (led by J. J. Döllinger) who did not accept the new dogma (⟡ *Pope*) of papal infallibility. They allow marriage of the clergy, and since 1932 have been in communion with the ⟡ *Church of England*.

Old Red Sandstone ⟡ *Devonian Period, Geological Time Scale*.

Old Stone Age ⟡ *Palaeolithic*.

Old Testament ⟡ *Bible*.

Old Vic. Originally, the Coburg Theatre, opened in 1818 near Waterloo Bridge, London; rechristened the Royal Victoria (hence 'Old Vic') Hall and Coffee Tavern (⟡ *Music Hall*) in 1880; it was taken over by Lilian Baylis in 1914, to bring Shakespeare to the poor, and achieved great local popularity, became a recognized

training-ground for actors and producers, and by the 1930s was nationally famous. The building was damaged early in the Second World War, but reopened on its original site in 1950, and in 1963 became the British National Theatre.

Olefines. ⟡ *Hydrocarbons* with the general formula C_nH_{2n} and (unlike the ⟡ *paraffins*) unsaturated, i.e. one or more pairs of ⟡ *carbon* atoms are linked by double ⟡ *chemical bonding*. The simplest member of the family is ethylene (C_2H_4), with the

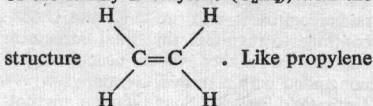

$$\text{structure} \quad \begin{array}{c} H \\ \diagdown \\ C = C \\ \diagup \\ H \end{array} \begin{array}{c} H \\ \diagup \\ \\ \diagdown \\ H \end{array} \quad . \text{ Like propylene}$$

(C_3H_6), this is a valuable by-product of the cracking (⟡ *Petroleum*) of paraffins of high molecular weight. Because of its unsaturated nature, ethylene is very reactive, and it has become an important raw material. By catalytic oxidation ethylene oxide is obtained, and from this, by ⟡ *hydrolysis*, the well-known ⟡ *antifreeze* compound ethylene glycol. Glycol is also used in the manufacture of ⟡ *Terylene*. Alcohol can be obtained cheaply from ethylene by catalytic combination with water, and under great pressure (also with a ⟡ *catalyst*) the valuable ⟡ *polymer* polythene is obtained. Propylene similarly gives the ⟡ *plastic* polypropylene and the important solvent acetone. Recent nomenclature shortens ethylene to ethene and propylene to propene.

Oligarchy. Rule by a few; the constitution of a state whereby a small minority hold all political power, e.g. Thebes and Corinth in the ancient Greek city-states. The Greeks distinguished oligarchy from aristocracy: the former signified ⟡ *government* by the wealthy for corrupt or selfish ends, the latter the rule of the best for the public good.

Oligopoly ⟡ *Monopoly*.

Olive. *Olea europaea*; a small tree with narrow greyish-green leaves, cultivated from early times in the Mediterranean region. The most important product is the edible oil extracted from the fruit, but they are also pickled for eating. Black olives are ripe, but green olives are pickled unripe, treated with alkali to destroy their bitterness, and stored in brine.

Olympic Games. In antiquity they were part of a Pan-hellenic festival in honour of ⟡ *Zeus*, held once in four years in

Greece at Olympia, where a sacred truce was observed whatever Greek States might be at war. Women were not allowed to compete or watch but had their separate games, the Herea, until Greece came under Roman rule. The first record of an Olympic victor is from 776 B.C. (the date used as a base by the Greeks for their chronology of four-year periods or Olympiads). At first there were only foot races; other contests e.g. boxing, wrestling, chariot-racing were added later. Professionalism crept in at an early date, but the Games continued in later centuries under Roman patronage till A.D. 394, when Emperor Theodosius brought them to an end. The Olympic Games were revived in 1896 by Baron Pierre de Coubertin (France) in Athens. Since then (except for the two World War periods) they have been held every four years; the 1964 Olympics were held in Tokyo. In 1896 there were 285 competitors from 13 nations, and in the Rome Olympics of 1960 nearly 6000 from 84 nations. Winter Olympics, purely for snow and ice sports, began at Chamonix in 1924 and have been held separately in each peace-time Olympic year. The Olympics are supposedly confined to ◊ amateurs, without prejudice of race, religion, or politics, but in practice the degree of amateurism varies from sport to sport. Control of the Games is by the International Olympic Committee, a self-electing body. In each Games, at least 15 of the following 22 sports must be held: Athletics, Archery, Basketball, Boxing, Canoeing, Cycling, Equestrian Sport, Fencing, Football, Gymnastics, Handball, Hockey, Judo, Modern Pentathlon, Rowing, Shooting, Swimming and Diving, Volleyball, Water-polo, Weight-lifting, Wrestling, and Yachting. In both men's and women's events gold, silver, and bronze medals are awarded to the winners. Intensive training is essential for success in the Games, at which international rivalry has reached a pitch alien to their original spirit. Many competitors, e.g. in the Soviet bloc, receive subsidies officially, and in several other countries, e.g. U.S.A., there are unofficial subsidies to permit lengthy training. ◊◊ Decathlon, Pentathlon.

Olympus ◊ Zeus.

Oman ◊ Muscat and Oman.

Ombudsman ◊ Administrative Law.

Omdurman (1898) ◊ Mahdi.

Ommayads. Arab dynasty of caliphs; the Ommayad leader Muawiya displaced Ali and his son from the ◊ caliphate, A.D. 661, and there resulted a permanent schism between the ◊ Sunnis and ◊ Shiahs. There were 14 Ommayad caliphs, whose capital was usually Damascus, a city of splendour and civilization, until the ◊ Abbasids in 750 almost wiped out the family. One member escaped to ◊ Spain, where he became ruler of the Moors as Abdul Rahman, Emir of Córdoba. Abdul Rahman III, who assumed the title of Caliph, conquered most of Spain in the 9th cent. and inaugurated an era of great architectural, literary, and scientific distinction. The Almoravides from Africa, allies of the Ommayads, supplanted them in 1031.

Onion. The common onion, *Allium cepa*, probably originated from a wild plant of C. Asia and was widely cultivated at the time of the Pharaohs. It is a biennial, producing an edible bulb in the first year. Apart from the many garden varieties, there are several distinctive types grown to a lesser extent: the Egyptian onion produces additional bulbs at the top of the flower stem. The Welsh onion is either a variety of *A. cepa* or another species; it is a perennial and makes a clump of small bulbs which may be used at any time. The shallot, *A. ascalonicum*, is a small onion, native to Palestine, from which a clump of bulbs grows by the end of the season; the potato onion is somewhat similar. Garlic, *A. sativum*, is another onion from central Asia which makes clumps of bulbs. Leeks and chives are also species of *Allium*.

Ontology. That main part of ◊ metaphysics which has to do with being or with the fundamental reality of the universe. ◊◊ Scholasticism.

ONTOLOGICAL ARGUMENT ◊ God.

Onyx ◊ Marble, Silica.

Oolite. < Gr. *oos*, egg; spherical-grain limestone, resembling fish roe. Of marine origin, probably formed in shallow water, the particles acquiring concentric layers of ◊ calcium carbonate as they were rolled over the sea bed. Also, stratigraphical divisions of the Middle Jurassic period, where oolitic limestones are typical. A prominent oolitic escarpment including the Lincoln heights, Edge Hill, and the Cotswolds crosses England NE to SW. The oolitic Bath-stone is one of the best-known building materials.

Opal ◊ *Silica*.

Open-hearth System ◊ *Siemens-Martin Process*.

Opera. Music played an important part in medieval religious drama, but opera in the modern sense derives from the attempt to revive Greek drama in the late 16th-cent. Florence. The first known opera is *Dafne*, with music (now almost all lost) by Peri and Corsi, the first important opera (still occasionally performed) was Orfeo 1607, by Monteverdi, and the first public opera-house was opened in Venice in 1637. Opera of this period depends for its emotional force on ◊ *recitative*.

Opera spread to France, with the work at Louis XIV's court of the Italian-born Lully, e.g. *Cadmus et Hermione* 1673; the first important English opera is Purcell's *Dido and Aeneas* 1689, a 'freak' composed for a girls' school. In the 18th cent. a new type of Italian serious opera, with emotional weight transferred to the formal aria, conquered Europe and was composed also by non-Italians, notably Handel (◊ *Oratorio*) who settled in London.

Gluck wished to make opera less formal and more truly dramatic, e.g. *Orfeo* 1762, but the earliest composer fully and regularly performed today is Mozart e.g. *Le Nozze di Figaro, Don Giovanni, Così fan tutte* in Italian and *Die Entführung aus dem Serail, Die Zauberflöte* in German, with spoken dialogue, all composed 1782–91. After Beethoven's one opera, *Fidelio* 1805, Weber's *Der Freischütz* laid the foundation for German romantic opera, which culminated in Wagner's tetralogy *Der Ring des* ◊ *Nibelungen*, first performed complete in 1876, at the opening of his festival theatre in Bayreuth.

French 19th-cent. opera produced Gounod's *Faust* 1859 and Bizet's *Carmen* 1875. The principal Italian opera composers from 1800 are: Rossini, *Il Barbiere di Seviglia* 1816, *Guillaume Tell* 1829; Verdi, a vast range – *Il Trovatore* and *La Traviata* 1853, to his final *Falstaff* 1893; and Puccini, *La Bohème* 1896. Russian opera was established by Glinka with *A Life for the Tsar* 1836; notable later works were Mussorgsky's *Boris Gudonov* 1874, Tchaikovsky's *Eugene Onegin* 1879, Borodin's *Prince Igor* 1890, and Rimsky-Korsakov's *Tsar Saltan* 1900. Czech opera produced Smetana's *The Bartered Bride* 1866.

Other important operatic composers were Debussy, *Pelléas et Mélisande* 1902; Richard Strauss, *Salome* 1905; Berg, *Wozzeck* 1925; Stravinsky, *Oedipus Rex* 1927; Britten, *Peter Grimes* 1945, etc.; and Menotti, *The Consul* 1950, etc.

OPERETTA: A light amusing form of opera, usually employing spoken dialogue. Its French master, Offenbach, inspired both Johann Strauss (the younger) in Vienna and Sullivan in Britain; later operetta composers include Franz Lehár and Oscar Straus. Its successor in more recent times is the musical comedy.

Ophthalmia. Any inflammation of the eye, esp. conjunctivitis. The inflammation is usually the result of bacterial infection by pneumococci, streptococci, gonococci, etc., but is sometimes caused e.g. by sunlight and ultraviolet light.

Opium. The dried juice of the capsules of *Papaver somniferum*, the opium ◊ *poppy*, which contain the alkaloids morphine, narcotine, and codeine. Opium was first obtained from the poppy of the Near East and Persia whence the habit of chewing and smoking the drug spread to India and China. An international effort to control traffic in opium has met with limited success, esp. as opium exports are a valuable source of foreign exchange to mainland China.

Opium Wars. 1839–42, 1856–60. Two wars between Britain and ◊ *China* consequent upon the Chinese government's attempt to stop importations of opium from India. After the first Opium War, China was compelled to cede ◊ *Hong Kong* and open five ports to foreign trade. In the second Opium War, the British and French captured Tientsin and Peking, and China was obliged to open treaty ports in the north, to accept western diplomatic representation at Peking, and to grant rights of travel in the interior. ◊ *Boxer Rebellion*.

Opossum. Members of two distinct groups of arboreal ◊ *marsupials*, one American, the other Australian. The American form is the more primitive and therefore more closely related to the true ◊ *mammals*. The Australian forms are very specialized, with various evolutionary lines adapted to numerous arboreal environments; they produce a single offspring annually. It is the American types that 'play possum' i.e. feign death when threatened.

Optics. Study of the nature and properties of light.

GEOMETRICAL OPTICS: Concerned with the geometry of the reflection and refraction of light. Generally speaking light rays travel in straight lines; when a ray of light strikes a reflecting surface at right angles, it is reflected back directly along the same path, but when the ray strikes the reflecting surface e.g. a plane mirror at an angle, it is reflected back at an angle and in the opposite direction. The law of reflection of light from a plane mirror (see fig. 1) states that the angle of reflection of a light ray (r) is equal to the angle of incidence (i). From the geometry of this

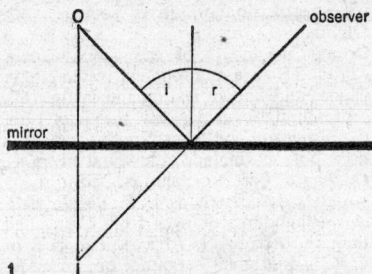

1

diagram it is clear that to the observer these rays appear to emanate from an image point (I) behind the mirror, and this image appears to be at a distance behind the mirror-surface equal to the distance between it and the object (O). A plane mirror thus reflects back an object and its setting with almost exact verisimilitude. The image it produces is known as a virtual image, i.e. the light rays do not actually go through it.

By a detailed application of this law to a spherical concave mirror, it can be shown (fig. 2a) that parallel incoming light rays are brought to an approximate focus at a point (f), the mid point of a line between the mid point of the mirror (p) and the centre (c) of the imaginary sphere of which the mirror is a part.

Similarly (fig. 2b), parallel rays of light reflected from a convex mirror are reflected in such a way as to appear to emanate from an approximate point f behind the mirror halfway between the mirror and its centre of curvature.

The distance between the mid point of the mirror (p) and the principal focus (f) is the focal length. When objects are placed in proximity to such mirrors, they cast images according to their position in relation to the principal focus and the centre of curvature. In a concave mirror the image is inverted and real, i.e. the light rays actually go through it, when the object is at a point farther from the mirror than c. When it is at c, the image is real, inverted, and the same size as the

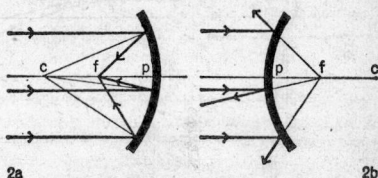

2a   **2b**

object. When the object is inside the principal focus, the image is virtual, right way up, and larger than the object. In a convex mirror the image is always virtual, upright, and smaller than the object.

REFRACTION: The bending of a ray of light when it passes obliquely from one medium to another of different density, e.g. from air to water or glass, owing to the fact that light travels faster in some media than in others. Thus, when a ray of light strikes a glass surface at an oblique angle, one side of it is slowed down first, and the ray turns off in a different direction (fig. 3). The angle of incidence is that which the incident ray makes with the normal (i): the angle of refraction is that between the refracted ray and the normal (r). Snell's law states that a constant ratio (the refractive index) exists between the sines of the angles of incidence and refraction for any two given media: this is also the ratio of the velocity of light in one medium to its velocity in the other.

The fact that a prism is capable of breaking up light into its component spectral colours is based on the fact that the refractive indices of most media depend upon the wavelength and hence the spectral colours of the light (fig. 4). The focusing of convex and concave lenses may be understood by regarding their curved surfaces as being built up of a sequence of prisms of gradually increasing angle (fig. 5a and b). A lens possesses a definite focal length, f, dependent upon the degree of curvature of its surfaces, and the refractive index of the material and that of the surrounding material. The image casting properties of lenses are based on the same principles as those governing spherical mirrors; i.e. the image is real or virtual, upright or in-

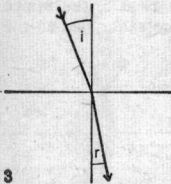

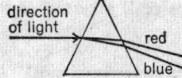

3

4

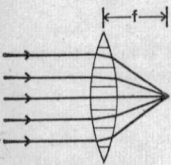

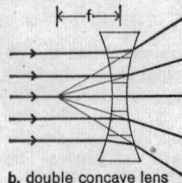

a. double convex lens   b. double concave lens

5a   5b

verted, the same size as the object or larger or smaller according to the type of lens, its focal length and the position of the object in relation to the principal focus.

PHYSICAL OPTICS: Based on the fact that on a microscopic scale light consists not of particles moving in straight lines but of wave motion; hence, under suitable conditions, the behaviour of light will deviate from that deduced from geometrical optics, owing to the phenomenon of wave-interference. This occurs when two light waves are so combined or superimposed as to reinforce (if in the same phase) or neutralize each other (if in the opposite phase). When two light-sources emit light of the same wavelength, with a constant phase relationship between them, alternate light and dark patterns may be produced, owing to alternate cancellation and reinforcement of light amplitude. The 'Newton's Rings' in colour photography also result from light interference, owing to the fact that if a slightly convex lens

touches a plane-glass plate, light will be reflected from the surfaces of both lens and glass. Where the optical-path difference between the two rays is an odd number of half wavelengths, the two reflected rays will cancel, and a dark fringe is produced; owing to the curvature of the lens, alternate dark and bright fringes result.

Oracle. In ancient mythology, a prophetic answer given by a god to a suppliant's question; also a place where an oracle may be requested. The priest or priestess would go into a trance or would interpret e.g. the rustling of leaves and give inspired but often ambiguous or misleading advice (◊ *Croesus*). Famous oracles were those of ◊ *Apollo* at Delphi, of ◊ *Zeus* at Dodona, and of Zeus Ammon in the W. Egyptian desert. Resort to oracles is also widespread in primitive societies. ◊ *Divination, Shaman.*

Orange. Members of the genus *Citrus,* wild in SE Asia and long cultivated e.g. in China, and known in England in the 16th cent. though rarities till the late 17th. *C. aurantium* (bitter or Seville orange) is used for marmalade and candied peel; *C. sinensis* (sweet orange) is used in many varieties as dessert, as is *C. nobilis deliciosa* (mandarin oranges from China and tangerines from N. Africa). The peel of *C. bergamia* gives bergamot oil, an essential ingredient in ◊ *eau de cologne.* At one time all mansions had their orangeries, ornate buildings with very long windows. Orange trees are remarkable in that flowers and fruit at all stages of development are borne throughout the year, although there is a peak fruiting season. Leading exporters are Spain, Italy, Israel, U.S.A., and Brazil. The flowers give oil of neroli, used in perfumery.

Orange Society. Militant anti-Catholic body, oath-bound and secret, organized in lodges on the ◊ *Freemasons* model; founded 1795 to counter the successes of the ◊ *United Irishmen* and to maintain the Protestant 'Ascendancy' in Ireland. Notorious in the 1790s for harsh repression of Irish peasant nationalism, and for corruption in connexion with the passing of the 1800 ◊ *Act of Union,* the Society subsequently became concentrated in NE ◊ *Ulster.*

Orang-outang. < Malay, 'man of the woods'; a species of aboreal fruit-eating ◊ *ape* restricted to SE Asia and now rare. The female weighs 80 lb. and the male about twice as much, also differing in having large flexible ear-like lobes and a beard. Unlike other ape ◊ *primates*, they show little social organization.

Oratorio. Term usually reserved for non-staged large-scale musical works on religious or solemn themes (other than settings for use in church services); the chorus is usually prominent. Bach's *St Matthew Passion* 1729, Handel's *Messiah* 1741, and Haydn's *Creation* 1798 are the best-known examples.

Orbit. 1. The path in space of a body moving under the gravitational attraction of other bodies. In the ◊ *solar system* the overwhelming gravitational influence of the sun on the planets makes each orbit an ellipse with the sun at one focus. This is the first law of planetary motion, formulated by Johannes Kepler 1571–1630. His second law states that a line joining the planet to the centre of the sun would sweep out equal areas in equal times, and his third law says that the square of the time to complete an orbit is proportional to the cube of the planet's distance from the sun ($T^2 \propto d^3$). Minor deviations from an orbit caused by secondary gravitational forces are known as perturbations. Orbits can be accurately calculated, and the putting up of ◊ *artificial satellites* has created great interest in orbital theory. Special factors affecting satellite orbits are the 'braking' effect of the earth's atmosphere, the earth's irregular shape, the pressure of sunlight, and the effect of the earth's magnetism on magnetic material in the satellite.

2. The path of electrons around the ◊ *atom*; also the equation describing this.

3. The ◊ *eye*-socket.

Orchestra. Although instruments had earlier often been grouped into 'consorts' of the same kind, e.g. viols or recorders, and consorts had occasionally played together, the orchestra as a regularly constituted body of mixed instrumentalists emerged only in 17th-cent. ◊ *opera* houses. Its basis, found also in the *concerti grossi* of Handel and Bach, is the string group, to which wind and percussion instruments were added at the composer's choice.

The so-called 'classical' orchestra is that of a late Haydn or Mozart symphony – strings plus a pair each of flutes, oboes, clarinets, bassoons, horns, and trumpets, plus kettledrums (timpani). In the 19th cent. this was customarily expanded, notably by the addition of trombones, harp, and various percussion instruments. The works of Richard Strauss and Mahler mark a climax in the employment of lavish orchestral forces. A modern reverse tendency is exemplified in Stravinsky's requirement of a huge orchestra (in practice at least 80) for *The Rite of Spring* (1913) but only 38 players to accompany the soloist in his Movements for Piano and Orchestra (1960). ◊ *Musical Instruments*.

Orchids. Members of the *Orchidaceae*, a vast family of 15,000 species found throughout the world (except in the coldest regions) but most abundant in the tropics, where the majority are ◊ *epiphytes* rooting in moss or dead wood on trees, with moisture-absorbing aerial roots also. In temperate regions most orchids have roots and underground tubers; these are more difficult to cultivate than the tropical epiphytes. The flowers occur in a bewildering variety of shape and size, from the minute to the very large, in every shade of colour including green and black, and are usually of great beauty. Orchids interbreed readily; as a result, many ◊ *hybrids* have been raised, and the cultivation of orchids is extremely popular. Among terrestrial orchids native to the British Isles are *O. fuchsii*, the common spotted orchid of wet places, and *O. mascula*, the early purple orchid of the meadows. Some orchids closely resemble insects e.g. fly, spider, bee. Those seen in flower-shops are tropical. One orchid gives ◊ *vanilla*.

Orders. 1. In biology ◊ *Biological Classification*.

2. In architecture ◊ *Architectural Orders*.

Orders of Chivalry. Originally founded as religious orders, e.g. the Knights Hospitaller were founded 1113 as a nursing order, but soon (like the Knights Templar, 1118) came to be a crusading order and acquired extensive possessions in Palestine and Europe. The Teutonic Order, founded 1191, became famous for its 13th-cent. onslaughts upon the Slavs. The knightly orders of the later Middle Ages were secular, e.g. the Order of the Garter, about 1348, and the Order of the Golden Fleece. In the 17th and 18th centuries categories were instituted to confer purely titular honours, e.g. the Order of the Bath, a revival of a medieval order dating

436

to 1399. The Knights Templar were dissolved in 1307, but the Knights Hospitaller still exist. ◊ *Malta.*

Ordnance Survey ◊ *Map.*

Orestes. In classical legend, son of ◊ *Agamemnon* and Clytaemnestra, brother of ◊ *Iphigenia* and Electra; when Clytaemnestra murdered Agamemnon, her children were spared, Electra remaining with her mother and Orestes going into exile at the court of his uncle Strophius, father of his great friend Pylades. At manhood Orestes returned to Mycenae with Pylades, to avenge his father. Spurred on by Electra, he killed his mother and her lover Aegisthus, but he was pursued by the avenging ◊ *Furies* for his crime of matricide. At last he came to Athens, where ◊ *Athena* set up the court of Areopagus to judge the case; he was acquitted and the curse on the house of ◊ *Pelops* dissipated. The legend, which may reflect the victory of patriarchy over matriarchy, was presented in dramatic form by Aeschylus in the *Oresteia* trilogy. ◊ *Tragedy (Greek).*

Organ ◊ *Keyboard Instruments.*

Organization for European Economic Cooperation (O.E.E.C.). Association of 17 European nations 1947 as a result of the Marshall Plan, to allocate U.S. financial aid and coordinate their economic and reconstruction programmes. The European Payments Union and a code of trade liberalization were introduced, and the rapid economic recovery of Europe after the war was largely due to the Marshall Plan and the O.E.E.C. which was replaced 1961 by the Organization for Economic Cooperation and Development (O.E.C.D.), joined by U.S.A. and Canada as full members. ◊ *Free Trade.*

Organization of African Unity. Set up in 1963 to promote the 'unity of African States' and rid Africa of 'all forms of colonialism'. It includes some thirty African states (including the Arab countries of N. Africa). At its Cairo meeting 1964 it refused to admit Tshombe of the ◊ *Congolese Republic* to its meetings.

Organization of American States ◊ *Pan-American Union.*

Original Sin. Christian doctrine that Adam (the first man), as a result of disobeying a command from God soon after his creation (see Gen. iii), transmitted to all human beings an innate tendency to depravity, which can be overcome only by participating in the merits of ◊ *Jesus Christ* through ◊ *baptism.* ◊ *Confirmation.*

Orion. 1. In Greek legend, a giant Boeotian hunter; subject of various contradictory legends. One is that while asleep he was blinded by Dionysus at the request of Oenopion of Chios, whose daughter he had ravished, but that he recovered his sight by exposing his eyes to the rays of the rising sun and then lived with ◊ *Artemis,* who eventually killed him with an arrow (either by accident or because he attempted to seduce her) and turned him into the constellation Orion, in which his sword and belt can be seen.
2. In astronomy ◊ *Nebulae.*

Ormolu. Originally a French 18th-cent. method of gilding furniture and clocks; *or moulu* (ground gold) amalgamated with mercury was brushed on, the mercury was volatilized by careful heating, and the gold was burnished. Now objects gilded with cheap modern alloys of e.g. copper and zinc are also called ormolu.

Ornithopter. Flapping-wing aircraft; ornithopters have engaged the attention of inventors mainly because flapping wings give both propulsion and lift by the same primary means as in nature, but practical difficulties have prevented the development of a successful design, though the Russians have built and successfully flown a ◊ *glider* with articulated wings.

Orpheus. In Greek legend, a Thracian bard whose playing on lyre or lute could excite even inanimate things; in the quest of the Argonauts (◊ *Golden Fleece*) he lulled the guardian dragon to sleep with his music. When his wife Eurydice died he went to ◊ *Hades* to recover her, and ◊ *Pluto* was so moved by his playing that he agreed to let her follow Orpheus back to earth, on condition he did not turn to look back until they emerged; but he did look back, she returned to Hades, and his grief so infuriated the Thracian women that they tore him to pieces in their orgies at the feast of ◊ *Dionysus.* In classical Greece the Orpheus legend was the nucleus of a mystical cult teaching asceticism, purity of life, and the immortality of the soul; some of its literature is still extant, e.g. the *Hymns of Orpheus,* and the Orphic mysteries influenced the philosophies of Plato and his successors in Greece and Alexandria.

Orthodox Church ◇ *Eastern Orthodox Church.*

Oscillation ◇ *Wave.*

Osiris. In Egyptian mythology, husband of ◇ *Isis* and father of ◇ *Horus*; the creator, god of the Nile, and ruler of Amenti, the land of the dead. Also the principle of goodness, in opposition to his evil brother Set (who killed him). Osiris personified the immortal part of man; his myth may represent the contest for supremacy between Upper and Lower ◇ *Egypt* and the introduction of a new cult in place of Set's older sky-and-sun cult. He is usually depicted as a mummy wearing the crown of Upper Egypt; the ◇ *Apis* bull was one of his incarnations.

Osmium ◇ *Platinum Metals.*

Osmosis. Process by which fluids pass through semipermeable membranes, the less dense fluid tending to pass into the more dense. In plants, osmosis permits the absorption of water through the roots; in animals, dissolved foodstuffs are absorbed into the bloodstream by the same process.

Ossian (Oison). Legendary 3rd-cent. Gaelic warrior-bard, son of ◇ *Finn.* In the mid 18th cent. James Macpherson published a prose collection of *Poems of Ossian* which he claimed to have translated from Scottish Highland originals; after much controversy as to their authenticity, it is now generally agreed that they were entirely or mainly his own work.

Osteomyelitis. Inflammation of the interior of a bone and of the bone marrow, usually caused by a blood-borne streptococcal infection; sometimes a complication of ◇ *typhoid fever*; in growing children it is likely to impair the growth of the long bones.

Ostrich. The largest living bird; its white frilly plumes were once so prized that it was hunted almost to extinction. It is now reared on ostrich farms in Africa and S. America. Its wings are small and useless for flying, but on its strong two-toed legs it can run at up to 40 m.p.h. It lays a white egg weighing about three lb. in a communal nest which the males guard by night and the females by day.

Ostrogoths ◇ *Goths.*

Otitis. Inflammation of the outer ◇ *ear*, *o. externa*, or middle ear, *o. media*, the latter usually following infection of the nose and throat and sometimes causing mastoiditis.

Ottawa Conference. 1932. Trade Conference at which it was agreed to adopt a policy of preferential ◇ *tariff* treatment between all members of the British Commonwealth and colonies.

Otter. A member of any of several genera of the Carnivora, related to the badger; found throughout the world (except Australia); the European otter *Lutra lutra* may weight up to 30 lb. and be three ft long. In the same way that the ◇ *seal* has evolved marine aquatic features, most genera of otters are superb freshwater swimmers, eat fish, and have webbed feet. There is also a sea otter, which weighs 70–80 lb.

Otterburn. 1388. Victory of the Scots (commanded by the Earl of Douglas) over a larger English army (under Henry Hotspur), remembered chiefly on account of the Scots ballad *Otterburn* and the English *Chevy Chase.*

Ottoman Empire. In the 10th cent. a number of Turkish tribes emerged from Central Asia; while the Seljuks occupied ◇ *Persia* and ◇ *Syria*, the Ottomans settled in Asia Minor during the 13th cent. at the expense of the ◇ *Byzantine empire*, the whole of which they took after the capture of Constantinople in 1453. Two sultans greatly extended the Ottoman empire, Selim the Grim into Syria and Egypt, Suleiman the Magnificent into Europe. The western conquests were checked before Vienna in 1529, but to the E. and S. the empire absorbed all Syria, Mesopotamia, and Egypt. For several hundred years the skill of the 'Sublime Porte' (as the government of Constantinople was styled) and the brutal efficiency of its army, with the influence of a common religion (◇ *Islam*), kept most of the empire intact; but in the 19th cent. pressure from Russia and the European powers (◇ *Navarino*) combined with internal dissension to make Turkey the 'sick man of Europe'. British foreign policy encouraged Turkey's westernization, and whilst Britain and Russia cooperated to bring about Greek independence conflicting Russo-British interests led to the ◇ *Crimean War.* Despite promises of more liberal rule for the subject peoples, Turkey faced continued unrest in the Balkans, Armenia, and Crete. Although after the ◇ *Russo-Turkish War* the Powers intervened to preserve Turkey's position (◇ *Berlin Congress*), her brutally repressive policy towards ◊ *Armenia* and her attack on ◊ *Greece* in 1897 left her with few friends. In 1908 the 'Young Turk' party attempted to check national decline by a revolt which instituted constitutional government. After defeat in the ◊ *Balkan Wars*, Turkey sided with Germany in the ◊ *First World War*; subsequently her boundaries were reduced to a small area in Europe around Istanbul (Constantinople) and Anatolia. In 1922–3 the sultanate was abolished and ◊ *Turkey* became a republic. ◊ *Caliphate, Janissaries.*

Ovary. 1. Female reproductive parts of a ◊ *flower* formed of one or several ◊ *carpels.* A fertilized ovary becomes a ◊ *fruit.*

2. ◊ *Reproduction (Human).*

Overdrive. In an automobile the speed of the propeller shaft (which decides the speed of the car) is normally, at the most, equal to the engine speed. For continuous high-speed running, however, it is more economical for the engine to be rotating more slowly than the propeller shaft, and therefore an additional gear called an overdrive is provided in some cars.

Overture. In the classical French operatic overture, e.g. Lully's, a slow section was followed by a fast, which was sometimes followed by another slow section. The Italian overture, established by Alessandro Scarlatti, preferred the order fast-slow-fast; this form merged into that of the ◊ *symphony.* Later operatic overtures, e.g. in Mozart's *Le Nozze di Figaro*, tended to be in a single ◊ *sonata*-form movement; this form in a short non-theatrical concert-piece, e.g. Mendelssohn's *The Hebrides*, may also be called an overture.

Ovule ◊ *Carpel.*

Oxalic Acid. A colourless crystalline substance, $(CO_2H)_2.2H_2O$, rather stronger than ◊ *acetic acid*, which contains two 'acidic' ◊ *hydrogen* atoms and gives both acid and normal ◊ *salts.* It occurs as a ◊ *potassium* salt ('salts of lemon') in the juices of *Oxalis*, wood sorrel, and is found also in the leaves of beet as the free acid and as the ◊ *sodium* or ◊ *calcium* salt in many other plants. Some of its salts e.g. calcium oxalate are insoluble in water; but some metals e.g. iron form soluble complexes with the oxalates of sodium or potassium, hence oxalate salts are used for removing ink or rust stains. The acid and its salts are poisonous.

Ox-bow Lake. Water remaining in the arc of a meander cut off and abandoned by a river flowing straight across the neck of the loop during flooding and shortening its course across the ◊ *flood plain.*

Oxford Movement. A 19th-cent. 'high-church' (◊ *Arminianism*) movement within the ◊ *Church of England* associated with Newman (later a Cardinal), Keble, and Pusey; also called Tractarian and Anglo-Catholic. In reaction against the ◊ *Evangelical movement*, its members emphasized spirituality, ritual, the sacraments, and tradition. With *Tracts for the Times* in the 1830s it achieved initial success; but Newman's emphasis on pre-Reformation doctrines, and in 1845 his secession (followed by that of other Tractarians) to the ◊ *Roman Catholic Church*, caused the decline and disappearance of the movement, though some Anglo-Catholicism survives here and there. In the 1850s the Broad Church (Latitudinarian) movement developed as a result of the clash between Evangelicals and Tractarians.

Oxford University ◊ *Universities.*

Oxygen. The most abundant element on the earth: as a gas it forms one fifth of the world's atmosphere; in combination with hydrogen it is 90 per cent by weight of all water and it is a major constituent in combination with a variety of elements of the majority of minerals and is present in all living matter. It was first isolated 1774 by Priestley and Scheele, working independently, and soon afterwards Lavoisier gave it its name and showed that a mixture of oxygen with ◊ *nitrogen* constitutes air, and that oxygen of the air takes an essential part in the burning of combustible material e.g. fuel, and in the other oxidations which take place in the animal body following respiration. In these reactions ◊ *carbon* and hydrogen, usually as compounds, are the chief elements to be oxidized, producing carbon dioxide and water. The oxidations are exothermal (heat-producing) reactions and the principal sources of energy. Oxygen is prepared in the laboratory by heating certain oxides or the salts of some oxy-acids, and commercially by liquefying purified air and separating it by fractional ◊ *distillation* into nitrogen (b.p. $-196°$ C), argon (b.p. $-186°$ C.), and oxygen (b.p. $-183°$ C). It is a colourless and tasteless gas, slightly soluble in water. The molecular weight is 32, corresponding to the diatomic molecule O_2; the liquid is light blue, the solid darker. It is mainly oxygen-16 and small amounts of two heavier isotopes. Ordinary oxygen is not very chemically active at room temperature, although most elements, when heated, combine with it to form oxides (exceptions are platinum, silver, and gold, the ◊ *inert gases*, and the ◊ *halogens*). Oxides are divisible into neutral (e.g. water), acidic (formed by most non-metals and soluble in water to give acids e.g. sulphur dioxide), and basic (formed by most metals, and when soluble giving alkalis e.g. sodium oxide). Because both ◊ *silicon* (next in abundance to oxygen) and ◊ *aluminium* (which follows silicon in abundance) readily combine with oxygen, the earth's crust is mainly aluminosilicates (e.g. ◊ *felspars* and ◊ *clay*) and ◊ *quartz*. Very many organic compounds, esp. those of biological significance, contain oxygen. The slight solubility of oxygen in water is of great importance, because it enables fish and other aquatic life to obtain a supply of the gas, and allows moist tissue to absorb it during the respiratory processes of the higher animals. The element follows a continuous biological cycle: animals use it to oxidize e.g. sugar to carbon dioxide, and thus obtain heat and muscular energy. Plants reduce the carbon dioxide back to sugar by ◊ *photosynthesis*, deriving the necessary energy from the sun; energy produced by the oxidation of food or fuel has been made available by the endothermal (heat-aborbing) processes of reduction whereby oxygen is removed as the result of solar radiation. Oxygen is an important commercial product; it is transported as liquid in large heat-insulated tanks and as compressed gas in cylinders. Very large quantities are now used in torches for cutting and welding steel in fabrication industries ranging from shipbuilding to general engineering. Its applications in extraction metallurgy are increasing, as is its use in the chemical industry, for medical purposes, and in research.

Oyster. A ◊ *hermaphrodite* shallow-water marine mollusc of the class *Lamellibranchia*, related to mussels and scallops; a delicacy (normally consumed alive, after thorough washing), it is becoming increasingly expensive, partly owing to the depredations wrought upon British oyster-beds by carnivorous boring molluscs accidentally imported from America. Pearls are produced when the oyster secretes nacre (mother-of-pearl) around a foreign body within the shell; the best pearls are obtained from the marine pearl oyster of the Pacific and Indian oceans, but pearls may also be obtained from freshwater ◊ *clams* or mussels and may be 'cultured' by the deliberate introduction of gritty matter.

Ozone. When molecular ◊ *oxygen* O_2 receives suitable energy (e.g. from ultra-violet light, radioactive bombardment, or electrical discharge), a molecular rearrangement takes place and a colourless gas O_3 with a characteristic smell is formed; this 'ozone' has strong oxidizing powers owing to its ready decomposition, whereby some of the oxygen is released in the active atomic condition. Commercially, it is produced by passing air or oxygen through a silent electrical discharge; it is used for bleaching, sterilizing, and smell removal e.g. from kitchens (by oxidizing the unwanted compounds). The seaside smell called 'ozone' is due to other causes, atmospheric ozone being found only at high altitudes.

P

Pacific Islands. 1. Gilbert and Ellice Islands. Area 360 sq. m. Pop. 50,000. British colony. Air-communications centre.
2. Solomon Islands. Area 11,500 sq. m. Pop. 133,000. British protectorate. Products cocoa, copra, timber.
3. New Hebrides. Area 5700 sq. m. Pop. 65,650. British-French condominium. Products cocoa, coffee, copra, fish, manganese, timber.
4. ◊ *French Polynesia.*
Pacific War. 1941–5. In the ◊ *Second World War*, after the Japanese attack on the American fleet in ◊ *Pearl Harbor*, within six months the Japanese had overrun the Philippines, Hong Kong, the Malay peninsula, Burma, and the Netherlands East Indies, and were threatening both India and Australia; only at ◊ *Bataan* was any prolonged resistance made. The U.S. navy and air force checked the Japanese in 1942 at the decisive battles of the ◊ *Coral Sea* and ◊ *Midway*; by 1943 U.S.A. was superior at sea and in the air, and with the U.S. landings at ◊ *Guadalcanal* the Japanese land forces received their first setback. Their advance in New Guinea and the Solomon Islands was halted; the Australian and U.S. troops began to regain ground as they became more proficient at jungle warfare. In 1944, after the battle of ◊ *Leyte Gulf*, and the reconquest of the Philippines, Japan itself suffered increasingly heavy aerial attack, and after the dropping of the first atom bombs (◊ *Hiroshima*) Japan surrendered.

Paediatrics. Science of the medical care of children, usually from birth to the age of puberty; it first became a subject of scientific study in the mid 19th cent. as a result of the efforts of Charles West, a London obstetrician who founded the Hospital for Sick Children in Gt Ormond Street. At first much attention necessarily had to be given to the consequences of ignorance, malnutrition, and poor housing. In the 20th cent. the most striking developments have been the reduction in infant mortality and the dramatic fall in the incidence of disease and death from infection esp. diphtheria. Latterly there has been much research into all aspects of child health and development, notably the biochemical aspects of disease, the disturbances of fluid and electrolyte ◊ *metabolism*, and the relationship of certain inborn errors of metabolism to forms of mental deficiency. There have been considerable advances in paediatric surgery, esp. in the repair of congenital lesions of the heart.

Paint. Liquid with pigment in suspension, usually containing three main ingredients: binder, thinner, and pigment. The binder is a natural drying oil, e.g. linseed oil or in recent developments a synthetic resin. The thinner is an organic solvent such as turpentine or white spirit. The pigment may be one or more from a vast range of colouring matters, natural or synthetic: earths, e.g. umber; plants, e.g. indigo; animal, e.g. carmine. White pigment is usually white lead, zinc white, or titanium dioxide. Artists' oil paints, basically the same as commercial paint, are made from the finest ingredients.
VARNISH: A solution of gum or resin in oil or spirits; shellacs and lacquers are distinctive types extensively used by the Chinese in very early times.
◊ *Gouache, Watercolour.*

Pakistan. Muslim State in the Indian subcontinent, resulting from the ◊ *partition* of 1947. It consists of two widely separated portions: W. Pakistan, area 310,403 sq. m., pop. 42.9 m.; E. Pakistan, area 55,126 sq. m., pop. 50.8 m. Cap. Rawalpindi (Karachi till 1960), but a new cap. at Islamabad is being built; also Lahore (W.) and Dacca (E.). A republic, member of the ◊ *British Commonwealth*. The republican constitution came into force in 1956, but was suspended under ◊ *martial law* 1958–62; the 1962 constitution vests all executive authority in the President, General Ayub Khan, Army C. in C. and Chief Martial Law Administrator. A new National Assembly was elected in 1962.
ECONOMY. Largely agricultural. E. Pakistan (i.e. E. Bengal) produces esp. jute (70 per cent of world production), oilseeds, rice, sugarcane. Since 1947 by rapid industrial expansion E. Pakistan has built 14 jute-manufacturing plants, and the

cotton, hydroelectricity, and natural-gas industries are also being rapidly developed. W. Pakistan produces esp. wheat, other cereals, cotton, etc. and there is some small-scale industry (textiles and food processing).

HISTORY. (For earlier history ◊ *East India Company, India, Indus Civilization*.) When British rule ended in 1947, the Indian Congress Party agreed to a separate Muslim state: the consequent exchange of Hindu and Muslim minorities caused acute sufferings and loss of life estimated in millions. India and Pakistan remain on bad terms over the ◊ *Kashmir* dispute. The first Pakistan Prime Minister was assassinated in 1951: six others held office 1951–8; the Constituent Assembly was suspended in 1954, and martial law was proclaimed in 1958. The present regime claims to be locally democratic and centrally paternalistic.

LANGUAGES. W. Pakistan, Urdu; E. Pakistan, Bengali. Both are ◊ *Indo-European* languages.

Palaeocene Period (Eozoic Era) ◊ *Geological Time Scale, Primates.*

Palaeolithic. Old Stone Age; the first and longest of the cultural stages in human development, covering much of the geological ◊ *Pleistocene epoch*, during which man developed an upright posture, articulate speech, conceptual thought, the use of fire, and tool-making. The earliest known form of ape-man, Australopithecus, living in S. and E. Africa about 600,000 years ago, may not have been a tool-maker; about 500,000 years ago, in SE Asia, China, and parts of N. Africa, another type of ape-man, Pithecanthropus, is associated both with fire and with crudely-shaped chopping tools. The standard implements of the Lower Palaeolithic of Africa, Europe, and W. Asia are the multi-purpose core tools (◊ *Flint*) called 'hand-axes', showing a very slowly improving sequence of development, over a period of about 400,000 years, through the Abbevillian and Acheulian (Chellean) industries during the second and third glacial and interglacial periods of the ◊ *Ice Age*. Flake tools were also used, sometimes by themselves, in the Clactonian tradition, until a new technique, the Levalloisian, was developed in the third interglacial period, about 200,000 to 100,000 B.C. All these Lower Palaeolithic remains come from 'open' hunting sites, buried in geological deposits esp. river gravels, and not from caves.

The Middle Palaeolithic cultures cover the onset and first peak of the fourth and last glaciation, about 100,000 to 30,000 B.C., and have two main components, the Levalloisian flake tradition and the Mousterian industry associated with Neanderthal Man; they show considerable improvement in flint technique, and have several specialized types of tool. Neanderthal Man was the first hominid to practise deliberate burial of the dead, and there is some evidence of ritual activities; many of the remains of this period come from caves. Neanderthal Man seems to have died out completely, and the Upper Palaeolithic cultures of the last glaciation about 30,000 to 10,000 B.C. are associated with true modern man, *Homo sapiens*. Technical advances became more rapid, and a variety of regional cultures developed, the classic sequence in Europe being Aurignacian, Gravettian, Solutrean, and Magdalenian. The flint work, based on the production of blade tools, is of very high standard, esp. in the Solutrean, and a wide range of specialized equipment in flint, bone, antler (and presumably wood and leather) was evolved. Personal ornaments were worn, and the dead were carefully buried. The most impressive remains of the Upper Palaeolithic are the works of ◊ *cave art* in W. Europe, and decorated small objects including female statuettes, all suggesting elaborate fertility and magico-religious concepts and ritual. ◊ *Geological Time Scale.*

Palaeontology. Study of extinct plant and animal life, mainly in the form of ◊ *fossils*, most frequently found as casts of infiltrated minerals formed within a sediment-mould about the animal's body; as satisfactory conditions for fossilization rarely occur, the fossil record is incomplete, and 'missing links' are the rule rather than the exception. Nevertheless fossils give the most direct support for the theory of ◊ *evolution*. The period of the earth's history for which we have no fossil record is 12 times as long as the fossil record; thus we have little knowledge of the arrangement of ◊ *sedimentary rocks* before the ◊ *Cambrian system*. The fossil record indicates that a few animals have changed little since their inception, that the life of each period was dominated by some transient animal type, and that animals have become more complex with time. The study of fossils also shows whether plants and animals lived on land or in the sea and at times the climatic conditions then prevailing e.g. plant remains and shells found in ◊ *London clay* show that the climate of what is now SE England was once warm and moist, like that of today's tropical rain belt. ◊ *Geological Time Scale*.

Palate. The roof of the mouth, consisting of the hard palate (front) and soft palate (back).

CLEFT PALATE: A congenital defect along the centre of the hard palate, resulting from failure of the two sides to join; often associated with hare lip, in which the two sides of the upper lip fail to unite.

Palatinate. Historically, two regions of Germany: (a) the Lower Palatinate on the Rhine; (b) the Upper Palatinate in Bavaria. It takes its name from the rank of Count Palatine, used in the Roman, Byzantine, and Holy Roman Empires, conferred on Count Conrad by the Emperor Frederick I in 1156. In 1214 the Wittelsbachs who had held the Bavarian Palatinate since 1115 acquired the Rhenish Palatinate also and members of the family held both until 1777 when the Upper was inherited by the ruler of the Lower. The Palatinate regions were devastated in the ◊ *Thirty Years War* and again in the wars of the 18th cent. After the ◊ *Napoleonic Wars* parts of the Lower Palatinate were integrated into ◊ *Bavaria*, which in 1871 joined the German empire. In 1946 the Rhenish Palatinate became part of the new state of Rhineland-Palatinate.

Pale ◊ *Ireland*.

Palestine. One of the districts of Syria, Falastin, into which Asia Minor was divided after the Arab conquest in A.D. 636; after varying fortunes (◊ *Crusades*), it became part of the ◊ *Ottoman Empire*. In the late 19th cent. the ◊ *Zionist* movement brought numbers of Jews back to the country. After its occupation by British troops during the First World War a British ◊ *mandate* was established, and under the imprecise Balfour Declaration (on a 'national home for the Jews') increasing numbers of Jews entered the country. Arab opposition culminated in the 1936-8 revolt. In the absence of any agreed settlement between Jews and Arabs, in 1948 a partition into ◊ *Israel* and ◊ *Jordan* was established, on the basis of recommendations of the U.N. General Assembly, and the British withdrew. ◊ *Arab League, Judaism*.

Palinurus. In Virgil's *Aeneid*, steersman of the ship bringing ◊ *Aeneas* from Troy. He went to sleep at his post, fell overboard, reached the shore, and was murdered by the local people. Later, Aeneas met his soul when visiting ◊ *Hades*. A cape on the S. Italian coast is said to be named after him.

Palladian Style. The architectural style evolved by Andrea Palladio 1508-80 in his buildings in Vicenza and Venice; also the work of his immediate followers in Italy, and in England that of Inigo Jones in the 17th cent. and in the early 18th cent. that of Lord Burlington, Colen Campbell, William Kent, and others who based their style on Palladio's. It was characterized by symmetry and the addition of free-standing classical columns to the façades.

Palladium ◊ *Platinum Metals*.

Palm. A large monocotyledon family, of about 1500 species, in tropical and subtropical countries, varying in height from a few feet in the only European species, *Chamaerops humilis* (the leaves of which make very tough bags) to over 100 ft for several tropical species e.g. royal palm, date palm. The large hard glossy leaves, usually on long stalks, may be palmate (fan-shaped) or pinnate (like the fronds of a fern). Many palms are of great economic importance, providing coconuts, dates, edible oils, and waxes. Sago is produced from food reserves stored in the stem of the sago palm, the sap from cut inflorescence-stalks of some species gives sugar and fermented drinks, the areca palm gives the betel nut chewed throughout Asia, and other palms give fibre for ropes, brushes, mats, brooms, and raffia.

Palsy ◊ *Paralysis*.

Pampas. Probably < Quechua *pampa*, a plain. Various plains in S. America, like the ◊ *prairies* in N. America; usually the vast almost treeless area round the Rio de la Plata in Argentina, with a natural covering of tall 'pampas grass', largely desert in the W., but with a heavier rainfall and more fertile in the E. Cattle and sheep are reared; alfalfa (for fodder), flax (for linseed), maize, and wheat are cultivated. The climate is warm temperate, but a strong cold S. wind, the Pampero, sometimes breaks the summer heat.

Pan. < Gr. 'everything'; in Greek mythology, god of flocks and herds and of nature in general, part man and part goat, wearing a leopard's skin, and esp. connected with Arcadia. He invented the musical instrument pan-pipes (called Syrinx after a nymph who became a reed in order to elude him), and was believed to cause the terror ('panic') felt by travellers in lonely places. According to legend, at the crucifixion of ◊ *Jesus Christ* a cry went up 'Great Pan is dead!' and every ◊ *oracle* ceased for ever. ◊◊ *Midas*.

Panama. Area 31,890 sq. m. Pop. 1.1 m. Cap. Panama City. Rel. Roman Catholic. Language Spanish. A republic in central America, between ◊ *Colombia* and ◊ *Costa Rica*, with a single-chamber legislature of 53 members, elected every four years.

ECONOMY. Wholly agricultural, with chief product bananas, also cereals, cocoa, coconuts, coffee, rubber, mahogany. Education is free and compulsory 7–15; there is one university.

HISTORY. Discovered by the Spanish in 1501, Panama remained a separate colony (though continually raided and part-occupied by buccaneers and pirates) until after the revolt of the Spanish-American colonies, in the 1820s, it became part of Colombia. After Colombia refused to ratify an 1878 concession treaty for the construction of a canal, Panama broke from Colombia, with U.S. aid, and declared itself a separate sovereign republic in 1903, granting U.S.A. a perpetual lease of the Canal Zone. In recent years there have been frequent demonstrations in Panama against the U.S. retention of the Canal Zone.

Panama Canal. Waterway connecting the Atlantic and Pacific oceans, 51 m. NW to SE across the Isthmus of ◊ *Panama*, built 1904–14 by U.S.A. on land leased in perpetuity by the Republic of Panama. The minimum depth is 41 ft, the maximum height to which vessels are raised in passing through the six locks is 85 ft. Responsibility for defence rests with U.S.A. but tolls are the same for all countries. The Canal Zone is administered by a U.S. Governor as a State Reservation.

Pan-American Union. Association of American republics founded 1890 to pro-

mote political and economic collaboration; a number of institutions were set up and agreements concluded on communications, trade, immigration, and defence, but in Latin-American countries the P.A.U. was long suspected of being a cloak for U.S.A. policy, esp. after e.g. American interventions in Panama 1903, Haiti 1915–34, and the Dominican Republic 1916–34. During F. D. Roosevelt's presidency 1932–45 the 'good-neighbour' policy began to put relations between U.S.A. and Latin America on a more friendly and equal basis; the 1947 Rio Treaty provided for mutual assistance should any signatory attack another. The P.A.U. was succeeded in 1948 by the Organization of American States, to foster mutual understanding and cooperation among the 21 states of the W. hemisphere; it is a regional agency within the ◊ *United Nations Organization*.

Pancreas. Large ◊ *gland* situated at the back of the abdomen just below the diaphragm, which discharges a digestive juice into the ◊ *intestine* through the pancreatic duct (◊ *Digestion*). This juice includes trypsin, which breaks down some ◊ *proteins*; lipase, which deals with fats; and others which split carbohydrates. The pancreas also contains scattered groups of cells (Islands of Langerhans) which produce the hormone insulin, which regulates ◊ *carbohydrate* metabolism. ◊◊ *Endocrine System*.

Panda. A carnivore which has become herbivorous. There are two genera, *Ailurus fulgens*, with red-brown body and black legs, arboreal in the E. Himalayas, and *Ailuropoda melanoleuca*, predominantly white but having black limbs, ears, and eye patches, found in central China. Both (like the ◊ *bear*) have secondarily evolved a herbivorous grinding dentition for their diet of fruit and bamboo-shoots.

Pandora. In Greek mythology, the first woman on earth; made from clay by ◊ *Hephaestus* at the order of ◊ *Zeus*, as a vengeance upon ◊ *Prometheus* and man, she was endowed with every charm, and also with deceit and curiosity. Zeus gave her a box, forbade her to open it, and sent her to marry Epimetheus, brother of Prometheus; she opened the box, from which emerged all the evils which have ever since afflicted mankind. Only one thing remained in the box: Hope.

Panslavism. Concept of cultural and possibly political unity of the Slav peoples, first put forward in the 17th cent. but not a potent force until the growth of nationalism in the 19th, when Russia was the only independent Slav State. It contributed to the collapse of ◊ *Austria-Hungary,* and provided Russia with an ostensible motive for her Balkan policy. The expansion of Soviet influence since the ◊ *Second World War* has been seen as a form of panslavism, although it affects non-Slav countries e.g. E. Germany, Hungary. ◊ *Soviet Union (History).*

Pansy. < Fr. *pensée*; the wild perennial, heartsease, *Viola tricolor,* grown in Elizabethan gardens, was greatly improved early in the 19th cent. by selective breeding, and by 1835 400 named varieties had been developed. Societies were formed to encourage the development of the Show Pansy, which had to conform to rigid rules as to shape and colour. The garden pansy is now raised annually from seed. VIOLA: More compact, free-flowering, and long-lived plants, originating from crosses between the garden pansy and the wild Pyrenean *V. cornuta.*

Pantheism. Belief that all that exists is divine and the universe and God are one. Broadly the outlook of ◊ *Hinduism* represented in the West by the teaching of such philosophers as Spinoza and Giordano Bruno. Excluding any personal deity, it is irreconcilable with any interpretation of orthodox ◊ *Christianity.* ◊ *Animism, Buddhism, Gnostics, Jains, Mysticism.*

Panther. Group of great cats, 'panther' now being chiefly used for the black leopard of S. India. *Panthera pardus,* the spotted leopard of Africa and Asia, hunts any animal weaker than itself; its fur is pale or reddish brown, with irregular dark rings. *Panthera onca,* the jaguar, is similar but has a characteristic black dot within the rings; the largest New World cat, six or seven ft long, short-legged, it hunts any quadruped but rarely attacks man, and is now found mainly in the tropical forests of S. America. The ocelot is a similar but smaller animal, with different marking. Cougar and puma are alternative names for closely related S. American varieties.

Pantomime. Strictly ◊ *mime*; in Britain, a traditional Christmas-time theatre show, loosely based on nursery-rhyme or fairy-tale material and incorporating song, dance, spectacle, juggling, acrobatics, and music-hall (variety, vaudeville) speciality acts: the 'Principal Boy' is an actress and the 'Dame' a comic actor.

Papacy ◊ *Papal States, Pope, Roman Catholic Church, Vatican.*

Papal Jubilee. Year during which Roman Catholics may obtain special spiritual favours and plenary ◊ *indulgences,* on condition of making pilgrimage to Rome, visiting certain churches, and saying appointed prayers. Jubilees may be proclaimed by the ◊ *Pope* at any time, but normally occur every 25 years ('Holy Year'); they are initiated by the opening of a special door ('Holy Doors') at St Peter's in Rome.

Papal States. Parts of Italy allegedly granted to the Popes in the 3rd cent. A.D. according to the Donation of Constantine, an 8th-cent. forgery; first recognized by Pepin of France in A.D. 754. In the 12th cent. Innocent III extended the frontiers to include the whole of central Italy (◊ *Guelphs and Ghibellines*). During the exile of the papacy to Avignon 1309–78 the papal states disintegrated; they were not finally brought under effective centralized control again until the 16th cent. (◊ *Counter-Reformation*). The abrogation of papal rule during the ◊ *Napoleonic Wars* emphasized the inadequacies of church administration; in 1846 Pius IX finally acceded to the demands for reform, but during the revolutions of 1848 he supported ◊ *Austria* against the nationalists of ◊ *Italy,* and lost all the papal lands except Rome, which in 1870 was also captured. The papal secular domain was reduced to the ◊ *Vatican* only, but the papacy refused to recognize the Italian kingdom, and the Popes remained legally 'prisoners of the Vatican' until 1929, when the Lateran Treaty established the Vatican as a separate state within the city of Rome. ◊ *Pavia.*

Paper. A thin sheet or web formed by the deposition of fibres (usually vegetable) from suspension in a liquid or vapour, in such a way that they intermesh; during or after manufacture it may be impregnated or coated to fill a wide variety of purposes e.g. newsprint, books, writing paper, wrapping paper, paper board (cardboard). Chinese records attribute the invention of paper A.D. 105 to Tsai Lun, who used plant fibres well boiled with other ingredients, pulped, spread on a straining frame, and subjected to pressure. Outside the Far East paper-making was unknown until the capture of Chinese prisoners by Arabs at Samarkand in the 8th cent. It was made by Chinese workmen at Baghdad A.D. 795 and in Damascus a little later, and was introduced into Europe 1150 by the Moors. The first British paper-mill was operating in Hertfordshire about 1490. All paper was made by hand until Louis Robert, a clerk in a French paper-mill, devised machinery 1798; the émigré brothers Fourdrinier in England developed his method and produced paper in continuous rolls. John Dickinson 1809 patented an invention leading to mass production of paper board. Popular newspapers and greater literacy in the late 19th cent. meant an enormous increase in newsprint and printing-paper consumption, which has continued in the 20th cent. even faster, with great advances in manufacturing and mass-production techniques.

The fibrous raw material is mainly cellulose obtained from a wide variety of plants, from grasses to large trees; the most widely used is wood pulp, produced mainly in Canada, Finland, Norway, Sweden, and U.S.S.R. Esparto grass (a speciality in British printing since 1856) produces fine-quality paper; other materials used are bagasse (sugar-cane stalk), bamboo, flax, rag, straw, and waste-paper for cardboard. Producing a ton of paper requires from one to five tons of coal, thousands of gallons of good clean water, cellulose fibres in a quantity depending on their quality and that of the paper being made, bleaching agents, resin and alum for ink-resistance, loading (e.g. china clay) to improve the surface, starch for stiffening and finish, mineral and synthetic dyes, and gelatine for durability.

BLOTTING-PAPER: An unglazed highly-absorbent paper.

WATERMARK: Produced by designs in the fine wire mesh on which paper is made.

◊ *Parchment.*

Paprika ◊ *Pepper (2).*

Papua ◊ *Melanesians, Race.*

Papyrus. A variety of sedge, ◊ *Cyperaceae*; also the form of paper made from it. Formerly abundant in the marshes of the Nile, it was of considerable symbolic importance to the ancient Egyptians and a common motif in their art and architecture, and also used for making rafts, matting, ropes, sails, baskets etc. Paper was made by slicing the pith and beating it with a hammer, laying the strips thus formed side by side, and beating them into sheets, which were then stuck together to form rolls.

Parachute. Umbrella-shaped canopy to break the fall of objects dropped from a height; now standard equipment for military flyers and also used for dropping stores and braking the re-entry speed of space capsules into the atmosphere. Designs for parachutes were made by Leonardo da Vinci in the 15th cent. The first recorded parachute descent is attributed to André Jacques Garnerin, Paris, 1797.

Paraffins. ◊ *Hydrocarbons* (general formula C_nH_{2n+2}) mainly derived from natural ◊ *petroleum.* 'Paraffin' < Lat. *parum affinis*, slight affinity; these compounds are chemically fairly inert. The simplest are gases: methane, ethane, propane, butane; the liquids are named from the number of carbon atoms in the molecule e.g. octane (C_8H_{18}). Those of high molecular weight are solids e.g. in paraffin wax.

HOUSEHOLD PARAFFIN: A mixture of paraffins corresponding to the kerosene fraction obtained by the fractional ◊ *distillation* of crude petroleum, including those with b.p. within the range 200–260° C.

OCTANE: Like all the higher members of the series, can exist in more than one form, by differing arrangements of the atoms in the molecule. Isooctane is used as a yardstick for fuel efficiency e.g. octane number or octane rating; in a standard ◊ *internal combustion engine* it does not 'knock' readily, and is given the arbitrary number of 100, whereas normal heptane (C_7H_{16}) knocks very easily, and is given the value 0. The octane number of liquid fuel is therefore defined as: 'The percentage by volume of isooctane in a mixture of normal heptane and isooctane which knocks to the same extent as the spirit under test.' Ordinary motor spirit has an octane rating of about 80, whereas special fuels for aero-engines have a rating much above 100. Propane and butane are gaseous fuels (propagas, butagas). ◊ *Methane.*

Paraguay. Area 157,000 sq. m. Pop. 1.8 m. Cap. Asunción. Rel. Roman Catholic. An inland state of S. America, between Argentina, Brazil, and Bolivia.

The President, elected for five years, has executive power; the legislature is a House of Representatives.

ECONOMY. The country consists of a plateau (where most of the population live) and the low-lying Chaco. Agriculture and industry are backward, but stock-breeding is important and there are exports of cotton, maté, and tobacco; most production is for home consumption.

HISTORY. Paraguay became a Spanish colony in 1535, and Asunción was the focal point from which Spanish colonization of S. America proceeded; it was here that the remarkable ◊ mission establishments ('reductions') of the Jesuits (◊ Society of Jesus) organized the Indians into successful communities. After declaring itself independent in 1811, Paraguay was involved in a disastrous war with Brazil, Argentina, and Uruguay 1865–70, after which only 22,000 males remained alive. The Chaco, long disputed with Bolivia, was the occasion of the Paraguay-Bolivia Gran Chaco War 1932–5.

LANGUAGE. Spanish; also ◊ Guarani.

Paraguay Tea ◊ Maté.

Paraldehyde. Product of the self-condensation of acetaldehyde caused by the action of acid; a liquid used in medicine as a non-toxic hypnotic drug. ◊ Aldehydes.

Parallax. Apparent change in the position of an object caused by an actual change in the position of the observer; also the angular measure of this change in position. An example of parallax in astronomy is the small ellipse which a nearer ◊ star appears to follow during the year when viewed against the background of distant stars; this movement is really caused by our own yearly orbit around the sun, and can be used to estimate the distance of the star. The parallax of a star is expressed as the angle subtended at the star by the mean radius of the earth's orbit, i.e. the average angle between its direction from the earth and its direction from the centre of the sun.

Paralysis. Loss of power of movement in parts of the body, caused by damage either to the brain (or spinal cord) or to muscle nerves or to the muscles themselves.

CEREBRAL PALSY: Paralysis resulting from brain injury sustained before or soon after birth.

SPASTIC PARALYSIS: Condition caused by brain damage where there is impaired control of the muscles, leading to involuntary and uncoordinated movements. The physical defects are not necessarily accompanied by mental abnormality, though this occurs in about half the cases.

Paranoia. A mental condition in which a permanent and unalterable system of delusions develops, without any other evidence of mental disorder; few cases in fact meet this definition, and the term is now largely replaced by 'paranoid' i.e. mental disorders in which delusions of persecution and/or grandeur predominate but in which there can be and usually is other evidence of mental illness, often ◊ schizophrenia.

Parapsychology ◊ Psychical Research.

Parasites. An organism which lives at the expense of another living organism (the host) drawing nourishment directly from it. Parasites may eventually cause the death of the host, and some esp. among bacteria and fungi can then continue to live as saprophytes. Many common human diseases are caused by parasitic bacteria, e.g. anthrax, ◊ cholera, diphtheria, ◊ leprosy, meningitis, plague, pneumonia, tetanus (lockjaw), ◊ tuberculosis, typhoid fever. Others are caused by minute parasitic animals e.g. ◊ dysentry, malaria, sleeping sickness. Hookworms and tapeworms are parasites as are the ◊ flea, louse, mosquito, and tick. Fungi are common parasites of plants and cause the majority of plant diseases, e.g. potato blight, mildews, rusts, smuts. Some flowering plants are parasites, e.g. ◊ dodder. Also parasitic are the ◊ viruses which cause many animal and plant diseases.

Parchment. Used for books and documents before the introduction of paper, and still in use for documents needing to be durable; prepared from skins of she-goats or sheep. The skin is split, the outer 'skiver' being used as leather and the inner part for parchment manufacture.

PARCHMENT PAPER: Tough semi-transparent paper obtained by treating bleached cellulose with chemicals.

Pardon ◊ Reprieve.

Parent-Teacher Association. A voluntary association to promote understanding and cooperation between parents and teachers for the welfare of the children. These associations have no official powers, but organize meetings at which educational topics are discussed or at which teachers have an opportunity of meeting parents. They are common in the U.S.A. but still rare (though increasing) in the U.K., and even rarer in other countries. Their influence can be greater than their unofficial status would suggest, and they often raise funds for additional facilities e.g. swimming baths and playing fields.

Parhelion ◊ *Halo*.

Paris. In Greek legend, son of ◊ *Priam* and ◊ *Hecuba*; warned in a dream that her coming child would bring disaster, his mother exposed him on Mt Ida at birth, but he was found by a shepherd and grew up extremely handsome. When called upon to judge the contest for the golden apple offered by Eris (strife) to the most beautiful of the three goddesses ◊ *Aphrodite*. ◊ *Athena*, and ◊ *Hera*, he awarded it to Aphrodite and earned the enmity of Hera and Athena (hence 'apple of discord'). He abandoned his wife Oenone for ◊ *Helen*, carrying her off to Troy and thus causing the Trojan war, in which his cowardice earned general contempt. At the fall of Troy he was killed by Philoctetes with a poisoned arrow, in some versions in the presence of Oenone, who hanged herself in grief.

Paris Commune. 1871. At the close of the ◊ *Franco-Prussian War* the Parisians, led by the ◊ *National Guard* and the officials of a suburban ◊ *commune*, in protest against the humiliating peace terms, refused to dismantle their artillery, and formed a provisional revolutionary government including many shades of political opinion. The Thiers government cooperated with the Prussian forces in a siege of the city which lasted three months. Finally the extremists gained control in Paris; the execution of hostages lowered the Commune's prestige, and the people capitulated. The Versailles and Prussian troops entered Paris and savage reprisals followed; 17,000 persons were shot in the streets during the 'Week of Blood'. The events inspired Marx's most vehement polemic, *The Civil War in France*, the only work which he wrote in English.

Paris Treaty (1856) ◊ *Berlin Congress, Crimean War*.

Paris Treaty (1898) ◊ *Philippines*.

Parliament. The legislature of the U.K. sitting normally for about 160 days a year (Commons) or 110 (Lords). It developed slowly out of the political and administrative expedients of the medieval kings (◊

Evesham, Norman Conquest) and took definite shape in the 14th cent. Its emergence as an effective legislature was a result of Tudor and Stewart conflicts (◊ *Commonwealth and Protectorate, Reformation, Restoration*), and it became the permanent regular mode of government after the ◊ *Glorious Revolution* of 1688. The ◊ *Reform Bills*, Parliament Acts, and Representation Acts of the 19th and 20th centuries gradually transformed it from an aristocratic to a democratic institution.

It consists of two Houses. The House of Lords (largely shorn of power by the Acts of 1911, 1949, 1962) is composed of about 800 hereditary peers (many of whom do not attend), with the two Archbishops, the Bishops of London, Durham, and Winchester, and about 21 other bishops, nine Law Lords, and an increasing number of Life Peers (under the 1958 Act). Women may sit as Life Peeresses and also, under the 1962 Act, as peeresses in their own right. Members receive no salary, but are entitled to an attendance allowance of $3\frac{1}{2}$ guineas a day. The chairman of the House is the ◊ *Lord Chancellor*. The House (in practice only the Lord Chancellor and the Law Lords) also acts as the Supreme Court of Appeal, this being a survival from the time when Parliament declared what the existing law was as well as enacting new laws (hence the phrase 'the High Court of Parliament').

The House of Commons consists of 630 Members (England 511, Scotland 71, Wales 36, N. Ireland 12) elected by direct universal manhood suffrage, in single-member constituencies. M.P.s receive a salary of £1750 p.a. The House elects its chairman, the Speaker.

The House of Commons must be dissolved, and a General Election held, within five years of the previous elections (except during a state of emergency e.g. war).

Legislation may be initiated by either House, except that Money Bills are a Commons prerogative and may not be introduced, amended, or delayed by the Lords. All Bills are read three times in each House and then receive the Royal Assent (the power to refuse which has not been exercised since the early 18th cent.) after which the Acts become law. A Bill rejected by the Lords but passed by the Commons in two successive sessions may be sent for the Royal Assent without further discussion in the Lords. A Bill involving taxation or public expenditure requires a Financial Resolution from the Government, which thus normally presents all Public Bills, though private Members on either side of the House of Commons may initiate Bills (for which special debating time is provided), as can peers in the House of Lords. In the Commons a special feature is 'question time' – a period set aside weekly when Ministers are called upon to reply to any question on which any M.P. has given notice.

By virtue of tight discipline within the Parliamentary parties, the ◊ *Prime Minister* and Cabinet have increased control over the House of Commons. Each party maintains discipline in voting amongst M.P.s through its 'Whips'; thus a party in power is assured of its majority when the House 'divides' (votes) on debates. A free vote (i.e. when the Whip is not applied) has become rare.

CAVALIER PARLIAMENT ◊ *Restoration*.
'MAD' PARLIAMENT ◊ *Evesham*.
MODEL PARLIAMENT ◊ *Evesham*.
PARLIAMENT OF SAINTS ◊ *Commonwealth and Protectorate*.
PARLIAMENT v. KING ◊ *English Civil Wars*.
RUMP PARLIAMENT ◊ *Commonwealth and Protectorate*.

Parliamentary Privilege. Right enjoyed by each House of Parliament, both the High Court of Parliament as such, and by individual Members of Parliament, which exceed the rights possessed by other bodies or individuals. As early as 1404 Members of Parliament were exempt from arrest for debt, breach of contract, or trespass; Parliamentary privilege now includes freedom of speech in debate (i.e. a member cannot be prosecuted for what he says in Parliament), the right of both Houses to control their own proceedings absolutely, and the right to prosecute others for 'constructive contempt' (i.e. reflexions verbally or in print on the character and proceedings of Parliament, or its Members, derogatory to its dignity). Breaches of privilege are dealt with by a Parliamentary Committee which can reprimand or expel members and fine or imprison non-members. ◊ *Defamation*.

Parnassians. 19th-cent. school of French poets led by Leconte de Lisle, seeking objectivity and impersonality, in opposition to the looser forms and subjective emotionalism of earlier French ◊ *romanticism*; their anthology *Le Parnasse contemporain* appeared in 3 vols. 1866–76. Baudelaire, Verlaine, Hérédia, Mallarmé, Catulle Mendès, Gautier, were associated with the movement.

Parody. A satirical imitation of the style of a particular work or author, usually by transferring it to a trivial or nonsensical subject either to reveal the pretentiousness or over-solemnity of the original or simply to achieve a comic effect. A method similar to that of ◊ *burlesque* or ◊ *pastiche*; used intelligently, it can be revelatory as well as deflating, an effective form of criticism. An outstanding English parodist (late 19th cent.) was J. K. Stephens.

Parrot. Large group of gaudy tropical birds varying considerably in size and plumage, including cockatoos, macaws, parrakeets; the budgerigar is a small parrakeet native to Australia. Some are able to mimic phrases and words, in a harsh voice. Most are gregarious and pair for life. The female lays up to twelve eggs in holes in trees or rocks or on the ground. Some parrots live as long as 60 years.

Parsec. The unit of distance most used in technical ◊ *astronomy*; the distance from the earth or a star whose mean annual ◊ *parallax* is one second of arc, i.e. the distance at which the mean radius of the earth's orbit would subtend an angle of one second. It is equal to 3.258 light-years (19 million million miles).

Parsifal (Percival). In ◊ *Arthurian legend*, the pure knight to whom the ◊ *Holy Grail* was revealed; the hero of Wolfram von Eschenbach's *Parzifal* and of Wagner's music drama *Parsifal*.

Parsnip. Root used for culinary purposes, developed from the wild *Pastinaca sativa*, a biennial native to Britain, S. and Central Europe to the Caucasus. Cultivated since Roman times, it is less used since the introduction of the potato, to which it is, however, superior in nutritive value.

Parthenogenesis. Type of asexual ◊ *reproduction*, occurring in the female sexual organs of potentially bisexual animals; common in some organisms e.g. ◊ *aphids* where several summer generations may be produced from unfertilized eggs, males not appearing until autumn, when sexual reproduction ensues. ◊ *Bees* have both parthenogenetic and fully sexual (biparental) reproduction, males being produced from unfertilized and females from ferti-lized eggs.

Parthenon ◊ *Athens.*

Parthians. Semi-nomadic people of the ancient world, famous as horsemen and archers, who occupied a country S E of the Caspian Sea in the 3rd cent. B.C. About 250 B.C. Arsaces won Parthian indepen-dence from the Seleucid Empire and founded the Parthian Empire, which rapidly extended its power until it occu-pied all of modern Iran and Iraq and most of Afghanistan. Mithridates I (about 170-138 B.C.) established the capital at Ctesi-phon. Parthians annihilated a Roman army at Carrhae in 53 B.C. and threatened the Roman power in Syria and Asia Minor, but they were defeated by Ven-tidius in 39-38 B.C. Thereafter the empire declined, finally succumbing in A.D. 224 to the revolt of Ardashir, who founded the Persian Sassanian Empire.

Particle Accelerator. Machines of various types used in nuclear research to produce beams of highly accelerated charged particles, usually ◊ *electrons* or ◊ *protons* needed to penetrate the ◊ *nucleus* of ◊ *atoms* to explore their structure. An early simple type is the ◊ *cyclotron*; more powerful is the linear accelerator, a tube-like structure designed so that the effective electric field down the tube progressively increases the velocity of the particles. ◊◊ *Subatomic Particles.*

Partition. The solving, usually temporary, of political problems or rivalries by the division of a country into two or more parts under distinct suzerainties. It has almost invariably resulted in continuing friction. ◊◊ *India, Ireland, Palestine, Poland.*

Partnership. The carrying-on of business by persons in common with a view to profit; unlike a company, a partnership acquires no rights or liabilities apart from the assets and liabilities of its members, and liability for partnership debts is not limited (as it is with companies). There may, however, be a 'limited partnership' consisting of at least one general partner whose liability is unlimited, and one or more limited partners who take no part in the management and whose liability is limited to their agreed contribution. A limited partnership must be registered as such with the Registrar of Companies.

Partridge. Medium-sized lowland ◊ *game* bird, related to the ◊ *pheasant*; the Euro-pean grey partridge, whilst able to fly rapidly for short distances (when the quick beat of its wings is very audible), usually runs swiftly along the ground in cover. It conceals its nest in hedges or growing corn. In Britain partridge shooting is legal from 1 Sept. to 1 Feb.

Passchendaele (1917) ◊ *Ypres.*

Passive Resistance. The refusal to obey laws or orders issued by a recognized authority; a considered act of defiance made by an individual or a community, which may have a constructive purpose or be a demonstration of protest, and may vary from deliberate negligence in the per-formance of duties to an absolute refusal to be bound by the regulations in question. ◊ *Civil Disobedience, Conscientious Ob-jectors.*

Passover. Jewish eight-day festival in the month Nisan (March-April) in com-memoration of the exodus of Israel from Egypt; marked by abstention from the use of leavened bread, and by a special domestic religious service, Seder, including a ritual meal. ◊◊ *Judaism.*

Pasteurization ◊ *Milk.*

Pastiche. Originally, a literary or artistic composition 'pasted up' from the work of various authors or artists or from differ-ent parts of given works; now commonly an imitation (usually satirical, ◊ *Burl-esque, Parody*) of the style of a particular author or school.

Patent. The exclusive right to use an in-vention, granted only for inventions re-lating to methods of manufacturing; anyone interested may oppose the grant of a patent on the grounds e.g. that the applicant is not the inventor. Infringement of a patent is a ◊ *tort*; the parties may by agreement refer a dispute to the comp-troller of the Patent Office, who may award damages normally of up to £1000. Or the plaintiff may seek damages before a court.

Pathology. Study of the changes occurring in the structure of the body as the result of disease. Tissues taken from the body at operation are examined microscopically, to determine the nature and extent of any disease present and provide information for further treatment. Post-mortem ex-aminations provide material for the study of disease processes in general and oppor-tunities for the assessment of any treat-ment the patient may have received; the medico-legal post-mortem enables the naturalness or otherwise of death to be determined, and provides evidence to assist the course of justice.

Patriarchy ◊ *Clan, Kinship.*

Patriliny ◊ *Kinship.*

Pavia. 1525. Town on the River Po in N. Italy where the Emperor Charles V beat Francis I of ◊ *France*, who was captured and for nearly two years imprisoned at Madrid. The crushing defeat of France altered the balance of power in W. Europe and consolidated Spain's supremacy in papal politics, which further stimulated the ◊ *Reformation* movement in England and the Netherlands. ◊ *Papal States.*

Pavlovianism ◊ *Conditioning, Psychology.*

PAYE ◊ *Income Tax.*

Payroll Tax ◊ *Income Tax.*

Pea. *Pisum sativum*, of the ◊ *Leguminosae*; an important vegetable. Members of this family were probably eaten in very early times, but the green pea approximating to that of today does not appear to have been in cultivation prior to the late 17th cent. ◊ *Sweet Pea.*

Peanuts. Groundnuts, monkey-nuts; a plant of the tropics and subtropics, one of the ◊ *legumes*, genus *Arachis*, of S. American origin, and a very valuable crop in suitable soil and climatic conditions, yielding a 'nut' with a high oil and protein content. The 'nut' is the seed, which is unusual in that after flowering the fertilized ovary bends down and enters the soil beside the plant, where the seed ripens in a rough-coated pod. A 'Groundnut Scheme' was sponsored by the British Government to introduce large-scale production in W. Africa, but the conditions of the area were unsuitable and the scheme failed.

Pear ◊ *Fruit.*

Pearl Harbor. 1941. Attack by the Japanese navy on the U.S. naval base at Pearl Harbor on 7 Dec. without any declaration of war. Midget submarines and carrier-borne aircraft inflicted heavy damage on the U.S. fleet and air force, which were taken completely by surprise; General Short and Admiral Kimmel were accused of dereliction of duty but were absolved. The Japanese attack was followed by a declaration of war on America by both Italy and Germany; U.S.A. was thus brought into the ◊ *Second World War.*

Pearls ◊ *Oyster.*

Peasants Revolt. 1381. Precipitated by resistance to the poll tax, but the deeper causes were longstanding grievances against the enforcement of villeinage (◊ *Feudalism*), exacerbated by the reduction in population caused by the ◊ *Black Death.* The rebels (mainly from East Anglia and Kent) marched on London, where they burned public buildings and broke open prisons. At Mile End their leader Wat Tyler persuaded the boy King Richard II to promise the abolition of villeinage; later (after several public officials had been killed) Tyler again met the King at Smithfield, where he was killed by the Lord Mayor of London. Richard managed to restrain Tyler's followers until the Lord Mayor returned with strong forces and dispersed them. The rebels were pursued and punished with great severity.

Peasants War. 1524–6. Widespread rising of peasants in Germany and Austria against their feudal overlords (often prince-bishops), whose exactions increased as their position decayed with the rise of the commercial classes and the ◊ *Reformation.* The rebels had expected support from Luther, but he violently denounced the rising and encouraged its ruthless suppression. As a result of its failure and that of the 'new Zion' of the ◊ *anabaptists* seven years later at ◊ *Münster*, serfdom and ◊ *feudalism* were prolonged in the German and Austrian lands until the time of the ◊ *French Revolution.*

Peat. Plant remains, less compressed than ◊ *coal.* Can be used as a fuel (e.g. in Ireland) and also for horticultural purposes. FENLAND PEAT: Similar, but formed from different plants and not so acid in chemical reaction.

◊ *Coal Measures.*

Pectins. A class of polysaccharide ◊ *carbohydrates* occurring esp. in fruit juices; in water they form a thick viscous solution, which jells by the action of acid and thus helps in the setting of ◊ *jams* etc. The structure is similar to that of ◊ *starch* or ◊ *cellulose* (i.e. from the union of sugar units), but the units forming the pectin ◊ *polymer* are of a sugar acid.

Pediment. The stone triangular member about the ◊ *entablature* which fills in and supports the gable-end of a classical building; the centre-piece is often filled with sculpture, as on the Parthenon. Also, loosely, any roof-end whether triangular, broken, or semi-circular; and any similar feature over a door or window or other opening. ◊ *Architectural Orders*.

Pegasus. In Greek legend, the winged horse springing from the blood of the ◊ *Gorgon* Medusa when ◊ *Perseus* killed her; the mount of Bellerophon, who killed the ◊ *Chimaera*, tried to fly Pegasus to heaven, and was unseated at the fountain of Hippocrene (dedicated to the ◊ *Muses*) on Mt Helicon, where Pegasus stamped when stung by a gadfly sent by ◊ *Zeus*.

Pelagianism. Christian heresy named after a Welsh or Breton monk Pelagius, about A.D. 400, who denied original sin, taught that baptism was therefore unnecessary for its removal but was merely a sign of union with Christ, and maintained that believers could live a life of perfect holiness without the aid of supernatural grace. His teachings, stoutly opposed esp. by St Augustine, were condemned at the General Council of Ephesus A.D. 431.

Pelican. Large white water-bird related to the cormorant, widely found in tropical and sub-tropical regions; it feeds on fish, which it stores in a large skin pouch, a downward extension of its bill. The N. American species has a wing spread of 8–10 ft.

Pellagra. Disease endemic among people whose diet is deficient in vitamin B_2 as a result of depending on maize as a staple article of food; it causes loss of weight, muscular weakness, dermatitis developing into atrophy of the skin, and psychological symptoms e.g. depression, irritability, and sometimes insanity. The remedy is to restore vitamin deficiency.

Peloponnesian War. 431–404 B.C. Conflict between the Greek states, recorded by Thucydides; ◊ *Athens* was the more powerful at sea, while ◊ *Sparta* and the Boeotian Confederation were predominant on land; the initiative frequently alternated, and the fighting ranged as far afield as Syracuse. Finally the destruction of her fleet at ◊ *Aegospotami* compelled Athens to surrender. The war left ineradicable hostilities between Greek states, and marked the end of the political hegemony of Athens, though it helped to stimulate her intellectual development.

Pelops. In Greek legend, ruler of Pisa in Elis; son of ◊ *Tantalus*, who boiled him for a banquet to the gods, most of whom recognized and refused the dish; ◊ *Demeter* inadvertently ate a shoulder; ◊ *Hermes* re-boiled what remained, restoring Pelops to life, and Demeter gave him an ivory shoulder. Later Pelops gained Hippodamia in marriage by winning a chariot race with the help of Myrtilus, her father's charioteer; but instead of paying Myrtilus the promised reward, he murdered him. This drew down on him and his line the curse pursuing his sons Atreus and Thyestes and his grandsons Menelaus (◊ *Helen*) and ◊ *Agamemnon*, which was eventually expiated by his great-grandson ◊ *Orestes*. The Peloponnese (S. Greece) is said to be named after Pelops.

Pelota. A game of Basque origin popular in Spain and S. France played with a hard rubber ball about 2 in. in diameter covered with goatskin; known in Central America as 'J'ai Alai' and played by professionals as a spectacle there and in U.S.A. and S. France. Two or four people play, each wearing a *cesta*, a long curved wicker basket attached to the arm; the ball is caught in this and thrown forward (often at nearly 150 m.p.h.) against the front wall of a court 176 ft long by 55 ft wide. As in all other court games, the object is to make it impossible for the opponent to return the ball.

Penal Laws. Legislation of Henry VIII and Elizabeth I harshly discriminating against Roman Catholics, who were e.g. forbidden to own property of more than minimal value, to enter any university or learned profession, to take any part in local or national government, to travel more than five miles without permits; failure to attend Anglican church service was punishable by heavy fines (this was directed against ◊ *nonconformists* also), and the celebration of Mass was a capital crime. In practice the penal laws were in general laxly administered except against the nonconformists in England in the ◊ *Restoration* period and esp. against the Roman Catholics in ◊ *Ireland*. ◊ *Catholic Emancipation Act*.

Penelope. In Greek legend the wife of ◊ *Ulysses*; wishing to remain faithful to him during his long absence, she kept her suitors at bay by promising to consider their claims when she had finished her weaving. Each night she unravelled what she had done during the day, so that it lasted till her husband's return; hence 'Penelope's web', a never-ending task.

Penguin. Swimming and diving bird, which lost the power of flight early in its evolution; on land, penguins sit upright on large webbed feet and waddle across the ice, but they swim excellently, their rigid wings being entirely modified for swimming. They feed on fish and breed in immense rookeries, the King Penguin in the depth of winter so that the young may be fully fledged by the next winter. They are found only in the S. hemisphere, from the Antarctic to the Galapagos Islands.

Penicillin. Substances produced by certain moulds (◊ *Fungi*) of the *Penicillium* group, with a powerful antibacterial effect (◊ *Antibiotics*) and low toxicity to man, effective against many infections (though not all). Organisms naturally sensitive to penicillin, if they encounter it in treatment, may develop resistant strains. The penicillins and their antibiotic effect were recognized by Sir Alexander Fleming in 1929; a culture of staphylococcus contaminated by spores of *P. notatum* showed areas in which the staphylococci had been killed. Subsequent research became an item of Anglo-American collaboration during the Second World War. Mould strains giving the antibiotic in the best yield, and nutrients for growth, were selected, and the antibiotic was isolated from the liquid in which the mould had grown, without destroying the rather sensitive penicillin molecule; hence the chemical structure of the penicillins was deduced. A purely chemical synthesis, since achieved, does not yet offer a useful method of preparation. The chemical structure of early penicillin strains was unstable; the development of a penicillin sufficiently stable to be effective when taken by mouth was a great practical advance.

Peninsular War. 1808–14. Napoleon's 'running sore' or 'Spanish ulcer'. During the ◊ *Napoleonic Wars* Britain's naval supremacy (◊ *Trafalgar*) enabled her to send support (via Portugal) for the resistance of ◊ *Spain* to French occupation. By skilful use of prepared lines at Torres Vedras, Wellesley (later the Duke of Wellington) kept superior French forces at bay during 1810, and then advanced and captured the key fortresses of Ciudad Rodrigo and Badajoz. The French were unable to overcome the Spanish guerrillas and also concentrate against the British, whose naval blockade denied supplies to the French except overland. At Talavera, Salamanca, and ◊ *Vitoria* the British defeated the hitherto invincible French; the Peninsular campaign had already been carried into France itself when Napoleon abdicated after Leipzig.

Penology ◊ *Criminology.*

Pentagon. A five-sided building on the outskirts of Washington housing the U.S.A. Department of Defence; hence U.S. defence officials.

Pentameter. A five-foot line, usually iambic (◊ *Metre*); since the 16th cent. the form predominant in English poetry (including blank verse and esp. ◊ *sonnets*). ◊ *Rhyme.*

Pentateuch ◊ *Bible.*

Pentathlon. A competition involving five events, in the ancient ◊ *Olympic Games* running, jumping, javelin, discus, and wrestling. Revived in the 1912 Olympics, it was superseded by the 10-event ◊ *Decathlon.* The women's Pentathlon, at championship level, comprises 200-metre sprint, 80-metre hurdles, high jump, long jump, and shot-put.

Peony. The herbaceous garden peony (Chinese peony) is descended from *Paeonia lactiflora*, a native of Siberia and Mongolia, perennial, with decorative foliage and large often fragrant flowers (red, pink, or white), developed in China and Japan since the 8th cent. Another group, the tree (Moutan) peonies, are shrubs with very large single or double flowers, in all shades of white, pink, red, crimson, and maroon, originally bred by the Japanese from the wild *P. suffruticosa* of China and Tibet. The roots of *P. officinalis*, of Crete and the Mediterranean, were used in medicine in the 16th and 17th centuries.

Pepper. 1. A ◊ *spice*, chiefly from the dried unripe berries of *Piper nigrum*, of the *Piperaceae*, a tropical Asiatic shrub. Black peppercorns are the whole berries; white peppercorns have been husked. Pepper was highly prized in the Dark and Middle Ages, when it was rare and costly; for instance as the ransom of Rome in the 5th cent. A.D. the ◊ *Huns* demanded pepper rather than gold. It became more available in Europe after the Cape trade routes had been established in the 16th cent.

2. Sweet peppers (capsicums, paprika, pimento); the fruits of *Capsicum annuum* and *C. frutescens*, of the *Solanaceae* (as are cayenne and chillies), native to S. America and introduced to the Old World after the 16th-cent. voyages of discovery.

Pepsin. Protein-splitting digestive ◊ *enzyme* secreted by the mucous membrane of the stomach; it requires an acid environment, provided by hydrochloric acid (◊ *Halogens*) released by specialized cells in the membrane. ◊ *Digestion*.

Perception. In philosophy, theories of perception ◊ *Phenomenalism, Realism*.

Perch. Olive-coloured black-striped bony freshwater fish with bright red pelvic and caudal fins, common in Europe and Britain; it is voracious, feeding on smaller fish and even on its own young.

Perennial. In horticulture, strictly any plant which flowers year after year, including trees and shrubs, but usually restricted to herbaceous perennials, i.e. plants producing new stems each spring from roots which remain alive year after year. Well-known examples are aquilegia, campanula, geum, michaelmas daisy, phlox, peony.

Perfume. Originally the aroma from burning incense; now ◊ *scents* of all kinds. In the past perfumes were made only from ◊ *essential oils* e.g. derived from jasmine, violets, roses, or from animal sources e.g. ◊ *musk*; modern perfumes are either made from relatively rare and costly natural substances or mass-produced from synthetic ingredients. Leading producers of perfume oils are S. France (rose-water, from Grasse), Bulgaria (attar of roses), and the E. Indies.

Perianth ◊ *Flower*.

Periodic Table ◊ *Elements*.

Peritonitis. Inflammation of the peritoneum, the membrane which lines the abdomen and covers the internal organs, usually developing from bacterial infection of one of the organs in the abdomen esp. the appendix. The peritoneum is so extensive and porous that peritonitis causes very severe toxaemia, which may quickly prove fatal; but ◊ *antibiotics* have greatly helped treatment.

Periwinkle. *Vinca*; creeping evergreen shrubs, native of Europe, prized in gardens for providing ground cover, with blue, burgundy, or white single or double flowers; not very free-flowering.

Permanganate of Potash ◊ *Manganese*.

Permian ◊ *Geological Time Scale*.

Permutation. In mathematics, one pattern (among several) of arranging a given number of objects. The digits 1, 2, 3 can be arranged in six possible ways e.g. 1 2 3; 1 3 2; 3 2 1; etc. The total of permutations possible with any stated number (N) of objects is factorial N (written N!), which is obtained by multiplying the number by all the consecutive whole numbers below it down to 1 (e.g. factorial 3 is $3 \times 2 \times 1 = 6$).

COMBINATION: A selection of a given number of different items from a larger specified number (e.g. three teams out of 20) when the order of selection is of no importance. This is given by the formula N! divided by r! multiplied by (N−r)! where N is the larger number and r the number selected from it. In a typical football-pool forecast, where eight draws are to be chosen from about 50 matches, the number of possible combinations (of which only one or a few are winning combinations) is therefore 50! divided by 42! multiplied by 8! i.e. 322,147,190.

Peroxide ◊ *Sodium*.

Perpendicular Style. The last phase of English ◊ *Gothic architecture*, following the ◊ *Early English* and ◊ *Decorated* styles; beginning about 1330, established by about 1360, and persisting until the ◊ *Reformation*; it is characterized by an emphasis on straight verticals and horizontals, by slender vertically subdivided supports and large windows, and by fan vaulting. Most typical is the panel motif i.e. narrow vertical panels used in rows and tiers, in traceries and as blank-wall decoration. The chancel of Gloucester Cathedral, the nave of Canterbury Cathedral, and St George's Chapel at Windsor illustrate the early, middle, and late phases.

Persephone (Proserpina). In Greek and Roman mythology, goddess of spring; daughter of ◊ *Zeus* and ◊ *Demeter*, wife of ◊ *Hades* (Pluto), who while she was gathering flowers carried her off to the underworld. Demeter wandered the earth in search of her, forbidding it to bear crops, and Zeus demanded her release for two thirds of every year. An obvious fertility year myth, the story was probably so interpreted in the annual mysteries and festival in honour of Persephone and Demeter at Eleusis near Athens.

Persepolis. Greek name ('Persian city') for capital of Achaemenian ◊ *Persia*, planned in the 6th cent. B.C. by Darius the Great and continued by later kings. Its spacious halls, with pillars often 60 ft high decorated with rich relief carvings, stand on an enormous man-made platform of limestone; the capitals of the pillars are often in the form of animals standing back to back, a feature unique to this period of architecture. The city was sacked by Alexander in 330 B.C. Its extensive ruins remain impressive.

Perseus. In Greek mythology, son of ◊ *Zeus* and ◊ *Danae*; it was prophesied that Danae's son would kill her father Acrisius, who therefore set her and the child adrift. They were rescued by Polydectes, who later sent Perseus to obtain the head of the ◊ *Gorgon* Medusa; returning, he rescued Andromeda from a sea monster, and married her. The prophecy was fulfilled when he accidentally killed Acrisius with a quoit during athletic games. He is usually represented wearing the winged sandals lent to him by ◊ *Hermes* in order to reach the Gorgons and carrying the shield lent to him by ◊ *Athena* in order to kill Medusa in safety. ◊▷ *Pegasus*.

Persia (Iran). Area 628,000 sq. m. Pop. (1962) about 21 m. Cap. Teheran. Rel. mainly ◊ *Shiah* Muslim. A hereditary monarchy, ruled by the Shah advised by the ◊ *Majlis* (national assembly). The present Shah, Mohammed Reza Pahlevi, has been hampered in his attempts to redistribute land to the peasants by the Majlis, largely composed of landowners.

ECONOMY. Main product ◊ *petroleum*; the oil resources were discovered in the early 20th cent. and developed by the Anglo-Persian (Anglo-Iranian) Oil Co. until 1951, when Prime Minister Mussadiq nationalized the oil industry. The ensuing dispute was settled 1954, when it was agreed the industry be operated by the National Iranian Oil Co. and a Consortium of 17 international oil companies, of which the British Petroleum Co. holds 40 per cent of the shares, the Persian government receiving 50 per cent of the earnings. Despite development plans (financed from oil revenues), some welfare legislation, and the Shah's enlightened leadership, economic and social progress has been slow. Most wealth remains with a small minority, corruption in both central and local government is widespread, and the extensive use of opium

(despite official prohibition) continues a major problem. Much of the country is barren, though irrigation can bring fertility; there is some coal, and Persia produces cotton and is self-supporting in food, but in the absence of land reform most of the rural population have a very low standard of living.

HISTORY. The Medes and Persians broke away from the Assyrian Empire in the 7th cent. B.C. and under Cyrus the Great established a far-reaching empire and founded the Achaemenid dynasty; Darius created a centralized administration with excellent communications, built ◊ *Susa* and ◊ *Persepolis*, adopted the cultures of contiguous empires, and conquered Egypt and NW India. This empire flourished until the 4th cent. B.C. when Alexander the Great destroyed it. Under ◊ *Parthian* rule there was a revival, followed in the 3rd cent. A.D. by the vigorous Sassanian line and a second powerful Persian empire when the splendours of Ctesiphon and Firuzabad outshone Byzantium, art and architecture reached great heights, and administration was good. The Sassanian period ended with the Arab invasions A.D. 641, and ◊ *Islam* replaced the age-old ◊ *Zoroastrianism*; the merging of cultures produced a distinctive style in miniature painting, extremely beautiful carpets, and superb buildings e.g. the Great Mosque of Isfahan. Persia again became an influential well-administered nation under the Safavid dynasty 1499–1736, but after the Afghan invasion 1722 its history was a sequence of varying fortunes and rulers. After the discovery of oil in 1901, Anglo-Russian rivalry persisted until 1907 when by agreement Persia was divided into British and Russian spheres of influence, later abandoned after the ◊ *First World War*. An Army officer, Reza Khan, overthrew the Kajar dynasty in 1921 and became Emperor as Reza Shah Pahlevi; in the ◊ *Second World War* he was suspected of pro-Axis sympathies, and British and Soviet forces occupied Persia, forced his abdication, and replaced him by his son the present Shah.

LANGUAGE. Persian descends from the Iranian branch of ◊ *Indo-European languages*: the sacred books of Zoroaster (about 600 B.C.) are in East Iranian. Pahlevi (late old Persian) was spoken until early Christian times. Modern Persian is a related form modified by the infusion of a rich ◊ *Arabic* vocabulary, written in Arabic script but Indo-European in structure and spirit, the language of present ◊ *Iran* and part of Afghanistan.

Persian Art. A wide term covering the arts of the Iranian plain through six millennia; pottery (◊ *Faience*) was produced in this region in the 5th millennium and coloured pottery in the 4th, followed by terracotta and carved stone statuettes in the 3rd. By about 1500 B.C. the Kassites in Luristan were making exceptionally fine bronze objects, usually incorporating animal forms of great elegance. Under the Sassanids A.D. 226–651 the desire for magnificence increased; hunting motifs esp. that of the emperor overcoming a lion predominate in the decoration of silver and gold wares, pottery, and textiles. Exported from Persia, these influenced ◊ *Byzantine* and Coptic art. Conversion to ◊ *Islam* did not impose a completely Islamic form on Persian art, which continued to portray human and animal figures in ◊ *miniature* paintings of great delicacy, despite the Koranic prohibition.

Personal Income. The wages and salaries, rents, profits (other than capital gains), and transfer payments e.g. pensions, received by individuals. Between 1954 and 1962 the statistical average income in the U.K. rose by some 20 per cent in real terms, i.e. a 60 per cent rise in money terms, modified by a 24 per cent increase in retail prices. The U.K. distribution of income in selected groups is shown below.

Income Group	Number of persons (in m.)	
	1962	1954
£500 or under	9.95	17.23
£500–1000	11.52	7.74
£1000–1500	4.28	.74
£1500–5000	1.23	.49
£5000–and over	.15	.06

The number of persons in the middle-income range (£500–£1500 a year) doubled between 1954 and 1962. Well over half of all incomes were in this bracket in 1962.

Perspective. Any method of representing three-dimensional space on a two-dimensional surface so as to reproduce an onlooker's impression of a scene from a given point; one form of perspective is the mathematical linear perspective which has as its object to bring the points and lines of an object on to the right position on the drawing surface and is a branch of geometry. The other form used in art aims at reproducing the impression of the distance of an object; perspective as used by artists is usually an approximation and may use two or more vanishing points. The use of variations of depth of colour (the darker ones indicating proximity) to simulate distance is known as aerial perspective.

Perspex ◊ *Ketones, Plastics.*

Peru. Area 531,000 sq. m. Pop. 12 m. of which some 12 per cent are of Spanish descent, the remainder mixed or pure Indian. Cap. Lima. Rel. Roman Catholic. A republic on the Pacific seaboard of S. America, with a President, Senate, and Chamber of Deputies all elected for six years by compulsory direct popular vote. After the inconclusive elections of 1962 a military junta deposed the President, but in 1963, after fresh elections, a new President and legislature were returned.

ECONOMY. A mountainous country with limited arable land, there is a generally low standard of living. There are varied mineral resources, worked by foreign companies, of which lead, copper, silver and iron are of most importance. The way of life of the majority of the Indians is little changed since the time of the ◊ *Incas.* Literacy is low except among the townspeople.

HISTORY. Peru, in particular the Cuzco valley, was the cradle of the Inca civilization which was destroyed in the early 16th cent. by the Spanish Conquistador Pizarro. Peru then remained a Spanish colony until the S. American wars of liberation in the 1820s, becoming independent in 1821.

LANGUAGES. Spanish; also Aymara, Quechua.

Pest. In early times, corruption or infection of the air; now any noxious creature, usually an insect. Pests are carriers of animal and plant diseases, e.g. mosquitoes, tsetse flies, aphids, or attack domestic animals, e.g. ox-warble flies, botflies, horseflies; the greatest damage is caused by insect pests attacking growing or harvested crops, e.g. ◊ *locusts,* the ◊ *colorado beetle,* and various ◊ *caterpillars.* Some insect larvae called ◊ *woodworms* feed on wood and often damage timber. Rats and cockroaches are also common pests.

Pesticides. Some natural products (arsenic, derris, nicotine oil, pyrethrum) have long been used in pest control. Recently numerous synthetic products have been introduced (DDT, gammexane, fluoride derivatives, etc.) which are highly efficacious. Some act upon contact; others (the systemic type) are absorbed, and kill by inhibiting the insect's ability to limit its nerve stimuli.

Insecticides have their dangers: in killing indiscriminately they may destroy beneficial insects necessary for flower and fruit-crop pollination, and may kill wild life and even domestic animals. Some insecticides accumulate in soil and tissue. Thus toxic chemicals are being accumulated in animal fat (including human), and the cumulative effect can be a serious hazard. Such accumulation is at the rate of six parts of insecticide per million of fat in America, half that rate in Britain; it represents so serious a hazard that steps are being taken to limit their use. On the other hand, insecticides enable greatly increased crops to be raised, and the adequate nutrition of the exploding world population may be impossible without them.

Petal ◊ *Flower*.

Peterloo Massacre. 1819. The repressively reactionary legislation and prosecutions in Britain after the ◊ *Napoleonic Wars*, coupled with the increasing hardships of the ◊ *Industrial Revolution*, and the ◊ *Corn Laws*, led to widespread protest demonstrations and hunger-marches, demanding redress of grievances and reform of Parliamentary representation. When 60,000 men, women, and children assembled in St Peter's Fields, Manchester, the local magistrates read the ◊ *Riot* Act to a part of the crowd and almost at once called on the militia to disperse the 'rioters'; several were killed and over 600 wounded. The name Peterloo is a bitter echo of ◊ *Waterloo*.

Petit Mal ◊ *Epilepsy*.

Petrel. Small dark wide-ranging ocean bird with a white rump patch; they live and feed over the seas of the world, visiting coasts and islands only to breed. Stormy Petrels, Mother Carey's Chickens, are commonest in the N. Atlantic.

Petrochemical Industry ◊ *Petroleum (Petrochemicals)*.

Petrol Engine ◊ *Internal Combustion Engine*.

Petroleum. Crude inflammable oil known since antiquity, chemically a complex mixture of hydrocarbons (which occur naturally in the form of oil, bitumen, and gas) with small amounts of other substances (nitrogen, oxygen, and sulphur compounds); probably formed by the decomposition of marine organisms buried and compressed under successive layers of sediments on the bed of the sea and transformed by chemical or bacterial action. In course of time oil was squeezed out from the original source-rock into more porous rocks, in some of which (where trapped below impervious layers and no longer able to move) it accumulated. Thus oil accumulations are usually found in porous ◊ *sedimentary rocks* (which can be of very different geological ages) and in traps formed by folds, faults, or the up-dip edges of porous layers which grade into impervious rock. The modern petroleum industry was born 1859 with the systematic drilling for oil in Pennsylvania, U.S.A. In spite of advanced exploration techniques, the location of exploitable oilfields remains a tedious and costly undertaking. Of the known reserves, 23 per cent of the world total are in U.S.A. and the Caribbean area, 62 per cent in the Middle East. 'PROVEN' RESERVES: Oil in already-discovered fields, known to be available by means of existing extraction methods. These have steadily increased as a result of intensive exploration. In m. metric tons: 1935, 3200; 1945, 7000; 1955, 22,000; 1961, 40,000. Even now, extraction techniques recover only about one third of the oil present in the oil reservoirs. Total world production in million metric tons was 490 in 1948, 868 in 1956, and 1173 in 1961; of this last, U.S.A. 408, S. and Central America 181, the Middle East 285. Annual production is now rising most rapidly in the Middle East. The major cost of the final products, about 50–70 per cent, occurs at the exploration, drilling, and production stage: refining and transport each account for about 20 per cent.

NATURAL GAS: The recent discovery of gas e.g. in Italy, the Sahara, Canada has proved a useful addition to the fuel supply and petrochemical requirements.

REFINING: Crude oil is initially refined by fractional distillation, since the various components (or 'fractions') of petroleum have different boiling points and can thus be separated. The first or more volatile products e.g. ◊ *methane*, ethane, propane, butane are gases; the next fraction serves as motor spirit (gasoline) but frequently requires 'up-grading' by various processes to improve its anti-knock quality; the middle distillate range contains ◊ *paraffins* (kerosene), gas-oil, and diesel fuel. The residue may yield heavy fuel-oil, bitumen, and lubricants. The pattern of products produced by distillation may bear little relation to the market needs for motor spirit, fuel-oil, etc. If there is a shortage of light products, 'cracking' (which breaks down the large molecules into small ones) may be applied; a well-known process is catalytic cracking, which mainly produces petrol (gasoline).

About half the refining capacity in the world is still in U.S.A., but there is a growing tendency to refine oil where it is consumed; since 1938 refinery capacity in Europe has increased tenfold, and the manufacture of chemicals from petroleum has grown rapidly into a major industry in U.S.A., Canada, Britain, and several European countries.

PETROCHEMICALS: Various processes applied at the refinery produce light gaseous hydrocarbons as by-products; these gases together with other specific hydrocarbons form the basis upon which a petrochemical industry has been built up, for the production of ◊ *synthetic resins* (◊ *plastics*), synthetic ◊ *rubber*, synthetic fibres (e.g. nylon, Terylene), and the basic constituents of ◊ *detergents*.

OIL INDUSTRY: Comprises a large number of undertakings, but the bulk of the production depends on a small number of large companies performing all functions from exploration to marketing. The Standard Oil Co. of New Jersey is the largest; the Royal Dutch Shell Group, the second largest, is much the most important non-American concern. Capital expenditure in the non-communist countries runs at about £400 m. annually.

TRANSPORT: The needs of the industry have called into being fleets of tankers, whose tonnage amounts to one third of all the world's shipping.

USES: By 1960 oil and natural gas together met 60 per cent (coal 38, hydro-electricity 2) of the power requirements of the non-communist world, and the share of petroleum is increasing. Motor vehicles consume one third of all petroleum fuels, ships and aircraft one eighth; the remainder is used mainly as industrial and domestic fuel. ◊ *Gas Industry, Oil Shales, Seismology*.

Petrology ◊ *Geology*.

Pewter ◊ *Alloys, Lead*.

Phaedra ◊ *Hippolytus, Theseus*.

Phagocyte. ◊ *Cell* with the power to engulf and then digest ◊ *micro-organisms*, ◊ *protozoa*, damaged blood cells, and finely-divided foreign substances, thus playing an important part in healing wounds and destroying infections. Phagocytes may move freely, as in the ◊ *blood*, or may occupy fixed positions in the tissues.

Phalanx. Infantry formation, first used by the Spartans and adopted by all Greek states, in which the soldiers were aligned 8–16 deep, to form a block; used for purely shock tactics in frontal attack. The phalanx of Alexander the Great of ◊ *Macedon* was 16 ranks in depth, armed with 24-ft spears. It remained effective until the Romans found tactics to defeat the Macedonians in 168 B.C.

Pharmacology. The study of the action of drugs on organs and tissues of the body. For centuries remedies were derived chiefly from ◊ *herbs*, though a few were based on minerals such as sulphur and iron. The first synthetic drug was chloral, in 1869, since when there has been a rapid development of synthetic drugs of increasing complexity and diversity of effect. Drugs are usually classified according to the system that they affect or according to the nature of their effect. Synthetic drugs must be rigorously tested before they are released for general use; such testing includes investigation of any side-effects or long-term dangers which may make them unacceptable. Recent experience with thalidomide has shown that the possibility of congenital malformation in offspring must also be tested. Since 1864 the *British Pharmacopoeia*, published by the General Medical Council, makes available authoritative lists and standards for approved drugs, by which pharmacists and doctors are guided.

Pharsalus 48 B.C. The decisive battle of the Roman civil war fought in Epirus between Pompey and Julius Caesar, whose use of highly-trained infantry defeated an army twice the size of his own. Pompey fled to Egypt, where he was assassinated. ◊ *Philippi*.

Pheasant. Large ◊ *game* bird with a long sweeping tail, the female brown but the male gaudily coloured with dark green head; solitary ground birds, feeding on arable land, nesting in a scrape in the ground, and laying 8–15 pale olive-brown eggs. The adults roost in trees, and fly clumsily when disturbed. They are bred specially for sport.

Phenol. A hydroxyl derivative (C_6H_5OH) of ◊ *benzene*; formerly called carbolic acid, for its slightly acidic reaction. It forms crystals somewhat soluble in water, with the characteristic 'carbolic' odour. A disinfectant, it was the surgical ◊ *antiseptic* introduced by Lister in 1867, but is poisonous if taken internally. It is obtained in quantity, in various processes, by chemical treatment of benzene, is consumed in large amounts in the manufacture of phenol ◊ *formaldehyde* and bakelite ◊ *plastics* (◊ *polymers*), and is one starting-point for the making of adipic acid, an intermediate for ◊ *nylon*. Useful derivatives include the chlorophenol antiseptics, the explosive picric acid, and dichlorophenoxyacetic acid, a selective ◊ *weed-killer*. When obtained from coal-tar ◊ *distillation* it is accompanied by cresols, rather stronger disinfectants, which are the basis of creosote.

Phenomenalism. The theory of radical ◊ *empiricism* that human knowledge is limited to or based on our sense impressions, phenomena. It is sometimes claimed, and often denied, that there is an unknowable reality behind phenomena. Recently phenomenalism has been advanced as an account not of all knowledge but of sense-perception: we experience only 'sense data', from which we make up the notion of a physical object.

PHENOMENOLOGY: The detailed description and comparison of mental states and processes e.g. perceiving and believing, considered as 'pure experience', i.e. without reference to their causes or their possible relation to things in the world. Edmund Husserl 1859–1938 founded the phenomenological movement in European philosophy.

Philippi. 42 B.C. The victory of Octavian (the future Emperor Augustus) and Antony over Brutus and Cassius, the murderers of Julius Caesar, in Macedonia; it consolidated the power of the Triumvirate, i.e. Octavian, Antony, and Lepidus. ◊ *Pharsalus, Rome.*

Philippines. Area 114,834 sq. m. Pop. 30.6 m. Cap. Manila. Rel. predominantly Roman Catholic. A group of 11 large and many small islands off S E Asia in the W.

Pacific. A republic since 1946, with a Senate of 24 elected for six years and a four-year-term President and House of Representatives, of 120 maximum.

ECONOMY. Mainly agricultural; chief products coconuts, fruit, hemp, maize, rice, sugar, timber, tobacco. Manufacturing and processing industries are increasing. Literacy is over 75 per cent, education taking 25 per cent of the budget; there are 24 universities, one dating to 1611.

HISTORY. Discovered in 1521 by Magellan, who was killed there; invaded, conquered, and named Filipinas by the Spanish from 1565. Manila was seized by the British in 1762 but restored to Spain in 1764. The 19th cent. brought continual rebellions esp. that of 1898 (just before the ◊ *Spanish-American War*), when the rebels destroyed the Spanish fleet in Manila Bay; U.S. troops defeated the Spanish, and by the Treaty of Paris 1898 the islands were ceded to U.S.A. Two months later an anti-American rebellion broke out and lasted until 1902, after which the U.S. President ruled the islands through an appointed Commission, granting some local autonomy in 1916, a form of 'Commonwealth status' in 1934, and complete independence after the Second World War. ◊ *Pacific War.*

LANGUAGES. Tagalog (Malayan). Also Spanish and English (which is the medium of instruction).

Philosophy. Short definitions – whether those recently fashionable, mentioning 'linguistic analysis', or older generalizations e.g. 'the science of sciences' – do not afford much real light; a clearer notion may be had by considering a few of the central problems of philosophy. Typical western philosophers have not dealt primarily with the very general questions about what attitude to life one ought to take up, although by tradition there is a part of philosophy called ◊ *ethics* devoted to establishing what is the 'good life' and (more often) what moral principles one ought to follow and which of them must be abandoned when they conflict. Kant would have us treat all men as ends and never as means, Bentham would have us seek the greatest happiness of all. Recent ethics has attempted to restrict itself to a morally uncommitted analysis of statements of principle and of particular moral judgements: are these essentially expressions of personal attitudes, and if they are, can any good reasons or arguments be given for them? It has also been concerned with ◊ *free will* (the question of whether men ordinarily choose and decide freely), related as it is to moral responsibility: if my decisions do not result from my character, my desires, or even my whims, are these curious events 'decisions' at all? But if, as it seems, they do so result, are they then determined in advance, and hence unfree? The theory of ◊ *knowledge*, a second part of philosophy, has asked questions of a quite general sort about the origin and extent of human knowledge and the claims of kinds of belief (notably that based on sense experience) to count as knowledge, and has also dealt with a host of more particular problems, as it does today. An empirical proposition, it is said, is true when it corresponds to the facts; but what are 'facts'? Not things, since many facts are in no sense things; but what then? Hence, what of the common theory that truth is correspondence to facts? ◊ *Logic*, whose increasing formalization and technicality make it difficult to express many of its problems in ordinary language, has been concerned with the analysis of types of statements and arguments (originally ◊ *syllogisms*) which it would be self-contradictory to deny, and has also sought to answer general questions about them. We need never see a man, or observe anything whatever, to know that he is not both over and under six feet tall; in virtue of what, exactly, is it true? There is also ◊ *metaphysics*, which has often been less than clear in both its questions and its answers; in its speculative and major part, its commonest assumption is that the universe is in some comforting sense an organized and coherent system, and its commonest question is about the nature of that system. It has also offered answers to questions on ◊ *God* and immortality, and in its critical part has inquired into the basis of human knowledge; what, it has recently been asked, are the necessary conditions of our having a language or conceptual system?

These are some of the problems of philosophy, distributed into its major parts, though the above artificial separation of these parts is misleading, since in fact they have been closely and sometimes inextricably related; questions of what we

can know have been bound up with metaphysical questions of what in fact exists, and conclusions in logic have led to the rejection of ethical views. Nor does philosophy today consist only of these parts. In the past 'philosophy' comprised the whole of human inquiry, including studies now established as separate sciences; today there are the philosophies of science, religion, and history, political philosophy, aesthetics, and an increasing number of still more specialized investigations e.g. the philosophy of mathematics. Perhaps as much as can be said briefly and usefully in general description is that most of the problems of philosophy share the characteristics of being questions neither strictly empirical nor strictly logical, they are not to be settled either by scientific investigation or by the deduction exemplified in logical or mathematical proofs. A first step at least toward their solution (or in some cases their dismissal as unreal or confused problems) seems to be what can be called conceptual analysis: is what we call a 'free' decision an unconstrained one, self-determination? and what do we mean by these suppositions? Such questions and their ramifications – sometimes thought to be peculiar to contemporary 'linguistic philosophy' – have in less explicit ways almost always been fundamental to philosophy.

PHILOSOPHY OF HISTORY: Includes the study of historians' procedures e.g. that they explain past events by showing them to be instances of general laws, perhaps of human nature or economics; and speculation about patterns in history e.g. that it is proceeding towards a classless society (Marx) or that civilizations result from challenge and response (Toynbee).

PHILOSOPHY OF RELIGION: Loosely, quasi-philosophical studies of religion which may also be of a theological, psychological, or anthropological nature; more precisely, it is an uncommitted analytic inquiry into religious concepts and claims, and more recently into the meaningfulness of religious language. ◊ *God, Logical Positivism*.

PHILOSOPHY OF SCIENCE: That part of philosophy concerned with the description and logical justification of scientific methods, e.g. kinds of inductive reasoning, and the analysis of scientific concepts, e.g. scientific law. One general view of method, that of Karl Popper, is that it involves (1) a general hypothesis, comparable to a guess; (2) deductions from the hypothesis, e.g. that certain experiments should have certain results; (3) the experiments, essentially rigorous attempts to prove the hypothesis wrong; (4) rejection of the hypothesis, or its acceptance as corroborated.

Phloem ◊ *Bast.*

Phlogiston. < Gr. *phlogistos*, inflammable; the German chemist G. E. Stahl 1660–1734 propounded the theory (which dominated 18th-cent. chemical thought) that everything combustible must contain an inflammable principle ('phlogiston') which escapes during combustion, leaving ash ('calx'), and therefore that to recombine the 'calx' and the 'phlogiston' would re-create the substance. Phlogiston was believed to pass freely from one body to another and to be the cause of heat and light.

Phlox. Almost exclusively a N. American plant genus; the half-hardy annual *P. drummondii* is the parent of the many coloured garden varieties, and the border phlox has developed from perennials e.g. *P. paniculata* and *P. carolina.*

Phoenicians. Semitic people of the Lebanon coast, organized in city-states e.g. Tyre, Sidon, Byblos about 3000–2000 B.C. now chiefly remembered as skilful navigators and traders and the inventors of the ◊ *alphabet.* In the 12th cent. B.C. with the decline of the power of ◊ *Egypt,* and under pressure from the ◊ *Assyrian* empire in their home territory, they spread their trading and colonizing activities all over the Mediterranean, their most famous outpost being ◊ *Carthage.* Their cities in the E. Mediterranean came within the Empire of ◊ *Persia* in the 6th cent. B.C. but after the battle of Issus in 333 B.C. passed to Alexander the Great of ◊ *Macedon*; after his death, anarchy ensued until Pompey brought the whole of Syria within the dominion of ◊ *Rome.*

Phoenix Park Murders. 1882. On the assassination of two British officials in the grounds of the Viceregal Lodge in Dublin, attempts were made to inculpate the Irish Nationalist Party in the House of Commons and its leader Parnell. ◊> *Home Rule.*

Phonetics. The study, classification, and recording of speech sounds; also, commonly, phonetic transcription. Sounds regarded by the speakers of a given language as separate and distinctive are classed as 'phonemes' and for the purpose of practical phonetic transcription it is thus necessary to have one symbol for each phoneme. The most widely adopted script on this principle is that of the International Phonetic Association, consisting of the Latin alphabet with extra symbols, which can accurately indicate the pronunciation of most living languages and which provides a useful aid in the teaching of foreign languages.

Phosgene ◊ *Carbonyls.*

Phosphorescence. The production of light by many chemical substances after exposure to light energy, esp. to ultraviolet light; e.g. if exposed to daylight for some time calcium sulphide will glow in the dark. The wavelength of the emitted light is different from that of the absorbed light. The name is mistakenly used to describe ◊ *luminescence* of organisms, and the phenomenon should not be confused with ◊ *fluorescence*: substances which fluoresce are luminous only when light falls upon them.

Phosphorus. A non-metallic element with two chief allotropes, white and red; in nature it always occurs combined, mainly as rock phosphate, a crude form of the mineral apatite, chief source of phosphorus and its compounds. Heating apatite with sand and ◊ *coke* in an electric furnace produces white phosphorus, a wax-like solid which glows feebly in air, is very poisonous, and must be kept under water to prevent spontaneous inflammation, since the ignition temperature is low. Phosphorus in the vapour state is tetraatomic; when heated to 270° C in the absence of air, it is converted to the red allotropic form, much more resistant to oxidation, non-poisonous, which can safely be kept in air. Both forms burn and (according to conditions) give phosphoric or phosphorous oxide, each of which dissolves in water to give respectively orthophosphoric or phosphorous acid. Industrially, red phosphorus and the sesquisulphide are used in match-making, and the chlorides are important reagents in organic chemistry. Nearly all the phosphorus now produced is burned to form the oxide for the preparation of phosphoric acid, from which can be prepared a variety of phosphates, used for rustproofing, in the manufacture of foodstuffs (e.g. soft drinks, jellies, cheese, baking-powders), and for water-softening, synthetic ◊ *detergents*, emulsion paints, fireproof materials, fertilizers, etc. Crude rock phosphate treated with 70 per cent sulphuric acid is rendered soluble and thus available as the fertilizer 'superphosphate'.

Photoelectric Effect. The emission of electrons by substances, esp. certain metals e.g. caesium, when exposed to light. Electrons liberated in this way constitute a photoelectric current, which can be utilized in e.g. photoelectric cells, serving various purposes; a common use is as a switch which operates when light falls on it, as in the 'electric eye' devices e.g. burglar alarms, automatic door-openers. ◊ *Quantum Theory*.

Photo-engraving. A technique invented in the 19th cent. which by the relief printing process makes possible the reproduction of drawings, paintings, and photographs. The image is exposed on a sensitized metal plate, and the non-printing areas are made lower than the printing areas by ◊ *etching*. Images containing tonal gradations (e.g. photographs) are divided into a fine pattern of regularly disposed dots, varying in size, by means of a half-tone screen. By using colour filters, separate plates for each of the three primary colours – yellow, red, and blue (to which a black plate is usually added) – can be made, and paintings and colour photographs reproduced by overprinting these in exact register with each other. Various methods of ◊ *electronic* scanning and engraving, which replace the photographic-chemical principle by electronic impulses and mechanical ◊ *engraving*, have recently been perfected; these can also be applied to non-metallic synthetic surfaces. Other methods combining electronics, photography, and chemistry are still at an experimental stage, but may revolutionize present photo-engraving techniques and eventually entirely supersede them. This method is best adapted to the reproduction of illustrations together with letterpress. ◊ *Photogravure*.

Photography. Process of producing pictures by the action of light on a chemically-prepared material; the ◊ *camera obscura* had long shown how a lens could cast an exact image, but it was not till the 18th cent. that attempts were made to register and preserve the image. Though the light-responsive qualities of silver salts

were discovered 1727, progress towards a practical application were slow, and not till Daguerre's experiments in the use of silver iodide deposited on silver-plated copper, about 1830, was a real advance made. Improvement both in the photographic plates and in the camera followed, but the equipment remained cumbersome until Eastman invented the roll film 1884 and in 1888 introduced the Kodak, a simple mass-produced camera which promoted the spread of amateur photography and led to the growth of a vast new industry, which expanded still further with the advent of the ◊ *cinema* and the increasing application of photography to industrial techniques. The photographic process consists in exposing a light-sensitive negative material (now silver bromide colloidally dispersed over gelatin) and developing, fixing, washing and drying the negative from which the final positive print is made.

Colour photography was at first possible only through multiple exposures, each for one colour, but became accessible to amateurs in 1935 when the Eastman Kodak Co. introduced a colour film with layers each sensitized for one of the primary colours but the whole acting as a single unit.

In astronomical photography the ◊ *telescope* itself is used as the camera. Although all star-images appear as points, the brighter stars produce larger images than the fainter ones, as a result of the spreading of light in the emulsion; this 'defect' is used to measure relative star-brightness. The use of coloured filters (photometry) allows the brightness of stars in the light of different wave-length regions to be measured. ◊ *Cinematography*.

Photogravure. An ◊ *intaglio* printing process, made possible by a number of 19th-cent. inventions; the image is exposed on a pigmented, gelatin-coated, sensitized carbon tissue, which is transferred to a copper-surfaced cylinder, and the reversed image is etched into the copper by using a screen which divides it into a number of regularly-disposed cells of varying size and depth, dark areas having large deep cells, light areas small shallow ones. After ink has been applied to the whole surface, the surplus is wiped from it, leaving the cells filled with ink and ready to be pressed on paper or other material. The process is mainly used for large-circulation magazine-printing, but is also capable of high-quality reproduction in art books, on postage stamps, etc. ◊ *Etching, Photoengraving.*

Photons ◊ *Subatomic Particles.*

Photosynthesis. The process by which all green plants (and some bacteria) convert light energy into the chemical energy fundamental to all life, by synthesizing ◊ *sugars* from ◊ *carbon dioxide* and ◊ *water*. It is the opposite process to ◊ *respiration.*

Light energy is absorbed by ◊ *chlorophyll* in plants and used to produce molecules with high potential energy (e.g. adenosine triphosphate) and high reducing power (capacity to give electrons or hydrogen ions, e.g. reduced coenzymes). These are used to convert carbon dioxide into organic carbon compounds (mostly ◊ *carbohydrates*) and eventually into all the other organic materials of plant cells. Many ◊ *enzymes* are involved in these complex processes. The carbon dioxide is absorbed by the plant from its surroundings. Water molecules are also involved chemically, and provide the hydrogen ions required. The surplus oxygen from water is usually given off as a gas. The process of carbohydrate synthesis can be summarized thus:

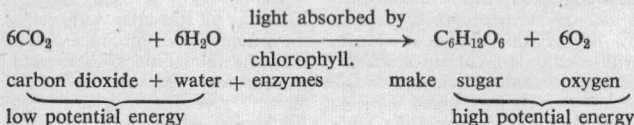

$$6CO_2 + 6H_2O \xrightarrow[\text{chlorophyll.}]{\text{light absorbed by}} C_6H_{12}O_6 + 6O_2$$

$$\underbrace{\text{carbon dioxide} + \text{water} + \text{enzymes}}_{\text{low potential energy}} \quad \text{make} \quad \underbrace{\text{sugar} \qquad \text{oxygen}}_{\text{high potential energy}}$$

Photosynthesis is of supreme importance as the primary synthetic process upon which all living organisms eventually depend. Also, many of the world's sources of energy e.g. coal, oil, gas derive from the photosynthetic products of past geological times.

Phrenology. 'Craniology'; theory popular in the 19th cent. (but now entirely discredited) that the brain consists of various localized organs, corresponding to faculties and propensities of the mind, allegedly indicated by protuberances on the skull. **Phtah** ◊ *Ptah.*

Phylum ◊ *Biological Classification.*

Physics. Once called natural philosophy; the whole range of science dealing with matter and energy and the relationships between them. It embraces mechanics, heat, light, sound, electricity, and magnetism, and nowadays merges with chemistry and mathematics and develops into specialized spheres such as astrophysics, atomic and nuclear physics, and particle physics. Physics endeavours to find a unifying principle to explain all natural phenomena. ◊ *Matter, Quantum Theory, Relativity.*

Physiocrats. A group of French thinkers and publicists of the 18th cent. led by Mercier de la Rivière and Dupont de Nemours, who preached an economic science based upon agriculture in preference to trade, and advocated the simplification of taxation. Believing firmly in the natural virtue and reasonableness of men, they advocated a policy of enlightened self-interest and implied that it was as easy to build institutions as to destroy them. Many prominent men of the period were associated with these ideas, including Turgot and Mirabeau. ◊ *Enlightenment.*

Physiology. The study of processes occurring in living organisms e.g. ◊ *respiration*, ◊ *excretion*, ◊ *metabolism*, etc. Medieval physiology, based on the teachings of Aristotle and Galen and closely bound up with theology, was semi-mystical, regarding the heart, liver, etc. as the 'seats' of the soul and other spirits of the body. Harvey revolutionized the study by his demonstration of the circulation of the blood and the function of the heart, 1628, but physiology was not put on to a truly scientific basis until the 19th cent. when Galvani first demonstrated the effects of electricity on muscle, Magendie established the need to base physiology on experiment rather than speculation, and Claude Bernard discovered most of the essential features of animal metabolism. Since then physiology has developed along specialized lines, the chief of which are biophysics, biochemistry, and physiological neurology, stimulated by developments in other sciences esp. physics and ◊ *electronics.*

Physiotherapy. The use of physical means e.g. exercise, massage, heat, light, electricity in the treatment of disease and the restoration of function after injury; one of the oldest forms of medical treatment, originating in the healing springs near which were built the temples of ◊ *Aesculapius*. Until the 19th cent., physiotherapy was virtually confined to hydrotherapy; later, medical gymnastics were introduced, and discoveries in the physical sciences made possible the therapeutic application of electricity and of radiant energy.

Pianoforte ◊ *Keyboard Instruments*.

Picaresque. A genre of prose ◊ *romance* or ◊ *novel*, consisting of a loosely-organized series of adventures, usually low-life, befalling the main character, a strolling rogue (Sp. *picaro*) with redeeming features; Cervantes' *Don Quixote* and Le Sage's *Gil Blas* are typical examples. In England Smollett's novels e.g. *Roderick Random* are the closest to the picaresque.

Picric Acid ◊ *Phenol*.

Picts. The painted people; tribes of obscure origin who in historic times inhabited parts of Scotland and Ireland; the Romans built Hadrian's Wall as a defence against Pictish incursions from Scotland into England, but after their departure in the 5th cent. A.D. the Picts raided far south; under Kenneth MacAlpin they united with the Scots and the two peoples fused into one.

Pidgin. Pidgin English (Chinese mispronunciation of 'business-English') is a widespread medium of communication along the coast of China and other parts of SW Pacific. The vocabulary is English, but the structure follows Chinese patterns.

Piedmont. Region in NW Italy, ruled by the ◊ *Savoy* dynasty from the 11th cent. although important cities like Turin enjoyed a large measure of independence. It was a major battlefield in the wars of the 16th–18th centuries and was long subject to French influence. By 1748 it had come completely under the rule of the dukes of Savoy, by then kings of Sardinia. It was annexed by France during the Napoleonic wars 1798–1814 (◊ *Marengo*), but by the 1815 settlement it once more became part of ◊ *Sardinia*. In the 19th cent. it was a centre of opposition to Austrian rule in Italy and of the Italian unification movement.

Piers Plowman. A 14th-cent. English poem in alliterative verse, attributed to William Langland; the most substantial piece of Middle English verse outside Chaucer's works. Through the convention of a succession of visions seen in a dream, it alternates religious and moral allegory with social and political satire.

Pietà. Representation of ◊ *Mary* with the body of the dead ◊ *Jesus Christ*, repeating the Madonna and Child image; first found in 14th-cent. German art, esp. sculpture.

Piezoelectricity ◊ *Electricity*.

Pig. Member of the ◊ *swine* family, early domesticated and bred for meat in most countries. In some religions (Islam, Judaism) its flesh is considered 'unclean'. Pigs are omnivorous feeders, and produce large litters. Some are bred for bacon and ham ('baconers') and others for fresh meat ('porkers'). Main exporters of bacon are Canada, Denmark, and Poland. ◊◊ *Swine*.

Pigeon. A world-wide family of strong swift flying birds, which pair for life; two white eggs are laid, in a notoriously flimsy nest, and the young are fed on a milky secretion of the crop. The European wood pigeon destroys large amounts of cultivated vegetables and corn. Pigeons have been domesticated since 3000 B.C. and over 200 strains have been produced, esp. the carrier pigeon, known for its speed and ability to fly long distances.

PIGEON-RACING: A sport pursued in many countries, developed after the telegraph had replaced the pigeon as a message-carrier, in the 1840s; races (which are timed flights to determine highest speed) can range from 50 to 700 m., a normal racing speed being 40 m.p.h. The Confederation of Long-distance Racing Pigeon Unions of Gt Britain and Ireland has some 120,000 members, with 85,000 of them within the National Homing Union (1897).

Pigmentation. In animals often has an attracting or warning or concealing function. In e.g. the ◊ *chameleon* and ◊ *octopus*, which change their colour, the various special cells in the skin (chromatophores) expand or contract to keep the coloration similar to that of their background. In higher animals a black pigment, melanin, occurs in the skin, the retina, and the hair, which protects them from the actinic rays of the sun, the amount of melanin determining the darkness of the skin (◊ *Albino*). Human skin also contains other pigments e.g. oxy-haemoglobin in superficial blood capillaries, responsible for the pinkish tints.

A main function of animal coloration is to provide protection, by resemblance to the normal background: ◊ *camouflage*. It can also serve to advertise the animal in the breeding sason. ◊ *Mimicry*.

Pike. Large voracious bony freshwater fish of Europe, Britain, and N. America, reaching a length of 5 ft and a weight of 50–70 lb. The mouth is very large, with numerous strong sharp teeth; they eat other fish, wildfowl, and small aquatic mammals, their voracity making it rare for more than one adult fish to be found in any one pool or stretch of river. Each pike lays some half million eggs on stream beds, the vast majority being eaten by other fish.

Pilaster. A rectangular column projecting only slightly from a wall and conforming to the design of the ◊ *architectural order* with which it is used; frequently found separating the windows in post-classical Italian buildings and in 17th and 18th cent. English buildings.

Pilgrim Fathers. 1620. A group of puritan objectors in the Church of England who to escape persecution joined with others wishing to settle in N. America, sailed in the *Mayflower*, and founded the Massachusetts Bay Colony; throughout the 17th cent. they were followed by similar groups (esp. after the ◊ *Restoration*) who settled the Atlantic seaboard as 'New England'. ◊ *United States History*.

Pilot. Person with special knowledge of local conditions who steers ships in and out of ports and harbours; on board only in an advisory capacity, the ship's master remaining responsible. Usually self-employed, although licensed by the port authority or by a special pilotage authority (◊ *Trinity House*), but in some countries a government servant. The pilot of an aircraft is in charge at all times; he is licensed by an appropriate national licensing authority.

Piltdown Man. Between 1908 and 1912 an amateur antiquarian, Charles Dawson, found in Piltdown (Sussex) a skull, jaw, and canine tooth thought to be those of an ancestral human type of the Lower Pleistocene (about 500,000 years ago). The reconstructed skull appeared to overthrow all the theories of human evolution held at that time, since it represented a creature with an entirely modern head and a thoroughly ape-like jaw. Some scientists were sceptical, but it was not until 40 years later that fluorine and other tests showed the skull to be not more than 50,000 years old and the jaw that of a modern ape, cunningly faked. The perpetrator of the hoax remains unknown.

Pineapple. *Ananas comosus*; a native of tropical America, introduced into Britain in the early 18th cent. as a decorative plant. It is grown commercially in the Azores and Australia.

Piquet. A card game for two, using 32 cards (ace to seven). Twelve cards are dealt to each player. The non-dealer (minor) may discard up to five cards and take new ones from the eight cards undealt, while the dealer (major) can then change with those still remaining in the pile. The two hands are then compared, and points are given for different combinations e.g. the greatest number in each suit, and for reaching a score of 30 before the opponent has scored (pique). After this, the cards are played (without trumps) in tricks of two, and a bonus is given for winning the last trick. The game dates to the 16th cent. and was given its name in the reign of Charles I.

Piracy. Acts of unlawful violence, detention, or depredation for private ends against shipping on the high seas; also applies to aircraft outside the jurisdiction of their country of origin; in English law, a ◊ *felony* punishable by imprisonment for life. In earlier times certain areas were notorious as pirate haunts. Pompey led an expedition against the Cilician pirates 67 B.C. and for a time freed the Mediterranean from piracy, which had threatened to starve Rome. Later notorious examples were the Barbary corsairs who sallied out from Algiers, Tunis, and Tripoli until the 19th cent. and the English buccaneers who preyed on Spanish shipping in the W. Indies in the 17th and 18th centuries, often with the tacit approval of their government. Piracy continued till recent years in the China Seas.

Pistol ◊ *Firearms*.

Pithecanthropus ◊ *Palaeolithic, Primates*.

Pituitary. Ductless ◊ *gland* in a recess in the sphenoid bone at the base of the brain, to which it is connected by a stalk; the hormones it produces regulate many bodily functions e.g. the growth and development of sexual characteristics.

Placenta. Organ by which, in placental mammals, the embryo is nourished. It is composed of tissue from both mother and embryo and acts as an organ of exchange and as an endocrine gland, producing hormones which adapt the uterus for pregnancy. At birth the umbilical cord joining it to the embryo is broken and it is discharged as the afterbirth.

Plague. Formerly, any widespread pestilence; now specifically infection with the organism *Pasteurella pestis,* which may affect the lungs (pneumonic plague), the lymph glands (bubonic plague), or the body generally (septicaemic plague). The disease is usually transmitted to man from rats by the bite of infected fleas, and was formerly almost invariably fatal; the ▷ *Black Death* wiped out perhaps half the population of Europe in the 14th cent. The Great Plague of London in 1665 was the last serious outbreak in Britain. In that of China in 1894 the plague bacillus was finally isolated; the disease has now been virtually eradicated, by the destruction of rats and by sanitary precautions. Effective treatment can be given by ▷ *antibiotics.*

Plainsong. The ritual chant used by the Roman Catholic Church in its services; the form named Gregorian chant after the 6th-cent. St Gregory (Pope Gregory I) is now considered standard. Melodically complete in itself, it requires no accompaniment; it is irregular in rhythm, and has its own system of notation. ▷ *Psalms.*

Plane-table. A land ▷ *surveying* instrument for precise work e.g. detailed mapping of country between points already fixed by theodolite (▷ *Geodesy*), consisting of a tripod supporting a drawing-table, on which rests an alidade (sighting-instrument).

Planetarium. Complicated instructional device using a great number of lenses to project a representation of the night sky on the inside of a hemispherical dome. Simulated movements of heavenly bodies can be speeded up to show otherwise imperceptible long-period effects e.g. the apparent paths of the planets, the movements of ▷ *stars,* and the changing appearance of the constellations over the centuries.

Planets ▷ *Astrology, Astronomy, Solar System, Star.*

Plankton. Minute floating organisms in fresh and salt water; the food of many marine creatures, esp. such commercially important fish as herrings. The principal fishing grounds of the world are situated on the continental shelf, where plankton abound. In winter months the planktonic animals and plants are relatively scarce, but a great increase occurs in the spring.

PHYTOPLANKTON: Of plant origin.

ZOOPLANKTON: Of animal origin.

Plantagenets. 1154–1485. The English ruling house, a branch of the Angevin dynasty, from Henry II to Richard III. Until the deposition of Richard II in 1399 the family's succession was direct; thereafter the crown passed to other branches of the family (▷ *Wars of the Roses*) until the defeat of Yorkist-Plantagenet Richard III by the remotely Plantagenet Henry Tudor. Thanks to Henry's marriage to the Yorkist heiress Elizabeth Plantagenet, the Tudor dynasty claimed direct succession, but various Yorkist-Plantagenet descendants e.g. the Poles and Courtenays continued to make claims until the mid 16th cent.

Plants. A wide range of organisms; most live by ▷ *photosynthesis,* but a few are ▷ *parasites* or ▷ *saprophytes* e.g. fungi. The most complex plants have roots, stems, and ▷ *leaves;* but the most primitive, with features in common with primitive animals, are aquatic, and many are only a single ▷ *cell,* which swims by fine threads called flagellae. Unlike animal cells, a plant cell has a more or less rigid wall round it, basically made of ▷ *cellulose* but often impregnated with ▷ *lignin* (as in ▷ *wood*) or waxes (as in ▷ *cork*). Plants continue to grow in size throughout their life, i.e. open growth, in contrast with the closed growth of animals. The plant kingdom is broadly divided into the following groups.

THALLOPHYTA: Algae, fungi, lichens, slimes, moulds, bacteria. The most primitive plants and primarily aquatic. They are unicellular, or multicellular as fine threads e.g. fungi or a flat thallus e.g. seaweeds, and reproduce by various types of ▷ *spore.*

BRYOPHYTA: Mosses and liverworts; the simplest land plants, small, with no vascular tissue, reproducing by spores. Most are found in moist places, but many can survive extreme desiccation.

TRACHEOPHYTA: With specialized conducting and supporting vascular tissue, in two groups. 1. *Pteridophyta:* Include ▷ *ferns,* ▷ *horsetails,* and many genera only known as ▷ *fossils;* they reproduce by spores, and formed the dominant vegetation during the Carboniferous period: much of our coal derives from them. 2. *Spermophyta:* Seed-bearing plants with roots, stems, and leaves, the simplest being the ◊ *gymnosperms* e.g. ◊ *conifers,* cycads, yew, and most complex the ◊ *angiosperms,* flowering plants with seeds enclosed within ◊ *fruits.* ◊◊ *Flower, Leaf.*

Plasma ◊ *Blood.*

Plassey. 1757. Victory in Bengal of the British under Clive, defeating Suraj-ud Dowlah, during the ◊ *Seven Years War,* by which Britain gained Bengal and ensured British supremacy in ◊ *India.* ◊◊ *Black Hole of Calcutta.*

Plastics. Natural or synthetic organic materials which can be moulded; now usually those ◊ *polymers* which are neither elastomers nor fibres. Plastics are mainly of two types: the thermoplastic soften on warming and harden on cooling (processes indefinitely repeatable); the thermosetting gradually harden when moulded, become rigid on cooling, and thereafter cannot be softened again by heating. The earliest synthetic plastic, celluloid (originally 'xylonite'), produced in 1855, was very inflammable. In 1894 the safer non-inflammable cellulose acetate was produced; casein-type plastics followed in 1897; and 10 years later Bakelite was produced from formaldehyde and ◊ *phenol.* Bakelite was dark brown, but a similar type made from formaldehyde and ◊ *urea,* first seen at the Wembley Exhibition of 1926, enabled bright colours to be used. Another important development of the 1920s was the introduction of injection moulding. In the 1930s appeared polystyrene, polyvinyl chloride (PVC), polymethyl methacrylate, polyethylene (polythene), and nylon; and since the 1940s the polyurethanes, the exceedingly useful polyethylene terephthalate (Terylene), and polypropylene have been added. CASEIN PLASTICS: Casein is a ◊ *protein* substance derived from skimmed milk; plastic made from it is used in the manufacture of e.g. buckles and buttons, and as a fibre it can be blended with cotton, wool, or rayon. CELLULOSE ACETATE: Used in ◊ *lacquers* and for wrapping materials, safety cinematograph film, and sound-recording tape. CELLULOSE NITRATE: Celluloid; despite its great inflammability, it is still used

in lacquers and for buttons, ping-pong balls, pen and pencil barrels, etc. NYLON: One of the most important plastics. As a fibre it is extensively used in textile fabrics and stockings. It has a far greater tensile strength than cotton or silk, and is widely used for bristles, parachutes, ropes, and motor tyres. As a solid it can be used for bearings and small structural parts which are impervious to corrosion. POLYETHYLENE: Polythene; much used for containers, bottles, stoppers, pipes and tubing, chemical apparatus, insulators, and protective sheeting. POLYETHYLENE TEREPHTHALATE: Terylene; much used as a clothing and upholstery-fabric material. POLYMETHYL METHACRYLATE: Transparent, thermoplastic; used as an alternative to glass e.g. perspex, plexiglas. Such products are less brittle but more easily scratched than glass, and are used for e.g. spectacle lenses, magnifying glasses, and for insulators, combs, and dentures. POLYPROPYLENE: Similar to polyethylene; less waxy, harder, and not so easily scratched. POLYSTYRENE: Transparent, thermoplastic; used as 'unbreakable glass', as an insulator, and in the manufacture of flooring, casters, and artificial leather. POLYURETHANES: Used in adhesives, and for giving highly polished insulating coatings to wire etc. Often used in the form of foam e.g. for cushioning and carpet underlays. POLYVINYL CHLORIDE (PVC): Hard, non-inflammable; and used for bristles, pipes and tubing, and to coat fabrics and sheath electric wiring (for which in domestic use it has displaced lead). PHENOL-FORMALDEHYDE RESINS: Usually moulded from powder, e.g. Bakelite (see above); used for many small castings and in varnishes, adhesives, packing materials, and for reinforcing rubber. UREA-FORMALDEHYDE RESINS: Also moulded from powder, into a colourless 'glass' which if required can be coloured with added pigments, used for e.g. tumblers, dishes, bathroom fittings, containers, adhesives.
    ◊ *Acetylene.*

Plataea. 479 B.C. Victory on the frontiers of Attica by which, with that of ◊ *Salamis,* the Athenians and Spartans under

Pausanias saved ◊ *Greece* from invasion by ◊ *Persia*.

Platinum Metals. Two trios of metallic ◊ *elements*: (a) ruthenium, rhodium, palladium; (b) osmium, iridium, platinum. With iron, cobalt, and nickel they make up Group VIII of the Periodic Classification. They all belong to the Transition Series and show characteristic properties of variable valency, catalytic power, etc. Their melting points are all above 1550° C, and they are very heavy – the first three a little denser than lead, the other three almost twice as dense. They usually occur in nature in the same ore; the complex copper ores of Sudbury, Ontario, are a valuable source. Though scarce and expensive they have valuable uses.

OSMIUM: The densest of all metals; very hard. Alloyed with IRIDIUM ('osmiridium') it is used for the tips of gold pen-nibs.

PALLADIUM: Similar to platinum but lighter in weight; used in the manufacture of jewellery, dental plates, and electrical contacts; also used as a ◊ *catalyst* because it readily adsorbs ◊ *hydrogen*.

PLATINUM: The most important. Very resistant to both acids and alkalis; used in chemical apparatus, spinnerets, resistance thermometers, thermocouples, as an industrial catalyst, and for jewellery.

RHODIUM: Can be electroplated on small expensive articles e.g. jewellery, or deposited on a glass or metal base to make mirrors; used as wire in thermocouples.

RUTHENIUM: Mainly used as a hardening additive for platinum or palladium.

Platonism. The philosophy of Plato, influenced by Socrates, presented in dialogue form; among the greatest of intellectual achievements, it includes the first outstanding characteristically philosophical analyses of many problems. It is best known for its doctrine of Ideas, developed most fully in the 'parable of the cave' in Plato's *Republic*, which may be said to have its origin in the notion that there is some one thing, e.g. Justice, in virtue of which many things of a particular kind, e.g. just actions, are alike. The Ideas are said to have some kind of objective reality – they are in fact more real than the physical world – and to be changeless and eternal. True knowledge, as distinct from mere opinions based on sense experience of the changing world (which imperfectly reflects the Ideas and even owes its existence to them), is to be had by intellectual acquaintance with the Ideas themselves. Philosophy is the study of the Ideas; hence, since acquaintance with them, esp. the Idea of the Good, is essential to the best government, philosophers would be the rulers of an ideal republic. ◊ *Neoplatonism*.

Playing-cards. There is no evidence of four-suited packs of playing cards prior to their appearance in Italy about A.D. 1320. The earliest packs had up to 78 cards, of which 56 were numerical and 22 were Tarot (emblematic, representing such things as the Wheel of Fortune and Temperance, and probably used first for fortune-telling) and were known as 'attutti', trumps, having a higher value than the others. From Italy playing cards spread to Spain, Germany, and France, and each country evolved typical designs which have remained substantially unchanged. The French simplified the symbols and the forms of the 'pips' and produced the present hearts, spades, diamonds, and clubs: this type, introduced into England about 1400, was copied by English makers and with slight modifications became the design now current. In 1463 imports of foreign cards into England were prohibited and card playing forbidden except to the nobility or at Christmas. By the end of the 16th cent. card playing was general, however, and in 1628 the Worshipful Company of Makers of Playing Cards was founded. The pack was not standardized at 52 cards until ◊ *whist* became widely popular, and only after 1870 did the double-headed court card with corner indices become general. The pack now consists of four suits of 13 cards numbered one to ten, and three court cards, King, Queen, and Knave. An extra card or 'Joker' is often used in gambling games.

Pléiade. Group of seven 16th-cent. French poets, of whom the best-known are Ronsard and Du Bellay, whose purpose was to use the French language, not Latin, and to establish for it a literature comparable with that of the classics. They adopted classical and Italian verse forms, esp. the ◊ *sonnet*.

Pleiades. Cluster of ◊ *stars* in Taurus (named the Seven Sisters, after the daughters of ◊ *Atlas* and Pleione), of which six are clearly visible to the naked eye. Long-exposure photographs show light reflected from clouds of dust and gas among the stars.

Pleistocene Epoch. < Gr. *pleistos,* most, *kainos,* recent; the opening of the Quaternary Period (the last million years of the ◊ *Geological Time Scale*), the main feature of which was the great ◊ *Ice Age.* Although the shortest, this Epoch is the most important, covering the formation of the present landscapes and the development of early man. ◊ *Neanderthal Man.*

Pleurisy. Inflammation of the pleura, membranes covering the lungs and chest, which often follows lung infections esp. tuberculosis and may also be associated with pneumonia. In the early stages breathing is painful, and friction between the inflamed surfaces can be heard by stethoscope; later the space between the pleural layers becomes filled with a fluid which masks pain and friction.

Plimsoll Line. 1876. The load-line painted on the side of all ships, to indicate the maximum draft (depth in the water) to which the vessel may be laden. Named after Samuel Plimsoll M.P. who after a long struggle secured the passing of the law enforcing it; previously, overloading had frequently led to the loss of ships with all hands. Equivalent legislation has since been introduced by all maritime countries.

Plough. Tool whose basic function is to break up the soil and expose it to the disintegrating activity of weather e.g. rain, frost, sun; originally simply a large forked stick dragged through the soil by men or later by animals, first used in Europe and Asia in the Bronze Age and unknown elsewhere until introduced by settlers. The modern plough consists of a coulter (a knife-like front blade), a ploughshare, and a mould board (for turning over the soil); it had evolved into substantially its present form by the early 19th cent. Through most of history the plough has been drawn by oxen, which were displaced by horses in some countries; today there is an increasing use of tractor-drawn ploughs, particularly in the U.K. and U.S.A.

Plover. A boldly patterned comparatively short-billed wading bird with various habitats; several varieties including lapwing, oystercatcher, grey plover, and golden plover breed inland on heaths and ◊ *tundra,* to which they return each year from the mud-flats and marshes, where they have gathered in flocks to feed on worms and small arthropods and molluscs. **Plum** ◊ *Fruit.*

Pluralism. 1. Any doctrine that the universe, or some part of it, is made up of a variety of substances or kinds of thing. ◊ *Dualism, Monism.* **2.** The holding of two or more profitable public offices or sinecures, esp. church appointments e.g. bishoprics and deaneries, historically a source of great public discontent against e.g. Cardinal Wolsey and other early 16th-cent. prelates, and various bishops and office-holders under the Stewart kings.

Pluto. 1. Planet ninth from the sun, with no known satellites, discovered photographically in 1930; because of its smallness and remoteness from the earth it can be seen only in a large ◊ *telescope* and even so without surface details. Regular changes in brightness revealed by photometry indicate a rotation period of six and a half days. ◊ *Solar System.* **2.** In mythology: ◊ *Hades.*

Plutonic. < Gr. Pluto, god of the underworld; ◊ *igneous rocks,* e.g. granite (which have a coarse crystalline structure from having cooled slowly within the earth's crust); also various deep-seated phenomena e.g. earthquakes (◊ *Seismology*).

Plutonium. ◊ *Actinides*; a soft grey metallic ◊ *element,* with a number of isotopes, all radioactive; discovered in 1940 and now made in quantity in nuclear reactors, from ◊ *uranium*-238. The plutonium isotope 239 is separated from unconverted uranium and fission products by chemical processes, which usually involve solvent extraction. It is used for certain nuclear reactors, and as the explosive in nuclear devices, in place of uranium-235: both suffer spontaneous fission, with the release of ◊ *energy* when the amount of the element reaches the critical mass. In smaller masses plutonium releases energy continuously, and is perceptibly warm when a piece is felt through a polythene bag; it is one of the most dangerous poisons, because of its alpha radioactivity and because it remains a long time in the bone after assimilation. Plutonium and uranium are technically the most important members of the actinide series.

Plymouth Brethren. Protestant Christian body founded about 1830 by J. N. Darby and others, called by themselves simply

'Brethren'; have no Church organization or formal ministry, but meet weekly in 'rooms' to celebrate the Lord's Supper (◊ *Holy Communion*). They practise adult ◊ *baptism*, are Fundamentalist (upholding the literal inerrancy of the Bible), and endeavour to withdraw as completely as possible from ordinary life; the stricter Brethren such as those known as 'Exclusive' will not even eat with non-members. They have undergone a succession of schisms, but are said to number about 80,000 in Gt Britain.

Pneumatic Appliances. Equipment which requires a source of compressed air for motive power, e.g. drills, rams, and other portable tools used on building sites. Pneumatic tools are also frequently used in mines, as the used air does not contaminate the atmosphere; they are frequently based on the piston-and-cylinder principle. Others are driven by small air ◊ *turbines*.

Pneumonia. Inflammation of the spongy tissue of the lungs, blocking the air spaces, which may be caused by various agents including viruses.

BRONCHO-PNEUMONIA: Esp. common as a complication of infectious disease e.g. influenza; also often results from chronic heart and kidney diseases.

LOBAR PNEUMONIA: Usually due to infection by one specific ◊ *micro-organism* (the pneumococcus).

Poet Laureate. From the Greek and Roman custom of crowning poets with laurel (bays); in Britain, the court poet, with the duty of writing verses e.g. for coronations, royal birthdays, etc. In the early 17th cent. Samuel Daniel, Ben Jonson, William Davenant, and John Denham were all more or less loosely described as 'poet laureate'; in 1668 the title was officially given to Dryden (shortly to be satirized by Buckingham as 'Mr Bays'). On the death of Tennyson 1892 the laureateship was unprecedentedly refused by William Morris. Since 1930 the Poet Laureate has been John Masefield, b. 1878.

Poetry. No single definition suffices; there are e.g. *The art of patterned language*; *Emotion put into measure*; *Language that implies more than it states*; *Emotion recollected in tranquillity*; etc. Poetry generally represents imaginative speech in its greatest concentration, from the use of 'overtones' and emotional connotations, multiple meanings, puns, ambiguities, ironies, metaphor, simile, imagery, the evocation of sense-impression by allusion, the stressing of words by ◊ *metre* or ◊ *rhyme*, alliteration or assonance, the emotive, musical, or kinesthetic effects of sound, etc. Poetry need not rhyme, but it differs from prose in having stricter forms, deliberate arrangements of recurrent rhythmical units, greater concentration, and more imaginative subject-matter and treatment, though many of these qualities are of course found in 'creative' and rhetorical prose also; the boundary between poetry and prose is far from rigid, the distinctions often being mainly formal.

High claims have been made for the poet and for poetry. The ancient view of the poet as a sacred priest or divinely inspired singer (◊ *Bard*), and of the poetic process as a state of possession or enthusiasm akin to madness, has perhaps its most eloquent expression in Shelley's *Defence of Poetry* 1821. Wordsworth, on the other hand, believed in inspiration but saw the poet as 'a man speaking to men'; he insisted that poetry should be written in 'a selection of the language really used by men'. Different ages have disagreed as to how far conscious judgement is employed in poetic composition or the imagination is paramount; the idea of poets as dreamers out of touch with 'reality' applies to few if any of the great poets, who have usually been men of unusual perception, expressing their own responsiveness and that of their times in language not vague but precise. ◊ *Elegy, Epic, Lyric, Ode, Sonnet*, etc.

Poinsettia ◊ *Euphorbiaceae*.

Point-Four Programme. 1949. U.S. programme for technical and financial aid to underdeveloped areas, based on the fourth point made during President Truman's inauguration address. It was subsequently absorbed into the U.S. foreign aid programmes.

Pointillisme. A technical development of ◊ *Impressionism* practised by Georges Seurat and others, based on the theory that juxtaposed dots of primary colours e.g. blue, yellow give an effect of brighter secondary colours e.g. green than is produced by mixing on the palette. The effectiveness of the technique depends on the size of the dots and how far from the canvas the spectator stands.

Poison. Certain chemical substances which, in certain dosages, have harmful or fatal effects upon organisms; some substances, e.g. quinine, become poisonous only when taken in large doses. Poisons are classified as corrosive, irritant, or systemic. Treatment is generally by the use of antidotes, where known, or of emetics (in the case of systemic poisons) or demulcents e.g. raw egg, in the case of corrosive poisons. ◊ *Lead, Pesticides, Snake.*

Poison Gas ◊ *Chemical Warfare.*

Poison Ivy. *Rhus toxicodendron*; a N. American semi-woody herb or shrub with three-lobed leaves. Some people are very sensitive to contact with it, which may cause extensive rashes and blisters similar to nettle stings but more persistent.

Poitiers. 1356. English victory during the ◊ *Hundred Years War*; Edward the Black Prince defeated and captured John II of France and his son Philip of Burgundy, and England exacted a huge ransom and in 1360 dictated the Treaty of Brétigny, confirming all her claims to e.g. Calais, ◊ *Gascony*, Poitou, etc. Most of the lands were, however, reconquered by the French by 1373. ◊◊ *Bannockburn.*

Poker. A card game for two to seven players, using a full pack of cards, in which all suits rank equally, the ace is the highest card (except in a straight 5-4-3-2-A), and the twos are often jokers; it dates to the 16th cent. In 17th-cent. England brag was played, and a similar game in Germany, from which came the French *poque*; this reached French America at the beginning of the 19th cent. and developed into its modern form, which reached England in 1871.

DRAW POKER: Five cards are dealt singly face down to each player, who puts up the same amount of money as the others. Each person can change up to four cards on his turn, and must then equal the bet of the first player, or go higher, if he wishes to remain in the game. The winner is the one who has the best hand of various established combinations of cards or who can bluff the others into thinking that he has so that they withdraw.

STUD POKER: One card is dealt face down and the other four face up.

Poland. Area 121,000 sq. m. Pop. 31 m. Cap. Warsaw. Rel. about 85 per cent Roman Catholic. Independent state, the Polish People's Republic, lying between U.S.S.R. and Germany. Under the 1952 Constitution supreme power is vested in the Sejm (the historic Parliament), elected by universal adult suffrage for a four-year term, which forms a 31-man Council of Ministers and elects five others to form the State Council (the supreme governing body and collective head of state). In the 1961 election the National Front (mainly the socialist-communist Polish United Workers Party, but also the Peasant Party and the Democratic Party) gained 98 per cent of the poll, though power rests largely with the political bureau of the P.U.W.P.

ECONOMY. Since the ◊ *Second World War* there has been considerable industrial development. Main industries and services have all been nationalized, but 86 per cent of the agricultural land is farmed by peasants on a cooperative basis (collectivization having been ended 1956 by the Gomulka administration); Poland was the only communist country with over-plan agricultural output 1962. The combined port of Gdańsk-Gdynia-Sopot has become a large ship-handling and ship-building centre. Huge deposits of ◊ *sulphur* have recently been discovered, and the return of the western provinces has given Poland large coal reserves and a considerable iron and steel industry.

HISTORY. In the Middle Ages Poland was a strong independent kingdom, of varying frontiers, which acquired most of Galicia and at one time the Ukraine. The 15th–16th centuries were Poland's golden age, with territories from the Black Sea to the Baltic and intellectual vitality which produced e.g. Copernicus. In the 17th cent. the state was weakened by external pressure from ◊ *Russia* and ◊ *Turkey* and internal rivalries; despite the liberation of Vienna from the Turks in 1683 by the Polish king Jan Sobieski, Poland declined, until by three successive partitions she was swallowed up by Russia, Austria, and Prussia. For 125 years Poland ceased to exist as a state, but triple foreign rule did not suppress national sentiment. After the ◊ *First World War*, Poland was re-established as a sovereign state in 1919, but the provinces of Pomorze and Mazuria (as E. Prussia) and Silesia were left in German hands. Poland had access to the sea only by the ◊ *Polish Corridor*, where the new port of Gdynia was built; Gdańsk (Danzig) was made an International Zone, and reclaimed by Germany on the rise of ◊ *Nazism*. The Second World War began by Germany's invasion of Poland 1939; Soviet forces occupied E. Poland and German the rest of the country. When Germany attacked U.S.S.R. all Poland was German-occupied. In 1943 the German forces sealed off and wiped out the Warsaw Ghetto, with all its inhabitants. After the rising in Warsaw (1944), doomed when the Soviet army did not rally to its help, the Germans systematically destroyed Warsaw. In 1945 the Soviet Army drove out the Germans and a left-wing provisional government was set up. By the ◊ *Potsdam Conference* Poland gave up part of E. Poland to U.S.S.R. and received previously German territories (◊ *Oder-Neisse Line*), in return. The 1947 elections gave the Stalinist-controlled 'Democratic Bloc' a majority, and in 1948 Poland became virtually a single-party state. However, on the eve of the 1956 revolt in ◊ *Hungary* the anti-Stalinist wing of the Party took command, releasing from prison both their leader Gomulka and the Primate, Cardinal Wyczinski. 'Destalinization' has been more thorough in Poland than elsewhere in the Soviet bloc: the economy shows great vigour, the standard of living has improved, and State and Church have established a *modus vivendi* (◊ *Concordat*). ◊◊ *Rapacki Plan*. LANGUAGE. Though a ◊ *Slavonic language*, Polish uses the Latin alphabet (without q), which has insufficient symbols to represent all the phonemes (◊ *Phonetics*), and thus requires various accents to modify both consonants and vowels. It is a highly inflected language (seven cases in nouns and adjectives, three genders of adjectives and pronouns, several tenses and aspects of verbs), with more Latin and French borrowings than other Slavonic languages.

Polarization. The restriction of light or other electromagnetic waves to one plane. Normally light-waves vibrate in all directions at right angles to the direction in which the light is travelling. When light is polarized, e.g. by passing through certain kinds of crystal such as Iceland spar, the waves vibrate in one plane only, owing to a process known as double refraction, in which the crystal splits the light ray into two parts.

Polaroid. A material for polarizing light,

cheaper than the Nicol prism, prepared by distributing oriented crystals of iodoquinine sulphate over a ◊ *plastic* e.g. polyvinyl alcohol; can be used to prevent glare e.g. in spectacles and car windscreens.

Polder. In the Netherlands, land reclaimed from the sea by first enclosing it with dikes and then draining it. Polder soil is extremely fertile, the country's richest agricultural land. By far the greatest scheme is the Zuider Zee land reclamation (begun 1924, main dam completed 1932); eventually there will be four large polders covering about 820 sq. m.

Pole. 1. In geography, the N. and S. ends of the earth's axis of rotation. ◊◊ *Antarctica, Arctic.*

2. In ◊ *magnetism*, the points near the ends of a magnet which are the apparent sources of the magnetic field. The poles of the earth, regarded as a huge magnet, do not coincide with the geographic poles, and the angular deviation of a ◊ *compass* needle from the true N/S at any point is called the ◊ *declination*. The pole of a magnet is termed N. or S. according to which of the earth's poles attracts it.

Police. Civil force for maintaining public order and preventing ◊ *crime*. In England in early times resort was had to 'hue and cry' (the pursuit of a suspect by calling upon all able-bodied men to assist), and in Tudor times the ◊ *sheriff* was responsible for order, with the help of constables and the watch; but it was not till Sir Robert Peel, in 1829, introduced an organized and uniformed body of men that a police force in the modern sense was created. In Britain the police are organized on a local basis, under the supervision of the Home Secretary in England and Wales and the Secretary of State in Scotland (though the creation of a centralized police force has been discussed). There are about 125 separate forces, the largest being the Metropolitan Police, which covers an area centred on Westminster with a radius of about 15 m. and has headquarters at New Scotland Yard, under the command of the Commissioner of Police; the City of London, however, has its own police force. In the rest of the country the counties (and in some cases the boroughs) maintain their own police forces. There are some 80,000 regular police in Britain;

members of the police force may not belong to a trade union. Obstructing a police officer in the execution of his duty is a misdemeanour, punishable at law. A police officer is entitled without a warrant to arrest a person reasonably suspected of a ◊ *felony*, if one has in fact been committed, or on a reasonable charge of felony even though it is later shown that no felony had been committed; on the other hand, a police officer is personally answerable at law for wrongful acts, must rely upon his own discretion and knowledge of the law in the discharge of his duties, and cannot act arbitrarily with impunity as the agent of the police authority (◊ *Judges Rules*). Chief constables are now vicariously liable for the torts of constables under their command. In most European countries police organization is much more centralized, but in U.S.A. the police are on a very local basis and there is no federal police force (but ◊ *Federal Bureau of Investigation*). The 1961 Royal Commission on the Police recommended the retention of independent police forces in the U.K. and suggested only minor changes at Scotland Yard. ◊◊ *Secret Police*.

Poliomyelitis. In its acute form, an infection of the ◊ *central nervous system* caused by a virus, of which there are three epidemic strains. The incubation period is usually 10–14 days, with a brief attack of fever followed by a latent period of 2–3 days during which the patient feels well, then there is a recurrence of symptoms, with muscular pain followed by varying degrees of paralysis. In many cases only the pre-paralytic stage occurs and the disease passes unrecognized. Formerly confined to children, the infection now chiefly affects adolescents and adults, but its incidence and mortality have greatly declined since immunization by vaccine became possible. ◊◊ *Salk's Vaccine*.

Polish Corridor. 1919–39. When the Polish state was re-created after the First World War (◊ *Versailles Treaty*) the historically disputed and ethnographically confused Baltic coastlands were allotted so that most of the province of Pomerania (Polish Pomorze) remained in German hands as E. Prussia, thus cutting Poland off from the Baltic to which she was given limited access, however, by a corridor about 10 m. broad and 100 m. long, over

which the Germans had frontierless transit; in it lay the Port of Dańzig (Gdansk), which was made an International Free City. Its citizens were largely German, and it became a centre of Nazi agitation. The Germans precipitated war in 1939 by the seizure of Danzig.

Pollen. Male ◊ *spores* (microspores) of seed plants. Pollen grains vary from 10 to 150 μ (microns) in diameter: most are about 20–30. Pollen-grain walls are very resistant to decay and are found preserved in peats and lake bottoms. The technique of extracting, identifying, and counting the pollen grains in these permits the reconstruction of vegetation which existed in the past. Pollen in deposits as old as 300 m. years has been analysed, but the technique is most commonly used for the more recent Quaternary deposits, up to 1 m. years old.

POLLINATION: The transfer of the pollen to the female organs (stigma in ◊ *angiosperms*, ovule in ◊ *gymnosperms*) by wind, insects, or water. Some flowers are highly specialized to attract insect pollination, by their structure, colour, or ◊ *nectar*, or all three. Those pollinated by wind are usually simpler and inconspicuous e.g. ◊ *catkins*. In many flowers the ovules ('embryo seeds') are fertilized by their own pollen. Bees and wind also carry the pollen of one flower to different ones but unless the two are closely related no fertilization results. If they are, cross-fertilization occurs and a ◊ *hybrid* will result. Cross-fertilization has long been used by man to develop crops, plants, and flowers with special characteristics.

Pollution. Two forms are serious consequences of modern industrial and domestic practice.

AIR POLLUTION: The incomplete combustion of fuels in homes, factories, and vehicle engines causes permanent pollution of the atmosphere in thickly populated and industrial areas, and periodic spectacular phenomena, e.g. the British 'smog' 1952, 1955, 1962, and similar 'smog' endemically in Los Angeles. In Britain the Smoke Abatement Act and smoke-free zones have brought some improvement, but progress is delayed by the reluctance of some local authorities to enforce the Act; such measures reduce the air's smoke content, but no means has yet been found of reducing the ◊ *sulphur* dioxide.

WATER POLLUTION: The discharge of industrial wastes pollutes rivers; local authorities may make controlling regulations. The discharge of waste oil and the cleaning of oil tankers pollutes the sea, damaging fisheries and fouling beaches; by international agreement, the discharge of oil in coastal waters is prohibited. ◊ *Fallout*.

Pollux ◊ *Castor and Pollux*.

Polo. A four-a-side sport in which mounted players propel a wooden ball with long-handled clubs towards opposing goals, the players individually (and therefore teams collectively) having handicaps of from -1 to $+10$ offset against the number of goals scored. The pitch is usually 300 by 200 yds. The modern game began in India 1853 and soon spread to England, but has been curtailed in the past 50 years by the rising costs of keeping ponies. The leading polo countries are now U.S.A. and Argentina.

Polonium. A metallic ◊ *element*, resembling both ◊ *tellurium* and ◊ *bismuth*, discovered by Pierre and Marie Curie in 1898; the first of the radioactive elements. It occurs in nature in minute amounts, but is now made in nuclear reactors by the neutron irradiation of bismuth; the longest-lived ◊ *isotope* has a half-life of only 138 days.

Poltava. 1709. Battle in which Peter I of Russia completely routed Charles XII of Sweden and the Cossack forces of Mazeppa; decisive in the Northern War for Baltic supremacy, 1700–21.

Polyandry ◊ *Polygamy*.

Polyanthus ◊ *Primrose*.

Polygamy. Various forms of plural marriage. When a man has several wives at the same time, polygyny; when a woman has several husbands, polyandry. Polygyny is common in many parts of the world and is permitted by many religions, but in any particular society most marriages are monogamous, since the numerical balance of the sexes is about equal and economic circumstances also operate to restrain polygyny, the encouragement of which sometimes sprang from particular historic or economic causes, as in Islam or Mormonism, and with changed circumstances has often become inoperative. The ◊ *Australian aborigines* practise various forms of polygyny, in which a man may have primary and secondary wives, the latter being also the primary wives of other men; these forms of marriage are all formally instituted and subject to strict rules of ◊ *exogamy*. Polyandry is rare and found mainly in parts of India, Assam, and Tibet; often a woman must marry only brothers (adelphic polyandry). The hypothetical 'group-marriage' so loved by Victorian and marxist ethnologists, conjectured to have been the earliest form of human marriage, has never been reliably reported from any part of the world.

Polymers. Compounds consisting of large ◊ *molecules* (macromolecules) formed from the union of two or more simple molecules of a single compound (addition polymer) or different compounds (condensation polymer). The polymerization process is theoretically capable of proceeding indefinitely, and the product always has regularly recurring structural units (groups of atoms). Thus, under pressure and with the help of a ◊ *catalyst*, ethylene C_2H_4 will form an addition polymer $(C_2H_4)_n$ known as 'polythene', of molecular weight up to 40,000. There are many natural polymers e.g. ◊ *cellulose*, but a large number are synthetic products. Polymers are of three main types: (a) elastomers e.g. rubber, with special elastic properties, (b) ◊ *plastics*, and (c) fibres e.g. silk.

Polynesians. The people of the Pacific from New Zealand to Easter Island, including the ◊ *Maori*, Hawaiians, Tongans, Samoans, Tahitians, and Marquesans. Traditionally, all had sacred chiefs or kings and elaborate systems of ranking, but outside Tonga the native rulers have either lost all power or no longer exist. The Polynesians lacked iron, but their culture was very elaborate; many of the islands have the remains of large stone buildings and monuments (the most famous being those of Easter Island). Polynesian origins and migrations have been subjects of much argument, but there is little doubt that they came from SE Asia and migrated eastwards; theories of an American origin, though energetically canvassed, are not seriously held by ethnologists. Almost all the Polynesian peoples have suffered disastrous depopulation since contact with Whites, by war, western diseases, or 'blackbirding' (slave-trading).

Polyphemus ◊ *Cyclopes*.

Polypropylene, Polystyrene ◊ *Plastics*.

Polytechnic. The original École Polytechnique, created during the ◊ *French Revolution* to prepare engineers and technicians of all kinds, was intended not as a specialized but as a general institute of technology (as it still remains); modern polytechnics at the highest level include e.g. the Massachusetts Institute of Technology, the Zurich Polytechnic, and many German Technische Hochschulen. In Britain the Polytechnic Institution in Regent Street, built originally to house an exhibition, was turned in 1882 into a technical-training ◊ *college* and recreational centre for young men and women (it subsequently developed into a leading centre for higher education); similar colleges were established in the 20th cent. by local education authorities and voluntary bodies to provide a wide variety of vocational and general courses. Many of those in London tend to specialize e.g. in domestic science, engineering, architecture; some prepare students for degree examinations. In communist countries 'polytechnization' means the educational theory that labour and study, action and theory, production and science should all be closely interconnected, and that schools should be inspired by the community's productive life rather than the traditions of the past. ◊ *Education.*

Polythene, Polyvinyl ◊ *Plastics.*

Pompeii. Ancient city near Naples at the foot of Mt Vesuvius; originally an Italian settlement, it came under Greek influence and was later occupied by Samnites. In the 1st cent. B.C. its inhabitants were made citizens of ◊ *Rome* and it became a flourishing city, but in A.D. 63 it was partly destroyed by an earthquake, and in A.D. 79 it was totally buried by an eruption of the ◊ *volcano*. The buried city was not rediscovered until 1748, when the buildings and decorations were found preserved with remarkable completeness.

Pontoon (Vingt-et-Un, Blackjack). A card game for 2–12 players, one holding the bank and dealing, played in 15th-cent. France and now the only card game of most American gambling houses. A player with a count of 21 in two or more cards wins (aces counting one or 11 and face cards 10). Special bonuses are given for ace and face (or 10), a 'natural', and for some other combinations. The bank deals one card to each player, who places his bet and receives one card more, and one or more cards to any player asking for them, in turn. Any player having a count of more than 21 automatically loses; a tie is a win for the bank. A winner by a 'natural' usually takes over the bank.

Poor Law. From 1601, the 'old poor law' recognized the need for relief to be paid to the poor, and made this a charge upon parish rates; the parish councils were also responsible for providing the able-bodied with work. A person without resources was entitled to relief only in his or her parish of origin. In the late 18th and early 19th cent. the 'Speenhamland system' of paying 'outdoor relief' as a supplement to low wages became prevalent; though in the short run this alleviated immediate hardship, it ultimately pauperized and demoralized the working class and absolved employers from paying a living wage. The Poor Law Amendment Act of 1834 put an end to 'outdoor relief', making the poor the responsibility of elected local boards subject to strong centralized control; the workhouse system, by which minimal shelter in return for compulsory unpaid work was provided, was reorganized and extended. After much protest against 'workhouse imprisonment', in 1871 the Local Government Board assumed control of the Poor Law Commissioners; increasingly, responsibility for the poor and the unemployed became a government concern, and Labour Exchanges were established in 1909. The 1911 National Insurance Act provided for contributory insurance against loss of work and for payments during unemployment; the Ministry of Labour was set up in 1916 and the National Assistance Board soon after. By the National Assistance Act of 1948 (◊ *Welfare State*) the state service of financial assistance according to need was unified and centralized under the Ministry of Pensions and National Insurance.

Pope. To the ◊ *Roman Catholic Church*, the successor of St Peter as the Vicar of Christ; elected by the College of ◊ *Cardinals*, he holds office till death, as Bishop of ◊ *Rome*, ruler of the ◊ *Vatican*, and patriarch of the Western church (apart from the Eastern Orthodox and the various Protestant churches). Since the Middle Ages every Pope (except the Dutchman Adrian VI, 1522–3) has been Italian; the present Pope – Paul VI, elected 1963 – is the 264th. The General Council of 1870 made papal infallibility a dogma by declaring any pronouncement on faith and morals made by a Pope *ex cathedra* (from his throne, i.e. by virtue of his office) to be infallible and therefore binding upon all Roman Catholics. ◊ *Old Catholics, Papal States, Reformation, Trent (Council of)*.

Pope's Line. 1494. After the discovery of the New World in 1492, Alexander VI (the Borgia Pope) proclaimed that all new lands subsequently to be discovered were to belong either to Spain or to Portugal, W. and E. respectively of a geographic demarcation line; by this Portugal gained ◊ *Brazil*. Other maritime nations esp. England, and later the Netherlands, strongly objected to the ruling, which proved a contributory factor in the rise of ◊ *Protestantism*.

Popish Plot. 1678–80. On the dissolution of the Cavalier Parliament (◊ *Restoration*), the new ◊ *Whig* Parliament drafted the ◊ *Exclusion Bill* to ensure a Protestant succession, in the midst of a spate of reports of plots to murder the King and Ministers. Many Roman Catholics were accused, fined, and imprisoned; some were executed esp. Jesuit priests, including the Queen's secretary. Of those executed, a few were proved agents of the ◊ *Counter-Reformation*, but there is no evidence of any murder plot. Many of the accused were wholly innocent.

Poplar. *Populus*, of the *Salicaceae*; a small genus of N. temperate shrubs and trees, with broad-stalked leaves and wind-pollinated hanging ◊ *catkins*. The leaf stalk is flattened, esp. in the aspen, *P. tremula*, and the leaves tremble readily; the seeds are enveloped in silky hairs, and some have resinous buds, esp. the balsam poplar, *P. balsamifera*, while *P. alba* and *P. nigra* give timber e.g. for chip baskets. The Lombardy poplar, *P. italica*, is easily recognized by its upright branches and tall narrow shape.

Poppy. Gĕnus *Papaver*, of several varieties mostly native in the Old World, with ephemeral brilliant flowers. The red or corn poppy grows widely in Europe and Asia; the oriental varieties include the opium poppy, *P. somniferum*, from the pod of which is extracted a milky juice which is the source of opium and contains the narcotics ◊ *morphine* and codeine. Opium-smoking originated in the Near East and was introduced to India by the Muslim conquest and carried to China (◊ *Opium Wars*). Addiction is still widespread in China, India, and Iran, in spite of legislation to check the habit and stamp out trade in the drug.

Popular Front. Name given to coalition governments which included all parties – from communist to centre – opposed to Fascism. Léon Blum in France formed the first such government in 1936: it continued in different forms till 1938. It broke up under Daladier after the ◊ *Munich Pact* which the Communists rejected. A similar coalition was the Spanish United Front Government. ◊ *Spanish Civil War*.

Population. The present world population is estimated at about 2500 m. It had increased from 1000 m. in 1850 and 1500 m. in 1900. If the present rate of increase continues it is expected to reach 3800 m. in 1975 and 6267 m. in 2000, the population of Asia accounting for well over half of both figures. A rapid increase in the population of Europe began in the 17th cent. with advances in medicine, sanitation, and technology; between 1650 and 1900 the population of Europe quadrupled (100 m. to 400 m.). From about 1900 the birthrate in Europe fell markedly, and the present rapid increase is mainly in the underdeveloped countries of Asia, Africa, and Latin America.

Porcelain. A translucent ◊ *ceramic* substance harder than earthenware (◊ *Pottery*), made from ◊ *kaolin* mixed with a pulverized ◊ *felspar* rock and set by baking at about 1450° C; invented in China and used there for decorative and household ware by the 8th cent. A.D. but not made in Japan till the 16th. In the Chinese T'ang and Sung dynasties very fine wares were produced, notably those with grey or green celadon glazes. Ming porcelain was of still finer texture, often elaborately decorated in blue on white or in gay enamel colours; porcelain figures appeared in the late Ming period esp. in Tê-Hua, where potters specialized in white statuettes of Kuan Yin and other deities. The production of such figures (in Europe called *blanc de Chine*) was greatly increased in the 17th–18th centuries; 'soft-paste' porcelain, a European imitation, was made in Italy and France before the secret of true 'hard-paste' porcelain was discovered at Dresden in 1708. The first

European porcelain factory was established in 1710 at Meissen near Dresden, and before the end of the 18th cent. there were factories in every European country; apart from Meissen (where Kändler was chief modeller) the most important was at Nymphenburg, where the other great modeller Bustelli worked; in Italy the Ginori factory at Florence and the Capodimonte factory at Naples produced fine porcelain. Until the mid 18th cent. the French continued to make 'soft-paste' porcelain, at Chantilly, Mennecy, and Vincennes, but later the royal Sèvres factory produced Europe's most exquisite 'hard-paste' porcelain. 'Soft-paste' production was maintained also in England, esp. at Bow, Chelsea, Derby, Worcester, and the Wedgwood factory in Staffordshire. ⟡ *China, Faience.*

Porcupine. Rodents, widely distributed, with coats bearing long spines which lie rearwards. They scamper backwards on their enemies and can seriously injure them with their spines, esp. if these are left to fester in the wound.

Porpoise. *Phocaena*; an aquatic mammal about five ft long, related to ⟡ *whales* and ⟡ *dolphins*; like dolphins, they have a pair of chest fins, a shark-like back fin, and a propulsive horizontally-arranged tail fin (unlike fish, whose tail-fin is vertical). They feed on small fish e.g. herring and mackerel, and their meat was eaten in England during the Tudor period.

Port. 1. A fortified wine about 20 per cent alcohol and 6–10 per cent sugar, developed over 300 years ago by British wine merchants settled in Oporto, and (like sherry) popular mainly in English-speaking countries; strictly, wines from the Douro valley in Portugal. The grapes (mainly red) are picked and trodden on the same day, to extract the maximum colour, a feature of port. While fermenting, the wine is mixed with grape brandy to stop the fermentation; the wine thus retains much natural sweetness. Vintage port can be made only in good years; 'from the wood' is blended port either ruby or tawny (left longer in barrel); 'white' ports have been developed and are used mainly as aperitifs. In Britain only wines from Portugal may be described as port; others (e.g. S. African, Australian) must be called 'port-style' or 'port-type'.

2. ⟡ *Docks and Harbours.*

Port of London. The tidal part of the Thames, 69 m. from the sea to Teddington, containing the London, St Katharine, Surrey Commercial, West India, Millwall, East India, Royal Victoria, Royal Albert, King George V, and Tilbury dock systems; under the 1908 Act, administered by the Port of London Authority (PLA), with 28 members (18 elected, 10 appointed), which also controls the Thames Conservancy Board.

Portraiture. The art of painting or carving human likenesses was practised in Egypt in the 3rd millennium B.C. The earliest Greek portrait statues and busts (as distinct from ideal representations) are chiefly from the 4th cent B.C. and numerous portraits were produced in the Hellenistic era, but it was left to the Romans to bring the art of portrait sculpture to its first peak of excellence on coins as well as in statues and busts. Byzantine portraits tend to be less lifelike and increasingly symbolic, and the medieval church (with its emphasis on the transience of individual personality) discouraged portrait likenesses, but portraiture returned in the ⟡ *Renaissance*, when individuality once more became an ideal. The earliest portraits of note are medals by Pisanello; later in the 16th and 17th centuries painted and sculptured portraits were produced throughout Europe, notably by Hilliard (⟡ *Miniatures*), Holbein, Rembrandt, Van Dyke, Velasquez (⟡ *Dutch Art, Flemish Art*), and Lely. The 18th cent. produced flattering society portraits by Reynolds and Gainsborough and the more realistic work of the Scot Raeburn and the American Benjamin West. In the 20th cent. 'lifelike' portraiture has become largely an art of the academies, except e.g. Augustus John and Epstein; major artists e.g. Picasso and Modigliani have used sitters chiefly as starting-points for works of ⟡ *cubism* or ⟡ *expressionism.*

Portugal. Area 34,500 sq. m. Pop. 9 m. Cap. Lisbon. Rel. preponderantly Roman Catholic. Since 1933 a ⟡ *corporative state* (Nova Estado) with an elected President, a single chamber of 120 members, having very limited powers, and a 'Corporative Chamber' of representatives of industry and local authorities. The 'oversea provinces' (fifth largest external possessions in the world) include: Madeira, the Azores, and Cape Verde Islands; Macao in China; and Portuguese Guinea, Angola, Mozambique in Africa.

(Goa was regained by India in 1962.) The standard of living is low and illiteracy high. Natural resources are scanty, though timber (◊ *Cork*), wine (◊ *Port*), sardines, and some scarce minerals (◊ *Wolfram*) are exported; the 'oversea provinces' contribute substantially towards the balance of payments. Colonial policy is assimilation with metropolitan Portugal, but progress has been exceedingly slow; there have been protests, with inconclusive rebellions, against conditions in Angola, Mozambique, and Portuguese Guinea.

HISTORY. Portugal is called 'England's oldest ally', the connexion dating to the Middle Ages and ◊ *Plantagenet* marriages. Portuguese power began to grow under John I in the 14th cent. and became extensive in the 15th as a result of the discoveries by the explorers sent out by Prince Henry the Navigator. Díaz rounded the Cape of Good Hope in 1488, da Gama reached India in 1498, and under the ◊ *Pope's Line* decision Portugal received ◊ *Brazil*. After the mid 16th cent. Portugal's power declined, and she lost much of her empire to the Dutch; Brazil became independent in 1822. Internally Portugal entered upon a period of unrest and instability. In 1910 the King was forced to abdicate, but the republic did not flourish; since 1932 Dr Salazar (previously Finance Minister) has been P.M. and virtually dictator. Portugal remained neutral in the ◊ *Second World War*, but is a member of the ◊ *North Atlantic Treaty Organization*.

LANGUAGE. One of the ◊ *Romance languages*, Portuguese is spoken by about 100 m. people; its vocabulary has been enriched by Arabic, French, and Spanish, and it has a rich and varied literature. By mutual agreement between Portugal and Brazil, the spelling was reformed in 1943.

Portuguese Art and Architecture. Though influenced by those of Spain (◊ *Spanish Architecture, Spanish Art*), the arts of ◊ *Portugal* have always preserved a certain independence. The reign of Manuel I, 1495–1521, a period of great prosperity and confidence, produced the exuberant Manueline architectural style (Boytac and the de Arrudas), showing the influence of Portugal's contacts with India, though the greatest painter of the mid 15th cent., Nuno Gonçalves, derived much of his intense realism from Flanders and esp. from Van Eyck (◊ *Flemish Art*). Portugal took more readily than Spain to

◊ *Renaissance* classicism esp. in architecture, and in the 17th cent. produced fine though austere Jesuit churches, later developing a lavish but harmonious ◊ *baroque* style, which was successfully transplanted to Brazil. ◊ *Portraiture* was a leading element in the work of Portuguese painters e.g. Cristovão de Figueiredo (16th cent.), Domingos Vieira (17th), and Domingos António Sequeira (late 18th). The greatest modern Portuguese artist was the sculptor Guillen Franco.

Poseidon. < Gr. 'earth-shaker'. In Greek mythology, god of earthquakes, horses, and the sea (equivalent of Roman Neptune) with a trident as emblem; godfather of ◊ *Theseus*. He disputed the possession of Attica with ◊ *Athena*, and asked the gods to allot it to the donor of the most useful gift; he presented a horse, Athena an olive-tree, and she was adjudged the winner.

Positivism. The view that all real or positive knowledge derives from sense experience and particularly from scientific observation and experiment. Thus Comte and other positivists disdained unempirical speculation and *a priori* claims about the world e.g. in ◊ *metaphysics*, and argued that human progress depended on a scientific study of society.

Positron ◊ *Beta Particles*.

Post-Impressionism. Loosely, the late 19th-cent. artistic reaction in France against ◊ *Impressionism* and its preoccupation with the purely visual; it implied a return to form, composition, and intellectual content. The most notable post-impressionists were Van Gogh, Cézanne, and Gauguin (whose use of non-naturalistic colour and firm outlines was violently anti-impressionist). Cézanne declared that he wanted to make Impressionism into 'something solid and durable, like the art of the museums'.

Post Office. In Tudor England there was a Master of the Posts responsible for royal despatches; the government Letter Office was created during the Protectorate, and later accepted private letters, which it conveyed by mail-coach. The first passenger-carrying mail-coach ran between London and Bath in 1784. The uniform penny post (a rate long maintained for letters) was established in 1840 by Sir Rowland Hill; the first air-mail letter was carried from Hendon to Windsor in 1911 to celebrate the coronation of George V.

The Post Office also runs a savings bank, the telegraph and telephone services, and the parcel post, and issues radio, television, car, and dog licences, old-age pensions, family allowances, premium bonds, etc. Expenses are met from and income goes into a self-contained fund created by the 1961 Post Office Act.

In U.S.A. the first postal system started 1639 at Boston; Benjamin Franklin was joint Postmaster-General 1775. The famous Pony Express of 1860–1 carried letters across the continent to the W. coast.

In France a state Post Office existed in the mid 15th cent. under Louis XI, but later it was farmed out, to become a national agency only after the ⟡ French Revolution.

The International Postal Union, created 1875, now includes almost every country in the world; its Congress meets every five years.

Potassium. A very soft silvery ⟡ alkali metal, which instantly tarnishes in air and is even more reactive than ⟡ sodium; it is the lightest element to have a natural radioactive ⟡ isotope; and potassium-40 (which emits ⟡ beta particles) is now used in its analytical determination. The name is derived from pot-ashes (wood ash), from which the carbonate was extracted with water, but until 1702 the compound was confused with sodium carbonate. It occurs in all land plants, but its industrial sources are salt deposits in Germany, U.S.A. and U.S.S.R. The amount in sea-water is low compared with sodium. Potassium hydroxide (caustic potash, KOH) is an important reagent in organic chemistry; the aqueous solution is used for absorbing carbon dioxide, the solid for drying gases. The carbonate, nitrate, and sulphate are ⟡ fertilizers with individual advantages for certain crops. Potassium nitrate (nitre, saltpetre) differs from sodium nitrate (Chile saltpetre) in not being deliquescent; it is used (with ⟡ charcoal and ⟡ sulphur) in the manufacture of ⟡ gunpowder, and also for pickling meat.

Potassium Permanganate ⟡ Manganese.

Potato. Solanum tuberosum, of the Solanaceae, a plant whose tubers have a large starch content; native of the Andes, where it was cultivated by the ⟡ Incas, introduced into Europe first in Spain about 1570, shortly afterwards brought to England by Francis Drake, and introduced into N. America in the 17th cent. It rapidly became a major crop throughout N. Europe and most parts of the temperate zone, where it is a staple carbohydrate food (the most important after the cereals). Potatoes are also used as fodder and for the production of alcohol.

Potsdam Agreement. 1945. Signed by the U.S.A., U.S.S.R., and Gt Britain to implement the principles agreed at ⟡ Yalta. It established complete Allied supervision of Germany and agreed to treat it as a single economy during the occupation. All former German territories east of the ⟡ Oder-Neisse Line were transferred to Polish and Russian administration 'pending a final peace treaty'. Reparations, war crimes, and many other points were dealt with, often in ambiguous terms, and France was not a party to the agreement. Owing to the antagonism which developed between U.S.S.R. and the Western powers (⟡ Iron Curtain), and since the Allies made no final peace treaty with Germany, much of the agreement remained a dead letter. ⟡ Berlin, Germany (Democratic/ Federal Republic).

Pottery. Objects made from fired clay; often classified as earthenware, stoneware, or ⟡ porcelain, according to the temperature of firing. The first making of pottery is one of the features of the ⟡ Neolithic age; it occurred in parts of W. Asia and Greece in the middle of the 7th millennium B.C. and was in general use throughout the Near East by about 5500 B.C. The earliest pots were hand-made; the potter's wheel was known in Iran and Mesopotamia about 3500 B.C. but did not reach Egypt until the early 3rd millennium. Its invention made possible a much higher standard of modelling and greatly increased output. The first pots were of plain ware, in imitation of leather, wood, basketwork, etc. Burnishing was introduced later, and then painting; superb painted vessels were produced in Iran and Mesopotamia in the 4th millennium B.C. and in the Mediterranean in the 3rd. Although a type of glaze was widely used in Egypt from the early 3rd millennium, the technique of applying a true glaze to earthenware pots was first developed in Assyria in the 17th cent. B.C. and by the 7th became widespread in W. Asia, whence it was probably adopted by the Chinese. China is esp. important, both for its superb glazed stoneware from the 3rd cent A.D. onwards, and also for the 9th or 10-cent. A.D. discovery of porcelain.

Even when very fragmentary, pottery is of outstanding importance in ◊ *archaeology*, because its manufacture, whether hand-made or mass-produced, is a strictly traditional craft; the almost infinite variety of methods of manufacture, fabric, shape, finish, and decoration make it a highly sensitive indicator of regional groups, chronological periods, and trade, e.g. the ◊ *Minoan* civilization and that of ◊ *Mycenae* were dated by linking their pottery with dated dynastic periods. ◊ *Ceramics, Faience.*

Poultry. Birds kept in a domesticated state, for egg production or meat; poultry farming (systematized large-scale poultry-keeping) is now so specialized that some firms raise and sell only young chicks, others raise poultry (some for meat, others for eggs) in flocks of thousands or tens of thousands, usually in the artificial conditions of 'batteries' (instead of ranging freely in search of food).

Poynings Law. 1495. Statutes under which any free Irish Parliament was made illusory by providing that no Parliament could be summoned or any legislation introduced without the prior assent of the English Privy Council; it also enforced the complete anglicization of the counties within the Pale. It was not repealed until 1782. ◊ *Penal Laws.*

Pragmatism. Originally (with C. S. Peirce) the view that the meaning of a statement such as that something is 'hard' contains ideas about effects, e.g. that it will dent other things; more commonly, philosophical attitude of judging the truth of a proposition by its results, i.e. by experience. It insists on the validity of empirical methods, and the necessity to alter hypotheses in the light of new discovery. William James introduced the term 1898 and J. Dewey further developed the doctrine.

Prague Peace (1635) ◊ *Thirty Years War.*

Prairies. < Fr. 'meadows'; the vast, undulating, grassy, generally treeless plains of N. America, covering the S. parts of Alberta, Saskatchewan, and Manitoba in Canada (the Prairie Provinces), and U.S.A. from the foothills of the Rocky mountains to about the longitude of Lake Michigan. Now one of the most important wheat-producing areas in the world. ◊ *Pampas.*

Prayer Book (Book of Common Prayer). Collection of official formularies for public worship, and for the administration of the ◊ *sacraments* and other rites, in the ◊ *Church of England*; originally drawn up largely by Archbishop Cranmer and issued in 1549, with more definitely Protestant revision in 1552 and further revisions in 1559, 1604, and 1662 (◊ *Clarendon Code, Savoy Conference*). A further attempted revision in 1928 was not approved by Parliament (◊ *Erastianism*), but parts are episcopally sanctioned. A number of churches deriving from the Anglican, e.g. in Scotland, S. Africa, U.S.A., and Canada, have produced their own revisions, departing little from its formularies while enriching it with new material and accommodating its style and directions (rubrics) to local needs, current circumstances, and advances in the study of the ◊ *Liturgy*. The text derives largely from pre ◊ *Reformation* Latin prayers, modified into majestic English. ◊ *Breviary.*

Praying Mantis. Orthopterous insect similar to the ◊ *locust* found in temperate and tropical climates; the name derives from the pose it assumes when preparing to catch its prey of insects and occasional small vertebrates.

Precedent. A case establishing a rule of law which must subsequently be followed, every court being bound by decisions of a court superior to itself, and the House of Lords, the Court of Appeal, and the Court of Criminal Appeal by the precedents they themselves create. Precedents established in other courts may still be treated as having persuasive authority, as may decisions of foreign and Commonwealth courts, esp. those in systems descended from English law. On the whole, Continental systems reject the doctrine of precedent and rely upon detailed legislative codes to a much greater extent than does English law.

Predestination. Doctrine of some Protestant Christians (◊ *Calvinism*) that God's inscrutable Will has chosen certain men and women for eternal salvation irrespective of their personal merit, and that these 'elect' cannot fall from grace; a continual subject of theological debate since St Augustine 354–430, and variously justified in repeated attempts to reconcile inevitability with ◊ *free will* and to define the relationship between Grace and human endeavour. ◊ *Arminianism*.

Premium Bonds. Though somewhat similar to the State ◊ *lottery* system prevalent in many countries, the bonds sold in the U.K. since 1956 are not a lottery, because they are redeemable at any time at their face value. Each month some hundreds of numbers are selected at random by the electronic computer ◊ *Ernie* to qualify for prizes from £25 to £5000.

Pre-Raphaelite Brotherhood. A group of English painters (originally, D. G. Rossetti, W. Holman Hunt, and J. E. Millais) who sought to emulate the earlier Italian schools, in reaction to contemporary taste for Raphael and late Italian artists. The first Pre-Raphaelite painting, exhibited by Rossetti 1849, was fiercely abused, but in 1851 the Brotherhood won the support of Ruskin, and it soon secured wide popularity in England; their works, usually illustrating moral themes, were painted with an exquisite attention to detail (often symbolic), in hard bright colours.

Presbyterians. Protestant Christian body without ◊ *bishops*, maintaining Church government by presbyters (elders), both clerical and lay, only the former administering the ◊ *sacraments* or (generally) preaching. Tracing their origin to Calvin, Presbyterians became predominant in Scotland at the time of the ◊ *Reformation*, and in the mid 17th cent. displaced the ◊ *Church of England* for a time. They are of importance in N. Ireland, the Netherlands, Switzerland, and U.S.A. ◊ *Calvinism, Covenant.*

Prester John. In medieval legend, a priest-king ('prester', priest) ruling a Christian people, in remote Asia or Africa (sometimes identified as the Ethiopians), traditionally expected to march his armies to the defence of western Christendom against ◊ *Islam*; the Byzantine Emperor Manuel Comnenus and Pope Alexander III both sent letters to him, without reply. The legend may reflect rumours of ◊ *Nestorian* communities.

Priam. In classical legend, king of Troy during the Trojan war; son of Laomedon, husband of ◊ *Hecuba*, and father of ◊ *Cassandra*, ◊ *Hector*, ◊ *Paris*, and many others. He was too old to take much part in the war, but after Hector's death he claimed his son's body from ◊ *Achilles*;

when, at the fall of the city, one of his sons was killed at his feet by Pyrrhus before the altar of ◊ *Zeus*, he hurled his spear at Pyrrhus, who killed him.

Price Control. The fixing of prices by a government or government agency; it can take the form of a general price freeze, at the level of prices ruling on a given day; but more often prices are fixed commodity by commodity. Price control occurs fairly widely in public utilities e.g. electricity and gas, or in transport undertakings, and is also used widely in agriculture, but otherwise in western countries it has mainly been a wartime expedient.

Priest. < Gr. *presbyteros*, elder. Authorized minister of religion, esp. one qualified to offer sacrifices. Among the greater religions, ◊ *Islam* and ◊ *Buddhism* have no priests; the priesthood of ◊ *Judaism* described in the Bible ceased to function after the fall of the Temple A.D. 70. The term is not used by Protestants (except Anglicans). Among other Christians, the priest alone (as the bishop's delegate) can celebrate ◊ *Holy Communion* and hear ◊ *confession*; he is ordained to his office by the laying-on of a bishop's hands (◊ *Holy Orders*). In the ◊ *Roman Catholic Church* a priest may not be married; in the ◊ *Eastern Orthodox Church* he may marry before ordination, but not after.

Primates. By this name Linnaeus (◊ *Biological Classification*) distinguished ◊ *monkeys*, ◊ *apes*, and men from the remaining mammals, secundates; they are now classified as members of one of 26 zoologically equivalent mammalian orders. The more primitive primates, grouped in the sub-order *Prosimii*, are the aye-aye, ◊ *lemur*, and indri of Madagascar, the loris and potto of India, and the African potto and bush-baby. Their close affinity with the *Insectivora* e.g. ◊ *hedgehog* indicates that they and the primates diverged from a common ancestor very early in mammalian evolution; prosimian fossils are known from the Paleocene Period, about 60 m. years ago. The group also contains the spectral ◊ *tarsier* of India. The more highly evolved primates are grouped in the sub-order *Anthropoidea*, of which there are four sub-divisions. The *Hominidae* contains one present-day genus, *Homo*, man, with two fossil genera Pithecanthropus and Australopithecus (though the relations of the last are doubtful). Our own genus has two fossil species,

H. neanderthalensis and *H. heidelbergensis*. The *Pongidae* comprise the ◊ *gibbon* and the great apes, the ◊ *orangoutang* of SE Asia and the ◊ *gorilla* and ◊ *chimpanzee* of Africa; these two groups are more closely related to the Old World prominent-nosed catarrhine monkeys e.g. ◊ *baboon*, ◊ *rhesus* (macaque), mandrill than to the New World flat-nosed platyrrhine monkeys e.g. marmoset, howler. The gestation period, blood groups, and menstrual cycle of the apes relate more nearly to those of man than those of the catarrhina. Among the particular features of the primates setting them apart from the other mammalian orders are acute stereoscopic vision, hands with opposable thumb and (generally) fingernails, and the great information-storage capacity of the cerebral cortex of the brain.

Prime Minister. The U.K. chief Minister, head of the government; appointed by the monarch, but in practice must have the support of a majority in the House of Commons (◊ *Parliament*), of which since 1902 he had invariably already been a member on taking office, until Lord Home became P.M. (1964) before renouncing his earldom and standing for election. The P.M. selects the Cabinet and leads his own party. Though not officially recognized by the Crown until 1905, the office is about 250 years old, Sir Robert Walpole being regarded as the first P.M. in virtue of his long ministry 1721–42; the term Prime Minister or Minister Premier had however been used of e.g. Buckingham, Danby, etc. in the 1670s, to which period the term 'Cabinet' (Charles II's study) also dates. The Hanoverian monarchs (from 1714) did not intervene in politics; during the Regency 1811–20 George III was unable to preside at Cabinet meetings, and no monarch has done so since. The office of P.M. includes the recommending of Regius Professors at universities and of dignitaries of the ◊ *Church of England*. The official residences are 10 Downing St (Whitehall) in London and Chequers, a country residence presented in 1917 by Lord Lee of Farnham.

Primitive Art. The art of primitive peoples e.g. ◊ *Australian aborigines*, ◊ *Polynesians*, and the Negroid ◊ *Melanesian* and ◊ *African peoples*, whose cultures correspond to those of the European Stone Age. (The famous bronzes of the W. African kingdom of Benin, also called 'primitive', are comparable with the sophisticated arts of the metal-using civilizations.) Primitive art has usually been said to be religious, and to lack individuality in the sense of there being only regional styles, rigidly adhered to and not changing with time. In fact much primitive art is secular, and although there are many defined regional styles the artist has considerable freedom for the expression of his own individuality. Primitive art differs from other forms largely in that there are rarely full-time specialists, that appreciation is found throughout the population, and that art is produced for specific social purposes rather than for its own sake. The most famous areas are W. Africa and the Congo basin for wood carvings, Melanesia for carvings esp. masks, NW America for carved utensils and totem poles, Central America and Polynesia for stone carvings, and Australia for rock engravings. The aesthetic merits of primitive art were discovered in the early 20th cent. by French artists, who in the distortions and uninhibited vitality of primitive masks, figurines, and so on found a stimulus to their own reaction against academic and naturalistic art. Most modern artists, from the *Fauves* onwards, have derived inspiration from this source. ◊ *Cave Art.*

Primitives. A 19th-cent. term for European painters of before about A.D. 1500, esp. of the Netherlands and Italian schools; also (in a quite unrelated sense) certain modern painters e.g. Douanier Rousseau, whose lack (or apparent lack) of professional training gives their work a sense of child-like wonder. Of 20th-cent. painters ('Sunday painters') the American 'Grandma' Moses is the best known.

Primrose. *Primula vulgaris*; a wild flower, native to Britain in the yellow variety. *P. vulgaris sibthorpii* from Greece, pink or red flowers, *P. vulgaris heterochroma*, from Persia, white, purple, blue, or yellow. The interbreeding of these forms, and selection of the resulting plants, has produced the modern varieties of coloured primrose (primula, polyanthus).

EVENING PRIMROSE. Plants of the genus *Oenothera*, originally the biennial *O. biennis*, from U.S.A. now naturalized in parts of the British Isles.

Printing. Process for producing identical copies on a press. The three principal methods are relief, intaglio, and planographic (◊ *Lithography*), in each of which the image appears reversed from left to right on the printing surface, so as to result in a 'right-reading' image when pressed upon paper or other material.

INTAGLIO PRINTING: Plates (usually copper) are engraved or etched, so that only the incised lines retain the ink, the rest being wiped off before printing. Invented in Italy in the late 15th cent.

RELIEF PRINTING: The characters stand out from the type or block, so that only they receive ink. It was known in China from the 9th cent. A.D. and reached Europe in the 14th, when it came to mean the letterpress process of taking impressions from a surface made up of printing types generally considered to have been invented by Gutenberg about 1440 and brought to England by Caxton. Type, the method of composing it, and the printing-press did not change materially until the early 19th cent. when the first all-iron hand-press and then the power-driven printing-machine were invented. Composing machines followed, first those which assembled previously-cast type, then those which both cast letters and assembled them in the order required. The rotary principle for printing-presses, in conjunction with reels of paper (made possible by the invention of the Fourdrinier paper-making machine), laid the basis for modern newspaper printing. More recently it has been applied to the printing of books.

STEEL-ENGRAVING: An intaglio printing-process, used mainly for producing banknotes, postage stamps, and stationery. ◊ *Engraving, Etching, Photogravure, Type, Xerography.*

Prism ◊ *Optics.*

Privateer. A privately-owned armed ship, employed in wartime (◊ *Letter of Marque*) to attack enemy shipping, with the object of taking prizes for the benefit of the owners and crew. During the Anglo-French wars of the 17th, 18th, and early 19th centuries, both sides fitted out large numbers of privateers; many of them subsequently took to ◊ *piracy.*

Privy Council. Her Majesty's Privy Council; in the U.K. now a large honorary body of eminent men, although some of its committees perform important functions. All Cabinet ministers are *ex officio* members. Its origins are in the 9th cent. and for centuries its members were the chief advisers of the king (the equivalent of the modern Cabinet).

Prize. Until the early 19th cent. enemy ships captured during war were sold with their cargoes, the proceeds being divided pro rata between owners, captain officers, and crew as 'prize money'; the system was a main inducement in the fitting-out of ◊ *privateers* and in navy recruitment. Some prize-money was paid also for enemy ships sunk.

Probability. 1. In mathematics, a precise estimate of the likelihood of an event occurring, i.e. the 'odds' that it will happen; e.g. a dice may fall on one of six sides, and the probability of a given number being uppermost is 1 in 6, but with two dice the probability of the same two numbers appearing at one throw is $\frac{1}{6} \times \frac{1}{6}$ i.e. one in 36. Various mathematically important deductions have been made regarding probability, one being Bernoulli's Theorem on the number of 'successes' likely in a given number of trials, and Gauss's 'error law' stating the magnitude of possible error in a given experiment. Probability in the sense of expectation is allied to ◊ *statistics*, e.g. the life-expectation figures used by insurance companies are obtained by estimating the mean age at which death occurs in large population groups.

2. In philosophy, two classes of theory. To say an event is probable, e.g. my paying the rent this month, is to say something about the frequency, given certain conditions, with which such events occur. Such an analysis does not seem to fit other kinds of probability-statement, e.g. about the probability of scientific theories being true; these, according to the second theory, seem to be claims that there is supporting evidence of some sort not having to do with frequency.

Procurator Fiscal. An official appointed in each Scottish county to act as public prosecutor in the sheriff's court and to inquire into suspicious deaths (there being no coroner in Scotland), the inquiry being private and not by means of an inquest; he reports to the ◊ *Lord Advocate.* He also makes preliminary investigations into serious crimes, and upon his report the Lord Advocate's office decides whether to prosecute. ◊ *Scots Law.*

Professional. In sport, broadly, a professional is one who plays for reward; professionalism ultimately appeared even in the ancient ◊ *Olympic Games*, and has existed ever since. The modern professional emerged after the late 19th-cent. reorganization of most major sports. Except in sports (e.g. rowing) which derived from an occupation, the ◊ *amateur* came first and then the professional. There are two types of professional: the teacher and the competitor. Financial rewards vary greatly between sports: some e.g. boxing and golf bring substantial returns; others are poorly paid. Recent significant changes in England have been the lifting of the wage ceiling for professional soccer players (◊ *Association Football*), some of whom now earn well over £100 a week, and the abolition of all barriers between amateur and professional in ◊ *cricket*.

Profit-sharing. A bonus in proportion to net profits; the principle of distributing income so that the workers receive a share in the profits of the concern, in addition to their regular wages. Alternatively, the employees may be given actual shares in the company. It does not, however, imply participation by workers in management. In the U.K. the Liberal Party advocates compulsory profit-sharing, which is not favoured by the trade-union movement in general.

Progression. A mathematical sequence of numbers.

ARITHMETIC: Each new term in the sequence is formed by adding a constant amount to the term before: thus 2, 5, 8, 11, etc. has first term 2 and 'common difference' 3. The general case is usually written a, $(a+d)$, $(a+2d)$, . . .

GEOMETRIC: Each new term in the sequence is formed by multiplying the term before by a constant quantity: thus 3, -6, $+12$, -24 . . . has first term 3 and 'common ratio' (-2). The general case is usually written a, ar, ar^2, . . .

Progressive Education. Since the early 20th cent. reformers in many countries have tried to transform traditional teaching and discipline methods, objecting to schools where teachers taught abstract subjects of little relevance to children's needs and maintained order by force and threat of punishment. Rudolf Steiner 1861–1925 introduced play-acting and spontaneous artistic activities into education, and Madame Montessori in Italy invented ways for children to teach themselves with carefully-designed play material, while others modified the methods of teaching older pupils. Dewey in the U.S.A. gave the new approach justification in terms of a theory of knowledge, and his influence encouraged experiments of all kinds. Curry at Dartington Hall, Carleton Washburne at Winnetka, A. S. Neill at Summerhill, and others ran schools which provided education described as 'child-centred' rather than 'teacher-centred' or 'subject-centred'. Most of these pioneers were men and women deeply concerned for the brotherhood of man and the maintenance of peace; feeling that schools everywhere tended to encourage a too narrow and exclusive patriotism in the young, they held that education should aim more at promoting international understanding.

Prohibition. 1919–33. Throughout the late 19th cent. various temperance organizations in U.S.A. esp. the Women's Christian Temperance Union agitated for legislation to prevent the selling of alcoholic liquor. By 1919 prohibition laws were in force in the States of Maine and Kansas, and after widespread political agitation the Volstead Act amended the Constitution to make prohibition nationwide. This 18th Amendment proved virtually impossible to enforce, esp. in the large cities, since outside the rural districts it lacked any wide measure of popular support. The manufacture and distribution of liquor was carried on by 'bootleggers', esp. in Chicago, and resulted in gangster disorders. In 1933 the 21st Amendment repealed the 18th; but several 'dry' States still maintain their own prohibition laws.

Some countries e.g. India, Saudi Arabia forbid alcohol on religious grounds.

Proletariat. In ancient Rome, the *proles* were the poorest class, whose main function was to beget children. Marx applied the term to the class of wageearners in an industrial society, whose sole means of existence is by the sale of their labour-power. Lenin expected that the class-conscious van of the proletariat would establish a dictatorship as a stepping stone to a classless society. The march of events belied this concept, but communist writers, misleadingly, continue to describe communist parties as parties of the proletariat.

Prometheus. < Gr. meaning forethought; in classical legend, one of the ◊ *Titans*, the bestower of fire, which he stole from heaven. ◊ *Zeus* chained him to a rock in the Caucasus, and sent an eagle to peck forever at his perpetually renewed liver; eventually ◊ *Hercules* killed the eagle and released him. The marriage of his brother Epimetheus ('Afterthought') to ◊ *Pandora* was part of the vengeance of Zeus. ◊◊ *Centaurs*.

Proof Spirit. An arbitrary standard mixture of ◊ *alcohol* and water, used in the U.K. and U.S.A. to compute the strength of alcoholic liquors for excise purposes. Spirits are usually sold at '30° under proof' and '70° proof' which mean the same; such liquor contains 40 per cent alcohol by volume, 33.3 per cent by weight.

Propeller. 1. The marine screw propeller was patented 1836 by Ericsson, a Swedish engineer, and rapidly superseded the paddle-wheel; twin-screw ships, in which the propellers assist steering, were introduced about 1860 in England.

2. Aeroplane propellers (airscrews) consist either of two, three, four, six, or eight blades; they propel the aircraft by pushing air backwards, and to do this the blades must have a twist (pitch). Propellers with a fixed pitch are efficient only for a limited speed range, and variable-pitch propellers superseded them. They enable the pilot to choose the optimum pitch for a variety of flying requirements; or they choose it automatically, as in constant-speed propellers. The limit to the speed at which a propeller can rotate and still be fully effective is when the speed of the tip approaches that of sound, and propeller aircraft are normally designed for speeds below 600 m.p.h. in level flight.

Property. Primitive societies have a concept of individual rights in personal property e.g. clothes, weapons, domestic equipment, and also a concept of joint or communal property in land and livestock, usually held in trust for his dependants by the head of a family or ◊ *clan*; a society having a chief or king considers him the ultimate owner of all land (◊ *Feudalism*). In modern society, property rights may be vested in individuals, shared with others e.g. in a joint stock company, or held on behalf of the community e.g. in public ownership; the development of the ◊ *welfare state* has meant a progressive restriction of property rights (e.g. those of manufacturers) considered inviolable at earlier stages of capitalism, though private-property rights remain extensive. In law property is classed as PERSONAL i.e. chattels (movable objects of all kinds and leasehold property) and REAL i.e. freehold land and buildings.

Proportional Representation. Electoral system designed as an improvement upon election by simple majority, in contests involving more than two candidates. One method allows the voter to state a second and third preference; candidates receiving a predetermined percentage of the votes are returned; and any votes they may receive over that percentage are distributed to other candidates, in line with the second or third choices given by the voters, and candidates receiving enough from the distribution of 'surplus' votes to reach the required minimum are also declared elected. This method is known as the single transferable vote. Another method bulks together the votes for minority candidates in all constituencies, and if any of the minority parties receives a sufficient number of votes candidates from a national party list are then returned to Parliament as members without constituencies. Supporters of P.R. argue that it is the most truly fair and democratic system of representation; its opponents object that it promotes political fragmentation by favouring numerous small parties and would result in unstable coalition governments.

P.R. should not be confused with the Alternative Vote system, which allows voters to indicate a second choice if more than two parties present candidates; if no candidate receives an absolute majority, the second choices are counted and added to the votes of the first two candidates, one of whom should then possess an absolute majority. Though endorsed by the Royal Commission of 1911 on electoral reform, this system has not been adopted in British elections.

Prostate. Secondary sex ◊ *gland* in the male, surrounding the neck of the bladder, producing an alkaline medium which mingles with the spermatozoa and enables them to resist acid conditions in the vagina of the female. In later life the prostate is liable to enlargement, and the resulting obstruction causes back-pressure in the urinary tract and may seriously damage the kidneys; the enlarged gland may be surgically removed.

Prostitution. Commerce in sexual relations, in which women or men offer sexual services in return for money; a practice of great antiquity. In western societies the law attempts to limit it by legislation against soliciting, which e.g. in Britain under the 1959 Street Offences Act is punishable by fines for the first two offences and by imprisonment up to three months for subsequent offences, and by legislation directed against those who organize and profit from prostitution. Prostitutes are far less numerous in London now than in the 19th cent. though the 1955 statistics of 11,900 convictions show an increase over the 1930s, and the Street Offences Act has resulted in the development of a 'call-girl' system. In France prostitution was previously legal in registered *maisons de tolérance* subject to police and medical inspection; the system ended in 1946 but the closing of brothels does not appear to have reduced prostitution, while the recorded incidence of ◊ *venereal disease* has increased.

Protactinium. ◊ *Actinides*; a natural radioactive ◊ *element* derived from uranium-235. In 1918 Hahn and Meitner proved it to be the precursor of ◊ *actinium* by the loss of an α-particle. The usual valency state is 4.

Protective Colouring ◊ *Pigmentation.*

Protectorate. 1. Country which while nominally independent cedes some of its functions to a stronger power in return for protection. In the past protectorates were frequently established over native states which would have been incapable without such protection of maintaining any semblance of sovereignty.

2. Cromwellian ◊ *Commonwealth and Protectorate.*

Proteins. Organic nitrogenous compounds of very high molecular weight, forming a large part of all living matter; either highly insoluble and fibrous (e.g. hair, skin, wool, silk) or soluble (e.g. egg albumen, serum globulin, and ◊ *enzymes*) and extremely difficult to synthesize. Analysis into their constituent ◊ *amino-acids* has been advanced by ◊ *chromatography*, although the chemical formulae of many remain unknown. The amino-acids may be regarded as the bricks building all protein structure by combining in different ways in tissue cells to form the characteristic proteins. Plants are able to synthesize all the amino-acids they require

from inorganic matter, but animals cannot do so and must obtain them by eating plants or other animals, from which e.g. the human body builds up its own special protein requirements out of some 20 specific amino-acids. ◊ *Diet, Digestion.*

Protestantism. Complex of Christian beliefs deriving immediately from the revolt of Martin Luther and others in the early 16th cent. against corruption in the doctrine and discipline of the western church, and ultimately from the long-standing doctrines of e.g. the ◊ *Albigenses*, etc. The name derives from the 1529 *Protestatio* (against the decree of the Diet of Spires that no innovations in religion were permissible). Protestants generally accept the ◊ *Bible* as the sole source of religious authority, uphold the principle of 'private judgement' in interpreting it, and have a less sacramentalist theology than Roman Catholics. Differences of opinion have led to great fragmentation; many of the larger Protestant bodies have split into several smaller sects. In general, Protestantism secured little permanent hold in the Latin countries, and is confined mainly to N. Europe and the parts of the world colonized therefrom. ◊ *Reformation, Thirty Years War.*

Proteus. In Greek mythology, guardian of the sea-caves of ◊ *Hephaestus*; an old man with the power of prophecy. Those wishing to consult him had to catch him asleep on the rocks at noon with his seals drowsing round him; he eluded pursuers by continually changing his shape, but if they persisted sufficiently, or could chain him down, he resumed his ordinary form and answered their questions.

Proton. Elementary particle with a positive electric charge, constituting the nucleus of the hydrogen atom and a constituent of all other atomic nuclei. Contrary to the unit negative charge of the atom (◊ *electron*), the proton represents the fundamental unit of positive charge of the atom. Every atomic nucleus contains one or more protons, the number of which gives the ◊ *atomic number* of the element and is different for every element. ◊ *Subatomic Particles.*

Protozoa. Microscopic unicellular or, rather, non-cellular organisms, considered the simplest and most primitive type of animal. The phylum Protozoa is divided into four classes, three of them distinguished essentially by their method of locomotion: the flagellates e.g. *Euglena* move by whip-like flagellae; the ciliates e.g. *Paramecium* by cilia (hair-like threads covering the surface of the cell); and the rhizopoda e.g. ⟡ *Amoeba* by pseudopodia (false feet). Although some members of each of these groups are ⟡ *parasites* e.g. tsetse-fly the majority are free-living. Many of the flagellates, like plants, have chloroplasts (⟡ *Chlorophyll*) enabling them to produce food. The fourth group, sporozoa, characterized by ⟡ *spore* formation, are all parasites. Many are disease-producing, e.g. the malarial parasite. ⟡ *Biological Classification*.

Provence. SE France; so named because in the 2nd cent. B.C. it was the first Roman province beyond the Alps. In the early Middle Ages it retained many Roman institutions, even after Frankish and Arab invasions; from A.D. 1033 it was nominally part of the ⟡ *Holy Roman Empire*, but largely independent and oriented towards Spain and Italy, with which it had extensive trade relations. After flourishing in the 11th and 12th centuries, it was the scene of the crusade against the ⟡ *Albigenses* in the 13th cent. but as the European trade centres moved NW it declined, passed to the Angevin kingdom of Naples 1246, and was incorporated as a province of France 1486.

LANGUAGE. Provençal, the *langue d'oc*; one of the ⟡ *Romance languages*, still spoken in S. France by about 10 m. It closely resembles ⟡ *Catalan*. Provençal literature (⟡ *troubadour*) is of considerable importance in medieval studies.

Proverb. A traditional short, memorable, and shrewd observation, allusive rather than explicit, and believed to summarize common experience; by nature and origin, proverbs tend to be sceptical and conservative, and one or two can usually be cited on either side of any particular question. Proverbs flourished in stable rural cultures, Arabic, Persian, and Indian literature being particularly rich in them, and notable early collections include the biblical Book of Proverbs, parts of the Welsh and Irish Triads, and the 'Proverbs of Alfred'; they remained popular throughout the later Middle Ages and the ⟡ *Renaissance*, e.g. Erasmus's *Adagia*, 1500, but tended to decline as the printed word displaced the spoken.

Prussia. Largest of the former German states, occupying the major part of N.

Germany. In the 13th cent. the Teutonic Knights (⟡ *Orders of Chivalry*) germanized the Prussians (originally Slavs) and largely replaced them by German settlers; later, when the Grand Master adopted ⟡ *Lutheranism*, the country became a hereditary duchy under Polish suzerainty, ruled by a branch of the ⟡ *Hohenzollerns*. In 1618 the country passed to the Elector of ⟡ *Brandenburg*. In 1701 the Elector Frederick III had himself crowned king of Prussia as Frederick I; the country quickly developed into a state with the most efficient army in Europe (⟡ *War of the Austrian Succession*), with which Frederick II (the Great) set Prussia on its course of aggressive expansion, conquering ⟡ *Silesia* and seizing W. Prussia at the first ⟡ *partition* of Poland in 1772. Under his successors Prussia declined, and in 1806 was defeated by Napoleon at ⟡ *Jena*; the Treaty of ⟡ *Tilsit* made Prussia a virtual dependency of France, but by the social, economic, and educational reforms of Stein and Hardenberg, the abolition of serfdom, and the introduction of universal education, Prussia re-asserted herself; her army, modernized by Scharnhorst and Gneisenau, played a decisive role at ⟡ *Waterloo*. By the ⟡ *Vienna Congress* Prussia recovered lost territories, gained the Rhineland (⟡ *Palatinate*) and Westphalia (which became important industrial centres). Between 1828 and 1835 she set up a customs union (⟡ *Zollverein*) which included most of the other German states (excluding Austria). Following the lead of the Austrian chancellor Metternich, government became reactionary; the 1848 attempt at revolution was ruthlessly crushed. Bismarck, who became Prussian Chancellor in 1862, pursued a policy which eliminated Austria from German affairs and led to Prussian leadership of the N. German Confederation and of the German empire after the ⟡ *Franco-Prussian War*; although thenceforward part of Germany, Prussia remained under the authoritarian influence of the *Junker* (land-owning) class until 1918. After the ⟡ *Second World War* Prussia was split between the new territorial divisions (*Länder*) which replaced the former states.

Psalms. 150 sacred poems in the ⟡ *Bible*, many traditionally attributed to King David, concerned with the praise of God and incidents in the history of Israel; they are a central feature of public worship among both Jews and Christians. The Biblical Psalms (the Hebrew texts of which were originally sung) have particular Western musical importance through their place in the Offices of the Roman Catholic church e.g. Matins, Vespers, and in the Morning and Evening Prayer of the Anglican Church, the traditional settings being respectively those of ◊ *plainsong* (in Latin) and Anglican chant (in English). The texts of psalms have also received many other musical settings by various composers, from Tallis to Stravinsky.

Psyche. In Greek legend, a beautiful maiden personifying the human soul. The tale of Cupid and Psyche (◊ *Eros*) has Cupid take her to live with him in a palace, where he visits her at night; he forbids her to look at him, because she is mortal and he a god. She disobeys, and loses him. Finally he relents; she is made immortal and restored to him for ever.

Psychiatry. The branch of medicine dealing with disorders of the mind and the promotion of ◊ *mental health*; for a long time psychiatry developed more slowly than the rest of medicine, but in the 20th cent. progress has been increasingly fast. Among the most important discoveries are Freud's work on ◊ *psychoanalysis*, the physical methods of treatment with insulin and electric shock, the drugs which have recently revolutionized the treatment of ◊ *schizophrenia* and depressive illness, and modern methods of treating patients in their own homes instead of in hospital.

General psychiatry is concerned with mental illness in adults and its treatment: other branches are child psychiatry ◊ *educational subnormality*, ◊ *psychotherapy*, and forensic psychiatry (psychiatric causes of crime). Social psychiatry, dealing with social aspects and the community treatment of mental illness, has recently become increasingly important, as has the psychiatry of old age. Some psychiatrists follow e.g. the 'school' of Freud, of Jung, or of Klein (each of which has its own theory of the causation of mental illness and its own method of psychotherapy), but most psychiatrists make use of ideas from more than one of these schools, and treat their patients with physical treatments, including drugs, as well as psychotherapy.

Psychical Research. The study of reported odd and unexpected events e.g. thought-transference, telepathy, hauntings, communications with the dead through ◊ *mediums*, etc. The possibility of the scientific study of such things was first suggested in the early 17th cent. by Sir Francis Bacon, but it was not undertaken until towards the end of the 19th cent. The Society for Psychical Research was founded in London 1882 for the purpose; similar societies have since been started in other countries. The term 'parapsychology' for the experimental side of psychical research was first suggested by the late W. McDougall, Professor of Psychology at Duke University in U.S.A. where a Parapsychological Laboratory has been organized under J. B. Rhine. ◊ *Extrasensory Perception.*

Psychoanalysis. Certain theories about the human mind, and also certain techniques for its treatment; both originated with Freud, and the term is commonly restricted to his theories and techniques, though it is also applied to those of Jung, Adler, and other post-Freudian psychologists. The therapeutic aim is to resolve mental conflict by bringing into consciousness thoughts and impulses which have been repressed; this is primarily effected by the analysis of ◊ *dreams* and by free association of ideas. The value of analysis is not conclusively established, but the underlying theories have considerable influence on ◊ *psychology*.

Psychology. < Gr. *psyche*, soul; the scientific study of behaviour, concerned with the 'higher functions' esp. in man. It was previously defined as the study of the mind, a definition still appropriate for some fields esp. ◊ *psychoanalysis* and related schools. Psychology proper deals chiefly with the normal mind, psychoanalysis and ◊ *psychiatry* with pathological behaviour, and parapsychology with supranormal mental phenomena. Present trends in the teaching of psychology are towards eclecticism in theory, with stress on experimentation, testing, and measurement.

ABNORMAL PSYCHOLOGY: Includes clinical psychology, and comprises ◊ *psychoanalysis*, behaviour therapy (based on the work of Pavlov), ◊ *hypnosis*, and psychopharmacology i.e. the study of the effects of drugs on mental states and behaviour.

ANIMAL PSYCHOLOGY: Study of animal behaviour, either by controlled laboratory experiments or by observation in the natural environment.

DEVELOPMENTAL PSYCHOLOGY: Study of mental development from birth to adolescence; now expanding to include later development e.g. aspects of gerontology (the general science concerned with old age) and geriatrics (the medical study of old age).

EDUCATIONAL PSYCHOLOGY: Concerned with the special problems of teaching and learning. ◊ *Educational Subnormality, Teaching Machines.*

OCCUPATIONAL PSYCHOLOGY: Originally confined to industrial problems; now includes all occupations e.g. administration, management, the armed services. ◊ *Ergonomics, Vocational Guidance.*

SOCIAL PSYCHOLOGY: The application of psychological theory and techniques to group behaviour.

There is no single theory of psychology; different schools of thought include the following:

BEHAVIOURISM: Holds that psychology is essentially the study of observable behaviour, and excludes concepts such as ◊ *consciousness* or mind.

GESTALT PSYCHOLOGY: Sees mental life in terms of configurations or wholes not reducible to sensations or other discrete elements; it has contributed much to the understanding of perception, ◊ *memory*, and intelligence.

PAVLOVIANISM: Based upon the materialistic theories of Pavlov; thus it is basically behaviourism (see above), but it includes classification into four basic types of ◊ *nervous system.*

PSYCHOANALYTICAL SCHOOLS: Stress the importance of the unconscious sources of motivation, and include Freudian theory, analytical psychology (Jung), and individual psychology (Adler). Allied to them is the 'Hormic' School (Gr. *horme*, urging) which stresses the importance of purposes or goals in mental life. ◊ *Psychoses, Psychosomatics.*

Psychopaths. Individuals who find it difficult to conform to the socially accepted norms of behaviour, their ability to form good personal relationships being disturbed; although they may be intelligent, and sometimes charming, their frequently irresponsible behaviour and lack of regard for others may lead them into conflict with the law. The disorder may result from a severe psychological illness in early life, from which there has been a partial recovery, or possibly (◊ *Deprivation*) from the denial of the normal affection and love of parents in childhood. ◊ *Psychoses.*

Psychoses. Severe mental disorders causing substantial changes in personality. It is impossible to distinguish a psychosis sharply from the less severe ◊ *neurosis*, but generally in a psychosis there is lack of awareness of the illness, thinking is disordered, and contact with reality is very poor.

FUNCTIONAL PSYCHOSES: As far as is known, the origin of the disorder is psychological; ◊ *manic depression, paranoia, schizophrenia.*

ORGANIC PSYCHOSES: The result of damage to the brain, chemical injury, or deterioration, including disorders of old age and brain damage: ◊ *alcohol, drug addiction, venereal diseases.*

Psychosomatics. The study of the relationship between psychological phenomena and bodily conditions, esp. psychological causes of physical illness, which can at times contribute to many kinds of illness and in some appear to play a major part, e.g. asthma, duodenal ulcer, migraine. Some personality structures are clearly more susceptible to psychosomatic illness than others; the reason remains uncertain.

Psychotherapy. The use of psychological as distinct from physical methods in the treatment of mental disorder, including e.g. behaviour therapy, based on research into learning, a method of helping the patient to 'unlearn' the symptoms of ◊ *neurosis*; group psychotherapy, in which several patients are treated together, their discussion of problems being an attempt to help them lead a normal life; ◊ *hypnosis*; ◊ *psychoanalysis*; psycho-drama, a method of developing the patients' insight by their acting-out given roles in improvised plays.

Ptah (Phtah). An Egyptian smith god, equivalent to ◊ *Hephaestus*; creator of the universe at the command of ◊ *Thoth*; usually represented in human (or mummy) form, and esp. honoured at Memphis.

Pterodactyl (Pterosaur). A fossil reptile adapted for gliding through the air by having a modified fourth little finger (◊ *Bat*) for supporting its membranous wing. These 'flying lizards' were contemporaries of ◊ *Archaeopteryx*, and like it evolved from the archosaurs, a group of 'old lizards'. From the Pterodactyl sprang numerous groups of reptile (◊ *Dinosaur, Crocodile*, etc.) at the beginning of the Triassic period 195 million years ago.

Puberty. The time of life when the reproductive organs begin to function and the individual becomes capable of procreation; secondary characteristics also develop, e.g. the growth of body hair, the deepening of the male voice, and breast changes in the female. Puberty usually begins between 13 and 17 in boys and somewhat earlier in girls; in England the legal ages of puberty are 16 for boys and 12 for girls.

Public Health. The provision by the community of care for the health of the individual. Responsibility is in the hands of Local Health Authorities, whose Public Health Committees are advised by a Medical Officer of Health with executive as well as advisory functions in regard to e.g. housing, air pollution, water supplies, waste disposal; executive responsibilities cover a large number of personal health services e.g. health education, maternity and child welfare, industrial hygiene, care of schoolchildren and mentally defective, deranged, aged, and handicapped persons. ◊ *Welfare State.*

Public Prosecutor. The official (in England and Wales the Director of Public Prosecutions) appointed to decide when criminal proceedings are to be instituted and to supervise prosecutions, in England under the supervision of the ◊ *Attorney-General.* Anyone is entitled to prosecute for a crime, and police officers and other officials frequently do so, but it is the Public Prosecutor's duty to undertake criminal proceedings in capital offences and where a case is referred to him by a government department and he considers that it should be brought to court. A judge may decide that facts which have come to light in the course of a trial make it necessary for him to refer the papers to the Public Prosecutor. ◊ *Procurator Fiscal.*

Public School. 1. In Britain a private school, independent of the State educational system, boarding or day, and charging fees. The formal test of whether a school is a 'public school' is membership of the Headmasters' Conference. Some are long-established collegiate foundations e.g. Eton and Winchester which were

always boarding. Others are town grammar schools which outgrew their local associations in the 19th cent. In the 17th and 18th centuries many of them fell into disrepute; the influence of Thomas Arnold, headmaster of Rugby about 1830, recast the whole system in more or less its present mould, by modernizing the curriculum, developing the prefect system, and concentrating on religion, the classics, and leadership-training. This gave an impetus for the founding of many similar schools, including a few for girls; most such schools charge high fees (though some scholarships are available) and are organized on the house system, with 50 to 70 boys under each housemaster. The curriculum is similar to that of a ◊ *grammar school*, but with greater emphasis on religious observance, organized games, and the prefect system. The public schools are independent of the Ministry of Education and of the local education authorities.

PREPARATORY SCHOOL: A similarly organized school catering for children between 8 and 12.

2. In U.S.A. a public school is one supported entirely out of public funds, coeducational and non-residential, while a preparatory school is the equivalent of a British public school ◊ *United States (Education).*

Pueblo Indians. American Indians, settled since 500 B.C. in what are now New Mexico and Arizona, living in stone or adobe houses in towns (pueblos) usually set on cliffs or ◊ *mesas.* Before the Europeans arrived they had an advanced agriculture based on irrigation, grew cotton, and produced colourful textiles; their silver working is also famous. Their religious ceremonies are extremely elaborate, those of the Hopi and Zuni being the most famous. Long exposed to Spanish influence, they still speak Spanish, and today number about 30,000 in some dozen pueblos.

Puerto Rico. Area 3435 sq. m. Pop. 2.5 m. (mainly of Spanish descent). Cap. San Juan. An island in the W. Indies, a U.S.A. commonwealth territory, locally self-governing since 1952; the Senate of 27 and House of Representatives of 51 are elected for four years and the Supreme Court appointed by the Governor.

ECONOMY. Agricultural; main crops coffee, cotton, fruit, maize, sugar, sweet potatoes, yams. Some industrialization is developing rapidly.

HISTORY. Discovered by Columbus in 1493, the island was seized by Spain in 1508 and remained a Spanish colony until during the ◊ *Spanish American War* in 1898 it was seized by U.S.A. and in 1899 ceded by Spain.

Puffin. N. European sea-birds of the ◊ *auk* family, black and white, with a large head emphasized by the triangular red, blue, and yellow parrot-like bill. They breed in colonies, perching in groups on rocks and ledges generally on islands near the shore, often inhabiting and enlarging old rabbit warrens.

Pulse. 1. In biology, the throbbing of the arteries as the ◊ *heart* pumps blood through them. The pulse rate in persons at rest varies with age and sex, but is normally 60 to 70 beats a minute; it is usually 'felt' at the radial arteries in the wrists or at e.g. the temporal artery in front of the ear, the carotid in the neck, or the femoral in the groin. In thin persons, with poorly developed abdominal walls, the pulse of the abdominal aorta may even be seen. Animal pulses vary widely, e.g. rabbits about 200 but camels about 30; between these extremes are cats 110–20, dogs 70–90, cattle 45–50, horses 35–40.
2. In botany, the edible seeds of ◊ *legumes* e.g. peas, beans, lentils.
3. In electricity, a short burst of current or voltage repeated many times a second; e.g. in pulsed ◊ *radar* very powerful bursts of energy lasting only about one millionth of a second may be produced at much longer intervals, e.g. one thousandth of a second; pulsating power is used for such high-energy applications because equipment to sustain this power continuously would be prohibitively large and expensive. Radar experience has led to the use of pulse techniques in ◊ *automatic data-processing* and communication systems.

Puma ◊ *Panther.*

Pumice. Stone formed by frothy ◊ *lava* light enough to float on water, with open spaces (vesicles) which are bubble-holes formed by the expulsion of gases and vapour from the viscous molten lava. Used from antiquity as an ◊ *abrasive*; the Romans are believed to have used it to remove facial hair in lieu of shaving.

Pumps. The need to lift and move water and other fluids is so frequent in many different machines that pumps of a wide variety have been developed. The ancient world used scoop wheels and the Archimedean screw to raise water for irrigation. Modern pumps owe their development to the demands of the mining industry. In Savery's pump of 1698 steam pressure was applied directly to the water, but pumps in which pressure was applied by a piston working in a cylinder became more common. The development of the steam engine by Newcomen between 1705 and 1711 was occasioned by the need to provide power for mine pumping. In general, pumps are of two types, reciprocating and rotary: the reciprocating are best suited for high-speed or high-pressure needs, the rotary for moving large volumes of fluid at lower speeds and pressures. Vacuum pumps are used to remove gas, vapour, or liquid from an enclosed space, to create a pressure below that of the surrounding atmosphere.

Punic Wars. 264–241, 218–201, 149–146 B.C. The word 'Punic' is a variant of ◊ *Phoenician*; the young Roman state came into conflict with the established power of ◊ *Carthage* in the W. Mediterranean, and in the first Punic War (waged mainly in Sicily) the Romans were compelled to build their first fleet. The success of its novel tactics compensated for the failure of the Roman armies, and ultimately brought Rome a favourable peace. In the second Punic War the Carthaginian general Hannibal invaded Italy, but despite his victory at ◊ *Cannae* the Roman confederation was too resilient to be reduced; when Scipio led a counter-attack to Africa, Carthage admitted defeat and surrendered its province in Spain. Fears of the economic supremacy of Carthage were not allayed, however; in 149 B.C. the Romans seized an excuse for war and completely destroyed Carthaginian power.

Pupa. Resting stage in the life of insects which undergo a complete ◊ *metamorphosis*, from the egg through the larva to the pupa; characteristic of the ◊ *beetle* (Coleoptera), ◊ *bee* (Hymenoptera), ◊ *fly* (Diptera), ◊ *butterfly* (Lepidoptera). In some of these the pupa encases itself in a cocoon, often of a silk-like nature but sometimes of hair or leaves; that of the butterfly is called a chrysalis. After the cocoon stage the imago (perfect insect) emerges. ⟡ *Silkworm*.

Purgatory. In Roman Catholic, Eastern Orthodox, and some minority Protestant Christian belief, a place (or state) in which the 'holy souls' of believers dying in grace but with sins still unexpiated are detained in suffering, before entering heaven; it is held that prayers or good works offered on their behalf (⟡ *Indulgence*) by the living can shorten their suffering.

Puritans. Radical members of the ⟡ *Church of England* in the 16th and 17th centuries, the name originally deriving from purity of doctrine rather than of behaviour, who opposed the ecclesiastical establishment, esp. in its use of Roman Catholic liturgy and vestments and its appointment of bishops. They advocated a simpler form of worship and a strict moral code, and the more extreme dressed plainly and disapproved of all forms of entertainment. They opposed Archbishop Laud's efforts to bring Anglican ritual closer to that of Rome, and gained ground esp. in Scotland (⟡ *Covenant*) and in London. They were in the ascendency at the beginning of the ⟡ *Commonwealth and Protectorate*; with the Restoration and the ⟡ *Clarendon Code* they merged into the general body of Dissenters and ⟡ *Nonconformists*. During the early 17th cent. many puritans emigrated to America (⟡ *Pilgrim Fathers*). The name remains a term for a continuing attitude to life – the virtues of piety, strict sexual morality, temperance, frugality. ⟡ *Calvinism*.

PVC (Polyvinyl chloride) ⟡ *Plastics*.

Pygmalion. In Greek legend, a sculptor (perhaps king of Cyprus) who made (or caused to be made) the marble statue of a woman, Galatea, so beautiful that he fell in love with it, persuaded ⟡ *Aphrodite* to bring it to life, and married his creation.

Pygmies. Negroid peoples of Africa and SE Asia, remarkable for their short stature; those of Africa, Negrilloes, live mainly in the Ituri forest region of the Congo basin, while those of Asia, Negritoes, include the Semang (Malaya), the Aëta (Philippines), and the Ayome (New Guinea). All are forest-dwellers, dependent upon hunting and food-gathering, living in small isolated bands with the simplest form of social organization and culture, frequently trading with surrounding peoples, who supply them with salt and other necessities in return for forest produce. They are probably dwindling in numbers, owing to disease from external contact and to destruction of the forests. ⟡ *Race*.

Pyramids. The tombs of the Pharaohs of ancient ⟡ *Egypt*, from the 3rd millennium B.C. The first Pharaoh to build a pyramid was Zoser, of the 3rd Dynasty, whose stepped pyramid at Saqqara stands 200 ft high; the three famous pyramids at Giza were built by Pharaohs of the 4th Dynasty, the Great Pyramid of Cheops (built of blocks averaging $2\frac{1}{2}$ tons) standing 481 ft high, a geometrical pyramid of extraordinary accuracy. There are many other large pyramids, and smaller ones for wives and officials. The burial chamber, constructed beneath or inside the pyramid, was reached by means of a passage. The method of building is not certain, but it seems likely that the courses were laid from the centre outwards, and that the massive stones were dragged up on ramps, perhaps by sledges. The motives prompting this gigantic labour are not clearly known, but the pyramid form probably had a symbolic significance, in connexion with the Pharaoh's function as sun-god; also it formed a massive structure of great permanence.

Pyrethrum. Early name for plants now included in the genus ⟡ *Chrysanthemum*. Garden pyrethrums are varieties of *C. coccineum*, hardy perennials with finely divided leaves and large red, pink, or white daisy flowers.

PYRETHRUM POWDER: A contact ⟡ *insecticide*, from the flowers of *C. coccineum*. S. Africa, Japan, and U.S.A. are the main producers.

Pyrites. Iron sulphide, pale brassy-yellow ore with brilliant lustre found in sedimentary, igneous, and metamorphic rocks, a common constituent of ore veins associated with many different metals; worthless as a source of iron but when roasted produces sulphuric acid and sulphur. Each of the leading producers, Japan and Spain, supplies about one fifth of the world's annual output of 4 m. tons.

Q

Qatar ◊ *Gulf Sheikhdoms.*

Quadrant ◊ *Astrolabe, Sextant.*

Quakers ◊ *Society of Friends.*

Quantum Physics. Newton's equations of motion and law of gravitation, and Maxwell's equations of electromagnetism, when used in conjunction with Einstein's special theory of relativity, appear to give a correct description of how visible matter responds to forces. On the atomic scale, however, these classic equations usually predict incorrect results, and phenomena occur which cannot be visualized in terms of a classic model. The classic equations can be used e.g. to determine to a high degree of accuracy the orbits of the bodies of the ◊ *solar system*, but they fail to explain even the simplest atomic planetary system; e.g. the hydrogen atom which consists of one 'sun' nucleus and only one 'planet' electron. About 1900 it was realized that a new set of laws would be needed to explain atomic phenomena. Although the quantum theory originated by Planck in 1900 accounted for some of these, by assuming that radiant ◊ *energy* is emitted from atoms only in discrete packets (quanta) and is not continuous, it was not until the 1930s that a consistent alternative to the classic laws was established. In this new approach, the mechanistic concept that the path of an object can be followed in detail is no longer valid. Instead, a new concept of the wave-function of a particle is introduced, the amplitude of the wave-function at a given position in space being related to the ◊ *probability* of finding the particle at that particular position. The fundamental function for calculating particular wave-functions is named after Schrödinger, who first formulated it. Like their counterpart, light-waves in ◊ *optics*, wave-functions are subject to interference and diffraction; e.g. an electron beam generates a diffraction pattern when it passes through the regular lattice of a crystal. The concepts of quantum mechanics imply the principle of indeterminacy (uncertainty), investigated by Heisenberg, according to which the principles of the conservation of energy and of momentum cease to have meaning when the time and position scales respec-tively become sufficiently small. The 'correspondence principle' states that when the laws of quantum mechanics are applied to a visible system they predict the same results as those obtained by the classic laws.

Quantum Theory. The theory that energy is propagated by a continuous wave motion was found not to satisfy certain undeniable phenomena associated with light e.g. the ◊ *photoelectric effect.* It was replaced by the theory that energy is transmitted in bursts of separate bundles or quanta (Planck 1900). Thus a corpuscular concept of the nature of light was re-introduced, combined with wave theory. Further elaborations of the theory have since been made. ◊ *Quantum Physics.*

Quarantine. Period during which persons, animals, and birds entering a country are kept in isolation after arrival, as possible carriers of certain infectious diseases; it varies according to the incubation period of the disease, but formerly was generally 40 days, hence the name. ◊ *Rabies.*

Quarterly Review. A journal founded in 1809 by the publisher John Murray at the suggestion of Walter Scott, the first editor being William Gifford; its principles were conservative and Tory, in opposition to the Whig ◊ *Edinburgh Review,* but it was never so brilliantly written as its rival, perhaps because of less assured editorial direction. It specialized in long and solid but slashing reviews: Southey was a principal contributor in the first numbers; and other famous contributors were J. W. Croker (author of the insensitive criticism 1818 of Keats's *Endymion,* said to have hastened the poet's death), Scott, and Gladstone.

Quartz. Silicon dioxide, a very common mineral, an original constituent of granite and similar acid ◊ *igneous rocks* e.g. sandstones; a common vein-stone, carrying many different metal ores. Extensively used as an abrasive e.g. in sandpaper, in iron-moulding, in the building industry, and in manufacturing glass, pottery, and fire-bricks. Quartz crystals are often coloured e.g. amethyst (violet, purple), cairngorm (yellow), rose quartz (pink).

'Rock crystal' is pure quartz, colourless and transparent. ◊ *Mica, Silica.*

Quaternary Era ◊ *Geological Time Scale, Pleistocene Epoch.*

Quatrain. A four-line stanza linked by ◊ *rhyme,* in English commonly the 'ballad stanza' rhyming *a b a b* or *a b c b*; or 'heroic quatrain' of iambic pentameters (◊ *metre*) rhyming *a b a b* e.g. Gray's *Elegy*; and the '*In Memoriam* stanza' of iambic tetrameters rhyming *a b b a.* Though Fitzgerald's *Omar Khayyam* is very popular, its *a a b a* quatrain has seldom been imitated.

Quebec. 1759. Town on River St Lawrence, capital of French Canadian province of the same name. During the ◊ *Seven Years War* the British general Wolfe, after two frontal attacks had failed, sent his army up the weakly defended Heights of Abraham (considered impregnable) by night, taking the French by surprise. He was killed at the moment of victory, but the victory won ◊ *Canada* for Britain.

Queen Anne Style. In architecture, typical not only of the reign of Anne 1702–14 but also of that of William and Mary 1688–1702, deriving partly from the 1630–60 semi-Dutch style and largely from the stringent domestic-architecture regulations of the 1667 Rebuilding Act after the ◊ *Fire of London*; characterized by the style of Christopher Wren 1632–1723 (Surveyor-General in charge of the post-Fire reconstruction). The plain brick frontage, uniformity of house sizes and heights, pedimented doorways, and hipped roofs are typical. The period also includes Hawksmoor and Vanbrugh, working in

the English ◊ *Baroque* style. The small-scale domestic 'Wren' style was revived about 1870 by Norman Shaw and others.

Quinine ◊ *Alkaloids.*

Quorum. The minimum number of members of a committee who must be present in order to conduct business and reach valid decisions. In the House of Commons the quorum is 40; for other bodies an arbitrary number is usually established by the rules.

R

Rabbit. Animal resembling the ⟡ *rodents*, but classified with the hare in the order *Lagomorpha*; rabbits are gregarious, living in burrows in warrens, and a pest owing to the rapidity with which they multiply (littering 5–10 young 4–6 times a year). They are bred as pets, for food, and for fur (coney). In Australia, where they have no natural enemies, their vast numbers and voracity have inflicted grave damage on agriculture and pastures. ⟡ *Myxomatosis*.

Rabies. Contagious disease in many animals and sometimes humans, caused by a filtrable virus; characterized by throat spasms, convulsions, eventual paralysis of all muscles, and death. Sufferers develop a fear of drinking water, hence the name hydrophobia. The virus gains access through open wounds, and the tendency of infected animals to become aggressive and bite spreads the disease. It does not occur in Britain, Australia, or New Zealand but is prevalent in many other areas; in S. America the annual incidence among cattle has been reported in hundreds of thousands. Very persistent, the disease is difficult to detect in isolated areas where spreaders abound, e.g. foxes, jackals, wolves. In some countries blood-lapping (vampire) bats are carriers; but dogs are chiefly responsible for human infection. Because the virus takes varying times to travel from the point of infection to the central nervous system, the incubation period may be from 10 days to several months; this facilitates the protection of humans by vaccination after infection. ⟡ *Quarantine, Scheduled Diseases*.

Race. All human beings belong to the species *Homo sapiens*, but isolation of some groups and the operation of natural selection in varying climatic conditions have produced 'races' with distinctive common physical characteristics differentiating them. Scientists are wary of the concept 'race' because of the way it has been abused (⟡ *Race Relations*); the different races shade off into one another, no definite lines of demarcation can be drawn, and there is probably no such thing as a 'pure' race. Some form of classification, however, is useful for anthropological description, and the criteria include limb sizes, head shape and features, skin and hair colouring. AUSTRALIFORMS: (see table).

Race	Subdivision	Distribution	Main Characteristics
Euripiform	Nordic	Chiefly N. and W. Europe	Slender; fair; narrow face; eyes close together; prominent chin; dolichocephalic or mesocephalic.
	Alpine	Chiefly central Europe.	Darker than Nordic; abundant hair; short nose; brachycephalic.
	Dinaric	Cent. Europe to Caspian Sea with outliers in S. Arabia.	Olive skin; tall; brachycephalic; meeting eyebrows; high-bridged 'Semitic' nose.
	Mediterranean	Mediterranean countries, N. Africa, Near and Middle East, NW India.	Elongated head; dark hair; sallow pigmentation; medium height; narrow nose.
	Erythriot	NE Africa.	Dark-skinned; wavy hair, sparse on body; thin lips; no prognathism.
	Ainu	Japan.	Euriforms absorbed by Mongols; esp. hirsute.

Race	Subdivision	Distribution	Main Characteristics
Mongoliform	Tungusian Sinian	Throughout Asia and Far East.	More or less typical Mongoloid.
	Polynesian	Polynesia and Micronesia.	Tall; mesocephalic.
	Arctic	Eskimo and other inhabitants of Arctic America.	Skin brownish; tend to epicanthic fold.
	Amerindian	Indigenous peoples of N. and S. America.	Skin reddish to yellowish; height and head shape vary; features Mongoloid.
Negriform	Negro (Sudanian, Guinean, Nilot, Zingian)	Throughout Africa.	Pigmentation varies from light brown to near black; head shape and stature variable; Nilotes esp. tall and slender; black 'woolly' hair; everted lips; slight prognathism; broad nose.
	Negrillo (pygmy)	African equatorial forests.	Short (less than 59 in. adult male); skin reddish-brown; hair rust-coloured; arms much longer than legs.
	Negrito	Andaman Islands forests of Malay Peninsula, some Philippine tribes (Aëta).	Full-lips, not everted; some pygmy characteristics.
	Papuan	In and around New Guinea.	Long, abundant black hair; prominent beaklike nose; dolichocephalic.
	Melanesian	From New Guinea to Fiji.	Shorter than Papuans; moplike hair.
Khoisaniform	Bushman	SW Africa, cent. Tanganyika.	Short; skin yellow to yellow-brown; short ('peppercorn') hair, sparse on body; marked female steatopygia (heavy fat on buttocks and thighs); dolichocephalic.
	Hottentot	ditto	ditto
Australiform	Veddian (pre-Dravidian)	Cent. and S. India and Ceylon.	Rather short; skin sallow to very dark brown; wavy dark hair; prominent supraorbital ridge; dolichocephalic.
	Australian aborigine (Blackfellow)	Australia.	ditto

NOTE: The following terms used in the table are based on a system of measurements and indices of the human head (anthropometry):

BRACHYCEPHALIC: Broad-headed.   MESOCEPHALIC: Round-headed.
DOLICHOCEPHALIC: Long-headed.   PROGNATHISM: Jutting-forward of the lower part of the face.

EURIPIFORMS: Of widely varying type; narrow noses, thin lips, wavy abundant face and body hair.

KHOISANIFORMS: (see table).

MONGOLIFORMS: The most numerous; prominent cheekbones, broad flat faces, skin yellow-white to red-brown, scanty straight hair, brachycephalic, epicanthic fold on upper eyelid, sacral spot on buttocks in early infancy.

NEGRIFORMS: Dark skin, spiralled hair, low broad noses, thick or everted lips, prognathous.

Race Relations. With the ending of colonialism, the greater mobility of population, and the 'westernization' of hitherto backward countries, race relations present problems in many areas. In Africa there is not only the case of S. Africa (◊ *Apartheid*) but the unresolved antagonisms between Africans, Asians, and Arabs, e.g. in ◊ *Zanzibar*, while in Britain trouble over West Indian immigrants has occurred, and in the U.S.S.R. African students have protested against discrimination. In U.S.A. after the Second World War liberal American opinion increasingly condemned the prolongation of the longstanding inequalities between Negro and white, esp. in the South, e.g. segregation in housing, employment, public transport, places of recreation, and the educational system. A series of ◊ *Supreme Court* decisions declared segregated educational systems illegal, but resistance to the Court's orders led to widespread disturbances in 1963, resulting esp. from the intransigeance of state authorities in Missouri and Alabama. As a result, more stringent powers to enforce integration are being sought, and have begun to be used in e.g. New York city. In 1964 the Supreme Court ruled the 1946 Hill-Burton Act (permitting segregation in hospitals) to be unconstitutional. Racism in the sense of the theories of Gobineau and Chamberlain, which proclaims belief in the superiority of the 'Aryan' races and the importance of preserving racial purity, and which was carried to its frightful conclusion by Hitler (◊ *Nazism*) against Jews and Slavs, no longer commands wide support; the problem of racial prejudice and of social and economic integration nevertheless remains considerable.

Rackets. A very fast game played by two or four men in a walled court 62 by 31 ft,

with rackets and a small hard ball. It originated as a tavern and prison game in the 18th cent. and was the forerunner of ◊ *squash rackets*, but is now little played except at certain British public schools. The British Championships are held at the Queens Club in London; there are also championships in Canada and U.S.A.

Radar. Radio Detection and Ranging, originally called radiolocation; designed to detect and find the range of moving objects, by sending a beam of electromagnetic waves towards them and measuring the time the 'echo' takes to return. Because the waves travel at the speed of light, and may return in only a few millionths of a second, measurements must be extremely quick and accurate. In his 1934–6 pioneer work Watson-Watt tried continuous radio waves of about 10-metre wavelength, but obtained better results with shorter waves transmitted in powerful short ◊ *pulses* (even then less than a million-millionth of the original power was returned in the echo). Britain's radar was a decisive factor in repulsing the German air offensive in 1940, and later in interception, night bombing, and location of rocket-launching sites. The formidable technical problems of radar were solved by teams of British and American scientists and engineers, who invented many new electronic devices and very-high-frequency techniques. These included the plan-position indicator, which presented a continuous picture of the target's position on the screen of a cathode-ray tube; search aerial arrays with accurately controlled movements and narrow beams; the ◊ *magnetron*, which produced very powerful bursts of high-frequency ◊ *energy* in transmitters; extremely fast ◊ *electronic* switches; sensitive and selective receivers; and waveguides. The peaceful uses of radar include air and ground and marine traffic control, automatic navigation and landing devices etc. Direction-finding and navigation by radar do not usually depend on echoes but on registering signals from specific transmitters. In ◊ *radioastronomy* wavelengths between 1 cm. and 30 metres are used, being the only ones able to penetrate the earth's ◊ *ionosphere*, and they have been successfully reflected back from the sun, the moon, some of the planets, auroras, meteor trails, and ◊ *artificial satellites*.

Radiation. Emission and transmission of energy in wave form, applied both to (1) electromagnetic energy and (2) particles from radioactive substances.

1. Electromagnetic radiation, of all wavelengths, travels through space at the speed of light (about 186,000 miles per second), its properties depending on its particular wavelength. The visible ◊ *spectrum* is only a small part of the complete electromagnetic spectrum, which varies from 'radio' waves many miles long to gamma and cosmic rays less than a millionmillionth of a cm. long. In addition to producing light, hot bodies (e.g. the sun, or electric bulbs) emit radiation of longer wavelength (◊ *Infrared Rays*), detectable by its heating effect. Immediately on the short-wavelength side of the visible spectrum are the ◊ *ultraviolet rays*, which are (generally) quickly absorbed in matter; and of still shorter wavelengths are the highly-penetrating ◊ *X-rays* and other rays produced in nuclear processes.

2. The process inherent in unstable ◊ *nuclides* of ◊ *elements* (the main ones that occur naturally are above 82 in the ◊ *Periodic Table*) whereby the atomic parent nucleus breaks up spontaneously to give a more stable product nucleus (daughter), together with the emission of particle (e.g. α-, β-particles) and/or electromagnetic e.g. γ-, X-rays) radiations.

Radioactive transformations, which are statistical in character, have thrown important light on the detailed structure of the nucleus.

With modern techniques using ◊ *particle accelerators* and ◊ *nuclear reactors*, the *nuclides* of any element may be made radioactive. The production of radioactive isotopes is of great value to the doctor (e.g. the treatment of cancer), the agriculturalist (e.g. the sterilization of pests and the development of sturdier strains of crops by genetic mutations), the engineer (e.g. material location and control, examinations of welded joints, etc.), the archaeologist, and even the criminologist.

Radiation Sickness. Study of casualties who escaped immediate death in the atom bombing of ◊ *Hiroshima* show that one of the principal effects of a single large dose of radiation is to destroy the capacity of the body to produce antibodies (◊ *Immunity*), so that the body's resistance to infection is greatly reduced. The bone marrow ceases to produce new blood cells; anaemia and massive gastro-intestinal haemorrhages follow; and the normal process of repair of body cells is interrupted. Vomiting, diarrhoea, inflammation of the mouth and throat, and fever lead inexorably to death usually within two weeks. Patients may recover very slowly from smaller doses, which produce chronic ill-health and anaemia. Prolonged exposure to repeated small doses may have delayed effects e.g. increased liability to ◊ *leukemia* and ◊ *cancer*. Similar effects result from breathing ◊ *fallout* dust. ◊ *Radiobiology*.

Radio. Wireless; the transmission of signals without wire, based on the discovery by Maxwell of electromagnetic waves (◊ *Radiation*) and of means to generate them by Hertz. In 1895 Marconi demonstrated a system of wireless communication. Further developments depended upon the invention of the vacuum tube by Fleming, a means of detecting radio waves by an electronic device, which made possible the transmission of sound and thus led to radio telephony and broadcasting. ◊◊ *British Broadcasting Corporation, Independent Television Authority, Radar.*

Radioastronomy. Recently developed branch of ◊ *astronomy* based on longwave radio radiation from heavenly bodies, whereas conventional optical astronomy depends for its information on light-waves in the visible, near ultraviolet and infrared parts of the electromagnetic spectrum. Radiation in other regions of the ◊ *spectrum* appeared to be absorbed by the earth's atmosphere, and it was not known that some long-wave radiation also reached the earth. Although Edison had drawn attention to the probability of this 'radio' radiation in the ◊ *solar system* as early as 1890, radioastronomy really began in 1932 when Jansky in U.S.A. first detected noise from outer space. Subsequent mapping of the sources showed that many did not coincide with known celestial bodies, but were invisible 'radio stars', at first explained as clouds of ◊ *hydrogen* evolving into new stars or as burnt-out stars deriving great radio energy from the effect of strong magnetic field and rapid rotation; many are now thought to be heavenly bodies too distant to be optically visible, and radioastronomy opens fresh possibilities for ◊ *space exploration.*

Among the known celestial bodies outside the solar system showing strong radio emission are the Crab ◊ *nebula* and the remains of other supernova explosions, the Andromeda nebula, and two galaxies in collision in Centaurus. Within the solar system, the sun, moon, and planets all emit short-wave radio radiation, whose variations can often be related to other phenomena, e.g. the sun's radio radiation increases enormously during flares. Radiation of 21 cm. wavelength is emitted by interstellar hydrogen, which is optically difficult to detect. Study of this radiation has been most fruitful in indicating the structure of ◊ *interstellar matter* within the ◊ *Galaxy*. ◊ *Radar*.

RADIO TELESCOPES are in the form of a large parabolic 'dish' of metal or wire e.g. the world's largest, at Jodrell Bank, or an extensive array of aerials.

Radiobiology. The study of the effect on living things of radiations, e.g. X-rays, gamma-rays, beams of electrons, alpha particles, and neutrons, and to a lesser extent ultraviolet light. Human beings receive radiations from both natural and artificial sources; the former include cosmic radiation, ultraviolet light from the sun, and radiation from decay of radioactive isotopes e.g. uranium and radium in the earth's crust. Artificial exposure results from the medical use of radiations, from occupational hazards, and from ◊ *fallout*; the dose of natural radiation received by the general population is negligible, and the dose from an X-ray examination is very small.

Radiations are always harmful to living things though tolerated in very small amounts. All organisms can be killed by radiation, although the dose required varies widely e.g. 30,000 roentgens of X-ray may be required to kill a bacterial cell, but about one hundredth of this is lethal to man, ◊ *Radiation Sickness*. Radiation can, however, be employed (under controlled conditions) to kill ◊ *cancer* cells. In 1926 Muller demonstrated that X-rays can cause ◊ *gene* mutations in fruit flies, an effect since found with other organisms. The critical dose appears to be very much less than a lethal dose. Dangerous but non-lethal doses may cause illness often revealed only years later, e.g. certain types of cancer. A further hazard is the ingestion of certain radioactive ◊

isotopes, e.g. radioactive ◊ *iodine* accumulates in the ◊ *thyroid* gland, radioactive ◊ *strontium* concentrates in developing bone-tissue, and exposure of bone-marrow cells to electrons emitted by disintegrating radiostrontium may induce ◊ *leukemia*. Bone tumours may also result from the same cause.

Radiocarbon Dating. Method of dating fossils and archaeological objects of wood, bone, textile, and other organic materials, developed by W. F. Libby in 1946. It is based on the presence in all organic matter of radioactive carbon-14 atoms, in the ratio of one to about 1000 m. normal atoms. As these disintegrate in dead organic materials by radioactive decay, with a ◊ *half-life* of 5530 years, it is possible to assess the age of an object by measuring the proportion of carbon-14 which remains. The method is still at an experimental stage, and there is room for error, e.g. owing to the contamination of specimens, but the dating in many cases has been corroborated by other evidence. The chronology for prehistory in the Near East and Europe is being revised in the light of new radiocarbon datings. Rocks may be dated by following a somewhat similar method based on the presence of uranium, in small quantities, which through a long chain of transformations disintegrates into lead.

Radium. With ◊ *polonium*, the first natural radioactive ◊ *element* discovered, by Pierre and Marie Curie in 1898; a metal found in ◊ *uranium* ores, similar in chemical properties to ◊ *barium*, from which it is derived by a chain of radioactive emissions. It owes its radioactive properties to the emission of ◊ *alpha particles*, and is used in medicine for the treatment of ◊ *cancer*, in industrial radiography for the non-destructive inspection of metal castings, and (mixed with ◊ *beryllium*) as a convenient small source of neutrons. Since the advent of the nuclear reactor, many much cheaper substitutes for radium have become available. The chief source is pitchblende from Canada, the Congolese Republic, and U.S.A.

Radon ◊ *Inert Gases*.

R.A.F. ◊ *Royal Air Force*.

Ragnarok. In Norse mythology, the destruction of the world and the gods (Götterdämmerung), when all things will perish by fire after a great battle with the powers of evil (who are also destroyed); after it, a new earth and heaven will come into being, Odin's sons Vali and Vidar, Balder and Hoder (◊ *Aesir*) will reappear, and a state of bliss will ensue.

Ragtime. An early type of ◊ *jazz* esp. for the piano; the 'ragging' (constant syncopation) of a straightforward tune. It was made widely famous in 1911 by Irving Berlin's song *Alexander's Ragtime Band*, and in 1918 was borrowed by Stravinsky in his *Ragtime for 11 Instruments*. ◊ *Dance.*

Railways. Originated as early as A.D. 1520 in mines, when it was realized that a horse could pull more wagons on rails than on a road, owing to the reduction in friction; steam traction was demonstrated in 1804 by Trevithick in S. Wales, but its first public use was Stephenson's Stockton–Darlington railway in 1825. In 1829 his Rocket locomotive attained a speed of 30 m.p.h. Steam-traction railways then developed rapidly in Britain and on the European continent, and a little later in U.S.A. The first trans-American line (Union Pacific Railway) was completed in 1869, the Montreal–Vancouver line (Canadian Pacific Railway) in 1885. In Russia the St Petersburg to Vladivostock line (Trans-Siberian Railway), linking the Baltic with the Pacific, was completed in 1905. Improvements in rolling-stock came early: Pullman sleeping-cars 1859, dining-cars 1879, corridor trains 1890. Practically all British, European, and U.S.A. railways are of the 4 ft 8½ in. narrow gauge, but the U.S.S.R. uses the 5 ft broad gauge. After 1900, electrification proceeded rapidly in thickly-populated areas; on other lines diesel or diesel-electric propulsion has since superseded or is superseding steam. Underground electric railways were pioneered in London, the Metropolitan line in 1863 and the 'tube' (City and S. London) in 1890. Under the 1921 Railways Act the numerous private railways in Britain were amalgamated in four main groups; the 1947 Transport Act brought these under public ownership as British Railways. The only major country where railways are still privately owned is U.S.A. In all countries railways have suffered from the competition of air and road transport, and in Britain the 1963 Beeching Plan has proposed the closing of many unprofitable lines. ◊ *Industrial Revolution.*

Rain. Water-vapour in the atmosphere condenses and forms clouds; the water droplets grow in size and finally fall. Various attempts have been made to produce rain artificially, e.g. 'seeding' the top of a cloud with solid carbon dioxide particles from aircraft to form ice crystals which produce raindrops; the process is expensive and of limited efficiency. ◊ *Weather.*

Rainbow. Coloured arch in the sky caused when sunlight passes through raindrops and is spread into its spectral colours by refraction and reflection. Light passing through spray or a waterfall often produces a rainbow effect. ◊ *Spectrum.*

Rain Forest. Tropical (equatorial) forest e.g. in the Amazon and the Congo basins, a region of constant heavy rainfall where owing to heat and moisture the vegetation is dense. Trees grow to great heights, ◊ *lianas* support themselves by climbing up other trees, and ◊ *epiphytes* e.g. orchids are abundant, but clearing is difficult and the soil impoverished; the Brazilian state of Amazonas, about 600,000 sq. m. of the Amazon basin, supports a population of less than ¼ m. The great variety of trees includes valuable hardwoods e.g. ebony and mahogany, and in S. America the wild rubber tree *Hevea brasiliensis*, but they are often too widely scattered to be of much economic value.

Ramadan. Ninth month of the Mohammedan year (◊ *Hegira*), during which the ◊ *Koran* was revealed to Mohammed; kept by Muslims as a strict fast, during which no food or drink (even water) may be taken from sunrise to sunset. The Mohammedan year being lunar, it may fall at any season of the solar year. ◊ *Religious Festivals.*

Ramayana. One of the Sanskrit epics of India which took its present form towards the 3rd cent. B.C. It recounts the adventures of Rama, 7th avatar (incarnation) of the god ◊ *Vishnu*. It is the story in the form of legend and allegory of the spread of the Aryans into southern India around 800 B.C. It deals with the tender and intimate aspects of family life and loyalties and has always had more popular appeal in India than the longer and more austere ◊ *Mahabharata.*

Ramillies (1706) ◊ *War of the Spanish Succession.*

Rapacki Plan. Proposal, first put forward in 1958 by the Polish Foreign Minister, to reduce tension in Europe by creating a European zone (to include Poland, Czechoslovakia, E. and W. Germany) in which the manufacture, stockpiling, and use of nuclear weapons would be banned, the prohibition to apply both to the forces of the states in the zone and to those stationed there by N.A.T.O. and Warsaw Pact states, and to be policed through aerial and ground inspection supervised by representatives of both blocs. The plan was supported by the U.S.S.R. but not accepted by the U.K. and U.S.A. because of the numerical superiority of the Warsaw Pact countries in conventional forces and because it did not provide for German reunification.

In 1964 Poland put forward a revision of the plan, by which existing stocks of nuclear weapons in central Europe would be frozen (under appropriate controls), stocks of conventional arms limited, and a non-aggression treaty concluded between N.A.T.O. and the Warsaw Pact states.

Rapallo Treaties. 1920, 1922. 1. 1920. The Italo-Yugoslav treaty whereby Italy received Triestino and Yugoslavia Dalmatia, while Fiume, seized by Italian troops in 1919, remained independent.

2. 1922. The Russo-German treaty which was the first international agreement recognizing the new Soviet state. The two signatories renounced all pre-war debts and war claims: Germany gained extensive trade facilities. The treaty was viewed with suspicion by the Allies, as the beginning of a German attempt to overthrow the ◊ *Versailles* settlement.

Rape. 1. A kind of turnip, genus *Brassica,* which develops leaves rather than root, used as green fodder for cattle, as a source of oil (from the seed), and as a green manure (ploughed under in full growth). ◊ *Cruciferae.*

2. Sexual intercourse with a woman without her consent, women being deemed legally incapable of consent if insane, mentally subnormal, or below the statutory 'age of consent' (16 in the U.K.); punishable by imprisonment.

'Rare-earth' Elements ◊ *Lanthanides.*

Rare Gases ◊ *Inert Gases.*

Raspberry. *Rubus idaeus;* the wild raspberry, a native of Europe, from which the cultivated varieties have been derived. Both white and red varieties were cultivated in England in the early 17th cent. In America other species of *Rubus* have also

been used in breeding, but the resulting varieties are not successful in Europe.

Rat. *Rattus,* larger species of the ◊ *rodent* family *Mus,* of world-wide distribution in many species, the smaller being known as mice. The females litter eight young five times a year, and the rate of reproduction is prodigious. The most abundant are *R. rattus,* black, and *R. norvegicus,* brown; both native to Asia. The more vigorous brown rat, spreading from Asia in the 18th cent., drove out the black from much of its territory both in Europe and America. The rat is virtually omnivorous and causes great damage to food stores and to crops. Flea-infested rats are carriers of several diseases and were responsible for disastrous epidemics in the Middle Ages.

Rationalism. In philosophy, the belief opposed to ◊ *empiricism,* that factual truths about the universe can be had by pure reasoning from self-evident premisses not themselves empirical: Descartes (◊ *Cartesianism*) begins with: 'I think; therefore I exist.' In another sense, rationalism is the view that religion ought not to be accepted on faith but rationally assessed.

Rattlesnake ◊ *Snake, Viper.*

Rayon. Various artificial fibres, not synthetics like e.g. nylon, but derived from vegetable ◊ *cellulose.* Pure cellulose is insoluble; its utilization depended on the discovery that partially-nitrated cellulose is soluble in organic solvents. The basic process, patented by Swan in 1883, consists in extruding a solution from a fine nozzle to form a filament, which is then 'regenerated' (solidified) in a precipitating fluid. The French cuprammonium process was next developed, in Germany, but was largely superseded by the viscose process, invented in England, whereby a soluble cellulose derivative is made by the action of carbon disulphide and caustic soda; the bulk of world production of rayon is now made by this process, the cellulose coming mainly from Canadian and Scandinavian wood pulp.

RAYON STAPLE: Filament cut into short lengths, similar to those of natural cotton or wool, suitable for use in cotton and woollen textile mills.

RAYON YARN: Continuous thread, made from filaments as they emerge in manufacture.

Realism. In art, the genre of several mid 19th-cent. painters esp. Courbet, reacting against the idealizing tendencies of neo-classicism and romanticism, who depicted harsh and sometimes squalid aspects of contemporary life.

In literature, detached presentation without the author's personal obtrusion, e.g. Flaubert's *Madame Bovary* 1857; also a determination not to flinch from life's unpleasant aspect; and sometimes 'an emphasis on sordid or unpleasant scenes'. In both art and literature, the term applies strictly to the subject-matter only; it is not to be confused with ◊ *naturalism*, the 'lifelike' or 'photographic' manner of painting or writing.

In philosophy, a theory of ◊ *universals*; also the common-sense view (as opposed to ◊ *idealism* and ◊ *phenomenalism*) that physical objects are not merely our 'ideas' but exist independently of our perception.

Real Tennis. As now played, a complex racket-and-ball game played across a net and also against the walls of an indoor court. The ball is small and hard, made of strips of cloth bound tightly with twine. It probably evolved from the medieval French game known as Royal Tennis from its popularity with several monarchs. Henry VIII built a court at Hampton Court Palace which is still in use. The game was originally played with the hand, first ungloved and then with gloves. The earliest rackets were of wood, introduced by the Italians, who called them *palettas*. These were followed by stringed rackets, which by 1700 were threaded vertically and horizontally to give a much tauter strike. The game was named from the French *tenez*, which a player called out before serving. Real tennis is still played, but to a limited extent, as the courts are very expensive.

Reaper. Tractor, or machine pulled by draft animals, for reaping ◊ *cereals*, to supplant cutting by scythe or sickle: early machines were invented in the 18th cent. but not developed, and the first practical machine was patented by Cyrus McCormick in 1834. A series of inventions followed, which permitted e.g. mechanical binding of the sheaves, and finally the 'combine', which both threshes and bags the grain.

Recitative. A kind of singing which in its rhythmic style is more nearly related to the irregularity of speech than to the regularity of formal song. It was invented in Italy shortly before 1600 and is most familiar as prefacing (often in conversational style) an aria in opera or oratorio e.g. of Handel, Mozart, or Rossini.

Recorder. Woodwind instrument belonging to the ◊ *flute* group, but end-blown, not side-blown like the modern standard flute. Current in W. European music from the 14th cent. to the 18th, when it began to be superseded by the side-blown flute; revived in modern times chiefly for the playing of old music and for educational use.

Rectifier. Substance or device which will pass electricity in one direction only and can therefore be used to convert alternating current to direct current. An arc maintained between a metal ◊ *electrode* and a pool of ◊ *mercury* has this property, and is the basis of the mercury-arc rectifier.

Red Cross. International organization, with headquarters in Switzerland, devoted to the relief of the wounded and prisoners during wartime. The International Committee of the Red Cross was created by the Geneva Conference of 1864, under the inspiration of the Swiss Henri Dunant; the Geneva Convention provided for the neutrality of the personnel of the medical services of the armed forces, the humane treatment of the wounded, the neutrality of civilians who voluntarily assisted them, and an international emblem to mark personnel and supplies. In honour of Dunant, the Swiss flag (with colours reversed) was adopted. There are 68 national Red Cross societies, and two international groups with headquarters in Geneva. In Muslim communities the cross is replaced by the crescent. ◊◊ *Solferino*.

Red Deer. *Cervus elaphus*, of the *Cervidae*, inhabiting Europe, N. Africa, Asia Minor, and N. Persia, and successfully introduced into New Zealand; a woodland animal, travelling in herds. The males (stags) alone bear antlers, which are shed annually, and may reach a shoulder-height of four ft six in. The coat is spotted in the young, and occasionally in the adult. In Britain the red deer has been confined to the Scottish highlands,

A single arrow before a word or phrase indicates a cross-reference to another main entry. A double arrow means *See also*.

Exmoor, and a few parks, but is in decline. ⟡ *Deer*.

Referendum. An official poll to ascertain the will of the voters on one or more specific proposals, used as a standard method in Switzerland and frequently employed in other countries e.g. France on issues of great national debate and importance e.g. ⟡ *French Community, Saar*. Its introduction into Britain has been proposed but never accepted.

Reformation. The explosive culmination in the early 16th cent. of centuries of 'heretical' opposition to the papacy (⟡ *Albigenses, Hussites, Lollards*), precipitated in 1517 by the 95 Theses of Martin Luther, objecting to papal malpractices and esp. the sale of ⟡ *indulgences*. Despite excommunication Luther persisted in his criticisms, and was widely supported, esp. in N. Europe; though he savagely opposed the ⟡ *Peasants War* (and later the ⟡ *Münster* rebellion), his call for Church reform was powerfully confirmed in 1529 when the Princes of the Holy Roman Empire issued the *Protestatio* from which ⟡ *Protestantism* takes its name. By the middle of the 16th cent. Protestantism had divided into two distinct branches: Lutheran and Calvinist, the latter comprising the followers of the Frenchman John Calvin, whose reforms, both in church government and in doctrine, were more extreme than Luther's. Calvinism was most successful in France (where its adherents were the ⟡ *Huguenots*), in Holland, and in Scotland. On the Continent, the struggle took long-lasting violent forms, and the policies of the ⟡ *Counter-Reformation* colour Europe's late 16th- and 17th-cent. history. In England the Reformation came about largely through political considerations. Henry VIII, unable to gain papal permission for a divorce from Catherine of Aragon, carried through a series of measures severing the English Church from Rome and establishing himself as its head, with the power to dissolve all monasteries and religious orders and dispose of their wealth. At the same time he opposed doctrinal reformation: a compromise between Roman Catholicism and Calvinism, close in many ways to the pre-Reformation Church, was established by Elizabeth, after the violent Catholic reaction of the reign of Mary. Literary results of the Reformation were the translation of the ⟡ *Bible* into vernacular languages (by Luther, Melancthon, Tyndale, Coverdale, etc.) and Cranmer's ⟡ *Prayer Book*. ⟡ *Arminianism, Moravians, Nonconformists, Thirty Years War*.

Reform Bills. Five statutes which reformed the British electoral system. Representation in Parliament (unchanged since the 16th cent.) had long ceased to reflect the distribution of population when the first Reform Bill of 1831 was introduced by the ⟡ *Whigs* under Earl Grey. After bitter resistance from the ⟡ *Tories* and rioting in favour of reform in several cities, it was passed in 1832; 141 seats taken from small boroughs were redistributed, mainly among the new industrial towns, 'rotten' boroughs were abolished, and the electorate (formerly 434,000 out of a population of 24 m.) was almost doubled (mainly by the addition of middle-class householders). The Reform Bill of 1867, a bid for working-class support by Disraeli, reallocated further seats and enfranchised the town-dwelling working class, again doubling the electorate. Gladstone's 1884 Bill removed the distinction between county and borough franchises and added about two m. rural voters. The 1885 Redistribution Act made representation nearly proportional to population, and the 1918 Representation of the People Act gave the vote (with short residence qualifications) to all men over 21 and all women over 30; the ratio of M.P.s to population was fixed at one to 70,000. The 1928 Act gave women the vote on the same terms as men; that of 1948 abolished plural representation (by which business-owners and University-members had voted both on a professional and a residential basis), and also abolished the few remaining double-member constituencies. Only peers, felons, and lunatics are now denied a vote. ⟡ *Chartism*.

Refraction ⟡ *Optics*.

Refrigeration. Keeping a cold chamber at a low temperature by continuously extracting and dissipating heat; basically an aspect of a pump-actuated ⟡ *heat* cycle. In a vapour-compression refrigerator, e.g. commercial and domestic types, a special fluid (often ammonia or 'Freon') is pumped through pipes in the cold chamber, where it absorbs heat and becomes a vapour, which a compressor recondenses into a fluid, the cycle continuing indefinitely. Used for manufacturing ice, for commercial cold storage in warehouses and ships, in domestic storage, in air conditioning, and for various engineering and industrial processes, refrigeration has e.g. revolutionized the preserving and transporting of meat, chilled beef remaining in good condition for 3 weeks at 28° to 30° F.

ACCELERATED FREEZE DRYING (AFD): A recent development combining the advantages of deep freeze and of dehydration, without loss of flavour or vitamin content.

DEEP FREEZE: Rapid freezing of fresh fish, fruit, vegetables, etc. which enables them to be kept in good condition for long periods.

Refugees. Throughout history people have fled from war and persecution, ◊ *Armenia, Huguenots, Jews*; but it was not until after the ◊ *First World War* that international action was taken to help them. The Norwegian Nansen 1861–1930 did much to develop aid for refugees and 'stateless' persons. The ◊ *Second World War* threw up a refugee problem of unprecedented size, when several million 'displaced persons' could not return to their homelands. The ◊ *United Nations* Relief and Rehabilitation Administration (UNRRA) was formed in 1943 to aid areas liberated from German and Japanese occupation; in 1948 its functions were taken over by the Food and Agriculture Organization and the International Refugee Organization, and in 1951 the office of the U.N. High Commissioner for Refugees was established. A vast amount of resettlement was carried out by these agencies; but persisting problems include e.g. Arabs obliged to leave Israel (itself having some of the millions of displaced Jews); Chinese who flee to ◊ *Hong Kong* from the mainland; Tutsi fleeing from ◊ *Rwanda* into Burundi; Christians and Hindus from ◊ *Pakistan* into India; etc. In 1956–7 there was a considerable exodus of refugees from ◊ *Hungary*. The United Nations Organization in 1958 passed a British resolution for a World Refugee Year, a campaign which in 1959–60 raised about £28 m. of which Britain contributed £9 m. By 1960 the number of refugees in Europe in need of assistance had been reduced to 160,000.

Regeneration. The power of replacing lost parts, which some living organisms possess to a high degree; e.g. certain species of flatworm, if cut in half, will form two individuals. In insects and mammals the regenerative powers are more limited, though particular tissues (e.g. skin, liver) can regenerate well.

Reichstag Fire. Fire which swept the German parliament building in Berlin in 1933. The Nazis exploited the fire to stir up feeling against the Communists and to justify decrees giving absolute power to the Nazi party. The instigator of the fire, a Dutchman, was executed; a Bulgarian Communist Dimitrov was tried for complicity but, after a brilliant defence, acquitted.

Reign of Terror. Period during the ◊ *French Revolution* when France was threatened by foreign invasion from spring 1793 to summer 1794, during which the Committee of Public Safety carried out several thousand hasty executions of 'counter-revolutionaries'.

Reindeer. *Rangifer*; a large Arctic and sub-Arctic ◊ *deer* with short ears and tail and a maned throat; both sexes bear antlers which are shed in winter, those of the male being larger and more complex. They have been domesticated by the Lapps and introduced as a domestic animal into arctic Canada and Alaska: the American species are called caribou.

Relativity. Theory concerned with the relationship between the observations of the same event made by different observers, moving relatively to one another. For instance, a passenger in a train moving at 60 m.p.h. may observe a second passenger walking along the corridor towards the engine at a speed of three m.p.h. relative to himself, but to an observer outside the train the walker's speed will appear as 63 m.p.h. Each description is valid for the system in which each observer finds himself. For such comparatively low velocities, a simple relationship can be readily established, but developing the idea leads to the question whether our world is moving relative to the universe, and whether, if so, the motion affects the laws of nature we deduce. Many problems of this kind were discussed in the late 19th cent. and esp. the idea that as light was considered to move in all-pervading 'ether', at a constant velocity with respect to it, the earth's motion through the 'ether' should be detectable by noting varying velocities of light-beams moving in different directions on the earth's surface. Despite the difficulties (light travels at about a fifth of a million miles a second), Michelson and Morley successfully carried out such an experiment; contrary to expectations, they found that irrespective of the observer's motion the velocity of light was always constant.

Working from this result, Einstein proposed his Special Theory of Relativity, which applies to observers moving at a constant velocity relative to one another, and assumes two main postulates: (1) All laws of nature are independent of the uniform relative motion of the observers; and (2) light, regardless of the velocity of the source, has the same velocity for all observers in uniform motion. From these postulates Einstein made many important deductions, one of the most fundamental being that ◊ *mass* and ◊ *energy* are equivalent, their relationship being expressible by the equation $E = mc^2$ (E energy, m mass, c velocity of light in cm. per second), which indicates that a small amount of matter is equivalent to a vast amount of energy, a phenomenon confirmed in the release of nuclear energy. This special theory also dealt with the effect of velocity upon length (◊ *Fitzgerald-Lorenz Contraction*), mass (the faster an object moves, in relation to an observer, the greater its mass), and time (if two observers are moving at a constant velocity relative to one another, the processes of each as observed by the other are slowed down). The application of the principles of relativity to most physical events ordinarily experienced on the earth's surface produces negligibly small discrepancies compared with classic principles; the differences become appreciable only at velocities approaching that of light, e.g. in high-energy electrons. In everyday life, an event can be adequately represented by three space coordinates (time is considered independently). In special relativity, reality can be mathematically translated only into four-dimensional ◊ *geometry*, taking account of time as well as space.

The General Theory of Relativity deals with phenomena as observed between systems not in uniform relative motion, and leads to a modification of the classic theory of gravitation; one calculation which it made possible, and which observation confirmed, was gravitational deflection of light.

Religion. The body of beliefs and practices by which man expresses his attitude to any superhuman power in whose existence he believes; defined by Frazer as 'a propitiation or conciliation of powers superior to man, which are believed to control the course of nature or of human life'. It was once thought that all primitive religions were forms of ◊ *animism*, and that the earliest was ◊ *totemism*; these views are now discarded.

Among primitive peoples, a belief in a creator god (or spirit) seems universal; this power is rarely personalized, and is often regarded as so remote and indifferent as to make propitiation by sacrifice unnecessary. Though traces of religious belief are found in prehistory, e.g. the Mother-Goddess figurines of the Late Stone Age, no one theory of origins has yet found general acceptance; probable factors were e.g. fear of the dead, awe at natural phenomena, fertility cults (as attempts to increase food supplies). The sacred beings propitiated by sacrifice include ancestor spirits, totemic spirits, spirits of particular places, the earth, and gods and goddesses in a pantheon or singly. Sacrifices and prayers are offered in sickness, disaster, harvest-times and at birth, death, and other crises. Specialist priests are rare, offerings being made by the head of a ◊ *clan* or family, often after contact with the divinity has been established by a ◊ *shaman*, diviner, or 'medicine-man'.

In general, the nature of a religion is closely associated with the form of the society, i.e. if the society is segmented into small groups, so is its body of sacred beings, each associated with a particular group. As a society changes, so does its religion, closely linked with which are beliefs and practices belonging to ◊ *magic, witchcraft and sorcery, oracles, divination*; the various aspects of this magico-religious complex vary in importance among different peoples, and the emphasis on them among one people changes with changing circumstances.

The beginnings of the 'higher' religions (◊ *Buddhism, Christianity, Judaism*), into which enters a strong ethical element, date to the 6th and 5th centuries B.C. The last world religion to arise was that of ◊ *Islam* in the 6th cent. A.D. Though since the 17th cent. organized religion has lost some ground to naturalist and materialist attitudes (⟡ *Atheism, Communism, Humanism, Marxism*), Christianity and Islam are still showing a high degree of viability and an ability to come to terms with contemporary thought (often in 'modernized' re-stated forms), without prejudice to their essentials. Most of the primitive religions are giving way to the world religions, mainly because of the breaking-up of the small primitive societies through contact with technologically advanced countries.

Religious Festivals. The chief Christian festivals are ⟡ *Easter*; ⟡ *Christmas*; Pentecost (Whitsun), 50 days after Easter, to commemorate the descent of the Holy Ghost on the Apostles (Acts ii); Ascension Day, 10 days before Whitsun; Epiphany, 6 Jan., marking Jesus Christ's baptism and the visit of the Wise Men (Magi) to his cradle; and among Roman Catholics Corpus Christi, in memory of the institution of the ⟡ *Eucharist*.

The chief Jewish holy days are ⟡ *Passover*; Pentecost, in Judaism the feast of Weeks or Harvest, 50 days after Passover, celebrating also the giving of the Law to Moses; New Year (Rosh Hoshanah) Sept. or Oct.; and Tabernacles (Succoth), 15 days later, commemorating the sojourn in the wilderness.

Buddhists celebrate Wesak, on the full moon in May, on which day the Buddha is said to have received enlightenment.

Main Muslim observances are ⟡ *Ramadan* and the pilgrimage to ⟡ *Mecca*.
Religious Orders ⟡ *Monasticism*.
Religious Wars ⟡ *Huguenots, Thirty Years War*.
Renaissance. The rebirth of classical forms and ideas in the arts, and the growth of secular culture, with the decline of the feudal, monastic, agrarian culture of the Middle Ages and the rise of urban mercantile civilization and a new ruling class, first evident in the 14th-cent. Italian city-states esp. Florence, Milan, and Venice; in literature and art, in Italy, the period from the death of Giotto 1337 to that of Michelangelo 1564, and in other parts of Europe a slightly later period, as Italian influence spread. Renaissance ⟡ *classicism* and ⟡ *humanism* contrast with the pietistic spirit of the Middle Ages; in literature the new ruling class, with their sympathy for the educational and political

theories of humanism, play an important part both as authors and patrons. Under their influence there developed a close relationship between literature and music; secular drama in place of morality and miracle plays; criticism rather than rhetoric; Platonism, Petrarchism, epics, pastorals, sonnets instead of courtly love and romances; a trend towards naturalism in the visual arts; an emphasis on individual subjectivity; vernacular literature; changes in prosody; a shift from the spoken word to the printed.

During the Renaissance, the most highly esteemed literary works were those of Petrarch and his followers (e.g. in England Thomas Wyatt), of the Pléiade and the Elizabethan sonneteers and of writers of epics (from Petrarch to Spenser). Today the most admired Renaissance literary works are those outside the then fashionable concepts, which most clearly show the old-new world conflict, e.g. Machiavelli's *Prince*, Cellini's *Memoirs*, Shakespeare's plays, Montaigne's *Essays*, and metaphysical poetry.

In art the same influences brought about great changes. In the 13th cent. Nicola and Giovanni Pisano had already made use of classical elements in their sculpture, and Giotto had painted with a vivid appreciation of the dignity and individuality of man; these two ideals first coalesced in the paintings of Masaccio, the buildings of Brunelleschi, the sculpture of Donatello, and esp. in the churches of Alberti, which employ the classical ⟡ *architectural orders*, are designed according to classical laws of proportion (derived from the human body), and are intended to glorify not only God but the artist's patrons. Artists revived all classical forms: the nude statue, the bronze statuette, the portrait, the medal, the engraved gem. At the same time the techniques of naturalistic representation were greatly improved by the development of e.g. ⟡ *perspective*. The 1420–1500 period in Italy is the early Renaissance; by about 1500 the great Italian artists were in full command of their techniques and had attained a pure and classically-balanced harmony. The 1500–27 period (up to the Sack of Rome) is the High Renaissance, to which belong Michelangelo's earlier works, Raphael's Roman works, and most of Leonardo da Vinci's works. In central Italy the pure Renaissance style gave way to ⟡ *mannerism*, but it lived on in Venice, where Titian emerged as the great painter of the mid 16th cent.

Rent. In law, what a tenant or user has to pay for using another's property. House-rent was traditionally a private bargain between owner and tenant; but in the U.K. during the First World War shortage of houses led to the passing of a Rent Act for temporary control of rents, subsequently perpetuated. The 1957 Rent Act removed from control (with some exceptions) premises whose rateable value on 7 Nov. 1956 was over £40 in London or £30 elsewhere; tenancies beginning after 6 July 1957 are not protected, and for houses still controlled a maximum rent was laid down, more in keeping with the current value of money and the costs of maintenance. In certain cases tenants may appeal to rent tribunals.

Reparations. The ⟡ *Versailles Treaty* fixed German reparations at 132,000 m. gold marks, despite warnings by economists e.g. Keynes that the problem of transferring such vast sums was insuperable. By 1923 Germany was in arrears, and also in the throes of currency ⟡ *inflation*. Both the ⟡ *Dawes Plan* and the later Young Plan, which eased the annuities, were unsuccessful. In 1931 reparations payments ceased and were never resumed. In all, Germany paid 20,000 m. marks, most of it borrowed. After the Second World War, no attempt was made to obtain monetary reparations; the ⟡ *Potsdam Conference* decided on massive confiscation of German plant, shipping, etc. The western powers removed equipment valued at $500 m. and the U.S.S.R. a far greater amount, estimated at $3700 m. The re-equipment of German industry with new machinery contributed greatly to the phenomenal recovery of the W. German economy after 1948.

Repoussé. Relief decorations on metals, produced by hammering from the under side; practised by the Assyrians and the Phoenicians, the art was brought to its highest peak in 4th-cent. B.C. Greece, the bronze cuirass from Siris in the British Museum being one of the finest examples. The most expert practitioners were Italian ⟡ *Renaissance* goldsmiths esp. Cellini, and Dutch silversmiths e.g. the Van Vianens.

Repression ⟡ *Defence Mechanism.*

Reprieve. The suspension of a sentence, which in the U.K. may be granted by the Crown on the Home Secretary's advice. The Crown may also grant a pardon either free or conditional e.g. the pardon of a person under sentence of death normally takes the form of a commutation to a term of imprisonment. A free pardon in effect negates the commission of the crime.

Reproduction. The process by which living things perpetuate their own species by the production of new individuals. The many ways in which this is done fall into two broad categories.

ASEXUAL REPRODUCTION: Common in the vegetable world, but in the animal kingdom found only in the lowest forms. The new generation is produced directly by a single individual; in its simplest form, a single cell divides into two and the two halves separate and become new individuals, but it may also occur by budding (in which small portions of the parent break off), by multiple fission (in which the parent breaks up into a number of new cells), or by the production of asexual ⟡ *spores*.

SEXUAL REPRODUCTION: Two sex cells (⟡ *gametes*) unite to form a zygote, from which arises the new individual. Sexual reproduction may be hermaphrodite, when the parent possesses both male and female sexual organs (e.g. most flowering plants, tapeworms, snails), or biparental, when it involves the union of two individuals of opposite sex, e.g. in mammals. ⟡ *Meiosis.*

HUMAN REPRODUCTION: The essential organs in which the germ-cells are kept segregated are the gonads (sex-glands), ovaries in the female, and testes in the male. The ovaries, small almond-shaped organs, lie in the pelvis; each contains some half million primordial germ-cells. These are dormant between birth and puberty; then (until menopause) one such cell matures once a month and passes into the cavity of the ⟡ *uterus*, where its subsequent history depends on whether fertilization has occurred (if not, it is discharged from the uterus within a few hours). The testis consists of a mass of small tubes in which great numbers of spermatozoa are constantly being produced; they are conveyed to the seminal vesicles, from which they may be discharged through the urethra in semen, a viscous liquid. In coitus, semen is ejaculated through the penis into the upper end of the vagina, bathing the cervix;

one c.c. of semen may contain several 100 m. spermatozoa, which move in a random manner, a few entering the uterus and fewer still the uterine (Fallopian) tube, where one spermatozoon may penetrate the layer of cells which surround an ovum and effect fertilization. It is also possible for fertilization to occur in the uterus. ⟡ *Fertilization, Gestation.*

Reptiles. Class of animals which arose in the late ⟡ *Carboniferous* period 300 m. years ago; the first fully terrestrial animals. During the Mesozoic Era they were the ruling animals of the earth, in forms fitted for life throughout the world, the icthyosaurs and plesiosaurs becoming adapted for aquatic life and the pterodactyls for flight; it was from the reptiles that ⟡ *mammals* evolved. Today there are four main groups, all cold-blooded and lung-breathing, the majority laying eggs in the ground. ⟡ *Alligator, Crocodile, Lizard, Snake, Tortoise, Turtle.*

Republicanism. Belief in or support of the government of a state by secular elected officers. The electorate of a republic may be of any size, and its institutions cast in any form, within the terms of this definition, except elective monarchy. The officers of a republican government are elected for a set term of years, not for life; making an elective headship of state permanent destroys the basis of republicanism, e.g. in Britain when Cromwell became Protector for life in 1653, and in France when Napoleon Bonaparte became First Consul for life in 1802 and when Louis Napoleon ceased to be President and became Emperor (Napoleon III) in 1852.

Republican Party, U.S.A. The present party was founded during the 1850s, to oppose slavery and Mormonism, and to build a railway to the Pacific. It was carried to victory by Abraham Lincoln, in the ⟡ *American Civil War*, and thereafter dominated the U.S. political scene for a quarter of a century. It became the party of industry and big business concentrated in the NE and Middle W. It erected a tariff wall behind which U.S. industry grew rapidly. Nevertheless the radical elements led it into trust-busting and the Sherman Act against monopolies, 1890. Particularly in the Middle West, a centre of Republican strength, its supporters were staunch isolationists, and their influence for long determined Republican attitudes to foreign affairs. In economic

matters the Republicans stand for the minimum of government control, to ensure 'fair competition'; in social affairs they have remained true to their early concept of racial equality. They have often been embarrassed by a 'lunatic fringe' of deep reactionaries such as the present John Birch Society. Since the depression of 1932, which began in the Republican Presidency of Hoover, it has been in office only under President Eisenhower 1952–60. The Eisenhower administration was faced with the task of containing the aggressive activities of U.S.S.R. and the war in ⟡ *Korea*; at home suspicion of communist subversion led to the investigations of Senator Macarthy's committee which for a time threatened the accepted freedoms of a democratic society. It lost the 1960 election by the narrowest of margins, and in 1964 its ultra-conservative candidate Goldwater was overwhelmingly defeated; he received 26 m. votes against the 42 m. for Lyndon Johnson. ⟡ *Congress, U.S.A.*

Requiem. The Roman Catholic ⟡ *Mass* for the Dead (Requiem Mass, *Missa pro defunctis*) has often been set to music, e.g. by Mozart, Berlioz, Verdi, Fauré. Also, settings of other 'commemorative' texts, e.g. Brahms, *A German Requiem*, and works by Delius, Hindemith, Britten.

Resale Price Maintenance. A requirement by a manufacturer or group of manufacturers that retailers sell specified goods at a fixed price; in the U.K. individual manufacturers may legally enforce the observance of price-maintenance undertakings, but group agreements were made subject to the Restrictive Practices Court established 1956 which requires that all agreements to fix prices or to allot specific shares of a market between firms should be registered with the Court, which might declare such agreements void if it found them contrary to the public interest. In 1965 a measure to abolish resale price maintenance became law.

Resins ⟡ *Synthetic Resins.*

Resonance. In any physical system having a natural mode of vibration or oscillation, this can be built up by periodic application of a small force, at the system's natural frequency; a child's swing may be given a large amplitude by a succession of small pushes of appropriate frequency; wine-glasses have been shattered by resonant vibrations excited by a violin, and troops have to break step when crossing a bridge to ensure that the marching frequency will not produce resonant oscillations of the bridge. Buildings subjected to vibrations have to be designed with great care, because relatively small sources of vibrational energy may produce catastrophic resonance in the structure. Radio receivers are 'tuned' by adjusting the freqency of an electrical oscillatory circuit, to achieve resonance with the transmission to be received.

Respiration. Process involving two aspects: external respiration i.e. breathing, either through the ◊ *lung* (as in man) or through gills (in fish) to take oxygen from the air (or water) and after its use to expel the resultant carbon dioxide and water. Internal respiration is the carrying in the blood of oxygen to the cells of the body, where it is used in chemical reactions which produce energy. An inherent rhythmic activity controls breathing, the depth and speed of which respond to changes in the oxygen or carbon dioxide content of the blood or to changes in the composition of the air breathed. Admixture of other gases or a severe drop in atmospheric pressure cause damage to tissues which may be fatal if prolonged. ◊ *Circulatory System.*

Restoration. 1660. After the death of Cromwell his son Richard became Lord Protector but was dismissed by the Army Council, and after six months of Army-Parliament wrangling General Monk was summoned to London to restore order; Monk seemed at first inclined to accept the Protectorate himself, but began secret negotiations for the return of Charles II, who returned in April 1660 after guaranteeing civil and religious liberty and constitutional government. After the King's return the 'Cavalier Parliament', which sat till 1679, was elected. The House of Lords was restored and the Church of England re-established. The King broke his guarantees in various ways: by the ◊ *Clarendon Code*, and by attempts to govern without Parliament. His reign was notorious for licentiousness and for violent politico-religious conflicts. ◊ *Covenant, Exclusion Bill, Popish Plot, Test Act.*

Restrictive Practices. Agreements in restraint of trade. (a) By firms; ◊ *Resale Price Maintenance* for the U.K. and Anti-Trust Laws for U.S.A. (b) By ◊ *trade unions*, to protect the jobs of skilled men; e.g. restrictions on numbers of apprentices allowed in a given trade, fixing the numbers employed on a given process, allowing only members of a specified union to do certain work. These union restrictions sometimes lead to strikes and inter-union disputes; in the U.K. there is in general no legislation against them.

Revisionism. Theory originally associated with Eduard Bernstein 1850–1932, a German Social Democrat who claimed that ◊ *marxism* was subject to evolution, declared revolution to be neither desirable nor inevitable, and thought ◊ *socialism* attainable by 'gradualism' ('reformism') i.e. a long series of partial reforms 'nibbling capitalism away' (◊ *Fabian Society*); all western social-democratic parties e.g. the British ◊ *Labour Party* have continued more or less Bernsteinian.

To orthodox ◊ *communism* 'reformism' is a dangerous backsliding frequently and virulently denounced. The term 'revisionism' is also constantly equated with 'deviationism' and 'diversionism', i.e. deviation or diversion from the current line of Soviet policy.

Revolution. A sudden change of government (or of the entire political system) by unconstitutional means, whether or not accompanied by violence, e.g. a 'palace revolution' is an abrupt change of government but not of system. A major political revolution frequently brings far-reaching changes in the social structure of the country concerned, e.g. the 1789 ◊ *French Revolution*, the 1917 ◊ *Bolshevik* revolution; or it may consolidate an already developing system, e.g. the English 17th-cent. ◊ *Glorious Revolution*, the 18th-cent. ◊ *American Revolution.*

More loosely, any far-reaching changes, e.g. the ◊ *Industrial Revolution.*

Rhea. 1. Flightless three-toed S. American bird, related to the ◊ *Ostrich*, but smaller and with less decorative feathers, about 4 ft tall and able to run at great speed; with other flightless birds, e.g. the Cassowary, it forms the primitive group of Ratites. They are polygynous, and rival males fight for possession of the harem. The male incubates 60 to 100 eggs in the common nest.

2. In mythology: ◊ *Cybele, Titans.*

3. In astronomy: ◊ *Saturn.*

Rhenium. A rare silvery metallic ◊ *element*, not discovered till 1925 though widely distributed; used in some ◊ *cata-*

lyst mixtures for hydrogenation processes; it forms a useful alloy with ◊ *molybdenum*.

Rhesus Factor. ◊ *Blood Groups*; a blood factor (also found in Rhesus monkeys) in 85 per cent of persons. A Rh-negative person transfused with Rh-positive blood suffers no ill-effects at the time, but the Rh-factor stimulates the recipient's tissues to produce antibodies (◊ *Immunity*), which may agglutinate transfused red cells in any second transfusion with Rh-positive blood, a dangerous possibility of great importance in obstetrics. If a Rh-negative woman becomes pregnant by a Rh-positive man, from the Rh-positive foetus (through the placenta) she receives an antigen stimulating Rh-antibodies, which may destroy the blood of any subsequent Rh-positive foetus, causing haemolytis of the newly born. This can often be cured by exchange transfusion, i.e. draining the blood of the baby and simultaneously replacing it by fresh Rh-negative blood of the correct ABO group.

Rhesus Monkey. Member of the widely distributed macaque family of monkeys (which includes the Barbary ape, still found on the Rock of Gibraltar). They are much used in medical research. ◊ *Rhesus Factor.*

Rheumatism. 1. Acute rheumatic fever, caused by streptococcal infection esp. in children; characterized by painful swollen joints and lesions in the heart valves, which may permanently cripple the heart. **2.** A painful condition of the joints, or their attached structures, in adults; usually due to unknown causes.

Rhinoceros. Massive animal found in Africa and India, weighing four or five tons, very thick-skinned, of low intelligence, with one or two horns made of modified hair; vegetarian, and inoffensive unless attacked. Its sight is poor, but it has very acute hearing and sense of smell. The white *R. simus*, the largest land mammal except the ◊ *elephant*, is found only in game reserves in Africa; it may reach a shoulder height of nearly 6 ft and be 15 ft long, but is capable of great speed. ◊ *Tapir.*

Rhizome. An underground stem, often swollen, with leaves reduced to small scales, characteristic of many perennial ◊ *herbs* (iris, couch-grass), which remains in the ground in winter and sends up new shoots in spring. Rhizomes produce ◊

roots very easily, and are a means of vegetative propagation.

Rhodesia (formerly Southern Rhodesia). Area 150,333 sq. m. Pop. 4 m. of whom only 221,000 are Europeans. Cap. Salisbury. A dominion within the British Commonwealth. After the dissolution of the Federation of Rhodesia and Nyasaland (◊ *Malawi, Zambia*) in 1963 the government began to press for complete autonomy which the British government refused to grant until satisfied that the Negro population would be democratically represented in the Rhodesian parliament. The Rhodesian Prime Minister threatened a unilateral declaration of independence but withdrew this threat in face of warnings from the British government in 1964.

Rhodium ◊ *Platinum Metals.*

Rhododendron. A vast genus of trees and shrubs, in about 500 species, widely distributed, the majority native to China, Tibet, and N. India; varying from dwarf moorland shrubs to large forest trees, with flowers of every shape and colour except blue, many of the less hardy ones being sweet-scented. Great numbers of hybrids have been raised, and generally flower earlier than the species. They will not grow on limy soils, and in Britain prefer the moister and milder regions. ◊◊ *Ericaceae, Azalea.*

Rhubarb. Descended from the wild *Rheum rhaponticum* of central Asia, modern varieties being probably hybrids of several species; first cultivated in England in the 16th cent. as a pot-herb, the leaves being considered superior to those of spinach or beet. The stalks were not used in cookery until the early 19th cent.

Rhyme. Ending lines of verse with syllables of the same sound; first adopted in 4th-cent. A.D. Latin hymns, and dominant in W. European poetry since the later Middle Ages. In English, usually one syllable, sometimes two for comic effect, occasionally three or more; in e.g. Italian two-syllable rhyme is normal. The rhyme-scheme of a poem is represented by *a, b, c,* etc. for each successive rhyme, e.g. 'Jack and Jill' rhymes *a a b c c b*. When the final syllable bears the stress, the rhyme is 'masculine', otherwise it is 'feminine'.

Ribesaceae. Currants; a small dicotyledonous family of shrubs, with one genus, *Ribes*; often included in the larger group of ◊ *Saxifragaceae*, important ornamentally for saxifrages, philadelphus (mock orange), hydrangea, escallonia, and astilbe. Some *Ribes* species have edible berries e.g. the red and black currant, with its cultivated varieties, including the white currant. *R. grossularia* is the gooseberry. All three, together with *R. alpinum*, the mountain currant, are wild in Britain.

Riboflavin ◊ *Vitamins (B₂)*.

Rice. *Oryza sativa*, of the *Gramineae*; a ◊ *cereal* of complex origins, in numerous varieties, one of the major food plants of the world esp. in Asia. World production at above 200 m. tons is about equal to wheat production. Cultivated in numerous varieties from early times, originally as a dry-land crop in humid climates, as it still is in a few favourable areas; but mainly planted under water in 'paddy fields', the ground gradually drying out as the grain ripens. Outside the Far East, a large amount is also grown in S. Europe e.g. the Po valley in Italy, and in the S. States of U.S.A. The grain contains about 8 per cent protein, 2 per cent oil, 78 per cent carbohydrate, and 12 per cent moisture. Polished rice (seedcoat and germ removed) is lower in protein, higher in carbohydrate, and has scarcely any vitamin content; if used as a staple food, it causes deficiency diseases e.g. ◊ *beri-beri*. 'Wild rice' comes from a different plant. In Japan an alcoholic beverage saké is made from rice. 'Rice paper' is made not from rice but from the pith of the ginseng plant.

Rickets. A disturbance of the calcium and phosphorus ◊ *metabolism* in young children, leading to general ill-health, proneness to infection, softening of bones, and deformity; caused by a deficiency of Vitamin D, resulting from inadequate diet or from insufficient sunlight, it is treated by making good the vitamin deficiency.

Rifle ◊ *Ballistics, Firearms, Shooting*.

Rift Valley. Depression formed when a block of the earth's crust drops down between two parallel ◊ *faults*. Central Scotland, between the Highlands and the S. uplands, is a rift valley; the deepest and longest in the world runs more than 4000 m. along the Jordan Valley, the Dead Sea, and the Red Sea to Lake Nyasa in E. Africa.

Rights of Man. 1. ◊ *Declaration of the Rights of Man*.

2. Pamphlet by Thomas Paine in English in defence of the ◊ *French Revolution*, published 1791–2.

Ringworm. Invasion of the skin by ◊ *fungi*, which produce lesions often in the shape of rings; the scalp, body, hair, nails, and the skin of the groin, hands, and feet are most likely to be affected. Special ◊ *antibiotics* are making it possible to deal more speedily with this very persistent disease. ◊◊ *Mycosis*.

Riot. A severe disturbance of the peace by three or more people who without authority assemble together for a common purpose and who actually carry out that purpose in such a way as to alarm a normal person; those taking part in a riot are guilty of a misdemeanour.

Under the Riot Act of 1714 when 12 or more persons refuse to disperse within one hour of a magistrate reading a Proclamation calling upon them to do so, they are guilty of a ◊ *felony* and are liable to be dispersed by the military. Those assisting the magistrate in dispersing the rioters are not liable for injuries inflicted on those resisting arrest. ◊◊ *Peterloo Massacre*.

Risorgimento. < Italian, 'resurgence'; the 19th-cent. national movement for the unification of Italy under Italian rulers, after the post-Napoleonic restoration of the old order by the 1815 ◊ *Vienna Congress*. Associated with the Carbonari revolts in ◊ *Sicily* 1820 and ◊ *Sardinia* 1821, and with further risings in the ◊ *Papal States* etc. 1831, after which Mazzini formed the ◊ *Young Italy* secret society. In 1848 during the Lombard revolt against ◊ *Austria-Hungary* Sardinia assumed the leadership of the Risorgimento, and in the 1850s Cavour achieved alliance with the French ◊ *Second Empire*. In the 1859–60 war Sardinia and France defeated Austria at ◊ *Magenta, Solferino*; after the conquest of Sicily by Garibaldi's redshirts, the kingdom of Italy was proclaimed in 1861.

Rites de Passage ◊ *Initiation Rites*.

River. A body of fresh water flowing in a natural channel, usually emptying into the sea; or a tributary of a large river. Some rivers, e.g. the Jordan, empty into salt lakes; some dry up in deserts. Rivers greatly modify the land by deposition and ◊ *erosion*; a great river e.g. the Mississippi annually wears away and carries off over 500 m. tons of soil and rock, much of which is deposited in the lower reaches (◊ *Delta, Flood Plain*). The erosion of the banks and destructive floods can be controlled e.g. by constructing artificial ▷ *levees*. Rivers serve for communication and transport, ▷ *irrigation*, hydroelectric power. The longest European river is the Volga, 2290 m. The world's longest is the Nile, about 4160 m. The Missouri-Mississippi and the Amazon (the greatest in volume of water) are slightly shorter.

RIVER BASIN: The area drained by a river system, varying tremendously in extent. A river rising in coastal highlands and flowing straight to the sea has a small basin, one rising far inland and traversing much of a continent has an immense basin e.g. the Amazon, which with its tributaries drains over 2.7 m. sq. m. (almost 29 times the area of the U.K.).

RIVER TERRACES: Portions of a former ▷ *flood plain* left along a valley after a rejuvenated river has cut a new bed at a lower level. Generally only fragments remain, but even if discontinuous they occur at the same height on opposite sides; if the process is repeated, a series of terraces may result, the highest being normally oldest.

▷ *Catchment Area, Valley.*

Roads. Paved roads, as distinct from tracks, were built in ancient Egypt, Babylon, Assyria, and Persia; they served administrative purposes as well as trade. The Greeks, with their self-contained, independent city-states, had little interest in road-building, but the Romans built enduring roads, primarily for military communications, to all corners of the Empire (▷ *Roman Roads*). It was not until the 19th cent. that road-building on a comparable scale was undertaken, stimulated first in Britain by the Industrial Revolution and by the techniques which Telford and John McAdam developed early in the 19th cent. With the coming of railways, highways were again neglected, but the invention of the motor car gave them a new importance. Road systems, however, developed haphazard, and it was not till the motorway was introduced (the *Autobahnen* of Germany and highways of the United States) that any specific provision was made to cope with the vast growth of road traffic, but like the older roads these were links between cities. Within cities the traffic congestion poses both social and economic problems of the greatest complexity. The serious and far-reaching effects upon housing conditions and amenities in both town and country in the U.K. are examined in detail in the Buchanan report, *Traffic in Towns* (1963). The disparity between road facilities and the growth of traffic is shown by the fact that over the ten years 1952–62 the public's purchases of motor vehicles (business and private) increased fourfold while capital expenditure by public authorities in the U.K. on roads only doubled. ▷▷ *Motor Car.*

'Roaring Forties'. Nautical name for region of stormy, wet, and comparatively mild weather in the S. hemisphere from about lat. 40° to 50° S. where the prevailing W. winds blow with great regularity and strength throughout the year.

Robbery ▷ *Larceny.*

Robbins Report ▷ *Education Acts and Reports, Universities.*

Robin. Small brown European passerine bird, with bright red breast; it lives in fields, woods, and gardens, and will fiercely defend its boundaries from encroaching neighbouring robins, but rapidly becomes accustomed to human beings. They lay five or six whitish eggs, in hedges, cracks in walls, or even tin cans. The American robin is a larger redbreasted bird of the ▷ *thrush* family.

Robin Hood. In English folklore, a 12th-cent. outlaw and brigand (possibly 'Rob in the Wood') who frequented Sherwood Forest in Nottinghamshire and robbed the rich for the benefit of the poor; alleged to be e.g. the outlawed Earl of Huntingdon, etc. Many popular ballads tell of his adventures with his band (Friar Tuck, Will Scarlett, Maid Marian, Little John, Allan-a-Dale, etc.) and there may be some historical foundation for the legends, which are, however, also more or less closely associated with ▷ *Beltane* May Day revels, ▷ *morris dancing*, and mythology e.g. ▷ *Odin*, the 'wild huntsman', Herne the Hunter, ▷ *Wayland*, etc.

Rock Crystal ▷ *Quartz.*

Rocket. Self-propelled ▷ *missile* working on the jet or reaction principle. Invented by the Chinese in about A.D. 1200, as first used it consisted of a paper tube filled with gunpowder, in which form it has persisted in fireworks. It was sporadically used in warfare; General Congreve (who had been subjected to Tippoo Sahib's rocket fire at Seringapatam in 1799) devised a military rocket used in the latter part of the ▷ *Napoleonic Wars*, but advances in artillery (◊ *Firearms*) cut short its development as a military weapon. In 1919 an American, Goddard, stimulated research into the possibility of using rockets in astronomical observation, and Oberth, a Rumanian, pursued the subject scientifically. Rockets were again used in the ◊ *Second World War*, as anti-aircraft missiles, and from ships against beach installations. The Germans devoted large sums to experiments, which led in 1944 to the V1 and then the V2, prototype of all modern rocket engineering.

A rocket differs from a ◊ *jet-propulsion* engine only in being independent of the air around it for its oxygen, which is contained in the propellant, so that rockets can produce thrust at great heights and in outer space; the speed depends on the rate of ejection (exhaust). Rockets may use solid or liquid fuel, the latter involving extremely difficult engineering problems, and may be single-stage or multiple (for attaining greater range).

Rococo. < Fr. *rocaille*, shell-work; originally, decorations in which shells and frothy wave-like patterns of curves predominated, not only applied to but determining the form of small porcelain objects, silver-ware, furniture, schemes of interior decoration, and occasionally whole buildings. As an artistic style, usually considered the last phase of ◊ *Baroque*, but unlike it in having no symbolic significance; it emerged in France about 1700, rose to popularity throughout Europe in the 1730s, and gradually went out of fashion after 1750 as the vogue for ◊ *neoclassicism* gained ground. Painters e.g. Boucher, Hogarth, Guardi attempted to catch transitory effects of flickering light and swirling movement, while sculptors sought to represent the graceful turns of the body and fleeting facial expressions. A highly sophisticated courtly style, it reached its summit of delicate if sometimes 'precious' and brittle refinement in France, and in German principalities dominated by French taste. Its most notable expressions were French interior decoration and furniture, French and English silver, German porcelain, and S. German architecture esp. the Amalienburg near Munich, by F. de Cuvilliès, and the pilgrimage church of Vierzehnheiligen by B. Neumann, where the twirly decorations echo the rhythmical curves of the ground-plans and the interiors are painted in colours as brilliantly fresh as a meadow of Alpine flowers.

Rodents. *Rodentia*, the largest and one of the most successful mammalian orders, in 1000 species, characteristically having well-developed gnawing incisors; many, e.g. ◊ *rats*, are considered pests.

Rodeo. Originally an incidental display of skill by cowboys when rounding up cattle, an aspect it still retains in remote areas e.g. the Australian Outback; now an exhibition of the skill of cowboys in various events such as roping cattle and riding broncos and steers, which in many cases has become as professional as a circus.

Rolling-mills. To obtain plate from steel ingots, the white-hot metal is squeezed between rollers (like a giant mangle) in several stages, the strip getting thinner and longer; during the rolling process the hot metal becomes covered with oxide scales, which have to be removed by 'pickling' in hot dilute sulphuric acid. In later stages it is rolled cold, giving an untarnished surface, more accurately controlled size, and a harder product.

Roman Architecture. A combination and adaptation of Greek and Etruscan architecture, in which the simple trabeated (post-and-lintel) style of the former was combined with the arch, vault, and dome of the latter; it is characterized by massive grandeur rather than simplicity and harmony, and ornament was often applied lavishly with little relation to the function of the building. It is to be found at its best chiefly in types of building unknown to the Greeks e.g. amphitheatres like the Colosseum (1st cent. A.D.) and the Pantheon, the basilicas, and the aqueducts (that at Pont du Gard remains an almost intact example) in which Roman architecture achieved buildings of great dignity and strength admirably adapted to the practical ends they were intended to serve. A striking contribution of the Romans was the invention of ◊ *concrete* (2nd cent. B.C.) and its application in spanning large areas by means of vaulting based upon ribbing of bricks; after its introduction they tended to abandon both the discipline and the restrictions of the cut-stone structure of the Greeks, and resorted to composite structure with plaster and thin stone facings.

Roman Art. Although always strongly influenced by the Greeks and the Greek-inspired ◊ *Etruscans*, the Romans nevertheless evolved their own version of the Greek style in painting and sculpture; vividly realistic busts, statues, and heads on coins reveal a preoccupation with realistic portraiture foreign to the Hellenic ideal and a much greater interest in narrative relief sculpture; the finest examples are those on the Column of Trajan, A.D. 113. The Romans resorted to opulent decoration of buildings with stone and stucco sculpture and produced handsome bronze furniture and elaborately wrought gold and silver vessels. Little remains of what must have been extensive paintings in the form of wall decorations, but an abundance of surviving ◊ *mosaics* found not only in Rome but throughout the Empire reveal the popularity and diversity of this form, in which Roman artists excelled, in which at times narrative realism and at others ornamental design predominates. A change came over Roman art towards the end of the 2nd cent. A.D. when a less naturalistic but more expressive style of sculpture was employed, perhaps occasioned by the spiritual unrest of the times, e.g. the column of Marcus Aurelius, and numerous Dionysiac and Christian sarcophagi. The classical tradition went into a decline, and by A.D. 312 (when the Arch of Constantine was carved) it was almost forgotten; symbols, often crudely executed, began to replace naturalistic elements, and the way was prepared for the ◊ *Byzantine* style.

Roman Catholic Church. Body of Christians owing spiritual allegiance to the ◊ *Pope*, with a celibate clergy, claiming to be the only true church of Jesus Christ perpetuating the faith he taught his followers. Its essential doctrines include the authority of ecclesiastical tradition, transubstantiation (◊ *Holy Communion*), papal infallibility, ◊ *purgatory*, and the immaculate conception and bodily assumption of ◊ *Mary*. Governed by the College of ◊ *Cardinals*, administratively it is divided into territorial dioceses, under archbishops or bishops, subdivided into parishes, under priests. The religious orders run colleges, hospitals, and ◊ *missions*. Some E. European groups e.g. the Uniates (◊ *Eastern Orthodox Church*) have non-Latin liturgies and a non-celibate clergy. After three centuries of civil disability, Roman Catholics in Britain have exercised their religion freely since 1829, but the sovereign and consort, and the Lord Chancellor, may not be Roman Catholics. ◊ *Oxford Movement, Papal States, Sacraments, Vatican City State.*

Romance. Fictitious or legendary narrative, loose in structure, remote from the settings and situations of common life; the 12th to 15th-cent. medieval romances applied the codes of chivalry and ◊ *courtly love* to Celtic myths (◊ *Arthurian Legend*), to classical legends (◊ *Mythology*), and to ancient and recent history (◊ *Chansons de Geste*). Romantic fiction of this sort remained popular until the early 19th cent. (◊ *Gothic Revival*), while much of Scott's work has the character of the romance as well as the ◊ *novel.* ◊ *Roman de la Rose.*

Romance Languages. Descended not from classical but from vulgar ◊ *Latin*, the speech of the common men and legionaries of the Roman Empire; they include five national languages (French, Spanish, Portuguese, Italian, Rumanian) and four regional tongues (Catalan, Rumansch, Galician, Sardinian, the last nearer to Latin than even Italian). The documents connecting vulgar Latin (before A.D. 500) with the derivative Romance languages are seldom continuous; the first linguistic record distinguishable as Old French rather than Gallo-Roman is the text of the Strasbourg Oaths, A.D. 842. In the following centuries the other Romance languages became separate and distinct; Rumanian is the latest, dating to the early 16th cent.

Roman de la Rose. A 13th-cent. French verse ◊ *romance*. The first part, by Guillaume de Lorris, about 1235, is an allegory of ◊ *courtly love*; the second and longer part, by Jean de Meung, about 1280, is mainly vigorous and often learned satire, with disquisitions on various subjects. The poem, frequently imitated (e.g. the English *Romaunt of the Rose*, partly by Chaucer), greatly influenced subsequent European literature.

Romanesque Architecture. A style which began at Cluny in France in the 10th cent. A.D. and lasted till the 13th, when it merged into the ◊ *Gothic*; characterized by conscious planning of the disposition of space, in contrast to the more sculptural spirit of classical architecture, and by the addition of chapels and ambulatories around the simple ground plan or ◊ *basilica*, it is technically distinguished by the round arch, tall shafts and columns, and massive construction. Vaulting in place of wooden ceilings remained rare until after 1050, when various systems – tunnel, groin, pointed vaults – were developed in different regions. The two-tower façade with a tower over the crossing is typical of 'churches in England and Normandy, screen façades with no tower are usual in S. France, and a multitude of towers over the W. as well as the E. ends characterizes German romanesque. Outstanding French examples are at Vézelay, Caen, and Autun. Italian romanesque, more than the northern varieties, retained a strain of ◊ *Byzantine* and ◊

Worms cathedral

Muslim influence, e.g. Monreale Cathedral in Sicily. In England the style is called Norman, and is the most consistent of the W. European romanesque; the cathedrals of Winchester, Ely, and Durham are supreme examples. In military architecture, the keeps of the Tower of London and of Rochester castle are typical of Norman simplicity and solidity.

Roman Law. The Romans were probably the earliest western people to evolve a comprehensive body of law with the characteristics now considered essential to a legal system. The traditional story of the codification of Roman law is that it was recorded in 12 tables in 450 B.C. and reached its fullest expression in the *Corpus Juris Civilis* of the Byzantine Emperor Justinian, about A.D. 530, though after the fall of Rome in A.D. 476 it survived mainly as the basis of ◊ *canon law*, and in local courts. Classical Roman law, as against the customary local adaptations, was revived in the 16th cent. and adopted by most European countries; it still exercises great influence on Continental law, e.g. the ◊ *Code Napoléon*. Though England deliberately rejected it, its influence is to be found in e.g. English commercial law.

Roman Numerals. Letters represent certain numbers: I=1, V=5, X=10, L=50, C=100, D=500, M=1000. Economy is achieved by addition e.g. VIII=5+3, or subtraction e.g. IX=10−1 (*after* a main figure meaning add, and *before* meaning subtract) Thus e.g. MD=1500, MDC= 1600, MDCCCC=1900, MDCCCCLX =1960, MDCCCCLXIV=1964; except that the Romans themselves wrote 4 as IIII, because IV (=JU) were the first letters of ◊ *Jupiter*, the chief deity; IV =4 is a medieval usage. The system is cumbersome for large numbers, and lacks a ◊ *zero*.

Roman Roads. The Romans built a vast network of roads to facilitate communications, esp. for their armies, between Rome and its many provinces. Their roads typically ran in straight lines and were well and solidly constructed: many existing roads follow the same routes in various parts of Europe. In Britain several roads are of Roman origin e.g. Watling Street from London to the N. and the Fosse Way from Lincoln to the SW.

Romanticism. A European late 18th cent. movement in philosophy and the arts, exalting imagination and intuition above reason, the spontaneous above the disciplined, the individual above society. It has been argued that there never was a single movement, but only different 'romanticisms'; indeed the term has been applied to the gothick novel, to exoticism and fantasy and unadorned description of the simple aspects of contemporary life; yet these different manifestations had in common a belief that society and its conventions restrict rather than liberate, a determination to express individual response to experience directly rather than by traditional styles and modes, the valuing of emotion for its own sake, and the view that the poet has no responsibilities except to his own vision. The movement continues throughout the 19th cent. from the German ◊ *Sturm und Drang* poets and self-styled Romantics, influenced by Idealist philosophy (e.g. of Schelling), to the 'alienated' French writers about 100 years later, out to '*épater les bourgeois*'; the ◊ *Parnassians* thought of themselves as anti-romantic, but continued the romantic tradition of extreme individualism, both in their response to experience and in their techniques of expression. If an ideal of formlessness seemed implicit in earlier romantic protest against strict ◊ *neoclassicism*, this was simply a stage in the development of a different and more organic conception of form, first developed by the German romantic writers and transcendental philosophers, and brought influentially into English critical thought by Coleridge. Romanticism tended to confuse self-expression with adequacy of expression, to overweight the personal, to make the poet always the naïve hero of his own poems, and to deprecate wit and irony. The 20th-cent. anti-romantic reaction attacked these weaknesses and brought astringency, irony, and wit back to poetry whilst retaining the highly personal and *ad hoc* nature of poetic forms. ◊ *Gothic Revival*.

In the fine arts romanticism was partly a revolt against neoclassicism, partly an expression of a new sensibility to nature, and partly a cult of hero-worship (esp. associated with Napoleon in the work of Delacroix, Géricault). Rejecting classical restraint, the romantic painters gave unbridled expression to their emotions, most of them abandoning the flat linear manner and ordered compositions of neoclassical painting, in favour of more dramatic and dynamic effects e.g. Turner; the movement reached its peak in the 1830s, and continued to influence later styles.

Romany. 1. A gipsy, or ◊ *gipsies* collectively.

2. The gipsy language: < *rom*, a man or gipsy. *Romani chiv*, gipsy tongue. Basically Indian, Romany is world-wide, has many dialects, and contains numerous borrowed words varying from region to region. ◊ *Indo-European Languages*.

Rome. City of the ancient world, according to legend founded by ◊ *Romulus* in 753 B.C. In the 5th cent. B.C. the Romans freed themselves from their ◊ *Etruscan* rulers, the Tarquins, and established a republic, though this was never a true democracy: under the patricians it began as an aristocracy, and as the people (the plebs) gradually acquired power it became an oligarchy, in which the Senate was all-powerful. During the republican era (despite the Sack of Rome by the Gauls 390 B.C.) the Romans gradually asserted their hold over all Italy, the conquest of which was completed by 275 B.C. They then turned to Sicily, which brought conflict with Carthage (◊ *Punic Wars*). The first

Punic War 264–241 B.C. led the Romans for the first time to become a naval power; in the second war 218–201 B.C. despite the brilliance of the Carthaginian general Hannibal, Rome by her pertinacity and her great resources completely defeated Carthage and became master of the Mediterranean and the lands around it. In 146 B.C. Rome destroyed Carthage itself, Greece became subject to Rome, and Greek influence, already strong since early contacts, further modified Roman culture. The riches which flowed in from the provinces sapped the simpler virtues of the old Romans, taxation was abolished, and gradually the citizen armies were replaced by professional soldiers from throughout the Roman territories, whose allegiance was primarily to the general they served not to the Republic. The city was torn with dissension, the mass of the people were restive, the slaves were treated with barbarity. After the Social War 91 B.C. against the Italian peoples, the Romans were obliged to extend citizenship to most of Italy, but the Republic was clearly in dissolution and the real power was in the hands of rival generals. In 60 B.C. Pompey, Caesar, and Crassus formed a triumvirate; 10 years later Caesar returned from his Gallic Wars to crush Pompey at Pharsala 48 B.C. and become master of Rome, Emperor in all but name. His conquests extended Roman civilization into the barbarian lands of Europe beyond the Alps. After his assassination in 44 B.C., his heir Augustus defeated Antony at ◊ *Actium* and with his proclamation as Imperator in 30 B.C. the era of the Empire began. In the Augustan Age triumphs at home and in the provinces brought Rome to the height of her power: the city was rebuilt with a new splendour, art and letters flourished, and the citizens enjoyed comforts and amenities not to be matched for over 1500 years: the population grew to over a million. For the next two centuries Rome ruled a vast area over which the Pax Romana was a reality, in spite of frequent wars at the frontiers and the barbarities of despots such as Caligula and Nero. The Christians though long persecuted began slowly to gain converts and increase their influence. Trajan, Hadrian, and the Antonines brought what is termed the Golden Age of the Empire, after which it went into decline. The Praetorian Guard and later the armies of the provinces increasingly came to choose the Emperors. Inroads by Germanic tribes began, and the Empire was thrown into confusion by the capture of Emperor Valerian by the Persians. In the 3rd cent. A.D. plague and a financial crisis further weakened the Empire; the political and financial reforms of Diocletian produced only a temporary respite. Constantine granted religious toleration to the Christians, and in 324 A.D. removed his capital to Byzantium. After the death of Theodosius in 395 the Empire was divided permanently into an Eastern and Western part, and the West quickly lost its importance (◊ *Holy Roman Empire*). Its capital was shifted repeatedly. Alaric the Visigoth took Rome in 410 and in 455 it was conquered by Gaiseric the Vandal. In 476 the last Emperor of the West, Romulus Augustulus, was deposed by Odoacer, who was himself murdered in 493 by Theodoric of the Ostrogoths. In the following centuries Rome disintegrated both politically and materially, and by the Middle Ages its population had fallen to 50,000. It was not to re-emerge as a centre of importance until the rise of the Papacy. ◊ *Roman Architecture/Art/Law*.

Rome Treaty (1957) ◊ *European Economic Community*.

Romulus. In classical legend, son of Mars (◊ *Ares*) and the Vestal Virgin Rhea Silvia; twin brother of Remus; and worshipped as Quirinus by the Romans. For her unchastity, Rhea Silvia was executed and her sons exposed, but a she-wolf (sacred to Mars) suckled them. At manhood, the brothers quarrelled over the building of their city; Romulus killed Remus, founded ◊ *Rome*, and eventually was taken to heaven in a fiery chariot by Mars.

Roncesvalles ◊ *Chansons de Geste*.

Rondeau. A short poem, with a refrain and only two rhymes; originally probably an accompaniment to a round dance. The basic rondeau (crystallized in France in the 16th cent.) has 15 lines rhyming *a a b b a a a b R a a b b a R*, the refrain (*R*) usually being the first few words of the poem.

RONDEL: An earlier form of rondeau.

ROUNDEL: An 11-line variant, devised in the 19th cent. by Swinburne.

ROUNDELAY: A round dance; a short simple song; or any verse-form using a refrain.

Root Crops. Plants cultivated for their edible roots, providing food for animal or human consumption; e.g. artichokes, beets, carrots, mangels, potatoes, swedes, turnips. A valuable source of ◊ *carbohydrate*, and of some ◊ *protein*, the food values varying widely according to weather conditions, e.g. low in a wet season.

Roots. The main underground organs of ◊ *plants*, serving as anchors and supports, and absorbing water and minerals from the soil. The primary root (radicle) emerges when a ◊ *seed* germinates, and may persist, develop lateral roots, and produce a tap-root system; but in many species e.g. grasses it is replaced by other roots growing from the stem base. Many roots have specialized functions, e.g. as secondary stems (banyans), aids to climbing (ivy), food stores (turnips, carrots); in many ◊ *epiphytes* they take part in ◊ *photosynthesis*.

Rosaceae. Rose family, cosmopolitan dicotyledons (the flowers usually having five sepals, five petals, large numbers of stamens, and numerous carpels), which includes many fruits e.g. almond, apricot, cherry, peach, plum (all *Prunus*), apple (*Malus*), blackberry, loganberry, raspberry (all *Rubus*), strawberry (*Fragaria*), medlar (*Mespilus*), pear (*Pyrus*), quince (*Cydonia*), and garden flowers or shrubs e.g. cotoneaster, japonica, laurel, rose, spiraea; also many British wild flowers e.g. agrimony, blackthorn (sloe), hawthorn.

Rose. The most prominent member of the *Rosaceae*, found wild throughout the N. temperate zone in many species; possibly the first flower to be cultivated, and certainly grown in ancient Egypt and Greece. The Romans made great use of roses, and even grew them under glass in winter; the expression *sub rosa* comes from their custom of hanging a rose above a council table to enjoin secrecy. The use of dried rose-hips as beads in the Middle Ages, to make a string of prayers, gave the word rosary. Most of the roses now cultivated derive from *R. chinensis, R. damascena, R. foetida, R. gallica (rubra), R. moschata, R. multiflora, R. odorata, R. rugosa*, and *R. wichuraiana*, most of which are Asian and were introduced into Europe from Roman times onward, but esp. in the 18th and 19th centuries, when more scientific methods of pollination and selection produced the longer-flowering hybrid-perpetual, hybrid-tea, and hardy floribunda types. The first yellow strain came from a Persian rose at the end of the 19th cent. and the number of varieties then increased rapidly. Many roses are grafted on to understocks, frequently briar or *R. canina* (dog rose) or *R. multiflora*; hybridization and the development of new varieties has become a very extensive specialized business esp. in Britain, France, Denmark, Germany, Netherlands, U.S.A. In Britain, the National Rose Society tests new hybrids, issuing certificates to those found acceptable.

ATTAR OF ROSES: A highly fragrant ◊ *essential oil*, from the autumn damask rose grown in the Balkans esp. Bulgaria.

ROSE-HIP SYRUP: A valuable source of Vitamin C, mainly from *R. canina*.

Rosemary ◊ *Labiatae*.

Rosetta Stone. A slab of black basalt now in the ◊ *British Museum*, found in 1799 by a French officer at Rosetta, in the W. delta of the Nile, during France's occupation of Egypt in the ◊ *Napoleonic Wars*, and handed to the British in 1801 after the French surrender; it bears inscriptions in Egyptian and Greek, the Egyptian in both hieroglyphic and demotic script, so that by study of the three scripts Thomas Young and Jean François Champollion succeeded in interpreting the previously indecipherable ancient Egyptian hieroglyphics.

Rotorcraft. Heavier-than-air aircraft, deriving lift from a rotor or rotors, e.g. ◊ *autogiro, helicopter*.

Rouge et Noir ◊ *Trente et Quarante*.

Roulette. A gambling game in which an ivory ball is made to travel round a revolving 'wheel' divided into 37 compartments (1–36 and zero) coloured alternately red and black (*rouge et noir*), finally coming to rest on one of these, which determines who wins. The game is of French origin, dating to the end of the 18th cent. It is a feature of the casino at Monte Carlo.

Round (musical) ◊ *Canon and Fugue*.

Roundel, Roundelay ◊ *Rondeau*.

Rowing. Boat races are of great antiquity. The oldest official rowing race in England is the Doggett Coat and Badge event for Thames watermen, 1716. The first University Boat Race between Oxford and Cambridge was virtually the start of amateur rowing, in 1829; Henley Regatta (1839) and the first ◊ *Olympic* Regatta (1908) are important milestones in the spread of the sport, which now has many types of boat and crew. Henley, the unofficial world championship, provides keen competition in races for eights, fours, coxless fours, pairs, and single sculls.

Royal Aeronautical Society. Founded in 1866 and granted the prefix 'Royal' in 1918; the oldest aeronautical society in the world, it confers fellowships and gives special awards. In 1868 it held the first air exhibition in Britain in the Crystal Palace, and its first Gold Medals were awarded to the Wright brothers in 1909 (◊ *Aeroplane*).

Royal Air Force. Formed in April 1918, by the amalgamation of the Royal Flying Corps, 1912, and the Royal Naval Air Service, 1914, and reorganized in 1919 by Lord Trenchard after the ◊ *First World War*; though it was not till 1934 that re-equipment was seriously undertaken. On the outbreak of the ◊ *Second World War* the R.A.F. was numerically inferior to the Luftwaffe, but in the Hurricane and Spitfire it possessed fighters equal or superior to those of the Germans. An independent military arm, unlike the air forces of the U.S.S.R. and Germany (which operated in close conjunction with the land forces), it rapidly expanded, and played a highly important role not only in the ◊ *Battle of Britain* and the defence of the sea approaches, but in the strategic bombing of Germany.

The R.A.F. is administered by the Air Council, headed by the Minister of Defence (Air). In addition to fighter, coastal, and transport commands, it has a V-bomber force capable of carrying stand-off nuclear bombs and also designed to carry air-launched ballistic ◊ *missiles*. The Skybolt missile was abandoned in 1963. ◊◊ *Aviation, Fleet Air Arm*.

Royal Automobile Club. Founded 1897 as the Automobile Club of Gt Britain and Ireland, the present title dating to 1907; the U.K. national motoring authority, affiliated to the Fédération Internationale de l'Automobile, its main function being to assist and defend the interests of private motorists and to control motor racing. It gives its members towing facilities and free breakdown service and legal advice. ◊◊ *Automobile Association*.

Royal National Lifeboat Institution. A body which maintains and operates the ◊ *lifeboats* round the U.K. coasts, in liaison with the Coastguard Service, an official organization; it relies entirely on voluntary subscriptions, and the lifeboat crews are volunteers. Since its foundation in 1824 it has rescued over 80,000 people.

Royal Naval College. Naval officers used to receive their initial training at sea, the last of the old training-ships being the wooden battleship *Britannia* and the brig *Martin*; Admiral Lord Fisher (First Sea Lord 1904) founded the Royal Naval College at Dartmouth in 1905, to train entrants to the executive and engineering branches of the Royal Navy and Royal Marines.

Royal Navy. After the Norman Conquest, the ◊ *Cinque Ports* were under obligation to furnish ships to the king in time of war; it was not till the 16th cent. that vessels were specifically constructed as ◊ *warships*, and the *Great Harry*, re-equipped in 1540 with two tiers of guns, may be considered the first battleship. The emergence of a faster, steadier, heavily-gunned vessel was an English development, and was basically the reason for the defeat of the Spanish ◊ *Armada*. Naval vessels were improved, but remained fundamentally similar until after Nelson's day and the 19th-cent. advent of steam. The Royal Navy took permanent shape in the mid 17th cent. under Cromwell and then Charles II; the Admiralty directed policy, while the Navy Commissioners maintained supplies and material, often negligently. Tactics remained stereotyped until Nelson reinvigorated them in the late 18th cent. Steam and the 'ironclad' coincided with a new era of growing competition in naval construction; but for about 200 years the Royal Navy was substantially unrivalled.

The administration of the Royal Navy is in the hands of the 11-man Admiralty Board (three members, political appointees, the rest naval officers), headed by the Minister of Defence (Navy); the First Sea Lord is the Chief of Naval Staff.

Royal Society. In full, the Royal Society for Improving Natural Knowledge; in effect the British National Academy of Sciences, but a private body; its earliest members were not specialists but wealthy amateurs united in pursuit of practical knowledge, and its diverse interests included e.g. concern for the English language. Founded in 1645 (during the ◊ *English Civil Wars*) as a 'philosophical-club' offshoot of the 16th-cent. Gresham College, it was active esp. at Oxford throughout the ◊ *Commonwealth and Protectorate*, and after the ◊ *Restoration* was incorporated by royal charter in 1662, 1663, and 1669, suffering from grave lack of funds until Newton's presidency 1703-26. Since 1665 it has published its proceedings, as the *Philosophical Transactions*, and since 1857 it has occupied part of Burlington House.

Royal Society for the Prevention of Cruelty to Animals (RSPCA). Founded in 1824 (60 years earlier than the ◊ *National Society for the Prevention of Cruelty to Children*); it maintains inspectors who investigate charges of cruelty to animals, and is supported by voluntary contributions.

Ruanda-Urundi ◊ *Burundi, Rwanda.*

Rubber. A product of the coagulated resilient ◊ *latex* of various tropical trees e.g. castilloa, ficus (◊ *Fig*), hevea, ◊ *manihot*, all but ficus being S. American, and commercial supplies coming almost exclusively from *Hevea brasiliensis*; the raw latex is tapped by cutting diagonally through the bark and collecting the exuded liquid. Various types of rubber were known to the American Indians, who used it for waterproofing, burned it in torches, and played with rubber balls. Crude coagulated latex waterproofing has been replaced by latex dissolved in various solvents, a method first used in 1823 by Mackintosh; later Goodyear discovered vulcanization (heating latex with sulphur and adding fillers), which greatly widened the range of rubber manufactures. Demand was at first met by collecting latex from wild trees in the Amazon basin, but the invention of tyres caused a vast increase in consumption, wild 'Para' rubber proved insufficient, and plantations of Brazilian rubber trees were started in Malaya and Indonesia in the late 19th cent. About 50 per cent of all rubber is used for tyres; the rest goes into a variety of products e.g. belting, footwear, tubing.

SYNTHETIC RUBBER: Chemically, substances composed of long-chain hydrocarbons, resembling certain types of synthetic resins, characterized by the particular kind of elasticity found in natural rubber. Synthetic rubbers are of two main classes. The first are general purpose rubbers which are used in most of the ways natural rubber is e.g. for tyres, wire and cable insulation and a wide range of domestic articles and are closely competitive in price with the natural product. Special purpose rubbers, which are more expensive, have been developed for use where some particular quality is highly desirable e.g. resistance to great heat, to oil or corrosive action, etc. Synthetic rubber was first developed in Germany in the 1930s. U.S.A. embarked on large-scale production of synthetic rubber when the loss of SE Asia in the ◊ *Second World War* cut off Allied supplies. Today more than a third of world consumption of rubber is filled by the synthetic product. ◊ *Silicones*.

Rubidium. A rare ◊ *alkali* metal, with chemical and physical properties very similar to those of ◊ *potassium*; with caesium, it was discovered by Bunsen about 1860, by spectrum analysis.

Ruby. Gem-stone; red variety of ◊ *corundum*.

Rugby League Football. A thirteen-a-side handling game with an oval ball, played by both amateurs and professionals, which began 1893 when 22 clubs in Lancashire and Yorkshire broke away from the ◊ *Rugby Union* because it forbade professionalism; today 32 professional clubs in these two counties and Cumberland compete in two divisions, with promotion and relegation, and also in a knock-out competition for the Rugby League Cup, the final of which is played at Wembley. Internationals are played against Australia, New Zealand, and France. Attendance figures support the claim that changed rules make the game faster and more entertaining to watch than that of Rugby Union. ◊ *American Football*.

Rugby Union Football. A fifteen-a-side handling and kicking game played with an oval ball, which must not be 'knocked on' or passed forward, on a field 110 by 75 ft, the basic aim being to score a 'try' by grounding the ball behind the opponents' line. The fact that the rules of the Roman game of *harpastum* were essentially the same is almost certainly coincidence; Rugby Union is regarded as an offshoot from the medieval village football games which preceded ◊ *association football*. Modern Rugby owes its name to Rugby School (where in a form of soccer match 1823 William Webb Ellis 'with a fine disregard for the rules . . . first took the ball in his arms and ran with it, thus originating the distinctive feature of the Rugby game'), and the first Rugby clubs were set up by former public-schoolboys. At its foundation 1863 the Football Association ruled against 'the carrying code'; Rugby Union developed separately, the Union itself being formed in 1871 by 17 clubs and three schools, the first international game (against Scotland) being played in the same year. It has remained solely an amateur game, and has spread to Australia, New Zealand, and S. Africa. The International Board, 1890, now comprises the four 'home' unions: Australia, S. Africa, New Zealand, France.

Rule of Law. The supremacy of law, as governing the actions of all citizens, and the exclusion of arbitrary action by the sovereign or his agents (◊ *Absolutism*). It also means that everyone is equal before the law and no one is exempt by virtue of position or office from obedience to law. In Britain the rule of law emerged from the long struggle between Parliament and Crown as to final power, which culminated in 1689 (◊ *Glorious Revolution*), when Parliament established that the legislature was supreme, and proscribed all arbitrary action by the Crown.

Rum. Alcoholic spirit, originally produced in the Caribbean, made by fermenting molasses for some days and maturing the resultant almost colourless alcohol in casks (usually oak) for 3–20 years; colour is taken up from the casks, and caramel is often added. Jamaica is the main producer; a light-coloured ('white') rum is also made in Cuba and the Virgin Isles. In the Royal Navy 90 per cent proof rum is a traditional free issue; the current daily ration is one eighth of a pint, but until 1824 it was half a pint.

Rumania. Area 91,600 sq. m. Pop. 18.8 m. Cap. Bucharest. Rel. Eastern Orthodox. A republic on the Black Sea, at the mouth of the Danube, between Bulgaria and U.S.S.R. The state is a socialist 'people's republic', the 1952 constitution being modelled on that of U.S.S.R. and the legislature being the single-party Grand National Assembly, elected for four years, which between sessions delegates its rights to the State Council.

ECONOMY. There are rich resources of petroleum and minerals, e.g. coal, gold, iron ore, lignite, mica, natural gas, salts, silver, uranium, with much timber and considerable agricultural output esp. grain; heavy industry, esp. chemical, iron and steel, and machine-building e.g. oil-drilling equipment, is developing rapidly, with overall annual increases of about 15 per cent. In 1962 petroleum output reached a record peak with 11.6 m. tons. The State plan for the creation of an all-round balanced economy has caused conflict with U.S.S.R. in ◊ *Comecon.*

HISTORY. In classical antiquity, the Roman provinces of Dacia and Scythia Pontica; also the later Danubian principalities of Moldavia and Wallachia. The principalities were ruled by ◊ *Turkey* until 1866, when the ◊ *Hohenzollerns* succeeded; the 1878 ◊ *Berlin Congress* made Rumania an independent kingdom, incorporating parts of Dobrudja, seized by Rumania from Bulgaria. After the ◊ *First World War,* Bessarabia, Bukovina, and Transylvania were added; but during the ◊ *Second World War,* on a Soviet ultimatum in 1940, Rumania ceded Bessarabia and N. Bukovina (20,000 sq. m.) to U.S.S.R. and returned S. Dobrudja (3000 sq. m.) to Bulgaria. In 1947 King Michael abdicated and a socialist-communist coalition proclaimed the republic; in 1952 and 1961 the Popular Democratic Front, the sole party, gained 98.8 and 99.7 of the votes cast. Recently Rumania has shown an increasing tendency to ignore Soviet guidance.

LANGUAGE. One of the ◊ *Romance languages,* though with many non-Latin borrowings; the earliest texts date to the 16th cent.

Rumansch ◊ *Romance Languages.*

Ruminants. Class of hoofed mammals which ruminate, i.e. chew the cud, first swallowing grassy food without mastication and later returning it to the mouth and chewing it till fully masticated; e.g. ◊ *antelope, camel, cattle, deer, giraffe, goat, llama, sheep.*

Rummy. Originally called rum (odd) poker; a card game for two to six players, with the full pack of cards. Each person receives seven cards; with two persons, each has 10 cards; with five or six, each has six. One card is turned up on the stockpile; each player in turn draws a card and discards one. The aim is to collect sets, i.e. three or four of the same value, or three or more of a suit sequence. The original version was popular early in the 20th cent. ◊ *Canasta.*

GIN RUMMY: For two players, with 10 cards each; popular in U.S.A.

'Rump' Parliament ◊ *Commonwealth and Protectorate, English Civil Wars.*

Runes. The letters of the old Teutonic alphabet, formed by straightening Greek or Roman letters to make them easy to carve on wood or stone. Used extensively by the Scandinavians, Frisians, and Anglo-Saxons, and linked with their religious beliefs; perhaps devised in Italy, and dating to the 2nd cent. A.D. Several runic monuments have been found in Britain.

Rushes. Strictly, members of the family *Junaceae;* many as tussocks of round, green, pith-filled, pointed stems, with clusters of small brownish flowers near the tip, growing in marshes and fens.

BULRUSH: Two British genera, *Typha* with cylindrical brown heads, and the giant reed used for baskets, thatching, etc.

Russia ◊ *Soviet Union (History).*

Russian ◊ *Slavonic Languages.*

Russian Architecture. In early times, ◊ *Byzantine;* the inscribed cross-plan with five domes typifies churches of the 11th–16th centuries, though ◊ *Renaissance* forms appeared before 1500. The earlier tradition survived Renaissance influence, under Ivan the Great 1440–1505, and culminated in the mid-16th-cent. cathedral of St Basil in the ◊ *Kremlin.* Full westernization came with ◊ *baroque* esp. Rastrelli's 18th-cent. Peterhof and the Winter Palace in St Petersburg; ◊ *neoclassicism* was introduced by Vallin de la Mothe and Rinaldi, and Russian architects esp. Starov and Zacharov made St Petersburg the neoclassical city *par excellence.* Mid-19th-cent. Russian architects followed western revivals, adding their own ancient-Russian revival. In the 20th cent. post-revolutionary architecture began with advanced modernism, was followed by reactionary academic classicism, and has recently made a tentative return to western fashions.

Russian Art. Until the end of the 17th cent. ◊ *Byzantine.* There were notable schools of ◊ *icon* painters in Moscow, Novgorod, Pskov, and Kiev; fine if sometimes barbarically rich silverwork and jewellery were also produced. Western influences were introduced in the early 18th cent. under Peter the Great, and inspired a number of painters notable mainly for their portraits. Later painters were influenced by ◊ *neoclassicism* and ◊

romanticism; in the early 20th cent. ◊ *impressionism* came in from France. In the revolutionary atmosphere 1907–24 a handful of avant-garde artists e.g. Malevich, Kandinsky, Pevsner, Gabo experimented with forms of ◊ *abstract art* esp. ◊ *constructivism*, but this movement was suppressed; 'socialist realism' is now the official Soviet style.

Russian Revolution (1917) ◊ *Bolsheviks, Soviet Union*.

Russo-Japanese War. 1904–5. Both Russia and Japan had aggressive designs on ◊ *Korea* and ◊ *Manchuria*; Russia refused compromise, believing that Japan would inevitably be defeated and counting on victory to avert internal revolt, but the Japanese attacked the Russian Pacific fleet in Port Arthur without warning, and the Russian armies, hampered by divided command and poor communications, were quickly beaten (◊ *Mukden*). At sea the Japanese routed Russia's Pacific fleet and then annihilated her Baltic fleet at ◊ *Tsushima*. As a result, Russia leased Port Arthur to Japan, evacuated Manchuria, and acquiesced in the Japanese occupation of Korea. The revelation of the Tsarist regime's weakness precipitated the 1905 revolution in Russia.

Russo-Turkish Wars. The expansion of Russia brought frequent conflict with Turkey. In the 16th and 17th centuries Russia was long involved in fighting to overcome the Tatars in the Crimea and win firm control of the Black Sea. In 1783 Catherine annexed the Crimea; war with Turkey ensued, ended in 1792 by the Treaty of Jassy which gave Russia substantial advantages. The further Russo-Turkish War in 1877 resulted from anti-Turkish uprisings in ◊ *Serbia*, Herzogovina, and Montenegro; intervening to help the latter, Russia invaded Turkey, on whom she forced the Treaty of San Stefano, but alarmed at her influence in the Balkans, Britain, France, and Austria intervened. There followed the ◊ *Berlin Congress* and Treaty, which placed ◊ *Bulgaria* under Turkish suzerainty, made

◊ *Rumania* a Hohenzollern Kingdom, and guaranteed the independence of Serbia, to demonstrate that Russia was not to be the sole arbiter of Balkan affairs.

Rust. 1. The familiar reddish-brown deposit on iron, a combination of the metal with oxygen in the air, facilitated by the presence of moisture: ◊ *Corrosion*.
2. In botany, various parasitic ◊ *fungi*, and the plant diseases caused by them.

Ruthenium ◊ *Platinum Metals*.

Rwanda (Ruanda). Area 10,169 sq. m. Pop. 2.6 m. (chiefly Hutu and Tutsi, with 50,000 ◊ *pygmies*). Cap. Kigali. A republic in central Africa, independent since 1962, formerly part of the Belgian Congo and after 1946 a Belgian trusteeship under the U.N. (Ruanda-Urundi).
ECONOMY. Almost wholly agricultural, esp. coffee, cotton, hides; some mining.
HISTORY. For many centuries the Tutsi (ethnically distinct from other African peoples) were the ruling caste in a rigid feudal economy, with the Hutu and pygmies as their serfs and slaves. When the U.N. trusteeship ended, Ruanda-Urundi split into ◊ *Burundi* (which remained a monarchy) and Rwanda, which voted overwhelmingly to abolish the Tutsi monarchy. During 1963 many of the Tutsi nobles fled to Burundi, where they organized an armed counter-revolutionary force, the 'Cockroach', which in 1963 and early 1964 made a number of forays into Rwanda; panic among the Hutu within Rwanda resulted in horrifying massacres of the remaining Tutsi. The Burundi-Rwanda tension is a matter of debate in the U.N. and the Organization for African Unity.

Rye. *Secale;* a relatively recent and very hardy ◊ *cereal*, probably originating in Asia, grown for food mainly in N. Europe and extensively used for malting in the production of rye whisky esp. in N. America. It tolerates poor soil and low winter temperatures but is very susceptible to ◊ *ergot* infection. Until the mid 19th cent. rye ('black') bread was the major food of about a third of Europe.

S

Saarland. Highly industrialized area on the W. frontier of Germany. Ceded to France, under the supervision of the League of Nations, after the ◊ *First World War*; returned to Germany, after a ◊ *referendum*, in 1935; after the ◊ *Second World War* again occupied by France. Under the 1956 agreement between France and W. Germany it was returned, with a special economic status to safeguard French commercial interests.

Sabbath. Seventh day of the Jewish week, on which by tradition God rested after creating the world and man (Gen. ii. 2–3) and which he commanded to be observed by complete abstinence from ordinary work (Exod. xx. 11). Its observance has remained a prominent feature of ◊ *Judaism*, but in remembrance of Jesus Christ's resurrection the early Christians transferred the weekly rest to the first day (Sunday), which is still consecrated to worship and rest by most Christians, and is often called the 'Sabbath' (though a few bodies e.g. Seventh-Day ◊ *Adventists* observe Saturday). In the U.K. a number of legal restrictions on Sunday work and leisure-time activities are still in force; the Lord's Day Observance Society exists to press for their continuance.

Saccharin. A synthetic sweetening agent derived from toluene; although it has no food value, it is esp. useful in the diet of diabetics.

Saccharose ◊ *Carbohydrates.*

Sacco-Vanzetti Case. 1920–7. Two Italian immigrants in U.S.A. were charged with the murder of the paymaster and guard of a Massachusetts factory; the defence claimed that they had not been properly identified, and there was widespread suspicion of victimization, both being known radicals of anarcho-syndicalist views. Appeals for a retrial were denied by the Massachusetts Supreme Court, though much of the evidence against them was discredited and in 1925 another Italian confessed to the murder. After world-wide protest meetings, in 1927 the Governor of Massachusetts postponed the execution and appointed a three-man advisory committee, which upheld the conviction. The two men were executed in Aug. 1927;

they are still widely considered to have been political martyrs.

Sacrament. In Christian theology, an external sign of the bestowal of an interior grace, instituted by ◊ *Jesus Christ* and in certain circumstances necessary for all men. The ◊ *Roman Catholic Church* and the ◊ *Eastern Orthodox Church* recognize seven sacraments: ◊ *baptism*; ◊ *Holy Communion* (the Sacrament *par excellence*); penance (◊ *Confession*); ◊ *confirmation*; the anointing of the sick; matrimony; and ◊ *holy orders*. The ◊ *Church of England* admits as sacraments only holy communion and baptism, though it uses most (or all) of the others as sacred rites. The 'matter' of a sacrament is the material vehicle of the grace conferred, e.g. water in baptism, bread and wine in communion; the 'form' is the words by which it is administered, which are strictly defined. Generally, sacraments must be administered by duly ordained priests, or in the case of confirmation (except in the Eastern Churches) and holy orders, by bishops; but baptism may in case of necessity be administered by the laity, and some hold that in matrimony the parties administer the sacrament to each other, the priest acting only as a necessary witness.

Sacrifice. Offering of a material thing, esp. a living creature, to a god in recognition of his power and to gain his goodwill. The offering is generally killed or destroyed, often by fire; if an animal, its flesh is eaten by the priests and worshippers. Sacrifice is a feature of many primitive religions and an important factor in ◊ *Hinduism* and in ancient ◊ *Judaism*. Roman Catholic theology teaches that the ◊ *Mass* is a sacrifice, in union with the sacrificial death of ◊ *Jesus Christ*, which itself fulfilled and completed the Jewish sacrifices offered under the Mosaic law. Neither ◊ *Islam* nor ◊ *Buddhism* contains any element of sacrifice.

Safavids ◊ *Persia.*

Safety Factor. In mechanical or civil engineering, the margin of strength, expressed as the ratio between the greatest load a component can carry without failure and the highest load (stress) it is expected to take; the factor varies for different materials and purposes, e.g. in aircraft the structure is in general required to be able to stand three times the maximum working stress expected, i.e. a safety factor of 3. In parts of buildings the factor may be as low as 1.5 but the hoisting cables of a lift require a safety factor of 10. ⬦ *Fatigue of Materials.*

Saffron. The powdered dried stigmas of the Mediterranean *Crocus sativus*, which yield a yellow dye and flavouring agent, used in food from early times. In the 15th cent. the main centre of cultivation in England was Saffron Walden. Spain is now the main supplier.

Saga. < Norse, 'something said'. A form of heroic literature (⬦ *Edda, Iceland, Norway*), with four main types: those dealing with early kings, e.g. the *Heimskringla*, by the Icelandic poet Snorri Sturluson; those dealing with the violent exploits of 10th- and 11th-cent. Icelandic families e.g. the *Njal's Saga*; those based on direct information about more or less contemporary heroes, e.g. the *Sturlunga Saga*; and purely fictitious works, dating to the late 12th and the 13th centuries but set in the remote past, e.g. the *Volsunga Saga*. Later Icelandic sagas, translations of French and other European ⬦ *romances*, replace the violent old heroic code by that of chivalry.

Sage ⬦ *Labiatae.*

Sago ⬦ *Palm.*

Sails and Sailing. A sail is an area of cotton, canvas, matting, or other material forming a soft aerofoil whereby the force of the wind is used to drive a ship; sails may be rigged square or fore-and-aft, square sails e.g. in Greek and Roman ⬦ *galleys*, Viking ships, and most medieval craft being rectangular and set at right-angles to the keel, the upper edge being bent to a horizontal spar suspended on the foreside of a mast. The square rig, ideal for sailing before the wind, was retained by ships using the ⬦ *trade winds* long after the introduction of fore-and-aft rigging; but it was dependent on fair winds. The Mediterranean lateen sail, forerunner of the fore-and-aft rig, was also slung from a spar, but was triangular, and the spar was tilted for greater manoeuvrability. Fore-and-aft sails e.g. the lugsail, the gaff mainsail, and the Bermuda sail have the forward edge secured

to a mast or stay; they permit sailing more or less directly into the wind which, blowing past the leeward side of the sail, creates a vacuum which pulls it against the direction of the wind, the jib acting like the slot on the wings of aircraft (see diagram) to guide the airflow and prevent

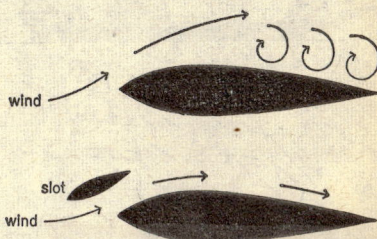

turbulence. Most large sailing ships of the 18th and 19th centuries carried both kinds of sail, e.g. a baque was square-rigged on the foremast and mainmast, the mizzenmast being fore-and-aft; while a barquentine was square-rigged on the foremast only. The sails were named according to position and purpose, from the topgallant and royal at the top of the mast to the mainsail at the bottom. ⬦ *Clipper, Yachting,* and illustration on next page.

St Bartholomew Massacre. 1572. The bloodiest episode in the long French struggle between growing Roman Catholic ⬦ *absolutism* and the numerous dissenting ⬦ *Huguenots.* A plan of the Cardinal the Duke of Guise, the Queen Mother Catherine de' Medici, King Charles IX, and the Duke of Anjou (Henri III) to exterminate the Huguenots had long been in existence; the 1572 plot was known in advance to e.g. William of Orange, who kept the secret. In Aug. 1572 many thousands of Huguenots were invited to Paris to celebrate the marriage of the Huguenot Henri de Navarre to his cousin Marguerite de Valois, sister of Charles IX. On 22 Aug. the Huguenot leader Coligny narrowly escaped assassination in a Paris street. Two days later, on St Bartholomew's Day, Coligny and tens of thousands of unarmed Huguenots were slaughtered at night, by sudden and concerted action not only in Paris but in many other cities. The Pope (Gregory XIII) publicly rejoiced and had a commemorative medal struck. Elizabeth I of England put her court, ministers, and

barque

barquentine

brig

brigantine

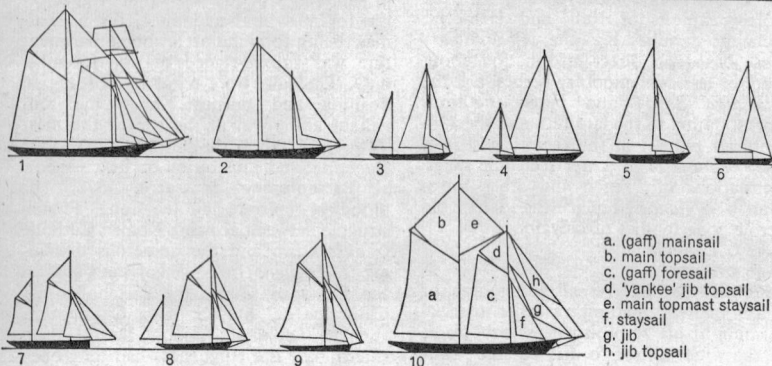

a. (gaff) mainsail
b. main topsail
c. (gaff) foresail
d. 'yankee' jib topsail
e. main topmast staysail
f. staysail
g. jib
h. jib topsail

1. topsail schooner 2. (bermudan) staysail schooner 3. bermudan ketch 4. bermudan yawl 5. bermudan cutter
6. bermudan sloop 7. gaff ketch 8. gaff yawl 9. gaff cutter 10. gaff schooner

Parliament into mourning, and the English attitude towards Mary Queen of Scots (niece and pupil of the Guises, Dowager Queen of France) hardened irrevocably. The French wars of religion broke out again with increased bitterness and continued another 20 years. ◊ *Edict of Nantes*.

St Cyr. Military school founded 1802 by Napoleon and transferred to St Cyr (near Versailles) 1808; the cadets follow a two-year course, with a third year at a specialized school of a particular branch of the army.

St Germain Treaties. 1570. Ended the first phase of the French Wars of Religion; ◊ *Huguenots*.
1679. Ended the third war between France, her ally Sweden, and the ◊ *Netherlands*, allied with Brandenburg.
1919. Peace treaty between the Allies and ◊ *Austria* after the ◊ *First World War*, which ended the Austro-Hungarian monarchy, the new Austrian republic recognizing the independence of ◊ *Czechoslovakia, Hungary, Poland, Yugoslavia*, and agreeing not to compromise its own, i.e. by economic or political union

with Germany. ⟡ *Anschluss, Versailles Treaty*.

St Helena. Area 47 sq. m. Pop. 4624. A solitary island in the S. Atlantic over 1000 m. from Africa and nearly 2000 m. from S. America. A British colony ruled by the Governor and a small executive Council. ECONOMY. Some flax-fibre production and lace-making industry; otherwise subsistence agriculture. HISTORY. Discovered by Portugal in 1502, and used as a general port of call until annexed in 1633 by the Dutch and then in 1659 by the British ⟡ *East India Company*; they loaned it to the Crown 1815–21 as the place of exile of Napoleon, who died there.

St John (Knights) ⟡ *Orders of Chivalry*.

St Lawrence Seaway ⟡ *Canal*.

St Pierre and Miquelon. Area 93 sq. m. Pop. 4900. Islands off Newfoundland; member of the French Community.

Salamander. Member of the tailed ⟡ *amphibian* group *Urodela*; the spotted salamander, black with yellow patches, is an example of warning ⟡ *pigmentation*, and resembles a small soft-skinned ⟡ *lizard*. The axolotl is remarkable in that under natural conditions it retains the ⟡ *larva* form, with external gills, but nevertheless is sexually mature. This is an example of neoteny, a process thought to have played an important part in ⟡ *evolution*.

Salamis. 480 B.C. Sea battle near Athens in which the Greeks lured the Persian fleet to attack them in the narrow straits between the island of Salamis and the mainland, and despite their inferior numbers destroyed 200 Persian vessels and removed the threat of invasion. ⟡ *Greece (Ancient)*.

Salic Law. A rule of succession banning royal and noble inheritance of office and title through the female line, allegedly part of the ancient Germanic Lex Salica. When on the death of Charles IV of France in 1328 both his daughter and his sister's son, Edward III of England, were barred from the throne by Salic law, Edward (as the nearest kin and already lord of more than half the French territories) declared himself King of France, and the ⟡ *Hundred Years War* began.

Salic law also caused the separation of ⟡ *Hanover* from the British crown in 1837, on the accession of Queen Victoria. It still applies in e.g. Belgium, Denmark, Norway, Sweden.

Salicylic Acid. A hydroxy-acid, derived from ⟡ *phenol*, used in medicine for treating skin diseases; a common ingredient in corn-plasters. ⟡ *Aspirin* is made from it. The ester methyl salicylate occurs in oil of wintergreen, used in liniments and toothpastes.

Salk's Vaccine. The first effective vaccine against ⟡ *poliomyelitis*, discovered in 1953; it is prepared by cultivating all the three serological types of poliomyelitis virus, in tissue cultures made from the renal tissues of monkeys, and has been successfully used on a large scale in U.S.A. Originally the virus was killed by treatment with formaldehyde; subsequently an improved vaccine using living viruses was developed.

Salmon. Strictly, the genus *Oncorhynchus*, the Pacific salmon, of the *Salmonidae*, the Atlantic salmon being a ⟡ *trout*; zoologically salmon are intermediate between ⟡ *cod* and ⟡ *shark*. Migrating from the sea to fresh water to spawn, they swim to the head-waters of the rivers, often covering distances up to 3000 m. After spawning, the 'kelt' usually die; a year later, the young fish migrate back to the sea, where they take up to seven years to reach maturity, passing through the successive stages of 'parr', 'grilse', 'maiden-fish'. The five commercially important species may reach weights of 70 to 100 lb. each, and the annual catch in U.S.A. and Canada is about 400 m. lb. Most of this is canned.

Salt. 1. Common salt; a chemical compound of the elements sodium and chlorine, transparent, in small cubic crystals; a very important part of human and animal diet, used as a preservative in the food industry, esp. for fish and meat, and as a condiment. To keep it free-flowing for table use, sodium carbonate and phosphate are added. Large deposits of rock salt are worked in Poland, Britain (Cheshire), and U.S.A. It is also extracted from sea-water by evaporation.
2. Compound in which the proton of an ⟡ *acid* has been replaced by a positive ion, so that the negative and positive charges exactly balance and the ⟡ *molecule* itself is without charge. From hydrochloric acid, chlorides Na^+Cl^-; from nitric acid nitrates $Na^+NO_3^-$; from sulphuric acid sulphates $Na_2^+SO_4^{2-}$; from phosphoric acid sulphates $Na^+_3PO_4^{3-}$; normal salts are sulphates and phosphates

from which all the protons have been removed; those in which some protons remain are hydrogen salts, e.g. sodium hydrogen sulphate. The ions may consist of a charged atom Ca^{2+} or a group of a few atoms e.g. $(NH_4)^+$ or $(SO_3)^{2-}$; salts composed of such ions are simple; in complex salts the ion is much more complex than sulphate e.g. Prussian blue, with ion $[Fe(CN)_6]^{4-}$. ⟡ *Valency*.

Saltpetre ⟡ *Potassium, Sodium*.

Salvador. Area 7722 sq. m. Pop. 2.5 m. (one of the most densely populated countries in the New World). Cap. San Salvador. Central American republic, on the Pacific coast of the isthmus, between Guatemala, Honduras, and Nicaragua.

ECONOMY. Very mountainous; volcanic and subject to earthquakes. Main crop coffee; also balsam, cotton, indigo, maize, rice, sesame-seeds, sisal, sugar. The illiteracy rate is about 50 per cent, but recent Budgets have granted a high percentage of revenue for educational purposes.

HISTORY. Conquered by Spain in 1526 and part of the Guatemala Viceroyalty until the revolt of the Spanish colonies in 1821, when it joined the Federation of Central American States, from which it seceded in 1839. The 1950 Constitution allows for an elected two-year legislature and six-year presidency; there were two coups d'état 1960–1, a new Assembly was elected, and in 1962 a single-candidate election confirmed Colonel Rivera as President for five years.

Salvation Army. Protestant Christian organization founded by 'General' William Booth (1829–1912) with the object of influencing the poor and depressed classes neglected by the 'respectable' churches; headed by a 'General' elected by a High Council of officers, who holds office till death or resignation, and conducted on quasi military lines, its members wearing a uniform and following a strict code of discipline; engages in a wide variety of social and rescue work among the underprivileged and criminal classes, and places much emphasis on emotional appeal and instantaneous 'conversion'.

Samarium ⟡ *Lanthanides*.

Samoa. Chain of Pacific islands midway between Hawaii and E. Australia.

AMERICAN SAMOA: Tutuila and six other small islands. Area 76.5 sq. m. Pop. 20,000. Cap Pago Pago. Chief exports copra, tuna fish. A U.S. dependency.

WESTERN SAMOA: Savaii, Upola, and other small islands. Area 1133 sq. m. Pop. 114,427. Cap. Apia. Chief exports bananas, breadfruit, cocoa, copra, pineapples. Member of the British Commonwealth.

Sanctions (Economic) ⟡ *Boycott, League of Nations*.

Sanctuary. A sacred place. **1.** In antiquity, the shrine of a god; in the Middle Ages, Christian churches and other consecrated buildings e.g. abbeys, monasteries. To remove anyone from a sanctuary or commit violence within its precincts was sacrilege, and runaway slaves, escaping prisoners, and fugitives from justice or from enemies frequently took refuge at shrines. They were frequently starved out; in England, felons were permitted to leave sanctuary unharmed on condition of going into permanent exile abroad. It was the sacrilege of violating sanctuary that gave the murder of Becket in 1170 its importance; his immediate canonization stressed the Church's determination to enforce its own powers against those of the secular law. By the 16th cent. the Church itself dared not violate sanctuary; e.g. the poet Skelton satirized Cardinal Wolsey and fled into sanctuary in Westminster Abbey in 1527, where he remained for two years, until his death. A century later, in 1623, during the early Parliamentary struggles against Stewart clericalism, sanctuary rights were abolished in Britain.

Today embassies sometimes act as sanctuaries for political fugitives, e.g. Cardinal Mindszenty has for several years been living in the U.S. Embassy in Budapest.

2. In a cathedral, the room where the sacred vessels are stored.

3. A nature reserve, where wildlife is protected.

Sandstone. Sedimentary rock formed by the cementing together of grains of ⟡ *quartz*, the detritus resulting from the denudation of granite and similar igneous rocks. The cement may be silica, clay, iron, or lime; hence there are siliceous, argillaceous, ferruginous, and calcareous sandstones; the siliceous is the strongest and most durable, as the cementing material has the same physical and chemical characteristics as the sand grains themselves. Used for building and paving material. ⟡ *Devonian Period, Geological Time Scale.*

Sandstorm. Mass of sand, rarely higher than 50–100 ft, carried not far from its source by a strong wind e.g. the hot dry Saharan and Arabian whirlwind called the simoom.

DUSTSTORM: Mass of fine dust, 10,000 ft high or more, filling the air and sometimes reducing visibility almost to zero, caused by turbulent wind over a dry dusty surface, e.g. in desert regions of N. Africa, Iraq, and NW India.

San Francisco Conference (1945) ⟡ *Dumbarton Oaks, United Nations.*

San Marino. Area 23 sq. m. Pop. 17,000. Cap. San Marino. A republic inside Italy near the Adriatic, governed by two Captains-Regent and a 10-man State Congress, with a 60-man legislative Council elected for five years by universal suffrage.

ECONOMY. Principal products cattle, ceramics, cereals, concrete, cotton yarn, paints, wine. The revenue and expenditure are balanced.

HISTORY. Founded by a stonecutter in the 4th cent. A.D. and always resistant to the claims of the papacy; Italy respects its integrity and sovereignty.

Sanskrit. One of the ⟡ *Indo-European languages*; the sacred tongue of ⟡ *Hinduism.* Indian languages descending from Sanskrit, spoken in India, include Bengali, Bihari, Gujarati, Hindi, Marathi, Oriya, Punjabi, Rajasthani, Sinhalese, and Urdu. ⟡ *Mahabharata, Ramayana.*

CLASSICAL SANSKRIT: A late form evolved by grammarians about 300 B.C.

PALI, PRAKRIT: The ancestors of the modern Indian languages. Pali (line, rule) was used in the canonical books of ⟡ *Buddhism.* Prakrit < *prakrta,* unrefined; a number of closely related dialects.

VEDIC SANSKRIT: < *Veda,* knowledge, *sanskrt,* refined. The ancient language of the 4 collections of hymns called Rig, Sama, Yajur, and Atharva ⟡ *Vedas.*

San Stefano Treaty ⟡ *Berlin Congress, Russo-Turkish Wars.*

Sapphics. Verses written in the ⟡ *metre* or stanza supposedly devised by the Greek poetess Sappho, one used in many of the Odes of Horace and occasionally attempted experimentally in English by poets exploring the possibilities of quantitative verse.

Sapphire. Gem-stone; blue variety of ⟡ *corundum.*

Saprophytes. Organisms which live on decaying organic matter, producing ⟡ *enzymes* which decompose tissues whose soluble products they absorb as nutrients. All ⟡ *fungi* which are not parasites are saprophytes, as are many bacteria and a few flowering plants e.g. the bird's-nest and coral-root orchids, native to Britain and living in humus-rich soils. Saprophytes cause decay and rotting of tissues, and may be economically important e.g. in spoilage of food and timber by wet rot, ⟡ *dry rot,* moulds, mildews, etc., but the majority are an essential part of the cycles of breakdown and resynthesis of all materials in living organisms, e.g. in the carbon cycle and ⟡ *nitrogen cycle.*

Saracens. Name applied indiscriminately in the Middle Ages to Muslim peoples, whether Arabs, Moors, or Turks. Strictly, the people of NW Arabia.

Sarajevo ⟡ *Serbia.*

Saratoga. 1777. In the ⟡ *American Revolution,* decisive defeat by the British army advancing from Canada under General Burgoyne, isolated from the forces intended to support him from the south; he attempted to retreat, but was surrounded and forced to capitulate.

Sarawak. Area 48,250 sq. m. Pop. 776,990 (multi-racial). Cap. Kuching. The NW coast of ⟡ *Borneo.*

ECONOMY. Chief products bauxite, gold, nuts, pepper, rice, rubber, sago, timber. There are deposits of coal.

HISTORY. 1841–1946 a sultanate hereditary in the Brooke family, and from 1888 a British protectorate; ceded to the Crown in 1946 and since then a British colony, adjacent to that of N. Borneo.

Sardinia. Area 9302 sq. m. Pop. about 1.2 m. Cap. Cagliari. Mediterranean island S. of Corsica; autonomous region of ⟡ *Italy.*

ECONOMY. Mainly agricultural: cattle, grain, grapes, olives, tobacco; lobster and tuna fisheries. Also rich mineral deposits: copper, iron ore, lead, lignite, salt, zinc. Hydroelectric power is beginning to be used.

HISTORY. Settled by ⟡ *Phoenicians*; in 238 B.C. conquered by ⟡ *Rome,* captured in the 5th cent. A.D. by the ⟡ *Vandals,* and from the 6th to 7th centuries part of Byzantium, then seized as a ⟡ *papal state,* and in the 14th cent. presented to Spain. By the 1713 ⟡ *Utrecht Treaty* it was ceded to Austria, Spain re-annexed it in 1717, and

1720 it was made a monarchy under the Duke of Savoy, as part of Piedmont (in exchange for Sicily), the capital being Turin. Feudal privilege was not abolished until 1836. Administrative autonomy was rescinded in 1847 but restored in the 20th cent. after the ◊ *Second World War*.

LANGUAGE. Sardinian, the ◊ *Romance language* nearest to ◊ *Latin*.

Saros. In ◊ *astronomy*, the interval of 6585 days (18 years and either 10 or 11 days according to the number of leap years included) at which ◊ *eclipses* of the sun or moon recur. This cycle was known to the Babylonians and enabled them to predict eclipses.

Sarsens. Large lumps of sandstone, some embedded in red clay, found on the chalk downs of SE England esp. near Marlborough; residual masses of the Reading beds (Tertiary sandstones) which once overlay the chalk, most of which has been worn away. Their popular name 'greywethers' derives from a supposed resemblance to sheep at rest. Enormous sarsens were used in the stone circles at ◊ *Avebury* and ◊ *Stonehenge*. ◊ *Geological Time Scale*.

Sassanians ◊ *Persia*.

Satan ◊ *Devil*.

Satellite ◊ *Artificial Satellite, Space Exploration*.

Satellite Astronomy. Astronomical observation is hampered by the fact that radiation from outer space in the medium and long wavelengths of ultraviolet, X, or gamma rays cannot penetrate the earth's atmosphere and only above a height of 100 m. can these radiations be observed. Instruments in ◊ *rockets* have carried out brief observations above Australia and U.S.A. Orbiting astronomical observatories containing telescopes with detecting devices designed to observe in the new wavelength regions and incorporating stabilization systems, so that the telescopes could be directed to chosen points in the sky, would be more effective, to make observations by photo-electric devices e.g. on magnetic tape and transmit them to the ground. Such observatories are being designed in the U.K. and U.S.A.

Satire. Any poem, writing, speech, or other expression ridiculing human follies, illusions, hypocrisies, or the like; the most notable Greek satires are the comedies of Aristophanes, but the Latin *satura* was originally a hotch-potch of rude abuse having little direct connexion with the more sophisticated work of such satirists as Horace, Juvenal, and Persius or with those of the modern genre e.g. Dryden, Molière, Pope, Voltaire, Swift, Byron, Orwell. ◊ *Burlesque, Parody*.

Saturn. The planet sixth from the sun in the ◊ *solar system*. Its main body is similar to that of ◊ *Jupiter*, a band structure being visible in a complete cloud cover; white spots can sometimes be seen, and also the polar flattening which results from the planet's rapid rotation. Spectroscopy reveals ammonia and methane. The rings of Saturn are estimated to be only 10 m. thick, but they have an extreme diameter of 171,000 m. They consist of a swarm of particles, possibly ice, thought to be of the order of one yard in diameter. There is a faint inner 'crape' ring, a main middle ring, and a somewhat less bright outer ring, separated from the others by the dark Cassini's Division. Saturn's nine satellites are (outwards): Mimas, Enceladus, Tethys, Dione, Rhea, Titan, Hyperion, Iapetus, and Phoebe; the largest, Titan, is bigger than the earth's moon, and has an atmosphere.

Saudi Arabia. Area 927,000 sq. m. Pop. 6 m. Cap. Mecca and Riyadh. Rel. Muslim. Covers most of Arabia and comprises the Hejaz, Nejd, and Asir, unified to form the Saudi Arabian kingdom by Ibn Saud, who drove Hussein from the Hejaz in 1925. His son Saud ibn Abdul Aziz succeeded him in 1953; in 1958 a 'Cabinet System' was instituted with some devolution of power to a Council of Ministers, headed by the Emir Faisal, a younger son, who replaced his brother as ruler in 1964.

ECONOMY. For revenue the country depends largely on royalties from oil companies, the chief being the U.S.-owned Arabian–American Oil Company (Aramco). Royalties rose from £3 m. in 1938 to £110 m. by 1954. A large proportion goes as grants to desert tribes and members of the royal family. Saudi Arabia is largely desert. Of the larger Arab countries it is the least Westernized, and remains technically and socially backward.

HISTORY. An independent state in the 18th cent. but under the rule of ◊ *Turkey* in the 19th until Ibn Saud started his revolt in 1917.

Sauria ◊ *Lizard*.

Savanna. Tropical region, the natural vegetation mainly grass and scattered trees; differs from the equatorial ◊ *rain forest* regions in having distinct hot-wet and cool-dry seasons. There are savanna regions N. and S. of the Amazon (◊ *campos, llanos*) in S. America, but the most extensive are in Africa, where vast numbers of wild animals still flourish. Savanna land is suitable for cattle-grazing, but only at low density, as forage is sparse.

Savoy. From the 11th cent. to the 19th an independent duchy, extending over parts of present-day ◊ *France, Italy, Switzerland*, and also ◊ *Burgundy, Piedmont*. Switzerland incorporated Geneva in the 15th–16th centuries and France the Bresse area in the 17th. In the 18th Savoy became part of the kingdom of ◊ *Sardinia*; annexed by France during the ◊ *French Revolution*, it was returned to Sardinia by the ◊ *Vienna Congress*, but after a ◊ *referendum* in 1860 most of it was ceded to France, under the Turin Treaty creating the new Italian state (◊ *Solferino*).

Savoy Conference. 1661. Body of 12 Anglican bishops and 12 Independent (◊ *Puritan*) divines, convened after the ◊ *Restoration* 1661 to negotiate agreed forms of worship for general use in England. The bishops rejected all offers of compromise over the ◊ *Prayer Book*, and the conference collapsed, after which the ◊ *Clarendon Code* made all non-Anglican preaching or teaching an offence punishable by severe penalties; 2000 divines who would not comply with the Act of Uniformity were ejected from their parishes on St Bartholomew's Day 1662 and with their congregations suffered much persecution for 25 years. ◊◊ *Nonconformists*.

Saxhorn, Saxophone ◊ *Brass Instruments*.

Saxifragaceae. Saxifrage; usually dwarf plants, widely spread throughout the Northern Hemisphere generally in mountainous regions where they make close moss-like tufts or 'cushions' of rosettes. The flowers are white, yellow, or red, plain or spotted, and may sit on the tuft or be carried on graceful sprays a foot or more in length. ◊◊ *Ribesaceae*.

Saxony. Originally, the land of the Saxons, in what is now NW Germany; later, at various times, a duchy, electorate, kingdom, province, and state. The Saxons began to expand southwards from Holstein in the 2nd cent. A.D. Conquered and converted to Christianity by Charlemagne, their territory formed one of the five duchies of early medieval Germany. After the fall of Henry the Lion in 1180 the duchy was divided; later the E. was joined to Meissen and Thuringia, the whole becoming known as Saxony, while the W. was Lower Saxony. The electors of Saxony adopted ◊ *Lutheranism*, but continued to support the ◊ *Hapsburgs*: until the ◊ *Thirty Years War* their state was more advanced than ◊ *Brandenburg*. Afterwards, though it remained the more important cultural centre, politically it lagged behind both ◊ *Prussia* and ◊ *Bavaria*. During the ◊ *Seven Years War* it was occupied by Prussia. For the support it gave Napoleon (who made it a kingdom) it was penalized by the loss of Thuringia and parts of Lusatia to Prussia, and later was easily compelled to join the N. German Confederation and in 1871 the German empire. It retained its separate administration, however, until the abdication of Frederick Augustus III in 1918. It now forms part of ◊ *Germany (Democratic Republic)*. Lower Saxony, however, is a province *(Land)* of ◊ *Germany (Federal Republic)*. ◊◊ *Guelphs and Ghibellines*.

Scabies. Skin disease caused by *Sarcoptes scabiei*, a tiny burrowing ◊ *mite*, causing intense itching esp. at night; infestation is readily transmissible and is associated with low standards of hygiene.

Scandium. A rare metallic ◊ *element* very similar in properties and chemistry to the ◊ *lanthanides*; like them, it is obtained from the mineral monazite, but neither it nor its compounds yet have commercial or technological applications.

Scarlatina (Scarlet Fever). Fever, mainly affecting children, caused by various strains of haemolytic streptococcus. Symptoms include inflammation of the throat and a bright red body-rash, which produces some scaling of the skin as it clears. Infection of the middle ear, arthritis, ephritis, and heart disease are possible complications. The incidence and mortality rate of the disease have declined greatly during the last 50 years.

Scent. Odour emanating from animals and plants esp. flowers, where it serves to attract pollinating insects. In many mammals scent is important for finding a mate, and also the scent gland may serve as a defence e.g. in the skunk, or as a means of recognizing their own kind. The scent of commerce (▷ *perfume*) is obtained from the ▷ *essential oils* of plants and the glands of certain animals.

Scepticism. Sometimes the argued attacks of the Sceptics, notably Pyrrho, on Graeco-Roman philosophies e.g. ▷ *Stoicism* claiming to have found truth; more commonly, a recurring attitude in the history of philosophy issuing in arguments against various beliefs and dogmatisms. In the theory of ▷ *knowledge*, scepticism involves the argument that belief in independently existing physical objects goes beyond the available evidence of subjective sense impressions.

Scheduled Diseases. Most countries have laws requiring certain serious diseases or very infectious diseases of animals to be reported immediately to the police or appropriate government department so that preventive measures may be taken; in Britain the scheduled diseases are ▷ *anthrax*, atrophic rhinitis of pigs, ▷ *foot-and-mouth disease*, contagious bovine pleuropneumonia, rinderpest, ▷ *glanders*, epizootic lymphangitis of horses, ▷ *rabies*, ▷ *mange* in horses, sheep scab (mange), sheep pox, swine fever, certain forms of tuberculosis in cattle, and meat measles (*Brucella melitensis*) in cattle.

Schists ▷ *Granite, Magma, Metamorphic Rocks*.

Schizophrenia. A serious ▷ *psychosis* in which disturbances of thinking, perception, and emotion lead to abnormal behaviour often with withdrawal from normal social activities, to ▷ *hallucinations* and delusions, and to a variety of other symptoms; persons suffering from it are said to be of a schizoid or 'split' personality. The cause is unknown, but recent research suggests that it lies in a biochemical disturbance in the brain, the exact nature of which has yet to be discovered. Modern treatment with drugs can do much to help patients.

Schlieffen Plan. Strategic plan drawn up in 1905 by the German Chief of Staff, Count von Schlieffen, for use in the event of a war on two fronts. It postulated a rapid German victory against France by a massive surprise attack through Belgium, to isolate Paris from the Channel ports, thus releasing the main German forces for the eastern front. It was followed in 1914 though with certain variations which may

or may not have been responsible for its failure (▷ *Battle of Marne*).

Schneider Trophy. Originally intended as a test of the seaworthiness and speed of seaplanes, it became a pure speed contest in which entries were sponsored and largely financed by governments. The first race, Monaco 1913, was won by M. Prévost for France in a Deperdussin at 46 m.p.h. Howard Pixton gave Britain her first win 1914 at 87 m.p.h. The rules laid down that three successive wins would conclude the series and give permanent possession of the trophy; Britain fulfilled these conditions with R.A.F. pilots, Venice 1927, S. N. Webster, 282 m.p.h., and the Solent 1929 H. R. D. Waghorn 329 m.p.h., and 1931 J. N. Boothman 340 m.p.h. The aircraft which won the last contest was the Supermarine S-6b designed by Spitfire-designer R. J. Mitchell and powered by a 2350-h.p. Rolls-Royce R engine.

Scholasticism. Medieval theologico-philosophical doctrinal movement, which sought a philosophy for Christianity by examining the relation between reason (esp. ▷ *Aristotelianism* and ▷ *Platonism*) and revelation; the early stages were marked by the controversy between nominalism (holding that ▷ *universals* are merely words) and ▷ *realism*. The supreme synthesis of Christianity and Aristotelianism was the Thomist philosophy of Thomas Aquinas (later canonized and now recognized as the official philosopher of the Roman Catholic church), as set forth in his *Summa Theologica* and other works in the 13th cent. Other leading scholastics were Erigena, a 9th-cent. exponent of ▷ *neoplatonism*; Anselm, founder of ontology; Abelard, who in the 12th cent. offered a solution to the problem of universals; Bonaventura (the 'Seraphic Doctor') and Duns Scotus, who offered a different synthesis from Aquinas, in the 13th cent.; and William of Ockham, who held that the existence of God was a matter of faith and not capable of proof by argument, 14th cent.

School Men ▷ *Scholasticism*.

Sciatica. Form of ▷ *neuritis* affecting the sciatic nerve, which runs down the back of the thigh and supplies the hamstring muscles, those below the knee, and those of the foot; it produces a burning pain and tenderness along the course of the nerve, and may cause wasting of the calf muscle often associated with prolapsed ◊ *invertebral disc*.

Sclerosis. Hardening and increase of tissue, esp. the connective tissue in the ◊ *central nervous system*, by degeneration, injury, or prolonged inflammation.

ARTERIO-SCLEROSIS: A degenerative change in artery linings; small masses containing ◊ *cholesterol* appear, and may obstruct the blood vessels and cause serious damage to the organs they supply. DISSEMINATED SCLEROSIS: A hardening of areas of the brain and spinal cord, resulting from replacement of nervous tissue by fibrous; it leads to weakness and heaviness in the limbs, muscle tremors, and impaired speech and eyesight.

Scorpion. Arthropods of the class *Arachnida*, related to ◊ *spiders*, like which they have a peculiar method of respiration, picking up oxygen from gill-like structures aptly called 'lung-books'; after seizing their prey, they arch the abdomen forward and paralyse the victim with venom injected through the tail-sting. Ovo-viviparous, the mother scorpion carries the young on her back in the early stages of their life-span. Scorpion venom is too little understood for safe generalization. Two types are known: one acts locally and causes pain but not human death, the other is a neurotoxic poison causing degenerative changes in various organs and frequently death.

Scotland. Area 29,795 sq. m. Pop. 5.2 m. Cap. Edinburgh. N. Kingdom of Gt Britain; part of the ◊ *United Kingdom*.

The early inhabitants were northern ◊ *Picts* and the Scots from Ireland; they resisted the Romans. They were converted to Christianity in the 6th cent. mainly by the Irish missionary Columba. In the 9th cent. the Picts and Scots were united by Kenneth MacAlpin, whose descendants Malcolm II and Duncan extended their rule southwards, over what are now the Lothians and the border counties. Under Malcolm III and his English queen, St Margaret, Scotland came under Norman influence, and the process of feudalization in the Lowlands continued until in the reign of William the Lion, 1165–1214, Scotland became a vassal of England. Richard I sold the Scots their freedom in 1189; but in the late 13th cent. Edward I used a disputed succession to the Scottish crown and re-

asserted the English claim to overlordship; an uprising under Wallace failed in 1298 (◊ *Falkirk*), and by 1303 Edward had conquered the country. Under Edward II the English were defeated by Robert Bruce at ◊ *Bannockburn*, and in 1328 Edward III acknowledged Scotland's freedom by a treaty.

Under her ◊ *Stewart* kings, from the mid 14th cent. Scotland continued to enjoy independence (◊ *Otterburn*); the Lowlands were fairly prosperous, and the court and universities produced a literary and intellectual culture at least as brilliant as that of England, thanks partly to friendly relations with France, but there was much faction and civil disorder, and the French alliance led to invasion by England and a heavy Scottish defeat at ◊ *Flodden*, where James IV, husband of Henry VII's daughter, was killed. The death of his son James V 30 years later made his week-old daughter Mary the Queen of Scots; the long regency of her mother Mary of Guise (sister of the Cardinal) was taken up with ◊ *Reformation* and ◊ *Counter-Reformation* struggles.

As Henry VII's great-granddaughter, Mary was next to Elizabeth in the English succession (or next to Mary Tudor, and before Elizabeth, if Henry VIII's divorce were not recognized). Despite France's adherence to the ◊ *Salic Law*, when Mary married the heir to the French throne in 1558 she was styled Queen of Scotland and of England, and thenceforward bore the English royal arms. In 1559 her husband became King of France, and for a year she claimed triple queenship, but on his death Catherine de' Medici and Cardinal de Guise (◊ *Huguenots*) sent her to Scotland. Her close links with the Counter-Reformation, her political ineptitude, her disastrous marriage to her cousin Darnley (soon afterwards murdered, possibly with her complicity, ◊ *Casket Letters*) caused civil war. Despite the warlike qualities of her third husband Bothwell (a Protestant) she had to flee from Scotland, taking refuge in England. Elizabeth maintained her, under 'house arrest', for 18 years, but after the ◊ *St Bartholomew Massacre*, and with increasing evidence of French, Spanish, and papal plots for Mary's accession as Queen of England, she was at last executed in 1587.

On the death of Elizabeth in 1603, Mary's son (by Darnley) James VI of

Scotland became James I of England, thus uniting the two crowns. Stewart rule in the 17th cent. was attended by the ◊ *English Civil Wars* and ultimately the ◊ *Glorious Revolution*; after the accession of Anne, the last Stewart monarch (when the succession of the house of ◊ *Hanover* became inevitable if the ◊ *Jacobites* were not to return), Scotland was made an integral part of Gt Britain by the 1707 ◊ *Act of Union*.

The Jacobite rebellions of 1715 and 1745 gained most of their support from Scotland, and after the second the Highlands were ruthlessly brought to order and the ◊ *clan* structure extirpated; in the 18th and 19th centuries they were depopulated by clearances. In the Lowlands, however, Edinburgh remained an intellectual capital respected throughout Europe; with the ◊ *Industrial Revolution*, Glasgow and other towns took on a fresh importance, but in general Scotland sank to provincial status. In the 20th cent. a separatist Scottish Nationalist movement developed but made little headway. ◊ *Church of Scotland, Gaelic, Lallans, Scots Law*.

Scotland Yard. Headquarters of the London Metropolitan Police, housed in New Scotland Yard, which provides a number of U.K. national services e.g. maintenance of criminal records, control of the Criminal Investigation Department and its Special (political) Branch, publication of the Police Gazette, and acts as the United Kingdom bureau of ◊ *Interpol*.

Scots Law. Before the Union of the two kingdoms 1707 the legal systems of England and Scotland had developed quite separately, Scotland having accepted a great deal of ◊ *Roman law*, while England rejected it, a difference subsequently reflected in both the content and the nomenclature of the two systems. The tendency is now towards assimilation, since Parliament frequently passes laws applicable to both England and Scotland and the House of Lords is the final court of appeal for both. The civil law of Scotland is administered largely in the Court of Session, consisting of an 'outer House', an 'inner House' (Court of Appeal), and the local sheriff courts: criminal cases go before the sheriff courts, but major cases are heard in the High Court of Justiciary

Sculpture. Both bas-relief and in the round was brought to a high pitch of excellence in many early civilizations – Babylon, the Indus valley, Egypt, China. In Europe it rose to its first great peak in 6th-cent. B.C. Athens, where Phidias and Praxiteles freed it from the limitations of Egyptian convention, to achieve unrivalled expression of the ideal beauty of the human figure. The Romans imitated and prolonged the Greek tradition without adding to it. In the ◊ *Romanesque* and ◊ *Gothic* periods religious sculpture of outstanding quality was produced, much of it in wood; ◊ *Renaissance* sculptors e.g. Donatello and Michelangelo revived classical forms. In the 17th cent. the ◊ *Baroque* artist Bernini created a style which persisted with slight modifications until the emergence of the ◊ *neoclassical* Canova. Towards the end of the 19th cent. Rodin emerged as one of the great masters of sculpture, esp. as portraiture. In the 20th cent. Epstein proved as consummate a portraitist, if less powerful. Notable among those 20th-cent. sculptors who have taken representational forms as their point of departure are Henry Moore, Zadkine, Marini, and Picasso. Various kinds of abstraction and purity of form characterize the work of Arp, Naum Gabo, Brancusi, and Barbara Hepworth. The ◊ *mobiles* of Alexander Calder set sculpture in motion in a most effective way. In addition to traditional materials, 20th-cent. sculpture employs such industrial materials as steel, aluminium, glass, and concrete. ◊ *Primitive Art*.

Scurvy. Disease caused by lack of ◊ *vitamin* C, the symptoms being anaemia, sponginess and ulceration of the gums, and haemorrhages into the skin, subcutaneous tissues, and joints: the remedy is to overcome the vitamin deficiency. In earlier times scurvy was common among sailors deprived of fresh vegetables and fruit during long voyages. It was discovered as early as 1601 that the juice of ◊ *limes* prevented the disease: this became a regular issue in the British Navy in 1795 – hence the nickname 'limeys' applied by Americans to the British.

Scylla. In Greek legend, a girl turned into a six-headed monster by ◊ *Circe*: she jumped into the Straits of Messina and became a group of rocks opposite the Charybdis whirlpool, making the passage extremely dangerous to shipping; hence 'between Scylla and Charybdis'.

Scyths. Nomadic conquerors of the steppes of what is now S. Russia, where the Scythian kingdom was established by the 8th cent. B.C. Although they were barbarians, the Scyths had close trading relations with China and also with the Greeks, whom they served as mercenaries, and were skilled craftsmen in metal, leather, and wood-carving. They invaded the ◊ *Assyrian* Empire and successfully resisted Alexander the Great, but their kingdom gave way to that of the Sarmatians in the 3rd cent. B.C.

Sea ◊ *Ocean.*

Sea Anemone. Sessile flower-like animal, in appearance an inverted thick-stalked ◊ *jellyfish*, found in shallow temperate and tropical waters; the mouth is surrounded with tentacles bearing stinging cells, used for stunning prey.

Sea-horse. Small bony marine fish, the free-moving head resembling that of a horse and set at an angle to the body; they live in the vertical position, the prehensile tail attaching them to seaweed stems and holding them stationary. The eggs are carried by the male in a pouch on the underside of the tail. There are some 50 species in tropical and warm-temperate seas.

Seal. 1. Several genera of intelligent marine carnivores with hind limbs modified as paddles, ungainly on land but marvellous swimmers, most numerous in Arctic and Antarctic waters; some have an undercoat of permanent fur ('sealskin'). They live in herds and communicate by barking; all but one species produce young in early summer. Seal meat, hides, blubber, and even bone and sinew are important in ◊ *Eskimo* economy. Sealing (which has already made one species extinct) is now controlled. Closely related are the ◊ *walrus* and sea lion.
2. Stamps of metal or semi-precious stone, usually engraved with some symbolical device which leaves an impression in wax or other plastic material, used as a mark of authority and ownership since very early times. Fine examples of cylinder seals (which roll a device on to wax) survive from the ◊ *Sumerian* civilization of the 3rd millennium B.C. and steatite seals of considerable artistic merit were made in the Indus Valley civilization 3000–1500 B.C. The discovery of these seals outside the country of their origin throws much light on trade in the ancient world.

Sea Mile (Admiralty Mile) ◊ *Nautical Mile.*

Sea-snake. Member of the poisonous family *Hydrophiidae*, related to the ◊ *cobra*, up to six ft long and adapted to a marine life by being viviparous; they have lost the belly-scales which enable other snakes to move on land, and propel themselves by an oar-like tail, sometimes swimming hundreds of miles from land.

Seasons. Periods of the year characterized by differing climatic conditions caused by changing position of the earth in relation to the sun. The inclination of the earth's axis remains more or less constant at about $23\frac{1}{2}°$ as the earth proceeds in its orbit. At the Equinoxes the vertical rays of the sun strike the earth at the equator and neither hemisphere is tilted towards the sun; at the solstices the vertical rays of the sun strike the earth at $23\frac{1}{2}°$ N. and $23\frac{1}{2}°$ S. and the N. and S. hemispheres are tilted in turn towards or away from the sun. In temperate regions there are thus four distinct seasons, from equinox to solstice, solstice to equinox, and so on. Where the inflence of the ocean is considerable, e.g. in the British Isles, the seasonal variations are not so great as in the interior of the continents and the change from season to season is more gradual. Ocean currents, prevailing winds, and altitude may also modify seasonal changes.

Outside the temperate regions, the year cannot be divided into four seasons. In polar regions the changes from winter to summer and summer to winter take place so abruptly that spring and autumn are scarcely recognizable. In the tropics the seasons depend more on rainfall than on the position of the sun, and the year is usually divided into dry and rainy seasons. In equatorial regions scarcely any seasonal changes can be distinguished: temperatures are high throughout the year, and much rain falls during every month, the only noteworthy change being from wet to very wet. ◊◊ *Climate, Monsoon, Rain Forest, Tundra, Weather.*

Sea-urchin. The class *Echinoidea* of the phylum Echinoderms ('hedgehog skin'); the body is covered by numerous articulated spines, for defence and locomotion, and most have a complicated masticatory apparatus, the 'Aristotle's lantern'. Common British species are the edible sea-urchin *Echinus esculentus*, found in the

sub-littoral zone on rocky shores, and the sand-burrowing heart-urchin E. cordatum.
Seaweed ⬦ Algae.
Secondary Era ⬦ Geological Time Scale.
Second Empire. 1852–70. In December 1852 Louis Napoleon, President of the ⬦ Second Republic, declared himself Emperor as Napoleon III. He reinforced his position by obtaining favourable results in plebiscites. His regime was absolutist till the 1860s, but was then forced to liberalize in order to gain support. A series of disasters at home and abroad culminated in the ⬦ Franco-Prussian War, when his Empire collapsed under defeat and German occupation. ⬦⬦ Paris Commune.

Second Republic. 1848–52. After the 1830 revolution in France and the installation of the Orleanist monarchy, King Louis Philippe set up a mild but narrow middle-class rule, but a working-class rebellion in 1848 (during which Marx produced the Communist Manifesto) caused the regime to collapse. The Second Republic was declared (the First Republic being that of the 1789–99 ⬦ French Revolution), under the first French government to be based on universal male adult suffrage. Continued conflict between the Paris socialists and the moderates from the provinces created widespread alarm, and there was relief and acquiescence when Louis Napoleon (nephew of Napoleon I) was elected President. ⬦⬦ Second Empire.

Second World War. 1939–45. The events precipitating war were the 1938 Nazi occupation of ⬦ Czechoslovakia to satisfy Hitler's demand for 'territorial revision', and the invasion of ⬦ Poland in Aug. 1939, which violated German undertakings and obliged ⬦ France and the ⬦ United Kingdom to honour their guarantees. Poland was overwhelmed in a few weeks, invaded also by U.S.S.R. from the east, and divided under the terms of the 1939 Soviet-German Neutrality Pact. After a winter of inactivity (the 'phoney war') on the W. front, in April–May 1940 the Germans overran ⬦ Denmark, Norway, the Netherlands, and Belgium, outflanked the Maginot Line, and in a 'blitzkrieg' of tank and air attacks (⬦ Schlieffen Plan) overwhelmed the Allied defences and in June invaded France. The British Expeditionary Force had to be rescued by the ⬦ Dunkirk evacuation, France capitulated on 21 June (⬦ Vichy France), and

Mussolini took ⬦ Italy into war on the German side. Britain was alone against Germany and Italy until U.S.S.R. (June 1941) and U.S.A. (Dec. 1941) became her allies; exile governments of all the nations overrun by Germany were set up in London. The Germans next attempted to obtain mastery of the air over the Channel preparatory to invasion of Britain, but the attempt was defeated in the ⬦ Battle of Britain. An Italian advance from Eritrea on Egypt was repulsed by British forces, but a protracted N. African campaign developed, German troops being sent there after ⬦ Greece and ⬦ Crete had been overrun.

In June 1941 the Germans abandoned the Soviet pact and invaded U.S.S.R. Great initial victories brought them within six m. of Moscow (the Soviet government removed to Kuibyshev), but they were then halted. Across the Atlantic, U.S.A. remained a friendly neutral (⬦ Lend Lease) until the Japanese attack on ⬦ Pearl Harbor was followed by Germany and Italy also declaring war on her. The Japanese gained remarkable successes on land, but in the ⬦ Pacific War the Americans established a growing superiority. Meanwhile the Russians had begun a vast counterattack, the high points of which were the battle of ⬦ Stalingrad and the raising of the 12-month siege of Leningrad. In N. Africa, British and U.S. forces defeated and eliminated all German and Italian resistance (⬦ Alamein), then carrying the war into Italy, which capitulated in Sept. 1943, though German troops continued a stubborn resistance.

At sea, the war was essentially a problem of keeping the sea lanes open, and of preventing sinkings of ships by German submarines; German surface raiders were quickly eliminated, but the Battle of the Atlantic was grim and protracted.

In 1944 the Germans bombarded Britain with V1 and V2 ⬦ rockets, but Allied forces under General Eisenhower landed in France (⬦ D-Day); in a long series of engagements, the German armies were pressed back, while on the E. front also they were in retreat. Early in 1945 the fighting reached Germany on both fronts, and various Allied armies began to meet on German soil. Hitler and Goebbels committed suicide; ⬦ Berlin surrendered to the Russians on 2 May, Germany's unconditional surrender being signed by General

Jodl on 7 May. On the Japanese front the Soviet Far Eastern Army was making headway in Mongolia and China (occupied by Japan); after atom bombs were dropped on ◊ *Hiroshima* and Nagasaki, Japan surrendered on 2 Sept. 1945. ◊ *Casablanca/Potsdam/Yalta Conferences, Nazism, Reparations, War Crimes.*

Secret Police. A special police force for the suppression of subversive political activity, often exempted from normal legal procedures; sometimes empowered to ignore the civil rights of suspects, or to operate their own secret courts and prisons. Celebrated examples are the Council of Ten in 14th-cent. Venice, the Oprichnina of Tsarist Russia, its Soviet successors, and the Gestapo of Nazi Germany.

The Oprichnina was replaced in 1918 by the CHEKA, for suppressing counterrevolution, then by the OGPU, for the defence of the Soviet State. Later this was incorporated into the NKVD (People's Commissariat for Internal Affairs); at the end of the ◊ *Second World War* all the People's Commissariats were renamed Ministries, hence the change of initials to MVD. Under Stalin, with Beria as head of the secret-police section of the Commissariat (or Ministry), the Soviet forced-labour camps had populations of over a million (many of these guilty of ordinary crime, but many simply politically suspect); after Stalin's death large numbers were released under a general amnesty in 1954, and the special police force was separated from the Ministry and reformed as the GBD (State Security Office).

In Germany the Gestapo (Secret State Police) in 1936 merged with the SS (Security Unit) of the SA (Storm Troopers), who wore a black uniform with death's-head insignia; it not only terrorized the general public and organized the mass exterminations (◊ *Genocide*), but kept close surveillance on Army officers, the government, and the Nazi party officials.

In U.S.A. the ◊ *Federal Bureau of Investigation* has a political section. In the U.K. the Special Branch of ◊ *Scotland Yard* deals with political cases, in cooperation with the Military Intelligence security department.

Secret Societies. Groups within a society whose members are pledged to strict secrecy as regards their proceedings and which usually have special rituals, secret signs, etc. The function may be religious (e.g. the Greek and Roman mysteries), social (e.g. modern Freemasons, college fraternities), or criminal (Ku Klux Klan, Mafia). Secret societies among primitive peoples often undertake the education of the young, provide forms of local government (e.g. the camp police of the Plains Indians in N. America), perform rituals on behalf of the whole tribe, or simply function as a social club from which women are excluded.

Securities and Exchange Commission. Agency of the U.S. government set up under an Act of 1934, following the Wall Street crash of 1929. It administers the laws for the protection of investors and the suppression of misrepresentation and other abuses which may occur in the securities market. A proposal for a similar body in the U.K. was considered by the Jenkins Committee, which reported in 1962, but was not recommended. ◊ *Stock Exchange.*

Security Council ◊ *United Nations Organization.*

Sedan. 1870. Decisive German victory during the ◊ *Franco-Prussian War*; MacMahon, the French commander, was wounded early in the battle, and the resulting confusion of command facilitated the German plan of surrounding the French. Napoleon III himself and 82,000 men were forced to surrender. ◊ *Paris Commune, Second Empire.*

Sedgemoor. 1685. On the accession of James II (◊ *Exclusion Bill*), Charles II's illegitimate son the Protestant Duke of Monmouth led a rebellion of almost unarmed West-country peasantry, which was defeated in part by artillery and in part by the defection or incompetence of its leaders. Monmouth was beheaded and thousands of his followers condemned to death or to life transportation at the 'Bloody Assize' under Jeffreys the 'hanging judge', previously notorious on the opposite side during the ◊ *Popish Plot*. Three years later James was deposed by the ◊ *Glorious Revolution.*

Sedimentary Rocks. Formed by the consolidation of sediment e.g. clays, sandstones, limestones; they cover the greater part of the earth's land surface, having for the most part accumulated in seas, where they are laid down as horizontal beds of strata on the sea floor. The earth's history can be interpreted by studying the different types of sediment and comparing the fossilized organic remains. ⟡ *Geological Time Scale.*

Seed. A complex reproductive body characteristic of higher plants. A seed develops from a fertilized ovule; as it is the product of the fusion of two sexual cells, it may develop into a plant differing somewhat from the parents (⟡ *Mendelism*). The seed consists of an embryo, often surrounded by nutritive tissue (endosperm) and within a hard protective seed coat (testa). The embryo has a tiny root, a shoot and one or more cotyledons, the first leaves modified for special functions during germination and usually differing in shape from the permanent foliage. If the seed has no endosperm the cotyledons may contain food reserves (e.g. pea, bean). Some cotyledons behave as true leaves – they turn green and photosynthesize; others simply absorb food from the endosperm and transfer it to the young plant. Most seeds need a resting period before germinating, which usually corresponds to winter, but some can germinate at once whilst a few (e.g. mangroves) begin germination on the tree and drop off as seedlings. Seeds can lie dormant and withstand extremes of heat, cold, and drought for varying periods, but being alive must metabolize and lose water, however slowly, and there is a limit to the time they remain viable. Some (chiefly tropical) live a short time, most several years, and the longest record is for the sacred lotus – at least 120 years.

Seeds are dispersed in various ways: often within a fruit, or individually by wind (seeds may be very small, winged, plumed, flattened, etc.) or by animals and birds to which they stick by barbs or other means of adhesion, or by which they are spread in droppings after being eaten. ⟡ *Cereals, Fruit.*

Segregation, Desegregation ⟡ *Apartheid, Race, Race Relations.*

Seismology. The study of earthquakes; the Seismological Society of Japan, founded in 1880 by John Milne (who devised the seismograph, for recording earthquake shocks), did much to give it the status of an exact science. A recent practical application is the seismic method of petroleum exploration by creating 'artificial earthquakes'; seismological techniques can be used to detect underground or other atom-bomb explosions.

Selenite ⟡ *Gypsum.*

Selenium. A rarish ⟡ *element* which (like sulphur) has several allotropes, a red non-metallic form soluble in carbon disulphide, and a grey metallic form to which it changes at about 130° C; widely distributed in sulphide minerals, from which it is recovered as a by-product. Its chemical properties are similar to those of sulphur, the vulcanizing power of which it improves. Selenium generates an electric current when exposed to light, and is used in the manufacture of photoelectric cells for film soundtracks, photographic exposure meters, burglar alarms, etc. It also has rectifying properties, and is used for converting alternating current to direct current. It is widely used in the ⟡ *glass* industry, small amounts for removing colour caused by iron, and larger amounts to produce red glass. Selenium and its compounds are toxic.

Seljuks ⟡ *Abbasids, Ottoman Empire.*

Selva ⟡ *Rain Forest.*

Semantics. Branch of semiotics (theory of signs) concerned with the meaning of words. Unlike direct signals, e.g. light flashes or flags, words are symbols (i.e. signs representing objects, ideas, or relationships), and except with onomatopoeic words, e.g. 'clatter', 'splash', their signification depends on tradition and agreement; in one aspect semantics is a branch of linguistics dealing with changes in meaning, in another it is related to psychology and deals with human responses to verbal symbols and the science of symbolism in general, while its concern with language as both a symbol-system and a mode of behaviour is relevant to anthropology and also to literary criticism in respect of the use of words by imaginative writers to convey or suggest moods or special awareness, the semantic distinction between lexical meaning and contextual sense being important here. ⟡ *Etymology, Language.*

Semaphore ⟡ *Code.*

Semi-conductors ⟡ *Conduction, Transistor.*

Semiramis. In Babylonian legend, widow of King Ninus, founder of Nineveh; she succeeded him, and by her magnificent buildings and prowess in war raised Nineveh to great glory, creating the renowned 'hanging gardens' of Babylon and conquering Egypt and Ethiopia. At death she went to heaven in the form of a dove. Some of the legends perhaps confuse her with ◊ *Ishtar*.

Semites. The speakers of ◊ *Semitic languages*. The word refers only to language, and its use to refer to so-called 'racial' groups e.g. the Jews, although common, is inaccurate.

Semitic Languages. Sub-group of the ◊ *Hamito-Semitic languages,* including Amharic, Arabic, Hebrew, and Maltese among living languages; a common characteristic is that words are almost invariably composed of three radical consonants, from which a wide variety of derivatives are made by variations of vowel-changes and prefixes, e.g. Ar. root *slm* > Islam, Muslim, salaam. This patterned change-ringing makes possible a rich vocabulary. The most ancient Semitic tongue was Akkadian (Assyrian, Babylonian), spoken in Mesopotamia 2800–100 B.C. and recorded in ◊ *cuneiform*. ◊ *Sumerians*.

Sempach (1386) ◊ *Switzerland (History)*.

Senegal. Area 78,000 sq. m. Pop. 3.1 m. Cap. Dakar. Independent Republic on the W. coast of Africa. The oldest French colony in Africa, Senegal became self-governing within the French Community in 1958. It was briefly federated with ◊ *Mali* (formerly French Soudan).

Senussi. Muslim sect founded in the early 19th cent. by an Algerian, Sheikh as-Sanusi, who settled in Cyrenaica, where the fraternity became accepted by the ◊ *Bedouin* and its holy men (marabouts) provided a stable form of government. The Senussi led the opposition to Italian rule, and cooperated with the British in the Second World War; after the war the head of the sect, the Emir Mohammed al-Idris, became King of ◊ *Libya*.

Sepal ◊ *Flower*.

Separation of Powers. The fundamental democratic principle that legislative, executive, and judicial powers should be exercised by separate and mutually independent authorities. None of the three powers should be able to control or interfere with the others; the same individuals should not hold posts in more than one of the three branches, and one branch of government should not exercise the functions of another. The possibility of an excessive concentration of power in one place is thus avoided.

The modern formulation of the principle derives from Locke and from Montesquieu, who felt that the stability of government in England was due to the separation of powers, which had been in existence since the ◊ *Glorious Revolution* of 1688. In the U.K. this separation has become blurred, the legislative to some extent controlling the other two; but in U.S.A. the distinctions between the three are very sharply drawn indeed, the system of 'checks and balances' at times interfering with government processes.

Sepsis. Originally, any form of putrefaction in the body; now only ◊ *infections* by fever-producing organisms. ◊ *Antiseptics*.

Septuagint ◊ *Bible*.

Sequoia. A genus of ◊ *conifers*. There are two species wild in California and Oregon: *S. sempervirens* (Wellingtonia, Redwood) grows in the conifer forests of the Pacific coast, the tallest known trees, reaching heights up to 364 ft; *S. gigantea* (giant sequoia), in the conifer forests in the foothills of the Sierra Nevadas, remarkable for its great size and the diameter of the trunk (up to 35 ft), the thick soft bark, which is resistant to burning, and the great age it reaches (estimated at 3,000 years). Both species are widely cultivated as ornamental trees esp. in parks.

Serapis. In Egyptian mythology, a sun god, a manifestation of ◊ *Apis* and thus of ◊ *Osiris*; husband of ◊ *Isis*, also god of the underworld, an equivalent of Asklepios (the healer) and of ◊ *Zeus*. The Serapeion, his temple at Alexandria, became the religious centre of Hellenistic Egypt; his cult (with that of Isis) was widespread in Ptolemaic Egypt and the Roman Empire.

Serbia. An ancient Slav kingdom in the Balkans, now a constituent republic of ◊ *Yugoslavia*. It was independent until subjugated by the Turks in 1389, and part of the ◊ *Ottoman Empire* until the 18th cent. The Austrians annexed it 1718–39, but it was repossessed by Turkey. At the end of the 18th cent. Russia encouraged Balkan independence movements, and in 1805 the Serbs revolted, under Karageorge; his murder in 1817 by Obrenovitch began a dynastic feud, which led to several violent changes of ruler (under nominal Turkish suzerainty). After the Turkish massacres of 1874, which resulted in the ◊ *Russo-*

Turkish Wars, Serbia became an independent kingdom by the ◊ *Berlin Congress* and Treaty. In the 1912–13 ◊ *Balkan Wars* Serbia's growth by the seizure of territory from Turkey and Bulgaria alarmed Austria-Hungary; when the heir to the Austrian throne was murdered in Sarajevo in 1914, as a result of a Serbian plot, Austria's demand for control of Serbia precipitated the ◊ *First World War.*

Serbian (Serbo-Croat) ◊ *Slavonic Languages.*

Serenade. Strictly, a piece of open-air evening music; Mozart and his contemporaries gave the name to a special type of composition for chamber orchestra in several movements. It has also been freely used for multi-movement works by later composers e.g. Brahms, Schoenberg, Britten. The Italian form *Serenata* was sometimes used, e.g. by Handel, for a cantata or short opera.

Serfdom. Serfs were those peasants in a state of hereditary bondage to their lord under the ◊ *manorial system.* In the Middle Ages serfdom was prevalent in most of Europe, and later it spread to Russia. In England, where the Norman Conquest reduced most of the freemen to serfs, serfdom disappeared before the end of the Middle Ages; in France its last vestiges were ended by the French Revolution. In Russia it lasted until Tsar Alexander II emancipated the serfs in 1861.

Serpentine. Hydrated magnesium silicate; one of the ◊ *metamorphic rocks,* formed by the alteration of impure ◊ *dolomites* or of ◊ *igneous rocks* rich in magnesium. Once used for ornaments and interior decoration because of its attractive lizard-skin appearance, dark green with red, yellow, and brown streaks. ◊ *Silica.*

CHRYSOLITE: A fibrous serpentine occurring in E. Canada, marketed as an ◊ *asbestos.*

Serum. The yellowish fluid which separates off when whole blood is allowed to clot, containing natural disease-resistant substances. Immune sera, derived from animals which have undergone an extensive immunization process against given infections, are used in the treatment of bacterial or virus diseases; they give the recipient a passive ◊ *immunity.*

Sestina. An intricate poetic form; six stanzas, each of six unrhymed lines: the end-words of the lines of the first stanza

(*a b c d e f*) also end those of all the others (in the second *f a e b d c,* in the third *c f d a b e,* and so on), and the poem may conclude with a three-line 'envoy' (◊ *Ballade*) using all the end-words. The invention of the sestina is attributed to the 13th-cent. Provençal poet Arnaut Daniel; it was imitated by Dante and cultivated by French poets both in the 16th-cent. ◊ *Pléiade* and in the 19th-cent. medieval revival.

Sevastopol. 1854–5. A Russian naval base in the Crimea, capturing which was a main objective in the ◊ *Crimean War.* Besieged, but ably defended by General Todleben, the city held out through the winter, but in the face of renewed French and British attacks in Aug. 1855 was set on fire and abandoned.

Seven Bishops. 1688. When James II (◊ *Exclusion Bill*), having revived the ecclesiastical High Commission (◊ *Court of Star Chamber*), ordered his declaration of ◊ *Indulgence* to Roman Catholics to be read from all pulpits, seven bishops refused. Their trial for treason aroused enormous public excitement, and their acquittal made James's deposition inevitable. ◊ *Glorious Revolution.*

Seven Wonders of the World. In the ancient world: the Pyramids of Egypt, the Hanging Gardens of Babylon, the Temple of Diana at Ephesus, Phidias's Statue of Jupiter at Athens, the Mausoleum at Halicarnassus, the Colossus at Rhodes, and the Pharos (lighthouse) at Alexandria. Only the Pyramids survive.

Seven Years War. 1756–63. Struggle which arose out of Anglo-French colonial rivalry, and the Austro-Prussian quarrel over ◊ *Silesia,* fought by a coalition of France, Austria, Russia against Britain and ◊ *Prussia.* Prussia, initially successful against Austria, was later forced on to the defensive by the converging attacks of the three Allies. Britain, under the premiership of the elder Pitt, took both Canada (◊ *Quebec*) and India (◊ *Plassey*) from France; Silesia was ultimately ceded to Prussia. The war consolidated the British empire in India and Canada. ◊ *Berlin, Black Hole of Calcutta, East India Company.*

Sewage, Sewers. Sewage is liquid-borne waste carried off by sewers. The sewers of ancient Rome were probably for the disposal of storm water, but at Mohenjodaro (◊ *Indus Civilization*) remains of waste-sewers proper have been found dating to 3000 B.C. Until the early 19th cent. sewers were either open or non-existent, waste matter often being discharged direct into rivers. The method of safe water-carriage of waste matter was suggested by Edwin Chadwick in the late 1830s as a means of combating disease, and the building of town sewers in Britain and other European countries followed rapidly. In London many small streams were converted into subterranean sewers. Sewage treatment consists of the separation of solids from liquids by screens, grit and sedimentation tanks, the biological oxidation of organic matter, and the destruction of bacteria by burning or by chemical means. The resultant sludge is dumped in the sea or converted into ⋄ *fertilizer*.

Sex ⋄ *Reproduction*.

Sex Determination. In most animals, and man, sex is genetically predetermined, at fertilization, by the sex-bearing ⋄ *gamete*; the female produces sex cells, gametes, which all have X-chromosomes, and the male sex cells of two sorts, X (female-determining factor) and Y (male-determining factor) in approximately equal numbers, the Y being dominant. At fertilization the egg or eggs may receive an X-bearing sperm and develop into a female or a Y-bearing sperm and develop into a male.

Sextant. Instrument for ascertaining the vertical angle of heavenly bodies from the horizon, which with the time of the observation noted from the ⋄ *chronometer* navigational tables, and the ⋄ *Nautical Almanac*, is used to calculate the ship's position in terms of ⋄ *latitude*. A more accurate and complex version of the quadrant, the sextant was invented independently by the Englishman John Hadley and the American Thomas Godfrey, 1731.

Seychelles. Area 156 sq. m. Pop. 44,000. Cap. Victoria. A group of 92 volcanic islands in the Indian ocean, settled by the French in the 18th cent. but later ceded to Britain. Now a British colony, exporting cinnamon, copra, guano, vanilla.

Shale ⋄ *Oil Shales*.

Shallot ⋄ *Onion*.

Shaman. Word of Siberian origin; a priest or magician in a primitive society, esp. one operating in a state of trance (induced by auto-suggestion, fasting, intoxicants, or self-torture) as healer, ⋄ *oracle*, rain-maker, and ritual-leader. Many shamans appear to possess remarkable powers imperfectly understood by western students, and it seems likely that they are intelligent men (and women) with considerable knowledge of the properties of drugs and skill as hypnotists.

SHAMANISM: A complex of beliefs and rites of people esp. in N. America and N. Asia who believe that contact with the supernatural is maintained through shamans. ⋄ *Animism, Divination*.

Shark. Marine cartilaginous fish, of many species ranging from the small dogfish found in British waters to the 50-ft long whale shark; the ⋄ *gills* are not covered by a single gill-cover, as in bony fish, each having its own opening or gill-slit. The skin is covered with tough, sharp scales. Many species are carnivorous, with razor-sharp teeth; others e.g. the whale shark feed on ⋄ *plankton*. Generally the mouth is on the under surface of the head. Unlike most fish, the shark introduces sperm into the body of the female, and in some cases the young are born alive. Oil is obtained from the liver; the flesh may be used as food e.g. rock salmon. Sharks are often hunted as big-game fish, the chief British centre being off Cornwall.

Sheep. *Ovis*, of the *Bovidae*; various wild and domesticated species valued for their meat, skins, and ⋄ *wool*, and in a few countries for their milk; one of the earliest animals domesticated, perhaps derived from the wild mouflon of Greece and the urial of Asia. During the Middle Ages sheep were a major economic asset in Britain and the basis of a thriving export trade in wool and cloth, and many of the principal breeds are native to England e.g. Cotswold, Devon, Kentish, Leicester (long wool); Clun, Dorset, Hampshire, Shropshire, Southdown, Suffolk (short wool); Blackface, Cheviot, Exmoor, Welsh (mountain breeds). Two other important breeds are Merino (Spain) and Karakul (Uzbekistan S.S.R.); no domesticated sheep were found in N. America; and in S. America their place was to some extent filled by the llama. Sheep were widely introduced by European colonists in S. America, Australia, and N. Zealand, which are now the principal exporters of wool.

SHEEP-POX: One of several pock diseases of domestic animals caused by filtrable viruses, with symptoms fever and skin eruptions, forming scabs within a few days; in the past it ravaged many flocks, and today it is one of the ◊ *scheduled diseases* in most countries. The virus is very resistant to ordinary germ-destroying conditions, and may survive for years in scabs on hides. ◊ *Cowpox.*

SHEEP-SCAB: ◊ *Mange.*

Sheffield Plate. An early form of silver plate still prized by collectors; in 1742 Thomas Bolsover of Sheffield discovered by chance that copper could be coated with silver merely by fusing the two metals together, and this led to the production of silver-plated tableware etc. as a substitute for solid silverware. Output was greatly increased when techniques were developed for producing silver-plated sheets by fusing silver to both sides of the copper strip before it was rolled out. Sheffield plate was rapidly superseded after the first patent for ◊ *electroplating* copper was granted 1840.

Shellac. An exudate on certain varieties of trees in India when attacked by the insect *Coccus lacca.* A wax and a red dye (cochineal) are first removed from the crude exudate leaving shellac as a yellow resin. It is used as a protective coating for wood and plaster. ◊ *Japanning, Lacquer.*

Sheriff. Originally the shire reeve (county governor); in England and Wales, a High Sheriff of each county is elected annually for one year, his duties being largely social e.g. entertaining the ◊ *assize* judges on circuit. In Scotland, 12 sheriffs control the sheriff courts, roughly equivalent in civil-law capacity to county courts in England and Wales. In the City of London the liverymen annually elect two sheriffs, one from their own number and the other from the aldermen.

Sherry. A fortified wine of alcohol content 16–22 per cent; true sherry, named after the town of Jerez, comes only from the province of Cadiz in Spain. The grapes are dried in the sun and then pressed, and the juice fermented for several months in casks; grape brandy is added. A complicated blending process is carried out by the solera system, in which rows of casks are stacked vertically, the uppermost containing new wine and the sherry being run off from the bottom cask, where it has matured for five or six years; this cask is then topped up from the cask next above, and so on. There are various kinds

of sherry; as drunk in Britain, Fino is usually pale and dry, Amontillado medium, Oloroso and Brown sweet and dark. Sherry has become predominantly a drink of English-speaking peoples; it has been imitated outside Spain, e.g. S. Africa makes a good sherry-type wine. Spain exports over two m. gallons to the U.K. annually.

Shiahs. < Ar. 'partisans'; the smaller of the two sects of ◊ *Islam.* The original unity of the Muslim faith was shattered in the 8th cent. by the struggle between the family of Ali, head of the ◊ *Caliphate*, and the ◊ *Ommayads*, which split Islam into the Shiahs (followers of Ali) and the ◊ *Sunnis.* The Shiahs, preponderant in Persia and India, and in some strength in Iraq, regard Ali and Hussein (close relatives of Mohammed) as almost divine, and expect the ◊ *Mahdi* (Messiah) again to lead them, as a true caliph.

Of the Shiah sects, the Assassins were famous in the Middle Ages for their fanaticism. The Ismailite sect regards the Aga Khan as its spiritual leader.

Shingles ◊ *Herpes.*

Shinto. National cult of Japan, in part patriotic as State Shinto, in part religious as Cult Shinto; originally a crude polytheism stressing veneration of ancestors, esp. those of the Imperial House (believed to be descended from the Sun-goddess Amaterasu), it is now a manifestation of patriotic feeling rather than a religion in the usual sense. Its ethics are largely borrowed from ◊ *Buddhism* and ◊ *Confucianism.*

Ship. Any decked seagoing vessel; before the advent of steam, strictly a ship-rigged vessel, i.e. with three or more masts all carrying square ◊ *sails.* ◊ *Battleship, Steamship, Warship,* etc.

Ship-money. A tax formerly levied by the English Crown from the coastal towns, for the provision of defences against piracy; it had developed from the Norman practice of requiring them to provide ships and men in time of war (◊ *Navy*). By levying ship-money in peace-time, without the sanction of Parliament (which had not sat for eight years), and extending it to inland areas as a means of increasing his personal revenues, Charles I provoked the resistance of John Hampden, who was tried and condemned in 1637 for his refusal to pay; the tax was a major cause of conflict between the King and the nation.

In 1640 Charles was forced to call Parliament, which abolished the tax: in 1641 the ◊ *English civil wars* began.

Shipping. Boats and ships have been important means of transport since prehistoric times, but the first great sea-going peoples were the Minoan-period Cretans and the Phoenicians (succeeded by the Greeks, Carthaginians, and Romans), who colonized the Mediterranean coasts by sea and ventured beyond the Straits of Gibraltar into the Atlantic. In the early Middle Ages the Hanseatic League had important fleets which controlled trade in the Baltic and the North Sea, and the Italian city states had a similar influence in the Mediterranean. With the discovery of the New World at the end of the 15th cent. Portugal, Spain, England, and Holland became great maritime nations. After the 1760–1840 ◊ *Industrial Revolution* Britain played a preponderant part in world trade, and her ◊ *merchant navy* achieved its highest share in 1895 when it was nearly half the total world tonnage. ◊ *Navigation.*

MERCHANT SHIPPING: Broadly divided into dry, or general cargo, and tanker shipping. The following countries had tonnages under their flags in 1962:

In millions of gross registered tons

	Dry Cargo	Tanker	Total
U.K.	12.9	7.5	20.4
U.S.A.	5.5	4.6	10.1
Norway	5.7	6.7	12.4
Liberia	3.8	6.8	10.6
Japan	5.9	2.2	8.1
Greece	5.0	1.7	6.7

FLAGS OF CONVENIENCE: The actual ownership of vessels is obscured by these. Many ships, esp. tankers, sail under Panamanian and Liberian flags to avoid taxation. These include ships of U.S. oil companies which would be uneconomic if operated with American crews.

The British share of world tonnage has declined from nearly 30 per cent in 1939 to below 17 per cent in 1962. Among various reasons for this is the urge felt by virtually all countries to possess a national fleet irrespective of their shipbuilding facilities or operating experience. Much of world shipping (but not British) is subsidized, directly or otherwise.

LINERS, TRAMPS, TANKERS: Liners run regular schedules on fixed routes. Some are passenger ships, but the majority are cargo liners. Tramps are chartered (hired) for a particular voyage. To reduce operating costs, the tendency is to build larger tramps, esp. those used for bulk cargoes. The same applies to tankers, which now include several of the largest vessels afloat. Passenger ships have suffered from the competition of air transport, and the great luxury liners (except some on the N. Atlantic route) are generally run at a loss. On the N. Atlantic the number of passengers carried by sea in 1962 was 819,403 as against 2.2 million by air

Shipping Conference. Association of shipping companies of various nationalities to maintain standardized rates for passenger and freight charges on liner i.e. regularly operated ocean routes; the rates do not apply to 'tramp' shipping i.e. vessels which do not follow established schedules.

Shiva (Siva). One of the chief trinity in the Hindu pantheon (◊ *Hinduism, Pantheism*); represents both the destructive and the reproductive powers of nature; though identified with asceticism, also worshipped with phallic symbols as god of reproduction. Shiva has three eyes and matted hair, and holds a trident and a drum shaped like an hour-glass; he is often depicted performing the dance by which he created the universe.

Shooting. Rifle-shooting as a sport became popular through the military volunteer movement in Britain and U.S.A. about 100 years ago; the National Rifle Movement (1860) has since then held annual championships, transferred from Wimbledon to Bisley 1890, the main award being the Queen's Prize. The programme includes shooting with a service rifle, a match rifle, and a sporting rifle or pistol. Small-bore (0.22 in. calibre) target-shooting is also very popular both in Britain and on the continent of Europe; the National Small-bore Rifle Association has about 4000 affiliated units. The International Shooting Union (reformed 1947) now includes some 70 countries, of which 60 compete in the ◊ *Olympic Games.*

Trap-shooting began in Britain in the 19th cent. when marksmen used sporting guns to fire at glass balls thrown into the air; these were replaced by clay pigeons in the 1880s. In America the variant skeet-shooting appeared 1910; two traps are used, 40 yds apart, the shooter moving round a circular track to different positions.

Game-shooting with shotguns is popular throughout the world. In Britain the seasons are: Grouse 12 Aug. to early Dec. Partridge 1 Sept. to 1 Feb. Pheasant 1 Oct. to 1 Feb.

Shop Steward. Originally a dues-collecting trade-union representative in a factory; as the scale of industry grew there arose a need for someone to represent the 'shop-floor' worker to the management and the local trade-union branch, and not the foreman but the shop steward assumed the new function of negotiating at 'shop' level. As a worker a shop steward is employed by the firm and as an official he is recognized by the trade union, but his first loyalty is to his fellow-workers in his own 'shop'.

Short Story. A short narrative; as legend, myth, parable, folk-tale, or joke it has existed as long as man, and it became a conscious art in the 19th cent., its range of subject-matter and treatment being limitless provided only that it says much in little, achieving its impact through compression. Its scope is revealed by e.g. Poe, Maupassant, Chekhov, Henry James, Conrad, Joyce, Katherine Mansfield, Kafka, S. V. Benét, J. D. Salinger, Frank O'Connor.

Show-Jumping. Horse-jumping over various gates and obstacles in an arena; the first recorded show-jumping competition was held in Paris 1866, and the sport quickly spread to Britain. After 1912, when jumping was included in the ◊ Olympic Games for the second time, the Fédération Équestre Internationale was founded. Under the British Show Jumping Association the sport has made great progress in Britain since the Second World War; the chief British meeting is the Royal International Horse Show at the White City.

Shrimps ◊ Crustacea.

Sial. From the first syllables of silica and alumina; the relatively light (sp. gr. 2.67) rocks e.g. ◊ granite forming the continental masses. ◊ Isostasy, Sima.

Siam ◊ Thailand.

Sibyl. In Greek and Roman legend, a prophetess inspired by a deity. Most famous were the Erythraean Sibyl, who prophesied regarding the Trojan War, and the Cumaean Sibyl, consulted by ◊ ◊ Aeneas before his visit to ◊ Hades. The latter offered nine books of prophecies to Tarquin, legendary king of early Rome; he rejected the offer, and she destroyed three of the books. A year later she offered the remaining six, at the original price. Again rebuffed, she destroyed three more, and then sold the last three for the price of the nine; preserved at Rome under the temple of ◊ Jupiter on the Capitol, they were ultimately destroyed by fire. There is a 2nd-cent. collection of spurious 'Sibylline Oracles', concerning ◊ Jesus Christ, still extant.

Sicilian Vespers. 1282. Popular rising in ◊ Sicily against its French rulers, on an Easter Monday. Several thousand French were killed; the crown was then offered to Peter III of Aragon, who evicted Charles of Anjou and restricted French rule to the Italian mainland.

Sicily. Area 9928 sq. m. Pop. about 4 m. Cap. Palermo. An autonomous region of ◊ Italy; the largest W. Mediterranean island.

HISTORY. The Greeks and Carthaginians established colonies in Sicily, but in the 3rd cent. B.C. the ◊ Punic Wars left it as a province of Rome; its prosperity declined, and it was overrun by the ◊ Vandals and in the 9th cent. A.D. by the Arabs. After its conquest by the ◊ Normans in the 11th cent. it prospered, with a Graeco-Arab-Norman civilization. After the failure of the last Hohenstaufen claimant to the throne, in the 13th cent. Pope Clement IV made Charles of Anjou King, as his vassal, but before long the French were expelled (◊ Sicilian Vespers) and the island came under Aragonese rule; its prosperity again declined. In the 18th cent. an independent ◊ Bourbon dynasty united the Two Sicilies, i.e. the island and the mainland area round Naples; in 1808 Napoleon made Marshal Murat King of Naples, but he did not conquer Sicily. After his defeat, the Two Sicilies kingdom was recreated. The first of the 1848 revolutions was the Sicilian rising; Ferdinand II was named King Bomba for his bombardment of Palermo and Messina. In 1860, after the successful invasion by Garibaldi, Sicily voted for incorporation into the kingdom of ◊ Sardinia. With the unification of Italy, Sicily became a part of the new state; its poverty, and the survival of the ◊ Mafia, are serious problems.

Siderite ◊ Iron, Meteor.

Siegfried ◊ *Nibelungenlied*.

Siemens-Martin Process. William Siemens introduced the regenerative furnace for steel-making in 1861; the French brothers Martin 1865 patented the full ('open-hearth') process widely adopted in which crude iron, usually molten, is heated on a shallow hearth with limestone and steel scrap, by the combustion of gas (derived from oil or coal) above the surface of the charge, the flow of gas and air being reversed about every 10 minutes. The process lasts several hours, but can be hastened by the use of oxygen, to facilitate the removal of unwanted elements (e.g. oxides, slag), and can use a much greater proportion of scrap than does the ◊ *Bessemer Process*. Electric-furnace steel-making has recently been gaining ground, at the expense of small open-hearth furnaces not using molten iron. ◊ *Blast Furnace, Gas Industry, Iron and Steel Industry, Petroleum*.

Sierra Leone. Area 27,925 sq. m. Pop. 2.2 m. Cap. Freetown. Independent W. African state, member of the British Commonwealth, with a House of Representatives and a Prime Minister. A small coastal strip is tropical rain forest, the interior is savanna. The coast produces palm kernels, an important export, and the staple food, rice. Other exports are diamonds and recently iron ore. The interior is administered in provincial regions, in which the population is largely tribal.

Sikhs. Religious sect, numbering about 6 m. mainly in the Punjab, founded by Nanuk 1469–1533, who sought to combine togeher ◊ *Hindus* and Muslims by creating a monotheistic religion opposed to idolatry and the caste system. In the 17th cent. the last of the gurus (teachers) in order to oppose the rule of the ◊ *Moguls* organized the Sikhs on a military basis. They have continued to value military virtues, and the men wear distinctive turbans to cover their hair. On ◊ *partition* the Sikhs strove for independent status without success.

Silage. Grass or other green fodder preserved by a controlled process of fermentation; the sugars are converted to acids, which act as preservatives, a process analogous to the pickling of domestic foodstuffs. Well-made silage has a high feeding value for stock, owing to its protein content. The process was known in

Roman times, but the modern process using tall 'silos' is about 100 years old.

Silenus. Minor Greek divinity, foster-father of ◊ *Dionysus*; sometimes a son of ◊ *Pan*; leader of the satyrs; usually represented as a hairy, robust old man with pointed ears, intoxicated, and riding on a donkey.

Silesia. Region of E. central Europe. Part of the earliest Polish state in the 10th cent. it was later split up into a number of petty states, and received a large number of German settlers; it came under ◊ *Hapsburg* rule after 1526. It suffered considerably from the enforcement of the ◊ *Counter-Reformation* during the ◊ *Thirty Years War*. Conquered from Austria by Frederick II of Prussia in 1740, its coal resources became important to Prussia's economy. In 1921, after an armed rising of Poles most of upper Silesia became part of ◊ *Poland*. At the ◊ *Potsdam Conference* substantially all Silesia became Polish and the German population was expelled (◊ *Oder-Neisse Line*).

Silica. Silica (the only oxide of ◊ *silicon*) occurs in several forms, and the numerous rock-forming silicates (chemically, salts of several silicic acids) include many minerals of economic value and several semi-precious stones e.g. agate, carnelian, onyx, garnets.

HYDRATED ALUMINIUM SILICATES: Include kaolin, fuller's earth, and many gem-stones e.g. topaz, tourmaline.

TALC (SOAPSTONE): A magnesium silicate widely used as an absorbent and as a filler in making paint, paper, and rubber.

Silicon. A non-metallic ◊ *element*, the second most abundant constituent of the earth's crust (25 per cent) where it occurs always as a chemical compound in the form of the oxide silica and as silicates taking various forms such as felspar, sandstone, quartz, granite, etc. The element has a valency state of 4, forms gaseous hydrides, a volatile chloride and a hard solid carbide ◊ *carborundum*. The silicates provide a great variety of minerals and synthetic materials e.g. earthenware, bricks, porcelain, and glass. The element itself is mainly used in the ◊ *alloy* ferro-silicon, for both ordinary and silicon steels; the latter have magnetic properties that make them suitable for the cores of electrical transformers. The oxide is used alone to make pure silica-ware, which is as clear as glass and can be worked like it but can be heated and cooled rapidly without fracture and does not soften below 1700° C; much of it is used in industry and in scientific research of all kinds. Very large quantities of sand are used in the glass and building industries and in horticulture; much of it is converted into the ◊ *abrasive* carborundum by heating with ◊ *coke* in an electric furnace. ◊ *Silicones*.

Silicones. ◊ *Polymers* formed from chains of alternating silicon and oxygen atoms, each silicon atom (tetravalent) also being linked to two other atoms or organic radicals; silicones can be liquid or solid, they are chemically inert and have found uses in many fields. Methylchlorosilicones are water-repellent and render fabrics waterproof. Methyl, ethyl, or phenal silicone polymers give short-chain oils or rubber-like solids. Silicone rubber, unlike natural rubber, retains its elasticity even at very low temperatures. Other uses of silicone preparations include anti-stick layers for baking tins, anti-foam preparations, heating-bath fluids, lubricants and greases.

Silk. A filament produced by the larva of *Bombyxmori*, the silk moth, which on approaching maturity spins silk threads of great length and fineness for its cocoon; a single cocoon yields 2000 to 3000 ft. At least 4 strands must be twisted together to make usable thread. The larvae feed solely on mulberry leaves, and silk comes mainly from China, India, and Japan, where it was a major export until the invention of nylon; silk reeling and weaving were closely guarded secrets in China for about 3000 years, until in the 15th cent A.D. Byzantium became famous for silk textiles; the Arabs introduced silk-making into Spain; later Lyons and Venice became renowned for exquisite fabrics. Although for many purposes displaced by the new synthetic fabrics, silk remains distinctive and esteemed. World silk production was 130 m. lb. 1938 but had fallen to 24 m. lb. 1945; recently it has fluctuated round about 70 m. lb. annually

SHANTUNG (TUSSORE SILK, WILD SILK): Made from filaments produced by the Tussah worm of India, woven into rather rough durable fabric.

Silkworm. The ◊ *caterpillar* of moths of the families Saturnidae or Bombycidae, the latter including the mulberry-feeding larva of the flightless *Bombyxmori*, from which the finest ◊ *silk* is obtained; the silk is spun from the modified glands and woven into a cocoon. Other arthropods also secrete silk, e.g. all ◊ *spiders*, pseudo-scorpions, and some ◊ *mites*.

Silurian ◊ *Geological Time Scale*.

Silver. A valuable ◊ *element*, early identified because it is often found in the pure state. It is easily recovered from its ores, much silver being extracted during the treatment of lead and copper ores; it resists corrosion by ordinary atmospheric agents (except ◊ *sulphur* compounds, which blacken the surface), and is used for jewellery, silverware, and electrical contacts, usually hardened by alloying with a little copper or gold, and also as a bearing metal, in ◊ *electroplating*, and for silvering mirrors. In its compounds, silver is usually monovalent. The halides e.g. silver bromide are used in photography, the nitrate and colloidal silver have medical uses. 'Standard' silver, 92.5 per cent silver, was formerly used for silver coinage in Britain; 'silver gilt' is silver plated with a thin layer of gold. ◊ *Hallmark*.

Sima. From the first syllables of silica and magnesium; the dark, heavy (sp. gr. over 3.0), deep-seated e.g. basaltic rocks which form the ocean basins and underly the continental masses (as distinct from ◊ *Sial*). ◊ *Isostasy, Plutonic*.

Simoom ◊ *Sandstorm*.

Sinanthropus ◊ *Palaeolithic, Primates*.

Singapore. An island off the S. lip of the Malay peninsula with which it is connected by a causeway. It was developed as the main British naval base in S E Asia and heavily fortified. When Japan entered the Second World War Japanese forces quickly overran Malaya and attacked Singapore from the landward side and rapidly overcame the defences. It was a military disaster for Britain; over 70,000 British and Australian troops surrendered. ◊ *Malaysia*.

Sinn Fein. < Irish, 'ourselves alone'; the late 19th and early 20th cent. separatist nationalist movement associated with the surviving ◊ *Fenians* and the Irish nationalists who after the Parnell debacle recreated national unity, refusing compromise with the British government. ◊ *Anglo-Irish 'Troubles', Home Rule, Partition*.

Sirocco. S. Wind from the Sahara in Sicily and Italy. Hot, dry, sometimes dust-laden when crossing the N. African coast, it picks up moisture in passing over the Mediterranean and reaches S. Italy hot, humid, and very enervating. Withers vegetation; often causes much crop damage esp. while vines and olives are in blossom. Also any warm S. wind, e.g. the ◊ *Khamsin*, along the N. coast of the Mediterranean.

Sisyphus. In Greek legend, a king of Corinth typifying trickery and malice, punished in ◊ *Hades* for his misdeeds by being condemned to roll a huge rock eternally uphill; whenever it reached the top, it fell back to the bottom, hence a 'Sisyphean task', useless labour.

Skalds. Ancient Scandinavian court poets who celebrated the old Norse gods, heroes, and kings in elaborate concentrated verse of great metrical virtuosity; the tradition culminated in ◊ *Iceland* in the 10th and 11th centuries.

Skating. As a means of travel on ice, skating dates to prehistoric times; the earliest skates were of bone or wood, superseded by blades of iron in the 17th cent. by which time skating as a pastime was widespread in Europe. Artificially-frozen rinks came into use in the late 19th cent. Britain's National Skating Association was formed 1879; the International Skating Union (1892) held the first World Championships 1896. It is now a pastime for millions of amateurs, and many champions turn professional, either to teach or to appear in ice-shows. Skating is judged in four categories: (a) figure-skating (the carrying out of compulsory figures) and free-skating (the competitor's own choice of movements to music); (b) pair-skating (a free programme by two people); (c) ice-dancing (a fairly recent development); (d) speed-skating (in which rivals compete two at a time in time-trials).

Skeleton. The bony or cartilaginous structure in vertebrates which protects the internal organs of the body, affords a framework for support of the soft tissue, provides attachment for muscles, contains the blood-forming tissue of the body, and stores the minerals calcium and phosphorus. In some invertebrates there is an external (exo-) skeleton, which supports and protects the body. The human skeleton consists of some 200 bones, comprising the ◊ *skull*, the spinal column (7 cervical vertebrae, 12 thoracic vertebrae, 5 lumbar vertebrae, sacrum, and coccyx),

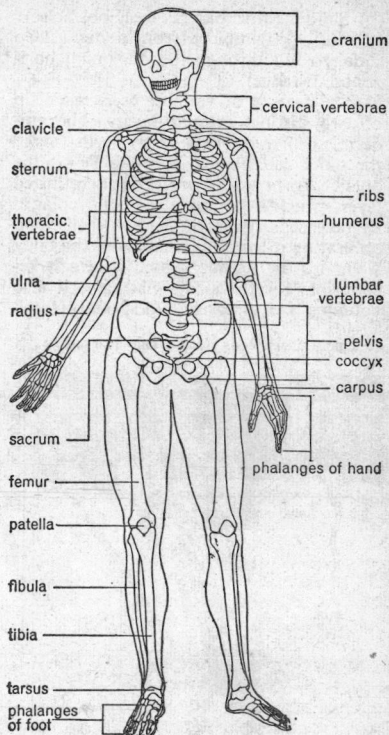

the sternum (breastbone), the thorax (12 pairs of ribs), the pelvic girdle, and the limbs.

Ski-ing. The art of moving over snow on two long skis (pointed wooden or plastic boards), originally devised by mountain dwellers, now the most widespread and popular of winter sports. Rock carvings in Scandinavia suggest that a primitive form of ski-ing existed some 5000 years ago. Skis were used in warfare in Sweden in the 13th cent. and in Finland in the Second World War. Racing began in Norway 200 years ago, and jumping in the late 19th cent. The impetus to ski-ing as a sport came from British enthusiasts of the 1900s, who held competitions in Switzerland and founded the Ski Club of Gt Britain 1903; the Fédération Internationale du Ski was founded 1910. Competitively ski-ing has three main forms: (a) Speed-racing (cross-country downhill);

(b) Slalom (downhill between obstacles);
and (c) Ski-jumping (from a high steep
slide, to fall through the maximum horizontal distance).

Skin. The skin of vertebrates is made up
of two distinct cellular layers. The epidermis (outer layer) is several cells thick;
the older cells, which come to lie on the
outside, form a dead protective keratinized
layer, which is continually being replaced
by new cells. Beneath the epidermis, and
separating it from the muscles of the body
wall, lies the dermis, which is largely responsible for the skin's elasticity. It also
contains fat reserves, blood and lymph

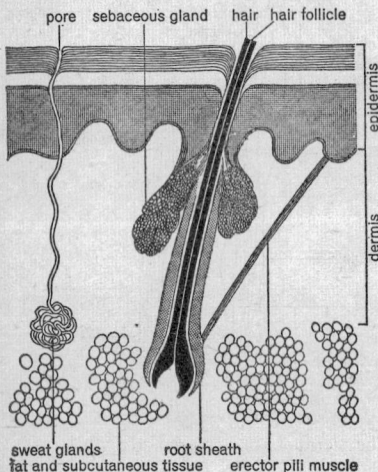

vessels, and nerves. Sebaceous, mucous,
and other glands are situated in the
dermis, and from modifications of the
dermis hair, feathers, horn, teeth, and
bones are formed. The skin of mammals,
in addition to its protective function, also
regulates water and heat loss. When the
skin of mammals is injured, epidermal
cells stretch under the blood clot, to close
the gap, and then begin to divide rapidly;
blood vessels enlarge, for increased transport of metabolites, and more fibres are
built up in the dermis until there is complete repair. ⟡ *Grafting.*

Skull. Bony structure in vertebrates which
protects and supports the head, consisting
in man of 8 cranial and 14 facial bones.
The brain is seated in the cranium,
through the base of which it communicates

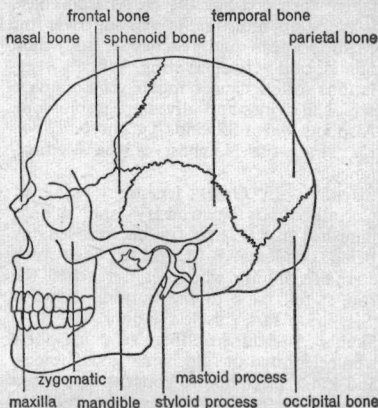

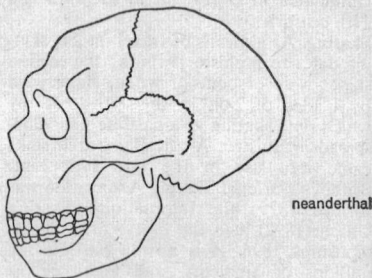

neanderthal

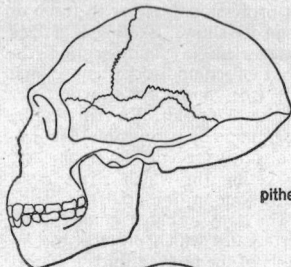

pithecanthropus

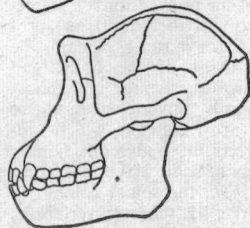

chimpanzee

with the spinal cord through a circular opening, the foramen magnum. In the newborn human infant several areas of the skull (fontanelles) are still soft membrane, but these ossify during development. In man the skull is distinguished from that of other vertebrates in having the face set below rather than in front of the cranium, and in having a high, smoothly-rounded cranial vault. It is possible to trace the development of these and other characters by comparison with fossil hominid skulls and with those of other primates.

Skunk. *Mephitis*; small mammal allied to the badger and native to N. and central America, capable of emitting a vile-smelling glandular secretion as a protection against enemies. It is about the size of a cat and has handsome fur of black boldly marked with white, which is of commercial value.

Skyscraper. A very high building of many floors (there is no precise definition as to the number) constructed on a steel frame, to achieve a maximum exploitation of restricted and costly urban areas; developed in America in the late 19th cent. esp. by L. Sullivan. The first genuine skyscraper was the 1883 Home Insurance Building in Chicago, but the great development of skyscraper architecture occurred in New York with the Flatiron Building 1902, the Woolworth Building 1913, and the Empire State Building, the highest building in the world (1248 ft, 102 storeys), 1931. This purely American style of architecture has spread to numerous other countries. In Brazil there are noteworthy examples in Rio, São Paulo, and Brasilia; Gio Ponti's ovoid Pirelli building in Milan is a new departure in skyscraper design.

Slander ◊ *Libel and Slander*.

Slang. Colloquial speech not fully 'recognized'; 'language on trial'. To be distinguished from substandard speech and vulgarity or profanity, it is appropriate in certain contexts, though out of place at literary or rhetorical level, and is used for intimacy, novelty, and vivacity, being lively and picturesque because often highly figurative, and friendly because it puts the speaker on familiar terms with his hearers. Many slang expressions are metaphorical (e.g. cut no ice, fly off the handle) and if they outlive the novelty phase pass into the language as idioms or colloquialisms.

CANT, CRYPTIC LINGO: Originally the secret language of vagrants; code slang used by criminals. It varies regionally; one of its derivatives is school slang, part generic and part localized.

RHYMING SLANG: Originally a cryptic lingo of the London Cockneys.

Slavery. An institution dating to prehistory, whereby persons were bound to a master, to work without recompense or freedom; its origins are obscure and varied, but undoubtedly the taking of prisoners in war was a principal source of slaves. The early Mesopotamian states used slaves, as did the early Hebrews and the Greeks. The conditions of slaves varied greatly from age to age and in different societies. In general the slave had no legal rights and was a chattel of his master, but the personal or skilled slave usually received better treatment than those on estates. When Rome expanded, slavery became vital to the working of the vast estates and agricultural slavery was brutal in the extreme. Through changing economic conditions, slaves in Rome and Europe were largely replaced by the serfs and villeins of medieval times, who had only meagre personal rights. A new development came in the 16th cent. after the discovery of America, when the need for labour on the new plantations was met by the transportation of great numbers of slaves from Africa; the British, French, Dutch, Portuguese, and Spanish all engaged in the slave trade. Britain made the trade illegal in 1811, but did not abolish slavery in British possessions till 1833. Other countries followed; in U.S.A. emancipation came after the ◊ *American Civil War*, in Brazil not till 1888. Some persisting examples of slavery are still to be found in Arabia and parts of Africa, but on a very small scale.

Slavonic Languages. Group of ◊ *Indo-European languages* descended from a Slavonic language spoken in prehistoric times in SE Europe, first recorded in the 9th cent. in Church Slavonic (Old Bulgarian); the main Slavonic languages are the Baltic group (Latvian, Lithuanian), the 3 dialects of Russian, the W. group (Polish, Czech, Slovak), and the S. group (Slovene, Serbo-Croat, Bulgarian). They have a high degree of inflection, comparable to Latin, in nouns, pronouns, adjectives, and verbs. Some are written in the Cyrillic alphabet. Existing Slavonic languages resemble one another; though speakers of one are not necessarily able to understand the others, adaptation is not comparable to learning a new language and many, e.g. Poles, Ukrainians, Czechs, can communicate without difficulty.

Sleep. Resting-period for body and mind, essential to all higher animals, in which consciousness sinks to a very low level, the real nature of which is unknown. Certain minimal periods and regularity are necessary, but they vary with individuals. In man deepest sleep occurs two or three hours after falling asleep. ◊ *Dreams, Hibernation.*

Sleeping Sickness ◊ *Tsetse Fly.*

Slide-rule. A mechanical means of performing calculations approximately and with great rapidity. With practice, three-figure accuracy is a normal accomplishment. The top pair of scales are graduated with the logarithms of numbers 1–100, and the bottom pair 1–10; squares and square roots may thus be read at sight. The invention of the modern slide-rule is ascribed to Wingate in 1872. Variations of the rule are made in cylindrical and circular forms; by these means greater accuracy is possible without the apparatus becoming too unwieldy.

'Slipped Disc' ◊ *Invertebral Disc.*

Sloth. S. American edentate, small two-toed or three-toed, leaf-eating, nocturnal, related to the ◊ *armadillo*; generally found hanging upside-down from branches, and slow and clumsy in gait. Its Pleistocene ancestors were ground-living animals, some larger than elephants.

Slow-worm (Blind-worm). Typical member of the family *Anguidae*, a snake-like ◊ *lizard* about a foot long and harmless, living under stones and capable of burrowing, one of the few ◊ *reptiles* found in Britain; viviparous, producing up to a dozen young in the autumn. Some members of the family have limbs.

Smallpox ◊ *Variola.*

Smoke Abatement ◊ *Pollution.*

Snail. Large and widely distributed group of molluscs, of the class *Gastropoda*, found chiefly on land but also in water; most have a spiral shell, usually with a right-handed coil. Although a few are carnivorous, most varieties live on plants. The common snail is very destructive in gardens esp. at night and after rain. An edible variety, *Helix pomatia*, is widely eaten in Europe.

Snake. ◊ *Reptile* of the order *Squamata*, which includes the ◊ *lizard*; limbless, except the ◊ *boa constrictor*, which has rudimentary hind legs. There are about 2500 species, most of which are of the family *Colubridae*. About one fifth of all snakes are poisonous, having grooved or hollow teeth through which the venom flows from the fangs; only a few are absolutely deadly (copperhead, rattlesnake, fer-de-lance, bushmaster), but many are highly dangerous (Old World ◊ *vipers*, ◊ *cobra*, ◊ *mamba*, ◊ *sea-snake*). The venomous snake often has an almost indistinguishable 'double' which is harmless (◊ *mimicry*). The largest snakes (anaconda, python, boa constrictor) kill by strangling; their jaws are so hinged that they can swallow prey of greater girth than their own. All snakes live on insects, birds, or animals. Fast locomotion is achieved by undulation of the body, slow by movements of the belly-scales. Most snakes lay eggs, but some are viviparous. Snake venoms are of two main kinds, one attacking the victim's blood system, the other his nervous system; anti-snake serum is available in countries where dangerous snakes occur. The only poisonous snake in Great Britain is the adder.

Snapdragon ◊ *Antirrhinum.*

Snipe. World-wide species of wading bird; the common snipe, pack snipe, and great snipe are European waders which migrate in winter to Africa. The brown and black stripes provide camouflage in the long marsh grass where they live. Their flight is zig-zag. The female incubates four spotted eggs in a hollow in the ground.

Snooker. A game derived from ◊ *billiards*, based on a variation called 'black pool' reputedly devised by Colonel Sir Neville Chamberlain in India 1875, introduced to Britain in the 1880s and for many years merely a diversion from billiards; in the 1930s billiards lost favour, snooker became more popular and since 1951 it has replaced billiards as a professional championship game, in which 22 balls are used: 15 red, 6 pool (yellow, green, brown, pink, blue, black), and one white.

Snow. When water-vapour in the atmosphere freezes it falls as snow, usually as flakes of delicate feathery structure, occasionally as crystals of powdery consistency, the crystal structure of snowflakes is of great complexity, variety, and beauty.

About 10 in. of snow is equivalent to an inch of rain. As snow is permeated with air, it serves as an insulating layer and protects the ground against cold.

Snowdrop. *Galanthus nivalis*, the common snowdrop, is not native to Britain but was introduced from France in the 16th cent. and became naturalized. Many snowdrops come from the Near East and S. Russia, where they have larger flowers and leaves. From Greece comes a snowdrop which flowers in October, and from the Caucasus one that flowers as late as March.

Soap. Animal and vegetable oils (i.e. compounds of fatty acids and glycerine) modified by the action of caustic soda or caustic potash. Chemically soaps are ◊ *salts*, usually of sodium or potassium with the longer chain fatty acids. Basically the process was discovered in antiquity. There are records of Phoenician trade in soap in the 6th cent B.C. Marseilles became famous for soap making in the 9th cent A.D.; the first factory in England began in Bristol in the 12th cent. Many oils and fats are used in modern manufacture. The chief animal fat (tallow) comes from the cattle and sheep industries of Argentina and Australia; vegetable oils are also widely used e.g. ◊ *coconut*, palm, and cottonseed oil. An important by-product is ◊ *glycerine*. ◊ *Detergents*.

Soapstone (Talc) ◊ *Silica*.

'Soccer' ◊ *Association Football*.

Social Contract. A class of political theories which assert that the state and society are the products of voluntary agreement among men, sometimes used to explain the historical origins of the state and society, or sometimes the nature and limits of political allegiance and social obligation. Social-contract theories can be found among the ancients (e.g. the theories of the sophists, Glaucon and Thrasymachus, as represented in Plato's *Republic*; they attained a peak of popularity in 17th- and 18th-cent. Europe, e.g. Hobbes, Locke, Rousseau.

Social Credit. A theory based on the belief of a Canadian, Major Douglas, that suitable manipulation of the monetary system could assure prosperity, basically by unorthodox injections of credit e.g. paying everyone his annual share of the 'national dividend' according to the country's prosperity – a proposal much resembling the current idea that wage increases should be related to those in national productivity. The small Social Credit Party of Canada is a protest group not closely wedded to the Douglas theory.

Socialism. A theory of political and economic organization in which the means of production, distribution, and exchange are removed from private control into 'social' or community control, and in which there is equality of opportunity for the individual to develop his talents and share in the wealth of the society. In practice there are many variants advocated by different socialist parties. Most agree in aiming at the elimination of economic inequality through State control of the main means of production. ◊ *Labour Party, Marxism, Revisionism.*

Society of Friends (Quakers). Protestant Christian religious body deriving from the teachings of George Fox 1624–91 that every man is directly guided by the 'inner light' of the ◊ *Holy Ghost*; all dogma, formalism, priesthood, and ◊ *sacraments* are rejected, and worship is simple and largely silent. Oaths and force are rejected: Quakers are distinguished by their refusal to take part in war and by their active concern to mitigate its results by social and charitable work. Early peculiarities (distinctive dress and the refusal to use either titles of honour in addressing others or the 'pagan' names for the days of the week or months) have now largely fallen into disuse. Though a small body, about 170,000 in Britain and America, their influence and example have been outstanding.

Society of Jesus (Jesuits). Roman Catholic religious order founded A.D. 1534 by Ignatius Loyola, a converted Spanish soldier (later canonized); in addition to the traditional three vows, of poverty, chastity, obedience, its members are bound by a fourth, to go unquestioningly wherever the Pope may order, for the salvation of souls. Governed autocratically by a General, they are now principally occupied in educational and missionary work and in the performance of the 'Spiritual Exercises' drawn up by the founder. Suspicions of their involvement in non-religious matters led to their suppression by the Pope in 1773 but in 1814 they were restored by Pius VII. Today, with about 35,000 members they are one of the largest religious orders, working in all parts of the world. There are about 700 Jesuits in England and Wales. ⇔ *Gunpowder Plot, Kulturkampf, Missions, Popish Plot.*

Socratic Method. Eliciting from a pupil, by skilful questioning, a general definition of a term e.g. Justice, and by further questioning establishing whether or not the definition fits, in two stages, first the ironic (destructive) and then the manuetic (constructive); attributed to Socrates (⇔ *Dialectic*). Also, any question-and-answer teaching method; the questioner's pretence of ignorance is 'Socratic irony'.

Soda. Washing soda is hydrated sodium carbonate. Soda-ash is anhydrous sodium carbonate. Caustic soda is sodium hydroxide (⇔ *Sodium*). Soda water ⇔ *carbon dioxide.*

Sodium. A very soft silvery ⇔ *alkali* metal which instantly tarnishes in air, reacts violently with water, and is highly electropositive (⇔ *Metals and Non-metals*). It has a terrestrial abundance of 2.62 per cent and occurs principally as the chloride (common salt) in sea-water and as rocksalt left by the evaporation of prehistoric seas. It also occurs as the carbonate found round inland lakes where evaporation is high (e.g. Dead Sea), the nitrate (Chile saltpetre), and the borate (borax), known since earliest times, but the element was not isolated until 1807, by Davy.

Common salt is either mined or dissolved from rock-salt beds, or obtained from sea water by evaporation; the crude salt from either source is purified by recrystallization. It forms the raw material of the great alkali industry in which metallic sodium is made by the electrolysis of fused salt, and sodium hydroxide (caustic soda) by the electrolysis of brine; chlorine is a valuable by-product from both processes. The industry also converts it to soda ash (sodium carbonate), washing soda, bicarbonate, and sulphate. Salt is an essential food; the bicarbonate is used in baking powders and fire-extinguishers; the hydroxide and carbonate, important industrial chemicals, are used in the bleaching, dyeing, soap, paper, and textile industries, and for water softening; both carbonate and sulphate are employed in the glass industry. Sodium cyanide (for gold and silver extraction, and for casehardening steel) and sodium peroxide (for oxidizing and bleaching) are also valuable. The element itself has many uses: as a heat-transfer liquid in some nuclear power

reactors; as a lead alloy for the manufacture of the anti-knock lead tetraethyl; in photoelectric cells; as a reagent in the organic chemical industry.

Sodium Hydroxide ⇔ *Chlorine.*

Sodium Perborate ⇔ *Boron.*

Soil Mechanics. Branch of civil engineering dealing with the behaviour of soils and its effect on earthworks and foundations. From such studies it is possible to determine safe loads for building foundations, safe slopes for cuttings and embankments, and suitable thicknesses for road and airfield pavings.

Solanaceae. The nightshade family; dicotyledonous plants of temperate and tropical regions, with many species native in central and S. America. The family is commercially important. There are several food plants, e.g. *Solanum tuberosum* (potato) and *S. lycopersicum* (tomato) both native to S. America. *S. melongena* is the egg-plant (aubergine), native to India. Capsicums are sweet peppers and chillies. *Nicotiana tabacum* gives tobacco. Many solanaceae contain alkaloids and are used medicinally, e.g. deadly nightshade (*belladonna*), thornapple, ⇔ *henbane* (also wild in Britain). Many are decorative, e.g. schizanthus, petunia, nicotiana, salpiglossis, and physalis (Cape gooseberry). The fruits of some physalis are edible. The *Solanum dulcamara* (woody nightshade), bitter-sweet with red berries, and *S. nigrum* (black nightshade) are wild in Britain. Although considered poisonous here, the young *S. nigrum* leaves are eaten as spinach in the tropics.

Solar System. Comprises the ⇔ *Sun,* planets (with their satellites) and ⇔ *asteroids* (all held in orbit by the Sun's gravitational force), and ⇔ *comets,* ⇔ *meteorites,* gas and dust, the Sun's mass amounting to 99.9 per cent of the whole.

The many theories put forward to explain the solar system fall into two main classes: that it evolved as a result of a heavenly catastrophe; and that it evolved from a nebula. The former includes (a) the close approach of another star caused tidal waves, which extended so far that they became detached from the Sun and solidified to form the planets; (b) the Sun was originally a double star; one component exploded like a nova, and material captured by the Sun formed the planets.

The nebular theories include (a) the Sun was formed from a rotating cloud of dust

Orbital and Physical Data of the Planets

Planet	Average distance from Sun (Earth 1)	Orbital period	Relative mass (Earth 1)	Equatorial diameter (miles)	Rotation Time
Mercury	0.39	88 days	0.05	3,000	88 days?
Venus	0.72	225 days	0.81	7,700	225 days?
Earth	1.00	365 days	1.00	7,900	23 hrs 56 min.
Mars	1.52	687 days	0.11	4,230	24 hrs 37 min.
Jupiter	5.20	11·9 yrs	317.80	88,700	9 hrs 50 min.
Saturn	9.55	29·5 yrs	95.20	74,200	10 hrs 14 min.
Uranus	19.20	84 yrs	14.50	29,500	10 hrs 49 min.
Neptune	30.09	165 yrs	17.20	27,700	15 hrs 40 min.
Pluto	39.44	248 yrs	0.80?	3,700	6½ days

and gas; the main central concentration formed the Sun, and the outer regions condensed to form the planets; (b) when the Sun was formed from a contracting nebula, a flat disc like the present rings of Saturn remained; this later broke up,

sun

0   100   200   300   400   500   600   700   800
thousands of miles

• mercury   • pluto   • mars   • venus   • earth

● neptune   ● uranus   ⬡ saturn   ● jupiter

planets compared with the diameter of the sun

• pluto
● neptune
uranus
jupiter
saturn
earth mars
mercury
venus

50   100   200   400   800   1600   3200
millions of miles

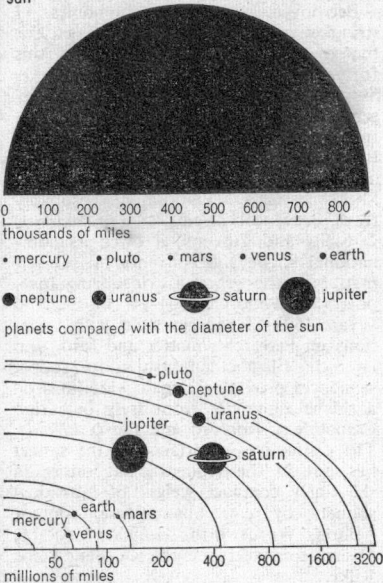

and condensations of the matter in it formed the planets.

Since the end of the First World War these and other theories have been examined in considerable detail. A satisfactory theory must allow for the angular momentum of the planets themselves and also for their angular momentum about the Sun, for the different densities and chemical composition of the planets, and for the fact that the planetary orbits are nearly coplanar. Although it seems unlikely that the exact details of the formation of the solar system can ever be proved, the fact that we can see stars in process of formation, in condensing clouds of interstellar matter, does lend considerable weight to the nebular theory. ◇ *Jupiter, Mars, Saturn*.

Solder. ◇ *Alloy* used for joining metals. Common soft solders, which have a low melting point, are alloys of ◇ *lead* and ◇ *tin* in varying proportions, usually with a small amount of antimony; e.g. plumber's solder is generally about 30 per cent tin and better-quality soft solders about 40 per cent. Brazing solder, which is often used for other metals as well as brass, has a higher melting point and is usually an alloy of copper, zinc, and some silver. Special-purpose solders may include any metal that amalgamates particularly well with the metals to be joined.

Solferino. 1859. Decisive defeat of Austria by the Franco-Sardinian army, under Napoleon III, in the war for the unification of ◇ *Italy*. The suffering of the wounded led a Swiss present at the battle to advocate a plan to alleviate the worst barbarities. ◇ *Red Cross*. ◇ *Savoy*.

Solicitor. The English legal profession is divided into two categories; a solicitor may argue a case in a lower court, but in higher courts he must brief (engage) a ◇ *barrister*. The training, admission and discipline of solicitors is under the control of the ◇ *Law Society*; they perform a great deal of legal business other than litigation (◇ *Conveyancing*). In Continental countries and in U.S.A. the legal profession is not differentiated, every lawyer being entitled to perform all the functions of the profession, though in practice specialization often occurs; the advantages and disadvantages of the English system are the subject of considerable debate.

Solicitor-General. The junior of the two Law Officers of the Crown, the senior being the ◊ *Attorney-General*. Not in fact a solicitor, but a Queen's Counsel (◊ *Barrister*) and usually an M.P.

Solstice. Time when noon sun is furthest N. (about 21 June) or S. (about 22 Dec.) of the equator; also the sun's position at these times (◊ *Celestial Sphere*). In the N. hemisphere, the June (summer) solstice brings the longest day and shortest night, the Dec. (winter) solstice the shortest day and longest night; in the S. hemisphere this is reversed. ◊◊ *Equinox*.

Solutrean ◊ *Palaeolithic*.

Somalia. Area 246,000 sq. m. Pop. about 2 m. (largely nomadic). Cap. Mogadishu. Rel. Muslim. An E. African republic on the Indian Ocean, between Ethiopia, French Somaliland, and Kenya; formerly British and Italian Somaliland. The legislature is 33 members of the British Somaliland Assembly sitting with 90 from the Somalia Assembly to form the United Assembly.

ECONOMY. Mainly pastoral; the climate is arid. Exports bananas, hides, live cattle.

HISTORY. The British protectorate over the NE part of the country lasted from 1888 to 1960. The Italians held the S. part as a colony from 1893 to 1941. During the ◊ *Second World War* the Italian section was occupied by British forces. In 1950 the United Nations placed the S. part under Italian trusteeship. When this ended in 1960, British and Italian Somaliland united as Somalia, which also claims French Somaliland and parts of Ethiopia and Kenya. Like the neighbouring Galla and Danakil, the Somali people are ◊ *Cushites*, originally from Arabia; many live in Ethiopia and Kenya, frequently wandering across the frontiers for grazing and water.

Somme. 1916. British and French offensive during the ◊ *First World War*, which broke through the German lines but was not followed up quickly enough. It achieved only limited objectives, at an enormous cost in lives.

Sonata. In the era of Haydn and Mozart, a substantial instrumental work, usually in three or four movements; later, e.g. Liszt's piano sonata, one long movement, supposedly equal in weight and variety to several shorter ones. The classic ◊ *symphony* is in effect a sonata for orchestra, the classic string quartet a sonata for strings, but 'Sonata' has generally been used of works for piano alone, or for one instrument with piano.

Almost always the first movement of such a multiple-movement sonata, symphony, etc. is in a particular form which has been labelled sonata-form. Essentially, such a movement first has a section in which music in one key is contrasted with music in another ('exposition') and then later, after 'development', has another section (the recapitulation) in which the same music is re-worked so as to emphasize only one key, the one in which the movement began.

Beethoven, with his 9 symphonies, 17 string quartets, 32 piano sonatas, etc., is the great master and developer of this form. ◊◊ *Chamber Music*.

Sonnet. A poem of 14 lines grouped by sense and ◊ *rhyme* into either two quatrains and two triplets (Italian or Petrarchan, and Miltonic) or three quatrains and a concluding couplet (English or Shakespearean). Elaborated, probably from Provençal origins ◊ *Troubadours*, in Sicily and Tuscany, it owed its international vogue and conventional subject-matter to the gracefully idealizing love-poetry of Petrarch 1304–74. In England Wyatt 1503–42 experimented with variations on Petrarch's matter and form, but later the Elizabethan fashion for sonnet sequences providing elegant variations on a theme came not from Italy but from France, e.g. Ronsard and the ◊ *Pléiade*. The distinctive importance of the sonnet lies not in the sequence but rather in the finely compact weight of individual sonnets by e.g. Shakespeare, Donne, Milton, Wordsworth, Hopkins; notable foreign sonneteers include e.g. Baudelaire, Rilke.

Sorbonne. The University of Paris, founded in the early 13th cent. and early the principal teaching centre in Europe esp. for theology; during the 15th cent. and later, it dabbled in ◊ *Renaissance* and ◊ *Reformation* politics and lost prestige, but in 1598 Henri IV (◊ *Huguenots*) gave

it a new statute, and later Cardinal
Richelieu built new colleges (finished
1627) on the present site. The Collèges
were abolished in 1793 during the ◊
French Revolution, but Napoleon founded
the Université de France in 1806; this
became the new Université de Paris, which
now has over 50,000 students.

Sorcery ◊ *Witchcraft*.

Sorghum. ◊ *Cereal* of the genus *Panicum*, in a great number of varieties,
resembling ◊ *millet*. The staple food-grain
of the tropical Old World esp. Africa,
containing about 10 per cent protein, 4
per cent oil, 70 per cent carbohydrate, and
11 per cent moisture.

S.O.S. The international distress signal for
use in wireless telegraphy; the letters have
no meaning, but in Morse code the
··· ─ ─ ─ ··· has a pronounced rhythm
attracting immediate attention. The S.O.S.
signal is transmitted on a 500-metre or
2000-metre wavelength; all ships observe
two silence periods each hour, listening on
these frequencies to ensure that any S.O.S.
signal however weak shall be picked up.
The word 'Mayday' is used in radio telephony.

Soudan (French) ◊ *Mali*.

Sound. A wave motion, detectable by
the ear, that requires a medium for its
transmission and cannot pass through a
vacuum. The wave motion is longitudinal,
the particles at any point in the transmitting medium being 'pushed forward' by
those behind them and in turn pushing
forward those in front before returning
to their mean position; in this way the
particles oscillate about their mean position while the wave travels forward
through the medium. The velocity of
sound (about 1100 ft a second in air) is
much less than that of light (186,000 miles
a second in free space) and this explains
the delay between the flash and sound of a
gun. When an aircraft is flying at a speed
greater than that of sound in air (760
m.p.h. at ground level and 660 m.p.h. at
36,000 ft) the air cannot 'get out of the
way' quickly enough and conical shock
waves similar to sound are created, particularly by the nose and tail, and are carried along with the aircraft. Where these
wave cones intersect with the ground a
boom is heard and the wave pressure may
be sufficient to break windows etc. Sonic
booms are not, however, a new phenomenon; the carter's whip, for example,

produces its crack by moving faster than
sound. ◊ *Supersonic Flight*.

Sound Barrier. Transitional period at
which an aircraft accelerates from subsonic to ◊ *supersonic flight* at speeds
greater than the speed of sound in air; the
drag-rise from compressibility effects was
formerly visualized as a 'barrier' to higher
speeds. ◊ *Mach Number*.

Sounding. Ascertaining the depth of
water, for many centuries by lowering a
lead weight on a long line marked in
fathoms.

ECHO-SOUNDER: An electronic instrument in the ship's bottom sends out
sound-waves, which bounce off the sea-
bed; since the speed of sound in water is
almost constant, the echo's return-time
establishes the water's depth. The device
was invented shortly before the Second
World War.

South Africa. Area 472,359 sq. m. Pop.
16 m. (African 10.9 m. White 3.1 m.
Coloured 1.5 m. Asian 0.5 m.). Cap. Pretoria and Cape Town. Independent republic. Government by Prime Minister and
Cabinet, with a Senate of 43 elected and
11 nominated members, and a House of
Assembly of 160 members elected by all
whites over 21.

ECONOMY. Varied resources both agricultural and mineral. The most valuable
exports are wool, gold, diamonds, and
copper; the Rand produces about one
half of the annual world production of
gold. Coal, iron, and uranium are other important products. There is some industry
based on steel works, but S. Africa is a
large importer of textiles, machinery, and
vehicles.

Of the total population about 3 m. are
of European origin, 60 per cent of them
Boers; the remainder are mainly Bantu,
with some Indian and mixed communities;
the legal system is based on Roman-Dutch
law.

HISTORY. The Dutch settlement at the
Cape dating from the 17th cent. was taken
by the British during the Napoleonic
Wars, as a base on the route to India. The
Dutch (Boers) were dissatisfied with
British rule and from 1835 many of them
trekked inland, settling in what became
the Independent Boer republics of the
Transvaal and Orange Free State; others
settled in Natal. Friction between the
British in Cape Colony and Natal and
the two Boer states became acute when

gold and diamonds were discovered in the latter. Local leaders on both sides acted provocatively (◊ *Jameson Raid*), and the ◊ *Boer War* broke out in 1899. The Boers at first were successful, besieging British troops in Ladysmith and ◊ *Mafeking*; Roberts and Kitchener defeated the main Boer forces by the end of 1900, but two years of guerrilla fighting followed before peace was made. After the war it was agreed that a single political unit in S. Africa was desirable; the Boer states were incorporated with the British provinces but given self-government in 1907. Considerable bitterness remained amongst the Boers, which Botha and Smuts tried to remove; in 1910 the various provinces united to form the Union of South Africa.

The United Party was in power (under General Smuts) 1933–48. The Nationalist Party tried to prevent S. Africa entering the ◊ *Second World War* on the Allied side. Dr Malan gained a majority for the Nationalist Party in 1948, which under Mr Strijdom and later Dr Verwoerd carried out the policy of ◊ *apartheid* and steadily increased its strength at each election. A clear majority was obtained in the referendum of 1960 on the proposal to make the Dominion a republic. Criticisms of apartheid at the Conference of Commonwealth Premiers in 1961 led to the withdrawal of S. Africa from the British Commonwealth.

LANGUAGE. Afrikaans, English.

South Arabian Federation. Group of Arab territories in southern Arabia, internally self-governing but under British suzerainty. Britain is pledged to help it become independent. The neighbouring State of ◊ *Yemen* is opposed to, and does not recognize, the Federation.

South-east Asia Treaty Organization (SEATO). Established in 1954 under a treaty between Australia, France, New Zealand, Pakistan, the Philippines, Thailand, the U.K., and U.S.A. which pledged economic cooperation and collective action in the event of either external aggression or internal subversion involving members in the Treaty area (which is so defined as to exclude ◊ *Formosa* and ◊ *Hong Kong* from the military provisions). The headquarters of SEATO is at Bangkok.

Southern Cross. Name for a prominent constellation visible in the S. hemisphere where it has served the same purpose in

navigation as the pole star in the N. hemisphere.

Southern Lights ◊ *Aurora*.

Southern Rhodesia ◊ *Rhodesia*.

South Sea Bubble. 1720. The South Sea Company was founded in 1711 as a rival to the Bank of England, with the intention of making a profit by taking over government debts. In return for the monopoly of the trade to S. America (thought to be fabulously wealthy) the company first took over a government debt of £9.5 m. and later £31 m. of the ◊ *National Debt*, on which it was to receive a guaranteed interest of 6 per cent. Its stock rose out of all proportion to its earnings, and fraudulent speculation was engendered. The company's attempt to stop fraudulent schemes burst the bubble: thousands were ruined. Robert Walpole initiated measures to restore the credit of the company and the government.

South Tyrol. Alto-Adige, Bolzano; an area south of the Brenner Pass acquired by Italy from Austria in 1919. Two thirds of the population is German-speaking, and Italy in 1946 guaranteed their rights equally with those of the Italian-speaking section. In 1948 the area was combined with Trentino into an autonomous region in which there is an Italian majority. Since then the treatment of the minority has been a source of recriminations between Austria and Italy.

Sovereignty. 1. Possession of supreme lawmaking power within a body politic. A distinction is often drawn between legal and political sovereignty. Legal sovereignty is possessed by an authority recognized by the courts as having an unrestricted right to make law, e.g. Parliament in the U.K. Political sovereignty refers to the authority considered to be the ultimate actual source of power within the body politic, commonly the electorate. The concept of sovereignty entered the realm of political theory in the 16th cent. with the rise of powerful national monarchies, and it both reflected and assisted the tendency to the centralization of power.

2. In ◊ *international law*, the possession of that full autonomy which is the essential prerequisite for entry into the comity of nations.

Soviet Union. Area 8.6 m. sq. m. Pop. 225 m. Cap. Moscow. The U.S.S.R. (Union of Soviet Socialist Republics) which united the Russian Soviet Federal

Socialist Republic with the Ukrainian, Byelorussian, and Transcaucasian Republics, came into existence in 1922. Other republics were subsequently added to the Union, which now comprises 15, each inhabited by a major nationality after which it is named. Under the 1936 Constitution the Soviet Union is 'a socialist state of workers and peasants'. The local and national government councils (soviets) are directly elected; the legislative organ is the Supreme Soviet, consisting of the Council of the Union and the Council of Nationalities, elected for four years. Between sessions the Supreme Soviet acts through its Presidium, and elects the Council of Ministers, the highest executive and administrative organ. (Each constituent S.S.R. has its own Republic Soviet also.) There is universal and secret suffrage, but the only legal political organization is the Communist Party, which must approve candidates for office. The practice has been to offer one preselected candidate for each vacancy, the choice to be ratified at the polls. The power of the Communist Party *apparat* permeates the whole life of the state although its full members form only about three per cent of the population. The U.S.S.R. is founded on state or collective ownership of the means of production. Personal property e.g. earned income and savings, dwelling houses for one's own use, furniture and chattels, and the right to inherit such personal property, are legally protected. The Constitution permits freedom both of religious worship and of anti-religious propaganda; the ◊ *Eastern Orthodox Church* is disestablished, and congregations must maintain their churches and clergy; few churches remain in use.

ECONOMY. Since the Revolution the U.S.S.R. has become a leading industrial country, and it now occupies second place in the world, after U.S.A. The economy has been rigidly planned since 1928, and for many years, under the influence of marxist doctrine and defence needs, heavy industry was emphasized at the expense of housing and consumer goods, while Stalin's policy of forcible ◊ *collectivization of agriculture* proved a costly failure. Since the Second World War very large sums have been invested in nuclear physics and space research. In both these fields notable successes have been achieved, including the first manned space flight,

accomplished by Yuri Gagarin on 12 April 1961 (◊ *Artificial Satellite, Space Exploration*). Now, however, first priority is being given to expansion of the chemicals industry, which, it is hoped, will assist both agriculture and the production of consumer goods. Khrushchev stressed the importance of material incentives and the 1961 party programme envisaged overtaking U.S.A. in *per capita* production during the present decade and building 'the material and technological base of communism' by 1980.

Education is provided only by public authorities; there are no private schools. Each Republic has its own Ministry of Education, which looks after teacher training and general education, from the age of seven, for eight (primary) or ten/eleven (secondary) years. The systems are centralized, with uniform curricula, and teachers are employed and paid by the Ministry. Methods of teaching are formal and traditional; great stress is laid on scientific and technological subjects. Admission to higher education depends primarily upon success in examinations though young people who have worked in industry or agriculture have certain privileges in gaining admission to a university or institute. There is a separate Ministry of Higher Education in the central Government, and others in the Republics; other Ministries e.g. Agriculture maintain advanced technological institutes. Scientific research, which is coordinated by an influential State Committee (headed by a Deputy Prime Minister), is carried out in a large number of institutes subordinated either to the Academy of Sciences or directly to government bodies. Interesting features of Soviet higher education are: (a) all full-time students receive stipends; (b) there are large numbers of correspondence-course and part-time students (approx. one-third of the total number); (c) a large proportion of the students attend specialized institutes (with an enrolment of over 2 m.) rather than universities. There are now 33 universities and 900 technological institutes.

HISTORY. The earliest rulers were Vikings, welcomed by the Slavs to halt the invasions from the East. By the 11th cent. the country (then a number of warring principalities stretching from Novgorod to Kiev) had adopted orthodox ◊ *Christianity*. For a time the princes became vassals of the Mongol empire; subsequently, in the struggle against the Tatars (Tartars), the princes of Moscow established their pre-eminence, and Ivan III (who took the title 'ruler of all the Russias') expelled the Tatars, and began to restrain the power of the boyars (nobles), a policy which his grandson Ivan the Terrible (1530–84) ruthlessly continued. During this period, till the 17th cent., the rulers of Russia were preoccupied with expansion and consolidation eastwards; it was not until the 18th cent. (Peter the Great (1672–1725) and Catherine II (1729–96)) that their interests turned westwards. St Petersburg was built and became the capital, and Russia began to play an important role in European affairs (◊ Poltava); but in spite of having taken a leading part in the ◊ Napoleonic Wars, 19th-cent. Russia failed to make progress. The administration was inefficient and often brutal, nothing was done to reform the land-holding system or the status of the peasants, who remained serfs until 1861, and internal order was maintained by repression. In foreign affairs Russia suffered reverses both in the ◊ Crimean War 1854 and in the ◊ Russo-Japanese War 1905. Home affairs were equally badly handled. A revolution broke out in 1905; concessions were made and a Parliament (Duma) set up, but once order was restored the Government reverted to repression. Many of the peasants, workers, and intelligentsia were deeply discontented and disposed to sympathize with the revolutionary aims of the Social Democratic and Social Revolutionary Parties; on the complete breakdown of the Tsarist government under defeat in the ◊ First World War, the Menshevik revolution of Feb. 1917 brought the Kerensky provisional government to power for a few months until its vacillations gave the ◊ Bolsheviks their chance to seize power under Lenin, who with Trotsky, Stalin, and others formed a Council of People's Commissars. A 'dictatorship of the proletariat' was set up, and peace was made with Germany at ◊ Brest Litovsk. A bitter civil war broke out between Bolsheviks and anti-Bolsheviks (Reds and Whites) in 1918 and was won by the former in 1922. Lenin died in 1924; in the ensuing struggle for power Stalin ousted Trotsky. The qualified reversion to private enterprise permitted by Lenin's ◊ New Economic Policy

(NEP) was reversed by Stalin in 1928 when the State Plan system was begun, with great hardship esp. to the peasants, of whom vast numbers died. The U.S.S.R. was recognized by Britain and other European states in 1924 and admitted to the League of Nations in 1934; but no cooperation developed between her and the other non-Fascist powers, and she concluded a non-aggression pact with Nazi Germany in 1939, despite which in the ◊ Second World War the latter invaded U.S.S.R. in 1941. Wartime cooperation between U.S.S.R. and the Allies changed to the antagonism of the 'cold war' shortly after Germany's surrender 1945. The dictatorial aspect of Stalin's leadership grew more oppressive, until in 1953 he died; and there ensued a period of 'collective leadership'. In 1956 at the 20th All Union Party Congress Khrushchev, already important as Chairman of the Central Committee of the Comunist Party, denounced the misrule and personality cult of Stalin and emerged as the dominating figure. He subsequently also became Chairman of the Council of Ministers. He supported a policy of 'peaceful co-existence' with capitalist countries (which led to a doctrinal quarrel with the Chinese Communists), changed the priority for industry from heavy equipment to consumer goods, and generally ameliorated the lot of the Soviet people through the policy of 'destalinization'. In October 1964 Khrushchev was unexpectedly shorn of office: A. N. Kosygin replaced him as Chairman of the Council of Ministers and L. I. Brezhnyev as Chairman of the Central Committee of the Communist Party.

LANGUAGE. Russian, the official language, one of the ◊ Slavonic languages, is spoken by about 115 m. Ukrainian and Byelorussian, spoken in the respective Republics, are closely related to Russian; in the other constituent Republics there are native languages unrelated to Russian, and in all some 120 languages are spoken within the U.S.S.R.

Soya ◊ Bean.

Space Exploration. Voyages to the moon and planets were envisaged by imaginative writers e.g. Jules Verne and H. G. Wells, but it was not until advances in rocket propulsion were achieved that 'space travel' entered the realm of possibility. Ziolkovsky in Russia was the first to publish a serious mathematically based study of the principles of space travel, 1903. Hermann Oberth, a German mathematics professor, examined the fundamental engineering problems involved, in a remarkable book *The Way to Space Travel*, 1929, which inspired the experimental work in Germany in the 1930s, exploited for military purposes by the Nazis, which resulted in the wartime V2 rocket; this subsequently served as the prototype space rocket.

No exact point at which 'space travel' begins can be fixed, since there is no clear boundary to gravitational fields, but orbital flight around the earth is a critical step. This was first achieved by Major Yuri Gagarin, in April 1961. Both U.S.A. and U.S.S.R. have plans for extensive space research; those of U.S.A. include a series of unmanned lunar vehicles, with instruments of increasing sophistication, which will make observations near the moon and eventually be 'soft-landed' on it; one scheme is to place mobile remote-controlled cameras with transmitters on the lunar surface. The next stage, manned flight, awaits the completion of more powerful rockets. ◊ *Artificial Satellites*.

Spain. Area 196,700 sq. m. Pop. 31.3 m. Cap. Madrid. Rel. almost entirely Roman Catholic. Independent sovereign State sharing the Iberian peninsula with ◊ *Portugal*. The present head of state is Generalissimo Franco (*el Caudillo*, the Leader). There is no constitution; the Caudillo appoints a cabinet and controls the Falange, the only political party allowed to function. The Cortes (National Assembly) was re-established 1942; roughly half of its members are *ex officio* as e.g. National Councillors of the Falange, and half are elected by the national syndicates, the municipalities, the professions, etc. Spain was declared a monarchy by a law of 1947 confirming Franco as head of state charged with naming his own successor (as king or regent). ECONOMY. About 70 per cent of the exports are agricultural products, notably sherry and citrus fruits; there are also important mineral resources, esp. coal and iron.

HISTORY. The original Iberian and Celtic inhabitants became civilized under Roman occupation. The country was later occupied by Visigoths and by the Moors (◊ *Ommayads*) who were eventually driven out by the Christian states of León, ◊ *Castile*, ◊ *Aragon*, and Navarre. The 1479 union of Aragon and Castile brought Spain under a central authority and prepared the way for her to become the richest and most powerful state in Europe, with a vast empire in the New World. Charles I (also Holy Roman Emperor as Charles V) was the leading Roman Catholic prince opposing the ◊ *Reformation*; his extensive European territories were soon redivided, leaving his son Philip II in possession of the ◊ *Netherlands*, the revolt of which and the difficulties created by the overseas empire led to Spain's decline. Despite military successes during the ◊ *Thirty Years War*, the Hapsburg alliance was worsted by France, and the death of the childless Charles II brought the ◊ *War of the Spanish Succession*, which placed the Bourbons upon the throne. Napoleon deposed the Bourbon monarch 1808 and made his own brother Joseph King of Spain; this provoked national revolt, and with British assistance in the ◊ *Peninsular War* the Spaniards liberated their country. The 1812 constitution ushered in a long period of constitutional and dynastic struggles, later exacerbated by the growth of anarchist parties. The empire disintegrated in the 1820s (◊ *Colombia*, *Ecuador*, etc.), and the last colonies were lost in the ◊ *Spanish-American War*. Ecclesiastical difficulties and the ◊ *Basque* and ◊ *Catalan* separatist tendencies prevented the dictator Primo de Rivera 1923–30 and the subsequent republic from creating a modern and stable state. Rebellion against a liberal government resulted in the ◊ *Spanish Civil War* 1936–9, General Franco's victory restoring stability at the cost of repressive dictatorship. Though sympathetic towards Hitler and Mussolini, Franco kept Spain neutral in the ◊ *Second World War*. His government has grown more acceptable to the Western powers since 1945, as excluding communist influence; Spain concluded an agreement with U.S.A. for economic and military aid 1953.

LANGUAGE. One of the ◊ *Romance languages*, spoken by about 110 m. in Spain and her dependencies, and throughout central and S. America (exc. Brazil). Standard Spanish comes from Castile, the land of the castles (*castillos*) around Burgos, whose influence caused Castilian to expand. King Alfonso X (1252–84) organized the language and gave it official status, confirmed by the foundation of the Royal Spanish Academy 1713.

Spanish-American War. 1898. The Spanish suppressed revolts in ◊ *Cuba* and the ◊ *Philippines* in 1895, afterwards granting a constitution to Cuba. American newspapers stirred up popular protests against the quelling of the revolts; the blowing-up of the American battleship *Maine* in Havana harbour gave President McKinley an occasion to begin war. Within 10 weeks Spain was completely defeated, and had to cede both Cuba and the Philippines to U.S.A. in return for an indemnity of $20 m.

Spanish Architecture. The earliest buildings of note are the 9th-cent. churches of non-Muslim Asturias, strongly influenced by Carolingian styles, and the Islamic ◊ *mosques*, of which the earliest example (8th cent.) is at Cordoba. The Islamic style continued until the 14th cent. (with a magnificent example in the Alhambra at Granada), though in the 9th to 11th centuries a combination of Christian and Muslim elements had resulted in the Mozarabic style. Of the ◊ *Romanesque* style which began in Catalonia in the 11th cent. the masterpiece is the pilgrimage church of Santiago de Compostella. The 13th-cent. ◊ *Gothic* cathedrals of Burgos, Toledo, and León show French influence; the most original Spanish Gothic is ◊ *Catalan*, in Barcelona Cathedral. The richly decorated late Gothic, introduced by architects from Cologne and the Netherlands, combined with ◊ *Renaissance* details, produced the Plateresque style. The Renaissance style is seen at the Alhambra and Escorial palaces; the ◊ *Baroque* developed exuberant national characteristics, esp. under the Churrigueras. Of 18th-cent. buildings the palace of Aranjuez is outstanding. The only modern architect of note was Gaudí, whose extravagant ◊ *art nouveau* buildings are in Barcelona.

Spanish Art. The first important works are the 11th- and 12th-cent. carvings on the great ◊ *Romanesque* cathedrals; in N. Spain, sculpture and painting were strongly influenced by France and Flanders, whilst in S. Spain the arts remained under Islamic domination until the 17th cent. A fusion of Muslim and Spanish motifs produced the Mozarabic style of decoration, popular for lustre pottery wares. The first great painter of the Spanish school was the 16th-cent. Cretan El Greco, whose mystically intense style reflects the ascetic character of the Spanish church; a similar intensity of feeling characterizes the statues of saints by Alonso Berruguete. The golden age of Spanish painting began in 1623, when Velasquez became Court painter, and ended in 1682 with the death of Murillo; it includes the work of Francisco Herrera the elder, Ribera, and Zurbarán. Although subject to Italian influences, they created a distinctively Spanish style, notable for its vivid colour and its striking contrasts between an earthy realism and an ethereal spirituality. The next great painter was Francisco de Goya, famous as much for his grotesque and terrible etchings ('The Horrors of War') as for his remarkably candid court portraits. After his death, Spain became an artistic backwater; her most notable modern painter, Picasso, works in France, and her two other major modern artists, Juan Gris and Joan Miró, are closely allied with the school of Paris.

Spanish Civil War. 1936–9. After the victory of the United Front (of republicans, socialists, syndicalists, and communists) in the 1936 elections, the right-wing elements rallied to General Franco, who started a rebellion in Morocco and took his troops to the mainland, where he occupied E. Spain and isolated Madrid. Hitler and Mussolini poured in supplies and some 'volunteers' to help Franco; Britain and France, by pursuing a policy of non-intervention, in effect hamstrung the loyalists, who received (from U.S.S.R. and the volunteer International Brigade) less effective help than the rebels did from the fascist powers. The Franco forces were united; the loyalists had in common only their opposition to fascism; and their political and regional antagonisms added to their handicaps. The war was notable for the tenacity and bravery of both sides, and for the brutality of the Franco forces (◊ *Guernica*). In 1937 the nationalists drove a wedge between the two main republican areas; after taking Madrid in 1939 Franco forced the unconditional surrender of the loyalists and set up the present dictatorship.

Sparta. City-state of ancient Greece, which concentrated on developing its military capacities. The ruling class were trained for war by hard physical discipline; the helots (serfs) who farmed the land had no legal or civil rights and paid tribute to the rulers. Sparta formed the Peloponnesian League, and in the war against Persia fought as the ally of Athens at ◊ *Plataea, Salamis, Thermopylae*; but later the two were rivals, and in the great ◊ *Peloponnesian War* of 431–404 B.C. Sparta defeated Athens and destroyed the Athenian empire. Persia supported the Athenian and Theban rebels, and in return for withdrawal of this support Sparta surrendered the Greek cities in Asia Minor. Thebes, however, defeated Sparta, which was soon conquered by Philip of ◊ *Macedon*.

Spastics ◊ *Paralysis*.

Species ◊ *Biological Classification*.

Spectrohelioscope. Instrument enabling the surface of the ◊ *sun* to be visually examined in light of a very restricted range of wavelength.

SPECTROHELIOGRAPH: Makes a photographic rather than visual recording.

Spectroscopy ◊ *Astronomy*.

Spectrum. Originally, the distorted coloured patch formed by sunlight (white light) after passing through a glass prism; now, more widely, all radiant-energy phenomena classifiable in terms of wavelength. The solar spectrum demonstrates that white light is composed of many shades of colour (for simplicity we think of seven main ones), which are refracted by different amounts depending upon wavelength (◊ *Dispersion*). Spectra from different sources are all characteristic of those sources, and the careful analysis of any spectrum is a useful tool for the identification of the ◊ *elements* present. Special instruments for this purpose are the spectroscope and (for quantitative work) the spectrometer. A modern way of analysing the light source is by means of a diffraction grating. Spectrum analysis has made it possible to learn what elements are present in the stars. ◊ *Radio-astronomy*.

Speenhamland System ◊ *Poor Law*.

Spelling. Orthography, i.e. the written recording of speech sounds. Ideal spelling would always represent any given speech-sound by the same symbol (◊ *Phonetics*), but this is rare, because pronunciation tends to change. The most phonetically spelt European language is Finnish, which went unrecorded until the 16th cent. and

has since undergone no phonetic changes. The ◊ *Romance languages* and the ◊ *Germanic languages* have had more sound-changes than the ◊ *Slavonic languages*; e.g. Czech and Russian spelling is near-phonetic, Italian, Portuguese, Spanish, and Swedish are almost so, French and English extremely unphonetic. Old English and Middle English spelling was fairly phonetic, though chaotic; with the spread of writing in the 15th cent. Caxton and his successors remodelled the spelling to bring it into line with classical originals (e.g. dette > debt, vittles > victuals), making it less phonetic. The growth of literacy encouraged a fixed orthography, which Johnson's *Dictionary* 1755 did much to further. Today both the *Shorter Oxford English Dictionary* (revised 1963) and *Webster's New International Dictionary* (3rd ed. 1962) show a surprising number of alternative spellings. Advocates of spelling reform have included Robert Bridges and Bernard Shaw. ◊ *Alphabet*.

Spermatozoa ◊ *Reproduction*.

Sphagnum. Bog moss, Irish moss, peat moss; a very distinctive genus of mosses, forming dense tussocks in swamps and bogs, esp. on moors. When decayed and compressed it forms sphagnum ◊ *peat*. The leaves are only one cell thick, but contain many dead empty cells, which absorb water: dried sphagnum is very absorbent, holding 10 times as much water as cottonwool. In Ireland and Scotland it was used as a surgical dressing from early times; sterilized sphagnum was used in both world wars.

Sphinx. 1. In Greek legend, daughter of Typhon and the ◊ *Chimaera*; a winged monster with a woman's head and a lion's body, who devoured everyone who could not answer the riddle she propounded: 'What goes first on four feet, then on two, then on three, and is the weaker the more feet it has?' When ◊ *Oedipus* correctly replied 'Man', the sphinx killed herself.

2. In Egypt, a statue of a woman-headed lion, symbolizing benevolent strength; the most famous is the huge sphinx near the Great Pyramid.

Spices. Aromatic fruits, nuts, etc. used for flavouring, perfuming, and pickling, e.g. allspice, aniseed, caraway, cinnamon, cloves, frankincense, ginger, mace, mustard, myrrh, pepper, turmeric, vanilla. The category overlaps with that of the aromatic herbs, but spices are mainly tropical esp. from the W. and E. Indies, S. America, and Africa. From ancient times they were in great demand as meat-preservatives, and in A.D. 408 the ransom of Rome from the Goths was pepper not gold. The spice-trade was a major incentive in the voyages of discovery after the land route to the Far East was closed by the Turks in the mid 15th cent. The immense profits derived from it were an important factor in the early overseas rivalry between England, Spain, France, and the Netherlands. Later, prices were kept high artificially; today, however, spices are no longer essential, owing to the use of refrigeration, and are often replaced by synthetic flavourings.

Spiders. Arthropods of the class *Arachnida*, in 40,000 species, with fossils known from the ◊ *Devonian* system and thus older than the ◊ *insects*, from which they differ in possessing four pairs of walking legs and a pair of leg-like palps, which in the male are used as copulatory organs. Like the ◊ *scorpions*, most have 'lungbooks' in addition to insect-like tracheal breathing tubes. Their unique feature is the possession of abdominal spinnerets which spin ◊ *silk*, used for nest building, fashioning cocoons and webs, and binding prey. The web is used to trap prey, as protection from adverse conditions, as camouflage, and in courtship. Many spiders e.g. ◊ *tarantula* spin no webs but hunt on the ground. Some spiders are blind, although most have some form of eye; some can emit sounds but none is known to hear. Most species are solitary, and all freely devour one another: the new-born separate by a flight ◊ *instinct*, some running away and others becoming airborne by spun-silk gossamer. After mating, the male either dies or is eaten by his mate. Almost all spiders have poison glands, but very few are lethal to man; an exception is the tropical Black Widow. Other members of the *Arachnida* are scorpions, ◊ *mites*, ◊ *ticks*, harvestmen, and king-crabs.

Spinach. *Spinacia oleracea*; a native of the E. Mediterranean, rich in Vitamin C. Not used by the Greeks and Romans, and first mentioned in England in 1568, when it was believed to have medicinal virtues; it was eaten both cooked and in salads.

Spine. The vertebral column (backbone); ◊ *Skeleton*.

Spinet ◊ *Keyboard Instruments.*

Spinning and Weaving. The making of textiles, whether of wool, linen, cotton, or other fibres, remained a hand process until the late 18th cent. when such pioneers as Kay, Hargreaves, Crompton, Arkwright made inventions which brought about increasing mechanization in all the textile industries and led to the rise of a vast factory industry in place of the old household artisan methods. By 1800 the introduction of steam power led to rapid expansion of spinning, though the use of power-looms for weaving developed more slowly. The principles of the processing techniques have remained basically unchanged; the matted fibres are loosened and cleaned, to form a fine web, which is then shaped into a soft continuous rope (sliver) about an inch in diameter, and this is passed through machines which draw the fibres parallel and ensure their uniform distribution; further processes draw out and reduce the sliver which is finally twisted into yarn at the spinning frame. Weaving is similar in principle to darning; lengthwise threads (warp) are interlaced with crosswise (weft) to form a fabric; complicated patterns and coloured effects can be produced by using coloured yarns in combination, with special mechanisms to control the lifting of the warp threads. Modern automatic looms weave at great speed with little supervision: a single weaver may be in charge of 40 or more machines producing simple cloths. Plain cloths of cotton, rayon, etc., may be bleached, dyed, roller-printed, or screen-printed to produce many beautiful effects. Fabrics may also be glazed or treated with synthetic resins or other chemicals to make them resistant to creasing, shrinkage, and fire as well as water-repellent; such processes are usually carried out at a separate finishingworks.

The advent of synthetic fibres has not led to any fundamental changes in manufacture, but rather to a greater variety or blending of materials; even in the manufacture of woollen fabrics there is now a considerable use of synthetics mainly blended with natural wool. Although the extrusion process for making synthetic fibre produces a continuous filament, this is seldom used as such, but is subjected to normal spinning processes. ◊ *Cotton Industry, Rayon, Synthetic Resins.*

Spiritual. Religious folksong, usually in solo-and-refrain form, developed by N. American Negro slaves in the 18th and 19th centuries, generally based on European ⟡ *hymns*. Also, analogous non-Negro American religious folksongs.

Spiritualism. Belief that the spirit or personality of man continues to exist after death and that communication may be established through mediums by such means as trance speaking, automatic writing, and even physical phenomena, e.g. ectoplasm, levitation, and the disturbances caused by poltergeists. Notable spiritualists were Daniel Dunglas Home and Mme Blavatsky. ⟡ *Psychical Research.*

Spleen. Organ on the left side of the stomach, full of veins; it acts as a filter for removing foreign matter and broken-down red cells from the blood, by extracting the haemoglobin and returning it to the bone-marrow for re-use. The spleen was formerly supposed to be the seat of ill-humour, spite, and melancholia; hence 'full of spleen' and 'splenetic'.

Split Personality ⟡ *Schizophrenia.*

Sponges. Members of the phylum Porifera; sessile aquatic animals, attached to the sea bed. Although multicellular, they have not yet been proved to possess specialized coordinating tissues e.g. a nervous or endocrine system. They feed on minute particles suspended in water, which is drawn into their bodies through a large number of small pores and expelled through one or a few large openings.

Spore. Minute, usually one-celled reproductive bodies of plants. In lower plants e.g. ⟡ *algae, fungi, mosses,* spores are liberated into the surrounding air or water and eventually grow into new plants. In seed-bearing plants, spores are both male and female. Only the male spores (pollen grains) are released: the female spores remain on the plant within an ovule (often in cones or flowers) and after fertilization and complex changes, a ⟡ *seed* is produced.

Spring. Water percolates through permeable rock to an impermeable layer, along which it flows underground, to gush out at the surface; or it sinks through fissures and is led to the surface at some distant point. It may sink to a sufficient depth to be heated and emerge as a hot or thermal spring, as commonly in volcanic regions (⟡ *Geyser*) but also e.g. at Bath, Wiesbaden, and other spas.

MINERAL SPRING: Contains a noticeable quantity of mineral matter (other than calcium carbonate or calcium sulphate), sometimes salt, sulphur, or iron (chalybeate springs), with a medicinal value.

Spruce ⟡ *Conifers.*

Sputnik. < Russian, 'fellow-traveller'; first Soviet earth-satellite, launched Oct. 1957. Sputnik I had a total weight of about four tons (including the instrumental sphere, 184 lb.); its orbital period was 96.2 minutes, with an apogee of 512 nautical miles. After orbiting for three months it disintegrated. Sputnik II carried a live dog, whose heartbeats, rate of respiration, and other details were relayed to the ground by radio, for the study of biological hazards in ⟡ *space exploration.*

Square Root. The square root of a number is that number which when multiplied by itself gives N. Thus 9 has two square roots, 3 and −3. There is a systematic method of extracting the square root of a number to any degree of accuracy. There is no square root of any negative number. Nevertheless, the mathematical application of the concept that some 'operator' – it cannot be an ordinary number – is the square root of minus one, has very useful applications in algebra, trigonometry, and particularly in the theory of electricity.

To understand the meaning of 'operator', let us consider the following diagram:

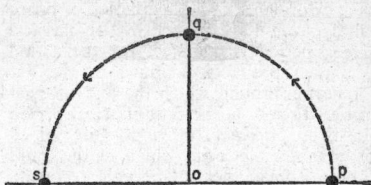

It will be seen that an anti-clockwise rotation through the right angle transforms the power p into the point q. If the operation is repeated, q becomes s. If we denote this operation by i, then the repeated operation at op can be written i.i.op=os, so that if op=1, and hence os =1, we have $i^2 = -1$.

Squash Rackets. A game played in an enclosed court, either as singles or doubles, with rackets and a small rubber ball; originated (⟡ *Rackets*) in the 1870s at Harrow, it was developed by the Queens

Club and the M.C.C. There are open amateur and professional championships, and 'squash' is popular in Canada, S. Africa, Pakistan, Egypt, and also in U.S.A. where the rules are somewhat different. The unofficial international body is the British Squash Rackets Association (1929).

Squid. Popular name for marine cephalopods (◊ *octopus*) of world-wide distribution, mostly aggressive, highly mobile, and carnivorous; a typical squid has a long slender body edged with triangular fins, a short square head with well-developed eyes, and ten arms with rows of suckers underneath for capturing and eating its prey. When in danger it emits an inky fluid (sepia). The giant squid may reach 50 ft in length.

Squirrel. Small rodent common in most parts of the world, with soft thick fur, much used by furriers; there are two main types, the red squirrel (native to Europe) and the N. American grey squirrel. The latter drives out the former when introduced to its habitat e.g. in Britain.

S.S. (Schutz Staffel) ◊ *Nazism, Secret Police.*

Stag. 1. ◊ *Deer.*

2. A speculator who applies for new issues of shares, not to hold as an investment but in the hope of reselling them immediately at a profit.

Stage. Often synonymous with ◊ *theatre*, but strictly the raised acting area on which the performance of a play, ballet, or opera takes place. Its existence in the classical Greek period is disputed, for the action was then probably confined to the flat 'orchestra' around which the audience sat in tiered rows. In the post-classical period the two *paraskene* or wings were joined by a raised platform, which in the more ornate Roman theatres became recognizably like the modern stage. Late medieval and ◊ *Renaissance* times saw the use of a platform or apron stage, projecting into the audience. From the ◊ *Restoration* onwards, the use of wings and movable scenery led to the 'picture stage': the action took place up-stage, and the part between the proscenium and the audience grew smaller. Modern 'flexible staging' means arranging the stage according to the demands of the play, and 'open staging' is a stage open on three sides, not hemmed in by the proscenium; ◊ *theatre-in-the-round* uses no stage at all, but simply an acting area, around which the audience sits.

STAGE SCENERY: Scenery was kept to a minimum by Greeks and Romans, although they used *periaktoi*, revolving prisms with a different scene indication on each face. The open-air theatres of Elizabethan times used only the simplest scenery, but Inigo Jones 1573–1652 was responsible for the decoration of many ◊ *masques* at the English court, and the extensive use of scenery in these performances influenced the indoor or 'private' theatres of the Jacobean period. He was, in fact, reflecting scenic arrangements which had long been fashionable in Italy, where e.g. Palladio, Peruzzi, Serlio, Neroni, and Buontalenti had applied to stage design the techniques of ◊ *perspective*. In effect the Italians developed the picture-frame stage, with the audience on one side only, which was to dominate the theatre for nearly five hundred years. In the 18th cent. the architectural settings of the Renaissance and baroque theatres gave way to landscaped backdrops or domestic interiors; in the 19th, scene-painters supplied a succession of 'cut-outs' and naturalistically painted canvases for e.g. Kemble, Kean, Macready, Irving. Lighting advanced from the concealed and coloured lights of the 16th cent. to the pioneer work in interpretative lighting of Adolphe Appia 1862–1928, who with E. G. Craig virtually founded the modern school of lighting and design, which supports a return to the open and uncluttered acting areas of classical times. 20th-cent. techniques include the revolving stage and the use of gauzes (made opaque or transparent by lighting) to effect rapid scene-changes. In arena theatre and theatre-in-the-round, however, scenery has been dispensed with entirely.

Stained Glass. The use of coloured glass arranged in patterns and held together by lead strips in windows dates to ancient times; the introduction of scenes from life was first made in the 9th cent. in France and Germany, the earliest extant examples being probably of the 11th cent. at Augsburg. The art reached its height in the ◊ *Gothic* cathedrals of the 12th and 13th centuries, and fine examples survive at Chartres, Bourges, Canterbury, and York; it declined in the 14th cent. and was little practised after the 16th till the 19th cent. ◊ *Gothic Revival*, when it tended towards imitativeness and lacked both the simplicity and the jewel-like quality of the medieval craft. A return to medieval principles in the 20th cent. has been much more successful, notably in Coventry cathedral.

Stainless Steel ◇ *Iron*.

Stakhanovite. A worker who considerably and consistently exceeds the work quota and is rewarded with higher wages, privileges, etc. From the Soviet miner Alexei Stakhanov, who regularly exceeded his norm and was held up as a model.

Stalactite. A pendant of limestone hanging from the roof of a cavern. Calcium carbonate is very soluble in water containing carbon dioxide; when such water, at pressure in the cracks of the rock, reaches an opening, the pressure is reduced and some of the lime held in solution is deposited round the opening, gradually forming stalactites, which develop exceedingly slowly and only if there are no air currents.

STALAGMITE: A similar lime stump rising upward as a result of deposits from dripping water; ultimately stalactite and stalagmite meet and form a complete column.

TUFA: Similar lime deposits on cavern sides, often like curtains.

◇ *Calcite, Karst Region*.

Stalingrad. 1942. The turning-point on the Soviet front during the ◇ *Second World War*. The Germans surrounded the city on three sides (the fourth being the Volga) in Aug. 1942, and actually entered it. In some of the fiercest fighting of the war, around and in the town, they were held at bay until the arrival of a relief army under General Zukhov. The Germans were encircled; in Feb. 1943 von Paulus surrendered with the remnants of his army. The Soviet Army went over to the offensive, and gradually drove back all German forces, continuing their advance through Poland and into Germany itself.

Stamen. Male reproductive organ of a ◇ *flower*. Consists of a ◇ *pollen* sac (anther) producing pollen grains, often on a stalk.

Stamp Act. 1765. Introduced by Grenville as a means of making the American colonists contribute to the cost of the ◇ *Seven Years War* by placing a duty on all legal documents. Such a storm of opposition was provoked that the Act had to be repealed, though in order to save its

face the government passed the Declaratory Act declaring its right to tax the colonists.

Star. Mass of gas held together by its own gravitational attraction, the ◇ *sun* being an average example. The diameter of the biggest stars (super giants) is many hundred times that of the sun, and the diameter of the smallest (white dwarfs) about a hundredth of that of the sun. Densities vary enormously. Temperatures and pressures are exceedingly high at the centre of a star, and nuclear reactions there produce the star's light and heat; all stars are emitting energy and consequently losing mass. Temperatures of the outer layers are lower and vary from about 50,000° C for some stars to 2000° C for others. The 'fixed' stars (so called to distinguish them from nearby stars and the planets, whose motion is apparent) are in fact streaming through space at enormous speed, and it is their remoteness that conceals their motion: light from the nearest star takes $4\frac{1}{2}$ years to reach earth, and that from some distant stars millions of years.

BINARY STARS: Most of the stars are single (like the sun), but perhaps as many as a third are double and others are multiple. True binaries are so close together that they are under the influence of each other's gravitational attraction and orbit around a common centre of gravity. In some the separate components can be detected visually by telescope, in others only by spectroscopic methods (◇ *Doppler Effect*).

MAGNITUDE: The apparent magnitude of a star is its observed brightness; its absolute magnitude is its intrinsic brightness irrespective of its distance and is defined as what its brightness would be if it were at a standard distance of 33 light years (10 parsecs). Thus the sun has an apparent brightness some 10,000 m. times that of Aldebaran, but its absolute brightness is only about one 100th. Determination of the apparent magnitude of a star is still based on Ptolemy's method of dividing the then visible stars into six magnitudes according to their apparent brightness, the brightest being called 1st magnitude and the faintest 6th magnitude.

NOVAE: These 'new' stars, one or two of which are detected each year in our ◇ *Galaxy*, are really existing faint stars which suddenly blow off a shell of matter and within hours increase many thousand-fold in brightness; they then gradually decrease in brightness to the original level. Supernovae are exceptionally bright novae, which may increase more than 100 m. times in brightness. Three have been recorded in the ◊ *Milky Way*, the Crab ◊ *nebula* (1054), Tycho's Star (1572), and Kepler's Star (1604).

SPECTRAL CLASSIFICATION: Spectra of the great majority of stars consist of a continuous band of radiation from the near ultraviolet through the conventional colours of the rainbow to the infrared. This 'continuum' is crossed by dark lines and bands caused by gases in the stars' outer layers, which not only enable the gases to be identified but also give information about the temperature and pressure of the stellar atmospheres. Our knowledge of stars comes mainly from the study of their spectra.

STAR CLUSTERS: Astronomical photographs show two distinct types of star cluster. The 400 or so galactic clusters in the spiral arms of the Milky Way consist of comparatively few stars, which are relatively close together and are assumed to have a common origin; the ◊ *Pleiades* is the best-known example. The very distant globular clusters, of which about 100 are known, contain several hundred thousand stars and show a high degree of spherical symmetry; the two brightest are just visible to the naked eye from the southern hemisphere.

VARIABLE STARS: Most stars are nearly constant in appearance and brightness, but some vary, e.g. the sun shows slight variations during its 11-year sunspot cycle. The variation may be so great that a star is visible at maximum brightness and invisible at minimum. Some stars e.g. novae vary irregularly, and others (of which the Cepheid variables are best known) pulsate with complete regularity.

Starch. A ◊ *carbohydrate* of formula $(C_6H_{10}O_5)_n$ which is an important constituent of many foods derived from plant sources; usually extracted from rice, potatoes, or maize. 'Soluble' starch is specially treated to make it water-soluble. When starch is hydrolyzed, e.g. by ◊ *enzymes* in the digestive juices, the simple sugar glucose $C_6H_{12}O_6$ is formed, and this is easily assimilated by the body. Starch is used as a source of glucose (and alcohol by fermentation from this), in laundry work, and for making paste. A simple test

for starch is the intense blue colour that it gives with ◊ *iodine*.

Starfish. Common marine *Echinodermata*, structurally intermediate between ◊ *sea-urchins* and sea-stars (*asteroidea*), slow-moving, with a very simple nervous system; they feed on molluscs e.g. mussels, which they pull apart. Echinoderms have a number of unique features e.g. their method of locomotion, a water-vascular system drawing water from the sea through the sieve-plate and using it to extend the tube-feet, which have terminal suckers.

State. 1. The authority at the apex of a body politic whose function it is to regulate public affairs and to promote the general temporal well-being of the citizens of the territory within its jurisdiction. **2.** A fully self-governing political unit having rights and obligations in ◊ *international law*. **3.** A regional government having a measure of independent law-making authority in certain federal systems, e.g. New York State.

◊ *Federalism, Parliament,* etc.

Statistics. The compilation of numerical records; also the technique for computation and sampling. The general purpose is to compare past performance with present trends and to 'project' future trends. A familiar statistical concept is the arithmetic mean, i.e. the average value for a group of observations (e.g. mean rainfall for a given month over a period of years). Much of the theory of statistics is based upon the assumption that the frequency in the occurrence of events which happen at random will follow a definite pattern fairly closely, e.g. if a record is kept of the series made by throwing four dice a very large number of times, then the frequency-patterns of the various totals at each throw will all bear a close resemblance; the larger the number of throws, the more closely will the frequency-pattern approximate.

All governments maintain organizations to collect statistics. In the U.K. a Central Statistical Office was set up in 1940 to provide a comprehensive statistical service on economic and financial matters. The availability of statistics is an important tool in ◊ *economic planning*, in estimating ◊ *population* trends, and in many aspects of insurance. ◊ *Automatic Data Processing*.

Statute of Westminster ◊ *British Commonwealth of Nations.*

Statutory Instrument. A form of delegated legislation; ◊ *Administrative Law, By-laws.*

Steam-engine. Piston-driven engine, in which the force exerted by steam moves the piston; it was the first practical source of mechanical power, apart from water wheels or windmills, which were limited to special localities. Throughout the 18th cent. all the early designs of engine were introduced to pump water from mines. The early engines of Savery and Newcomen were superseded by the Watt beam-engines, in which higher steam pressures were used. The steam engine provided the first power-unit which could be mounted on wheels, and led both to the ◊ *railway* locomotive (George Stephenson) and to ◊ *steamships* (Robert Fulton). It provided the essential power-plant for the ◊ *Industrial Revolution*; now it is being superseded by steam ◊ *turbines, internal combustion engines, electric motors.* ◊ *Boiler, Pumps.*

Steamship. The first experiments in applying steam power for ship propulsion came at the end of the 18th cent. A boat propelled by a jet of water generated by steam attained a speed of 4 m.p.h. on the Potomac (U.S.A.) 1787; Symington demonstrated the first steamer in Britain 1788, and his *Charlotte Dundas*, launched 1802, was used as a tug. Fulton's famous *Clermont* covered the 150 m. from New York to Albany in 30 hours, 1807. Henry Bell's *Comet* started the earliest regular steamship service (on the Clyde) 1812, and shortly afterwards steamships were used on the Atlantic. The early steamships used paddlewheels, but these were displaced by the screw propeller; the first large screw-driven ship to cross the Atlantic was the *Great Britain,* 1845. With the coming of iron ships, steam rapidly supplanted sail. As to speed, the *Servia* in 1881 made the Atlantic crossing in seven days; the fastest modern liners have reduced this to something under four days. Early steamships had simple expansion engines, which evolved into the more efficient compound-expansion and triple-expansion engines, the latter still being common. Steam turbines, first installed by Parsons in the *Turbinia* 1894, came into general use in large vessels and permit the development of enormous horse-power. The first ocean craft to use Diesel engines was the Danish *Selandia* 1912; diesels have since become increasingly favoured for engines of up to 20,000 h.p. In other vessels oil has largely superseded coal as fuel. Whilst nuclear power has been used esp. for specialized purposes (esp. in submarines), it has not yet been shown to be economic for commercial vessels. ◊ *Shipping.*

Steel ◊ *Bessemer Process, Blast Furnace, Iron and Steel Industry, Metallurgy, Siemens-Martin Process.*

Stem. The main aerial axis of a ◊ *plant,* which supports the leaves and reproductive structures and conducts water and mineral salts to them, and carries food materials from the leaves to other parts of the plant. Stems are kept erect in various ways. Trees and shrubs are supported entirely by masses of xylem (◊ *Wood*). Most herbaceous dicotyledonous plant stems have an outer cylinder of vascular tissue with pith or a hollow in the centre. When stems are cut, callus (usually corky tissue) grows out over the wound. In pruning, branches should be cut off the main stem; otherwise the stumps, which die when not supplied with food, will decay before the wound is healed, and decay may extend back into the centre and kill the tree. Similarly, twigs should be pruned near a bud. Vegetative reproduction by stems is common, e.g. underground stems (◊ *rhizomes*) and runners which root at the nodes (strawberry, mint, couch grass). Some rhizomes are also storage structures (iris, ginger), as are tubers (potato) and corms (crocus). Some aerial stems also store food, e.g. the sago palm. Water-storage is common in the stems of succulents. Stems may also be protective and modified into spines (gorse).

Steppes. Generally treeless, grassy plains extending over the lower Danube basin and in a broad belt over S. European Russia and SW Siberia, with a climate resembling that of the ◊ *prairies* and ◊ *pampas,* i.e. high annual range of temperature and light rainfall largely in spring and early summer. One of the world's main wheat-growing areas, e.g. the Ukraine (◊ *Black Earth*), where the soil has a high humus content, and is esp. fertile and productive. ◊ *Agriculture.*

Sterility. Inability to produce offspring. In both plants and animals it may be caused by changes of environment or by hybridization, and interbreeding at first impairs and finally precludes reproduction; in man it may result from disease (esp. venereal), malformation of organs, hormone disturbances, or exposure to radiation (◊ *Fallout*).

Sterilization. Deprivation of the power of ◊ *reproduction*, without removal of the ability for sexual intercourse. (a) Female: normally by tying the Fallopian tubes, thus preventing spermatozoa from reaching the ovaries; (b) male: a simple operation to block the passage of spermatozoa from the testis to the seminal vesicles.

In English law, sterilization on eugenic grounds is virtually prohibited, being held contrary to the public interest. For the insane, feeble-minded, and epileptic it is legal in a number of non-Catholic countries, esp. Scandinavia and some States in U.S.A. In Denmark, it may be carried out at the individual's express wish, if he or she is a possible carrier of mental abnormality.

Sterling Area. Those countries which hold their currency reserves in London and conduct their international trade in sterling, including Australia, India, New Zealand, Pakistan, S. Africa.

Sterling Balances. U.K. net liabilities to overseas countries; amounted to about £500 m. in 1939 but had risen to £3600 m. in 1945 as a result of the war, and has subsequently reached slightly over £4000 m. of which £2700 m. is held by ◊ *Sterling Area* countries.

Stewart Architecture. The style began with Inigo Jones's Palladio-inspired Queen's House at Greenwich and Banqueting House in Whitehall (◊ *Palladian Style*),

Queen's House, Greenwich

and was continued by John Webb, Sir Roger Pratt, and Hugh May; the great architect of the latter part of the period was Christopher Wren, and apart from his numerous London churches examples of the style in churches are rare. Most Stewart architecture is domestic and influenced by Holland. The country houses, of which many survive, are usually simple tall brick buildings with dormered roofs, ornamented only by elaborate stone mouldings around the main doors and windows and occasionally by pediments or Dutch gables on the main façade, Belton House in Lincolnshire being one of the best surviving examples; they are distinguished by very rich interiors, with both wood carving (Grinling Gibbons) and stucco.

Stewarts. The Stewart family, whose name derived from their office of hereditary stewards to the king of ◊ *Scotland*, succeeded to the Scottish throne in 1371, and (by descent from Henry VII, ◊ *Tudors*) ruled both Scotland and England 1603–49, Scotland alone 1651–60, and both kingdoms 1660–88 (◊ *English Civil Wars, Glorious Revolution*). The French spelling Stuart was used by Mary Queen of Scots, half French by birth and briefly Queen of France. After the deposition of James II his daughter Mary and nephew William of Orange, in a dual monarchy, ruled both kingdoms, as did James's second daughter Anne, on whose death the crowns passed to her distant cousin the king of ◊ *Hanover*. James's son the Old Pretender and grandson the Young Pretender continued to claim the throne; ◊ *Jacobites*.

Stigma ◊ *Carpel, Flower.*

Stock Exchange. Market for buying and selling ◊ *stocks and shares*; the earliest, that in London, began in the 17th cent., when the government and trading companies first began to raise money by public subscription and 'stock jobbers' met in the Royal Exchange and in City coffee-houses to act as brokers. In 1773 a special building, the Stock Exchange, was acquired. Today there are about 3500 members, of two sorts: the 2800 brokers act for individuals, and the 700 jobbers act as wholesalers in securities and do not deal with the public. Transactions between brokers and jobbers are simply recorded in notebooks, the Stock Exchange motto being *Dictum Meum Pactum*, my word is my bond. The London Stock Exchange list about 9000 different securities with a nominal value of £50,000 m. and a survey in 1962 showed about 3.5 m. individual investors in the U.K. Roughly one half of all investments are held by 'institutional investors': insurance companies, building and friendly societies, trade unions, investment trusts, etc. Other important stock exchanges are Paris, Brussels, Amsterdam, and New York (which now transacts more business than any other and is subject to laws administered by the Federal Securities and Exchange Commission).

Stocks and Shares. Investments of various types; stocks include government and municipal securities and the loan debt of commercial companies, and the interest on them is fixed, while shares are of two basic kinds, (a) ordinary shares (sometimes called common stock or equities), which specifically risk capital and on which interest fluctuates with the fortunes of the company; (b) preference shares, the holders of which are entitled to receive their dividends, usually fixed, as a prior charge against any profits. Holders of ordinary shares may vote at the company's annual general meeting, but not holders of preference shares. Other funds lent to a company (rather than invested in it, as ordinary shares) are classed as debentures and loan stock. These have a claim prior to that of preference shares against the assets of a company if it goes out of business. ⟡ *Stock Exchange, Investment Trusts.*

Stoicism. A philosophy founded by Zeno in the 4th cent. B.C. and probably the principal comprehensive philosophy of the Graeco-Roman world; its basic ethical doctrine was that man's purpose, happiness, is to be achieved through a life in which all desires are subordinated to virtue, by living in accord with the ruling force of the universe, *logos,* cosmic reason. Nevertheless it does attach some value to the realization of natural desires, unlike ⟡ *Cynicism* (which influenced it greatly).

Stone Ages ⟡ *Mesolithic, Neolithic, Palaeolithic.*

Stonecrop. Common name of the genus *Sedum*; originally, the yellow Sedum acre, native to Britain. All sedums have fleshy leaves, and many exotic species are cultivated. *S. anglicum* was a Saxon remedy for 'foot addle' (gout).

Stonehenge. Prehistoric stone circle on Salisbury Plain in Wiltshire, surrounded by a low bank with outer ditch, consisting of an outer circle of ⟡ *sarsen* stones, an inner circle of smaller bluestones, and two central horseshoes, the outer composed of massive sarsen trilithons (pairs of stones each supporting a lintel) and the inner of bluestones. The technical achievement of the whole is remarkable: the horizontal stones are fitted to the uprights of the sarsen circle by mortise-and-tenon joints, and the uprights have entasis (a slight convexity) to correct the distortion of perspective. The bluestones were almost certainly brought from Pembrokeshire, probably part of the way by sea, and the monument was built and altered over a period of several centuries. The earliest stage (the surrounding bank and ditch) was constructed in late ⟡ *Neolithic* times about 1900–1700 B.C. The ⟡ *Beaker People* were associated with a double bluestone circle, later dismantled and incorporated into the more ambitious final version, constructed between 1600 and 1400 B.C. and associated with the early ⟡ *Bronze Age* Wessex culture, whose people are known to have had trade contacts with ⟡ *Mycenae.* It has been suggested that some elements in the conception of Stonehenge stemmed ultimately from the Mycenaean world, and even that a wandering Mycenaean architect may have supervised the building.

'Stones' ⟡ *Calculus (2), Gallstones.*

Storm Troopers ⟡ *Nazism.*

Strategy. The general direction of military operations: the art of bringing an enemy to battle under the most favourable conditions. In its modern sense the word was first used by writers at the end of the 18th cent. In his *Précis de l'Art de Guerre* Jomini laid down the broad divisions of strategy, but in his subsequent analysis of Napoleon's campaigns he was often at fault. Klausewitz's *Vom Kriege,* 1831, exerted much influence on military thinking, but his precepts were frequently misinterpreted. In its broad principles strategy should in theory remain unaffected even though weapons and ⟡ *tactics* change, since the art of the commander is concerned with a general plan of campaign, the choice of major objectives, the selection of bases and lines of communication, and the combination of surprise and concentration of superior forces, at a time and place of his choosing, with the object of overcoming the enemy's will to resist. The term 'grand strategy' is sometimes applied to the overall plan of war, which calls for close cooperation between the military command and political leaders and for the organization of the morale, resources, and industry of a nation as a whole.

Strawberry ◊ *Fruit (Soft Fruits)*.

Strike. Refusal of employees to work, with the aim of securing rectification of grievances. The right of workers to combine in trade unions was long opposed. In the second half of the 19th cent. there were many strikes both in Europe and U.S.A. esp. in the coal-mining and iron-and-steel industries, and in the railways. Most strikes have as their objective improvements in wages or hours, but some occur over demarcation disputes e.g. when a trade union claims a certain type of operation as its particular preserve; prolonged strikes have been the exception since the end of the Second World War. The number of days lost by strikes varies considerably in different countries, as do the conciliation procedures provided by law. In communist countries the right to strike is not recognized, and trade unions bear little resemblance to their counterparts in other countries. ◊ *Arbitration, General Strike, Trade Union*.

Stringed Instruments. Apart from ◊ *keyboard instruments* with strings, three classes may be distinguished. (a) Instruments with open strings only, each note having its own string, e.g. harp, lyre, and also the dulcimer group (e.g. the Hungarian cimbalom), which are essentially harps laid flat and played with hammers. Harps are of ancient origin and dominated the music of Mesopotamia and Egypt, but the modern concert harp, with a mechanism shortening the strings (and thus raising the pitch), dates only to the early 19th cent. (b) Instruments in which the pitch of the strings is raised by manual 'stopping' while the other hand sets the strings vibrating either directly or by means of a plectrum, e.g. guitar, lute, banjo, Japanese *samisen*. (c) Instruments in which the pitch of the strings is raised by manual 'stopping' but which are played by a horsehair bow. The violin, viola, violoncello ('cello), and double-bass (the string basis of the European orchestra) are called the 'violin family'; from 1700 they gradually superseded the earlier 'viol family' (e.g. viola da braccio, viola d'amore, viola da gamba), which differed in having frets across the fingerboard and a flat back, and whose tone is

softer and less brilliant and versatile than the violin's.

Strontium. A scarce readily oxidized alkaline earth metallic element, which occurs in strontianite and celestine; its properties are similar to those of ◊ *barium*, and it has little use except in pyrotechnics (for crimson colour). It is readily assimilated and incorporated into bone, where it is retained; hence the danger of ingestion of strontium 90, a radioactive ◊ *fall-out* product from nuclear fission, which contaminates grass and can be a danger (esp. to children) from the milk of cows using such pasture.

Strychnine. Alkaloid obtained from the seeds of *Strychnos nux vomica*, an Indian tree; although a poison it was once used in tonic medicines.

Stuarts ◊ *Stewarts*.

Student Christian Movement. Body of British university students who desire to understand the Christian faith and live the Christian life, closely associated with the World Student Christian Federation; it includes members from most Christian churches (except the Roman Catholic), works through conferences and study circles, and has given its name to an important religious publishing house.

Sturgeon. Bony fish found in temperate seas and rivers of the N. hemisphere, in about 20 species; they show a mixture of primitive features and a tendency for the bony structure of the skeleton to be replaced by cartilage. One species is found in Britain, where by an act of Edward II it is a royal fish. The largest species is the beluga, found mainly in the Caspian Sea, where it may attain a weight of a ton. The eggs (caviare) are an expensive delicacy, the flesh is eaten (similar to salmon), and ◊ *isinglass* is obtained from the air-bladders.

Sturm und Drang. Storm and Stress; a late 18th-cent. German literary movement, named after von Klinger's play of 1776, stressing the claims of feeling and intuition (◊ *Romanticism*) as against the rationalism of the ◊ *Enlightenment*, and including the young Goethe, Herder, Jakob Lenz, von Klinger, Heinrich Leopold Wagner, and Schiller. The favourite literary form of the *Sturm und Drang* writers was ◊ *tragedy*, and their favourite aesthetic quality the sublime; their intuitionist and psychological approach to literature helped to direct critical attention to the origins and nature of language, the nature of human expression and communication, and therefore to ◊ *folk literature*.

Styx ◊ *Cerberus, Hades*.

Subatomic Particles. Particles of matter, smaller than the ◊ *atom*, thought to be the fundamental particles from which all matter is formed. The chief of these are ◊ *electrons*, which orbit round the ◊ *nucleus* of the atom, and ◊ *protons* and ◊ *neutrons*, which form the nucleus. (Photons, the fundamental units of ◊ *radiation*, sometimes described as particles, are strictly quanta of energy.) Since the beginnings of atomic physics many other forms of subatomic particles have been produced and discovered. Some are in existence only for a minute fraction of a second; some (e.g. electron and proton) are stable. The paths of subatomic particles may be detected by such devices as the cloud chamber, the bubble chamber, and the spark chamber.

Subjectivism. In ◊ *ethics* and ◊ *aesthetics*, the view (comparable to the opinion that 'beauty is in the eye of the beholder') that making a value judgement is merely the expression of an attitude. In philosophy (◊ *Phenomenalism, Idealism*), the view that qualities of physical objects amount to our subjective sense impressions.

Sublimation. The process, according to Freudian theory, whereby the psychological energy necessary for the 'higher' human activities is obtained by deflecting energy away from primitive instinctive outlets, esp. sexual ones. Thus sexual impulses may be sublimated in art, the maternal instinct in social work, aggression in competitive games, etc.

Sublime Porte ◊ *Ottoman Empire*.

Submarines. Experiments with submersible craft can be traced back to the first practical submarine built by Drebbel, a Dutchman, about 1620, made watertight with leather and propelled by oars. More effective was Robert Fulton's *Nautilus* (early 19th cent.) which could remain submerged for six hours, using first an air tube and later a tank of compressed air. In the American Civil War the Confederates employed a number of submarines; one of them managed to blow up a Union vessel but was herself destroyed by the explosion. The modern submarine was developed at the beginning of the 20th cent. by two Americans,

Holland and Lake, who used petrol engines for surface propulsion and electric motors under water. All naval powers recognized their potentialities esp. the Germans, who used them in large numbers in both world wars, concentrating upon sinking merchant shipping. Despite new weapons e.g. depth-charges and locating devices, developed to counter the U-boats, the allies and neutrals lost 4770 ships to submarines in the Second World War. A German development now in general use is the schnorkel, to draw fresh air into the vessel without surfacing. Internal-combustion engines and electric motors are now being superseded by nuclear power, which does not consume air and can be used during submersion. Nuclear submarines can remain on patrol submerged for several weeks at a time.

Subpoena. An order to a witness to attend at a specified place and time to give evidence, under penalty ('*sub poena*') of punishment for contempt of court if he does not do so.

Succulents ◊ *Cactus, Euphorbiaceae*.

Sucrose ◊ *Carbohydrates, Lactose*.

Sudan. Area 976,750 sq. m. Pop. 12.1 m. (Muslim and largely Arab in the N., Christian and Negro in the S.) Cap. Khartoum. African republic, S. of Egypt. The legislature is a Central Council partly elected and partly nominated by the Army Council.

ECONOMY. Agricultural; main export crop cotton. Also gum arabic (the bulk of the world's supply), groundnuts, livestock, millet, oilseeds. The Sennar Dam on the Blue Nile irrigates the Gezira Scheme, which produces high-quality long-staple cotton. Two important new dams are under construction.

HISTORY. After 1899, the Sudan was administered by a Governor-General as a condominium of Britain and ◊ *Egypt*. This was reaffirmed in the 1936 Treaty, but by the 1953 Agreement the Sudan was guaranteed self-determination, and a House of Representatives was elected which in 1955 voted unanimously for independent sovereignty. In 1958 the Sudanese army seized control by a coup d'état. ◊ *Mahdi*.

Sudd. Tightly packed mass of floating reeds, papyrus, and other aquatic plants and vegetation, on the main stream of the upper Nile; seriously impedes navigation, sometimes forming a mass 20 m. long and

20 ft thick, strong enough to support an elephant.

Sudetenland. An area in Czechoslovakia bordering on Germany, previously part of Austria-Hungary, which in 1919 contained about 3 m. German-speaking people. After the Nazis obtained power they instituted intensive propaganda amongst the Sudeten Germans to press for union with Germany. This was achieved by the ◊ *Munich Pact* 1938. After the Second World War the Sudetenland was returned to Czechoslovakia, who expelled the German-speaking population.

Suez Canal. Built by a largely French company on plans by de Lesseps, and opened in 1869, to connect the Mediterranean with the Red Sea, enabling ships to reach the East without rounding Africa. The British Government under Disraeli bought a controlling interest in 1875. The canal, which includes dredged passages through lakes, is 100 m. long with a minimum depth of 84 ft. The average time of passage is 12 hours.

In the ◊ *First World War* Turkish attempts to reach the canal were repulsed; in the ◊ *Second World War* it was the strategic objective of the German N. African campaign, and was at times blocked by German bombing. Nationalization of the canal by President Nasser of ◊ *Egypt* was announced on 26 July 1956, and after a period of negotiations to secure the rights of users, a Franco-British invasion of the Canal Zone took place in Oct. shortly after ◊ *Israel* had launched an attack on Egypt. Intervention by the United Nations led to a cease-fire, and by Dec., U.N. troops had replaced the Franco-British forces. Meanwhile the canal had been blocked by the Egyptians; it was cleared by the U.N. during 1957, and compensation was paid to the shareholders at the rate originally suggested by President Nasser, i.e. the Paris Stock Exchange closing prices for the Company's shares on 26 July.

Suffragette Movement. The demand for the enfranchisement of women and their representation in Parliament goes back to the late 18th cent. and during the 19th cent. was supported by such important figures as Cobden, J. S. Mill, and Disraeli. By the first decade of the 20th cent. the movement took an extreme form in the demonstrations of Mrs Pankhurst and her daughters, e.g. burning letter-boxes, assaulting prominent opponents, and breaking windows; this, however, won little sympathy from the public. More effective work was done by the National Union of Suffrage Societies. The First World War, though it brought the campaign to an end, gave obvious justification for the suffragettes' demands by demonstrating the extent to which women could undertake work previously done only by men, and in 1918 a Bill allowing women of 30 to vote and to sit in Parliament was passed with little opposition. Lady Astor was the first woman to take her seat in the House of Commons. A parallel movement in the U.S. gave women the vote in 1920. In the U.K. women of 21 were enfranchised 1929.

Sufis. < Ar. *suf*, wool (because of their rough woollen garments); Mohammedan mystics who seek union with Allah by ascetic and other special devotional practices, including religious dances, and organized in orders whose members are known as faqirs or dervishes. The claims of some to have reached a state of near-identity with the divinity led in certain cases to their persecution as heretics; some are honoured by Mohammedans as saints. Outstanding were al-Ghazali, the Persian mystical poet 1059–1111; Hallaj, executed 922; Ibn Arabi 1165–1240, who influenced Dante; and al-Jilani, d. 1166. ◊◊ *Gnostics, Mysticism.*

Sugar. Originated in the East and was known to the Romans. In Europe it remained a scarce imported luxury during the Middle Ages. The Arabs introduced the sugar-cane to the Near East, and the Portuguese disseminated it throughout the tropics in the 15th cent. At about the same time a method of making sugar from beet-root was discovered in Germany. The wide cultivation of sugar-cane led to its becoming a cheap and popular food; it is widely produced in semi-tropical countries: large exporters are Cuba, U.S.A., and Brazil. Sugar is made from both sugar-cane and ◊ *sugarbeet* by somewhat similar processes of crushing and refining, which also result in various by-products e.g. ◊◊ *Molasses.*

Chemistry of sugar: ◊ *Carbohydrates.*

Sugarbeet. A ◊ *root crop* developed by selective breeding to have a high sugar content, in modern varieties as high as 20 per cent; the sugar is extracted from the chopped roots, and when dried the remaining pulp forms a feed of almost as high feeding value as oats, while the 'tops' (leafy parts) are cut off at harvest and also form a useful feed. Sugarbeet provides about one half of the world's requirements of sugar and is extensively grown in France, Germany, Russia, U.S.A., and to some extent in the U.K. (East Anglia). The garden or red beet is a near relative: both have been bred from the wild *Beta vulgaris*, a plant common in coastal areas of Europe.

Suicide. Until recently although suicide in some societies, e.g. ancient Rome, modern Japan, was considered honourable, in England it was a ◊ *felony*. Under the Suicide Act 1961 it is now, however, no longer a crime to commit or attempt to commit suicide. The survivor of a suicide pact who kills the other party is nevertheless guilty of manslaughter, and a person who encourages another's suicide is also guilty of an offence punishable by up to 14 years' imprisonment. The British suicide rate is fairly constant at about 5000 annually.

Suite. A piece of music composed in several movements but not corresponding to one of the supposedly closer-knit forms e.g. symphony, concerto. In the 17th and 18th centuries, e.g. in Bach and Handel, the suite was characterized by the inclusion of dance-forms e.g. *allemande* and *gigue*. Later, the suite was increasingly made up of a selection of movements arranged from a ◊ *ballet* or ◊ *opera* (e.g. Tchaikovsky's *Nutcracker Suite*).

Sulphonamides. Drugs useful in combating several bacterial diseases (pneumonia, meningitis, dysentery) by their action in preventing the growth of bacteria. They developed from the observed anti-bacterial effect of a dye-stuff, prontosil red, first used in 1935.

Sulphur. A solid non-metallic yellow ◊ *element* ('brimstone'). Found in the craters or crevices of active or extinct volcanoes, or bedded with layers of ◊ *gypsum* on salt domes (where it is often associated with ◊ *petroleum* deposits). An essential constituent of many animal and vegetable substances e.g. ◊ *protein*. It was first recognized as a natural element in 1777 by Lavoisier. Common (rhombic) sulphur, the allotrope stable at ordinary temperatures, changes at 98.6° C into the other common allotrope, prismatic sulphur; there is also an elastic plastic form, ob-

tained by pouring liquid sulphur into water. All forms revert to rhombic when kept at room temperature. Sulphur burns in air to give sulphur dioxide gas (SO_2) which when passed over heated vanadium catalysts, with more air, is converted to the solid trioxide (SO_3); the oxides dissolve in water to give respectively sulphurous (H_2SO_3) and sulphuric (H_2SO_4) acids, the latter being manufactured in enormous quantities all over the world as one of the cheapest and most useful industrial chemicals, used for making fertilizers, celluloid, dyes, rayon, accumulators, and in the explosives, petroleum, paper, and chemical industries. Sulphuric acid consumption is a significant indication of a nation's industrial activity. Sulphur itself is used as a fungicide, an insecticide, and a plant food, in the rubber industry, and in pharmacy. Sulphur dioxide gas (also available in liquefied form) is used for the preparation of sulphites and bisulphites (for papermaking), for fumigating and bleaching, and for the preparation of sodium thiosulphate (photographers' 'hypo'). Sulphur combines with ◊ *hydrogen* to produce the unpleasant-smelling gas hydrogen sulphide H_2S, an important chemical reagent. The organic chemistry of sulphur includes the manufacture of many valuable dyes, detergents, drugs, and lubricants. The chief sources of supply of mined sulphur are the Gulf States of U.S.A. (45 per cent) and the Etna region in Sicily (4 per cent); further large deposits recently discovered in Poland are being exploited, and large quantities are obtained from the hydrogen sulphide that occurs in the natural gas at Lacq in S. France.

Sumerians. The earliest civilized people of Mesopotamia, non-Semitic, originally from the Iranian plateau, who settled in S. Mesopotamia in the 5th millennium B.C. Their earliest culture is called Ubaid, from the main site at the head of the Persian Gulf. The demands and opportunities of an irrigation economy led to a remarkably rapid development of literate urban civilization, fully established about 3500 B.C. The plough, the potter's wheel, and the chariot were used, and the Sumerians had wide contacts e.g. with the ◊ *Indus civilization* and invented ◊ *cuneiform* writing; the most conspicuous feature of their cities was the ziggurat, an artificial hill containing a temple and storehouses, the centre of their economy. Dynastic Sumer's chief cities were the capital Ur, Erech (Uruk), and Kish. A great flood, perhaps that of the ◊ *Bible*, is prominent in Sumerian legend. The Akkadians in 2350 B.C. established Semitic rule over both Akkad and Sumer; under the 3rd dynasty Sumerian rule was briefly revived at Ur, but fell to the Elamites and then to ◊ *Babylon*.

LANGUAGE. Not one of the ◊ *Indo-European languages*, Sumerian is the most ancient of all recorded languages and unrelated to any other known tongue; although it ceased to be used after the 3rd Ur dynasty, ancient cuneiform texts were copied for educational and religious purposes until the Christian era. Agglutinative in type, it had no finite verbs : Rawlinson and others deciphered it from dictionaries made by the Akkadians. ◊ *Gilgamesh*.

Summit Conference. 1955. Meeting between President Eisenhower (U.S.A.), Mr Khrushchev (U.S.S.R.), Sir Anthony Eden (U.K.), and M. Faure (France) to discuss German reunification, disarmament, and related problems. Its main success was that it ended amicably with provision for a fuller meeting of Foreign Ministers.

Sun. The sun is a sphere of gas held together by its own gravitational attraction. It contains neither solid nor liquid matter. The gas is almost entirely in atomic form, although a few molecules are present in its outermost layers. Solar energy is produced by nuclear processes in its central regions, where the conversion of ◊ *hydrogen* into ◊ *helium* takes place at a steady rate, at a temperature of about 20,000,000° C. This energy slowly filters to the outside of the star and escapes into space in the form of heat and light.

The effective 'surface' of the sun that we see is known as the photosphere and has a temperature of about 6000° C. Photographs of this taken under optimum conditions show the photosphere as having a changing, mottled appearance. This granulation is the outward evidence of turbulence in the solar surface. Above the photosphere is a thin layer of gas, the chromosphere, which may be considered as the solar atmosphere, also in turbulent movement. It was first observed at solar ◊ *eclipses*, when its red appearance gave it its name. It has a thickness of some thousands of miles. As light from the sun streams through the relatively cool gases of the chromosphere, absorption lines characteristic of the individual gases are imprinted on it. These are the ◊ *Fraunhofer lines* which enable us to identify the gases and ions present in the solar surface.

Above the chromosphere and spreading far out into space is the corona, whose light comes from highly excited rarefied gases and also contains sunlight scattered from dust particles and electrons. The coronal temperature is of the order of 1,000,000° C. It forms an impressive sight at total eclipses of the sun.

SUNSPOTS: These are dark areas to be seen on the photosphere which are not fully understood. They are of all sizes up to 20,000 miles in diameter and are transient phenomena, having lifetimes usually of days, although large ones have lasted several months. The study of sunspot lifetimes is confused by the unequal rotation of the sun, which not being that of a solid body is about 25 days at the equator and about 29 days near the ◊ *poles*. The number and distribution of sunspots varies over a cycle of 11 years, and at a minimum the surface of the sun may be clear of spots.

When the sun is examined by means of a spectroheliograph or ◊ *spectrohelioscope* its surface appears quite different from pictures of the photosphere. In particular, if it is examined in the wavelength emitted by ◊ *hydrogen* we see the distribution of this gas above the photosphere. The sunspots are still dark against the background, but large areas called *flocculi* appear bright.

On spectroheliograms, prominences are also to be seen. These are enormous masses of gas high above the photosphere. They show as dark lines or patches on the surface of the solar disc or as bright clouds above it. Some prominences are static and long-lived, but others have rapid and continuous movement which is appreciable to visual observation inside a few minutes.

The spectrohelioscope shows a further transient phenomenon of flares or eruptions. Occasionally, in red hydrogen light, an intensely bright spot may develop within a few minutes and then die away again. Such spots are usually associated with active sunspot groups. What they are is not certain, but they may be considered as gigantic explosions on the sun. When they take place, strong ultraviolet radiation is emitted simultaneously with the visible radiation; both reach the earth at the same time. This ultraviolet light affects the D-layer (one of the gas layers in the earth's upper atmosphere) and causes a radio fadeout. One to two days later, further radio interference occurs, as well as magnetic storms and ♢ *auroras*, when ionized particles, shot out from the eruption and travelling much more slowly than the radiation, impinge on the earth's atmosphere.

In addition to giving out ultraviolet light, visible light, and infrared radiation, the sun also emits X-rays (very short wavelength) and radio waves (long wavelength). As the X-rays are absorbed in the upper atmosphere, they have to be studied by means of rockets and satellites. They are always present, but become stronger when flares occur. They are associated with the inner corona rather than the sun itself. Some radio radiation too is always emitted from the 'quiet' sun, but during flares or other solar activity it greatly increases. ♢ *Solar System*.

Sundial. Device for telling time from the sun's shadow cast by an arm (gnomon) on a plate marked in hours. It measures apparent solar time: to obtain mean time, allowance has to be made for ♢ *longitude* and the equation of time. The forerunners of sundials were merely upright stones or poles, conveniently placed for measuring their time-revealing shadows. Later, pyramids and obelisks were used. Sundials as such were probably developed in ancient Egypt and Mesopotamia, and dial markings became increasingly accurate as astronomy and mathematics progressed. Sundials remained a common means of telling time until ♢ *clocks and watches* became generally used. The heliochronometer is a particularly accurate form of sundial, in which the shadow is cast by a fine wire.

Sunflower. Plants of the genus *Helianthus*, in the *Compositae*. *H. annuus* is grown on a small scale for the huge decorative yellow flowers and on field scale for the seeds, which are eaten as a delicacy in the east and give an industrially used oil. *H. tuberosus* (the Jerusalem artichoke) has tuberous edible roots.

Sunnis. < Ar. *sunna*, tradition; the largest sect of Muslims, adherents of the 'Sunna'

i.e. accepting as valid certain traditions of belief not enshrined in the ♢ *Koran*, and approving of the succession of the four first caliphs. They are the majority sect in Turkey, Arabia, and Africa. ♢ *Caliphate, Ommayads, Shiahs.*

Superego ♢ *Ego.*

Supersonic Flight. At sea level under standard atmospheric conditions the waves which carry sound travel at 760 m.p.h. When aircraft reached speeds greater than this, after the Second World War, aircraft design had to meet many new requirements. At subsonic speeds the molecules forming the air, though somewhat crowded together on impact with the aircraft, had no great difficulty in flowing around and past it, but at supersonic speeds the air molecules pile up in the path of the aircraft and form a shock wave or 'sound barrier'. The effect of this is most pronounced as the aircraft is accelerating through the speed of sound; at higher speeds the air is thrust aside so rapidly that no pressure wall builds up. To overcome some of these problems the shape of the wings and fuselage have been modified to present as little air resistance as possible e.g. in swept-back wings. At very high speeds the heat generated by friction creates a further set of problems. Normal plastics and aluminium alloys do not remain strong enough at the high temperatures generated, and new, stronger materials e.g. titanium alloys, stainless steel, and special plastics, have to be used. ♢ *Fatigue of Materials.*

Supreme Court of the U.S.A. Established 1789 as part of the system of checks and balances designed to prevent either the legislative or the executive branch of the government gaining absolute control; now consists of nine members, with the Chief Justice as President, its decisions being reached by majority vote. Its two basic functions are to interpret Congressional enactments when they are challenged and to act as the final court of appeal. Its rulings can be changed only by a Constitutional amendment which requires a two-thirds majority in both houses of Congress. Twenty-two such amendments have been passed to date (1964).

Surfactant ♢ *Detergents.*

Surfing. Riding a rolling wave breaking on to a beach, on a wooden board. The sport began about 1907 in Australia, where many annual competitions are held, and has a growing popularity in other countries.

Surgery. This has a long history. Even in Neolithic times, operations on the skull (trepanning) were performed; the Greeks and Romans had skilful surgeons, with some knowledge of how to avoid sepsis and the use of soporifics to reduce pain, and their skill was inherited by the Arabs. After the fall of Rome surgery in Europe declined and fell into the hands of unskilled charlatans. In England and France the barber-surgeon became a well-known figure, and not until the 18th cent. did the profession gain any standing. The high mortality from infection discouraged surgical intervention except in desperate cases. Modern surgery owes its development to the introduction of ether as an anaesthetic by Morton in 1846 and Lister's techniques for avoiding sepsis: ◊ *anti-septics*. In the 20th cent. there has been great progress, based on the work of the 19th-cent. pioneers, and the extension of surgery to new fields – the nervous system, the heart and lungs (facilitated by mechanical appliances to maintain circulation during interruption of the heart's action). The scope of surgery of blood vessels has been widened by the use of plastic substitutes for weakened vessel walls; successful transplantation of kidneys has taken place, with the help of immunology and chemistry. In ophthalmic surgery corneal grafting has become a commonplace; in diseases of the ear, nose, and throat improved instruments and techniques have simplified the removal of foreign bodies from the respiratory tract, and have brought relief in some forms of deafness. Orthopaedic surgery, developed largely by the work of Sir Robert Jones, is now less concerned with correcting deformities caused by poor hygiene and nutrition than with the treatment of fractures and bodily injuries resulting from accidents.

Surrealism. A literary and artistic movement founded in France in the early 1920s as the heir in some respects of ◊ *dadaism*; dedicated to the matching of the irrational in experience by a deliberately shocking and arbitrary irrationalism in the content and medium of literature and art. Influenced by Freud, and in general by the recognition of the part played by the unconscious and the irrational in determining sensibility, it looked to the dream, to automatic writing, to the non-logical associations that spring out of the unregulated consciousness, as a guide to the choice of both technique and subject-matter. There was also an anti-bourgeois element in surrealist attitudes, derived partly from ◊ *marxism* and partly from a more generalized feeling of the need to destroy conventional values. The literary movement flourished chiefly in France between the wars, under the leadership of the French poets Aragon and André Breton. The artistic movement was led by the sculptor Hans Arp, joined later by artists from all over the world: Max Ernst, de Chirico, Joan Miró, Dali, Tanguy, and the sculptor Giacometti. Most surrealist works show objects depicted realistically but juxtaposed in an unexpected and sometimes horrifying manner. There was also a short-lived surrealist cinema, exemplified 1929 by Buñuel's *Un Chien d'Andalou*.

Surveying. The measurement and mapping of the earth's surface. Surveys of a local nature need not take account of the curvature of the earth, and are known as plane surveys. The comprehensive large-scale mapping of whole countries dates to the end of the 18th cent. The common method was to establish a base-line several miles long, which was measured with a high degree of accuracy. Triangulation stations were then set up, forming a network of triangles covering the area to be mapped. All angles were measured by theodolite, and the whole system related to the base-line. The curvature of the earth was taken into account, and positions fixed by star observations. This branch is known as geodetic surveying (◊ *Geodesy*). Detailed mapping between triangulation points was often done with the ◊ *plane-table*. Aerial photographs are now used extensively for detailed mapping. Stereoscopic photography, in conjunction with a few 'ground-control' measurements, enables ◊ *contour* maps to be made. Instruments have recently come into use which enable distances to be found by timing the travel of light or radio waves. With these it is possible to make geodetic surveys by measuring the sides of the triangles (trilateration) instead of their angles.

Survival of the Fittest ◊ *Evolution.*

Susa. City of ancient ◊ *Persia*, capital of the region known in the Old Testament as Elam, now represented by three mounds or tells. The earliest levels date to about 3800 B.C. Susa seems to have been captured by Sargon of Akkad about 2360 B.C. and was for a time under Akkadian domination. Its period of greatest splendour was in the 12th cent. B.C. Later it declined, but it became an important city again as part of the Achaemenid Empire of the Persians.

Suttee. < Sanskrit *sati*, 'true' wife; immolation of a widow on the funeral pyre of her dead husband, among Hindus, by whom it was believed that the pair would be reborn together in subsequent reincarnations (◊ *Transmigration*). It was the practice mainly of princely families, and was made a statutory offence in 1829; it is still occasionally reported, but the reliability of the reports is doubtful.

Swahili ◊ *African Languages.*

Swaziland. Area 6705 sq. m. Pop. 280,300. Cap. Mbabane. A British protectorate; like Basutoland and Bechuanaland, an enclave geographically within ◊ *South Africa.* Exports esp. asbestos; also citrus fruits, cotton, rice, sugar, tobacco. There are rich iron deposits.

Sweden. Area 173,436 sq. m. Pop. 7.6 m. Cap. Stockholm. Rel. Lutheran. Constitutional monarchy, with Council of Ministers responsible to a Parliament (Riksdag) of two chambers, elected by proportional representation, the Upper of 150 members sitting for eight years and the Lower of 230 members for four.

ECONOMY. Great forests in the north and agricultural land in the south. Rich mineral resources (excellent iron ore, lead, zinc, sulphur, and manganese). Large output of timber and wood pulp, dairy and agricultural produce; the considerable industrial production is distinguished by precision and quality. The standard of living is high; state-provided social services and educational facilities are excellent. There is considerable state control of major industries (railways, mining, utilities, refineries) and a record of good employer–union relations.

HISTORY. The early inhabitants were Swedes and Goths; Sweden was united with Norway and Denmark in the 14th cent. Gustavus Adolphus made extensive conquests in the 17th cent. in the Baltic states and beyond; Sweden played an important part in the ◊ *Thirty Years War*, but subsequently was attacked by both Russia and Denmark in the Great Northern War and deprived of all lands on the eastern shore of the Baltic, losing ◊ *Finland* to Russia in the later 18th cent. Napoleon made the French Marshal Bernadotte King of Sweden, and his line became the ruling family. ◊ *Norway* was united with and ruled by Sweden from 1814 to 1905, when the connexion was peaceably dissolved. Sweden remained neutral through both world wars, but has a strong military establishment; though a member of the ◊ *United Nations Organization*, she is uncommitted to any group of treaty powers. A Socialist government has been in power, alone or in coalition, since 1932.

LANGUAGE. One of the ◊ *Germanic languages*; spoken by about 6.5 m. Modern Swedish has been simplified and regulated (on the basis of the cultivated speech of Stockholm) by the Swedish Academy (founded 1786) through its 1836 *Grammar*, its still unfinished *Dictionary* (begun 1893), and its 1906 reform of the spelling.

Swedenborgianism. System of beliefs based on the teachings of Emanuel Swedenborg 1688–1772, Swedish scientist and mystic, who claimed to have been admitted to direct contact with the angelic world, and to have been commissioned to found the 'New Church', which accepts as divinely revealed his numerous writings in which the spiritual world is minutely described. His church still exists in England (*c.* 7000 members), Sweden, and U.S.A., and is active in distributing his writings. ◊ *Gnostics, Mysticism.*

Swedes. Swedish turnips (in U.S.A. rutabaga); a ◊ *root crop* once grown extensively for human and animal consumption. The considerable labour-requirement for its cultivation has led to its decline as a crop.

Sweepstake ◊ *Lottery.*

Sweet Pea. Annual flower, of the ◊ *Leguminosae*, developed from the strongly scented *Lathyrus odoratus*, a wild plant of S. Italy and Sicily, introduced into England at the end of the 17th cent. The wild plant has small maroon flowers. After Henry Eckford started to cross the few existing varieties in 1870, many new varieties were developed, with larger flowers and a greater range of colour. In 1900 a sport with waved and frilled petals appeared, which immediately became very popular. From then on this form was developed with larger flowers, clearer colours, more blooms to a stem, and every variety of colour except yellow and true blue.

Sweet Potato. *Ipomoea batatas*, of the *Convolvulaceae*; a creeping plant native to S. America, with large edible tubers weighing up to 5 lb. each, containing more sugar and less starch than ordinary potatoes. There are several cultivated varieties, white, red, or yellow; the tubers are sometimes dried and ground to make a flour, e.g. Brazilian arrowroot. Carried from Brazil to other tropical countries by the Portuguese, it is now widely used in human diet, often replacing the ◊ *yam*.

Swimming. Swimming was popular in ancient Greece and Rome, but fell into disfavour in Europe in the Middle Ages through a belief that it was responsible for spreading epidemics. It was revived as a sport in London about 1837; the Metropolitan Swimming Association (1869) laid down rules for competition, and the sport rapidly spread abroad. Men's swimming was included in the 1896 ◊ *Olympic Games*, and women's in 1912; the International Federation was formed 1908. Modern competitive events are: Breaststroke; Butterfly stroke (developed from the breaststroke 1935); Backstroke; Freestyle. There are also ◊ *water polo* and diving (springboard, plain, and high).

Swine. Mammals of the family *Suidae*; the wild European *Sus scrofa*, still found in parts of Europe and Asia, was early domesticated (◊ *Pig*). Boar hunting and pig-sticking were and to some extent still are favourite forms of hunting.

SWINE FEVER: A serious virus disease of pigs, spread by excreta and infected straw etc. as well as by direct contact; difficult to control, as the virus survives in cold storage and imported carcases can introduce the disease. Rigorous controls introduced 1963 by the British Ministry of Agriculture provide for slaughter of infected and in-contact animals, safe disposal of carcases, and compensation to owners. ◊ *Scheduled Diseases*.

Swiss Brethren ◊ *Mennonites*.

Swiss Guards. Regiments of Swiss mercenaries served in various European armies from the 15th cent. to the 19th; they were not volunteers, but were Swiss troops who served foreign powers, by agreement of the Swiss government, in return for payment. The French in particular hired Swiss troops; the Swiss Guards' defence of the Tuileries during the ◊ *French Revolution*, when 500 were massacred by the mob, is a memorable incident in their history. Swiss regiments served France under Napoleon and up to 1830. In 1874 the Swiss constitution forbade Swiss mercenary service abroad, with the exception of the ceremonial Swiss Guard of the Vatican, the Pope's bodyguard, recruited from the Roman Catholic cantons.

Switzerland. Area 15,950 sq. m. Pop. 5.8 m. Cap. Berne. Rel. Protestant 53 per cent, Roman Catholic 46 per cent. Federal republic of 22 cantons (three subdivided) each with its own parliament and government. The official languages are German, French, and Italian, with Rumansch as a regional language. The Federal Assembly consists of the National Council, 196 members elected by direct adult male vote for four years, and the Council of States, 44 members, two from each canton. The Assembly elects the Federal Council of seven men from different cantons (at least two from the French- and Italian-speaking areas) for four years. The President is elected annually from the government. Swiss women have no vote.

ECONOMY. Few resources except timber and hydroelectric power; exports include precision machinery, watches, cheese, chemicals. The tourist industry and banking are important economic adjuncts.

HISTORY. Occupied from early times by the Celtic Helvetii, the area became Roman in 58 B.C. and after various later invasions was Frankish in the 6th cent. A.D. In the 11th cent. it came under the ◊ *Holy Roman Empire*, but in 1291 Uri, Schwyz, and Unterwalden (the 'Forest Cantons') founded the Swiss Confederation, which in 1315 defeated an attempt by the ◊ *Hapsburgs* to reassert their rule, and was then joined by Lucerne, Zurich, Berne, Zug, and the district of Glarus. In a second conflict with the Hapsburgs the Swiss won a great victory at Sempach in 1386, which led to recognition of their independence by the Peace of Basle in 1389. The ◊ *Reformation*, led in Switzerland by Zwingli and Calvin, divided Switzerland into Catholic and Protestant sections (a division which persisted for 300 years, until the forcible suppression of the Catholic 'Sonderbund' in 1847). In 1798, after the ◊ *French Revolution*, Napoleon conquered Switzerland and set up the Republic of Helvetia, which lasted until 1803, when he created 19 fresh cantons under French domination; the forest cantons continued to oppose him. The ◊ *Vienna Congress* in 1815 declared Switzerland neutral, gave it a new federal constitution, and added the Geneva part of ◊ *Savoy*. Switzerland remained neutral in both World Wars, and her traditional neutrality led to the choice of Geneva as headquarters of the League of Nations, the International Labour Organization, the Red Cross, and various other international bodies. ◊ *Westphalia, Treaty of.*

Swordfish. Large bony deep-sea fish, related to the mackerel; the bones of the upper jaw are prolonged in a serrated sharp structure, which (with its tremendous swimming speed) makes the swordfish a very formidable creature. It feeds on other fish, and is a favourite big-game fish.

Sycamore ◊ *Maple.*

Syllogism. An argument, of the kind first classified by Aristotle, comprising two premisses sharing a common term, and a conclusion that must be true if the premisses are true: e.g. If no politicians are idealists, and some good men are politicians, then some good men are not idealists. ◊ *Logic.*

Symbiosis. The living together of dissimilar organisms, in a relationship which appears to be of mutual benefit by providing e.g. protection, shelter, food; ◊ *lichens* are symbiotic associations of ◊ *algae* and ◊ *fungi*. Root nodules on *Leguminosae* contain symbiotic nitrogen-fixing bacteria, and some of the nitrogen compounds they produce are absorbed by the plant: ◊ *Nitrogen Cycle*. The hollow stem of the tropical tree *Cecropia* is inhabited by ants, which feed on special nodules produced on the leaf stalks, but attack leaf-cutter ants and probably protect the tree. ◊ *Parasites.*

Symbolism. In literature, specifically the movement away from realism and ◊ *classicism* begun in the late 19th cent. by the French poets Rimbaud, Corbière, Mallarmé, Verlaine, and Laforgue under the influence of Poe and Baudelaire. Employing private rather than public symbols, and working by suggestion rather than by direct statement, the Symbolists decisively influenced the later Imagist and Surrealist movements and the poetry of Valéry, Yeats, and Eliot. Symbolism, however, is a fundamental artistic process, which may be formalized (e.g. in ◊ *allegory* where each symbol relates to a single deducible meaning) or more often arises spontaneously, or is created within an individual context, at once conveying to the reader its explicit meaning and affecting him by the range and force of its suggestions. One of the most famous examples is the whale in *Moby Dick*, both a specific creature and a symbol of indefinable but powerful significance.

Symphony. In standard modern use, an extended orchestral composition, the orchestral form of the ◊ *sonata*. Haydn is regarded as the 'father' of the symphony, which became the chief orchestral expression of abstract musical ideas for e.g. Mozart, Beethoven, Brahms, Bruckner, Tchaikovsky. It was combined with a narrative idea by Berlioz ('Fantastic Symphony' 1830) and with voices notably by Beethoven ('Choral Symphony', No. 9, 1824) and Mahler. An important modern exponent is Shostakovich, who has written 13 symphonies.

The symphony is most often in four movements but e.g. Sibelius's No. 7, 1924, concentrates it into one movement. The importance of the symphony in the 19th cent. created the term 'symphony orchestra' to describe the modern concert-hall orchestra, with its four sections of strings, woodwind, brass, and percussion (and occasionally such unclassified extras as piano, harp).

Synagogue. Building in which Jews meet for public prayer and often other communal and educational activities; usually oblong, it is oriented towards Jerusalem and furnished with the Ark, a chest containing the scrolls of the Mosaic Law (before which a lamp perpetually burns), a pulpit, a reading-desk, and in older and strictly traditional synagogues a gallery for women worshippers. ◊ *Judaism.*

Synchrotron. Type of ◊ *particle accelerator.*

Syncline. Downfold of ◊ *sedimentary rock* layers, the contracted strata on each side of the depression dipping towards each other in a trough along the line of the central axis of the fold. In areas where former mountain chains have been worn down to plains and re-elevated into plateaux, the toughened rocks of former synclines often offer the greatest resistance to ◊ *erosion* and ◊ *exfoliation*, and a synclinal structure can be seen in some of Britain's highest peaks e.g. Snowdon.

ANTICLINE: The arch of the fold, where the less compacted strata dip away from the line of the fold's crest or axis, in opposite directions. The Weald and the S. Pennines are of anticlinal structure, the lower older beds being exposed by the denudation of the arch. ◊ *Geosyncline*.

Syndicalism. Form of ◊ *socialism* in which ownership and control of the means of production and distribution are in the hands of the workers themselves, not in the hands of the State. Under syndicalism (as in theoretical marxism) the State would wither away and be replaced by a federation of economic units. It has a close affinity to ◊ *anarchism*, reached its peak in the late 19th cent. and was of some importance in Italy and Spain, but is now virtually extinct.

Synthetic Resins. Chemically, these are of two distinct groups. (a) Those made by bringing various chemicals together and producing a chemical reaction, by heat or a catalyst (or both), to form long chains of macromolecules (polycondensation reactions). These typically furnish thermosetting resins i.e. those which remain rigid when heated, e.g. Bakelite and similar types. (b) Those produced by polymerization reactions, in which high ◊ *polymers* are made usually by linking them together into long chains in various patterns. These are typically thermoplastic resins i.e. they soften on heating but become rigid again on cooling. Well-known products are polyvinyl chloride (PVC), used in bags, raincoats, piping, and the acrylic resins, from which Perspex and Plexiglas are made. ◊ *Rubber (synthetic)*.

SYNTHETIC FIBRES: Made from a range of synthetic resins which are convertible into fibres by an extrusion process. The resin, either molten or in solution, is forced at great pressure through a fine spinneret and solidifies rapidly on emerging into the air as a continuous filament. Fibres of this kind are made from a wide variety of materials, many of which are petroleum-based, e.g. nylon, perlon, Terylene, Dacron, orlon. ◊ *Rayon*.

Syphilis ◊ *Venereal Disease*.

Syria. Area 70,800 sq. m. Pop. 4.8 m. Cap. Damascus. Rel. Muslim.

ECONOMY. An essentially agricultural country, esp. cotton; poor in mineral resources, although the search for petroleum continues, and the government receives some revenue from the Iraq Petroleum Company, whose pipelines cross Syria.

HISTORY. Part of the ◊ *Ottoman Empire* until 1920, and thereafter under a French mandate until 1941, when Allied Forces (including Free French) granted its independence, promised since 1939. In 1958 President Nasser of ◊ *Egypt* and President Kuwatly of Syria announced the complete political union of the two countries as the ◊ *United Arab Republic*; a provisional constitution was proclaimed, declaring the country to be a 'presidential democracy'. In November 1961, a coup aimed at the restoration of Syrian independence was successfully carried out by high-ranking Army officers. This was reversed in 1963, when Syria again joined the U.A.R.

Syriac ◊ *Aramaic, Semitic Languages*.

Syringa ◊ *Lilac, Mock Orange*.

T

Table-tennis. Version of tennis played on a table 9 ft by 5 ft, originally known as ping pong, developed in Britain about 1880, but not regarded as a serious game till 1920. An English open championship was held in 1922 and a world championship in 1926. Now of world-wide popularity.

Taboo. < Polynesian 'tabu', something set apart from the ordinary, forbidden, sacred, or mystically dangerous, which may harm or pollute ordinary people who come in contact with it; in Polynesia such persons as kings and priests, and objects intimately associated with them, were *tabu*. Also actions mystically forbidden which place the doer in a state of ritual pollution.

Tactics. Methods and organization of actual combat in war, as distinct from ◊ *strategy.* Fighting first was the confused personal combat of the tribe or horde; discipline and training produced the Greek ◊ *phalanx* and the Roman ◊ *legion,* whose tactics were based upon shock attack. Infantry remained the decisive factor in battle, until the heavy mailed cavalry of the Goths appeared, and subsequently in medieval times the armoured knights, not the infantry, were the shock troops. With the development of the long-bow and ◊ *firearms,* cavalry became again a subsidiary arm, to be brought into action after preliminary infantry and artillery action. Frederick the Great introduced tactics in which fire-power played a greater part, a system successfully developed by the British Army in the ◊ *Napoleonic Wars.* Napoleon continued to use close columns of infantry flanked by skirmishers, and also used artillery and cavalry in mass in the final stages of a battle. Head-on charges remained the classic arbiter of battle until the increasing fire-power of riflemen and artillery fundamentally changed tactics, in the ◊ *American Civil War.* The devastating fire-power of machine-gun and magazine rifle, in conjunction with trenches and barbed wire, despite the vast increase in the weight of artillery, brought about a static form of warfare in the First World War, and neither the Allied nor German generals found tactics to restore the elements of mobility and surprise. In the Second World War the use of ◊ *tanks* and highly mobile artillery, and the close cooperation of aircraft, brought back a war of movement. The bayonet and cavalry charge finally disappeared in the era of mechanized warfare. The advent of the atomic warhead for heavy artillery and short-range ◊ *rockets* has introduced an incalculable potential into battle tactics.

Tadpole. The immature young of certain animals, notably ◊ *frogs,* anatomically very different from the adults; the duration of the tadpole phase varies from species to species and from individual to individual, some remaining tadpoles for less than a day, others e.g. those of frogs for months.

Taff Vale Judgement ◊ *Trade Union.*

Taft-Hartley Act (Labor Management Relations Act). 1947. The Act modified earlier U.S. legislation about the rights of labour unions. It empowers the Government to obtain an 80-day injunction against threatened strikes likely to be damaging to national welfare (known as the 'cooling-off' period). It prohibited the 'closed shop', increased the list of unfair labour practices and specified a term of 60 days' notice for both employers and employees before the termination of labour contracts. A clause forbidding union contributions to political parties was later quashed by the Federal courts. This Act which reversed the liberal trend of New Deal policy was passed by the U.S. Congress over President Truman's veto.

Taj Mahal ◊ *Indian Architecture, Moguls, Muslim Architecture.*

Talc ◊ *Silica.*

Talmud. The codification of centuries of Jewish oral commentary on the Torah (Pentateuch ◊ *Bible*), constituting a massive encyclopedia of Jewish law and traditions developed largely by means of inference from the biblical text in accordance with specific logical, analogical, and textual rules. It is divided into Mishnah (< Hebrew *shanah,* to repeat) and Gemara (completion), the latter being debate and commentary on the laws, precepts, and principles enunciated by the former. After the material in the Mishnah was codified, between about A.D. 120 and 220, when the Patriarch Judah I completed the work, oral discussion and elaboration went on among the 'Amoraim' (speakers or interpreters) who thus produced the Gemara. The best-known version is the Babylonian Talmud, containing (with the Mishnah) the Gemara produced by the Amoraim, who worked in Mesopotamia in the 4th and 5th centuries, the whole finally committed to writing by the Saboraim (reasoners) of the immediately following generations. The language of the Mishnah is ◊ *Hebrew*, that of the Gemara is largely ◊ *Aramaic*.

Tammany Hall. The Democratic Party's organization in the city of New York; founded in 1789 to represent middle-class opinion, in opposition to the city aristocracy. It had grown corrupt even as early as 1807, and by the 1860s 'Tammany' was synonymous with political graft; but its considerable welfare work among the late 19th-cent. immigrants led large numbers of them to join the Democratic Party. In 1934 the Tammany candidate for the mayoralty, James Walker, was forced to resign, and the independent LaGuardia was elected on a reform platform; but despite this setback Tammany Hall is still one of the most powerful U.S. political organizations.

Tammuz. Mesopotamian god; lover of ◊ *Ishtar*; his ritual death and resurrection at the harvest was celebrated by a great feast in the autumn (see Old Testament, Ezek. viii. 14) and as ◊ *Adonis* his cult became widespread throughout the eastern parts of the Roman empire in the early centuries A.D.

T'ang ◊ *China, Porcelain*.

Tanganyika. Area 362,688 sq. m. Pop. 10 m. (mainly Bantu and ◊ *Masai*); Cap. Dar-es-Salaam. Republic in E. central Africa, with a President, elected by universal suffrage, who is head of both government and state, the presidency being linked to the majority party in the National Assembly of 71 elected members and up to 70 nominated by the President.

ECONOMY. Mainly agricultural; exports coffee, cotton, hides, oilseeds, sisal; also minerals esp. diamonds, gold, lead, mica. Light industry is developing. The country is mountainous; Kilimanjaro is the highest peak in Africa, 19,340 ft. The Serengeti National Park is a 6000 sq. m. game reserve and sanctuary, famous for its great variety of wildlife.

HISTORY. Lake Tanganyika was discovered by Burton and Speke in 1858. The area to the sea was a German protectorate from 1891 to 1918. Subsequently a mandate, it became a self-governing member of the British Commonwealth in 1961. Since early 1964 it has been united with ◊ *Zanzibar*, an Enabling Act having promulgated a new state of Tanganyika and Zanzibar (Tanzania).

Tank. In 1492 Leonardo da Vinci wrote of covered chariots mounting guns, but the idea of combining the armoured car with the caterpillar tractor was not developed until 1915, when Colonel Swinton, with the support of Churchill and Sir John French, got official backing for tank trials; the prototype 'Little Willie' was produced in January 1916. Contrary to the advice of Swinton who wanted to launch a massive attack, a mere 49 were used on the ◊ *Somme* in September 1916, achieving surprise but not mass effect. Greater success at Cambrai late in 1917 established the tank's importance, and the Tank Corps was formed in that year. All countries experimented with increasingly effective versions, and the study of tank strategy and tactics was notably advanced by Fuller, MacArthur, De Gaulle, and the Germans Guderian and von Eimannsberger. In the Second World War the German Panzer (tank) Divisions were largely responsible for the success of the 'Blitzkrieg' campaigns. The Allies quickly developed efficient tanks (British 'Churchill', American 'Sherman', Soviet 'Stalin'), which played a decisive role in the eventual victory. British ingenuity was responsible for many special uses e.g. flame-thrower, flail mine-clearer, bridge-layer, petard strong-point destroyer, etc. Since the war tank development has been directed at sophistication of design and weapon systems, culminating at the present time in the British 'Chieftain' (120 mm. gun), American T95 (105 mm. gun) and M107 (175 mm. gun with 35-ft barrel), French AMX30 (105 mm. gun), and Swedish S (turretless, with 105 mm. gun). The development of tanks as fallout-proof nuclear missile-carriers is under experiment in most armies.

Tanker. Ship specially constructed for the carriage of liquids in bulk, the cargo space being divided into numerous tanks, to limit the distance the cargo can shift when the vessel rolls, and the engines usually being right aft, to limit the fire risk. The first tankers were built at the end of the 19th cent. and today they form a very large proportion of the world's merchant fleets (◊ *Shipping*). They vary in size from quite small ships, engaged in coastal and inland-water traffic, to giants of over 100,000-ton carrying capacity. The commonest cargo is oil, but molasses, wine, and chemicals are also shipped in tankers.

Tannenberg. 1410. A village in E. Prussia. Also called Grünwald; decisive victory whereby Poland expelled the Teutonic Knights (◊ *Orders of Chivalry*) from the Baltic lands.
1914. Scene of a decisive German victory early in the First World War. Two Russian armies were advancing into E. Prussia. Hindenburg surrounded and destroyed that of Samsonov at Tannenberg and subsequently routed the second Russian army in Masuria. The Germans were then able to transfer the weight of their forces to the Western front.

Tannins. A diverse group of compounds with the property of hardening collagen, the ◊ *protein* of hides; obtained from various parts of certain trees and plants e.g. the bark of oak, leaves of sumac and tea, wood of quebracho, horse chestnut, and wattle (acacia). Gallic-acid tannins (from the galls produced on oak leaves by parasites) form a complex with an iron salt, which by oxidation darkens on paper, and they have long been the basis of writing inks. Tannic acid ('tannin') in combination with tartar emetic (◊ *tartaric acid*) is a mordant in cotton dyeing. ◊◊ *Bast*.

Tantalum. A dark grey metallic ◊ *element* occurring with ◊ *niobium* in columbite crystals in veins in granite rocks and in resulting stream deposits. Ductile and resistant to corrosion and to high temperatures, it is very important as an ◊ *alloy* in manufacturing special chromium steels (◊ *Iron and Steel Industry*), for electrolytic rectifiers, and for surgical and dental instruments because of its very slight foreign-body reaction. It is also used in the exhaust systems of high-speed aircraft and the supercharger systems of petrol engines, and was formerly used for electric-lamp filaments. Tantalum carbide is extremely hard and industrially important. The U.S.S.R. has large deposits, but the output is unknown; 95 per cent of the remaining world supply comes from Nigeria.

Tantalus. In Greek mythology, son of ◊ *Zeus*; father of ◊ *Pelops* and Niobe. There are varying legends of his punishment for an offence against the gods: a large rock was suspended over his head at a banquet, continually threatening to fall on him; or in ◊ *Hades* he was made to stand in a pool of water which always receded when he tried to drink, or under trees whose branches bent away from him when he tried to pluck their fruit.

Tanzania ◊ *Tanganyika, Zanzibar*.

Taoism. Chinese cult based on the philosophy of Lao-Tse, dating to the 6th cent. B.C. as set forth in the *Tao Te Ching* and the writings of Lao's pupil Chuang-Tse; teaches a high and compassionate morality and stresses the virtue of *wu-wei*, withdrawal or non-action. Affected by degenerate ◊ *Buddhism* and popular superstition, it later became much contaminated with spiritualism and magical practices such as the search for an 'elixir of life' (◊ *Philosopher's Stone*) to procure longevity.

Tape-recording. A compact and economical method for storing information. It is usually made by coating tough narrow plastic ribbon with specially prepared magnetic powder which records sound or coded numerical information. It may be stored indefinitely. Magnetic tape recorders are now widely used for musical reproduction, in television, and for scienticific, industrial, and educational purposes. A recent important development is their use in ◊ *artificial satellites*, for exchanging information between satellite and earth.

Tapestry. Wall-hanging, usually of wool or silk, into which a pictorial design has been woven; tapestries were made in ancient Egypt and China, and probably also in the classical world. In France the art has been practised to a high degree of perfection since the 14th cent. esp. at Arras and in the great factories of Aubusson and of the Gobelins in Paris, which Louis XIV purchased in 1662 and made into the State manufactory. A notable English school of the 17th cent. was that at Mortlake. In the 19th cent. tapestry declined in artistic merit, but a 20th-cent revival has taken place in the Aubusson and Gobelins factories, and major artists e.g. Picasso, Braque, Miró have produced tapestry designs; Jean Lurçat has led a school of young artists working exclusively in tapestry. In England, ◊ *embroidery* was for long the preferred medium, but William Morris's 19th-cent. ventures into tapestry created an interest which has continued into the 20th cent. Graham Sutherland's design for the great hanging at Coventry Cathedral 1962 was executed at the Gobelins factory. ◊ *Bayeux Tapestry, Carpet (Rugs)*.

Tapeworm. Parasitic flat-worm commonly infecting man and domestic animals; the adult is attached to the interior of the victim's intestine, by suckers through which it absorbs nourishment from the host. Its body, which may be 30 ft long, consists of a chain of flattened segments, giving a ribbon-like appearance; each segment contains both male and female reproductive organs, and produce thousands of fertilized eggs, which pass out of the body with the waste. Each egg can give rise to an intermediate stage, the bladder-worm; if eaten by an appropriate intermediate host e.g. cattle, this passes into the muscle; if not killed in cooking, the worm may pass from meat into the human intestine, where it assumes the adult form.

Tapioca ◊ *Manihot*.

Tapir. Robust pig-like creature with a pronounced mobile snout living in marsh land in SE Asia and central and S. America, nocturnal and herbivorous. Its geographical distribution is explained by its descent from a numerous and widely-distributed group of Eocene *Perissodactyla* (horse-like animals) also ancestral to the ◊ *rhinoceros*.

Tarantula. Large, hairy ◊ *spider* from S. Italy and S. America, whose supposedly lethal bite was believed to cause a kind of St Vitus' Dance prior to death (hence 'tarantella'). There are several species, some of which prey on birds. Their bite is painful to man, but not lethal.

Tardenoisian ◊ *Mesolithic*.

Tariff, Customs. A list of goods on which duty is levied on importation; also the rate of duty on a particular commodity, either specific, a certain sum according to quantity by weight or volume, or more commonly *ad valorem*, a certain per-

centage of the assessed value of the article. The purpose of a tariff is either to provide revenue, e.g. the tariff on tobacco imported into Britain, or to protect home industries. ◊ *Free Trade, General Agreement on Tariffs and Trade*.

Tariff Reform. A policy of protection, advocated by Joseph Chamberlain in 1903, to reverse Britain's longstanding ◊ *free trade* policy. The customs tariff was to be reformed to give preference to colonial products. It did not at first find favour at the polls but the Conservative Party continued to support it, and in 1915 the McKenna duties on luxury goods became the first tariff on goods (i.e. other than revenue duties). It was followed by the 1921 Safeguarding of Industries Act, which imposed duties on the products of key industries. After the ◊ *Ottawa Conference* of 1932, ◊ *Imperial Preference* superseded free trade.

Tarsier. A prosimian ◊ *primate*, about the size of a rat, considered intermediate between the ◊ *lemur* and ◊ *monkey*, found in SE Asia; arboreal and nocturnal, its night vision is facilitated by the light-collecting power of its enormous eyes, hence the name spectral tarsier.

Tartaric Acid. A colourless solid somewhat soluble in water and optically active (◊ *Isomerism*); present in grapes as its acid potassium salt, a deposit of which (cream of tartar) forms during wine-making. It is used as a mild acid e.g. in baking-powder or effervescent salts; tartar emetic (potassium antimonyl tartrate) acts in conjunction with tannic acid (◊ *Tannins*) as a mordant for dyeing cotton with basic dyes.

Tartars ◊ *Tatars*.

Tartarus. In Greek and Roman mythology, the place of punishment after death for the specially evil, cut off from the rest of ◊ *Hades* by Pyriphlegethon, a river of perpetual flames. Homer makes Tartarus the prison of the ◊ *Cyclopes* and ◊ *Titans* after their defeat by ◊ *Zeus*.

Tasmania. Area 26,215 sq. m. Pop. 0.4 m. Cap. Hobart. A large island in the S. Pacific, off ◊ *Australia*, of which it is one of the constituent States. Discovered by the Dutchman Tasman 1642; settled by the British 1804. The economy is mainly agricultural, esp. fruit and live-stock.

Tasmanian Wolf. The largest of the marsupial carnivores, once widespread in

Australia but now restricted to its name-place; dog-like in appearance and habit.
Tatars. Incorrectly, Tartars; a Turkic tribe of nomads who fused with Mongols under Jenghis Khan in the 13th cent. A.D. and overran much of China, Turkestan, Afghanistan, and Persia. Under Batu Khan they became known as the Golden Horde, and raided as far afield as Hungary and Germany. After their invasions had receded, they continued to dominate much of Russia and Siberia, though their power disintegrated in the 15th cent. About 4 m. Tatars, Turkish-speaking Muslims, remain in the U.S.S.R.

Tate Gallery. A gallery in London provided by Sir Henry Tate opened in 1897 and subsequently enlarged, containing two collections of paintings: the British School (from the 18th cent. onwards) and modern foreign schools since 1850; and some modern sculpture.

Taxation. The right to and manner of levying taxes has often caused long and violent political struggles; in Britain since Tudor times ◊ *Parliament* has gradually asserted control over taxation and expenditure, and in U.S.A. the 17th-cent. slogan 'no taxation without representation' was powerful at the time of the ◊ *American Revolution*. Taxation takes many forms, but can be divided into two main types, indirect and direct.

Indirect taxes, levied on goods and services, include: customs duties; excise duties e.g. on tobacco, spirits, petroleum products; entertainment tax; purchase tax. Until recent times indirect taxes predominated, since machinery for direct taxation was lacking; e.g. the salt tax, the window tax, and 'sumptuary' taxes were important sources of revenue, now superseded. Indirect taxes bear more severely on the poor than on the rich. In some Continental countries, the indirect-tax burden is often more widely spread, the main form of indirect taxation being an 'added value' tax on all transactions.

Direct taxes are those levied upon the individual. They have taken various forms, e.g. the medieval poll tax (so much per head) or a property tax (long used in U.S.A.) but in most developed countries tax on income, both of individuals and of companies, has become the most prevalent form. The 'principles of taxation' are generally accepted to be that the tax burden should be spread fairly on the basis of ability to pay; that taxes should be equitable as between one individual and another; that they should be easy to administer and simple to understand. ◊ *Budget, Death Duties, Income Tax.*

Tea. A beverage from the dried leaves of *Camellia sinensis*, of which there are many varieties native in China and India, an evergreen shrub constantly pruned to stimulate the formation of the new shoots required for tea. The flavour and quality of tea depends on the age of the leaf, climate, soil, rate of growth, time of picking, and method of preparation. Green tea is produced by allowing the leaves to wilt and drying them rapidly. In black tea the tissues are bruised before the leaves are dried; the leaves darken, change flavour, and lose some astringency. India and Ceylon produce mostly black tea, Japan mostly green, and China both kinds. Some China teas are scented with flowers e.g. jasmine. Tea contains the stimulant ◊ *caffeine*, also some theobromine and ◊ *tannins*. Caffeine is produced commercially from tea dust. The volatile oil and caffeine are more soluble than the tannins, more of which dissolve the longer the tea is brewed, causing it to become increasingly bitter. In about 1825 tea plants were discovered in Assam, after which large tea plantations developed and India became the leading producer. Tea-drinking originated in China, perhaps 4000 years ago, and was brought west by the Arabs; it first reached Europe early in the 17th cent. and although expensive became popular in England. The ◊ *East India Company* retained the monopoly of importation until 1833, after which consumption mounted rapidly. London is the centre of the world tea trade. Tea consumption per capita is highest in the U.K. and Ireland, followed by Australia and New Zealand. Russians and Persians are also tea-drinkers; India, Ceylon, and China are the main producers.

Teaching Machines. A method of incorporating 'programmed instruction' in machines, which replace some of the more routine functions of a living teacher by presenting the student with the first stage of a course of instruction and then (according to his answer to a test question) either leading him on to the next stage or (if he has given a wrong answer) providing him with further instruction. Its effectiveness depends on the quality of this 'programme' ($\Diamond$ *Automatic Data Processing*) rather than on the machine, which is simply a mechanism to ensure that the student cannot progress to the second stage until his has mastered the first.

Teak. Hard durable timber, from *Tectona grandis* and related species native to SE Asia and Malaysia; it sinks in water, unless thoroughly dried.

Technetium. A metallic element in the manganese group; does not occur naturally, but was made in 1937 by bombarding $\Diamond$ *molybdenum* with high-energy deuterons, and later discovered in the fission products of uranium in a $\Diamond$ *nuclear reactor*. Its properties and chemistry are very like those of $\Diamond$ *rhenium*, another member of the group.

Teeth. Composed mainly of dentine (chiefly calcium phosphate) covered with enamel. In the centre is the pulp cavity, into which blood-vessels and nerves enter through a canal opening at the apex of the roots. Reptile, fish, and amphibian teeth are constantly replaced, but the 20 deciduous ('milk') teeth in mammals appear between the 6th or 9th month of life and the 24th and later fall out, to be replaced by the 32 permanent teeth, a process completed in man by the age of 20. Mammalian teeth are arranged in bilaterally symmetrical groups, those of the upper occluding against similar teeth in the lower jaw. The teeth of carnivores are sharp and pointed for tearing flesh, those of herbivores are flattened for crushing grass and leaves. Invertebrates do not have true teeth, but may have cone-shaped projections. $\Diamond$ *Dentistry*.

Telegraph. Method of sending messages in $\Diamond$ *code* (e.g. morse) as a series of electrical impulses, either by radio or by wire. Wire telegraphy is based on the invention of Samuel Morse, who demonstrated it in 1844 by sending a message between Washington and Baltimore. The first successful transatlantic cable was laid in 1866, and in the 1870s Stearns and Edison developed methods of sending more than one message over the wire at the same time. In the simple telegraph the encoding and decoding are done by a human operator; teleprinters automatically turn the received impulse into printed form, the operator using a typewriter keyboard. The same principles are involved in transferring information in and between electronic computers with no human intervention.

Telepathy $\Diamond$ *Extra-sensory Perception, Psychical Research*.

Telephone. Device for communication by means of wires in an electric circuit, developed from a system patented by Alexander Graham Bell in 1876. At the transmitting end, sound waves picked up by a microphone induce variations in a diaphragm (resembling the human eardrum). These are converted into fluctuations in an electric current, which are transmitted to the receiver diaphragm, where sound waves corresponding to those picked up by the transmitting microphone re-create the same sounds. The wireless telephone follows the same principle, radio waves replacing wire-conveyed waves as the form of transmission. The U.S.A. has more telephones per head (40 per 100 of population) than any other country, followed by Sweden (1 telephone for 3). In Britain the ratio is 1 telephone to 8 people.

Telescope. Instrument used for producing a magnified image of distant objects; probably invented in Holland 1608, and

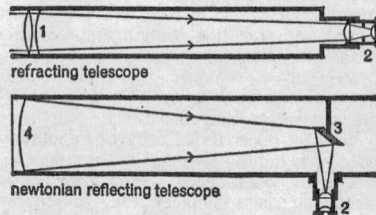

refracting telescope

newtonian reflecting telescope

| 1. object glass | 3. flat mirror |
| 2. eyepiece | 4. parabolic concave mirror |

first used in $\Diamond$ *astronomy* by Galileo 1609. Optical telescopes are of two main types: in the refracting telescope the objective is a large lens at one end of a hollow tube and the eyepiece a series of small lenses at the other: in the reflecting telescope a large mirror at the bottom of the tube collects the light and reflects it with a small mirror in the centre at the top, which in the Newtonian form directs it to an eyepiece at the side of the tube. The advantage of mirrors over lenses is that they can be larger and they avoid chromatic aberration ($\Diamond$ *aberration of light*). The objectives of telescopes may be used to collect light from a $\Diamond$ *star* and feed it to a recording instrument e.g. a spectrograph or photo-electric cell. Telescopes are also often used as cameras, by placing a photographic plate at the focal plane of the objective. The Schmidt telescope is specially designed for sky photography; it uses both mirrors and lenses and produces high-definition photographs of large areas of sky (up to 20° in diameter). The size of a telescope is expressed as the diameter of the objective. The largest telescopes are the 200-in. Hale (reflecting) and the 48-in. Schmidt, both at Mount Palomar, and the 40-in. (refracting) at Yerkes, U.S.A. ⬦ Optics.

A radio telescope is a directional aerial system which collects radio energy emitted by heavenly bodies. ⬦ Radioastronomy.

Television. Transmission by ⬦ radio of visual images. The process consists of converting a picture or scene by a special camera into a pattern of electric impulses which can be reconstructed in the receiver to form a picture.

The first successful system was demonstrated by Baird in England in 1926, using mechanical scanning, subsequently improved by electronic scanning. Much experimentation and development went on between 1930 and 1940, and by 1945 television as an entertainment had become a reality. Colour television has also been realized. In addition to its use in entertainment, television has uses in industry etc. where human observation is impossible e.g. in observing processes in nuclear reactors. The techniques and apparatus for transmission are similar in essentials to those used in radio transmission. ⬦ British Broadcasting Corporation, Independent Television Authority.

Telex. Service provided by the British Post Office for quickly transmitting printed messages over subscribers' telephone lines. A typewriter device is used at both transmitting and receiving ends. When a given key at the transmitter is depressed, a signal is sent along the line and activates a corresponding key at the receiver. Similar systems operate in many other countries.

Tells. Mounds found in countries of the Near and Middle East, the remains of a succession of brick-built cities or towns of the ancient world. The nature of sun-baked brick is such that it is easier to flatten buildings and build on top of the rubble than to dismantle them, and thus tells contain remains of buildings over a span of several centuries and offer un-

paralleled opportunities for archaeological excavation and stratigraphy.

Tellurium. A silvery brittle rare ⬦ element, occurring as tellurides in sulphide ores; one of the ⬦ sulphur family, its chemistry is similar to that of ⬦ selenium, although it is more metallic. It is used in small quantity for improving the qualities of lead and for making ruby glass; its oxide is valuable for making glass with an unusually high dielectric constant.

Tempera. Painting medium composed of powdered pigments mixed with fresh egg-yolk, thinned with water, to produce a quick-drying durable film of colour; used by the ancient Egyptians, the Greeks, and the Romans, it was the medium normally used for painting until the development of ⬦ oil painting in the 15th cent. The method has been revived by some modern artists e.g. the American Mark Tobey.

Temperament. A technical term in music. Suppose a string or air-column, when vibrated along its whole length, gives the note C; then if it is vibrated for a third of its length, it will sound the note G at the interval of a fifth above that C. Thus the musical interval of a fifth may be mathematically determined. In theory, it should be possible to tune an instrument on this basis, arriving eventually at B sharp, which as a semitone above B natural should be identical with C; in fact this B sharp would not be C but a note slightly higher, by a tiny interval called 'the comma of Pythagoras'. In order to bring this B sharp down to C, it is convenient to subtract a minute fraction from each of the fifths; this is the system called equal temperament, which came into use in the 18th cent. It is necessary for music using all the major and minor keys, e.g. Bach's Forty-Eight Preludes and Fugues or (for this reason) The Well-Tempered Clavier.

Temperature. A measure of the degree of hotness or coldness of a body; this determines the direction of · ⬦ heat flow. A change in temperature indicates a change in the amount of heat (total thermal energy of the vibrating atoms and molecules) held by the substance. An actual temperature is expressed as a fraction of the difference between two fixed and accurately reproducible temperatures.

As the total thermal energy decreases, so do the amplitudes of the vibrating atoms and molecules. Theoretically, therefore, the volume will decrease as the temperature falls, and the Absolute Zero is the temperature at which an ideal gas would occupy zero volume.

TEMPERATURE SCALE. The method of subdividing the distance between two fixed points on the type of thermometer under consideration. Two internationally-agreed fixed points are the ice point (temperature of pure melting ice) and the steam point (temperature of the steam immediately above pure boiling water). The Fahrenheit scale assigns 32° and 212° to the ice and steam points respectively, and the distance between these is divided into 180 equal parts. The Celsius (Centigrade) scale has 0° and 100° as the two fixed points, the region between being divided into 100 equal parts. Scientists use only the Celsius scale.

Templars ⬦ *Orders of Chivalry.*

Tennessee Valley Authority (TVA). Federal organization set up in 1933 during the ⬦ *New Deal* to reclaim the Tennessee River valley, which had suffered severely from floods and soil ⬦ *erosion*; it built dams and reservoirs and an extensive hydroelectric scheme to bring electric power to a large impoverished area. Designed to act as a 'yardstick' for private enterprise in the efficient and economical supply of light and power, as it involved government operation of electric supplies, it was violently criticized as socialistic but has since been generally recognized as a valuable scheme.

Tennis ⬦ *Lawn/Real/Table Tennis.*

Ten-pin Bowling. An indoor game in which contestants roll a heavy wooden ball of up to 16 lb., along a walled alley, at ten skittles 60 ft away. Of ancient Egyptian origin like most other bowling games, it was known in Germany in the 3rd cent. A.D. Luther helped to popularize it and is said to have decided on nine pins as the target. The game became widespread among 16th-cent. settlers in America, where the tenth pin was added in the 1840s, to circumvent laws against ninepins. In recent years the conversion of cinemas to bowling alleys in both America and Britain has brought a boom in the sport. The rules of the game are those of the American Bowling Congress, 1895.

Terbium ⬦ *Lanthanides.*

Termites. In many ways termites resemble ⬦ *ants* in appearance and social habits,

but they are of a quite different order, *Isoptera*, with over 2000 species, chiefly confined to the tropics. They are unlike ants in colour and in having thick waists. The most highly-organized colonies have queens (of enormous size); others produce winged males and females. They reproduce by an ant-like nuptial flight. Workers and soldiers are sterile. In Africa termites build mounds which may be as much as 20 ft high. They cause enormous damage by reason of their voracious appetite for wood, particularly dry wood in buildings.

Terms of Trade. The relationship between the prices at which a country sells its goods abroad and the prices which it pays for imports. Terms of trade are said to improve when the prices of imports fall in comparison with those received for exports. In the case of a country with a large international trade such as the U.K. changes in terms of trade are of considerable significance. Countries which sell goods in high demand in international trade tend to 'improve' their terms of trade, and in the 20th cent. the terms of trade have improved in general for industrial producers as against agricultural and raw material producers. ⬦ *Commodity Agreements.*

Territorial Army. Trained reserve of the British Army, organized on a county basis, established by Lord Haldane in 1907; merged with the Regular Army in 1939, it became an independent self-contained body again in 1947. Active membership is now voluntary, each unit carrying out 15 days' training in camp annually, in addition to weekly evening training sessions and occasional week-end camps.

Territorial Trusteeship. With the end of the Second World War and the founding of the United Nations Organization the system of ⬦ *mandates* of the League of Nations was replaced by a system of Trustee Territories whereby the administration of various non-selfgoverning territories was entrusted to certain members of the United Nations under the supervision of its Trusteeship Council. These territories are: Nauru Island, New Guinea, and the Trust Territory of the Pacific Islands.

Territorial Waters. Coastal waters under the jurisdiction of the state to which the coast belongs, peaceful passage through which is normally permitted to vessels of all nations; the traditional width, measured from the mean low-water mark, was one marine league i.e. three miles, the old cannon range. Bays, gulfs, and estuaries have been generally agreed to be territorial if the width of the entrance does not exceed six miles, but territorial rights are often claimed for much wider entrances. In ◊ *international law*, under the Freedom of the Seas principle, no state may claim sovereignty over the high seas outside its territorial waters except in respect of its own ships. Since the Second World War some states have sought to extend the three-mile limit; to control ◊ *fishing* rights, the government of Iceland in 1958 declared that its territorial waters extended 12 miles, and the legality of this claim was disputed by countries whose fleets fished these waters, esp. the U.K. Many other states wished to adopt the 12-mile limit, however, and Chile claimed exclusive fishery rights up to 200 miles out. United Nations conferences on the Law of the Sea, Geneva 1958 and 1960, failed to agree on the limits of territorial waters. The U.K. negotiated a bilateral agreement with Norway by which British fishermen are to fish in the 6–12 mile zone for 10 years, and accepted a similar three-year agreement with Iceland.

Tertiary Era ◊ *Geological Time Scale*.

Terylene. A synthetic fibre; so named from being a ◊ *polymer* from terephthalic acid. ◊ *Plastics, Synthetic Resins*.

Test Act. 1673. Passed by Parliament in repudiation of Charles II's ◊ *Indulgence*, enacting that anyone holding public office must publicly show himself to be a communicant member of the ◊ *Church of England*; Roman Catholics and Protestant Dissenters were thus excluded from office. Charles II and James II used their dispensing power to obviate the consequences of the Act to Roman Catholics, but not to Dissenters. After the ◊ *Glorious Revolution* of 1688 the position was reversed, and the ◊ *penal laws* were enforced. No general relief was granted until the ◊ *Catholic Emancipation* of 1829; posts at Oxford and Cambridge were restricted to members of the Church of England until 1871. ◊ *Exclusion Bill, Seven Bishops*.

Testes. Two sperm-forming glands in the scrotum of the male, also producing endocrine substances responsible for the development of the male sex-organs and of secondary sex characteristics e.g. the deepening of the voice and the growth of hair on the face. ◊ *Reproduction*.

Tetanus ◊ *Lockjaw*.

Teutonic Knights ◊ *Orders of Chivalry, Tannenberg (1410)*.

Teutonic Languages ◊ *Germanic Languages*.

Thailand. Area 198,247 sq. m. Pop. 30 m. Cap. Bangkok. Rel. mainly Buddhist. A kingdom in SE Asia bordered by Laos, Cambodia, Malaysia, and Burma; until 1949 it was called Siam. In 1946 King Ananda Mahidol was murdered and succeeded by the present king, Bhumibol Adulvadej: Marshal Pibul Songgram, who had been Prime Minister during Siam's alliance with Japan in the ◊ *Second World War*, became virtual ruler until overthrown by Field Marshal Saret in 1957, when a constitutional assembly was formed to draft a permanent constitution. Saret was deposed in 1958, and under the 1959 temporary constitution the king governs by the advice and consent of an appointed Constituent Assembly.

ECONOMY. The country is entirely agricultural. Rice is the main crop; the northern forests furnish teak. The government receives substantial financial aid from the U.S.A. Trade is mainly in the hands of an influential Chinese minority. Primary and secondary education is compulsory, free and widely available.

HISTORY. Siamese migrants from Asia arrived in the 13th cent. and overcame the original Mon and Khmer inhabitants, and set up a kingdom which united the country. Neither the Portuguese, who were the first Europeans to arrive, nor later the British, French, or Dutch, conquered Siam, which managed to remain the one independent state between British India and French ◊ *Indo-China*. Siam sided with the allies in the First World War but joined Japan in the Second.

LANGUAGE. Basically a tonal monosyllabic tongue of the Indo-Chinese family.

Thalidomide ◊ *Pharmacology*.

Thallium. A rare metallic ◊ *element* occurring in the dust from ◊ *pyrites* burners; grouped with aluminium, though its properties are more like those of lead, it has few uses. Its compounds are poisonous.

Thallophyta ◊ *Plants*.

Thanksgiving Day. American holiday inaugurated in 1621 by the Plymouth Colony of Massachusetts to commemorate their first successful harvest; made a U.S.A. national holiday by George Washington 1789, fixed as the fourth Thursday in November.

Theatre. The organized theatre of the western world has its origins in ancient Greece, where it grew out of communal ritual, the increasingly dramatized enactment of the community's activities and anxieties, e.g. hunting, fertility, warfare. At some unknown period the spectators gradually separated from the participants (dancers and reciters), who became actors, at first still religious but increasingly secular in function. By classical Greek times, festivals of drama in honour of ◊ *Dionysus* lasted nearly a week. The theatres seated up to 16,000 spectators in the open air, the audience sitting in a raked semicircle around the flat area (*orchestra*) where the chorus danced. Behind this acting space was the *skene*, a building which provided changing rooms for the actors and a setting for the action; it was later flanked by two *paraskene* (wings), and eventually a low ◊ *stage* connected these. Stage machinery included *periaktoi* (which seem to have been three-sided prisms which revolved to show different scenes), the *eccyclema* (a movable platform), and a kind of crane, used for 'flying' and the appearance of the *deus ex machina*. The actors wore masks, representational and life-size; the massive exaggerated masks belong to the 4th cent. B.C. and later. There is no evidence that Greek actors of the classical period wore thick-soled boots, as was once thought

In the Hellenistic period the theatres grew more ornate and complex. Roman theatres, although they followed Greek models, were even more sumptuous, and designed for spectacles, such as miniature sea-fights. The *orchestra* was replaced by a *cavea* (stage), in front of a magnificent permanent architectural 'set'. The audience, as before, sat in a tiered semicircle.

The Dark Ages were truly dark as far as the theatre was concerned. On its revival in medieval times it became the responsibility of the craft guilds, who produced the cycles of Mystery and ◊ *Miracle plays* on 'pageants' (small four-wheeled carts). Each section of the cycle

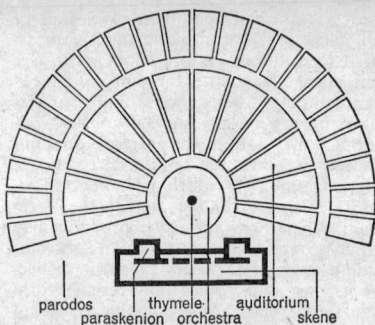

parodos   thymele   auditorium
     paraskenion orchestra   skene
greek

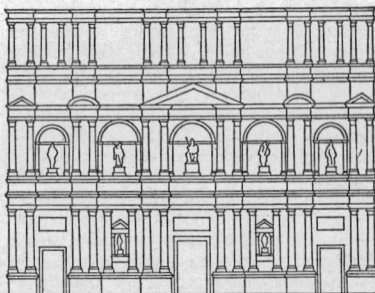

roman

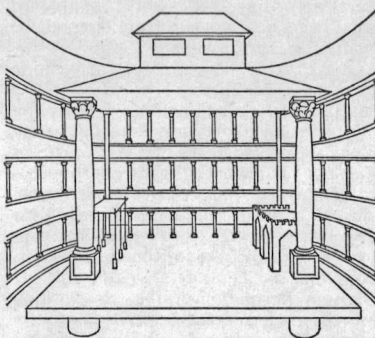

elizabethan

was entrusted to a guild, which mounted it on a pageant. Other plays were produced in 'mansions' (booths) around the market place, each booth representing a different scene. 'Round' plays were also produced, in theatres consisting of a circular area of flattened earth surrounded by a bank and ditch, with 'mansions' and a wooden 'castle' in the centre.

By the 16th cent. indoor theatres of classical design were being built in Italy, modelled largely on the Roman theatres. One of the finest examples of these ◊ *Renaissance* theatres is Palladio's Teatro Olimpico at Vicenza, 1580–84.

Elizabethan times brought the first permanent public (and commercial) theatres to England. The form of the Elizabethan theatre indicates its inn-yard origins. The audience stood or sat in galleries on three sides of the stage, which was left open to the sky for the sake of light, performances generally beginning at 2 p.m. At the back of the stage were the tiring rooms, an inner acting room, and a small gallery. The theatres were generally owned by businessmen like Henslowe or by joint-stock companies of actors like that of Burbage and Shakespeare. Since actors had no legal status in society, they were nominally the 'servants' of a nobleman, e.g. the Admiral's Men. Open theatres gave way to the indoor and more expensive 'private' theatres early in the 17th century.

The apron retreated during Restoration times, under the influence of Italy, and the stage area behind the proscenium became increasingly important; movable stage scenery (first used during the Interregnum) came into general use, and specialist stage designers, e.g. the Bibiena family in Italy, became prominent. Footlights and the proscenium curtain were introduced, and lighting advanced alongside the decorative arts. Early in the 19th cent. gas-lighting and the limelight came into use, to be displaced gradually by electricity, whose use was extended to emphasize the action, by the Swiss Adolphe Appia, 1862–1928. At the same time Gordon Craig advocated scenery which would interpret the drama rather than serve merely as a background.

At present most theatres conform in general to the pattern set in the late 17th cent. and the 'picture frame' stage still predominates, but the last few years have brought considerable advances in open staging and ◊ *theatre-in-the-round*. In this sense the development of the physical theatre may be said to have come full circle.

Theatre-in-the-Round. Many modern theatres esp. in U.S.A. are breaking away from the conventional proscenium style, and exploring afresh the relationship between acting area and audience. This movement is reflected in apron, arena, and open staging and above all in theatre-in-the-round, where the audience surrounds the acting area on all sides. Margo Jones pioneered this arrangement in her Dallas theatre, and Stephen Joseph has been responsible for much of the interest in Britain. ◊ *Theatre.*

Theism. The belief that there exists a good, omniscient, and omnipotent ◊ *God*, who (unlike the God of ◊ *Deism*) intervenes in the world.

Theodolite ◊ *Geodesy, Plane-Table, Surveying.*

Theosophy. Movement begun in 1875 by Madame H. P. Blavatsky, in New York, and after her death developed by Annie Besant in Britain. Based on Hindu and Buddhist teachings, it finds inspiration in the existence of certain 'mahatmas' or 'adepts', of high spiritual attainments, who have preserved a special mystical tradition through the ages; it upholds the doctrines of ◊ *karma* and reincarnation (◊ *Transmigration*) and the universal brotherhood of man, and expects the coming of a new 'World Teacher'. Its headquarters are at Adyar, Madras; it is mainly active in English-speaking countries. ◊ *Anthroposophy, Bahaism, Gnostics, Mysticism.*

Therapeutics. Branch of medicine concerned with the treatment of illnesses, formerly mainly by use of medicines, ointments etc., but now including an increasing number of physical methods, e.g. physiotherapy, manipulative treatment, radiation therapy, and, in mental disorders, psychotherapy.

Thermionic Valve (Tube). Originally a vacuum tube containing two electrodes, one of which (normally the cathode) is heated to cause the emission of electrons, and the other (normally the anode) would act as a collector. The actual difference in voltage between anode and cathode determines the strength of the electron current flowing. The effect was first discovered by Edison (U.S.A.) 1883: in 1904 Fleming in England invented the thermionic valve itself, which led to rapid developments in radio and television, and was basic to the whole new field of ◊ *electronics*. Today, valves often have more than two electrodes. Basically, they all, except the necessary anode and cathode, enable the electronics engineer to have special and delicate control over the electron current as it passes between the anode and the cathode.

Thermite. Mixture of finely-powdered aluminium with iron oxide or some other metallic oxide, producing great heat (about 3000° C) when ignited. It has been used for reducing oxides resistant to other methods, for welding and for incendiary bombs.

Thermocouple. An electrical device often used as a ◊ *thermometer*. It consists of two wires of different metals joined together to form a circuit. When one junction is heated to raise its temperature above that of the other one, a very small thermoelectric current flows in the circuit (Seebeck effect); a calibrated galvanometer capable of measuring the current would then give the difference in temperature between the junctions. Conversely, if a current of electricity is passed across the junction of two wires, heat will either be generated or absorbed according to the direction of the current (Peltier effect); the effect can be used to produce refrigeration.

Thermodynamics. Branch of physics dealing with ◊ *heat* as a form of energy. Joule first determined the mechanical equivalent of heat. It has three laws. (1) Heat and work are interchangeable, the amount of work always being equal to the quantity of heat, and heat can be expressed in terms of energy. (2) Heat energy always flows from a hotter to a colder body. (3) Every substance has a limited availability of energy to perform work (entropy), which approaches zero as its temperature nears absolute zero, which can never be reached.

Thermometer. An instrument for measuring ◊ *temperature*, first devised by Galileo about 1600. It may be constructed by making use of any physical property of a substance known to vary regularly with change of temperature. The type of instrument depends on the actual temperature or the range and accuracy of temperatures to be measured. The commonest one for measuring ordinary temperatures depends on the expansion of a small reservoir of liquid (e.g. mercury or coloured alcohol) along a closed glass capillary tube sealed on to it. The constant-volume gas thermometer has the

widest range; pyrometers, which are remote from the heat source and measure the intensity of radiation (light or heat) incident on them, are used for the extremely high temperatures of furnaces. The thermometer used for general scientific work for temperatures below 660° C depends upon the variation in resistance of a piece of platinum, and above 660° C upon the generation of thermoelectric electromotive force. ◊ *Thermocouple*.

Thermoplastic, Thermosetting ◊ *Plastics*.

Thermopylae. 480 B.C. A large Persian army invaded ◊ *Greece* and was marching S. towards Athens. At the vital pass of Thermopylae, Leonidas, the Spartan king, held the Persians long enough to give the Athenians time to organize a successful resistance. Leonidas and his band of 300 were all killed.

Thermostat. Device for turning off and on a source of heat in order to maintain a constant temperature. The expansion or contraction of some material sensitive to temperature changes, e.g. a column of mercury rising or falling in a tube, can be used to make or break an electric circuit. Strips of two metals with different coefficients of expansion are also often used; distortion resulting from the different response of the two metals to temperature changes causes the control to cut off or restore the heat source, at predetermined levels.

Theseus. In Greek legend, an Athenian hero, godson of ◊ *Poseidon*; destroyer of e.g. Procrustes, who amputated or stretched his victims to fit a bed. After Medea (◊ *Golden Fleece*) had tried to poison Theseus, he slew the Cretan bull brought to Greece by ◊ *Hercules*, which was devastating Marathon, and then went to Crete, where he killed the Minotaur (◊ *Minos*) and abducted Ariadne, who had given him the thread by which he had found his way through the Labyrinth (◊ *Daedalus*). He left her on Naxos (where ◊ *Dionysus* married her), and as king of Athens defeated the ◊ *Amazons*, married their queen Hippolyta, and had a son ◊ *Hippolytus*; after Hippolyta's death he married Ariadne's sister Phaedra. He died in Scyros; bones said to be his were brought to Athens after the Persian wars for burial in the Theseion, a sanctuary which became a principal centre of his cult.

Thiamin ◊ *Vitamins (B)*.

Third Reich. 1933–45. Period of Nazi rule in Germany. After 1933 Hitler rapidly established a brutal dictatorship, and became both head of state and of the army; the Nazi Party was the sole legal party, and all government posts of importance were awarded to Nazis. In 1934, Hitler eliminated all opposition within the Party by having Röhm and his supporters murdered. He instituted repressive legislation against Jews and suspended all civil rights. In foreign policy he flouted the restrictions of the ◊ *Versailles Treaty*, courted Mussolini, left the ◊ *League of Nations*, intervened in the ◊ *Spanish Civil War*, annexed Austria and humiliated France and Britain first by the ◊ *Munich Pact* and then by seizing ◊ *Czechoslovakia*. In 1939 after making a non-aggression pact with U.S.S.R., he precipitated the ◊ *Second World War* by invading ◊ *Poland* after which the terrors of concentration camps and the merciless elimination of ◊ *Jews* were intensified. Late in the war an attempt to assassinate Hitler by a group of army officers failed. In spite of intensive bombing and defeats on all fronts, the Nazi regime collapsed only in the hour of total defeat. ◊ *Genocide, Nazism, War Crimes.*

Third Republic. 1871–1940. The French government formed after the defeat in the ◊ *Franco–Prussian War*; its features were a President elected for seven years by the Senate and Chamber of Deputies, an indirectly elected Senate, and an Assembly elected by universal suffrage, to which the Premier and Cabinet were responsible. Owing to the multiplicity of French parties and their inability to form stable coalitions, there was a succession of weak and shortlived governments, 99 between 1873 and 1940, of which only eight lasted more than two years. The Third Republic was shaken by the ambitions of generals, scandals, the ◊ *Dreyfus affair*, and the disasters of the ◊ *First World War*, which it survived largely by virtue of the basic economic strength of the country and the efficiency of the professional administrative services. When France capitulated to the Germans in 1940 (◊ *Vichy France*) the Third Republic came to an end, to be succeeded in 1944 by the ◊ *Fourth Republic.*

Thirty-nine Articles. Doctrines of the ◊ *Church of England*, formulated in 1571, which its clergy are required to accept

and not to criticize in their public teaching. Worded in general and often negative terms, and open to wide variety in interpretation, they deal with e.g. the ◊ *Trinity*, ◊ *free will* and ◊ *predestination*, the authority of the Church, the ◊ *sacraments*, and Church–State relations. ◊ *Erastianism, Prayer Book.*

Thirty Years War. 1618–48. Touched off by the demands of German Protestants for religious toleration, the war soon became a struggle for political domination in Europe, between the ◊ *Hapsburgs*, the German Protestant states, ◊ *Bourbon* France, Sweden, Denmark, and the ◊ *Netherlands*. In 1618 the Protestant nobles of ◊ *Bohemia* offered the crown to the Lutheran prince the Elector Frederick of the ◊ *Palatinate*, whom the Imperial forces immediately deposed, annexing the territory. The Hapsburg aim was to possess Germany and regain the territory lost to Catholicism by the ◊ *Reformation*. Denmark, under Christian IV, who feared Hapsburg power on the Baltic, launched an attack on N. Germany, but after a series of defeats by Tilly and Wallenstein he withdrew from the war after the Treaty of Lübeck in 1629. In the same year the Emperor Ferdinand II issued the Edict of Restitution, which heavily oppressed the Protestants. Gustavus Adolphus of Sweden now entered the war, avowedly as the champion of Protestantism, but in fact in hopes of conquests in N. Germany; backed by Cardinal Richelieu in France, he was later joined by Saxony. Tilly captured the Protestant stronghold of Magdeburg in 1631, but was twice defeated by the Swedish army (1631 Breitenfeld, 1632 Lech, where he was killed). At the battle of ◊ *Lützen* in 1632 Wallenstein was defeated, but Gustavus Adolphus was killed and his army disorganized. The Peace of Prague in 1635 might have ended the war, for it was accepted by most German princes; but Richelieu was unwilling to sanction a settlement which left Imperial power almost intact, and France openly entered the war. In the last phase there was fighting all over Europe, and the Imperial forces were defeated on all sides. Peace negotiations were begun in 1640; the final Peace of ◊ *Westphalia* recognized the independence of the German princes in 1648. The war was the first great international struggle for power; it destroyed what authority the ◊ *Holy*

Roman Empire had retained. It caused great loss of life and devastation esp. in Germany, where large areas were left underpopulated and unproductive.

Thor ◊ *Aesir.*

Thorax. The part of the trunk between the neck and the abdomen, i.e. the chest; the cavity is bounded at the back by the 12 dorsal vertebrae and at the front by the 12 pairs of ribs and the sternum, and is separated from the abdomen by the diaphragm. ◊ *Skeleton.*

THORACOPLASTY: The surgical removal of ribs, in order to reduce the size of the chest cavity and induce collapse of a tuberculous lung.

Thorium. ◊ *Actinides*; a silvery metal which rapidly tarnishes in air, occurring as phosphate in monazite sand found in India, U.S.A. and U.S.S.R. It shows only the valency state of 4, and its chemistry is simple. In the days of gas-lighting, large quantities of the nitrate mixed with a little cerium nitrate were used for impregnating cotton gas-mantles. Since 1940 the principal interest in it has arisen from the fact that it can absorb neutrons to give uranium-233, which is fissionable and can be used in a nuclear reactor.

Thorn. *Crataegus (Rosaceae)*; large genus of N. temperate regions, many from N. America. They are usually spiny and have flat heads of white flowers (more rarely, pink or red) and red or orange berries. *C. monogyna* (may, hawthorn), with heavily scented flowers in May and June, is found commonly in Britain in hedgerows or as small rugged trees in open places. There are many superstitions about it, esp. in Ireland. The Glastonbury Thorn, which flowers in mid-winter, and is alleged to open its first flowers on Christmas Day, is a variety of *C. monogyna*, supposed to have sprung from the staff of Joseph of Arimathea. Blackthorn (sloe) is *Prunus spinosa.*

Thoth. In Egyptian mythology, originally a moon god, adviser and arbiter to the other gods, inventor of mathematics. The Greeks identified him with ◊ *Hermes.* He is represented with the head of one of his sacred animals, the ibis and ape.

Thrombosis. The formation of an obstructing clot (thrombus) in the heart or in a blood vessel. The most common causes are infection and impairment of the circulation or of the bodily mechanisms which prevent coagulation of the ◊

blood. A clot in the brain is likely to cause paralysis, and one in the heart to result in heart seizure. Thrombosis in a blood vessel may cause ◊ *gangrene* of the area which the vessel serves.

Thrush. 1. A world-wide family including the song-thrush, missel-thrush, and blackbird. The song-thrush feeds on snails, breaking the shells by beating them against 'anvil' stones, and on worms; it breeds early in the year, building a mud-lined nest for four to five blue-green eggs. **2.** In medicine, an infection of the mouth and throat caused by fungi of the species *candida*, commonest in delicate babies and in old people. ◊ *Mycosis.*

Thugs. Secret fraternity of murderers in India, devotees of Kali, the Hindu goddess of destruction. They travelled in gangs disguised as merchants, and ingratiated themselves with wealthy travellers, whom they killed by strangling; the corpses were plundered and buried. The fraternity was suppressed 1829–36 and 300 of its members executed.

Thulium ◊ *Lanthanides.*

Thunderstorm. When strong upward currents of moist air form very deep cumulonimbus clouds, shedding rain and sometimes hail, static electricity builds up in the clouds and discharges as lightning ('forked' when the discharge itself is seen, 'sheet' when it merely lights up the clouds); sound waves (created by rapid expansion of the heated air) produce thunder. Most frequent and severe in equatorial regions, where the moist air is sufficiently warm near the ground to cause violent up-currents, e.g. the lower Amazon basin has thunderstorms about 170 days in the year.

Thyme ◊ *Herbs, Labiatae.*

Thymol ◊ *Eucalyptus.*

Thyroid. Ductless gland in the neck, which utilizes iodine to form the hormone thyroxin which it secretes in the blood. Its main function is to control the body's rate of metabolism. ◊ *Cretinism, Glands, Goitre.*

Tibet. Area 463,000 sq. m. Pop. 1.3 m. Cap. Lhasa. Rel. Buddhist (about 20 per cent of the male population are monks). Autonomous province of China, N. of the Himalayas.

ECONOMY. Agricultural, exporting borax, musk, salt, wool to India and herbs, horn, musk to China.

HISTORY. In the 9th cent. A.D. Tibet was

military power, but after conversion to Buddhism it remained for centuries in isolation. After intervention in the 18th cent. China claimed suzerainty, but this was often of a shadowy nature. In 1904 the British Younghusband expedition forced Tibet to open its doors to British trade, and prevented other foreign powers having commercial relations there. During the 1911 Revolution in China, Tibet maintained its independence and retained it until 1950, when the country was occupied by the forces of communist China. External affairs were surrendered to China, but autonomy was nominally retained in internal affairs. The religious leader, the Dalai Lama, at first appeared to support the Chinese regime, but after a Tibetan rising in 1959, which was rapidly overcome, he fled to India. In 1962 the Chinese attacked India, seeking rectification of the Tibetan frontier ($\Diamond$ *MacMahon Line*).

Tick. Bloodsucking arachnid somewhat larger than a $\Diamond$ *mite*, parasitic esp. on dogs, sheep, and other mammals, but also on birds and reptiles, and spreading many animal diseases by injecting the germs into the blood of new hosts. Some attack the ears of domestic animals; failing treatment, this can cause injury or death.

Tides. The rise and fall in the level of oceans caused by the gravitational attraction of the moon and to a lesser extent

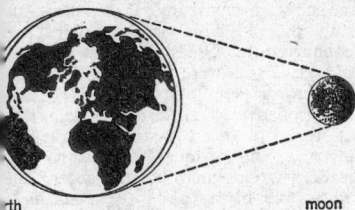

earth   moon

the sun; one bulge of water is drawn up on the side of the earth under the moon and a secondary one is created on the opposite side of the earth, where, however, the pull is less. Two high and two low tides thus occur at any particular point during the moon's period of rotation round the earth (about 24 hours, 50 min.). When the moon is new or full, its pull is assisted by that of the sun, and tides of maximum range (spring tides) occur; at first or third quarter the moon's

pull is opposed by that of the sun, and less pronounced neap tides result. In the open ocean the tidal rise and fall is only two or three feet, but it is greatly increased by certain configurations of the coasts. In the Bay of Fundy the rise and fall is 50 feet. In funnel-shaped estuaries the tide gives rise to a bore – a wall of water which advances upstream at rising tide.

Tiger. Great cat, one of the carnivora, found throughout Asia, some e.g. the Bengal Tiger (10 ft long) larger than $\Diamond$ *lions*; the beautiful red-brown coat is marked by vertical black stripes and the belly-surface is white. The mother shows maternal care in the feeding, protection, and instruction of the young, three or four being born at a litter. Tiger-hunting has long been an aristocratic sport in India; the tiger's ferocity and strength are such that 10 to 30 men armed with rifles and mounted on elephants are considered fair odds.

Till Eulenspiegel. German peasant of the 14th or 15th cent. famous throughout Europe as a practical joker; known as Owlglass in Britain.

Tilsit Treaty. 1807. Treaty whereby Napoleon secured the cooperation of Russia in the $\Diamond$ *Continental System*, in return for Prussia's consent to ceding half her territory to Russia. It marked the zenith of Napoleon's career.

Time. Man's subjective experience of time is often relative: eventful periods appear shorter than equally long but uneventful periods. The measurement of the passage of time, however, can be placed upon an objective basis, and there are various methods of measurement. $\Diamond$ *Atomic Clock, Calendar, Chronometer, Clocks and Watches.*

SIDEREAL TIME: The time required for the earth to rotate once on its axis with a particular star as reference point, the sidereal day being about 4 min. shorter than a solar day. There are thus slightly more than 366 such days in a year.

SOLAR TIME: Measured by the hour angle of the sun exactly as given by the sundial. The length of the day so defined varies in the course of the year: resort therefore is made to a fictitious mean solar day which is the sum of all the actual solar days of a year divided by 365. The difference between apparent time and mean solar time is known as the equation of time ranging from a maximum of about 16½ min. to zero four times a year. The mean solar time on the meridian of Greenwich formerly known as Greenwich Mean Time (GMT) is now termed Universal Time.

EPHEMERIS TIME: The rate of rotation of the earth is not quite regular, however, and the invention of very accurate quartz, atomic, and molecular clocks has made it possible to use Ephemeris Time based on the period of the earth's revolution around the sun for very precise work. The various measures of time are tabulated in the yearly Astronomical Ephemeris.

Tin. A metallic element which does not easily tarnish. Ordinary tin is 'white' tin, but this allotrope is not stable below 13° C; at lower temperatures a grey allotrope forms, and this change ('tin plague') can in extremely cold conditions cause crumbling of the metal. Smelted from tin-stone, readily reduced to metal by heating together with ◊ carbon, the metal has been known since antiquity; it is used for coating (tinning) metals e.g. copper, brass, and iron (◊ tinplate) to protect them from oxidation or corrosion (provided the coating remains unbroken). Tinning allows iron to be soldered, and prevents poisonous metals e.g. copper from dissolving and contaminating food. Tin forms two series of compounds in the respective valency states of 2 and 4; the oxide is a base and gives stannous salts, while the dioxide (stannic) is acidic ('putty powder') and is used for polishing, for white glaze for ceramics, and for milk-white glass. ◊ Alloys.

Tinplate. Sheets of iron or steel coated with tin to prevent corrosion, widely used for making food containers. It was formerly prepared mainly by the 'hot dip' process, in which sheets were passed through a bath of molten tin. Since 1930 this method has been giving way to an electrolytic process which gives a thinner but nevertheless effective coating, making possible fine-gauge tinplate; it also plates articles of irregular shape more evenly. So great is the demand for tinplate in the canning industry that techniques have been developed by which it is produced as a continuous strip for feeding into can-making machines, some of which are capable of turning out several thousand cans a minute.

Tiresias. In Greek legend, a Theban wh was temporarily transformed into woman for killing a female snake. When Zeus and ◊ Hera asked him whether ma or woman experienced greater pleasu in carnal love, his answer displeased Her who struck him blind; but Zeus compe sated him with long life and the gift prophecy, to which ◊ Athena afterwar added a staff and the ability to interpr the language of birds. In one of the mar versions he became a man again when I killed the female snake's mate.

Titania ◊ Uranus (1).

Titanic. Largest vessel of the White St Line, 45,000 tons, which on her maide voyage from Southampton to New Yo in 1912 collided with an iceberg and san with a loss of 1513 lives; the tragec caused amendments to be made in t International Regulations for the Safe of Life at Sea with regard to ship co struction and to lifeboat requirements.

Titanium. A bright grey metallic ◊ el ment forming 0.6 per cent of the earth crust, used in the manufacture of light b highly tensile alloys, resistant to corr sion by many chemicals. The most in portant compound is the dioxide, prepar in large quantities as a white pigme used in paint, in enamels for domest iron goods, and in rubber, linoleum, ar cosmetics.

Titans. In Greek legend, the predecesso of the Olympian gods, typifying u measured strength and lawlessness; po sibly the old gods of an earlier peop conquered by Greek invaders (◊ Myt ology). They were the offspring of Uranus, heaven, and Gaea (Ge), eart Imprisoned in ◊ Tartarus by their fathe at their mother's instigation they d throned and dismembered him; their leader Cronos married his sister Rhe who gave birth to e.g. ◊ Demeter, Hera, ◊ Pluto, ◊ Poseidon. Warned th one of his children would displace hir Cronos swallowed them all, but Rhe went to Crete to give birth to ◊ Zeu who when adult gave Cronos a potic which made him disgorge his offspring. the War of the Titans, Zeus and h brothers and sisters defeated their fath and his followers, who were hurled into prison below Tartarus; Zeus assumed ru over earth and heaven. ◊ Hecate.

T.N.T. (Trinitrotoluene) ◊ Explosive Nitrogen.

Toad. Rough-skinned ◊ *amphibian*, with short legs which do not permit a frog-like leap; the skin, with both mucous and serous glands, is unpalatable to predators, and the life-cycle is similar to that of the ◊ *frog*. Toads hibernate in burrows. Some species show rudimentary parental care. They are found throughout the world, two species being native to Britain.

Toadstools. Fruiting bodies of ◊ *fungi*, commonly held to be inedible, unlike ◊ *mushrooms*; in fact most toadstools are edible, e.g. truffles (produced underground), edible Boletus (the main 'mushroom' in mushroom soup), chanterelles, blewits, lactarius, etc. Some are unpleasant (stinkhorn) and some very poisonous (death cap, fly agaric). Toadstools have various shapes and sizes, often with a smooth cap, and gills, pores, or teeth carrying the spores. Some form hard brackets on trees. Puffballs are almost circular, and when ripe shed clouds of brown spores through a hole in the top. Toadstools are esp. common in woods.

Tobacco. Broad-leaved plant with scented flowers opening at night, native to tropical America. The U.S.A. remains a major source of production, and chief exporter: it is now also grown in China, India, U.S.S.R., Europe, and the Near East, and is an important export crop for some E. African countries. The characteristics of different tobaccos depend not only on type but on soil and climate. Pipe smoking, copied from the Indians, was popularized in Britain by Ralegh and Drake; the taking of snuff was introduced by Jean Nicot (hence nicotine), a French diplomat, into the court of France where it became fashionable. Subsequently smoking was severely repressed almost everywhere; in Britain the Great Plague 1665 gave fresh impetus as smoking was held to confer immunity to infection. The most rapid increase occurred after the adoption of the cigarette habit from the Turks during the Crimean War. In the U.K. the sale of cigarettes rose from negligible in the 1880s to 36,000 m. in 1920 and 113,000 m. in 1961, Virginia tobacco replacing Turkish in popularity over the same period. A similar increase occurred in the U.S.A. (from 50 in 1900 to 4000 in 1961 per head of those over 15 years of age). A striking growth in deaths from lung cancer and respiratory diseases in recent years led to investigations in U.K. and U.S.A. and the U.S. Surgeon-General after careful study found evidence of 'a causal link' between smoking and higher mortality rates in a number of diseases. He summed up: 'Cigarette smoking is a health hazard of sufficient importance for the U.S.A. to warrant prompt remedial action'. The U.K. study reached similar conclusions.

Tobago ◊ *Trinidad and Tobago.*

Tobogganing. Racing down ice-slopes on sleighs or toboggans, on a time-trial basis; the first organized races were held in Switzerland about 1890, and the famous Cresta Run at St Moritz was first marked out for bobsleighs (longer toboggans for two or four people) in 1895 and rebuilt in 1904 as an artificial run. The first World Championships were held 1927. Present classifications are as follows. (1) Cresta: the sleigh is a skeleton on which a single person lies prone. (2) Luge: ridden by one or two men, seated. (3) Bobsleigh: a two- or four-man event; modern bobsleighs can travel at up to 90 m.p.h. In the 1964 Olympics the two-man bobsleigh was the one event won by Britain.

Togo. Area 21,000 sq. m. Pop. 1.5 m. (several African races esp. Ewe). Cap. Lamé. A republic in W. Africa (between Dahomey and Ghana), set up 1960 by the U.N.

ECONOMY. Mainly agricultural; chief exports cocoa, coffee, copra, cotton, manioc, pinekernels. Teak plantations have been started, and French firms are developing phosphate mines.

HISTORY. A German colony till the First World War, between the wars a French mandated territory, a U.N. trusteeship under French administration 1946–60. In 1963 a military junta assassinated President Olympio and seized control, dissolving the National Assembly, suspending the constitution, and declaring a provisional government under Mr Granitsky. Under a fresh constitution a new Assembly was elected and Mr Granitsky took office as President. ◊ *Ghana.*

Tolpuddle Martyrs. 1834. Six farm labourers of Tolpuddle, Dorset, formed a friendly society of agricultural labourers to try to obtain a weekly wage of 10s. since the repressive legislation against trade unions had been repealed in 1824. They were prosecuted for 'administering an illegal oath' and sentenced to transportation to Australia. The iniquity of the procedure aroused widespread and effective protest, which secured their release in 1836.

Tomato. *Lycopersicum esculentum*, also called love-apple; an annual, probably derived from one of the 10 species native to Peru, either *L. esculentum*, or *L. galeni* with small cherry-like fruits. It came to Europe at the end of the 16th cent. from Mexico, where several wild and cultivated varieties exist. It is only within the last 50 years that it has become so popular in Britain as to be the basis of a large glasshouse industry, though in Italy it was cultivated widely from about 1600, for use with spaghetti.

Tonnage. In medieval times a ship's size was expressed as the number of tons (tuns) of wine that could be carried in the hold; various formulae based on the vessel's length and beam were devised to calculate this figure, but early in the 19th cent. Moorsom's system of measuring the full internal capacity of the hull (not including open or partly open deck erections) in cubic ft, and expressing it in tons of 100 cubic ft as the Gross Register Tonnage (GRT) came into use. The space occupied by crew accommodation, propelling machinery, etc. being deducted, the remainder is the Net Register Tonnage (NRT). The displacement tonnage, the usual way to indicate a naval vessel's size, is her actual weight. ⟫ *Shipping.*

Topaz ⟡ *Silica.*

Torah ⟡ *Bible, Talmud.*

Tornado. Extremely violent revolving storm (whirlwind) usually not over a quarter of a mile in diameter and accompanied by a column of cloud, heavy rain, and thunder; a local phenomenon advancing more or less in a straight line, normally north-eastwards at 20–40 m.p.h. Often dies out in less than an hour, but causes great destruction along its narrow track, demolishing buildings and uprooting trees by wind speeds probably over 200 m.p.h. near the centre. Frequent east of the Rocky Mountains in U.S.A. esp. in the Mississippi basin, where hot moist air from the Gulf of Mexico meets cool dry air from the north.

WATERSPOUT: Tornado at sea, usually in the tropics; a funnel-shaped portion descends from a heavy cloud till it meets a cone of spray raised from the sea and forms a column of water from 20 to ove? 200 ft across and several hundred ft high. As the top often travels at a differen? speed from the base, a waterspout usuall? breaks and disappears within half an hour.

Torpedo. An underwater projectile, whic? can be launched from a ship, submarine or aeroplane. The first effective torped? was designed by Robert Whitehead 186? ⟫ *Destroyer, Submarines.*

Torres Vedras ⟡ *Peninsular War.*

Tort. A civil wrong (other than breac? of trust or of ⟡ *contract*), e.g. assault negligence, trespass, wrongful detentio? of goods, for which damages may b? claimed in remedy.

Tortoise. Terrestrial member of the rep? tilian order *Chelonia*, closely related t? the ⟡ *turtle*, having a hard protective cas? of horn-covered bone; the longest-live? of vertebrates, they may live for 125 year and range in size from ounces to hundred weights, the largest being the rare gian? tortoise of the Galapagos Islands.

Tory. Originally Irish for a Catholic out? law. During the stormy debates in Par? liament on the ⟡ *Exclusion Bill* of 167? those in favour of the measure called thei? opponents 'tory', a term of abuse whic? gained currency, being applied next t? the ⟡ *Jacobites*; subsequently, when th? Whigs welcomed the French Revolution 'tory' came to mean anti-republican, re? actionary. In the 1870s Disraeli reconsti? tuted the Tory Party under the name ? *conservative*; 'tory' still survives as ? jocular or pejorative title.

Totemism. A form of religion in whic? the sacred object, the totem, is represente? in the form generally of an animal o? plant. Totems may be associated with an? worshipped by clans, local groups, or in? dividuals. Offerings may be made to them and dramas representing the mystical re? lationship between them and men enacte? periodically, often in order to perpetuate the particular species. The most famous form of group totemism is that of the ⟡ *Australian aborigines*. Ethnologists onc? thought totemism to be the most 'primi? tive' and so the original form of religion but this seems to be conjecture, ther? being no evidence to support it. The wor? 'totem' comes from the language of th? Ojibwa of North America, where th? totem is regarded as an individual guard? ian. In British Columbia the Indians carved the totem animals on totem poles o indicate ancestry or to depict clan myths.

Tourmaline ◊ *Silica*.

Tours. A.D **732.** Frankish victory which checked the advance of the Moors, who had taken Bordeaux and Poitiers and were advancing on Tours when they were met by the Franks under Charles Martel. They attacked the Frankish defensive position, and lost heavily; with their retreat to Spain, the threat of further Muslim advance into Europe was removed.

Town Planning. Planned towns were known in antiquity, and one outstanding example survives in the ruins of Pompeii. In the Dark Ages and medieval times towns were largely determined by defensive considerations; the Renaissance produced magnificent avenues and sections rather than integrated cities. Wren produced an admirable plan for the rebuilding of London after the Great Fire of 1666, which was not carried out. In the 19th cent. Washington, U.S.A., and Haussmann's remodelling of Paris were instances of town planning, and subsequently other planned cities – usually capitals – have been built, notably at Canberra, New Delhi, and Brasilia. In Britain 'model villages' for workers were built by Cadbury Bros. at Bourneville 1879) and by Lever Bros. at Port Sunight (1888). Shortly after came the first ◊ *garden city*. Sir Patrick Geddes in Britain and Lewis Mumford in U.S.A. were important advocates of town planning in the sense of an integrated, urban community – fully provided with amenities – physical, cultural, recreational, etc. But acceptance by public authorities of responsibility for such planning came slowly in Europe and later still in the U.S.A. In the U.K. the principal relevant acts are the Town and Country Planning Acts of 1947, 1959, and 1962, which require local planning authorities to submit comprehensive plans for their areas to the Minister of Housing. Most plans were ready by 1961, but few have been executed. ◊ *New Towns*.

Trace Elements. For healthy growth, plants and animals need (besides the normal nutrients e.g. nitrates, phosphates, and potash) minute amounts of compounds containing such elements as boron, manganese, and cobalt; deficiency of any one of these 'trace elements' can result in specific diseases e.g. 'heart rot' in sugar-beet

(boron deficiency) or the wasting disease in sheep known as 'pining' (cobalt deficiency).

Tracer Elements. Radioactive isotopes which can be introduced into a system to accompany a stable isotope and thus enable its course and destination to be traced, the minute radioactive emissions from such isotopes being detectable by a ◊ *Geiger counter*. Tracers are used in biochemical investigation e.g. of metabolic processes, for studying chemical reactions, and in metallurgy, geology, archaeology, and other fields of study.

Tracheophyta ◊ *Plants*.

Tracheotomy. Surgical opening of the trachea (windpipe). Before immunization and antibiotic treatment had reduced the severity of ◊ *diphtheria*, tracheotomy was often used to relieve the difficulty in breathing. Nowadays the operation is usually to bypass obstruction caused by malignant disease of the throat.

Trade Cycle. The tendency for economic activity to fluctuate. It is inherent in the free enterprise system, which, if totally undirected, tends to fluctuate between boom and depression. Fluctuations in fixed investment or stockbuilding are particularly liable to cause trade cycles. If business men on an optimistic view of trends decide to increase plant capacity (that is, their investment) they increase employment and so increase incomes. This increase in incomes will lead to more spending and possibly to higher prices, and will encourage business men to expand capacity even further. So a cumulative process is set in train of rising investment, rising incomes, and possibly of inflation – rising prices. This process, if it goes on long enough, can lead to hyperinflation, in which prices begin to rise very fast indeed.

In the same way, the cumulative process can work downwards. Business men for some reason invest less, thus reducing employment, incomes, and consumer spending. This may lead to further cuts in investment and this process also can become cumulative. This is the downward phase of the trade cycle, generally known as ◊ *deflation*.

Business cycles of this kind are not limited to one country, but – through international trade – are transmitted from one country to another. As production and incomes fall in the industrial countries, for example, their purchases of raw materials and foodstuffs from the primary producing countries are reduced. This brings down the prices of primary products, so in turn these primary producers reduce their purchase of manufactured goods, and further worsen the position in the industrial countries. In this way, too, tendencies upwards or downwards can be cumulative on an international scale.

Governments have increasingly discovered that they are not powerless in face of the trade cycle; they can intervene to stop the cumulative movement e.g. by spending more themselves if private investment is falling, or by increasing taxation if the economy is moving towards a boom. In European countries today, therefore – although some items of national expenditure, like stockbuilding or fixed investment, may move in a cyclical fashion – there is no full trade cycle, because the Government intervenes. In a number of countries there has not been a single year since the war in which national output was lower than the year before. In U.S.A. there are still cyclical movements, up and down, of economic activity as a whole, but on a much smaller scale than before the war. ✿ *Keynes, Unemployment*.

Trademark. A mark on goods distinguishing them from others. It may be a device or an invented word. A registered trademark is protected by law.

Trades Union Congress. Federation of the major British ◊ *trade unions*, founded 1868. Some 18 large unions or federations of unions with a membership of over 8 m. are affiliated, though many small unions are not. A main function of the T.U.C. is to bring union representatives together to discuss matters of common concern, the annual conference being the supreme authority. It elects an executive, the General Council, recognized by the Government as the channel for consultation with government departments on matters of general concern to employers. The T.U.C. itself is a non-political body, and the affiliated unions remain autonomous, the T.U.C. having no control over their actions in wage negotiations, etc.

Trade Union. An organization of workers for the purpose of protecting their interests and obtaining higher wages, shorter hours, and better working conditions. The early history of trade unionism in the U.K. is essentially that of the struggle to legalize their position. The Combination Acts of 1799 and 1800 and the Common Law were used to hamper the early attempts of textile workers and miners to form unions. After their repeal in 182 there was a rapid development but a period of poor trade and unemployment slowed unionization; it was not till legislation during the years 1871–6 that their activities received full legal recognition. Membership grew rapidly after 1890. By the judgement in the Taff Vale case 190 it was decided that trade unions could be collectively sued for losses occasioned by strikes. The Trade Disputes Act 190 passed by the Liberals granted trade unions immunity from legal suits for damages and permitted peaceful picketing. A further decision in 1909 ruled that unions could make grants to political parties and in 1913 a law was passed whereby union members could 'contract out' i.e. decline to subscribe for political purposes. After the 1926 General Strike the Trade Disputes Act of 1927 made a general strike illegal and substituted 'contracting-in' (i.e. positively indicating a wish to contribute to political ends) for 'contracting-out'. This remained in force until 1946, when the Act was repealed in its entirety by the Labour Government. The 'closed shop' i.e. the requirement that all workers belong to a trade union is now found in a number of industries or in individual factories. The main function of trade unions is collective bargaining with employers, with strike action as a final resort. In the U.K. bargaining tend to be at national level, whereas in U.S.A. negotiations with individual plants or firms are frequent. Unions were also once important as friendly societies, providing sickness and unemployment benefits these functions have been largely superseded in the U.K. by national insurance. There is a wide variety of size and type of union. In the U.K. there are craft unions e.g. plumbers; industrial unions i.e. all employees of one industry e.g. the Tobacco Workers Union; and general unions e.g. the Transport and General Workers Union, originally for unskilled workers but now including clerical workers. There are some 650 unions in the U.K. with membership varying from 6 (London Jewish Bakers) to $1\frac{1}{4}$ m. (Transport and General Workers Union). The majority are affiliated to the ◊ *Trades Union Congress*.

FRANCE: Unions were given legal recognition only in 1884 and were organized under the Confédération Générale du Travail. This was split over the question of communist influence between 1918 and 1925 and on its reunification became dominated by the communists. In 1947 the movement again split in 2 parts, Force Ouvrière (non-communist) and the C.G.T. A third, smaller confederation, originally founded by Roman Catholic workers, dropped 'Chrétien' from the title in 1964 to become the Confédération Française et Démocratique du Travail.

GERMANY: There were various competing trade union organizations all of which were suppressed in 1933 by the Nazis. In Western Germany after the Second World War labour was organized on the basis of a small number of large industrial unions; in this way German industry avoids the demarcation disputes which arise with craft unionism.

U.S.A. ◊ *American Federation of Labor, National Labor Relations Act, New Deal, Taft-Hartley Act*.

Trade Winds. Regular winds of great importance in the days of sailing-ships, blowing throughout the year from subtropical high-pressure belts towards the equator (in the northern hemisphere from the NE, in the southern hemisphere from the SE) esp. over oceans. Weather in trade-wind regions is usually fine, but tropical cyclones sometimes occur (◊ *Tornado*). ◊◊ *Latitude*.

ANTI-TRADES or COUNTER-TRADES: Steady winds of the upper air at heights of several thousand ft above the trade winds blowing in the opposite direction. DOLDRUMS: Belt of light winds and calms around the equator where sailing-ships were sometimes becalmed for weeks between the NE and SE trade winds.

Trafalgar. 1805. Cape off SW coast of Spain where during the ◊ *Napoleonic Wars* the British under Nelson defeated the combined French and Spanish fleets. Collingwood, with the larger squadron, cut off and overwhelmed part of the French and Spanish fleets, while Nelson, keeping the enemy in doubt about his tactics by his daring approach in line ahead, broke through the centre and prevented any help being given to the rear. Of the 33 French and Spanish ships 17 were captured. The battle, in which Nelson was killed, ended French hopes of victory at sea. ◊◊ *Continental System*.

Tragedy. A form of serious drama in which the hero suffers and often dies, but in a context which leaves the audience with feelings of exaltation rather than despair. In the western world Aristotle based himself on the great 5th-cent B.C. tragedies of Aeschylus, Sophocles, and Euripides (see below) and defined tragedy as 'a representation of an action . . . which through arousing pity and fear achieves the catharsis [purging] of such emotions'. Though it attempts to explain both the 'peculiar pleasure' and the value of tragedy, Aristotle's definition is limited by his concentration on the Greek examples. Greek tragedy developed from rituals and derives its plots from myths, behind many of which lies the idea of redemptive suffering, most concretely symbolized in the widespread myths of the dying god.

Tragedy re-emerged in Europe out of medieval drama (◊ *Miracle Play*) and reached its peak in Shakespeare in the late Elizabethan and early Jacobean period. Religious, popular, and academic streams all flowed into Elizabethan tragedy; though the mythic and ritual elements are not always as obvious as they are in much Greek tragedy they are deeply embedded, and modern criticism with its interest in archetypes and symbols has located them in e.g. *Hamlet*, *Macbeth*, and *King Lear*. Shakespearean tragedy, with its deep humanist interest in psychologico-moral problems, its profoundly exploratory use of language, and its combination of popular entertainment with great subtlety and individuality of technique and insight, provides the spectator, and more especially the reader, with an almost infinite richness of meaning.

A much more precisely formulated kind of tragedy developed in 17th-cent. France, where the attempt by Corneille and Racine to devise a tragedy which would adhere to the neoclassic unities resulted in tragedies of concentrated conflict, presenting the last phase of a complex emotional situation in tightly knit action expressed in language of most carefully turned poetic rhetoric. The conflict between love and honour is a favourite theme. In Corneille, this sometimes seems to be the playing of a complex game of moral chess, with a given problem to solve in so many moves; but in Racine it often results in a sharp and moving illumination of the human inwardness of what might at first sight appear a mechanical or conventional pattern of action.

European romantic tragedy, esp. German and English of the late 18th and early and mid 19th centuries, concentrated on the conflict between the hero and society, and was essentially literary rather than theatrical.

Modern tragedy owes much to Ibsen, having learned from him both to investigate problems of social morality and to employ a conscious symbolism in both plot and language, but no great tragedy in the classic sense has appeared in the 20th cent. O'Neill's attempt in *Mourning Becomes Electra* to write tragedy on the Greek model was manifestly unsuccessful; Arthur Miller's *Death of a Salesman* perhaps comes closest to greatness.

GREEK TRAGEDY: Invented and brought to perfection by the Athenians in the 6th and 5th centuries B.C. and possibly a fusion of a ritual dance with a hero-cult; associated throughout its history with the cult of ◊ *Dionysus*. The traditional founder, Thespis (about 554 B.C.), appears to have interspersed his series of choral odes with an actor's speeches, sometimes narrative and sometimes in dialogue with the chorus leader. Aeschylus, the first of the three great Attic tragedians, appeared early in the 5th cent. B.C. and brought the form to maturity by various innovations of which the most important was the introduction of a second actor. Dialogue thus became independent of the chorus, and Greek tragedy began to resemble drama as we know it, stressing the conflict between human wilfulness and eternal universal laws, between human psychology and natural destiny. The Aeschylus trilogy the *Oresteia* superbly combines powerful lyric poetry and a sombre preoccupation with moral dilemmas and theology, attempting to discover a pattern in the conflict. Aeschylus's successor, Sophocles 495–406 B.C., introduced a third actor, and in his last play a fourth, and reduced the chorus from its Aeschylean proportions; his art is noted for its formal perfection, his acknowledged masterpiece, *Oedipus Rex*, being sometimes regarded as the perfect archetypal tragedy, in which the hero, by dramatic irony, from being the father of

his people becomes their scapegoat. In contrast with his two great predecessors, the genius of Euripides (*c.* 485–407 B.C.) was for irony and speculation; he shocked Athenian audiences by introducing into his tragedies persons in dirty ragged dress, but his great emotional powers are well shown in his most famous work the *Medea*, and perhaps even more powerfully in the *Troades*, while *Ion* may be taken as the first romantic drama and *Hippolytus* shows natural laws as immoral and the conflict between natural desires and human codes of honour as a subject for ironical contemplation. In Euripides, the choruses are reduced still further, until they are little more than decorative interludes. ◊ *Drama*, *Theatre*.

Tramp Ship. A vessel carrying any cargo it can obtain to any destination, not operated to a schedule but chartered to any merchant who can provide a cargo, at fluctuating freight rates. ◊ *Shipping*.

Transcendentalism. In philosophy, a vague term variously used for doctrines of ◊ *metaphysics* which suppose the existence of an unknowable reality or a reality immanent in or beyond the ordinary appearances of the world. More specifically, a movement in New England (U.S.A.) 1830–60 under the influence of German ◊ *idealism* and English ◊ *romanticism*, esp. Emerson, Bronson, and William Alcott, Margaret Fuller, Theodore Parker, and George Ripley (chief founder of the Brook Farm experiment in agriculture, education, and communal living). The movement's periodical was *The Dial* 1840–4, ed. Margaret Fuller and then Emerson.

Transformer. Unit of equipment widely used in electrical engineering for changing the voltage of an A.C. supply, consisting essentially of two windings around the same core of magnetic material. The current in the input (primary) coil creates a varying magnetic field which induces an alternating current in the output (secondary) winding; ◊ *Induction*. The ratio of input to output voltage depends on the relative number of turns in the two windings. Long-distance transmission of electricity being cheaper at high voltage, the voltage is usually stepped-up by transformers before transmission, and then reduced by other transformers before the supply reaches consumers.

Transistor. Small electronic device invented in U.S.A. 1948, consisting of a very thin wafer of a crystalline semiconductor sandwiched between two layers of similar material processed to carry the opposite kind of electric charge. It has the valuable property that a small current flowing in one section can control a much larger current flowing in the other. No heat energy is required to start this action (in contrast to thermionic valves), and the enclosure need not be evacuated or gasfilled, as the movement of electrons takes place inside the solid crystal structures. The transistor is much smaller, lighter, more durable, and more efficient than an equivalent valve, with a longer life. Since it works from very small batteries for long periods, it makes possible light, portable, and compact radio, television, and other electronic equipment, and is rapidly replacing valves in these. ⋄ *Conduction.*

Transition Elements. Mendeleev in his Periodic Classification of the elements (*c.* 1870) called three trios of elements which did not fit conveniently into his table 'Transition Elements'. These nine and nearly all those in the sub-groups of the Mendeleev scheme – all metals – are now classed as transition elements because of their special atomic structure. The atom of any transition metal has, besides the usual valency electrons of the outer shell, an incomplete penultimate shell containing at least one unpaired electron. This irregular arrangement gives all the transition elements specially interesting properties e.g. variable valency, catalytic power, paramagnetism, coloured ions, etc. The first transition series includes elements of atomic number from 21 to 29: scandium, titanium, vanadium, chromium, manganese, iron, cobalt, nickel, copper; the second series includes those from atomic number 39 to 47: yttrium, zirconium, niobium, molybdenum, technetium, ruthenium, rhodium, palladium, silver; among those in the third series are tungsten, iridium, platinum, and gold.

Transmigration (Metempsychosis). Transfer of the soul at death into another body, whether human (reincarnation), animal, or even plant. Belief in it is a feature of most Oriental religions (⋄ *Hinduism, Buddhism, Jains*); it was held by Plato, Pythagoras, and the Orphics in the classical world, and some modern thinkers maintain its truth. It has never been ac-

cepted by official Christianity or Judaism, though Origen taught something closely approaching it and there are traces of the idea in the ⋄ *Kabbalah.* ⋄⋄ *Karma.*

Transmutation of Elements. Transformation of one element into another, in which alchemists believed. It can now be achieved in a limited way by the bombardment of elements with high-speed particles. ⋄⋄ *Cyclotron.*

Transuranic Elements. Those which have a higher atomic number than uranium (atomic number 92). The elements up to and including uranium occur in nature; the transuranic elements are artificially created, and as their atomic number becomes greater their ⋄ *half-life* becomes progressively shorter. Since the first, neptunium, was produced in 1940 the list of such elements has reached eleven, from atomic number 93 to 103.

Trappists ⋄ *Cistercians.*

Trasimene. 217 B.C. Lake in N. Italy beside which during the Second ⋄ *Punic War* the Roman consul Flaminius rashly led his army between the shore of the lake and the nearby hills in pursuit of Hannibal and the Carthaginian army; aided by mist, Hannibal ambushed the Romans in the defile and annihilated them.

Trauma. < Gr. 'a wound'; any physical injury or emotional shock which causes serious physical or mental effects. In ⋄ *psychoanalysis*, a primal trauma is a serious shock in early life, leading to permanent psychological injury, and a traumatic ⋄ *neurosis* a disorder in which the symptoms are related to the original and earlier physical or mental trauma, e.g. in ⋄ *hysteria.*

Trawler. A fishing vessel employed in catching white fish e.g. cod, haddock, etc. which feed on the sea-bottom, by means of a triangular net towed along the seabed; usually a steamship, or a diesel-driven steel-built vessel 100 to 170 ft long, of exceptionally seaworthy design.

Treason. An act by a person owing allegiance to a particular sovereign state which gravely endangers the highest interests of that state. A British subject,

---

A single arrow before a word or phrase indicates a cross-reference to another main entry. A double arrow means *See also.*

or the holder of a British passport, owes allegiance to the British sovereign wherever he may be, and an alien under the protection of the Crown owes 'local allegiance' while in the dominions of the Crown. In practice in the U.K. and in U.S.A. no prosecution for treason is likely except in time of war. In some countries e.g. U.S.S.R. the concept of what is treason is more broadly interpreted and may cover various activities inimical to the state such as economic sabotage. ◊ *Capital Punishment*.

Trent, Council of. 1545–63. To meet the challenge of ◊ *Lutheranism* a reforming party developed within the Roman Catholic Church which after overcoming many obstacles, at last obtained the General Council which met at Trent in 1545 under the reformer Pope Paul III and sat at intervals until 1563 under several Popes. After the death of Paul III the Jesuits took the lead in the Council, and the accession of Paul IV meant a turn towards greater conservatism, but all dogmas, doctrines, jurisdiction, disciplines, regulations, etc. were clarified and precisely defined, and many abuses were banned. The modern ◊ *Roman Catholic Church* is organized on the basis of the decisions of this Council. ◊ *Reformation*.

Trente et Quarante (Rouge et Noir). A card game using six packs shuffled together, in which the player bets against the bank; common in casinos. The dealer lays out a row of cards (*noir*) until the count equals or exceeds 31 (court cards count 10, aces one) and a second row (*rouge*) in the same manner. The row with a count nearer to 31 wins. Bets are on *rouge* or *noir*, or on the first card being of the winning or losing colour (*couleur* and *inverse*). If both totals are equal, a tie or *refait* is called and all bets are called off, except if 31, when all stakes are 'imprisoned' and released if at the next deal they would have been successful.

Trial. The deciding of a criminal or civil case by a court. A civil action normally begins with the plaintiff's issue and service of a ◊ *writ*, followed by an exchange of documents (pleadings) between him and the defendant, or their solicitors, to ensure that each party knows the case that will confront him when the matter comes to court. The plaintiff, or his counsel, usually opens the case by explaining the questions in dispute, and how he will seek

to establish his case, to the judge and (if any) the jury, before calling his witnesses (◊ *Evidence*). The defence then opens, calls its evidence, and addresses the court with arguments in support of its case, and the plaintiff or his counsel makes a closing speech. If there is a jury, the judge sums up, indicating the law and reminding them of the evidence, after which they find their verdict; if there is no jury, the judge gives judgement. In indictable criminal proceedings there is no preliminary exchange of documents; the case is first brought before a ◊ *magistrate*, who hears the prosecution witnesses and decides whether or not there is sufficient evidence for him to commit the accused for ◊ *jury* trial, and at this stage the accused rarely offers evidence or calls witnesses; the prosecution presents an indictment setting out its allegations, a copy of which the accused has a right to receive, and he is not required to state what form his defence will take. Unless the accused pleads Guilty, the order of trial is similar to that in civil cases, the prosecution standing as plaintiff, except that defending counsel now always has the right to address the jury last. If the verdict is Guilty, the judge passes sentence. Thus each side has an opportunity of commenting on the other's case and the court hears both before judgement; in English law, the court simply decides between the cases presented and does not go beyond them to seek broader truths. ◊ *Felony, Judges Rules, Public Prosecutor*.

Trinidad and Tobago. Area: Trinidad 1864 sq. m. and Tobago 116 sq. m. Pop. 0.83 m. (total). Cap. Port of Spain (Trinidad); Scarborough (Tobago). Trinidad is the second largest of the W. Indian islands, close to the N. coast of S. America near Venezuela; Tobago is 20 miles to the N. An independent state, a member of the British Commonwealth since 1962, with a legislature of an elected House of Representatives and a Senate appointed half by the Governor-General, one third by the Prime Minister, and the remainder by the Opposition and several religious, economic, and social bodies.

ECONOMY. Principal exports asphalt (from the 114-acre natural lake, producing about 160,000 tons p.a.) and petroleum; also citrus fruits, cocoa, coconuts, coffee, molasses, sugar, rum.

HISTORY. Trinidad was discovered by Columbus in 1498 and colonized by Spain 1532, but annexed by Britain in 1797 and formally ceded to her in 1802 by the Peace of Amiens, as was Tobago in 1814; the two were amalgamated as a Crown Colony in 1888.

Trinitrotoluene (T.N.T.) ◊ *Explosives, Nitrogen*.

Trinity. By a dogma accepted by most Christians, God is one but exists in three Persons, the Father, the Son, and the ◊ *Holy Ghost*, coeternal and coequal, though the Son is begotten by the Father and the Holy Spirit 'proceeds' from Father and Son (or according to the ◊ *Eastern Orthodox Church*, from the Father only). The dogma was first promulgated at the first Council of Nicaea A.D. 325 and most of the ◊ *heresy* in the early Church (◊ *Arianism, Nestorianism*) arose from attempts to explain it in varying and unaccepted senses. Groups of three specially important divine or semi-divine persons are found in many religions (in ◊ *Hinduism*, Brahma-Vishnu-Shiva, in ancient Egyptian religion, Osiris-Isis-Horus), but these have little resemblance to the Christian Trinity. ◊ *Creed*.

Trinity House. The U.K. national ◊ *lighthouse* authority and chief pilotage authority, founded in Deptford as a guild of mariners 1514 and granted its first charter by Henry VIII; licenses ◊ *pilots* and also maintains about 60 lighthouses and 40 lightships, buoys, and lights, the cost of the service being defrayed from a fund raised by 'light dues' paid by ships using U.K. ports. It is administered by a Board of Wardens, elected by the Elder Brethren. In Scotland and N. Ireland lighthouses are maintained by separate commissioners.

Tristram (Tristan). Knight of ◊ *Arthurian legend*. In one version, Tristram was sent to Ireland by his uncle King Mark of Cornwall to bring back Yseult, Mark's bride, but the two unknowingly drank a potion which made them lovers for life; after his marriage, Mark discovered their love, and banished Tristram to Brittany, where he married another Yseult (Blanchemains, the Whitehanded). When mortally wounded, Tristram sent for Yseult of Ireland to heal him; her ship was to carry a white sail if she were on board, a black sail if she were not. The sail was white, but his wife Yseult told

him it was black, and he died of grief; Yseult of Ireland, finding him dead, killed herself. In another version, the jealous Mark kills Tristram.

Tritium. A radioactive isotope of ◊ *hydrogen* used in the hydrogen bomb. ◊ *Lithium*.

Trolls. In Germanic folklore, a race of misshapen dwarfs, living in hills and caves and addicted to stealing human children and substituting their own. They were particularly averse to noise, because Thor threatened them with his hammer (◊ *Aesir*).

Trombone ◊ *Brass Instruments*.

Trompe l'Œil. Fr. 'deceive the eye'; paintings which give an illusion of reality. At Pompeii houses were decorated with *trompe l'œil* still-life groups and windows framing landscapes. During the ◊ *Baroque* period artists made use of every illusionistic device, including a mixture of painted and relief figures; certain 17th- and 18th-cent. northern artists specialized in painting panels which appear to be pieces of wood with documents, prints, pens, etc. pinned to them. This style was revived in 19th-cent. America.

Tropics. Parallels of latitude approx. $23\frac{1}{2}°$ N. (Tropic of Cancer) and S. (Tropic of Capricorn) of the equator, representing respectively the most N. and S. positions on the earth's surface where the sun appears vertically overhead at noon.

Trotskyites. Dissident communists who uphold the views of Leon Trotsky, esp. his emphasis on the international aspect of communism and his belief in a continuing world revolution, in opposition to Stalin's insistence on 'socialism in one country'. Trotsky was defeated in the struggle for power, exiled 1928, and murdered in Mexico 1940. His numerous intelligent and polemical works contained effective criticism of Stalinist policy. 'Trotskyite' subsequently became a term of abuse for any communist who deviates from the current party line.

Troubadours. The 12th- and 13th-cent. composers of both words and music of highly elaborate Provençal love-lyrics in S. France (◊ *Provence*) and neighbouring parts of Spain (◊ *Catalan*) and Italy, who originated the composed solo song as distinct from ◊ *folk song*; they developed and disseminated the conventions of secular ◊ *courtly love*, and their technical refinements were adopted by later writers in Sicily, Tuscany, Germany (◊ *Minne-singers*), and N. France, where the Trouvères who wrote the ◊ *Chansons de Geste* were influenced by their poetry from the 12th cent. onwards, and developed courtly lyric poetry together with the local narrative tradition. A troubadour was usually a man of some standing, as distinct from the jongleur or wandering minstrel; about 500 of them are known by name.

Trout. Bony freshwater and marine fish of the family Salmonidae; the brook trout, *Salmo fario*, is common in the rivers and streams of Europe and has been introduced into other parts of the world e.g. New Zealand. In ponds and streams it may grow only to seven or eight in. long before reaching maturity, in large lakes to about three ft. An excellent ◊ *game* fish, it is closely related to the N. Atlantic ◊ *salmon*, *S. salar*, the lake trout, *S. trutta*, and the American brook trout, *Salvelinus fontinalis*.

Troy. City of the ancient world famous from Homer's *Iliad*; also called Ilium. There were in fact several successive cities of Troy, the site of which was identified by Heinrich Schliemann as the mound now called Hissarlik in Turkey near the mouth of the Dardanelles, and excavated by him and Dörpfeld 1871–94. Excavation revealed the remains of nine superimposed towns, dating from the Neolithic period onwards. It is now agreed that the level known as Troy VII a represents the Homeric Troy, and that it was destroyed about 1260 B.C. or a little before.

Troyes (Treaty) ◊ *Hundred Years War*.

Trucial States ◊ *Gulf Sheikhdoms*.

Truffle. A totally underground fungus usually growing in woodland; a much esteemed delicacy in Roman times, it has been used in cookery in France and Italy since the 16th cent. The black truffle of France is used in *pâté de foie gras*. Dogs and pigs are used to find truffles, which can be located by a slight odour above the soil.

Trumpet ◊ *Brass Instruments*.

Trust. Arrangement whereby property owned by one person is administered by another person, for the benefit of a third designated by the original owner. The duty of the trustee is to make the capital earnings of the property available to the beneficiary as prescribed by the settler, and to administer the trust honestly. Increasingly banks and similar corporate organizations are appointed trustees. New trustees may be appointed by previous trustees; in default, the Court will appoint them. A trust established for charitable, educational, and similar purpose enjoys certain advantages e.g. exemption from income tax.

In U.S.A. business organizations took advantage of the trust arrangement by persuading stock-holders to appoint a board of trustees to handle their stock for them, thereby permitting such a board to handle a number of business enterprises simultaneously, and trusts came to mean arrangements between companies whose objective is to fix and maintain prices, and in some cases to limit production, centralize selling, and allocate quotas between firms or sections of an industry (◊ *Restrictive Practices*). By the 1890s American public opinion became extremely hostile to trusts and saw them as a menace to small business and inimical to fair competition. The Sherman Anti-Trust Law of 1890 declared all such combinations illegal. In practice it proved difficult to enforce, and the Clayton Act of 1914 was devised to strengthen the power of the government to take action against monopolies. ◊◊ *Cartel, Monopoly*.

Trusteeship Council ◊ *United Nations Organization*.

Truth. Traditional philosophical theories of the nature of truth, or of what 'true' means, are briefly: (1) the Correspondence theory, that the truth of a proposition consists in correspondence to facts; (2) the Coherence theory, that a proposition is true if it coheres or hangs together with other accepted propositions; (3) the Pragmatist theory, that a proposition is true if in some sense it satisfies. Correspondence is thought the least objectionable, but has the difficulty (among others) that facts themselves seem 'true' propositions. ◊ *Pragmatism*.

Tsetse Fly. Bloodsucking African fly, larger than the house fly, which bites both men and animals. It is a carrier of the trypanosomes, parasitic protozoa which cause sleeping sickness (trypanosomiasis) in man and nagana in animals, diseases causing fever, anemia, enlargement of the glands and, unless treated early, usually fatal. Long a scourge of large areas of Africa, it has been largely brought under control by ◊ *pesticides*.

Tsushima. 1905. Island between Japan and Korea off which the Japanese defeated the Russian fleet during the ◊ *Russo-Japanese War*. Though Admiral Rozhestvensky's fleet was equal in numbers to that of the Japanese Admiral Togo, it had suffered by its long voyage from the Baltic, and its crews lacked training. Togo was able to execute a daring tactical manoeuvre (rather similar to Nelson's at ◊ *Trafalgar*) and to annihilate the Russian fleet, in one of the most complete of modern naval victories.

Tuareg. 'People of the Veil'; long-civilized ◊ *Berber* people of the Sahara, who still retain their own ancient alphabet. Nominally ◊ *Sunni* Muslims. The men wear a turban which covers most of the face, whilst women go unveiled and enjoy respect and freedom. They have always been fiercely independent.

Tuba ◊ *Brass Instruments.*

Tuberculosis. Infectious disease, caused by the bacillus *Mycobacterium tuberculosis*, characterized by the formation of lesions (tubercles) in the tissues. It mainly affects the lungs, but may also attack the lymph glands, alimentary tract, bones and joints, kidneys, and the central nervous system. Minor lung infections in childhood are common, but are usually benign and tend to create immunity. Artificial immunity can be created with B.C.G. vaccine. A recent dramatic fall in the death rate from tuberculosis can be attributed to improved methods of treatment rather than to any great lowering in the incidence of infection.

Tudors. 1485–1603. The ruling dynasty of England after the ◊ *Wars of the Roses*. Tudor, originally a Welsh Christian name, was adopted as a surname by Owen Tudor, second husband of Henry V's widow, Katherine of France. Their son Edmund Tudor married a distant descendant of Edward III; his son Henry Tudor ended the Wars of the Roses when he defeated Richard III at ◊ *Bosworth* and was crowned as Henry VII. He married the eldest daughter of Edward IV, thus 'uniting the roses'. Under his son Henry VIII and his grandchildren Edward VI, Mary I, and Elizabeth I strong and stable government, which during the 15th cent. the country had lacked, was restored. The subsequent dynasty, the ◊ *Stewarts*, derived their claim from Margaret Tudor, daughter of Henry VII.

Under the Tudors, large numbers of spacious manor houses were built, in the style known as Tudor or Elizabethan. Buildings of this period showed a marked increase in comfort and in the number and variety of separate rooms. Externally they frequently combined brickwork with half-timber and made use of modified Perpendicular forms, such as square mullioned windows and the so-called Tudor arch. Hampton Court Palace is a prime example of the Tudor style. Under Elizabeth there was an increasing tendency towards symmetry and considerable use of ◊ *Renaissance* and Flemish decorative motifs.

Tulip. *Lileaceae*; genus of wild bulbous plants, most of them native in the Near East and central Asia; they were prominent in Turkish gardens in the 16th cent. in many cultivated varieties, which were introduced first into Holland and later to England. At the time of the Dutch tulip mania bulbs fetched fantastic prices, and these tulips had to conform to rigid rules as to shape and arrangement of colours. Innumerable types are now grown, some derived from the old tulips, others from crosses with more recently introduced species.

TULIP TREE ◊ *Magnolia.*

Tumulus ◊ *Barrow.*

Tundra. Originally, the treeless plains of N. Eurasia, bordering the Arctic Ocean; now also the corresponding region of Canada and Alaska. The mean monthly temperature is below f.p. most of the year, the winters are long and severe, the summers short and warm. From about one ft below the surface the soil remains perpetually frozen. This and the intensely cold strong winter winds make tree growth impossible. There are dwarf birches and willows, and mosses and lichens are abundant in summer, but much of the flat ground becomes marshy. The fauna are mainly reindeer, caribou, musk-ox, and small fur-bearing animals, whose pelts are sought by hunters. Transport used to be principally by dog-sleigh in winter and canoe in summer, but air transport is now increasingly used.

Tungsten. Important metallic ◊ *element*, obtained mainly from the mineral wolframite, major deposits of which occur in China and U.S.A. Having great tensile strength and the very high m.p. of 3380° C, it is used for the manufacture of electric-lamp filaments (now replacing ◊ *tantalum*). The alloy ferro-tungsten is of great importance in the manufacture of special steels for high-speed cutting tools (◊ *Iron and Steel Industry*), and the extremely hard compound tungsten carbide is used for the tips of high-speed machine-tools and of ball-point pens. ◊◊ *Wolfram*.

Tunisia. Area 45,000 sq. m. Pop. 4.2 m. Cap. Tunis (near the site of ancient Carthage). N. African republic, between Algeria and Libya. Government is by a President and a Legislative Assembly. The first P.M. was Habib Bourguiba, now President.

ECONOMY. Mainly agricultural, exporting cereals, citrus fruits, dates, olive oil, wine, and some iron ore, lead phosphates. HISTORY. Occupied after A.D. 670 by the Arabs, who intermarried with the original ◊ *Berber* inhabitants, it subsequently became nominally Turkish, but the Bey was virtually independent. Fearing for the safety of Algeria, and suspicious of Italian ambitions in N. Africa, the French invaded the country to establish a protectorate in 1880. Tunisia had a real identity, a land-holding peasantry, relatively few nomads, and a substantial middle class. French rule was restored after the expulsion of Axis forces in the Second World War, and the Nationalist party (Néo-Destour) led by Bourguiba campaigned for independence, granted in 1956. The Bey was deposed and the monarchy abolished in 1957. Tunisia is a member of the ◊ *Arab League*, and supported the Algerian nationalists; nevertheless its relations with France remained amicable, and it enjoys greater stability and prosperity than its neighbours.

Tunnels. Passages cut through hills (sometimes under rivers) to facilitate communications. Short rock tunnels were constructed in Greek and Roman times. Earth tunnels (the one on the St Quentin canal, 1810, is perhaps the first) are more recent. Methods of construction differ according to the nature of the ground. Rock tunnels are usually driven with the aid of explosives. The first very long tunnel was the Mont Cenis, 1857–71, 8 m. long. Other notable rock tunnels are the St Gotthard, 9 m. and the Simplon, 12¼ m., in the Alps, the Severn, 4.3 m. and the Mersey rail (1886) and road (1936) tunnels. Earth tunnels present various problems. The use of timber sheeting and frameworks, care-fully placed as excavation proceeds, continues to the present day, but for large tunnels and those in bad ground other techniques are used. In such cases the tunnel is circular and lined with segmental rings of cast iron or pre-cast ◊ *concrete*. Shield driving, in which a circular ring is pressed forward by hydraulic jacks, was used by M. I. Brunel under the Thames in 1824 and perfected by J. H. Greathead about 1870. This method of tunnelling was used extensively in the London underground-railway system.

Turbine. Any motor the shaft of which is caused to rotate by the force of a stream of water, steam, or gas acting upon blades set on the shaft. Essentially, all turbines work in the same way as a water-wheel.
WATER TURBINE: There are two types: the impulse turbine, a direct development from the water-wheel, of which the Pelton Wheel is typical; and the reaction turbine, where the water flows outwards between the blades (e.g. somewhat like a rotary lawn sprinkler). Water turbines are extensively used for the generation of electricity in hydroelectric power stations.
STEAM TURBINE: In this, steam at high pressure and temperatures replaces water. Parsons in 1884 invented the first really successful steam turbine, in which the expansion of the steam actuated successive turbines of gradually increasing size. The efficiency of this and further refinements on it at the end of the 19th cent. revolutionized water transport and led the way to cheap electrical-power production. In most modern turbines expansion takes place through both nozzles and blade passages, in a combination of the impulse and reaction effects.

gas turbine engine

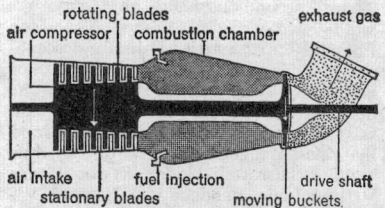

GAS TURBINE: Its principle is the same as that of the steam turbine; in it the fuel (commonly an oil fuel e.g. paraffin), instead of generating steam, is burned with air in a combustion chamber, from which hot gas erupts at great speed. ⟡ *Jet Propulsion.*

Turkey. Large wildfowl, of the genus *Meleagris*, in its wild form, common to N. and central America, where it was domesticated by the ⟡ *Aztecs.* It was introduced to Europe in the 16th cent. and is now bred to give maximum meat production with minimum size. Difficult to rear in its early stages after hatching, it is later less of a problem; large turkey farms are now being developed in many countries. The name originally applied to the guinea-fowl, introduced to W. Europe via Turkey.

Turkey. Area 294,502 sq. m. Pop. 27.8 m. Cap. Ankara. Rel. Muslim. It extends over the whole of Asia Minor and a small area beyond the Bosphorus (Turkey in Europe), which includes Istanbul (Constantinople) the cap. until 1922. The legislature is the National Assembly, consisting of the Senate, 150 members, and the Assembly of Deputies, 450 members, under a President. The present government is a coalition of the People's Republican Party and the Justice Party (formerly Democratic Party).

ECONOMY. About 75 per cent agricultural, mainly cereals, cotton, fruit (esp. figs and sultanas), nuts, oilseeds, opium, pulses, sugarbeet (now self-supporting in sugar), tobacco, wool. There are 17 sugar factories, as against only four in 1949. The considerable mineral wealth is under-exploited, but output of coal (about 40 per cent lignite) is increasing, as are exports of antimony, chromite, copper, manganese, wolfram. Heavy and light industries are being rapidly developed.

HISTORY. Formerly the centre of the ⟡ *Ottoman Empire*, which was broken up after the First World War. The Sultanate was abolished in 1922; Kemal Ataturk (Gazi Mustafa Kemal) became President and pursued a policy of rapid westernization. Until the end of the Second World War his People's Republic Party was unopposed, but in 1950 the Democratic Party gained power and remained in office until 1960. It was overthrown by a military coup d'état and the Committee of National Union; Prime Minister Menderes, the Foreign Minister, and the Finance Minister were executed and the President imprisoned for life. Elections in 1961 made General Gürsel President and returned a balance of parties which re-

sulted in the coalition government. Turkey is a member of the ⟡ *Central Treaty Organization* and the ⟡ *North Atlantic Treaty Organization.* In 1964 friction with Greece over ⟡ *Cyprus* again became an international issue.

Turkish Languages ⟡ *Altaic Languages.*

Turpentine. Fluid resins, from various conifers and other trees. On distillation, oil of turpentine passes over and resins are left. It has important industrial uses, particularly in paint and varnish manufacture.

Turquoise. Sky-blue gem-stone, hydrated aluminium phosphate; found in thin veins in Iran and in New Mexico, U.S.A.

BONE TURQUOISE: Made by polishing fossil bones stained blue by iron phosphate.

Turtle. Member of the *Chelonia*, a class of land and sea ⟡ *reptiles* which have changed little in their evolutionary history of 175 m. years; they breathe by means of lungs, are toothless but have a bird-like beak, and are carnivorous. All turtles lay their eggs on land, indicating that the aquatic turtles had terrestrial ancestors. Turtles are caught for making soup; the material known as tortoiseshell comes from the hawksbill turtle. ⟡ *Tortoise.*

Tutsi ⟡ *Burundi, Rwanda.*

Twins. Of two distinct types: identical twins result from a single egg which has divided into two halves, each of which has developed into a separate child, and the resemblance of such twins (always of the same sex) in appearance and fundamental characteristics is extremely close. The incidence of such twins is entirely accidental, unrelated to any hereditary factors, and occurs at a fairly constant rate of about 3–4 cases per 1000 births in all races and societies. Fraternal twins (dizygotic) result from two separate fertilized eggs and are not likely to be more similar than single offspring of the same parents. Hereditary factors cause such twinning to be more frequent in some families than others, and its incidence also becomes greater with older mothers, reaching a peak at ages 35–9.

Type. The small blocks of cast metal with raised letters used in ⟡ *printing*, introduced by Gutenberg. The earliest types were cut in imitation of the formal Gothic scripts current in Europe in the 15th cent. but within 50 years a multiplicity of designs had emerged, among them the first

raph aim. Cōſuluit autē dauid d
Hi aſcendā cōtra philiſteos: ꝛ tra
cos in manus meas: Qui rñdit.

Formal Gothic, from the 42-line Bible printed by
Gutenberg, Mainz, 1452-6 (reduced)

totius generis origo Habraam numerād
iuſtitiā quā non a moſaica lege(ſeptima
Moyſes naſcitur)ſed naturalı fuit ration

First true roman: Jenson, Venice, 1470
(reduced)

C ur tamen hoc libeat potius decurrere cam
P er quem magnus equos A uruncæ flexit a
S i uacat,et placidı.rationem admittitis,eda

First italic: Aldus, Venice, 1501
(slightly reduced)

Garicum vt fungus naſcitur in arboribu
glandiferæ præſertim arbores hoc ferun
phorum quoqꝫ prouenit colore candido.

Typical 16th-century roman:
De Colines, Paris, 1536 (reduced)

Quouſque tandem abutêre, Catilina, pa-
tientia noſtra ? quamdiu nos etiam fu-
ror iſte tuus eludet? quem ad finem ſe-

Caslon, London, 1734 (reduced)

lic of Learning has great obligatio
nuity has left a fairer copy for m
than any other maſter. In his gre

Baskerville, Birmingham, 1758 (reduced)

tro sta in certa disinvoltura di trat
franchi, risoluti, spediti, e nondim
no così nelle forme esatti, così degr

Bodoni, Parma, 1818 (reduced)

Note : an employee is entitled by the Contra
months' continuous service, two weeks afte
continuous service. An employee is require
notices can be waived by either party. Paym

Typical 19th-century sans serif in wide use today

true roman of Jenson, a Frenchman working in Venice, and Aldus's italic by Griffo
of Bologna. Except in Germany and Scandinavia, roman type was almost universally adopted in the occidental world ; the
beautiful versions produced in Italy,
France, and the Low Countries before
1600 have not fundamentally changed to
this day. Later versions of roman type
e.g. those of William Caslon, 1734, and
John Baskerville, 1757, both Englishmen
whose influence was widespread upon
typographers abroad, and of the Italian
Giambattista Bodoni, about 1806, merely
reflected growing technical mastery and
changes in taste. In the last 50 years many
historical designs have been revived
(sometimes in a slightly modified form)
for mechanical composition, and new ones
have been created. Of these, Times New
Roman, first cut for *The Times* in 1932,
has found the widest acceptance. In addition to types used in books there are many
types of highly individual design and
varying merit specifically devised for
use in display, advertising, etc.

Type-metal ◊ *Alloys.*

Typhoid Fever. Acute and highly contagious disease resulting from infection
with the bacillus *Salmonella typhi*, taken
into the system either in contaminated
food or water or by contact with a carrier (◊ *Fly*). The incubation period is
about 14 days, and the onset of the fever
brings lassitude, headaches, and either
constipation or diarrhoea. A red rash is
followed by enlargement of the spleen,
severe inflammation and ulceration of the
bowel, and general toxaemia. Haemorrhage from and perforation of a bowel
ulcer are dangerous complications. Unless
adequately treated, a patient may continue to harbour the causal organism
after recovery and so be a danger to
others. Typhoid is preventable : ◊ *Immunity.*

Typhoon ◊ *Hurricane.*

Typhus. Acute infectious and contagious
disease caused by a large virus-like organism (a species of Rickettsia), characterized
by fever, depression, severe headaches,
and a rash which appears from the third
to the seventh day of the fever, which
lasts about two weeks. It is spread by
lice, and epidemics are likely to occur in
crowded areas where standards of hygiene
are low. It was once known as 'gaol fever'.

U

Uganda. Area 93,981 sq. m. (of which 3,600 sq. m. are water). Pop. 6.5 m. Cap. Kampala. A republic in E. central Africa, between Sudan, Kenya, Tanganyika, and Rwanda. A member of the British Commonwealth, independent since 1962 and a republic since 1963, with a President, Prime Minister, and Cabinet, and a National Assembly of 92 elected members. The present Government is a coalition of the People's Congress Party and the Kabaka Yekka movement of ◊ *Buganda*; there is a federal relationship between Buganda and the central administration.
ECONOMY. Mainly agricultural; chief exports coffee, cotton. Also groundnuts, hardwoods, maize, oilseeds, sisal, sugar. Some mineral resources, with exports of beryl, copper, tin. The Owen Falls hydro-electric scheme supplies substantial electric power to Kenya.

Uillean Pipes ◊ *Bagpipe.*

Uitlanders ◊ *Jameson Raid.*

Ulcer. Lesion of the skin or mucous membrane, often suppurating, caused by persistent irritation or infection. Stomach ulcers largely result from corrosion of areas of the intestinal wall by overactive gastric juices; they may become sufficiently serious to perforate the wall and cause peritonitis.

Ulm (1805) ◊ *Napoleonic Wars.*

Ulster. One of the original five kingdoms (later the four provinces) of ◊ *Ireland*; partly conquered by the Anglo-Normans in the 12th cent. it was not fully so until the defeat and banishment of the Earl of Tyrone in 1603. In the 1650s Cromwell planted Ulster with large numbers of English and Scottish ◊ *Presbyterians*, forcibly expelling the native Irish (◊ *Penal Laws*) and forming a Protestant stronghold; the process was continued and accelerated under William of Orange and later (◊ *Orange Society*). In the late 18th cent. many of the leaders of the United Irishmen were from Ulster, then stronghold also of the principles of the ◊ French Revolution, but such activities were ended by the crushing of the 1798 Rebellion and the passing of the 1800 ◊ Act of Union. The bitter struggles over landlordism e.g. with the ◊ *Land League* were frequently based on the demand for 'Ulster Custom' (or 'tenant right' i.e. security of tenure) to be extended to all Ireland. There was considerable opposition in Ulster esp. in Belfast to the ◊ *Home Rule* proposals and ◊ *Sinn Fein*; in 1914 armed revolt threatened. In 1920, under the Amending Act and the Government of Ireland Act, the ◊ *partition* of Ireland made the six of Ulster's nine counties with a Protestant majority into N. Ireland. ◊ *Anglo-Irish 'Troubles', Easter Rebellion.*

Ultrasonic Waves. Similar to sound waves, but of higher frequencies and thus of shorter wavelength; inaudible to the human ear. An early example was the ultrasonic whistle, audible to a dog but not to man. They now have various uses in industry, science, and medicine, e.g. to detect flaws in metal without harming it. The ultrasonic waves in cleansing fluids subject objects to intense local vibration, effective for cleaning small and intricate articles. The study of such waves, which find increasing practical use, is termed ultrasonics.

Ultraviolet Rays. Invisible rays with a wavelength below that of visible violet rays, down to very short wavelengths where X-rays begin; a component of the sun's radiation (also produced artificially in the mercury arc-lamp), most of which is absorbed before reaching the earth by the ◊ *ozone* layer of the atmosphere. Excessive absorption of ultraviolet rays is harmful to the human body, but moderate dosage is beneficial. Ultraviolet rays have germicidal properties.

Ulysses (Odysseus). In Greek legend, king of Ithaca, a wise and crafty leader in the Trojan war, who devised the wooden horse by means of which Troy was captured. Homer's *Odyssey* describes his long journey home, during which he was captured by the ◊ *Cyclopes*, helped by ◊ *Aeolus*, and delayed by ◊ *Circe*, avoided the dangers of ◊ *Scylla* and Charybdis, spent seven years with ◊ *Calypso*, and at last reached Ithaca and his faithful wife ◊ *Penelope*.

Umbelliferae. The carrot family; a large dicotyledonous family, of wide distribution, predominantly in the N. Hemisphere. Most are aromatic herbs with hollow or pith-filled stems, much-divided leaves, and leaf-stalks sheathing the stems. The inflorescence is an umbel, usually of white flowers but also yellow, pink, or blue. Many umbelliferae are used for food, e.g. carrot, parsnip, celery, celeriac. Some yield ◊ *essential oils* valuable as condiments, e.g. angelica, aniseed, caraway, chervil, dill, fennel, lovage, parsley. The commonest drug plant is ◊ *hemlock*. Many species are ornamental. Many umbelliferae are common wild flowers, and several hedgerow species with lacy flowers and foliage are known generally as cowparsley.

Unconscious Mind. A postulate of Freudian psychology which envisages a part of our mind, of which we are unaware, as a reservoir of thoughts, feelings, and wishes some of which may once have been conscious but which have been forgotten or repressed, and which may be brought to ◊ *consciousness* again under special conditions e.g. in ◊ *dreams,* under ◊ *hypnosis,* or during ◊ *psychotherapy.* It is also said to contain thoughts and feelings which have never been conscious. ◊ *Collective Unconscious.*

Undulant (Malta) Fever. Infection with any of the organisms known as *brucella,* transmissible from animals (cattle, goats) to man, usually by infected milk. Characterized by prolonged and recurrent bouts of fever, with headache and muscular pains.

Unemployment. Persistent lack of work for those in search of it, statistically ascertainable in industrial countries but less easy to estimate in agricultural countries. It may be general (owing to a trade ◊ *depression*), seasonal (as in holiday resorts), or structural i.e. due to a decline in an industry e.g. cotton manufacturing in U.K. or the silk industry in Japan. Both structural and seasonal unemployment may be highly localized, so that unemployment can be 9 or 10 per cent in one area when it is only 3 per cent in another. Unemployment was widespread in the inter-war years; since 1945 all governments have striven to maintain full employment, with considerable success. ◊ *Development Area, Trade Cycle.*

Uniate Church ◊ *Eastern Orthodox Church.*

Uniform. In armies, standardized costum to distinguish combatants from civilian (an important distinction in ◊ *inter national law*), to differentiate betwee regiments etc. and to encourage *esprit d corps.* In Europe, military uniform bega to appear in the mid 17th cent. at abou the same time as the abandonment o armour and the establishment of nation armies. Uniforms of the 17th and 18t centuries were a standardized version o contemporary civilian costume (as nava officers' uniform still is) with minor addi tions e.g. the gorget (a plate worn at th throat). The mitre-like grenadier's cap o the 18th cent. was one of the few speci fically military developments. Uniform was at its most ornate in the period of th Napoleonic wars, when the cocked ha began to give way to the shako, the bear skin, and various other forms of headgear Thereafter, economies were introduce and uniforms became less elaborat though still colourful. William IV dresse the whole of the British army (except th artillery and riflemen) in red, already lon in use for some regiments; this con spicuous colour remained in force unti the Boer War when the concept of ◊ camouflage influenced the choice of a inconspicuous colour already used i India (khaki, < Hindustani 'dusty'). I the First World War the British an American troops wore khaki, the Frenc 'horizon blue', and the Germans 'fiel grey'. Naval officers wore uniform dres of dark blue with white or gold from th late 18th cent. but lower-deck uniform was not prescribed by regulation unti 1857, when it was based on the practica costume already in use. The uniform o the Royal Navy was adopted (with mino modifications) in other navies.

Uniformity. The Elizabethan Act of Uni formity in 1559 brought back into use th ◊ *Prayer Book* of Edward VI's reign (wit some revisions), and imposed a shillin fine for non-attendance at church. The ◊ Restoration Act of Uniformity in 1662 re introduced the Prayer Book (disused dur ing the Interregnum), with further revi sions, and laid down that all ministers o religion were to be ordained by ◊ *Churc of England* bishops. ◊ *Clarendon Code Nonconformists, Test Act.*

Unionists ◊ *Conservative Party.*

Union Jack. More correctly, the Grea Union; the national flag of the U.K. It made up from the flags of England (St George, white with a red cross), Scotland (St Andrew, blue with a white saltire i.e. diagonal cross), and Ireland (St Patrick, white with a red saltire). When James VI of Scotland became James I of England in 1603 the red cross of England was superimposed on the white saltire and blue field of Scotland. The red saltire and white field of Ireland were incorporated after the Act of Union in 1800.

Unitarianism. Form of Protestant Christianity rejecting the doctrine of the ◊ *Trinity* and upholding the personal unity of God. Spread after the ◊ *Reformation* esp. in Poland and Hungary) by Faustus Socinus 1539–1604 and others; as Socinianism, it was taught in England first by John Biddle 1615–62 and then by Theophilus Lindsay 1723–1808, who formed it into a denomination to which many English ◊ *Presbyterians* became attached. Arising independently in America, it became influential esp. in New England through the works of Emerson, Longfellow, and others. Undogmatic, it appeals to reason and conscience as the standards or belief and action.

United Arab Republic. ◊ *Egypt, Iraq, Syria, Yemen.* In Feb. 1958 Egypt and Syria proclaimed the union of the two countries under one head of state, President Nasser of Egypt, with a common legislature, a unified army, and one flag. In March 1958 the Kingdom of the Yemen joined the federation. Syria left the U.A.R. in 1961 but rejoined in 1963, when Iraq joined also. It was temporarily called the United Arab States, but has reverted to the name Republic. ◊ *Arab League.*

United Kingdom. The United Kingdom of Great Britain and Northern Ireland, capital London, has an area of 93,053 sq. m., pop. 53.3 m. The Church of England is the established Church; there are large Free Church communities and a Roman Catholic minority. The U.K. is the parent state of the British Commonwealth, a member of the North Atlantic and South-East Asia Treaty Organizations, and one of the five permanent members of the Security Council of the United Nations Organization. It is also a member of E.F.T.A., but not of the European Common Market. Since 1945 most overseas territories of colonial status have been granted independence (India, Nigeria, Ghana, etc.). The U.K. still has extensive military commitments, besides the army maintained in Germany, both in the Near and Far East, and military expenditure remains high. At the last General Election in 1964 a Labour Government was elected by a narrow majority (seats in Parliament: Labour 317, Conservative 304, Liberal 9). ECONOMIC AND SOCIAL. The U.K. produces about one half of its food requirements and apart from coal and some iron has few mineral resources; it is a major importer of foodstuffs and raw materials, for which it has to pay by extensive exports of manufactured goods, a pattern of trade developed since the ◊ *Industrial Revolution.* With growing industrialization overseas the pattern of industry in the U.K. has gradually changed from emphasis on textiles and coal to a more diversified range, esp. engineering and technical products. British agriculture is highly mechanized and employs only 4 per cent of the working population. London remains an important financial centre, but the strains of the Second World War have caused recurrent difficulties over the ◊ *balance of payments.* (◊ *Sterling area, Merchant Marine.*) Employment has remained at high levels and the ◊ *gross national product* has roughly doubled since the War. The ◊ *cost of living* has risen steadily as a result of ◊ *inflation,* but this has been offset by a relatively greater rise in wages. Health services, pensions, education, and all forms of social welfare have developed extensively (◊ *Welfare State, Education,* etc.).

HISTORY. The U.K. is a monarchy whose origin and development is bound up with the history of the four separate national parts: England, Wales, Scotland, and Northern Ireland. Details will be found in separate articles amongst which, in addition to the cross-references in this article, the following are esp. relevant: *Wessex, Anglo-Saxons, Norman Conquest, Magna Carta, Wars of the Roses, English Civil Wars, Commonwealth and Protectorate, Napoleonic Wars, Tariff Reform, First/Second World Wars.*

United Nations Organization. Successor to the League of Nations, set up by fifty nations at the San Francisco Conference 1945. Its principal organs are: The General Assembly; The Security Council; The Economic and Social Council; The Trusteeship Council; ◊ *The International Court of Justice*; The Secretariat. The General Assembly comprises all members of the United Nations (now over 110 member states). Its decisions are made by a two-thirds majority. It works, however, mainly through committees, some of which (e.g. political and security, economic and financial) are permanent and some ad hoc. The Security Council consists of 11 member states each with one representative and one vote. There are five permanent members (China, France, U.K., U.S.A., and U.S.S.R.) and six non-permanent elected by the General Assembly for two-year terms. Procedural matters may be decided by the assent of any seven members, but on all other proposals unanimity of the permanent members is required. The chief duty of the Security Council is to maintain or restore international peace; it may organize military forces, supplied by the member states, either for police action (as in Egypt 1956) or for armed intervention (as in the Congolese Republic 1961). The U.N. Secretariat is headed by the Secretary-General (U Thant of Burma), whose position has become one of considerable influence, due in no small part to the outstanding qualities of the first two Secretaries-General, Trygve Lie and Dag Hammarskjöld. A Soviet proposal, on the death of Hammarskjöld in 1962, to replace the Secretary-General by a committee of three ('troika') was dropped. Membership is open to all peace-loving states sponsored by the Security Council and accepted by the Assembly. There have been disputes over certain cases; applications e.g. from communist China and Korea have been rejected.

◊ *Food and Agriculture*/*International Civil Aviation* / *International Labour* / *World Health Organization.*

United Provinces ◊ *Netherlands.*

United States of America. Area 3,548,974 sq. m. Pop. 180 m. (almost entirely English-speaking, 10 per cent Negro, about 0.5 m. Red Indians). Cap. Washington. Federal Republic of 50 States, the Federal District of Columbia (i.e. Washington), and one Territory. The constitution of 1787, modified by amendments, provides for the election of a President every four years through an electoral college, which usually but not always results in the election of the candidate of the party polling the majority of votes. The President may serve for only two terms;

in the event of his death or incapacity h is succeeded by the Vice-President (who i elected with him and is a member of ·hi party). The President appoints members o the executive, including the Cabinet, wh are subject to Senate approval. Neither h nor his Cabinet are members of ◊ *Con gress*, the legislative branch of the govern ment, and he can initiate legislation onl through his supporters in Congress. T become law, all Congressional measure require his signature.

The ◊ *Supreme Court* is virtually a independent organ, since it may interpre the constitutional meaning of federal an state legislation and annul laws which i finds contrary to the constitution. Sinc the 1930s there has been a great expansio in the size and duties of the Executive but since the President as Chief Executiv is constitutionally empowered to act o his own initiative in military and diplo matic matters, Congress has only limite control over his activity in these increas ingly crucial fields, in which his duties an activities have multiplied. Nevertheless Congress remains one of the most power ful popular assemblies in the world; it members continue to initiate and enact great deal of legislation (in contrast to th few private-member's Bills passed by th British Parliament).

Each State in the Union has its ow Governor, legislature, judiciary, and stat militia. Governors and legislatures ar elected by majority vote, for periods vary ing from two to four years. States dea with all matters not reserved to Congres by the Constitution, e.g. police, loca government, education, marriage laws and social welfare. Federal interventio occurs, however, in matters of constitu tional concern such as ◊ *race relations* and is often much resented. There is n established church. The largest singl denomination is Roman Catholic (39.5 m in 1958), followed by Baptist and Method ist. The Episcopalian church correspond to the Church of England.

ECONOMY. The U.S.A. is rich in natura resources: oil, coal, iron, and a variety o other minerals, great forests. Except fo areas in the W. it has climatic and soi conditions suitable for a wide variety o crops, and a river system valuable both for communications and for hydroelectri power. Between the ◊ *American Civi War* and the end of the 19th cent. U.S.A was transformed from a largely agricultural economy into a great industrial power. U.S. industry was built up behind tariff walls, which reached a formidable peak in the Smoot-Hawley Tariff of 1930. (Since the Trade Agreement Act of 1934, many tariff rates have been reduced.) Massive immigration from Europe, and two world wars, spurred industrial development and inventiveness. Today, with less than 10 per cent of the world's population, the U.S.A. accounts for nearly half the world's output of goods, and its inhabitants enjoy the highest material standards of living. The U.S. economy is to a great extent self-contained. Though imports and exports amount in value to less than 10 per cent of the national income, this makes U.S.A. the largest single trading nation in the world. In 1962 when the national income was estimated at $450,000 m. U.S. exports were $21,000 m. and imports $16,000 m. The U.S.A. is the largest single producer of steel, coal, automobiles, electric power, and petroleum; it was the pioneer of mass production methods, and leads the world in the mechanization and automation of industry, and in industrial and scientific research.

FINANCE. The 1963 U.S. Federal Budget provided for an expenditure of $86,000 m. Of this, defence expenditure absorbed over one half, and large sums were also spent on economic and military aid to foreign countries. The U.S. budget covers a narrower field than does that of the U.K. since each separate State assumes the main responsibility for education and social services etc.

EDUCATION. The vast majority of Americans attend publicly provided free day schools. Although the school system is decentralized in the hands of local and State authorities, with inevitable differences in standards, a substantially homogeneous pattern has developed of free and compulsory schooling between the ages of 7 and 16. There are 12 grades, 1–8 being in elementary schools, 9–12 in high schools. There are a few schools outside the public system; those corresponding to British 'public schools' are known as 'preparatory schools'. A large proportion of students proceed to State universities where tuition is free. Universities vary in standards and esteem; degrees are granted in a great variety of subjects, some of which are vocational. There are wholly independent institutions of long standing e.g. ◊ *Harvard* 1636, Yale 1701, Princeton 1746, for men, and Vassar 1861 and Wellesley 1870 for women; many are State universities for men and women (Alabama 1831, California 1868).

United States History. After its discovery by Columbus in 1492, the first Europeans to settle were Spaniards in the 16th cent. followed by the English colonies in Virginia and New England, and the French in the Mississippi valley. In the 18th cent. the French ambition to unite their territory with Canada, and so isolate the 13 British colonies, led to their defeat in the ◊ *Seven Years War*. With the end of effective French power in N. America, the colonials came increasingly to resent the restrictions imposed by Britain, and in 1776 the ◊ *American Revolution* broke out. On gaining independence, the 13 states were faced with the problem of forming an effective central government, which was resolved by the adoption of a federal constitution in 1787. The purchase from Napoleon of the French Mississippi holdings (◊ *Louisiana Purchase*) more than doubled American territory. In the early years of the Union, unified rather than imperilled by the ◊ *War of 1812*, little cause for friction between the States arose, and the cotton-growing south retained its traditional predominance. Slowly the importance of the industrial north began to outstrip the agricultural slave-owning south; differences between them were intensified by the question whether new states should be admitted to the Union as 'free' or 'slave' (◊ *Mason-Dixon Line*). The Missouri Compromise, 1820, setting latitude 36° 30′ N. as the line between slave and free territory, was accepted for a time, during which Texas (1845), New Mexico, and S. California (1848) were taken from Mexico; but it broke down over Kansas (1854). The passing of control of the federal government to the 'free' party by the election of Lincoln as President in 1860 led to the ◊ *American Civil War*. After 1864, the new Republican Party remained in power, with two brief breaks, until 1912. Industry grew rapidly in the N. and W. though the problems of reconstruction in the S. were largely neglected. Railways were built, agriculture developed, and immigration from Europe swelled the population as the

Union spread from east to west. The acquisition of Puerto Rico and the Philippines in the ◊ Spanish-American War made U.S.A. a colonial power, and it became increasingly interested in Latin-America. In 1917 U.S.A. declared war on Germany and played a decisive part in the closing Allied campaign. President Wilson was a chief architect of the ◊ Versailles Treaty and of the ◊ League of Nations, but his policy was rejected by a hostile Senate, which refused to accede to the League, and it was not until the Second World War that the U.S.A. finally abandoned isolationism. The period after 1918 was one of unprecedented prosperity until the onset of the great depression in 1929. Recovery was guided after 1932 by Roosevelt's ◊ New Deal policy, which led to increased intervention in economic matters by the federal government. The U.S.A. played a major part in the ◊ Second World War, from which it emerged as indisputably the most highly productive and militarily powerful nation, and continued to assume a leading role in post-war reconstruction and international affairs: ◊ Berlin, Cuba Crisis, Marshall Plan, N. Atlantic Treaty Organization. For internal affairs ◊ Democratic/Republican Party.

Unit Trusts ◊ Investment Trusts.

Universals. In philosophy, the quality things must have if a general word, e.g. 'warm', is to apply to them; the problem of universals may be formulated as: How are we able to use general words? The theory of ◊ realism is that we name entities, e.g. warmth, which exists in some sense if not in the individual way of e.g. warm things; nominalism holds that only particular things exist, and that we apply the same general word to some of them because of resemblances; conceptualism (a middle road) holds that we form general ideas or concepts which do in some sense exist, and apply them to similar things. ◊ Scholasticism.

Universities. The modern university can be traced to medieval origins in Paris and Bologna. Outside the West other forms of higher learning have flourished, e.g. in Islam, but the Western pattern is now established throughout the world. Oxford came into being in the 12th cent. and Cambridge in 1209. The German universities were influential in the 19th cent., and the University of Berlin (1810) was a model for many new universities founded in the expanding industrial cities towards the end of the 19th cent. During the 20th cent. universities all over the world have been under mounting pressure to expand, to incorporate new and more specialized branches of teaching and research, and to adapt their organization to the demands of industrial societies. In most countries universities are financed directly or indirectly by the State, though in some e.g. U.S.A. there are many purely private institutions. The British universities, though they rely increasingly on State funds, are nevertheless independent of direct State control though linked to government through the University Grants Committee. British and American universities value highly academic freedom: i.e. the principle that professors alone should decide what to teach, and that appointment, promotion, and dismissal should be decided upon academic grounds alone, independent of racial, religious, or political considerations. The universities of Oxford, Cambridge, London, and Wales consist of loosely federated colleges, each of which retains a great deal of independence. The other 27 universities of Britain are unitary institutions, each under the academic control of a Senate (mainly of professors). They are divided into faculties of Arts, Science, Medicine, etc. and further into departments e.g. mathematics, geography, the head of which usually has the title of Professor; then come Readers, Senior Lecturers, Lecturers, Assistant Lecturers, and Demonstrators. About one in nine of university teachers is a professor. Students are admitted selectively after passing public examinations and normally pursue their studies for three or four years; the passing of a final examination is marked by the award of a degree.

About 85 per cent of students at British universities qualify for a maintenance grant from the State or county authority. Students may live in college or in a student hostel. About a quarter live in lodgings and another quarter at home.

Teaching consists of lectures, seminars (discussion groups of 10 to 20 students) conducted by lecturers, individual tutorials, and directed reading; and where appropriate practical work in laboratories, workshops, or hospitals. The 'tutorial' system is a special feature of the Oxford and Cambridge colleges. There are many differences between the organization and student life of British universities and those in other countries, yet the similarities are important. Two great problems face universities today – specialization and increasing size. The Robbins Report 1963 envisages an increase in the proportion of the relevant age group going on to full-time higher education in the U.K. from 8.5 per cent in 1961 to 17 per cent by 1980, and expects that higher education will include a wide range of institutions catering for a growing number of special fields, with increasing emphasis on the natural and social sciences. In U.S.A. there are already more than 3 million students in roughly 2000 degree-granting institutions. In Britain existing universities have plans for expansion, and new ones are being founded at York, Norwich, Colchester, Brighton, Canterbury, etc. The latter plan to experiment with new forms of organization and with degree courses which avoid the rigidity of the single-subject honours degree which have long been a feature of British universities. Universities are not only for teaching but for the extension of knowledge: post-graduate and research studies have become an important and growing aspect of university activity, esp. in the natural sciences. ⟡ *Academic Degree, College, Education, Examination, Soviet Union, United Kingdom, United States of America, etc.*

Universities of Oxford and Cambridge. Oxford is the oldest English university; there was already a centre for teaching in 1133, and the first college (University College) was founded 1249. Like Cambridge (where the first college, Peterhouse, dates to 1284) it is organized on the basis of some 20 residential colleges, corporate entities governed by their own Fellows and distinct from the University (which controls the main libraries, laboratories, and so on). For centuries the universities of Oxford and Cambridge were entirely self-supporting, but since 1915 they have received government grants; today about 70 per cent of the students also receive some state assistance. There are some 9000 students at each university, the tutorial system of individual tuition being a traditional feature. Women's colleges were first built in the late 19th cent., but although women took examinations, they were not granted ⟡ *academic degrees* until recently. The normal duration of the university course is three years, leading to a B.A. degree; the M.A. degree is awarded without further examination, but research work must be done for other degrees e.g. Ph.D. or B.Litt. ⟡ *Education.*

Untouchables ⟡ *Caste.*

Upanishads. Sanskrit treatises on metaphysics and theology, the oldest examples of Hindu thought attached to the ⟡ *Vedas* and to the dicta on matters of Hindu faith and worship, dating probably to before A.D. 500. Translated into European languages in the 19th cent. they influenced German and English ⟡ *romanticism,* American ⟡ *transcendentalism,* and the poet Yeats.

Upper Volta ⟡ *Voltaic Republic.*

Ur. City of the ancient ⟡ *Sumerians*; in the Old Testament, the home of Abraham. Ur was probably founded as early as the 4th millennium B.C. and was at one time overlaid by a thick water-laid clay deposit, representing a great flood such as is prominent in Sumerian legend, possibly that of the Old Testament. Flourishing by 2500 B.C. it was captured by Sargon of the ⟡ *Akkadians* about 2350 B.C. After the Akkadian ascendancy it continued to be an important city through different empires until the 6th cent. B.C. The site was discovered in the 19th cent. and excavated in the 20th by Leonard Woolley.

Uraemia. Form of poisoning caused by accumulation of urea and other nitrogenous end-products in the blood after failure of the excretory mechanism of the kidneys. The symptoms are nausea, headaches, dimness of vision, and coma or convulsions. Most serious kidney lesions e.g. chronic ⟡ *nephritis* lead to uraemia.

Uranium. ⟡ *Actinides*; a grey, ductile, malleable metal occurring in pitchblende (U_3O_8) and other minerals; more abundant than e.g. silver and bismuth. Discovered by Klaproth in 1789, it was little regarded until Becquerel made observations on it in 1896 which led to the discovery of the radioactive elements and of the various natural radioactive series. The discovery of uranium fission as a source of energy by Hahn and Strassman 1938 led to its use in nuclear reactors and bombs; for these purposes the ⟡ *isotope* uranium-235 has to be separated from natural uranium. Before the advent of nuclear energy, uranium had limited uses as an alloying metal, in the preparation of catalysts, and for colouring glazes. An intensive world-wide search for uranium is taking place: leading sources are S. Africa, Canada, U.S.S.R. ⬦ *Plutonium*.

Uranus. 1. The planet seventh from the sun (mean distance about 1783 m. miles) and the first of the 'new' planets discovered, by William Herschel 1781. It is barely visible to the naked eye, and even large telescopes reveal little detail. The rotation period (about 10¾ hours) has been determined from photoelectric measurements of brightness. It has five moons: Miranda, Ariel, Umbriel, Titania, and Oberon. ⬦ *Solar System*.

2. In Greek mythology, heaven, the oldest of the gods, husband and son of Gaea (Ge) the earth, and father of the ⬦ *Titans* and the ⬦ *Cyclopes*. When his children were born he confined them in ⬦ *Tartarus*; ultimately the Titan Cronos dismembered him, whereupon from his blood sprang the ⬦ *Furies* and from the foam round parts of his body thrown in the sea sprang ⬦ *Aphrodite*. Probably the Greeks evolved such legends in order to absorb the deities of the peoples they conquered (⬦ *Mythology*).

Urdu ⬦ *Indo-European Languages, Sanskrit*.

Urea. NH_2CONH_2; the amide of carbonic acid, a white water-soluble crystalline substance, the medium by which nitrogen formed by protein metabolism in the body of mammals, birds, and some reptiles is excreted in the urine. An adult human excretes 20 to 70 grammes a day, according to the protein content of the diet. Urea is also present in milk and blood. It was the first organic compound to be prepared artificially. Large quantities are now synthesized from ammonia and carbon dioxide for use as fertilizer and for the manufacture of urea-formaldehyde resins (⬦ *polymers*). Barbiturate drugs make use of urea or urea derivatives as intermediates.

Ureter, Urethra ⬦ *Bladder*.

Urticaria. Nettlerash; a vascular reaction of the skin, characterized by intensely itchy weals which occur in crops and usually quickly disappear. The commonest cause is an allergy (⬦ *Histamine*), but it sometimes follows the injection of foreign proteins during immunization.

Uruguay. Area 72,180 sq. m. Pop. 2.6 m Spanish speaking, predominantly of Euro pean descent. Cap. Montevideo. Rel Roman Catholic. Between Brazil an Argentina; the smallest republic in S America and its only welfare state. The standard of living and literacy are high Under the 1952 Constitution governmen is by a unique system, designed as guarantee against dictatorship, by National Council composed of six mem bers from the majority party and three from the opposition; its members may not serve again in successive terms. The legislature is a 99-man Chamber of Depu ties and 30-man Senate, elected for fou years by direct vote of all literate adul citizens. An arbitration tribunal mediate in any dispute between Council and legis lature.

ECONOMY. Mainly pastoral, with cattle and wool as the main exports. The trenc to expand wheat and other agricultura production has not been entirely satisfac tory. There is some light industry, bu mineral resources are scanty.

HISTORY. The story of Uruguay is a long struggle between the Spanish of Argentina and the Portuguese from Brazil for possession, followed (once independence was gained in 1828) by factional struggles between two opposed parties, the Blancos and Colorados. In 1903 President Ordonez put the country on a new course which brought order and prosperity and was consolidated by the constitution of 1952 **U.S.S.R.** ⬦ *Soviet Union*.

Uterus. The womb; a pear-shaped ex pandable organ of ⬦ *gestation* in mam mals, which holds the fertilized ovum or embryo during its development and ther expels it through the vagina. In woman it expands during pregnancy by about three times. It is lined by a soft membrane (endometrium) which undergoes cyclica changes each month (⬦ *Menstruation*) to prepare it for the possible reception of a fertilized ovum. ⬦ *Reproduction*.

Utilitarianism. The 18th- and 19th-cent doctrine that we ought to seek the greates happiness of the greatest number of people: an action is 'right' if it is likely to produce greater happiness than any other possible action. Bentham 1748–1832 thought we should compare actions solely as to the quantities of pleasure they would produce; John Stuart Mill 1806–73 complicated the doctrine by arguing that we should take into account that one quantity of pleasure may be of higher quality than another. Utilitarianism was the outstanding philosophical foundation for 19th-cent. reform movements of many kinds; Bentham had originally considered it a means of assessing particular laws, and Mill applied it widely in the many causes he supported. ◊ *Enlightenment*.

Utopia. < Gr. *ou-topos*, no place, deliberately confused with *en-topos*, good place. An impossibly ideal society, usually dependent upon far-fetched schemes for happiness and welfare, from the imaginary island of More's political essay *Utopia*, 1516 (English translation 1551). More probably intended his Utopia not to be perfect but to shame Christians into his ideal of right behaviour.

Utrecht Treaty. 1713. Concluded the ◊ *War of the Spanish Succession*; King Philip of Spain renounced all rights of succession to the French throne, while Louis XIV of France recognized the King of ◊ *Hanover* as heir to Britain. The ◊ *Hudson's Bay* Territory and other French possessions were ceded to England, together with ◊ *Gibraltar* and Minorca from Spain; the ◊ *Netherlands* were secured against French aggression by a chain of barrier fortresses (they later passed under Austrian control), and ◊ *Savoy*, enlarged by the addition of ◊ *Sicily*, was made a kingdom.

V

Vaccination ◊ *Immunity*.

Vagina. Passage in the female which runs from the uterus to the vulva (◊ *Reproduction*). It has an inner folded membranous coat and an outer muscular coat. The vagina, which receives the male organ in coitus, is normally 3–3½ in. long, and is capable of great distension to allow the passage of a child at birth.

Valency (Valence). The power of an atom or group of atoms to link with another atom or group; the valency of an element can be simply defined as the number of atoms of hydrogen (or chlorine) which one atom of the element will combine with or replace. Thus sodium is univalent (monovalent) in sodium chloride NaCl, oxygen is bivalent (divalent) in water H_2O, nitrogen is tervalent (trivalent) in ammonia NH_3, etc. The valency of an element does not usually exceed seven, but some elements esp. the transition ones can have more than one valency, e.g. iron is bivalent in the ferrous compounds but tervalent in the ferric. ◊ *Chemical Bonding*.

Valhalla. In Norse mythology, the home of ◊ *Odin* and those killed in battle; part of the palace of Gladsheim in Asgard, the realm of the gods, it had 540 doors through each of which 800 men could march abreast. The heroes went out from Valhalla each morning to fight, and each evening feasted there attended by the ◊ *Valkyries*, their wounds being miraculously healed.

Valkyries. In Scandinavian mythology (◊ *Aesir*), the nine or more daughters of ◊ *Odin*, originally priestesses of Freya, sent to choose which heroes shall fall in battle and to conduct the fallen to ◊ *Valhalla*; the Valkyries Hrist and Mist are Odin's cupbearers.

Valley. A depression in the earth's surface caused by a river system; broad and gentle in soft rock or steeper-sided and ravined in hard rock, sometimes modified by the passage of a glacier. Or the sinking of land between two roughly parallel faults or fractures: ◊ *rift valley*. The rivers provide easy communication and the soil is usually deep and fertile; the valleys of the Indus, the Nile, the Tigris-Euphrates, and the Yangtse were cradles of the earliest civilizations.

Valmy. 1792. The first victory of the army of the ◊ *French Revolution* over the forces of the First Coalition (Austria, Britain, Holland, Prussia, Spain). Forced to retreat by the Duke of Brunswick's Prussians, the French General Dumouriez managed to join Kellermann and threaten the Prussian advance; after a long artillery duel, Brunswick withdrew.

Value, Theory of. In economics, the study of the process by which the free market settles on the price of a particular commodity. Early theories suggested that the value of goods depends on the amount of labour incorporated in an object; but this failed to explain the high value of natural diamonds, or of a loaf of bread in a beleaguered city. The classic 19th-cent. economists held that price is determined by the interaction of demand and supply, the 'two blades of scissors' (Alfred Marshall), based on the law of diminishing utility that the addition of each unit of a commodity adds less to the consumers' satisfaction than the previous unit did; thus if the output of a commodity is increased, the price will normally have to be lower if the market is to absorb it. The theory also holds that, in the long run, in a perfectly competitive market, prices settle at the lowest cost of production, including normal profits. ◊ *Marxism*.

Valve. 1. Device (e.g. water tap) to regulate the flow of a gas or liquid. For precise control (e.g. of the amount of petrol passing through a carburettor) a needle valve may be used.

SAFETY VALVES: On boilers etc. Designed to open when a dangerous pressure is approached.

2. ◊ *Thermionic Valve*.

Vanadium. A silvery malleable metallic ◊ *element* which does not tarnish readily; about as abundant as copper, the chief sources being patronite, carnotite, and vanadinite. It is widely used in steel manufacture, to refine the grain and improve mechanical properties and tempering characteristics; the product is known as ferrovanadium. The compounds most in demand are vanadium pentoxide (V_2O_5) and sodium metavanadate ($NaVO_3$), now the chief ◊ *catalysts* in the contact process for manufacturing sulphuric acid.

Van Allen Belts. Two radiation belts around the earth, composed of charged particles moving near the speed of light. They were discovered by Van Allen from data collected by the first U.S. satellites (◊ *Space Exploration*). The smaller belt forms a band about 1000 miles above the earth's magnetic equator, and the larger one almost encloses the earth some 20,000 miles up. Outer limits are being continuously changed by incoming streams of particles and variations in solar radiation. The belts affect radio transmission and play a part in visible ◊ *auroras* and magnetic storms.

Vandals. Teutonic tribe long settled in the Oder valley who in about A.D. 400 moved into Gaul. Refused permission to settle, they invaded Spain where they were allowed to stay by Emperor Honorius. They later crossed to Africa under Gaiseric and took Carthage, which was regained in A.D. 533 by the Roman general Belisarius; and they then disappeared from history. Their brief successes and their depredations by sea (they sacked Rome in A.D. 455) contributed to the decline of the Roman Empire.

Vanilla. Aromatic substance used for flavouring and perfumes, from the pods of the Mexican climbing orchid *Vanilla planifolia* and related species, brought to Europe via the W. Indies in 1800. The Aztecs used vanilla to flavour chocolate. ◊ *Spices*.

Variola. Smallpox; a severe infectious disease caused by a filterable virus. The incubation period is about 12 days, and the early symptoms include fever followed by a rash. The lesions turn into scabs, which may leave permanent scars (pock marks). Once a great scourge, it has been largely wiped out by vaccination (◊ *Immunity*).

Vatican. Area 109 acres. Pop. 940. An enclave within Rome, containing the Lateran Palace (city residence of the ◊ *Pope*), the central administrative offices of the ◊ *Roman Catholic Church*, the Vatican Library and Museum, the cathedral church of St Peter, and Castel Gandolfo (the Pope's country residence). Formerly the capital of the ◊ *Papal States*, by the Lateran Treaty of 1929 it was recognized as an independent sovereign state with its own citizenship, coinage, diplomatic corps, and postal system. Its civil government is conducted by a Governor and Council appointed by the Pope, whose chief advisers are the College of ◊ *Cardinals* and the administrative Curia Romana. The General Council which opened in 1962 is the second in history to be held in the Vatican. ◊ *Swiss Guards.*

Vault. An arched covering in stone, brick, or concrete resting on walls, piers, or arches; brick vaulting was used in Babylonia and Egypt 6000 years ago and highly

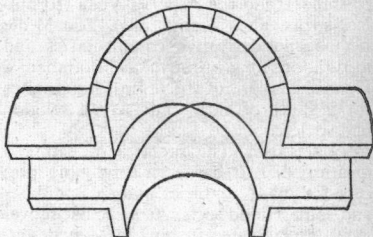

roman intersecting vault

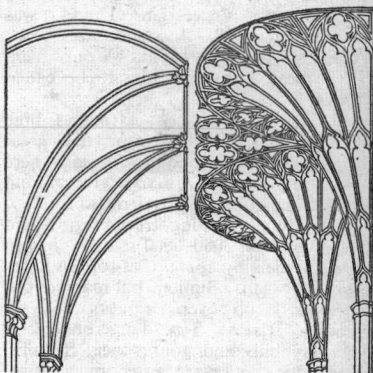

gothic vaulting   fan vaulting

developed by the Sassanids in Persia between 600 and 400 B.C. The Romans used intersecting barrel vaults, combining concrete with brick arches. Later ◊ *Romanesque* architects developed intersecting vaults, while ◊ *Gothic* architects applied the pointed arch to vaulting and invented a new system consisting of a framework of stone ribs supporting panels; Gothic fan vaulting, however, is built on a solid centring, and the ribs are not structural.

Vedanta. Term in Hinduism with three main applications. (1) Certain of the Upanishads (◊ *Vedas*). (2) The six *Darshanas*, philosophical systems founded on the Vedas. (3) One of these systems, dealing with the relation between the individual soul and ultimate reality (*Brahma*) and the means of achieving their identification.

Vedas. The sacred ◊ *Sanskrit* writings of ◊ *Hinduism*, consisting of four main collections of hymns, the Rig Veda (the oldest, containing over 1000), Sama Veda and Yajur Veda (containing stanzas from the Rig Veda accompanied by ritual formulas), and the Atharva Veda (formulas, spells, and incantations). The Vedic hymns and derivative commentaries and meditations (e.g. Aranyakas, Brahmanas, Upanishads) are of the utmost importance for a study of early Indo-Aryan religion and society.

Vegetarianism. The practice of eating a meatless diet. It has been a religious precept for many centuries among Buddhists and some Hindu sects. As a secular movement, it originated in 1847 in Manchester, and has spread to other countries. The International Vegetarian Union was founded in 1908. A stricter sect, the Vegan, started in 1944, allows only fruit, nuts, wheat, and vegetables to be eaten. ◊ *Diet*.

Veld. Dutch, 'a field'. In Afrikaans, high open grazing country esp. the great Transvaal tableland in S. Africa, where sheep are pastured, maize grown, and citrus fruits cultivated by irrigation.

HIGH VELD: Rolling treeless grassland like ◊ *prairies*, 5000–6000 ft high, broken here and there by *kopjes* (flat-topped hills). MIDDLE VELD: Similar, but marked also by *rands* (scrub-covered ridges).

Venereal Disease. Two dangerous forms exist: syphilis and gonorrhoea. Syphilis, a contagious disease caused by a spirochete, starts as a local sore two to four weeks after infection, during which time it spreads widely throughout the body. If not treated, the secondary stage, characterized by a transient rash and glandular enlargement, appears in from six weeks to six months. After this there is an indefinite latent period of a few weeks or many years before the onset of the tertiary stage, which causes degeneration of the blood vessels and nervous system, often leading to insanity and death. An infected mother may transmit syphilis as a congenital infection to her offspring, who commonly die at an early age or suffer from grave injury to the bones, eyes, and nervous system.

Gonorrhoea is an acute inflammation of the genital passages in either sex, due to the gonococcus. Immediate symptoms are painful and include the passage of a highly infective discharge. Untreated, the infection may spread to other and less accessible areas and may cause a crippling arthritis. Infants born to infected mothers are liable to develop gonococcal ophthalmia, once a frequent cause of blindness. Treatment of venereal disease is by means of antibiotics; penicillin-resistant strains, however, present difficulties.

The origin and history of venereal disease is obscure and disputed, but it seems clear that it swept Europe in epidemic form shortly after 1493; its virulence diminished later, but it remained a major disease until energetic measures were taken to combat it in the 20th cent. It has not been entirely eliminated, and there is evidence of a rising incidence amongst adolescents. Under the National Health Service Act 1946, provision of facilities for the treatment of venereal disease have become a statutory responsibility of the Regional Hospital Boards in the U.K.

Venezuela. Area 352,051 sq. m. Pop. 8.3 m. Cap. Caracas. Rel. Roman Catholic. Language Spanish. The most northerly S. American republic, between Colombia, British Guiana, and Brazil. The constitution as modified in 1958 provides for the popular election of a president and of a National Congress consisting of a Senate and a Chamber of Deputies, all elected for a term of five years.

ECONOMY. Venezuela is the world's largest exporter of petroleum, which is 90 per cent of the exports by value; it also produces iron ore, asbestos, cement, diamonds, foodstuffs. All major industrial concessions are owned by foreign companies, paying 50–70 per cent of their profits to the government. A government-owned steel mill is now in production.

HISTORY. A Spanish colony from the 16th cent. until the Wars of Liberation in the 1820s; the Republic of Venezuela was founded in 1830 and subsequently ruled largely by military dictators, esp.

General Castro 1899–1908 and General Gómez 1908–35. In 1945 Betancourt's left-wing but anti-communist Democratic Action Party came to power, after a revolt against the conservative government of General Medina, but was overthrown in 1948 by a military junta. Betancourt fled to Cuba. After a further revolt in 1958 the Democratic Action Party returned to power and Betancourt again became President.

Venice. A city-state founded in the Middle Ages among the lagoons of Venice as a refuge from the barbarians on the mainland. Its importance increased as Venice cleared the Adriatic of pirates and became one of the main centres for European trade with the east; its participation in the fourth ◊ *Crusade* increased its possessions, which included the Dalmatian coast, part of Greece, and Crete. Oligarchic rule replaced the democracy of the republic, and the Doge was reduced to a figurehead. The 15th cent. saw the height of Venetian power and influence; the rivalry of other Italian states, the fall of Constantinople to the Turks in 1453 (which cut off Levantine trade), and the discovery of the Cape route to the east led to its decline. In 1797 it fell easily to Napoleon; by the ◊ *Vienna Congress* in 1815 it was ceded to Austria, but after the Austro-Prussian war of 1866 it became part of the kingdom of Italy.

Venus. 1. The planet second from the sun (mean distance 67 m. miles). Its orbit is between those of ◊ *Mercury* and the earth, and it comes nearer to the earth than any other planet. Venus is sometimes very conspicuous in the west at sunset (evening star) and in the east at sunrise (morning star), being outshone only by the sun and moon. It shows phases, like the moon, and is invisible when between the earth and the sun and brightest when showing only a thin 'new moon' phase. The planet is obscured by thick cloud, and its surface cannot be seen. Spectroscopy shows much carbon dioxide, a little water vapour, but no oxygen. Venus, which has no satellite, has been detected by radar on a frequency of 2388 megacycles per second. ◊◊ *Solar System.* **2.** In mythology: ◊ *Aphrodite.*

Verdun. 1916. A series of fortresses at Verdun, guarding the approach to Paris, were the object of heavy German attacks in the ◊ *First World War*; owing to novel tactics and superior artillery support, the Germans captured some forts, but under General Pétain, with his slogan *Ils ne passeront pas*, the French threw them back. Both sides lost heavily; one million men were killed.

Vermouth. Wine containing up to 16 per cent alcohol, to which are added various herbs, chiefly wormwood (hence the name). Italian or sweet Vermouth can be white or red; French Vermouth is white and dry. Both types are made mainly in Italy and France, but similar products are now made in other countries. A number of apéritifs, e.g. Dubonnet, Byrrh, are based on vermouth; they frequently contain quinine. Alcohol content for all these is about 30° proof.

Vernalization. Treatment of partially germinated seeds by exposure to temperatures just above freezing, before they are sown; this shortens the time taken for the plants to flower and seed. It is important agriculturally and was developed esp. in Russia, where vernalized cereals can be sown in spring to avoid the severe winters. Vernalization is one of several types of physiological preconditioning of plants, e.g. influencing the time of flowering by artificially changing the day length (photoperiodism), and hardening-off of plants before planting out in early spring. The breaking of dormancy in seeds and bulbs (to make them flower earlier) is also important agriculturally, but is a different physiological process.

Versailles Treaty. 1919. Treaty signed on 28 June 1919, after lengthy negotiations between Clemenceau, Lloyd George, and Woodrow Wilson, intended to solve the problems that had caused the ◊ *First World War*. For the French, the chief aim was to reduce the power of Germany: accordingly German territory west of the Rhine was demilitarized and occupied, limitations were placed on German armaments, and heavy ◊ *reparations* were imposed (though never collected). Poland was reconstituted, from territory detached from Germany, Russia, and Austria. Wilson hoped to set up a world organization to maintain peace; and thus the Covenant of the ◊ *League of Nations* became the first part of the Treaty. The British aims were imprecise, but they secured the destruction of the German fleet and the liquidation of German colonies. Wilson's failure to persuade U.S.A. to join the League of Nations, the reversion of U.S.A. to isolationism, and the failure of France and the U.K. to act in concert rapidly emasculated the Treaty. The majority of Germans regarded it as unjust and oppressive, and Hitler (◊ *Nazism*) was able to rally support by his denunciations of the 'Diktat' of Versailles. ◊ *Fourteen Points.*

Vertebrates. Largest and most important sub-phylum of the Chordata, including fish, amphibians, reptiles, birds, and mammals, and differing from the other chordates in having a skull, a well-developed brain, and a skeleton; the latter feature has made the vertebrates one of the two most successful groups of land animals (the other being the insects). Vertebrates are not alone in showing numerous examples of varying evolutionary mechanisms, but because of their success they show such mechanisms very clearly. Their numerous adaptations have enabled them to fill every possible ecological niche. Thus, whales have secondarily evolved mechanisms for submarine aquatic life; birds are adapted for flight; the terrestrial mammals include ground-living ruminants, arboreal primates, subterranean insectivores and so on. The fossil remains of vertebrates supply the best evidence for ◊ *evolution.* The larger size possible for a vertebrate (as against invertebrates) permits great development of the nervous system and the elaboration of sense organs, and hence the capacity for large information-storage and versatile behaviour.

Vertigo. Giddiness or a sense of instability, usually resulting from disturbance of the 'balance' mechanism in the middle ear or from a brain lesion affecting muscular activity. It may be temporarily produced by a sudden drop in blood pressure, or by toxaemia from alcohol or drugs.

Vesta. In Roman mythology, virgin goddess of the hearth; equivalent to the Greek Hestia, who however plays no great part in Greek legend. At Rome, Vesta guarded the sacred fire brought by ◊ *Aeneas* from Troy. Her priestesses, the six Vestal Virgins who tended it in a sanctuary on the Forum, were girls of noble family sworn to serve for 30 years, and strictly supervised: loss of virginity was punished by burial alive.

Vestigial Organs. Remnants of organs, e.g. appendix and third eyelid in man, which have long lost biological significance and thus any (natural) selective value. Their reduction has resulted from a genetic mechanism in which ◊ *genes* affecting them have by chance been lost from animal populations. That they are not lost by disuse alone is shown by the presence of eyes in some cave-dwelling animals.

Vesuvius ◊ *Caldera, Pompeii, Volcano.*

Vetch. Species of *Vicia* (*Leguminosae*), many wild in Britain and some planted as an alternative to clover. *V. faba*, the broad ◊ *bean*, is a distinct type.

Veto. The prohibition or checking of a bill or other political measure by some competent person or body, e.g. the President of U.S.A. can veto any bill or legislative resolution passed by Congress, though his veto can be overridden by a two-thirds majority in both Houses of Congress. Any one of the five permanent members of the Security Council of the ◊ *United Nations Organization* (the U.K., U.S.A., U.S.S.R., France, and Nationalist China), through the use of the veto, can prevent the Council from operating effectively.

Vichy France. 1940–4. In the ◊ *Second World War*, after the defeat of France by the Germans in 1940, that part of France not subjected to German occupation (roughly, S. France) was governed from Vichy, under Pétain and Laval.

Victorian Art ◊ *Biedermeierstill, Genre Painting, Gothic Revival.*

Victory. The flagship of Lord Nelson at the battle of ◊ *Trafalgar.* Built at Chatham 1759–65 and first commissioned in 1778, her dimensions were 153 ft keel, 186 ft gun-deck, and 51.5 ft beam, with ◊ *tonnage* (old measurement) 2162 burthen and armament thirty 32-pounders, twenty-eight 24-pounders, and forty-two 12-pounders. *Victory* ended her seagoing service in 1812; she has since lain at Portsmouth, where she is the flagship of the Commander-in-Chief of the Royal Navy.

Vicuña ◊ *Llama.*

Vienna, Congress of. 1815. After the ◊ *Napoleonic Wars* the main European powers met to reach a general settlement. The Austrian Chancellor Metternich, whose guiding principles were 'legitimacy' (i.e. the restoration of the rightful hereditary rulers) and a return to the pre-revolutionary borders, played an important role, as did Castlereagh for Britain and Talleyrand for France. ◊ *Holy Roman Empire* was replaced by a German Confederation led by Prussia (which acquired new territories); Poland was redivided, chiefly in favour of Russia, who also acquired Finland; Italy remained divided into small states, the kingdom of Sardinia being enlarged to include Savoy and Piedmont. Holland and the Austrian Netherlands were united under the House of Orange; Austria gained Lombardy and Venetia; Norway passed from Denmark to Sweden. Switzerland was permanently neutralized. The Bourbons were restored in France, Naples, and Spain. Britain secured Dutch Ceylon and the Cape Colony, and made gains in the W. Indies. But the general tenor of the Congress was reactionary, and in the following decades its spirit infused European politics and repressed the rise of nationalism. The Congress however made some liberal gestures; it introduced free navigation of the Rhine and Meuse, condemned the slave trade, recommended extending rights granted to Jews. It also laid down the procedures of international diplomacy which are still valid.

Vietminh ◊ *Vietnam (North)*.

Vietnam. Eastern coastal strip of ◊ *Indo-China*, largely tropical forest and mountains. The fertile valleys and deltas are highly cultivated and densely populated. Rice is the main crop. There are some mineral sources, including coal, and some light industry. It includes the previous French territories of Tonkin, Annam, and Cochin China. During the Second World War it was occupied by the Japanese, and after the war French efforts to reassert their authority were widely opposed. In 1954 the nationalist Vietminh defeated the French at ◊ *Dien Bien Phu*. Subsequently Vietnam was divided into two as North Vietnam and South Vietnam. Elections scheduled for 1956 to reunify the country have not been held.

NORTH VIETNAM: A people's (communist) republic. Area 63,000 sq. m. Pop. 17 m. Cap. Hanoi.

SOUTH VIETNAM: Area 66,281 sq. m. Pop. 16 m. Cap. Saigon. Republic. Government is by a president and a single-chamber National Assembly, both elected by universal suffrage; real power is largely in the hands of the President. The country has received considerable Ameri-

can financial aid. In 1963 dissatisfaction amongst the Buddhist community at the treatment received from the Catholic minority (the President and his family being Catholic) led eventually to an army coup and the overthrow and execution of President Ngo-dinh Diem. The efforts of the Vietcong (communist party) to dominate S. Vietnam led in 1965 to increased U.S. military aid and intervention.

Vikings. Norsemen (or Danes) from Scandinavia who between the 8th and 10th centuries A.D. raided the coasts of Europe, crossed the Atlantic to become the first discoverers of America, and penetrated deep into Russia. They settled in England and France: Alfred the Great in a treaty about 885 ceded to Guthrum a large part of England (the Danelaw); it was early reconquered by ◊ *Wessex* but retained a distinctive character until the 12th cent. A second wave of Vikings (980–1016) harried the ◊ *Anglo-Saxons*, and Ethelred the Unready tried to buy them off with the 'Danegeld', but in 1016 the Danes established Canute as king, and he and his sons ruled until 1042. In France, Rollo and his followers took over the area which became Normandy, where the French-speaking Normans under William sailed to conquer England in 1066. ◊ *Norman Conquest*.

Villanelle. A poem of five stanzas of three lines each, with a final quatrain, having only two rhymes throughout, the first and third lines of the first stanza being re-used to conclude alternate stanzas and forming the last two lines of the quatrain. ◊ *Ballade*.

Vine. Any climbing plant; more specifically, the grape-vine, *Vitis vinifera*, possibly originating in the Caucasus, early introduced to Europe. On its transplantation to America it was attacked by the pest *Phylloxera*, which was carried to Europe, where it wiped out vast areas of vineyards; they had to be replanted with resistant rootstocks developed from the native N. American grapes, upon which *V. vinifera* was successfully grafted. ◊ *Grape, Wine*.

Vinegar ◊ *Acetic Acid*.

Viol, Viola, Violin, Violoncello ◊ *Stringed Instruments*.

Viper. Family of poisonous ◊ *snakes*, in two groups, one in the Old World and the other in America, including the rattlesnake, a desert snake whose tail has scaly cups which rattle. Rattlesnakes, copper-heads, and water moccasins are pit vipers, with a heat-sensitive pit in front of the eye, to sense warm-blooded animals. The Old World group includes the adder, the only poisonous snake found in Britain.

Virginals ◊ *Keyboard Instruments.*

Virginia Creeper. Two climbing vines, of N. American origin, *Parthenocissus quin-quefolia* and *P. vitacea* (ampelopsis). The former climbs by cup-like suckers; the latter, a very handsome plant, requires support. They belong to the same family as the grape-vine.

Virgin Lands ◊ *Wheat.*

Viruses. Sub-microscopic bodies only observable by means of the electron microscope; they stand uncertainly be-tween inanimate and living matter, but they can multiply only within living tissue, vegetable or animal. They are smaller than ◊ *bacteria.* Viruses are responsible for many diseases (in man, measles, polio, smallpox; in animals, foot-and-mouth disease, ◊ *rabies*; in plants, tobacco mosaic). There are no drugs (including the antibiotics) effective in combating the virus-caused diseases, but in some cases e.g. polio, rabies, smallpox, immunization provides protection. Certain cancers in animals have been traced to viruses. A natural defence substance 'interferon' made by the cells of organisms has been isolated. ◊◊ *Immunity.*

Viscose Rayon ◊ *Cellulose.*

Vishnu. One of the chief trinity in the pantheon of ◊ *Hinduism.* Preserver of the world (created by ◊ *Brahma*) and husband of Shri Lakshmi, he is often de-picted with four arms, holding a club, a lotus, a shell, and a disk; the river Ganges springs from his feet. Today his cult is largely that of ◊ *Krishna*, his eighth incarnation; the story of the seventh, as Rama, is told in the *Ramayana.*

Visigoths ◊ *Goths.*

Vision. Sense in animals enabling them to perceive light and colour. Vision ranges from the eyespots of some invertebrates, through the compound mosaic eyes of in-sects, to the complex eyes of octopus and vertebrates. In vertebrates vision depends on the nervous layer of the eyeball called the retina, on which light rays are focused and from which images are conveyed to the brain via the optic nerve. Within the retina are light-sensitive neurones, known (from their shape) as *rods* and *cones.*

Rods predominate in nocturnal and cones in diurnal animals. Man, in common with the higher primates, has fully developed binocular or stereoscopic vision, which en-ables him to distinguish depth and dist-ance accurately. Colour vision is present in some fish and reptiles, in birds, and in all higher primates, though in some verte-brates e.g. cats and dogs it is poorly developed.

Visual Teaching Aids. Adjuncts to oral teaching, to enliven the work and eluci-date difficulties: e.g. maps, diagrams, charts, tape-recordings, films, television, radio. In Britain, the National Committee for Visual Aids in Education and the Local Education Authorities coordinate the work and stimulate the production of material. The BBC and ITA broadcast television and sound-radio programmes for schools and for adult-education classes; over 3000 schools are equipped with TV receiving sets. Similar facilities exist in other countries; recent develop-ments include closed-circuit TV in uni-versity teaching (e.g. surgery and teacher-training), language courses with tape-recorders etc., and ◊ *teaching machines* enabling pupils to teach them-selves at their own rate.

Vitamins. Organic compounds of highly complicated chemical composition which whilst not part of the substance of cells are essential agents in the processing of cellular matter and thus for the growth and maintenance of the body. They are effective in minute quantity. The human body itself builds up very few vitamins, so that the majority must be obtained from specific foods. The existence and role of vitamins were discovered only in 1912, although the importance of specific elements in diet was known earlier in the case of ◊ *scurvy.* The table opposite lists a few typical vita-mins (of which a great number have now been isolated) and their functions; whilst all are present in foodstuffs, they are now available as synthetic substances also.

Vitoria. 1813. One of the last battles of the ◊ *Peninsular War.* With 80,000 Eng-lish and Spanish troops, Wellington as-saulted the over-extended position occu-pied by Joseph Bonaparte, King of Spain; abandoning their guns, the French re-treated. The defeat marked the end of their rule in the peninsula.

Vitamin	Use	Foods containing it (best sources first)
A	Hemi-carotene (Axerophthol) Synthesized 1947	Aids growth. Prevents 'night blindness'.	Cod-liver oil. Milk, eggs, butter, carrots, tomatoes.
B₁	Thiamin (Aneurin) Synthesized 1936	Aids utilization of carbohydrates. Prevents nervous disorders and 'beri-beri'.	Brown bread. Milk, yolk of egg. Rice husks.
B₂ (G)	Riboflavin (Lactoflavin) Synthesized 1934	Respiration of cells. Prevents photophobia.	Milk, yeast, liver, brown bread.
B₄ or B₅ (N)	Nicotinic acid (Niacin) Synthesized before 1900	Prevents pellagra.	Yeast, liver, meat, milk, green vegetables.
C	Ascorbic acid (Cevitamic acid) Synthesized 1933	Promotes healing, increases resistance to disease. Prevents scurvy.	Blackcurrants, oranges, lemons, rose-hips. Green vegetables. Potatoes.
D₂ *	Calciferol Synthesized 1935	Helps bone formation. Prevents rickets.	Formed in body by sunshine. Cod-liver oil, milk, butter.

* D_1 and D_3 have similar activity.

Vocational Guidance. The process of helping young people to choose a career; all Local Education Authorities have Youth Employment Officers, who interview pupils wishing for help, try to discover their abilities and temperament, and suggest work in which they will find happiness and satisfaction. The National Institute of Industrial Psychology has prepared aptitude tests, and arranges interviews for those needing guidance.

Vodka. Spirituous drink, of Russian origin, also made in Poland. The best quality is made from a grain malt, cheaper kinds from potatoes. It is colourless and almost flavourless. In Russia and Poland it is frequently sold with a very high percentage of alcohol. As sold in the U.K. it is comparable in strength with gin.

Volcano. A vent in the earth's crust ejecting steam, gases, and ◊ *lava*, either as a gentle flow of e.g. basaltic lava from a fissure, or as a violent explosion carrying millions of tons of ashes and rocks into the atmosphere, to fall back round the vent and build up a conical mountain. The cones of e.g. Vesuvius and Etna (11,000 ft high, the biggest in Europe) are built up of ash and lava-flows around central vents or craters, with neither smoke nor fire; steam and fine dust rise, and the red glow of molten rock is reflected by night on the clouds of condensed steam. When lava in the central vent cools and solidifies, pressure builds up, and unless a new side-outlet is found the mountain will explode, as with e.g. Monte Somma A.D. 79, destroying Pompeii, and Krakatoa in 1883, with enormous loss of life and destruction, the debris spreading for thousands of miles. Volcanoes are active, dormant, or extinct; there are 500 active volcanoes in existence.

◊ *Brecchia, Caldera, Magma, Pumice.*

Volleyball. A six-a-side game in a court 60 ft by 30 ft, in which teams volley a ball across an 8-ft net with their hands, aiming to ground it in their opponents' half. Invented in U.S.A. 1895, it was brought to Europe by American troops in the First World War, but only since the Second World War has its popularity spread rapidly. The International Volleyball Association (1947) has over 70 member countries, and received ◊ *Olympic Games* status for 1964.

Volstead Act ◊ *Prohibition.*

Voltaic Republic. Area 106,011 sq. m. Pop. 3.6 m. Cap. Ouagadougou. Republic in W. Africa near the Ivory Coast. Formerly a French colony; a member of the Conseil de l'Entente. The legislature is a single-house National Assembly, under a president.

ECONOMY. Mainly livestock-breeding; also exports of cotton, groundnuts. There are deposits of bauxite, copper, gold, graphite, manganese. Its sea-outlet is Abidjan, cap. of ◊ *Ivory Coast*.

HISTORY. Part of the Mossi empire until annexed by France in 1896; the Niger and Upper Senegal colony, created in 1904, became Upper Volta in 1919, and was part of the Ivory Coast 1932–47 and part of French W. Africa 1947–58. ◊ *Ghana*.

Voodoo. Voodun; religion of Haitian Negroes of W. African origin. As in other variants of W. African cults (found among all descendants of slaves in central and S. America), a major feature is ritual by drumming, chanting, and dancing, to induce the spirits of various gods to possess the participants; but the rites – despite popular belief – are not sexual orgies. The gods have African names and also those of Roman Catholic saints, originally adopted to conceal their paganism.

CANDOMBLÉ, MACUMBA: Similar cults in Brazil.

Vorticism. Derived in art from ◊ *cubism* and ◊ *futurism*, and in literature from ◊ *Imagism*; initiated 1912 by Wyndham Lewis and publicized by his paper *Blast*, and intended 'to build up a visual language as abstract as music'. In art, its characteristics are the use of machine-like forms and motifs in dynamic vortex-like compositions; in literature, it combined romantic emphasis on intensity and freshness of feeling with a classical demand for self-discipline and economy of expression. Its chief literary exponent was Ezra Pound.

Vulcan ◊ *Hephaestus*.

Vulgate ◊ *Bible*.

Vulture ◊ *Eagle*.

W

Wagner Act ◊ *National Labor Relations Act.*

Wagram. 1809. On 5 July Napoleon crossed from the island of Lobau in the Danube (near Vienna) and advanced to meet the Austrians under the Archduke Charles. The following day the Austrians attacked but were forced back by the concentrated fire of his 'grand battery' of 100 guns, and retreated with heavy losses. ◊ *Napoleonic Wars.*

Waitangi Treaty (1840) ◊ *Maori.*

Wakefield. 1460. A Lancastrian victory over the Yorkists during the ◊ *Wars of the Roses.* The Duke of York was killed, and the Lancastrian forces, under Queen Margaret, marched south to rescue King Henry VI, after a further victory at St Albans.

Wakefield Cycle ◊ *Miracle Play.*

Waldenses (Vaudois). Christian sect, similar to the ◊ *Albigenses,* founded about 1170 in SE France by Peter Waldo, a merchant of Lyons, in protest against the worldliness of the official Church, which severely persecuted them; spread widely in parts of France, Germany, and Italy and in the 16th cent. became allied with the Protestant reformers. Their persecution in Savoy in the 17th cent. aroused much sympathy in Britain, and led to Protector Cromwell's intervention on their behalf, the writing of Milton's well-known 'Avenge . . .' sonnet, and the public donation of a very large sum of money for their relief. A Waldensian Church still exists in Italy, esp. in Piedmont, with about 25,000 members. ◊ *Protestantism, Reformation.*

Wales. Area 8000 sq. m. Pop. 2.7 m. Cap. Cardiff. Rel. preponderantly ◊ *nonconformist.* A principality of Gt Britain, the monarch's eldest son being traditionally Prince of Wales. The British government includes a minister for Welsh Affairs. Wales elects 36 members to the House of Commons.

ECONOMY. Wales is mountainous; much of the country is agricultural, sheep rearing being important. Glamorgan has important coal deposits and is the centre of an industrial area with large iron and steel, chemical, and tinplate works. With the decline of the coal-mining industry Wales was for long beset with unemployment. There are many famous resorts, castles, and beauty spots which attract tourists. ◊ *Eisteddfod.*

HISTORY. In prehistoric times Wales was settled by ◊ *Celts.* Under Roman control by A.D. 78, it was Christianized by the 6th cent. notably by St David. In the 11th cent. the Normans established earldoms on the Welsh borders, but the real conquest of Wales came in 1282 when Edward I defeated and killed the last native Welsh prince, making his own newborn son Prince of Wales in 1301. There were several revolts, notably that of Glendower 1400–9. Welsh support helped to put the part-Welsh Henry Tudor on the English throne in 1485, and Wales was formally united with England by the 1536 ◊ *Act of Union.* Nonconformism took firm root in Wales, which later became a stronghold of ◊ *Methodism.* After the ◊ *Reform Bills* the Welsh returned many Liberals to Parliament and achieved some nationalist aspirations, e.g. the 1914 disestablishment of the Church of England in Wales, with autonomy in education. The disputed border county of Monmouthshire was added to the principality for administrative purposes after the Second World War. LANGUAGE. Cymraeg, one of the Celtic languages; it has a rich and varied literature dating to the 6th cent. A.D. and is spoken by about half the population, though virtually all speak English also.

Wallaby ◊ *Kangaroo.*

Wallflower ◊ *Cruciferae.*

Wall Street. Street in lower part of Manhattan island; one of the major financial centres of the world. It houses the New York Stock Exchange, and the American Stock Exchange, the head offices of leading banks and insurance companies, and commodity exchanges. The 'Wall Street crash' of 1929, when share prices tumbled and many banks went bankrupt, ushered in the long years of the ◊ *depression* of the 1930s.

Walnut. *Juglans regia*; a tall deciduous tree, with pinnate leaves, native in SE Europe and Asia. The male flowers are in ◊ *catkins* and the female in short spikes.

The fruit is not a true nut but a stone fruit (drupe) like plums, cherries, and peaches, covered by a soft husk which gives a brown juice. As the fruit ripens the green husk turns black and decomposes. Pickled walnuts are prepared from whole unripe fruits, husk and all, before the shell has hardened. Walnut timber is valuable and was very popular for furniture in Europe in the late 17th and early 18th centuries.

Walrus. Arctic aquatic carnivore, up to 12 ft long, related to the ◊ *seal*; sparsely haired, with bristles on the snout and ivory tusks (for which it was once hunted) up to two ft long, serving as weapons and to dig up shellfish.

Wandering Jew. The central figure in a legend extant in many variant forms; perhaps the best known is that of the artisan Ahasuerus, at whose door Jesus Christ paused to rest while carrying his cross, and who angrily urged him on. Jesus said: 'I go, but you shall await my return.' Ahasuerus has ever since trudged the world, unable to die, restored to the age of 30 after each 100 years. The story dates to the 13th cent. or earlier and has often been used in poems and fiction.

War. As organized conflict, distinct from mere primitive fighting, war dates to the emergence of organized states, e.g. the ancient empires of Assyria and Egypt. It became an instrument of policy, and its nature changed further with the development of the modern nation-state and the progress of technology. In medieval times and up to the 18th cent. wars (apart from those of religion) tended to be limited both in objective and in extent, e.g. to the acquisition of a province or the resolving of a dynastic quarrel. The size of armies was also limited, and the life of the bulk of the population as a whole, despite the hazards of pillage and massacre, continued comparatively unchanged. In the 19th and 20th centuries, with the commitment of more and more of the resources of industrialized nations to war, it tended to become total, involving the whole population and economy of the belligerent countries. The objective ceased to be limited and became the unconditional surrender of the enemy. The increased effectiveness of explosives, the advent of aircraft and submarines, added enormously to the destructiveness of military operations. The application of nuclear technology to weapons threatens not only total war but total destruction. The long-held concept of war as a mere extension of the peaceful pursuit of policies of national interest becomes meaningless when resort to war involves the likelihood of complete mutual destruction. War has been seen by some writers (e.g. Lewis Mumford) as a stimulus to social and technological progress (the development of international finance, mass-production, radar, rocket propulsion, etc.) and even (e.g. by Nietzsche) as an ennobling experience. Others (like Norman Angell and Arnold Toynbee) condemn war as a destroyer of material wealth, of moral standards, and ultimately of civilizations. ◊ *Strategy, Tactics*.

LAWS OF WAR: Rules and conventions concerning the conduct of war, first formulated by the Dutch jurist Grotius in *Rights of War and Peace* in 1625, the general theme of which was that civilians should be well treated and that military action should not proceed beyond that necessary to attain 'just' ends. The wars of the 18th cent. were in this sense 'limited'. In the 19th cent. a variety of formal limitations were agreed: at sea, no privateering; on land, no bombardment of open towns, no dum-dum bullets, humane treatment of prisoners (rules accepted in the Geneva Conventions). Nations issued manuals to their troops embodying the rules as they saw them. In the stress of total war nations abandoned restraints as it suited them. Of the agreed conventions, hardly a single one was consistently observed by all belligerents of the two world wars, though the restraining influence of their existence was undoubtedly of value. ◊ *Atom Bomb, Chemical Warfare, Red Cross, War Crimes*.

Warblers. Large world-wide family of active insectivorous song-birds, usually building small nests in low vegetation. Warblers of Britain and Europe include the blackcap, whitethroat, chiff-chaff, and the willow, garden, sedge, reed, and wood warblers, all migrant species returning northwards in the spring from the Mediterranean and Africa.

War Crimes. These are of two kinds: (1) breaches of the traditional laws of welfare e.g. maltreatment of prisoners; (2) crimes against peace e.g. waging an aggressive war. This second category is of recent origin and compared with the first, established, category is controversial. The Nazi leaders of the Second World War were charged with both types of crimes before the International Military Tribunal at Nuremberg established by agreement amongst the Allies in 1945. They were further charged with crimes against humanity e.g. murder, enslavement, deportations, and other inhumane acts committed against the civilian population. ◊ Genocide.

Amongst those sentenced to death were Göring, Ribbentrop, and Streicher. Similar but less publicized trials of Japanese war criminals were also held. In all some 8000 persons were tried of whom 2000 were executed. Criticism has been made of the Nuremberg Tribunal on the grounds *inter alia* that the offence of waging an aggressive war was not one known to international law before the 1945 agreement and that it was therefore retrospective, and also that the jurisdiction of the tribunal extended only to the defeated and not to all combatant countries. Such criticism is far from universally accepted. Subsequent trials of war criminals e.g. the Auschwitz trial of 1964 were held in W. Germany under a law of the Federal Republic.

Ward of Court. In English law infants (persons under 21) may be made wards of court to safeguard those in need of care and protection. The court makes any necessary orders as to its ward's education and the management of his or her property.

War of 1812. War between Britain and U.S.A. during the ◊ *Napoleonic Wars*, caused by a variety of factors, of which British search of American ships (and impressment of their sailors), and the ambitions of American frontiersmen to seize land from the Indians and British, were the most important. The Americans invaded Canada but were repulsed. The British, after initial naval setbacks, won control of the sea after the defeat of the U.S. *Chesapeake* by the *Shannon*, marched on Washington, and burned the White House; but neither side gained decisive advantage. Peace was restored by the Treaty of Ghent, 1814, which provided for a return to prewar positions. As the news of the peace travelled slowly, one final battle was fought in Jan. 1815, when the Americans under Jackson (later

President) defeated the British at New Orleans. ◊ *Continental System*.

War of Jenkins' Ear. 1739. An English sailor, Robert Jenkins, told the House of Commons that the Spaniards had cut off his ear; the story increased indignation against Spain, already high at the Spanish claims to a right to search British ships. War resulted, and became merged in the wider ◊ *War of the Austrian Succession*.

War of the Austrian Succession. 1740–8. Struggle between ◊ *Prussia* and the ◊ *Hapsburgs*, which began when Frederick II refused to recognize Maria Theresa's right to succeed to the Hapsburg lands, and seized ◊ *Silesia*. It involved all the major European nations. British forces fought on land and sea against Spain and France. The Peace of Aix-la-Chapelle restored the prewar boundaries, except that Prussia retained Silesia. ◊◊ *Dettingen*.

War of the Spanish Succession. 1701–13. The quarrel between France and Austria over the successor to the childless Charles II of Spain flared up into a European war. France occupied the Netherlands, and with Bavarian help was at first victorious. At ◊ *Blenheim* Marlborough put the initiative in the hands of the allies, and at Ramillies he drove the French from the Netherlands. Meanwhile in Spain allied expeditions twice reached Madrid, but were forced to retire. The war considerably modified the standing of the European powers. France and Holland, though neither lost any territory, found their prestige diminished, while Britain emerged with a strengthened reputation both on land and at sea. ◊◊ *Malplaquet, Utrecht Treaty*.

Warrant. A written authorization by a Justice of the Peace (a) for a specified person to search specified premises for specified property; or (b) for the arrest of a specified person. General terms are not sufficient for a search warrant, and entering private property otherwise than in pursuance of a warrant is trespass, except that a person may enter to arrest a felon, if a felony has been committed, or to prevent the commission of a felony. A police officer is entitled to arrest without a warrant any person reasonably suspected of a felony, as is any member of the public if a felony has in fact been committed. Anyone arrested without a warrant except under these conditions may claim damages for false imprisonment.

Warsaw Pact. A 20-year treaty of friendship, collaboration, and mutual assistance signed in Warsaw in 1955 by Albania, Bulgaria, Czechoslovakia, the German Democratic Republic, Hungary, Poland, Rumania, and U.S.S.R. It provided for immediate assistance to any member state attacked in Europe and for a unified military command for the armed forces of the member states. The treaty is open to any state irrespective of its political regime, and is to lapse in the event of a system of collective security being established in Europe. It is often regarded as a response to the incorporation of the German Federal Republic in the ◊ *N. Atlantic Treaty Organization.* ◊◊ *Rapacki Plan.*

Warship. In the Middle Ages there was little difference between warships and merchant vessels, the former generally being merchant ships temporarily fitted with a 'castle' at each end as a strongpoint for archers and soldiers; an exception was the ◊ *galley*, a special war vessel of little use for cargo. With the coming of artillery, warships and merchant vessels began to develop along slowly diverging lines, until steam and steel-plating made the differences so great that with rare exceptions they became unable to exchange roles. Warships were classified in the early 19th cent. as line-of-battle ships, ◊ *frigates*, sloops, and corvettes; they are now divided into a much wider range of specialized types e.g. ◊ *aircraft-carriers*, *cruisers*, *destroyers*, minelayers, ◊ *submarines*, etc.

Wars of Religion ◊ *France (History)*, *Huguenots*, *Thirty Years War*.

Wars of the Roses. 1455–85. A long intermittent struggle between the Houses of Lancaster (red rose) and York (white rose) to secure the throne for their claimant. It arose from the claim of Richard, Duke of York, to take the throne from King Henry VI since he was descended from Henry IV, his grandfather, who had usurped the throne. The fortunes of war fluctuated as different combinations of nobles rallied to a particular claimant, the Earl of Warwick (nicknamed 'the Kingmaker') being a most powerful factor. The Duke of York's eldest son was crowned as Edward IV during Henry VI's lifetime, and in 1483 Edward's son became Edward V but was displaced by Edward's brother, the Duke of Gloucester, as Richard III. A further rival (distantly Lancastrian), Henry Tudor, succeeded in defeating Richard, who was killed at ◊ *Bosworth* 1485, and founded the Tudor line; he strengthened his title by uniting the conflicting factions through his marriage to Edward IV's daughter Elizabeth. The wars exhausted and discredited the nobility and paved the way for the strong, central 'middle-class' government of the ◊ *Tudors.*

Washington Conference (1921) ◊ *Disarmament.*

Wasp. Winged member of the *Hymenoptera*, mainly carnivorous. Like ◊ *bees*, wasps have both solitary and social forms; in the latter there are three castes – queens, workers, and drone males. Wasps serve to keep down insect pests. Most wasp nests (the clay nest of the potter wasp is an exception) are of a paper-like substance composed of finely chewed wood. The wasp, unlike the bee, can sting repeatedly.

Watercolour. A medium composed of ground pigments and gum, which when applied to paper produces a distinctive transparent effect quite different from oil colours. The oldest paintings found are Egyptian watercolours. In the Middle Ages artists produced brilliant illuminated manuscripts in this medium. Its use as a complete technique developed in the 18th and 19th centuries and was esp. popular in England where Turner, Girtin, Bonington, and Cotman excelled. ◊◊ *Gouache, Tempera.*

Waterfall. A perpendicular drop in a river at a sudden change of gradient, usually caused by the outcrop of a layer of hard rock above an easily eroded layer; the rocks are horizontal, or dip gently upstream. (A downstream dip causes rapids.) Hydroelectric stations at falls throughout the world produce vast amounts of electric power. The Niagara falls in N. America, the Iguassu falls in S. America, and the Victoria falls in Rhodesia are famous for volume, height, and beauty.

Water-hyacinth. *Eichhornia crassipes*; a tropical water-plant either rooted or (more usually) free floating. The leaf-stalks are swollen and bladderlike. It may multiply rapidly in lakes and slow-flowing rivers, forming dense mats which seriously hinder navigation.

Water-lily. Aquatic plants, of the family *Nymphaeaceae* rooting in the mud at the bottom of pools, shallow lakes, and slow-moving streams, with floating leaves and beautiful flowers in many colours. Some are hardy, e.g. the common British water-lily *N. alba*. The giant Brazilian lily, *Victoria regia,* has circular floating leaves over a yard in diameter. ⬦ *Lotus.*

Waterloo. 1815. Battle near Brussels which ended the Hundred Days rule of Napoleon after his return from exile in Elba. Napoleon had hoped to defeat the Allies by attacking them singly, and his first objective was to prevent the junction of the British and Prussian armies. He defeated but did not rout the Prussians under Blücher at Ligny; meanwhile the British repulsed the French army at Quatre Bras, falling back towards Brussels when Napoleon's forces arrived. Wellington took up a strong position at Waterloo, against which on 18 June Napoleon launched a massive attack. The Anglo-Dutch army stood firm, and at dusk the Prussian forces arrived and ensured the defeat of Napoleon's army. Napoleon fled, and signed his second abdication. ⬦ *Napoleonic Wars.*

Water Polo. A sort of water 'football' in which teams of seven swimmers with four reserves oppose each other in a pool up to 30 yds long by 20 yds wide. Begun in Britain about 1870, it became an ⬦ *Olympic Games* event 1900 and is governed by the International Water Polo Board. There are home internationals among England, Scotland, Ireland, and Wales; overseas, Eastern European nations dominate international competition.

Watershed (Divide). The boundary line marking the limits of the ⬦ *catchment area* of a river system; it does not necessarily follow the highest ridge, but skirts the headstreams of the system's tributaries and is thus very irregular.

Water Ski-ing. Ski-ing in the wake of a towing motor-boat. Its precise origin is obscure; experiments were conducted in America and Europe throughout the 1920s. The World Water-Ski Union (1946) now has over 30 member countries; European Championships began 1947 and World Championships 1949. Competitive ski-ing comprises slalom, jumping, and figure ski-ing. Over 50 clubs are affiliated to the British Water-Ski Federation.

Water-softening ⬦ *Ion Exchange.*

Waterspout ⬦ *Tornado.*

Water-table. Level below which the rocks of the earth's crust are saturated with water; the depth depends a great deal on climate, e.g. in an arid region it may be over 100 ft down, in a wet one it may be at the surface of low-lying areas and create swamp. It varies with the seasons, rising in wet weather and falling in dry, the lowest level being the permanent water table. The water table may be lowered, and an area's water reserves impaired, by high demand for water for household and industrial purposes.

Waterways ⬦ *Canal, River.*

Wattle ⬦ *Acacia, Tannins.*

Wave. The phenomenon typified by the up-and-down motion of water, as a cork bobbing on ripples shows the movement of the water to be an up-and-down periodic movement: the cork itself does not travel, although the ripples are propagated horizontally across the surface. The horizontal movement of the wave results from the fact that the water is everywhere oscillating vertically with the same frequency, but with a progressively increasing phase-lag the further the waves are from the source. Terms involved in the description of all forms of wave motion can be illustrated by the same example. The distance between crests is the wavelength; frequency is the number of crests passing a given point (i.e. oscillations) per second; the distance a given crest appears to travel in a second gives its velocity, and the intensity of the oscillation is the amplitude. In wave motion the medium through which the wave passes does not move along with the wave. Waves may be either transverse or longitudinal, in the sense that the periodic displacement of the medium may be at right angles to the direction of propagation of the wave (e.g. waves on water) or along the direction of propagation (e.g. sound waves). All electromagnetic waves (e.g. light, radio waves) are longitudinal oscillations and all travel in free space at the same speed i.e. that of light. Light waves travel in various media at differing speeds, e.g. more slowly in air than in free space and more slowly still in water and glass. Sound waves are longitudinal pressure waves which travel at different speeds through different media, e.g. much more rapidly through iron than through air.

Wave Mechanics. A recent theory of matter which modifies the earlier concept of the structure of atoms as miniature planetary systems (◊ *atom*) and conceives of it as consisting of ◊ *subatomic particles* whose movements are similar to those of electromagnetic waves.

Wayland (Weiland). In Scandinavian and English legend, a lame smith, resembling ◊ *Hephaestus*; his sword Balmung was so sharp that when one of its victims was cleft to the thighs he did not know he had been hit until he moved and fell apart. An old stone near Lambourne in Berkshire was said to be his smithy; traditionally, if a horse was left there, with a few coins on the stone, its rider would find it newly shod.

Weasel ◊ *Ferret.*

Weather. State of atmosphere for given limited period in terms of pressure, temperature, humidity, rain or snow, cloud, wind speed and direction; in temperate latitudes greatly influenced by movement of ◊ *depressions*, which usually follow an E. track. ◊ *Climate, Meteorology.*

Weathering. Mechanical or chemical disintegration of rocks. Surface expansion under hot sun and contraction during cold nights cause strain in e.g. granite (all the constituent minerals having different expansion and contraction rates), water-filled cracks expand if frozen, and the rock mass breaks up. ◊ *Erosion, Exfoliation, Karst Region, Laterite.*

Weaver-bird. Sparrow-like birds found in the tropics, remarkable for their neatly woven nests, usually round with a tubular entrance, which they sling from branches. The sociable-weavers build a communal roof over their individual nests, each with a separate entrance and egg chamber.

Weaving ◊ *Spinning and Weaving.*

Weed-killers. Chemical preparations (a) general, to kill all plants indiscriminately, used simply to clear ground before cultivation, or (b) selective, to over-stimulate the growth hormones of certain plants, causing them to die; particularly toxic to broad-leaved plants, and thus useful to rid lawns, grassland, and cereal crops of weeds. Some early lawn weed-killers were 'selective' simply because broad-leaved plants collected more of the toxic spray than grass. ◊ *Pesticides.*

Weevil ◊ *Beetle.*

Weightlessness. Weight is perceptible only when one body rests upon another or resists gravity; thus weightlessness occurs in a spacecraft in free orbit (i.e. once the rocket propulsion has ceased) since the gravitational pull of the earth is exactly offset by the centrifugal force of the spacecraft. Weightlessness will occur wherever a spacecraft may be outside an atmosphere; it does not result from the equalization of two opposing gravitational fields (e.g. of the earth and the moon). The experience of Soviet and American astronauts has shown that weightlessness is tolerable for a period of days, but its effect over prolonged periods is unpredictable.

Weight-lifting. The lifting of weights competitively is an ancient sport revived in the 19th cent. and included in the 1896 ◊ *Olympic Games*; the International Weight-lifting Federation (1920) governs the World Amateur Championships. The competitive two-handed lifts are (1) Clear-and-press; (2) Snatch; and (3) Clean-and-jerk, contested in seven weight divisions (Bantam $123\frac{3}{4}$ lb., Feather $132\frac{1}{4}$ lb., Light $148\frac{1}{4}$ lb., Middle $165\frac{1}{4}$ lb., Light-heavy $181\frac{7}{8}$ lb., Middle-heavy $198\frac{3}{8}$ lb., Heavy more than $198\frac{3}{8}$ lb.).

Weights and Measures. In crude form, measures date to prehistory, when simple units such as the hand, arm, or pace were used. The Babylonians, Phoenicians, and Egyptians achieved some similarity in their measures, and a high degree of standardization was obtained throughout the Roman Empire. There is a vast multiplicity of systems in different parts of the world. Of these, two predominate: the ◊ *metric system*, introduced in France in 1795, and the older traditional British (and American) system. The metric system has been widely adopted for scientific purposes. In the U.K. the legal standards are set out in the Weights and Measures Act, 1963, based on standards kept by the Board of Trade, for the yard, pound, metre, and kilogram. There are a few differences between the U.S.A. and the U.K. in some units of weight and capacity. The U.K. or long ton (2240 lb.) is 20 cwt of 112 lb., the U.S. short ton (2000 lb.) is 20 cwt of 100 lb. The British Imperial gallon = 1.2 U.S. gallons.

Weimar Republic. 1919–33. Name by which the first German federal republic is known, after the city in which its constitution was adopted. This provided for an elective president with a seven-year term, a two-chamber government (Reichstag, elected by universal suffrage, and Reichsrat, representing the various states). The first President, Ebert (1919–25), was a socialist, but his successor, Field-Marshal von Hindenburg, was a nationalist and monarchist at heart. Post-war difficulties and inflation handicapped the young Republic, which failed to secure wide popular support or the real loyalty of the German army. The depression of 1930 led to mass unemployment and the growth of communist and Nazi movements. Both parties deliberately fomented disturbances, to produce a situation of tension, from which the Nazis eventually benefited most, to emerge as the largest single party in 1932. Hindenburg appointed Hitler Chancellor in 1933; by intimidating the Reichstag, he quickly secured an amendment to the Constitution giving him dictatorial power, which brought the Weimar Republic to an end. ⟡ *Nazism, Third Reich.*

Welding. The joining of two metal (or plastic) surfaces by heating them until they fuse together. In oxyacetylene welding the heat is produced by an intense gas flame. Two electrical methods are also used. In arc-welding the heat is produced by maintaining an ⟡ *electric arc* between an electrode and the workpiece. In resistance-welding a strong current is passed through the surfaces to be joined, until they are melted by heating owing to ⟡ *electrical resistance.*

Welfare State. The phrase was coined to describe the new social-insurance and health-service regulations introduced in the U.K. by the Labour Government after the Second World War, which derived largely from the Beveridge Plan (*Full Employment in a Free Society*) of 1944, but it has since been applied also to other nations where similar provisions exist. The Welfare State organization includes considerably extended terms of reference for the National Assistance Board, compulsory social insurance (to which both workers and employers contribute) covering not only unemployment benefits (as previously) but also e.g. sick pay, maternity benefits, and superannuation pay (in addition to the existing old-age pensions). The National Health Service, which is free (apart from small charges for medical prescriptions and dental services, etc.), is not financed by the social-insurance payments, but is a charge upon the national budget. The statutory obligation to give workers a minimum of two weeks paid holiday a year, the raising of the school-leaving age, and the organization of e.g. home-help, child-welfare, and foster-mother services are also part of the Welfare-State legislation.

Wends ⟡ *Brandenburg.*

Werewolf. In medieval legend, a man who was turned (or could turn himself) into a wolf, proof against armed attack, and who ranged by night to dig up and eat corpses and devour children. Similar stories are found in Greek and Roman legend; the belief persisted in the Balkans until recent times. It may derive from the masked animal-men of prehistory (depicted in cave-paintings e.g. at ⟡ *Lascaux* and Pech-Merle), possibly adherents of an animal cult or members of a secret society, like the leopard-men and lion-men of Africa.

Wessex. The kingdom of the West Saxons in the ⟡ *Anglo-Saxon* heptarchy, founded upon the earlier pre-Roman and Romano-British organization of Britannic tribes. Alfred the Great, King of Wessex A.D. 871–99, checked the Danish invasions and made Wessex synonymous with England. Subsequent Kings of Wessex controlled the whole country, including the Danelaw, until the 11th-cent. invasions of the ⟡ *Vikings.* When Hardicanute's reign ended 1042, Edward the Confessor was recalled and ruled until his death in 1066, when William of Normandy invaded England to claim the throne: ⟡ *Norman Conquest.*

In the late 19th cent. the novelist Thomas Hardy revived the term Wessex, to describe Dorset and adjoining counties.

West Indies. Area 90,060 sq. m. Archipelago extending from Florida to Venezuela, in three main groups: (a) Greater Antilles (⟡ *Cuba, Jamaica, Puerto Rico*); (b) ⟡ *Bahamas*; (c) Lesser Antilles. Independent: 72,000 sq. m. British: 12,300 sq. m. U.S.A.: 3890 sq. m. French: 1350 sq. m. Netherlands: 430 sq. m. Venezuelan: 90 sq. m. ⟡ *Netherlands West Indies, West Indies Federation.*

West Indies Federation. From 1958 to 1962, ten British colonies, but in 1962 ⟡ *Jamaica* and ⟡ *Trinidad* became independent within the British Commonwealth; the present eight-member Federation consists of Barbados, the Leeward Islands (Antigua, St Kitts, Montserrat); the Windward Islands (Dominica,

Grenada, St Lucia, St Vincent), and the dependent Cayman Islands and Turks-and-Caicos Islands. Total area 1597 sq. m. Total pop. 698,000. Cap. Bridgetown (Barbados).

Westminster Abbey. The collegiate church of St Peter, in Westminster; originally Edward the Confessor's church of 1050, consecrated in 1065. In 1245 Henry III began rebuilding and enlarging it, and the work continued until the 18th cent. It is cruciform in design; the eastern Lady Chapel, called the Henry VII chapel, has a famous tracery roof over 35 ft long and 100 ft high, in the Pointed style. The octagonal chapterhouse dates to the reign of Henry III. Since William the Conqueror every English sovereign has been crowned in Westminster Abbey (where also Cromwell was inaugurated as Lord Protector). The Coronation Chair contains the Stone of Scone, brought from Scotland in 1297 by Edward I, alleged to be ultimately the Tara Stone of ancient Ireland. The Abbey is the traditional burial-place of the famous, and has many memorial monuments, e.g. Poets' Corner in the S. transept.

Westminster Cathedral. Roman Catholic Cathedral in London, built 1895–1903; in early Christian ◊ *Byzantine* style, with fine interior mosaics and a campanile over 280 ft high.

Westminster Hall. The only building of the ancient Palace of Westminster (◊ *Houses of Parliament*) now surviving. Built by William Rufus and completed in 1097; the fine Gothic timber roof, with an unsupported span of 68 ft, begun by Richard II, was completed in 1399. For centuries Westminster Hall served as the chief law court of England; those tried there include Sir Thomas More, Charles I (and later his judges), Guy Fawkes, and Warren Hastings.

Westminster, Statute of ◊ *British Commonwealth of Nations.*

Westphalia, Treaty of. 1648. A religious and territorial settlement between the Hapsburgs, Spain, France, Sweden, and the German states, which concluded the ◊ *Thirty Years War.* It ended the ◊ *Holy Roman Empire* as an entity, replacing it by a number of independent states. France emerged as the dominant power, obtaining control of ◊ *Alsace* and the bishoprics of Metz, Toul, and Verdun. Sweden received W. Pomerania and Stettin. The Upper

◊ *Palatinate* went to ◊ *Bavaria*, which became an independent state, as did ◊ *Austria, Brandenburg, Savoy.* The Confederation of ◊ *Switzerland* and the independent ◊ *Netherlands* were given formal recognition. Religious toleration was granted to Calvinists as well as Lutherans in Germany, although the principle was not established in the Hapsburg territories.

West Point. The U.S.A. Military Academy, founded 1802 as a school for military engineers and greatly expanded after 1812; all branches of the army are covered, in four-year courses, and the cadets number over 2500. The equivalent Navy and Marine Academy is Annapolis, founded 1845; the Air Force Academy, founded 1954, is in Colorado.

Whale. With ◊ *porpoises* and ◊ *dolphins*, whales form the mammalian aquatic order Cetacea; like the Icthyosaurs, they are secondarily adapted to an aquatic life, and are believed to have originated in the Mesozoic Era. They suckle their young, have vestigial hair, are warm-blooded (about 36° C), and breathe with lungs; most whales have a gestation period of 10 months, producing a single offspring. Existing whales fall into two groups, the baleen (whalebone) and the odontoceti (toothed); both types can sustain a speed of 15 knots. They range in size from the 35-ft sperm-whale to the 90-ft fin-whale (blue whale), and are the largest animals in existence. Their blubber is a thick subcutaneous coat of fibrous connective tissue and fat, an inch thick in porpoises and dolphins and a foot thick in whales; it acts as an insulator and a food store. In search of food, sperm and bottle-nose whales may dive to 3000 ft (where the pressure is 1300 lb. per sq. in.). The 'blow' of a surfaced whale is a means not of disposing of water but of exhaling; the apparent geyser is condensed water-vapour. Whales may dive for 50 minutes and on surfacing 'blow' at 10-second intervals for five minutes. Migratory movements are connected with reproduction: as the newborn whale lacks blubber, birth in temperate or even tropical waters is necessary.

WHALING: Hunting whales for their blubber has a long history, going back perhaps to the Basques in the 10th cent. From the early 17th cent. American whalers from New England hunted the sperm whale in the S. Atlantic and the

Pacific, catching them by hand-harpooning from rowing-boats, based on ships or coast stations. Modern whaling is a highly technical operation carried out with harpoon guns from small rapid vessels attached to a whaling factory-ship. International conventions have attempted to lessen the threat of extinction to the whale, and recently the whaling nations have accepted observers to accompany whaling expeditions in order to see that the limits of the catch are observed.

Wheat. *Triticum*; the oldest and most valuable cereal, probably developed from the wild *emmer* or *einkorn* in the Near East, widely cultivated in all temperate climates. There are several varieties, which produce flour with different qualities. The presence of gluten (a protein) in flour makes it particularly well adapted for bread. The softer wheats, richer in starch, are used for biscuit, cake, and pastry flours, and the harder for bread; the hardest is used for macaroni. The outer layers of the grain are richest in protein; these, together with the bran, are removed in milling white flour. Wheat is also used in the manufacture of whisky and beer.

Production is widely spread and many countries are self-sufficient (major producers are Canada, China, U.S.A., and U.S.S.R.); but only a few have substantial export surpluses e.g. U.S.A., Canada, Australia, Argentine: the U.S.S.R. is trying to increase production for internal needs, but her efforts to exploit the 'Virgin Lands' (hitherto uncultivated steppes of central Asian Russia) have not been very successful. In temperate climates some types of wheat may be planted in autumn (winter wheats); in cold climates this is impossible but special quick-growing seed can be used (◇ *Vernalization*). Improvements in seed, cultivation, and control of pests have led to an immense increase in wheat production in the 20th cent.

Wheel. In the Old World the wheel first appeared in ◇ *Bronze Age* civilizations, about 3000 B.C., when its use is established by remains of wheel-made pottery, as well as by wheeled vehicles. The earliest wheels probably developed from rollers and were solid discs; spoked wheels were introduced about 1800 B.C., and made possible the rapid horse-drawn chariot as a weapon of war. In the New World the wheel was not used until the European conquests.

Whig. < Scots Gaelic, 'raider', 'cattle-thief'; first used at the time of the ◇ *Exclusion Bill*, and later applied to ◇ *Scotch Presbyterians*. The Whigs stood for Protestant and constitutional monarchy, and came to power in 1688 (◇ *Glorious Revolution*) After the reign of Queen Anne, with the accession of the house of ◇ *Hanover*, they remained the predominant party until the resurgence of the Tories about 1760. After the ◇ *French Revolution* they were representative of the middle-class trade interests, and espoused the cause of political reform, which culminated in the ◇ *Reform Bill* of 1832. Under Gladstone the party changed its name to Liberal, but for some 20 years continued to consist of 'new Liberals' and 'old whigs'.

Whisky. < Gaelic *usquebaugh*, 'water of life'; spirit distilled from a mash of grain. Malt whisky is made solely from barley, which is moistened, allowed to sprout, dried above a peat fire, and then ground and mixed with water to form the mash. Distilled in a pot-still, this produces a spirit with an alcohol content of 60–70 per cent. Grain whisky is made by processing a mixture of malted and unmalted ground grain in a patent still; Irish whisky is mainly grain. By law, all Scotch whisky must be matured for at least three years; as usually sold it is a roughly equal blend of malt and grain whiskies, reduced to about 70 per cent proof. American and Canadian whiskies are rye or bourbon. Rye is made by malting rye and saccharifying more rye with the malt. Bourbon whisky is made in the same way but from the action of a malted wheat or barley on a maize mash. The distinctive qualities of various whiskies depend upon the local water, the quality of peat used in curing the malt, the kind of casks used for maturing, and age.

Whist. A four-handed card game played by pairs of partners, in which each player receives 13 cards. The aim is to win tricks, each trick consisting of a card from each player, played in turn. The highest card of the suit led, or the highest trump, wins the trick; trumps (one particular suit) depend on the last card dealt, which is shown face up. The game is of English origin, dating to the 17th cent. Hoyle published a treatise on it in 1742, and it spread widely to the Continent and to America in the 19th cent. ◇ *Bridge* developed from it at the end of the 19th cent. and although as a result the parent game lost its popularity, the whist drive is still a favourite form of competition. Solo whist is of later invention. The individual bids are: abundance (to take eight tricks); misère (to take none); solo (to take five); and 'prop and cop' (to take seven tricks in partnership).

Whitby Synod. A.D. 664. Called by King Oswy of Northumbria to settle the difference of usage between the Roman and the Celtic Churches in England. By accepting the arguments of the English St Wilfrid rather than those of the Celtic St Colman, esp. concerning the date of Easter, the Synod brought the Northumbrian and Mercian Christians within the organization of the Roman Church.

White Dwarfs ◊ *Star*.

White Gold ◊ *Alloys*.

Whooping-cough. Infectious disease, mainly of children, characterized by respiratory catarrh and paroxysms of coughing, often ending in long and noisy inspiration ('whoops'). Vomiting may follow. There is no satisfactory treatment, but prevention by immunization is now widely practised.

Will. Statement of a person's desire as to the disposal of his property on his or her death; to be valid, a will must be properly executed, i.e. signed by the testator and two witnesses, all in each other's presence. A member of the armed forces on active service may make a valid will without these formalities, or even orally, and unlike others he may make a will while under 21. A will is revoked (a) by making a new one with inconsistent provisions; (b) by destroying it with the intention of revoking it; (c) by intentional obliteration of its contents, in part or whole; (d) by marriage, unless the will is made in contemplation of the marriage. Where no will is left, or where the testator fails to make reasonable provision for a wife, an infant, a disabled son, or an unmarried or disabled daughter, the Court may within certain limits order provision to be made out of the estate.

Willow. *Salix*, of the *Salicaceae*; deciduous dicotyledonous shrubs and trees, partial to damp places. Male and female plants are separate, with erect insect-pollinated ◊ *catkins*: the seeds are plumed and wind-dispersed. A variety of *S. alba* is the cricket-bat willow. *S. babylonica*,

the weeping willow, is native to China. Osiers are shrubby willows, with flexible shoots used for baskets etc. Willow bark was used medicinally before synthetic salicyl compounds (e.g. aspirin) were common.

Willowherb. Many plants of the genus *Epilobium*; also the Rosebay Willowherb (Fireweed), *Chamaenerion angustifolium*, found in most parts of Europe, Asia, and N. America, which may become a pest, as it spreads very rapidly in waste and open places by means of its plumed seeds and ◊ *rhizomes*. Of many *Epilobiu* native to Britain the commonest is the Great Willowherb, *E. hirsutum*, which has deep purple-rose flowers and grows in moist places.

Winds. Movement of air over the earth's surface, their force being measured on the Beaufort Scale, a series of numbers from 0 (calm) to 12 (hurricane), devised by Admiral Sir Francis Beaufort, adopted by the British Admiralty 1838, and recognized internationally 1874. ◊ *Föhn, Harmattan, Hurricane, Khamsin, Mistral, Monsoon, Sirocco, Tornado, Trade Winds*.

Windward Islands ◊ *West Indies Federation*.

Wine. The fermented juice of the fresh grape. There is evidence that wine-making was already known some 10,000 years ago; it was certainly common in Egypt by 2000 B.C. Ancient literature and the Bible abound in references to it, and through the Greek and Phoenician colonies the grape ◊ *vine* was introduced into France and Spain; the Romans took it to the Rhine and the Danube. There were vineyards in England at the time of Domesday Book, but these virtually disappeared in the late Middle Ages, by which time a large international trade in wine had developed and England was a large importer.

France and Germany make the top-quality table wines. The grape vines are derived from a single species, *Vitis vinifera*. There are hundreds of different varieties in use, and each wine district grows those which by long experience and tradition are best suited to its soil and climate. After picking, the grapes are crushed, or pressed, and placed in vats to ferment. Red wines are made from black grapes, the colour coming from the skins, white wines from white grapes or from black whose skins are removed, and rosé-wines by leaving the skins in the vat for a short time. Most table wines naturally contain 6–14 per cent alcohol by volume; fortified wines e.g. ◊ *sherry* have further alcohol added.

France has over 3 m. acres of vine-yards, mainly S. of Paris (apart from the ◊ *Champagne* and Alsace districts), and produces annually between about 700 and 1300 m. gal. of wine. The Bordeaux region contributes many fine wines, the red be-ing known in England as claret. White Bordeaux ranges from dry to very sweet. Of the wines of Burgundy, the red comes strictly from a small area, the Côte d'Or, with a large number of small vineyards. White Burgundy (invariably dry) comes from a larger area. The Rhône valley pro-duces some good red wines, and a great quantity of poor wine for conversion into commercial alcohol. The Loire valley wines are mainly white. The naming and labelling of French bottled wines is strictly controlled by law; an *Appellation d'Origine Contrôlée* indicates its origin and nature, the year or vintage also being of importance, since the weather plays a large part in determining the character of a wine. In sunnier lands (Spain, Italy, U.S.A.) the vintage is less important. Most French wine sold in the U.K. is bottled from bulk shipments, but sales of expensive château-bottled wine remain im-portant.

Italy has extensive vineyards, but is a smaller exporter than France. The best-known wines are the Tuscan Chiantis, and those of Orvieto, Apulia, and Piedmont; there is also a large production of ◊ *ver-mouth*.

Germany is a minor producer but much of her wine is of high quality. Most of it is grown in small, terraced vineyards on the banks of the Rhine, Main, and Moselle, the most northerly in Europe. Labelling is strictly regulated, and the better wines are designated by the name of particular vineyards. Broader descriptions e.g. Niersteiner and Liebfraumilch cover a wide range of quality. Grapes are left late to ripen and this is indicated by descriptions such as *Spätlese* (from late gathered grapes), *Beerenauslese* (from choice grapes left till they are berries), and *Trockenbeerenauslese* (from a still later gathered crop of raisin-like fruit). The wine of the Rhineland is known in

Britain, but not elsewhere, as 'Hock', after Hochheim near Mainz.

Spain, Algeria, Argentine, Portugal, Yugoslavia, U.S.A. are also considerable producers, and Austria and Hungary pro-duce some good wines. Increasing U.K. imports, almost invariably red, come from Spain and Algeria, cheap wines compar-able with the *vin ordinaire* of France but with rather more strength and body. Yugoslav 'Riesling' resembles German white wines. Portugal produces some good wines, esp. rosé, which have their own characteristics.

Consumption of wine in the U.K. has varied considerably. In 1795 (when the population was under 10 m.) some 10 m. gal. were imported. Per head consump-tion thereafter declined, and it is only since 1946 that there has been any sub-stantial increase. England has always been a major consumer of ◊ *port* and ◊ *sherry*. ◊ *Madeira*.

Wistaria. Climbing genus of the ◊ *Leguminosae*, with hanging racemes of pea-shaped flowers, usually lavender but also purple, rose, or white. Two species come from N. America and five from China and Japan; that often grown on house walls, where its twisted branches frequently reach a great height, is *W. sinensis*. The showy *W. floribunda*, most often seen on pergolas in Italy and other Mediterranean countries, has magnificent racemes up to 4 ft long.

Witchcraft and Sorcery. Much confusion exists in the usage of these and related terms, but anthropologists have now generally adopted the following termin-ology.

SORCERY: The use of spells and material objects ('medicines' e.g. hair-clippings, nail-parings, or effigies) for malevolent purposes.

WITCHCRAFT: The possession of an in-nate mystical power harmful or fatal to other people, often accompanied by the possession of the 'evil eye' and the ability to take on the forms of animals, and identifiable by certain physiological or psychological characteristics.

WITCH-DOCTOR: A person thought able to identify witches, often by 'smelling them out', who in many primitive societies directs the witch-hunt and conducts an autopsy in which the signs of witchcraft are sought in the entrails of the supposed witch. Whereas witches and sorcerers are considered evil, the witch-doctor is regarded as a socially benevolent person (◊ *Shaman*). It has been argued that European witchcraft was the survival of a pre-Christian religion centred on the 'horned god' (◊ *Pan*), who had become the Christian devil. This form of witchcraft involved the conjuring of demons and spirits, and should properly be called demonology. In general, however, it may be assumed that true witches do not exist, and that the phenomenon of witchcraft accusation has arisen at varying times and in most societies because people in times of stress have found a cathartic relief in ascribing their ills and misfortunes to malevolent persons who may then be sought out and killed; the persons accused are generally the solitary, the eccentric, or the deformed. Modern antisemitism and anticoloured feelings are similar phenomena. Witch-hunts of this kind in Europe and in the American colonies resulted in the deaths of thousands of probably harmless people. The last execution for witchcraft took place in Scotland in 1722.

Witenagemot. < Moot, meeting of the king's Council, in the various kingdoms of ◊ *Anglo-Saxon* England, made up from the chief magnates, prelates, and household officers (*witan*, wise men), summoned by the king to give advice on laws, taxes, etc. The king could call upon whom he liked; it resembled the modern Privy Council rather than Parliament. The Norman Great Council developed from it.

Woad. Blue dye obtained from the leaves of the herb *Isatis tinctoria*, which contains indigo, native to Britain. It was used by the ancient Britons to dye their bodies.

Woden ◊ *Odin*.

Wolf. Several genera of wild dog, ranging in size from the Alsatian-like grey wolf *Canis lupus* of N. America to the fox-like Antarctic wolf *Dusicyon* of the Falkland Islands. Wolves are also found in Europe and Asia. They mate in winter, the gestation period of 63 days permitting litters of about 10 to be born in spring. Pairing may be for life. Wolves frequently hunt in small groups.

Wolfram. The chief source of ◊ *tungsten*, occurring in veins on the edges of large bosses of granite; in Cornwall often associated with tinstone. The leading supplier is China, but Bolivia, Portugal, and U.S.A. are important producers.

Wood. Xylem; a complex vascular tissue in plants, which conducts water and mineral salts upwards from the roots and is the main supporting tissue in woody plants. The cells are impregnated with ◊ *lignin*. In large tree-trunks the outer and softer sapwood conducts water, but the cells of the central region (heartwood) become filled with tannins and resins. Heartwood yields the more valuable timber. Softwood is from conifers e.g. pine, spruce. Hardwood is from deciduous trees (oak, lime); it is not always hard, e.g. ◊ *balsa*. The hardest and heaviest woods are obtained from tropical trees e.g. mahogany, ebony, teak. Some, e.g. ironwood, is heavier than water. ◊ *Carbon, Paper, Rayon*.

Woodcut. A print made from a wooden block; the oldest graphic medium which is reproducible, a technique developed in the 15th cent. It was widely practised until the mid 16th cent. and revived in the 19th. As most woods are absorbent, blocks for woodcuts have to be carved by the tricky black-line (relief) process, in which the white (negative) parts of the block are carved away, a task usually entrusted to craftsmen. Artists famous for woodcuts e.g. Dürer, Holbein designed but rarely executed them.

WOOD ENGRAVING: A similar process, in which the end-grain section of a block of wood (rather than the long grain, as in wood-cutting) is manually incised by means of graver and gouge; the perfecting of the technique is generally ascribed to Thomas Bewick 1753–1828. As the principal method of illustrating books, magazines, and catalogues it has been superseded by photo-engraving and photogravure, but it remains an important artistic technique.

Woodpecker. *Picidae*; a widely distributed group of birds, including the green woodpecker, spotted woodpecker, and wryneck, with short stiff tails used as props in climbing tree-trunks; with their chisel-bills they bore into the trunk with a loud drumming action, to extract grubs with their long tongues. They lay four to eight eggs, in holes which they excavate and fill with wood chips.

Woodwind ◊ *Bassoon, Clarinet, Flute, Oboe, Recorder*.

Woodworm. The larvae of *Anobiidae*, beetles which infest furniture and the wood of buildings to obtain food; usually the larvae of the furniture beetle, whose activity produces wood-dust, a sign of their presence. The larvae becomes a tiny beetle, which bores its way to the surface and escapes; the resulting small holes indicate past infestation rather than present occupation. Various control methods are available.

Wool. Fibre from the fleece of the domesticated sheep; it is elastic, an excellent insulator, and has a tensile strength superior to that of cotton. Chemically it is mainly protein (keratin). It was probably the first fibre to be spun and woven into textiles: examples of woollen materials are found in early tombs in Egypt and Babylon. Improved breeds of sheep developed by the Romans led to the merino, which furnishes the finest grade. It is noticeable that no wild animal produces true wool: the fine hair of goats, camels, vicuña, etc. is however commercially also classed as wool. In the Middle Ages England became a leading producer of wool, exporting it widely throughout Europe; despite the encouragement of the Norman kings weaving and dyeing did not become an important industry until Tudor times. British woollens gained high repute, and wool manufacturing remained the staple industry of Britain until it was displaced by cotton. It is still a leading industry with a valuable export section. Other woollen manufacturing countries of importance in world trade are Japan, France, and Italy. Woollen fabrics are made from soft yarns; worsteds, e.g. gaberdines, whipcords, serges from smoother and more tightly woven yarns. Admixtures of synthetic fibres are now commonly used in woollen textiles. The main exporters of wool are Australia, Argentina, New Zealand, Uruguay, and S. Africa. Considerable quantities are produced in Gt Britain.

Worcester. 1651. Final battle of the ◊ *English civil wars*; Cromwell's 'crowning mercy'. Charles II, having been crowned King of Scots, entered England with a Scottish army, but was completely routed. He subsequently reached the Continent, after weeks of remarkable narrow escapes.

Workers Educational Association ◊ *Education.*

World Council of Churches. International organization, founded in 1948, of Protestant Christian churches which 'accept our Lord Jesus Christ as God and Saviour', for the purpose of common action and witness; it includes about 150 bodies. Its headquarters are in Geneva.

World Health Organization. An agency of the United Nations, founded in 1948, operating (a) by providing advisory services which help countries to combat diseases e.g. malaria, tuberculosis, cholera, typhus, to improve sanitation and nutrition, and to train their own health services; and (b) by standardizing the classification and nomenclature of drugs and diseases, and providing health statistics. There are about 100 member states, whose representatives meet annually in the World Health Assembly, to review the policy and establish the budget of the organization.

World Series ◊ *Baseball.*

World Wars ◊ *First/Second World War.*

Worm. Any elongated, soft-bodied, legless, creeping animal. Mainly in three phylae, the annelids (◊ *Earthworm*), the platyhelminthes (e.g. flatworms, ◊ *tapeworm*), and the nematodes (e.g. threadworms, round-worms). Many other groups contain worm-like forms e.g. certain insect ◊ *larvae*, shipworms (◊ *molluscs*), and ◊ *slow-worms.* Many worms and grubs destroy plants, wood, and other tissues by feeding upon them. ◊◊ *Caterpillar, Reptiles, Silkworm.*

Worms. 1521. Meeting of the German Diet at which Luther defended his 95 Theses before the Emperor Charles V against the papal legate. Refusing to recant, he was placed under the Imperial and ◊ *Papal Ban*, and the breach between his followers and the papacy was irrevocably widened. ◊◊ *Lutheranism, Reformation.*

Wrestling. A sport in which two men try to throw each other to the ground; popular among the ◊ *Sumerians* about 3000 B.C. and an important though very rough part of the ancient ◊ *Olympic Games.* The Romans combined their style with the Greek to produce Graeco-Roman, still widely practised, though several countries e.g. Japan have their own traditional styles. The International Amateur Wrestling Association (1921) controls the amateur sport. Graeco-Roman (holds above the waist only) and Freestyle (of American origin) are competed in the Olympics at various weights. In Britain the National

Amateur Wrestling Association was formed in 1904.

Writ. Document issued by a court, commanding the recipient to obey the instructions in it. Most civil actions in the High Court are begun by a writ ordering the defendant to enter an appearance, by completing a form indicating that he proposes to defend and giving an address for service of all future documents in the action; failing this, judgement may be given against him in his absence. There are also writs of execution and prerogative writs (◊ *Certiorari*).

X

Xenon ◊ *Inert Gases.*

Xerography. An electrical photographic method based on the fact that the conductivity of selenium is directly related to the amount of light falling on it. A selenium coating on a metal plate is given a charge of static electricity; when the object to be 'photographed' is projected on to it, it forms an electrostatic image of the original. What in ordinary photography would be a black-and-white negative is in this case a plate consisting of areas of varying electrostatic charge. When oppositely charged powder containing graphite and resin is spread over the plate, the powder is attracted to particular areas according to the charge; i.e. it forms an image of the original in powder, which is then transferred to copying-paper and fixed by heat. Xerography is widely used for simple and quick copying of documents, and also for the rapid preparation of paper or metal plates for offset lithography.

XERORADIOGRAPHY: Xerography applied to the taking of X-ray photographs in medicine and industry; by permitting repeated use of the same plate after decharging, it is likely to play an important part in extending mass radiography.

X-rays. In 1895 Röntgen observed a type of ◊ *radiation* which made a barium platinocyanide screen glow brightly, even when the discharge tube was covered with material opaque to light. He called this 'unknown' radiation X-rays. These are now known to form part of the electromagnetic spectrum, but are hundreds of times shorter in wavelength than visible light. They are generated when fast electrons are stopped at a target, usually the anode of a tube across which a high voltage is applied. X-rays have the property of being able to penetrate matter, but not without some absorption, which increases with the density of the material. This property was early applied in medical diagnosis, to explore the 'inside' of a patient. X-rays harm living cells, and must be used with great care. They are, however, used in large doses where (as in cancer) the aim is to destroy abnormal cells. Other uses include testing of metals and other materials, detection of 'fakes' (jewellery, paintings, etc.), and research into the structure of matter. X-ray crystallography, now a powerful research tool, makes use of the fact that X-rays have a wavelength of the same order as the spacing between the atoms of a crystal; thus it is possible to obtain diffraction and interference from a crystal in the same way as a diffraction-grating produces these effects with ordinary light. By observing the direction and intensity of the 'reflections' of X-rays from the different layers of atoms in a crystal, the structure can be deduced. ◊ *Cancer, Radiobiology.*

Y

Yachting. Sailing for sport probably originated with boat races for wagers between rival 'watches' aboard 15th-cent. men-of-war; later Charles II fostered yachting; and clubs and competitions existed in England and Holland in the 18th cent. Early in the 19th cent. the formation of the Yacht Club (now the Royal Yacht Squadron) helped to increase the sport; the Royal Yachting Association was formed 1875 and the Royal Ocean Racing Club 1924. Yachting has been an ◊ Olympic Games event since 1900. There are several forms e.g. class-racing, cruising, ocean-racing, etc., and many yacht classes. Increasing costs have restricted the building of large yachts, and the sport has rapidly changed from a rich man's prerogative to a universal sport dominated by the 27 classes of racing dinghies, most of which are cheap to buy and maintain. The most famous race for big yachts is the ◊ America's Cup. Other well-known races are the Rhode Island to Bermuda Race, the Round-the-Island Race (Isle of Wight), and the Fastnet Race (S. coast of England to the Irish coast and back), and the Cowes Meeting at the Isle of Wight is renowned.

Yak. *Bos grunniens*; the wild and domesticated ox of Tibet, allied to the bison, one of the largest of the ox family, characterized by long shaggy hair on the flanks and under parts of the body and by its bushy tail. Wild yaks are black and stand 6 ft high at the shoulder.

Yalta Conference. 1945. Meeting between Roosevelt, Churchill, and Stalin in the Crimea, at the end of the ◊ Second World War; it was agreed to demand unconditional surrender from Germany, to divide it into occupation zones, liquidate all its munitions industry, bring war criminals to trial, de-Nazify the country, and demand ◊ reparations. France was to participate in the Control Commission for Germany and occupy a fourth zone. A ◊ United Nations Organization was discussed, as were new frontiers for ◊ Poland. The U.K. and U.S.S.R. agreed to withdraw support from the Polish government-in-exile in London. Under a secret clause, the U.S.S.R. undertook to declare war on Japan two months after the end of the European war, in return for certain Japanese islands and concessions over Chinese territories. ◊ Potsdam Conference.

Yam. Fleshy tubers containing starch produced by various species of *Dioscorea*, a large genus mostly of tropical and subtropical climbers, cultivated as food esp. in tropical America. Their use is declining, as they are being replaced by ◊ *manihot* and ◊ *sweet potatoes*, which are easier to grow and prepare. The *Dioscorea* species contain poisons e.g. alkaloids and saponins, and some yams (esp. those producing tubers nearer the soil surface) are poisonous unless grated and washed to remove the sap.

Yaws. Tropical disease resembling syphilis, involving widespread ulceration of the skin and caused by the spirochaete *Treponema pertenue*; it may be spread by flies.

Yeasts. Unicellular ◊ *fungi*, the best-known genus being *Saccharomyces*. Yeasts secrete ◊ *enzymes*, which bring about the alcoholic fermentation of sugar. The genus *S. cerevisia* has two forms, which produce 'top' and 'bottom' fermentation, employed in the manufacture of English and German type beer. The action of yeast converts sugar into alcohol and carbon dioxide (fermentation). In brewing and wine-making the alcohol is the important product, whilst in baking it is the escaping carbon dioxide which causes the dough to rise.

Yemen. Area 74,000 sq. m. Pop. 4 m. Cap. Taiz. Rel. Muslim. The Arabic name means 'on the right hand', i.e. lucky; it is the *Arabia Felix* of the ancient geographers. A republic in SW Arabia, near Aden.

ECONOMY. Mainly mountainous, but fertile; exports coffee, cotton, hides, oilseeds, raisins, salt.

HISTORY. The Yemen Kingdom formed part of the ◊ United Arab Republic 1958-61, but was temporarily expelled from it by Egypt after Syria's defection. In 1962, on the death of Imam Ahmad, an army coup d'état under General Sallal deposed his son, with Egyptian aid. The republic under Sallal is not recognized by Britain, but is a member of the United Nations and of the re-formed U.A.R.

Yeoman. A class of small freeholders which emerged in late feudal times, superior to the serfs but below the gentry, and was a name long used for small farmers between the labourer and the large landowner.

YEOMEN OF THE GUARD: Ancient royal bodyguard recruited from old soldiers with meritorious service; their uniform is a survival of Tudor times. Those at the Tower of London are distinct from the guard proper and have specific permanent duties. The name 'Beefeater' comes from the French *bouffetier* – the man who served at the (royal) buffet.

YEOMANRY: An irregular cavalry force in Gt Britain raised in the 18th cent. amongst those willing to provide their own horses. It was occasionally called out to help the civil authorities. They formed the nucleus of the Imperial Yeomanry which served in the Boer War, becoming after 1907 the cavalry of the ◊ *Territorial Army*.

Yeti ◊ *Abominable Snowman*.

Yew. *Taxus baccata*; a very long-lived slow-growing evergreen tree, important in medieval times as providing the wood for the English long bow. Its leaves are poisonous to man and animals. Because of its dense branching system, it is easily trimmed to any shape and has long been used for topiary work. It is a ◊ *Gymnosperm*.

Yggdrasil. In Scandinavian legend, the world ash-tree, its roots in hell, its trunk and branches on earth, its summit in heaven. Under it sat the three Norns (Fates), who spun the thread of destiny for men and gods. An eagle perched at the top, a dragon lay at the foot, and a squirrel ran between them creating discord. ◊ *Odin* hung from its branches to acquire wisdom.

Y.M.C.A. ◊ *Young Men's Christian Association*.

Yoga. Systems in ◊ *Hinduism*, the aim of which is to bring about union with Reality, the Absolute, and which involve various techniques of developing inner powers; the version for which a certain vogue developed outside India involves special breathing exercises and postures combined with prolonged meditation (Hatha Yoga). The various systems are explained in the Yoga Sutras of Patanjali (about 300 B.C.) and in the Bhagavad Gita.

Yom Kippur ◊ *Day of Atonement*.

York Cycle ◊ *Miracle Play*.

Yorktown. 1781. The closing campaign of the ◊ *American Revolution*. The British troops under General Cornwallis retreated to Yorktown, Virginia, and fortified it to await reinforcements. The French fleet blockaded Chesapeake Bay, and finally, outnumbered and surrounded, Cornwallis capitulated and hostilities were brought to an end.

Yoruba ◊ *African Languages, Nigeria*.

Young Italy. *Giovine Italia*; republican and anticlerical secret society for the unification of Italy, founded in the 1830s by Mazzini and influential both in the revolts against the ◊ *Papal States* and also, by example, in the 1848 revolutions all over Europe. The name was widely copied, e.g. Young Ireland, Young Poland, Young Turks. ◊ *Risorgimento*.

Young Men's Christian Association (Y.M.C.A.). Undenominational Protestant organization, founded in London in 1844, by George Williams, to provide young men with educational and recreational facilities in a Christian atmosphere. The movement spread to the U.S.A. and later to other countries. There are over 75,000 members in the U.K. and the World Alliance constituted in Paris in 1855 claims a world membership of well over a million. The Y.W.C.A. (for girls and women), founded in 1855, is now a world-wide association with over 500,000 members.

Young Plan (1929) ◊ *Reparations*.

Young Turks ◊ *Ottoman Empire*.

Ypres. 1914, 1915, 1917. Three battles of the ◊ *First World War*. In 1914 the British held out against superior German forces, thwarting their drive to the sea. In 1915 the Germans used chlorine gas for the first time against the British, inflicted 60,000 casualties, but failed to achieve a decisive break-through. In 1917 Haig launched a massive and costly attack at Passchendaele, which achieved negligible success.

Yseult (Iseult, Isolde, Isoud) ◊ *Tristram*.

Ytterbium ◊ *Lanthanides*.

Yttrium. A rare ◊ *element* which occurs in gadolinite (◊ *Lanthanides*); the first member of the Second Transition Series. No important use for it has yet been found.

Yucca ◇ *Liliaceae*.

Yugoslavia. Area 98,725 sq. m. Pop. 19 m. Cap. Belgrade. Rel. 49 per cent Eastern Orthodox, 37 per cent Roman Catholic, 12 per cent Muslim. A federal republic comprising ◇ *Serbia*, Croatia, Slovenia, ◇ *Montenegro*, Bosnia-Herzegovina, and part of ◇ *Macedonia*. After the 1944 liberation from German occupation, the leader of the communist resistance Marshal Tito was elected President. Supreme federal authority is vested in the People's Assembly, consisting of a Federal Council elected by popular suffrage and a Council of Producers representing the workers. Apart from making military and economic agreements with U.S.S.R. President Tito has pursued an independent course. The U.S.S.R. broke off relations with Yugoslavia 1948, after which her commercial and financial dependence on western powers increased. Relations with U.S.S.R. were resumed 1955, but Yugoslavia remains uncommitted; President Tito has been prominent among leaders of 'non-aligned' countries.

ECONOMY. About 50 per cent of the population are engaged in agriculture and forestry; there is an important mining industry, and manufacturing has grown considerably since 1947. Heavy industry was nationalized in 1945 and is conducted by state agencies, but most enterprises are run by locally autonomous workers' councils, and the official polic is decentralization. Wages and prices ar fixed by the individual enterprises. Abou half the land is privately owned, an foreign companies (e.g. French, Italian produce goods under licence. The selling market is competitive.

HISTORY. Yugoslavia was created i 1918, after the dissolution of the ○ *Austria-Hungarian Empire*; Serbia exer cised the preponderant influence in th new state, and antagonism between Serb and Croats resulted 1929 in King Alex ander's assumption of dictatorial powe Alexander was assassinated in Marseille 1934, and as his son Peter was under ag Prince Paul became regent. He turne increasingly to Germany in an attempt t solve economic difficulties. Disliked fo his pro-Nazi leanings, he was depose 1941 by a coup d'état, whereupon th Germans invaded and occupied th country, but two rival groups – one unde General Mikhailovic, the other unde 'Tito' (Josip Broz) – organized resistance movements; the Allies at first supportec Mikhailovic, but later sent help to Tito whose movement was the more effective of the two.

LANGUAGE. Croatian, Slovenian (both using the Latin alphabet), and Serbian (using the Cyrillic alphabet); all are ◇ *Slavonic languages*.

Y.W.C.A. ◇ *Young Women's Christian Association*.

Z

Zambia. Area 288,130 sq. m. Pop. 3.5 m. (3.4 m. Africans). Capital Lusaka. Independent country of central Africa, member of British Commonwealth, formerly N. Rhodesia. After the 1962 elections, held under the 1962 constitution, the first African-dominated legislature came to power, 21 seats being held by Kenneth Kaunda's United National Independence Party and Harry Nkumbula's African National Congress and 16 by the (European) United Federal Party.
ECONOMY: Zambia is the world's second largest producer of copper, on which the economy depends. Other mineral products are cobalt, zinc, lead, and manganese.
HISTORY: In 1953, the former British protectorate of Northern Rhodesia became part of the Federation of Rhodesia and Nyasaland. In face of African demands for political representation (they outnumber Europeans by 30 to one), negotiations for a new constitution began in 1960. The Federation was dissolved in 1963, and full independence, as Zambia, was achieved in 1964.

Zanzibar. Area 1020 sq. m. Pop. 299,111 (Negroes, Indians, an Arab minority). Cap. Zanzibar. Rel. predominantly Muslim. Two islands (Zanzibar and Pemba) of E. Africa, off the coast of Tanganyika; as a sultanate, a British protectorate until Dec. 1963, then very briefly a member of the British Commonwealth; now an autonomous part of the new state of Tanganyika and Zanzibar (Tanzania), with its own government under President Karume and a Revolutionary Council.
ECONOMY. Almost wholly dependent on cloves, of which it produces the bulk of the world's supply; other exports are coconuts, coir, copra.
HISTORY. A very early trading-centre for Arabs and Persians, seized by Portugal in 1565 but later retaken by the Arabs. In 1890 it became a British protectorate. Under the sultanate the Arabs were dominant. The 1963 elections returned left-wing members only (Afro-Asian party 54 per cent, Nationalist 35, People's Party 11). A few weeks after the granting of independence, an anti-Arab revolution

by the Afro-Shirazi party deposed the Sultan, who fled to Britain with his family; the republican government at once nationalized all land (except the valuable clove plantations) and public buildings. It has received loans from China and technological aid from E. Germany, has close relations with Uganda and Kenya, and has been recognized by the U.K. and many other states.

Zarathustra ◊ *Persia, Zoroastrianism.*

Zebra ◊ *Horse.*

Zebu. *Bos indicus*; the humped cattle of India, resistant to heat and ticks but having a poor yield of milk and meat. It has been introduced into southern U.S.A. and S. America (known there as Bramah), where useful cross-breeds with other cattle have been developed.

Zen. School of Japanese Mahayana ◊ *Buddhism,* deriving from Bodhidharma, a 6th-cent. A.D. Chinese teacher. It holds that by meditation (often on *Koans,* paradoxical phrases) and bodily training one may attain *satori,* a sudden illumination and enlightenment on the nature of the self and of the emptiness or void of which all things are manifestations. In recent years Zen has attained some popularity in Europe and America, sometimes in rather distorted forms. It was cultivated by the Samurai, the knightly order of pre-westernized Japan. ◊ *Mysticism.*

Zenith. Point on the ◊ *celestial sphere* directly overhead. Because the earth is not a true sphere, and also rotates, the geographical zenith (point where a line joining the centre of the earth to the observer would cut the celestial sphere) does not always coincide with the astronomical zenith (point where a plumbline extended upwards would cut the sphere). The zenith distance of a heavenly body is its angular distance from the observer's zenith.

Zephyr (Zephyrus) ◊ *Aeolus.*

Zeppelin. The greatest advance in the development of large ◊ *airships* was attributable to Count Ferdinand von Zeppelin 1838–1917, whose design enabled a large lighter-than-air aircraft to maintain a sound aerodynamic shape by using a girder form with fabric outer covering and independent gas bags inside; before the First World War his airships had carried 35,000 passengers without serious mishap. Zeppelin and Schütte-Lanz airships were used 1914–18 for reconnaissance and bombing but proved very vulnerable and ineffective. The *Graf Zeppelin*, launched 1928, completed 590 flights and over a million miles without accident, but the *Hindenburg*, used on transatlantic and other services, caught fire disastrously when going to her moorings in 1937.

Zero. 0; the symbol for nought. Its introduction to Europe (from India, via the Arabs) during the Middle Ages made it possible to accord a positional value to the symbols 1 to 9, and thus to represent any number whatsoever. This was a turning-point in the evolution of a number system permitting calculations with large numbers, essential to modern science. With the concept of negative as well as positive numbers, zero took its place between -1 and $+1$ on the scale of integers (e.g. in temperature scales).

ABSOLUTE ZERO: The theoretically lowest possible ◊ *temperature* (approximately $-273°$ C) at which all molecular movement and chemical reaction would cease.

Zeus. In Greek mythology, supreme god of heaven; originally the Indo-European sky-god Dyaus. In one legend, born in Crete and suckled by the goat Amalthea; husband of ◊ *Hera* but perpetually unfaithful, and son of Cronos whom he overthrew (◊ *Titans*) and succeeded as ruler of the upper world, his brothers ◊ *Poseidon* and ◊ *Hades* taking the sea and the underworld. Honoured as the father of gods and men, and mainly a benevolent deity guarding justice, punishing perjury, endowed with foreknowledge and sometimes revealing the future to men by oracles or dreams, his power was limited only by destiny or the ◊ *Fates*. He and the other chief gods lived on Mount Olympus on the borders of Thrace.

Ziggurat. Form of temple common in the ◊ *Sumerian*, ◊ *Babylonian*, and ◊ *Assyrian* civilizations, square in ground-plan with high walls inclining inwards; the flat summit was used for astrological observations, and the building contained a temple and storehouses for grain, part of which was distributed among the craftsmen who worked near by and part stored against times of famine.

Zinc. A white metallic ◊ *element*, occurring with ◊ *copper* and other sulphide ores as zinc-blende and early known in the form of brass, its copper alloy. It is obtained by oxidizing the sulphide to oxide and reducing this by heating with ◊ *carbon* in retorts: the metal volatilizes and is subsequently condensed. A freshly cut surface is bright but rapidly becomes coated with oxide, which makes the colour greyish and prevents further attack. As a building material it is used for flashings, weatherings, and roof covering. For protecting iron, the sheet (after cleaning) is dipped in or sprayed with molten zinc ('galvanized iron'). Zinc is a major constituent of some die-casting alloys e.g. 'Mazak' and is used in dry electric batteries; as a fine powder it is an industrial chemical, and with copper it gives the important series of alloys known as the brasses. Its chemistry is very simple, because the valency state is always two; the oxide provides a white pigment and a filler for rubber, the chloride is a flux in soldering, the sulphate is used in the textile industry and the sulphide in the pigment lithopone (◊ *Barium*), and the carbonate is also a pigment. Some zinc compounds are employed in medicine.

Zinjanthropus. Type of primitive hominid, known from fossil bones discovered by Dr L. S. B. Leakey in Olduvai Gorge, Tanganyika, in 1959, and belonging to the wider group of African ape-men known as the Australopithecines. The remains belong to the Lower Pleistocene period, over 1 m. years ago. Although ape-like in brain-size and in other respects, *Zinjanthropus* walked upright on two feet and his dentition resembled that of man. In 1964 Leakey announced that he had found the remains of a much more advanced hominid, contemporary with *Zinjanthropus*, but belonging to the genus *Homo*; he proposed the name *Homo habilis*, to indicate that this type of early man used tools.

Zionism. Movement for the establishment of a Jewish state in Palestine, founded by Theodor Herzl in the late 19th cent. It gathered strength under leadership of Chaim Weizmann, and during the First World War, by the Balfour Declaration of 1917, the British government supported the idea of a 'Jewish national home' in Palestine. During the British mandate over Palestine, this was implemented by allowing quotas of Jewish settlers, which led to increasing friction with the indigenous Arab population, to Arab and Jewish terrorism against the British forces, and finally to the partition of Palestine into ◊ *Israel* and ◊ *Jordan*. Zionist activities still continue, esp. in the U.S.A. where large sums of money are raised to help the State of Israel. ◊ *Jewish Agency*.

Zirconium. A grey ductile metallic ◊ *element*, which remains bright in air because of a film of oxide; fairly abundant in nature, but difficult to obtain pure. Because it has a low absorption of neutrons, the pure metal is used for 'canning' uranium rods for the graphite-moderated nuclear reactors. It is also used as a deoxidizer, and in some special alloys e.g. with magnesium, for steel.

Zodiac. The band of the ◊ *celestial sphere*, on either side of the sun's apparent yearly path amongst the stars, containing the paths of the moon and planets. Since Babylonian times it has been divided into 12 'signs' or 'houses' named Aries, Taurus, Gemini, Cancer, Leo, Virgo, Libra, Scorpio, Sagittarius, Capricorn, Aquarius, and Pisces (after the constellations in them). These divisions no longer completely correspond to the constellations of the same names – owing to gradual shift in the position of the stars as we now see them, as a consequence of the axis of rotation of the earth not being absolutely constant. The stars will be back in their rightful houses after the complete cycle of precession (25,868 years). ◊ *Astrology*.

Zodiacal Light. A faint cone of light, with its base on the horizon, sometimes seen in the west after sunset and in the east before sunrise. It is caused by the scattering of sunlight by dust particles and electrons which lie in the ecliptic plane.

Zollverein. German, 'customs union'. The Treaty of Vienna, 1815, set up a large number of separate German states, and Prussia, the largest, found itself hampered economically by a diversity of tariffs and by enclaves of other states. Prussia between 1828 and 1835 persuaded some of these to agree to tariff unification; other groups of German states formed their own zollvereins, but gradually these and most other German states joined the Prussian-dominated zollverein, thus facilitating economic and political integration in 1870.

Zoo. Zoological gardens were first founded to facilitate the detailed study of the behaviour, life history, and physiology of many species of animals; whilst retaining this function, they have become also institutions of popular interest. Only a proportion of animals born in captivity survive although breeding in captivity is becoming more successful, and zoos replenish their stock with animals captured in their native habitat.

Zoology ◊ *Biology, Birds, Ecology, Evolution, Fish, Fossils, Insects, Physiology, Primates, Reptiles, Vertebrates, etc.*

Zoroastrianism. Religion of the old Persian empire, from about 600 B.C. Named after Zoroaster (Zarathustra), who preached an ethical dualism by which a good god (Ahura Mazda, Ormazd) and an evil god (Angramainyus, Ahriman) are eternally at war, though the final victory will be with the good. The good principle was symbolized by fire, which was greatly honoured; physical and moral purity were highly esteemed, and Zoroastrian ethics and beliefs probably influenced the later parts of the Old Testament. After the Islamic conquest of Persia, fugitives went to India carrying the sacred fire; their descendants the Parsis play a prominent part in Hindu industrial life in and around Bombay. Some have returned to Persia, where they are now tolerated. The sacred writings of the cult are known as the (Zend) Avesta.

Zulu. Bantu-speaking people of Natal, S. Africa. The Zulu nation was formed between 1818 and 1822 by the king Shaka, who conquered the surrounding tribes by his remarkable military ability and his adoption of the short stabbing spear, which proved more effective in close combat than the traditional throwing spear. Shaka's power was based on his control of the army regiments, consisting of young men taken from their homes and owing personal loyalty to him alone. He was assassinated 1828; the Zulu were later defeated by both Boers and British and restricted to N. Natal, under a Paramount Chief whose traditional powers have been greatly curtailed. ◊ *Apartheid, Basutoland*.

Zygote ◊ *Meiosis*.

A modern dictionary for every Penguin reader

THE PENGUIN ENGLISH DICTIONARY

Containing more than 45,000 main entries, from the most colloquial words to the most formal, *The Penguin English Dictionary* has been specially prepared and written for Penguins by a team led by Professor G. N. Garmonsway, Professor of English in the University of London (King's College) and is the result of seven years' work.

The emphasis in this new dictionary is on current usage and the entries include many hundreds of post-war words and senses, in addition to the established vocabulary in English. Definitions are given in the most direct and simple form possible, and the dictionary introduces a new and immediately understandable system for pronunciation, which is likely to be of the greatest use to foreign students of English.

We believe *The Penguin English Dictionary* can justifiably claim to be an unrivalled catalogue of English words as they are used today in print and speech.

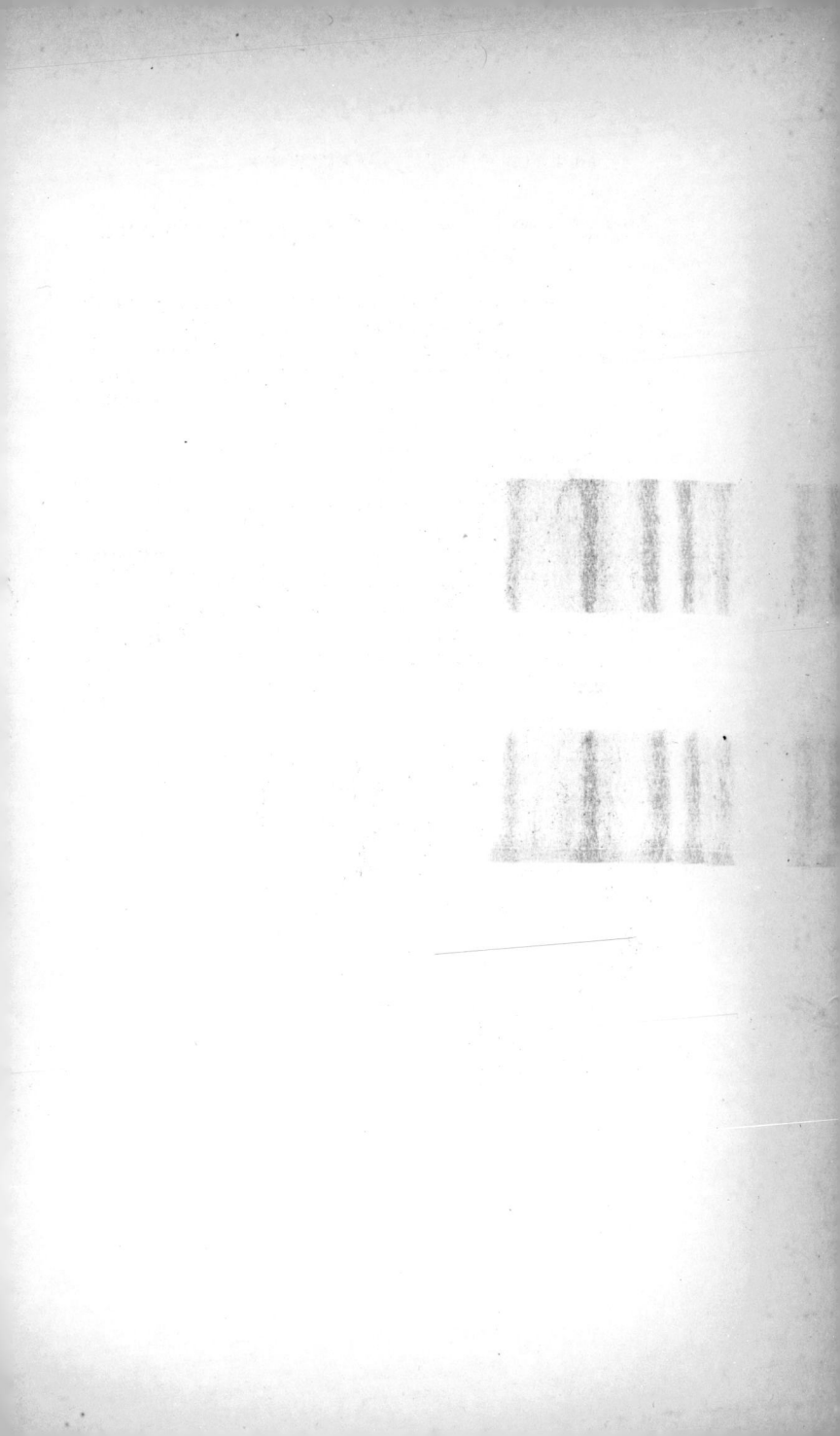